WINCHESTER STUDIES

General editor: Martin Biddle

1

WINCHESTER IN THE EARLY MIDDLE AGES

AN EDITION AND DISCUSSION OF THE WINTON DOMESDAY

Liber de terris Regis red
dentibz langablas ⁊ brug
imlovre. Sicut solebant Red
dere. Tempore Regis Edwar
di.

Henric rex volens scire
quid rex Edwardus ha
buit omnibz modis winto
me in suo dñico: burgensi
um suorz sacramento hoc co
probari iussit. Volebat ēnim
illud inde penitus habe. sed
Rex edwardus suo tempe
inde habuit. hoc g sacram
tum factu fuit de quart xx
⁊ vi. Burgensibz meliorib;
Wint psente Willo epo ⁊ her
bto cameraio ⁊ Rad basset
⁊ Goisfrido ridel ⁊ Willo de
pomearchar. hoc ante bur
genses pacto sacramto apor
ta orientali exeunte inqui
rere etbergingis.

¶ Alwin sideslone tenuit tpr
regis Eadwardi. i. domu reddeñ
tem de langabulo vi d ⁊ omne
alia consuetud regis ⁊ rex eam
tenuit in dñio qm eam tenet fil
Rad Roselli. qa dimissa fuit
ei a patre ⁊ nulla consue inde
ungua reddidit ⁊ reddit L. s.

¶ Edwinus Godeswale tenu
it j domu T.R.E. reddentem
de langabulo vi d ⁊ retro illa
domu deconsue iii d ⁊ om
ne aliam consue in teñ Ric
capell com de mleut ⁊ nulla
consue inde reddidit ñ in hoc
anno ⁊ reddidit pannu xx s.

¶ Brumañ delaforda tenuit
j domu T.R.E. reddente om
ne consue in eam tenet Srb
tus saluagi ⁊ nulla consue
inde reddidit ⁊ banc Osbtus
fil Alberede p viii s.

¶ Leuret de essewem tenu
it j domu T.R.E. reddente
omne consue qm tenet Osbt
fil alberede ⁊ nulla consue
ungq inde reddidit ⁊ de eade
tra ht herebtus canis i man
sura que reddit xv s ⁊ nulla

Winton Domesday, fo. 1ʳ: Survey I, preface and entries 1–4 (251 × 174 mm)

WINCHESTER STUDIES · 1

WINCHESTER IN THE EARLY MIDDLE AGES

AN EDITION AND DISCUSSION OF THE WINTON DOMESDAY

FRANK BARLOW, MARTIN BIDDLE
OLOF von FEILITZEN *and* D. J. KEENE
with contributions by
T. J. BROWN, H. M. NIXON
and FRANCIS WORMALD

EDITED BY

MARTIN BIDDLE

OXFORD
AT THE CLARENDON PRESS
1976

Oxford University Press, Walton Street, Oxford OX2 6DP

OXFORD LONDON GLASGOW NEW YORK
TORONTO MELBOURNE WELLINGTON CAPE TOWN
IBADAN NAIROBI DAR ES SALAAM LUSAKA ADDIS ABABA
KUALA LUMPUR SINGAPORE JAKARTA HONG KONG TOKYO
DELHI BOMBAY CALCUTTA MADRAS KARACHI

ISBN 0 19 813169 0

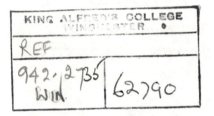
*Printed in Great Britain
at the University Press, Oxford
by Vivian Ridler
Printer to the University*

FOR
DILYS AND ERIC NEATE
ONCE ALDERMEN OF
WINCHESTER

GENERAL EDITOR'S PREFACE

THE programme of archaeological excavations carried through in Winchester under my direction from 1961 to 1971 was first undertaken at the instigation of the late Mr. Roger Quirk, C.B. In that first campaign in 1961 our objectives were limited to a single site and essentially to a single problem: to recover in the face of impending destruction whatever remained in one particular spot of the buildings of the Anglo-Saxon New Minster. It was impossible in those days to work in Winchester for a long summer and not to realize the untapped wealth of the city's archaeology, and the extent to which it was threatened with elimination through the demands of modern development for roads and buildings. With this in mind the Winchester Excavations Committee was formed at my suggestion the following year, under the chairmanship of the mayor of 1961–2, Councillor (later Alderman) Mrs. E. C. Neate, J.P., who remains chairman to this day. The Committee undertook excavations in Winchester for ten successive years from 1962 to 1971, and from 1964 to 1970 was fortunate to enjoy the collaboration of the University of North Carolina and Duke University.

By 1966 the results of the Committee's work were such that their evaluation and publication could only be secured by the creation of a full-time unit charged with this task. The Winchester Research Unit was set up in the autumn of 1968 with the support of the Calouste Gulbenkian Foundation, the British Academy, the Department of the Environment, the Hampshire County Council, the Winchester Corporation, I.B.M., and many other bodies. The results of its work will be published in the series 'Winchester Studies', of which this is the first volume.

The original impetus for the excavations of 1961 was Roger Quirk's study of the documentary evidence for the location and architectural character of the Old and New Minsters, published in 1959 and 1961 (see below, pp. 307 and 315). From the start, therefore, a proper combination of documentary and archaeological evidence was a basic principle of our work. This approach was soon extended. On the one hand we tried to study the city's origins and subsequent development through a use of all relevant evidence, whether derived from documents, archaeology, or the natural sciences. On the other hand we expanded our work to an intensive inquiry into the historical evolution and over-all topography of the medieval and early modern city, on the basis of the written records and the surviving structures and townscape. Only on these foundations could we have hoped to approach any real understanding of the urban community in its succeeding patterns; and only thus could the evidence of the detailed yet inevitably limited archaeological investigations be extrapolated to a wider canvas, while at the same time being controlled by a framework of different but convergent knowledge.

Already in the interim report on the first season of excavations use was made of the twelfth-century surveys of the city, collectively known as the Winton Domesday. They were quarried by us on several subsequent occasions, as indeed they had been by others since their first publication by the Record Commission in 1816. But it was soon obvious that the surveys required extensive study if they were to contribute fully to our knowledge of late Saxon and Norman towns and Winchester in particular.

In 1966 I asked Professor Frank Barlow, in whose department in the University of Exeter I was then teaching, if he would edit the text, the proposal being that we should collaborate in its annotation and topographical analysis. Professor Barlow at once agreed. When the time came to make a start in 1969, after the establishment of the Research Unit, the affair began to expand. Dr. Derek Keene, historian on the Unit, was ideally placed through his study of the later medieval topography and history of Winchester to elucidate many problems concerning its earlier development, land-tenure, and personalities. He agreed to join the team. It was shortly afterwards that Professor Barlow suggested we should seek the collaboration of a student of personal names to deal with 'an *onomasticon* without parallel for the period and of the utmost importance' (see below, p. 14). Professor Dorothy Whitelock suggested Dr. Olof von Feilitzen of the Royal Library in Stockholm, who agreed to undertake the task and produced his manuscript so rapidly that it was possible for the three other principal collaborators to make use of it from an early stage in their own work. My task as editor and contributor has been greatly eased by this interchange of ideas at all times between the various authors. It has, we believe, resulted in an edition of the manuscript and a discussion of its problems which individually we could never have achieved.

There remained other technical problems which needed discussion. As was most appropriate, the then President of the Society of Antiquaries, the late Professor Francis Wormald, agreed to edit the fragments of a tenth-century sacramentary found in the binding of the Winton Domesday in the late eighteenth century. It was one of his last works, and I am most grateful to Mr. B. C. Barker-Benfield and Professor Julian Brown for helping to see it through the press. Professor Brown also agreed to write about the palaeography of the Domesday. Mr. H. M. Nixon undertook a major study of the group of twelfth-century bindings of which the Winton Domesday is an important example, as well as contributing to our knowledge of the pedigree of the manuscript in the eighteenth century.

My role as general editor allows me to thank my fellow collaborators in a way which would not perhaps usually be open to an editor and contributor to a volume. I am indeed deeply conscious how much I have learned from them all and of the hard work they have undertaken. In a personal sense I am especially grateful to Frank Barlow for his characteristically generous agreement to my original suggestion and to Derek Keene for his illuminating companionship through this volume, as well as for readily undertaking more editorial chores than anyone had any right to expect. If there is one single impression that remains it is of the generosity with which so many have helped. I think particularly of the numismatists and of the place- and personal-name scholars, especially Olof von Feilitzen.

The economics of publishing are such today that books of this kind cannot proceed without a considerable subvention. The dedication of this volume expresses our indebtedness to two of my friends who made it possible. This was indeed only the latest in a series of actions by which severally and jointly they have supported our work throughout fourteen years. They deserve the best that we can offer.

MARTIN BIDDLE

Winchester
St. Valentine's Day 1974

CONTENTS

LIST OF PLATES

LIST OF FIGURES

LIST OF TABLES

LIST OF ABBREVIATIONS

THE list is not intended to be more than a key to the short titles and other abbreviations used in this volume. It makes no pretence to be a bibliography of the subject, for abbreviations have normally been used only where a title occurs more than five times in the text, and many important items are thus omitted. Apart from their usual short title, a few works have been given a second and greatly abbreviated form to facilitate reference in the personal- and place-name entries of Parts II and III (for example, *P* instead of *Pipe Roll*); these specially shortened forms appear in the following list with an appropriate cross-reference. For further explanation of the abbreviations used in Parts II and III, see below, p. 143, n. 1.

a	*ante*
AB	*Analecta Bollandiana*
Abbreviatio Placitorum	G. Rose and W. Illingworth (eds.), *Abbreviatio Placitorum Richard I–Edward II* (Rec Comm, 1811)
AC	J. H. Round (ed.), *Ancient charters, royal and private, prior to A.D. 1200* (PRS, 10, 1888)
Ælfric	G. I. Needham (ed.), *Ælfric: Lives of Three English Saints* (London, 1966), 60–81 [Life of Swithun]
Adigard	J. Adigard des Gautries, *Les Noms de personnes scandinaves en Normandie de 911 à 1066* (Nomina germanica, 11, Lund, 1954)
AGC	L. Musset (ed.), *Les Actes de Guillaume le Conquérant et de la reine Mathilde pour les abbayes caennaises* (Mém. de la Soc. des Antiquaires de Normandie, 37, Caen, 1967)
Agric HR	*Agricultural History Review*
Anglia Sacra	H. Wharton (ed.), *Anglia Sacra sive Collectio Historiarum* (2 vols., London, 1691)
Antiq J	*Antiquaries Journal*
Arch J	*Archaeological Journal*
arr.	*arrondissement*
ASC	C. Plummer (ed.), *Two of the Saxon chronicles parallel* (2 vols., Oxford, 1892–9, reprinted 1952)
AS Ch	A. J. Robertson (ed.), *Anglo-Saxon Charters* (Cambridge, 1939)
Ass	Assize Rolls: PRO, Just 1
AS Wills	D. Whitelock (ed.), *Anglo-Saxon Wills* (Cambridge, 1930)
AS Writs	F. E. Harmer (ed.), *Anglo-Saxon Writs* (Manchester, 1952)
Barlow *English Church*	F. Barlow, *The English Church 1000–1066: A Constitutional History* (London, 1963)
Bayeux	V. Bourrienne (ed.), *Antiquus cartularius ecclesiae Baiocensis* (2 vols., Rouen and Paris, 1902–3)
BCS	W. de Gray Birch (ed.), *Cartularium Saxonicum* (3 vols. and index, London, 1885–99)
BEH	B. E. Hildebrand, *Anglosachsiska mynt i svenska kongliga myntkabinettet* (Stockholm, 1881)
Bergh	Å. Bergh, *Études d'anthroponymie provençale*, i (Göteborg, 1941)

BHL	*Bibliotheca Hagiographica Latina Antiquae et Mediae Aetatis* (Socii Bollandiani, Subsidia Hagiographica, 6, 2 vols., Brussels, 1898–1901; Supplement-ibid. 12, 1911)
Birch *Ancient Manuscript*	W. de Gray Birch (ed.), *An Ancient Manuscript* (HRS, London and Winchester, 1889)
Björkman	See *NPN*
Black Book	W. H. B. Bird (ed.), *The Black Book of Winchester* (Winchester, 1925)
Bl Bk	See *Black Book*
BM	British Museum
BMC	See *BMC Anglo-Saxon kings* and *BMC Norman kings*
BMC Anglo-Saxon kings	C. F. Keary and H. A. Grueber, *A catalogue of English coins in the British Museum. Anglo-Saxon series* (2 vols., London, 1887–93)
BMC Henry II	D. F. Allen, *A catalogue of English coins in the British Museum. The Cross-and-Crosslets* ('*Tealby*') *Type of Henry II* (London, 1951)
BMC Norman kings	G. C. Brooke, *A catalogue of English coins in the British Museum. The Norman kings* (2 vols., London, 1916)
BNJ	*British Numismatic Journal*
Boehler	M. Boehler, *Die altenglischen Frauennamen* (Germanische Studien, 98, Berlin, 1931)
Book of Fees	H. C. Maxwell-Lyte (ed.), *Liber Feodorum. The Book of Fees commonly called the Testa de Nevill* (2 vols. and index, London, 1920–31)
Brooke *Missionary*	C. N. L. Brooke, 'The missionary at home: the church in the towns, 1000–1250', in G. J. Cuming (ed.), *The Mission of the Church and Propagation of the Faith* (Studies in Church History 6, Cambridge, 1970), 59–83.
BT	J. Bosworth and T. N. Toller, *An Anglo-Saxon dictionary* (Oxford, 1898–1921)
Bury	D. C. Douglas (ed.), *Feudal documents from the abbey of Bury St. Edmunds* (London, 1932). See Addenda.
Bury S	R. H. C. Davis (ed.), *The kalendar of Abbot Samson of Bury St. Edmunds* (Camden 3rd ser. 84, London, 1954)
byn.	byname
CA	*Current Archaeology*
Cal Chart R	*Calendar of Charter Rolls* (6 vols., London, 1903–27). For earlier charter rolls, see *Rot Chart*.
Cal Close R	*Calendar of Close Rolls* (in progress, London, 1900–). For earlier close rolls, see *Close R*.
Cal Mem R 1326–7	*Calendar of Memoranda Rolls 1326–1327* (London, 1968)
Cal Pat R	*Calendar of Patent Rolls* (in progress, London, 1891–). The first two vols. for Henry III print the full texts.
Camden OS, NS, and 3rd ser.	Camden Society, old series and new series; Royal Historical Society, Camden third series
Campbell	A. Campbell, *Old English grammar* (Oxford, 1959)
cant.	*canton*
Clark Hall	J. R. Clark Hall, *A concise Anglo-Saxon dictionary* (3rd edn., Cambridge, 1960)
Close R	*Close Rolls, Henry III* (14 vols., London, 1902–38). For later rolls, see *Cal Close R*
Colvin (ed.) *King's Works*	R. Allen Brown, H. M. Colvin, and A. J. Taylor, *The History of the King's Works*, i–ii, *The Middle Ages* (ed. H. M. Colvin, 2 vols. and portfolio, London, 1963)
cont.	continental

Cur	See *Curia Regis R*
Curia Regis R	*Curia Regis Rolls* (in progress, London, 1923–)
DaGP	G. Knudsen and M. Kristensen (eds.), *Danmarks gamle Personnavne* (Copenhagen, 1936–64)
Dauzat	A. Dauzat, *Dictionnaire étymologique des noms de famille et prénoms de France* (Paris, 1951)
Dauzat–Rostaing	A. Dauzat and C. Rostaing, *Dictionnaire étymologique des noms de lieux en France* (Paris, 1963)
DB	Domesday Book (the manuscript)
DB	A. Farley and H. Ellis (eds.), *Liber censualis vocatus Domesday-Book* (Rec Comm, 4 vols., 1783–1816)
DB Ex	*Exon Domesday*, see *DB*, vol. iv.
DBS	P. H. Reaney, *Dictionary of British surnames* (London, 1958)
DB StP	W. H. Hale (ed.), *The Domesday of St. Paul's of the year 1222* (Camden OS 69, London, 1858)
DEPN	E. Ekwall, *The concise Oxford dictionary of English place-names* (4th ed., Oxford, 1960)
Deville *Ste Trinité*	J. A. Deville (ed.) *Cartulaire de l'abbaye de la Ste Trinité du Mont de Rouen* (Paris, 1841, being pp. 402–87 of B. Guérard (ed.), *Cartulaire de l'abbaye de Saint Bertin*)
DGSEE	H. C. Darby and E. M. J. Campbell (eds.), *The Domesday Geography of South-East England* (Cambridge, 1962)
Dialogus de Scaccario	Charles Johnson (ed.), *Dialogus de Scaccario* (London, 1950)
DM	D. C. Douglas (ed.), *The Domesday Monachorum of Christ Church, Canterbury* (London, 1944)
DNB	*Dictionary of National Biography*
Drevin	H. Drevin, *Die französischen Sprachelemente in den lateinischen Urkunden des 11. und 12. Jahrhunderts* (dissertation, Halle, 1912)
Du Cange	C. Du Cange, *Glossarium mediae et infimae Latinitatis* (Niort, 1883–7)
Earle	J. Earle (ed.), *A handbook to the land-charters and other Saxonic documents* (Oxford, 1888)
Econ HR	*Economic History Review*
EDD	J. Wright, *The English dialect dictionary* (Oxford, 1888–95)
EETS	Early English Text Society
EHR	*English Historical Review*
Ekwall	See *DEPN, ELPN*
Ekwall *Genitive*	E. Ekwall, *Studies on the genitive of groups in English* (Lund, 1943)
Ekwall *PNLa*	E. Ekwall, *The place-names of Lancashire* (Manchester, 1922)
Ekwall *SNCL*	E. Ekwall, *Street-names of the City of London* (Oxford, 1954, corr. reprint 1965)
Ekwall *Studies*	E. Ekwall, *Studies on English place-names* (Stockholm, 1936)
Ekwall *Subs R*	E. Ekwall, *Two early London subsidy rolls* (Lund, 1951)
el.	element
Ellis	The printed text of the Winton Domesday published by Sir Henry Ellis in 1816 in *DB* iv. 531–63
Ellis *Introduction*	H. Ellis, *A general introduction to Domesday Book accompanied by indexes* (2 vols., London, 1833)
ELPN	E. Ekwall, *Early London personal names* (Lund, 1947)

English Binding	G. D. Hobson, *English Binding before 1500* (Cambridge, 1929)
English Coins	G. C. Brooke, *English Coins* (3rd edn., London, 1950)
English Hammered Coinage	J. J. North, *English Hammered Coinage*, i, *Early Anglo-Saxon to Henry III, c. 650–1272* (London, 1963)
EPN	A. H. Smith, *English place-name elements*, i–ii (EPNS 25, 26, Cambridge, 1956)
EPNS	English place-name society. Publications.
f.	feminine (when placed after a personal name or noun)
Fellows Jensen	G. Fellows Jensen, *Scandinavian personal names in Lincolnshire and Yorkshire* (Copenhagen, 1968)
FEW	W. von Wartburg, *Französisches etymologisches Wörterbuch* (in progress, Bonn, 1928–)
FF	Feet of Fines, PRO, CP 25 [Hampshire]
Fine R	T. D. Hardy (ed.), *Rotuli de Oblatis et Finibus . . . temp. Regis Johannis* (Rec Comm, 1835)
Finn *Norman Conquest*	R. Welldon Finn, *The Norman Conquest and its effects on the economy 1066–86* (London, 1971)
Forcellini	Ae. Forcellini, *Totius Latinitatis lexicon* [and] *Onomasticon* (Prato and Padova, 1858–1940)
Forssner	T. Forssner, *Continental-Germanic personal names in England* (Uppsala, 1916)
Förstemann	E. Förstemann, *Altdeutsches Namenbuch* (2 vols., Bonn, 1900–16)
France	J. H. Round (ed.), *Calendar of documents preserved in France*, i, *918–1206* (London, 1899)
Fransson	G. Fransson, *Middle English surnames of occupation 1100–1350* (Lund, 1935)
Furley *City Government*	J. S. Furley, *City Government of Winchester From the Records of the XIV & XV Centuries* (Oxford, 1923) [titled on spine *Winchester Records*]
Furley *Usages*	J. S. Furley, *The Ancient Usages of the City of Winchester* (Oxford, 1927)
Gesta Pontificum	N. E. S. A. Hamilton (ed.), *Willelmi Malmesbiriensis monachi de gestis pontificum Anglorum* (RS, 1870)
Gesta Regum	W. Stubbs (ed.), *Willelmi Malmesbiriensis monachi de gestis regum Anglorum . . .* (2 vols., RS, 1887–9)
Gesta Stephani	K. R. Potter (ed.), *Gesta Stephani* (London, 1955)
Godefroy	F. Godefroy, *Dictionnaire de l'ancienne langue française* (Paris, 1880–1902)
Godstow Cart	The MS. (PRO, E164/1/20) and not the English abstract printed by EETS, for which see *Godstow Cart*.
Godstow Cart	A. Clark, *The English Register of Godstow Nunnery* (3 vols., EETS, 129–30, 142, London, 1905–11)
Goodman *Chartulary*	A. W. Goodman (ed.), *Chartulary of Winchester Cathedral* (Winchester, 1927)
Goodman *Goodbegot*	A. W. Goodman, *The Manor of Goodbegot in the City of Winchester* (Winchester, [1923])
Gröhler	H. Gröhler, *Über Ursprung und Bedeutung der französischen Ortsnamen* (2 vols., Heidelberg, 1913, 1933)
Hallqvist	H. Hallqvist, *Studies in Old English fractured 'ea'* (Lund, 1948)
Harl. MS.	Harleian manuscript [British Museum]
HBS	Henry Bradshaw Society
HE	Bede, *Historia Ecclesiastica Gentis Anglorum*, in C. Plummer (ed.), *Venerabilis Baedae Opera Historica* (2 vols., Oxford, 1896)

Hemmeon *Burgage Tenure*	M. de Wolf Hemmeon, *Burgage Tenure in medieval England* (Cambridge, Mass., 1914)
Historia Novella	K. R. Potter (ed.), *The Historia Novella by William of Malmesbury* (London, 1955)
HMC	Historical Manuscripts Commission
HMC vi	HMC, *Sixth Report*, part 1 (London, 1877), Appendix, pp. 595–605 [the Corporation of Winchester], with many extracts from the medieval archives of the city
Hobson	See *English Binding*
Holtzmann	W. Holtzmann (ed.), *Papsturkunden in England* (3 vols., Berlin and Göttingen, 1930–52)
HRO	Hampshire Record Office
HRS	Hampshire Record Society
Huguet	E. Huguet, *Dictionnaire de la langue française du 16ᵉ siècle* (Paris, 1925–67)
Hyde Cart	BM, Harl. MS. 1761
I Interim, II Interim, etc.	Martin Biddle, Interim reports on the Winchester excavations 1961–71, in *Arch J* (*I Interim*) and *Antiq J* (*II–X Interim*) as follows:

I Interim (1961 season), *Arch J*, 119 (1962), 150–94 (with R. N. Quirk)
II Interim (1962 and 1963 seasons), *Antiq J* 44 (1964), 188–219
III Interim (1964 season), ibid. 45 (1965), 230–64
IV Interim (1965 season), ibid. 46 (1966), 308–32
V Interim (1966 season), ibid. 47 (1967), 251–79
VI Interim (1967 season), ibid. 48 (1968), 250–84
VII Interim (1968 season), ibid. 49 (1969), 295–329
VIII Interim (1969 season), ibid. 50 (1970), 277–326
IX Interim (1970 season), ibid. 52 (1972), 93–131
X Interim (1971 season), ibid. 55 (1975), 96–126, and forthcoming

Inventory	J. D. A. Thompson, *Inventory of British Coin Hoards, A.D. 600–1500* (Royal Numismatic Society, Special Publications 1, London, 1956)
Ipm	*Inquisitio post mortem* [cf. PRO, C 132–6 and 142]
Jackson	K. H. Jackson, *Language and history in early Britain* (Edinburgh, 1953)
Jacobsson	H. Jacobsson, *Etudes d'anthroponymie lorraine* (Göteborg, 1955)
*JBAA*¹	*Journal of the British Archaeological Association* (1st ser. etc.)
Jordan	R. Jordan, *Handbuch der mittelenglischen Grammatik* (2. Aufl. bearb. von H. C. Matthes, Heidelberg, 1934)
JTS	*Journal of Theological Studies*
Jumièges	J. J. Vernier (ed.), *Chartes de l'abbaye de Jumièges* (2 vols., Rouen and Paris, 1916)
Kalbow	W. Kalbow, *Die germanischen Personennamen des altfranzösischen Heldenepos und ihre lautliche Entwicklung* (Halle, 1913)
Kaufmann *Erg.-Bd*	H. Kaufmann, *Ernst Förstemann: Altdeutsche Personennamen, Ergänzungsband* (Munich, 1968)
Kaufmann *Unters.*	H. Kaufmann, *Untersuchungen zu altdeutschen Rufnamen* (Munich, 1968)
KCD	J. M. Kemble (ed.), *Codex diplomaticus aevi saxonici* (6 vols., London, 1839–48)
Keene *Brooks Area*	D. J. Keene, 'The Brooks Area of Medieval Winchester' (unpublished, Oxford D.Phil. thesis, 1972)
Ker *Catalogue*	N. R. Ker, *Catalogue of Manuscripts containing Anglo-Saxon* (Oxford, 1957)
Ker *Libraries*	N. R. Ker, *Medieval Libraries of Great Britain* (2nd ed., London, 1964)
King's Serjeants	J. H. Round, *The King's Serjeants and Officers of State* (London, 1911)

Knowles and Hadcock	D. Knowles and R. N. Hadcock, *Medieval Religious Houses: England and Wales* (London, 1953)
Kökeritz	H. Kökeritz, *The place-names of the Isle of Wight* (Uppsala, 1940)
Langlois	E. Langlois, *Table des noms propres de toute nature compris dans les chansons de geste* (Paris, 1904)
Lantfred	E. P. Sauvage (ed.), *Sancti Swithuni . . . Translatio et Miracula auctore Lantfredo . . .* (Brussels, 1885, separately [pp. 1–52], and in *AB* 4 (1885), 367–410)
Lasch–Borchling	A. Lasch and C. Borchling, *Mittelniederdeutsches Handwörterbuch* (in progress, Hamburg 1928–)
Latham	R. E. Latham, *Revised medieval Latin word-list from British and Irish sources* (London, 1965)
Lebel	P. Lebel, *Les Noms de personnes en France* (5e éd., Que-sais-je?, 235, Paris, 1962)
Le Neve *Monastic Cathedrals 1066–1300*	John Le Neve, *Fasti Ecclesiae Anglicanae 1066–1300*, ii, *Monastic Cathedrals* (compiled by Diana E. Greenway, London, 1971)
Le Neve *St. Paul's, London, 1066–1300*	John Le Neve, *Fasti Ecclesiae Anglicanae 1066–1300*, i, *St. Paul's, London* (compiled by Diana E. Greenway, London, 1968)
Liber de Hyda	E. Edwards (ed.), *Liber Monasterii de Hyda* (RS, 1866)
Lib. Land.	J. Rhys and J. G. Evans (ed.), *Liber Landavensis* (Oxford, 1893)
Löfvenberg	M. Löfvenberg, *Studies on Middle English local surnames* (Lund, 1942)
Loyd	L. C. Loyd, *The origins of some Anglo-Norman families* (Harleian Soc. 103, Leeds, 1951)
Luick	K. Luick, *Historische Grammatik der englischen Sprache* (Leipzig, 1914–40)
LVD	J. Stevenson (ed.), *Liber Vitae ecclesiae Dunelmensis* (Surtees Soc. 13, London, 1841; facs. ed., London, 1923)
LVH	W. de Gray Birch (ed.), *Liber Vitae: Register and Martyrology of New Minster and Hyde Abbey, Winchester* (HRS, London and Winchester, 1892)
LW	*Liber Wintoniensis* [used in Part II only, to indicate the printed text of the Winton Domesday published in this volume]
m.	masculine
Malmesbury Reg	J. S. Brewer and C. T. Martin (eds.), *The Register of Malmesbury Abbey* (2 vols., RS, 1879–80)
Mansion	J. Mansion, *Oud-Gentsche naamkunde* (The Hague, 1924)
MED	H. Kurath *et al.* (eds.), *Middle English dictionary* (in progress, Ann Arbor, 1956–)
Med Arch	*Medieval Archaeology*
Mensing	O. Mensing, *Schleswig-holsteinisches Wörterbuch* (Neumünster, 1927–35)
MGH	*Monumenta Germaniae Historica*
Michaëlsson	K. Michaëlsson, *Études sur les noms de personnes françaises d'après les rôles de taille parisiens* (2 vols., Uppsala, 1927–36)
Milner[1–3]	John Milner, *The History Civil and Ecclesiastical, & Survey of the Antiquities, of Winchester* (1st edn., Winchester, i (1798), ii (1799)). The second edition, corrected and enlarged to 1809, appeared in that year; and a third edition, with supplementary notes to 1839, was published in 1839.
MLN	*Modern Language Notes*
mon.	moneyer
Monasticon	William Dugdale, *Monasticon Anglicanum* (eds. J. Caley, H. Ellis, and B. Badinel, 6 vols. in 8 parts, London, 1817–30)
Morlet	M.-T. Morlet, *Les Noms de personnes sur le territoire de l'ancienne Gaule du VIe au XIIe siècle*, i (Paris, 1968)

Morlet *Étude*	M.-T. Morlet, *Étude d'anthroponymie picarde* (Coll. de la Soc. de linguistique picarde, 6, Amiens, 1967)
MRSN	T. Stapleton (ed.), *Magni rotuli scaccarii Normanniae sub regibus Angliae* (2 vols., London, 1840–4)
MS.	manuscript
NED	*A New English Dictionary* (Oxford 1888–1933)
Niermeyer	J. F. Niermeyer, *Mediae Latinitatis lexicon minus* (in progress, Leiden, 1954–)
NoB	*Namn och bygd. Tidskrift för nordisk ortnamnsforskning*
NPN	E. Björkman, *Nordische Personennamen in England* (Halle, 1910)
Nth Ass	D. M. Stenton (ed.), *The earliest Northamptonshire assize rolls, A.D. 1202* (Northampton, 1930)
Nth Ch	F. M. Stenton (ed.), *Facsimiles of early charters from Northamptonshire collections* (Northampton, 1930)
Num Chron[1]	*Numismatic Chronicle* (1st ser., etc.)
Obedientiary Rolls	G. W. Kitchen (ed.), *Compotus Rolls of the Obedientiaries of St. Swithun's Priory, Winchester* (HRS, London and Winchester, 1892)
Obed R	See *Obedientiary Rolls*
OE	Old English
ONFr	Old Northern French
OS	Ordnance Survey
P	See *Pipe Roll*
p	*post*; patronymic
Pachnio	R. Pachnio, *Die Beinamen der Pariser Steuerrolle von 1292* (dissertation, Königsberg, 1909)
patr.	patronymic
pers.n(s)	personal name(s)
Pipe Roll 31 Henry I, etc.	The printed Pipe Rolls (PRO, E372) published by the PRS from 5 Henry II onwards (in progress, London, 1884–) and by the Rec Comm, 31 Henry I, 2–4 Henry II, and 1 Richard I (ed. J. Hunter, 1833 and 1844). In Parts II and III of the present volume, *P* and P refer to printed and manuscript Pipe Rolls respectively.
pl.n(s)	place-name(s)
PNC, etc.	*The Place-Names of Cambridgeshire* and other county monographs of the EPNS [for county abbreviations, see below, pp. 143, n. 1]
PNDB	O. von Feilitzen, *The pre-Conquest personal names of Domesday Book* (Uppsala, 1937)
Pokorny	J. Pokorny, *Indogermanisches etymologisches Wörterbuch* (2 vols., Bern, 1949–69)
Pope	M. K. Pope, *From Latin to modern French* (2nd edn., Manchester, 1952)
PRBW	MS. Pipe Rolls of the Bishopric of Winchester in HRO
PRBW	See *PRBW 1210–11* [this abbreviation used only in Part II]
PRBW 1208–9	H. Hall (ed.), *The Pipe Roll of the Bishopric of Winchester, 1208–1209* (London, 1903)
PRBW 1210–11	N. R. Holt (ed.), *The Pipe Roll of the Bishopric of Winchester, 1210–11* (Manchester, 1964)
PRO	Public Record Office
	The following classes have been referred to in this volume by their official call numbers:
C 132–6, 142	Chancery, Inquisitions *post mortem*
C 143	Chancery, Inquisitions *ad quod damnum*

PRO (*cont.*):
CP 25	Court of Common Pleas, Feet of Fines
E 101	Exchequer, Accounts, Various
E 159	Exchequer, King's Remembrancer, Memoranda Rolls
E 164	Exchequer, King's Remembrancer, Miscellaneous Books, Series I
E 179	Exchequer, King's Remembrancer, Subsidy Rolls, etc.
E 198	Exchequer, King's Remembrancer, Documents Relating to Sergeanties, Knight's Fees, etc.
E 326	Exchequer, Augmentations, Ancient Deeds, Series B
E 372	Exchequer, Pipe Office, Pipe Rolls
Just 1	Justices Itinerant, Eyre Rolls, etc.
SC 6	Special Collections, Ministers' and Receivers' Accounts

Proc Hants FC	*Proceedings of the Hampshire Field Club and Archaeological Society*
PRS	Pipe Roll Society
PRS	Publications of the Pipe Roll Society
Quirk *OM*	R. N. Quirk, 'Winchester Cathedral in the tenth century', *Arch J* 114 (1957), 28–68
RADN	M. Faroux (ed.), *Recueil des actes des ducs de Normandie de 911 à 1066* (Mém. de la Soc. des Antiquaires de Normandie, 36, Caen, 1961)
RAH	É. Berger (ed.), *Recueil des actes de Henri II, roi d'Angleterre et duc de Normandie* (3 vols. and introd., Chartes et diplômes relatifs à l'histoire de France, Paris, 1909–27)
RBE	H. Hall (ed.), *The Red Book of the Exchequer* (3 vols., RS, 1896)
RCHM	Royal Commission on Historical Monuments
Reaney	See *DBS*
Reaney *Origin*	P. H. Reaney, *The Origin of English Surnames* (London, 1967)
Rec Comm	Record Commissioners
Redin	M. Redin, *Studies on uncompounded personal names in Old English* (Uppsala, 1919)
Reg	See *Regesta*
Regesta	H. W. C. Davis, R. H. C. Davis, H. A. Cronne, and C. Johnson (eds.), *Regesta regum Anglo-Normannorum* (4 vols., Oxford, 1913–69)
Reg Pontissara, etc.	Registers (both MS. and printed) of the bishops of Winchester in chronological order of bishops, as follows:
Reg Pontissara	C. Deedes (ed.), *Registrum Johannis de Pontissara Episcopi Wyntoniensis* (Canterbury and York Society, London, 19 (1915) and 30 (1924))
Reg Sandale ⎱ *Reg Assier* ⎰	F. J. Baigent (ed.), *The Registers of John de Sandale and Rigaud de Asserio, Bishops of Winchester* (HRS, London and Winchester, 1897)
Reg Stratford	HRO, MS. Register of John de Stratford
Reg Edington	HRO, MS. Register of William of Edington, 2 vols.
Reg Wykeham	T. F. Kirby (ed.), *Wykeham's Register* (2 vols., HRS, London and Winchester 1896–9)
Reg Wolsey	F. T. Madge and H. Chitty (eds.), *Registrum Thome Wolsey Cardinalis Ecclesie Wintoniensis Administratoris* (Canterbury and York Society, London, 32 (1926))
RH	W. Illingworth and J. Caley (eds.), *Rotuli hundredorum* (2 vols., Rec Comm, 1812–18)
Richardson and Sayles	H. G. Richardson and G. O. Sayles, *The Governance of Mediaeval England* (Edinburgh, 1963)
Rom.	Romance

Rot Chart	T. D. Hardy (ed.), *Rotuli Chartarum in Turri Londinensi asservati, 1199–1216* (Rec Comm, 1837). For later rolls see *Cal Chart R.*
Rot Litt Claus	T. D. Hardy (ed.), *Rotuli Litterarum Clausarum in Turri Londinensi asservati* (2 vols., Rec Comm, 1833–44)
RS	Rolls Series
Rubin	S. Rubin, *The phonology of the Middle English dialect of Sussex* (Lund, 1951)
Rymer's Foedera	T. D. Hardy (ed.), *Rymer's Foedera: Syllabus, in English, with Index* (3 vols. PRO, 1869–85)
s.a.	*sub anno*
Sanders *Baronies*	I. J. Sanders, *English Baronies. A Study of their Origin and Descent 1086–1327* (Oxford, 1960)
Sawyer (followed by number of charter)	P. H. Sawyer, *Anglo-Saxon Charters* (London, 1968)
SCBI	*Sylloge of the coins of the British Isles,* 1– (in progress, London, 1958–)
Schiller–Lübben	K. Schiller and A. Lübben, *Mittelniederdeutsches Wörterbuch* (Bremen, 1875–81)
Seals	L. C. Loyd and D. M. Stenton (eds.), *Sir Christopher Hatton's Book of Seals* (Northampton Record Society, 15, Oxford, 1950)
Searle	W. G. Searle, *Onomasticon Anglo-Saxonicum* (Cambridge, 1897)
Selborne Charters	W. D. Macray (ed.), *Charters and Documents relating to Selborne and its Priory* (HRS, London and Winchester, 1891)
Sievers–Brunner	K. Brunner, *Altenglische Grammatik nach der angelsächsischen Grammatik von Eduard Sievers* (3rd edn., Tübingen, 1965)
SMS	*Studier i modern språkvetenskap* (Stockholm)
SMW	D. J. Keene, *Survey of Medieval Winchester* (Winchester Studies 2, in preparation). When *SMW* is followed by a key word, reference should be made to the index of *SMW*; when followed by a number, the reference is to a gazetteer entry in the body of the text.
s.n.	*sub nomine*
S NPh	*Studia neophilologica*
Souter	A. Souter, *Glossary of later Latin* (Oxford, 1949)
Southwick Cart	HRO, Southwick MS. Registers, nos. i–iii
StAug	G. J. Turner and H. E. Salter (eds.), *The Register of St. Augustine's abbey, Canterbury* (2 vols., London, 1915–24)
St. Catharine's Hill	C. F. C. Hawkes, J. N. L. Myres, and C. G. Stevens, *Saint Catharine's Hill, Winchester* (Winchester, 1930), separately and in *Proc Hants FC* 11 (1930)
St. Denis Cart	St. Denis cartulary: BM, Add. MS. 15314
Stenton *ASE*	F. M. Stenton, *Anglo-Saxon England* (3rd edn., Oxford, 1971)
Stephenson *BT*	Carl Stephenson, *Borough and Town. A study of urban origins in England* (Medieval Academy of America, publication 15, Cambridge, Mass., 1933)
StGreg	A. M. Woodstock (ed.), *Cartulary of the priory of St. Gregory, Canterbury* (Camden 3rd ser., 66, London, 1956)
Stowe 846	BM, Stowe MS. 846 [abstracts of enrolments of deeds in the Winchester city court, *c.* 1300 to *c.* 1500]
St. Wandrille	F. Lot, *Études critiques sur l'abbaye de Saint-Wandrille* (Paris, 1913)
Sundby	B. Sundby, *The dialect and provenance of the Middle English poem 'The Owl and the Nightingale'* (Lund, 1950)
Survey	The Winchester survey of 1285 printed below, Appendix I. 2, pp. 511–19
s.v.	*sub verbo* or *sub voce*

Tait *Medieval Borough*	J. Tait, *The Medieval English Borough* (Manchester, 1936)
Tavernier-Vereecken	C. Tavernier-Vereecken, *Gentse naamkunde van ca. 1000 tot 1253* (Tongres, 1968)
Tax	S. Ayscough and J. Caley, *Taxatio Ecclesiastica . . .* (Rec Comm, 1802)
Templars	B. A. Lees (ed.), *Records of the Templars in England in the twelfth century* (London, 1935)
Tengvik	G. Tengvik, *Old English bynames* (Uppsala, 1935)
Thuresson	B. Thuresson, *Middle English occupational terms* (Lund, 1950)
Tobler–Lommatzsch	A. Tobler and E. Lommatzsch, *Altfranzösisches Wörterbuch* (in progress, Berlin, 1925–)
TRE	*Tempore regis Edwardi*
TRW	*Tempore regis Willelmi*
Urry	See Urry *Canterbury*
Urry *Canterbury*	W. Urry, *Canterbury under the Angevin kings* (London, 1967)
Vallet	A. Vallet, *Les Noms de personnes du Forez et confins aux XIIe, XIIIe et XIVe siècles* (Paris, 1961)
var(r).	variant(s)
VCH	*The Victoria History of the Counties of England*
VCH Essex	i (1903)
VCH Hants	i (1900), ii (1912)
VCH Oxon.	ii (1907)
VCH Som.	ii (1911)
VCH Suffolk	ii (1907)
VCH Surrey	ii (1905)
VCH York	*City of York* (1961)
VE	J. Caley and J. Hunter (eds.), *Valor Ecclesiasticus temp. Henrici VIII . . .* (6 vols. and introd., Rec Comm, 1810–34)
Vetusta Monumenta	Society of Antiquaries of London, *Vetusta Monumenta quae ad rerum Britannicarum memoriam conservandam Societas . . . curavit* (London, 1747–1893; Indexes, 1810, 1897). Reference to this work in the present volume denotes the fascicule forming Pls. I–III with accompanying text [17 pp.] of vol. iii (1796), 'Description of the Hospital of St. Mary Magdalen, near Winchester . . . 1788'.
Vita Dunstani (auct. B)	See W. Stubbs (ed.), *Memorials of St Dunstan* (RS, 1874)
Waverley ann	*Annales monasterii de Waverleia*, in H. R. Luard (ed.), *Annales Monastici*, ii (RS, 1865), 127–411
WCA	Winchester City Archives (MSS. quoted by title of series and individual number or year, as applicable). Now housed in HRO
WCL	Winchester Cathedral Library (MSS. quoted by title of series and individual number, where applicable. 'Records' refers to vols. of this title into which medieval deeds have been pasted. 'Register' refers to an individual volume of the Registers of the Common Seal)
WCM	Winchester College Muniments (MSS. quoted by number)
Welbeck MS.	Titchfield register; Welbeck MS. I. A. 2 (BM, Loans 29/55 and 58)
William of Malmesbury	See *Historia Novella*, *Gesta Pontificum*, and *Gesta Regum*
Winchester ann	*Annales monasterii de Wintonia*, in H. R. Luard (ed.), *Annales Monastici*, ii (RS, 1865), 1–125
Winchester 1949–60, i	Barry Cunliffe (ed.), *Winchester Excavations 1949–60*, i (Winchester, 1964)
Winchester 1949–60, ii	John Collis (ed.), *Winchester Excavations 1949–60*, ii (Winchester, forthcoming)

Winchester Studies 2	See *SMW*
Winchester Studies 3. i	Martin Biddle, *Pre-Roman and Roman Winchester*: i, *Venta Belgarum* (Oxford, in preparation)
Winchester Studies 4	Martin Biddle and Birthe Kjølbye-Biddle, *The Old and New Minsters in Winchester* (Oxford, in preparation)
Winchester Studies 5	Martin Biddle and Edward Harris, *The Brooks and other town sites in medieval Winchester* (Oxford, in preparation)
Winchester Studies 7	Martin Biddle, Katherine Barclay, Suzanne Keene, *et al.*, *The Crafts and Industries of medieval Winchester* (Oxford, in preparation)
Winchester Studies 8	Yvonne Harvey *et al.*, *The Winchester Mint and other medieval numismatic studies* (Oxford, in preparation)
Withycombe	E. G. Withycombe, *The Oxford dictionary of English Christian names* (2nd edn., Oxford, 1950)
Worcester ann	*Annales monasterii de Wigornia* in H. R. Luard (ed.), *Annales Monastici*, iv (RS, 1869), 353–569
Wulfstan *Narratio Metrica*	Alistair Campbell (ed.), *Frithegodi monachi breuiloquium vitae beati Wilfredi et Wulfstani Cantoris narratio metrica de sancto Swithuno* (Thesaurus Mundi, Zürich, 1950)
c. 1110	Winton Domesday, Survey I
1148	Winton Domesday, Survey II
*	a reconstructed form [Parts II and III]
~	identical with the preceding form of the name [Parts II and III]

ACKNOWLEDGEMENTS

WE incurred many obligations in the writing of this book and have received every courtesy in reply to the demands we placed on our friends and colleagues and on the learned institutions in which we worked. We are most grateful to them all.

Our particular thanks are due to the President and Fellows of the Society of Antiquaries of London, among whose manuscripts the Winton Domesday has been preserved since 1790, for permission to undertake its publication, and for every facility during our work upon it. We would like especially to thank Mr. F. H. Thompson, Assistant Secretary, and Mr. John Hopkins, Librarian, for the ready help we have received from them.

Those who assisted us with place-names and numismatic matters are acknowledged in the appropriate places, but we would like to thank here those who allowed us to benefit from their knowledge and advice in other ways: Miss Anne Oakley, Mr. T. A. M. Bishop, Mr. J. M. G. Blakiston, Mr. Christopher Blunt, Professor Donald Bullough, Professor Kenneth Cameron, Dr. Pierre Chaplais, Mr. A. R. A. Hobson, Professor N. R. Ker, Dr. Michael Lapidge, Dr. Walter Oakeshott, Mr. Derek Renn, Mr. Alexander Rumble, Dr. Daniel Sheerin, Dr. William Urry, Professor Dorothy Whitelock, and Mr. Patrick Wormald.

We are especially grateful to Professor Dorothy Whitelock and Professor R. H. C. Davis for reading the proofs and for their extensive comments on Parts IV and V. We have tried to take full account of their remarks but we are entirely responsible for the errors that remain.

The librarians, archivists, and staff of the Bodleian Library, the British National Library, the Department of Manuscripts in the British Museum, the Hampshire Record Office, the Public Record Office, Winchester Cathedral Library, Winchester City Archives, and Winchester College Fellows Library and Muniments, have given us every assistance, as have the Hampshire County Library Service, Southampton University Library, and the Winchester City Library, upon all of whom we have placed particularly heavy demands. Philippa Stevens, of the Hampshire County Library, with the generous agreement of the Chief Librarian, compiled the index, a contribution for which we are especially grateful.

We would acknowledge also the generosity of the Trustees of the British Museum and the Dean and Chapter of Winchester Cathedral in allowing us to publish photographs and other illustrations of the bindings of manuscripts in their possession, and the Keeper of the Public Records and the Controller of Her Majesty's Stationery Office for permission to publish the manuscripts edited in Appendix I. Lastly, for emphasis, so far from being last, our own colleagues who have assisted at every stage in the production of the book: Marjorie Bowen for her interest in the work and unfailing help; Caroline Raison for her constant encouragement and cheerful revision of what had already been revised; and Kathleen Brown and Dorothy Gaukroger who helped out as deadlines approached.

To these, and to the many others whose thoughts at times must have followed those of the Winchester scribe who wrote *Explicit hoc totum, pro Christo da mihi potum*, our best thanks and appreciation.

PART I

THE WINTON DOMESDAY

I

INTRODUCTION

i. THE MANUSCRIPT

THESE two twelfth-century surveys of the borough of Winchester are contained in a contemporary vellum manuscript which now belongs to the Society of Antiquaries of London (MS. 154). There is no obvious indication of the whereabouts of the manuscript during the Middle Ages, but the marginal *notae* and other comments may be suggestive (Table 1). In each case the annotations refer to a property wholly or partly in the fee of the prior of St. Swithun's, and the word *sacrista'* against **II, 928** can only mean one of the sacristans of the priory, who had a wider interest in that area of the city.[1] It seems a reasonable assumption that the manuscript was kept in the cathedral priory during the Middle Ages and that it there received the few marginal annotations it now contains.[2]

When the manuscript was rebound in the first half of the nineteenth century a new vellum paste-down and facing end-leaf were inserted at each end. On the first paste-down is the bookplate of the Society of Antiquaries, with the shelf-mark 40.h., and above it, in ink in a nineteenth-century hand, is written 'Num. 154', the number the manuscript has borne since the publication of Sir Henry Ellis's *A Catalogue of Manuscripts in the Library of the Society of Antiquaries of London* in 1816. On the facing leaf is the number 120. After the first end-leaf and before the first leaf of the text are a pair of folio paper leaves folded and attached to a guard, with five compensating stubs. They bear a description of the manuscript in the hand of Charles Lyttleton (1714–68), dean of Exeter from 1748 to 1762, and subsequently bishop of Carlisle, who became President of the Society of Antiquaries in 1765. This is dated 'February 10th 1756'.

Beneath this date, at the foot of the recto of the second leaf of the pair, is a note signed

---

[1] See below, **II, 791,** n. Here and throughout the present volume, **I** and **II** refer to the surveys of *c.* 1110 and 1148 respectively.

[2] The reference by Thomas Rudborne (*Anglia Sacra*, i. 257) to a copy of Domesday Book in the cathedral treasury at Winchester might conceivably be taken as an elliptical reference to the present manuscript, but is more likely a confused memory of one of the now famous references to the keeping of Domesday Book in the royal treasury at Winchester.

'Gustavus Brander ["X^t church Hants" added in another hand] 17 May 1776' which reads:

> By a Memorandum which I have in my possession, I find that this Manuscript belongd formerly to Dean Young, made Dean of Winchester by King James Ist; who was son of Sir Peter Young of Seatoun in Scotland; preceptor to King James—Patricius Junius the famous Grecian was the Deans Brother, Library Keeper to King Charles Ist.[1]

At the upper right hand corner of the first leaf of the text is written 'J. West. 1756' (Frontispiece).

John Young (1585–1655) was appointed to the deanery of Winchester in 1616 and remained there until he was expelled in 1645. If, as seems possible, the Winton Domesday

TABLE 1
Marginal notes in the Winton Domesday

Folio	Entry	Sign	Property/tenant	In whose fee
Survey I				
2^v	23	Pointing hand	Godbegot	Prior of St. Swithun's
Survey II				
14^v	42	Pointing hand and *Godebiete*	Godbegot	Prior of St. Swithun's
22^v (Pl. III)	478	*Nota* and marginal line	*Herbertus Westman*	Prior of St. Swithun's and the bishop of Salisbury
22^v (Pl. III)	479	*Nota* and marginal line	*Emma uxor Roberti*	Prior of St. Swithun's and Adelaide
24^r	551	*Nota*	*Anschetillus Buclar'*	Prior of St. Swithun's
25^r	603	*Nota*	*Heredes Gunt'*	Prior of St. Swithun's
26^v	674	*pratum*	*Turstinus*	Prior of St. Swithun's and the bishop of Winchester
26^v	687	*.w. monat'*	*Robertus Pinguis*	Prior of St. Swithun's
30^v	928	*sacrista'*	King's Gate	Prior of St. Swithun's

had formerly been preserved among the cathedral muniments, the dean may have borrowed it or taken it into safe keeping during the troubles of the 1640s.[2] It is not listed among the records recovered by John Chase, the chapter clerk, after the Muniment House had been 'defaced and spoyled and divers writings taken away' by the army in 1642 and 1646,[3] but this is not surprising for the dean at one time had one of the Chapter Books in his possession which he apparently never returned.[4] This too was the case with the present manuscript. It descended among a large trunkful of the dean's papers to his grand-daughter, and then to her nephew, John Bailey, rector of South Cadbury, Somerset, who discovered and identified the manuscript in 1739. Announcing his find

[1] The memorandum referred to was probably the original or a copy of the letter of 11 Sept. 1739 (see below, p. 3, n. 1) which contains most of this information. The rest could have been added from Brander's general knowledge.

[2] There is no reference to the Winton Domesday in Patrick Young's list of books in the cathedral library compiled c. 1622 (WCL, MS. XIX). The list contains only fifteen items and does not include volumes of a financial character. For the date and provenance of this and other lists by Young of the contents of cathedral libraries, see Ivor Atkins and Neil R. Ker (eds.), *Catalogus Librorum Manuscriptorum Bibliothecae Wigorniensis . . . by Patrick Young . . .* (Cambridge, 1944).

[3] W. R. W. Stephens and F. T. Madge, *Documents relating to the history of the Cathedral Church of Winchester in the seventeenth century* (HRS, 1897), 57.

[4] F. R. Goodman (ed.), *The diary of John Young S.T.P. Dean of Winchester* (London, 1928), 28.

to Browne Willis that September, Bailey inquired whether 'you think this a piece of antiquity worth your notice'.[1]

The manuscript next emerged when it was exhibited to the Society of Antiquaries on 29 January 1756 by Dean Lyttleton,[2] as he then was, who also delivered a paper still preserved among the Society's correspondence.[3] From this it appears that the manuscript was now in the possession of James West. West, who had been elected a Fellow of the Society of Antiquaries in 1726, was not present at the meeting, for which he must have loaned the manuscript. It was perhaps for this occasion that he wrote his name in it over the date 1756.

James West (? 1704–72) held the office of joint-secretary to the Treasury from 1741 to 1768, was recorder of Poole, President of the Royal Society, and a Fellow of the Society of Antiquaries, but is now best remembered as a collector of pictures, prints, coins, antiquities, and books. His printed books were sold in a notable sale by Langford beginning on 29 March 1773, but his collection of early state papers and other records was bought privately by Lord Shelbourne, first Marquess of Lansdowne, and is now among the Lansdowne Manuscripts in the British Museum.[4] By contrast his illuminated manuscripts were dispersed at Langford's sale of West's 'Large and justly Admired Museum of Curiosities' commencing on 27 February 1773. '*Henry I. Domesday Book* for *Winchester*, with an Account thereof, by Bp. *Lyttleton, on vellum, very curious*' formed Lot 62 on the fourth day of the sale (3 March), and was purchased by Brander for six guineas.[5] Gustavus Brander (1720–87) was a London merchant, a Director of the Bank of England, and a Trustee of the British Museum. His books were sold by Leigh and Sotheby on 8 February 1790. The manuscript was lot 1170 and was bought on behalf of the Society of Antiquaries by John Topham, their treasurer, for five guineas.[6]

The text was printed by Sir Henry Ellis in 1816 together with other Domesday satellites in the fourth volume of the Record Commission's edition. It was accompanied by a facsimile of the first page of Survey I (fo. 1ʳ) and a brief introduction.[7] Already on its discovery in 1739 the manuscript was described as being 'in the same Manner as Domesday Book'.[8] Lyttleton called it 'K. H. 1st. Domesday of Winton City' in 1756;[9]

---

[1] Copy of a letter dated 11 Sept. 1739 from John Bailey to Browne Willis, in Antiquaries' Common Place Book, Soc. of Antiquaries, MS. 264, fo. 33 (new foliation). For Bailey, see Joseph Foster, *Alumni oxonienses . . . 1500–1714* (Oxford, 1891–2), s.n. Bayly.

[2] Soc. of Antiquaries, Minutes, vol. vii, p. 239.

[3] Soc. of Antiquaries, 1756 Papers. This paper, in the customary form of a letter addressed to the Fellows of the Society, is a slightly lengthier version of the note signed by Lyttleton on 10 Feb. 1756, which is now bound with the Winton Domesday. The note omits the last paragraph of the letter, dealing with *Sapalanda* (see below p. 238 s.n.), and replaces it with some conjectures as to why the survey was compiled. The substance of the letter and note was printed, with additional comments, by Richard Gough, *British Topography*, i (2nd edn., London, 1780), 388–9.

[4] S. de Ricci, *English collectors of books and manuscripts* (Cambridge, 1930), 51.

[5] One of the two copies of Langford's catalogue in the Dept. of Printed Books in the British Museum (C. 119. h. 3 (65)) has been annotated with the buyers' names and prices. Lot 62 has the additional manuscript note '24 Saxon Deeds were pasted on the Cover', presumably a reference to the Sacramentary leaves which Brander later detached, see below, pp. 526–7; cf. also p. 541, where Brander's own account of the acquisition of the manuscript and his subsequent investigation of its binding is quoted in full.

[6] Soc. of Antiquaries, Council Minutes, vol. iii, 19 Feb. 1790.

[7] Henry Ellis (ed.), *Liber Censualis vocatus Domesday-Book*, iv, *Additamenta ex Codic. Antiquiss* (London, 1816), xv–xvi, 531–62. His introduction relies heavily on Lyttleton via Gough (see above, n. 3).

[8] See above, n. 1.

[9] Soc. of Antiquaries, 1756 Papers.

at West's sale in 1773 it was 'Henry I. Domesday Book for Winchester';[1] and when the Society of Antiquaries acquired it in 1790 it was recorded as 'Winchester Domesday Book'.[2] Ellis turned these to its modern title, the Winton Domesday, in his introduction of 1816 and on his facsimile page, although his text is headed Liber Winton'. The manuscript has been referred to on many subsequent occasions, but the only study of any length devoted to it since 1816 has been J. H. Round's discussion of Survey I in the Victoria County History of Hampshire in 1900.[3]

The manuscript seems to have been written shortly after the date of Survey II (1148).[4] It consists of 33 leaves of vellum, 251 × 174 mm, the written space 185 × 125 mm., with 29 lines to the page in double column (Frontispiece, Pls. I–III). The 4 gatherings, each of 4 bifolia, have signatures a–f. There is one additional leaf (fo. 33). The pages are ruled on both sides in plummet, with vertical lines for the columns, those on the extreme left and right being double. The text is written in minuscule in a similar hand which occurs throughout the manuscript. The first column on fo. 1 and the first seven lines of col. 1 on fo. 13ᵛ (the beginning of Survey II) are in red. Sometimes the scribe's indication to the rubricator can be seen in the outer margin. The headings, names of streets, etc., are in red rustic capitals. Initials in Survey I are in red, in Survey II alternately red and blue. As Survey I ends on fo. 12ᵛ and Survey II begins on fo. 13ᵛ, the book was planned as a whole. It was copied, it seems, without much change from drafts which were occasionally incomplete: in Survey II gaps were left now and then for some missing information. Moreover, although the extant manuscript has been extensively corrected, some obvious errors remain and the gaps have not been filled.[5] Marginal crosses sometimes draw attention to a defect, but the rarity of marginal Notae, pointing fingers, or other annotations (Table 1), suggests that the manuscript was neither a working copy nor very much used. This is perhaps surprising in view of the magnificent binding with which it was provided, and may indicate that the production of the book was soon overtaken by other events, perhaps by the departure of Bishop Henry into exile in France in 1155.[6]

ii. THE EARLY TWELFTH-CENTURY BOROUGH[7]

Winchester was one of the fortified boroughs which Alfred and his successors had created to serve as defensive strongholds against invaders and as secure administrative and trading centres. Like other ancient boroughs it had no charter or any other formal authorization for its privileges. The king was the lord of the whole borough: it was a

---

[1] See above, p. 3, n. 5.   [2] See above, p. 3, n. 6.

[3] J. H. Round, 'The Survey of Winchester temp. Henry I', VCH Hants i. 527–37, with a facsimile of fo. 1ʳ, and photographs of the binding.

[4] For a full discussion of the manuscript and the handwriting, see below, p. 520. The manuscript is also described in N. R. Ker, Medieval Manuscripts in British Libraries, i, London (Oxford, 1969), 307; and in The New Palaeographical Society, 1st ser., vol. ii, pt. 1 (London, 1903–12), Pl. 212.

[5] For an account of the corrections, see below, pp. 522 ff.

[6] The binding and the binding leaves are discussed in full below, pp. 526 ff., by Mr. H. M. Nixon, who has also contributed to the account of the recent history of the manuscript in this section. The fragmentary tenth-century sacramentary written on the binding leaves is described below by Professor Francis Wormald, pp. 541 ff.

[7] The standard work is Tait Medieval Borough. See also F. W. Maitland, Township and Borough (Cambridge, 1898); Hemmeon Burgage Tenure; Urry Canterbury.

royal city. But kings had granted much of the property away, especially to the Church. In the twelfth century (and, no doubt, in the eleventh) the largest landholders in the city were the bishop of Winchester, the prior of the cathedral church, the abbot of New Minster (Hyde Abbey), and the abbess of St. Mary's. Other religious houses owned some property, and a few tenements were attached to rural manors and baronial fiefs. This 'tenurial heterogeneity' is characteristic of the Domesday borough.

The royal revenue came from ground-rents (landgable) and the profits of tolls, the borough court, and possibly of moneyers. It was collected by the king's servants in the city, two or more reeves. There is no evidence that by 1148 the citizens had acquired the privilege of electing their own reeves, but they may have managed their own affairs in other minor ways.[1] The reeves paid what they had collected, probably less customary deductions, to the sheriff or other 'farmer' who had agreed with the king on a fixed render (the 'farm'), and expected to make a profit on the transaction. The farm of Winchester is not known for the Norman period because the city is omitted not only from Domesday Book but also, owing to mutilation, from the Pipe Roll of 1130. In the early twelfth century it seems to have been £80 blanch (£84 by tale).[2] This can be compared with London's traditional farm of £300, and the £100 which both York and Lincoln rendered in 1086. The sheriff was actually farming the city for about £140 in the later 1150s, but even so the king then drew from the city in lands and profits only £20 more than the holders of the six other great fiefs received from lands alone.

A borough, like a rural township, had fixed boundaries and fell into two parts, the buildings with their curtilages and the surrounding agricultural lands. The borough's centre was protected by a bank and ditch, sometimes strengthened by a wall, so that there was a sharp physical distinction between the intra- and extra-mural areas. But the land enclosed by the walls was not completely covered by houses, shops, and industrial buildings: there were gardens, orchards, paddocks, yards, and waste spaces as well. And outside the walls, especially near the gates and along the approach roads, there were suburban developments. The borough, however, differed from the rural township because of the privileges it enjoyed, rights which, presumably, had once been granted by the king. The most important of these in the early twelfth century were, as in the pre-conquest period, possession of a market, a mint, and a borough court, and the enjoyment of a type of free tenure peculiar to boroughs. There was also an economic difference. The eleventh- and twelfth-century boroughs were trading and industrial centres, not farming communities. In the rural village there was usually a regular apportionment of agricultural land to the farmhouses—strips in the open fields, a share of the meadow, rights in the woodland, and pasture rights over the open fields and the waste. In the boroughs by the twelfth century the agricultural land was relatively unimportant, and, although some men still held both urban and agricultural property, the regular pattern

---

[1] See below, pp. 422–6.
[2] Tait *Medieval Borough*, 171. This is the allowance made for it in the county farm in the Pipe Rolls of Henry II, and represents an older state of affairs. But since the sheriff was actually farming the city for £142. 12s. 4d., it is possible that the earl's Third

Penny should be added to the £80 to give the total farm: £80 + £40 = £120 blanch (£126 by tale). As will be seen below, p. 27, landgable and stall tolls produced only about £10 of this. See further below, pp. 499–500.

had broken down. Specialization of interest and a free land market had produced variety and inequality. These two twelfth-century Winchester surveys seldom mention agricultural land;[1] and, indeed, Winchester is an extreme case, for the city seems never to have possessed open fields or common meadows. Although some of the wealthier citizens may have owned farms as well as urban tenements, and some of the poorer inhabitants of the suburbs may have found work as agricultural labourers, in the circumstances there could be no agricultural holdings or common rights attached to the tenements in the way found in some boroughs.

The Domesday terms for urban property are *masura* or *mansura* (manse), *mansio* (mansion), *domus* (house), and *haga* (haw). At Winchester, especially in Survey **II**, we have also *terra* (land) and *managium* (another noun from *manere*, to dwell). These terms can be translated tenements, messuages, land-holdings, properties, etc. They are often called by modern historians 'burgages', although the term *burgagium* occurs rarely in this sense in the twelfth century and does not occur in these Winchester surveys. Most of the Latin words suggest dwelling-houses rather than building plots; but they could be applied indifferently to the bare land, the house or houses on it, or to both.[2] They were also used for any part or parcel of the original messuage. Although the traditional property boundaries were very persistent, and at Winchester were hardly ever obliterated, urban property, because of the lack of restraints on the land market, economic changes, and the cheapness of labour and building materials, was most unstable. Within this basic framework tenements could be accumulated or divided in any way. Buildings could be moved or thrown down and rebuilt. Their use could be changed: dwelling-house, shops, booths, workshops, industrial yard, garden, a close for grazing animals—all these are possible uses to which a *domus* or *terra* could be put at different times or by successive owners. A building could be separated from its garden (*curtilagium*), and a house—cellar, solar, and attics—could be divided, horizontally, vertically, or in both ways, into a number of smaller tenements.[3] Houses could be broken up into, or faced by, shops. Shacks could be built in gardens. Contrariwise, several properties could be joined together, and a large house built where before were a number of smaller buildings.[4] By the twelfth century, therefore, properties were unequal in size and value, clear evidence that there was already a long history of true urban development. The properties varied from, at the one extreme, an attic room or a shop with a very narrow frontage and nothing behind in the shape of a garden, to, at the other, a large stone house with stabling and out-houses,

---

[1] Meadows are mentioned outside North Gate (**II, 357**) and in *Bucchestret* (**II, 674**).

[2] The same property is described as *mansurae* in *c.* 1110 (**I, 223**) and *terrae* in 1148 (**II, 680**). At Canterbury, Rental B (mid-twelfth century) has *mansurae*, Rental D (*c.* 1200) has *terrae*: Urry *Canterbury*, 187. But see also below, p. 7, n. 1, and further, pp. 13–14.

[3] In the Winchester surveys multiple rents (see below, p. 378 and Table 27) may frequently indicate the presence of a number of different occupiers, and sometimes we are told that the tenement has been divided (e.g. **I, 8, 14, 36,** and **42**). Outside West Gate properties had been turned into building plots

(e.g. **I, 82** and **86**), but there was no reason to record how individual buildings were divided up. However, the cellars in High Street, some of which had become forges (**I, 38** and **61–3**), must have been the basements of houses, or more likely their massively built and perhaps vaulted ground-floor levels. In Survey **II** there seems to be a list of rents of solars in High Street (**II, 152–8**).

[4] In *Brudenestret*, for example, Cheping, or his father Alwin, had put two messuages together and taken in the lane which had divided them (**I, 135**). Similarly Elsi the clerk had joined two messuages together (**I, 148–9**). For the evidence of Survey **II** in this respect, see below, p. 344.

set in spacious gardens, with a paddock for the horses and a wide gate out of which carts could be driven. Sometimes in these surveys it would appear that *domus*, *mansura*, *mansio*, *managium*, and *terra* are used as well in a more restricted, even technical, sense.[1] And there are some unequivocal technical terms, such as *bordellum* (shack or hut), *escheop* (shop), *estal*, *eschamel*, and *selda* (stall), *cellarius* (cellar, probably storehouse),[2] and *forgia* (forge).

What all these urban properties had in common (and the privilege seems to have been attached to all property within the boundaries, even to fractions of tenements and to agricultural land) was their 'burgage' tenure. This was designed to encourage the growth of a trading and manufacturing community. Land could be bought and sold,[3] even left by will, divided and accumulated, with the greatest freedom. In this respect it was in sharp contrast to land held in villeinage or by any feudal tenure. As a result of the active land market a large population developed which soon exhibited the mobility characteristic of big urban conglomerations of people. Relatively few properties can be identified from their holders (whether the same person or his heir) in both Survey I and Survey II, and there is only limited coincidence between the surveys and Winchester witness-lists of the period.[4] Bernard, a royal scribe who is known to have held Winchester property in Henry I's reign, does not occur in the surveys. The occupation of urban property seems to have been as transitory in the twelfth century as it is today.

The freeholder who held urban property in demesne as of fee was in theory the tenant of a lord. (Both Winchester surveys, like Domesday Book, are organized in a pattern which is a compromise between topographical and feudal forms.[5] The urban surveys are street by street; but everyone holds of someone, and all property pertains to somebody's fief. There is the royal fief or demesne, the bishop's fief, and so on. We also read of the king's burgesses; and obviously there are too the bishop's burgesses and the burgesses of other lords, both ecclesiastical and lay. It is to these lords that the tenement pays (and this is how it is expressed) landgable, the low, fixed, perpetual money-rent, often 5*d.* or 6*d.* a year, which is one of the main features of burgage tenure. These sums had never been large, and by the twelfth century with the depreciation of the currency they bore no relation to the rentable value of the tenement, which, indeed, was usually very much more. Landgable could be divided as the property was divided,[6] or could be attached in whole or in part to any fraction of the original messuage. Although

---

[1] Cf. 'L. held one *domus TRE* . . . Now . . . from that *terra* H. has one *mansura* . . .' (I, 4). In Survey II *managium* clearly has a technical meaning (see II, 197, 230, 245, 250, 293, 403, 421, 465, and 806); but no one has yet been able to give the word a precise significance. For further discussion of these technical terms, see below, p. 337.

[2] For this word, see above, p. 6, n. 3 and also below, p. 339.

[3] A good example of such a Winchester sale is in J. H. Round, 'Bernard the King's Scribe', *EHR* 14 (1899), 424. Thezo and his wife Rohesia, daughter of Ailric *de Cleindona*, sold their land and tenements (*domos*) in *Bucchestret*, which they held of the king,

for 2 marks of silver. The transaction took place in Henry I's reign, and the property may be identified with II, 669. Of the twenty-six persons who witnessed the payment for this property, four, and a close relative of a fifth, may be identified in the surveys; see I, 234 and II, 360, 669, 698, and 817.

[4] Round, *EHR* 14 (1899), 424; V. H. Galbraith, 'Royal Charters to Winchester', *EHR* 35 (1920), 382–400.

[5] For Domesday Book, see most recently Sally Harvey, 'Domesday Book and its predecessors', *EHR* 86 (1971), 735 ff.

[6] e.g. II, 226, where 4*d.* has been divided into 1¼*d.* and 2¾*d.*

it was not a very profitable custom, it was carefully recorded for boroughs in Domesday Book and is entered, although not often by name, in the Winchester surveys. Probably its special value was that it was an acknowledgement of dependency—it indicated whose burgess the man was—and so served to pin the responsibility for other liabilities. In the twelfth century, Winchester landlords probably levied small charges on the sale and purchase of properties on their fiefs;[1] but it is possible that escheat (for lack of an heir) and forfeiture (for crime) were the most lucrative perquisites of lordship. In this there is again sharp contrast with tenure in villeinage or feudal tenure. And although the tenements attached to extra-mural manors or baronial fiefs form a special category,[2] they were the means by which the outside world participated in borough privileges. Such tenements could serve as town houses or lodgings and were also valuable trading outlets. Through them agricultural produce could be sold in the borough and manufactured goods and luxuries bought there at the advantage reserved for burgesses.

Indeed it makes little economic, social, or political sense to describe the urban community in feudal terms. The Winchester surveys, since the first was made for the king, the second for the bishop, are concerned almost exclusively with the lords and their burgesses. This form, however, obscures the true picture, or at least the economic situation. It describes a relatively stable pattern which had little influence on the changing scene at the lower levels. Men bought and sold urban property at economic prices without much or any of the profit going to the feudal lord. When it was sold for a lump sum (*gersuma*), the vendor usually also retained a perpetual rent, either large or small. These rents could be bought and sold, or assigned, often to a religious house. Any rent could be burdened with a rent-charge to a third party, usually a religious corporation. An urban capitalist could, therefore, invest his money variously in the borough. He could buy tenements (intra- or extra-mural), rents, or rent-charges; he could put out money on mortgage. He could break properties up or join them together. It was a relatively sophisticated world in which lords had little more than rentrolls and estates varied from a shop of a few square feet to a portfolio of lucrative properties. By 1148, and indeed by 1110, most of these features can be seen at Winchester. What is more, there seems to be very little tenurial distinction at the burgess level. There is no clear division between on the one hand freeholders, burgesses 'owning' property, and on the other their tenants, holding at will or for a term of years. All men, except a few exceptionally favoured owners, paid rent to somebody for their property. And the one clear economic, and perhaps social, distinction was between those who only paid out—the occupiers—and those who also drew in—the landlords—although, of course, an occupier of one property could draw rents from other tenements. Social classes may have owed something to the presence of many royal and ecclesiastical officials in the city, but, beyond this, they owed most to wealth.

---

[1] The episcopal pipe rolls show that the bishop did this according to a standard scale both in the city and suburbs in the early thirteenth century (*PRBW 1208–9*, 77–8; *PRBW 1210–11*, 161–2). But the bishop was a landlord of exceptional authority in Winchester.

[2] e.g. **I, 152** and **156–7**: see below, p. 382 and Table 28.

iii. SURVEY I

The earlier survey has a heading and an explanatory preface. According to the latter, King Henry I (1100–35), wishing to recover those royal rights in his demesne in Winchester which King Edward had enjoyed, ordered the bishop of the city and four lay courtiers to put the burgesses on oath and make inquiry into the matter. Eighty-six of the more important burgesses were empanelled and sworn, and after they had taken the oath they began to make the inquiry. The report they produced is described as a list of the royal lands in Winchester which paid landgable and brewgable, just as they had done in Edward the Confessor's day. The survey can be dated fairly closely. William Giffard was appointed bishop of Winchester in 1100 and consecrated in 1107. Roger, bishop of Salisbury, mentioned in entry **75**, was given his bishopric in 1102 and likewise consecrated in 1107. The *terminus a quo* would seem to be 1102 × 1107. Bishop William died in 1129; Geoffrey Ridel, another of the commissioners, was drowned in the White Ship in 1120; and Bernard, the queen's chancellor, mentioned in entry **83**, became bishop of St. David's in 1115. It would seem, therefore, that the survey was made at some time between 1102 and 1115. There have been two attempts to obtain a closer dating. It has been suggested that a royal writ, which cannot be later than 1107 and could be earlier than 1105, postdates this inquest.[1] And it is also possible to argue that, if the moneyer Wimund was already dead when the survey was made, it cannot be earlier than 1116.[2] But since the evidence of the writ is inconclusive and our knowledge of Henry I's coinage is still imperfect, it seems best to date Survey **I** *c.* 1110.

The investigation of the royal revenue by royal commissioners or judges on circuit has a history from the Domesday survey of 1086 through the General Eyres of the Norman and early Angevin period to the *Quo Warranto* proceedings which became common under Henry III. The kings of this period were all interested in concealments and purprestures, the witholding of and encroachment on their financial rights. And the usual method employed by the royal agents was to put local communities, or their representatives, on oath to tell the truth, and ask them questions. This is the sworn inquisition. Winchester, like London, is omitted from Domesday Book; but probably only because the task of transferring one set of records to the other was never completed. It is now realized that various official records, especially assessment lists, existed before Domesday Book and indeed made the great survey possible. The form of Survey **I** makes it almost certain that it was based on one of these. In each entry the *TRE* holder is put first, and

---

[1] Richardson and Sayles, 218, n., 429–30. The writ (*Regesta*, ii, no. 729; text, p. 311, no. xxviii) is a notification that the king has awarded to Hawise, widow of William Mauduit I, her dowry, namely two estates and the demesne mansion (*dominicum managium*) at Winchester outside the city gate, *et terram que est in vico Fullonum et domos similiter*. Richardson and Sayles argue that as Robert Mauduit is holding this property in Survey **I**, the survey is earlier than the writ. It is true that Hawise is not mentioned in Survey **I** (or Survey **II**). But the property held in Survey **I** by Robert Mauduit consisted of three tenements in High Street, two of which he had inherited from his father (**I**, 45, 53, and 56). A demesne mansion (?) outside one of the gates and held by a Mauduit is not listed, and a *vicus Fullonum* finds no place (for this street-name, see below, p. 234, s.v.). The unspecified houses of the writ might be the three in High Street; but there are too many discrepancies for a clinching argument. It is possible that Hawise, having won her case and obtained the writ, was bought off by her stepson.

[2] See below, p. 410.

the 'twelfth-century details appear both second and secondary'.[1] Survey **I** is essentially a modernization of an Edwardian list of tenements. The only way of dating this earlier list is from the *TRE* holders of lands. In fact moneyers are the only datable persons; and, on the evidence they provide, two dates are possible—*c.* 1047 or *c.* 1057.[2] In the circumstances the latter seems the more likely.

The commissioners employed by Henry I at Winchester were servants high in his confidence and favour. The bishop and the two men closely associated with the royal treasury, Herbert the chamberlain and William of Pont de l'Arche, had local connections and knowledge. Ralf Basset and Geoffrey Ridel were probably more independent of the city and most likely had that to recommend them.[3] At all events, Henry's use of such weighty men shows how much importance he attached to the inquiry. It is not obvious from the findings of the inquest exactly how the survey was carried out. The itinerary is straightforward: first High Street, then the northern side-streets from west to east followed by the southern side-streets from east to west, the lands outside each gate being surveyed when that point was reached on the circuit (Fig. 4).[4] It seems that the survey takes us up one side and down the other side of each street. The account of High Street is in four parts: the king's demesne from east to west and then from west to east; and the lands of the 'barons and tenants' from east to west and the lands of the 'rent-payers' from west to east. We may conclude that the last two categories are the same and that we are twice taken up and down High Street. As J. H. Round realized,[5] on each occasion the north side was surveyed first. The Godebiete tenement, now Godbegot, known to be on the north side of High Street on the corner with *Alwarnestret*, is described (**I, 23**) on the way from East Gate to West Gate; and the destruction of twelve tenements for the building of the king's house, which was on the south side of the street, is recorded (**I, 57**) on the way back. Moreover, whereas the surveyors counted thirty-eight royal and eight baronial properties on the journey from east to west, they counted in the reverse direction only twenty-five royal properties and five belonging to the rent-payers. On the south side of the street was not only the king's house, but also St. Mary's Abbey and consequently, no doubt, fewer burgess tenements.

Although the survey of High Street is presented as two separate journeys, this may be an editorial device. Indeed, it is not clear who moved around and in what fashion. The commissioners themselves could easily have remained stationary and confined their duty to hearing and evaluating the evidence. Only one jury, possibly the eighty-six better burgesses of the preamble, seems to speak: 'Forges have been made here; but we do not know by whom.' (**I, 64**); 'He has incorporated some of the king's road into his house; but we do not know how much.' (**I, 78**); 'The lane has been blocked up; but we do not know [by whom].' (**I, 91**); 'And know that . . .' (**I, 103** and **105**). It may be, therefore, that the eighty-six burgesses carried out a preliminary investigation and declared to the commissioners what they had found, but it seems unlikely that they all walked around in

---

[1] Sally Harvey, *EHR* 86 (1971), especially p. 770. The existence of an earlier written survey finds some corroboration in the detail and extent to which the names and other facts of the period *TRE* were still ascertainable when Survey I was compiled more than

forty years later: cf. below, e.g. pp. 179–91, 402–3, 449.

[2] See below, p. 407 and Table 37.

[3] For these commissioners, see below, p. 33.

[4] For further discussion of the order of survey, below, p. 243.

[5] *VCH Hants* i. 529–30.

a single group. Table 3 summarizes the changes in terminology and in the forms of the entries which suggest that different parts of the town could have been surveyed by separate groups, but the total of eighty-six cannot be broken down into a number of equal-sized panels.

TABLE 2

The tenements on the king's fief in Surveys I and II

Streets	Survey I (c. 1110)	Survey II		
		On the king's fief	The remainder	Total
High Street	62[1]	76[4]	92	168
Outside West Gate	43[2]	58	70	128
Outside North Gate	—	1	52	53
Snidelingestret	7	7	28	35
Brudenestret	9[3]	9	26	35
Scowrtenestret	8	7	38	45
Alwarnestret	7	7	30	37
Flesmangerestret	3	2	29	31
Sildwortenestret	—	7	20	27
Wunegrestret	13	5	35	40
Tannerestret	18	15	44	59
Bucchestret	26	24	17	41
Colobrochestret	—	1	23	24
Outside East Gate	—	—	57	57
Mensterstret	—	3	30	33
Calpestret	25	17	12	29
Goldestret	16	10	39	49
Outside South Gate i	—	—	101	101
Outside South Gate ii	—	—	67	67
Gerestret	14	13	6	19
Totals	251	262	816	1,078

[1] Including twenty-seven tenements on the king's fief which had rendered custom *TRE* but no longer rendered any custom *c.* 1110. The twelve tenements which had been taken into the royal palace (**I, 57**) and the following entries, which do not represent properties existing *c.* 1110, are excluded: **I, 35, 58, 60, 66**, and **67**. The thirteen tenements 'on the lands of the barons' which had rendered custom to the king *TRE*, three of which had ceased to render any custom to the king by *c.* 1110, are also excluded.

[2] Including six properties which had rendered custom *TRE*, but no longer rendered any custom *c.* 1110.

[3] Excluding twenty-two tenements 'on the lands of the barons', three of which had rendered custom *TRE*, but no longer rendered any custom *c.* 1110.

[4] Excluding stalls and the *balchus*.

The inquiry was confined geographically to the royal demesne, the *feudum regis*, in the borough, or, as it is once expressed (**I, 80–1**), to the king's burgesses. The distinction between *terra regis* (the king's land) and *terra baronum* (the land of the barons) was, for the king, basic, and determined the arrangement of Domesday Book itself. That Survey **I** is concerned only with *terra regis* is easily proved by comparing it with Survey **II**. The later survey, undoubtedly comprehensive, lists about 1,100 properties; Survey **I** runs to no more than 300. In Table 2 the properties listed in Survey **II** are divided into those on the king's fief and the remainder, for comparison with the total number of properties listed in Survey **I**. The order followed is that of Survey **II**.

There are, of course, difficulties in these statistics. It is not always obvious, especially outside the gates, how the properties should be counted. There are also apparent contradictions in Survey I to the thesis being advanced. Under High Street there are sections labelled 'the lands of the barons and tenants' (I, 68–75) and 'the lands of the (?) rent-payers' (I, 76–80).[1] Similarly under (or after) *Brudenestret* is a section headed 'the lands of the barons' (I, 140–62). These tenements cannot be *terra regis*, but are included because, although *terra baronum*, they are still burdened with royal customs. The total of thirty-two tenements recorded in *Brudenestret*, including 'the lands of the barons', is very close to the total of thirty-five tenements in Survey II, which presumably lists all the properties in the street. Thus, 'the lands of the barons' in *Brudenestret* in Survey I may simply have been all the tenements in the street apart from those on the king's fief. But this argument cannot be applied to High Street, where the discrepancy between the numbers of properties recorded in Surveys I and II remains large. In any case only some forty properties are involved. The general import of the statistics is clear, and the absence from Survey I of all areas described in Survey II as outside the royal demesne is most impressive.

The royal commissioners for Survey I must therefore have had, or devised, some way of distinguishing property on the royal demesne from the rest. Perhaps the first question was 'Of whom is this land held?' There may also have been a formal question about unauthorized changes and encroachments, especially encroachments on the streets. Apart from these there were three main questions put by the commissioners in respect of each holding surveyed: (1) Who held it in the time of King Edward (*TRE*) and who holds it now (*modo*)? (2) What royal customs were rendered by the tenant then and what are rendered now? (3) What is it worth (to the tenant)? But if the last question was asked for all properties, the answers were omitted from the report after High Street and the lands outside West Gate, with the exception of a few entries among 'the lands of the barons' in *Brudenestret*.

The information obtained by the inquest is not presented uniformly. There are three main formulations. The first, with which the survey begins, is as follows:

I

Wulfric the priest held 1 tenement (*domus*) *TRE* which paid every custom. Now Robert son of Wimund holds it and likewise pays every custom. And it yields 15s. (I, 7)

With entry 43, and for no obvious reason, for we are some way down High Street on our return from West Gate to East Gate, we change to a new formula:

II

The tenement (*domus*) of Almod paid the custom *TRE*. Now Robert son of Ralf holds it and likewise pays the custom. And it yields 45s. (I, 47)

---

[1] There is a practical reason for thinking that these two expressions refer to the same categories (above, p. 10). As the *censuales*, the men who pay *census*, are probably the men who pay *gafol* (the two being synonymous), each heading may give us half the story: we are concerned with those barons and their tenants who pay landgable to the king. Some items, e.g. I, 15–16, although listed under *terra regis*, should have been transferred to this category.

This formula is used almost consistently[1] until, with *Snidelingestret* (**I, 124**), we return to a variation of Type I:

III

Theoderic the king's cook paid 6*d.* and the custom and Farman 6*d.* and the custom *TRE*. Now Herbert Giddy owes the same for the 2 messuages (*mansurae*). (**I, 185**)

For *Brudenestret* and 'the lands of the barons' (**I, 131–61**) there is a mixture of Types I, II, and III; but from *Scowrtenestret* until the end of the survey (**I, 166–295**) Type III is used consistently (Table 3).

TABLE 3

The different forms of the entries and units of rent in Survey I

	Normal units of rent to the king	Type of entry	Account of rent other than that due to the king	Use of *domus* and *mansura*
High Street, north side		Type I	Yes	*domus*
High Street, south side		Types I and II	Yes	*domus*
High Street, barons and tenants, east to west	Customs (Units of 6*d.* in Survey II)	Types I and II	Yes	*domus*
High Street, taxpayers, west to east		Type I	Yes	*domus*
Outside West Gate	Customs and/or units of 4*d.*	Type I	Yes	*domus*
Snidelingestret		Type III	No	*
Brudenestret		Types I, II, and III	No	*domus*
Lands of the barons		Types I and II	Not usually	*domus*, *mansura*
Scowrtenestret		Type III	No	*
Alwarnestret		Type III	No	*
Flesmangerestret	Units of 5*d.* or 4*d.* and/or customs	Type III	No	*
Wunegrestret		Type III	No	*mansura* (once)
Tannerestret		Types I and III	No	*domus* (once), *mansura*
Bucchestret		Type III	No	*mansura*
Calpestret		Type III	No	*mansura*
Goldestret		Type III	No	*domus*, *mansura* (once each in the same entry)
Gerestret		Type III	No	*mansura* (once)

* Neither term used under these streets.

Broadly it seems that Types I and II are used on the one hand to describe tenements called *domus* (houses), and that Type III is applied on the other hand to tenements called *mansurae* (manses). Although these are often alternative names for burgage tenements, Survey **I** appears to draw a technical distinction between them.[2] The former, situated mainly in High Street, *Brudenestret*, and outside West Gate, seem to have paid 6*d.* or 4*d.* landgable, sums corroborated by the evidence of Survey **II**. The latter apparently paid a varying sum, often a fraction or multiple of 5*d.* or 10*d.* But these different rates of landgable assessment may rather have reflected the ranking of High Street, the side-streets within the walls, and the western suburb, than the relative values of the *domus* and the *mansura* (Table 3).[3]

[1] Except that with entry **81** the formula becomes 'all customs' instead of the singular forms.

[2] See above, p. 7 and below, p. 337.
[3] See below, pp. 375–82.

There are two references to manses standing on a house-property (**I, 23** and **103**), and it is clear from the rents paid that a manse, although often burdened with more landgable, was smaller and less valuable than a *domus*. It is a complication, but causes no real difficulty, that *domus* is also used in the narrower sense of a domestic building, especially in the context of a recent urban development outside West Gate (**I, 98, 100, 107,** and **117–22**).

Besides the two main types of property, *domus* and *mansurae*, some other kinds of building and estate are mentioned. In High Street there were stalls of different sorts: eight *estals* (**I, 20–1**), two *eschamel*, shambles (**I, 23**; cf. **I, 19**), and one *selda* (**I, 71**); there were also a few shops i.e. *escheopes* (**I, 27**), the guildhall of the *cnihtas* (**I, 34**), a market (**I, 35**), several cellars, and at least seventeen forges, some of which had formerly been cellars (**I, 38, 59,** and **61–5**). Outside West Gate houses had been built on *terrae* (**I, 100, 107, 117,** and **122**), on gardens (**I, 98**), and on curtilages (*curtilla*) (**I, 118–21**). In addition nine huts (*bordella*) had been put up on *domus* (**I, 84** and **101**).[1]

The survey seems to list the owner and perhaps the most substantial tenants. When it is recorded that, below the king, A held of B (and there are only about half a dozen cases) we are presumably concerned with sub-infeudation and an additional step in the tenurial ladder. For example, William of Pont de l'Arche held a messuage in High Street from the son of William fitzGilbert (**I, 49**; cf. also **I, 33, 64, 102, 117,** and **144**). Wazo held a tenement of the monks of St. Swithun who held it of the king (**I, 28**). Herbert the chamberlain had developed some property outside West Gate, and we are told what rents he received from three of the houses (**I, 117**; cf. **I, 118–22**). The statement that 'on the lands of the barons', probably in *Brudenestret*, Geoffrey the clerk held or holds two messuages *de dominio regis* and two messuages *de Lessam* (**I, 157**) has been interpreted as meaning that he held two tenements on lease,[2] but little confidence can be put in this ungrammatical solution. There are references to occupiers in connection with arrangements for paying custom (cf. **I, 116**) or to lament the substitution of poor men for a good burgess household (**I, 16–18**). The commissioners' purpose was to record the pre-1066 and the present owners and tenants, the persons who at the different periods were legally responsible for landgable and the other customs. And, although occasionally a name could not be put to a woman or a widow, the commissioners were remarkably successful. Moreover they tried to individualize all persons by recording a byname or other distinguishing feature. The result is an *onomasticon* without parallel for the period and of the utmost importance (see Part II, pp. 143 ff.).

The survey is called a list (*liber*) of the royal lands paying *langabulum* and *brug'* (elsewhere usually spelled *brueg'*) in Winchester. The latter was explained by W. H. Stevenson[3] as *bru(e)-gablum*, 'brew-gable', payment for licence to brew—correctly, for the same impost was collected from certain properties belonging to the bishop, under the name of *brugabulum* or *burgabulum*.[4] Since, however, there are few references to this custom by name in the text, and it does not seem to have been very lucrative, it was given special

---

[1] For further discussion of these technical terms, see below, p. 337.

[2] Hemmeon *Burgage Tenure*, 89.

[3] *VCH Hants* i. 529.

[4] *PRBW 1208–9*, 77; *PRBW 1210–11*, 161.

mention presumably only because it was a feature of the earlier administrative records which lie behind the present text.¹ *Langabulum* (OE *land-gafol*), landgable, is the commonest name for burgage rent. In the text of the survey, however, there are few explicit references to it. For High Street the usual answer is that the house pays (or does not pay) every custom. For 'outside West Gate' the formula changes to 'pays all customs'. Sometimes the shortened phrase 'pays the custom(s)' is used. All these seem to be stylistic variations, for more limited liabilities are expressed by specifying the actual customs rendered or by excepting those not rendered. It also seems that landgable, if not brewgable, is included among these customs, for the first two items in the survey are in this form:

> Edwin Good-soul held 1 tenement *TRE* which paid 6*d.* landgable (and the area behind the tenement paid 3*d.* for custom) and every other custom. Now Richard, chaplain of the count of Meulan, holds it; and he has never paid any custom in respect of it except this year . . . **(I, 2)**

It appears, therefore, that landgable was one of the customs for which the house properties were responsible and that in the survey after the first two items it was included in the general formula.² Some support for this view is to be found in Survey **II**, where royal tenants in High Street mostly owed the king 6*d.*

With *Snidelingestret* the formula changes to 'Burewold paid 2*d.* and the customs *TRE*. Now Brithwold the priest owes the same' **(I, 124)**. Occasionally the entry is more specific: 'The tenement of Leving the Dolt paid 6*d.* landgable and every custom *TRE*. Now his son Wulfward does the same' **(I, 139)**. So it is more than likely that all payments of this type were *langabulum*. Presumably the formula changes because for *mansurae* the payment was not standard. Fractions and multiples of 10*d.* are most common: 2½*d.* (once), 5*d.* (7 times), 10*d.* (31 times), 15*d.* (13 times), 20*d.* (four times), and 30*d.* (9 times). But nineteen different rates between 1*d.* and 32*d.* are mentioned, and 6*d.* occurs 29 times. Because landgable is the ground rent, holdings could be defined as so many penceworth of land. For example, Odo Ticchemann's son held eight-pennyworth of royal land **(I, 133)**.³

The obligation on the tenements ran from all customs to nothing (*domus quieta*). Besides landgable and brewgable only two customs are commonly mentioned by name: *wata* or *waita*, watch-duty,⁴ and geld, liability to the royal tax, *here-geld* or Danegeld.⁵ Watch duty suggests that the city was divided into wards, *custodiae*, to which the service was due.⁶ Three other customs occur once: *fripene* (?frithpenny) **(I, 193)**,⁷ *avra* (carrying-service) **(I, 28)**,⁸ and *pascere prisonem* (? victualling the prison) **(I, 144)**. Soke and sake, private jurisdiction, is also mentioned once **(I, 279)**.

---

¹ From the bishop's tenements in 1208, the earliest date for which we have a figure, it produced 13*s.* 11*d.* and receipts thereafter showed a fairly steady decline: *PRBW 1208–9*, 77.

² There seems nothing to support Hemmeon's view, *Burgage Tenure*, 159, n. 2, that as soon as the term *omnes consuetudines* creeps into the survey, 'the totals [? money totals] go up'. This is to confuse payments and receipts. The amount of landgable is always stated or implied. It can be combined with brewgable (e.g. **I, 81–2**), but seems never to be added to rents.

³ By West Gate, Henry de Port had incorporated eight-shillings worth of *terra regis* into his *domus*: this presumably was the economic rent.

⁴ N. Neilson, *Customary Rents* (Oxford Studies in Social and Legal History, 2, Oxford, 1910), 131 ff., under *Wardsilver*.

⁵ Ibid. 115 ff.

⁶ F. W. Maitland, *Township and Borough* (Cambridge, 1898), 50. There is reference to the bishop of Salisbury's *custodia* in **I, 108**.

⁷ Neilson, *Customary Rents*, 166. ⁸ Ibid. 60 ff.

These obligations lay on the tenement and were, presumably, enforceable against the person who held the messuage in demesne—the virtual owner of the property who had no freeholder beneath him. This is the person who is named first in the description of the tenement. But the burden was probably often transferred to the occupiers. One tenement, we are told, was quit, but the dwellers on it performed the customs (**I, 205**), presumably to the profit of the owner, for in another case it is the owner who holds all the customs since he pays nothing (**I, 12**). On one tenement the men pay the geld (**I, 45**). In three cases Herbert the chamberlain, probably because he was a baron of the Exchequer, acquits his men of the geld (**I, 13b, 24**, and **33**). Two houses outside West Gate belonged to Aubrey the chamberlain. Wirstan held one of them from Aubrey for 5s. 2d. a year and performed the royal customs. Judicel held the other for 28d. and paid the king landgable and brewgable (**I, 102**). By Henry I's reign some owners only rendered the customs when these were demanded by the reeves (**I, 27, 29, 32**, and **44**). One estate paid geld only when required to by the king's writ (**I, 80**).

A strange feature revealed by the survey is that whereas in the side streets the obligations on the messuages had not changed between *TRE* and Henry's reign and, apparently, were still being enforced, there were many exemptions or evasions in High Street, some outside West Gate, and a few on 'the lands of the barons' in *Brudenestret*. It is for these latter areas that the rent or rents paid by the tenement is stated at the end of each item. The usual expressions are, e.g., 'and it yields 49s.' or 'he receives from it 6s.' Sometimes there are more elaborate statements. Occasionally it is clear that it is the profit to the owner which is being declared, for example 'and this tenement and his other tenements yield £6. 16s.' (**I, 53**). Properties apparently occupied by their owners were not valued, however, possibly because there was no procedure for doing so. The document thus supplies only partially the information which could have led to a revision of the ground rents, or a re-imposition of all the liabilities of burgage tenure. It would appear, however, that at least in High Street the king did recover some of the dues which he had lost.[1] In *Brudenestret* he probably failed to recover those he had lost from 'the lands of the barons', and the landgable receipts from his other tenements there actually fell.[2] Further speculation seems fruitless at present for no one knows for certain even why Domesday Book itself was compiled or what use, if any, was made of its statistics at the time.

The Winchester valuations are nevertheless of interest to us. Sometimes they disclose quite elaborate financial arrangements. In High Street the abbot of Hyde had a house which produced the following rents: to the abbot £3. 5s.; to Robert the baker, the son of William, 8s.; to Cheping[3] son of Alveva £2; to Hubert son of William £2. 5s.; to Roger the abbot's brother 18s. (**I, 73**). The *cnihtas* guildhall, also in High Street, was held by Godwin Prison and Godwin Green's son. They drew 25s. in rents, the wife of Ascelin 12s., and Henry of Dummer 10s. Cheping son of Alveva took 5s. in rent, possibly from a church on the estate (**I, 10**). Also considerable values are revealed. A house of one of the

---

[1] See Table 2 and below, p. 350.
[2] See Tables 2 and 12 a.
[3] In this Introduction, in the notes to Parts II and III, and in Parts IV and V, the spelling of this name

has been normalized to the form most often used of the individual concerned. For the preferred forms, see **I, 10**, n. 6.

'rent-payers' in High Street, owned by Bernard of St. Valéry, yielded £12 (**I, 77**), two other houses in the street yielded £9 (**I, 19** and **49**), and a further 18 yielded £3 and above.

From Survey **I** it is possible to get some idea of what changes had occurred in the city since 1057(?)–66. In connection with the destruction of property for the building of the king's house, the survey gives twelve names and adds, 'these men held tenements [or, were house-holders] and were burgesses and performed the customs' (**I, 57**). Elsewhere there are laments that now there were only poor men where once there had been a solid burgess household.[1] It would seem that the city fathers believed that in the good old days there were as many burgesses as houses and that each burgess kept an appropriate household, whereas now speculators had moved in, estates were being broken up for profit, and property was 'going down'. Although there probably never was a time when the city consisted of a community of burgesses each maintaining a household in his own undivided house, it is likely that economic prosperity and a free land market was having the effects described. Men were able to treat property commercially; and this soon disrupted the original pattern and made boroughs look quite unlike the rural village. In Survey **I** all except nine of the messuages in High Street produced substantial rents and must have been sub-let. Of the nine, two were uninhabited (**I, 22** and **55**), and it is by no means certain that the rest were occupied by their owners. Two were held by the same man, Robert Mauduit (**I, 45** and **56**), son of William Mauduit, a Hampshire tenant-in-chief;[2] and with reference to a third messuage he held (**I, 53**), it is stated that this and his other houses brought in £6. 16s. Apparently all three houses were accounted for together and would appear to have been sub-let. In later medieval terminology **I, 53** would perhaps have been described as his capital tenement. The remaining five were in the hands of Thomas of St. John and Osbert [son of] Thiard (**I, 30**), Ralf Brito (**I, 31**), the wife of Hugh fitzAlbuchon (**I, 40**), Herfrid, the king's sergeant (**I, 44**), and Emma de Percy, Henry de Port's sister (**I, 68**). These are all important people, mostly high in the favour of the king. Osbert held other properties outside West Gate (**I, 101** and **122**), on one of which he had built lodging houses for poor men. He and some of the others may indeed have had town houses in High Street, but it is obvious that the number of these, at least on the king's demesne, was not large. Outside West Gate, of forty-three properties listed, perhaps seven had owner-occupiers (**I, 85, 88–9, 92, 104, 109**, and **114**). As values are not given for properties beyond this point, the inquiry cannot be pursued.

We can also identify some substantial property owners. Herbert the chamberlain, either the Domesday Hampshire tenant-in-chief or his son, held five whole tenements and one part in High Street, worth altogether £25. 14s. (**I, 4, 13b, 24, 33, 48**, and **74**). Outside West Gate he had four properties. No value is put on two of these (**I, 116** and **123**); one produced £1. 2s. (**I, 111**); and the fourth had been broken up for housing and produced 8s. 11d. (**I, 117**). From another messuage he drew 5s. (**I, 118**). Herbert also had a piece of land in *Brudenestret* which yielded 10d. (**I, 152**). Thus on royal demesne Herbert had a rent roll of £27. 10s. 9d. His son Geoffrey had two tenements in High Street which together produced £9. 9s. 6d. (**I, 27** and **32**). His steward had a tenement in

---

[1] **I, 16–18**; cf. **I, 13a**. It is not obvious what caused this isolated group of complaints.

[2] For Robert, see also above, p. 9, n. 1, and below, **I, 45**, n. 1.

High Street (**I, 55**); his cook drew 24*s.* from an estate outside West Gate (**I, 107**), and his vassal had a messuage in *Gerestret* (**I, 292**). A less important man, the son of Ralf Rosell, owned seven houses on royal demesne, three in High Street worth £11. 16*s.* (**I, 1, 5,** and **19**), three adjacent properties in *Tannerestret* (**I, 199–201**), and one in *Bucchestret*, all in the north-east corner of the city. At least one of the tenements (**I, 1**) had come from his father, and in one case he had encroached on the king's road.

iv. SURVEY II

The second survey, dated 1148,[1] in the third quarter of Stephen's reign, was carried out by a different authority, the bishop of Winchester, covered the whole city, and had different terms of reference. According to the preamble four questions were asked about the lands (*terrae*) of Winchester: (1) Who is the tenant? (2) How much does he hold? (3) From whom does he hold it? (4) How much does each person get out of it? The occasion of the survey may have been the destruction wrought in the city by the civil war. In 1141 there had been fighting in and around Winchester; and in the survey some thirty-four lands are reported as 'waste'.[2] By 1148 the Angevin cause in England seemed lost and the church and barons began to put their estates in order again. Bishop Henry was interested in estate management,[3] and it is possible that in 1148 he held special responsibility for the city under the king. He was also by far the largest landlord in the city and may have been looking to his own revenues on the eve of an important and potentially expensive visit to Rome which he was probably obliged to undertake that year.[4] But, as with the earlier survey, the exact purpose of Survey **II** is not self-evident.

With this survey, unlike Survey **I**, we are not told how it was made. It is called an inquisition, and the questions must have been put by commissioners to juries. One entry, unfortunately slightly corrupt, reads, 'William Durage should pay the abbot 2*s.* according to the neighbours and the abbot's servants' (**II, 349**). In another case a man would not disclose the payment he made (**II, 270**). There are several entries such as 'but we do not know what they pay' (**II, 357**; cf. **II, 465, 517–18, 563, 783, 808,** and **810**). A sprinkling of gaps in the text, so that missing information could be filled in later, also suggests the collection of verbal information rather than a search of records. The topographical order of the survey is almost exactly the same as before: High Street, the

---

[1] Presumably 1148–9, modern style. The occurrence of named individuals is consistent with this date, but cf. **II, 2,** n. 1.

[2] See below, p. 386.

[3] As soon as he became abbot of Glastonbury Henry of Blois recovered the alienated properties of the abbey and had the recoveries recorded in a *libellus* (Thomas Hearne (ed.), *Adami de Domerham, Historia de rebus gestis Glastoniensibus* (Oxford, 1727), ii. 304). As bishop of Winchester he took many of the cathedral estates into his own hands, and probably set them on a firmer footing (Goodman *Chartulary*, nos. 7, 10, and 14). He may even have commissioned the great cathedral cartulary, the *Codex Wintoniensis* (BM, Add. MS. 15350). In the 1150s he rescued the abbey of

Cluny from insolvency and had made a survey of the abbey's rents (A. Bernard and A. Bruel, *Recueil des chartes de l'abbaye de Cluny*, v (Collections des documents inédits sur l'histoire de France, Paris, 1894), 488–505). Henry's recorded opinion, that Domesday Book had been made in order that everyone should be content with their own rights (*Dialogus de Scaccario*, 63), expresses a sufficient motive for the compilation of the survey of Winchester in 1148.

[4] If, as is probable, the year 1148 was considered to have begun on 25 March, the survey is very likely to have been undertaken after Bishop Henry's suspension and summons by the Pope at the Council of Rheims during March and April. See below, pp. 492–3.

northern side-streets from west to east, the southern side-streets from east to west, and the lands outside the gates at the appropriate points in the circuit (Fig. 4).[1] It also seems that the streets were surveyed systematically from end to end, first one side then the other. The various 'fiefs', the royal demesne, the bishop's fief, etc., have to be sorted out. It is a topographical, not a feudal, survey.

In this document there are two descriptive terms which cannot be explained. From the 402 tenements which make up the bishop's fief, sixty-two payments to the bishop are described as *de terra Baronum*, *de terra .B.* or *de t' .B.*, and sixty-nine as *de .B.* (Table 12). There are in all sixty-five examples of the various forms of *de terra Baronum* (including three on properties not in the bishop's fief), and seventy-six examples of *de .B.* with its variants (including four on the king's fief, one on the prior's, and two on the properties of other landlords). The two terms can be listed in a descending order (Table 4).

TABLE 4

The various forms of the term(s) de terra Baronum *and* de .B. *in Survey II*

de terra Baronum	1 *example*	d. terra .B.	1 *example*	đ. t' .B	1 *example*
de terra .Barō.	1	de. t' .B.	7	de. .B.	1
de. t' .Bar'.	1	de t' .B.	10	de .B.	60
de. terra .B.	3	de t' .B	1	de B.	13
de terra .B.	25	de. t .B	1	đ. .B.	1
de terra B.	4	de t .B.	2	.B.	1
đ. terra .B.	1	đ. t' .B.	6		

(where *terra* has been silently expanded unless written as *t'* or *t*)

This list might give the impression that we have a single term, ever more abbreviated by the scribe. Two points argue against this. The 'preferred' forms (and indeed the correct forms, palaeographically speaking) are *de terra .B.*, *de t' .B.*, and *de .B.*, the last twice as common as the other two combined. This is a frequency that may suggest a real distinction. Second, the order in which the terms occur in the manuscript is strikingly different from the above list. This order is briefly set out in Table 5 normally grouping the minor variants under the 'preferred' forms, and expanding *terra* unless written as *t'* or *t*.

This second list shows that scribal practice did indeed vary in succeeding entries, as in **II, 211, 213–18, 219,** and **220–5,** but it also shows that the scribe was not progressively shortening the term or terms. The *de .B.* entries at the beginning of Survey **II,** in High Street, form a notable group; they are followed by a block of longer forms up to **II, 427** (including only one *de .B.*); and these are followed by a third and final block of shorter forms (including three isolated examples of *de terra .B.*). All this might suggest scribal vagaries, were it not for the initial group of *de .B.* entries. It is possible that the scribe was following separate returns for different areas of the city, one of them relating to High Street alone, and that in these original returns the phrase was couched in different ways, sometimes *de .B.*, sometimes in a form of *de terra Baronum*.

[1] For further discussion of the order of survey, see below, p. 243.

There are perhaps four possibilities: one, that all the forms are scribal variants, more or less abbreviated, of *de terra Baronum*; second, that scribal practice in the survey as we have it reflects the varying expressions used in the original returns to express *de terra Baronum*; third, that the real form was *de .B.* (as at the beginning of the survey), and that all subsequent variations are an attempt on the part of the scribe to explain it; fourth, that there were two distinct terms with different meanings, and that the scribe has more or less faithfully reproduced them, varying his abbreviation of the longer term.

TABLE 5

The order of occurrence in Survey II of the various forms of the term(s) de terra Baronum *and* de .B.

Entry	Term	Examples	Entry	Term	Examples
21	de .B.	1	424–6	de t' .B.	3
26	.B.	1	427	de. t' .Bar'.	1
36 ff.	de .B.	39	437 ff.	de t' .B.	4
211	de terra Baronum	1	445	de terra .B.	1
213–18	de terra .B.	6	448, 480	de t' .B.	2
219	de. t .B.	1	483, 492–7	de .B.	6
220–5	de terra .B.	4	501	de. terra .B.	1
230	de .B.	1	504–5	de .B.	2
263 ff.	de terra .B.	11	525	de t' .B.	1
368–71	de t' .B.	4	545, 564, 570	de .B.	3
372 ff.	de terra .B.	4	574	de t' .B.	1
383–6	de t' .B.	4	611–13, 615 ff.	de .B.	11
388–9	de terra .B.	2	663	de t' .B.	1
390	de terra .Barō.	1	665 ff.	de .B.	9
395–7	de terra .B.	3	1,069	de terra .B.	1
398 ff.	de t' .B.	7	1,074–5, 1,085	de .B.	3
423	de terra .B.	1			

Typical examples of the use of these terms are: 'S. pays the bishop 1 mark *de .B.*' (**II, 162**); 'B. pays the bishop 7*s. de .B.* and receives 9*s.*' (**II, 137**); 'S. pays the bishop 30*d. de. t' .B.*' (**II, 412**); 'T. pays the king 2*d.* and the bishop 6*s. de. t .B.* And he himself receives . . . 4*s.*' (**II, 219**). The meaning of *de* is clearly 'from': it is unlikely to identify the collecting agent, for whom *per* would be expected; and it cannot refer to the recipient. It indicates the source of the rent.

The geographical distribution of the two terms is complex (Fig. 19), although there are areas—notably the eastern and southern suburbs, the latter with 117 episcopal properties —completely free from both labels. Nevertheless there are some distinctive features to be seen in their distribution, notably the concentration of *de .B.* on the presumed site of the former royal palace, and these are discussed in more detail below.[1] It is true that there are some cases where *de .B.* and *de terra .B.* are found in close juxtaposition, but these are few and appear insignificant compared with the broadly different distribution of the two terms. They never both come from the same tenement and no payment has both labels. They are, therefore, alternatives—obviously of the same kind—and this again

[1] See below, pp. 23 and 353–5.

suggests that they could be no more than variant forms. There are also a few anomalous cases: two payments by the bishop to the king *de .B.* (**II, 60** and **168**), both from tenements in High Street and both of 6*d.*, were obviously landgable; and in one case a woman, Iveta, who seems essentially a royal burgess, draws a rent *de terra .B.* (**II, 223**). These are possibly mistakes: in the first two cases the label could have been transferred from the receipt to the payment.

'The lands of the barons' find a place in Survey **I**,[1] and the phrase has a clear meaning: sub-infeudated land as opposed to royal demesne. In the context of Survey **II** it could refer to the land held by the bishop's barons and be equivalent to 'thegnland', a term which actually appears in Survey **I** (**I, 74**). And the only way in which it is conceivable that burgesses paid rents 'from the land of the barons' (and the phrase is always in the singular in Survey **II**) is if the bishop had taken land away from his feudal vassals and taken it into his own demesne. Although tenants usually pay and rarely receive *de terra .B.* (but cf. **II, 223**), the phrase can be compared with 'S. pays the bishop 26*d.* and receives 33*d. de feudo de Odiham*' (**II, 387**; cf. **II, 392**). Nevertheless, this explanation is by no means convincing.

Since the phrase 'from the land of the barons' does not at first sight make much sense, it is possible, as suggested above, that the scribe, not having understood *de .B.*, had a flash of inspiration when he reached **II, 211**, decided that it stood for *de terra Baronum*, and made the substitution on most ensuing occasions. The variety cannot, however, be explained by different scribes. On fo. 26 occurs *de .B.* (**II, 638**), *de t' .B.* (**II, 663**), and *de .B.* (**II, 665**).

Unfortunately, even if we regard *de terra Baronum* as a rationalization of *de .B.* we are no closer to a solution, for *de .B.* cannot be deciphered with certainty. From its form it could denote a person or a territorial source, like *de feudo regis* or *de feudo de Odiham*, or it could identify the type of payment, like *de langabulo* (**II, 63**) or *de thelonio* (**II, 56–9**). The form *.B.* should be an initial; but *de Baldewino*, or *de Bernardo* does not make sense in the context. Who could such a person be? Nor do *de Baronibus*, *de Bedellis*, or *de Ballivis* fit (although more must be said below of *de Baronibus*), for no more than individuals could these classes of men have provided the money. It is just possible, however, that *de .B.* indicated a special method of collection; that the money went through the hands of royal bailiffs instead of episcopal servants. If *de .B.* has a territorial sense, *de Basingestoches* (**I, 11**; cf. **II, 434**) would be a likely identification. One entry certainly points that way: 'R. pays the bishop 5*s. de B.* and receives 11*s.* from that same royal fief' (**II, 67**), but this may only be a reference to the royal fief mentioned in the preceeding entries of the survey. And in several contexts *de .B.* seems to describe the land from which the rent was due. For example, 'H. pays the bishop 10*d. de .B.* He also pays the bishop 29*d.* and W. M. 7*s.*' (**II, 492**). 'S. pays the king 6*d.* and the bishop 15*s.* 3*d. de B.* and 7*s.* And A. receives 8*s.*' (**II, 112**). But it is difficult to understand how payments to the bishop out of urban tenements could be derived from a royal manor, and no other records of Basingstoke property in Winchester suggest that it was worth more than a few shillings. Or the scribe who began substituting *de terra Baronum* could have been

---

[1] See above, p. 12.

right. In which case we have to accept that a special category of sub-infeudated land was scattered throughout the city. To this point we will return.

For the moment we may continue to discuss *de .B.* If *.B.* is parallel with *langabulum* and *thelonium*, of the various possibilities, *burgum*, *borda*, *bordellum*, *burgabulum*, *bruegabulum*, only the last two seem at all likely.[1] In the Pipe Rolls of the bishopric of Winchester the episcopal collectors render account for *brugabulum* collected from three streets and outside the five gates. In 1208–9 this toll yielded 13s. 11d., in 1210–11, 17s. 5d.[2] The *de .B.* payments of Survey **II** are, however, substantial. They amount to £18. 9s. 8¾d. and the *de terra .B.* payments to £7. 13s. 6d., 1 bizant,[3] and a half-pound of pepper,[4] out of a total rentroll of some £70 (Table 14, cf. Fig. 14a). There is no coincidence between the areas from which brewgable was collected in the twelfth century and the *de .B.* and *de terra .B.* areas.[5] Moreover, brewgable does not usually fit the context very well. The payments described are rents. *Burgabulum*, as a synonym for landgable, is at least as likely. For instance it fits quite well into the unusual entry, **II, 60**: 'The bishop pays the king 6d. *de .B.* And he receives 17s. and D. receives 6s. and M. 6s.' It also suits the simple entries like 'D. pays the bishop 10s. *de .B.*' (**II, 149**), except that 10s. would seem an economic rather than a ground rent. In many cases the *de .B.* payment is a second charge, distinct from landgable: for example, 'Peter the mercer pays the king 6d., the bishop 9s. *de .B.*, and William Martel 40s.; and Peter receives 12s.' (**II, 35**). Here the 6d. to the king is the landgable.

None of the straightforward explanations appears to fit all the contexts. Indeed both expressions, *de .B.* and *de terra Baronum*, seem superfluous and in nearly every case could be omitted without difficulty.[6] What we require is something which can apply to any sum of money paid to the bishop of Winchester (and, perhaps, by him), and something which is outside the context. One possibility is that *de .B.* stands for *denariis blancis*, 'in blanch pennies', and indicates that the amount was rectified according to the silver content of the money. It is indeed likely that the bishop's exchequer was already modelled on the royal exchequer and it would not be surprising if the bishop had introduced blanch payments. But there do not seem to be any references to this practice in the bishop's Pipe Rolls which are extant from 1208–9. And the difficulty of the capital 'B' still remains.

Another possibility is that *de .B.* is a perversion of *deb.*, and stands for *debet*, 'it is owing'. There are some unambiguous statements in the text that payments to the bishop are in arrears—*debet reddere*, *deberet reddere*, *solebat reddere*—and in four cases, High Street (**II, 9**), outside West Gate (**II, 187**), outside North Gate (**II, 310**), and in *Bucche-*

---

[1] For brewgable, see above, pp. 14–15.

[2] Brewgable was collected in 1209 and 1211 as follows: outside East Gate, outside King's Gate, outside South Gate (1211 only), Gar Street (1211 only), outside West Gate, outside North Gate, Wengare Street, Tannere Street, Sparkford. From Tannere Street 2s. was collected in 1209, 10d. in 1210: *PRBW 1208–9*, 77; *PRBW 1210–11*, 161.

[3] A bizant was worth 2s. and was associated with Jews: L. F. Salzman, *English Trade in the Middle Ages* (Oxford, 1931), 16.

[4] A pound of pepper was worth about 7d.: Hemmeon *Burgage Tenure*, 87–8.

[5] See above, n. 2.

[6] There is one case where a *de terra .B.* entry may be connected with a Survey I entry. In *Gerestret* in 1148 Simon the dispenser paid the bishop 2s. for a waste 'land of the barons' (**II, 1069**). In the earlier survey Simon held a messuage in *Gerestret* for which his *antecessor* had paid the king 6d. and custom. Unfortunately, Simon's obligation or performance is not stated (**I, 283**).

stret (**II, 682**), these occur in the description of the first tenement in which the bishop is interested and are followed by *de .B.* or *de t .B.* entries. In two other cases, however, *Wunegrestret* (**II, 595**) and *Mensterstret* (**II, 797**), they occur after the contracted labels. In any case *de .B.* is not a contraction of *debet reddere* and, if given this sense, has to be explained differently. The draft survey could have been used, either originally or subsesequently, for accounting purposes, and *debet* was written against payments to (and occasionally from) the bishop which were in arrears. The copyist of Survey **II** misunderstood these notes, imagined they were descriptive in a different way, brought them integrally into his text, and also changed some of them into *de terra Baronum*. One obvious objection to this theory is that, out of a rentroll of some £70, about a third was in arrears. But this difficulty is easily surmountable. At Canterbury there were different rent days,[1] and a third of the total outstanding is neat enough.

By the early thirteenth century the episcopal revenues from most parts of the city had fallen considerably below the level recorded in 1148. This could be largely explained by the loss of the rents *de .B.* and *de terra Baronum*. If this was so, it raises the possibility that these rents were not properly the bishop's, or were exceptional charges. In either case this would reflect the extent of the bishop's authority in the city in 1148. Most of the rents *de .B.* came from properties on or near the palace site (Fig. 19), and thus suggest that this rent at least was associated with the bishop's quasi-royal position, or was in some way connected with events which centred on the palace during the siege of 1141.

Whether or not the two terms meant the same, we still have to decide who these barons were. If the bishop held these properties by virtue of his quasi-royal authority in the city, the barons need not necessarily have been his own. Yet there appears to be no coincidence between the 'lands of the barons' (presumably the king's barons) in Survey **I** and the 'land of the barons' in Survey **II**.

In the twelfth century the leading citizens of London were known as the 'barons of London',[2] but there are no clear instances in which their fellows at Winchester were distinguished by the same title.[3] There is, however, a remote possibility that on this occasion a body of leading Winchester citizens was in fact being referred to as 'barons'. These barons may have constituted a property-owning association, and the reason that their properties come into the bishop's possession by 1148 could be connected with his exceptional authority in the city. A parallel contemporary case of an association of leading citizens owning a substantial estate of urban property would be the guild of English *cnihtas* in London.[4] The early guilds of leading Winchester citizens are discussed below.[5]

---

[1] In the middle of the twelfth century there were two great settlement days, Mid-Lent and Michaelmas, although landgable fell due on seventeen different days: Urry *Canterbury*, 38–9.

[2] F. M. Stenton, 'Norman London' in D. M. Stenton (ed.), *Preparatory to Anglo-Saxon England* (Oxford, 1970), esp. p. 23 and note. In time the term became more restricted in meaning and by the fourteenth century the barons of London were taken to be the aldermen alone: Gwyn Williams, *Medieval London from Commune to Capital* (London, 1963), 48.

[3] Henry I addressed several writs to 'the barons of Hampshire and Winchester' and 'the barons and faithful of Hampshire and Winchester': *Regesta*, ii, nos. 1255, 1378, and 1380. These cases perhaps indicate the lack of distinction at a certain level between the chief men of the county and of the city. When the men of Winchester alone are addressed they are called *burgenses*: *Regesta*, ii, nos. 803 and 804.

[4] See Stenton, op. cit., 32–3; *AS Writs*, 231–5; and G. A. J. Hodgett (ed.), *The Cartulary of Holy Trinity Aldgate* (London Record Society, 1971), nos. 871–5.

[5] See below, pp. 335–6 and 427.

There are some possible instances of a topographical association between tenements from which rents *de .B.* or *de terra Baronum* were due and the evidence for the guilds themselves. The largest single group of rents *de .B.* occurs close to the *gihalda* (**II, 140, 143,** and **155**) on the south side of High Street. On the north side of High Street there was one rent *de .B.* from a tenement (**II, 35**) very close to property where there was probably a guildhall in the thirteenth century, and where there was probably a guild of *cnihtas* in the reign of Edward the Confessor (**II, 32–4,** cf. **I, 34**). On the same side of the street the bishop had rents *de .B.* from property next to Chapman's Hall (**II, 67–9**). There was a pre-conquest guild of the men outside West Gate (**I, 105**), in an area where the bishop had many rents *de terra Baronum*. There do not appear, however, to have been any rents *de .B.* or *de terra Baronum* from properties near the *hantachenesele* in *Colobrochestret* (**II, 712**).

What would have happened to these properties after the bishop lost possession of them, as he appears to have done? They may have reverted to the heirs of members of the defunct guild and so rapidly have lost their original identity. They may alternatively have been recovered by the original association or some evolving form of it. The guild merchant does not seem to have been significant as a property-owning body,[1] and the community of citizens or city corporation did not acquire tenements on any scale until the later fourteenth century.[2] The Hospital of St. John the Baptist, which had a fundamental and close association with the government of the city in the later Middle Ages, is recorded as a property-owner in the city in 1219, and in 1294 had a portfolio of properties with a net annual value of £52.[3] There is a possible link between this hospital and the *hantachenesele*,[4] but these associations are altogether too circumstantial for any categorical conclusions to be drawn.

Could the bishop in 1148 have held the land of any other group of 'barons'? The defeat of the empress's party at Winchester in 1141 may have resulted in the seizure of Winchester properties belonging to her supporters among the leading men of the city and county. Technically these could have been regarded as the confiscated properties of rebels held by the bishop on the king's behalf, or Henry of Blois may simply have seized the tenements of his opponents in the heat of victory, as he seized the treasures of Hyde Abbey, or as the Londoners ransacked the cellars of the Winchester burgesses.[5] It is not really clear, however, how the term 'barons' might be applied to this group of people, unless it was being used very loosely in the sense of 'holders of land' or 'tenants', as its use in Survey I suggests was possible.[6] If *de .B.* is to be considered as an extreme abbreviation of *de terra Baronum* it does not seem likely that properties on the site of the former royal palace, which was probably in the possession of the bishop before 1141, could have been confiscated in this manner. On the other hand the palace site may already have been colonized on its northern and western margins before 1141, and the bishop may have resumed these properties during or after the siege. Strong arguments against

---

[1] See **I, 105,** n. 1; and *SMW*.

[2] See *SMW*, s.v. 'corporate landlords'.

[3] See below, pp. 335–6 and note. The hospital rental of 1294 is WCA, St. John's Rolls 1.

[4] See below, p. 336.

[5] For these events, see below, pp. 318–19 and 339–40.

[6] The first rubric for the 'lands of the barons' in Survey I refers to the *terris baronum et ten[en]tium*, the second to the *terris chens[ual]ium*: see above, pp. 10 and 12.

the identification of these barons as in some way representative of the opposition in 1141 are the tendency of the two terms to occur in groups of successive entries in the survey, as if they referred to properties in a single fief, and the apparent connection between the distribution of these properties and those on the king's fief. Neither of these characteristics, to be discussed in further detail below,[1] would appear to be typical of groups of properties whose owners had no more than a political interest in common. The terms appear, in fact, to reflect a pattern of territorial lordship, rather than the ownership of tenements on the rentrolls of private landlords in mid twelfth-century Winchester.

This long discussion has resulted in no firm conclusion. But some positive points do emerge. There is sufficient variation of scribal practice in the recording of the terms *de .B.* and *de terra Baronum* for there to be a real possibility that the two forms mean the same. The bishop was the principal recipient of both rents, but he appears to have lost possession of them before the early thirteenth century. There is a strong territorial association between the properties from which these rents were due and the royal fief in the city, but there is no sign that these rents were at any time in the possession of the king. Finally, their occurrence appears to suggest a pattern of territorial lordship rather than one of private ownership.

Since, however, the most obvious interpretations do not fit and the more plausible reconstructions are in opposition to each other, the problems must be regarded as unsolved. In the text printed here the terms have been normalized as *de B.* and *de terra baronum*. In the translation *de B.* has been left as it is and *de terra baronum* and its contractions have been translated 'from the land of the barons'.[2] In discussion, however, both in this introduction and elsewhere in the volume, the forms *de .B.* and *de terra Baronum* have been retained, with their variants if required, as being closer to the original manuscript.

The preamble to Survey **II** expresses the scope of the inquiry in feudal terms. The inquest was into who held what of whom. The information, however, is presented almost entirely in financial terms, and this no doubt comes much closer to reality. The rights which men had in the burgage tenements were almost entirely fiscal. We are concerned with rents and rent-charges, not with lords and vassals, fealty and services. Nevertheless, the four questions are usually answered directly or indirectly, and, although the information is not presented in absolutely standard form, there is less variety than in Survey **I** and the variations seem to be without significance. The simplest form is 'A. pays the bishop x*d*.' Usually the entry adds, 'and receives y*s*.' The more complicated items then list the various rent-charges. The first name in the entry is the freeholder who holds the messuage in demesne. And he holds it of the next man named, the person to whom he pays landgable or a rent. The amount of land he holds is not usually given explicitly; but it seems to have been one land (*terra*) unless otherwise stated. The fourth question seems always to be answered in full detail. All rents arising from the tenement are noted together with the recipient. The payer, however, is usually not named if he is a tenant by lease or at will.

[1] See below, pp. 354–5.
[2] For further discussion, see below, p. 353, Tables 11, 14, and Fig. 14*a*.

The information presented by the survey is more conveniently considered in an order different from that of the questions listed in the preamble: first the tenements, then the rents, and finally the tenants and the fiefs.

Whereas in Survey **I** the tenements are mostly *domus* or *mansurae*, the basic unit in 1148 is the *terra* (land). Although continuity of layout cannot be proved from the surveys —indeed relatively few properties can be identified in both lists (Table 9)—we are probably concerned only with a change of name. Since *terra* has replaced both *domus* and *mansura* it is probably an even less technical term, and its use may signify that some tenurial niceties have been abandoned. Survey **II** is also even less interested than Survey **I** in the buildings on the *terrae*. There are a few references to *mansiones* (but none to *mansurae*); a *domus* has become a stall (**II, 48**); stalls (*estals, seldae, scammels*) are plentiful; the forges remain; but cellars and other parts of a dwelling house are not mentioned.

The rental pattern seems unaltered in essentials. Landgable, although named even less frequently than in Survey **I,** can still be identified throughout the survey; and the liability appears to be unchanged. We can also see that the bishop and prior of Winchester received money payments which look like landgable. There are almost no references to other customs or to services in Survey **II.** This probably does not mean that they have disappeared, merely that they were not investigated. The superstructure of economic rents and rent-charges is probably more complicated than before, but has developed no new features. There are in 1148 some very complicated arrangements. Herbert the chamberlain, the son of the Herbert of Survey **I,** had one tenement in High Street (**II, 38**) and paid the king 6*d.* (for landgable) and the monks of Tewkesbury 12*d.* Herbert received the following rents: 10*s.* from Odgar's son, 6*s.* from Richard Bagnor, 15*s.* from Roger of La Haye, 6*s.* from Drew, 6*s.* from Hervey, and 6*s.* from Herbert son of Westman. Roger of La Haye also paid the prior of Winchester 5*s.*, but on the credit side received 33*s.* in rent from the tenement. Herbert son of Westman received 6*s.* in rent which cancelled his own liability. Thus the owner, Herbert the chamberlain, in return for royal landgable and a rent-charge to Tewkesbury, a total of 1*s.* 6*d.*, drew 49*s.* Among the sub-tenants Roger made a profit of 13*s.* Herbert son of Westman simply passed on the rent he received but may have retained some land for his own use. The other three were probably occupiers, getting either living accommodation or a place of business in return for an economic rent.

Although the heading to the survey is in feudal form and assumes that everyone held of someone else, there are few references to fiefs and few relationships described which are not economic. In fact we are concerned more with estates or rentrolls than with fiefs. Apart from the king, who drew little more than landgable from his burgesses, there were four principal landlords in Winchester: the bishop, the prior, the abbot of Hyde, and the abbess of Winchester. These drew all kinds of rents from the inhabitants of Winchester and were occasionally burdened with payments out of the tenements. For example, Ansgod Tresor paid the bishop 2*s.*, and the bishop was responsible for paying the 6*d.* (? landgable) which Ansgod owed the king (**II, 437**). Geoffrey the Deaf paid the prior 2*s.* 6*d.*, and the prior paid the bishop 1*s.* (**II, 629**).

The largest fiefs were scattered throughout the city; the smaller were usually more compact (Fig. 19). The abbot of Hyde's estate was in the northern part of the city, the area closest to the abbey. More curious is the way in which the fiefs of the abbesses of Winchester, Wherwell, and Romsey were segregated in different streets. Wherwell's fief was within a solid block, *Brudenestret*, *Scowrtenestret*, *Alwarnestret*, and *Flesmangerestret*; and Romsey had only one property beyond the compact *Calpestret*, *Goldestret*, and *Gerestret* area. In the various streets, the fiefs are usually formed of blocks of tenements rather than scattered messuages. When the property had been granted to the churches it had been transferred in units larger than the tenements of 1148.[1]

The king drew rents from all areas of the city except *Colobrochestret*, *Mensterstret*, and outside the East and South Gates. The bulk of his property was in the most populous areas, High Street and outside West Gate. As he rarely received anything more than landgable, he drew only £7. 3s. 4¾d. in annual rents from 262 properties (Table 12, cf. Fig. 14a). Seventy-six tenements in High Street brought him £1. 11s. 0d. The bishop drew over £40 from nearly as many. The king, however, had at least £3. 1s. 4d. a year in weekly rents or tolls from stalls in High Street, an indication that, as the later detailed evidence for the fee farm shows, the major part of the royal revenue from Winchester was derived from the commerce of the city.[2]

By far the largest and most valuable fief was the bishop's, which at almost £70 a year, including rents *de .B.* and *de terra Baronum*, was worth ten times that of the king (Tables 13 and 14, cf. Fig. 14a). The prior's fief, at more than £28, was worth four times, and the abbot of Hyde's fief, at more than £11, one and a half times the value of the king's. The abbess of Winchester received a little less than the king and the abbesses of Wherwell and Romsey received about £2 and £1 respectively (Table 11, cf. Fig. 14a).

Nearly all the tenements in the city and suburbs lay in one or other of these seven fiefs. Their territorial and financial distribution, further evidence for their size and value in the eleventh, twelfth, and thirteenth centuries, and the implications of this pattern of lordship are discussed in detail below.[3]

At a lower level were the estates of the burgesses. As an example we can take the estate of Martin of Bentworth, possibly a butcher, who took his name from a place fourteen miles north-east of Winchester. Although he is twice listed as though he was alive (**II, 56** and **487**), his heirs occur and it is his wife who appears most often. It seems that in 1148 the family was in fact represented by his widow, whose Christian name is never stated, his sister, and his heirs. It was not uncommon for women to be property-holders in Winchester; and Martin's wife was, perhaps, one of the richest of these. The family held a number of stalls in High Street. In one place Martin received 3s. 6d. from one and his wife 16s. from five. Their landgable to the king was 1d. a stall a week (**II, 56**). The heirs received 2s. from another stall (**II, 17**), and the wife held a further stall from the king for 2d. a week (**II, 28**), and a shambles for 1d. a week to the king and 5d. (? a year) to the prior. From the shambles she received 1½d. a week (**II, 43**). The family also held urban tenements or interests in them. Martin's sister paid the bishop 3s. for a tenement in High Street (**II, 144**). His wife held a High Street property on the fief of the earl of Gloucester

---

[1] For discussion of these large early tenements, see below, p. 340 and cf. Fig. 12.

[2] For the fee farm, see above, p. 5, below, pp. 499 ff.,

and Appendix I.

[3] See below, pp. 349–69, Tables 11–19, 21, 22, and Figs. 14–16 and 19.

and received 67s. 6d. from two tenants (**II, 139**). In *Alwarnestret* Martin paid the king 1s. 3d. and received 4s. (**II, 487**). In *Sildwortenestret* Martin's wife took 3s. and 2s. 4d. from two adjacent properties (**II, 565–6**). In *Mensterstret* she collected 4s., 5s., and 2s. (**II, 795, 808, and 809**). One of these messuages was on Baldwin's fief; of another it is recorded 'it is not known from whom she holds it' (**II, 808**). In *Calpestret* she paid 3s. to the prior and received 14s. (**II, 825**). From a property in *Goldestret* she paid the abbess of Romsey 1s. 8d. (**II, 854**). Outside South Gate the heirs held a vacant plot for which they paid the bishop 1s. 8d. and from which they obtained 5s. They also had house property which yielded 5s. (**II, 1058**). The whole family drew £6. 18s. 8½d. in rents and paid out £2. 5s. 6d. They had too, of course, the use of some of the property, probably for trading purposes.

Survey **II** depicts a thriving commercial and industrial city.[1] Some characteristic features of the state of development achieved by 1148, such as the complexity of tenure, were already evident half a century before, in Survey **I**. We may compare, for example, the thirteen trade bynames recorded for *c.* 1110, with the twenty-three recorded in 1148 on the king's fief (which represents approximately the same sample of the whole city as Survey **I**), and wonder whether this reflects a considerable mercantile and industrial development in Winchester during the first half of the twelfth century. Yet in Survey **I** as a whole, both *TRE* and *c.* 1110, twenty-six trade bynames were recorded, nineteen of which did not occur on the king's fief in 1148. Eight of the trade bynames occurring in *c.* 1110 did not appear on the king's fief in Survey **II**. These statistics appear inconclusive, and may reveal changes in patterns of nomenclature rather than industrial development, yet it would be possible to argue that the variety of trades present in the city by the end of the eleventh century was as great as in the middle of the twelfth. It is clear at least that the troubles of Stephen's reign had little long-term effect on the city.[2] Winchester, the seat of the treasury and the headquarters of so many royal clerks and sergeants, had every stimulus to develop its good geographical position as a trading and industrial centre. The city may have lost some of its importance as a royal residence after the first decade of Henry I's reign,[3] but the accession in 1129 of Bishop Henry of Blois with his great wealth, his administrative dynamism, and his royal and continental connections, may have discounted this to some extent.

V. THE METHOD OF EDITING

The orthography of the manuscript has been followed except that *i* is used as the equivalent of *i* and *j*, and *v* is used for the consonant, *u* for the vowel. The letter *e* with a cedilla has been extended to *ae*. Proper names, however, except for the rationalization of the initial letter, have been presented as far as possible as written. Abbreviated name-forms, if unambiguous, have as a rule been silently extended. Obvious errors have been corrected in the printed text and the manuscript reading given in the footnotes. Accidental omissions have been supplied in square brackets. The punctuation and capitalization are the editor's.

The manuscript text is much abbreviated, but, although there is variation in the formulas employed and much scribal carelessness, it is usually clear how words should be

---

[1] See below, pp. 427–39.   [2] See below, pp. 386, 489–90.   [3] See below, pp. 295–7.

extended. Hence in Survey **I** *redd'*, *fac'*, and *ten'* have regularly been extended to *redd-it/ unt/ebat/ebant*, *fac-it/iunt/iebat/iebant*, and *ten-et/ent/uit/uerunt* according to the context. Where the editor has been in doubt the extension is shown in italic type. In Survey **I** *cons'* and *consuet'* have been extended to *consuetudinem* or *consuetudines* usually without indication, according to what seems to be the scribe's usage in that section. In any case, since the singular and plural forms were apparently used in the same sense, little harm can have been done.

The items in each survey have been numbered in order to facilitate reference. Normally the paragraph signs in the manuscript or the commencement on a new line and the use of a coloured majuscule have been accepted as separating one item from another. But, occasionally, obviously connected information has been divided in the manuscript and, conversely, the description of two tenements has been run together. When the confusion is obvious, the presentation has been rectified in the text. But there are not a few other cases where it can be suspected that successive entries refer to the same tenement.

vi. NOTES ON THE TRANSLATION

Although J. H. Round's view that the text of Survey **I** (he was not concerned with the other survey) was 'unfortunately too corrupt and, consequently, too obscure for satisfactory translation',[1] can only be regarded as a far from candid excuse, his reluctance to undertake the task is understandable. The text is indeed obscure. Not because it is corrupt—it is hardly inferior to Domesday Book—but because it is written in a technical language. To translate business records from Latin jargon into English jargon is not exciting work and the sense given to the phrases largely depends on the general interpretation of the document. If the purpose of the survey, the terms of reference, or the import of the several parts of the returns have been misunderstood, the translation will be misleading.

The purpose and meaning of the surveys have already been discussed. It remains to state how some of the key phrases are translated and how they should be understood. In Survey **I** *TRE* (*Tempore Regis Edwardi*) has been retained in the translation in order to save space. It means 'In the time of King Edward', i.e. before 1066 and perhaps in this case *c.* 1057.[2] The tenurial units, *domus*, *terra*, *mansio*, *mansura*, *managium*, cannot usually be differentiated and may not always have had any special technical significance (see above, pp. 13–14, and below, p. 337). Where it is clear that *domus*, *mansio*, or *managium* means a building or living accommodation, the word has been translated 'house' or 'living accommodation'. Usually *domus* has been translated 'tenement', *terra* 'land', and *mansio/mansura* 'messuage'. In Survey **I** to pay, render, to perform the custom/all customs, etc. means to pay those customary financial dues and perform those customary services for which the tenement was responsible. Most of the phrases are thought to be synonymous (see above, pp. 15 ff.). The compiler of Survey **I** used various phrases to indicate that the obligations were the same *TRE* and *modo* (now): *debet/facit similiter*, *debet/facit idem*, *debet facere similiter/idem*. They are no more than stylistic variations and have been translated 'owes/does the same' or 'should do the same'.

[1] *VCH Hants* i. 527.   [2] See above, p. 10.

Sums of money have been expressed in arabic figures, but have not been reduced to
£. s. d., i.e. 40d. has been retained in preference to 3s. 4d. A mark of silver is 13s. 4d.
A bizant, a gold coin first struck at Byzantium, was worth about 2s. The final sentence in
most of the early items in Survey **I**, *et reddit . . .*, literally, 'And it pays', has been translated 'And it (the tenement) yields . . .' It is probably equivalent to Domesday Book's
et valet ('it is worth'); but, with its clear connection with *redditus* and *renta*, could equally
well be translated 'And the rent is . . .' It states the value of the whole property (or sometimes of the part defined) to the owner or other named persons. In Survey **II** we are told
for each tenement what rents are paid, essentially from and to the freeholder. The
standard formula is probably *Episcopus reddit regi vii d. et obolum et habet ix s. de eadem
terra* (**II, 876**; cf. **II, 43, 258, 270, 332, 359, 381, 439, 484, 661,** and **838**), 'The bishop
pays the king 7½d. and receives 9s. from that land.' But most often *reddit* is omitted.
Whenever a proper name in the dative follows one in the nominative case, 'pays' has been
inserted in the translation. Other expressions, *debet/deberet reddere* (**II, 2, 9,** and **436**)
and *solebat reddere* (**II, 16, 310,** and **838**), state the obligation but infer that the rent is
not being paid, usually because the tenement is waste or vacant. When a payment was
made in respect of several tenements (*de iii mansuris*) *de* could be translated 'from' or
'for'. The latter has been preferred. Elsewhere the choice has depended on the context.

In Survey **II** two phrases *de .B.* and *de terra Baronum* cannot be explained with certainty (see above, pp. 19 ff.). In the translation the former has been left as it stands, the
latter has been translated 'from the land of the barons', although this is unlikely to be
its true meaning.

The translation of the personal names has been particularly difficult. No one can be
sure what vernacular forms the Latin versions represent. And, even if we did know, there
would be no point in reproducing them. It seemed desirable therefore to give names in a
familiar form whenever possible. The post-conquest names cause the least trouble.
Henricus appears as Henry (but not Harry), *Theodericus* as Theoderic (not Terry). Most
Old-English names have no modern equivalents. *Aluredus* is translated as Alfred; but
where there is no modern form the Latinized version of the manuscript has been left.
Even more difficult are the bynames. Here the interpretations given by Dr. von Feilitzen
have been followed as far as possible (below, pp. 143 ff.). Latin words have been translated:
e.g. *pinguis* = Fat. Wherever a vernacular byname can easily be modernized this has been
done: e.g. *watmaungre* = wet-monger. But few French nicknames have been translated:
Petit, for example, has not been turned into 'Little'. With local bynames the modern
spelling of the place has been given, e.g. *de Inglesh'* = of Inglesham. Where the place
cannot be identified the manuscript reading has been kept in italic type. *Filius* has usually
been translated 'son of', not 'fitz'. 'Henry son of William' may look as strange as 'Godric
fitzEaldred', but it seemed sensible here to apply a single rule. All the same it must be
admitted that a few inconsistencies have been allowed for one reason or another.

2

TEXT, TRANSLATION, AND NOTES

(i) THE SURVEY OF *c.* 1110

(SURVEY I)

Liber de terris regis reddentibus langabulum et bru-*gabulum* in Wint*onia*, sicut solebant reddere tempore regis Edwardi.

Henricus rex volens scire quid rex Edwardus habuit omnibus modis Wintonie in suo dominico, burgensium suorum sacramento hoc comprobari iussit. Volebat enim illud inde penitus habere quod*ᵃ* rex Edwardus suo tempore inde habuit. Hoc igitur sacramentum factum fuit de quattuor viginti et vi burgensibus melioribus Wint*onie*, presente Willelmo episcopo[1] et Herberto camerario[2] et Radulfo Basset[3] et Goisfrido Ridel[4] et Willelmo de Pontearchar'.[5] Hoc autem burgenses peracto sacramento a porta orientali ceperunt inquirere ether-gingis.[6]

[1] Alwinus Sidessone tenuit tempore regis Eadwardi i*ᵇ* domum reddentem de langabulo vi d. et omnem aliam consuetudinem regis; et rex eam tenuit in dominio. Modo eam tenet filius Radulfi Roselli,[1] quia dimissa fuit ei a patre; et nullam consu[e]tudinem inde unquam reddidit; et reddit l s.

[2] Edwinus Godeswale tenuit i domum T.R.E. red-dentem de langabulo vi d. et retro illam domum de con-suetudine iii d., et omnem aliam consuetudinem. Modo tenet Ricardus capellanus comitis de M*e*llent;[1] et nullam consuetudinem inde reddidit nisi in hoc anno; et reddidit per annum xx s.

ᵃ sed *MS.*   *ᵇ* ii *MS.*

A record of the lands of the king which pay landgable and brewgable in Winchester, just as they used to pay in the time of King Edward.

King Henry, wishing to know what King Edward had in every way in his demesne at Winchester, ordered this to be declared by the oath of his burgesses. For he wanted to have from it everything that King Edward had had there in his time. This oath, therefore, was taken by eighty-six of the more important burgesses of Winchester in the presence of Bishop William,[1] Herbert the chamberlain,[2] Ralf Basset,[3] Geoffrey Ridel,[4] and William of Pont de l'Arche.[5] After the burgesses had taken the oath, they began to make their inquiry, going up and down[6] from the East Gate.

[HIGH STREET (NORTH SIDE, EAST TO WEST)]

[1] Alwin Scid's son held 1 tenement *TRE* which paid 6d. landgable and every other royal custom; and the king held it in demesne. Now the son of Ralf Rosell[1] holds it, because it was left to him by his father; and he has never paid any custom in respect of it. And it yields 50s.

[2] Edwin Good-soul held 1 tenement *TRE* which paid 6d. landgable (and the area behind the tenement paid 3d. for custom) and every other custom. Now Richard, chaplain of the count of Meulan,[1] holds it; and he has never paid any custom in respect of it except this year. And it yielded 20s. a year.

PREFACE 1. William Giffard: dean of Rouen; chancellor to William II; nominated to Winchester by Henry I, 1100; owing to Henry's difficulties with Anselm, not conse-crated until 1107; died 1129. *DNB* xxi. 298.

2. See also **4, 13b, 24, 33, 35, 48, 74, 111, 116–17, 123, 152,** and **292.** See also above, pp. 17–18. A royal chamberlain; a tenant-in-chief in Berks. and Wilts. and an extensive mesne-tenant; a married clerk (his position in this list proves his clerical status); but possibly there were father and son of the same name. Chamberlain of the treasury under William II, royal treasurer under Henry I. Died before 1130, possibly in 1128. His son, Herbert fitzHerbert, in Survey **II** likewise called Herbert the chamberlain, was fined 353 marks of silver (£235) for his father's land in 1130. Also in 1130 Gervase fitzOsbert owed the king 20 marks for recovering his land which Herbert had had with Gervase's father's sister, and Robert de Venuiz paid 16s. 8d. for Herbert's daughter and her dowry; *Pipe Roll 31 Henry I*, p. 37. For Herbert's son, Geoffrey, see **I, 27.** Richardson and Sayles, 217–23, 422 ff.

3. A royal justiciar: *DNB* iii. 385; Richardson and Sayles, 174 ff.

4. A royal justiciar, drowned in 1120: *DNB* xlviii. 274; Richardson and Sayles, 174 ff. But to be distinguished from his descendant and namesake, Henry II's justiciar, who died as bishop of Ely in 1189.

5. See also **49, 82, 143, 173, 259; II, 171, 671,** and **830.** William, sheriff of Hants and Berks., possibly a widower and the father of Robert (see **II, 270** and **830**), bought c. 1130 the daughter of Robert Mauduit I and his office of chamberlainship of the treasury. He had a a chequered history under Stephen. See *Historia Novella*, p. 16; *Gesta Stephani*, pp. 5, 100–1. Cuckolded by his wife and imprisoned by her lover in his own castle (? Winchester) in 1143, he was dead by 1148 (**II, 171, 671,** and **830**): Richardson and Sayles, 221–2, 431–3, and elsewhere; H. A. Cronne, *The Reign of Stephen* (London, 1970), 202–3.

6. Cf. below, **80–1,** *hesterdinges.*

1 1. See also **5, 19, 199–201,** and **216.** For his father, see **20** and **80.**

2 1. Robert, count of Meulan, lord of Pontaudemer and Beaumont in Normandy, earl of Leicester in England, died 1118; a friend of Henry I. In 1130 his twin son, Waleran, count of Meulan, was pardoned 25s. when the city of Winchester paid an aid of £80: *Pipe Roll 31 Henry I*, p. 41. Henry de Beaumont, earl of Warwick (see **279**), was Robert's younger brother.

[3] Brumanus de la Forda[1] tenuit i domum T.R.E. reddentem omnem consuetudinem. Modo eam tenet Wibertus Saluagius; et nullam consuetudinem inde reddidit. Et hanc Osbertus filius Alberede[2] [. . .] per[a] viii s.

[4] Leuret de Essewem tenuit i domum T.R.E. reddente[m] omnem consuetudinem. Modo tenet Osbertus filius Alberede;[1] et nullam consuetudinem unquam inde reddidit. Et de eadem terra habet Herebertus camerarius[2] i mansuram que reddit xv s. et nullam [fo. 1ᵛ] consuetudinem reddidit.

[5] Climehen tenuit i domum T.R.E. reddentem omnem consuetudinem. Modo eam tenet filius Radulfi Roselli;[1] et nullam consuetudinem inde unquam reddidit; et reddit vi sol.

[6] Lewinus sutor tenuit i domum T.R.E. reddentem omnem consuetudinem. Modo tenet eam Audoenus napparius;[1] et nullam consuetudinem inde unquam reddidit preter geldum; et reddit xviii sol. et vi d.

[7] Wluricus presbiter tenuit i domum T.R.E. reddentem omnem consuetudinem. Modo tenet eam Robertus filius Wimundi;[1] et similiter reddit omnem consuetudinem; et reddit xv sol.

[8] Huneman tenuit i domum T.R.E. reddentem omnem consuetudinem. Et de illa tenet abbatissa Wint'[1] i partem; et similiter reddit omnem consuetudinem; et reddit viii sol. Et de illa terra tenet adhuc Hugo Oillardus[2] i partem; et nullam[b] consuetudinem inde facit; et reddit ii sol.

[9] Wido[c] tenuit i domum T.R.E. reddentem omnem consuetudinem. Modo tenet eam Anschetillus de Iorz;[1] et nullam consuetudinem inde facit; et reddit xxx s.

[10] Et ibi deiuxta[d] fuit chenictehalla,[1] ubi chenictes potabant gildam suam, et eam libere tenebant de rege

[3] Brunman of Fordingbridge[1] held 1 tenement *TRE* which paid every custom. Now Wibert the Wild holds it; and he has not paid any custom in respect of it. And Osbert son of Albereda[2] [? holds] it [of Wibert] for 8s.

[4] Leuret *de Essewem* held 1 tenement *TRE* which paid every custom. Now Osbert son of Albereda holds it;[1] and he has never paid any custom in respect of it. And Herbert the chamberlain[2] holds 1 messuage of that land which yields 15s. And he has not paid any custom.

[5] Climehen held 1 tenement *TRE* which paid every custom. Now the son of Ralf Rossell[1] holds it; and he has never paid any custom in respect of it. And it yields 6s.

[6] Lewin the shoemaker held 1 tenement *TRE* which paid every custom. Now Oin the napier[1] holds it; and he has never paid any custom in respect of it except geld. And it yields 18s. 6d.

[7] Wulfric the priest held 1 tenement *TRE* which paid every custom. Now Robert son of Wimund[1] holds it, and likewise pays every custom. And it yields 15s.

[8] Hunmann held 1 tenement *TRE* which paid every custom. The abbess of Winchester[1] holds one part of it, and likewise pays every custom, and it yields 8s. And moreover Hugh Oillard[2] holds one part of it, and performs no custom in respect of it. And it yields 2s.

[9] Guy held 1 tenement *TRE* which paid every custom. Now Anschetil de Jort[1] holds it, and performs no custom in respect of it. And it yields 30s.

[10] And nearby was the hall of the *cnihtas*,[1] where the *cnihtas* used to drink their guild; and they held it freely

---

[a] pro *Ellis*   [b] et nullam *repeated and underlined MS., 'near by'*; cf. [28]

[c] *Wuido MS., u crossed out by rubricator*   [d] deiusta

3 1. Possibly 'of the Ford': cf. below, pp. 194 and 237, s.n.
2. See also **4** and **69**.
4 1. See **3**.
2. See I, Preface.
5 1. See **1**.
6 1. For napiers, see *Constitutio Domus Regis*, printed in *Dialogus de Scaccario*, 130; *King's Serjeants*, 222–7. A payment under London to the wife of Oin the napier in 1130 is in *Pipe Roll 31 Henry I*, p. 143.
7 1. See also **41, 62**, and **65**. A Robert fitzWimund was pardoned 10s. of Danegeld in Sussex in 1130: *Pipe Roll 31 Henry I*, p. 72. Wimund was a moneyer of William I, William II, and Henry I. For this tenement cf. **II, 73**, where there were forges, and see below, p. 399 and Table 39.
8 1. For this tenement, cf. **II, 72**.

2. See also **17**. Probably a royal constable, see *King's Serjeants*, 6. In 1130 the sheriff of Surrey accounted for the relief which William fitzHugh owed for his father's land and office: *Pipe Roll 31 Henry I*, p. 50. See also *Regesta*, ii, no. 1685a.
9 1. See also **12, 187**, and **279**. Cf. Ansger de Iorz (**182**). *King's Serjeants*, 291, suggests that the family derived their name from Jort (Calvados), and mentions some other members.
10 1. For this guildhall, which is presumably distinct from that described in entry **34**, and early guilds, see J. H. Round, *VCH Hants* i. 530–2; Tait *Medieval Borough*, 119–23, 136; Urry *Canterbury*, 124 ff. The order of survey suggests that **I, 10** may be the same as **II, 69**, Chapman's Hall. For guildhalls and guilds in Winchester, see below, pp. 335–6 and 427.

Edwardo. Modo eam tenent Godwinus Prison[2] et Godwinus Grenessone,[3] et clamant regem inde ad warant per eius breve quod habent; et domus illa reddit eis xxv sol., et uxori Azelini xii sol., et Henrico de Domera[4] x sol. Et in eadem terra est quedam aecclesia[5] quam habet Chepingius filius Alueue,[6] et clamat inde regem ad warant; et eius filius habet ibi de renta v sol.

of King Edward. Now Godwin Prison[2] and Godwin Green's son[3] hold it; and they vouch the king to warranty by his writ which they have. And the tenement yields them 25s., the wife of Ascelin 12s., and Henry of Dummer[4] 10s. And on that land is a certain church[5] which Cheping the son of Alveva[6] holds, and he vouches the king to warranty in respect of it; and her/his son has there 5s. of rent.

[11] Alwinus Aitardessone[1] fuit quidam monetarius T.R.E., et tenuit i domum que pertinuit Basingestoches.[2] Modo tenet eam Godefridus de Tolcha; et nichil consuet*udinis* reddidit; et reddit xl sol.

[11] Alwin Aitard's son[1] was a moneyer *TRE* and held 1 tenement which pertained to Basingstoke.[2] Now Godfrey of Touques holds it and paid nothing in the way of custom. And it yields 40s.

[12] Paganus de la medehalla[1] tenuit i domum T.R.E. reddentem omnem consuetudinem. Modo tenet eam Anschetillus de Iorz;[2] et tenet omnem consuetudinem, quia nichil inde dedit; et reddit xii sol. et [fo. 2] suum estagium.[3]

[12] Pain of the mead-hall[1] held 1 tenement *TRE* which paid every custom. Now Anschetil of Jort[2] holds it, and he holds every custom because he gave nothing in respect of it. And it yields 12s. and [the profit of] its upper storey (?)[3]

[13a] Goderun Litteprot tenuit i domum T.R.E. reddentem omnem consuetudinem. Modo tenet eam Radulfus de Felgeriis;[1] et nullam consuetudinem inde reddidit preter geldum. Et tunc T.R.E. erat i domus. Modo manent ibi iiii homines; et redd*it* xxix sol.

[13a] Godrun Litteprot held 1 tenement *TRE* which paid every custom. Now Ralf of Fougères[1] holds it, and paid no custom in respect of it except geld. And *TRE* there was 1 house there. Now 4 men live there. And it yields 29s.

[13b] Alestanus*a* Douetessone[1] tenuit i domum T.R.E.

[13b] Alestan Dovet's son[1] held 1 tenement *TRE* which

a There is no break or paragraph sign in the MS.

10 2. See also **228** and **238**. He seems to have been dead by 1148: **II, 690**. He was a neighbour of the other Godwin in *Bucchestret*. A Godwine was a moneyer of Henry I. Godwin Prison's properties seem to have had moneying connections: see below, Table 39. See also **172**.
    3. See also **233**.   4. See also **87** and **137**.
    5. If the identification with **II, 69** is correct, this church would be that known as St. Mary *de linea tela* or St. Mary *de la Wode* in the thirteenth and fourteenth centuries.
    6. See also **71, 73**, and **134**. As he is associated with Henry of Dummer, he may be Cheping the Rich of **87**. He is probably not Chiping the son of Alwin (**135**; cf. **241**). He is clearly distinguished from Chiping of Keynsham (**71**). And he is not connected with Chiping of Worthy, the important *TRE* tenant (see **141**). Cheping son of Alveva was probably the moneyer of Henry I and Stephen. Hugh son of Chepping, also a moneyer of Stephen, appears to have succeeded him in two of his tenements by 1148: see **73, 134**, and below, Tables 39 and 44.
11 1. Ælfwine was a Winchester moneyer from Cnut to Harold II: *English Coins*, 77. For his brother, Alward, also a moneyer, see **107**, and for both moneyers see below, pp. 401 ff. and Table 34.
    2. Basingstoke was a royal manor. See also **II, 434**. In 1212 a messuage in Winchester had previously rendered 2s. to the manor of Basingstoke: *Book of Fees*, i, 77.

12 1. Possibly a Winchester locality, see below, pp. 195 and 238 s.n.   2. See **9**.
    3. This word also occurs in **43, 46, 75**, and **82**. Houses yield a sum of money *et* or *preter suum estagium*. This seems to mean 'besides its *estagium*'. In the context *stagium* (a stage, or storey) seems better than *lastagium* (lastage, a customs duty); and the phrase may mean 'without taking the upper storey into account'. For similar expressions concerning *managium*, see **II, 197**.
13a 1. The original benefactor of the monks of Savigny: *Regesta*, ii, no. 1015. For his family, see L. Delisle, 'Digest of two letters illustrative of the family of Clemence, Countess of Chester', *JBAA*[1] 7 (1852), 123–51, and *Seals*, no. 236. His son, Henry, became a monk at Savigny in 1150. In 1150–73 his grandson, Ralph, a benefactor of the canons of Fougères and of Missenden Abbey, granted his land in Winchester, which his father had held in the reign of Henry I, to Missenden via Hamo Boterel. William son of Arfast quitclaimed in the tenement *cum quatuor bordellis iuxta domum suam* shortly afterwards: J. G. Jenkins (ed.), *The Cartulary of Missenden Abbey*, iii (HMC, JP1, 1962), nos. 700–4, 893, and 895. The abbey had 23s. annual rent in Winchester in the thirteenth century: BM, Harl.MS. 3688, fo. 194[v].
13b 1. See also **39**. As he was succeeded in one tenement by a chamberlain and in the other by the sheriff, he may have been a royal servant.

reddentem omnem consuetudinem. Modo tenet Herebertus camerarius;[2] et nullam consuetudinem inde reddidit preter hoc quod homines suos adquietavit de geldo;[3] et reddit lxi sol.

[14] Godwinus Elmeressone[1] tenuit i domum T.R.E. reddentem consuetudinem. Modo tenent monachi de Sancto Swithuno;[2] et reddunt similiter consuetudinem; et reddit xxiii sol. Et de eadem domo habet Willelmus de Albinneio[3] [. . .]; et nullam consuetudinem inde reddit; et reddit per annum xiii sol.

[15] Godwinus Socche[a1] fuit T.R.E. magister monetarius, et tenui[t] i domum de feudo episcopi Wint'.[2] Modo tenent eam monachi de Sancto Swithuno.[3] Faciunt consuetudinem; et reddit xxxvii[b] sol.

[16] Winestaham[c] Escitteport[1] tenuit i domum T.R.E. reddentem omnem consuetudinem. Et hanc dedit Hugo lardarius[2] monachis de Sancto Swithuno; et modo reddunt consuetudinem.[3] Sed tunc ibi manebat i bonus civis, modo pauperes; et reddit lxiiii sol.

[17] Brunestanus[1] et Alestanus Flathege tenuerunt duas domos T.R.E. red[d]entes omnem consuetudinem. Modo tenet eam Hugo Oilardus;[2] et nullam consuetudinem reddit; et de venta regis retinuit c sol.[3] Et tunc ibi manebant duo boni burgenses, modo nullus nisi pauperes; et reddit xliiii sol.

[18] Fulges[1] tenuit i domum T.R.E. reddentem omnem consuetudinem. Modo tenet eam Henricus lardarius;[2] et nullam consuetudinem reddidit. Et solebat ibi manere i bonus civis, modo nullus; et reddit xxvi sol.

---

paid every custom. Now Herbert the chamberlain[2] holds it, and paid no custom in respect of it except that he acquitted his men of geld.[3] And it yields 61s.

[14] Godwin Elmer's son[1] held 1 tenement *TRE* which paid custom. Now the monks of St. Swithun[2] hold it, and likewise pay custom. And it yields 23s. And William d'Aubigny[3] holds [one messuage (?)] of that land, and pays no custom in respect of it. And it yields 13s. a year.

[15] Godwin Sock[1] was a master moneyer *TRE* and he held 1 tenement of the fief of the bishop of Winchester.[2] Now the monks of St. Swithun hold it.[3] They perform the custom. And it yields 37s.

[16] Winstan Shut-gate[1] held 1 tenement *TRE* which paid every custom. And Hugh the larderer[2] gave it to the monks of St. Swithun, and now they pay the custom.[3] But then one good citizen lived there, now only poor men. And it yields 64s.

[17] Brunstan[1] and Alestan Flat-hedge held 2 tenements *TRE* which paid every custom. Now Hugh Oilard[2] holds it and pays no custom and retains 100s. from the king's toll.[3] Two good burgesses used to live there, now no one but poor men. And it yields 44s.

[18] Fulges[1] held 1 tenement *TRE* which paid every custom. Now Henry the larderer[2] holds it and paid no custom. And one good citizen used to live there, now none. And it yields 26s.

---

[a] Godwinus So(cche) *over an erasure*   [b] *Erased* i *after* xxxvii?   [c] Wuinestaham *MS.*, u *crossed out by rubricator*

13b 2. See **I**, Preface.

3. See also **24** and **33**. Herbert the chamberlain was excused paying Danegeld as a member of the Exchequer Board: *Dialogus de Scaccario*, 56.

14 1. See also **48**, **87**, and **196**.

2. For this tenement, cf. **II**, **64**.

3. See also **33**. Probably the master-butler, William d'Aubigny *pincerna*, and presumably the father, not the son who married Henry I's widow and became earl of Arundel: *King's Serjeants*, 141–2; *Regesta*, ii, p. xiii. Only the son is in *DNB*.

15 1. Not to be identified, as W. H. Stevenson and J. H. Round suggested, *VCH Hants* i. 536, with Godwine Ceoca, the Winchester moneyer, for whom see **171**. For moneyers' interests in property here, cf. **II**, **64–5**, and for Godwinus Socche as a moneyer see below, p. 422 and Table 34.

2. For the bishop's fee, cf. **II**, **63**.

3. This tenement is on the fief of the bishop of Winchester (assigned to the monks), and like **16** and **28** it

could have appeared under 'the land of the barons and tenants'. For this tenement, cf. **II**, **62**.

16 1. A Wynstan was a moneyer of Edward the Confessor: see **175** and below, Table 35.

2. William II and Henry I confirmed Hugh the larderer's grant of lands and houses to the prior and monks in precepts to be dated 1096 and 1100/1103–6. In one, Hugh's son Henry is mentioned: *Regesta*, ii, nos. 803–4. For larderers, see *Constitutio Domus Regis*, in *Dialogus de Scaccario*, 131; *King's Serjeants*, 233ff. For this tenement, cf. **II**, **61**. Cf. **18**.

3. In Rufus's confirmation charter to the monks (V. H. Galbraith, *EHR* 35 (1920), 382 ff., no. XI), it is expressly stated, *et [monachi] reddent mihi et prepositis meis consuetudines quas ipsi reddebant qui eas ecclesiae dederunt*.

17 1. Cf. **90** and **131**. Perhaps the moneyer of Edward the Confessor: see also **256**, and below, Table 35.

2. See **8**.   3. Cf. **42**.

18 1. If a mistake for Fugel, see **155**.

2. See also **59**; cf. **16**.

[19] Ailwardus chenicte tenuit i domum T.R.E. red-dentem omnem consuetudinem. Modo habet filius Radulfi Roselli;[1] et nullam consuetudinem reddidit. Et de calle regis preoccu[fo. 2v]pavit duos pedes de lati-tudine et de longitudine quantum domus durat.[2] Et cum illa terra preoccupavit le balcheus regis, ubi latrones ponebantur in prisone.[3] Et in illa eadem terra manent viii carnifices,[4] unde prepositus solebat habere unaquaque dominica die viii d.; et reddit ix lib.

[20] Leuingius et Got habebant T.R.E. duas estals. Modo habet Rogerus filius Armerlanc;[1] et facit consue-tudinem. Sed preoccupavit duos pedes de calle regis in longitudine,[2] sicut Radulfus Rosell'[a3] fecerat; et hoc fecit per Warinum prepositum.[4] Et Gesordus prepositus[5] debet habere xxx sol., quia Rogerus tenet estals de eo.

[21] vi estals[1] sunt modo qui reddunt xi s. et viii d.[2]

[22] Sideloc tenuit i domum T.R.E. reddentem omnem co[n]suetudinem. Modo habet uxor Wimundi monetarii;[1] et reddit de langabulo vi d. et nullam aliam consuetudi-nem; et est deospitata.[2]

[23] [b]Domus Godebiete[1] fuit T.R.E. quieta, et modo

[19] Ailward the *cniht* held 1 tenement *TRE* which paid every custom. Now the son of Ralf Rosell[1] has it and paid no custom. And he has encroached on the king's road 2 ft. in width and in length as far as the tenement extends.[2] And with that land he has appropriated the king's *balchus* where thieves used to be put in prison.[3] And on that land live 8 butchers[4] from whom the reeve used to have every Sunday 8d. And it yields £9.

[20] Leving and Got had 2 stalls *TRE*. Now Roger son of Amerland[1] has them and performs the custom. But he has appropriated 2 ft. of the king's road in length[2] just as Ralf Rosell[3] had done; and he did this with the permission of Warin the reeve.[4] And Gesord the reeve[5] ought to have 30s. because Roger holds the stalls from him.

[21] There are now 6 stalls[1] which yield 11s. 8d.[2]

[22] Sideloc held 1 tenement *TRE* which paid every custom. Now the wife of Wimund the moneyer[1] has it, and she pays 6d. landgable and no other custom. And it is unoccupied.[2]

[23] The Godebiete tenement[1] was quit *TRE* and is

[a] -i erased   [b] A (late medieval?) hand pointing to this entry in margin

19 1. See 1.
2. The encroachment was perhaps on to the entry to *Flesmangerestret*, cf. 20, n. 2, below. For encroachments, see also 20, 23 (*bis*), 52, 59, 64, 65, 73, 78, 83, 90, 101, 122, and perhaps 165, and cf. II, 17, n. 2, and below, pp. 280–2.
3. *Balchus* in II, 52, presumably a balk- or beam-house (? one constructed of strong timber), perhaps a cage for prisoners. See also J. H. Round, *VCH Hants* i. 532, n. 8, and cf. below, p. 236 s.v.
4. Although associated with the prison, more likely butchers than executioners, especially since the butchers were perhaps congregated at the entry to *Flesmangerestret*, cf. I, 20 and 21; II, 54, 55, 56, 58, and 59.
20 1. Probably the Roger Amberlang of 249.
2. Perhaps next to 19, in the entry to *Flesmangerestret*; cf. also 19, n. 2.
3. See 1.
4. For Warin, see also 59 and 78–9. The names of a number of royal reeves in Winchester in Henry I's time have been preserved, see below, pp. 422 ff., and Table 46.
5. Gesord does not seem to have been noticed else-where. Geoffrey the reeve occurs at about this time: *Regesta*, ii, no. 503; V. H. Galbraith, *EHR* 35 (1920), 382 ff., no. XXII. A *Ger' prepositus* occurs ibid., no. XXXI. See also below, p. 423.
21 1. Cf. II, 56.
2. This item is possibly the conclusion to 20.
22 1. A Winchester moneyer under William I and II

and Henry I: *English Coins*, 85, 90, and see below, p. 410 and Table 39.
2. Cf. 55.
23 1. See also II, 42. For this tenement, see Goodman *Goodbegot*. It was confirmed to the monks of St. Swithun by William II in September 1096, free and quit of all service: V. H. Galbraith, *EHR* 35 (1920), 382 ff., no. XI. Good-man's reconstruction of the bounds of the charter of 1012 by which King Æthelred granted an extensive property here to Queen Emma (Sawyer 925) may be modified (Fig. 12). The measurements suggest that the modern frontages on to High Street and St. George's Street are the same as in 1012. The E. boundary, however, may now be represented by a line on the E. end of the earliest excavated phase of St. Peter's church. Tenth- and eleventh-century pits were found to the N. of the church, but none dated by the excavator as earlier than the thirteenth century were found to the E. of this line. The encroachments mentioned in the survey probably occupied the strip 16 feet in width between this suggested boundary of 1012 and the modern frontage of St. Peter's Street. In this reconstruc-tion, the W. boundary fits better with modern tenement divisions on the High Street frontage. Cf. *Winchester 1949–60*, i. 19–48, where Goodman's reconstruction is accepted. The property known as Godbegot in the later Middle Ages appears to have occupied only that part of the land within the boundaries of 1012 to the E. of the modern Royal Oak Passage, and so may represent the 'messuage which one calls Ælfric's good acquisition'

est quieta. Et tunc tempore R.E. Adelwoldus prepositus Wint'² dedit parentibus suis de calle regis iii mansuras quas hospitaverunt.³ Modo he iii mansure preoccupate sunt in domo Godebiete; et de his mansuris quae sunt occupate in domo monachorum*a* ii mansuras tenent Rogerus siccus et Ainolfus⁴ i domum. Et in aecclesia⁵ que pertinet domui sunt preoccupate duo eschamel quae erant in calle regis,⁶ et que unaquaque ebdomada reddebant de consuetudine ii d.; et reddit vi lib. et xvi*b* sol.

[24] Godwinus cheni[cte] tenuit i domum T.R.E. reddentem omnem consuetudinem. Modo habet Herbertus camerarius,¹ et nullam consuetudinem reddit preter hoc quod adquietavit homines suos de geldo;² et reddit vii lib. et xv sol.

[25] Leflet Ecregeles docter tenuit i domum T.R.E. reddentem omnem consuetudinem. Modo tenent moniales;¹ consuetudinem fac*iunt*; et reddit iiii lib.

[26] Algar Godesbranesson¹ tenuit i domum T.R.E. reddentem omnem consuetudinem. Modo tenent monachi de Sancto Swithuno;² et [fo. 3] reddu[n]t*c* similiter consuetudinem; et reddit iiii lib.

[27] Aluricus de Canesham¹ tenuit i domum T.R.E. reddentem omnem consuetudinem. Modo tenet Goisfridus filius Hereberti;² similiter reddit consuetudinem per deprecationem prepositorum, preter langabulum. Et abante [. . .] escheopes que fuerunt Edde regine;³ et similiter reddit consuetudinem; et reddit c et ix sol. et vi d.

[28] Burewoldus¹ tenuit i domum T.R.E. reddentem consuetudinem. Modo tenent monachi, et Gazo de eis. Et iuxta*d* istam domum erat vicus² qui preoccupatus est

quit now. And *TRE* Adelwold, reeve of Winchester,² gave to his parents 3 messuages from the king's road which they occupied.³ Now these three messuages are appropriated to the Godebiete tenement. And of the three messuages which are included in the tenement of the monks, Roger the Lean holds 2 messuages and Ainolf⁴ 1 tenement. And to the church⁵ which pertains to the tenement are appropriated 2 market-stalls which were on the king's road⁶ and which each week used to pay 2*d.* custom. And it yields £6. 16*s.*

[24] Godwin the *cniht* held 1 tenement *TRE* which paid every custom. Now Herbert the chamberlain¹ has it and pays no custom except that he acquitted his men of geld.² And it yields £7. 15*s.*

[25] Leflet, Ecregel's daughter, held 1 tenement *TRE* which paid every custom. Now the nuns¹ hold it and perform the custom. And it yields £4.

[26] Algar Godesbrand's son¹ held 1 tenement *TRE* which paid every custom. Now the monks of St. Swithun² hold it and likewise pay the custom. And it yields £4.

[27] Aluric of Keynsham¹ held 1 tenement *TRE* which paid every custom. Now Geoffrey son of Herbert² holds it and likewise pays the custom when requested by the reeves, except landgable. And in front are the shops which belonged to Queen Edith;³ and he likewise pays the custom. And it yields 109*s.* 6*d.*

[28] Burewold¹ held 1 tenement *TRE* which paid the custom. Now the monks hold it, and Wazo from them. And next to that tenement was a street² which has been

---

a monachi *MS., final* -s *erased*   *b Erasure before* xvi   *c Corrected from* reddit   *d* iustam *MS.; cf.* [10]

which Emma bequeathed to Old Minster. The house of Queen Emma mentioned in entry **75** may have been that part of her original property which she retained for her own use. For the interpretation of *Godebiete*, see below, p. 158, s.v.

2. See also **38**, and below, p. 424, and Table 46.
3. Cf. **19**, n. 2.
4. Possibly a moneyer of Henry I: see below, Table 40.
5. St. Peter *in macellis*, erected by the prefect Æthelwine before 1012: Goodman *Goodbegot*, 2. The church was evidently enlarged at the expense of two neighbouring shambles between the time of King Edward and the date of the survey.
6. Cf. **19**, n. 2.
24 1. See I, Preface.
2. See **13b**.
25 1. For this tenement, cf. II, **40**.
26 1. See also **78**; cf. **79**.

2. For this tenement, cf. **II, 39**.
27 1. See also **43**.
2. See also **32**. He is probably the son of Herbert the chamberlain. See *Regesta*, ii, no. 1000 (to be dated 1111). For this tenement, cf. **II, 38**.
3. King Edward the Confessor's wife.
28 1. Cf. also **124** and **199**. A property confirmed to the priory by William II in September 1096: V. H. Galbraith, *EHR* 35 (1920), 388. See above, entry **16**, n. 2. For this tenement, cf. **II, 37**.
2. Probably a lane running N. from High Street in the vicinity of *Scowrtenestret* into, or across, the block between High Street and the back street. Entirely lost. For its approximate location, cf. the correspondences in Table 9 with the positions of Survey **II** entries shown on Figs. 18 or 19, and see discussion on pp. 244–5. For other blocked streets and lanes, see **40, 45, 53, 60, 81, 91, 107, 135,** and **163**; cf. **II, 716**; and see below, pp. 278–81.

in illa domo; et facit similiter consuetudinem preter avram; et reddit*a* c et xii sol.*b*

appropriated to that tenement. And he likewise renders the custom (except carrying-service). And it yields 112*s*.

[29] Andrebodus[1] fuit monetarius T.R.E. et tenuit i domum. Modo tenet eam Rualdus filius Faderlin;[2] et facit omnem consuetudinem per deprecationem prepositorum; et reddit xlviii sol.

[29] Andrebode[1] was a moneyer *TRE* and held 1 tenement. Now Ruald son of Faderling[2] holds it and performs every custom when requested by the reeves. And it yields 48*s*.

[30] *c*Alg' har*engarius* tenuit i domum T.R.E. reddentem vi d. de langabulo et consuetudinem. Modo tenent Thomas de sancto Iohanne[1] et Osb' Tiart[2] et faciunt similiter.

[30] Algar the herring-monger held 1 tenement *TRE* which paid 6*d*. landgable and custom. Now Thomas of St. John[1] and Osbert Thiard[2] hold it and do the same.

[31] *c*Almodus presbiter tenuit i domum T.R.E. reddentem vi d. de langabulo et omnem consuetudinem. Modo tenet Radulfus Brito et reddit similiter.

[31] Almod the priest held 1 tenement *TRE* which paid 6*d*. landgable and every custom. Now Ralf Brito [the Breton] holds it and pays the same.

[32] Wlwardus bed*ellus* tenuit i domum T.R.E. reddentem consuetudinem. Modo tenet Goisfridus filius Hereberti;[1] et reddit langabulum et alias consuetudines per deprecationem prepositorum; et reddit iiii li.

[32] Wulfward the beadle held 1 tenement *TRE* which paid the custom. Now Geoffrey son of Herbert[1] holds it and pays landgable and the other customs when requested by the reeves. And it yields £4.

[33] Wlwardus harengarius tenuit i domum T.R.E. reddentem consuetudinem. Modo tenet Willelmus de Albinneio,[1] et Herbertus camerarius[2] de eo; et nullam*d* reddit consuetudinem preter watam, et [hoc quod] homines suos*e* adquietat de geldo;[3] et reddit lxxii sol.

[33] Wulfward the herring-monger held 1 tenement *TRE* which paid the custom. Now William d'Aubigny[1] holds it and Herbert the chamberlain[2] from him. And he pays no custom but Watch except that he acquits his men from geld.[3] And it yields 72*s*.

[34] Chenictes tenebant la chenictahalla[1] libere de rege Edwardo. Modo tenet Rogerus filius Geroldi;[2] et nullam consuetudinem inde facit preter watam et geldis;*f* et reddit vi li. et ii sol.

[34] The *cnihtas* held the hall of the *cnihtas*[1] freely from King Edward. Now Roger son of Gerold[2] holds it, and he performs no custom in respect of it except Watch and gelds. And it yields £6. 2*s*.

---

a preter avram *cancelled and* et reddit *in another hand in the margin the whole entry is written over an erasure*   *d* *Suspension mark added*   *b* d. MS.   *e* Add quos MS.   *c* *No paragraph sign:*   *f* Cf. [45]

29 1. A Winchester moneyer from Cnut to Harold II: *English Coins*, 77. He is presumably identical with the *Andrebode cangeor* of I, 212. For the tenement, cf. II, 36 in which *Ailwardus*, probably a moneyer of Henry I, had an interest: see below, p. 403 and Tables 34 and 42.
2. Faderling was a Domesday under-tenant of Hugh de Port: J. H. Round, *VCH Hants* i. 481, 534. See also II, 473.
30 1. One of Henry I's new men: Round, *VCH Hants* i. 535. He was sheriff of Oxon. *c.* 1110–7 and frequently witnessed Henry's writs: *Regesta*, ii, no. 885 and *passim*. In 1130 his brother, John, paid 160 marks to inherit his lands: *Pipe Roll 31 Henry I*, p. 3, cf. pp. 38, 124.
2. Also called Osbert son of Thiard: see also **101** and **122**.
32 1. See **27**.
33 1. See **14**.
2. See I, Preface.
3. See **13b**.

34 1. Presumably distinct from the guildhall in entry 10. See J. H. Round, *VCH Hants* i. 530–2. In the late thirteenth century a building in private possession known as *la Gialde* stood back from High Street, near St. Peter Whitbread church. The abbot of Hyde was patron of the church and had rights in this and adjacent properties: see *VCH Hants* v. 75; WCM, 1302, 1303, and 1305; Stowe 846, fos. 5*v*, 43*v*, and 47*v*; and Harl. MS. 1761, fo. 25*v*; WCA, Stake Rolls, m. 3. For this property, cf. **II, 32, 33, and 34**.
2. Roger granted the land of Asgarby to St. Mary of Lincoln as a prebend for the benefit of Robert de Grainville, a grant which Henry I confirmed 1100 × 1105 at Winchester: *Regesta*, ii, no. 731, cf. no. 1841. Robert (a Domesday tenant-in-chief) and Roger were sons of Gerold de Roumare. Roger's son, William de Roumare, eventually inherited his uncle's lands and became earl of Lincoln. For the family, see J. H. Round, *VCH Hants* i. 424–5.

[35] Apud tres monasterios¹ allevatum est mercatum² quod non fuit ibi T.R.E.; et est supra terram abbatis³ et Herberti camerarii.⁴

[36] Godeman Brunechingessone¹ et Godricus savonarius tenuerunt ii domos T.R.E. reddentes consuetudinem. Et de his domibus tenet partem abbatissa Wint';² et reddit quantum suae parti pertinet [fo. 3ᵛ] de consuetudine; et reddit xx sol. Et aliam partem tene[n]t Ricardus tailator et Sawalus presbiter;³ et nullam consuetudinem faciunt; et reddit xv sol.

[37] Golsewanus presbiter tenuit i domum T.R.E. reddentem omnem consuetudinem. Modo tenet Iohannes filius Ernuceon; et nullam consuetudinem reddit; et reddit xxiii sol. et iiii d.

[38] Adelwoldus prepositus Wint'¹ habuit T.R.E. unum cellarium regis Edwardi. Modo habet Escorfan;² et nullam consuetudinem inde reddit; et reddit xv sol.

ᵃA PORTA OCCIDENTIS USQUE AD PORTAM ORIENTISᵇ

[39] ᶜAlestanus Douetessone¹ tenuit T.R.E. unam domum reddentem consuetudinem. Modo tenet Henricus de Port;² et nullam consuetudinem facit inde. Et in domo illa preoccupavit de terra regis quae erat iuxta portam³ vi solida*tas*; et reddit xxxix sol.

[40] Gilebertus Bochenel tenuit T.R.E. i domum reddentem consuetudinem. Modo eam tenet uxor Hugonis filiiᵈ Albuchon et non reddit consuetudinem. Et erat ibi vicus¹ quem Hugo filius Albuchon et Henricus de Port² preoccupaverunt in domo sua.

[35] By the three minsters¹ a market² has been established which was not there *TRE*. It is on the land of the abbot³ and Herbert the chamberlain.⁴

[36] Godman Brown-king's son¹ and Godric the soapmaker held 2 tenements *TRE* which paid the custom. The abbess of Winchester² holds part of these 2 tenements and pays the amount of custom which pertains to her share; and it yields 20*s*. Richard the tailor and Sawal the priest³ hold the other part, and they perform no custom; and it yields 15*s*.

[37] Colsvein the priest held 1 tenement *TRE* which paid every custom. Now John son of Ernuceon holds it and pays no custom. And it yields 23*s*. 4*d*.

[38] Adelwold, reeve of Winchester,¹ held 1 cellar of King Edward. Now Escorfan² has it and pays no custom in respect of it. And it yields 15*s*.

FROM THE WEST GATE TO THE EAST GATE

[HIGH STREET (south side)]

[39] Alestan Dovet's son¹ held 1 tenement *TRE* which paid the custom. Now Henry de Port² holds it and performs no custom in respect of it. And he has appropriated to that tenement six shillings-worth of royal demesne which lay next to the Gate.³ And it yields 39*s*.

[40] Gilbert Bochenel held 1 tenement *TRE* which paid the custom. Now the wife of Hugh, son of Albuchon, holds it and pays no custom. And here was a street¹ which Hugh son of Albuchon and Henry de Port² appropriated to their tenement.

ᵃ *Whole rubric written over an erasure which appears to correspond to the first two lines of* [39]   ᵇ *In margin, for rubricator:* a porta occidentis usque ad orientis   ᶜ *First two lines written over an erasure*   ᵈ filius *MS.*

---

35 1. For this locality, see **II, 25**, n. 1.

2. Fish were sold near here in the early fourteenth century. See *SMW*.

3. For the abbot's land, cf. **II, 10–24**.

4. See **I**, Preface.

36 1. Presumably the Godman Brincigesone of entry **96**. Before 1130 two men had been fined for the land of their uncle Brunching in Sussex: *Pipe Roll 31 Henry I*, p. 68.

2. For this tenement, cf. **II, 8**. The abbess had a garden near here in 1417: *SMW* 8.

3. See also **105, 215**, and **219**; cf. **287**.

38 1. See **23**.

2. See also **195**, and **II, 563**. An Escorfan occurs in 1130: *Pipe Roll 31 Henry I*, pp. 4, 5, 76, 108.

39 1. See **13b**.

2. See also **40** and **51**. Sheriff of Hants 1101–?6. He was followed by William of Pont de l'Arche in 1106. For the Port family, see J. H. Round, *VCH Hants* i. 423–4, 534. Adelaide (Adelidis) (**239**) and Emma de Percy (**68**) were his sisters. For his son John, see **II, 2**.

3. See **40**, n. 1.

40 1. Cf. **39**. The adjacent properties **39** and **40** appear to have encroached over the king's ground next to West Gate and over an adjacent street. An internal street leading towards West Gate from the south was blocked by the construction of the castle in 1067, see *VIII Interim*, 285–9. See also below, p. 303, and for other blocked streets and lanes, see **28**, n. 2, and below, pp. 278–81.

2. See **39**.

[41] Alwinus presbiter[1] tenuit[a] i domum T.R.E. et faciebat consuetudinem. Modo tenet Robertus filius Wimundi;[2] et similiter reddit consuetudinem; et reddit xx sol.

[42] Terra monial*ium* reddebat T.R.E. consuetudinem; et de ea tenet[b] Willelmus filius Odonis[1] dimidiam partem, et Willelmus Brunus[2] dimidiam partem, unde ventam regis retinuit;[3] et nullam consuetudinem inde faciunt; et domus reddit lxviii sol.

[43] [c]Domus Alurici de Cainesham[1] T.R.E. reddebat consuetudinem. Modo tenet Rogerus Patinus; et non facit consuetudinem; et reddit xxxiii sol. preter estagium suum.[2]

[44] Domus cuiusdam vidue reddebat T.R.E. consuetudinem. Modo tenet Herfridus regis serviens[1] et facit consuetudinem per deprecationem prepositorum.

[45] Domus Stanulfi presbiteri erat quieta T.R.E. preter watam et geldis.[d] Modo tenet Robertus Maleductus[1] [fo. 4] et similiter est quieta. Sed pater eius[2] preoccupavit viculum[3] i et[e] postea eum implacitavit Ricardus de Curci;[4]

[41] Alwin the priest[1] held 1 tenement *TRE* and performed the custom. Now Robert son of Wimund[2] holds it and likewise pays the custom. And it yields 20*s*.

[42] The land of the nuns paid the custom *TRE*. William son of Odo[1] holds half of it, and William Brown[2] the other half, from which he retained the king's toll.[3] And they perform no custom. And the tenement yields 68*s*.

[43] The tenement of Aluric of Keynsham[1] paid the custom *TRE*. Now Roger Patten holds it and does not perform the custom. And it yields 33*s*. apart from its upper storey (?).[2]

[44] The tenement of a certain widow paid the custom *TRE*. Now Herfrid, the king's sergeant,[1] holds it and performs the custom when requested by the reeves.

[45] The tenement of Stanulf the priest was quit *TRE* except for Watch and gelds. Now Robert Mauduit[1] holds it and likewise is quit. But his father[2] appropriated a lane,[3] and afterwards Richard de Courcy[4]

---

[a] ten'et *MS.*   [b] *Followed by an erasure, probably of* Will', *at end of line*   [c] *No paragraph sign, first line written over an erasure*   [d] *Cf.* [34]   [e] unum *crossed out*

41 1. See also 172–3 and 289.
2. See 7. For a later moneyer's interest in or near this property, cf. II, 172.
42 1. See also 107, his interest in which suggests that he is the member of the family of goldsmiths which held the office of cutter of dies for the coinage as a hereditary sergeanty. For Odo, his grandfather, dead by 1098, and Odo, his father, see *Regesta*, ii, p. xxv. Odo *monetarius*, who occurs in 129, may have been William's father. His epithet must have been due to his control of the dies, rather than to a direct involvement in the production of coins, for he struck no Winchester money. He may have been identical with the Odo who was active as a moneyer at Bury St. Edmunds within the period *c.* 1131–4, for Odo the goldsmith was a tenant and benefactor of the abbey of St. Edmund and had extensive properties in Suffolk and Essex (*English Hammered Coinage*, 146; *VCH Essex* i. 350–1). The Bury moneyer, however, was active a little too late to be conclusively identified with Odo the goldsmith and may perhaps have been an otherwise unrecorded member or associate of the family. William son of Odo, confirmed in his father's properties between 1116 and 1127 (*Regesta*, ii, no. 1524) and pardoned 11*s*. of the Winchester Aid in 1130 (*Pipe Roll 31 Henry I*, p. 41), was a royal sub-constable in *c.* 1136 (*Constitutio Domus Regis*, in *Dialogus de Scaccario*, 133). The Richard son of Odo of II, 351 and 380 was probably, in view of the identity of the latter tenement with I, 129, another son of Odo the moneyer. In 133 we have a William son of Odo son of Ticcheman whose

sons probably appear in II, 405, but this seems to have been a different family. See Addenda.
For moneyers' interest in this and the adjacent tenement, cf. II, 172, and for the numismatic aspects of this problem, see p. 409, below.
2. See also 294.   3. Cf. 17.
43 1. See 27.
2. See 12.
44 1. Cf. 76. As he has left no trace in *Pipe Roll 31 Henry I* and *Regesta* he was, presumably, a minor servant.
45 1. See also 53 and 56. For Robert and the Mauduit family, see above, p. 9, n. 1, and I, Preface, n. 5; Richardson and Sayles, 429–33; *Dialogus de Scaccario*, pp. xxv–xxvi; J. H. Round, *VCH Hants* i. 533. Robert, a royal chamberlain, was the son of William Mauduit I (died *c.* 1100), and died *c.* 1129. His son Robert Mauduit II was drowned in the White Ship disaster in 1120. His daughter married William of Pont de l'Arche and proved an unsatisfactory wife.
2. William Mauduit I (see last note).
3. Probably a lane running S. from High Street somewhere between *Mensterstret* and *Gerestret*, and W. of the lane mentioned in entry 53, below. Presumably lost, but cf. St. Nicholas's Lane (now lost) and Hammond's Passage, in the block between *Goldestret* and *Calpestret*. For the method of location and for other blocked streets and lanes, see 28, n. 2, and below, pp. 278–81.
4. See also 53. A tenant-in-chief in Oxon., who also acted as a royal justice in Normandy: J. H. Round, *VCH Hants* i. 533.

sed finem fecit[5] de antea[a] iusti[ci]am regis; et homines domus geldant et reddunt [. . .]

impleaded him; and he made a fine[5] before the king's justiciar. And the men of the tenement pay geld and pay [. . .].

[46] Domus Aldrecti fratris Odonis[1] fuit quieta T.R.E. Modo eam tenet Willelmus filius Anschetilli et similiter est quieta preter watam et geld*is*; et reddit xxiiii sol. preter suum estagium.[2]

[46] The tenement of Aldred the brother of Odo[1] was quit *TRE*. Now William son of Anschetil holds it and likewise is quit except for Watch and gelds. And it yields 24*s*. apart from its upper storey (?).[2]

[47] Domus Almodi[1] reddebat consuetudinem T.R.E. Modo tenet Robertus filius Radulfi[2] et similiter reddit consuetudinem; et reddit xlv sol.

[47] The tenement of Almod[1] paid the custom *TRE*. Now Robert son of Ralf[2] holds it and likewise pays the custom. And it yields 45*s*.

[48] Domus Godwini Elmeressone[1] reddebat consuetudinem T.R.E. Modo tenet eam Herebertus camerarius[2] et nullam consuetudinem reddit; et reddit lx sol.

[48] The tenement of Godwin Elmer's son[1] paid the custom *TRE*. Now Herbert the chamberlain[2] holds it and pays no custom. And it yields 60*s*.

[49] Domus Lewini Chane[1] reddebat consuetudinem T.R.E. Modo tenet eam Willelmus de Ponte Archar'[2] de filio Willelmi filii Gisleberti et nullam consuetudinem reddit; et reddit ix li.

[49] The tenement of Lewin Chane[1] paid the custom *TRE*. Now William of Pont de l'Arche[2] holds it from the son of William son of Gilbert, and pays no custom. And it yields £9.

[50] Domus Aldrecti[1] reddebat T.R.E. consuetudinem. Modo eam tenet Herebertus de Sancto Quintino[2] et non facit consuetudinem; et reddit lxxiii sol. et vi d.

[50] The tenement of Aldred[1] paid the custom *TRE*. Now Herbert of St. Quentin[2] holds it and performs no custom. And it yields 73*s*. 6*d*.

[51] Domus Burewoldi Frefhewini[b] reddebat T.R.E. consuetudinem. Modo tenet eam Henricus de Port[1] et non facit consuetudinem; et reddit iiii li.

[51] The tenement of Burewold Frethewin paid the custom *TRE*. Now Henry de Port[1] holds it and performs no custom. And it yields £4.

[52] Domus Ulueue reddebat T.R.E. consuetudinem. Modo tenet eam Robertus filius Fulcheredi[1] et non facit consuetudinem. Preoccupatum est de calle regis iiii pedes de latitudine et de longitudine quantum domus durat;[2] et reddit c et xvii sol.

[52] The tenement of Ulveva paid the custom *TRE*. Now Robert son of Fulchered[1] holds it and performs no custom. There is appropriated to it 4 ft. in width of the king's road, and in length as far as the tenement extends.[2] And it yields 117*s*.

[53] Domus Siwardi Leuerunessone[c] reddebat T.R.E. consuetudinem. Modo tenet Robertus Maleductus[1] et facit similiter consuetudinem. Sed pater ipsius Roberti[1] preoccupavit vicum[2] i in illa domo. Unde

[53] The tenement of Siward Leofrun's son paid the custom *TRE*. Now Robert Mauduit[1] holds it and likewise performs the custom. But his father[1] incorporated one street[2] in that tenement. Richard de

---

[a] *? Correct to* ante; *cf.* [53]   [b] *Possibly altered to* frethewini   [c] Lenerunessone (*incorrectly*) Ellis

---

45 5. For this early use of the formula (and see **135**), see Round, ibid. 533–4.
46 1. Aldred and Odo of Winchester were important royal thegns. See Round, ibid. 427–8. For the same or other Aldreds, see **50**, **151**, and **179**.
  2. See **12**.
47 1. Cf. **115**.
  2. See also **54**. He cannot be identified with any other Robert fitzRalph of the period.
48 1. See **14**.
  2. See **I**, Preface.
49 1. See *LVH* 70.
  2. See **I**, Preface. For this tenement, cf. **II, 171**.
50 1. Cf. **46**.
  2. See also **149–51**. Hugh of St. Quentin was a Domesday tenant-in-chief. Herbert followed Robert fitzHamo

(see **96**) to South Wales and established his family in Glamorgan: J. H. Round, *VCH Hants* i. 535; *Regesta*, ii, no. 1307.
51 1. See **39**.
52 1. Fulchered was a Hampshire Domesday tenant of New Minster: *VCH Hants* i. 471, where he occurs next to Hugh de Port. In 1130 Robert fitzFulchered accounted for the fine he had made for his father's office: *Pipe Roll 31 Henry I*, p. 122. See also *Regesta*, ii, no. 1550.
  2. Cf. **19**, n. 2.
53 1. See **45**.
  2. Probably a lane running S. from High Street, somewhere between the lane mentioned in entry **45**, above, and *Mensterstret*. Presumably lost, but cf. **45**, n. 3. For the method of location, and for other blocked streets and lanes see **28**, n. 2, and below, pp. 278–81.

Ricardus de Curci[1] eum inplacitavit, qui erat tunc iusticia regis, et tunc ante[a] iusticiam regis de hoc placito[b] fecit finem;[1] et hec domus et aliae suae domus reddunt vi li. et xvi sol.[3]

Courcy,[1] who was then the king's justiciar, impleaded him, and afterwards Robert made a fine[1] before the king's justiciar in this plea. And this and his other tenements yield £6. 16s.[3]

[54] Domus Godwini Porriz reddebat T.R.E. consuetudinem. Modo tenet eam Robertus filius Radulfi[1] et similiter reddit consuetudinem; et reddit xlix sol.

[54] The tenement of Godwin Porriz paid the custom *TRE*. Now Robert son of Ralf[1] holds it and likewise pays the custom. And it yields 49s.

[55] Domus Godwini francigene[1] reddebat consuetudinem T.R.E. Modo eam tenet Ranulfus dapifer Her-[fo. 4ᵛ] berti camerarii[2] et reddit langabulum et non facit aliam consuetudinem; et terra est dehospitata.[3]

[55] The tenement of Godwin the Frenchman[1] paid the custom *TRE*. Now Ranulf, the steward of Herbert the chamberlain,[2] holds it and pays landgable but does not perform any other custom. And the land is unoccupied.[3]

[56] Domus Vulurici reddebat T.R.E. consuetudinem. Modo eam tenet Robertus Maleductus;[1] et similiter facit consuetudinem.

[56] The tenement of Wulfric paid the custom *TRE*. Now Robert Mauduit[1] holds it and likewise performs the custom.

[57] Lethmerus,[c1] et Alwi Chasiessone, et Hizeman, et Godwinus francigena,[2] et Lewinus Balloe,[3] et Godwinus Sarz, et Godwinus Sorz, et Gonnod,[4] et Lesweda, et Sonricus hosarius, et Alestanus Hwit, et Edewa: hi tenebant domus et erant burgenses et faciebant consuetudinem; et pars erat de dominio[d] et pars de dominio[d] abbatis; et hoc totum est preoccupatum in domo regis.[5]

[57] Lethmer,[1] Alwi Chasi's son, Hizeman, Godwin the Frenchman,[2] Lewin Ballock,[3] Godwin Sarz, Godwin Sorz, Godnod,[4] Lesweda, Sonric the hosier, Alestan White, and Edeva—these held tenements and were burgesses and performed the custom. And part was on royal demesne and part on the abbot's demesne. And all this was incorporated into the king's house.[5]

[58] Et in mercato fuerunt v monete que sunt diffacte precepto regis.[1]

[58] And in the market were 5 mints which were destroyed by order of the king.[1]

[59] Et in capite coquine[1] regis tenet Henricus lard*a*-*rius*[2] ii forgias;[3] sed unam examplavit de duobus pedibus in calle regis,[4] ita quod inde requisivit Warinum prepositum,[5] et ipse dedit licentiam ei; et reddunt xvi sol.

[59] And at the end of the king's kitchen[1] Henry the larderer[2] holds 2 forges;[3] but he extended one by 2 ft. into the king's road.[4] So he approached Warin the reeve[5] in this matter and Warin gave him permission. And they yield 16s.

[60] Et ibi erat unus vicus qui stupatus est pro coquina regis.[1]

[60] And here was a street which was blocked up for the king's kitchen.[1]

---

a antea, *final a expunged, MS.; cf.* [45]   *b* placita *corrected to* placito *MS.*   *c* Lechmerus *Ellis*   *d* *Superscript* i *added for* -i(o); *cf.* [72–3]

53 1. See No. 45.   3. See 45 and 56.
54 1. See 47.
55 1. See also 57.
   2. See I, Preface.
   3. Cf. 22.
56 1. See 45.
57 1. Probably a moneyer of Edward the Confessor: see below, Table 35.
   2. See 55.
   3. Cf. 138.
   4. Perhaps a moneyer of William I: see 182 and below, p. 415.
   5. For discussion of the Norman royal palace, see below, pp. 292 ff.
58 1. For discussion, see below, pp. 397–9.
59 1. See 60.
   2. See 18.

3. See 61–5 and cf. II, 73 and 90. The forges were probably moneyers' workshops, see below, pp. 399–400.
   4. Cf. 19, n. 2.
   5. See 20.
60 1. The succession of entries in this survey shows that the kitchen lay between the main block of properties removed to make way for the Norman extension of the palace (I, 57) and Thomas Gate to the E. (I, 64). The blocked street ran thus in a position which suggests that it was perhaps one of the main north–south streets of the late Saxon layout, leading S. from High Street to the Old and New Minsters and the royal palace (Fig. 9, *c.* 963–1066). After the extension of the palace the street was apparently replaced by an entry further E. leading direct to Thomas Gate (Fig. 9, *c.* 1110). See further below, p. 294, and for blocked streets and lanes, 28, n. 2, and below, pp. 278–81.

[61] Et iterum in capite coquine[1] habebant burgenses cellarios suos; et reddebant langabulum. Modo monachi habent i forgiam,[2] et similiter reddunt consuetudinem; et reddit vi sol.

[62] Et ibidem habet Robertus filius Wimundi[1] i forgiam,[2] que fuit cellarius T.R.E.; et reddit iiii sol.

[63] Et ibidem Gisl' Gibart [habet] iiii forgias,[1] que fuerunt T.R.E. cellarii; et reddunt xii s.

[64] Et desubtus Thomeseiete[1] preoccupatus est,[2] et sunt facte ibi forgie;[3] sed nescimus per quem; et de illis tenet Walterus Chibus[4] iiii forgias de filio Boselini; et reddunt xii sol.

[65] Et ibidem Robertus filius Wimundi[1] [habet] vi forgias,[2] et reddunt xxviii sol.; et de his forgiis preoccupatis in calle rex nullam consuetudinem habet.[3]

[66] Et ubi Merewenehaia[1] est ibi fuit i domus quam tenuit [fo. 5] Edwinus[2] T.R.E. Sed Goisfridus clericus[3] eam defecit.

[67] Et eodem modo defecit aliam domum quam tenuit Alwoldus T.R.E.

Hic de domibus existentibus in cons*uetudine* T.R.E.; et supra eius terram sunt.[a] Modo incipit de terris baronum et ten[en]tium, a porta orientis usque ad portam occidentis.[1]

[a] finit *MS.*

[61] And also at the end of the kitchen[1] the burgesses used to have their cellars and paid landgable. Now the monks have a forge[2] and likewise pay the custom. And it yields 6*s.*

[62] And Robert son of Wimund[1] also has a forge[2] there, which was a cellar *TRE.* And it yields 4*s.*

[63] And Gilbert Gibart has 4 forges[1] there, which were cellars *TRE.* And they yield 12*s.*

[64] And below Thomas Gate[1] there is encroachment,[2] and forges[3] have been made there; but we do not know by whom. And Walter Chibus[4] holds 4 of these forges of the son of Boselin. And they yield 12*s.*

[65] And in the same place Robert son of Wimund[1] has 6 forges,[2] and they yield 28*s.* And from these forges built by encroachment on the road the king has no custom.[3]

[66] And where Merewen's enclosure[1] is there was a tenement which Edwin[2] held *TRE.* But Geoffrey the clerk[3] threw it down.

[67] And in the same way he threw down another tenement which Alwold held *TRE.*

The account so far is about the tenements liable to pay custom *TRE*; and they are on his [Edward's] land. Now begins an account of the lands of the barons and tenants, from the East Gate to the West Gate.[1]

61 1. See **60**.
 2. See **59**.
62 1. See **7**, and for a later moneyer's interest in this area, **II, 111**.
 2. See **59**.
63 1. See **59**.
64 1. A gateway to the New Minster and subsequently to the cathedral precinct, situated in the modern Market Street probably at the end of Market Lane (Fig. 9, *c.* 1110). See *SMW*, and below, p. 238, for the place-name.
 2. Cf. **19**, n. 2.
 3. See **59**.
 4. *Walterius Kiburs* was cured of infirmities, including a flux of the belly which had laid him low for six years, by contact with relics of the Virgin in 1113. The relics were displayed by a group of canons from Laon who were in Winchester trying to raise money for their cathedral. Walter foreswore the practice of usury and paid a handsome sum to the canons from a fortune which exceeded 3,000 pounds. See S. Martinet, 'Le voyage des Laonnois en Angleterre en 1113', *Fédération des sociétés d'histoire et d'archéologie de l'Aisne, Mémoires*, 9 (1963), 81–92. We are grateful to Mrs. Pamela Johnston for the reference to this article. See also J. S. P. Tatlock, 'The English Journey of the Laon Canons', *Speculum*, 8 (1933), 454–65.
65 1. See **7**. After the date of this survey John de Recham granted to Stephen de Bendenges a *fabrica* next to the

gate called *Thomeshet* worth 5*s.* a year in rent, and land worth 2*s.* rent *inter muros atrii*, which had been in the fief of Robert son of Wimund. These properties, later described as the *forgia que est iuxta portam que dicitur Thomasgate* were granted to the priory of St. Denis next to Southampton by Maurice de Bendeng'. This entry may thus be identified with **II, 111**. John de Recham had reserved from the property an annual rent of 1 lb. of pepper which William de Colevile later granted to the canons. St. Denis Cart., fos. 120[v] and 121[v].
 2. See **59**.
 3. The forges of this and the previous entry appear to have been erected on open ground between *Thomeseiete* and High Street. Cf. **19**, n. 2.
66 1. In the fourteenth century a tenement on the N. side of High Street, just W. of the entry to Tanner Street, was *contra merewenehay*. At the same date, a tenement on the S. side of High Street, just W. of the entry to Colebrook Street, was *ex opposito merwenhay*. The *fossatum de Merwenhaye* was the water-channel in the middle of High Street at this point, and *merewenehaia* itself was evidently in the middle of the street. See *SMW* 116, 119, and 120; Stowe 846, fo. 102; and below, p. 238, s.n.
 2. Probably a moneyer of Edward the Confessor: see below, Table 35.
 3. See also **67** and **130**.
67/8 1. See above, pp. 10–12.

[HIGH STREET (NORTH SIDE, EAST TO WEST)]

[68] Domus Lewingii Mandingessone[1] fuit quieta T.R.E. Modo eam tenet Emma de Perci[2] et est similiter quieta.[a]

[68] The tenement of Leving Manding's son[1] was quit *TRE*. Now Emma de Percy[2] holds it and it is likewise quit.

[69] De feudo abbatis fuit quaedam domus T.R.E. que faciebat watam et geld*um* reddebat. Modo eam tenet Osbertus filius Alberede;[1] et non facit consuetudinem; et reddit xl sol.

[69] There was a certain tenement on the fief of the abbot which performed Watch and paid geld *TRE*. Now Osbert son of Albereda[1] holds it and does not perform the custom. And it yields 40s.

[70] Alfed tenuit i domum T.R.E. de feudo episcopi Wint' et faciebat consuetudinem. Modo eam tenet Helias dapifer episcopi;[1] et non facit consuetudinem; et reddit xxv sol.

[70] Alfled held 1 tenement *TRE* of the fief of the bishop of Winchester and performed the custom. Now Helias, the bishop's steward,[1] holds it and does not perform the custom. And it yields 25s.

[71] Ailwardus de Chainesham tenuit de feudo abbatis Wint' i domum et fuit quieta preter watam et geld*um*. Et de hac tenet Robertus filius Dur*andi*[1] i partem et habet[b2] lviii sol. et iiii d., et Chipingus filius Alueue[3] viii sol., et Chipingus de Cainesham xv sol., et ipse abbas xxii d. Et Elsi presbiter[4] habet de quadem aecclesia[5] que pertinet domui et de seld*a* xxviii sol., et Lewinus[6] xxiiii sol.; et faciunt sicut T.R.E.

[71] Ailward of Keynsham held 1 tenement of the fief of the abbot of Winchester and was quit except for Watch and geld. Robert son of Durand[1] holds one part of it; and he has[2] 58s. 4d., Chiping son of Alveva[3] 8s., Chiping of Keynsham 15s., and the abbot 22d. And Elsi the priest[4] has from a certain church[5] which pertains to the tenement and from a stall 28s. and Lewin[6] 24s. And they do just as was done *TRE*.

[72] Rogerus frater abbatis[1] tenuit[2] i domum et facit de consuetudine tantum quantum solebat fieri T.R.E. Et est de dominio abbatis et reddit xxxvi sol.

[72] Roger, the abbot's brother,[1] held[2] 1 tenement and performs as much custom as used to be performed *TRE*. And it is on the abbot's demesne. And it yields 36s.

[73] Abbas habet in dominio i domum et facit consuetudinem sicut solebat T.R.E. fieri; et reddit lxv sol. Et de eadem terra habet Robertus pistor filius Willelmi viii sol., et de eadem terra habet Chipingius filius Alueue[1] xl sol., et de eadem terra habet Hubertus filius Willelmi xlv sol., et de eadem terra habet Rogerus frater abbatis[2] xviii sol.; et habet ibi domum ubi non solebat esse T.R.E. et vicus regis ibi est strictior.[3]

[73] The abbot has in demesne 1 tenement and performs the custom just as it used to be performed *TRE*. And it yields 65s. And from this land Robert the baker, son of William, has 8s., Chiping son of Alveva[1] has 40s., Hubert son of William has 45s., and Roger the abbot's brother[2] has 18s. And the abbot has there a house where there was not one *TRE* and the king's street is narrower there [because of it].[3]

---

[a] T.R.E. Modo eam tenet *repeated, crossed out by rubricator*   [b] reddit *MS.*

68 1. Possibly a moneyer of Edward the Confessor: see below, Table 36.

2. Henry de Port's sister: see **39**.

69 1. See **4**.

70 1. Witnessed a charter of Bishop William: J. H. Round, *EHR* 14 (1899), 430.

71 1. See also **267**. A Durand was sheriff of Hampshire in 1096: *Regesta*, ii, pp. 403, 407.

2. Reading *habet* for *reddit*; cf. **73** and **75**.

3. See **10**.

4. An Elsi *clericus* is in **148–9**.

5. Hyde Abbey subsequently had the patronage of at least three churches in High Street: St. Peter Whitbread, St. Laurence, and St. George. St. Laurence was in the possession of the abbey of Tiron in 1147 and before that was probably incorporated in the royal palace. St. Peter

Whitbread was at the W. end of High Street. St. George lay towards the E. end of High Street, a feature in common with the church in this entry with which it may be identified. *VCH Hants*, v. 75, 76; *France*, 98, 527. For the Hyde Abbey property near here, cf. II, 77.

6. Probably a moneyer of Henry I: see below, Table 39.

72 1. See also **73**. The abbot of New Minster was Geoffrey (1106–24).

2. Probably a mistake for *tenet*, holds.

73 1. See **10**.

2. See **72**. Since this tenement apparently lay towards the W. end of High Street and was in the fee of the abbot, it may be identical with **II, 23**, which Hugh son of Chepping held from the abbot.

3. Cf. **19**, n. 2.

[74] [fo. 5ᵛ] De feudo episcopi Wint' tenet Herbertus camerarius¹ iᵃ theinlandam et facit eandem consuetudinem quam solebant facere eius antecessoresᵇ T.R.E.; et reddit vii li. et xi s.

[75] Domus Emme regine¹ fuit quieta T.R.E. et modo est quieta. Et de hac terra habet Rogerus episcopus Salesberie² xxxvii sol., et Turstinus vi s. et suum estagium,³ Robertus filius Osberti de Auco xx sol.

ᶜModo incipit de terris chens[ual]iumᵈ a porta occidentis usque ad portam orientis.¹

[76] ᵉDomus Aluini fuit quieta T.R.E. Modo [est] similiter quieta preter waitam quam fecit; et reddit lxxv s.; et habet ibi in vadimonio de terris Herefridi¹ xvii s.

[77] Domus Odonis de Esperchefort¹ fuit quieta T.R.E. preter watam. Modo eam tenet Bernardus de Sancto Walarico,² et non facit watam; et reddit xii li.

[78] Domus Algari Godesbranesson¹ fuit quieta T.R.E. preter watam. Modo tenet eam Warinus prepositus,² et est similiter quieta. Sed ipse preoccupavit de calle regis³ in sua domo, sed nescimus quantum; et reddit vi li.

[79] Domus Godesbrani¹ fuit quieta T.R.E. preter watam. Modo tenet eam Warinus prepositus,² et est similiter quieta; et reddit Willelmo filio Ansgeri³ l sol.

[74] Herbert the chamberlain¹ holds a thegnland of the fief of the bishop of Winchester and performs the same custom as his predecessors used to perform *TRE*. And it yields £7. 11*s*.

[75] The tenement of Queen Emma¹ was quit *TRE* and is quit now. And from this land Roger bishop of Salisbury² has 37*s*., Thurstin 6*s*. and his upper storey (?),³ and Robert son of Osbert of Eu 20*s*.

Now begins an account of the lands of the rent-payers (?) from the West Gate to the East Gate.¹

[HIGH STREET (SOUTH SIDE, WEST TO EAST)]

[76] The tenement of Alwin was quit *TRE*. Now it is likewise quit except for Watch, which he performed. And it yields 75*s*. And he has there in pledge from the lands of Herefrid¹ 17*s*.

[77] The tenement of Odo of Sparkford¹ was quit *TRE* except for Watch. Now Bernard of St. Valéry² holds it and does not perform Watch. And it yields £12.

[78] The tenement of Algar Godesbrand's son¹ was quit *TRE* except for Watch. Now Warin the reeve² holds it and it is likewise quit. But he incorporated some of the king's road³ into his tenement, although we do not know how much. And it yields £6.

[79] The tenement of Godesbrand¹ was quit *TRE* except for Watch. Now Warin the reeve² holds it and it is likewise quit. And it yields to William son of Ansger³ 50*s*.

ᵃ *7 MS.*   ᵇ *antecessorem MS.*   ᶜ *Whole rubric written over an erasure*   ᵈ *thensiũ MS.: possibly, as*
[67/8], *another garbled form of* tenentium   ᵉ *No paragraph mark: whole entry (except* Herefridi xvii s.) *written over*
an erasure

74 1. See I, Preface.
75 1. The widow of kings Æthelred and Cnut, and mother of Harthacnut and Edward the Confessor. She died in 1052. The house apparently lay towards the W. end of the N. side of High Street, and so may represent a part of the extensive tenement which Æthelred granted to his queen in 1012, cf. entry 23, esp. n. 1. The present entry is evidence that the *TRE* tenant did not actually hold in 1065.
   2. Roger le Poer, bishop of Salisbury 1102–39, Henry I's chancellor and chief justiciar: Richardson and Sayles, *passim*; *DNB* xlix. 103. See also 108 and, for his successor's properties in Winchester, II, 51, 268–9, and 691. In 1130 he was pardoned £6. 15*s*. 8*d*. of the city's aid: *Pipe Roll 31 Henry I*, p. 41. See also E. J. Kealey, *Roger of Salisbury, viceroy of England* (Berkeley, Calif., 1972), esp. app. iv, p. 277.
   3. See 12.

75/6 1. See above, pp. 10–12.
76 1. Cf. 44.
77 1. See also 143.
   2. See also 143; cf. 209. He made a grant of a rent-charge to the prior and monks of Winchester for the soul of his son: *Regesta*, ii, no. 1379. He could have taken his name from the church of St. Valery which was outside West Gate. See 93, n. 1, and 107.
78 1. See 26.
   2. See 20.
   3. Cf. 19, n. 2.
79 1. See 26; cf. 250.
   2. See 20.
   3. See also 138 and 170. Possibly a justiciar in Sussex: *Regesta*, ii, no. 1238, cf. no. 1022. He died *c.* 1122. Henry I addressed a Winchester precept to *W. filio Ansgeri et omnibus ministris portuum maris*: V. H. Galbraith, *EHR* 35 (1920), 382 ff., no. XXXII.

[80] Rannulfus*a* Crispus porrexit[1] de consuetudine regis in terra Radulfi Roselli,[2] et non geldavit postea nisi per breve regis.

*b*Summa in hesterdinges.[1] In hoc vico habuit rex Edwardus lxiii burg*enses* reddentes consu*etudinem*. Postea fuerunt vastati xii, quia in eorum terris fuit facta domus regis.[2] Et de aliis non habet rex cons*uetudinem* nisi de xvii;*c* et in his terris xvii burg*enses regis* consu*etudinem* reddentes*d* manent.

*e*EXTRA PORTAM DE WEST

[81] *f*Domus Safugel reddebat T.R.E. omnes consuetudines; et modo est in elemosina;[1] et reddit regi de langabulo et brue*gabulo* viii d. et elemosine viii sol. Et ibi iuxta fuit quidam vicus,[2] sed fuit diffactus quando rex fecit facere suum fossatum.[3]

[82] *f*Domus Edrici ceci[1] reddebat omnes consuetudines T.R.E. Modo tenet eam Rannulfus Pasturellus et reddit langabulum et brue*gabulum* et nullam aliam consuetudinem; et reddit ii s. et suum estagium.[2] Et de eadem terra tenet Willelmus de Pontearch'[3] i terram, et non facit consuetudines, et est vasta. Et super eandem terram habet Albericus coquus[4] i domum et non facit consuetudines, et reddit ei vi s.

[83] *f*Domus Alestani Coppede reddebat omnes consuetudines T.R.E. Et modo habet Bern*ardus* cancellarius regine[1] [fo. 6]*g* et non facit consuetudines; et pars illius domus est super terram regis et pars super terram episcopi. Et ipse preoccupavit i pedem de vico regis[2] et habet inde xxiiii s.

[80] Rannulf Curly transferred (?)[1] some of the king's custom on to the land of Ralf Rosell,[2] and afterwards did not pay geld except when ordered to by the king's writ.

The total on both sides.[1] In this street King Edward had 63 burgesses paying the custom. Afterwards 12 were destroyed because the king's house was built on their lands.[2] And of the rest [i.e. 51] the king has no custom except from 17. And on these lands dwell 17 burgesses paying the king's custom.

OUTSIDE WEST GATE

[81] The tenement of Safugel paid all customs *TRE* and now is held in alms.[1] And it pays to the king for landgable and brewgable 8*d*. and in alms 8*s*. And next to it was a street[2] which was destroyed when the king had his ditch made.[3]

[82] The tenement of Edric the Blind[1] paid all customs *TRE*. Now Rannulf Pastorel holds it and pays landgable and brewgable and no other custom. And it yields 2*s*. and [the profit of] its upper storey (?).[2] And of that land William of Pont de l'Arche[3] holds 1 land and does not perform the customs. And it is waste. And on that land Alberic the cook[4] has a house and does not perform the customs, and it yields him 6*s*.

[83] The tenement of Alestan Coppede paid all customs *TRE*. And now Bernard, the queen's chancellor,[1] has it and does not perform the customs. And part of that tenement is on the land of the king and part on the land of the bishop. And [Bernard] encroached 1 ft. on the king's street.[2] And he has from it 24*s*.

---

a This entry starts on a new line but is not given a paragraph sign or a rubricated initial letter   *b* Whole paragraph rubricated over an erasure   *c* xviii Ellis   *d* reddentibus MS.; paragraph mark before manent   *e* Whole heading written over an erasure   *f* [81], [82], and [83], lines 1 and 2, occupying the remainder of fo. 5*v*, col. b, are written over an erasure   *g* The remainder of this entry is written over an erasure occupying the first four lines of fo. 6, col. a

80 1. This expression is also found in **108**.
2. See **1**.
80–1 1. Cf. *ethergingis* in **I**, Preface. The 63 *TRE* custom-paying burgesses can be counted. The 17 existing custom-paying burgesses are not so easy to identify. Presumably the clerk has omitted, besides those entirely quit, tenements held by religious persons (**14–16, 25–6,** and possibly **72–3**), and tenements from which less than all the customs were paid (**6, 13a, 13b, 22, 24, 27, 33–4, 45–6, 55, 71, 76,** and **80**). But seventeen can be reached in several slightly different ways.
2. See **57**.
81 1. This may mean that the rent was employed for a charitable purpose.
2. Outside and perhaps to the S. of West Gate. The continuation of the sentence shows that it was presumably

destroyed when the castle ditch was dug in 1067: see the next note and p. 263, below. For other blocked streets and lanes, see **28**, n. 2, and below, pp. 278–81.
3. Probably a reference to the construction of Winchester castle by William I early in 1067; see below, p. 302.
82. 1. Cf. below, p. 209, n. 2.
2. See **12**.
3. See **I**, Preface.
4. See also **191**, and for his son, **II, 562**. For royal cooks, see *Constitutio Domus Regis* in *Dialogus de Scaccario*, 131–2.
83 1. Bernard, chaplain and chancellor of Queen Matilda, bishop of St. David's (cons. 19 Sept. 1115, died 1148): *Regesta*, ii, p. xi. For his properties in Winchester, see **II, 516, 669,** and **680**.
2. Cf. **19**, n. 2.

[84] Domus Auici reddebat omnes consuetudines T.R.E. Modo habet Girardus barrat*us* et nichil inde reddit regi. Et super illam terram sunt iiii bardelli; et reddunt iiii sol. et omnes consuetudines regi.

[85] Domus Alrici[1] omnes consuetudines reddebat T.R.E.; et modo habet filius eius, et facit consuetudines.

[86] Domus Wenestani reddebat omnes consuetudines T.R.E.; et modo sunt in ea iii domus, et reddunt consuetudines.

[87] Domus Godwini filii Elmari[1] reddebat omnes consuetudines; et Henricus de Dunmera[2] et Chepingius dives[3] habent inde per annum ix s.

[88] Domus Wenestani Sotebord reddebat omnes consuetudines T.R.E. Modo habent illam Sawardus et Ingulfus et[a] faciunt consuetudines.

[89] Domus Liwoldi reddebat consuetudines T.R.E. Modo tenet quedam vidua et reddit consuetudines.

[90] Domus Brunestan[1] et Babbi et Welestani Opchieher et Engelr*ici* redd*ebat* consuetudines T.R.E. Modo tenet Gilebertus archarius et non facit consuetudines; et posuit domum suam in vico regis iiii p*edes*;[2] et habet inde xlii sol. per annum.

[91] Domus Elmeri[1] et Godwini Clawecuncte et Godwini Capel[2] redd*ebat* omnes consuetudines T.R.E. Modo tenet Hugo de Chiuilli[3] et facit consuetudines et reddit regi iiii d. et recipit[b] inde xviii sol. Et ibi iuxta [est] i venella[4] in qua manebant Fulcardus[5] et Elfegus tornator, et fac*iebant* consuetudines regi. Modo est obstupata,[4] sed nescimus [a quo].

[92] Domus Godwini filii[c] Chetel reddebat[d] omnes consuetudines T.R.E. [Modo] tenet quedam vidua et facit consuetudines.

[93] Domus Alurici Penipurs reddebat omnes consuetudines T.R.E. Modo tenet Willemus potarius[1] et facit consuetudines; et habet inde i marcam argenti.

---

[84] The tenement of Avic paid all customs *TRE*. Now Girard Barrat has it and pays nothing from it to the king. And there are 4 shacks on that land; and they pay 4*s*. and all customs to the king.

[85] The tenement of Alric[1] paid all customs *TRE*. Now his son has it and performs the customs.

[86] The tenement of Winstan paid all customs *TRE*. And now there are 3 houses on it and they pay the customs.

[87] The tenement of Godwin son of Elmer[1] paid all customs; and Henry of Dummer[2] and Cheping the Rich[3] have from it 9*s*. a year.

[88] The tenement of Winstan Soot-board paid all customs *TRE*. Now Seward and Ingulf have it and perform the customs.

[89] The tenement of Liwold paid the customs *TRE*. Now a certain widow holds it and pays the customs.

[90] The tenement of Brunstan,[1] Babba, Wilstan Opchieher, and Engelric paid the customs *TRE*. Now Gilbert the archer holds it and does not perform the customs. And he put his house 4 ft. on the king's street.[2] And he has from it 42*s*. a year.

[91] The tenement of Elmer,[1] Godwin Claw-cunt, and Godwin Capel[2] paid all customs *TRE*. Now Hugh of Quevilly[3] holds it and performs the customs and pays the king 4*d*. and receives from it 18*s*. And next to it is a lane[4] in which Fulcard[5] and Elfege the turner used to live and perform the customs to the king. It is now blocked up,[4] but we do not know [by whom].

[92] The tenement of Godwin son of Chetel paid all customs *TRE*. Now a certain widow holds it and performs the customs.

[93] The tenement of Aluric Pennypurse paid all customs *TRE*. Now William the potter[1] holds it and performs the customs. And he has from it 1 mark of silver [13*s*. 4*d*.].

---

[a] et *repeated*   [b] recepit *MS.*   [c] filius *MS.*   [d] reddit *MS.*

85 1. Cf. 170. An Alric and his father held land in Hants both *TRE* and *TRW*. Here is a clear case of an Englishman succeeding his father in a Winchester tenement.
87 1. See 14.
2. See 10.
3. See 10. Cheping was probably a moneyer of Henry I: for this and other moneying associations of the area see below, Table 39.
90 1. Cf. 17.
2. Cf. 19, n. 2.
91 1. See also 103.
2. Cf. 121.

3. In 1130, under Essex and Herts., Robert fitzSiward accounted for the 15 marks he had offered for the office and wife of Hugh Chivilli: *Pipe Roll 31 Henry I*, p. 53.
4. Probably a lost minor lane in the western suburb in the area to the N. of *Wodestret* (Romsey Road), or on the N. side of that street. Cf. 107 and 122. For the method of location and for other blocked streets and lanes, see 28, n. 2, and below, pp. 278–81.   5. Cf. 101.
93 1. See also 255. William, described by Henry I as *serviens meus*, gave the property, which was in front of the minster of St. Valery, to the monks of St. Swithun: V. H. Galbraith, *EHR* 35 (1920), 382 ff., no. XXIX. For the locality, cf. 107.

[94] Domus Edwini fabri reddebat omnes consuetudines T.R.E. Modo tenet Emma uxor Roberti[1] et facit consuetudines; et inde recipit[a] xx s.

[95] Domus Siremani et Alurici Toi et Godwini Penifeder reddebat consuetudines T.R.E. Modo tenet [fo. 6ᵛ] abbas[1] et facit consuetudines; et inde habet xxiiii sol.

[96] Domus Godmani Brincigesone[1] reddebat omnes consuetudines T.R.E. Modo tenet Alwinus de Hodiam[2] et facit consuetudines et habet inde viii sol. Et tenet aliam domum de feudo Roberti filii Hamonis[3] et non facit consuetudines.

[97] Domus Alwini fenarii reddebat consuetudines T.R.E. Modo tenet Robertus et facit consuetudines; et inde habet ii sol.

[98] Gardini Lipestani Bittecat reddebant xii d. T.R.E. Modo sunt quatuor domus super illam terram et reddunt similiter regi xii d. et faciunt consuetudines; et habet[1] de rentis xi sol. et vi d.

[99] Domus Godwini Goce et Gode reddebat consuetudines T.R.E. Modo tenet Emma uxor Roberti filii[b] Wasferi[1] et facit consuetudines; et inde recipit[a] v sol.

[100] Super terram abbatis sunt v domus que nullam consuetudinem reddunt regi; et inde habet iii s. et iii d.; et est de terra regis.

[101] Domus Fulcardi[1] reddebat consuetudines T.R.E. Modo tenet Osbertus filius Thiardi,[2] et reddit regi viii d. Et ipse Osbertus posuit ibi v bordellos partim[c] in vico regis,[3] et fecit eos pro amore dei ad hospitandum pauperes.

[102] Domus Ulfchetilli et Wlfori reddebant consuetudines T.R.E. Modo tenet Wirstanus i domum de Alberico camerario[1] pro v s. et ii d. per annum et facit consuetudines regis; et Iudicellus[2] tenet alteram et dat regi langabulum et bruegabulum et Alberico camerario xxviii d.

[a] recepit MS.   [b] filius MS.   [c] partem MS.

94 1. Wife (probably widow) of Robert fitzWasfer. See also 99.
95 1. More likely the abbot of New Minster than the abbess of Winchester.
96 1. See 36.
    2. See also II, 330 and 468.
    3. See 50, n. 2.
98 1. Possibly Lefstan.
99 1. See 94.
101 1. See 91.

[94] The tenement of Edwin the blacksmith paid all customs TRE. Now Emma, the wife of Robert,[1] holds it and performs the customs, and receives from it 20s.

[95] The tenement of Sireman, Aluric Toi, and Godwin Pennyfather paid the customs TRE. Now the abbot (?)[1] holds it and performs the customs and has from it 24s.

[96] The tenement of Godman Brown-king's son[1] paid all customs TRE. Now Alwin of Odiham[2] holds it and performs the customs and has from it 8s. And he holds another tenement of the fief of Robert fitzHamo[3] and does not perform the customs.

[97] The tenement of Alwin the hay-merchant paid the customs TRE. Now Robert holds it and performs the customs and has from it 2s.

[98] The gardens of Lefstan Bittecat yielded 12d. TRE. Now there are 4 houses on that land and they yield likewise 12d. to the king and perform the customs. And he[1] has in rents 11s. 6d.

[99] The tenement of Godwin Goze and Goda paid the customs TRE. Now Emma, wife of Robert son of Wasfer,[1] holds it and performs the customs and receives from it 5s.

[100] On the land of the abbot are 5 houses which pay no custom to the king. And he [? the abbot] has from them 3s. 3d. And it is on royal demesne.

[101] The tenement of Fulcard[1] paid the customs TRE. Now Osbert son of Thiard[2] holds it and pays the king 8d. And Osbert placed there 5 shacks partly on the king's street,[3] and made them for the love of God to provide lodgings for poor men.

[102] The tenements of Ulfchetil and Wulfhere paid the customs TRE. Now Wirstan holds 1 tenement of Alberic the chamberlain[1] for 5s. 2d. a year and performs the king's customs; and Judicel[2] holds the other and gives the king landgable and brewgable and Alberic the chamberlain 28d.

    2. See 30.
    3. Cf. 19, n. 2.
102 1. There was an Aubrey the chamberlain in Hampshire in 1086, who, according to J. H. Round, may have been the queen's chamberlain: VCH Hants i. 425, 503b.
    2. Juthekel de Wintonia witnessed a Winchester deed of this period: EHR 14 (1899), 424. He may still have held this property in 1148, cf. II, 275; but there could have been another person of the same name, cf. II, 864, n. 1.

[103] Domus Elmeri[1] reddebat consuetudines T.R.E. Modo tenet Gisla uxor Gardini et non facit consuetudines. Et sciatis ibi esse ii mansuras; et inde habet viii sol.

[104] Domus Lewini Gulee reddebat consuetudines T.R.E. Modo tenet Bretfol et facit consuetudines.

[105] Domus Alwini Poplestan et Alwini[a] heuere reddebant consuetudines T.R.E. et reddebant hominibus destre gilda[b][1] xxxv d. Modo tenet Sawalo presbiter[c][2] et non facit consuetudines; et inde recipit[d] xii s. Illa[m] terram sciatis fuisse T.R.E. hominum extra portam de West.[1]

[106] Domus Alueredi Taddebelloc[e] [fo. 7] reddebat omnes consuetudines T.R.E. Modo tenet Hoellus et facit consuetudines et inde recipit[d] vi s.

[107] Terra Alwardi filii Etardii reddebat omnes consuetudines T.R.E., et fuit monetarius regis E.[1] Super illa[m] terram manebant v domus et fac*iebant* consuetudines. Et hec sunt nomina illorum qui tenebant domus: Liwin',[2] Dodesmere, Godemannus,[3] Godwinus, Liuuinus;[2] et illi qui modo tenent terram illam reddunt Willelmo filio Odonis[4] et Roberto de Seifrewast[5] vi sol. et iiii d.; et coquus Herberti[6] inde recipit[d] xxiiii s. et facit consuetudines. Et inter illam terram et monasterium Sancti Walarici[7] erat i venella[8] que pertinebat ecclesie; et Erchembaldus regis serviens[9] coniunxit eam aecclesie pro amore dei.

[103] The tenement of Elmer[1] paid the customs *TRE*. Now Gisla, wife of Gardin, holds it and does not perform the customs. And know that there are there 2 messuages. And she has from it/them 8*s*.

[104] The tenement of Lewin Gulee paid the customs *TRE*. Now Bretfol holds it and performs the customs.

[105] The tenements of Alwin Pebble and Alwin the hewer paid the customs *TRE* and paid the men of the Easter Guild[1] 35*d*. Now Sawal the priest[2] holds them and does not perform the customs. And he receives from them 12*s*. Know that *TRE* that land belonged to the men outside West Gate.[1]

[106] The tenement of Alfred Toad-ballock paid all customs *TRE*. Now Hoel holds it and performs the customs and receives from it 6*s*.

[107] The land of Alward the son of Aitard paid all the customs *TRE*. And he was a moneyer of King Edward.[1] On that land were 5 houses and they performed the customs. These are the names of those who held the houses: Lewin,[2] Dodesmere, Godman,[3] Godwin, and Lewin.[2] And those who now hold that land pay William son of Odo[4] and Robert of Chiffrevast[5] 6*s*. 4*d*. And the cook of Herbert[6] receives from it 24*s*. and performs the customs. And between that land and the minster of St. Valery[7] was a lane[8] which pertained to the church. And Erchembald, the king's sergeant,[9] joined it to the church for the love of God.

---

[a] Alwinus *MS.*   [b] Des-/tregilda *MS., with hyphen following* Des *at end of line*   [c] prb'to *MS.*   [d] recepit *MS.*   [e] caddebelloc *Ellis*

103 1. See **91**.

105 1. See the last sentence. This may be a guild of the men living outside West Gate, and so called because of the association of the western suburb with the liturgical celebration of Easter, see below, p. 268. Before 1330 the Winchester merchant guild owned a croft in the western suburb, and in the reign of Edward I a guild of palmers was tenant of a property there: Stowe 846, fo. 33[v]; Furley *City Government*, 70. The church of St. James at the limit of the W. suburb was a station in the Palm Sunday procession from the cathedral and Hyde Abbey (*Reg Pontissara* 439–41). The obscure dedication of the other church at the limit of the suburb, St. Anastasius or St. Anastasia, may originally have commemorated the Anastasis, the Resurrection. In any case the W. suburb was sufficiently associated with the Easter liturgy in Winchester for the guild there to be dedicated to that feast. This interpretation depends on reading *destre* as a form of *de Ēastran*, where *e* of *de* has been elided before the *e* of the OE f. pl. 'Easter'. Elsewhere in Survey **I** we have *de Auco* (**I**, 75) and *de Esperchefort* (**I**, 77), and in Survey **II** *de Est* (**II**, 731/2). The evidence is thus on the whole against elision, but since *destre* seems otherwise to make no sense, the interpretation has been accepted here.

2. See **36**.

107 1. Ælfwerd was a Winchester moneyer under Harold Harefoot: *English Coins*, 77. For his brother Alwin, see **11**, and for both see below, pp. 401 ff. and Table 34.

2. A Leofwine was a moneyer of Edward the Confessor: see below, Table 35.

3. Probably a moneyer of Edward the Confessor: see below, Table 35.

4. See **42**.

5. See also **II**, 288. In 1166 his son William held the two knights' fees of the bishop of Winchester which his father had held (*RBE* i. 205).

6. See **I**, Preface.

7. The church of St. Valery stood outside West Gate in what is now Sussex Street. See *Reg Pontissara* 441; HRO, Mottisfont Priory Rental, 1340. For this locality, cf. **93**.

8. Probably a lost minor lane in the western suburb, running W. from Sussex Street. Cf. **91** and **122**. For the method of location and for other blocked streets and lanes, see **28**, n. 2, and below, pp. 278–81.

9. An unidentified royal servant.

[108] Domus Tochi reddebat consuetudines T.R.E. Modo tenet Herluinus, et reliquit illam domum pro rectit*udine*[1] et porrexit[2] in custodia[3] episcopi Salesberie;[a][4] et inde recipit[b] x sol.

[109] Domus Bictrici Bade reddebat consuetudines T.R.E. Modo tenet Edricus et facit consuetudines.

[110] Domus Ficelli reddebat consuetudines T.R.E. Modo [tenet] abbatissa[1] et facit consuetudines.

[111] Domus Leurici reddebat consuetudines T.R.E. Modo tenet Herbertus camerarius,[1] et facit consuetudines; et inde recipit[b] xxii s.

[112] Domus Hedrici reddebat consuetudines T.R.E. Modo tenet Unfridus Parfait,[1] et facit consuetudines, sed non geldat; et inde recipit vi s.

[113] Domus Elmari Picteurte reddebat consuetudines T.R.E. Modo tenet Ricardus prepositus,[1] et facit consuetudines; et inde recipit xxxii d.

[114] Domus Tutel reddebat consuetudines T.R.E. Modo tenet Simon,[1] et non facit consuetudines, nisi langabulum.

[115] Domus Almodi[1] reddebat consuetudines T.R.E. Modo tene[n]t Edmundus et Sawinus,[2] et faciunt consuetudines; et inde recipit Willelmus de Anesi[3] x s.

[116] Domus Godemanni et Lutemanni et Edwi reddebat consuetudines T.R.E. Modo tenet Herbertus camerarius,[1] et non facit consuetudines. Et in illa terra manet Algotus vir Alwii, et non facit consuetudines.

[108] The tenement of Toky paid the customs *TRE*. Now Herlwin holds it; and he gave up that tenement because of a legal judgement[1] and transferred[2] it/ himself into the custody[3] of the bishop of Salisbury.[4] And he receives from it 10*s*.

[109] The tenement of Brictric Bad paid the customs *TRE*. Now Edric holds it and performs the customs.

[110] The tenement of Ficel paid the customs *TRE*. Now the abbess[1] holds it and performs the customs.

[111] The tenement of Leofric paid the customs *TRE*. Now Herbert the chamberlain[1] holds it and performs the customs. And he receives from it 22*s*.

[112] The tenement of Edric paid the customs *TRE*. Now Unfrid Parfait[1] holds it and performs the customs, but he does not pay geld. And he receives from it 6*s*.

[113] The tenement of Elmar Pick-wort paid the customs *TRE*. Now Richard the reeve[1] holds it and performs the customs. And he receives from it 32*d*.

[114] The tenement of Tutel paid the customs *TRE*. Now Simon[1] holds it and performs no custom except landgable.

[115] The tenement of Almod[1] paid the customs *TRE*. Now Edmund and Sawin[2] hold it and perform the customs. And William d'Anesi [Anizy][3] receives from it 10*s*.

[116] The tenement of Godman, Luteman, and Edwi paid the customs *TRE*. Now Herbert the chamberlain[1] holds it and does not perform the customs. And on that land lives Algot, Alwig's man, and does not perform the customs.

---

[a] *rubricator has corrected* a   [b] *recepit MS.*

108 1. *rectitudo* also means customary right or service; but the sense of the passage is obscure.
2. See 80.
3. Perhaps this just means custody or wardship. But since we meet with watch duty in Survey **I**, *custodia* may have the technical sense of a Ward. See Tait *Medieval Borough*, 60, n. 3; Urry *Canterbury*, 92 ff.
4. See 75, n. 2; for this property, cf. **II, 268–9**.
110 1. For this tenement, cf. **II, 261**.
111 1. See **I**, Preface.
112 1. See also **120**.
113 1. See also **189, 204**, and cf. **20**, n. 4. He is addressed in a precept of Henry I to be dated 1100 × 1106: *Regesta*, ii, no. 804.

114 1. Cf. **283**.
115 1. See **47**.
2. There were *TRE* and later tenants of this name in Winchester and Hampshire: cf. entries **180** and **217**; *VCH Hants* i. 458, 465, 507, 513; and see also **212**.
3. He was present, between 1108 and 1113, at the treasury in Winchester on that now famous occasion when Abbot Faricius of Abingdon proved his case by Domesday Book: *Regesta*, ii, no. 1000; J. H. Round, *Feudal England* (London, 1895), 142 ff.; V. H. Galbraith, *The Making of Domesday Book* (Oxford, 1962), 209.
116 1. See **I**, Preface. This tenement may have been part of a block of Herbert's property on the W. side of Sussex Street; cf. **117** and **123**.

[117] Ante portam Herberti camerarii¹ erat vasta terra super fossatum² [fo. 7ᵛ] T.R.E. Modo sunt v domus; et quedam vidua tenet i, et reddit camerario xxiii d.; et Alwinus le feller tenet aliam, et dat camerario ii s.; et Radulfus Holinessone tertia[m] pro v sol.; et quedam lauandaria*ᵃ* quartam; et i hospitale pro amore dei [. . .]

[118] Curtillum¹ Wnprice reddebat ii d. T.R.E. Modo tenet Radulfus Escouell' i mansuram, et facit consuetudines excepto langabulo, et reddit camerario² v sol. Et super curtillum sunt vi domus, et faciunt*ᵇ* consuetudines reg*is*; et inde recipit Radulfus de Tuberilli viii sol.

[119] Curtillum Godwini Cimel reddebat*ᶜ* ii d. T.R.E. Et super illud curtillum sunt iii*ᵈ* domus, et reddunt regi iiii d.; et Herbertus presbiter¹ inde recipit xv sol. et facit consuetudines reg*is*.

[120] Curtilla Godwini et Brictwi reddebant iiii d.*ᵉ* T.R.E. Et super illa curtilla sunt iii domus et reddunt regi viii d. et omnes consuetudines; et Unsfridus Parfait¹ inde recipit i. marcam argenti.

[121] Curtillum Capel¹ reddebat ii d. T.R.E. Et super illud curtillum sunt iii domus; et Osbertus frater Maiesent² reddit inde regi viii d. et omnes consuetudines.

[122] Et ibi iuxta erat quedam vasta terra; et Brumannus fecit super illam terram i domum quae non fuit T.R.E. Modo tenet eam Osbertus filius Tihardi,¹ et reddit regi v d. de langabulo et omnes consuetudines. Et Osbertus frater Maiesent² tenet illam de eo, reddens ei vii solidatas ferrorum per iii adden*arios.* Et pars illius domus sedet super fossatum et pars in vico regis.³

[123] Domus Hauoc¹ reddebat omnes consuetudines

[117] In front of the gate of Herbert the chamberlain¹ was *TRE* a waste land within/above the ditch.² Now there are 5 houses there. A certain widow holds one and pays the chamberlain 23*d*. Alwin the feller holds another and gives the chamberlain 2*s*. Ralf Holin's son holds the third for 5*s*.; and a certain washerwoman the fourth. And [the fifth is] a hospital for the love of God.

[118] The curtilage¹ of Wnprice paid 2*d*. *TRE*. Now Ralf Escovell holds 1 messuage and performs the customs except landgable and pays the chamberlain² 5*s*. And on the curtilage are 6 houses which perform the king's customs. And Ralf *de Tuberill* receives from it/them 8*s*.

[119] The curtilage of Godwin Cimel paid 2*d*. *TRE*. And on that curtilage are 3 houses, and they pay the king 4*d*. And Herbert the priest¹ receives from it/them 15*s*. and performs the royal customs.

[120] The curtilages of Godwin and Brictwi paid 4*d*. *TRE*. And on those curtilages are 3 houses which pay the king 8*d*. and all customs. And Unfrid Parfait¹ receives from them 1 mark of silver [13*s*. 4*d*.].

[121] The curtilage of Capel¹ paid 2*d*. *TRE*. And on that curtilage are 3 houses. And Osbert the brother of Maiesent² pays the king for them 8*d*. and all customs.

[122] And there was adjacent a certain waste land on which Bruman built a house which was not there *TRE*. Now Osbert son of Thiard¹ holds it and pays the king 5*d*. landgable and all the customs. Osbert the brother of Maiesent² holds it from him, paying him 7 shillingsworth of irons [? horse-shoes] at three account-days. And part of that house rests on the ditch and part on the king's street.³

[123] The tenement of Havoc¹ paid all customs *TRE*.

ᵃ lauanclaria *Ellis*   *ᵇ* facit *MS*.   *ᶜ* reddit *MS*.   *ᵈ* in *MS*.   *ᵉ* iii d. *corrected to* iiii d.

117 1. See **I**, Preface.
  2. This property was perhaps on the E. side of Sussex Street against the city ditch and opposite Herbert's tenements on the W. side of the street; cf. **I**, **116** and **123**. For the city ditch, see also **163**, **164**, and below, p. 274.
118 1. The word is consistently contracted to *curtill'* in entries **118–21**. The use of *illud* and *illa* shows that it is a neuter noun; but it is impossible to say whether *curtillum* or *curtillagium* is intended.
  2. See **I**, Preface.
119 1. There is also a Herbert the priest in 1148: see below, **II**, **632**.
120 1. See **112**.
121 1. Perhaps Godwin Capell, see **91**.
  2. See also **122**.
122 1. See **30**.

  2. See **121**.
  3. Cf. **19**, n. 2, and see below, p. 274. The street in question may be a lost minor lane in the western suburb (cf. **91** and **107**), rather than the extramural *twichen*, now Sussex Street. In which case the ditch may be one of those mentioned in **123**, rather than the city ditch, for which see **117**, **163**, and **164**.
123 1. This is probably a personal name (see below, p. 238, s.v.). Ralph Havoc appears to have succeeded his father as a royal falconer by 1130: *Pipe Roll 31 Henry I*, p. 148. By 1180–1 the royal hawk mews at Winchester stood outside West Gate on the W. side of this property. It is possible that this was the establishment of the royal falconers at Winchester from at least the latter part of the eleventh century. See Colvin (ed.) *King's Works*, ii. 1006, and *SMW* 716.

T.R.E. Modo ten[e]t Herbertus camerarius,[2] et facit omnes consuetudines. Et illa domus inter ii fossatum.[a3]

Now Herbert the chamberlain[2] holds it and performs all the customs. And that tenement is between the two ditches (?).[3]

SNITHELINGA STRET[b]

[124] Burewoldus[1] reddebat ii d. et consuetudines T.R.E. Modo Brithwoldus presbiter debet similiter.

[125] Leouingus[1] reddebat[c] iiii d. et consuetudines T.R.E. Modo Gilebertus debet similiter.

[126] Brithwen vidua reddebat viii d. et consuetudines T.R.E. Modo [fo. 8] Osbertus filius Iuonis debet idem.

[127] Lufmancat reddebat iiii d. et consuetudines T.R.E. Modo Ricardus faber debet similiter.

[128] Godricus Chingessone[1] reddebat iiii d. et consuetudines T.R.E. Modo Hardi[n]gus faber[2] debet similiter.

[129] Alnodus Stud' reddebat vi d. et consuetudines T.R.E. Modo Odo monetarius[1] debet similiter.

[130] Almarus reddebat iiii d. et consuetudines T.R.E. Modo Goisfridus clericus[1] debet similiter.

IN BREDENESTRET

[131] Domus Brunestani[1] reddebat xxx d. et consuetudines T.R.E. Modo Arnulfus Burdin et Ulf debe[n]t idem.

[132] Eustachius reddebat viii d. et consuetudines T.R.E. Modo Godwinus Withmundin debet idem.

[133] Odo Ticchemannessone tenuit terram liberam preter waitam T.R.E., et de terra regis viii denarratas. Modo Willelmus filius eius[1] debet similiter.

SNITHELINGA STREET [TOWER STREET]

[124] Burewold[1] paid 2d. and the customs *TRE*. Now Brithwold the priest owes the same.

[125] Leving[1] paid 4d. and the customs *TRE*. Now Gilbert owes the same.

[126] The widow Brithwen paid 8d. and the customs *TRE*. Now Osbert son of Ivo owes the same.

[127] Lufman Cat paid 4d. and the customs *TRE*. Now Richard the blacksmith owes the same.

[128] Godric King's son[1] paid 4d. and the customs *TRE*. Now Harding the blacksmith[2] owes the same.

[129] Alnod Stud paid 6d. and the customs *TRE*. Now Odo the moneyer[1] owes the same.

[130] Almar paid 4d. and the customs *TRE*. Now Geoffrey the clerk[1] owes the same.

IN *BREDENE* STREET [STAPLE GARDENS]

[131] The tenement of Brunstan[1] paid 30d. and the customs *TRE*. Now Arnulf Burdin and Ulf owe the same.

[132] Eustace paid 8d. and the customs *TRE*. Now Godwin Withmunding owes the same.

[133] Odo Ticchemann's son held a land which was free except for Watch *TRE*, and from the royal demesne 8 pennyworth of land. Now his son William[1] owes the same.

---

[a] ? *for domus est inter ii fossata*   [b] *In lower margin text for rubricator almost entirely cut off*   [c] reddit *MS.*

123 2. See I, Preface.
   3. The two ditches were perhaps the suburban boundary ditch and the partly silted-up N. ditch of the Iron Age settlement. This would place the property very close to the known site of Henry II's hawk mews. 116 and 117 may have been adjacent.
124 1. Cf. 28.
125 1. Possibly a moneyer of Edward the Confessor: see below, Table 36.
128 1. Possibly a moneyer of Edward the Confessor: see

below, Table 36.
   2. For his son, who seems to be holding the same property, see II, 379.
129 1. He is not listed in *English Coins*, but cf. 42, n. 1, and below, p. 409. For the tenement, cf. II, 380 held by Richard son of Odo.
130. 1. See 66.
131 1. Cf. 17.
133 1. Cf. 42.

[134] Petrus reddebat x d. et consuetudines T.R.E. Modo Chepingus filius Alueue[1] debet idem.

[135] [a]Alwinus pater Chepingi[b1] habuit duas domos T.R.E. Modo tenet eas Chipingus eius filius similiter quietas. Et inter has duas domos erat vicus[2] quem sui anticessores [sic] hospitaverunt cum alia terra; et de hoc fuit Chippingus inplacitatus, sed non fecit finem[3] ante iusticiam regis; et adhuc tenet Chipingus, [et reddit] iiii d. et facit consuetudines inde.

[136] [c]Domus Hachechasse reddebat xv d. de langabulo et omnem consuetudinem tempore R.E. Modo Gaufridus cler*icus*[1] tenet eam et facit consuetudinem similiter.

[137] [c]Domus Poti[1] reddebat xii d. et omnem consuetudinem T.R.E. Modo tenet eam Henricus de Dommere[2] et facit similiter.

[138] [c]Domus Edwacre et Balloc[1] redd*ebat* xii d. et omnem consuetudinem T.R.E. Modo Willelmus filius Ansgeri[2] facit similiter.

[139] [c]Domus Lewingi Dol reddebat T.R.E. vi d. de langabulo et omnem consuetudinem. Modo Ulwardus eius filius facit similiter.

DE TERRIS BARONUM[d]

[140] Domus Lewine Waterpotes et eius filii de terra abbatis redd*ebant* x d. de langabulo et omnem consuetudinem T.R.E. Modo eas tene[n]t Ascelinus Casier et Alwinus Bollochessege[1] et non fac*iunt* consuetudinem.

[141] Chipingus de Ordia[1] reddebat consuetudinem [fo. 8[v]] T.R.E. de i domo. Modo tenet eam Radulfus de Mortu[o]mari[2] et non facit consuetudinem.[e]

[134] Peter paid 10d. and the customs TRE. Now Cheping son of Alveva[1] owes the same.

[135] Alwin the father of Cheping[1] had two tenements TRE. Now his son Chiping holds them likewise quit. And between these two tenements was a street[2] which his predecessors occupied with the other land. Chipping was impleaded about this matter, but he did not make a fine[3] before the king's justiciar; and Chiping still holds it/them. And he pays 4d. and performs the customs for it/them.

[136] The tenement of Hachechasse paid 15d. landgable and every custom TRE. Now Geoffrey the clerk[1] holds it and likewise performs the custom.

[137] The tenement of Pot[1] paid 12d. and every custom TRE. Now Henry of Dummer[2] holds it and does the same.

[138] The tenement of Edwacer and Ballock[1] paid 12d. and every custom TRE. Now William son of Ansger[2] does the same.

[139] The tenement of Leving the Dolt paid 6d. landgable and every custom TRE. Now his son Wulfward does the same.

CONCERNING THE LANDS OF THE BARONS

[140] The tenements of Lewin Waterpot and his son on the land of the abbot paid 10d. landgable and every custom TRE. Now Ascelin Casier and Alwin Bullock's-eye[1] hold them and do not perform the custom.

[141] Chiping of [Headbourne] Worthy[1] paid the custom from 1 tenement TRE. Now Ralf of Mortemer[2] holds it and does not perform the custom.

---

[a] *Whole entry, except possibly* (fa)cit consuetudines inde., *written over an erasure*   [b] -us *MS.*   [c] *Original paragraph marks for* [136–9] *have been erased and repositioned (partly cut away)*   [d] *In margin, for rubricator;* de terris baronum   [e] *Last two lines written over an erasure*

134 1. See 10, n. 6. Cheping had probably been succeeded in this property by his son Hugh, also a moneyer, by 1148: cf. II, 403.
135 1. See 10, n. 6.
  2. A lost lane, probably running W. from *Brudenestret* into or across the block between that street and *Snidelingestret*. For the method of location and for other blocked streets and names, see 28, n. 2, and below, pp. 278–81.
  3. See 45.
136 1. Cf. 157.
137 1. Possibly God' Pot; see 174. For his son, William, see II, 488.
  2. See 10.
138 1. Possibly Lewinus Balloe; see 57.
  2. See 79.
140 1. Cf. 232.
141 1. See also 142. For this royal thegn, see J. H.

Round, *VCH Hants* i. 421, 428. He also held three houses in Southampton, which passed to Ralf de Mortemer, ibid. 516b. Chiping's estate at Headbourne Worthy included eight *hagae* in Winchester and had been purchased from the Old Minster for the term of three lives of which Ralf de Mortemer's was the last. The estate had reverted by 1148 when the rents from the Winchester properties (II, 406–9 in *Brudenestret*; II, 502 in *Alwarnestret*; and II, 608 in *Tannerestret*) were being paid to the reeves of Worthy. See *VCH Hants* i. 489b, and below, p. 383.
  2. See also 142 and 148. For this important baronial family, which took its name from Mortemer-sur-Eaulne, arr. and cant. Neufchâtel, Seine-Mme, see Sanders *Baronies*, 98; J. H. Round, *VCH Hants* i. 416, 420–1, 428, 434–5, 534; *DNB* xxxix. 130. Of Ralf I's sixteen Hampshire manors, thirteen had belonged to Chiping. For Ralf's son, Hugh I, see II, 421.

[142] ᵃEx alia parte Chipingus¹ reddebat consuetudinem T.R.E. de iiii mansuris. Modo tenet eas Radulfus de Mortuomari¹ et facit consuetudinem.

[143] ᵃOdo de Esp[er]chefort¹ habebat iiii mansuras T.R.E. et faciebant consuetudinem. Modo tenet Bernardus de Sancto Walarico,¹ et illi qui manent intus faciunt consuetudinem, preter hec² queᵇ Willelmus de Pontearch'³ tenet.

[144] Godwinus de Ordia tenuit i terram T.R.E. Modo tenet eam Henricus frater Debou',¹ et Willelmus de Salesberie de eo, et facit similiter consuetudinem preter pascere prisonem.²

[145] Abbatissa de Warewella¹ faciebat consuetudinem T.R.E. de parva terra.ᶜ Modo facit similiter.

[146] Godwinus Cederli' tenebat de terra abbatisse T.R.E. et faciebat consuetudinem. Modo tenet eam Wimundus presbiter, et tota consuetudo est retro.

[147] Alwinus Watmaungre tenuit de terra abbatis¹ T.R.E. Modo tenet eam Constantinus et facit consuetudinem.

[148] ᵈAlestanus tenuit [i] terram T.R.E. et faciebat consuetudinem. Modo tenet eam Elsi clericus¹ et facit consuetudinem. Et reddit Radulfo de Mortuomari² ii sol.³

[149] Wluricus tenuit i terram T.R.E. et dabat langabulum et faciebat omnem consuetudinem. Modo [tenet] eam Elsie clericus¹ et facit similiter consuetudinem. Et reddit Herberto de Sancto Quintino² xv d.³ Et he ii mansure sunt in una.

[150] Leuret tenuit i terram T.R.E. et faciebat omnem consuetudinem. Modo tenet eam Alestanus¹ eius filius

[142] On the other side Chiping¹ paid the custom for 4 messuages *TRE*. Now Ralf of Mortemer¹ holds them and performs the custom.

[143] Odo of Sparkford¹ had 4 messuages *TRE* and performed the custom. Now Bernard of St. Valéry¹ holds them and the men who live within perform the custom except those things² which William of Pont de l'Arche³ holds.

[144] Godwin of Worthy held 1 land *TRE*. Now Henry, the brother of Debou¹ holds it, and William of Salisbury from him, and he likewise performs the custom except provisioning the prison (?).²

[145] The abbess of Wherwell¹ performed the custom *TRE* from a small piece of land. Now she does the same.

[146] Godwin Chitterley held of the land of the abbess *TRE* and performed the custom. Now Wimund the priest holds it and the whole custom is in arrears.

[147] Alwin Wet-monger held of the land of the abbot¹ *TRE*. Now Constantine holds it and performs the custom.

[148] Alestan held [1] land *TRE* and performed the custom. Now Elsi the clerk¹ holds it and performs the custom. And he pays Ralf of Mortemer² 2s.³

[149] Wulfric held 1 land *TRE* and gave landgable and performed every custom. Now Elsie the clerk¹ holds it and likewise performs the custom. And he pays Herbert of St. Quentin² 15d.³ These 2 messuages are joined together.

[150] Leuret held 1 land *TRE* and performed every custom. Now his son Alestan¹ holds it and performs the

---

ᵃ *Whole entry written over an erasure*   ᵇ quod *MS.*   ᶜ paruo terre *MS.*   ᵈ *The whole of fo. 8ᵛ, col. b, containing* **[148]**–**[154]**, . . . Wigot, *has been erased and rewritten. Erased paragraph marks can be seen in their original positions opposite* **[148]**, *line 4, and* **[150]**, *line 7, of MS. See below, p. 523.*

142 1. See **141**.
143 1. See **77**.
    2. It is not clear what William holds.
    3. See **I**, Preface.
144 1. Alternatively, it means, 'Henry de Bou', his brother.
    2. By the early thirteenth century the king's gaol stood on the W. side of *Scowrtenestret*, possibly adjacent to this property. See *SMW*.
145 1. For this property, cf. **II**, 418–19.
147 1. For this property, cf. **II**, 420.

148 1. See also **149**; cf. **71**.
    2. See **141**.
    3. For this tenement, cf. **II**, 421.
149 1. See **148**.
    2. See **50**.
    3. In *c.* 1160 Herbert of St. Quentin granted three messuages in Winchester to Godstow Nunnery. Of the two within the walls one rendered a rent of 15d. and the other a rent of 12d. (cf. **150**). See *Godstow Cart*, 180.
150 1. Possibly a moneyer of Henry I: see below, Table 40.

et facit consuetudinem. Et de eadem terra habet Herbertus de Sancto Quintino² xii d.,³ et Chippingus xxxiii d., et alius Chipingus⁴ xii d., et Blundel xii d.

custom. And from that land Herbert of St. Quentin² has 12*d*.,³ Chipping 33*d*., another Chiping⁴ 12*d*., and Blondel 12*d*.

[151] Et iuxta illam terram tenebat Aldret¹ i terram T.R.E. reddentem omnem consuetudinem. Modo tenet eam Herbertus de Sancto Quintino.²

[151] And next to that land Aldred¹ held 1 land *TRE* which paid every custom. Now Herbert of St. Quentin² holds it.

[152] Et est ibi iuxta quaedam terra de Ouettona de feudo regis,¹ unde Herbertus camerarius² habebat x d. et faciebat consuetudinem.

[152] And next there is a certain land pertaining to Overton (?) on the royal demesne,¹ from which Herbert the chamberlain² had 10*d*. and performed the custom.

[153] Et est ibi iuxta quaedam mansura quae redd*it* monachis de Sapalanda¹ xxx d. et fac*it* consuetudinem quam*ᵃ* solebat facere T.R.E.

[153] And next there is a certain messuage which pays to the monks from Sheepland¹ 30*d*. and performs the custom which it used to perform *TRE*.

[154] Alestanus fuit monetarius¹ T.R.E. et habuit quandam terram. Modo tenet eam Wigot [fo. 9] de Lincolnia*ᵇ²* et facit omnem consuetudinem preter waitam; et reddit monachis de Sapalanda³ xxx d.

[154] Alestan was a moneyer¹ *TRE* and had a certain land. Now Wigod of Lincoln² holds it and performs every custom except Watch. And it/he pays the monks from Sheepland³ 30*d*.

[155] Fugel¹ tenuit i terram T.R.E. et fac*iebat* omnem consuetudinem. Modo tenet eam filius e[i]us et facit similiter consuetudinem.

[155] Fugel¹ held 1 land *TRE* and performed every custom. Now his son holds it and likewise performs the custom.

[156] Quedam domus de Polametona reddebat consuetudinem T.R.E. [Modo] tenet eam Willelmus Bertram¹ et facit similiter.

[156] A certain tenement pertaining to Polhampton paid the custom *TRE*. Now William Bertram¹ holds it and does likewise.

[157] Gaufridus clericus¹ ten*uit* ii mansuras de dominio regis, et idem ten*uit* ii mansuras de Lessam² que reddebant de langabulo xxx d. et omnem aliam consuetudinem T.R.E. Modo debent similiter facere.

[157] Geoffrey the clerk¹ held/holds 2 messuages of the royal demesne and also held/holds 2 messuages pertaining to Lasham² which paid 30*d*. landgable and every other custom *TRE*. Now they should do likewise.

[158] Domus*ᶜ* Ulueue Betteslaf¹ fuerunt quiete T.R.E. Modo tenet eas comes de Mellent² et sunt similiter quiete preter waitam.

[158] The tenements of Ulveva Betteslaf¹ were quit *TRE*. Now the count of Meulan² holds them and they are likewise quit except for Watch.

ᵃ quae *MS*.　　　*ᵇ* Delinc *MS*.　　　*ᶜ* Ddomus *MS*., d *duplicated in rubrication*

150 2. See **50**.　　　3. See **149**, n. 3.　　　4. Cf. **10**.
151 1. Cf. **46**.
　　2. See **50**.
152 1. Possibly Overton (see **156**), which was an episcopal manor. Upton (*Optune*) and Wooton (*Odetone*) were royal demesne in 1086. Cf. **157**, n. 2.
　　2. See **I**, Preface.
153 1. See also **154**, and **159–61**. As no monastery of this name has been recorded, the monks are probably those of Winchester (St. Swithun) and *Sapalanda* (sheep-land) may have been one of their estates. Alternatively this sheep-land may have been a locality in the city near *Brudenestret*, perhaps the area or market-place within the walls to the W. of North Gate; see below pp. 285–6.
154 1. Æthelstan was a Winchester moneyer from Æthelred to Edward, and Æthelstan Loc occurs under Cnut and Edward: *English Coins*, 77; cf. below, p. 407 and Tables 34 and 37.

2. Sheriff of Lincs. (1115–21). See J. H. Round, *VCH Hants* i. 535; *Regesta*, ii, no. 1116, etc.
3. See **153**.
155 1. See also **270** and **18**. Fulghel held land in Southampton *TRE*: *VCH Hants* i. 516b.
156 1. In 1086 William Bertram held Polhampton in Overton (cf. **152**) of the king: *VCH Hants* i. 491b. The tenement in Winchester presumably went with the manor. William's *antecessor* at Polhampton was Tostig. Cf. **157**, n. 2.
157 1. Cf. **136**.
2. *Esseham* in Domesday Book, *VCH Hants* i. 452b, a royal manor. For city tenements attached to rural estates, see entries **152** and **156**, and cf. the list and discussion below, pp. 382 ff., Fig. 20, and Table 28. Hemmeon *Burgage Tenure*, 89, translated *de lessam* 'on lease'.
158. 1. An important female landholder in Hampshire and thereabouts *TRE*. See J. H. Round, *VCH Hants* i. 429.
2. See **2**.

[159] Borewoldus Horloc tenuit i domum T.R.E. et fac*iebat* omnem consuetudinem. Modo tenent monachi et faciunt similiter consuetudinem; et reddit eis xxx d. de Sapalanda.¹

[160] Lowricus presbiter de Sapalanda¹ monacorum tenuit i domum T.R.E. et reddebat omnem consuetudinem et xxx d. Modo tenet eam eius uxor et facit similiter.

[161] Hunbric tenuit quandam terram de Sapalanda¹ T.R.E. et fac*iebat* omnem consuetudinem. Modo tenet eam Alwinus Barbitre et facit similiter.

[162] Summa: in hoc vico de terra regis fuerunt T.R.E. x burgenses. Modo sunt ibi viii.¹

[163] Extra portam de Nort Hugo de Menes habet domum super fossatum¹ regis que non fuit T.R.E., et reddit langabulum episcopo Wirec'.² Et ibi fuit vicus T.R.E. per quem burgenses ducebant equos suos ad aquare.³ Et habet vicum preoccupatum⁴ episcopus Durelmensis⁵ in domo sua. Modo eam domum habet epicopus Wirec'.

[164] Et supra fossatum regis¹ sunt ix domus et ii curtil*la*ᵃ unde episcopus Wint' habet langabulum.

[165] Et apud Palliesputte¹ sunt ix domus in calle regis² unde abbas langabulum habet.

IN SCOWERTENESTRET*ᵇ*

[166] Brithmarus¹ aurifaber reddebat x d. de langabulo et omnem consuetudinem T.R.E. Modo Deria debet similiter.

[159] Burewold Hoar-lock held 1 tenement *TRE* and performed every custom. Now the monks hold it and they likewise perform the custom. And it yields them from Sheepland¹ 30*d*.

[160] Leofric the priest of Sheepland¹ *Monachorum* held 1 tenement *TRE* and paid every custom and 30*d*. Now his wife holds it and does likewise.

[161] Hunbric held a certain land pertaining to Sheepland¹ *TRE* and performed every custom. Now Alwin Barbitre holds it and does likewise.

[162] Total: in this street on the royal demesne there were *TRE* 10 burgesses. Now there are 8 there.¹

[163] Outside North Gate Hugh of Meon has a house, which did not exist *TRE*, on the king's ditch,¹ and pays landgable to the bishop of Worcester.² And there was a street there *TRE* along which the burgesses used to lead their horses to water.³ And the bishop of Durham⁵ incorporated⁴ that street into his tenement. Now the bishop of Worcester holds the tenement.

[164] And on the king's ditch¹ are 9 houses and 2 curtilages from which the bishop of Winchester has landgable.

[165] And at Palliesputte¹ are 9 houses/tenements on the king's road² from which the abbot has landgable.

IN *SCOWERTENE* STREET [JEWRY STREET]

[166] Brithmar the goldsmith¹ paid 10*d*. landgable and every custom *TRE*. Now Deria [? Diera] owes the same.

ᵃ curtilz *MS.* ᵇ *In margin, for rubricator:* In Scowertenestret

159 1. See **153**.
160 1. See **153**.
161 1. See **153**.
162 1. This refers, presumably, to entries **131–9**. But not all those were custom-paying burgesses (cf. **135**). It is not clear how ten has been reduced to eight.
163 1. The city ditch; see also **117, 164** and below, p. 274.
    2. Either Wulfstan's successor, Bishop Samson (1096–1112), or his successor, Bishop Theulf (1113 (consecrated 1115)–1123). For the former as a royal servant, and his possible association with Domesday Book, see V. H. Galbraith, 'Notes on the career of Samson, bishop of Worcester (1096–1112)', *EHR* 82 (1967), 86–101.
    3. The street perhaps led downhill towards the running water on the E. and formed a continuation of the external *twichen* now known as Swan Lane; see below, pp. 263 and 274, and for other blocked streets and lanes, **28**, n. 2, and below, pp. 278–81.
    4. Understanding *habet preoccupatum* in the sense of

preoccupavit.
    5. Probably Rannulf Flambard, bishop 1099–1128. There are good reasons for the chief agent of William Rufus to have maintained a substantial house in Winchester, of which he perhaps lost possession on the accession of Henry I. Cf. below, p. 389. New Minster was apparently committed to Rannulf in 1088 and was presumably held by him until the appointment of Robert Losinga as abbot in 1090/1 (*Winchester ann*, s.a. 1088; cf. D. Knowles, C. N. L. Brooke, and V. C. M. London (eds.), *The Heads of Religious Houses: England and Wales, 940–1216* (Cambridge, 1972), 82).
164 1. See **117** and **163**.
165 1. In the thirteenth and fourteenth centuries this area lay at the limits of the city liberty, on the E. side of the road to Basingstoke: see *SMW*, and p. 264 below.
    2. If this does imply encroachment, cf. **19**, n. 2.
166 1. Probably a moneyer of Edward the Confessor: see below, p. 407 and Table 35. See also **217**.

[167] Alwinus reddebat x d. et omnem consuetudinem T.R.E. Modo Robertus scaldeator[1] debet similiter.

[168] Luwoldus Gustate[1] reddebat iiii d. [de] langabulo et omnem consuetudinem T.R.E. Modo Alwinus bedellus[2] facit idem.

[169] Durandus reddebat xiiii d. et omnem [fo. 9[v]] consuetudinem T.R.E. Modo filius Almari presbiteri debet idem.

[170] Lowinus presbiter[1] reddebat xxx d. et consuetudinem T.R.E., et Alricus[2] xx d. et consuetudinem, et Lewinus Wrtwos x d. et omnem consuetudinem. Modo Willelmus filius Ansgeri[3] debet similiter facere de his iiii[4] mansuris.

[171] Ceca[1] reddebat ii d. et omnem consuetudinem T.R.E. Modo habet Baluert et facit similiter.

[172] Alwinus presbiter[1] reddebat xx d. et omnem consuetudinem T.R.E. Modo tenet Godwinus[2] et facit similiter.

[173] Idem Alwinus[1] reddebat consuetudinem T.R.E. Modo Willelmus de Ponthearcar'[2] debet idem.[a]

IN ALWARENESTRET[b]

[174] Lewinus Scottelauessone reddebat xv d.[1] et consuetudinem T.R.E. Modo uxor God' Pot[2] debet idem.

[175] Sawinus frater Wnstani[1] reddebat xv d.[2] et consuetudinem T.R.E. Modo Rannulfus de Curleio et Saieua debent similiter.[c]

[176] Aluricus archidiaconus[1] reddebat viii d. et consuetudinem T.R.E. Modo Robertus frater Warini[2] debet similiter.

[177] Alwoldus et Wndai reddebant de ii mansuris xii d.[1] et consuetudinem T.R.E. Modo Radulfus presbiter debet idem.

[167] Alwin paid 10d. and every custom *TRE*. Now Robert the scalder[1] owes the same.

[168] Luwold Gustate[1] paid 4d. landgable and every custom *TRE*. Now Alwin the beadle[2] does the same.

[169] Durand paid 14d. and every custom *TRE*. Now the son of Almar the priest owes the same.

[170] Lewin the priest[1] paid 30d. and custom *TRE*, Alric[2] 20d. and custom, and Lewin Wurtwos 10d. and every custom. Now William son of Ansger[3] should perform the same for these 4[4] messuages.

[171] Ceca[1] paid 2d. and every custom *TRE*. Now Baluert holds it and does the same.

[172] Alwin the priest[1] paid 20d. and every custom *TRE*. Now Godwin[2] holds it and does the same.

[173] The same Alwin[1] paid the custom *TRE*. Now William of Pont de l'Arche[2] owes the same.

IN *ALWARENE* STREET [ST PETER'S STREET]

[174] Lewin Scottelaf's son paid 15d.[1] and the custom *TRE*. Now the wife of God' Pot[2] owes the same.

[175] Sawin the brother of Wunstan[1] paid 15d.[2] and the custom *TRE*. Now Ranulf of Corlay (Courlay?) and Saieva owe the same.

[176] Aluric the archdeacon[1] paid 8d. and the custom *TRE*. Now Robert the brother of Warin[2] owes the same.

[177] Alwold and Wundai paid for 2 messuages 12d.[1] and the custom *TRE*. Now Ralf the priest owes the same.

---

[a] idem *over an erasure*   [b] *In margin, for rubricator*: in alwarenestret   [c] similiter *in another hand* (?)

167 1. *King's Serjeants*, 252 ff. gives some account of a scalding sergeanty.
168 1. Possibly a moneyer of Edward the Confessor: see below, Table 36. See also **209**.
    2. See also **221**. He was possibly the moneyer of Henry I: see below, Table 40.
170 1. Cf. also **190** and **257**.
    2. Cf. **85**.   3. See **79**.
    4. Possibly a mistake for '3'.
171 1. Possibly the Winchester moneyer, Godwine Ceoca: see *English Coins*, 77, and cf. below, Table 36.
172 1. See **41**.

2. A Godwine was a moneyer of Henry I: see below, Table 39. See also **10**.
173 1. See **41**.   2. See I, Preface.
174 1. For this tenement, cf. II, **486** or **487**.
    2. Cf. **137**.
175 1. A Sæwine and a Wynstan were moneyers of Edward the Confessor: see **16** and below, Table 35.
    2. For this tenement, cf. II, **486** or **487**.
176 1. See below, p. 392.
    2. See also II, **479**. Just possibly Robert fitzGerald, the brother of Henry and Warin. See *Regesta*, ii, p. 403.
177 1. For this tenement, cf. II, **500**.

[178] Alwinus filius Tartere[a] reddebat vi d.[1] et consuetudinem T.R.E. Modo Godefridus debet similiter.

[179] Leueua reddebat iiii d. et consuetudinem T.R.E. Modo Aldredus[1] debet similiter.

[180] Sawinus reddebat x d. et consuetudinem T.R.E. Modo tenet Turstinus clericus[1] et facit idem.

IN FLESMANGERESTRET[b]

[181] Burewoldus filius Wnstani reddebat xv d.[1] et consuetudinem T.R.E. Modo Robertus Fresle[2] debet idem.

[182] Gonnodus[1] reddebat ii s. et consuetudinem T.R.E. Modo abbatissa Warewelle et Ansger de Iorz[2] debent idem.

[183] Quedam vidua reddebat iiii d.[1] et consuetudinem T.R.E. et modo eadem est similiter [sic].

IN WENEGENESTRET[c]

[184] Henricus[d] thesaurarius[1] reddebat de i mansura vi d. et consuetudinem, et i aliam tenuit[e] quietam T.R.E. Modo uxor eius debet similiter.

[185] Theodricus coquus regis reddebat vi d. et consuetudinem, et Farmanus[1] vi d. et consuetudinem T.R.E. Modo Herbertus Gidi debet similiter de ii mansuris.

[186] Leovricus Abeaham reddebat vi d. et consuetudinem T.R.E. Modo Alwinus facit similiter.[1]

[187] Pilluc reddebat viii d. et consuetudinem [fo. 10] T.R.E. Modo Anschetillus de Iorz[1] debet similiter.

[188] Martinus reddebat iiii d. et consuetudinem T.R.E. Modo tenet Theodricus presbiter et facit idem.

[189] Wlwoldus reddebat consuetudinem T.R.E. Modo Ricardus prepositus[1] debet similiter.

[178] Alwin son of Tartere paid 6d.[1] and the custom TRE. Now Godfrey owes the same.

[179] Leofgifu paid 4d. and the custom TRE. Now Aldred[1] owes the same.

[180] Sawin paid 10d. and the custom TRE. Now Thurstin the clerk[1] holds it and does the same.

IN FLESMANGERE STREET [PARCHMENT STREET]

[181] Burewold the son of Wunstan paid 15d.[1] and the custom TRE. Now Robert Fresle[2] owes the same.

[182] Godnod[1] paid 2s. and the custom TRE. Now the abbess of Wherwell and Ansger of Jort[2] owe the same.

[183] A certain widow paid 4d.[1] and the custom TRE and now she does the same (?).

IN WENEGENE STREET [MIDDLE BROOK STREET]

[184] Henry the treasurer[1] paid 6d. and the custom for 1 messuage, and another he held quit TRE. Now his wife owes the same.

[185] Theoderic the king's cook paid 6d. and the custom and Farman[1] 6d. and the custom TRE. Now Herbert Giddy owes the same for the 2 messuages.

[186] Leofric Abeaham paid 6d. and the custom TRE. Now Alwin does the same.[1]

[187] Pilluc paid 8d. and the custom TRE. Now Anschetil of Jort[1] owes the same.

[188] Martin paid 4d. and the custom TRE. Now Theoderic the priest holds it and does the same.

[189] Wulfwold paid the custom TRE. Now Richard the reeve[1] owes the same.

---

[a] tart'e MS., *suspension mark added*   [b] *In margin, for rubricator:* in flesmangerestret (*obscured by binding*)
[c] *In margin, for rubricator:* [in wenegenestret] (*almost totally obscured by binding*)   [d] *Suspension mark after* i
erased   [e] tenet *MS.*

178 1. For this tenement, cf. **II, 484** or **501**.
179 1. Cf. **46**.
180 1. See also **289** and **II, 221**. He was pardoned 12s. in 1130 when Winchester paid an aid: *Pipe Roll 31 Henry I*, p. 41. For this tenement, cf. **II, 493**.
181 1. For this tenement, cf. **II, 512**.
     2. Engaged in a Norman lawsuit in 1118: W. Farrer, *An Outline Itinerary of King Henry the First* (Oxford, 1920), 83; dead by 1130: *Pipe Roll 31 Henry I*, p. 37.
182 1. Perhaps a moneyer of William I, see **57** and below, p. 415, n. 2. For a later moneyer's interest in the property,

cf. **II, 511–12**, and below, p. 415 and Table 43.
     2. Cf. **9**. For this tenement, cf. **II, 511** between properties identifiable with **I, 181** and **I, 183**.
183 1. For this tenement, cf. **II, 510**.
184 1. See Richardson and Sayles, 219–20; J. H. Round, *VCH Hants* i. 430.
185 1. Farman's son occurs in 1148: below **II, 130**.
186 1. For this tenement, cf. **II, 570**.
187 1. See **9**.
189 1. See **20**, n. 4, and **113**.

[190] Leuwinus presbiter¹ reddebat viii d. et consuetudinem T.R.E. Modo filius eius debet similiter.

[191] God' Clenehand reddebat consuetudinem T.R.E. Modo Albericus coquus¹ debet similiter.

[192] Brucstanus Banne reddebat x d. et consuetudinem T.R.E. Modo Siuardus Mus debet similiter.

[193] Urandus presbiter reddebat de langabulo xiii d., et de bru*gabulo* iiii d., fripene¹ et consue[tudinem] T.R.E. Modo Godefridus filius Emeline debet similiter.

[194] Helbingus reddebat xiiii d.¹ et consuetudinem T.R.E. Modo Bricthwinus bedellus debet similiter.

[195] Ulgarus wantar' reddebat xxxii d. et consuetudinem T.R.E. Modo Scorphanus¹ debet similiter.

[196] God*winus* Ælmeressone¹ reddebat viii d. et consuetudinem T.R.E. Modo Willelmus de Hoctona² debet idem.

^aIN TANNERESTRETE^b

[197] Adam Witegos et Godwinus faciebant consuetudinem T.R.E. de ii mansuris. Modo Osbertus filius Oini¹ debet idem.

[198] Smiewinus reddebat vi d. et consuetudinem T.R.E. Modo Goisbertus debet idem.

[199] Burewoldus¹ reddebat ii s. et consuetudinem T.R.E. Modo filius Radulfi Russel² debet similiter.

[200] Aldied reddebat consuetudinem preter langabulum et brue*gabulum* T.R.E. Modo idem filius Radulfi Russel¹ debet idem.

[201] Ancild^c reddebat x d. et consuetudinem T.R.E. Modo idem filius Radulfi Russel¹ debet idem.

[202] Godesman reddebat x d. et consuetudinem T.R.E. Modo Sueta debet similiter.

[190] Lewin the priest¹ paid 8*d.* and the custom *TRE.* Now his son owes the same.

[191] God' Cleanhand paid the custom *TRE.* Now Alberic the cook¹ owes the same.

[192] Brunstan Banne paid 10*d.* and the custom *TRE.* Now Siward Mouse owes the same.

[193] Urand the priest paid 13*d.* landgable, 4*d.* brewgable, frithpenny,¹ and the custom *TRE.* Now Godfrey son of Emeline owes the same.

[194] Helbing paid 14*d.*¹ and the custom *TRE.* Now Brithwin the beadle owes the same.

[195] Wulfgar the glover paid 32*d.* and the custom *TRE.* Now Escorphan¹ owes the same.

[196] Godwin Elmer's son¹ paid 8*d.* and the custom *TRE.* Now William of Houghton² owes the same.

IN *TANNERE* STREET [LOWER BROOK STREET]

[197] Adam White-goose and Godwin perfomed the custom *TRE* for 2 messuages. Now Osbert son of Oin¹ owes the same.

[198] Smiewin paid 6*d.* and the custom *TRE.* Now Goisbert owes the same.

[199] Burewold¹ paid 2*s.* and the custom *TRE.* Now the son of Ralf Russel² owes the same.

[200] Aldith paid the custom except landgable and brewgable *TRE.* Now the same son of Ralf Russel¹ owes the same.

[201] Ancild paid 10*d.* and the custom *TRE.* Now the same son of Ralf Russel¹ owes the same.

[202] Godesman paid 10*d.* and the custom *TRE.* Now Sweta owes the same.

---

^a *Paragraph mark erased*   ^b *In margin, for rubricator:* [in tannerestret] (*partly cut away*)   ^c *The third letter is blotched, probably in correcting from* e *to* c

190 1. See **170**.
191 1. See **82**. For this tenement, cf. **II, 562** in *Sildwortenestret*.
193 1. This is one of the rare references to brewgable and the only mention of the amount paid. The mention of frithpenny is unique.
194 1. For this tenement, cf. **II, 572**.
195 1. See **38**. For this tenement, cf. **II, 563** in *Sildwortenestret*.
196 1. See **14**.

2. See also **245**, **273**, and **278**. A royal chamberlain: *Regesta*, ii, pp. xv, xix. In 1130 he was accounting for the fines he had made for himself to marry the widow of Geoffrey de Favarches and for his son, Pain, to marry the daughter of Edward of Salisbury: *Pipe Roll 31 Henry I*, pp. 81, 94. There is a reference to his son in **II, 74**.
197 1. Possibly the son of Oin the napier; see **6**.
199 1. Cf. **28**.   2. See **1**.
200 1. See **1**.
201 1. See **1**.

[203] Leowingus reddebat de iii mansuris xl d. et consuetudinem T.R.E. Modo filius eius debet similiter facere.

[203] Leving paid 40*d*. and the custom for 3 messuages *TRE*. Now his son ought to do likewise.

[204] Alwinus reddebat vi d. et consuetudinem T.R.E. Modo Ricardus prepositus[1] debet similiter.[a]

[204] Alwin paid 6*d*. and the custom *TRE*. Now Richard the reeve[1] owes the same.

[205] [b]Raimbaldus tenuit i domum quietam T.R.E. Modo Nigellus de Cholcham[1] habet eam similiter. Tamen intus manentes faciunt consuetudinem *regis*.

[205] Rainbald held 1 tenement quit *TRE*. Now Nigel of *Cholcham*[1] holds it in the same way. Yet those dwelling on it perform the king's custom.

[206] Colling'[1] reddebat x d. et consuetudinem T.R.E. Modo Wiburg'[2] debet similiter.

[206] Colling[1] paid 10*d*. and the custom *TRE*. Now Wiburg[2] owes the same.

[207] [fo. 10[v]] [c]Godricus reddebat viii d. et consuetudinem T.R.E. Modo Foxpriche debet similiter.

[207] Godric paid 8*d*. and the custom *TRE*. Now Foxprick owes the same.

[208] Alwoldus reddebat vi d. et consuetudinem T.[R.]E. Modo Radulfus taneator Cattessone debet idem.

[208] Alwold paid 6*d*. and the custom *TRE*. Now Ralf the tanner, Cat's son, owes the same.

[209] Lewoldus[1] reddebat vi d. et consuetudinem T.R.E. Modo Bernardus facit idem.

[209] Lewold[1] paid 6*d*. and the custom *TRE*. Now Bernard does the same.

[210] Godwinus reddebat vi d. et consuetudinem T.R.E. Modo Walderus taneator debet idem.

[210] Godwin paid 6*d*. and the custom *TRE*. Now Walder the tanner owes the same.

[211] Lursius reddebat vi d. et consuetudinem et Uctredus vi d. et consuetudinem de ii mansuris T.R.E. Modo Wiburg'[1] debet idem.

[211] Lursi paid 6*d*. and the custom and Uhtred 6*d*. and the custom for 2 messuages *TRE*. Now Wiburg[1] owes the same.

[212] Andrebode cangeor[d][1] reddebat vi d. et consuetudinem T.R.E. Modo Sawinus debet similiter.

[212] Andrebode the money-changer[1] paid 6*d*. and the custom *TRE*. Now Sawin owes the same.

[213] Lewinus reddebat ii d. et consuetudinem T.R.E. Modo God' debet idem.[1]

[213] Lewin paid 2*d*. and the custom *TRE*. Now God' owes the same.[1]

[214] God' reddebat x d. et consuetudinem et God' ix d. et consuetudinem T.R.E. Modo Bruning de his ii mansuris debet idem.

[214] God' paid 10*d*. and the custom and God' 9*d*. and the custom *TRE*. Now Bruning owes the same for these 2 messuages.

[e]IN BUCCHESTRET[f]

IN *BUCCHE* STREET [BUSKET LANE]

[215] [g]Edwinus Wridel reddebat xv d. et consuetudinem T.R.E. Modo Sewal presbiter[1] debet idem.

[215] Edwin Wridel paid 15*d*. and the custom *TRE*. Now Sewal the priest[1] owes the same.

---

[a] *Second and third lines of MS. possibly over an erasure point, at the start of a new page (fo. 10[v]), the items are not distinguished by a paragraph sign* [b] *First line written over an erasure* [c] *From this* [d] gangeor *MS.* [e] *Written over an erased line of the main text* [f] Succhestret *Ellis, without MS. authority. In margin, for rubricator:* [in bucchestret] *(obliterated and partly cut away)* [g] *Whole entry written over an erasure*

---

204 1. See 20, n. 4, and 113.
205 1. Possibly a mistake for *Tolcha*, Touques (Calvados), but more likely an English place-name, see below, p. 193, s.v. For this tenement, cf. II, 608.
206 1. Possibly a moneyer of Edward the Confessor: see below, Table 36.
   2. See also 211.
209 1. Possibly a moneyer of Edward the Confessor:

see below, Table 36. See also 168.
211 1. See 206.
212 1. See 29. For the tenement, in which a later moneyer may have had an interest, cf. II, 644 and see below, p. 416 and Table 44.
213 1. For this tenement, cf. II, 646.
215 1. See 36.

[216] Godingus reddebat consuetudinem et Brunwif x d. et consuetudinem T.R.E. Modo filius Radulfi Russel[1] debet idem.

[217] Brithmarus[1] reddebat x d. et consuetudinem et Eldredus iiii d. et consuetudinem et Sawinus[2] x d. et consuetudinem T.R.E. Modo uxor Baldrici debet similiter.

[218] Lepstanus[1] reddebat v d. et consuetudinem T.R.E. Modo Blachem'[2] debet idem.

[219] Hiechsi reddebat ii d. et obolum et consuetudinem T.R.E. Modo Sawale presbiter[1] facit idem.

[220] Edtie Mase reddebat viii d. et consuetudinem T.R.E. Modo Aldied vidua[1] debet similiter.

[221] Luwen reddebat iiii d. et consuetudinem T.R.E. Modo Alwinus bedellus[1] debet idem.[a]

[222] Alwinus reddebat x d. et consuetudinem T.R.E. Modo Alur' Iola debet similiter.

[223] Luwinus[2] reddebat v d. et consuetudinem et Lepstanus[2] xii d. et consuetudinem T.R.E. Modo Gisulf' debet idem de ii mansuris.[3]

[224] Brithsuid reddebat vi d. et consuetudinem et Bolle vi d. et consuetudinem T.R.E. Modo Atser debet idem de ii mansuris.

[225] Brithmarus reddebat v d. et consuetudinem T.R.E. et God' vi d. et consuetudinem. Modo Edwardus presbiter debet idem de ii mansuris.

[226] Chitebaue reddebat viii d. et consuetudinem T.R.E. Modo Edwinus facit similiter.

[227] Brithwinus reddebat vi d. et consuetudinem T.R.E. Modo Godwinus Nalad debet idem.

[228] Godman Helteprest[1] reddebat x [fo. 11] d. et consuetudinem T.R.E. Modo Godwinus Prison[2] debet similiter.

[216] Goding paid the custom and Brunwif 10d. and the custom *TRE*. Now the son of Ralf Russel[1] owes the same.

[217] Brithmar[1] paid 10d. and the custom, Eldred 4d. and the custom, and Sawin[2] 10d. and the custom *TRE*. Now the wife of Baldric owes the same.

[218] Lefstan[1] paid 5d. and the custom *TRE*. Now Blacman[2] owes the same.

[219] Hiechsi paid 2½d. and the custom *TRE*. Now Sawal the priest[1] does the same.

[220] Edtie Titmouse paid 8d. and the custom *TRE*. Now the widow Aldith[1] owes the same.

[221] Lewen paid 4d. and the custom *TRE*. Now Alwin the beadle[1] owes the same.

[222] Alwin paid 10d. and the custom *TRE*. Now Alur' Iola owes the same.

[223] Lewin[1] paid 5d. and the custom and Lefstan[2] 12d. and the custom *TRE*. Now Gisulf owes the same for the 2 messuages.[3]

[224] Brithswith paid 6d. and the custom and Bolla 6d. and the custom *TRE*. Now Atser owes the same for the 2 messuages.

[225] Brithmar paid 5d. and the custom and God' 6d. and the custom *TRE*. Now Edward the priest owes the same for the 2 messuages.

[226] Chitebaue paid 8d. and the custom *TRE*. Now Edwin does the same.

[227] Brithwin paid 6d. and the custom *TRE*. Now Godwin 'No-harm' owes the same.

[228] Godman Halt-priest[1] paid 10d. and the custom *TRE*. Now Godwin Prison[2] owes the same.

[a] *Second line of MS. entry written over an erasure*

216 1. See **1**.
217 1. Perhaps the moneyer of Edward the Confessor: see **166** and below, Table 35.
　2. A Sæwine was a moneyer of Edward the Confessor: see below, Table 35.
218 1. Cf. **223**. Possibly a moneyer of Edward the Confessor: see below, Table 36.
　2. Cf. **236** and II, **688**.
219 1. See **36**.
220 1. See also **247**.
221 1. See **168**.

223 1. A Leofwine was a moneyer of Edward the Confessor: see below, Table 35.
　2. See **218**.
　3. For this property, see also II, **680**, where Gisulf is identified as the king's scribe. For Gisulf, see J. H. Round, *EHR* 14 (1899), 418 ff.
228 1. It is possibly more than a coincidence that in **229** the byname Haliprest occurs on its own. One man's name may have been given in two different forms. See also **291**.
　2. See **10**.

[229] Haliprest[1] reddebat x d. et consuetudinem T.R.E. Modo Ulfus debet idem.[2]

[230] Mandode reddebat x d. et consuetudinem T.R.E. Modo filius Roberti Marmion[1] debet idem.

[231] Eilaf reddebat viii d. et consuetudinem T.R.E. Modo Alueua de Mapeldreham debet idem.

[232] Bullochesiega[1] reddebat vi d. et consuetudinem T.R.E. Modo Lupsida debet idem.

[233] Lupsone reddebat xii d. et consuetudinem et Ailwardus viii d.[a] et consuetudinem T.R.E. Modo God-*winus* Grenesune[1] debet idem de ii mansuris.

[234] Steinulfus reddebat xxx d.[1] et consuetudinem T.R.E. Modo Seburga[2] debet similiter.

[235] Theodricus reddebat vi d. et consuetudinem T.R.E. Modo Edredus taneator[b] debet similiter. Et habet ibi i terram preoccupatam domui suae que non reddit langabulum.

[236] Lowinus reddebat v d. et consuetudinem T.R.E. Modo Blachem'[1] debet idem.

[237] Aluredus reddebat viii d. et consuetudinem T.R.E. Modo Edeua debet idem.

[238] Alwoldus reddebat viii d. et consuetudinem T.R.E. Modo God*winus* Prison[1] debet idem.

[239] Alwinus Ieltfange reddebat x d. et consuetudinem et Alwinus Childebroder iiii d. et consuetudinem et Alur' v d. et consuetudinem T.R.E. Modo Adelidis soror Henrici de Port[1] debet similiter facere de iii mansuris.

[240] [I]uxta murum habet abbatissa ii mansuras de terra regis.[1]

[229] Holy-priest[1] paid 10*d*. and the custom *TRE*. Now Ulf owes the same.[2]

[230] Mandode paid 10*d*. and the custom *TRE*. Now the son of Robert Marmion[1] owes the same.

[231] Eilaf paid 8*d*. and the custom *TRE*. Now Alveva of Mapledurham owes the same.

[232] Bullock's-eye[1] paid 6*d*. and the custom *TRE*. Now Lupsida owes the same.

[233] Lupsone paid 12*d*. and the custom and Ailward 8*d*. and the custom *TRE*. Now Godwin Green's son[1] owes the same for the 2 messuages.

[234] Steinulf paid 30*d*.[1] and the custom *TRE*. Now Seburg[2] owes the same.

[235] Theoderic paid 6*d*. and the custom *TRE*. Now Edred the tanner owes the same. And he has there 1 land taken into his tenement which does not pay landgable.

[236] Lewin paid 5*d*. and the custom *TRE*. Now Blacman[1] owes the same.

[237] Alfred paid 8*d*. and the custom *TRE*. Now Edeva owes the same.

[238] Alwold paid 8*d*. and the custom *TRE*. Now Godwin Prison[1] owes the same.

[239] Alwin Jeltfange paid 10*d*. and the custom, Alwin Childbrother 4*d*. and the custom, and Alfred 5*d*. and the custom *TRE*. Now Adelaide, sister of Henry de Port,[1] should do the same for the 3 messuages.

[240] The abbess has 2 messuages on royal demesne hard by the wall.[1]

---

[a] *Erasure before* viii d.   [b] taneāt *MS*.

229 1. See 228.
  2. For the property, see also II, 690.
230 1. The Marmions inherited many of the lands which Robert Dispensator held in 1086. Roger Marmion died *ante* Mich. 1129, and Robert I *c*. 1144. His son and heir was Robert II: Sanders *Baronies*, 145. As Robert I was not yet knighted in 1130, *Pipe Roll 31 Henry I*, p. 117, we may here be concerned with another member of the family.
232 1. See 140.

233 1. See 10.
234 1. For this tenement, cf. II, 705.
  2. She witnessed the sale of II, 669, to Bernard the Scribe: *EHR* 14 (1899), 424.
236 1. See 218.
238 1. See 10. For the property, see also II, 690.
239 1. See 39.
240 1. For the king's ground within the wall, see below, p. 279; and for the city wall, see below, pp. 273–4.

IN CALPESTRET

[241] Chepingus reddebat vi d. et consuetudinem et Ailwinus vi d. et consuetudinem T.R.E. Modo Suein' debet idem.

[242] Edricus reddebat consuetudinem T.R.E. Modo Stigandus clericus[1] debet idem.

[243] Godwinus Gretsud[1] reddebat de ii mansuris xii d. et consuetudinem T.R.E. Modo Radulfus clericus debet similiter.

[244] Coleman presbiter reddebat vi d. et consuetudinem T.R.E. Modo Spileman' presbiter debet idem.

[245] Willelmus reddebat xii d. et consuetudinem et Brun vi d. et consuetudinem et Brunmannus v d. et consuetudinem T.R.E. Modo Willelmus de Hoctona[1] debet similiter de ii mansuris.[2]

[246] Adelardus et Laue reddebant x d. et consuetudinem T.R.E. Modo Gaufridus camerarius[1] debet similiter de ii mansuris.

[247] Totelbied[a] reddebat vi d. et consuetudinem[b] [fo. 11v] T.R.E. Modo Aldied vidua[1] debet similiter facere.

[248] Leuingus[1] reddebat x d. et consuetudinem T.R.E. Modo Warinus de Hantona debet similiter.

[249] Alueua reddebat viii d. et consuetudinem T.R.E. Modo Rogerus Amberlang'[1] debet similiter.

[250] Godesbrandus[1] reddebat xii d. et consuetudinem T.R.E. Modo Godefridus Sar' debet idem.

[251] Lefflet reddebat viii d. et consuetudinem T.R.E. Modo Edwine presbiter debet idem.

[252] God' reddebat x d. et consuetudinem T.R.E. Modo Herbertus filius Edwini[1] debet similiter.

[253] Alwoldus reddebat xii d. et consuetudinem T.R.E. Modo Robertus filius Nunne debet similiter.

IN *CALPE* STREET [ST. THOMAS STREET]

[241] Cheping paid 6*d.* and the custom and Ailwin 6*d.* and the custom *TRE*. Now Svein owes the same.

[242] Edric paid the custom *TRE*. Now Stigand the clerk[1] owes the same.

[243] Godwin Great Bag[1] paid 12*d.* and the custom for 2 messuages *TRE*. Now Ralf the clerk owes the same.

[244] Coleman the priest paid 6*d.* and the custom *TRE*. Now Spileman the priest owes the same.

[245] William paid 12*d.* and the custom, Brun 6*d.* and the custom, and Brunman 5*d.* and the custom *TRE*. Now William of Houghton[1] owes the same for the 2 [*sic*] messuages.[2]

[246] Adelard and Lafa paid 10*d.* and the custom *TRE*. Now Geoffrey the chamberlain[1] owes the same for the 2 messuages.

[247] Totelbied paid 6*d.* and the custom *TRE*. Now the widow Aldith[1] should do the same.

[248] Leving[1] paid 10*d.* and the custom *TRE*. Now Warin of Southampton owes the same.

[249] Alveva paid 8*d.* and the custom *TRE*. Now Roger Amerland[1] owes the same.

[250] Godesbrand[1] paid 12*d.* and the custom *TRE*. Now Godfrey of Salisbury owes the same.

[251] Lefflet paid 8*d.* and the custom *TRE*. Now Edwin the priest owes the same.

[252] God' paid 10*d.* and the custom *TRE*. Now Herbert son of Edwin[1] owes the same.

[253] Alwold paid 12*d.* and the custom *TRE*. Now Robert son of Nunna owes the same.

---

[a] *An initial G has been changed to* T   [b] *The latter part of this line over an erasure*

242 1. Archdeacon Stigand occurs in Survey II: see II, **688**, and cf. below, p. 392.
243 1. Also in *LVH* 74.
245 1. See **196**.
    2. For this tenement, cf. II, **838**.
246 1. See also **270** and **272**. Like William of Houghton (**245**), a royal chamberlain: *Regesta*, ii, p. xv.

247 1. See **220**.
248 1. Possibly a moneyer of Edward the Confessor: see below, Table 36.
249 1. See **20**.
250 1. Cf. **79**.
252 1. See also **258**. He was probably a moneyer of Henry I: see below, Table 39.

[254] Burewoldus Crul reddebat x d. et consuetudinem T.R.E. Modo Eilwardus[1] filius Chiwen debet facere similiter.

[255] Algarus reddebat xii d. et consuetudinem T.R.E. Modo Willelmus potarius[1] debet similiter.

[256] Brunstanus Blachebiert[1] reddebat xi d. T.R.E. Modo Saiet[2] debet similiter.

[257] Lewinus presbiter[1] reddebat x d. et consuetudinem T.R.E. Modo Alwinus clericus[2] debet similiter.

[258] Herbertus filius Edwini[1] debet reddere de terra regis iiii d. et consuetudinem in alia parte.

[259] Ailflet reddebat iiii d. et consuetudinem T.R.E. Modo Willelmus[a] de Pont'[1] debet similiter.

[260] Leouingus et Brithwif reddebant l d. et consuetudinem. Modo Baldewinus de Rediuers[1] debet similiter.

[261] Bolle et Ailsi reddebant xiiii d. T.R.E. et consuetudinem. Modo Stigandus[1] debet similiter.

[262] Euerwinus reddebat de ii mansuris xl d. et consuetudinem T.R.E. Modo abbas de Westminist' [debet similiter].[1]

[263] Victricus reddebat vi d. et consuetudinem T.R.E. Modo Aluricus[1] debet similiter.

[264] Aluricus Fulebiert et Huni et Sewardus[1] et God' reddebant consuetudinem T.R.E. de iiii mansuris [et] ii sol. Modo Iohannes Bensetoure debet idem.

[265] Pucheshele reddebat xxx d. et consuetudinem T.R.E. Modo debet similiter.[1]

[254] Burewold Curly paid 10d. and the custom TRE. Now Ailward[1] son of Chinwen should do the same.

[255] Algar paid 12d. and the custom TRE. Now William the potter[1] owes the same.

[256] Brunstan Blackbeard[1] paid 11d. TRE. Now Saiet[2] owes the same.

[257] Lewin the priest[1] paid 10d. and the custom TRE. Now Alwin the clerk[2] owes the same.

[258] Herbert son of Edwin[1] should pay 4d. and the custom somewhere else for his holding on royal demesne.

[259] Ailflet paid 4d. and the custom TRE. Now William of Pont [? de l'Arche][1] owes the same.

[260] Leving and Brithwif paid 50d. and the custom. Now Baldwin of Reviers[1] owes the same.

[261] Bolla and Ailsi paid 14d. and the custom TRE. Now Stigand[1] owes the same.

[262] Everwin paid 40d. and the custom for 2 messuages TRE. Now the abbot of Westminster [owes the same].[1]

[263] Wictric paid 6d. and the custom TRE. Now Aluric[1] owes the same.

[264] Aluric Foulbeard, Huni, Seward,[1] and God' paid the custom and 2s. for 4 messuages TRE. Now John Bensetoure owes the same.

[265] Pucheshele paid 30d. and the custom TRE. Now it/he owes the same.[1]

[a] Willelmi MS.

254 1. Possibly the moneyer of Henry I: see below, Table 40.
255 1. See 93.
256 1. Probably a moneyer of Edward the Confessor: see also 17, and below, Table 35.
2. Saiet, the moneyer, and his nephew Aluric, apparently a goldsmith, occur in 1130: Pipe Roll 31 Henry I, p. 40. Saiet's heirs and his son Herbert appear in II, 848 (which possibly concerns this property) and 1078. The discrepancy in the figures between I, 256 and II, 848 suggests that one or both are mistaken. For Saiet and Aluric as moneyers, see below, p. 419, and Tables 40 and 44.
257 1. See 170. A Leofwine was a moneyer of Edward the Confessor: see below, Table 35.
2. Possibly the moneyer of Henry I: see below, Table 40.
258 1. See 252.
259 1. Probably an abbreviation for Pont de l'Arche, because in II, 830, we meet Robert de Ponte and a reference to William of Pont de l'Arche. For William,

who had a son Robert, see I, Preface.
260 1. A humble situation in which to find the future earl of Devon: DNB iii. 34.
261 1. Perhaps the moneyer of Henry I. For this tenement, cf. II, 826 which also owed 14d. rent to the king and was held by John the goldsmith. For Stigand as a moneyer, see below, p. 410, and Table 39. He may have been identical with the later reeve of the city: see II, 88, n. 1.
262 1. The Westminster Abbey estate at Eversley included a haga in Winchester worth 7d. in 1086. The abbey acquired Eversley from King Edward the Confessor: VCH Hants i. 472b; AS Writs, no. 85. For this tenement, cf. II, 827.
263. 1. Possibly the moneyer of Henry I: see below, Table 40.
264 1. Probably a moneyer of Edward the Confessor: see below, Table 35.
265 1. The continuity makes it likely that Pucheshele is a place-name.

IN GOLDESTRET[a]

[266] Alestanus Braders reddebat xv d. [fo. 12] et consuetudinem T.R.E. Modo Alueua filia eius debet idem.

[267] Ailsi[b] bedellus reddebat xv d. et consuetudinem T.R.E. Modo Robertus filius Durandi[1] debet idem.

[268] Alueua de Chrichelada reddebat x d. et consuetudinem T.R.E. Modo Willelmus Tardif[1] debet similiter.

[269] God' reddebat x d.[1] et consuetudinem T.R.E. Modo Hamo filius Erneis debet idem.

[270] Fugel[1] reddebat viii d.[2] et consuetudinem T.R.E. Modo Gaufridus camerarius[3] debet similiter.

[271] God'[c] Softebred reddebat viii d.[1] et consuetudinem T.R.E. Modo Gaufridus burgeis[2] debet idem.

[272] God' Cunnebried reddebat viii d.[1] et consuetudinem T.R.E. Modo Gaufridus camerarius[2] debet idem.

[273] Issiran reddebat iiii d. et consuetudinem T.R.E. Modo Willelmus de Hoctona[1] debet idem.

[274] Alwinus reddebat x d. et consuetudinem T.R.E. Modo Godefridus debet idem.

[275] Odo reddebat x d. et consuetudinem T.R.E. Modo Astcelinus Godeman debet idem.

[276] Godricus presbiter reddebat v d. et consuetudinem T.R.E. Modo monachi debent idem.

[277] Alfere reddebat x d. et consuetudinem T.R.E. Modo Willelmus de Meleford' debet idem.

[278] Edricus Chuet et Luuingus bedel et Ulmarus reddebant xv d.[1] et consuetudinem T.R.E. Modo Willelmus de Hoctona[2] debet idem.

[279] Ibi est una mansura que [est] data in escangio al*ias* [cum] socca et sacca et omni[d] consue*tudine* pro

IN *GOLDE* STREET [SOUTHGATE STREET]

[266] Alestan Broad-arse paid 15*d.* and the custom *TRE.* Now his daughter Alveva owes the same.

[267] Ailsi the beadle paid 15*d.* and the custom *TRE.* Now Robert son of Durand[1] owes the same.

[268] Alveva of Cricklade paid 10*d.* and the custom *TRE.* Now William Tardif[1] owes the same.

[269] God' paid 10*d.*[1] and the custom *TRE.* Now Hamo son of Erneis owes the same.

[270] Fugel[1] paid 8*d.*[2] and the custom *TRE.* Now Geoffrey the chamberlain[3] owes the same.

[271] God' Softbread paid 8*d.*[1] and the custom *TRE.* Now Geoffrey the burgess[2] owes the same.

[272] God' Cunnebried paid 8*d.*[1] and the custom *TRE.* Now Geoffrey the chamberlain[2] owes the same.

[273] Issiran paid 4*d.* and the custom *TRE.* Now William of Houghton[1] owes the same.

[274] Alwin paid 10*d.* and the custom *TRE.* Now Godfrey owes the same.

[275] Odo paid 10*d.* and the custom *TRE.* Now Ascelin Goodman owes the same.

[276] Godric the priest paid 5*d.* and the custom *TRE.* Now the monks owe the same.

[277] Alfere paid 10*d.* and the custom *TRE.* Now William of Milford owes the same.

[278] Edric Chuet, Leving the beadle, and Wulfmar paid 15*d.*[1] and the custom *TRE.* Now William of Houghton[2] owes the same.

[279] Here is a messuage which was given in exchange with soke and sake and every custom for a tenement of

---

[a] *In lower margin, for rubricator:* in goldestret   [b] Aisil *MS.*   [c] *Initial G rubricated over an erased capital* G *of text hand*   [d] omne *MS.*

267 1. See **71**.
268 1. In 1148 his widow was holding **II, 858**.
269 1. For this tenement, cf. **II, 859**.
270 1. See **155**.
  2. For this tenement, cf. **II, 860**.
  3. See **246**. Herbert the chamberlain held this tenement in 1148.
271 1. For this tenement, cf. **II, 861**.

  2. The heirs of Hugh *burgensis* held this tenement in 1148. *Gaufridus burgensis* appears in **II, 128**.
272 1. For this tenement, cf. **II, 865**.
  2. See **246**.
273 1. See **196**.
278 1. For this tenement, cf. **II, 875–6**.
  2. See **196**.

domo comitis de Warwich;[1] et inde facere debet An-schetillus de Iorz[2] consuetudinem.

[280] Terra abbatis de Sancto Edmundo reddebat x d· T.R.E. Modo debet idem.[1]

[281] Ranulfus filius Roberti Dop redd*it* [. . .] et con-suetudinem de terra regis.

IN GERESTRET[a]

[282] Huchelinus parcherius reddebat xx d. et con-suetudinem T.R.E. Modo Iwen parm*entarius*[1] debet idem.

[283] Luuingus scalarius reddebat vi d. et consuetudi-nem T.R.E. Modo Simon disp*ensator*[1] [. . .].

[284] Ulwardus[b] Cheppe reddebat xviii d. et consue-tudinem T.R.E. Modo Willelmus scruta*rius* debet idem.[c]

[285] Estanus Scodhe reddebat x d.[1] et consuetudinem T.R.E. Modo Anschetillus palm*arius* [fo. 12ᵛ] debet idem.

[286] Lancdelere[1] reddebat xxx d. et consuetudinem T.R.E. Modo Iohannes filius Fulcher' debet similiter.

[287] Alwinus Ruffus reddebat viii d. et consuetudi-nem T.R.E. Modo Sawalo debet idem.

[288] Suot et Edwinus filius Aluredi reddebant xxx d. et consuetudinem T.R.E. Modo Radulfus filius Rain-gard' debet similiter.

[289] Ediwinus Gule et Alwinus presbiter[1] reddebant xxx d. de ii mansuris et consuetudinem T.R.E. Tur-stinus clericus[2] similiter. Et de eadem fecit Ailwi consuetudinem.[3] Modo Edricus debet similiter.

[290] Burwoldus presbiter reddebat xv d. et consue-tudinem T.R.E. Modo Ricardus Dublel et Essulfus presbiter debent similiter.

the earl of Warwick.[1] Anschetil of Jort[2] ought to per-form the custom for it.

[280] The land of the abbot of St. Edmunds paid 10d. *TRE*. Now it owes the same.[1]

[281] Ranulf son of Robert Dop pays [. . .] and the custom for his holding on the royal demesne.

IN *GERE* STREET [TRAFALGAR STREET]

[282] Hugelin the park-keeper paid 20d. and the cus-tom *TRE*. Now Iwen the tailor[1] owes the same.

[283] Leving the ladder-maker paid 6d. and the custom *TRE*. Now Simon the dispenser[1] [. . .].

[284] Wulfward Cap paid 18d. and the custom *TRE*. Now William the ragman owes the same.

[285] Estan Scodhe paid 10d.[1] and the custom *TRE*. Now Anschetil the palmer owes the same.

[286] Lanc de Lere[1] paid 30d. and the custom *TRE*. Now John son of Fulcher owes the same.

[287] Alwin the Red paid 8d. and the custom *TRE*. Now Sawal owes the same.

[288] Swot and Edwin son of Alfred paid 30d. and the custom *TRE*. Now Ralf son of Raingard owes the same.

[289] Edwin Gule and Alwin the priest[1] paid 30d. and the custom for 2 messuages *TRE*. Thurstin the clerk[2] [owes] the same. And Ailwi performed the custom for it [*sic*].[3] Now Edric owes the same.

[290] Burwold the priest paid 15d. and the custom *TRE*. Now Richard Dublel and Essulf the priest owe the same.

---

[a] *Text in margin for rubricator almost entirely cut away*

[b] r *over an erasure*   [c] idem *over an erasure*

279 1. Henry de Beaumont, earl of Warwick, died in 1119. He was the younger brother of Robert, count of Meulan, for whom see **2**. There may have been some connection between the earl's tenement and one of the two properties which his nephew, the earl of Leicester, held in the same street in 1148 (**II, 857** and **892**).
  2. See **9**.
280 1. Benedictine abbey in Suffolk: *VCH Suffolk* ii. 56 ff. For the tenement, cf. **II, 880**.
282 1. In 1148 his heirs seem to have been holding **II, 1071** in *Goldestret*.

283 1. For Simon and his office and family, see *King's Serjeants*, 186 ff. Cf. **114**. For the tenement, cf. **II, 1069**.
285 1. For this tenement, cf. **II, 1068** or **1072**.
286 1. For a possible explanation, see below, p. 164, s.v. *Lancdelere*.
289 1. See **41**.   2. See **180**.
  3. If Alwin and Ailwi are the same person, it is possible that Edwin paid the landgable and Alwin was responsible for the service. But it seems probable that Alwinus (OE Ælfwine) and Ailwi (OE Æðelwīg) are different persons.

[291] Ailwinus Hieltepreost[1] reddebat xv d. Modo Picot pincerna debet similiter.

[292] Leuingus Drache reddebat xv d. Modo Radulfus homo Herberti camerarii[1] debet similiter.

[293] Dalphin reddebat vi d. Modo filius eius [debet] similiter.

[294] Spilemanus Brandwirchte reddebat xv d. Modo Willelmus Brun[1] debet similiter.

[295] Uluricus redd*it* xxx d. et consuetudinem.[a]

[291] Ailwin Halt-priest[1] paid 15*d*. Now Picot the butler owes the same.

[292] Leving Dragon paid 15*d*. Now Ralf the vassal of Herbert the chamberlain[1] owes the same.

[293] Dalphin paid 6*d*. Now his son [owes] the same.

[294] Spileman the sword-maker paid 15*d*. Now William Brown[1] owes the same.

[295] Wulfric pays 30*d*. and the custom.

[a] *Remainder of fo. 12[v] and fo. 13[r] blank*

291 1. See **228–9**.   **292** 1. See **I**, Preface.   **294** 1. See **42**.

(ii) THE SURVEY OF 1148

(SURVEY II)

[fo. 13ᵛ] Haec est inquisitio de terris Winton': quisquis tenet, et quantum tenet, et de quocunque tenet, et quantum quisque inde capit, precepto episcopi Henrici anno ab incarnatione domini MCXLVIII.

This is an inquest, held in 1148 by order of Bishop Henry, concerning the lands of Winchester. The questions were: what is the name of the landholder? how much does he hold? from whom does he hold it? and how much does each person receive from the land?

IN MAGNO VICO

[1] Robertus de Ingl'[1] regi vi d., et God' presbiter[2] tenet de eo, et habet inde xviii s.

[2] Iohannes de Port[1] debet reddere regi vi d.

[3] Et intus portam de west est quedam logia.[1]

[4] Herbertus camerarius[1] regi vi d., et habet vii s.

[5] Godefridus filius Willelmi[1] tenet iii terras et dicit esse[a] quietas, et habet inde xxxix s. Et[b] Peni habet inde iiii s. et Robertus ii s. et Osbertus xii d.

[6] Iua regi vi d. et habet xviii s.

[7] Ricardus de Baiaco[1] regi vi d.

[8] Abbatissa Wint' regi vi d.[1] et habet xiii s. et vi d. Et idem Ricardus[2] habet viii s.

[9] Robertus Mart'[1] tenet i mans*ionem* de feudo Willelmi filii Manne quietam[c] et i aliam de feudo regis que debet reddere regi vi d.; et de hac[d] debet reddere episcopo vii s. et ad hospitalem[2] xx s. et habet xxv s.

IN HIGH STREET

[1] Robert of Inglesham[1] pays the king 6d. God' the priest[2] holds it of Robert and (?) Robert receives from it 18s.

[2] John de Port[1] should pay the king 6d.

[3] And within the West Gate is a lodge.[1]

[4] Herbert the chamberlain[1] pays the king 6d. and receives 7s.

[5] Godfrey son of William[1] holds 3 lands and says they are quit. He receives from them 39s., Penny receives 4s., Robert receives 2s., and Osbert receives 12d.

[6] Iva pays the king 6d. and receives 18s.

[7] Richard of Bayeux[1] pays the king 6d.

[8] The abbess of Winchester pays the king 6d.[1] and receives 13s. 6d. And the same Richard[2] receives 8s.

[9] Robert the Weasel[1] holds 1 messuage quit of the fief of William son of Manni and 1 other of the king's fief which should yield the king 6d. And from this he should pay the bishop 7s. and the hospital[2] 20s.; and he receives 25s.

---

[a] et dicit esse *over an erasure part of* [5]   [c] quietem *MS.*   [b] *Although* Et ... xii d. *is given as a separate item in the MS., it clearly forms*   [d] hoc *MS.*

1 1. See also **26**, **55**, **66**, **127**, **417**, **506**, **549**, **553**, **555**, **579**, **580**, and **602**. He was the richest of the private landlords in 1148: see below, Table 24. A Master Robert of Inglesham was archdeacon of Surrey from c. 1155×59, and witnessed a Winchester deed of that date: Le Neve *Monastic Cathedrals 1088–1300*, 94 and Goodman *Chartulary*, no. 453. Cf. Osbert of Inglesham, probably also one of the clerical retinue of Henry of Blois, for whom see **715**, n. 1.
2. Presumably not the deceased Godwin of **241** and **325**. He may be the God' priest of Alton, **733**.
2 1. See also **84**, **138**, **270**, **439**, **474**, and **685**. Probably the son of Henry de Port (see I, **39**), lord of Basing. This survey indicates that he succeeded his father by 1148–9; he died in 1167, Sanders *Baronies*, 9. The evidence that he succeeded about 1153 is uncertain, cf. *Complete Peerage*, xi. 318. His daughter Clemencia married Henry Husey III: see **138**, n. 3. Ralf de Port occurs in **138** and **473**, Hugh de Port in **314** and **932**, and Roger de Port in **580**–**3**.
3 1. In the later Middle Ages the porter's lodge was

contained within the N. part of the structure of West Gate. See discussion below, pp. 276–7.
4 1. See also **38**, **542**, **828**, **841**, **860**, and **873**. Herbert fitzHerbert: see I, Preface. In 1156 he was pardoned Scutage as a knight of the abbots of Abingdon and Hyde: *Pipe Roll 2 Henry II*, pp. 35, 56.
5 1. See also **36**, **95**, **174**, **321**, **327**, **445–6**, and **573**.
7 1. See also **8** and **10**. For Robert of Bayeux, see **1001**. A Richard of Bayeux was a king's champion under Henry I: *Regesta*, ii, no. 626.
8 1. For this tenement, cf. I, **36**.   2. See **7**.
9 1. See also **67**, **310**, **443**, and **517**. Witnessed a royal notification, c. 1128: *Regesta*, ii, no. 1562. In 1130 he was pardoned Danegeld in Oxfordshire and a fine in Yorkshire: *Pipe Roll 31 Henry I*, pp. 5, 30.
2. See also **910** and **1081**, and for the Hospital of Jerusalem, **584** and **720**. The Hospital of St. Cross was founded c. 1136 by Henry of Blois, bishop of Winchester, and put under the care of the Order of the Knights Hospitallers: *VCH Hants* ii. 193 ff. See below pp. 328–9.

[10] Herebertus Corneilla[1] abbati de Hida[2] viii s. et Ricardus de Baiaco[3] eidem abbati ix s. et habet vi s.

[10] Herbert Crow[1] pays the abbot of Hyde[2] 8s.; and Richard of Bayeux[3] pays the same abbot 9s. and receives 6s.

[11] Gilebertus cum barba eidem abbati ix s.

[11] Gilbert with the Beard pays the same abbot 9s.

[12] Andreas eidem abbati ix s. et habet xii s.

[12] Andrew pays the same abbot 9s. and receives 12s.

[13] Turstinus Danais[1] eidem abbati ix s.

[13] Thurstin the Dane[1] pays the same abbot 9s.

[14] Radulfus clericus[1] eidem abbati ix s.

[14] Ralf the clerk[1] pays the same abbot 9s.

[15] Ade corduan*us* eidem abbati xi s.

[15] Adam the cordwainer pays the same abbot 11s.

[16] Cuppingus cord*uanus* solebat reddere eidem abbati xiiii s.; sed [est] vast'.

[16] Cupping the cordwainer used to pay the same abbot 14s.; but the land is waste.

[17] Heredes Martini[1] habent ii s. de i estal quod est in calle regis.[2]

[17] Martin's heirs[1] receive 2s. from 1 stall which is on the king's road.[2]

[18] Hugo Haccemus[1] eidem abbati iiii d. et habet iiii s.

[18] Hugh Hack-mouse[1] pays the same abbot 4d. and receives 4s.

[19] Adelardus acul*arius*[1] eidem abbati iiii s. et Hangere eidem abbati iiii s.

[19] Adelard the needle-maker[1] pays the same abbot 4s. and Hangman pays the same abbot 4s.

[20] Ricardus acul*arius* eidem abbati iiii s.

[20] Richard the needle-maker pays the same abbot 4s.

[21] Paganus pic'[1] eidem abbati xii d. et episcopo iiii s. de B.[2] et habet xvii s.

[21] Pain [son of] Picard[1] pays the same abbot 12d. and pays the bishop 4s. *de B.*[2]; and he receives 17s.

[22] Item Adelardus acul*arius*[1] eidem abbati xxx d. et habet viii s.

[22] Again Adelard the needle-maker[1] pays the same abbot 30d. and receives 8s.

10 1. It is possible that the Cornilla (Crow) of **23** is the same person.

2. The fee of the abbot of Hyde, extending from **10** to **24** inclusive, may have been in the neighbourhood of St. Paul's church, where the abbot's interests are recorded in the fourteenth century: see *SMW* 13.

3. See **7**.

13 1. See also **710** and **727**.

14 1. See also **654**, **659**, and **1001**.

17 1. For Martin of Bentworth, his widow, sister, and heirs, see above, pp. 27–8. For Martin, see also **56** and **487**. For his widow, see also **28**, **43**, **56**, **139**, **565–6**, **795**, **808–9**, **825**, and **854**. For his sister, see **144**. For his heirs, see also **1058**.

2. For encroachments, see also **43**, **56**, **87**, **88**, **98**, **105**, **106**, and **925**, and cf. I, 19, n. 2 and below, pp. 280–2.

18 1. Or Hatchmouse. See also **164**, **434**, **458**, **482**, and **539**. For Goda Hack-mouse see **70**, **457**, **518**, and **568**. As Hugh and Goda appear in adjacent entries (**457–8**), they were presumably closely related. Goda's brother, Robert, also occurs (**568**). In 1158 Hugh settled a debt to the king in Winchester: *Pipe Roll 4 Henry II*, p. 176. The family appears to have survived into the

thirteenth century. Geoffrey *Hachemuz* witnessed a Winchester document of the late twelfth or early thirteenth century: *Proc Hants FC* 20 (1956), 51, n. 22. For later members of the family, see **434**, n. 3, **457**, n. 1, and p. 517.

19 1. See also **22**.

21 1. See also **92**, **364–5**, **367**, **370–1**, **377**, **406**, and **431**; and *Paganus filius picardi* in **323** and **552**, who is probably the same person. He was pardoned two marks of the city's aid in 1161: *Pipe Roll 7 Henry II*, p. 57. On becoming a monk at Malmesbury in the late twelfth century, *Radulfus filius Pagani Pichard* endowed the abbey with the following properties in Winchester: land outside North Gate of the fee of the abbot of Hyde (cf. **323**): half a seld on St. Giles's Hill; land in *Snipelingestrate* of the fee of the Earl of Leicester (cf. **364–5**, **367**, **370–1**, and **377**); and a house *in vico iuxta murum versus prioratum*. Abbot Robert of Malmesbury granted these properties to Hugh Camberlane in return for 12s. annual rent. Hugh granted Winchester properties, including a seld on St. Giles's Hill, in the street of Northampton, and three houses in *Sniplegestrate* to Hugh Pichard in the 1220s: *Reg Malmesbury*, 35, 36, 37.

2. The first occurrence of this phrase. See above, p. 19.

22 1. See **19**.

[23] Hugo filius Chepping'[1] eidem abbati iiii s. et habet i m*arcam* de Cornilla[2] et Cornilla habet inde xl d.

[24] Turstinus acular*ius*[1] eidem abbati vii s.

[25] Ricardus filius Turoldi templo[1] ii s. et est de feudo Roberti de Oili[2] et regis.

[26] [fo. 14] De feudo Turoldi de Estuna episcopus habet xix s. [de] B. et Robertus de Ingl'[1] habet de eadem terra xx s. et Laurentius habet inde de Rogero iiii s. et idem Rogerus habet inde iiii s. similiter. Et*a* Durandus habet xii d.

[27] Rogerus pic*tor*[1] tenet i estal wast*um*. Alwinus*b* et Ernaldus regi unaquaque ebdomada ii d. preter quadragesimam.

[28] Et uxor Martini[1] regi ii d. in ebdomada similiter preter quadragesimam.

[29] Episcopus regi vi d. Et habet de Rogero filio Gunt'[1] xxx s. et ipse Rogerus habet xx s. et iiii d.

[30] Herebertus filius Gunt'[1] regi vi d. et habet de Pagano xxi s. et de Ansgero xxi s. et Anser habet viii s.

[23] Hugh son of Chepping[1] pays the same abbot 4s. and receives 1 mark [13s. 4d.] from Cornilla,[2] and Cornilla receives from the land 40d.

[24] Thurstin the needle-maker[1] pays the same abbot 7s.

[25] Richard son of Turold pays the Temple[1] 2s.; and the land is on the fief of Robert d'Oilli [Ouilly][2] and of the king.

[26] From the fief of Turold of Easton the bishop receives 19s. [de] B. and from that land Robert of Inglesham[1] receives 20s., Laurence receives from Roger 4s., and the same Roger receives likewise 4s. And Durand receives 12d.

[27] Roger the painter (?)[1] holds 1 stall which is waste. Alwin and Ernold pay the king 2d. a week except in Lent.

[28] And Martin's wife[1] likewise pays the king 2d. a week except in Lent.

[29] The bishop pays the king 6d. And he receives from Roger son of Guncelin[1] 30s.; and Roger receives 20s. 4d.

[30] Herbert son of Guncelin[1] pays the king 6d. and receives from Pain 21s. and from Ansger 21s. Ansger receives 8s.

---

a Et . . . xii d. *is presented as a separate item in the MS.*

23 1. See also **172**, **294**, **362**, and **403**. For Ralf son of Chepping, see **466**; for Robert son of Chepping, see **395**; for Roger son of Chepping, see **462**. For the tenement, cf. **I, 73**, in which Hugh's father probably had an interest. Hugh and his father were probably both moneyers of Stephen: see below, pp. 416–19 and Table 44.
  2. Cf. **10**.
24 1. See also **203**.
25 1. In *c*. Dec. 1139 Edith, wife of Robert d'Oilli II, granted to the Templars a rent of 2s., *quam dedit michi churoldus de Wintonia de tribus monasteriis*: A. M. Leys (ed.), *The Sandford Cartulary* (Oxfordshire Record Society, 19 and 22, 1938 and 1941), 50. This locality lay on the N. side of High Street, possibly between the church of St. Paul and the church of St. Peter Whitbread (cf. **I, 34**, n. 1; **II, 10**, n. 2, and **32**, n. 2), but the identity of the 'three minsters' is uncertain: cf. **I, 35**.
  The Templars also had rents in **II, 578**, **586**, and **838**, totalling 9s. 2d. (net). According to the 'Templars' Inquest of 1185, a rent of 8s. 4d. was collected from Winchester: *Templars*, 52. The Inquest also records the benefactions of the Port family in Hampshire. The royal farmer of Winchester accounted for 'newly established alms to the Knights of the Temple' of 1 mark from *Pipe Roll 2 Henry II*, p. 52 onwards.

b Ellis makes a new item without MS. authority

2. A royal constable. Robert I (d. *c*. 1091–2), a large Domesday tenant in Oxfordshire, was succeeded by his brother Nigel (d. *c*. 1115), who left a son and heir Robert II, who went over to the empress in 1141, and died in the following year. William of Chesney (**512**) seems to have held the d'Oilli fief at this date, and until 1153–4 or thereabouts. He was succeeded by his son Henry I: *Regesta*, ii, p. xvi; iii, pp. xix–xx. *King's Serjeants*, 81. A Ralf d'Oilli occurs in **122**.
26 1. See **1**.
27 1. See also **379**.
28 1. See **17**.
29 1. There are a good number of references to Guncelin, the sons and heirs of Guncelin, and the heirs of his sons; and it is possible that we are concerned with three generations, although there were other Guncelins in Winchester, e.g. the son of Hugh (**833**), and Guncelin Dore (**857**). For Guncelin, see **153**, **611–12**, and **896**; for his heirs, **583** and **603**; for his son, **320**; and for his son Conan **179**; for his son Roger, this entry and **415**; for his son Herbert, **30** and **454**; for Herbert's heirs, **502** and **895**; for the wife of Guncelin's son Hugh, **183**; for Hugh's heirs, **167**; for Hugh's sons, **180** and **424**.
30 1. See **29**.

[31] Hereuicus clericus[1] et sorores eius regi vi d. et Hereuicus habet xxvi s. de i selda. Et sorores eius habent xxxvi s. et vi d. et de istis xxx s. et vi d.[2] habet Robertus de Sancto Pancratio[3] xxii s.

[32] Filii Thome clerici[1] abbati de Hida[2] iii s. et habent inde xxxiii s.

[33] Rogerus de Wdecota[a] eidem abbati ii d. et habet xvi s.

[34] Haroldus de Chenesham eidem abbati vi d. et habet de Goscelino lv s. et de eadem terra habet idem Haroldus de filia Roberti de Diua xviii s. et ipsa habet inde xx s. et Iohannes nepos Petri[1] habet inde de eadem iii s.

[35] Petrus merciarius[1] regi vi d. et episcopo ix s. de B. et Willelmo Martel[2] xl s. et habet xii s.

[36] Godefridus filius Willelmi[1] regi vi d. Et habet xliiii s. et iiii d. de Ailwardo.[2] Et Ailwardus habet xxv s. et iiii d.

[37] Prior Wint' regi vi d.[1] et habet lxxviii s.

[38] Herbertus camerarius[1] regi vi d. et monachis de Teochesb' xii d. et Odgaressune[2] eidem Hereberto x s. et idem Edgar Ricardo Nigro[3] v s. et ipse Edgarus habet xvii s. et Ricardus Baganorus reddit eidem vi s. et

[31] Herewic the clerk[1] and his sisters pay the king 6d. and Herewic receives 26s. from 1 shop. His sisters receive 36s. 6d. and from this 30s. 6d.[2] Robert of St. Pancras[3] receives 22s.

[32] The sons of Thomas the clerk[1] pay the abbot of Hyde[2] 3s. and receive 33s.

[33] Roger of Woodcote pays that abbot 2d. and receives 16s.

[34] Harold of Keynsham pays that abbot 6d. and receives from Goscelin 55s.; and from that land the same Harold receives from Robert of Dives's daughter 18s. and she receives 20s. John, Peter's nephew,[1] receives from the same land/woman 3s.

[35] Peter the mercer[1] pays the king 6d., the bishop 9s. de B., and William Martel[2] 40s.; and Peter receives 12s.

[36] Godfrey son of William[1] pays the king 6d. And he receives 44s. 4d. from Ailward.[2] And Ailward receives 25s. 4d.

[37] The prior of Winchester pays the king 6d.[1] and receives 78s.

[38] Herbert the chamberlain[1] pays the king 6d. and the monks of Tewkesbury 12d. Odgar's son[2] pays that same Herbert 10s. and the same Edgar pays Richard Black[3] 5s. Edgar receives 17s. and Richard Bagnor pays him

---

[a] *MS. possibly reads* Wrlecota

31 1. See also **40, 220,** and **284.** In 1158 a Hervey, clerk of *Brunham,* who owed the king 1 mark, occurs in the Pipe Roll under Norfolk and Suffolk. The debt was pardoned two years later: *Pipe Roll 4 Henry II,* p. 127; *6 Henry II,* p. 2.

2. There is an arithmetical discrepancy.

3. See also **260, 283, 316, 345, 356, 670, 692–3, 700,** and **705.** He witnessed a charter of Henry, duke of Normandy, dated Devizes 1149: *Regesta,* iii. no. 795, and was a canon of Sarum *c.* 1150–60: W. R. Jones and W. D. Macray (eds.), *Charters and Documents Illustrating the History of the Cathedral City and Diocese of Salisbury* (RS, 1891), 16, 18, 19.

32 1. For his wife (widow), see **317.**

2. Cf. **33** and **34.** This second group of Hyde Abbey properties on the N. side of High Street, coming from West Gate, might represent the group owned by Hyde in the neighbourhood of St. Peter Whitbread church in the later Middle Ages: *SMW*; **I, 34,** n. 1; **II, 10,** n. 2, and **25,** n. 1.

34 1. Nephew of Peter the mercer. See also **154, 359,** and **859.** For Peter, see **35.**

35 1. See also **136, 200, 210, 238, 265, 515, 557,** and **863.** He occurs in *Pipe Roll 2, 3,* and *4 Henry II,* pp. 53, 108, 176, **as** *merciarius.* He owed the king £100 for having

his peace. He seems to have paid this sum in three years. For his brother, Ernald, see **135,** ?**138,** ?**842, 904,** ?**977,** ?**981,** ?**1045,** and ?**1060.** For his nephew John, see **34.**

2. See also **41, 51, 54, 467,** and **488-92.** William was one of King Stephen's stewards, served as sheriff of Surrey, and witnessed many royal documents: *Regesta,* ii, p. xii; iii, pp. xviii, xxii, xxiii, xxv. For Edith Martel, not apparently a relative, see **460.** In 1160–2 Geoffrey Martel granted a rent of 1 mark in Winchester held by John, the brother of William son of Martin, to the nunnery of St. Mary, Clerkenwell. The grant was confirmed by Geoffrey's son, William: W. O. Hassall (ed.), *Cartulary of St. Mary Clerkenwell* (Camden 3rd ser. 71, 1949), 27–8.

36 1. See **5.**

2. Probably a moneyer of Henry I: see below, Table 42. For an earlier moneyer's interest in this tenement, see **I, 29,** n. 1.

37 1. For this tenement, cf. **I, 28.**

38. 1. See **4.**

2. Apparently a mistake for Edgar's son, who is immediately contracted to Edgar. There is an Edgar's son in **132** and **307.**

3. See also **224** and **251.**

Rogerus de Haia⁴ reddit eidem xv s. et priori v s. et idem Rogerus habet xxxiii s. et de eadem terra habet ipse Herebertus de Drogone vi s. et [ipse]ᵃ Drogo habet vi s. et preterea habet Herebertus de Hereuico vi s. et de Hereberto filio Westman⁵ vi s. et idem Herebertus habet vi s.

[39] Prior regi vi d.¹ et habet Godefridus vi s. et Godefridus habet viii s.² et prior habet de Radulfo vi s. et Radulfus [fo. 14ᵛ] habet xi s. et vi d.ᵇ et prior habet de Radulfo Cuinta³ vi s. et Radulfus habet iiii s. et prior habet de Durando vi s. et Durandus habet vii s.

[40] Abbatissa Wint' regi vi d.¹ et Robertus Oisun² eidem abbatisse vi s. et habet x s. et Reimundus parmentarius³ eidem vii s. et habet xiii s. et Godefridus Niger eidem ii s. et Willelmus eidem ii s. et habet iiii s. et Paganus Gall'⁴ eidem iiii s. et habet ix s. et Aldit eidem iii s. et Gunnild eidem iiii s. et Petita eidem iiii s. et Morgellor eidem iiii s. et Hervicus clericus⁵ abbatisse xxv s.

[41] Willelmus Martel¹ regi vi d. et habet iiii li. et xvi. s et ix d.

[42] ᶜTerra Godebieta¹ semper quieta et est quieta.

[43] Et sunt ibi iuxta in calle regis¹ vi scamell² unde rex habet in unaquaque ebdomada de unoquoque i d. preter quadragesimam et uxor Martiniᵈ³ habet i ex istis⁴ et reddit priori v d. et habet in unaquaque ebdomada iii obolos preter quadragesimam et tria festa annalia.

[44] Ricardus clericus¹ priori v d. et habet v s.

6s. Roger of La Haye⁴ pays him 15s. and the prior 5s.; and the same Roger receives 33s. And from that same land the same Herbert receives 6s. from Drew and Drew receives 6s. Moreover Herbert receives 6s. from Hervey and 6s. from Herbert son of Westman.⁵ And the same Herbert [? son of Westman] receives 6s.

[39] The prior pays the king 6d.¹ and Godfrey receives 6s. and Godfrey receives 8s.² The prior receives 6s. from Ralf and Ralf receives 11s. 6d. And the prior receives 6s. from Ralf Cuinte³ and Ralf receives 4s. And the prior receives 6s. from Durand and Durand receives 7s.

[40] The abbess of Winchester pays the king 6d.¹ Robert Oison² pays the abbess 6s. and receives 10s. Raymond the tailor³ pays her 7s. and receives 13s. Godfrey Black pays her 2s. William pays her 2s. and receives 4s. Pain the Frenchman⁴ pays her 4s. and receives 9s. Aldith pays her 3s., Gunnhild pays her 4s., Petita pays her 4s., Morgellor pays her 4s., and Hervey the clerk⁵ pays the abbess 25s.

[41] William Martel¹ pays the king 6d. and receives £4. 16s. 9d.

[42] The Godebiete land¹ was always and is quit.

[43] And next in the king's road¹ are 6 shambles² from each of which the king receives 1d. a week except in Lent. Martin's wife³ has 1 of them⁴ and pays the prior 5d., and she receives 1½d. a week except in Lent and on the three annual festivals.

[44] Richard the clerk¹ pays the prior 5d. and receives 5s.

ᵃ Space left   ᵇ et vi d. *repeated and cancelled by rubricator in margin, both late medieval. The entry itself is written over an erasure*   ᶜ *A hand pointing to this entry and* Godebiete   ᵈ Martinus *MS.*

38 4. See also **73, 90–1, 104, 903, 913,** and **1043.** Robert *de Haia* and his son Richard were officers of the Norman Exchequer under Henry I and Stephen: *EHR* 14 (1899), 424, 427–8. Roger's interest in forges and property which may formerly have belonged to a moneyer suggests that he may be identical with King Stephen's moneyer *Rogier*, see below, p. 419 and Table 44. For Richard of La Haye, see **1067.**

5. See also **463, 478,** and **506.** Between 1155 and 1180–2 he granted 16s. 9d. rent in Winchester to Godstow Nunnery. His rents in 1148 totalled 21s. With other moneyers he was fined 100s. in 1166 *quia fabricauerunt simul in una domo*: Godstow Cart, fos. 163ᵛ, 164, 180, 181; *Pipe Roll 13 Henry II*, p. 193. Elyas Westman was the first mayor of Winchester whose name is known: Furley *City Government*, 16. For this tenement, cf. **I, 27,** and for Herbert as a moneyer of Henry II, and the long succession of moneyers' interests in this area, see below, Tables 42–5. See Addenda.

39 1. For this tenement, cf. **I, 26.**

2. The second receipt is either a correction or a careless repetition. There is another error in this item.

3. See also **890, 896, 974, 995,** and **1021.**

40 1. For this tenement, cf. **I, 25.**

2. See also **870, 877, 881–2,** and **983.** The family was mayoral in the thirteenth century; see also below, p. 447. For Thomas Oysun, perhaps Robert's son, see **139,** n. 2.

3. See also **85, 734,** and **777.** See Addenda.

4. See also **428.**

5. See **31.**

41 1. See **35.**

42 1. See **I, 23.**

43 1. See also **17,** n. 2.

2. These are nos. **43–7/9,** although the totals are 5 or 7.

3. See **17.**

4. See Addenda.

44 1. See also **48** and **53.**

[45] Panta priori v d. pro i estal.

[45] Panta pays the prior 5d. for 1 stall.

[46] Emma priori v d. et habet iii s.

[46] Emma pays the prior 5d. and receives 3s.

[47] Lacchewei¹ priori v d. et habet iii s.

[47] Lacchewei¹ pays the prior 5d. and receives 3s.

[48] Item Ricardus clericus¹ priori v d. de i domo quae solebat esse stal unde rex solebat habere unaquaque ebdomada i d. et ipse Ricardus habet modo inde iii s.

[48] Again Richard the clerk¹ pays the prior 5d. for 1 tenement which used to be a stall and from which the king used to receive 1d. a week. And Richard now receives from it 3s.

[49] Iohannes frater Richer'ᵃ¹ priori pro i terra v d. et rex solebat habere de illa quando fuit stal i d. et modo ipse Iohannes habet iiii s.

[49] John, Richer's brother,¹ pays the prior 5d. for 1 land, from which, when it was a stall, the king used to receive 1d. And John now receives 4s.

[50] Canonici Mert'¹ habent ibi iuxta i terra[m] de feudo regis unde Ansfridus burgensis² reddit eisdem xii d.

[50] The canons of Merton¹ have next 1 land of the king's fief from which Ansfrid the burgess² pays them 12d.

[51] Willelmus Martel¹ habet i terram wastam unde Nicholaus reddit episcopo Sar'² ii s. et est de feudo regis.

[51] William Martel¹ has 1 waste land from which Nicholas pays the bishop of Salisbury² 2s. And it is on the king's fief.

[52] Rogerus tinctor¹ tenet i terram de Balchus² et reddit bedell*is* regis iiii d. et habet xviii d.

[52] Roger the dyer¹ holds 1 land belonging to the *Balchus*² and he pays the king's beadles 4d. and receives 18d.

[53] Item Ricardus clericus¹ tenet i terram de feudo regis et habet iii s.

[53] Again Richard the clerk¹ holds 1 land of the king's fief and receives 3s.

[54] Willelmus Martel¹ habet ibi iuxta i vasta[m] terra[m] que solebat esse stal² et rex habebat i d.³

[54] William Martel¹ has next 1 waste land which used to be a stall² and from which the king used to receive 1d.³

[55] Robertus de Ingl'¹ tenet i terram de feudo regis et habet xliii s. Et Willelmus de Piro² habet de eadem terra xi s. et Bernardus carnifex³ habet x s. et [fo. 15] viii d. et Sewi⁴ habet de eadem terra xxxiii s. cum catall*is* que ipsi tenent de illo.⁵

[55] Robert of Inglesham¹ holds 1 land of the king's fief and receives 43s. From that land William *de Piro*² receives 11s., Bernard the butcher³ 10s. 8d., and Sewi⁴ 33s. together with the chattels which they hold from him.⁵

ᵃ Richer' . . . vd. *over an erasure*

---

47 1. See also 617 and 802; possibly Ralf Lacchewei, for whom see 74 and 420. Ralf seems to have been a royal servant: *Pipe Roll 2 and 3 Henry II*, pp. 54, 105.
48 1. See 44.
49 1. See also 943.
50 1. See also 516, 669, 680, and 1074. A house of Augustinian canons in Surrey, dioc. Winchester, founded in 1114: *VCH Surrey* ii. 94.
2. See also 449 and 1082. For his wife, see 476.
51 1. See 35.
2. Jocelin de Bohun, consecrated 1142, and formerly archdeacon of Winchester: see 688, n. 1. and below, p. 392, n. 7. For his other properties, see 268–9 and 691, and for the properties of his predecessor as bishop, I, 75.
52 1. See also 77–8, 639, and 663.
2. Cf. I, 19.

53 1. See 44.
54 1. See 35.
2. See I, 19, n. 4.
3. As toll (*de thelonio*).
55 1. See 1.
2. By 1191 his land in Winchester had come into the king's hands by escheat. Peter son of Walder was to pay 1 mark to have part of it: *Pipe Roll 3 Richard I*, p. 91.
3. See I, 19, n. 4.
4. Cf. also 751 and 964; for Eva, Sewi's wife, see 699; for Godfrey his son, see 532, 764, and 780.
5. This is the first of several references to chattels and equipment. See also 62, 401, 414, 496, 591, 696, 699, and 856. Sewi's wife hires out chattels in 699. For discussion, see below, p. 431.

[56] *Et ibi iuxta sunt vi stal unde rex habet in unaquaque ebdomada de unoquoque i d. preter quadragesimam et Martinus de Bintewrda[1] habet de i stal iii s. et vi d. et est de feudo regis. Et uxor Martini[1] habet de v stals xvi s. preter quadragesimam. Et in calle regis[2] Willelmus Piec[3] reddit prepositis vi d. et unaquaque ebdomada i d. de thelon*io* preter quadragesimam.[4]

[57] Rogerus Mercherel regi vi d. et habet de thelon*io* i d.

[58] Doisel regi vi d. pro suo stal'[1] et i d. de thel*onio.*

[59] Herebertus lardinarius regi vi d. et habet xvii s. et Robertus Trotardin habet ibi v s. Et Herebertus habet ibi vi d. Et in eodem tenore Ricardus carnifex[1] regi i d. de thelon*io* preter quadragesimam.

[60] Episcopus regi vi d. de B. Et habet xvii s. Et Durandus habet vi s. et Murta habet vi s.

[61] Prior regi vi d.[1] et habet xlviii s. et uxor Roberti unctarii iii s. et Robertus de eadem iiii so. et Edwinus ii s. et infirmarius habet de eadem xii s. Et Ingulfus Besmere[2] habet de eadem vi s. et Siluester habet iii s. Et Radulfus cocus habet xx s. et vi d.

[62] Prior regi vi d.[1] et habet xxxii s. et vi d. et Siluester habet vi s. et quedam femina est in domo sua et habet catalla Siluestri[2] et braciat et Giboda habet xi s.

[63] Episcopus[1] habet de ii terris que fuerunt Radulfi de Wingeham xlviii s. et iiii d. et de i terra desubtus debet rex habere vi d. de langabulo.

[64] Sanson monetarius[1] regi vi d. et priori xx s.[2] Et habet xiiii s.

[65] Item Sanson[1] regi vi d. et episcopo xx s. de B. et habet xliiii s.

[56] And next are 6 stalls, from each of which the king receives 1d. a week except in Lent. Martin of Bentworth[1] receives from 1 stall 3s. 6d. And it is on the king's fief. Martin's wife[1] receives from 5 stalls 16s. except in Lent. And on the king's road[2] William Peak[3] pays to the reeves 6d. and 1d. a week for toll except in Lent.[4]

[57] Roger Mercherel pays the king 6d. and receives from toll 1d.

[58] Doisel pays the king 6d. for his stall[1] and 1d. for toll.

[59] Herbert the larderer pays the king 6d. and receives 17s. Robert Trotardin receives there 5s. And Herbert receives there 6d. And in the same manner Richard the butcher[1] pays the king 1d. for toll except in Lent.

[60] The bishop pays the king 6d. *de B.* And he receives 17s. and Durand receives 6s. and Murta receives 6s.

[61] The prior pays the king 6d.[1] and receives 48s. Also from it Robert the grease-seller's wife receives 3s., Robert 4s., Edwin 2s., the infirmarer 12s., Ingulf the besom-maker[2] 6s., Silvester 3s., and Ralf the cook 20s. 6d.

[62] The prior pays the king 6d.[1] and receives 32s. 6d. And Silvester receives 6s. A certain woman is in his house and has Silvester's chattels[2] and brews. And Giboda receives 11s.

[63] The bishop[1] has from 2 lands, which used to be Ralf of Wingham's, 48s. 4d. And from 1 land [next] down [the street?] the king should receive 6d. landgable.

[64] Samson the moneyer[1] pays the king 6d. and the prior 20s.[2] And he receives 14s.

[65] Again Samson[1] pays the king 6d. and the bishop 20s. *de B.* And he receives 44s.

---

^a *The text runs on, but the division is indicated by a paragraph sign*

56 1. See **17**.
     2. See also **17**, n. 2.
     3. He witnessed a conveyance of property in High Street (cf. **43**) and *Alwarnestret* (cf. **487**) *c.* 1155–60: Southwick Cart iii, fos. 123ᵛ, 136ᵛ.
     4. For the stalls and encroachment, cf. I, **19–21**.
58 1. See I, **19**, n. 4.
59 1. See I, **19**, n. 4.
61 1. For this tenement, cf. I, **16**.

     2. See **712**.
62 1. For this tenement, cf. I, **15**.
     2. See **55**.
63 1. For the property, cf. I, **15**.
64 1. See also **65** and **118**, and below, p. 415 and Table 43; cf. **128–9**. For an earlier moneyer's interest in property near here, cf. I, **15**.
     2. For this property, cf. I, **14**.
65 1. See **64**.

[66] Robertus de Ingl'¹ regi vi d. et Willelmo filio Warin'² x s. et habet inde xvii s. et Willelmus filius Bos³ habet inde viii s.

[67] Robertus la Martra*ᵃ¹* episcopo v s. de B. et habet xi s. de eodem feudo regis.

[68] Baldewinus pistor¹ episcopo xv s. de B. et habet xii s. Et idem de alia terra regi vi d. et episcopo ii libras piperis*ᵇ* et habet xxviii s.

[69] Sewi tenet seld*am* ubi linei panni venduntur¹ et domos cum [fo. 15ᵛ] eis reddunt et reddit episcopo xii marcas et Alwine Bierd² habet iiii s. et Peitewinus³ v s. et est de feudo regis.

[70] Goda Hachemus¹ tenet ii terras de feudo regis, sed rex inde nil habet, et ipsa*ᶜ* Goda habet xxxvii s.*ᵈ* et vi d.

[71] Auitia regi vi d. et habet v s.

[72] Abbatissa Wint' regi vi d.¹ et habet de heredibus Radulfi camerarii² vi s. et ipsi habent xvi s.

[73] Girinus pincerna¹ regi vi d. et habet de Rogero de Haia² de istis et de forgiis³ xxv s. et idem Rogerus habet de hac terra nominat*a* xxi s.⁴ Et de istis xxi s. reddit Rogerus Roberto Norreis⁵ iiii s. et Emma habet ibi vi s.

[74] Radulfus Lacchewei¹ regi vi d. et episcopo iii s. de B. et habet xii s. Et de eadem terra reddit Rogerus de

[66] Robert of Inglesham¹ pays the king 6d. and William son of Warin² 10s. and receives from it 17s. And William son of Bos³ receives from it 8s.

[67] Robert the Weasel¹ pays the bishop 5s. *de B.* and receives 11s. from that same royal fief.

[68] Baldwin the baker¹ pays the bishop 15s. *de B.* and receives 12s. And for another land he pays the king 6d. and the bishop 2 lb. of pepper and receives 28s.

[69] Sewi holds a shop/shops where linen cloths are sold.¹ And it/they and the houses (?) yield [. . .]. And he pays the bishop 12 marks [£8]. And Alwin Beard² receives 4s. and Peitevin³ 5s. And it is on the king's fief.

[70] Goda Hack-mouse¹ holds 2 lands on the king's fief, but the king receives nothing from them. Goda receives 37s. 6d.

[71] Avice pays the king 6d. and receives 5s.

[72] The abbess of Winchester pays the king 6d.¹ and receives from Ralf the chamberlain's heirs² 6s. And they receive 16s.

[73] Girin the butler¹ pays the king 6d. and receives from Roger of La Haye² from these lands [*sic*] and from the forges³ 25s. And Roger receives from the said (?) land 21s.⁴ And from these 21s. Roger pays Robert Norreis⁵ 4s. And Emma receives there 6s.

[74] Ralf Lacchewei¹ pays the king 6d. and the bishop 3s. *de B.* and receives 12s. And from that land Roger of

---

ᵃ Martra *over an erasure*   *ᵇ* periperis *MS.*   *ᶜ* ipsam *MS.*   *ᵈ* xxx(vii s.) *over an erasure*

66 1. See **1**.

2. Possibly the son of Warin, sheriff of Dorset and Somerset: *Regesta*, iii, no. 189, cf. pp. xxiv–xxv.

3. See also **99** and **564**. Bernard the king's scribe had a legal dispute over a property in Launceston Castle, Cornwall, with a man named Bos: J. H. Round, *EHR* 14 (1899), 422. William was probably the moneyer of Henry II: see below, Table 45.

67 1. See **9**.

68. 1. See also **998–9**, **1020**, and **1027**.

69 1. This is Chapman's Hall, from which the king received 20 marks a year (usually well in arrears): *Pipe Roll 31 Henry I*, p. 40; *Pipe Roll 2, 3, 4 Henry II*, pp. 52–3, 108, 176. In 1156 Godfrey of Winsor (see **567**) and Wulfwin accounted for an old debt and Godfrey and Alwin Beard for the current year. The descent of this property, later known as the *linea selda* or *la Clothselde*, can be traced through the thirteenth century. When the tenement was granted to the cathedral priory in 1330, the private jurisdiction of the lord of *la Clothselde* over his tenants there, and his rights over the sale of linen cloth, still survived. The property occupied an extensive site

on the W. side of the entry to Middle Brook Street, and included the church of St. Mary *de la Wode*. If any property in Survey I represents Chapman's Hall it is, on topographical grounds, I, 10. See below, pp. 335, 435, and Appendix I. 1 and 2. See also *SMW* 93–100; Furley *City Government*, 77, 181–5; *VCH Hants* i. 531.

2. See also **502**. Possibly a moneyer of Henry I: see below, Table 42.

3. See also **82**.

70. 1. See **18**.

72 1. For this tenement, cf. I, 8.

2. See also **806**, **812**, and **918**. For his widow, see **978**. Ralf witnessed a doubtful Glastonbury charter (1115–27): *Regesta*, ii, p. xv.

73. 1. Not a royal butler.

2. See **38** and below, p. 419.

3. For this tenement, cf. I, 7 and for forges, cf. II, 90 and I, 59, and below, pp. 399–400.

4. There may be some confusion between this property and **90**.

5. See also **659–61**, **672–8**, **710**, and **717**.

74 1. See **47**.

Sagio filio Willelmi de Hoctun'² ii d. et Rad*ulfo* Lacchewei ii d. et habet iiii s.

[75] Tailebroc¹ regi [. . .] et habet vi s. sed calumpniat
istos.*a*

[76] Herebertus prepositus¹ episcopo vi s. de B. et habet
xxxvi s. et viii d.

[77] Rogerus tinctor¹ Hersie filio Warner'*b* ii d. et
habet ii s. et idem Rogerus Hereberto² ii d. et idem*c*
Rogerus abbati³ vi d. et filia eius abbati vii s.

[78] Filia Gupill'¹ tenet i terram de terra Geruasii et
habet de Rogero² iiii d. et ipse Rogerus habet iii s.

[79] Episcopus tenet i terram de feudo regis que debet
reddere regi vi d. et habet i marcam de Tiecia. Et ipsa
habet iii s.

[80] Osmoda¹ tenet i terram de feudo regis et habet
servientes*d* intus et ii bracins.

[81] Edmundus dapifer¹ regi vi d. et abbatisse vi d.

[82] Abbatissa regi vi d. et habet de Peiteuin'¹ xx s. et
Peiteuin regi iii d. et habet xxii s. et de quodam homine
ii s.

[83] Drogo tinctor¹ regi vi d. et Hugoni i marcam et
habet xvii s.

[84] Herebertus palm*arius*¹ tenet i terram quietam de
feudo Iohannis de Port² et reddit ei iii s. et habet ix s.
et vi d.

[85] Raimundus parm*entarius*¹ abbatisse iii s. et habet v s.

[86] Hudo mol*endinarius* episcopo*a* [. . .]

[87] Bernardus faber tenet i terram [fo. 16] quietam de
episcopo et est in calle regis.¹

Sées pays William of Houghton's son² 2d. and Ralf
Lacchewei 2d. and receives 4s.

[75] Tailebroc¹ pays the king [. . .] and receives 6s.
But he disputes that.

[76] Herbert the reeve¹ pays the bishop 6s. *de B.* and
receives 36s. 8d.

[77] Roger the dyer¹ pays Hersie son of Warner 2d.
and receives 2s. And the same Roger pays Herbert²
2d. And the same Roger pays the abbot³ 6d.; and his
daughter pays the abbot 7s.

[78] Gupill's daughter¹ holds 1 land of Gervase's land
and receives from Roger² 4d. And Roger receives 3s.

[79] The bishop holds 1 land of the king's fief which
should pay the king 6d. And he receives 1 mark [13s.
4d.] from Tiecia. She receives 3s.

[80] Osmoth¹ holds 1 land of the king's fief and has
servants within and 2 breweries.

[81] Edmund the steward¹ pays the king 6d. and the
abbess [of Winchester] 6d.

[82] The abbess pays the king 6d. and receives from
Peitevin¹ 20s. Peitevin pays the king 3d. and receives
22s. and from a certain man 2s.

[83] Drew the dyer¹ pays the king 6d. and Hugh 1 mark
[13s. 4d.], and receives 17s.

[84] Herbert the palmer¹ holds 1 land quit of the fief
of John de Port.² He pays him 3s. and receives 9s. 6d.

[85] Raymond the tailor¹ pays the abbess 3s. and receives 5s.

[86] Hudo the miller pays the bishop [. . .].

[87] Bernard the blacksmith holds 1 land quit of the
bishop. It is on the king's road.¹

---

a *Marked with a cross in the margin* (? *because defective*)
d senuientes *MS.*

b (War)ner' *over an erasure*   *c* idem *over an erasure*

74 2. For his father, see **838** and **I, 196**.
75 1. See also **470**, **608**, and **651**.
76 1. See also **77** and **157**. Between 1155 and 1180–2
Herbert granted 5s. rent in Winchester to Godstow
Nunnery: Godstow Cart. fos. 163, 164, 165.
77 1. See **52**.
  2. Cf. **76**.
  3. For this Hyde Abbey property, cf. **I, 69** and **71–3**.
78 1. Cf. **740**.
  2. Cf. **52**.

80 1. Cf. **160**, **372**, **404**, **433**, **666**, **894**, and **970**.
81 1. See also **723**.
82 1. See **69**.
83 1. See also **653**.
84 1. See also **720**.
  2. For John, see entry **2**. It is not clear how Herbert
holds the land quit if he pays 3s. rent.
85 1. See **40**.
87 1. See also **17**, n. 2.

[88] Stigandus¹ regi vi d. et est in calle regis.²

[89] Stephanus Mucheto¹ regi vi d. quamdiu iusticia episcopi voluerit.²

[90] Rogerus de Haia¹ tenet [. . .] forgias² in feudo regis de Girino et habet xxi s.³

[91] Oinus*a* ten*uit* i terram de iii s. de B. Modo tenet Rogerus de Haia¹ et est vasta.

[92] Pag*anus* pic'¹ episcopo vi s. de B. et habet x s. et vi d.

[93] Baldewinus episcopo xii d. et habet v s.

[94] Barill' et Anschetillus episcopo viii d.

[95] Godefridus filius Willelmi¹ tenet i terram de feudo regis et habet xv s.

[96] Girinus regi vi d. pro Roberto mac*one* et habet x s.

[97] Anschetillus regi vi d. et priori vi s. et ii d.

[98] Siluester regi vi d. et habet iiii s. et sunt in calle regis.¹

[99] Willelmus filius Bos¹ regi vi d. et habet iii s.

[100] Brifald regi vi d.

[101] Gaufridus¹ regi vi d.

[102] Ailwinus faber regi vi d.

[103] Uxor Nicholai¹ regi vi d. et habet xviii s.

[104] Rogerus de Haia¹ regi vi d. et habet vi s.

[88] Stigand¹ pays the king 6d. It is on the king's road.²

[89] Stephen Mucheto¹ pays the king 6d. for as long as the bishop's justiciar shall allow.²

[90] Roger of La Haye¹ holds [. . .] forges² on the king's fief from Girin and receives 21s.³

[91] Oin held [?] 1 land worth 3s. de B. Now Roger of La Haye¹ holds it and it is waste.

[92] Pain [son of] Picard¹ pays the bishop 6s. de B. and receives 10s. 6d.

[93] Baldwin pays the bishop 12d. and receives 5s.

[94] Barill and Anschetil pay the bishop 8d.

[95] Godfrey son of William¹ holds 1 land of the king's fief and receives 15s.

[96] Girin pays the king 6d. for Robert the mason and receives 10s.

[97] Anschetil pays the king 6d. and the prior 6s. 2d.

[98] Silvester pays the king 6d. and receives 4s. And they are [sic] on the king's road.¹

[99] William son of Bos¹ pays the king 6d. and receives 3s.

[100] Brifald pays the king 6d.

[101] Geoffrey¹ pays the king 6d.

[102] Ailwin the blacksmith pays the king 6d.

[103] Nicholas's wife¹ pays the king 6d. and receives 18s.

[104] Roger of La Haye¹ pays the king 6d. and receives 6s.

a O *over an erasure*

88 1. A Stigand was farming the city in 2 and 3 Henry II: *Pipe Roll 2* and *3 Henry II*, pp. 52, 107. He was probably the reeve (*prepositus*) of Winchester who issued a writ acknowledging a mid-twelfth-century conveyance: see 111, n. 2. He was dead by 1159 when his son Gervase rendered account for his debt: *Pipe Roll 5 Henry II*, p. 46. This property lay in an area associated with moneying and a Stigand was a Winchester moneyer late in the reign of Henry I: see below, Tables 41 and 42. In *c.* 1110 a Stigand held property in *Calpestret* which also had moneying connections: see below, Table 39. If the Stigand who held property in *c.* 1110, the moneyer, and the reeve were one man, he would have been aged at least 70 at the time of his death.
  2. See also 17, n. 2.

89 1. Perhaps the moneyer of Stephen, see Table 44 and cf. 644 and 865.
  2. Cf. 665, and see below, pp. 328 and 425.
90 1. See 38.   2. See 73, n. 3.   3. Cf. 73.
91 1. See 38.
92 1. See 21.
95 1. See 5.
98 1. See 106, n. 1, and also 17, n. 2.
99 1. See 66. William was probably the moneyer of Henry II. For the moneying connections of the area, see below, Table 45.
101 1. Probably the moneyer of Stephen: see below, Table 44.
103 1. See also 880.
104 1. See 38.

[105] Trauetier regi vi d. et est in calle regis.¹

[106] Mactilda regi pro calle regis¹ vi d. et habet ii s.

[107] Godwinus regi vi d.

[108] Sitcelane¹ regi vi d.

[109] Herdi[n]g' brachia*tor*¹ regi vi d.

[110] Ricardus Pinguis regi vi d.

[111] Cano[ni]ci de Sancto Dionisio¹ regi vi d. et habent de Osberto² viii s. et Osbertus habet xii s.

[112] Siwardus monetarius¹ regi vi d. et episcopo xv s. et iii d. de B. et vii s. et Ertur'ᵃ² habet viii s.

[113] Bernardus episcopo ii s. de B. et habet x s.

[114] Turoldus carnifex episcopo v sol. de B.

[115] Radulfus auri*faber* episcopo v s. de B.

[116] Seman' episcopo v s. de B.

[117] Hereman' episcopo vi s. de B.

[118] Sanson monetarius¹ episcopo iii sol. de B.

[119] Pupelina episcopo iiii s. de B. et habet iiii s.

[120] [fo. 16ᵛ] Willelmus pinctor episcopo ii s. de B. et habet x s.

[121] Willelmus filius Herberti¹ episcopo iii s. de B.

[122] Radulfus de Oili¹ episcopo iii s. de B.

ᵃ Ercur' *MS*.

[105] Travetier pays the king 6*d*. and it is on the king's road.¹

[106] Matilda pays the king for the king's road¹ 6*d*. and receives 2*s*.

[107] Godwin pays the king 6*d*.

[108] Sitcelane¹ pays the king 6*d*.

[109] Harding the brewer¹ pays the king 6*d*.

[110] Richard the Fat pays the king 6*d*.

[111] The canons of St. Denis¹ pay the king 6*d*. and receive from Osbert² 8*s*. Osbert receives 12*s*.

[112] Siward the moneyer¹ pays the king 6*d*. and the bishop 15*s*. 3*d*. *de B*. and 7*s*. And Arthur² receives 8*s*.

[113] Bernard pays the bishop 2*s*. *de B*. and receives 10*s*.

[114] Turold the butcher pays the bishop 5*s*. *de B*.

[115] Ralf the goldsmith pays the bishop 5*s*. *de B*.

[116] Seaman pays the bishop 5*s*. *de B*.

[117] Herman pays the bishop 6*s*. *de B*.

[118] Samson the moneyer¹ pays the bishop 3*s*. *de B*.

[119] Popelin pays the bishop 4*s*. *de B*. and receives 4*s*.

[120] William the painter pays the bishop 2*s*. *de B*. and receives 10*s*.

[121] William son of Herbert¹ pays the bishop 3*s*. *de B*.

[122] Ralf d'Oilli [Ouilly]¹ pays the bishop 3*s*. *de B*.

105 1. See 106, n. 1, and also 17, n. 2.
106 1. The encroachments of this entry, and of 98 and 105, may be identical with some of those recorded in Survey I near *Thomeseiete*, cf. I, 59, 64, and 65, and also II, 111. See also 17, n. 2.
108 1. See below, p. 172. This property lay towards the E. end of High Street, where there were streams.
109 1. See also 379.
111 1. See also 203, 420, 607, and 617. A house of Augustinian canons at Southampton founded *c*. 1127: *VCH Hants* ii. 160–4. This property was probably near *Thomeseiete*, and may be identified with I, 65.
　2. Probably the moneyer of Henry II, especially in view of the location of the property: see below, p. 419 and Table 45. The property may have been the one referred to in the writ which Stigand the reeve of Winchester (see 88, n. 1) addressed to the citizens, acknowledging that

William son of Rikefemme (cf. 181) had released to the canons of St. Denis by Southampton his claim in the land which Osbert *cerearius* held from the canons of the fief of Robert *Unnellus*: St. Denis Cart, fo. 124. The evidence of the writ suggests that the Osbert *cerarius* of 828 (and presumably 888) was identical with the Osbert of this entry.
112 1. See also 511–12. A Winchester moneyer under Stephen: *English Coins*, 90; see below, p. 416 and Table 43.
　2. See also 767.
118 1 See 64.
121 1. See also 618. Probably not the king's and Bishop Henry's nephew who was appointed archbishop of York in 1141. But their nephew Hugh of Le Puiset, who was associated with William, occurs in 494.
122 1. See 25.

[123] Robertus de Hungerford[1] episcopo iii s. de B. et habet iiii s.[a]

[124] Radulfus filius Suarling' episcopo iii s. de B.

[125] Radulfus filius Ulfi episcopo iii s. de B.

[126] Uxor Sauar' episcopo iii s. de B.

[127] Robertus de Ingl'[1] tenet i terram quietam de feudo regis et habet l s.

[128] Gaufridus burgensis[1] tenet i terram que fuit Alwini camerarii[2] quietam et reddit Sansoni[3] xlix s. et iiii d. et habet c s. et x s. et viii d.

[129] Et idem Sanson[1] reddit episcopo iiii s. de B. et habet xx s.

[130] Filius Fareman[1] episcopo xv s. de B. et habet xii s.

[131] Serlo et Gilebertus episcopo x s. de B.

[132] Edgaresune[1] episcopo v s. de B. et habet v s.

[133] Henricus pictor episcopo xviii d. de B.

[134] Robertus taleator[1] episcopo xviii d. de B.

[135] Ernoldus frater Petri[1] episcopo xvi s. de B. et habet xi s.

[136] Petrus merciarius[1] episcopo ii s. de B. et habet xiiii s.

[137] Bartholomeus episcopo vii s. de B. et habet ix s.

[138] Iohannes de Port[1] regi vi d. et Radulfus de Port[2] habet xl s. et Ernoldus[3] habet xxvi s.

[123] Robert of Hungerford[1] pays the bishop 3s. de B. and receives 4s.

[124] Ralf, Swartling's son, pays the bishop 3s. de B.

[125] Ralf, Ulf's son, pays the bishop 3s. de B.

[126] Savaric's wife pays the bishop 3s. de B.

[127] Robert of Inglesham[1] holds 1 land quit of the king's fief and receives 50s.

[128] Geoffrey the burgess[1] holds 1 land, which used to be Alwin the chamberlain's,[2] quit. And he pays Samson[3] 49s. 4d. and receives 110s. 8d.

[129] And the same Samson[1] pays the bishop 4s. de B. and receives 20s.

[130] Farman's son[1] pays the bishop 15s. de B. and receives 12s.

[131] Serlo and Gilbert pay the bishop 10s. de B.

[132] Edgar's son[1] pays the bishop 5s. de B. and receives 5s.

[133] Henry the painter pays the bishop 18d. de B.

[134] Robert the tailor/tally-cutter[1] pays the bishop 18d. de B.

[135] Ernold, Peter's brother,[1] pays the bishop 16s. de B. and receives 11s.

[136] Peter the mercer[1] pays the bishop 2s. de B. and receives 14s.

[137] Bartholomew pays the bishop 7s. de B. and receives 9s.

[138] John de Port[1] pays the king 6d. and Ralf de Port[2] receives 40s. and Ernold[3] receives 26s.

[a] iii *altered to* iiii

123 1. See also 738.
127 1. See 1.
128 1. Cf. I, 271. See also 139, n. 2.
  2. Probably Aldwin, Queen Matilda's chamberlain: *Regesta*, ii, p. xiv. An Ailwine was a moneyer of Henry I: see below, Table 42.
  3. Cf. 64.
129 1. Cf. 64.
130 1. See I, 185.
132 1. Cf. 38.
134 1. Round thought that he, like Gilbert (682), took his name from the exchequer tallies: *VCH Hants* i. 536.

135 1. Peter the mercer's brother: see 35.
136 1. See 35.
138 1. See 2.
  2. See also 473. Cf. 2.
  3. See 135. In his charter of 1189–96, Henry Husey III confirmed to the abbey of Durford the grant by his wife Clemencia, from her dowry, of the tenement which *Ernaldus le Burguin' tenuit de feodo Johannis de Port patris sui* in Winchester High Street. This is the only property in which John and Ernold occur together (cf. 473, where Ralf de Port is associated with Ernold the priest): BM, Cotton MS. Vesp. E. xxxii, fo. 8ᵛ; H. M. Colvin, *The White Canons in England* (Oxford, 1951), 88, 89.

[139] Uxor Martini¹ tenet de feudo comitis Glec'² et habet lxvii s. et vi d. de Ricardo et de Hugone et Ricardus habet x s.

[140] Iohannes filius Radulfi¹ episcopo vii s. de B. pro gihald*a*.²

[141] Uxor Edrici vinet*arii*¹ episcopo ii s.

[142] Rogerus palm*arius* episcopo viii s.

[143] Atscelina*a* episcopo viii s. et ipse Iohannes filius Radulfi¹ habet de gihald*a*¹ x s.

[144] Soror Martini¹ episcopo iii s.

[145] Uxor Edrici¹ episcopo xiii s.

[146] Fulco episcopo x s.

[147] Osbertus episcopo x s.

[148] Iohannes episcopo pro i selda x s.

[149] Drogo episcopo x s. de B.

[150] Filia Henrici¹ episcopo xv s. et monacis xxx s. et habet xxxvi s.

[151] Petrus Tresor¹ episcopo xvi s. et habet xv s.

De soliis desuper*b*¹

[152] Clemens Treisor episcopo v s. et viii d. et obolum.

[153] [fo. 17] Guncelinus¹ episcopo v s. et viii d. et obolum et habet xi s.

---

[139] Martin's wife¹ holds of the fief of the earl of Gloucester² and receives 67s. 6d. from Richard and Hugh, and Richard receives 10s.

[140] John son of Ralf¹ pays the bishop 7s. *de B*. for the guildhall.²

[141] Edric the vintner's wife¹ pays the bishop 2s.

[142] Roger the palmer pays the bishop 8s.

[143] Atscelina pays the bishop 8s., and that same John son of Ralf¹ receives from the guildhall¹ 10s.

[144] Martin's sister¹ pays the bishop 3s.

[145] Edric's wife¹ pays the bishop 13s.

[146] Fulk pays the bishop 10s.

[147] Osbert pays the bishop 10s.

[148] John pays the bishop 10s. for 1 shop.

[149] Drew pays the bishop 10s. *de B*.

[150] Henry's daughter¹ pays the bishop 15s. and the monks 30s. and receives 36s.

[151] Peter Tresor¹ pays the bishop 16s. and receives 15s.

From the solars above¹

[152] Clement Treisor pays the bishop 5s. 8½d.

[153] Guncelin¹ pays the bishop 5s. 8½d. and receives 11s.

---

a Erased stroke over t   *b* Given as an ordinary item. Ellis takes it as completing [151], but it is probably the heading for [152–8]

139. 1. See **17**.

2. Robert, earl of Gloucester, died in 1147. This property was probably associated with the land next to the house of Thomas Oysun, on the S. side of High Street, which William, earl of Gloucester, granted to the canons of Keynsham between 1166/7 and 1183. *Galfridus burgeus* (or *burgensis*) (cf. **128**) had held this land from Earl Robert and a rent of 20s. a year was due to the earl: Robert B. Patterson (ed.), *The Earldom of Gloucester Charters: the Charters and Scribes of the Earls and Countesses of Gloucester to A.D. 1217* (Oxford, 1973), no. 103. For Thomas Oysun's knowledge of Sparsholt before 1172, see *Curia Regis Rolls 1203–5*, p. 118, and for his mayoralty and family, see entry **40**, n. 2. For the earl of Gloucester's other property in Winchester, see entry **475** and below, p. 398 and cf. p. 299, n. 4. In 1130 the earl was pardoned £5. 16s. 8d. of the city's aid, *Pipe Roll 31 Henry I*, p. 41. **140** 1. See also **143, 155**, and ?**159**. He and Gervase (of Cornhill) accounted as sheriffs for London in 1158 and were probably both responsible for the farm of London before King Stephen's death: *Pipe Roll 2 Henry II*,

p. 3, *4 Henry II*, p. 111, and *7 Henry II*, p. 17. He witnessed a charter of Stephen in 1149–52: *Regesta*, iii, no. 938. After 1168 there was a reeve of Winchester of this name: J. G. Jenkins (ed.), *The Cartulary of Missenden Abbey*, iii (HMC, JP1, 1962), no. 703.

2. See also **143** and **155**. These references are probably all to the same guildhall, perhaps the guildhall on the S. side of High Street, just W. of the church of St. Laurence, where the city court met in a hall on the first floor until 1361: see p. 336 below and *SMW* 186.

141 1. See also **145**.

143 1. See **140**.

144 1. See **17**.

145. 1. See **141**.

150. 1. Henry's daughter Matilda occurs in entry **815**.

151 1. Perhaps the same as the Peter *thesaurus* who held a stone house in *Brudenestret* in c. 1170–80 (St. Denis Cart, fo. 122).

151–2 1. Items **152–8** with rents of 5s. 8½d. represent as nearly as possible the division of 40s. by 7.

153 1. See **29**.

[154] Iohannes nepos Petri[1] episcopo v s.[a] et viii d. et obolum.

[154] John, Peter's nephew,[1] pays the bishop 5s. 8½d.

[155] Item Iohannes filius Radulfi[1] episcopo v s. et viii d. et obolum et habet [de] gihalla[1] xxviii s.

[155] Again John son of Ralf[1] pays the bishop 5s. 8½d. and receives from the guildhall[1] 28s.

[156] Reginaldus de Sagio[1] episcopo v s. et viii d. et obolum.

[156] Reginald of Sées[1] pays the bishop 5s. 8½d.

[157] Herebertus prepositus[1] episcopo v s. et viii d. et obolum.

[157] Herbert the reeve[1] pays the bishop 5s. 8½d.

[158] Conanus episcopo v s. et viii d. et obolum.

[158] Conan pays the bishop 5s. 8½d.

[159] Episcopus regi vi d. et habet de Iohanne x s.

[159] The bishop pays the king 6d. and receives from John 10s.

[160] Osmoda[1] episcopo i marcam[2] de B. et habet xx s.

[160] Osmoth[1] pays the bishop 1 mark[2] [13s. 4d.] de B. and receives 20s.

[161] Alexander episcopo i marcam de B. et habet i marcam.

[161] Alexander pays the bishop 1 mark de B. and receives 1 mark.

[162] Selida episcopo i marcam de B.

[162] Selida pays the bishop 1 mark de B.

[163] Ebrardus[1] episcopo i marcam.

[163] Ebrard[1] pays the bishop 1 mark.

[164] Hugo Hacchemus[1] episcopo dimidiam marcam.

[164] Hugh Hack-mouse[1] pays the bishop ½ mark.

[165] Godefridus de ii seldis episcopo i marcam.

[165] Godfrey pays the bishop for 2 shops 1 mark.

[166] Ebrardus[1] et Brictwinus episcopo dimidiam marcam.

[166] Ebrard[1] and Brictwin pay the bishop ½ mark.

[167] Heredes Hugonis Guncel'[1] regi vi d. et Willelmo clerico[2] xxx s. et habent xviii s.

[167] Hugh Guncelin's heirs[1] pay the king 6d. and William the clerk[2] 30s. and receive 18s.

[168] Episcopus regi vi d. de B. et habet de Godehald[1] ii marcas et Godehald habet xxviii s.

[168] The bishop pays the king 6d. de B. and receives from Godehald[1] 2 marks, and Godehald receives 28s.

[169] Godehald[1] episcopo xx s. et habet xv s.

[169] Godehald[1] pays the bishop 20s. and receives 15s.

[170] Conanus episcopo i marcam et habet xix s.

[170] Conan pays the bishop 1 mark and receives 19s.

---

[a] episcopo v s. *over an erased sum of money*

154 1. See **34**.
155 1. See **140**.
156 1. See also **186, 226, 228, 411, 417, 440**, and **621**. See Addenda.
157 1. See **76**.
160 1. Cf. **80**.
  2. The sudden introduction of marks, and the fact that entries **160–6** add up to 6 marks, and, with entries **168** and **170**, to 9 marks, must have some significance. The royal property known as the Old Mint or Drapery, which had once been part of the royal palace, was valued at 9 marks in the thirteenth century. It lay on the High Street frontage: see below, Appendix II. But the survey seems here to be dealing with properties well to the W. of the palace site, so that the 9 marks probably have

some other meaning.
163 1. Cf. **166**.
164 1. See **18**.
166 1. Cf. **163**.
167 1. See **29**.
  2. See also **286** and **1084**. There was a William, clerk of Henry of Blois, bishop of Winchester (Goodman *Chartulary*, nos. 14 and 453), possibly identical with William, clerk of the hospital (? St. Cross): Lena Voss, *Heinrich von Blois* (Berlin, 1932), 175. Before 1162–3 a William the clerk witnessed a conveyance of **508**: Southwick Cart iii, fo. 134.
168 1. See also **169**, and cf. **856, 873**, and **1057**.
169 1. See **168**.

[171] Et ibi iuxta est quedam terra vacua de feudo Willelmi Pont'.[1]

[171] And next is a vacant land of the fief of William Pont.[1]

[172] Drogo tenet i terram quietam de Hugone filio Cheppingi[1] et habet li s. et iiii d.

[172] Drew holds 1 land quit of Hugh son of Chepping[1] and receives 51s. 4d.

[173] Robertus Wint' reddit regi xii d. de ii terris et habet xxiiii s.

[173] Robert of Winchester pays the king 12d. for 2 lands and receives 24s.

[174] Godefridus filius Willelmi[1] regi vi d. et habet iiii s.

[174] Godfrey son of William[1] pays the king 6d. and receives 4s.

[175] Henricus de Traci[1] tenet i terram de feudo regis et deberet[a] rex habere vi d., et habet viii s. et iiii d.

[175] Henry de Tracy[1] holds 1 land of the king's fief and the king should have received 6d.; and [Henry] receives 8s. 4d.

[176] Fulco regi vi d. et Anschetillo x s. et habet iii s.

[176] Fulk pays the king 6d. and Anschetil 10s. and receives 3s.

EXTRA PORTAM DE WEST

[177] Robertus faber[1] tenet i terram de feudo regis unde reddit regi iiii d.

OUTSIDE WEST GATE

[177] Robert the blacksmith[1] holds 1 land of the king's fief for which he pays the king 4d.

[178] Robertus Rust [tenet] i terram unde reddit regi ii d. et monachis de Lira[1] iiii s.

[178] Robert Rust [holds] 1 land from which he pays the king 2d. and the monks of Lyre[1] 4s.

[179] Conannus filius Guncel'[1] regi ii d. et hisdem monachis[2] iiii s., et Willelmus faber[3] reddit inde Conano viii s.

[179] Conan son of Guncelin[1] pays the king 2d. and the same monks[2] 4s.; and from the land William the blacksmith[3] pays Conan 8s.

[180] Filii Hugonis filii Guntsel'[1] regi [fo. 17[v]] ii [d.] et episcopo x d., et Ricardus le Meddere manet ibi et reddit eis xii s., et Sunabella tenet inde i seldam et reddit eisdem v s.

[180] The sons of Hugh son of Guncelin[1] pay the king 2d. and the bishop 10d. Richard the mead-seller lives there and pays them 12s. And Sunabella keeps 1 shop on the land and pays them 5s.

[181] Willelmus filius Richefemme[1] episcopo v d. et habet inde xxi s.

[181] William son of Richefemme[1] pays the bishop 5d. and receives from the land 21s.

[182] Ricardus fundor[1] episcopo xiii d. et habet xviii s. et viii d.

[182] Richard the fusour[1] pays the bishop 13d. and receives 18s. 8d.

---

[a] et deb'et MS., the Tironian sign for the second et over an erasure

171 1. Probably Pont de l'Arche: see I, Preface and 259. For this tenement, cf. I, 49.
172 1. See 23. For possible earlier moneyers' interests in this property, cf. I, 41–2, and see below, p. 409 and Table 44.
174 1. See 5.
175 1. See also 258. Married a sister and co-heiress of Alfred of Totnes, and was succeeded in his barony of Barnstaple before 1165 by their son Oliver: Sanders Baronies, 104.
177 1. See also 220.
178 1. See also 179. Benedictine monastery founded c. 1046 in arr. and diocese of Évreux by William fitzOsbern, lord of Breteuil and later of the Isle of Wight, and earl of Hereford. It was subordinated to the abbey of St. Évroul. FitzOsbern's grant of English lands to Lyre in 1070

included in ipsa civitate (Winchester) duos burgenses. In 1257 the abbey owned in suburbio Wynton' duo burgagia: C. Guéry, Histoire de l'abbaye de Lyre (Évreux, 1917), 16, 17, 568; BM, Egerton MS. 3667, fos. 25, 79[v].
179 1. See 29.
     2. See 178.
     3. See also 769, and for his wife 253.
180 1. See 29.
181 1. See also 111, n. 2.
182 1. See also 229, 231, and 255. Probably the fusor (fusour) of the Exchequer. See Pipe Roll 3 Henry II, p. 104: 'Et Ricardo fundori 46s. 8d. ad negocia scaccarii'. Richard fusor owed 10 marks of the city's aid in 1164–5: Pipe Roll 15 Henry II, p. 158. For the Exchequer melter (fusor), see Dialogus de Scaccario, 36–8. A Richard Fusor was a citizen of Winchester in 1207, Fine R 452.

[183] Uxor Hugonis filii Guncel'¹ episcopo viii d. et habet inde x d.

[183] Hugh son of Guncelin's wife¹ pays the bishop 8d. and receives from the land 10d.

[184] Picot sannarius¹ episcopo iiii d. et habet viii s. et viii d.

[184] Picot the salt-boiler¹ pays the bishop 4d. and receives 8s. 8d.

[185] Drogoᵃ Blundus¹ episcopo ii s. et habet inde vii s. et vi d.

[185] Drew Blond¹ pays the bishop 2s. and receives from the land 7s. 6d.

[186] Reginaldusᵇ de Sagio¹ de terra i vasta episcopo iiii d. et nil inde capit.

[186] Reginald of Sées¹ pays the bishop 4d. for 1 waste land and gets nothing from it.

[187] Alanus scutarius deberet reddere episcopo iiii s.

[187] Alan the shield-wright should have paid the bishop 4s.

[188] Willelmus Bruwere¹ tenet i terram que fuit Pagani et reddit filio Pagani iii s. et ix d.ᶜ

[188] William Brewer¹ holds 1 land which used to be Pain's, and he pays Pain's son 3s. 9d.

[189] Alexander filius Gollan'¹ episcopo viii d. et habet inde v s. et viii d.

[189] Alexander son of Goislan¹ pays the bishop 8d. and receives from the land 5s. 8d.

[190] Turoldus pr' episcopo iiii d. etᵈ habet de Hereuic' parmentario iiii s. et ipse Hereuic' habet inde xxxii d.

[190] Turold the priest (?) pays the bishop 4d. and receives from Herevic the tailor 4s., and Herevic receives from the land 32d.

[191] Godefridus cornem' episcopo v d. et manet ibi.¹

[191] Godfrey the corn-monger pays the bishop 5d. and lives there.¹

[192] Henricus Gladewin'¹ episcopo v d. et habet inde ii s.

[192] Henry Gladwin¹ pays the bishop 5d. and receives from the land 2s.

[193] Ansgier' de Diua episcopo xii d. et habet inde xi d. et curtilla sua.

[193] Ansgar of Dives pays the bishop 12d. and receives from the land 11d. and [the profits of (?)] his curtilages.

[194] Morell' paginan' episcopo xiiii d. et habet inde ex una parte xviii d. et ex alia ix d. Et item de alia xiiii d. et de Warin' Rusmangre viii d. et obolum.

[194] Morel Paignon (?) pays the bishop 14d. and receives from one part of the land 18d. and from the other 9d. And again from the other part he receives 14d. and from Warin Rush-monger 8½d.

[195] Willelmus de Rotomag' episcopo iii d. et obolum et habet inde xix d.

[195] William of Rouen pays the bishop 3½d. and receives from the land 19d.

[196] Alexander homo Godefridi episcopo iii d. et obolum et habet inde xii d.

[196] Alexander, Godfrey's vassal, pays the bishop 3½d. and receives from the land 12d.

[197] Stigandus filius Goscelini priori v d. et habet inde xxi d. et managium¹ suum quietum.

[197] Stigand son of Goscelin pays the prior 5d. and receives from the land 21d. and has his dwelling-house (?)¹ quit.

ᵃ Erasure after Drogo   ᵇ Suspension mark over g erased   ᶜ Followed by a blank line   ᵈ et repeated

183 1. See 29.
184 1. See also 644.
185 1. See also 381, 635, 899, and 905.
186 1. See 156.
188 1. See also 199. He was probably an ancestor of William Brewer the justiciar who died in 1226, since this property appears to have been in *Wodestret* where the later Brewer was a landowner: St. Denis Cart. fo. 119ᵛ; *SMW*; *DNB* vi. 297.

189 1. See also 209.
191 1. This is to explain why he draws no rent. It is an exception which may prove the rule.
192 1. See also 289.
197 1. The meaning of *managium* is not clear: perhaps it is not constant. For other occurrences, see 230, 245, 250, 293, 403, 421, 465, and 806. The expressions in Survey I concerning *estagium* can be compared: see I, 12.

[198] Willelmus de Corbulio priori iiii d.

[199] Willelmus Briwere[1] priori [. . .]*a* et habet inde xii s.

[200] Petrus mer*ciarius*[1] regi ii d. et habet inde vi s.

[201] Aluricus gener Henrici regi ii d.

[202] Walterus Martre tenet i terram de rege et habet v s. et nichil inde reddit.

[203] *b*Turstinus acularius[1] canonicis de Sancto Dionisio[2] xxxii d. et habet inde vi s. et vi d.

[204] *b*Turstinus de Aisel'[1] [tenet] ii mans*iones*[c] et habet inde xvi d. de langabulo.

[205] [fo. 18] *b*Crabeleg[c1] habet de renta xxxvii d. de terra Walteri filii Ricardi[2] et reddit Turstino de Aisel'[3] iiii d.

[206] Iuelot regi iiii d. et habet xxvii d.

[207] Uxor Ingulf[i] Long'[1] regi iiii d. et habet inde xii d.

[208] Robertus Mieta regi iiii d. et habet inde ii d. de Ansch*etillo* serviente*d* episcopi[1] et Ansch*etillus* habet inde xii s.

[209] Alexander Goisl'[1] regi de iii mans*ionibus* viii d. et habet inde v s. et x d.

[210] Petrus mer*ciarius*[1] regi ii d. et habet inde vi s.

[211] Walterus Meroie regi ii d. et episcopo ii s. de terra baronum.[1]

[212] Uxor Ingulfi[1] regi iiii d.

[213] Willelmus Pinguis[1] regi vi d.*e* et episcopo ii s. de terra baronum et ipse habet inde vi s. et vi d.

[198] William of Corbeil pays the prior 4*d*.

[199] William Brewer[1] pays the prior [. . .] and receives from the land 12*s*.

[200] Peter the mercer[1] pays the king 2*d*. and receives from the land 6*s*.

[201] Aluric, Henry's son-in-law, pays the king 2*d*.

[202] Walter the Weasel holds 1 land of the king and receives 5*s*. and pays nothing for it.

[203] Thurstin the needle-maker[1] pays the canons of St. Denis[2] 32*d*. and receives from the land 6*s*. 6*d*.

[204] Thurstin of Ashley[1] holds 2 messuages and receives from them 16*d*. landgable.

[205] Crableg[1] receives 37*d*. of rent from the land of Walter son of Richard[2] and pays Thurstin of Ashley[3] 4*d*.

[206] Ivelot pays the king 4*d*. and receives 27*d*.

[207] Ingulf Long's wife[1] pays the king 4*d*. and receives from the land 12*d*.

[208] Robert Miete pays the king 4*d*. and from the land receives 2*d*. from Anschetil, the bishop's servant;[1] and Anschetil receives from it 12*s*.

[209] Alexander Goislan[1] pays the king for 3 messuages 8*d*. and receives from them 5*s*. 10*d*.

[210] Peter the mercer[1] pays the king 2*d*. and receives from the land 6*s*.

[211] Walter Meroie pays the king 2*d*. and the bishop 2*s*. from the land of the barons.[1]

[212] Ingulf's wife[1] pays the king 4*d*.

[213] William the Fat[1] pays the king 6*d*. and the bishop 2*s*. from the land of the barons. And he himself receives from it 6*s*. 6*d*.

---

a Space left for amount   *b [203], [204], and [205] erased and rewritten, the original position being shown by the initial C of [205] for rubricator, in margin opposite line 2 of [204], at the bottom of fo. 17[v], col. b*   *c Followed by a space*   *d* seruientem *MS.*   *e* vi *over an erasure*

199 1. See **188**.
200 1. See **35**.
203 1. See **24**.
  2. See **111**.
204 1. See also **205**.
205 1. See also **520**.
  2. See also **559** and **562**. Possibly Walter fitzRichard, lord of Clare, Suffolk, who died childless in 1138. His lands passed to his nephew Gilbert fitzGilbert de Clare,

who was created earl of Pembroke in that year: Sanders *Baronies*, 111; *DNB* x. 375.   3. See **204**.
207 1. See also **212**.
208 1. See also **442**.
209 1. See **189**.
210 1. See **35**.
211 1. For this phrase, see above, pp. 19–25.
212 1. See **207**.
213 1. See also **422** and **849**.

[214] Alwinus lignator[1] episcopo iiii s. de terra baronum.

[214] Alwin the wood-cutter[1] pays the bishop 4s. from the land of the barons.

[215] Spiring[1] regi xii d. et episcopo vi s. et vi d. de terra baronum et habet inde xvi s.

[215] Spiring[1] pays the king 12d. and the bishop 6s. 6d. from the land of the barons and receives from it 16s.

[216] Fugel episcopo ii s. de terra baronum.

[216] Fugel pays the bishop 2s. from the land of the barons.

[217] Selida batar' episcopo v s. de terra baronum et habet vi s. et ix d.

[217] Selida the coppersmith(?) pays the bishop 5s. from the land of the barons and receives 6s. 9d.

[218] Willelmus lorimer[1] episcopo vi s. de terra baronum.

[218] William the lorimer[1] pays the bishop 6s. from the land of the barons.

[219] Terri Trauet' regi ii d. et episcopo vi s. de terra baronum et ipse habet inde iiii s.

[219] Terry Travetier pays the king 2d. and the bishop 6s. from the land of the barons. And he himself receives from it 4s.

[220] Hereuic' clericus[1] regi ii d. et [episcopo] ii s. de terra baronum et habet inde iiii s. de Roberto fabro[2] et Robertus habet inde xlii d.

[220] Herewic the clerk[1] pays the king 2d. and [the bishop] 2s. from the land of the barons. And from it he receives 4s. from Robert the blacksmith.[2] And Robert receives from it 42d.

[221] Turstinus clericus[1] regi iiii d. et habet xii s. de Rogero Macher' et Macher'[a] habet inde xl d. et de eadem terra habet Willelmus archidiaconus[2] ii s.

[221] Thurstin the clerk[1] pays the king 4d. and receives 12s. from Roger Macher. And Macher receives from the land 40d. and from the same land William the archdeacon[2] receives 2s.

[222] Willelmus archidiaconus[1] reddit regi de i terra iiii d. et de alia terra iiii d. et de tercia terra iiii d. et habet inde vii s. et reddit abbati de Hida v s.

[222] William the archdeacon[1] pays the king for 1 land 4d., and for another land 4d., and for a third land 4d. And he receives from it/them 7s. and pays the abbot of Hyde 5s.

[223] Iueta[1] Roberto filio Hunfridi[2] v d. et habet in[de] iiii s. de terra baronum.

[223] Iveta[1] pays Robert son of Humphrey[2] 5d. and from the land receives 4s. from the land of the barons.

[224] Ricardus Niger[1] episcopo x d. de terra baronum et habet inde v s.

[224] Richard Black[1] pays the bishop 10d. from the land of the barons and receives from it 5s.

[225] Rucche regi iiii d. et episcopo v s. de terra baronum.

[225] Ruche pays the king 4d. and the bishop 5s. from the land of the barons.

---

[a] Ma(cher) over an erasure

214 1. This property was probably in the street known in the thirteenth century as *Wodestret*: see below, pp. 235, 246–7, and 433–4.
215 1. Cf. 927.
218 1. In 1158 he was paid 40s. for harness supplied to the king: *Pipe Roll 4 Henry II*, p. 175.
220 1. See 31.
2. See 177. This may mean that the property was near, probably opposite, 177.
221 1. See also 385, 493–4, 496, 510–11, 572, 673, 696, 701, ?707, 749, and 785; cf. I, 180. He was excused 12s. of the city's aid in 1130 and was the clerk of William of Pont de l'Arche, the king's chamberlain (cf. I, Preface, n. 5). He held Faringdon and Popham in Hants, and was the ancestor of the Popham family:

Regesta, ii, no. 1872, and iii, no. 897. He was sheriff of Hants in 1155–9 and was succeeded in the office by his son, Richard: *Pipe Roll 2, 3,* and *4 Henry II*, pp. 54, 104, 171; *5 Henry II*, p. 48; *6 Henry II*, p. 48. For his nephew Edulf see **489** and **674**; for his wife's sisters, **496**. See Addenda.
2. See **222, 262, 277, 281,** and **667.** William is not listed in Le Neve *Monastic Cathedrals 1066–1300*, under Winchester, but there was at this period a well-known William, archdeacon of London (? c. 1127–after 1152): Le Neve *St. Paul's, London 1066–1300*, 9. See below, p. 392.
222 1. See **221.**
223 1. See also **228** and **254.**
2. See also **870, 873,** and **898–9.**
224 1. See **38.**

[226] Ricardus filius Robert[i] Petit regi i d. et i quadrantem; et de eadem terra reddit Reginaldus de Sagio[1] regi ii d. et iii quadrantes[2] et ipse habet inde iii s.

[227] Philippus[a] filius Sanson' regi iiii d. et habet v s.

[228] [fo. 18ᵛ] Iveta[1] regi de ii terris viii d. et habet xviii s. et Reginaldus de Sagio[2] habet de eadem terra xix s. et ipse Reginaldus reddit inde vi s.

[229] Ricardus fundor[1] regi iiii d. et abbatisse Wilton' v s. et habet inde vii s.

[230] Herefast regi xii d. de iii terris et episcopo xxii s. de B. et habet inde xvii s. et iiii d. et managium[1] suum quietum; et Willelmus filius Estmer'[2] habet inde xii d.; et de eadem terra Willelmus Gall' habet inde ii s.

[231] Ricardus fundor[1] abbati de Hida iii s. et ix d. et habet inde xvi s.

[232] Cuuache abbati xv d.

[233] Et bona filia abbati xii d.

[234] Uxor Bargelo' abbati xxviii d.

[235] Turb' cocus abbati vi d. et habet xii d.

[236] Robertus Putheld' priori Winton' iii s. de iiii terris et habet inde xxxii d.

[237] Seman harangarius priori xii d.

[238] Petrus merciarius[1] priori iiii d.[b] et habet vi s.

[239] Agemund' priori xii d.

[240] Spileman'[1] priori xii d.

[241] Heredes Godwini presbiter[i][1] priori viii d.

[242] Saieua priori xii d. et habet inde iiii d.

[226] Richard son of Robert Petit pays the king 1¼d.; and from the same land Reginald of Sées[1] pays the king 2¾d.[2] and receives from it 3s.

[227] Philip son of Samson pays the king 4d. and receives 5s.

[228] Iveta[1] pays the king for 2 lands 8d. and receives 18s. Reginald of Sées[2] receives from that same land 19s. and Reginald pays from it 6s.

[229] Richard the fusour[1] pays the king 4d. and the abbess of Wilton 5s. and receives from the land 7s.

[230] Herefast pays the king for 3 lands 12d. and the bishop 22s. de B. and receives from them 17s. 4d. and has his dwelling-house(?)[1] quit. William son of Estmer[2] receives from it/them 12d. and from the same land William the Frenchman receives 2s.

[231] Richard the fusour[1] pays the abbot of Hyde 3s. 9d. and receives from the land 16s.

[232] Cwache pays the abbot 15d.

[233] And Bonne-Fille pays the abbot 12d.

[234] Bargelo's wife pays the abbot 28d.

[235] Turbert the cook pays the abbot 6d. and receives 12d.

[236] Robert Putheld pays the prior of Winchester for 4 lands 3s. and receives from them 32d.

[237] Seaman the herring-monger pays the prior 12d.

[238] Peter the mercer[1] pays the prior 4d. and receives 6s.

[239] Agemund pays the prior 12d.

[240] Spileman[1] pays the prior 12d.

[241] Godwin the priest's heirs[1] pay the prior 8d.

[242] Saieva pays the prior 12d. and receives from the land 4d.

---

[a] -hi- over an erasure   [b] Whole entry written over an erasure to this point

226 1. See 156.
  2. An example of how 4d. landgable could be divided.
228. 1. See 223.
  2. See 156.
229 1. See 182.
230 1. See 197.
  2. For Robert son of Estmer, see 369.

231 1. See 182.
238 1. See 35.
240 1. In 1157–8 this or another Spileman purchased saddlery and harness for the king in Winchester worth £5. 14s.: Pipe Roll 4 Henry II, p. 175.
241 1. See also 325, and cf. 1.

[243] ^aErnold' Adeli[n]g'¹ priori ii s. et habet inde vi s.

[244] ^aAlebast et frater eius priori xxx d. et habent inde iiii s. et iii d.

[245] ^aUxor Godwini de Fuleflot¹ priori iiii s. et habet inde xxxiiii d. et ma[na]gium² suum quietum.

[246] Raulot priori x d. et uxori Iuonis¹ v d.

[247] Philippus^b priori [. . .]^c et habet xxviii d.

[248] Item Ern*oldus* Adeling'¹ priori xii d. et habet xvi d.

[249] Duchet¹ priori x s. et habet xi s. et ix d.

[250] Gunter' parm*entarius* tenet i managium¹ unde nil reddit.

[251] Ricardus Niger¹ regi ii d.

[252] Gilebertus regi ii d. et habet x s.

[253] Uxor Willelmi fabri¹ regi iiii d.

[254] Iueta¹ regi iiii d. et habet viii s.

[255] Ricardus fund*or*¹ regi iiii d.

[256] Duchet¹ regi iiii d.

[257] Hoel regi iiii d.

[258] Henricus de Traci¹ et Simon tenent i terram de feudo regis unde nil reddunt et episcopi habent inde xxx d. de Henrico filio Herefast' et ipse Henricus habet inde xv s.

[259] [fo. 19] Herebert^d regi iiii d. et habet inde ii s.

[260] Robertus de Sancto Pancratio¹ regi iiii d.

[261] Abbatissa Wint' regi iiii d.¹

---

[243] Ernold Atheling¹ pays the prior 2*s*. and receives from the land 6*s*.

[244] Alebaster and his brother pay the prior 30*d*. and receive from the land 4*s*. 3*d*.

[245] Godwin of Fulflood's¹ wife pays the prior 4*s*., and she receives from the land 34*d*. and has her dwelling-house (?)² quit.

[246] Raulot pays the prior 10*d*. and Ivo's wife¹ 5*d*.

[247] Philip pays the prior [. . .] and receives 28*d*.

[248] Again Ernold Atheling¹ pays the prior 12*d*. and receives 16*d*.

[249] Duchet¹ pays the prior 10*s*. and receives 11*s*. 9*d*.

[250] Gunter the tailor holds 1 dwelling-house (?)¹ for which he pays nothing.

[251] Richard Black¹ pays the king 2*d*.

[252] Gilbert pays the king 2*d*. and receives 10*s*.

[253] William the blacksmith's wife¹ pays the king 4*d*.

[254] Iveta¹ pays the king 4*d*. and receives 8*s*.

[255] Richard the fusour¹ pays the king 4*d*.

[256] Duchet¹ pays the king 4*d*.

[257] Hoel pays the king 4*d*.

[258] Henry de Tracy¹ and Simon hold 1 land of the king's fief and pay nothing for it. From it the bishops receive 30*d*. from Henry son of Herefast, and Henry receives from it 15*s*.

[259] Herbert pays the king 4*d*. and receives from the land 2*s*.

[260] Robert of St. Pancras¹ pays the king 4*d*.

[261] The abbess of Winchester pays the king 4*d*.¹

---

^a [243], [244], *and* [245] *erased and rewritten. Initials for rubricator in the margin indicate the original position of entries* ^b Philippi *MS.* ^c *Space left for amount* ^d *Followed by a space*

---

243 1. See also 248 and 271. A street outside West Gate was known as *Hathelinges'ret, Athelyngestret*, by the thirteenth century: see below, p. 233.
245 1. See Addenda.   2. See 197.
246 1. See also 383, and for Ivo's brother Richard, 384.
248 1. See 243.
249 1. Cf. 256 and 306. *Rannulfus Duchet* was pardoned 3*s*. when the city paid an aid in 1129: *Pipe Roll 31 Henry I*, p. 41.

250 1. See 197.
251 1. See 38.
253 1. For William, see 179.
254 1. See 223.
255 1. See 182.
256 1. Cf. 249.
258 1. See 175.
260 1. See 31.
261 1. For this tenement, cf. I, 110.

[262] Willelmus archid*iaconus*[1] regi de ii[a] terris viii d.

[263] Hunfridus Palefrei[1] et Alured' episcopo xxxii d. [de] terra baronum et Palefr' habet inde iiii s. et viii d. et Alured' habet inde xlii d.

[264] Walder' episcopo xvii d. de terra baronum et habet x s.

[265] Petrus merc*iarius*[1] regi de ii terris viii d. et habet inde xix s.

[266] Turoldus Scuuel'[1] regi ii d.

[267] Palefrei[1] regi ii d.

[268] Gilebertus cord*wanarius*[1] episcopo Sal'[2] ii s.

[269] Piterun episcopo Sal'[1] ii s.

[270] Robertus de Pont'[1] tenet i terram et i hospicium de Iohanne de Port;[2] sed non[b] vult dicere quid reddit inde.

[271] Ern*oldus* Adeling[1] regi de iiii terris viii d. et habet inde ii s.

[272] Turoldus Scuueil'[1] regi ii d. pro terra patris sui.

[273] Nicholaus regi ii d.

[274] Herebertus regi iiii d. et habet x d.

[275] Iudichel[1] regi ii d.

[276] Gilebertus cord*wanarius*[1] regi ii d. et leprosi[2] habent inde v s.

[262] William the archdeacon[1] pays the king for 2 lands 8*d.*

[263] Humphrey Palfrey[1] and Alfred pay the bishop 32*d.* from the land of the barons, and Palfrey receives from it 4*s.* 8*d.* and Alfred receives from it 42*d.*

[264] Walder pays the bishop 17*d.* from the land of the barons and receives 10*s.*

[265] Peter the mercer[1] pays the king for 2 lands 8*d.* and receives from them 19*s.*

[266] Turold Scuvel[1] pays the king 2*d.*

[267] Palfrey[1] pays the king 2*d.*

[268] Gilbert the cordwainer[1] pays the bishop of Salisbury[2] 2*s.*

[269] Piterun pays the bishop of Salisbury[1] 2*s.*

[270] Robert of Pont [de l'Arche][1] holds 1 land and 1 hospice of John de Port;[2] but he does not want to say what he pays for them.

[271] Ernold Atheling[1] pays the king for 4 lands 8*d.* and receives from them 2*s.*

[272] Turold Scuveil[1] pays the king 2*d.* for his father's land.

[273] Nicholas pays the king 2*d.*

[274] Herbert pays the king 4*d.* and receives 10*d.*

[275] Iudichel[1] pays the king 2*d.*

[276] Gilbert the cordwainer[1] pays the king 2*d.* and the lepers[2] receive from that land 5*s.*

---

[a] *Over an erasure*   [b] sed non *over an erasure*

262 1. See 221.
263 1. See also 267.
265 1. See 35.
266 1. See also 272.
267 1. See 263.
268 1. See also 276.
  2. See 51. For the property, cf. I, 108. From the succession of entries in Survey II the property appears to have been in the modern Sussex Street, where the medieval church of St. Valery (cf. I, 107) was situated.
269 1. See 51 and cf. I, 108.
270 1. See also 830. Probably Robert of Pont de l'Arche, son of William (for whom see I, Preface), as 830 suggests.
  2. See 2.
271 1. See 243.
272 1. See 266.

275 1. Perhaps the same person and property as in I, 102, but cf. 864, n. 1.
276 1. See 268.
  2. See also 447 and 641. The inmates of the Hospital of St. Mary Magdalen, on the down to the E. of Winchester, usually said to have been founded by Bishop Richard of Ilchester (1173–88), were known as *leprosi* and *infirmi super montem*. A sum of 60*s.* was paid annually to the hospital from the revenues of the city (*VCH Hants* ii. 197–200; *Vetusta Monumenta*, iii, 1–17). This payment was being made by 1155–6 (*Pipe Roll 3 Henry II*, p. 107), but is not mentioned in the Pipe Roll of 31 Henry I. The entries in Survey II show that the hospital had been founded by 1148. There was a fourteenth-century tradition that Henry of Blois had endowed the hospital with income (Goodman *Chartulary*, no. 422) and it seems most likely that he was indeed its founder. See below, pp. 328–9.

[277] Willelmus archid*iaconus*[1] regi ii d.

[278] Porcell' regi iii d.

[279] Cristianus regi iii d.

[280] Geruasius presbiter[1] regi ii d. et habet iiii s. et vi d.

[281] Item Willelmus archid*iaconus*[1] regi ii d. et habet x s.

[282] Hereuicus Freschet[1] regi ii d.

[283] Anschetillus lor*imer*[1] regi ii d. et Rob*er*to de Sancto Pancratio[2] ii s.

[284] Hereuicus clericus[1] episcopo viii s. de terra baronum et habet xii s.

[285] Uxor Ricardi filii Gunfridi regi ii d.

[286] Willelmus clericus[1] regi ii [d.] et episcopo ii s. de terra baronum et habet inde ii s.

[287] Aelricus faber regi ii d. et episcopo vi s. de terra baronum.

[288] Gunnora Roberto de Sifrewast[1] xii d.

[289] Henricus Gladewin'[1] regi iiii d. et habet vii s.

[290] Filius Hereberti turtellarii episcopo ix d.

[291] Philippus de Fuleflod'[1] episcopo v d. et habet iiii s.

[292] Mona*c*us de infirma*rio* Sancti Swithuni episcopo iii. et viii d. et habet de Radulfo filio Burewoldi*a* ii s. et de uxore [fo. 19ᵛ] Gifardi[1] xx d.; et uxor Gifardi habet inde xx d. et de Philippo[2] xxxii d.; et ipse Philippus habet inde vi s. et de Selid' Ruffo xx d. et [de] filia Godrici cum barba iiii s.; et ipsa habet inde xliiii d. et de Turb' War' iiii s.

[277] William the archdeacon[1] pays the king 2*d*.

[278] Porcel pays the king 3*d*.

[279] Christian pays the king 3*d*.

[280] Gervase the priest[1] pays the king 2*d*. and receives 4*s*. 6*d*.

[281] Again William the archdeacon[1] pays the king 2*d*. and receives 10*s*.

[282] Herewic Freschet[1] pays the king 2*d*.

[283] Anschetil the lorimer[1] pays the king 2*d*. and Robert of St. Pancras[2] 2*s*.

[284] Herewic the clerk[1] pays the bishop 8*s*. from the land of the barons and receives 12*s*.

[285] Richard son of Gunfrid's wife pays the king 2*d*.

[286] William the clerk[1] pays the king 2*d*. and the bishop 2*s*. from the land of the barons and receives from it 2*s*.

[287] Aelric the blacksmith pays the king 2*d*. and the bishop 6*s*. from the land of the barons.

[288] Gunnor pays Robert of Chiffrevast[1] 12*d*.

[289] Henry Gladwin[1] pays the king 4*d*. and receives 7*s*.

[290] Herbert the confectioner's son pays the bishop 9*d*.

[291] Philip of Fulflood[1] pays the bishop 5*d*. and receives 4*s*.

[292] The monk of St. Swithun's infirmary pays the bishop 3*s*. 8*d*. and receives from Ralf son of Burewold 2*s*. and from Giffard's wife[1] 20*d*. Giffard's wife receives from the land 20*d*. and from Philip[2] 32*d*. The same Philip receives from the land 6*s*. and from Selida the Red 20*d*. and from Godric with the Beard's daughter 4*s*. And she receives from the land 44*d*. and from Turbert War' 4*s*.

a Followed by an erasure

277 1. See 221.
280 1. He witnessed a conveyance of property in High Street (cf. 43) and *Alwarnestret* (cf. 487) *c*. 1155–60: Southwick Cart, iii, fos. 123ᵛ, 136ᵛ.
281 1. See 221.
282 1. See also 492. With *Eua uxor Freschet* he witnessed a conveyance of property in High Street (cf. 43) and *Alwarnestret* (cf. 487) *c*. 1155–60: Southwick Cart iii, fos. 123ᵛ, 136ᵛ.

283 1. See also 339.　　2. See 31.
284 1. See 30.
286 1. See 167.
288 1. See I, 107.
289 1. See 192.
291 1. See also 292–3. Philip's properties were probably near the Fulflood. Cf. 245.
292 1. See also 295 and 297.
　　2. See 291.

[293] Philippus de Fuleflod'¹ priori pro managio² suo vi s. et i d. et habet inde xliiii d.ᵃ

[294] Hugo filius Cupping'¹ priori v s. et vii d. et habet xviii s.

[295] Uxor Giffardi¹ priori vii s. et habet vi s. et vi d.

[296] Baganora priori xii d. et habet iii s.

[297] Selid' maco¹ uxori Giffardi² ii s. et habet iii s.

[298] Abbas de Hida habet [de] quadam terra xlii d.

[299] Oinus parmentarius abbati ix d. et habet iiii s.ᵇ

[300] Radulfus sacrista abbati xxiii d. et habet inde xi d.

[301] Edricus Puttuc abbati vi d.

[302] Quedam femina paupercula abbati ii d.

[303] Truued abbati viii d.

[304] Baf abbati vi d.ᶜ

ᵈEXTRA PORTAM DE NORTᵉ

[305] Robertus sellarius episcopo vi d.

[306] Radulfus Duchet¹ episcopo ix d. et obolum.

[307] Edgarᶠ sune¹ episcopo viii d.

[308] Hugo scriniarius episcopo vi d.

[309] Ricardus de Braio episcopo viii d. et habet inde xvi d.

[310] Robertus Martre¹ tenet i terram de episcopo et Turbertus de eo et solebat reddere episcopoᵍ ix d.

[311] Simphorianus episcopo xvi d.

[312] Emma uxor Sermonar'¹ episcopo iii d.

[293] Philip of Fulflood¹ pays the prior for his dwelling-house (?)² 6s. 1d. and receives from it 44d.

[294] Hugh son of Chepping¹ pays the prior 5s. 7d. and receives 18s.

[295] Giffard's wife¹ pays the prior 7s. and receives 6s. 6d.

[296] Bagnor pays the prior 12d. and receives 3s.

[297] Selida the mason¹ pays Giffard's wife² 2s. and receives 3s.

[298] The abbot of Hyde receives from a certain land 42d.

[299] Oin the tailor pays the abbot 9d. and receives 4s.

[300] Ralf the sacristan pays the abbot 23d. and receives from the land 11d.

[301] Edric Puttock pays the abbot 6d.

[302] A certain poor woman pays the abbot 2d.

[303] Truved pays the abbot 8d.

[304] Baf pays the abbot 6d.

OUTSIDE NORTH GATE

[305] Robert the saddler pays the bishop 6d.

[306] Ralf Duchet¹ pays the bishop 9½d.

[307] Edgar's son¹ pays the bishop 8d.

[308] Hugh the cabinet-maker pays the bishop 6d.

[309] Richard of Bray pays the bishop 8d. and receives from the land 16d.

[310] Robert the Weasel¹ holds 1 land of the bishop and Turbert holds of him; and he used to pay the bishop 9d.

[311] Symphorian pays the bishop 16d.

[312] Emma, Sermoner's wife,¹ pays the bishop 3d.

ᵃ i d. . . . xliiii d. *over an erasure*   ᵇ iii *changed to* iiii   ᶜ *Entry followed by an erasure*   ᵈ *Rubric written over an erasure*   ᵉ *In upper margin, text for rubricator rubbed and partly cut away*   ᶠ *Followed by an erasure*   ᵍ *Rubricator has extended contraction mark over* episcopo

293 1. See 291.   2. See 292.
  2. See 197.   306. 1. Cf. 249.
294 1. See 23.   307. 1. See 38.
295 1. See 292.   310. 1. See 9.
297 1. See also 340. Presumably distinct from Selida the   312 1. See also 601.
Red of 292.

[313] Hugo tornitor episcopo vi d.

[313] Hugh the turner (?) pays the bishop 6*d*.

[314] Iohannes faber[1] episcopo viii d. et Hugo[ni] de Porta[2] viii d.

[314] John the blacksmith[1] pays the bishop 8*d*. and Hugh de Port[2] 8*d*.

[315] Isabel de Diua[1] episcopo xxx d. et habet inde ix s. et vi d.*[a]* et Willelmus marescallus[2] habet de eadem terra xii s.

[315] Isabel of Dives[1] pays the bishop 30*d*. and receives from the land 9*s*. 6*d*. And William the marshal[2] receives from the same land 12*s*.

[316] Stephanus de Crichelad'[1] episcopo xxv d. et habet de Roberto de Sancto Pancratio[2] ii s.; et Robertus habet inde xii s. et Robertus bell' de eadem ii s.; et Robertus Crassus reddit eidem Stephano [. . .] et habet inde ii s.*[b]*

[316] Stephen of Cricklade[1] pays the bishop 25*d*. and receives from Robert of St. Pancras[2] 2*s*.; and Robert receives from the land 12*s*. and Robert the Fair from the same land 2*s*. And Robert the Fat pays that Stephen [. . .] and receives from the land 2*s*.

[317] Uxor Thome clerici[1] reddit predicto Stephano[2] xii d. et habet inde de Turoldo ii s.

[317] Thomas the clerk's wife[1] pays the aforesaid Stephen[2] 12*d*. and from the land receives from Turold 2*s*.

[318] Isabel de Diua[1] inclusis[2] Wint' [fo. 20] reddit xxx d. et habet inde iiii s. et Viuianus habet inde viii s.

[318] Isabel of Dives[1] pays the hermits[2] of Winchester 30*d*. and receives from the land 4*s*. Vivian receives from it 8*s*.

[319] Durandus Gumbold' Stephano de Crech'[1] vi d. et habet inde ii s.

[319] Durand Gumbold pays Stephen of Cricklade[1] 6*d*. and receives from the land 2*s*.

[320] Fil*ius* Gunt'[1] episcopo iiii d. et hord*ario*[2] ii s. et habet inde iiii s.

[320] Guncelin's son/daughter[1] pays the bishop 4*d*. and the hordarian[2] 2*s*. and receives from the land 4*s*.

[321] Godefridus filius Willelmi[1] abbati l d. et habet iii s.

[321] Godfrey son of William[1] pays the abbot 50*d*. and receives 3*s*.

[322] Ricardus presbiter[1] abbati xv d. et habet inde iiii s. et iii d.

[322] Richard the priest[1] pays the abbot 15*d*. and receives from the land 4*s*. 3*d*.

[323] Uxor Rogeri aurifabri tenet de Pagano filio Picard'*[c]*[1] v solida*tas* terre et de Osmod[2] v solida*tas* et vi d. et uxor Rogeri habet xi s. et viii d. et Paganus reddit inde abbati xv d.

[323] Roger the goldsmith's wife holds of Pain son of Picard[1] 5 shillingsworth of land and of Osmod[2] 5*s*. 6*d*. worth; and Roger's wife receives 11*s*. 8*d*. and Pain pays the abbot from the land 15*d*.

[324] Osmod[1] abbati xxxii d. et habet inde xv s. et x d.

[324] Osmod[1] pays the abbot 32*d*. and receives from the land 15*s*. 10*d*.

---

[a] d *over an erasure* (?)   *[b]* ii s. *corrected; correction mark in margin subsequently erased*   *[c]* Ricard' *Ellis*

314 1. See also **426**.
  2. See also **932**. Cf. **2**.
315 1. See also **318**.
  2. See also **529** and **1033**. He appears under Hampshire, together with John the Marshal, in *Pipe Roll 4 Henry II*, p. 173.
316 1. See also **317** and **319**; cf. **736**.
  2. See **31**.
317 1. See **32**.
  2. See **316**.
318 1. See **315**.
  2. From 1187 the crown made an annual payment of 30*s*. 5*d*. to the *incluso de sancto Æderedo extra Wintoniam*: *Pipe Roll 33 Henry II*, p. 200; *34 Henry II*, p. 178.

319 1. See **316**.
320 1. See **29**.
  2. He could have been an official at any of the monasteries, perhaps most likely of St. Swithun's or of Hyde, but since there were several granges and barns outside North Gate in the later Middle Ages, he might simply have been a custodian of such a store.
321 1. See **5**.
322 1. See also **590**. He was perhaps identical with the Richard, priest of Meon, who witnessed a charter of Henry of Blois (Goodman *Chartulary*, no. 10).
323 1. See **21**, n. 1.
  2. See also **324**.
324 1. See **323**.

[325] Heredes Godwini presbiter[i]¹ abbati vi d.

[326] Willelmus Mordant abbati xv d. et habet inde ix d.

[327] Godefridus filius Willelmi¹ abbati ii d.

[328] Edit Ruffa abbati xii d.

[329] Goduinus iunior abbati ii s. et habet inde iiii s.

[330] Alwinus de Odiam^{a¹} abbati iii s. et habet iiii s. et vi d.

[331] Ansgod mol*endinarius* abbati xviii d. et habet inde vii d.

[332] Godard' carp*entarius* et Wimund' reddunt abbati pro terra Petri Lancel' xviii d. et ipsi habent viii d.

[333] Herebertus pincerna abbati vi d. et habet inde ii^{b} s.

[334] Sired parm*entarius* abbati xviii d.

[335] Wluiua abbati xviii d.

[336] Uxor Oslac abbati xii d.

[337] Segrim¹ abbati vi d. et habet inde xxvi d.

[338] Symon de Hangelt' abbati iiii s. et habet viii s.

[339] Anschetillus lor*imer*¹ abbati xvi d. et habet^{c} iii s.

[340] Selid' maco¹ abbati iii s.

[341] Nicholaus presbiter abbati ix d.

[342] Rogerus pistor abbati ix d.

[343] Willelmus de Suttun'¹ abbati xiiii d. et habet xi s. et viii d.

[344] Anschetillus maco¹ tenet terram suam quietam de monacis et habet inde iiii s.

[345] Robertus^{d} de Sancto Pancratio¹ abbati x d. et habet inde iiii s.

[325] Godwin the priest's heirs¹ pay the abbot 6d.

[326] William Mordant pays the abbot 15d. and receives from the land 9d.

[327] Godfrey son of William¹ pays the abbot 2d.

[328] Edith the Red pays the abbot 12d.

[329] Godwin junior pays the abbot 2s. and receives from the land 4s.

[330] Alwin of Odiham¹ pays the abbot 3s. and receives 4s. 6d.

[331] Ansgod the miller pays the abbot 18d. and receives from the land 7d.

[332] Godard the carpenter and Wimund pay the abbot for Peter Lancelin's land 18d. and they receive 8d.

[333] Herbert the butler pays the abbot 6d. and receives from the land 2s.

[334] Sired the tailor pays the abbot 18d.

[335] Wulviva pays the abbot 18d.

[336] Oslac's wife pays the abbot 12d.

[337] Segrim¹ pays the abbot 6d. and receives from the land 26d.

[338] Simon of Hangleton pays the abbot 4s. and receives 8s.

[339] Anschetil the lorimer¹ pays the abbot 16d. and receives 3s.

[340] Selida the mason¹ pays the abbot 3s.

[341] Nicholas the priest pays the abbot 9d.

[342] Roger the baker pays the abbot 9d.

[343] William of Sutton¹ pays the abbot 14d. and receives 11s. 8d.

[344] Anschetil the mason¹ holds his land quit of the monks and receives from it 4s.

[345] Robert of St. Pancras¹ pays the abbot 10d. and receives from the land 4s.

---

^{a} O *over an erasure*　　　^{b} ii *preceded by an erasure*　　　^{c} et habet *over an erasure*　　　^{d} Roberto *MS.*

325 1. See **241**.
327 1. See **5**.
330 1. See **I, 96** and **II, 468**.
337 1. Cf. **725**.
339 1. See **283**.

340 1. See **297**.
343 1. See also **511** and **672**.
344 1. See also **346**.
345 1. See **31**.

[346] Uxor Anschetilli mac*onis*[1] abbati ii s.

[347] Aoulf' carpent*arius* abbati xii d.

[348] Watso abbati iii s.

[349] Willelmus Durage[1] debet reddere [fo. 20ᵛ] abbati ii s. sicuti vicini et ministri*[a]* abbatis dicunt.

[350] Item Durage[1] tenet i terram quietam de feudo Walteri de Grainuill'.[2]

[351] Ricardus*[b]* filius Odonis[1] regi vi d. et habet ii s.

[352] Drogo tenet i terram de Gaufrido de Masiaco quietam. Et habet inde iii s.

[353] Wdia[1] abbati vi d.

[354] Terricus vigil abbati iii s. et habet inde v s.

[355] Uxor Almodi[1] abbati ii d. et obolum et habet inde ii s.

[356] Robertus de Sancto Pancratio[1] episcopo i marcam de terra baronum et habet inde viii s. et vi d.

[357] Reimundus et Radulfus tenent i terram et i gard*inum* et pratum; sed nescimus quid reddunt inde.

SNIDELINGESTRET

[358] Monachi Wint' episcopo v s. de terra baronum et habent [. . .]

[359] Iohannes nepos Petri merc*iarii*[1] reddit eisdem monachis iiii s. et habet inde xiii s.; et Radulfus de Bosco eisdem monachis xiii d.*[c]* et habet inde iii s.; et Symon eisdem monachis ii s. et habet vi s.

[360] Willelmus de Tocho[1] eisdem monachis xii d. et habet iiii s.

[361] Rogerus Lippe regi xii*[d]* d. et episcopo iiii s. de terra baronum.

[346] Anschetil the mason's wife[1] pays the abbot 2s.

[347] Aculf (?) the carpenter pays the abbot 12d.

[348] Wazo pays the abbot 3s.

[349] William Durage[1] should pay the abbot 2s. according to the neighbours and the abbot's servants.

[350] Again Durage[1] holds 1 land quit of the fief of Walter of Grainville.[2]

[351] Richard son of Odo[1] pays the king 6d. and receives 2s.

[352] Drew holds 1 land quit of Geoffrey of Massy (?) and receives from it 3s.

[353] Widia[1] pays the abbot 6d.

[354] Terry the watchman pays the abbot 3s. and receives from the land 5s.

[355] Almod's wife[1] pays the abbot 2½d. and receives from the land 2s.

[356] Robert of St. Pancras[1] pays the bishop 1 mark from the land of the barons and receives from it 8s. 6d.

[357] Raymond and Ralf hold 1 land and 1 garden and meadow. But we do not know what they pay for them.

SNIDELINGE STREET [TOWER STREET]

[358] The monks of Winchester pay the bishop 5s. from the land of the barons and receive [. . .].

[359] John, Peter the mercer's nephew,[1] pays those monks 4s. and receives from the land 13s. Ralf of Bosc pays the same monks 13d. and receives 3s. And Simon pays them 2s. and receives 6s.

[360] William of Touques[1] pays those monks 12d. and receives 4s.

[361] Roger Lip pays the king 12d. and the bishop 4s. from the land of the barons.

[a] ministris *MS.*   *[b]* a *erased after* Ric'   *[c]* xii *changed to* xiii (?)   *[d]* xii *repeated and crossed out by rubricator*

346 1. See **344**.
349 1. See also **350**.
350 1. See **349**.
    2. Possibly Walter de Grenville, brother of Nicholas, one of Henry I's barons: Sanders *Baronies*, 41.
351 1. Probably a moneyer of Henry II: see also **380** and cf. **I, 42**, n. 1. He was pardoned 3s. of the shire's aid in 1158: *Pipe Roll 4 Henry II*, p. 172.

353 1. Cf. **429**.
355 1. See also **422**.
356 1. See **31**.
359 1. See **34**.
360 1. William de Thoca and Robert his son witnessed the sale of **669**: J. H. Round, *EHR* 14 (1899), 424.

[362] Hugo filius Cupp*ingi*[1] episcopo iii s. de terra baronum et habet iii s.

[363] Uxor Haccheselt episcopo viii d. de terra baronum et habet inde vi s.

[364] Paganus pic'[1] abbati xxviii d. et habet inde xii s.

[365] Idem Pag*anus*[1] episcopo xii d. de terra baronum et habet ii s.

[366] Iohannes ioculator regi iiii d.

[367] Item Pag*anus* pic'[1] regi iiii d.

[368] Rogerus Blundus episcopo ii d. de terra baronum.

[369] Robertus filius Estm'[1] episcopo vi d. de terra baronum.

[370] Item Pag*anus* pic'[1] episcopo iiii d. de terra baronum.

[371] Et item Pag*anus*[1] episcopo xii d. de terra baronum.

[372] Osmoda[1] episcopo de iii terris iii sol. de terra baronum.

[373] Robertus*a* parm*entarius* regi iiii d.

[374] Warinus filius Blachem' episcopo de terra baronum*b*[1] xviii d. et habet ii s.

[375] Alueua filia Estan'[1] episcopo x d. de terra baronum.

[376] Ricardus filius Rainer'*c* regi iiii d. et habet viii d.

[377] Et iterum Pag*anus*[1] episcopo xii d. et habet ii s.

[378] [fo. 21] Hoppecole episcopo iii s.

[379] *d*Fil*ius* Herdi[n]g*e* fabri[1] tenet i terram de rege de iiii d. quietam pro servicio suo et habet xviii d.; et de

[362] Hugh son of Chepping[1] pays the bishop 3s. from the land of the barons and receives 3s.

[363] Hack-salt's wife pays the bishop 8d. from the land of the barons and receives from it 6s.

[364] Pain [son of] Picard[1] pays the abbot 28d. and receives from the land 12s.

[365] The same Pain[1] pays the bishop 12d. from the land of the barons and receives 2s.

[366] John the jester pays the king 4d.

[367] Again Pain [son of] Picard[1] pays the king 4d.

[368] Roger Blond pays the bishop 2d. from the land of the barons.

[369] Robert son of Estmer[1] pays the bishop 6d. from the land of the barons.

[370] Again Pain [son of] Picard[1] pays the bishop 4d. from the land of the barons.

[371] And again Pain[1] pays the bishop 12d. from the land of the barons.

[372] Osmoth[1] pays the bishop for 3 lands 3s. from the land of the barons.

[373] Robert the tailor pays the king 4d.

[374] Warin son of Blacman pays the bishop from the land of the barons[1] 18d. and receives 2s.

[375] Alveva, Estan's[1] daughter, pays the bishop 10d. from the land of the barons.

[376] Richard son of Rainer pays the king 4d. and receives 8d.

[377] And again Pain[1] pays the bishop 12d. and receives 2s.

[378] Hoppecole pays the bishop 3s.

[379] Harding the blacksmith's son[1] holds 1 land of the king worth 4d. quit in return for his service and receives

---

a o *erased after* Robt'   *b* baronum et *MS.*   *c* R *over an erasure*   *d Initial* F *in red erased and rewritten in blue*   *e Suspension mark after* d *erased*

362 1. See **23**.
364 1. See **21**, n. 1.
365 1. See **21**, n. 1.
367 1. See **21**, n. 1.
369 1. Cf. **230**.
370 1. See **21**, n. 1.
371 1. See **21**, n. 1.
372 1. See **80**.

374 1. This is a case where *de terra baronum* precedes instead of following a sum of money; but there is evidence for derangement of the MS.
375 1. Possibly a moneyer of Henry I: see below, Table 42.
377 1. See **21**, n. 1. This tenement probably backed on to II, **406** in *Brudenestret*. See below, Figs. 18 and 19.
379 1. For the father, see I, **128**.

eadem habet Rogerus pic*tor*[2] iiii s. et vi d.; et de eadem habet[a] Hardingus brachiator[3] ii s.

[380] Ricardus filius Odoni[s][1] regi vi d. et habet ii s.

[381] Dr[o]go Blundus[1] reddit Hugoni de Hahela vi d. de i terra quam Hugo tenet quietam.

[382] Ricardus pic*tor* episcopo xii d. de terra baronum et habet ii s.

[383] Uxor Iuonis[1] episcopo x d. de terra baronum.

[384] Ricardus frater Iuonis[1] episcopo xii d. de terra baronum.

[385] Turstinus clericus[1] episcopo xii d. de terra baronum.

[386] Radulfus filius Petri[1] episcopo iiii d. de terra baronum.

[387] Stigandus parm*entarius* episcopo xxvi d. et habet xxxiii d. de feudo de Odiham.[b][1]

[388] Reginaldus Longus episcopo xiii d. de terra baronum.

[389] Filie Walerand' episcopo xi d. de terra baronum et habe[n]t v d.

[390] Benedictus presbiter episcopo ii d. de terra baronum.

[391] Rogerus Pofil[1] episcopo v d. Et sunt ibi iii mansion*es* vacue.

[392] Baldewinus[c] parm*entarius* episcopo xiii d. et habet iiii s. hucusque de feudo de Odiham.[d][1]

BRUDENESTRET

[393] Philippus de Vallo[1] priori Wint' xxx d. et habet inde xx d. et de Baldewino xii d.; et Baldewinus habet inde vi d. de Beatric'.

18*d*. And from the same land Roger the painter[2] receives 4*s*. 6*d*.; and from the same land Harding the brewer[3] receives 2*s*.

[380] Richard son of Odo[1] pays the king 6*d*. and receives 2*s*.

[381] Drew Blond[1] pays Hugh *de Hahela* 6*d*. for 1 land which Hugh holds quit.

[382] Richard the painter pays the bishop 12*d*. from the land of the barons and receives 2*s*.

[383] Ivo's wife[1] pays the bishop 10*d*. from the land of the barons.

[384] Ivo's brother, Richard,[1] pays the bishop 12*d*. from the land of the barons.

[385] Thurstin the clerk[1] pays the bishop 12*d*. from the land of the barons.

[386] Ralf son of Peter[1] pays the bishop 4*d*. from the land of the barons.

[387] Stigand the tailor pays the bishop 26*d*. and receives 33*d*. from the fee of Odiham.[1]

[388] Reginald Long pays the bishop 13*d*. from the land of the barons.

[389] Walerand's daughters pay the bishop 11*d*. from the land of the barons and receive 5*d*.

[390] Benedict the priest pays the bishop 2*d*. from the land of the barons.

[391] Roger Pofil[1] pays the bishop 5*d*. And there are there 3 vacant messuages.

[392] Baldwin the tailor pays the bishop 13*d*. and hitherto has received 4*s*. from the fee of Odiham.[1]

BRUDENE STREET [STAPLE GARDENS]

[393] Philip of Val[1] (?the Vale) pays the prior of Winchester 30*d*. and receives from the land 20*d*. and from Baldwin 12*d*. And Baldwin receives from it 6*d*. from Beatrice.

---

a habet *over erasure and correction mark in margin*
c *Over an erasure*   *d* h *over an erasure; cf.* [387]

b h *over erasure and correction mark in margin; cf.* [392]

379 2. See **27**.
  3. See **109**.
380 1. See **351**. He was probably a moneyer of Henry II: see below, Table 45. For the tenement, cf. **I, 129** and for the moneying connections of the family, **I, 42**, n. 1.
381 1. See **185**.
383 1. See **246**.

384 1. See **246**.
385 1. See **221**.
386 1. See also **397**.
387 1. A royal manor. See also **392** and **830**, and below, p. 383, and Table 28.
391 1. Cf. **400**.
392 1. See **387**.
393 1. See below, p. 239.

[394] Siluester priori xxx d.

[395] Robertus filius Cupp*ingi*'¹ episcopo vi d. et obolum*ᵃ* de terra baronum.

[396] Pauie episcopo xiii d. et obolum de terra baronum et habet iiii s. et vi d.

[397] Radulfus filius Petri¹ regi xv d. et episcopo xii d. de terra baronum.

[398] Filia Henrici filii Turstini¹ episcopo xii d. de terra baronum et priori i marcam et habet inde i marcam.

[399] Ansger'*ᵇ* episcopo xxx d. de terra baronum.

[400] Hugo Pofile¹ priori v s. et vi d. et Turstino de Ordia² vi d.

[401] Turstinus de Wordia*ᶜ*¹ priori ii s. et habet inde vii s. de Drogone et Drogo habet inde v s.; et preterea Dr[o]go habet mansionem i ibi et servientes suos et catella sua.²

[402] Ebrardus priori xxx d. et habet inde iiii s.

[403] Hugo*ᵈ* filius Chepp*ingi*¹ regi pro coquina sua [fo. 21ᵛ] iiii d. et habet inde managium² suum quietum*ᵉ* et ipse Hugo habet inde v s.

[404] Osmoda¹ regi viii d.

[405] Filii Willelmi filii Odonis¹ regi viii d.

[406] Pag*anus* pic'¹ prepositis de Wordie² xxiiii s. et habet inde v s.

[407] Willelmus palm*arius* debet reddere eisdem prepositis xxv d. sed terra est vasta.

[408] Wasco clericus eisdem p[re]positis xxv d.

[409] Stephanus frater Iohannis¹ eisdem prepositis xxxii d.

[394] Silvester pays the prior 30*d*.

[395] Robert son of Chepping¹ pays the bishop 6½*d*. from the land of the barons.

[396] Pavie pays the bishop 13½*d*. from the land of the barons and receives 4*s*. 6*d*.

[397] Ralf son of Peter¹ pays the king 15*d*. and the bishop 12*d*. from the land of the barons.

[398] The daughter of Henry son of Thurstin¹ pays the bishop 12*d*. from the land of the barons and the prior 1 mark and receives from it 1 mark.

[399] Ansger pays the bishop 30*d*. from the land of the barons.

[400] Hugh Pofil¹ pays the prior 5*s*. 6*d*. and Thurstin of Worthy² 6*d*.

[401] Thurstin of Worthy¹ pays the prior 2*s*. and from the land receives 7*s*. from Drew, and Drew receives from it 5*s*. And moreover Drew has 1 messuage there and his servants and chattels.²

[402] Ebrard pays the prior 30*d*. and receives from the land 4*s*.

[403] Hugh son of Chepping¹ pays the king for his kitchen 4*d*. and has from it his living-accommodation (?)² quit; and Hugh receives from it 5*s*.

[404] Osmoth¹ pays the king 8*d*.

[405] The sons of William son of Odo¹ pay the king 8*d*.

[406] Pain [son of] Picard¹ pays the reeves of Worthy² 24*s*. and receives from the land 5*s*.

[407] William the palmer ought to pay the same reeves 25*d*.; but the land is waste.

[408] Wazo the clerk pays the same reeves 25*d*.

[409] Stephen, John's brother,¹ pays the same reeves 32*d*.

ᵃ obolum et *MS*.   ᵇ *Suspension mark after g erased*   ᶜ Wordia *over correction*   ᵈ *o erased after* Hug'
ᵉ quietam *MS*.

395 1. Cf. 23.
397 1. See 386.
398 1. See also 414.
400 1. Cf. 391.
  2. See also 401.
401 1. See 400.
  2. See 55.
403 1. See 23. For the tenement, cf. I, 134.

  2. See 197.
404 1. See 80.
405. 1. Perhaps the sons of William son of Odo son of Ticcheman in I, 133; but cf. I, 42, n. 1.
406 1. See 21, n. 1. For the location of this tenement, cf. 377.
  2. See also 407–9, 502, and 608; and cf. I, 141, n. 1.
409 1. See also 1068.

[410] Terra Ulf regi xv d.

[411] Reginaldus de Sagio¹ regi xv d.

[412] Siluester episcopo xxx d. de terra baronum.

[413] Willelmus de Cadumo episcopo xxx d. [de] terra baronum.

[414] Filia Henrici filii Turstini¹ episcopo iiii s. de terra baronum. Eadem iterum episcopo ii s. de terra baronum et habet iiii s. de reddit*ibus* et in alia domo habet servientes suos et catella sua.²

[415] Rogerus filius Gunt'¹ Hunfrido ii s. et habet iii s. et di*midium* d*enarium*.

[416] Robertus de Turwill' regi vi d. et habet iii s.

[417] Reginaldus de Sagio¹ regi viii d. et Roberto de Inglesh'² x s. et habet inde xvii s. et vi d.

[418] Alexander regi viii d. et abbatisse de Warwll'¹ xxx d.

[419] Ansg[o]d Tresor¹ abbatisse de Warwll'² xv d. et Matilde*ᵃ* vii s.; et ipsa Matilda reddit abbatisse [de] Warwll' xv d. et abbati Wint' v d.

[420] Radulfus Lacchewei¹ canonicis de Sancto Dionisio² iii s. et canonici reddunt in[de] abbati de Hida³ xx d. et Radulfus habet xix s.

[421] Atscelina Hugoni de Mortem*er*¹ ii s. et episcopo de managio² suo xv d. de terra baronum.*ᵇ*

[422] Uxor Almodi¹ Willelmo Pingui² iii s. et habet viii d.

[423] Herefridus presbiter episcopo xii d. de terra baronum.

[410] Ulf's land pays the king 15*d*.

[411] Reginald of Sées¹ pays the king 15*d*.

[412] Silvester pays the bishop 30*d*. from the land of the barons.

[413] William of Caen pays the bishop 30*d*. from the land of the barons.

[414] The daughter of Henry son of Thurstin¹ pays the bishop 4*s*. from the land of the barons. She again pays the bishop 2*s*. from the land of the barons and receives 4*s*. in rents. And on another tenement she has her servants and chattels.²

[415] Roger son of Guncelin¹ pays Humphrey 2*s*. and receives 3*s*. 0½*d*.

[416] Robert of Tourville pays the king 6*d*. and receives 3*s*.

[417] Reginald of Sées¹ pays the king 8*d*. and Robert of Inglesham² 10*s*. and receives from the land 17*s*. 6*d*.

[418] Alexander pays the king 8*d*. and the abbess of Wherwell¹ 30*d*.

[419] Ansgod Tresor¹ pays the abbess of Wherwell² 15*d*. and Matilda 7*s*. Matilda pays the abbess of Wherwell 15*d*. and the abbot of Winchester 5*d*.

[420] Ralf Lacchewei¹ pays the canons of St. Denis² 3*s*. And the canons pay from it to the abbot of Hyde³ 20*d*. And Ralf receives 19*s*.

[421] Atscelina pays Hugh of Mortemer¹ 2*s*. and the bishop for her dwelling-house(?)² 15*d*. from the land of the barons.

[422] Almod's wife¹ pays William the Fat² 3*s*. and receives 8*d*.

[423] Herefrid the priest pays the bishop 12*d*. from the land of the barons.

ᵃ Matilda *MS.*   *ᵇ* de Mort(em') *in first line and all second line of MS. written over an erasure*

411 1. See **156**.
414 1. See **398**.
  2. See **55**.
415 1. See **29**.
417 1. See **156**.
  2. See **1**.
418 1. See also **419**, and for the property, cf. **I, 145**.
419 1. See also **437**, **592**, and **624**.
  2. See **418**.
420 1. See **74**.

  2. See **111**.
  3. For this property, cf. **I, 147**.
421 1. See also **609**. An important baron; for his father, Ralf I, see **I, 141**. For this tenement cf. **I, 148**. Hugh of Mortemer granted all his rent in Winchester *infra burgum* to Reading Abbey: BM, Egerton MS. 3031, fo. 36ᵛ.
  2. See **197**.
422 1. See **355**.
  2. See **213**.

[424] Filii Hugonis filii Guntscel'[1] episcopo viii d. de terra baronum.

[425] Chuuing' habuit i terram de terra baronum[1] unde solebat reddere xv d.; sed est vasta.

[426] Iohannes faber[1] Willelmo de Ipingis iiii s. et habet xii d. de terra baronum.[2]

[427] Pauida episcopo xv d. de terra baronum et habet xli d.

SCOWRTENESTRET

[428] Emma abbatisse Warewoll'[1] viii d. et P*aganus* Gall'[2] eidem abbatisse vi d.

[429] [fo. 22] Widie[1] eidem abbatisse iiii s.

[430] Ansfridus de Hacche[1] eidem abbatisse viii d. et habet iiii s.

[431] Pag*anus* pic'[1] eidem abbatisse xiiii d. et habet iii s.

[432] Filia Ricardi Budel eidem abbatisse vi d. et obolum.

[433] Osmoda[1] eidem abbatisse xv d. et obolum et habet xv d. et obolum.

[434] Willelmus filius Rogeri[1] habet iii terras vastas de feudo de Basingestoc'[2] et Hugo Haccemus[3] i et nichil redd*unt* vel cap*iunt*.

[435] Geruasius filius Burewoldi tenet i terram de feudo de Ulferet'[1] et nichil inde reddit et est vasta.

[436] Herebertus filius Watsconis tenet i terram ibi iuxta vacuam et deberet reddere xxx d. sed est vasta.

[424] The sons of Hugh son of Guncelin[1] pay the bishop 8*d.* from the land of the barons.

[425] Cuving had 1 land from the land of the barons[1] from which he used to pay 15*d.*; but it is waste.

[426] John the blacksmith[1] pays William of Iping 4*s.* and receives 12*d.* from the land of the barons.[2]

[427] Pavie pays the bishop 15*d.* from the land of the barons and receives 41*d.*

SCOWRTENE STREET [JEWRY STREET]

[428] Emma pays the abbess of Wherwell[1] 8*d.* and Pain the Frenchman[2] pays the same abbess 6*d.*

[429] Widia[1] pays the same abbess 4*s.*

[430] Ansfrid of Hatch[1] pays the same abbess 8*d.* and receives 4*s.*

[431] Pain [son of] Picard[1] pays the same abbess 14*d.* and receives 3*s.*

[432] Richard Beadle's daughter pays the same abbess 6½*d.*

[433] Osmoth[1] pays the same abbess 15½*d.* and receives 15½*d.*

[434] William son of Roger[1] has 3 waste lands of the fief of Basingstoke[2] and Hugh Hack-mouse[3] has 1; and he/they neither pay(s) nor take(s) anything.

[435] Gervase son of Burewold holds 1 land of the fief of Wolverton;[1] and he pays nothing for it, for it is waste.

[436] Herbert son of Wazo holds next 1 land which is vacant; and he should have paid 30*d.*; but it is waste.

424 1. See **29**.
425 1. This is a case where *de terra baronum* does not follow a sum of money. It may, of course, have slipped by a copyist's error from after 15*d.*
426 1. See **314**.
  2. This is a case where the bishop does not seem to be concerned with 'the land of the barons'.
428 1. See also **429–33**. In the thirteenth century Wherwell Abbey owned a block of property within North Gate at the N. end of *Scowrtenestret*: SMW 271.
  2. See **40**.
429 1. Cf. **353**.
430 1. See also **456** and **556**.
431 1. See **21**, n. 1.

433 1. See **80**.
434 1. See also **464–5, 508,** and **519**. He and his son Henry were pardoned 10*s.* 6*d.* of the shire's aid in 1158: *Pipe Roll 4 Henry II*, p. 172. See Addenda.
  2. A royal manor. Cf. **I, 11**. According to Domesday Book, *VCH Hants* i. 456a, 'In Winchester four inhabitants of the suburbs used to pay 12*s.* 11*d.*'
  3. See **18**. Walter Hake*mus* had a house on the W. side of this street in *c.* 1249: PRO, Just1/776, m. 22.
435 1. Perhaps a property belonging to the manor of Wolverton, Hants: see below, p. 383 and Table 28. Early forms of the place-name are *Ulvretune, Ulfretun,* and *Wulfertona, DEPN,* s.n.

[437] Ansgod Tresor¹ episcopo ii s. de terra baronum et episcopus debet illam aquietare erga regem de vi d.ᵃ

[438] Ricardus de Exonia regi xxii d.ᵃ

[439] Alexander reddit Iohanni de Port¹ xx d. et habet inde ii s. et vi d.

[440] Reginaldus de Sagio¹ regi xii d. et habet xi s.

[441] Robertus e[l]emosinarius¹ regi x d.

[442] Anschetillus serviens episcopi¹ regi iiii d. et episcopo xv d. de terra baronum et habet xvii s. et iiii d.

[443] Robertus Matre¹ episcopo iii s. de terra baronum et habet de Ricardo lorimer² ii marcas et de Urselino iudeo³ xxx s. et Ricardus lorimerᵇ habet inde vi s.

[444] Deulecreisse iudeius¹ episcopo xii s. et i bizantium de terra baronum.

[445] Godefridus filius Willelmi¹ episcopo xxx d. de terra baronum.

[446] Item Godefridus¹ regi x d.

[447] Brictwinusᶜ regi x d. et leprosis de Mont'¹ x s.

[448] Isabel episcopo xv d. de terra baronum et Turstino de Fisliaᵈ xvi s. et habet xiiii sol.

[449] Ansfridus burgensis¹ abbati de Hida² i d. et habet v s.

[450] Herebertus de Sale[s]b'¹ eidem abbati viii d. et habet inde i marcam.ᵉ

[437] Ansgod Tresor¹ pays the bishop 2s. from the land of the barons; and the bishop should acquit the land to the king for 6d.

[438] Richard of Exeter pays the king 22d.

[439] Alexander pays John of Port¹ 20d. and receives from the land 2s. 6d.

[440] Reginald of Sées¹ pays the king 12d. and receives 11s.

[441] Robert the almoner¹ pays the king 10d.

[442] Anschetil the bishop's servant¹ pays the king 4d. and the bishop 15d. from the land of the barons and receives 17s. 4d.

[443] Robert the Weasel¹ pays the bishop 3s. from the land of the barons and receives from Richard the lorimer² 2 marks and from Urselin the Jew³ 30s. And Richard the lorimer has from the land 6s.

[444] Deulecreise the Jew¹ pays the bishop 12s. and 1 bezant from the land of the barons.

[445] Godfrey son of William¹ pays the bishop 30d. from the land of the barons.

[446] Again Godfrey¹ pays the king 10d.

[447] Brithwin pays the king 10d. and the lepers on the hill¹ 10s.

[448] Isabel pays the bishop 15d. from the land of the barons and Thurstin of Fishleigh 16s. and receives 14s.

[449] Ansfrid the burgess¹ pays the abbot of Hyde² 1d. and receives 5s.

[450] Herbert of Salisbury¹ pays the same abbot 8d. and receives from the land 1 mark.

ᵃ *Marginal* N[ota] *shows through from verso, see* [478] *and* [479]   ᵇ *Followed by an erasure*   ᶜ *Over an erasure*   ᵈ *Eislia (wrongly) Ellis*   ᵉ *The marginal line against this entry is a show-through from the line on fo.* 22ᵛ *against* [464]

437 1. See 419.
439 1. See 2.
440 1. See 156.
441 1. See also 451, 495, 716, and 726. See Addenda.
442 1. See also 208.
443 1. See 9.
   2. See also 745.
   3. See also 444. This is the earliest evidence of Jews in Winchester. Subsequently the Winchester Jews had most of their properties in *Scowrtenestret*, which came to be known as Jewry Street, and in the neighbouring streets to E. and W.
444 1. Richard of Anstey borrowed money from Deule-

creise in the 1160s: Patricia M. Barnes, 'The Anstey Case', in Patricia Barnes and C. F. Slade (eds.), *A Medieval Miscellany for Doris Mary Stenton* (Pipe Roll Soc., 1962), 22.
445 1. See 5.
446 1. See 5.
447 1. See 276.
449 1. See 50.
   2. See also 450–72. Hyde abbey had an interest in a number of the properties on the E. side of this street in the later Middle Ages and was also patron of the church of St. Michael there: *SMW* 274, 276–8, and 278–9. See below, p. 357.
450 1. See also 451.

[451] Robertus elem*osinarius*[1] abbati de Truarz[2] x s. et abbati de Hida xl d. et habet ii marcas de Samuele; et Samuel reddit Herberto de Sar'[3] pro eadem terra xx s.;[a] et ipse Herebertus reddit predicto Samueli iiii s.; et de eadem terra tenet Rogerus v solidat*as* de Samuele et ipse [fo. 22[v]] Rogerus recipit inde v s.

[452] Henricus filius Roberti scoter' abbati[1] xiiii d. et habet vii s.; et Manig'[b] habet inde ii s.

[453] Stephanus filius Hugonis abbati xliiii d. et habet xvi s.

[454] Herbertus[c] filius Gunt'[1] abbati ii s.

[455] Heredes Trentem'[1] abbati ii s.

[456] Ansfridus de Hecche[1] abbati xv d.

[457] Goda Hacchemus[1] abbati xv d.

[458] Hugo Haccemus[1] abbati ii s.

[459] Uxor Buroldi abbati iii s.

[460] Edit Martel[1] eidem abbati xviii d.

[461] Matildis filia Godefridi abbati xviii d. et habet iii s.

[462] Rogerus filius Cheppingi[1] abbati de Hida ii s.

[463] Herebertus filius Westman[1] eidem abbati xxxi d. et habet viii s. et vi d.

[464] Willelmus[d] filius Rogeri[1] eidem[e] abbati iiii s. et habet viii s.[f]

[451] Robert the almoner[1] pays the abbot of Troarn[2] 10s. and the abbot of Hyde 40d. and receives 2 marks from Samuel. And Samuel pays Herbert of Salisbury[3] for the same land 20s., and Herbert pays the aforesaid Samuel 4s. Roger holds 5 shillingsworth of that same land from Samuel and Roger receives from it 5s.

[452] Henry son of Robert Archer pays the abbot[1] 14d. and receives 7s., and Manni receives from the land 2s.

[453] Stephen son of Hugh pays the abbot 44d. and receives 16s.

[454] Herbert son of Guncelin[1] pays the abbot 2s.

[455] Trentemars's heirs[1] pay the abbot 2s.

[456] Ansfrid of Hatch[1] pays the abbot 15d.

[457] Goda Hack-mouse[1] pays the abbot 15d.

[458] Hugh Hack-mouse[1] pays the abbot 2s.

[459] Burwold's wife pays the abbot 3s.

[460] Edith Martel[1] pays the same abbot 18d.

[461] Matilda, Godfrey's daughter, pays the abbot 18d. and receives 3s.

[462] Roger son of Chepping[1] pays the abbot of Hyde 2s.

[463] Herbert son of Westman[1] pays the same abbot 31d. and receives 8s. 6d.

[464] William son of Roger[1] pays the same abbot 4s. and receives 8s.

---

[a] xx *over an erasure*   [b] *Suspension mark after* i *erased*   [c] Rerbertus *MS.*   [d] Fill' *MS.*   [e] eidem *over an erasure*   [f] *There is a marginal line against this entry which calls attention to the* Nota *in the inner margin against* [478] *and* [479]

451 1. See **441**.
2. Founded by Roger of Montgomery in 1022 in the arr. Caen, diocese of Bayeux, and made a Benedictine monastery, following the observances of Fécamp, by his son Roger in 1050. Roger gave his abbey 5 hides in Hayling Island: *VCH Hants* i. 478a. John son of Gilbert *alias marescallus* granted *terram et domos* in Winchester on the fief of the abbot of Hyde to the abbey of Troarn by 1153–April 1154. In 1148 the abbey of Troarn had *unam domum* in Winchester (*Regesta*, iii, no. 902; R. N. Sauvage, *L'Abbaye de Saint Martin de Troarn au diocèse de Bayeux des origines au seizième siècle* (Mémoires de la Société des Antiquaires de Normandie, 4e série, 4, Caen, 1911), 371, 372, 373). The property lay on the E. side of *Scowrtenestret* (Jewry Street), near the junction with St. George's Street. A considerable part of it was in Jewish hands until at least as late as 1241, when Lumbard the Jew held a plot there of the abbot of Troarn (*Cal Close R 1237–42*, pp. 375–6; *Cal Chart R 1226–57*, p. 264; PRO, Just 1/775, m. 9d. and Just1/778, m. 59d). See also *SMW* 285.
3. See **450**.
452 1. The reference here and in the next nine entries is, presumably, to the abbot of Hyde.
454 1. See **29**.
455 1. For Trentemars, see **907** and **940**; for his sons **486** and **514**.
456 1. See **430**.
457 1. See **18**. *Galfridus Hachemus* held property on the E. side of *Shortenestret* in 1285: see below, p. 517, and *SMW* 278–9.
458 1. See **18**.
460 1. For William Martel, see **35**.
462 1. See also **1080**, and cf. **23**.
463 1. See **38**.
464 1. See **434**.

[465] Et item Willelmus[1] tenet quandam terram ubi managium[2] suum est; sed nil inde scimus.

[466] Radulfus filius Cheppi[n]gi[1] eidem abbati x d.

[467] Ormerus eidem abbati x d. et Willelmo Mart'[1] iii s.

[468] Odiham[1] eidem abbati xii d. et est vasta.

[469] Tochi eidem abbati v d.

[470] Tailebroc[1] abbati ii d.

[471] Ailricus Chie et Burewoldus abbati viii d.

[472] Brustinus abbati xii d. et est vasta.

ALWARNESTRET[a]

[473] Ernoldus presbiter[1] Radulfo de Port[2] vi d. et idem filio Federling'[3] vi d.

[474] Iohannes de Port[1] habet ii terras vastas.

[475] Et Osbertus Waspail habet ibidem i aliam terram de feudo comitis Gloec'[1] et est vasta.

[476] Episcopus Bathon' habet terram Petri de Valuin'[1] et reddit uxori Amfridi burgensis[2] xii d.; et ipse episcopus habet preterea ibi de suo feudo i aliam et habet de suo hospite dimidiam marcam.

[477] Monachi[b] de Egglessam[1] tenent quandam terram vacuam.

[478] Herbertus Westman[1] priori xx d. et episcopo Sar' ii s. et habet ibi xviii d.[c]

[465] And again William[1] holds a certain land where his dwelling-house(?)[2] is; but we know nothing about it.

[466] Ralf son of Chepping[1] pays the same abbot 10d.

[467] Ormer pays the same abbot 10d. and William Martel[1] 3s.

[468] Odiham[1] pays the same abbot 12d.; and the land is waste.

[469] Toky pays the same abbot 5d.

[470] Tailebroc[1] pays the abbot 2d.

[471] Ailric Chie and Burewold pay the abbot 8d.

[472] Brustin pays the abbot 12d.; and the land is waste.

ALWARNE STREET [ST PETER'S STREET]

[473] Ernold the priest[1] pays Ralf de Port[2] 6d. and Faderling's son[3] 6d.

[474] John de Port[1] has 2 lands which are waste.

[475] And Osbert Waspail has there another land of the fief of the earl of Gloucester,[1] and it is waste.

[476] The bishop of Bath has the land of Peter of Valognes[1] and pays Amfrid the burgess's wife[2] 12d. And the same bishop has there moreover 1 other land of his own fief and receives from his tenant ½ mark.

[477] The monks of Eynsham[1] hold a certain land which is vacant.

[478] Herbert Westman[1] pays the prior 20d. and the bishop of Salisbury 2s. and receives there 18d.

---

[a] *In upper margin, for rubricator:* alwarnestrat (= *in margin against heading directs to text for rubric above*)   [b] *Not rubricated as a separate item*   [c] *Marked with a marginal* N[ota]

---

465 1. See 434.
   2. See 197.
466 1. Cf. 23.
467 1. See 35.
468 1. See 330, and I, 96.
470 1. See 75.
473 1. Cf. 138.
   2. See 138.
   3. See I, 29.
474 1. See 2.
475 1. See 139.
476 1. Peter I, a Domesday tenant, was succeeded *post* 1109 by his son Roger, who died 1141–2. Roger's son, Peter II, died without offspring in 1158: Sanders *Baronies*, 12. Peter's tenements were in the hands of the bishop of

Bath because he had defected to the empress: *Regesta*, iii, nos. 275, 643. The bishop of Bath, Robert of Lewes, was possibly the author of *Gesta Stephani*: R. H. C. Davis, *EHR* 77 (1962), 209–320. He had also been deputy abbot for Henry of Blois at Glastonbury.
   2. See 50.
477 1. Benedictine monastery finally established in 1094/5: *VCH Oxon.* ii. 65 ff. Bishop Henry took a piece of land in Winchester from the monks of Eynsham *in confinio hospitii nostri* in exchange for three marks and granted the land back to them between 1143 and 1166: H. E. Salter (ed.), *The Eynsham Cartulary*, i (Oxford Historical Society, 49, 1907), 65.
478 1. See 38.

[479] Emma uxor Roberti fratris Warini[1] priori xii d. et habet iii s. Et Adeleis[2] habet de eadem terra xviii d.[a]

[480] Rogerus Witepe priori xvi d. et episcopo ii s. de terra baronum et habet xviii d.

[481] Rand' Bonus homo priori xv d. et habet iii s.

[482] Hugo Hacchemus[1] habet terram que [fo. 23] fuit Willelmi pro lang*abulo regis*[2] et reddit xxx d.

[483] Ricardus Loer'[1] episcopo xxx d. de B. et habet xv s.

[484] Item Ricardus[1] reddit regi vi d.[2] et habet x s. de Saiero.

[485] Emma[1] regi ii d.

[486] Filii Trentem'[1] regi xv d.[2] et habent vi s.

[487] Martinus de Binteword'[1] regi xv d.[2] et habet iiii s.

[488] Willelmus filius Pot[1] Willelmo Mart'[2] xv d.[b] et habet xix s. et iiii d.

[489] Edulfus nepos Turstini[1] Willelmo Mart'[2] vii s. et habet xix s.

[490] Willelmus Mart'[1] habet i terram.

[491] Adeliz[c][1] Willelmo Mar'[2] xv d.[3]

[492] Heruic' Freschet[1] episcopo x d. de B. Idem episcopo xxix d.[2] et Willelmo Mart'[3] vii s.

[493] Turstinus clericus[1] episcopo vi d. de B. et idem regi x d. et habet xl d.[2]

[479] Emma the wife of Robert, Warin's brother,[1] pays the prior 12*d.* and receives 3*s.* And Adelaide[2] receives from that land 18*d.*

[480] Roger White-peacock pays the prior 16*d.* and the bishop 2*s.* from the land of the barons and receives 18*d.*

[481] Randolf Goodman pays the prior 15*d.* and receives 3*s.*

[482] Hugh Hack-mouse[1] has a land which was William's for the king's landgable.[2] And he pays 30*d.*

[483] Richard Loer'[1] pays the bishop 30*d. de B.* and receives 15*s.*

[484] Again Richard[1] pays the king 6*d.*[2] and receives 10*s.* from Saiher.

[485] Emma[1] pays the king 2*d.*

[486] Trentemars's sons[1] pay the king 15*d.*[2] and receive 6*s.*

[487] Martin of Bentworth[1] pays the king 15*d.*[2] and receives 4*s.*

[488] William son of Pot[1] pays William Martel[2] 15*d.* and receives 19*s.* 4*d.*

[489] Edulf, Thurstin's nephew,[1] pays William Martel[2] 7*s.* and receives 19*s.*

[490] William Martel[1] has 1 land.

[491] Adelaide[1] pays William Martel[2] 15*d.*[3]

[492] Herewic Freschet[1] pays the bishop 10*d. de B.* He also pays the bishop 29*d.*[2] and William Martel[3] 7*s.*

[493] Thurstin the clerk[1] pays the bishop 6*d. de B.* and he also pays the king 10*d.* and receives 40*d.*[2]

---

[a] *Marked with a marginal* N[ota]   [b] *Erasure before* xv   [c] *Followed by a space*

479 1. For Warin's brother Robert, see **I, 176**. He may have been Robert fitzGerald. Emma (see also **485**) is presumably distinct from the Emma wife of Robert in **I, 94**.

2. See also **491**. As we are close to the Port family (**473–4**), this may be the sister of Henry de Port: see **I, 239**.

482 1. See **18**.

2. Perhaps William was responsible for the landgable.

483 1. See also **484**.

484 1. See **483**.

2. For this tenement, cf. **I, 178**, but note **II, 501**.

485 1. See **479**.

486 1. See **455**. See Addenda.

2. For this tenement, cf. **I, 174 or 175**.

487 1. See **17**.

2. For this tenement, cf. **I, 174 or 175**. See Addenda.

488 1. For Pot see **I, 137** and **174**.

2. See **35**.

489 1. See also **674**. Probably the nephew of Thurstin the clerk: see **221**. For his mother, see **496**.

2. See **35**.

490 1. See **35**.

491 1. Cf. **479**.

2. See **35**.

3. It is not clear why **490** and **491** are separated.

492 1. See **282**.

2. Here a *de B.* payment is apparently distinguished from an ordinary rent.

3. See **35**.

493 1. See **221**.

2. Possibly the same tenement as **I, 180**.

[494] Item Turstinus[1] Hugoni de Pusat[2] v s. et episcopo vii d. et obolum de B.

[494] Again Thurstin[1] pays Hugh of Le Puiset[2] 5s. and the bishop 7½d. de B.

[495] Robertus elemosinarius[1] episcopo xi d. et quadrantem de B.

[495] Robert the almoner[1] pays the bishop 11¼d. de B.

[496] Turstinus clericus[1] tenet i terram quietam et habet i marcam; et soror uxoris Turstini manet in una parte cum catellis sue sororis.[2]

[496] Thurstin the clerk[1] holds 1 land quit and receives 1 mark. And Thurstin's wife's sister lives on one part with the chattels of her sister.[2]

[497] Girinus clericus[1] episcopo ii s. de B.

[497] Girin the clerk[1] pays the bishop 2s. de B.

[498] Rogerus de Forest habet terram suam quietam et habet inde iiii s.

[498] Roger of Forest has his land quit and receives from it 4s.

[499] Edwardus de Stanam[a] habet terram suam quietam et habet inde iiii s.

[499] Edward of Stoneham has his land quit and receives from it 4s.

[500] Godard' regi xii d.[1] et habet vii s.

[500] Godard pays the king 12d.[1] and receives 7s.

[501] Bernardus Hubold[1] abb[at]isse de Warewoll' xxx d. et habet iii s. Et Ricardus qui manet intus habet ii s. Et idem Bernardus eidem abbatisse xx d. et idem Bernardus episcopo vi d. de terra baronum et regi vi d.[2]

[501] Bernard Hubold[1] pays the abbess of Wherwell 30d. and receives 3s. And Richard who dwells within receives 2s. And the same Bernard pays the same abbess 20d.; and the same Bernard pays the bishop 6d. from the land of the barons and the king 6d.[2]

[502] Heredes Herberti filii Gunt'[1] prepositis de Ordia[2] ii s. et Alwinus Bierd[3] eisdem xii d.[b]

[502] Herbert son of Guncelin's heirs[1] pay the reeves of Worthy[2] 2s. and Alwin Beard[3] pays them 12d.

[503] Girinus clericus[1] habet xii d. de quadam terra.

[503] Girin the clerk[1] receives 12d. from a certain land.

[504] Iohannes presbiter episcopo vi d. de B.

[504] John the priest pays the bishop 6d. de B.

[505] Baldewinus presbiter episcopo xx d. de B. et habet xii d.

[505] Baldwin the priest pays the bishop 20d. de B. and receives 12d.

[506] Herbertus filius Westman[1] abbati de Hida xx d. et habet v s.; et de eadem Robertus de Ingl'[2] habet vi s.

[506] Herbert son of Westman[1] pays the abbot of Hyde 20d. and receives 5s. And from the same land Robert of Inglesham[2] receives 6s.

[507] Colbrandus[1] eidem abbati xx d. et habet xx d.[c] Et Colbrandus reddit fratri Olaf[2] iii s. et vi d. et Willelmo de Bradeia vi d. et [fo. 23ᵛ] habet vi s.

[507] Colbrand[1] pays the same abbot 20d. and receives 20d. And Colbrand pays brother Olaf[2] 3s. 6d. and William of *Bradeia* [? Bradley] 6d. and receives 6s.

---

[a] *Suspension mark after* n *erased, and (?) replaced after* a

[b] xii *over an erasure*   [c] xx *over an erasure*

494 1. See 221.
2. Bishop of Durham (1153–95). The son of Hugh III of Le Puiset, the nephew of King Stephen and Henry, bishop of Winchester, he came to England *c.* 1130, occurred as archdeacon of Winchester 1139 (? 1142) × 1153, and, through the influence of William fitzHerbert, archbishop-elect of York, became *c.* 1143 treasurer and archdeacon of the East Riding: G. V. Scammell, *Hugh du Puiset bishop of Durham* (Cambridge, 1956); *DNB* xlvii. 10; Le Neve *Monastic Cathedrals 1066–1300*, 92; see below, p. 392.
495 1. See 441.
496 1. See 221.
2. One of these sisters is presumably the mother of Edulf: see 489. For chattels, see 55.

497 1. See also 503.
500 1. For this tenement, cf. I, 177.
501 1. See Addenda.
2. For this tenement, cf. I, 178, but note II, 484.
502 1. See 29.
2. See 406.   3. See 69.
503 1. See 497.
506 1. See 38. Elyas Westman had a house in this street in the early thirteenth century: Southwick Cart i, fo. 38.
2. See 1.
507 1. He witnessed a conveyance of property in High Street (cf. 43) and *Alwarnestret* (cf. 487) *c.* 1155–60: Southwick Cart iii, fos. 123ᵛ, 136ᵛ.
2. Or, his brother Olaf, or Olaf's brother.

[508] Willelmus filius Rogeri[1] tenet i terram quietam et habet x s. et vi d.

[509] Gaufridus filius Petri[1] habet i terram vastam que est de feudo abbatisse Winton'.

IN FLESMANGERESTRET[a]

[510] Turstinus clericus[1] regi iiii d.[2] et abbatisse de Warewolla v s. et habet xxviii s. et God' fullo et Toli xiiii s. qui manent in eis.[3]

[511] Et idem Turstinus[1] eidem abbatisse x s. ab aecclesia Sancti Martini[2] usque ad domum Siwardi monetarii[3] et habet inde x s.; et rex habet [. . .][b] sicut dicunt.[4] Et Willelmus de Sotton'[5] habet xviii s.

[512] Siwardus monetarius[1] regi xv d.[2] et Willelmo[c] de Chaisneto[3] ospicium salem et aquam[4] et Willelmo de Chateleia vi s. et habet inde ii s.; et idem abbatisse de Warew[o]lla xv d. et habet viii s.

[513] Osbertus Cod[1] eidem abbatisse xv d.; et dimidia pars illius domus[d] est vasta et deberet[e] reddere xv d.[f]

[514] Filii Trentem'[1] eidem abbatisse xxv d., sed abbatissa calumpniat iii s. et i d.

[515] Petrus merciarius[1] eidem abbatisse iii d. et habet vii s.

[516] Petrus sellarius canonicis de Merton'[1] xii d.

---

[508] William son of Roger[1] holds 1 land quit and receives 10s. 6d.

[509] Geoffrey fitzPeter[1] has 1 waste land which is of the fief of the abbess of Winchester.

IN *FLESMANGERE* STREET [PARCHMENT STREET]

[510] Thurstin the clerk[1] pays the king 4d.[2] and the abbess of Wherwell 5s. and receives 28s. And God' the fuller and Toli who dwell on them [receive (?)] 14s.[3]

[511] And the same Thurstin[1] pays the same abbess 10s. from the church of St. Martin[2] as far as the tenement of Siward the moneyer,[3] and receives from the land 10s. And the king receives [. . .], so they say.[4] And William of Sutton[5] receives 18s.

[512] Siward the moneyer[1] pays the king 15d.,[2] owes William of Chesney[3] lodgings, salt, and water,[4] and pays William *de Chateleia* 6s. He receives from the land 2s. He also pays the abbess of Wherwell 15d. and receives 8s.

[513] Osbert Cod[1] pays the same abbess 15d., and half that tenement is waste and should have paid 15d.

[514] Trentemars's sons[1] pay the same abbess 25d. but the abbess claims 3s. 1d.

[515] Peter the mercer[1] pays the same abbess 3d. and receives 7s.

[516] Peter the saddler pays the canons of Merton[1] 12d.

---

[a] *Text in margin for rubricator almost entirely cut away*
[d] domi *MS.*   [e] debet et *MS.*   [f] x *over an erasure*

[b] *Space left for amount*   [c] W *over an erasure*

---

508 1. See **434**. This was probably the land in *Alwarestret* which William purchased from *Bochardo carpentario* and granted to Southwick Priory before 1162–3. In the early thirteenth century the priory had 12d. rent from this property, which was said to be *iuxta murum aquilonis in capite vici*, and a further 12d. from an adjacent property: Southwick Cart i, fo. 38 and iii, fo. 134.
509 1. Witnessed a charter of Duke Henry (1153): *Regesta*, iii, no. 823. Presumably not the great royal servant who died in 1213.
510 1. See Addenda.
  2. For this tenement, cf. **I, 183**.
  3. Or, 'receive 14s. from the inhabitants'.
511 1. See **221**.
  2. The church of St. Martin, in the patronage of the abbey of Wherwell, was situated on the W. side of this street near its S. end: *SMW* 317, 318.
  3. See **112**.
  4. For this tenement, cf. **I, 182**.   5. See **343**.
512 1. See **112**. For a possible earlier moneyer's interest

here, cf. **I, 182**.   2. For this tenement, cf. **I, 181**.
  3. Brother of Robert, bishop of Lincoln, and uncle of Gilbert Foliot, bishop of Hereford and then London. A prominent supporter of King Stephen, at this date and until 1153–4 he seems to have held the d'Oilli fief, cf. **25**. See H. E. Salter, 'The Family of Chesney', *Cartulary of the Abbey of Eynsham* (Oxford Hist. Soc. 49 (1906)), i, Appendix I, pp. 411 ff.
  4. This expression is without parallel in these surveys.
513 1. See also **696**.
514 1. See **455**.
515 1. See **35**.
516 1. See **50**. Stephen, count of Mortain, quitclaimed to Bernard the scribe (see **I, 83**, n. 1) his right in 12d. rent from his land in *Flesshmongerestret*. Bernard granted the rent to Merton Priory, and subsequently the priory granted the land in *Flesshmongerestret*, which Robert de la Huche had held, to Herbert son of William of Winchester for 2s. rent: BM, Cotton MS. Cleopatra C. vii, fos. 68[v], 69, 76[v], 77; *EHR* 14 (1899), 424.

[517] Robertus Marc'[1] tenet i terram vastam de i mans*ione*, sed nescimus inde.

[518] Et Goda Hacchemus[1] tenet ibi iii mans*iones* vastas, sed nescimus quo ten*entur* vel quid reddat.

[519] Willelmus filius Rogeri[1] abbatisse de War*ewolla* xv d. et habet iii d.

[520] Crabeleg[1] eidem abbatisse viii d.; et est i terra vacua et reddit regi iii d.

[521] De feudo abbatisse de War*ewolla* sunt ii vacue terre, quas nemo tenet, que solebant reddere viii d.

[522] Golburg' eidem abbatisse ii d.

[523] Eduinus et frater eius priori Wint' vii d.

[524] Brufald' ei[dem] priori iiii d.

[525] Drogo*a* de Calp'[1] episcopo xv d. de terra baronum et habet iiii s.

[526] Gilebertus presbiter priori Wint' xii d. et Willelmus Danzel[1] habet de eadem iii s. et vi d.

[527] Et idem Willelmus Danzel[1] eidem priori xii d. et habet iii s.

[528] Erneis bedel eidem priori xii d. [fo. 24] et habet xv d.

[529] Willelmus mareschallus[1] episcopo xii d. et habet v s. Et Algerus habet de eadem ii s.

[530] Eldit episcopo viii d. et priori Winto' ii s. et habet xiii d.

[531] Siluester[1] episcopo xv d. et habet ix s.

[532] Godefridus filius Sewi[1] episcopo xx d. et habet x s.

[533] Robertus Pinguis[1] episcopo xiii d. et est vast*a*.

[534] Ricardus Longus clericus[1] episcopo vi d. et habet iiii s.

[517] Robert the Weasel[1] holds 1 waste land of 1 messuage, but we do not know about it.

[518] And Goda Hack-mouse[1] holds there 3 messuages which are waste; but we do not know from whom they are held or what he pays.

[519] William son of Roger[1] pays the abbess of Wherwell 15*d.* and receives 3*d.*

[520] Crableg[1] pays the same abbess 8*d.* And there is [also] one vacant land which yields the king 3*d.*

[521] There are 2 vacant lands of the fief of the abbess of Wherwell which no one holds, but which used to yield 8*d.*

[522] Golburg pays the same abbess 2*d.*

[523] Edwin and his brother pay the prior of Winchester 7*d.*

[524] Brifald pays the same prior 4*d.*

[525] Drew *de Calp'*[1] pays the bishop 15*d.* from the land of the barons and receives 4*s.*

[526] Gilbert the priest pays the prior of Winchester 12*d.* and William Danzel[1] receives from that land 3*s.* 6*d.*

[527] And the same William Danzel[1] pays the same prior 12*d.* and receives 3*s.*

[528] Erneis the beadle pays the same prior 12*d.* and receives 15*d.*

[529] William the marshal[1] pays the bishop 12*d.* and receives 5*s.* And Alger receives from the same land 2*s.*

[530] Aldith pays the bishop 8*d.* and the prior of Winchester 2*s.* and receives 13*d.*

[531] Silvester[1] pays the bishop 15*d.* and receives 9*s.*

[532] Godfrey son of Sewi[1] pays the bishop 20*d.* and receives 10*s.*

[533] Robert the Fat[1] pays the bishop 13*d.* and the land is waste.

[534] Richard Long the clerk[1] pays the bishop 6*d.* and receives 4*s.*

a Rrog' *MS., blue initial* R *for* D, *cf.* [653]

517 1. See 9. The MS. reading is *Marc'*, but this may be a mistake for *Mart'*.
518 1. See 18.
519 1. See 434.
520 1. See 205.
525 1. See also 838.
526 1. See also 527 and 549–50.
527 1. See 526.

529 1. See 315.
531 1. *Siluester alderman* witnessed a conveyance of property in this street (see 510, n. 1) before 1155: Southwick Cart iii, fos. 133, 141ᵛ.
532 1. See 55.
533 1. See also 559, 566, 687, 698, and 996.
534 1. See also 535.

[535] Idem Ricardus¹ priori Wint' xxx d. et habet viii s., et preterea habet de Ricardo de Limesia² ii s.

[536] Ricardus de Limesia¹ eidem priori liii d.

[537] Prior Wint' episcopo xxv d. et habet xvi s.

[538] Terra Willelmi elemosinarii¹ episcopo xxv d. et est vasta.

[539] Hugo Hacchemus¹ abbatisse de Warewolla² viii d.

[540] Et de eadem Edwardus clericus eidem abbatisse iiii d.

IN SILDWORTENESTRET[a]

[541] Robertus Quadde regi vi d.

[542] Uxor Talazin Hereberto camerario¹ xii d. et habet ii s.

[543] Rand' presbiter regi iii d.[b] et habet vi d.

[544] Ebrardus de Carnot'¹ regi xiiii d. et Ricardo de Limesia[c]² ii s. et habet iii s.

[545] Anschetillus Bucl'¹ episcopo iii s., regi x d. de B.

[546] Siluester episcopo vi d. et abbatisse xii d.

[547] Edmundus bulengarius episcopo xii d.

[548] Uxor Gaufridi de Sancto Laudo episcopo iii d.

[535] The same Richard¹ pays the prior of Winchester 30d. and receives 8s. And moreover he receives from Richard of Limésy² 2s.

[536] Richard of Limésy¹ pays the same prior 53d.

[537] The prior of Winchester pays the bishop 25d. and receives 16s.

[538] The land of William the almoner¹ pays the bishop 25d. and is waste.

[539] Hugh Hack-mouse¹ pays the abbess of Wherwell² 8d.

[540] And from the same land Edward the clerk pays the same abbess 4d.

IN SILDWORTENE STREET [UPPER BROOK STREET]

[541] Robert Quadde pays the king 6d.

[542] Talazin's wife pays Herbert the chamberlain¹ 12d. and receives 2s.

[543] Randulf the priest pays the king 3d. and receives 6d.

[544] Ebrard of Chartres¹ pays the king 14d. and Richard of Limésy² 2s. and receives 3s.

[545] Anschetil the buckle-maker¹ pays the bishop 3s. and the king 10d. de B.

[546] Silvester pays the bishop 6d. and the abbess 12d.

[547] Edmund the baker pays the bishop 12d.

[548] Geoffrey of St. Lô's wife pays the bishop 3d.

---

[a] *In lower margin, text for rubricator almost entirely cut away*   [b] *iii over an erasure*   [c] *Over an erasure*

535 1. See **534**.

2. See also **536** and **544**. Possibly a member of the baronial family which held Cavendish (Suffolk). Ralf I (died *c.* 1093) was succeeded by Ralf II (died *c.* 1129), who was succeeded by Alan. Robert of Limésy was bishop of Chester, 1085–1117. Another Robert of Limésy held land in Winchester in 1130 (*Pipe Roll 31 Henry I*, p. 41), and was the first master of the Hospital of St. Cross: *VCH Hants* ii. 194, 196. A Henry of Limésy witnessed a Winchester document of the late twelfth or early thirteenth century, *Proc Hants FC* 20 (1956), 51, n. 22. A Nicholas of Limésy held property in the city at about the same date: see below, p. 510.

536 1. See **535**.

538 1. In 1130 he held land in Leics., Bucks., Berks., and

Middx.: *Pipe Roll 31 Henry I*, pp. 89, 102, 126, 152. He witnessed Winchester charters of this period: J. H. Round, *EHR* 14 (1899), 423, 429–30, and may have been a royal almoner.

539 1. See **18**.

2. Cf. **540**. Wherwell Abbey had property on the W. side of *Shuldwortenestret* in the thirteenth century (BM, Egerton MS. 2104, fos. 93ᵛ, 182ᵛ), which may have been opposite the main block of Wherwell property in this street, see **510–15**.

542 1. See **4**.

544 1. See also **855** and **891**.

2. See **535**.

545 1. See also **551**.

[549] Willelmus Danzel[1] Roberto de Ingl'[2] viii d. et habet xii d.

[550] Et idem Willelmus[1] Baldewino de Portesia i d. et habet xxviii d.

[551] Item Anschetillus Buclar'[1] priori Wint' viii d.[a]

[552] Paganus filius Picardi[1] priori iiii d. et est vasta.

[553] Robertus de Ingl'[1] debet reddere Briauello xii d. et abbati de Hida xlii d. et habet iiii s.; et de alia terra habet i marcam.

[554] Hunfridus monacus[1] abbati xii d. et habet viii s.

[555] Ricardus filius Lambricht[1] tenet iii terras que solebant reddere Willelmo filio Oin[2] xxx d. [fo. 24ᵛ] Unde modo reddit Roberto de Ingl'[3] xviii d., et est de feudo regis. Et habet inde xxviii d.

[556] Amfridus de Hacche[1] priori Winton' xviii d. et habet v s.

[557] Petrus merciarius[1] priori Winton' x d. et abb[at]isse Wint' xiiii d. et habet ix s.

[558] Pontius eidem abbatisse xviii d.

[559] Robertus Pinguis[1] tenet i terram de feudo Walteri filii Ricardi.[2]

[560] Ricardus Cuillebrant episcopo xviii d.

[561] Hugo filius Brum' regi viii d.

[562] Hunfridus monacus[1] regi viii d. et Waltero filio Ricardi[2] xv d. et idem filio Alberici coci[3] iii d. et regi ii [d.] et habet viii s.[b]

[563] Scorfan[1] habebat iiii denaratas de terra in illa; sed nescimus ubi sit.[2]

[549] William Danzel[1] pays Robert of Inglesham[2] 8d. and receives 12d.

[550] And the same William[1] pays Baldwin of Portsea 1d. and receives 28d.

[551] Again Anschetil the buckle-maker[1] pays the prior of Winchester 8d.

[552] Pain son of Picard[1] pays the prior 4d. and the land is waste.

[553] Robert of Inglesham[1] should pay Briavel 12d. and the abbot of Hyde 42d. and he receives 4s. And from another land he receives 1 mark.

[554] Humphrey the monk[1] pays the abbot 12d. and receives 8s.

[555] Richard son of Lambert[1] holds 3 lands which used to yield William son of Oin[2] 30d. Now from these he pays Robert of Inglesham[3] 18d. And it is on the king's fief. And he receives from them/it 28d.

[556] Ansfrid of Hatch[1] pays the prior of Winchester 18d. and receives 5s.

[557] Peter the mercer[1] pays the prior of Winchester 10d. and the abbess of Winchester 14d. and receives 9s.

[558] Pons pays the same abbess 18d.

[559] Robert the Fat[1] holds 1 land of the fief of Walter son of Richard.[2]

[560] Richard Cuillebrant pays the bishop 18d.

[561] Hugh son of Brunman pays the king 8d.

[562] Humphrey the monk[1] pays the king 8d. and Walter son of Richard[2] 15d. And he also pays the son of Alberic the cook[3] 3d. and the king 2d. and receives 8s.

[563] Escorfan[1] used to have 4 pennyworths of land in it; but we do not know where it is.[2]

---

[a] *Marked with a marginal* N[ota]   [b] *Marginal* N[ota] *shows through from recto, see* [551]

549 1. See **526**.
  2. See **1**.
550 1. See **526**.
551 1. See **545**.
552 1. See **21**, n. 1.
553 1. See **1**.
554 1. See also **565**.
555 1. See also **564** and **916**.
  2. Possibly the son of Oin the napier: cf. **I, 197**.
  3. See **1**.
556 1. See **430**.

557 1. See **35**.
559 1. See **553**.
  2. See **205**.
562 1. See **554**.
  2. See **205**.
  3. See **I, 82** and **I, 191** in *Wunegrestret*, for this tenement, which might therefore be on the E. side of the street.
563 1. See **I, 38**, and **I, 195** in *Wunegrestret* for this tenement. Cf. **562**.
  2. This item should probably have been included in **562**.

[564] Willelmus filius Bos[1] episcopo iiii d. de B. et habet xi s. et ii d.; et Ricardus filius Lambricht[2] habet de eadem v s.

[565] Humfridus monacus[1] uxori Mart*ini*[2] iii s. et habet v s. et vi d.*a*

[566] Robertus Pinguis[1] uxori Mart*ini*[2] xxviii d.*b* et habet v s.

[567] Godefridus de Windelesor[1] priori xxvi d. et habet xii s.

IN WUNEGRESTRET*c*

[568] Robertus frater Goda Hacchemus[1] episcopo x d. et priori xxxiiii d. Et de quadam domo*d* ubi quedam femina facit bracinium suum habet v s., et de alia renta illius terrae habet viii s.

[569] Radulfus Lupus de ii mans*ionibus*e iii s. et i d.

[570] Alwinus brac*iator* regi v d.[1] et episcopo v d. Et idem Alwinus episcopo iii s. de B.

[571] Rogerus vinet*arius*[1] regi viii d.[2] et Dulzan' tenet illam.

[572] Turstinus clericus[1] regi xiiii d.[2]

[573] Godefridus filius Willelmi[1] tenet de feudo regis et habet de quadam parte illius terrae ii capones de Rogero vinet*ario*;[2] et Rogerus habet x d. de Luuingo*f* et preterea Godefridus habet v s.

[574] Herebertus filius Radulfi[1] episcopo dimidiam libram piperis de terra baronum.

[575] Helewisa[1] episcopo vi d.

[576] Walwain episcopo viii d.

[564] William son of Bos[1] pays the bishop 4*d. de B.* and receives 11*s.* 2*d.* And Richard son of Lambert[2] receives from that same land 5*s.*

[565] Humphrey the monk[1] pays Martin's wife[2] 3*s.* and receives 5*s.* 6*d.*

[566] Robert the Fat[1] pays Martin's wife[2] 28*d.* and receives 5*s.*

[567] Godfrey of Winsor[1] pays the prior 26*d.* and receives 12*s.*

IN *WUNEGRE* STREET [MIDDLE BROOK STREET]

[568] Robert, the brother of Goda Hack-mouse,[1] pays the bishop 10*d.* and the prior 34*d.* And from a certain tenement where a certain woman has a brewery he receives 5*s.*; and from another rent from that land he receives 8*s.*

[569] Ralf the Wolf pays for 2 messuages 3*s.* 1*d.*

[570] Alwin the brewer pays the king 5*d.*[1] and the bishop 5*d.* And the same Alwin pays the bishop 3*s. de B.*

[571] Roger the vintner[1] pays the king 8*d.*[2] and Dulzan holds the land.

[572] Thurstin the clerk[1] pays the king 14*d.*[2]

[573] Godfrey son of William[1] holds of the king's fief and receives from a certain part of that land 2 capons from Roger the vintner.[2] And Roger receives from Leving 10*d.* and moreover Godfrey receives 5*s.*

[574] Herbert son of Ralf[1] pays the bishop ½ lb. of pepper from the land of the barons.

[575] Heloïse[1] pays the bishop 6*d.*

[576] Walwain [Gawain] pays the bishop 8*d.*

---

a Second line of MS. written over an erasure   *b xxviii d. over an erasure*   *c In upper margin for rubricator:* In Wunegenstret (?)   *d ho' MS.*   *e Followed by a space*   *f de Luuingo over an erasure; correction mark in margin*

564 1. See 66.
  2. See 555.
565 1. See 554.
  2. See 17.
566 1. See 533.
  2. See 17.
567 1. See also 686 and cf. 69, n. 1.
568 1. See 18.
570 1. For this tenement, cf. I, 186.
571 1. See also 573.

  2. This rent was still being paid in 1285 and came from a property on the W. side of the street. See below, p. 517 and n. 2, and *SMW* 380.
572 1. See 221.
  2. For this tenement, cf. I, 194. This rent was still being paid in 1285, see below, p. 517 and n. 3.
573 1. See 5.
  2. See 571.
574 1. See also 596 and 829.
575 1. See also 577 and 1055.

[577] Item Helewisa¹ episcopo x d. et habet xx d.ᵃ

[577] Again Heloïse¹ pays the bishop 10d. and receives 20d.

[578] ᵇServientes de Templo¹ episcopo ii d.² et h[abe]nt iii s.ᶜ

[578] The servants of the Temple¹ pay the bishop 2d.² and receive 3s.

[579] [fo. 25] Robertus de Ingl'¹ episcopo vi d. et habet dimidiam marcam.

[579] Robert of Inglesham¹ pays the bishop 6d. and receives ½ mark.

[580] Item Robertus¹ Rogero de Port² xii d. de i terra.

[580] Again Robert¹ pays Roger de Port² 12d. for 1 land.

[581] Henricus mercator Rogero de Port¹ xii d.

[581] Henry the merchant/mercer pays Roger de Port¹ 12d.

[582] Durandus Cornet eidem Rogero¹ xii d. et habet xvi d.

[582] Durand Cornet pays the same Roger¹ 12d. and receives 16d.

[583] Heredes Gunt'¹ eidem Rogero² xii d. et habent vi d.

[583] Guncelin's heirs¹ pay the same Roger² 12d. and receive 6d.

[584] Willelmus Novus magistro hospitali[s] de Ierusalem¹ ii s.

[584] William New pays the Master of the Hospital of Jerusalem¹ 2s.

[585] Petrus Agnell' comiti de Clara¹ xii d. et Alwinus Stiward solebat ei reddere vi d. et ex alia parte iiii s.; et Osbertus filius Stiwardi habet de bordello viii d.

[585] Peter Agnel pays the earl of Clare¹ 12d., and Alwin Steward used to pay him 6d. and for another part 4s. And Osbert son of Steward has from a shack 8d.

[586] Seward' serviens abbatisse hominibus de Templo¹ ii d.

[586] Seward, the abbess's servant, pays the men of the Temple¹ 2d.

[587] Siluester episcopo xxviii d. et filie Herlebaldi¹ viii d. et habet iiii s.

[587] Silvester pays the bishop 28d. and Herlebold's daughter¹ 8d. and receives 4s.

[588] Ulf Niwem' episcopo xiii d. et filie Herlebaldi¹ iiii d.

[588] Ulf Newman pays the bishop 13d. and Herlebold's daughter¹ 4d.

[589] Engelramus¹ episcopo ii d.

[589] Engelram¹ pays the bishop 2d.

[590] Ricardus presbiter¹ episcopo ii d. et habet xii d.; sed heredes Hugonis Friedai² calumpniant illam.

[590] Richard the priest¹ pays the bishop 2d. and receives 12d. But Hugh Friday's heirs² claim the land.

ᵃ xx d. *over an erasure*   ᵇ *Whole entry written over an erasure*   ᶜ *Catch-word at end of quire, in bottom margin, partly cut away*

577 1. See 575.
578 1. See 25.
  2. In 1209 6d. rent due to the bishop in this street was in default, *terre Templariorum: PRBW 1208–9*, 77.
579 1. See 1.
580 1. See 1.
  2. See also 581–3. Lord of Kington (Herefordshire), who died before 1161. His father was Adam I, brother of Henry de Port, and son of Hugh de Port: see 2; Sanders *Baronies*, 57.
581 1. See 580.
582 1. See 580.
583 1. See 29.
  2. See 580.
584 1. See also 720. Items 9, 910, and 1081 probably

refer to the Hospital of St. Cross at Winchester. The Hospital of St. John of Jerusalem owned land on the W. side of this street in the later Middle Ages: *SMW* 391.
585 1. Gilbert, first earl of Hertford.
586 1. See 25.
587 1. For Herlebald, see 721; for his wife, 795; for his daughter, see also 588.
588 1. See 587.
589 1. Possibly a moneyer of Henry I: see below, Table 42.
590 1. See 322.
  2. See also 616. In *c.* 1220 Margaret Fridei granted land in this street, owing rents to the bishop and St. Swithun's Priory, to the canons of St. Denis: St Denis Cart, fo. 123; cf. *Selborne Charters*, ii. 74.

[591] Radulfus de Bichint' episcopo xvi d. et habet de Durando de iii bracinis et pro domo et pro ustiliis[1] unaquaque ebdomada viii d.

[591] Ralf of Bighton pays the bishop 16*d*. and receives from Durand for 3 breweries, a house, and utensils (?)[1] 8*d*. a week.

[592] Ansgod Tresor[1] episcopo xxix d.

[592] Ansgod Tresor[1] pays the bishop 29*d*.

[593] Ailricus Verbula priori Wint' xii d.

[593] Ailric Verbula pays the prior of Winchester 12*d*.

[594] Reginaldus filius Edulfi priori viii d.

[594] Reginald son of Edulf pays the prior 8*d*.

[595] Robertus presbiter[a] priori Wint' vi d. et episcopus debet habere inde iiii d.

[595] Robert the priest pays the prior of Winchester 6*d*. and the bishop ought to receive from the land 4*d*.

[596] Herebertus filius Radulfi[1] priori x d. et habet ix s.

[596] Herbert son of Ralf[1] pays the prior 10*d*. and receives 9*s*.

[597] Siluester[1] priori x d. et habet v s. et xi d.

[597] Silvester[1] pays the prior 10*d*. and receives 5*s*. 11*d*.

[598] Idem Siluester[1] priori v d.

[598] The same Silvester[1] pays the prior 5*d*.

[599] Willelmus presbiter priori de iii terris xv d.[1]

[599] William the priest pays the prior for 3 lands 15*d*.[1]

[600] Udelina priori viii d.

[600] Udelina pays the prior 8*d*.

[601] Uxor Sermonar'[1] priori xviii d.

[601] Sermoner's wife[1] pays the prior 18*d*.

[602] Robertus de Ingl'[1] abbatisse de Rumes' x d. et habet dimidiam marcam de Eduino Coppa;[2] et ipse Eduinus habet xi s. et vi d. ibidem.

[602] Robert of Inglesham[1] pays the abbess of Romsey 10*d*. and receives ½ mark from Edwin Coppa.[2] And the same Edwin receives 11*s*. 6*d*. in that same place.

[603] Heredes Gunt'[1] priori xx d.; sed est vasta.[b]

[603] Guncelin's heirs[1] pay the prior 20*d*.; but the land is waste.

[604] Beatric regi viii d.[1]

[604] Beatrice pays the king 8*d*.[1]

[605] Uxor Rogeri coci[1] episcopo xvi d. et de alia priori xviii d.

[605] Roger the cook's wife[1] pays the bishop 16*d*. and for another land pays the prior 18*d*.

[606] Diera priori iiii s. et habet iiii s.

[606] Diera pays the prior 4*s*. and receives 4*s*.

[607] Canonici de Sancto Dionisio[1] priori xiiii d. et habe[n]t v s. et ii d.

[607] The canons of St. Denis[1] pay the prior 14*d*. and receive 5*s*. 2*d*.

---

[a] *Over an erasure*   [b] *Marked with a marginal* Nota

591 1. This word also occurs in **696**. See **55** and below, p. 431.
592 1. See **419**.
596 1. See **574**.
597 1. See also **598**.
598 1. See **597**.
599 1. Between 1155 and 1182 William *sacerdos de Sancto Pancracio* granted a rent of 2*s*. from outside East Gate to Godstow Nunnery: Godstow Cart, fos. 163ᵛ, 164, 165. If he is identical with the William of this entry, this part of the survey may be near the church of St.

Pancras on the E. side of *Wunegrestret*. The church was in the patronage of St. Swithun's Priory by 1172: Goodman *Chartulary*, no. 42.
601 1. See **312**.
602 1. See **1**.
   2. See also **1029**.
603 1. See **29**.
604 1. This rent was apparently still being paid in 1285, see below, p. 517 and n. 4, and *SMW* 411.
605 1. For Roger see **803** and **931**.
607 1. See **111**.

IN TANNERESTRET[a]

[608] Tailebroc[1] prepositis de Ordia[2] xvi d. et ecclesiae S[anct]i Aldelmi[3] xx d. [fo. 25[v]] et habet iii s.

[609] Patricius priori vi s. et prior Hugoni de Mortemer[1] ii s.; et Patricius [habet] xxii s.

[610] Pag*anus* fullo[1] Ernaldo coco xi s. et habet iiii s.

[611] Guncelinus[1] episcopo vi d. de B. et habet ix s.

[612] Et[b] item Guncelinus[1] episcopo xv d. de B. et habet iii s.

[613] Porcus episcopo xv d. de B.

[614] Ailwardus[1] episcopo vii s. et habet ix s.

[615] Item Ailwardus[1] episcopo x d. de B.

[616] Heredes Fridai[1] episcopo xv d. de B.

[617] Lacchewai[1] episcopo xv d. de B. et Sancto Dionisio[2] ix d. et[c] habet xii s.

[618] Willelmus filius Hereberti[1] episcopo xv d. de B. et priori x s. et habet xix s. et iiii d.

[619] Girardus filius Brand[d] episcopo xvi d. de B. et habet iii s.

[620] Siwardus de Hedeleia priori xx d.

[621] Reginaldus de Sagio[1] priori xv d.

[622] Mainard' parm*entarius* priori xv d. et habet xvi d.[e]

IN TANNER STREET [LOWER BROOK STREET]

[608] Tailebroc[1] pays the reeves of Worthy[2] 16d. and the church of St. Aldhelm[3] 20d. and receives 3s.

[609] Patrick pays the prior 6s. and the prior pays Hugh of Mortemer[1] 2s.; and Patrick receives 22s.

[610] Pain the fuller[1] pays Ernold the cook 11s. and receives 4s.

[611] Guncelin[1] pays the bishop 6d. *de B.* and receives 9s.

[612] And again Guncelin[1] pays the bishop 15d. *de B.* and receives 3s.

[613] Pork pays the bishop 15d. *de B.*

[614] Ailward[1] pays the bishop 7s. and receives 9s.

[615] Again Ailward[1] pays the bishop 10d. *de B.*

[616] Friday's heirs[1] pay the bishop 15d. *de B.*

[617] Lacchewei[1] pays the bishop 15d. *de B.* and St. Denis[2] 9d. and receives 12s.

[618] William son of Herbert[1] pays the bishop 15d. *de B.* and the prior 10s. and receives 19s. 4d.

[619] Girard son of Brand pays the bishop 16d. *de B.* and receives 3s.

[620] Siward of Headley pays the prior 20d.

[621] Reginald of Sées[1] pays the prior 15d.

[622] Maynard the tailor pays the prior 15d. and receives 16d.

---

[a] *In lower margin, text for rubricator almost entirely cut away*   [b] *Ct MS.; cf.* [1030]   [c] *et repeated*
[d] *Over an erasure*   [e] *xvi over an erasure, with text for correction in margin*

608 1. See 75.
    2. See 406.
    3. There is no record of a parish church dedicated to St. Aldhelm in Winchester and so this reference is probably to the abbey of Malmesbury. By 1151 the abbey possessed lands in Winchester granted by *Daniele* (cf. 627) and by *Nigellus*. *Nigellus de Cholcham* had property in Tanner Street *c.* 1110 (I, 205), but cf. 938: *Malmesbury Reg* i. 350.
609 1. See 421.
610 1. For his daughter, see 637.
611 1. See 29.
612 1. See 29.
614 1. See also 615.
615 1. See 614.
616 1. See 590.
617 1. See 47.

2. See 111. Before 1172–3 Henry II confirmed the canons of St. Denis, near Southampton, in the possession of land in Tanner Street granted by Hugh the priest, as they had held it on the death of Henry I. In 1205–19 the earl of Winchester acknowledged that he owed the canons a rent of 12d. for land which *magister herbertus elemosinarius* granted them in Tanner Street adjacent to the S. side of the chapel of St. Mary. In 1278–9 St. Denis Priory granted its 6d. rent from this land to the bishop of Winchester: St. Denis Cart, fo. 119[v]; PRO, E326/9149. For St. Mary in Tanner Street, see *SMW*. According to the schematic reconstruction of properties in Survey II, entry 617 is very close to the site of St. Mary's church (Fig. 19). 618 1. See 121. Perhaps the son of Herbert the almoner, see 617, n. 2.
621 1. See 156.

[623] Ansgerus Gruti[1] episcopo iii s. et habet viii s. et viii d.

[624] Ansgod Tresor[1] episcopo xii d. et habet v s.

[625] [T]uroldus episcopo v s.

[626] Godefridus filius Giroldi episcopo xii d. et habet vi s. Et item Godefridus episcopo xii d. et habet vi s. Et item Godefridus episcopo iii s. de B.

[627] Edwinus Etsinemeta episcopo x d.[a] de B.; et idem episcopo ex alia parte xix d. et obolum. Et Daniel[1] pro quadam parte episcopo xx d., et ipse Daniel habet v s. Et ipse Eduinus habet de renta de hoc toto xii s.

[628] Andreas filius Ricardi cordwanarii[1] episcopo v d.

[629] Godefridus surdus priori Wint' xxx d. et prior episcopo xii d.

[630] Rand' de Morsteda[1] episcopo viii d.

[631] Ernoldus filius Ascor[1] episcopo v d. et habet v s.

[632] Herebertus presbiter[1] tenet i terram quietam que pertinet ad aecclesiam Sancti Iohannis.[2]

[633] Ficheldene abbati Wint'[1] ii s. et abbas episcopo v d.

[634] Siluester episcopo v d. et idem [de] i alia xxi d. et habet xii s. et vi d.

[635] Drogo Blundus[1] episcopo xxii d. et habet viii s.

[636] Radulfus filius Amfridi parmentarii episcopo x d. et habet de Siluestro xv d. et Sil[fo. 26]uester habet viii s.

[637] Filia Pagani fullonis[1] episcopo xlv d. et habet viii s.

[a] d. repeated

[623] Anser Gruty[1] pays the bishop 3s. and receives 8s. 8d.

[624] Ansgod Tresor[1] pays the bishop 12d. and receives 5s.

[625] Turold pays the bishop 5s.

[626] Godfrey son of Girold pays the bishop 12d. and receives 6s. And again Godfrey pays the bishop 12d. and receives 6s. And again Godfrey pays the bishop 3s. de B.

[627] Edwin Etsinemeta pays the bishop 10d. de B.; and the same man pays the bishop for another share 19½d. And Daniel[1] pays the bishop for a certain share 20d. and Daniel receives 5s. And that same Edwin receives in rents from the whole 12s.

[628] Andrew son of Richard the cordwainer[1] pays the bishop 5d.

[629] Godfrey the Deaf pays the prior of Winchester 30d. and the prior pays the bishop 12d.

[630] Randolph of Morestead[1] pays the bishop 8d.

[631] Ernold son of Ascor[1] pays the bishop 5d. and receives 5s.

[632] Herbert the priest[1] holds 1 land, which pertains to the church of St. John,[2] quit.

[633] Figheldean pays the abbot of Winchester[1] 2s. and the abbot pays the bishop 5d.

[634] Silvester pays the bishop 5d. and for another land 21d. and receives 12s. 6d.

[635] Drew Blond[1] pays the bishop 22d. and receives 8s.

[636] Ralf son of Ansfrid the tailor pays the bishop 10d. and receives from Silvester 15d.; and Silvester receives 8s.

[637] Pain the fuller's daughter[1] pays the bishop 45d. and receives 8s.

623 1. See also 672.
624 1. See 419.
627 1. The only occurrence of this name in the two surveys. Before 1151 a *Daniele* granted land in Winchester to Malmesbury Abbey: see 608, n. 3.
628 1. Richard *cord'* may be identical with Richard *corves'*, for whom see 926.
630 1. In 742 he is called Ralf of Morestead.
631 1. For Ascor's wife, see 1050 and 1053. We are possibly concerned with Ascor the goldsmith of 792, but an Atsur or Azar was sheriff of Oxon. *c.* 1150–2: R. H. C.

Davis, 'An Oxford Charter of 1191', *Oxoniensia* 33 (1968), 60 and n.
632 1. See also 908 and 912; cf. I, 119. He is presumably the priest of St. John's church.
   2. Probably the church of St. John *de Edera* at the N. end of *Tannerestret*. See *SMW*.
633 1. Hyde Abbey had land near the church of St. John *de Edera*: *SMW* 444, 445.
635 1. See 185.
637 1. For Pain, see 610.

[638] Erenburg episcopo xiiii d. de B.

[638] Erenburg pays the bishop 14*d. de B.*

[639] Rogerus tinctor[1] abbati vi d.

[639] Roger the dyer[1] pays the abbot 6*d.*

[640] Siluester eidem abbati vi d.

[640] Silvester pays the same abbot 6*d.*

[641] Radulfus de Dummera' et Hunfridus Pancheuot[1] deberent habere v s. et vi d. Modo habent xlii d. et obolum et de his terris habent leprosi[2] vi s. et Colbrand et Turstinus abbati de Hida ii d.

[641] Ralf of Dummer and Humphrey Pancevolt[1] should have received 5*s.* 6*d.* Now they receive 42½*d.* And from these lands the lepers[2] receive 6*s.* and Colbrand and Thurstin pay the abbot of Hyde 2*d.*

[642] Radulfus nepos Godefridi eidem abbati xx d.

[642] Ralf, Godfrey's nephew, pays the same abbot 20*d.*

[643] Stephanus[1] abbati xx d.

[643] Stephen[1] pays the abbot 20*d.*

[644] Item Stephanus[1] tenet i terram de Pic*oto* saln*ario*[2] que est de feudo regis.

[644] Again Stephen[1] holds 1 land from Picot the salt-boiler[2] which is of the king's fief.

[645] Canonici Porcest'[1] tenent ii terras vast[as], que fuerunt Brunild Prichelus et sunt de feudo regis, et habent xviii d.

[645] The canons of Portchester[1] hold 2 waste lands, which used to be Brunhild Pricklouse's, and are of the king's fief; and they receive 18*d.*

[646] God' clericus regi ii d. et est vast*a.*[1]

[646] God' the clerk pays the king 2*d.* and the land is waste.[1]

[647] Lichesuster regi ii d. et est vast*a.*

[647] Lichesuster pays the king 2*d.* and the land is waste.

[648] Luinus Budel regi ii d. et est vast*a.*

[648] Lewin Beadle pays the king 2*d.* and the land is waste.

[649] Blithild[1] et soror eius regi vi d. et est vast*a.*

[649] Blithild[1] and her sister pay the king 6*d.* and the land is waste.

[650] Heredes Hugonis de Auco[1] regi x d. et habent ix s. de renta.

[650] Hugh of Eu's heirs[1] pay the king 10*d.* and receive in rent 9*s.*

[651] Tailebroc[1] regi iiii d. pro terra Walder'.

[651] Tailebroc[1] pays the king 4*d.* for Walder's land.

[652] Godelina[1] regi iiii d. et i quadrantem.

[652] Godelina[1] pays the king 4¼*d.*

[653] Drogo[a] tinctor[1] [. . .][b] vi d. et iii quadrantes.

[653] Drew the dyer[1] pays [. . .] 6¾*d.*

[a] Rrogo *MS., blue initial* R *for* D; *cf.* [525] [b] *Space left for recipient*

639 1. See 52.
641 1. Among Bernard Pancevolt's Hampshire possessions in 1086 was land at Worthy to which a messuage in Winchester was attached: *VCH Hants* ii. 494.
    2. See 276.
643 1. See also 644.
644 1. See 643. He may have been the moneyer of King Stephen and an earlier moneyer had an interest in the property, cf. I, 212. See below, p. 416, Tables 34 and 44, and perhaps II, 89 and 865.   2. See 184.
645 1. See also 925. A house of Augustinian canons founded in 1133 and subsequently transferred to Southwick. The priory rental of 1219 records three properties in this street, none of which can be identified with this entry: Southwick Cart i, fo. 38; Knowles and Hadcock, 153, 159.
646 1. For this tenement, cf. I, 213.
649 1. See Addenda.
650 1. See also 850, where Hugh would seem to be alive. One of the same name is listed in *Pipe Roll 31 Henry I*, p. 85, under Northants., owing 300 marks for the daughter and forest sergeanty of Richard Ingaine.
651 1. See 75.
652 1. See also 655.
653 1. See 83. As 652–3 probably represent the division of a property, the recipient most likely was the king.

[654] Radulfus clericus¹ regi vi d.

[655] Godelina¹ regi ii d.

[656] Canonici de Ciricestria¹ habent i terram vacuam.

[657] Radulfus caret*arius*¹ regi vi d. et priori v d. et habet x s.

[658] Ailware*ª* tinctor priori v d.

[659] Radulfus clericus¹ priori v d. et Roberto Norreis² xviii d.

[660] Et idem Robertus Norreis¹ priori iiii s. et viii d. pro terris que fuerunt Oini filii Erepulfi.

[661] Et Anschetillus de Sancta Maria¹ Roberto² reddit xii d.

[662] Odo presbiter regi xl d. et habet xix s. et vi d.

[663] Rogerus tinctor¹ regi xvi d., episcopo ii s. de terra baronum, et habet viii s.

[664] Ricardus cocus regi xxii d.

[665] Willelmus Ulpis episcopo vi d. de B. et habet illam de prestito quamdiu iusticia episcopi*ᵇ* voluerit.¹

[666] Osmoda¹ tenet i terram de episcopo quam tenuit de Geruasio et habet inde xvi s.

[fo. 26ᵛ] IN BUCCHESTRET

[667] Willelmus arch*idiaconus*¹ regi x d. et habet vi s et Oinus habet inde iiii s.

[668] Humfridus de Sutton'¹ regi x d. et [habet] xx s. et manentes in eadem terra habent viii s. et vi d.

---

[654] Ralf the clerk¹ pays the king 6*d.*

[655] Godelina¹ pays the king 2*d.*

[656] The canons of Cirencester¹ have 1 vacant land.

[657] Ralf the carter¹ pays the king 6*d.* and the prior 5*d.* and receives 10*s.*

[658] Ailware the dyer pays the prior 5*d.*

[659] Ralf the clerk¹ pays the prior 5*d.* and Robert Norreis² 18*d.*

[660] And the same Robert Norreis¹ pays the prior 4*s.* 8*d.* for the lands which used to be Oin son of Erepulf's.

[661] And Anschetil of St. Mary¹ pays Robert² 12*d.*

[662] Odo the priest pays the king 40*d.* and receives 19*s.* 6*d.*

[663] Roger the dyer¹ pays the king 16*d.* and the bishop 2*s.* from the land of the barons and receives 8*s.*

[664] Richard the cook pays the king 22*d.*

[665] William Fox pays the bishop 6*d. de B.* and holds it on loan for as long as the bishop's justiciar shall allow.¹

[666] Osmoth¹ holds 1 land of the bishop which she held from Gervase, and she has from it 16*s.*

IN *BUCCHE* STREET [BUSKET LANE]

[667] William the archdeacon¹ pays the king 10*d.* and receives 6*s.* and Oin receives from the land 4*s.*

[668] Humphrey of Sutton¹ pays the king 10*d.* and [receives] 20*s.* and the dwellers on that land receive 8*s.* 6*d.*

ª Ailwart *Ellis,*   *ᵇ* episcopus *MS.*

654 1. See **14**.
655 1. See **652**.
656 1. Reformed as an Augustinian canonry in 1131: *VCH Glos.* ii. 80; Knowles and Hadcock, 134. The canons had *iii maisuras terre* in Winchester in 1133 and still had Winchester property in the thirteenth century: C. D. Ross (ed.), *The Cartulary of Cirencester Abbey, Gloucestershire* (London, 1964), xxi, xxii, 21–4, 131, 138, 151.
657 1. See also **822**.

659 1. See **14**.
   2. See **73**.
660 1. See **73**.
661 1. Cf. **731**, n. 1.
   2. Probably Robert Norreis: see **73**.
663 1. See **52**.
665 1. Cf. **89**.
666 1. See **80**.
667 1. See **221**.
668 1. See also **675** and **705**.

[669] Turb[er]tus carnifex[1] priori Meret*one*[2] xvi d. pro terra de feudo regis; et Bonefacius[3] reddit eidem priori xxx d. et Bonefacius habet xvi s.

[669] Turbert the butcher[1] pays the prior of Merton[2] 16*d.* for a land on the king's fief; and Boniface[3] pays the same prior 30*d.* and Boniface receives 16*s.*

[670] Robertus de Sancto Pancratio[1] regi [. . .]*a* et habet xi s.

[670] Robert of St. Pancras[1] pays the king [. . .] and receives 11*s.*

[671] Et ibi iuxta est quedam terra quam episcopus habet que fuit Willelmi de Pont;[1] et est de feudo regis et est vasta.

[671] And next is a certain land which the bishop has and which used to be William of Pont [de l'Arche]'s.[1] It is of the king's fief and is waste.

[672] Ansgerus Gruti[1] Willelmo de Sutt'[2] iii s.; et Willelmus Roberto Norreis[3] iii s.; et Ansgerus habet vi s.

[672] Anser Gruty[1] pays William of Sutton[2] 3*s.*, and William pays Robert Norreis[3] 3*s.* And Anser receives 6*s.*

[673] Turstinus clericus[1] regi ii d. et quadrantem, et idem Turstinus regi iii d. et habet iiii s. et iii d., et idem Turstinus Roberto Norreis[2] iii d.

[673] Thurstin the clerk[1] pays the king $2\frac{1}{4}d.$, and the same Thurstin pays the king 3*d.* and receives 4*s.* 3*d.* And the same Thurstin pays Robert Norreis[2] 3*d.*

[674] Edulfus nepos Turstini[1] regi iiii d. et Roberto Norreis[2] iiii d. de i morsella; et idem Turstinus regi viii d. et priori xii d. pro gardino. Item priori iiii d. pro prato et episcopo vi d. pro alio prato.*b*

[674] Edulf, Thurstin's nephew,[1] pays the king 4*d.* and Robert Norreis[2] 4*d.* for 1 bit of land. And the same Thurstin pays the king 8*d.* and the prior 12*d.* for a garden. Again he pays the prior 4*d.* for a meadow and the bishop 6*d.* for another meadow.

[675] Humfridus de Sutt*on*'[1] Roberto Norreis[2] xix d. et habet iiii s.

[675] Humphrey of Sutton[1] pays Robert Norreis[2] 19*d.* and receives 4*s.*

[676] Robertus Norreis[1] deberet reddere xviii d. de i terra; modo est vasta.

[676] Robert Norreis[1] should have paid 18*d.* for 1 land. But now it is waste.

[677] Radulfus carnifex eidem Roberto[1] xviii d.

[677] Ralf the butcher pays the same Robert[1] 18*d.*

[678] Et idem Robertus Norreis[1] deberet habere de i terra viii d. Modo est vasta.*c*

[678] And the same Robert Norreis[1] should have received for 1 land 8*d.* But now it is waste.

[679] Robertus Abendon' regi x d. et habet ii s.

[679] Robert of Abingdon pays the king 10*d.* and receives 2*s.*

[680] Gisulfus scriba[1] regi xvii d. de ii terris. Modo sunt vaste et prior de Moret*one*[d2] habet [. . .]

[680] Gisulf the scribe[1] pays the king 17*d.* for 2 lands. Now they are waste; and the prior of Merton(?)[2] receives [. . .].

---

a Space left for amount   *b pratum in margin in a late medieval hand*   *c est vasta repeated*   *d -re- over an erasure*

669 1. He witnessed a conveyance of property in High Street (cf. 43) and *Alwarnestret* (cf. 487) *c.* 1155–60: Southwick Cart iii, fos. 123*v*, 136*v*.

2. See 50. Presumably granted to Merton by Bernard the scribe. This property was the land and houses in *Bukerestreta* which Bernard purchased from Thezo and his wife Rohasia, the daughter of Ailric *de Cleindona*, for two marks of silver: *EHR* 14 (1899), 424.

3. *Bonifacius filius Asmundi* was among the local witnesses to the sale of this property: see ibid.

670 1. See 31.
671 1. See I, Preface and 259.
672 1. See 623.   2. See 343.   3. See 73.
673 1. See 221.   2. See 73.
674 1. See 489.   2. See 73.
675 1. See 668.

676 1. See 73.
677 1. See 73.
678 1. See 73.
680 1. See I, 223.

2. See 50. On this evidence J. H. Round, 'Bernard the King's Scribe', *EHR* 14 (1899), 418, considered that Bernard was dead. Round regarded him as Gisulf's successor in Winchester, but he may merely have acquired and bequeathed to Merton property in which Gisulf had a continuing interest. The need for this complex explanation would be avoided, however, if the clerk had omitted *deberet reddere* in transcribing this entry; cf. 676, 678. This property was the house *super aquam* belonging to Anselm the clerk, then to Gisulf, which William of Pont de l'Arche granted to Bernard the scribe (ibid. p. 422). Bernard was a benefactor to Merton Priory.

[681] Ailwardus¹ tinctor regi xii d. de ii terris.

[682] Gilebertus taleator¹ solebat reddere*ᵃ* episcopo vii d. Modo est vasta.

[683] Ainulfus parcheminus episcopo xiii d.

[684] Miles *clericus* episcopo ix d.

[685] Bonefa*cius* tannator Iohanni de Port¹ pro i curtilla vi d.

[686] Godefridus de Windes'¹ priori vi d.

[687] Robertus Pinguis¹ priori viii d. pro coiteburi.*ᵇ*²

[688] Stig*andus* archidiaconus¹ regi pro i terra que fuit Blachemani*ᶜ*² vi d. et idem de aliis terris xvi d. et habet inde ii d.

[689] Adam de Brudefort et Gilebertus frater eius regi xii d. pro ii terris.

[690] [fo. 27] Abbatissa Wint' regi x d. pro terra God*wini* Prison;¹ et eadem abbatissa regi x d. pro terra Ulf';² et abbatissa habet iiii d.

[691] Gaufridus Cole episcopo Sar'¹ ii d. et est de feudo regis; et domus illa sedet supra murum.²

[692] Robertus de Sancto Pancratio¹ regi ii d. et domus est iuxta murum.²

[693] Et idem Robertus¹ regi x d. et episcopo xviii d. de B. et habet vii s. et vi d.

[694] Asa¹ regi ii d. et illa domus est iuxta murum.²

[681] Ailward the dyer¹ pays the king 12*d*. for 2 lands.

[682] Gilbert the tailor/tally-cutter¹ used to pay the bishop 7*d*. Now the land is waste.

[683] Ainulf the parchment-maker pays the bishop 13*d*.

[684] Miles the clerk pays the bishop 9*d*.

[685] Boniface the tanner pays John de Port¹ for 1 curtilage 6*d*.

[686] Godfrey of Winsor¹ pays the prior 6*d*.

[687] Robert the Fat¹ pays the prior 8*d*. for Coiteburi.²

[688] Stigand the archdeacon¹ pays the king for 1 land which used to be Blackman's² 6*d*. And the same man pays for other lands 16*d*. And he receives from it/them 2*d*.

[689] Adam of Bridford and Gilbert his brother pay the king 12*d*. for 2 lands.

[690] The abbess of Winchester pays the king 10*d*. for the land of Godwin Prison,¹ and the same abbess pays the king 10*d*. for Ulf's land;² and the abbess receives 4*d*.

[691] Geoffrey Cowl pays the bishop of Salisbury¹ 2*d*., and the land is on the king's fief. And that tenement/house is on the wall.²

[692] Robert of St. Pancras¹ pays the king 2*d*., and the tenement is next to the wall.²

[693] And the same Robert¹ pays the king 10*d*. and the bishop 18*d*. *de B.* and receives 7*s*. 6*d*.

[694] Asa¹ pays the king 2*d*. and that tenement is next to the wall.²

ᵃ solebat reddere *over an erasure*   *ᵇ* .w. monat' *in margin in a late medieval hand*   *ᶜ* -us *MS.*

681   1. Cf. 658.
682   1. See 134.
685   1. See 2. See Addenda.
686   1. See 567.
687   1. See 533.
   2. In the thirteenth and fourteenth centuries this was an area of meadow in the NE. corner of the walled area, to the W. of Tanner Street. Part of it was enclosed within the Black Friars' precinct and in the later Middle Ages the name was applied to the narrow strip of 'king's ground' between the Black Friars and the city wall: *SMW*.
688   1. See also 762 and 783–4. Not listed in Le Neve *Monastic Cathedrals 1066–1300*. Stigand's properties were mostly outside East Gate. He was perhaps identical with the Stigand the chaplain who held the advowsons of the chapels of St. John and St. Peter outside East Gate when, before 1142, Jocelin de Bohun, archdeacon of Winchester (first occ. 1139), invested the canons of St.

Denis by Southampton with them: St. Denis Cart fo. 118. See also I, 242.
   2. For this property, cf. I, 218 and 236.
690   1. See I, 10. Probably a moneyer of Henry I: see below, Table 42. For this property, see I, 238.
   2. For this property, see I, 229.
691   1. See 51.
   2. The city wall, see also 692, 694, and 797, and cf. below, pp. 272–5.
692   1. See 31. Pope Alexander III (1159–81) confirmed Southwick Priory in the possession of *domum . . . iuxta orientalem portam* in Winchester granted by Robert of St. Pancras: Southwick Cart i, fo. 3ᵛ.
   2. See 691.
693   1. See 31.
694   1. Cf. also 846.
   2. See 691.

[695] Iuxta portam de Est solebat esse quedam logia et quidam gradus ad ascendendum ad aecclesiam super portam.[1] Et Willelmus portarius[2] fecit ibi iuxta quandam domum et tenet eam cum porta.

[696] Turstinus clericus[1] episcopo xv d. de B.; et idem Turstinus liberavit Osberto Cod[2] x s. de renta et iii bracinas[a] et ustilia sua,[3] unde ipse Osbertus reddit Turstino xxxvi s. Et idem Turstinus habet de eadem terra viii s. de Hoppere.

[697] Abbatissa Wint' solebat ibi habere i molendinum[1] et i terram ad illum[b] molendinum; sed est vacua.

[698] Robertus Pinguis[1] episcopo xxii d. de ii terris de B.; et Patricius Cachastra[2] habet v s.

[699] Eva uxor Sewi[1] episcopo xvi d. de B. et ipsa Eva habet inde xvi s. pro catellis que homini illius domus commendat[1] et pro domo.

[700] Robertus de Sancto Pancratio[1] regi viii d.

[701] Turstinus clericus[1] regi vi d. et habet x s.

[702] Bonefacius regi xii d.

[703] Eva regi viii d.

[704] Selieua Roberto de Campesiet xx d.; [sed est][c] vasta.

[705] Hunfridus de Sutton'[1] regi xxx d.[2] et habet de Roberto de Sancto Pancratio[3] xiii d.; et moniales de Godestowa[4] habent illam terram in sua saisina.

[706] Wilward' regi vi d.

[707] Et Turstinus[1] regi ii d. et habet inde xviii d.

[695] Next to the East Gate there used to be a certain lodge and steps for going up to the church above the gate.[1] And William the porter[2] made there a house next to it and holds it with the gate.

[696] Thurstin the clerk[1] pays the bishop 15d. *de B.*; and the same Thurstin conveyed to Osbert Cod[2] 10s. of rent, 3 breweries, and his utensils(?),[3] for which Osbert pays Thurstin 36s. And the same Thurstin receives from that same land 8s. from Hoppere.

[697] The abbess of Winchester used to have there 1 mill[1] and 1 land belonging to that mill. But it is vacant.

[698] Robert the Fat[1] pays the bishop 22d. for 2 lands *de B.*, and Patrick Cachastra[2] receives 5s.

[699] Eve, Sewi's wife,[1] pays the bishop 16d. *de B.* And Eve receives 16s. for the chattels which she hires to the tenant of that tenement[1] and for the tenement/house.

[700] Robert of St. Pancras[1] pays the king 8d.

[701] Thurstin the clerk[1] pays the king 6d. and receives 10s.

[702] Boniface pays the king 12d.

[703] Eve pays the king 8d.

[704] Selieva pays Robert of Kempshot 20d.; but the land is waste.

[705] Humphrey of Sutton[1] pays the king 30d.[2] and receives from Robert of St. Pancras[3] 13d.; and the nuns of Godstow[4] have that land in their seisin [possession].

[706] Wulward pays the king 6d.

[707] And Thurstin[1] pays the king 2d. and receives from the land 18d.

[a] bracinis *MS.* [b] illam *MS.* [c] *Space left*

695 1. See below, pp. 275–6. The church was probably dedicated to St. Michael, see below, pp. 276 and 330.
  2. See also **708**, **713**, and **716**.
696 1. See **221**.
  2. See **513**.
  3. See **55** and **591**.
697 1. See below, p. 283.
698 1. See **533**.
  2. *Adheliz uxor Cacast'* was one of the local witnesses to the sale of **669**: *EHR* 14 (1899), 424.
699 1. See **55**.
700 1. See **31**.

701 1. See **221**.
705 1. See **668**.
  2. For this tenement, cf. **I, 234**.
  3. See **31**.
  4. Benedictine nunnery founded near Oxford in 1133 by, according to tradition, Dame Ediva, a resident of Winchester, widow of Sir William Launcelene, *VCH Oxon.* ii. 71 ff. Before 1145 Ambrose son of Gerold granted 5s. rent in Winchester to Godstow. The nunnery acquired no other Winchester properties until after 1155: Godstow Cart, fos. 163v, 164, 180v, 181.
707 1. Thurstin the clerk (?), for whom see **221**.

IN COLOBROCHESTRET[a]

[708] Willelmus portarius[1] tenet i domum iuxta portam[2] que pertinet porte.

[709] Emma abbatisse Wint' xii d. et habet ii s.

[710] Turstinus Deneis[1] abbatisse iii d., et Robertus Norreis[2] habet iiii s.

[711] Ailwardus besmer'[1] abb[at]isse ii d. et habet ii s.

[712] [fo. 27ᵛ] Ingulfus[1] abbatisse vi d.; et hantachenesele solebat ibi esse ubi probi homines Wint' potabant Gildam suam; et remansit in manu regis.[2]

[713] Willelmus portarius[1] abb[at]isse Wint' x d.

[714] Watsco abbatisse iiii d.

[715] Osbertus magister[1] abbatisse xii d. et habet viii d.

[716] Willelmus portarius[1] tenet i terram ubi callis regis solebat esse,[2] et dicit quod de Roberto elemosinario[3] tenet. Et idem Willelmus portarius tenet terram que fuit Luini[b] Child. Et de toto reddit iii s. et idem Robertus xii d. ad hidam.[4]

[717] Et idem reddit Roberto Norreis[1] vi d., et est de feudo comitis Legrecestre.[2]

[718] Radulfus filius Sewala[1] abbatisse ii d. et habet ii d.

a *Text in margin for rubricator almost entirely cut away*

708 1. See 695.
    2. The East Gate, see 695.
710 1. See 13.   2. See 73.
711 1. See also 776.
712 1. Perhaps this is Ingulf the besom-maker (cf. 711), for whom see 61.
    2. Cf. I, 10. For the term, see below, p. 237, s.n. See also below, p. 336.
713 1. See 695.
715 1. See also 728 and 941. Perhaps a schoolmaster, cf. 864, n. 1. *Magister Ossebertus de Inglesham* witnessed two charters of Bishop Henry, 1158–71: A. Watkin (ed.), *The Great Chartulary of Glastonbury* (Somerset Record Soc. 59 (1947), 63 (1952)), i. 17; ii. 259. Osbert of Inglesham was a canon of Salisbury in *c.* 1160: W. R. Jones and W. D. Macray (eds.), *Charters and Documents illustrating the history of the Cathedral, City and Diocese of Salisbury* (RS, 1891), 19. Cf. Robert of Inglesham, for whom see entry 1.

IN COLEBROOK STREET

[708] William the porter[1] holds 1 house/tenement next to the gate[2] and this pertains to the gate.

[709] Emma pays the abbess of Winchester 12d. and receives 2s.

[710] Thurstin the Dane[1] pays the abbess 3d. and Robert Norreis[2] receives 4s.

[711] Ailward the besom-maker[1] pays the abbess 2d. and receives 2s.

[712] Ingulf[1] pays the abbess 6d.; and the 'guildhall' used to be there where the honest citizens of Winchester used to drink their guild. And it has remained in the king's hand.[2]

[713] William the porter[1] pays the abbess of Winchester 10d.

[714] Wazo pays the abbess 4d.

[715] Osbert the master[1] pays the abbess 12d. and receives 8d.

[716] William the porter[1] holds 1 land where the king's road used to be[2] and says that he holds it of Robert the almoner.[3] And the same William the porter holds the land which used to be Lewin Child's. And for the whole he pays 3s. And the same Robert pays 12d. per hide.[4]

[717] And the same man pays Robert Norreis[1] 6d.; and it is of the fief of the earl of Leicester.[2]

[718] Ralf son of Sawalo[1] pays the abbess 2d. and receives 2d.

b -us *MS.*

716 1. See 695.
    2. The blocked lane was possibly a southward continuation of the eastern portion of Colebrook Street: see below, p. 279 and for other blocked streets and lanes, I, 28, n. 2, and below, pp. 279–81.
    3. See 441.
    4. The translation of the last two sentences is doubtful.
717 1. See 73.
    2. Robert de Beaumont, earl of Leicester (d. 1168), was the son of Robert, count of Meulan, for whom see I, 2, n. 1. One of his other two properties in Winchester (857 and 892) may have been connected with the house which his uncle, the earl of Warwick, seems to have held in *Goldestret* in *c.* 1110: see I, 279. In 1130 the earl of Leicester was pardoned £1. 15s. of the city's aid: *Pipe Roll 31 Henry I*, p. 41. In 1175 the sheriff of Hampshire rendered account for £1. 0s. 10d. rent from the earl's land in the city: *Pipe Roll 20 Henry II*, p. 131.
718 1. See also 719.

[719] Et Radulfus¹ episcopo viii d.

[719] And Ralf¹ pays the bishop 8*d.*

[720] *ª*Herebertus palm*arius*¹ hospitali de Ierusalem² vi d.

[720] Herbert the palmer¹ pays the hospital of Jerusalem² 6*d.*

[721] Herleboldus¹ episcopo v d. et h[abe]t viii d.

[721] Herlebold¹ pays the bishop 5*d.* and receives 8*d.*

[722] Ailwinus sacrista abbatisse vi d. et habet x d.

[722] Ailwin the sacristan pays the abbess 6*d.* and receives 10*d.*

[723] Edmundus dapifer¹ abbatisse x d. et habet xlii d.

[723] Edmund the steward¹ pays the abbess 10*d.* and receives 42*d.*

[724] Simenel abbatisse vi d.

[724] Simenel pays the abbess 6*d.*

[725] Segrim¹ abbatisse vi d.

[725] Segrim¹ pays the abbess 6*d.*

[726] Robertus elem*osinarius*¹ abbatisse xix d. et obolum*ᵇ* et habet ix s. et vi d. Sed Robertus elem*osinarius* calumpniat inde iiii d.

[726] Robert the almoner¹ pays the abbess 19½*d.* and receives 9*s.* 6*d.* But Robert the almoner disputes 4*d.* of that.

[727] Turstinus Daneis¹ abbatisse xii d. et obolum.

[727] Thurstin the Dane¹ pays the abbess 12½*d.*

[728] Osbertus magister¹ abbatisse vii d. et obolum et abbatissa habet ibi i vastam plateam.*ᶜ*

[728] Osbert the master¹ pays the abbess 7½*d.* and the abbess has there 1 area which is waste.

[729] Enoc abbatisse x d. et habet iii s.

[729] Enoch pays the abbess 10*d.* and receives 3*s.*

[730] Willelmus Blundus abbatisse v d.

[730] William Blond pays the abbess 5*d.*

[731] Anschetillus¹ abbatisse vii d. et Brichtwen xl d.

[731] Anschetil¹ pays the abbess 7*d.* and Brithwen 40*d.*

EXTRA PORTAM DE EST*ᵈ*

[732] Edwinus faber episcopo ii s.

OUTSIDE EAST GATE

[732] Edwin the blacksmith pays the bishop 2*s.*

[733] God'*ᵉ* presbiter de Auelton'¹ episcopo viii d.

[733] God' the priest of Alton¹ pays the bishop 8*d.*

[734] Raimundus parm*entarius*¹ episcopo xxxii d. de v terris et habet xvi s. et*ᶠ* vi d.

[734] Raymond the tailor¹ pays the bishop for 5 lands 32*d.* and receives 16*s.* 6*d.*

[735] Rogerus parm*entarius* episcopo iii s.

[735] Roger the tailor pays the bishop 3*s.*

[736] Crichel¹ episcopo ii s.

[736] Crichel¹ pays the bishop 2*s.*

ª Initial H *over an erasure*   *ᵇ Blue initial* R *in error for* Rob[ertus] *erased: cf.* [990]   *ᶜ* placeam (*wrongly*) Ellis   *ᵈ In lower margin, text for rubricator almost entirely cut away*   *ᵉ* G *over erased red initial,* (?) B *ᶠ* xvi s. et *written over an erasure: correction note in margin erased*

719 1. See **718**.
720 1. See **84**.
  2. See **584**. After 1148 Hugh of Worthy, his wife, Emma, and his son, Peter, granted 6*d.* rent from *terram quam Herbertus palmarius tenuit in Colbrokenestret* to the Hospital of St. John of Jerusalem. Herbert, father of Emma, had previously rendered the rent: Welbeck MS., I D I (= BM, Loan 29/57), no. ciii.
721 1. See **587**.
723 1. See **81**.
725 1. Cf. **337**.
726 1. See **441**.

727 1. See **13**.
728 1. See **715**.
731 1. Possibly the same as the *Anschetillus de Sancta Maria* (the byname suggests that he was in the employment of St. Mary's Abbey) of **661**, who also owned property in *Colobrochestret*: St. Denis Cart, fo. 123ᵛ.
733 1. Cf. **1**.
734 1. See **40**. Houses outside East Gate *que fuerunt Reimundi* were granted to Gervase during the episcopate of Richard of Ilchester (1174–88): *PRBW 1208-9*, 76.
736 1. Cf. Stephen of Cricklade, **316**.

[737] Alueua episcopo iiii d. et habet iiii s.

[738] Aschetillus sell*arius* episcopo xii d. et Roberto de Hungerfort¹ iii s. de eadem.

[739] Marieta filia Alurici episcopo xii d. et habet v s.

[740] Ingolfus de Auiton' episcopo pro terra Geruasii xx s. et habet x s. et iiii d. Et Basset¹ habet de eadem [fo. 28] x s. et vi d.; et Gupill'² habet de eadem xii d.

[741] Sewinus¹ episcopo iiii d. et habet ii s.

[742] Terra Sewini de Pol prepositis de Alresford¹ v s. et Radulfus de Morsted'² habet ii s.

[743] Uxor Burn' priori xviii d.

[744] Sewinus de Barra¹ priori iii d.

[745] Ricardus lor*imer*¹ priori x d.

[746] Wlueua priori vi d. et obolum.

[747] Radulfus Soggera priori xviii d.

[748] Dicheuin priori xii d. et habet xx d.

[749] Turstinus clericus¹ priori iii s.ᵃ et habet xv s. et iiii d.

[750] Herebertus vigil priori x d. pro terra Ailmeri Longi.

[751] Udelot Sewico¹ xii d.

[752] Muriel priori vi d.

[753] Aldredus priori xiiii d. et habet vi d.

[754] Robertus priori viii d. et obolum.

[755] Ailricus priori iiii d. et obolum.

[756] God' et Serlo priori ix d.

[757] Scerpt priori vii d.

[758] Nicholaus priori vi d.

[759] Radulfusᵇ de Ouint' priori ii s. et habet xxxiii d.

[737] Alveva pays the bishop 4*d*. and receives 4*s*.

[738] Aschetil the saddler pays the bishop 12*d*. and pays Robert of Hungerford¹ 3*s*. from the same land.

[739] Marieta, Aluric's daughter, pays the bishop 12*d*. and receives 5*s*.

[740] Ingulf of Avington pays the bishop for Gervase's land 20*s*. and receives 10*s*. 4*d*. And Basset¹ receives from the same land 10*s*. 6*d*. and Gupill² receives from it 12*d*.

[741] Sawin¹ pays the bishop 4*d*. and receives 2*s*.

[742] The land of Sawin of Pool pays the reeves of Alresford¹ 5*s*. and Ralf of Morestead² receives 2*s*.

[743] Bernard's wife pays the prior 18*d*.

[744] Sawin of La Barre¹ pays the prior 3*d*.

[745] Richard the lorimer¹ pays the prior 10*d*.

[746] Ulveva pays the prior 6½*d*.

[747] Ralf Sogre pays the prior 18*d*.

[748] Dichwin pays the prior 12*d*. and receives 20*d*.

[749] Thurstin the clerk¹ pays the prior 3*s*. and receives 15*s*. 4*d*.

[750] Herbert the watchman pays the prior 10*d*. for Ailmer Long's land.

[751] Udelot pays Sewi¹ 12*d*.

[752] Muriel pays the prior 6*d*.

[753] Aldred pays the prior 14*d*. and receives 6*d*.

[754] Robert pays the prior 8½*d*.

[755] Ailric pays the prior 4½*d*.

[756] God' and Serlo pay the prior 9*d*.

[757] Scerpt pays the prior 7*d*.

[758] Nicholas pays the prior 6*d*.

[759] Ralf of Ovington pays the prior 2*s*. and receives 33*d*.

ᵃ iii s. *over an erasure: correction note in margin erased*

738 1. See **123**.
740 1. See also **764**.   2. See **78**.
741 1. Possibly either of Pool (**742**) or of La Barre (**744**).
742 1. An episcopal manor. See below, p. 383.
    2. See **630**, where he appears as Randolph.

ᵇ *Partly over an erasure*

744 1. Since the property lay outside the wall this may be a reference to a suburban bar; cf. below, p. 264.
745 1. See **443**.
749 1. See **221**.
751 1. See **55**.

[760] Suift episcopo vii d. et habet ii s. et God' mare-scallus habet xv d. Et*a* idem God' episcopo ix d. et Colsueinus presbiter episcopo iii obolos.

[760] Swift pays the bishop 7*d*. and receives 2*s*. And God' the marshal receives 15*d*. And the same God' pays the bishop 9*d*. and Colsvein the priest pays the bishop 1½*d*.

[761] Colerun et socia eius episcopo vi d.

[761] Colerun and her woman companion pay the bishop 6*d*.

[762] Stig*andus* arch*idiaconus*[1] episcopo x d. et habet xx d.

[762] Stigand the archdeacon[1] pays the bishop 10*d*. and receives 20*d*.

[763] Toche episcopo ii d.

[763] Toky pays the bishop 2*d*.

[764] Prior*b* Wint' et Godefridus filius Sewi[1] episcopo xv d. et habent inde xi s. Et Basset[2] habet inde v s. et iiii d. Et Siluester[3] adquietat priorem erga episcopum de xii d. et obolum de istis xv d., et habet inde xx d.

[764] The prior of Winchester and Godfrey son of Sewi[1] pay the bishop 15*d*. and receive from the land 11*s*. And Basset[2] receives from it 5*s*. 4*d*. And Silvester[3] is responsible for paying 12½*d*. of the 15*d*. due from the prior to the bishop and receives from the land 20*d*.

[765] Item prior Wint' episcopo viii d. et habet xii d.

[765] Again the prior of Winchester pays the bishop 8*d*. and receives 12*d*.

[766] Willelmus Waranc'[1] episcopo vi d. et pro via[2] ii d.

[766] William Waranc[1] pays the bishop 6*d*. and for a right of way[2] 2*d*.

[767] Ertur'[1] episcopo ii d. et pro via retro suam domum[2] i d.

[767] Arthur[1] pays the bishop 2*d*. and for a right of way behind his tenement[2] 1*d*.

[768] Item Siluester[1] episcopo vii d. et pro via retro[2] ii d.

[768] Again Silvester[1] pays the bishop 7*d*. and for a right of way behind his tenement[2] 2*d*.

[769] Willelmus faber[1] episcopo ii d. pro via retro.[2]

[769] William the blacksmith[1] pays the bishop for a right of way behind his tenement[2] 2*d*.

[770] Edwardus Waranc'[1] episcopo xx d. et habet x d.*c*

[770] Edward Waranc[1] pays the bishop 20*d*. and receives 10*d*.

[771] Edricus Buriman episcopo xxii d. et habet xvi d.

[771] Edric Buriman pays the bishop 22*d*. and receives 16*d*.

[772] Herebertus Papanholt episcopo xxi d.

[772] Herbert Papanholt pays the bishop 21*d*.

[773] Edred episcopo x d.

[773] Edred pays the bishop 10*d*.

[774] Pieferret episcopo xviii d.

[774] Pieferret pays the bishop 18*d*.

---

a et repeated *b On a fresh line, indented, but not rubricated, since initial P is written in black as part of main text* *c x over an erasure*

762 1. See **688**. Stigand's interest in the property suggests that it may have been near the church of St. John: cf. **688**, n. 1 and **783**, n. 1.
764 1. See **55**.
  2. See **740**.
  3. See also **768**.
766 1. Cf. **770**.
  2. Cf. **767-9**. This road may represent the modern Magdalen Hill, parallel to St. John's Street (see below, p. 263), but since it occurs well in the second half of the

entries outside East Gate it is more likely to have been parallel to Chesil Street.
767 1. See **112**.
  2. Cf. **766**.
768 1. See **764**.
  2. Cf. **766**.
769 1. See **179**.
  2. Cf. **766**.
770 1. Cf. **766**.

[775] Et Letard episcopo xviii d.

[775] And Letard pays the bishop 18*d*.

[776] [fo. 28ᵛ] Ailwardus besmera¹ episcopo v d. de ii terris et habet ii d.

[776] Ailward the besom-maker¹ pays the bishop for 2 lands 5*d*. and receives 2*d*.

[777] Raimundus parm*entarius*¹ episcopo v s. et habet v s.

[777] Raymond the tailor¹ pays the bishop 5*s*. and receives 5*s*.

[778] Bonefacius priori v d. et habet ii s. et vi d.

[778] Boniface pays the prior 5*d*. and receives 2*s*. 6*d*.

[779] Rogerus dispens*ator* priori v d. et Ricardus Galne habet inde iii s. et vi d.

[779] Roger the dispenser pays the prior 5*d*. and Richard Galne receives from the land 3*s*. 6*d*.

[780] Godefridus filius Sewi*ᵃ*¹ priori v d. et habet v s. Et de eadem terra h[abe]t Edwinus xii d.

[780] Godfrey son of Sewi¹ pays the prior 5*d*. and receives 5*s*. And from that same land Edwin receives 12*d*.

[781] Cristescoc priori ii d. et obolum et habet xvi d.

[781] Cristescock pays the prior 2½*d*. and receives 16*d*.

[782] Hunfridus capellanus¹ priori ii d. et obolum et habet v s. et x d.

[782] Humphrey the chaplain¹ pays the prior 2½*d*. and receives 5*s*. 10*d*.

[783] Chetel Stig*ando* arch*idiacono*¹ viii d. et habet ix d. Et Stig*andus* reddit priori: sed nescimus quid.

[783] Chetel pays Stigand the archdeacon¹ 8*d*. and receives 9*d*. And Stigand pays the prior, but we do not know what.

[784] Et item Stig*andus*¹ habet ii s.*ᵇ* et viii d. Et Robertus reddit Stig*ando* vi d. et habet xviii d.

[784] And again Stigand¹ receives 2*s*. 8*d*. And Robert pays Stigand 6*d*. and receives 18*d*.

[785] Turstinus clericus¹ episcopo vii d. et habet iii s.

[785] Thurstin the clerk¹ pays the bishop 7*d*. and receives 3*s*.

[786] Terra Alexandri de Walt' episcopo iii s. et vi d.

[786] The land of Alexander *de Walt'* pays the bishop 3*s*. 6*d*.

[787] Nicher episcopo x d. et quadrantem.

[787] Nicher pays the bishop 10¼*d*.

[788] *ᶜ*Basilia episcopo iiii d. et iii quadrantes.

[788] Basilia pays the bishop 4¾*d*.

*ᵈ*IN MENSTERSTRET

IN MINSTER STREET [LITTLE MINSTER STREET]

[789] *ᵉ*Iva priori ii s. et habet xxviii s. et vi d. et Godefridus carp*entarius* habet de eadem terra ii s.

[789] Iva pays the prior 2*s*. and receives 28*s*. 6*d*. and Godfrey the carpenter receives from that land 2*s*.

[790] Petrus Estreis episcopo vi d. de B.

[790] Peter the Easterling pays the bishop 6*d*. *de B.*

ᵃ filius Sewi over an erasure   *ᵇ d. MS.*   *ᶜ Whole entry over an erasure*   *ᵈ Rubric over an erasure*
ᵉ First line and part of second line written over an erasure

776 1. See **711**.
777 1. See **40**.
780 1. See **55**.
782 1. *Umfredus*, chaplain of the abbess of Winchester, granted 9*s*. 5½*d*. rent *super cheshullo* to Godstow Nunnery between 1155 and 1182: Godstow Cart, fos. 163–5.
783 1. See **688**. Stigand's interest in the property and

its position among the second half of the entries outside East Gate suggest that this property and **784** may have been near the church of St. Peter: cf. **688**, n. 1; **762**, n. 1; and **782**, n. 1.
784 1. See **688**.
785 1. See **221**.

[791] Duo sacriste[1] episcopo iiii s. de B.

[792] Atscor aurifaber[1] priori viii s. et habet iiii s.

[793] Turchetillus butar'[1] priori x d. et habet dimidiam marcam.

[794] Osmundus habet de eadem xii d.

[795] Uxor Martini[1] de feudo Baldewini habet iiii s. et uxor Herleboldi[2] habet iiii s.

[796] Strod habet i domum pro servitio suo de sacrista quietam.[1]

[797] Et sacrista tenet i alteram domum iuxta murum[1] et deberet reddere episcopo vi d.

[798] Robertus Grifin tenet i domum de sacrista pro servicio suo.[1]

[799] Walterus de 'Ticheb'[1] tenet i domum que[a] fuit Rogeri de Meleford'.[2]

[800] Willelmus filius Raimundi[1] tenet terram suam de Hereberto filio Gaufridi; et ipse Herbertus reddit priori et Willelmus eidem Herberto iii s.

[801] Et Matildis[1] priori xx d. et habet ii s.

[802] Et Lachewei[1] habet x s. et est de feudo regis.

[803] Rogerus cocus[1] priori v d.

[804] Portereue priori v d.

[805] Girardus priori v d.

[791] Two sacristans[1] pay the bishop 4s. *de B.*

[792] Ascor the goldsmith[1] pays the prior 8s. and receives 4s.

[793] Thurkell the cooper[1] pays the prior 10d. and receives ½ mark.

[794] Osmund receives from the same land 12d.

[795] Martin's wife[1] receives from Baldwin's fief 4s. and Herlebold's wife[2] receives 4s.

[796] Strod has 1 tenement of the sacristan quit in return for his service.[1]

[797] And the sacristan holds another tenement next to the wall[1] and should have paid the bishop 6d.

[798] Robert Grifin holds 1 tenement of the sacristan in return for his service.[1]

[799] Walter of Tichborne[1] holds 1 tenement which used to be Roger of Milford's.[2]

[800] William son of Raymond[1] holds his land of Herbert son of Geoffrey, and Herbert pays the prior, and William pays Herbert, 3s.

[801] And Matilda[1] pays the prior 20d. and receives 2s.

[802] And Lachewei[1] receives 10s., and it is of the king's fief.

[803] Roger the cook[1] pays the prior 5d.

[804] The portreeve pays the prior 5d.

[805] Girard pays the prior 5d.

[a] qui *MS.*

791 1. For the sacrist's interests in the area of Minster Street and King's Gate, cf. **796, 798, 818,** and **928.** Three years' arrears of rent due from the sacrist of St. Swithun's to the bishop amounted to 16s. 4d. in 1211: *PRBW 1210–11,* 158. The sacrist's rents to the bishop in 1148 totalled 4s. 6d. In the thirteenth century the sacrist of the cathedral priory played a leading part in the disputes over King's Gate and South Gate: *Abbreviatio Placitorum,* 147.
792 1. See **631.**
793 1. He was pardoned Danegeld in 1130: *Pipe Roll 31 Henry I,* p. 16.
795 1. See **17.**

2. See **587**; cf. **966.**
796 1. Cf. **798.**
797 1. See **691.**
798 1. Cf. **796.**
799 1. See also **827.** In 1166 his son Roger held two knight's fees of the bishop of Winchester which his father had held: *RBE* i. 205.

2. Witnessed a charter of William Giffard bishop of Winchester, J. H. Round: *EHR* 14 (1899), 430.
800 1. See addenda.
801 1. For the tenement, cf. **800,** n. 1.
802 1. See **47.** For the tenement, cf. **800,** n. 1.
803 1. See **605.**

[806] [fo. 29]*a* Heredes Radulfi camerarii[1] regi vi d. et Stigando maconi[2] iiii s. et est de feudo regis; et totum managium[3] Stigandi est de feudo regis.

[807] Stigandus maco[1] habet de Henrico presbitero v d. quos rex debuit habere quia est de feudo regis.

[808] Uxor Martini[1] habet v s.; sed nescimus de quo tenet.

[809] Willelmus Caddus[1] uxori Martini[2] ii s.

[810] Hugo Bel tenet i terram; sed*b* nescimus de quo tenet.

[811] Edmundus de Mitlinget' tenet [i] terram de priore et reddit vi d. et habet v s.

[812] Heredes Radulfi camerarii[1] priori iiii d. et habent viii s.

[813] Turstinus Mansel[1] priori vii d. et habet iiii s.

[814] Willelmus de Hotot[1] priori v d. et habet viii d.

[815] Mathilda filia Henrici[1] priori xv d. et habet iii s. et viii d.

[816] Willelmus de Hotot[1] priori v d. et habet ii s.

[817] Terra Stephani arch*idiaconi*[1] priori v d. et Burnard' de Braiosa[2] habet ii s.

[818] Ailwinus palmar*ius* sacriste xxi d.

[819] Willelmus Surlaf[1] priori iiii d.

[806] Ralf the chamberlain's heirs[1] pay the king 6d. and Stigand the mason[2] 4s., and it is of the king's fief. And Stigand's whole estate(?)[3] is of the king's fief.

[807] Stigand the mason[1] receives from Henry the priest 5d. which the king should have had because it is of the king's fief.

[808] Martin's wife[1] receives 5s. But we do not know of whom she holds.

[809] William Cade[1] pays Martin's wife[2] 2s.

[810] Hugh the Fair holds 1 land. But we do not know of whom he holds it.

[811] Edmund of Midlington holds 1 land of the prior and pays 6d. and receives 5s.

[812] Ralf the chamberlain's heirs[1] pay the prior 4d. and receive 8s.

[813] Thurstin Mansel[1] pays the prior 7d. and receives 4s.

[814] William of Hotot[1] pays the prior 5d. and receives 8d.

[815] Matilda, Henry's daughter,[1] pays the prior 15d. and receives 3s. 8d.

[816] William of Hotot[1] pays the prior 5d. and receives 2s.

[817] The land of Stephen the archdeacon[1] pays the prior 5d. and Bernard of Briouze[2] receives 2s.

[818] Ailwin the palmer pays the sacristan 21d.

[819] William Sour-loaf[1] pays the prior 4d.

---

a The entire leaf, both recto and verso, now bearing the text of [806]–[861], has been erased and rewritten. The paragraph marks of the erased text, a few of which can still be made out, show that it formed part of Survey I. Some of the erased marginal letters for the original rubricator can still be identified, and some have been left untouched or simply crossed out. See below, pp. 523–4.   b nos MS.

806 1. See **72**.
  2. See also **807**.
  3. See **197**.
807 1. See **806**.
808 1. See **17**.
809 1. The Christian Flemish financier, employed by Henry II and others, who died *c.* 1166. See Hilary Jenkinson, *EHR* 28 (1913), 209–27, 522–7, 730–2; H. W. C. Davis (ed.), *Essays in History Presented to R. L. Poole* (Oxford, 1927), 190–210. Cf. below, p. 438–9.
  2. See **17**.
812 1. See **72**.

813 1. See also **836**.
814 1. See also **816** and **1009**, and cf. **936**.
815 1. Cf. **150**.
816 1. See **814**.
817 1. Listed as archdeacon of Surrey 1107–*c.*1128: Le Neve *Monastic Cathedrals 1066–1300*, 91–2. The church of St. Swithun over King's Gate was in the patronage of the archdeacon of Surrey: *VCH Hants* v. 76.
  2. See also **872**. He is not in the direct descent of the lords of Bramber. He witnessed the sale of **669**: J. H. Round, *EHR* 14 (1899), 424.
819 1. See also **961**.

[820] Pag*anus* episcopo x d. et habet xx d.

[821] Em*ma* tenet hospi*cium* quod fuit Ricardi de Ricarduill'.

IN CALPESTRET

[822] Radulfus caret*arius*[1] priori xxix d. et habet xv s. et iiii d.

[823] Ricardus Grailepeis pri[ori] x d. et habet x s.

[824] Episcopus priori xxx d. et habet xviii s. de B.

[825] Uxor Martini[1] priori iii s. et habet xiiii s. Et de eadem terra Goduinus Bar[2] habet x s.

[826] Iohannes aurifaber[1] regi xiiii d.

[827] Walterus de Ticheb'[1] tenet i terram que fuit abbatis de Westmustier et i aliam partem que fuit Grimbaldi medici;[2] et est de feudo regis et debet reddere regi xl d.[3]

[828] Herebertus camerarius[1] priori xxii d. et habet v s. Goduinus habet de eadem viii s., et Osbertus cerarius[2] reddit eidem Herberto xii d., et Osbertus habet de eadem iiii s.

[829] Herebertus filius Radulfi[1] priori iiii d. et habet iii s.

[830] Robertus de Ponte[1] priori xi d. Et est quedam vasta terra de Odiam[2] que solebat reddere Willelmo Pon[fo. 29[v]][a]tearch' x d.[3]

[831] Ricardus furbar' priori xiii d.

[832] Godard' priori x d.

[833] Guncel' filius Hugonis[1] priori x d.

[834] Hadewis priori viii d. et habet ii s.

[820] Pain pays the bishop 10*d.* and receives 20*d.*

[821] Emma holds the hospice which used to be Richard of Ricarville's.

IN *CALPE* STREET [ST. THOMAS STREET]

[822] Ralf the carter[1] pays the prior 29*d.* and receives 15*s.* 4*d.*

[823] Richard Grailepeis pays the prior 10*d.* and receives 10*s.*

[824] The bishop pays the prior 30*d.* and receives 18*s. de B.*

[825] Martin's wife[1] pays the prior 3*s.* and receives 14*s.* From the same land Godwin Boar[2] receives 10*s.*

[826] John the goldsmith[1] pays the king 14*d.*

[827] Walter of Tichborne[1] holds 1 land which used to be the abbot of Westminster's and another part which used to be Grimbald the doctor's.[2] And it is of the king's fief and should pay the king 40*d.*[3]

[828] Herbert the chamberlain[1] pays the prior 22*d.* and receives 5*s.* Godwin receives from the same land 8*s.* and Osbert the chandler[2] pays the same Herbert 12*d.* And Osbert has from it 4*s.*

[829] Herbert son of Ralf[1] pays the prior 4*d.* and receives 3*s.*

[830] Robert of Pont [de l'Arche][1] pays the prior 11*d.* And there is a certain waste land pertaining to Odiham[2] which used to pay William of Pont de l'Arche 10*d.*[3]

[831] Richard the furbisher pays the prior 13*d.*

[832] Godard pays the prior 10*d.*

[833] Guncelin son of Hugh[1] pays the prior 10*d.*

[834] Hadewis pays the prior 8*d.* and receives 2*s.*

[a] *See note to fo. 29, above.*

822 1. See **657**.
825 1. See **17**.
  2. Possibly a moneyer of Henry I: see below, Table 42.
826 1. See also **847** and **852**. For the tenement, cf. **I, 261**.
827 1. See **799**.
  2. Henry I's doctor, see *Regesta*, ii, no. 528a and *passim*. He was dead by 1137/8, leaving a wife Azelina, and a daughter Emma: *Regesta*, iii, no. 579.

  3. For these two tenements see also **I, 262**.
828 1. See **4**.
  2. See also **888**. Probably a moneyer of Henry II: see **111**, n. 2 and below, Table 45.
829 1. See **574**.
830 1. See **I, Preface**, and **II, 270**.
  2. See **387**.
  3. For the tenement, cf. **I, 259**.
833 1. See **29**.

[835] Richild regi xii d. et habet vi d.

[835] Richild pays the king 12d. and receives 6d.

[836] Turstinus Mansel[1] regi xv d. et habet viii s.

[836] Thurstin Mansel[1] pays the king 15d. and receives 8s.

[837] Gunterus filius Berengarii[1] regi xii d. et habet iii s.

[837] Gunter son of Berengar[1] pays the king 12d. and receives 3s.

[838] Terra Willelmi de Hoctune,[1] quam servientes de Templo[2] tenent, solebat reddere regi x d.; et Drogo de Calp'[3] reddit eisdem v s.

[838] The land of William of Houghton,[1] which the servants of the Temple[2] hold, used to pay the king 10d. And Drew de Calp[3] pays them 5s.

[839] Seburg' regi iiii d. pro dimidia mansione.

[839] Seburg pays the king 4d. for a half messuage.

[840] Fulcho sellarius regi iiii d.

[840] Fulk the saddler pays the king 4d.

[841] Herbertus camerarius[1] regi xvi d. et habet iii s. et viii d.

[841] Herbert the chamberlain[1] pays the king 16d. and receives 3s. 8d.

[842] Ernaldus frater Petri[1] regi xiiii d. de ii terris et habet xxviii s.

[842] Ernald, Peter's brother,[1] pays the king for 2 lands 14d. and receives 28s.

[843] Reimboldus regi x d. et habet x s.

[843] Rainbold pays the king 10d. and receives 10s.

[844] Edredus regi viii d. et habet ii s.

[844] Edred pays the king 8d. and receives 2s.

[845] Drogo regi x d.

[845] Drew pays the king 10d.

[846] Asa[1] regi x d. et habet iiii s.

[846] Asa[1] pays the king 10d. and receives 4s.

[847] Iohannes aurifaber[1] regi xv d. de i terra et dimidia et habet xii s.

[847] John the goldsmith[1] pays the king for 1½ lands 15d. and receives 12s.

[848] Heredes Saieti[1] regi xiii d. et Ebrardo iii d.

[848] Saiet's heirs[1] pay the king 13d. and Ebrard 3d.

[849] Willelmus Pinguis[1] regi x d. et episcopo xx s. de B. et habet xxxii s. et iiii d.

[849] William the Fat[1] pays the king 10d. and the bishop 20s. de B. and receives 32s. 4d.

[850] Hugo de Aucho[1] abbatisse de Rumesie[2] xviii d.

[850] Hugh of Eu[1] pays the abbess of Romsey[2] 18d.

IN GOLDESTRET[a]

IN GOLDE STREET [SOUTHGATE STREET]

[851] Robertus filius Hugonis abbatisse de Rumesie xv d.

[851] Robert son of Hugh pays the abbess of Romsey 15d.

[a] In upper margin, for rubricator: [in] goldestret (partly cut away)

836 1. See 813.
837 1. For Berengar's wife, see 884 and 887.
838 1. For his son, see 74; and see I, 196 for William and I, 245 for this tenement.
   2. See 25. This tenement, on the W. side of Calpestret, eventually came into the possession of the Hospital of St. John of Jerusalem. By a lease of 1285 the hospital's tenant was to provide accommodation for the fratres milicie templi vel eorum clerici when required: Welbeck MS., I D I (= BM, Loan 29/57), no. cxxi; SMW 616.
   3. See 525.

841 1. See 4.
842 1. See 135.
846 1. Cf. 694.
847 1. See 826.
848 1. For Saiet, probably to be identified as the moneyer of Henry I and Stephen, and possibly for this tenement, see I, 256, and below, Tables 39 and 44.
849 1. See 213.
850 1. For his heirs, see 650.
   2. Cf. 851–5 in Goldestret. The abbess's property here evidently occupied a block fronting on to the two streets.

[852] Iohannes aurifaber[1] abbatisse de Rumesie xii d. et obolum et habet vi s.

[852] John the goldsmith[1] pays the abbess of Romsey $12\frac{1}{2}d$. and receives 6s.

[853] Muriel eidem abbatisse de Rumesie xii d. et obolum et habet xx s.

[853] Muriel pays the same abbess of Romsey $12\frac{1}{2}d$. and receives 20s.

[854] Uxor Martini[1] abbatisse de Rumesie xx d.

[854] Martin's wife[1] pays the abbess of Romsey 20d.

[855] Ebrardus de Carnot'[1] abbatisse de Rumesie xxviii d.

[855] Ebrard of Chartres[1] pays the abbess of Romsey 28d.

[856] Godehald[1] et Rogerus regi x d. et habent xviii d. Et in eadem domo habe[n]t servientes et suum bracinium.[2]

[856] Godehald[1] and Roger pay the king 10d. and receive 18d. And on that same tenement they have servants and their brewery.[2]

[857] Guncel' Dore[1] tenet i domum de feudo comiti[s] Legrecest',[2] et est in manu episcopi.

[857] Guncelin Dore[1] holds 1 tenement of the fief of the earl of Leicester[2] and it is in the hand of the bishop.

[858] Uxor Tardif'[1] regi x d. et habet xl d.

[858] Tardif's wife[1] pays the king 10d. and receives 40d.

[859] Iohannes nepos Petri[1] regi x d.[2] et habet vi s.

[859] John, Peter's nephew,[1] pays the king 10d.[2] and receives 6s.

[860] Herbertus camerarius[1] regi viii d.[2] et abbatisse de Rumes[ie] xxii d. et habet i marcam; et Drogo habet de eadem terra xv s.

[860] Herbert the chamberlain[1] pays the king 8d.[2] and the abbess of Romsey 22d. and receives 1 mark. And Drew receives from that same land 15s.

[861] Heredes Hugonis burgensis[1] regi viii d.[2] et habent xii s.

[861] The heirs of Hugh the burgess[1] pay the king 8d.[2] and receive 12s.

[862] [fo. 30][a] Robertus abbatisse de Rumesie xxvi d. et habet i marcam.

[862] Robert pays the abbess of Romsey 26d. and receives 1 mark.

[863] Petrus merciarius[1] eidem abbatisse x d.

[863] Peter the mercer[1] pays the same abbess 10d.

[864] Iudichel[1] eidem abbatisse xxii d.

[864] Judichel[1] pays the same abbess 22d.

[a] *The whole of the first col. and two-thirds of the second col. of fo. 30[r], now containing the text of* [862]–[889], *have been erased and rewritten exactly as in the case of fo. 29, above, q.v.*

852 1. See 826.
854 1. See 17.
855 1. See 544.
856 1. See 168. 2. Cf. 55.
857 1. See 29. 2. See 717.
858 1. For William Tardif and this tenement, see I, 268.
859 1. See 34. 2. For this tenement, cf. I, 269.
860 1. See 4. Geoffrey the chamberlain held this tenement in c. 1110. 2. For this tenement, cf. I, 270.
861 1. Geoffrey *burgeis* held this tenement in c. 1110.
2. For this tenement cf. I, 271.
863 1. See 35.
864 1. See I, 102. He may, however, be identical with the Master John Joichel who was in dispute with Jordan Fantosme, the historian, both of them clerks of Bishop Henry, over the running of the schools in Winchester in c. 1154–9: W. J. Millor, H. E. Butler, and C. N. L. Brooke (eds.), *The Letters of John of Salisbury*, i, *The Early*

Letters (London, 1955), 95–6. As *Magister Iohannes Iudicalis* he had a rent of 2s. in *Mensterstret* next to the land of Jordan Fantosme (BM, Add. MS. 15314, fo. 117), and a house in *Goldestret* in front of which the Hospitallers acquired land from Hugh of Wyngeham (Welbeck MS., I D I (BM, Loans 29/57), no. xcviii). See also 1048. Master John *Iekel* (alias *Iukel*) administered the vacant abbey of Hyde for the crown 1171–5; witnessed a Winchester document of c. 1200; and subsequently (but before c. 1225) granted a house in *Goldestret*, from which a rent of 20d. was due to Romsey abbey, to his nephew Wimarc and Reiner son of Everard: *Pipe Roll 17 Henry II*, p. 42, *19 Henry II*, p. 56, *20 Henry II*, p. 136, *21 Henry II*, p. 199; *Proc Hants FC*, 20 (1956), 51, n. 22; Southwick Cart iii, fos. 128, 136. The houses in *Goldestret* were almost certainly identical with this property and came into the possession of Southwick Priory in the thirteenth century, see *SMW*. For a possible earlier Winchester schoolmaster see 715. See also below, pp. 328, 492.

[865] Stephanus¹ regi viii d.² et habet iiii s.

[866] Warinus aurifaber¹ priori viii d. et habet ii s.

[867] Prior habet ibidem i terram vastam que deberet reddere xx d.

[868] Beatric' priori iiii s. et habet ii s.

[869] Uxor Godefridi priori x d.

[870] Robertus Oisun¹ Roberto filio Hunfridi² xv d.

[871] Prior Wint' solebat habere de i domo v s.; sed est vasta.

[872] Burnardus de Braiosa¹ Petro filio arch*idiaconi* x d. et [est] de feudo regis.

[873] Herbertus camerarius¹ Roberto filio Hunfridi² xii d. et habet ii s.; et Godehal'³ habet xi s.

[874] Rogerus molend*inarius* episcopo xiiii d.

[875] Robertus de Columbiers tenet i terram que solebat reddere regi vii d. et obolum;¹ sed nil reddit.

[876] Episcopus reddit regi vii d. et obolum¹ et habet ix s. de eadem terra; et Caper' habet de eadem viii s.

[877] Robertus Oisun¹ [. . .]ᵃ x d.

[878] Warinus aurifaber¹ tenet i terram que solebat reddere regi x d. Idem Warinus regi reddit viii d.

[879] Radulfus de Walteruile tenet i terram de feudo episcopi.

[880] Uxor Nicholai¹ abbati de Sancto Edmundo xii d.²

[881] Robertus Oisun¹ tenet terram suam de Ricardo Tistede.

ᵃ *Space left for recipient*

[865] Stephen¹ pays the king 8*d.*² and receives 4*s.*

[866] Warin the goldsmith¹ pays the prior 8*d.* and receives 2*s.*

[867] The prior has there 1 waste land which should have paid 20*d.*

[868] Beatrice pays the prior 4*s.* and receives 2*s.*

[869] Godfrey's wife pays the prior 10*d.*

[870] Robert Oisun¹ pays Robert son of Humphrey² 15*d.*

[871] The prior of Winchester used to receive from 1 tenement 5*s.*; but it is waste.

[872] Bernard of Briouze¹ pays Peter the son of the archdeacon 10*d.*; and it is of the king's fief.

[873] Herbert the chamberlain¹ pays Robert son of Humphrey² 12*d.* and receives 2*s.* And Godehald³ receives 11*s.*

[874] Roger the miller pays the bishop 14*d.*

[875] Robert of Columbiers holds 1 land which used to pay the king 7½*d.*;¹ but it pays nothing.

[876] The bishop pays the king 7½*d.*¹ and receives 9*s.* from that same land; and Caperun receives from it 8*s.*

[877] Robert Oisun¹ pays [. . .] 10*d.*

[878] Warin the goldsmith¹ holds 1 land which used to pay the king 10*d.* The same Warin pays the king 8*d.*

[879] Ralf of Vatierville holds 1 land of the fief of the bishop.

[880] Nicholas's wife¹ pays the abbot of St. Edmunds 12*d.*²

[881] Robert Oisun¹ holds his land of Richard Tisted.

865 1. Possibly a moneyer of Stephen, see Table 44 and cf. 89 and 644, n. 1.
  2. For this tenement, cf. I, 272.
866 1. See also 878.
870 1. See 40.   2. See 223.
872 1. See 817.
873 1. See 4.
  2. See 223.
  3. See 168.

875 1. The rents due to the king from this tenement and
876 total 15*d.* This suggests that the properties were identical with I, 278.
876 1. See 875.
877 1. See 40.
878 1. See 866.
880 1. See 103.
  2. For this tenement, cf. I, 280.
881 1. See 40.

[882] Et idem Robertus[1] priori xii d.

[882] And the same Robert[1] pays the prior 12*d*.

[883] Gaufridus de Sancto Nicholao[1] priori*[a]* vi d.

[883] Geoffrey of St. Nicholas[1] pays the prior (?) 6*d*.

[884] Uxor Beren*garii*[1] priori xii d. et habet iii s.; et idem Gaufridus[2] habet viii s.

[884] Berengar's wife[1] pays the prior 12*d*. and receives 3*s*. And the same Geoffrey[2] receives 8*s*.

[885] Turpin priori ii s. et habet ii s.

[885] Turpin pays the prior 2*s*. and receives 2*s*.

[886] Tellebiene priori xviii d.

[886] Tellebiene pays the prior 18*d*.

[887] Uxor Beren*garii*[1] priori xii d.

[887] Berengar's wife[1] pays the prior 12*d*.

[888] Osbertus cerarius[1] priori v s.

[888] Osbert the chandler[1] pays the prior 5*s*.

[889] Gilebertus de Meleford tenet i terram quietam unde habet i marcam.*[b]*

[889] Gilbert of Milford holds 1 land quit from which he receives 1 mark.

[890] Radulfus Cointe[1] priori xxx d. et habet xvii s. et vi d.

[890] Ralf Cointe[1] pays the prior 30*d*. and receives 17*s*. 6*d*.

[891] Ebrardus de Carnot'[1] priori iiii s. et habet xxix s.

[891] Ebrard of Chartres[1] pays the prior 4*s*. and receives 29*s*.

[892] Robertus filius Radulfi[1] tenet i terram de feudo comitis Legrec'[2] et habet xii d.

[892] Robert son of Ralf[1] holds 1 land of the fief of the earl of Leicester[2] and receives 12*d*.

[893] Rotrogus priori xii d.

[893] Rotrou pays the prior 12*d*.

[894] Osmoda[1] priori xxx d. et habet iii s.

[894] Osmoth[1] pays the prior 30*d*. and receives 3*s*.

[895] Heredes Herberti filii Gunt'[1] priori v s. et habe[n]t v s.

[895] The heirs of Herbert son of Guncelin[1] pay the prior 5*s*. and receive 5*s*.

[896] ᶜGuncel'[1] et Radulfus Cointe[2] priori [fo. 30ᵛ]*[d]* xv d., et Guncel' habet de Radulfo viii s.

[896] Guncelin[1] and Ralf Cointe[2] pay the prior 15*d*. and Guncelin receives from Ralf 8*s*.

[897] Willelmus Post' priori xii d. et habet i marcam.

[897] William Post pays the prior 12*d*. and receives 1 mark.

[898] Conanus Roberto filio Hunfridi[1] i libram piperis et habet iiii s.

[898] Conan pays Robert son of Humphrey[1] 1 lb. of pepper and receives 4*s*.

[899] Drogo Blund[1] Roberto filio Hunfridi[2] vii s. et habet xiii s.

[899] Drew Blond[1] pays Robert son of Humphrey[2] 7*s*. and receives 13*s*.

---

[a] Petri MS. *[b]* The erasure beginning with [806] on fo. 29 ends at this point *[c]* Initial G over an erasure
[d] The poor appearance of fo. 30ᵛ is due to the extensive erasure of fo. 30ʳ

882 1. See **40**.
883 1. See also **884**.
884 1. See **837**.
  2. See **883**.
887 1. See **837**.
888 1. See **828**.
890 1. See **39**.
891 1. See **544**.
892 1. There was a London merchant of this name: *Pipe Roll 31 Henry I*, pp. 148–9; the same or another was

rewarded by the king in Kent, *Pipe Roll 3 Henry II*, p. 101.
  2. See **717**.
894 1. See **80**.
895 1. See **29**.
896 1. See **29**.
  2. See **39**.
898 1. See **223**.
899 1. See **185**.
  2. See **223**.

EXTRA PORTAM DE SUD*a*

[900] *b*Mulier episcopo iiii d. et habet ii s. de Stephano; et Stephanus habet viii s.

[901] Et eadem mulier habet de Henrico fabro ii s. et de Godrico iiii d.

[902] *c*Ailmerus episcopo ii s.

[903] Rogerus de Haia*1* episcopo vi d. et habet iii s.

[904] Ernaldus frater Petri merc*iarii*1 episcopo viii d. et habet v s.

[905] Drogo Blundus*1* episcopo ix d. et habet iii s.

[906] Sewardus episcopo viii d.

[907] Trentemars*1* episcopo v d. et habet iii s.

[908] Herbertus presbiter*1* episcopo xii d. et habet de Godrico*d* xii d. Et Godricus habet xvi d.

[909] Lodewis*1* episcopo vi d. et habet xiii d.

[910] Hospitale*1* episcopo xxx d. et habet ix s. et i d.

[911] Osmod' episcopo iii s.

[912] Herbertus presbiter*1* tenet i terram quietam.

[913] Rogerus de Haia*1* episcopo xii d.

[914] Merwn*1* episcopo xxv d. et habet ii s. et iii d.

[915] Gaufridus de Cell' episcopo iiii s.

[916] Ricardus Lambert*1* episcopo iii s. et habet vi s.

[917] Imma priori ii s.

[918] Heredes Radulfi camerarii*1* episcopo xii d. et habent iii s.

[919] Ailwardus coruesar*ius* episcopo xii d.

OUTSIDE SOUTH GATE [i]

[900] A woman pays the bishop 4*d*. and receives from Stephen 2*s*. And Stephen has 8*s*.

[901] And the same woman receives from Henry the blacksmith 2*s*. and from Godric 4*d*.

[902] Ailmer pays the bishop 2*s*.

[903] Roger of La Haye*1* pays the bishop 6*d*. and receives 3*s*.

[904] Ernald, brother of Peter the mercer,*1* pays the bishop 8*d*. and receives 5*s*.

[905] Drew Blond*1* pays the bishop 9*d*. and receives 3*s*.

[906] Siward pays the bishop 8*d*.

[907] Trentemars*1* pays the bishop 5*d*. and receives 3*s*.

[908] Herbert the priest*1* pays the bishop 12*d*. and from Godric receives 12*d*. And Godric receives 16*d*.

[909] Lodewis*1* pays the bishop 6*d*. and receives 13*d*.

[910] The hospital*1* pays the bishop 30*d*. and receives 9*s*. 1*d*.

[911] Osmod pays the bishop 3*s*.

[912] Herbert the priest*1* holds 1 land quit.

[913] Roger of La Haye*1* pays the bishop 12*d*.

[914] Merwen*1* pays the bishop 25*d*. and receives 2*s*. 3*d*.

[915] Geoffrey *de Cell'* pays the bishop 4*s*.

[916] Richard [son of] Lambert*1* pays the bishop 3*s*. and receives 6*s*.

[917] Emma pays the prior 2*s*.

[918] The heirs of Ralf the chamberlain*1* pay the bishop 12*d*. and receive 3*s*.

[919] Ailward the shoemaker pays the bishop 12*d*.

a In upper margin, text for rubricator almost entirely cut away has been erased and not replaced; both m *and* a *in margin*   *b Initial* M *over an erasure*   *c A blue initial*   *d* habet *repeated*

903 1. See **38**.
904 1. See **135**.
905 1. See **185**.
907 1. See **455**.
908 1. See **632**.
909 1. See also **1007**.

910 1. See **9**, but cf. **1054**.
912 1. See **632**.
913 1. See **38**.
914 1. See Addenda.
916 1. See **555**.
918 1. See **72**.

[920] Hugo de Goi episcopo xii d. et habet iii s.

[920] Hugh of Gouy pays the bishop 12d. and receives 3s.

[921] Alured Herra episcopo v d.

[921] Alfred Herra pays the bishop 5d.

[922] Wluricus parmentarius episcopo iiii d.

[922] Wulfric the tailor pays the bishop 4d.

[923] Raimerus episcopo v s. et habet xii s. et xi d.

[923] Raimer pays the bishop 5s. and receives 12s. 11d.

[924] Semannus bolengarius episcopo v s.

[924] Seaman the baker pays the bishop 5s.

[925] Canonici Porcestr'¹ habent de i domo xvi d., et illa domus est in calle regis posita.²

[925] The canons of Portchester¹ receive from 1 house 16d. And that house is placed on the king's road.²

[926] Ricardus coruesarius¹ episcopo iiii d. et habet ii s.

[926] Richard the shoemaker¹ pays the bishop 4d. and receives 2s.

[927] Spiringus¹ episcopo xxvi d. et habet v s.

[927] Spiring¹ pays the bishop 26d. and receives 5s.

[928] In porta de Chingeta¹ habet sacrista² xv d.ᵃ

[928] In the gate of King's Gate¹ the sacristan² receives 15d.

[929] Aluricus cocus priori iii obolos et habet ii s.

[929] Aluric the cook pays the prior 1½d. and receives 2s.

[930] Lucelina priori iii d. et habet vi s.

[930] Lucelina pays the prior 3d. and receives 6s.

[931] Rogerus cocus¹ priori v d. et habet vi s.

[931] Roger the cook¹ pays the prior 5d. and receives 6s.

[932] Hugo de Porta¹ priori v d. et habet [fo. 31] xviii d.

[932] Hugh de Port¹ pays the prior 5d. and receives 18d.

[933] Herbertus campion priori v d.

[933] Herbert the champion pays the prior 5d.

[934] Urluid priori viii d.

[934] Urluid pays the prior 8d.

[935] Selida priori ii d.

[935] Selida pays the prior 2d.

[936] Hotot¹ priori v d.

[936] Hotot¹ pays the prior 5d.

[937] Petrus napier priori iii d. et habet xii s. Et Ingelbertus habet iii s. Et de eademᵇ habet Godeboldus¹ de Roberto Bontens v s.

[937] Peter the napier pays the prior 3d. and receives 12s. And Ingelbert receives 3s. And from the same land Godebold¹ receives from Robert Bontemps 5s.

[938] Nigellus presbiter¹ priori x d. et habet xl d.

[938] Nigel the priest¹ pays the prior 10d. and receives 40d.

[939] Stephanus priori v d. et habet iii s.

[939] Stephen pays the prior 5d. and receives 3s.

ᵃ sacrista' *in margin in a late medieval hand*   ᵇ *Line over* Et de eadem (? *in cancellation*) *erased*

925 1. See **645**. In 1219 Southwick Priory had 40d. rent outside King's Gate and 4s. rent in *Sewinestwichene* next to the church of St. Michael (Southwick Cart i, fo. 38). Cf. **1001**.
2. See also **17**, n. 2.
926 1. See **628** and also **1010** and **1024**.
927 1. Cf. **215**.

928 1. One of the two gates in the south wall of the city, see below, pp. 236, s.n., 263, 275.   2. See **791**.
931 1. See **605**.
932 1. See **314**.
936 1. See **814**.
937 1. See also **979** and **982**.
938 1. Cf. **608**, n. 3.

[940] Trentemars[1] priori v d. et habet xxviii d.

[941] Osbertus magister[1] priori v d.

[942] Girinus episcopo x s.

[943] Iohannes frater Richer'[1] priori v d. et habet iiii s.

[944] Willelmus filius Girardi tenet de episcopo [. . .];[a] et manentes reddunt ei iii s. et ipsi habent inde ii s.

[945] Walterus draper episcopo ii d. et obolum et uxori Radulfi de Clera xii d. Et idem[b] Walterus habet iii s.

[946] Willelmus Peuerel[1] tenet i terram de episcopo quietam; et Brictwen tenet illam quietam de eo. Et de eadem tenet Alduinus[2] i alteram quietam.[c]

[947] Walterus de Andeleio tenet i terram de episcopo et habet inde vii s. et ii d.

[948] Adeliz episcopo ii s.

[949] Ailwinus saponarius episcopo xviii d.

[950] Aldwinus Spich[1] prior ivi d.[d] et pater eius priori xii d.; et Aluinus habet iii s. et vi d.

[951] Stephanus Sarazinus[1] priori xx d. et habet ii s.

[952] Episcopus Exon'[1] priori xliiii d.

[953] Goda priori xii d.

[954] Goda Lamart' priori x d.

[955] Herbertus hosatus[1] [. . .][e] v d. et habet iiii s.

[956] Filia Iohannis priori iii d. et Ricardus habet iii s.

[957] Walterus presbiter abbatisse Wint' iii d.

[940] Trentemars[1] pays the prior 5d. and receives 28d.

[941] Osbert the master[1] pays the prior 5d.

[942] Girin pays the bishop 10s.

[943] John, Richer's brother,[1] pays the prior 5d. and receives 4s.

[944] William son of Girard holds of the bishop [. . .], and the inhabitants pay him 3s. and they have from the land 2s.

[945] Walter the draper pays the bishop 2½d. and Ralf of Clere's wife 12d. And the same Walter receives 3s.

[946] William Peverel[1] holds 1 land of the bishop quit, and Brithwen holds it quit of him. And of that same woman/land Aldwin[2] holds another land quit.

[947] Walter of Les Andelys holds 1 land of the bishop and receives from it 7s. 2d.

[948] Adelaide pays the bishop 2s.

[949] Ailwin the soap-maker pays the bishop 18d.

[950] Aldwin Spich[1] pays the prior 6d. and his father pays the prior 12d. And Alwin receives 3s. 6d.

[951] Stephen the Saracen[1] pays the prior 20d. and receives 2s.

[952] The bishop of Exeter[1] pays the prior 44d.

[953] Goda pays the prior 12d.

[954] Goda the Weasel pays the prior 10d.

[955] Herbert Hosed[1] pays [. . .] 5d. and receives 4s.

[956] John's daughter pays the prior 3d. and Richard receives 3s.

[957] Walter the priest pays the abbess of Winchester 3d.

---

a Space left for holding   *b item MS.*   *c Second and third lines of MS. written over an erasure*   *d vi d.*
over an erasure   *e Space left for recipient*

940 1. See 455.
941 1. See 715.
943 1. See 49.
946 1. Possibly William (II) Peverel of the Peak, an important baron and an adherent of Stephen, or William Peverel of Dover.   2. Possibly Aldwin Spich, see 950.
950 1. Cf. 946 and see also 993.

951 1. Between 1160 and 1184, when he died, he received an annual payment from the Crown of 30s. 5d. out of the Winchester revenues: *Pipe Roll 6 Henry II*, p. 49: *30 Henry II*, p. 85.
952 1. See Addenda.
955 1. Perhaps a member of the Husey family, cf. 138, n. 3.

[958] Albreda eidem abbatisse viii d.

[958] Albreda pays the same abbess 8*d*.

[959] Ulfild*ᵃ* eidem abbatisse iiii d.

[959] Wulfhild pays the same abbess 4*d*.

[960] Hubertus clericus tenet i terram, sed pertinet*ᵇ* ad ecclesiam.¹

[960] Hubert the clerk holds i land, but it pertains to the church.¹

[961] Willelmus Surlaf¹ eidem abbatisse x d. et habet xii d. Et abbatissa habet ibi i domum ubi ortolanus suus² manet.

[961] William Sour-loaf¹ pays the same abbess 10*d*. and receives 12*d*. And the abbess has there i house where her gardener² lives.

[962] Conanus¹ priori iiii d.² et habet viii d.

[962] Conan¹ pays the prior 4*d*.² and receives 8*d*.

[963] Monachi Glaston'¹ episcopo iiii s.

[963] The monks of Glastonbury¹ pay the bishop 4*s*.

[964] Sewi¹ episcopo i bizantiam de i terra.

[964] Sewi¹ pays the bishop i bezant for i land.

[965] Surpap¹ episcopo xx d.

[965] Sour-pap¹ pays the bishop 20*d*.

[966] Uxor Heleboldi¹ episcopo iiii d. et habet xviii d.

[966] Helebold's¹ wife pays the bishop 4*d*. and receives 18*d*.

[967] Mallardus episcopo xiiii d. et habet xl d.

[967] Mallard pays the bishop 14*d*. and receives 40*d*.

[968] [fo. 31ᵛ] Fati episcopo*ᶜ* iii s. et habet vi d.

[968] Fatty pays the bishop 3*s*. and receives 6*d*.

[969] Turneteil episcopo ii s.

[969] Turntail pays the bishop 2*s*.

[970] Osmoda¹ priori iiii d.

[970] Osmoth¹ pays the prior 4*d*.

[971] Rogerus Abonel¹ priori [. . .]*ᵈ* et habet iiii s.

[971] Roger Abonel¹ pays the prior [. . .] and receives 4*s*.

[972] Giroldus Furwatel priori iiii d.

[972] Girold Furwatel pays the prior 4*d*.

[973] Item Rogerus Abonel¹ [. . .].

[973] Again, Roger Abonel¹ [. . .].

[974] Radulfus*ᵉ* Cuinte¹ episcopo v d. et habet xviii d.

[974] Ralf Cuinte¹ pays the bishop 5*d*. and receives 18*d*.

ᵃ Ulsild *MS.*   *ᵇ* *Over an erasure*   *ᶜ* Fati episcopo *over an erasure* (?)   *ᵈ* *Space left for amount*
ᵉ a *over an erasure* (?)

960 1. The adjacent properties, **957–9** and **961**, each owed a rent to St. Mary's Abbey. The abbey was patron of the church of All Saints *in vineis*, which stood on the E. side of Kingsgate Street: Reg Stratford, fo. 90; *SMW*.
961 1. See **819**; cf. **965**.
2. He may have tended the abbess's vineyard: cf. **960**, n. 1.
962 1. See **963**, n. 1.
2. This rent may be the same as the 4*d*. due to St. Swithun's Priory from the land of Alured Foliot, next to the church of All Saints, which had lapsed by 1287 (WCL, Custumal, fo. 31; cf. entry **960**). Robert of Limésey granted this land, which was on the W. side of the church, to St. Denis Priory, Southampton: St. Denis Cart, fo. 124.
963 1. Benedictine abbey of which Bishop Henry was

still abbot: *VCH Somerset* ii. 82 ff. About 1137, Bishop Henry purchased land and houses at Winchester from *Conanus fenerator* (cf. **962**), rebuilt the property, and granted it as a hospice to Glastonbury Abbey. Conan was paid 6 marks and was later provided with lodgings at St. Cross Hospital until the end of his life. Rent and services were owed from the property to St. Swithun's Priory: A. Watkin (ed.), *The Great Chartulary of Glastonbury* (Somerset Record Soc. 64 (1956)), iii. 703, 704.
964 1. See **55**.
965 1. Cf. **961**.
966 1. Cf. Herlebold's wife, **795**.
970 1. See **80**.
971 1. See also **973** and **991**; cf. **1059**.
973 1. See **971**.
974 1. See **39**.

[975] Hugo pistor¹ priori x d. et habet ii s.

[975] Hugh the baker¹ pays the prior 10*d*. and receives 2*s*.

[976] Radulfus presbiter priori xii d. et habet xliii d.

[976] Ralf the priest pays the prior 12*d*. and receives 43*d*.

[977] Ernoldus frater Petri¹ episcopo xxvii d.

[977] Ernold, Peter's brother,¹ pays the bishop 27*d*.

[978] Uxor Radulfi camerarii¹ episcopo xviii d.

[978] Ralf the chamberlain's wife¹ pays the bishop 18*d*.

[979] Godeboldus¹ episcopo viii d. et habet iiii sol.

[979] Godebold¹ pays the bishop 8*d*. and receives 4*s*.

[980] Hugo pistor¹ episcopo xii d.

[980] Hugh the baker¹ pays the bishop 12*d*.

[981] Ernoldus frater Petri¹ episcopo iiii s. de ii terris.

[981] Ernold, Peter's brother,¹ pays the bishop 4*s*. for 2 lands.

[982] Godeboldus¹ episcopo x d. et habet iii s.

[982] Godebold¹ pays the bishop 10*d*. and receives 3*s*.

[983] Robertus Oison¹ episcopo xxix d.

[983] Robert Oison¹ pays the bishop 29*d*.

[984] Froggemore episcopo xviii d.

[984] Frogmore pays the bishop 18*d*.

[985] Uxor W. de Glauston'¹ episcopo xii d. et habet vi d.

[985] William of Glastonbury's¹ wife pays the bishop 12*d*. and receives 6*d*.

[986] Oricus episcopo ii d. et habet xii d.ᵃ

[986] Oric pays the bishop 2*d*. and receives 12*d*.

[987] Herdingus episcopo ii s. et habet xviii d.ᵇ

[987] Harding pays the bishop 2*s*. and receives 18*d*.

[988] Rualdus priori xii d.

[988] Ruald pays the prior 12*d*.

[989] ᶜRicher' presbiter priori xii d.

[989] Richer the priest pays the prior 12*d*.

[990] Teodericus mol*endinarius* episcopo vi d. et obolum*ᵈ* et habet xl d.

[990] Theoderic the miller pays the bishop 6½*d*. and receives 40*d*.

[991] Rogerus Abonel¹ episcopo ii d. et habet xxvi d.

[991] Roger Abonel¹ pays the bishop 2*d*. and receives 26*d*.

[992] Walterus parm*entarius*¹ episcopo ii d.

[992] Walter the tailor¹ pays the bishop 2*d*.

[993] Aldwinus Spich¹ episcopo xii d.

[993] Aldwin Spich¹ pays the bishop 12*d*.

[994] Hugo drapier episcopo xii d.

[994] Hugh the draper pays the bishop 12*d*.

[995] Radulfus Cuinte¹ episcopo xii d. et habet ii s.

[995] Ralf Cuinte¹ pays the bishop 12*d*. and receives 2*s*.

ᵃ (x)ii *over an erasure*   ᵇ s. et habet xviii *over an erasure*   ᶜ *There are erased red marks to one side or the other of most entries on fo. 31ᵛ, col. b, which begins at this point. These correspond to red initials on fo. 32ʳ and must have been caused by closing the MS. when the initials were still wet*   ᵈ *Blue initial R in error for* Rob[ertus] *erased; cf.* [726]

975 1. See 980.
977 1. See 135.
978 1. See 72.
979 1. See 937.
980 1. See 975.
981 1. See 135.
982 1. See 937.
983 1. See 40.

985 1. Probably William of Glastonbury, who succeeded his uncle Walkelin as chamberlain of Normandy before 1130: *Pipe Roll 31 Henry I*, p. 13; *Regesta*, ii, no. 1579, etc. He adhered to Stephen: *Regesta*, iii, nos. 293, 594.
991 1. See 971.
992 1. See Addenda.
993 1. See 950.
995 1. See 39.

[996] Robertus Pinguis¹ episcopo ix d. et habet xxxv d.

[997] Duresumer episcopo xii d.

[998] Baldwinus pistor¹ habet [i] terram quietam de episcopo et habet inde xiiii s.

[999] Et item Baldewinus¹ episcopo xii d. de alia.

[1000] Ansere episcopo xii d.

ᵃEXTRA PORTAM DE SUDᵇ

[1001] Robertus de Baioc'¹ episcopo v s. et habet in Sevetuichne² iii s. Et Edwardus cancellarius³ habet xii d. Et item Robertus de Baioc' habet in Seuetuichena xlii d. et Radulfus clericus⁴ v s. Et idem iuxta domum Sewlfi servientis⁵ viii s.

[1002] Alanus de Cellar'¹ episcopo xviii d.

[1003] Radulfus capellanus¹ episcopo xii d.

[1004] Forst episcopo xviii d.

[1005] [fo. 32] Willelmus vigil episcopo xviii d. et habet xx d.

[1006] Willelmus Polanus episcopo xii d.

[1007] Lodewis¹ episcopo iii s. et habet xii d.ᶜ

[1008] Ailwardus Rus episcopo v s. et habet iiii s.

[1009] Willelmus Hotot¹ episcopo iiii d.

[1010] Ricardus corvesarius¹ episcopo v s.

[1011] Michael episcopo iiii s.

[1012] Chawete¹ episcopo xii d.

[1013] Baldewinus maco episcopo xii d.

[996] Robert the Fat¹ pays the bishop 9d. and receives 35d.

[997] Duresumer pays the bishop 12d.

[998] Baldwin the baker¹ has 1 land of the bishop quit and receives from it 14s.

[999] And again Baldwin¹ pays the bishop 12d. for another land.

[1000] Ansere pays the bishop 12d.

OUTSIDE SOUTH GATE [ii]

[1001] Robert of Bayeux¹ pays the bishop 5s. and receives in *Sevetuichne*² 3s. And Edward the chancellor³ receives 12d. And again Robert of Bayeux receives in *Seuetuichena* 42d. and Ralf the clerk⁴ receives 5s. And Ralf receives next to the house of the servant/sergeant Sewulf⁵ 8s.

[1002] Alan of Cellier (? the cellar)¹ pays the bishop 18d.

[1003] Ralf the chaplain¹ pays the bishop 12d.

[1004] Forst pays the bishop 18d.

[1005] William the watchman pays the bishop 18d. and receives 20d.

[1006] William the Colt pays the bishop 12d.

[1007] Lodewis¹ pays the bishop 3s. and receives 12d.

[1008] Ailward Rush pays the bishop 5s. and receives 4s.

[1009] William Hotot¹ pays the bishop 4d.

[1010] Richard the shoemaker¹ pays the bishop 5s.

[1011] Michael pays the bishop 4s.

[1012] Chawete¹ pays the bishop 12d.

[1013] Baldwin the mason pays the bishop 12d.

ᵃ *Partly over an erasure of first line, before* xii   ᵇ *In lower margin, text for rubricator almost entirely cut away*   ᶜ xi *erased at end*

996 1. See **533**.
998 1. See **68**.
999 1. See **68**.
1001 1. See **7**.
2. This lane ran W. from Kingsgate Street to the road leading from South Gate. The church of St. Michael in Kingsgate Street stood on the N. side of the lane: *SMW*. Cf. **925**, n. 1, and for the name, below, p. 235, s.n.
3. Possibly the bishop's chancellor.   4. See **14**.

5. See also **1041**. This may mean that the property was adjacent to **1041**.
1002 1. See below, p. 193, n. 4.
1003 1. He witnessed the grant of two mills in the south suburb in c. 1155: Goodman *Chartulary*, no. 453.
1007 1. See **909**.
1009 1. See **814**.
1010 1. See **926**.
1012 1. See also **1039**.

[1014] Henricus [. . .]*ᵃ* episcopo [. . .]*ᵃ* vi d.

[1014] Henry [. . .] pays the bishop [. . .] 6*d*.

[1015] Isabel episcopo vi s. et habet xvi d.

[1015] Isabel pays the bishop 6*s*. and receives 16*d*.

[1016] Aluredus episcopo xii d.

[1016] Alfred pays the bishop 12*d*.

[1017] Aldelmus tela*rius*¹ episcopo xii d.

[1017] Aldhelm the weaver¹ pays the bishop 12*d*.

[1018] Hospic*ium* cancell*arii*¹ quietam [*sic*].

[1018] The hospice of the chancellor¹ is quit.

[1019] Wluricus care*tarius* episcopo xii d.

[1019] Wulfric the carter pays the bishop 12*d*.

[1020] Baldewinus pistor¹ episcopo ii s. et habet xii d.

[1020] Baldwin the baker¹ pays the bishop 2*s*. and receives 12*d*.

[1021] Radulfus Cuinta¹ episcopo iiii s. et habet xl d.

[1021] Ralf Cuinte¹ pays the bishop 4*s*. and receives 40*d*.

[1022] God' camerarius episcopo xii d.

[1022] God' the chamberlain pays the bishop 12*d*.

[1023] Pag*anus* medicus episcopo xii d.

[1023] Pain the doctor pays the bishop 12*d*.

[1024] Ricardus corueis*arius*¹ episcopo ii s. et habet xii d.

[1024] Richard the shoemaker¹ pays the bishop 2*s*. and receives 12*d*.

[1025] Robertus sutor episcopo xii d.

[1025] Robert the shoemaker pays the bishop 12*d*.

[1026] Osbertus monacus episcopo xii d. et habet iii s.

[1026] Osbert the monk pays the bishop 12*d*. and receives 3*s*.

[1027] Item Baldewinus¹ episcopo vi s., et item Baldewinus Gileberto de Chinai pro Richer' ii s.

[1027] Again, Baldwin¹ pays the bishop 6*s*. and again Baldwin pays Gilbert *de Chinai* on Richer's behalf 2*s*.

[1028] Willelmus medicus episcopo xxx d. et habet iiii s.

[1028] William the doctor pays the bishop 30*d*. and receives 4*s*.

[1029] Coppa¹ episcopo vi d.

[1029] Coppa¹ pays the bishop 6*d*.

[1030] Et*ᵇ* quatuor curtill*a* sunt ibi vast*a* et solebant reddere episcopo vii s.

[1030] And four curtilages are waste there, and they used to yield the bishop 7*s*.

[1031] Radulfus Sciteliure episcopo xviii d.

[1031] Ralf Sciteliure pays the bishop 18*d*.

[1032] Fil' Osberti episcopo iiii d.

[1032] Osbert's son/daughter(s) pays the bishop 4*d*.

[1033] Willelmus marescallus¹ episcopo xv d. et obolum.

[1033] William the marshal¹ pays the bishop 15½*d*.

[1034] Uxor Hunfridi episcopo xliiii d. et habet ii s.

[1034] Humphrey's wife pays the bishop 44*d*. and receives 2*s*.

[1035] Turstinus episcopo xvi d. et habet xl d. de Dauid; et Dauid habet inde iiii s. et ii d.

[1035] Thurstin pays the bishop 16*d*. and receives 40*d*. from David. And David receives from the land 4*s*. 2*d*.

ᵃ Blank space   *ᵇ* Ct *MS*. (e *in margin*); *cf*. [612]

1017 1. There was a weavers' guild in Winchester: *Pipe Roll 2 Henry II*, p. 52.
1018 1. Presumably lodgings for the king's chancellor on his visits to the city.
1020 1. See 68.

1021 1. See 39.
1024 1. See 926.
1027 1. See 68.
1029 1. See 602.
1033 1. See 315.

[1036] Ulgerus episcopo xvi d. et habet ii s.

[1037] Ailwardus vine*tarius* episcopo xxxii d. et habet vi s.*ᵃ*

[1038] Bittuc episcopo xii d.

[1039] Chawete¹ episcopo xii d.

[1040] Dora episcopo xii d. et habet ii s.

[1041] Sewlf serviens¹ episcopo ii s.

[1042] Muriel episcopo v d.

[1043] Rogerus de Haia¹ episcopo v d. et habet v s. et iiii d. et obolum.

[1044] Ricardus medicus¹ priori iii s. et habet xii d.

[1045] [fo. 32ᵛ] Ernaldus frater Petri¹ priori iii s.

[1046] Gaufridus filius Segar' priori xxviii d. et habet xviii d.

[1047] Willelmus tana*tor* priori xx d. et habet xxx d.

[1048] Briwer' priori v s. et habet dimidiam marcam de Iudichell'.¹

[1049] Et in venella subtus¹ reddunt homines priori vii s.

[1050] Ricardus et uxor Atscor¹ priori ii s.

[1051] Uxor Multun priori vii d.

[1052] Et Trewa priori xii d.

[1053] Et eadem uxor Atscor¹ [. . .]*ᵇ* v d. et habet xvi d.

[1054] Et ibi iuxta est quedam terra vasta, que solebat reddere episcopo xiiii d.; et monachi habent illam in hospital*i*.¹

ᵃ Followed by an erasure   *ᵇ Space left for recipient*

[1036] Wulfgar pays the bishop 16*d.* and receives 2*s.*

[1037] Ailward the vintner pays the bishop 32*d.* and receives 6*s.*

[1038] Bittuc pays the bishop 12*d.*

[1039] Chawete¹ pays the bishop 12*d.*

[1040] Dora pays the bishop 12*d.* and receives 2*s.*

[1041] Sewulf the servant/sergeant¹ pays the bishop 2*s.*

[1042] Muriel pays the bishop 5*d.*

[1043] Roger of La Haye¹ pays the bishop 5*d.* and receives 5*s.* 4½*d.*

[1044] Richard the doctor¹ pays the prior 3*s.* and receives 12*d.*

[1045] Ernald, Peter's brother,¹ pays the prior 3*s.*

[1046] Geoffrey son of Segar pays the prior 28*d.* and receives 18*d.*

[1047] William the tanner pays the prior 20*d.* and receives 30*d.*

[1048] Brewer pays the prior 5*s.* and receives ½ mark from Judichel.¹

[1049] And in the lane below,¹ the men pay the prior 7*s.*

[1050] Richard and Ascor's wife¹ pay the prior 2*s.*

[1051] Multun's wife pays the prior 7*d.*

[1052] And Trewa pays the prior 12*d.*

[1053] And the same Ascor's wife¹ pays [. . .] 5*d.* and receives 16*d.*

[1054] And next is a certain waste land, which used to yield the bishop 14*d.* And the monks have it in the hospital.¹

1039 1. See **1012**.
1041 1. See **1001**.
1043 1. See **38**.
1044 1. *Ricardus medicus* held land in *Seftwichene* during the episcopate of Richard of Ilchester (1174–88): *PRBW 1208–9*, 77.
1045 1. See **135**.
1048 1. See **864**.
1049 1. Unidentified, but possibly running S. from College Street, W. of the site of the later college; cf. **1054**.

1050 1. See **631**.
1053 1. See **631**.
1054 1. This was probably the 'Sustren Spital', the hospital of the cathedral priory whose inmates were a community of sisters, situated on the S. side of College Street. For its function in the later Middle Ages and its site, see G. W. Kitchin (ed.), *Obedientiary Rolls of St. Swithun's, Winchester* (HRS, 1892), 76, 397–454; and T. F. Kirby, *Annals of Winchester College* (London, 1892), 6–9, 134–6.

[1055] Helewisa¹ episcopo vi d. et habet x d.

[1056] Licgard*a* episcopo ii s.

[1057] Godehald¹ episcopo de ii terris xi d. et habet vi s.; et Ansgodus habet vi s. et vi d.

[1058] Heredes Martini¹ episcopo xx d. et habent v s. de terra vacua; et iidem*b* habent v s. de suis domibus preterea. Et Girardus habet inde x d.*c*

[1059] Abonel¹ episcopo iii d. et obolum et habet iiii s. et vi d.

[1060] Ernoldus frater Petri¹ episcopo v d. et habet v s.

[1061] Theduinus episcopo iiii d.

[1062] Warinus episcopo viii d. et Willelmus barrar' habet iiii s. et Gaufr[idus] Bal' habet xviii d.

[1063] Iohannes cord*wanarius* episcopo vi d. et obolum et habet xii d. Et quedam femina habet ii s.

[1064] Willelmus de Templo episcopo ii d. et obolum et habet xii d.

[1065] Iohannes episcopo v d. et habet iiii s.

[1066] Wluricus de Windes' episcopo ii s.*d*

[1067] Ricardus de Haia¹ episcopo xii d. et habet*e* x s. et Hunfridus habet xii d.

IN GERESTRET*f*¹

[1068] Stephanus frater Iohannis¹ regi x d.²

[1069] Simon dispensator¹ episcopo ii s. de terra baronum vasta.

[1070] Berengarius sell*arius* regi xviii d.

[1055] Heloïse¹ pays the bishop 6*d*. and receives 10*d*.

[1056] Licgard pays the bishop 2*s*.

[1057] Godehald¹ pays the bishop for 2 lands 11*d*. and receives 6*s*.; and Ansgod receives 6*s*. 6*d*.

[1058] Martin's heirs¹ pay the bishop 20*d*. and receive 5*s*. from a vacant land; and they receive besides 5*s*. from their tenements/houses. And Girard receives from it/them 10*d*.

[1059] Abonel¹ pays the bishop 3½*d*. and receives 4*s*. 6*d*.

[1060] Ernold, Peter's brother,¹ pays the bishop 5*d*. and receives 5*s*.

[1061] Theduin pays the bishop 4*d*.

[1062] Warin pays the bishop 8*d*. and William the gate-keeper receives 4*s*. and Geoffrey Ball receives 18*d*.

[1063] John the cordwainer pays the bishop 6½*d*. and receives 12*d*. And a certain woman receives 2*s*.

[1064] William of the Temple pays the bishop 2½*d*. and receives 12*d*.

[1065] John pays the bishop 5*d*. and receives 4*s*.

[1066] Wulfric of Winsor pays the bishop 2*s*.

[1067] Richard of La Haye¹ pays the bishop 12*d*. and receives 10*s*. and Humphrey receives 12*d*.

IN *GERE* STREET [TRAFALGAR STREET]¹

[1068] Stephen, John's brother,¹ pays the king 10*d*.²

[1069] Simon the dispenser¹ pays the bishop 2*s*. from the land of the barons which is waste.

[1070] Berengar the saddler pays the king 18*d*.

---

a Unclear: MS. possibly reads Liegard *over* Lig' *erased. Ellis gives* Lisgard   *b* eadem *MS.*   *c Lines 4(?) and 5 of MS. written over an erasure*   *d* s. *over an erasure (?)*   *e* et habet *over an erasure (?)*   *f In lower margin, text for rubricator almost entirely cut away*

1055 1. See **575**.
1057 1. See **168**.
1058 1. See **17**.
1059 1. Cf. **971**.
1060 1. See **135**.
1067 1. The grants of Robert of La Haye (Henry I's chief steward in Normandy), Muriel his wife, and their sons Richard and Ralf to the abbey of the Holy Trinity, Lessay, are rehearsed in a royal charter of 1126: *Regesta*,

ii, p. 353–4. Richard was steward to Duke Henry: *Regesta*, iii, p. xxxvi. See also **38**, n. 4.
1067/8 1. Three properties (**1069**, **1071**, and **1078**) seem connected with properties listed in Survey **I**. As they appear in the reverse order it is possible that the street was surveyed from the opposite end.
1068 1. See **409**.
   2. For the tenement, cf. **I, 285**.
1069 1. For Simon and the tenement, see **I, 283**.

[1071] Fil' Iwein'¹ regi vi d.

[1071] Iwein's son/daughter(s)¹ pay(s) the king 6d.

[1072] Posta¹ regi x d.²

[1072] Posta¹ pays the king 10d.²

[1073] Idem Posta¹ tenet i terram que fuit hominibus de Cadum' et habet inde dimidiam marcam. Et Iohannes Longus habet inde iiii s. Et est de feudo regis.

[1073] The same Posta¹ holds 1 land which used to be held by the men of Caen and receives from it ½ mark. And John Long receives from it 4s. And it is of the king's fief.

[1074] Robertus Turlux regi vi d., et Muriᵃ[fo. 33]el habet inde viii d. Et canonici de Meretone¹ habent xxvi d. de B.

[1074] Robert Turlux pays the king 6d. and Muriel receives from the land 8d. And the canons of Merton¹ receive 26d. de B.

[1075] Muriel regi vii d. de B.

[1075] Muriel pays the king 7d. de B.

[1076] Heredes Hereberti¹ regi iiii d. et [. . .]ᵇ

[1076] Herbert's heirs¹ pay the king 4d. and [. . .]ᵇ

[1077] Monachi regiᶜ xiiii d. et habent v s.

[1077] The monks pay the king 14d. and receive 5s.

[1078] Et Muriel habet xii s. et Herebertus filius Saieti¹ habet iiii d.

[1078] And Muriel receives 12s. and Herbert son of Saiet¹ receives 4d.

[1079] Alexander filius asinarii regi xv d.

[1079] Alexander son of the donkey-driver pays the king 15d.

[1080] Rogerus filius Chupping'¹ regi xii d. et habet pro ii bracinsᵈ et pro domo i marcam.

[1080] Roger son of Chepping¹ pays the king 12d. and receives for 2 breweries and a house 1 mark.

[1081] Willelmus Exon' regi vi d. et hospitali¹ xviii d.

[1081] William of Exeter pays the king 6d. and the hospital¹ 18d.

[1082] Ansfridus burgensis¹ regi viii d. et idem priori xv d.; sed est vastᵃ.

[1082] Ansfrid the burgess¹ pays the king 8d. and the prior 15d. But the land is waste.

[1083] Seiherᵉ et Willelmus priori ii s., et Willelmus habet xii d.

[1083] Seiher and William pay the prior 2s. and William receives 12d.

[1084] Semitonius et Willelmus clericus¹ priori xvi [d.] et habent v s.

[1084] Semitone and William the clerk¹ pay the prior 16[d.] and receive 5s.

[1085] Erdrea episcopo vii d. de B.

[1085] Erdrea pays the bishop 7d. de B.

[1086] Abbatissa de Rumesie habet ibi iii terras et debet habere inde xliiii d.ᶠ

[1086] The abbess of Romsey has there 3 lands and should receive from them 44d.

ᵃ Catch-word at end of quire, in bottom margin, mostly cut away as separate items, perhaps, with Ellis, we should read them together   ᵇ Although [1076] and [1077] are rubricated   ᶜ Monachi regi over an erasure   ᵈ s over an erasure   ᵉ -ih- over an erasure   ᶠ Remainder of fo. 33ʳ and fo. 33ᵛ blank

1071 1. For the property, see I, 282.
1072 1. See also 1073.
   2. For the tenement, cf. I, 285.
1073 1. See 1072.
1074 1. See 50.
1076 1. Possibly the heirs of Herbert son of Guncelin:
see 29.
1078 1. See I, 256.
1080 1. See 462.
1081 1. See 9.
1082 1. See 50.
1084 1. See 167.

PART II

THE PERSONAL NAMES AND BYNAMES OF THE WINTON DOMESDAY

1

INTRODUCTION

THE importance of the Winchester surveys as sources for the history of late Old English and early Middle English personal nomenclature has not hitherto been fully recognized by students of onomastics. It is true that the two surveys have been drawn upon from time to time for illustrative material but they have never been systematically utilized. In Searle's *Onomasticon*,[1] that classic and indispensable repertory of English names up to *c*. 1100, there are no references to the Winton Domesday. The same is true of Boehler's book on Old English women's names. Some forms culled from our record are cited by Björkman in his book on Scandinavian names in England (*NPN*),[2] and a handful are adduced in Forssner's study of the Continental Germanic element.[3] Redin included nineteen instances from the Winton Domesday in his monograph on Old English uncompounded names.[4]

In his book on Old English bynames Tengvik claims (p. 7) to have excerpted the relevant material in the **1066** and *c*. **1110** surveys, but there are not a few omissions and the etymologies are sometimes unsatisfactory. Finally, Reaney, in his *Dictionary of British Surnames* (*DBS*), has collected from the Winton Domesday many instances of such Christian names and bynames as have survived as modern surnames and has suggested a considerable number of good etymologies.[5]

[1] For the full titles and dates of the publications referred to in this contribution, see pp. xxiff., above. To save space some especially abbreviated references have been used here (e.g. *P* for *Pipe Roll*), but these shortened forms will also be found in the list on pp. xxiff. The abbreviations for languages, grammatical terms, and counties are those used in the publications of the English Place-Name Society, and are not included in this list. References to printed sources and other publications are always to pages except in the case of *AS Ch*, *AS Wills*, *AS Writs*, *BCS*, *KCD*, and *Reg* where reference is made to the number of the document. The MS. date of charters and other records is sometimes added in brackets after the main date, e.g. (12th c.) for '12th century'. Coins are referred to by reigns and numbers in the coin-catalogues (*BEH*, *BMC*, *SCBI*).

[2] *Asa, Atser, Colbrand, Gunnild, Gunnora.*

[3] *Gazo, Godesbrand, Hizeman, Huchelinus, Maiesent.*

[4] *Babbi, Bolle, Brun, Ceca, Chep(p)ing, Colling, Hauoc, Laue, Leouing, Suot* (all **1066**), *Sueta* (*c*. **1110**), *Coppa, Diera, Dora, Goda, Suift, Trewa, Wdia, Widie* (**1148**).

[5] It may be added that Fransson, in his book on Middle English occupational bynames, includes two examples from the *LW*: *Spilemanus brandwirchte* **1066** (p. 152f.) and *Walter draper* **1148** (p. 89). Thuresson's Ha material consists only of excerpts from the Subsidy Rolls of 1327 and 1333.

M

However, in view of what has been said above, a full survey and analysis of the ono-mastic material in the Winchester lists seemed worth while. In the following pages an attempt has been made to provide a complete index of the personal names and bynames of various types occurring in our record and to deal with some of the problems raised by them.[1]

The first part of the work presents a consolidated alphabetical list of all Christian names and other forenames that occur at the three dates in the surveys, including variant and abbreviated forms. The list serves as an *Index Nominum* to the *Liber Wintoniensis* as a whole. Apart from that, its main object is etymological, i.e. to trace, as far as possible, the origin of each name and to explain the form or forms in which it appears in the *LW*. The index is followed by a section which provides separate lists of the names in each survey and discusses the conclusions that emerge from a study of them.

The second part of the work deals with the bynames, which are arranged under four main heads: (1) local bynames; (2) occupational bynames; (3) bynames of relationship; (4) other bynames, chiefly nicknames.

By way of conclusion a brief chapter on the phonology of the names is added, followed by notes on latinization, anglicizing, inflexion, and vocabulary.[2]

[1] An investigation similar in object and character to the one attempted here, although of course of much greater scope, was carried out for medieval London by Ekwall, who published his findings in *Early London Personal Names* (Lund, 1947, abbr. *ELPN*). This excellent work has in many ways served as a model for the present paper.

[2] The author is much indebted to Professor Kenneth Jackson for valuable advice on the Celtic names, to Professor Mattias Löfvenberg for help with some *cruces*, notably the *Godebiete* problem, and to Mr. J. E. B. Gover for information on Hampshire place-names. He also wishes to thank Mr. Martin Biddle for check-ing a large number of doubtful readings against the manuscript, for devising the diagrams (Figs. 1 and 2), and for many helpful suggestions. Dr. Derek Keene gave much important topographical and historical information and also prepared the map (Fig. 3).

2

PERSONAL NAMES

i. ALPHABETICAL AND ETYMOLOGICAL INDEX

Arrangement of the index

THE index lists the material in one alphabetical sequence. Each entry groups all the forms of the relevant name; these are followed by a brief statement of the etymology. Old English etyma are quoted in the standard West Saxon spelling,[1] Old Scandinavian names in that of classical Old Icelandic and/or Old Danish. For dithematic names of Old English origin a general reference to Searle's *Onomasticon* should be taken as implied. Otherwise references have usually been given to the standard monographs, i.e. Redin for uncompounded names, Forssner and Morlet[2] for the Continental Germanic ones, Björkman (*NPN*), Adigard des Gautries, and Fellows Jensen for those of Scandinavian origin. For names dealt with by Reaney (*DBS*) references are supplied to the relevant entry in his dictionary where supplementary material can usually be found.

Unrecorded etyma or, in the case of English names, those not recorded in pre-conquest sources, have been marked with an asterisk.[3]

For each name the *LW* form has been used as head-word. No normalization has been attempted, but abbreviated name-forms, if unambiguous, have as a rule been silently extended. If a name occurs in more than one survey, the forms have been grouped in chronological order, the earliest one(s) being placed at the head of the main entry. These chronological groups are separated by semicolons. The 1066[4] material has not been given a date in this section, whereas entries from the two later surveys are preceded by the dates *c.* 1110 and 1148 printed in bold face (as here).

Within each date the forms are further subdivided into two main categories, (*a*) name only, (*b*) name followed by a byname or epithet of some kind or other.[5] The arrangement of the forms under (*b*) is based entirely on these added epithets, which are listed in strict alphabetical order irrespective of the possible variant spellings or case-endings of the relevant Christian name. An exception to this rule is made for such (*a*)-cases as refer to

---

[1] For the el. *-ræd*, which is practically always written *-red* in OE sources, West Saxon as well as non-West-Saxon, the latter form has been used throughout. The quantity has been left unmarked.

[2] For the shortcomings of Morlet's book and the need for caution in using it, see E. Ewig, *Beitr. zur Namenforschung*, N.F. 5 (1970), 89–90; C. Wells, *Medium Aevum*, 39 (1970), 358–64. Vol. 2, with the subtitle 'Les Noms latins ou transmis par le latin', appeared in the summer of 1972. References to Morlet in the present contribution are to vol. 1 only.

[3] Etyma first recorded in the *TRE* portion of DB have not been starred.

[4] i.e. the *TRE* of the text. The actual date of the presumed Edwardian survey may be *c.* 1057. See above, p. 10 and below, p. 407. The date 1066 (in bold face) is thus used in subsequent sections of this contribution with the meaning '*TRE, v.* 1057 (?)'.

[5] Note that occupational bynames have been written with lower-case initials throughout, whereas initial capitals have been used for the bynames of group (4), i.e. other bynames, chiefly nicknames.

a person in the (*b*)-category. These are placed immediately after the (*b*)-entry to which they refer. Identity with the preceding form of the name is indicated by the symbol ~.

Although cross-references are given from variant *LW* spellings of the same name, the arrangement of the index inevitably results in the breaking up of groups of related names. However, reference to the classified synchronic lists on pp. 179–83, in which the *LW* forms of Old English and Scandinavian names are placed under their respective etyma, will enable the reader to verify easily enough if a given name is represented in the material and under what head-form it appears in the index.

Comparative material of Hampshire provenance has been drawn from the *Liber Vitae* of Hyde Abbey (*LVH*),[1] Domesday Book (DB), the charters printed by Round and Galbraith,[2] the Pipe Rolls (*P*) of 1130 and 1155/8, the 1210–11 Pipe Roll of the bishopric of Winchester (*PRBW*), and the list of *c.* 400 Winchester pledges of 1207 in the *Rotuli de Oblatis et Finibus* (*Fine R*).[3] In dealing with names of Scandinavian and Continental origin, various Norman sources have been used, including the cartularies of Bayeux, Caen (*AGC*), Jumièges, and St. Wandrille, the pre-conquest charters of the Norman dukes (*RADN*), the Norman acts of Henry II (*RAH*), and the *Magni Rotuli Scaccarii Normanniae* (*MRSN*).

---

[1] Many of the persons figuring in the *LVH* were not residents of Winchester or inmates of the local monastic foundations but benefactors, living or departed, of New Minster (later Hyde Abbey) from other parts of the country, perhaps even foreigners. Still, since masses were regularly said for them, their names were bound to become more or less familiar to the congregation and hence likely to influence local fashions in name-giving.

[2] J. H. Round, 'Bernard, the king's scribe', *EHR* 14 (1899), 417–30; V. H. Galbraith (ed.), 'Royal charters to Winchester', *EHR* 35 (1920), 382–400.

[3] The 1207 list numbers 394 entries referring to 389 persons of whom 383 are mentioned by name. See further below, p. 184.

A

Abonel 1148 1059, (Rogerus) ~ 971, 973, 991.—OFr *Ab(b)onel* (Morlet 13), a derivative of OG *Abbo*; also in the Norman pl.n. *Abonelvilla* 1079–83 *AGC* 101. In *LW* the name is used in a patronymic function; see further below, p. 206.

Adam Witegos 197; **1148** ~ de Brudefort 689.— The biblical name; Withycombe 3.

Ade corduanus **1148** 15.—OE *Ad(d)a*, on which see Redin 81f., Ekwall, *Beiblatt zur Anglia*, 33 (1922), 78, or perhaps a pet-form of *Adam*; cf. Forssner 5f., *DBS* s.n. Ade.

Adelardus 246; ~ acularius **1148** 19, 22.—OG *Adel(h)ard*, on which see Forssner 8, Morlet 16f., or, in the *TRE* case, OE *Æðelheard*.

Adelidis soror Henrici de Port *c.* 1110 239; **1148** *Adeleis* 479, *Adeliz* 491, 948.—OG *Adelheid*, (Rom.) *Adelidis*, *Adeliz* f.; Forssner 6ff., Morlet 16.

Adelwoldus prepositus Wint' 23, 38.—OE *Æðelwald*. See also *Alwoldus*.

Ælmer, see *Almarus*.

Aelricus, see *Ailricus*.

Agemund' 1148 239.[1]—ON *Ǫgmundr*, OSw *Aghmund*; *PNDB* 141, Fellows Jensen 2f.

Ailflet 259.—OE *Æðelflæd* f.; see also *Alfed* below. The spellings *Ail-*, *Eil-* in this and the following seven entries reflect late OE *Ægel-* < *Æðel-* by a native sound-change, on which see *ELPN* 197, *SCBI* xi. 9, n. 1.

Ailmerus 1148 902, (terra) *Ailmeri* Longi 750.— OE *Æðelmær*. See also *Almarus*.

Ailricus 1148 755, ~ Chie 471, *Aelricus* faber 287, *Ailricus* Verbula 593.—OE *Æðelrīc*. See also *Alricus*.

Ailsi 261, *Aisil* bedellus 267.—OE *Æðelsige*. In the second form *l* has been misplaced by the scribe. See also *Elsi*.

---

[1] Cf. *Agamund* 11th- or early 12th-c. *LVH* 73, ~ æt þære stræt late 12th-c. *LVH* 124. One *Agemundus* was a *conversus* at Hyde Abbey *c.* 1130, *LVH* 41.—The name may also have occurred in ODan; see Fellows Jensen 3 and, for the OSw name, *Sveriges medeltida personnamn*, H. 1 (Stockholm, 1962), 20–3.

[2] Aitard's two sons were both moneyers *TRE* (see below, pp. 400f., Tables 34 and 37).

[3] *Thesaurus linguae latinae*, i, col. 1497.

[4] Gröhler i. 231f. Aubusson (Creuse) is *castrum Albucione* in an early medieval source; see A. Holder, *Altceltischer Sprachschatz*, i (Leipzig, 1896), 87. Note also

Ailwardus 233, ~ chenicte 19, ~ de Chainesham 71; *c.* 1110 *Eilwardus* filius Chiwen 254; **1148** *Ailwardus* 36, 614, 615, (de) *Ailwardo* 36, *Ailwardus* besmer' 711, ~ besmera 776, ~ coruesarius 919, ~ Rus 1008, ~ tinctor 681, ~ vinetarius 1037.—OE *Æðelweard*. See also *Alwardus*.

Ailware tinctor **1148** 658.—OE *Æðelwaru* f.

Ailwi 289.—OE *Æðelwīg*. See also *Alwi*.

Ailwinus 241, ~ Hieltepreost 291; **1148** ~ faber 102, ~ palmarius 818, ~ sacrista 722, ~ saponarius 949.—OE *Æðelwine*. See also *Alwinus*.

Ainolfus *c.* 1110 23; **1148** *Ainulfus* parcheminus 683.— OG *A(g)inulf*; Forssner 15, Morlet 25.

Aisil, see *Ailsi*.

(*Alwinus*) **Aitardessone** 11, (*Alwardi* filii) *Etardii* 107.[2]—OG *Aitard*, *Etard*; Forssner 17f., Morlet 26. One *Ægteard* was a lay brother at Romsey (Ha) *c.* 1130, *LVH* 64.

Alanus de Cellar' **1148** 1002, ~ scutarius 187.— OBret *Alan*.

(*Osbertus* filius) **Alberede** *c.* 1110 3, 4, 69; **1148** *Albreda* 958.—OG *Albereda* f.; Forssner 21f., Morlet 29.

Alberico (abl) camerario *c.* 1110 102, ~ (dat) camerario 102, *Albericus* coquus 82, 191; **1148** (filio) *Alberici* (gen) coci 562.—OG *Alberic*; Forssner 18f., Morlet 29, Michaëlsson ii. 65–8.

(*Hugo* filius) **Albuchon** *c.* 1110 40, (uxor Hugonis filii) ~ 40.—Lat **Albūciō, -ōnem*, a derivative of *Albūcius*,[3] attested by the pl.n. Aubusson (Creuse, Orne, etc.).[4] The *LW* form has Norman [tʃ] written *ch*, for Central French [ts].[5] A contemporary Norman example is *Albuchin* (var. *Albukun*) 1025 (18th c.) *RADN* 135 (Fécamp). Note also Herb' *Aubuco[n]* 1198 *MRSN* 483.

Alclied, see *Aldied*.

Aldelmus telarius **1148** 1017.—OE *Ealdhelm*.

Aldied 200; *c.* 1110 ~ vidua 220,[6] 247; **1148** *Aldit* 40, *Eldit* 530.—OE *Ealdgȳð* f.

Obsonville (Seine-et-Marne), *Albutionis villa* 1198 (Dauzat–Rostaing s.n.).

[5] Strictly speaking one would have expected the spelling *Albucheon*, but cf. Norman forms like *Ernucon*, *Arnuchon*, for which see *Ernuceon* below. In names hailing from the [ts] area, on the other hand, the suffix normally appears as *-ceon*, e.g. *Phanceon* 1086 DB Nf 144 < OFr *fançon* 'small child', Osmundus *Escanceon* 1130 *P* 125 < OFr *escançon* 'cupbearer'.

[6] In this and the preceding entry the manuscript has *Alclied* by scribal error.

Aldrectus, see *Aldredus.*

(domus) **Aldredi** 50, (domus) ∼ fratris Odonis 46,[1] *Aldret* 151, *Eldredus* 217; *c.* **1110** *Aldredus* 179; **1148** ∼ 753.—OE *Ealdred.*

Alduinus 1148 946, *Aldwinus* Spich 950, 993.—OE *Ealdwine.* See also *Alwinus.*

Alebast 1148 244.—Short for *Alebaster,* as in Roger *Alebaster* 1231 *Cur 1230-32,* 384 (Mx), a variant form of ME *arblaster, al(e)blaster* 'crossbowman', OFr *arbalestier* (*MED*), with dissimilatory loss of the second *l.* Note also Anglo-Lat *alabastarius* by the side of *arbalistarius,* etc.,[2] and cf. *DBS* s.n. Alabastar, Thuresson 162.

Alestanus 148, ∼ Braders 266,[3] (domus) *Alestani* Coppede 83, *Alestanus* Douetessone 13b, 39, ∼ Flathege 17, ∼ Hwit 57, ∼ fuit monetarius T.R.E. 154;[4] *c.* **1110** ∼ 150.[5]—In most cases probably OE *Ælfstān,* but OE *Æðelstān* is an alternative base; cf. *PNDB* 180f., 188.

Alexander 1148 161, 418, 439, (terra) *Alexandri* de Walt' 786, *Alexander* filius Asinar' 1079, ∼ filius Gollan' 189, ∼ Goisl' 209, ∼ homo Godefridi 196.— The Greek name. An early Norman example is *Alexander* de Tenechebraio 1066-83 *AGC* 95 (Tinchebray, Orne). Cf. also Jacobsson 124f.

Alfed 70.—For *Alfled* with omission of the second *l* by dissimilation and hence OE *Ælfflǽd* or *Æðelflǽd* f. Note that OE *Ælfred* is always *Alu(e)red* in *LW.* See also *Ailflet.*

Alfere 277.—OE *Ælfhere.*

Algarus 255, *Algar* Godesbranesson 26, (domus) *Algari* Godesbranesson 78, *Alg'* harengarius 30; **1148** *Algerus* 529.—Probably OE *Ælfgār,* but OE *Æðelgār* and *Ealdgār* are possible alternatives. On OE *Ælf-, Æðel-, Eald- > ME Al-,* see *PNDB* §§ 92, 103 and p. 106.

Algotus vir Alwii *c.* **1110** 116.—ODan, OSw *Algut, Algot; PNDB* 146, *ELPN* 74f.

Almarus 130, (Godwinus) *Elmeressone* 14, 48, (Godwini filii) *Elmari* 87, (domus) *Elmeri* 91, 103, (domus) *Elmari* Picteurte 113; *c.* **1110** (filius) *Almari* presbiteri 169, (God') *Ælmeressone* 196.—OE *Ælfmǽr* or *Æðelmǽr.* See also *Ailmerus.*

(domus) **Almodi** 47, 115, *Almodus* presbiter 31; **1148** (uxor) *Almodi* 355, 422.—OE *Æðelmōd.*[6]

Alnodus Stud' 129.—OE *Ælfnōð, Æðelnōð,* or *Ealdnōð,* on the last of which see *PNDB* 241.

Alricus 170, (domus) *Alrici* 85.—OE *Æðelrīc* or *Ælfrīc.* See also *Ailricus, Aluricus.*

Alueua 249, ∼ de Chrichelada 268; *c.* **1110** (Chepingus filius) *Alueue* 10, 134, (Chipingus filius) ∼ 71, (Chipingius filius) ∼ 73, *Alueua* filia eius [sc. Alestanus Braders] 266, ∼ de Mapeldreham 231; **1148** ∼ 737, ∼ filia Estan' 375.—OE *Ælfgifu* f.

Alur' Iola *c.* **1110** 222.—For *Aluredus* or *Aluricus* (qq.v.).

Aluredus 237, *Alur'* 239, (Edwinus filius) *Aluredi* 288, (domus) *Aluredi* Taddebelloc 106; **1148** *Aluredus* 263 bis, ∼ 1016, *Alured* Herra 921.—OE *Ælfred.* See also *Alur'.*

Aluricus archidiaconus 176,[7] ∼ de Canesham 27, (domus) *Alurici* de Cainesham 43, *Aluricus* Fulebiert 264, (domus) *Alurici* Penipurs 93, (domus) ∼ Toi 95; *c.* **1110** *Aluricus* 263; **1148** (Marieta filia) *Alurici* 739, *Aluricus* cocus 929, ∼ gener Henrici 201.—OE *Ælfrīc.* See also *Alricus* and *Alur'.*

(terra) **Alwardi** filii Etardii 107.[8]—OE *Ælfweard.*

Alwi Chasiessone 57; *c.* **1110** (Algotus vir) *Alwii* 116.— Probably OE *Ælfwīg,* alternative etyma being *Æðelwīg* and *Ealdwīg.* See also *Ailwi.*

Alwinus 167, 204, 222, 274, (domus) *Aluini* 76, *Alwinus* Aitardessone 11,[9] ∼ Childebroder 239, (domus) *Alwini* fenarii 97, *Alwinus* filius Tartere 178, (domus) *Alwini* heuere 105, *Alwinus* Jeltfange 239, ∼ pater Chepingi 135, (domus) *Alwini* Poplestan 105, *Alwinus* presbiter 41, 172, 289, idem ∼ 173,

---

[1] In entries, **I, 46** and **50** the manuscript has *Aldrecti* with *ct* miswritten for *d.*

[2] Latham s.v. *arbalista.*

[3] His daughter was called *Ælfgifu* (Alueua).

[4] He may be identical with either of two Winchester moneyers under Edward Confessor, *Elfstan,* BMC 1375, or *Æðelstan,* who appears as *Æðestan,* BMC 1407, 1444, *Æstan,* BMC 1372, 1386, 1404-6, 1443 (see below, pp. 400f., Table 34).

[5] Son of *Leuret < Lēofred.*

[6] There is no safe evidence for an OE **Ælfmōd.* The form *Elemod* on some Chester coins under *Æðelred II, BEH* 1511-13, *SCBI* v. 112, 116, vii. 486, may be an error for *Elfnoð, Ælfnoð, BEH* 1482-7, 1518; cf. also *Elenod, BEH* 1514. *Elemod* in a charter of 1011 (14th-c.) printed by F. Barlow, *Edward the Confessor* (London, 1970), 328f., is a very doubtful case. It may stand for *Æðelnoð.*

[7] Perhaps *Ælfric* decanus *c.* 1030 *LVH* 31.

[8] *... et fuit monetarius regis E.* Probably *Ælfwerd,* mon. Winchester, Harold I, *BEH* 1000 (see below, pp. 400f., Table 34).

[9] *... fuit quidam monetarius T.R.E.* He is *Ælfwine,* mon. Winchester, Edw. Conf., *BMC* 1401-3, 1440-2, 1460-3, 1482, 1496-9 (see below, pp. 400f., Tables 34 and 37).

~ Ruffus 287, ~ Sidessone 1, ~ watmaungre 147; *c.* 1110 ~ 186, ~ Barbitre 161, ~ bedellus 168, 221, ~ Bollochessege 140, ~ clericus 257, ~ de Hodiam 96, ~ le feller 117; 1148 ~ 27, *Aluinus* 950, *Alwine* Bierd 69, *Alwinus* Bierd 502,[1] ~ braciator 570, ~ 570, *Alwini* (gen) camerarii 128,[2] *Alwinus* de Odiam 330, ~ lignator 214, ~ stiward 585.—Mainly OE *Ælfwine.* In some cases we may have OE *Æðelwine* or *Ealdwine.* See also *Ailwinus, Alduinus.*

Alwoldus 67, 177, 208, 238, 253.—OE *Ælfwald* or *Æðelwald.*

(Rogerus) **Amberlang'** *c.* 1110 249, (Rogerus filius) *Armerlanc* 20.—OG *Amerland.*[3] The first form shows intrusive *b* between *m* and *r*.[4] In the second, the first *r* is due to anticipatory dittography. *-lang, -lanc* for *-land, -lant* probably arose through scribal confusion of *-c* and *-t* and subsequent association with the adj. *lang.* Cf. also Pope § 1232.

Amfridus, see *Ansfridus.*

Ancild 201.—OE **āncild* 'only child'; cf. *ān-cenned* 'only-begotten'.

Andreas 1148 12, ~ filius Ricardi cordwanarii 628.— The Greek name. An early native instance is *Andreas,* mon. Eadgar, *SCBI* i. 608; for post-conquest examples see Withycombe 22.

Andrebode cangeor 212,[5] *Andrebodus* fuit monetarius T.R.E. 29.[6]—OG **Anderbodo,* OHG *Antirpoto;* Forssner 28. Both entries probably refer to the same person.

(Willelmus filius) **Anschetelli** *c.* 1110 46, *Anschetillus* de Iorz 9, 12, 187, 279, ~ palmarius 285; 1148 ~ 94, 97, 731, *Anschetillo* (dat) 176, *Anschetillus* buclarius 545, 551, ~ de Sancta Maria 661, ~ lorimer 283, 339, ~ maco 344, (uxor) *Anschetilli* maconis 346, *Aschetillus* sellarius 738, (de) *Ansch'* serviente 208, *Ansch'* 208, *Anschetillus* serviens episcopi 442.— ON *Áske(ti)ll,* ODan *Eskil; PNDB* 167f., *ELPN* 75. *Anschetillus* is the usual form in Normandy, where the name is very common; see Adigard 287–93.

Ansere 1148 1000.—OG *Anshere;* Förstemann 127f., Morlet 39.[7]

Ansfridus burgensis 1148 449, 1082, *Ansfr'* burgensis 50, (uxor) *Amfridi* burgensis 476, *Ansfridus* de Hacche 430, ~ de Hecche 456, *Amfridus* de Hacche 556, (Radulfus filius) *Amfridi* parmentarii 636.—OG *Ansfrid; PNDB* 161. For Norman examples, some of which may go back to ODan *Asfrith,* ON *Ás(f)røðr,* see Adigard 348–56. *Amfrid* shows AN effacement of pre-consonantal *s,* on which see *PNDB* § 112, and subsequent assimilation of *n > m* before *f.*

(Willelmus filius) **Ansgeri** *c.* 1110 138, 170, *Ansgerus* de Iorz 182; 1148 ~ 30, 399, (de) *Ansgero* 30, *Ansgierus* de Diua 193, *Ansgerus* Gruti 623, 672, ~ 672.—OG *Anser* or, in some cases, ON *Ásgeirr,* ODan *Esger,* which also occurs in Normandy; Morlet 38, Adigard 186–9, 359.

Ansgodus 1148 1057, *Ansgod* molendinarius 331, ~ Tresor 437, 592, 624, *Ansg[o]d* Tresor 419.—OG *Ansgaud, -got;* Morlet 38. ON *Ásgautr,* ODan *Asgut,* which was common in Normandy, is a possible alternative; cf. Adigard 183–6, 356–8. On *-god* for *-got* see *PNDB* § 97.

Aoulf' carpentarius 1148 347.—Perhaps for *Aculf <* OE *Ācwulf,* on which see *PNDB* 140.

Armerlanc, see *Amberlang.*

Arnulfus Burdin *c.* 1110 131.—In view of the French byname the etymon is probably OG *Arnulf* (Morlet 41) rather than OE *Earnwulf.*

Asa 1148 694, 846.—ON, ODan *Ása* f.; *PNDB* 165.

Ascelinus Casier *c.* 1110 140, *Astcelinus* Godeman 275, (uxor) *Azelini* 10.—OG *Azelin,* a derivative of *Azo;* Forssner 38f., *PNDB* 170. Common in early Norman charters; *RADN,* Index. See also *Atscelina.*

Aschetillus, see *Anschetellus.*

Ascor, see *Atser.*

---

[1] Probably *Alfwin' berd* 1155/6 *P* 52 (Winchester).

[2] Probably *Ealdwine.* He seems to be identical with *Aldwin,* Queen Matilda's chamberlain, *Reg* ii, 1090, 1108, A.D. 1115.

[3] Cf. *Amarlandus* 961 *Cart. St. Bertin* (Morlet 35), *Amerland* 1086 DB 250b (St), (Vitalio filio) *Amerlandi* 1137 *Reg* iii, 298 (Falaise), (de) *Amerlant* (filio Frederici), (pro morte Rad.) *Amerlant* 1180 *MRSN* 10, *Amellandus* 1072–9 *France* 429 (Bellême). The first el. is either an original variant of the theme *Amal-* or due to dissimilation of *l–l > r–l.* In the second el., *-land* ultimately goes back to *-nand* in which *n–n > l–n.* See further Forssner 27f., 281, Kaufmann *Erg.-Bd* 225f., and on *Amar-,*

Förstemann 98, Kaufmann, *Unters.* 89 and *Erg.-Bd* 32f.

[4] As in OE *Amerdene,* DB *Amberdana,* Amberden (E), etc.; cf. Ekwall *Studies,* 84.

[5] Manuscript has *Gangeor.*

[6] He appears as *Anderboda, -bode, -bod* on Winchester coins under Edw. Conf. and Harold II and continued to work under Wm. I; for details see *BMC* under the mint in question and also below, pp. 400f. and Tables 34 and 37. One *Anderboda* was a lay brother at New Minster *c.* 1030, *LVH* 63.

[7] Cf. *Anserus* de Falesham 1112 *Bury* 154 (Sf). Norman examples are (Ricardus fil.) *Ansere* 1180 *MRSN* 49, (de Roberto) *Ansere* 1195 *MRSN* 172.

(Alexander filius) **Asinar'** 1148 1079.—Lat *asinarius* 'donkey-driver'.[1]

Astcelinus, see *Ascelinus.*

Atscelina 1148 143, 421.—OG *Azelina* f.; Forssner 39, Morlet 19. See also *Ascelinus.*

Atscor, see *Atser.*

Atser *c.* 1110 224; 1148 (Ernoldus filius) *Ascor* 631, (uxor) *Atscor* 1050, 1053, ∼ *aurifaber* 792.—ODan *Azur,* ON *Ǫzurr; PNDB* 170f. For Norman examples see Adigard 90f., 303f.[2]

Audoenus *napparius c.* 1110 6.[3]—This is the traditional latinized form of OFr *Ouen* < OG *Audwin,* a name familiar to Normans as that of their famous local saint, the seventh-century bishop of Rouen. It was occasionally, as in the case under notice, used unetymologically as a latinization of OFr *Oin* < OG *Audin, Odin;* see further *Oinus* below.

(domus) **Auici** 84.—OE *Æfic; PNDB* 172.

Auitia 1148 71.—Lat *Avitia* f., OFr *Avice;* Michaëlsson ii. 79ff., *DBS* s.n. Avis.[4]

Azelinus, see *Ascelinus.*

B

(domus . . .) **Babbi** (gen) 90.—OE *Babba;* Redin 83. Note also Rob' *Babbe* 1207 *Fine R* 457 (Winchester). ODan *Babbe* is a late loan from MLG; see *DaGP* 89, 1644.

Baf 1148 304.—Later examples are (Ivo) *Baf* 1186–8 *BuryS* 45 (Sf), (Adam) *Baf* 1275 *RH* ii. 154, 158 (Sf). Probably to be associated with the onomatopoetic stem *baff-* in ME *baffen* 'to scold, bark' (*MED* s.v.), OFr *baffe* 'a box on the ear', ModFr dial. *baffer* 'to eat greedily'; see *FEW* i. 203f.

Baganora 1148 296.—This is the pl.n. Bagnor (Brk), DB *Bagenore,* here used elliptically, perhaps for *Ricardus Baganorus* 1148; see below, pp. 193, 199.

Baldewinus de Rediuers *c.* 1110 260; 1148 ∼ 93,

393, (de) *Baldewino* 393, (de feudo) *Baldewini* 795, *Baldewino* (dat) de Portesia 550, *Baldewinus* maco 1013, ∼ *parmentarius* 392, ∼ *pistor* 68, 1020, ∼ 999, 1027 *bis, Baldwinus pistor* 998, *Baldewinus presbiter* 505.—OG *Baldwin; PNDB* 191.

(uxor) **Baldrici** *c.* 1110 217.—OG *Baldric; PNDB* 191.

Balloc 138.—An original byname, OE *bealluc* 'ballock, testicle'. Cf. *Matað̄an Balluc,* mon. Lincoln, Cnut, *BEH* 1658, and see also the bynames *Balloe* (for *Balloc*) and *Taddebelloc* below.

Baluert *c.* 1110 171.—OG *Baldfrith,* on which see Förstemann 237f., Morlet 50, with anglicizing of the second el. On *-frið* > *-ferð* [verþ], see *PNDB* §§ 14, 87. OE **Bealdfrið* is not on record but would be a possible alternative.

(uxor) **Bargelo'** 1148 234.—Possibly an abbreviation of *Bargelonensis* 'a man from Barcelona', a latinized adj. formed from OFr *Bargelone, Bargeloingne* 'Barcelona'.[5] This is a variant of *Barcelona, Barzelone,* the more usual OFr name for the city. Note also *comes Bargelini* 'the count of Barcelona' in a Norman charter of 1160.[6]

Barill' 1148 94.—An original byname, OFr *baril* 'barrel, cask'; *DBS* s.n. Barrell. Earlier examples are (Odo) *Barrillus* 1064 *Cartulaire de Marmoutier pour le Dunois* (Paris, 1874), 27 (Eure-et-Loir), (Gisleberti) *Barilli* 1130 *P* 44 (Sr ?).

Bartholomeus 1148 137.—The biblical name; Withycombe 41, Michaëlsson ii. 108ff., *DBS* s.n. Bartholomew.

Basilia 1148 788.—Lat *Basilia,* OFr *Basile* f.; Michaëlsson ii. 88, *DBS* s.n. Baseley.[7]

Basset 1148 740, 764.—An original byname, OFr *basset* 'of low stature'; Tengvik 286f., *DBS* s.n.

Beatric 1148 604, *Beatric'* 868, (de) ∼ 393.—Lat *Beatrix* f., OFr *Beatris, Bietriz,* etc.; Withycombe 42f., Michaëlsson ii. 126–8.

Benedictus *presbiter* 1148 390.—Lat *Benedictus,* OFr *Bene(o)it;* Michaëlsson ii. 98 ff., *DBS* s.n. Bennet.

---

[1] An early French example of the use of the word as a pers.n. is *Asinarius abbas* 852 G. Devailly (ed.), *Cartulaire de Vierzon* (Paris, 1963), 123.

[2] On the ultimate etymology of the name see H. Andersen, 'Navnet Asser og beslægtede navne', *Arkiv för nordisk filologi,* 80 (1965), 200ff.

[3] As Round points out, *VCH Hants* i. 536, he is identical with *Oini* (gen) *naparii* 1130 *P* 143 (London).

[4] The earliest occurrence in England (not noted by Reaney) seems to be *Avicia uxor Colemani* 1130 *P* 50

(Sr). Norman instances are (signum) *Avitię uxoris Ricardi* 1051–66 *RADN* 390, (pro) *Avicia . . . monacha facta c.* 1080 *AGC* 87.

[5] Langlois 69, L. F. Flutre, *Tableau des noms propres dans les romans du Moyen Âge* (Poitiers, 1962), 203. The normal Lat adj. is of course *Barcinonensis.*

[6] *RAH* i. 253.

[7] The earliest occurrence in England seems to be *Basilia uxor Odonis de Dommartino* 1130 *P* 94 (not in *DBS*).

Gunterus filius) **Bereng'** 1148 837, (uxor) ~ 884, 887, *Berengarius* sellarius 1070.—OG *Berengar*; Forssner 44f., Michaëlsson ii. 103f.

Bernardus c. 1110 209, ~ cancellarius regine 83, ~ de Sancto Walarico 77, 143; **1148** *Bernardus* 113, ~ carnifex 55, ~ faber 87, ~ Hubold 501, idem ~ 501 *bis*, *Burnard* de Braiosa 817,[1] *Burnardus* de Braiosa 872, (uxor) *Burn'* 743.—OG *Bernard*; Forssner 46. *Burn-* for *Bern-* in *Burnard* reflects anglicized *Beorn-*, as in *Beorn[ar]di de Nouo Mercato* (Neufmarché, Seine-Maritime) 1121 *AC* 8; see further below, p. 224, n. 1.

(Willelmus) **Bertram** c. 1110 156.—OG *Bertram*, used here as a patronymic; Forssner 47f.

(domus) **Bictrici** Bade 109.—OE *Beorhtrīc* with dissimilatory loss of the first *r*.

Bittuc 1148 1038.—Perhaps an OE **Byttuc* from OE *bytt(e)* f. 'bottle, flagon, cask' with the diminutive suffix *-uc*.[2] Cf. OE *Byttic*, Redin 151.

Blachem' c. 1110 218, 236; **1148** (Warinus filius) ~ 374, *Blachemanus* 688.—OE *Blæcmann*; *PNDB* 203.

Blithild 1148 649.—OG *Blidhild* f.; Förstemann 315, Morlet 59. An OE **Blīðhild* f., which is, however, not on record, would be a possible alternative.[3]

Blundel c. 1110 150.—OFr *blondel*, a diminutive of *blond* 'fair of hair or complexion'; *DBS* s.n. Blondel. See also *Nigellus*.

Bolle 224, 261.—OE *Bolla*; *PNDB* 205f. One *Bolla* was a *leuita* at New Minster c. 1030 *LVH* 61.

Bona filia 1148 233.—The latinized form of OFr *Bon(n)efille* f., on which see Jacobsson 184, Vallet 81, 108. Cf. also the byname (Lambert) *Bonne-Fille* 1292, Paris; Pachnio 38.

Bonefacius 1148 669 *bis*, 702, 778, *Bonefac'* tannator 685.[4]—Lat *Bonifatius*; *DBS* s.n. Boniface, Michaëlsson ii. 135f.

Borewoldus, see *Burewoldus*.

(Willelmus filius) **Bos** 1148 66, 99, 564.—OFr *Bos*, a variant of *Boson, Bueson*, from OG *Bōso*; Langlois 106, Kalbow 73.[5]

(de filio) **Boselini** c. 1110 64.—OG (Rom.) *Boselin*; Forssner 52.

(Girardus filius) **Brand** 1148 619.—ON *Brandr*, ODan *Brand*; *PNDB* 207. For some occurrences in Normandy see Adigard 95f.

Bretfol c. 1110 104.—An original nickname, ME *bredful, bretful* 'filled to the brim' (c. 1200, *MED*). A later Ha instance is (de) *Bretful* 1210–11 *PRBW* 122 (E. or W. Meon).

Briauello (dat) 1148 553.—OWelsh *Briauail* (*Lib. Land.*), MWelsh *Briafael*; Smith, *PNGl* iii. 242f., Jackson 448, 648f. Cf. also *Briauel* clericus 1165/6 *P* 111 (K).

Bric(h)twen, see *Brithwen*.

Brict(h)winus, see *Brithwinus*.

Brictwi 120.—OE *Beorhtwīg*.

Brifald' 1148 100, *Brufald'* 524.—OFr *brifalt* 'glutton'; cf. the OFr surname *Brif(f)aut* (c. 1300), on which see Michaëlsson ii. 148, and ModFr *Brif(f)aud* (Dauzat 67). If not a mere scribal error, *u* for *i* in the second *LW* form may reflect a sporadic tendency in OFr to round *i* before labial consonants.[6]

Brincigesone, see *Brunechingessone*.

Brithmarus 217, 225, ~ aurifaber 166.—OE *Beorhtmær*.

Brithsuid 224.—OE *Beorhtswīð* f.

Brithwen vidua 126; **1148** *Brichtwen* 731, *Brictwen* 946.—OE *Beorhtwynn* f.

Brithwif 260.—OE **Beorhtwīf* f. This is the only known example of the name.

---

[1] *Bernardus* de Braosa c. 1120–30, *EHR* 14 (1899), 424.

[2] On the suffix see F. Kluge, *Nominale Stammbildungslehre der altgerm. Dialekte* (Halle, 1926), § 61a, *EPN* ii. 224, Redin 152ff. It is added to an *i*-mutated base in OE **hylluc*, ME *hillok* (*EPN* i. 275), and OE *lyttuc* 'particle, small piece' (only in the plur. *lyttuccas*).

[3] The el. *Blīð-* is found only in *Blīðuald LVD* and *Blīðher* 968 *BCS* 1216 (W). There is also some ME evidence for an OE **Blīðwine*; see my note *NoB* 33 (1945), 75.

[4] One *Bonifacius* filius Asmundi is mentioned in a Winchester charter of 1100–35, *EHR* 14 (1899), 424.

[5] Note also *Bos* capicerius de Faia 1125–38 C. Urseau (ed.), *Cartulaire noir de la cathédrale d'Angers* (Paris, 1908), 274 (Indre-et-Loire), *Bos* de Sugnio 1125–48 ibid.

330 (Suegné, Vienne). *Bos, li quens d'Oxineford, Bos d'Oxenefort* in Wace's *Roman de Brut*, ed. I. Arnold, vol. ii (Paris, 1930), lines 10260, 11651, *Bos passim*, is *Boso ridochemsis, Boso de uado boum* in Wace's source, the *Historia regum Britanniae* of Geoffrey of Monmouth, ed. A. Griscom (London, 1929), 454, 474, 475. The byname *Bos*, on the other hand, is evidently Lat *bos* 'ox', a translation of OFr (le) *Bof, Buef*, examples being Anfridus *Bos* 1156–61 *RAH* i. 271 (Calvados), magistro Hunfrido *Bove* (abl.) 1165 *Bayeux* i. 142, and Gilebertus *Bos* c. 1180–90 G. H. Fowler (ed.), *The Cartulary of the Cistercian Abbey of Old Wardon, Bedfordshire* (Manchester, 1931), 180 (Bd), who is also called Gilebertus *le Bof*, ibid.

[6] Jacobsson 55f.

Brithwinus 227; *c.* 1110 *Bricthwinus* bedellus 194; 1148 *Brictwinus* 166, 447.—OE *Beorhtwine*.

Brithwoldus presbiter *c.* 1110 124.—OE *Beorhtwald*.

Briwer' 1148 1048.—ME *brewere, briwere* 'brewer'. Perhaps the same man as *Willelmus briwere* 1148; see below, pp. 177, 200, 205.

Brucstanus Banne 192.—For *Brunstanus* (see *Brunestanus* below) or *Bricstanus* < OE *Beorhtstān*.

Brufald, see *Brifald*.

Bruman(n)us, see *Brunmannus*.

Brun 245.—OE *Brūn*; Redin 11, *PNDB* 209. See also *Brun,* byn.

(Godeman) **Brunechingessone** 36, (Godmani) *Brincigesone* 96.—OE **Brūncyng* 'brown king', an original nickname; Tengvik 151. Note also *Brunchingi* (gen) 1130 *P* 68 (Sx), perhaps the same person.[1] The second *LW* form is badly blundered.

Brunestanus 17, (domus) *Brunestan* 90, (domus) *Brunestani* 131, *Brunstanus* Blachebiert 256.—OE *Brūnstān*;[2] *DBS* s.n. Brunsdon. See also *Brucstanus*.

Brunild Prichelus 1148 645.—OE **Brūnhild* f. This is the earliest recorded occurrence of the name. Note also *Brunild* late 12th c. *LVH* 124.

Bruning *c.* 1110 214.—OE *Brūning*; Redin 165, *PNDB* 210.

Brunmannus 245, *Brumannus* 122, *Brumanus* de la Forda 3; 1148 (Hugo filius) *Brum'* 561.—OE *Brūnmann*.

Brunstanus, see *Brunestanus*.

Brunwif 216.—OE **Brūnwīf* f. This is the only known example of the name.

Brustinus 1148 472.—A Norman byname, later examples of which are (Hugonem) *Brostin* 1147–9 *St. Wandrille* 145, 1169–70 *Jumièges* i. 239, (Paganus) *Brostin* 1196–7 ibid. ii. 121, 123. It survives in the ModFr surname *Broutin* (Dauzat 71) and should no doubt be associated with OFr *broster, brouster,* tr.

& itr., 'to graze, eat (also of persons)', OF *brout* 'nourishment', or with the cognate OFr (AN) *brouz,* early ModFr *broust* 'young shoot (of brushwood), sprout', etc.[3] Note also 'Hugo . . . a cognatione sua *Brustins* denominatus', a Frenchman, mentioned *c.* 1172 in *Materials for the History of Thomas Becket,* i (RS 67: 1, London, 1875), 304.

Bullochesiega 232.—An original byname, OE **bulluces-ēage* 'bullock's eye', and used in that function in (Alwinus) *Bollochessege c.* 1110 (q.v.); Tengvik 295. On *LW ie* for OE *ēa* see below, p. 224.

Burewoldus 28, 124, 199,[4] ∼ Crul 254 ∼ filius Wnstani 181, (domus) *Burewoldi* Frefhewini 51, *Borewoldus* Horloc 159, *Burwoldus* presbiter 290; 1148 *Burewoldus* 471 (Geruasius filius) *Burewoldi* 435, (de Radulfo filio) ∼ 292, (uxor) *Buroldi* 459.—OE *Burg-, Burhwald*.

Burnardus, see *Bernardus*.

Bur(w)oldus, see *Burewoldus*.

C

(curtillum) **Capel** 121, (domus Godwini) ∼ 91.—OFr *chapel,* ONFr *capel* 'hood'. An OE **cæppel,* a diminutive of *cæppe* 'cap, cope, hood', would be a possible alternative.

Caper' 1148 876.—An abbreviation for *Caperun* from OFr *chaperon,* ONFr *caperon* 'hood, cap'; *DBS* s.n. Capron.[5]

(Radulfus taneator) **Cattessone** *c.* 1110 208.—An original byname, OE *catt* 'cat', as in *Lufman Cat LW* 1066 (q.v.). Note also (obitus) *Byrhferði Cat sacerdotis c.* 1040 *LVH* 273.

Ceca 171.—OE *Cēoca*;[6] Redin 27f., 88.

(Alwi) **Chasiessone** 57.—An OE name in *-sige,* but the first el. is doubtful. Perhaps an error for *Chensie* < OE *Cynesige*.

Chawete 1148 1012, 1039.[7]—An original nickname, OFr *cauete,* a northern variant of *choete* f. 'owl'

---

[1] The passage runs: . . . [lacuna in MS.] *erboldus & Reimbertus debent . . . pro terra Brunchingi auunculi eorum*.

[2] One *Brunstan* was a lay brother at New Minster *c.* 1030 *LVH* 63.

[3] See the detailed treatment of this group of words, *FEW* xv. 311ff., and note also the use of the verb in the byname (Hugo) *broste salz,* (Hugo) *brustans salicem* 'Hugh who grazes willows' in a French 11th-c. charter noticed by A. Darmesteter, *Traité de la formation des mots composés dans la langue française* (Paris, 1894), 190.

[4] His house is mentioned in a post-conquest Winchester charter: domum *Burnuoldi* (for *Buruuoldi*), 1096

EHR 35 (1920), 388.

[5] Contemporary bearers of the name are *Caperun,* a London citizen *c.* 1130 *ELPN* 112, and Rob' *Caperun* 1130 *P* 126 (Br).

[6] Recorded as the byname of Godwine *Ceoca,* a Winchester moneyer under Cnut, his sons, and Edw. Conf., who may in fact be identical with the *LW* man. See below, pp. 400f. and Tables 36 and 37.

[7] Cf. also Adam *Gawet'* 1207 *Fine R* 457 (Winchester) with G miswritten for C, and (de Henrico) *Kawet,* (de Hugone) ∼ 1285 *Survey*.

(Tobler–Lommatzsch s.v.). Cf. ModFr dial *cauvette* 'owl' (Normandy, Picardy); *FEW* xvi. 304.

Chepingus, see *Chipingus.*

(Godwini filii) **Chetel** 92; 1148 ∼ 783.—ON *Ketill,* ODan *Ketil; PNDB* 304f., *ELPN* 78. For Norman examples see Adigard 119f., 404f., 466.

(Godricus) **Chingessone** 128.—OE *Cyng,* an original nickname from OE *cyning* 'king'; *PNDB* 221, n. 5, *DBS* s.n. King.

Chipingus 142, *Chepingus* 241, (Alwinus pater) *Cheping'* 135, *Chipingus* de Ordia 141; *c.* 1110 *Chippingus* 135, 150, *Chipingus* 135, alius ∼ 150, ∼ eius filius [i.e. of Alwinus] 135, ∼ de Cainesham 71, *Chepingius* Dives 87, ∼ filius Alueue 10, *Chepingus* filius Alueue 134, *Chipingus* filius Alueue 71, *Chipingius* filius Alueue 73; 1148 (Hugo filius) *Chepping'* 23, (de Hugone filio) ∼ 172, (Hugo filius) *Cupping'* 294, (Hugo filius) *Cupp'* 362, (Hugo filius) *Chepp'* 403, (Radulfus filius) *Cheppi[n]g'* 466, (Robertus filius) *Cupp'* 395, (Rogerus filius) *Chepping'* 462, (Rogerus filius) *Chupping'* 1080, *Cuppingus* corduanus 16.—OE *Cypping; PNDB* 221f.[1]

Chitebaue 226.—Unexplained. The second el. can hardly be identical with *Baue, LVH* 59, the name of an eleventh-century benefactress of New Minster, which is probably OSax *Bava* f.; see W. Schlaug, *Die altsächsischen Personennamen vor dem Jahre 1000* (Lund, 1962), 57.

(Eilwardus filius) **Chiwen** *c.* 1110 254.—For *Chinwen* < OE *Cyn(e)wynn* f.

Chuuing' 1148 425.—OE *Cūfing,* an *ing*-derivative of *Cūfa,* recorded as the byname of Wlfrice (dat) *Cufing* 955–8 *AS Wills* 4 (Ha); Tengvik 142f.

Clemens Treisor 1148 152.—Lat *Clemens; DBS* s.n. Clem.[2]

Climehen 5.—Unexplained.

Colbrand 1148 641, *Colbrandus* 507 *bis.*—ON *Kolbrandr,* OSw *Kolbrand; PNDB* 306.

Coleman presbiter 244.—OG *Coleman; PNDB* 218.

Colerun 1148 761.—A hybrid compound of the OE fem. el. -*rūn* and Scand or OG *Kol-, Col-,* for which

see *Colbrand, Coleman* above, and *Colsuein* below. Other examples are *Coleruna* uxor [Hermanni], ∼ uxor [Wlfrici], both late 11th c., *LVH* 30.[3]

Colling' 206.—OE *Colling,* which was also used as a byname; Redin 166, Tengvik 141f., Ekwall, *PNLa* 175. It is an *ing*-derivative of the stem represented by OE *coll 'hill', on which see *DEPN* s.n. Coleshill.

Colsueinus presbiter 1148 760;[4] *Golsewanus* presbiter 1066 37.—ON *Kol(l)sveinn; PNDB* 307, *ELPN* 79, Fellows Jensen 179f. The second form has *G-* for *C-,* a common scribal error, and an intrusive vowel in the consonant cluster. Later Ha examples are (de) *Colswano* de Wadedene, (de Roberto) *Colswein* 1210–11 *PRBW* 12, 114.

Conanus 1148 158, 170, 898, 962, *Conano* (dat) 179, *Conannus* filius Guncel' 179.—OBret *Conan;* Jackson 666, *DBS* s.n. Conan.

Constantinus *c.* 1110 147.—The Latin name; *DBS* s.n. Constantine, Bergh 101, Withycombe 69.

Coppa 1148 1029, (de Eduino) ∼ 602.—An original byname, OE **Coppa,* a derivative of OE *copp* 'top, summit; cup', ME also '(crown of the) head'.[5] It is recorded as the first el. of the OE pl.ns *Coppanford,* Copford (E), *Coppanleigh,* Copley Wood (So), *Coppanstan,* Copstone (K); see *PNSx* 179f., *PNE* 385, *DEPN* s.n. Copford.

Cornilla 1148 23 *bis,* (Herebertus) *Corneilla* 10.—OFr *corneille, cornille* 'crow'; *DBS* s.n. Cornell.

Crabeleg 1148 205, 520.—An original nickname, 'crab-leg', from OE *crabba,* ME *crab(be)* 'crab' and ME *leg* 'leg'. Cf. *DBS* s.n. Crabb.

Crichel 1148 736—This is probably an abbreviation for *Crichelad,* Cricklade (W), perhaps used elliptically for *Stephanus de Crichelad'* 1148; see below, p. 194. If, however, the form is to be taken at its face value, we may have an OFr **criquel,* an unrecorded suffixal variant of OFr *criquet* (dim. *criquillon*) 'cricket', from the onomatopoeic stem **krikk-,* which is also represented in West Germanic.[6] Cf. the synonymous MDu *kri(e)kel,* Du *krekel,* Germ dial *krichel,*[7] which may, alternatively, be the etymon of the *LW* name.

---

[1] The property of *Robertus filius Cupping* is mentioned in 1210–11: terra *Roberti Cuppinge, PRBW* 160. Note also Joh' *Cuppi[n]g',* Nicol' ∼ 1207 *Fine R* 452 (Winchester), (de) *Cupping'* Gunz 1210–11 *PRBW* 94 (Ha).

[2] Withycombe (p. 65) and Reaney (loc. cit.) have only ME examples, but a pre-conquest bearer of the name is *Clemens* abbas 959 *BCS* 1030 (W).

[3] Cf. also the Scand names listed by Björkman, *NPN* 83–6, and in his *Zur englischen Namenkunde* (Halle, 1912),

56f., Fellows Jensen 177ff., and note further the previously unrecorded *Colþegn,* mon. Chester, Edw. Conf., *SCBI* v. 282.

[4] MS. *Colsuem'.*

[5] The name is not recorded in DB 1086 as is incorrectly stated by Reaney, *PNE* 385.

[6] *FEW* ii. 1337.

[7] J. Müller, *Rheinisches Wörterbuch,* iv (Berlin, 1938), 1488f.

Cristescoc 1148 781.—An original byname, *Cristes cocc* 'Christ's cock, servant of Christ', as in Johannes *Cristescoc* 1185 (L); Reaney *Origin*, 268f.

Cristianus 1148 279.—Lat *Christianus*; Bergh 99f., *DBS* s.n. *Christian*.

Cuppingus, see *Chipingus*.

Cuuache 1148 232.—Probably an OE **Cwaca* 'one who quakes or trembles', from the stem in OE *cwacian* 'to quake, tremble'. Cf. also Ricard *Quac c.* 1150 *ELPN* 163 (Colchester) and Godwinus *Quachehand* 1130 P 146 (London).

D

Dalphin 293.—Lat *Delphinus*,[1] OFr *Dalfin, Daufin*, from Lat *delphinus* 'dolphin',[2] The name seems to have been used mainly in the south of France; *FEW* iii. 35, Dauzat 178. Early English occurrences include *Dalfin c.* 1130 Earle 257f. (D), (Roberto filio) ∼ *c.* 1150 *Seals* 208 (Nth).

Daniel 1148 627 *bis*—The biblical name; Withycombe 74f.

Dauid 1148 1035, (de) ∼ 1035.—The biblical name; Withycombe 75f.[3]

(Henricus frater) **Debou'** *c.* 1110 144.—Unexplained.[4]

Deria *c.* 1110 166.—Possibly, as Redin suggests (p. 47, n. 3), an incorrect spelling for *Diera* (q.v.) < OE *Dēora*.[5]

Deulecreisse Iudeius **1148** 444.—An OFr phrase-name, *Deu le creisse* 'may God make him grow,

prosper' (Pachnio 67), perhaps a translation of Hebrew *Gedaliah*.[6]

Dicheuin 1148 748.—OE **Dīcwine*, first el. *dīc* 'dike, trench'. This is the only known example of the name.[7] On personal names whose first el. indicates a locality see *PNDB* 15f., *NoB* 33 (1945), 93f.

Diera 1148 606.—OE *Dēora*; Redin 47. On *ie* for OE *ēo* see below, p. 224. *Deria c.* 1110 (q.v.) may be a garbled form of the same name.

Dodesmere 107.—An unidentified pl.n. used in a personal-name function; cf. below, p. 199.

Doisel 1148 58.—OFr *doisil* 'bung, spigot'.

Dora 1148 1040, (Guncel') *Dore* 857.—OE *dora* 'humble-bee'. A pre-conquest instance is (Aluuardus) *Dore* 1066 DB E 94; Tengvik 361f. Note also (Sawinus filius) *Dore* 1168/9 P 82 (Br).

(Alestanus) **Douetessone** 13b, 39.—Unexplained.

Drogo 1148 38, 149, 172, 352, 401 *bis*, 845, 860, (de) *Drogone* 38, 401, *Drogo* Blund 899, ∼ Blundus 185, 381, 635, 905, ∼ de Calp' 838, *Rrog'* de Calp 525, *Drogo* tinctor 83, 653.—OG *Drogo*; Forssner 60f.

Duchet 1148 249, 256, (Radulfus) ∼ 306.—An original byname, a diminutive of OFr *duc* 'leader, duke; eagle-owl', attested by Fr dial. (Gascon) *ducquet* 'small owl' (*FEW* iii. 196) and the surname *Du(c)quet* (Dauzat 216, s.n. Duchet). Note also (Rann') *Duchet* 1130 P 41 (Ha), (Ric') *Duket* 1205 *Fine R* 258 (Wa).[8]

Dulzan' 1148 571.—A derivative of OFr *dolz, dulz* 'sweet, gentle' with the suffix *-ānu(m) > -ain*, attested by ModFr *Doussain* (Dauzat 210).[9] Cf. also *Dulzelina* f. 1184/5 P 35 (Sf), and the ME byn. (le) *Duz, Douz*, on which see *DBS* s.n. Douce.

---

[1] Early bearers were a Christian in Rome and two 4th-c. bishops of Numidia and Bordeaux. The latter became a saint. Cf. *Inscriptiones Latinae christianae veteres*, ed. E. Diehl, ii (Berlin, 1927), no. 3780, *Thesaurus linguae latinae, Onomasticon*, iii (Leipzig, 1918), 93.

[2] According to P. Fouché, *Phonétique historique du français*, ii (Paris, 1958), 446, OFr *a* for *e* in *Dalfin* is due to a Gallo-Roman sound-change.

[3] Withycombe errs in stating (p. 76) that the name is not found in England before the Conquest; note *David* presbyter 996 *KCD* 695 (Wo).

[4] *Debou'* should perhaps be read *de Bou'*, i.e. Latin *de* with an abbreviated pl.n., perhaps *Bovecome* DB, Bowcombe (Ha) or *Boviete* DB, Boyatt (Ha); cf. *Wigot Delinc LW c.* 1110 **I, 154** for *Wigot de Lincolnia*.

[5] But cf. perhaps *Derianus* (< OBret *Dergen, Derian*), a lay brother at New Minster *c.* 1078–91 *LVH* 37. On the Bret name see K. H. Jackson, *A Historical Phonology of Breton* (Dublin, 1967), p. 98, n. 4.

[6] In England the name seems to have been used mainly

by Jews as in the present case; note also *Deulecreise* Judeus *c.* 1160 P. Barnes and C. F. Slade (eds.), *A Medieval Miscellany for Doris M. Stenton* (PRS 76, London, 1962), 22, a *Deulecressio* iudeo *c.* 1190–1210 *St Greg* 108 (Canterbury; a famous money-lender), *Deulecrese* le Eveske 1205 *Fine R* 315 (D). Cf. also the Norman byname (Will') *Deulecroisse* 1195 *MRSN* 152.

[7] Unless (Rad') *Dikenin* 1207 *Fine R* 457 (Winchester) is a misreading for *Dikeuin*.

[8] Reaney, *DBS* s.n. Ducket, prefers to derive ME *Duchet, Duket*, pers.n., and surname, from an unrecorded diminutive of OE **Ducca* or *dūce* 'duck', but this is an improbable alternative. OFr *duc* occurs as a byname in Ha: (de Roberto) *Duc* 1210–11 *PRBW* 46, (de Willelmo) ∼ ibid. 114.

[9] On the suffix see further K. Nyrop, *Grammaire historique de la langue française*, iii (2nd edn., Copenhagen, 1936), §§ 160–2. *-an* for normal *-ain* in the *LW* form is due to latinization.

Durage 1148 350, (Willelmus) ~ 349.—Possibly an unrecorded OFr adj. *durage*, a derivative of *dur* 'hard' with the suffix *-age*, which may conceivably survive in Norman dial. (19th c.) *durache* 'tough, leathery, hard', *FEW* iii. 193.[1] The evidence for such an adjectival formation is, however, scanty and uncertain. Possible parallels would be OFr *hautage* (late 12th c.) 'high',[2] *marinage* 'situated on the sea'.

Durandus 169; *c.* 1110 (Robertus filius) *Durandi* 267, (Robertus filius) ~ 71; 1148 *Durandus* 26, 39, 60, (de) *Durando* 39, 591, *Durandus* Cornet 582, ~ Gumbold' 319.—OFr *Durand, Durant*, from the present participle of Lat *durare* 'to persevere, endure, etc.'[3] For additional examples in OE and ME records see Forssner 62, *DBS* s.n. Durrand.

Duresumer 1148 997.—This may be an original nickname from OE *duru*, ME *dure* 'door' and ME *sumer* (< OFr *somier*, AN *sumer, somer*) 'beam' (in structure; *NED* s.v. *summer* sb. 2, 1324ff.); hence 'doorbeam'.

E

Ebrardus 1148 163, 166, 402, *Ebrardo* (dat) 848, *Ebrardus* de Carnot' 544, 855, 891.—OG *Eberhard, Ebrard*; Forssner 63f., Morlet 77.

(Leflet) **Ecregeles** (docter) 25.—Unexplained.

Edde (gen) regine 27.—OE **Eadde* or **Edde* f., a short form of *Ēadgȳð*. The reference is to King Edward's consort. Cf. OE *Eada, Ed(d)a* m., Redin 47f., 65; ME *Eda* f., *DBS* s.n. Ead. *Eda* (lat. nom.), *Eade* (gen), early 13th-c., *Seals* 221, is a pet-form of *Eadiua* (< OE *Ēadgifu* f.) in the same charter.

Edewa 57; *c.* 1110 *Edeua* 237.—OE *Ēadgifu* f.

Edgar 1148 38, *Edgarus* 38, *Edgar* sune 307, *Edgaresune* 132, *Odgaressune* 38.—OE *Ēadgār*. The last form, if not merely due to scribal error, shows association with OG *Odgar*; cf. Forssner 197.

Edit Martel 1148 460, ~ Ruffa 328.—OE *Ēadgȳð* f.

Edmundus *c.* 1110 115; 1148 ~ bulengarius 547, ~ dapifer 81, 723, ~ de Mitlinget' 811.—OE *Ēadmund*.

Edredus taneator *c.* 1110 235; 1148 *Edred* 773, *Edredus* 844.—OE *Ēadred*.

Edricus 242, (domus) *Hedrici* 112, (domus) *Edrici* Ceci 82, *Edricus* Chuet 278; *c.* 1110 ~ 109, 289; 1148 (uxor) *Edrici* 145, *Edricus* buriman 771, ~ Puttuc 301, (uxor) *Edrici* vinetarii 141.—OE *Ēadrīc*.

Edtie Mase 220.—For *Edsie* < OE *Ēadsige*?

(Reginaldus filius) **Edulfi** 1148 594, *Edulfus* nepos Turstini 489, 674.—OE *Ēadwulf*.

(domus) **Edwacre** 138.—OE *Ēadwacer*; Forssner 85, Reaney, *SMS* 18 (1943), 89f.[4]

(rex) **Edwardus** 80, (regis) *Edwardi* 38, (de rege) *Edwardo* 10, 34; *c.* 1110 *Edwardus* presbiter 225; 1148 ~ cancellarius 1001, ~ clericus 540, ~ de Stanam 499, ~ Waranc' 770.—OE *Ēadweard*.

(domus . . .) **Edwi** 116.—OE *Ēadwīg*.

Edwinus 66, (domus) *Edwini* fabri 94, *Edwinus* filius Aluredi 288, ~ Godeswale 2, *Ediwinus* Gule 289, *Edwinus* Wridel 215; *c.* 1110 ~ 226, (Herbertus filius) *Edwin'* 252, (Herbertus filius) *Edwini* 258, *Edwine* presbiter 251; 1148 *Edwinus* 61, 780, *Eduinus* 523, (de) *Eduino* Coppa 602, ipse *Eduinus* 602, *Edwinus* Etsinemeta 627, ipse *Eduinus* 627, *Edwinus* faber 732.—OE *Ēadwine*.

Eilaf 231.—ODan *E(i)laf*, ON *Eileifr*; *PNDB* 246. One *Eilauus* was a *puer* at New Minster *c.* 1080, *LVH* 36.

Eilwardus, see *Ailwardus*.

Eld-, see *Ald-*.

Elfegus tornator 91.—OE *Ælfhēah*.

Elmarus, *Elmerus*, see *Almarus*.

Elsi clericus *c.* 1110 148, *Elsie* clericus 149, *Elsi* presbiter 71.—OE *Ælfsige* or *Æðelsige*. See also *Ailsi*.

(Godefr' filius) **Emeline** *c.* 1110 193.—OG (Rom.) *Emelina* f.; Forssner 67f., Morlet 34f., *DBS* s.n. Emblem.

(domus) **Emme** regine 75; *c.* 1110 *Emma* uxor Roberti filii Wasferi 99, ~ uxor Roberti 94, ~ de Perci 68; 1148 ~ 46, 73, 428, 485, 709, *Em'* 821, *Emma* uxor Roberti fratris Warini 479, ~ uxor Sermonar' 312.—OG *Emma* f.; Forssner 69. See also *Imma*.

---

[1] On the early unvoicing o ⌊ʤ⌋ > ⌊tʃ⌋ in various French dialects see P. Fouché, *Phonétique historique du français*, iii (2nd edn., Paris, 1966), 938.

[2] See A. J. Greimas, *Dictionnaire de l'ancien français* (Paris, 1969), s.v. haut.

[3] Cf. A. Dauzat, 'Durand et Durandal', *Rev. internat. d'onomastique* 4 (1952), 39, O. Brattö, *Nuovi studi di antroponomia fiorentina* (Stockholm, 1955), 85–7, Morlet

Étude, 121, Lebel 57, n. 3. For additional OFr material see Jacobsson 199f., Vallet 59f., 83ff. The latter also records the derivatives *Durantetus, Durantinus* (13th c., p. 85), *Durantonus* (14th c., p. 92), and the fem. form *Duranda, Duranta* (13th–14th cc., pp. 75, 106).

[4] To the material adduced by Reaney we may add *Edwacer c.* 1100 Earle 264 (Exeter), *Edwakeres* (gen) ibid. 259.

Engelramus 1148 589.—OG *Engelram*; Forssner 73f.

(domus) Engelr[ici] 90.—OG *Engelric*; Forssner 74.

Enoc 1148 729.—The biblical name.

Erchembaldus regis serviens *c.* 1110 107.—OG *Erchembald*; Forssner 76, Morlet 80.

Ercur, see *Ertur*.

Erdrea 1148 1085.—Probably OG *Hardrada* f. (Morlet 124), which would become OFr **Hardrée*; cf. OFr *Hardre(us)*, *Erdré* m. < OG *Hardrad*, for which see Drevin 36, Langlois 325, Kalbow 92. The *LW* form shows loss of initial *h* and *er* for *ar*, both AN features. Final *a* is the Lat fem. ending. A good parallel is ME *Albrea*, OFr *Auberée*; Forssner 21, Michaëlsson ii, 65.

Erenburg 1148 638.—OG *Erenburg* f.; Forssner 82, Morlet 79, Jacobsson 228f. Early Ha instances are *Erenburch*, wife of Godwinus presbiter, *c.* 1100 *LVH* 30, 12th-c. ~ *LVH* 138.

(Oini filii) Erepulfi 1148 660.—OG *Erpulf*; Förstemann 489. The second vowel in the *LW* form is inorganic; see below, p. 225. An earlier Ha example is *Herpul* 1086 DB 52b, who held in Swainston.

Ernaldus 1148 27, *Ernoldus* 138, *Ernold*' Adeling 243, *Ern*' Adeling 248, 271, *Ernaldo* (dat) coco 610, *Ernoldus* filius Ascor 631, ~ frater Petri 135, 977, 981, 1060, *Ernaldus* frater Petri 842, 1045, ~ frater Petri merciarii 904, *Ernoldus* presbiter 473.—OG *Ernold*; Forssner 33f.

(Hamo filius) Erneis *c.* 1110 269; 1148 ~ bedel 528.—OG *Ernegis*, OFr *Erneïs*; Forssner 82f.

Ernoldus, see *Ernaldus*.

(Iohannes filius) Ernuceon *c.* 1110 37.—Possibly, as Tengvik suggests (p. 181), an OFr diminutive of OG *Ernust*.[1] The *LW* man may be identical with (Johannes filius) *Ernucuñ* 1086 DB E 84. Other early examples are *Ernucion* 1086 DB Sx 24b, 25, Sa 259, *Ernuzon* Br 59b, (Hugo filius) *Ernuceoñ* 1130 *P* 55 (E), (Robertus filius) ~ ibid. 147–8 (London).[2] See Addenda.

Ertur' 1148 767, *Ercur*' 112.—OBret *Arthur*[3] or

possibly Anglo-Scand *Ar(n)ður* < ON *Arnþórr*, ODan *A(r)ndor*. On the latter name see *NPN* 8f., *PNDB* 163. The second *LW* form has *c* for *t* by scribal error. *Er*- for *Ar*- is an AN feature (*PNDB* § 1). Later Winchester examples are (Bartholomeus filius) *Arthur*' 1207 *Fine R* 452, (Petrus filius) *Artur*' ibid. 453. Cf. also *Artur* quidam francigena 1086 DB Wo 174 b; *Erturo* (abl) a 1070 *AGC* 127 (Calvados) by the side of *Arturo* (abl) *c.* 1080 *AGC* 110 (the same person); *Arturus* 1104, 1115, *Erturus* 1111, a canon of St. Paul's, London (*ELPN* 106); *Erturo* (dat) fratri Warin 1130 *P* 41 (Ha). In all these cases we probably have the Breton name.

Escorfan, see *Scorphanus*.

Essulfus presbiter *c.* 1110 290.—OE *Æscwulf*.

Estanus Scodhe 285; 1148 (Alueua filia) *Estan*' 375.—OE *Ēadstān* or *Æðelstān*;[4] see *PNDB* 182 s.n. *Æstan*.

(Willelmus filius) Estmer' 1148 230, (Robertus filius) *Estm*' 369.—OE *Ēastmǣr*. For later ME instances see *ELPN* 37, Reaney, *SMS* 18 (1953), 91.

Etard, see *Aitard*.

Euerwinus 262.—OG *Everwin*; Forssner 85, Morlet 78.[5]

Eustachius 132.—Lat *Eustachius*, of which this seems to be the earliest occurrence in England; *DBS* s.n. Eustace, Withycombe 106.

Eva 1148 703, ~ uxor Sewi 699, ipsa ~ 699.—The biblical name.

F

(Rualdus filius) Faderlin *c.* 1110 29; 1148 (filio) *Federling*' 473.—Note also *Faderlin* 1086 DB Ha 45, 45b, 46b, 48b, perhaps identical with the *LW* man. No corresponding name is found in Continental sources, and Forssner's suggestion (p. 87) that we have here a Cont *-līn*-derivative of OG *Fader* is unlikely. The form *Federling* shows that the suffix

---

[1] Forssner 83, Morlet 85. A Norman example is *Ernostus* clericus a 1066 *AGC* 55.

[2] Norman examples are *Ernucio*, father of William of Danestal, 1108–18 *Reg* ii, 1188, (de Roberto) *Ernucon* 1180 *MRSN* 174, 177, (de) *Arnuchon* ibid. 174.

[3] The ultimate source of the Celtic name is Lat *Artorius*. There is virtually no evidence for the use of *Arthur* as an ordinary personal name in medieval Welsh sources, whereas it is well attested in Brittany. See J. S. P. Tatlock, *The Legendary History of Britain* (Berkeley, Calif., 1950), 215ff., and, for a list of occurrences of the name in Breton and OFr charters *c.* 850–1215, P. Gallais in *Moyen Âge*

et littérature comparée (Paris, 1967), 61ff. (with map). A recent authoritative survey of the Arthurian problem is that by K. H. Jackson, 'The Arthur of History', *Arthurian Literature in the Middle Ages* (Oxford, 1959), 1–11 (on the name, p. 2).

[4] Note the following series of spellings on Winchester coins under Cnut which illustrate the progressive reduction of the form *Æðelstān*: *Æðelstan SCBI* xv. 4042, *Æðestan* 4044–54, *Æðstan* 4056, *Æstan BEH* 3694.

[5] For additional examples see Reaney, *SMS* 18 (1953), 91f., who thinks there may have existed a native OE **Eoferwine*.

is -*ling*, not -*lin*, and that the first syllable had original æ. Hence possibly an OE *fæderling, a noun which, if not merely a diminutive of *fæder*,[1] may have denoted a relative on the father's side. Formal and semantic parallels would be OE *fædera* 'paternal uncle', which also occurs as the byname of *Osbern fadera c.* 1100 Earle 259, *fædering-mæg, fæderen-mæg* 'paternal kinsman', *sibling* 'kinsman'.

Farmanus 185; **1148** (filius) *Fareman* 130.—ON *Farmann*, ODan *Farman*; *PNDB* 250. One *Farman* was a lay brother at Romsey (Ha) *c.* 1030 *LVH* 63. Also in Normandy; Adigard 361.

Fati 1148 968.—A nickname, OE (*ge*)*fættig* 'fat, rich', ME *fatti* 'fat, obese' (*MED*). Cf. OE *Fætta*, byn.; Tengvik 312.

Federling, see *Faderlin*.

domus) **Ficelli** 110.—If *c* stands for *t* we have *Fitel*(*lus*), an anglicized form of Lat *Vitalis*; see *PNDB* 405f.[2]

Ficheldene 1148 633.—The pl.n. Figheldean (W), *Ficheldene* 1115.[3] On the occurrence of place-names in a personal-name function see below, p. 199.

Forst 1148 1004.—OE *forst* 'frost', an original byname, as in (Aluuinus) *Forst* 1066 DB Ha 52b; Tengvik 376.

Foxpriche *c.* **1110** 207.—An original byname, OE *fox* 'fox', and *prica* 'point, dot', here perhaps in the sense of 'instrument or organ having a sharp point', which, though not recorded until *c.* 1300 (*NED* s.v. *prick*), may be inferred for the OE word from the cognates *pricel*(*s*) 'goad, sharp point', *prician* 'to pierce'. The meaning of the compound is not apparent.[4]

(Burewoldi) **Frefhewini** 51.—For *Frethewini*, the latinized genitive of OE *Freðewine* < *Freoðuwine*, a back-mutated variant of *Friðuwine, Friðewine*.[5] The name is used here in a patronymic function.

(heredes) **Fridai 1148** 616, (Hugonis) *Friedai* 590.—OE *Frīgedæg* 'Friday', an original byname.[6]

Froggemore 1148 984.—The pl.n. Frogmore (Ha); cf. *Ficheldene* above.

Fugel 155, 270;[7] **1148** ~ 216.—OE *Fugel*; *PNDB* 256. See also *Fulges*.

Fulcardus 91, (domus) *Fulcardi* 101.—OG *Fulcard*; *PNDB* 256.

(Iohannes filius) **Fulcher'** *c.* **1110** 286.—OG *Fulcher*; Förstemann 551, Morlet 95. At New Minster *c.* 1080 there were one *Folchier*, a *puer* or *laicus*, and a monk named *Fulcerius*; *LVH* 36, 37.

(Robertus filius) **Fulcheredi** *c.* **1110** 52.—OG *Fulchered*; Forssner 98f., Drevin 31, *ELPN* 113.

Fulco 1148 146, 176, *Fulcho sellarius* 840.—OG *Fulco*; Forssner 98.

Fulges 18.—For *Fulger* from OG *Folcger*, (Rom.) *Fulger*, on which see Förstemann 550, Morlet 95, or an error for *Fugel* (q.v.).

G

(Gisla uxor) **Gardini** *c.* **1110** 103.—OG (Rom.) *Gardin*[8] or perhaps ONFr *gardin* 'garden' used as a nickname.[9]

Gaufridus *clericus* 157; *c.* **1110** ~ *burgeis* 271, ~ *camerarius* 246, 270, 272, ~ *clericus* 136; **1148** ~ 101, (Hereberto filio) *Gaufridi* 800, *Gaufridus Bal'* 1062, ~ *burgensis* 128, ~ *Cole* 691, ~ *de Cell'* 915, (de) *Gaufrido de Masiaco* 352, (uxor) *Gaufridi de Sancto Laudo* 548, *Gaufridus de Sancto Nicholao* 883, idem ~ 884, ~ *filius Petri* 509, ~ *filius Segar'* 1046.—OG (Rom.) *Gaufrid*; Forssner 101f., Morlet 105.

Gazo *c.* **1110** 28.—OG *Wazo*, with Central French *g*(*u*)- for initial *w*-; Forssner 249, Morlet 212. See also *Watso*.

(Rogerus filius) **Geroldi** *c.* **1110** 34; **1148** (Godefridus filius) *Giroldi* 626, *Giroldus Furwatel* 972.—OG *Gerold*, (Rom.) *Girold*; Forssner 103f., Morlet 100.

---

[1] Cf. the ModE nonce-word *fatherling* 'little father' (1625; *NED*).

[2] One *Phitelet* held in Ha *TRE*, DB 44b, and *Vitalis presbiter* was a tenant at Hurstbourne Tarrant (Ha) in 1086, DB 39. Note also *Fithel, Vithel* 12th-c. *LVH* 136, 52.

[3] *PNW* 365f.

[4] OE *prica* could perhaps also mean 'penis', although this sense does not happen to be recorded until 1592 (*NED* s.v. *prick*, 17). For a semantic parallel cf. *Taddebelloc*, byn. (q.v.).

[5] Note for example *Freðewine* by the side of *Friðewine* on Steyning coins, Cnut, *SCBI* xv. 3484, 3485.

[6] Recorded as a pers.n. in the boundary-mark *on Frigedæges tr*[*e*]*ow* 959 *BCS* 1047 (Ginge, Br) and as the first el. of Fridaythorpe (YE), DB *Fridagstorp*. A post-Conquest instance is *Friendai* 1086 DB 230b (Lei). As a byn. in Ketel *F*[*r*]*iedai* 1086 DB 135b, Chetel *Friedai* 273b (both Nf). See also *PNSr* 278f., 410f., Tengvik 218f., *DBS* s.n. Friday.

[7] One *Fulghel* held in Ha *TRE*, DB 52.

[8] Recorded once in the Annals of Verdun 1014-23, *MGH, Scriptores*, iv. 8: *Gardinus abbas*.

[9] Cf. (feodum Radulfi) *Gardin* 1184-8 *RAH* ii. 305, (Ricardus) *Gardin*, early 13th-c., *Recueil des historiens des Gaules*, 23 (Paris, 1876), 242 (Vimont, Seine-Maritime).

(terra) **Geruasii** 1148 78, 740, (de) *Geruasio* 666, *Geruasius* filius Burewoldi 435, ~ presbiter 280.— The earliest bearers of the name *Gervasius* were a third-century Italian saint, martyred at Milan, and a late sixth-century deacon of Le Mans who was martyred in France and subsequently canonized.[1] The ultimate etymology of the name is obscure.[2] See also Förstemann 586 and, for ME examples, Forssner 110f., *DBS* s.n. Jarvis.

Gesordus prepositus *c.* 1110 20.—For *Gesoldus*, an OFr form of OG *Gis(w)ald*, on which see Morlet 110, with AN confusion of the liquids.

(Gisl') **Gibart** *c.* 1110 63.—OG *Gebehard*, (Rom.) *Gibard*; Forssner 113f., Morlet 108. In the *LW* example the name is used in a patronymic function. Cf. the ModFr surname *Gibard* (Dauzat 291) and *Gifard* below.

Giboda 1148 62.—OG *Wigbodo*; Förstemann 1581. On the initial *g-* see *Gazo* above.

(uxor) **Gifardi** 1148 292 *bis*, (uxor) *Giffardi* 295, (uxori) ~ 297.—OG (Rom.) *Gifard*, a variant of *Gibard* (q.v.). An alternative and perhaps preferable etymon is OFr *gifart* 'chubby-cheeked, bloated', which was often used as a byname in Normandy and England; see Forssner 113f., *DBS* s.n. Giffard, and Tengvik 219f.

Gilebertus Bochenel 40; *c.* 1110 (filio Willelmi filii) *Gisleberti* 49, *Gilebertus* 125, ~ archar' 90, *Gisl'* Gibart 63; 1148 *Gilebertus* 131, 252, ~ frater eius [i.e. of Adam de Brudefort] 689, ~ cordwanarius 268, 276, ~ cum barba 11, *Gileberto* (dat) de Chinai 1027, *Gilebertus* de Meleford 889, ~ presbiter 526, ~ taleator 682.—OG *Giselbert*, OFr *Gilebert*; Forssner 115f.

Girardus Barrat' *c.* 1110 84; 1148 ~ 805, 1058, (Willelmus filius) *Girardi* 944, *Girardus* filius Brand 619.—OG *Gerard*, OFr *Girard*; Forssner 104f.

Girinus 1148 96, 942, (de) *Girino* 90, *Girinus* clericus 497, 503, ~ pincerna 73.—OG *Gerin*, OFr *Girin*; Forssner 108, Morlet 101.

Giroldus, see *Geroldus*.

Gisla uxor Gardini *c.* 1110 103.—OG *Gisla* f.; Morlet 111.[3]

Gislebertus, see *Gilebertus*.

Gisulf' *c.* 1110 223; 1148 *Gisulfus* scriba 680.[4] — OG *Gisulf*; Forssner 117.

(Henricus) **Gladewin'** 1148 192, 289.—OE *Glædwine*, used here as a patronymic, like *Goce* in the next entry; *PNDB* 261f., Reaney, *SMS* 18 (1953), 92f.

(Godwini) **Goce** 99.—OG *Goz(z)o*; Forssner 129f.

God' 214 *bis*, 225, 252, 264, 269, ~ Clenehand 191, ~ Cunnebried 272, ~ Softebred 271; *c.* 1110 ~ 213, (uxor) ~ Pot 174; 1148 ~ 756, ~ camerarius 1022, ~ clericus 646, ~ fullo 510, ~ marescallus 760, idem ~ 760, ~ presbiter 1, ~ presbiter de Auelton' 733.—In most cases clearly an abbreviation for a name in *God-*, chiefly *Godwine* (q.v.). Some instances may, however, represent OE *God*, on which see *PNDB* 262.

Goda, see *Gode*.

Godard' 1148 500, 832, ~ carpentarius 332.—OG *God(h)ard*; Forssner 120.

(domus . . .) **Gode** 99; 1148 *Goda* 70, 953, ~ Hachemus 70, ~ Hacchemus 457, 518, 568, ~ Lamart' 954.— OE *Goda* m. or Gode f.; *PNDB* 263.

(domus) **Godebiete** 23 *bis*; 1148 (terra) *Godebieta* 42.—These entries refer to a property in Winchester described in a writ of Edward Confessor as *se haga þe man hæt Ælfrices Godebegeaton* 1052–3 *AS Writs* 111 (BM, Add. MS. 29436, 13th c.).[5] W. H. Stevenson, who took *Godebegeaton* to be Ælfric's byname, explained it as the gen. of an OE **gōda-begēata* 'an acquirer of property', the first el. being the gen. plur. of *gōd* 'goods, property, wealth' and the second an unrecorded agent noun formed from the OE verb *begietan* 'to acquire'.[6] To this etymology it may be objected that strong verbs of the fifth class do not form agent nouns with the long vowel of the past plural but with the short vowel of the present stem or past participle, examples being *giefa*, *spreca*, etc.

[1] See *Bibliotheca sanctorum*, vi (Rome, 1965), 298ff.

[2] Cf. Tavernier-Vereecken 150. J. Hartig, *Münsterländische Rufnamen* (Cologne, 1967), 241, takes it to be Greek. The name has in fact been associated with Greek γερούσιος 'pertaining to the old man'; see J. van der Schaar, *Woordenboek van voornamen* (Utrecht, 1968), 105, s.n. Gervaas. However, although Γερβάσιος sometimes occurs as the name of Greek Orthodox bishops and monks, it is probably not of Greek origin (*ex. inf.* Prof. N. P. Andriotis, University of Salonika), nor can it, for reasons of phonetic chronology, be a hybrid of PrGerm **Gaiza-* and Celtic **vassus*, as

suggested by Forssner (p. 111) and Withycombe (p. 126).

[3] Early Norman examples are *Gisla* filia Turstini *c.* 1080–5 *AGC* 87, 131, *Gisla* uxor Willelmi Patrici *c.* 1080–3 *AGC* 107.

[4] Both entries refer to the same man; J. H. Round, *EHR* 14 (1899), 422.

[5] In a charter of 1096 printed by V. H. Galbraith, *EHR* 35 (1920), 388, William II confirms the grant: *domum vero Alurici Godebegete confirmo*.

[6] Stevenson's opinion is quoted at length by Goodman *Goodbegot*, 68–9.

Professor Mattias Löfvenberg suggests[1] that the passage in question should be translated 'the messuage which one calls Ælfric's good acquisition (property)' and that the crucial word is an unrecorded weak fem. noun *begēate, a variant of the recorded neut. noun begeat[2] and with the same meaning. Gode begeatan (-on)[3] would be the normal acc.sg. form of the adj. and noun. Löfvenberg's etymology has the advantage of providing a simple explanation of the numerous cases in medieval sources in which Gode begeate, Godebiete, etc., occur independently as the name of this property.[4] These forms no doubt reflect an OE nom. *sēo gōde begēate, ME *þe gōde biyēte, meaning something like 'the good bargain'. See Addenda.

Godeboldus 1148 937, 979, 982.—OG Godebold; Forssner 118.

Godefridus c. 1110 178, 274, ∼ de Tolcha 11, ∼ filius Emeline 193, ∼ Sar' 250; 1148 ∼ 39 bis, 165, (Alexander homo) Godefridi 196, (Matildis filia) ∼ 461, (Radulphus nepos) ∼ 642, (uxor) ∼ 869, Godefridus carpentarius 789, ∼ cornem' 191, ∼ de Windelesor 567, ∼ de Windes' 686, ∼ filius Giroldi 626, ∼ 626 bis, ∼ filius Sewi 532, 764, 780, ∼ filius Willelmi 5, 36, 95, 174, 321, 327, 445, 573, item ∼ 446, ∼ 573, ∼ Niger 40, ∼ Surdus 629.—OG Godefrid; Forssner 118f.

Godehald 1148 168 bis, 169, 856, 1057, Godehal' 873.—OG Godehild f.; Forssner 120. The second el. shows the OFr development -il- > -el- > -al-.[5]

Godelina 1148 652, 655.—OG (Rom.) Godelina f.; Morlet 114. Cf. Forssner 120.

Godemannus 107, (domus) Godemanni 116, Godeman Brunechingessone 36, (domus) Godmani Brincigesone 96, Godman Helteprest 228.—OE Godmann; PNDB 265f. See also Godeman, byn.

Goderu[n] Litteprot 13a.—OE Godrūn f.; ELPN 41, Reaney, SMS 18 (1953), 93.

Godesbrandus 250, (domus) Godesbrani 79, (Algar) Godesbranesson 26, (domus Algari) ∼ 78.—OG *Godesbrand; Forssner 120f. Note also Godesbrand 11th c. LVH 64.

Godesman 202.—OG Godesman; Forssner 121, Morlet 112, DBS s.n. Godsman.

Godingus 216.—OE Goding; PNDB 265.

Godman, see Godemannus.

Godricus 207, ∼ Chingessone 128, ∼ presbiter 276, ∼ savonarius 36; 1148 ∼ 908, (de) Godrico 901, 908, (filia) Godrici cum barba 292.—OE Godrīc.

Godwinus 107, 197, 210, (curtilla) Godwini 120, (domus) ∼ Capel 91, Godwinus Cederli' 146, ∼ chenicte 24, (curtillum) Godwini Cimel 119, (domus) ∼ Clawecuncte 91, Godwinus de Ordia 144, ∼ Elmeressone 14, (domus) Godwini Elmeressone 48, God' Ælmeressone 196, (domus) Godwini filii Chetel 92, (domus) ∼ filii Elmari 87, Godwinus Francigena 57, (domus) Godwini Francigenę 55, (domus) ∼ Goce 99, Godwinus Gretsud 243, (domus) Godwini Penifeder 95, (domus) ∼ Porriz 54, Godwinus Sarz 57, ∼ Socche 15,[6] ∼ Sorz 57; c. 1110 ∼ 172, ∼ Grenessone 10, God' Grenesune 233, Godwinus Nalad 227, ∼ Prison 10, God' Prison 228, 238, Godwinus Withmundin 132; 1148 ∼ 107, Goduinus 828, ∼ Bar 825, (uxor) Godwini de Fuleflot 245, Goduinus iunior 329, (heredes) Godwini presbiteri 241, 325, God' Prison 690.[7]—OE Godwine. The Frenchman Godwinus Francigena bore the OG name Godoinus; Morlet 113. See also God'.

Goisbertus c. 1110 198.—OG (Rom.) Goisbert; Forssner 124, Morlet 104.[8]

Goisfridus clericus c. 1110 66, 130, ∼ filius Hereberti 27, 32.—OG (Rom.) Goisfrid; Forssner 125f., Morlet 104.

---

[1] Personal communication.

[2] The existence of an OE fem. noun *begēat may be inferred from two passages in Laȝamon: for þære muchele biȝæte, MS. Caligula, line 609 (Madden's edn.; MS. Otho: for þare mochele bi-ȝeate), 'on account of the great booty' (not in MED), mid baldere bi-ȝeate, Caligula 27083 (Otho: mid baldere biȝæte), 'with bold booty' (MED, s.v. biyēte, c). On the second instance see also P. Hoffmann, Das grammatische Genus in Laȝamons Brut (Halle, 1909), 46. A weak variant of the noun seems in fact to be attested in the Ancrene Riwle: He biȝet þeos þreo biȝeaten, MS. Nero 71/5, 'He acquired these three benefits, advantages' (MED, ibid., b). Cf. A. Zettersten, Studies in the Dialect and Vocabulary of the Ancrene Riwle (Lund, 1965), 190.

[3] On late WS -on for -an see Campbell § 377.

[4] These include the rubric de terra Gode begeate added to KCD 720 (Cod. Wint., 12th c.), the LW forms under notice, in terra Gode Beatę 1160/1 P 57, and the spellings quoted by Goodman.

[5] See O. Schultz in Abhandlungen Adolf Tobler dargebracht (Halle, 1895), 187f. Note also Godehildis 1010, Godeheldis 1100, Godoholdis 1100, Godehaldis 1180, in French charters; Drevin 32.

[6] ...fuit T.R.E. magister monetarius. He is not identical with the pre-Conquest Winchester moneyer Godwine Ceoca as W. H. Stevenson assumed, VCH Hants i. 536; see Ceca above. Cf. also below pp. 400f. and 422, and Tables 34 and 37.

[7] Clearly the same man as Godwinus Prison, c. 1110.

[8] For the history of the el. Gois- < *Gautsi- see now E. Felder in Beiträge zur Namenforschung, N.F. 5 (1970), 14ff., esp. 20-1.

(Alexander) **Goisl'** 1148 209, (Alexander filius) *Gollan'* 189.—OFr *Goislain* (*Joislain*), a suffixal variant of *Goislin*, *Goislen* < OG (West Frankish) *Gauziolen*, *Gauzilin*, *Gaucilen*; see Förstemann 612f., Forssner 128f., Morlet 104, Kaufmann, *Erg.-Bd*, 142.[1]

Golburg' 1148 522.—OE *Goldburh f. See my note *NoB* 33 (1945), 81, *DBS* s.n. Goldburg. This is the earliest recorded occurrence of the name.

Gollan', see *Goisl'*.

Golsewanus, see *Colsueinus*.

Gonnod 57, *Gonnodus* 182.—OE *Godnōð.[2] These are the earliest examples of the name.

(de) **Goscelino** 1148 34, (Stigandus filius) *Goscelini* 197.—OG (Rom.) *Gautselin*, *Goscelin*; Forssner 128f., *DBS* s.n. Jocelyn.

Got 20.—ON *Gautr*, ODan *Gøt*. On *o* for Scand *au* see *PNDB* § 37. The corresponding weak form *Gauti* is well evidenced in English sources; *PNDB* 258.

(Godwinus) **Grenessone** c. 1110 10, (God') *Grenesune* 233.—OE *Grēne*, an original byname from OE *grēne* 'green, young, immature'; *PNDB* 274f.

(Robertus) **Grifin** 1148 798.—A pet form of OWelsh *Grifud*, MWelsh *Gryffud* with the Rom. suffix -*īn*, here used as a patronymic; *PNDB* 275, Jackson 346, *DBS* s.n. Griffin. The name also occurs in Normandy.

Grimbaldi (gen) medici 1148 827.—OG *Grimbald*; Forssner 130f.

(Durandus) **Gumbold'** 1148 319.—OG *Gundbald*, *Gumbald*, here used in a patronymic function; Förstemann 698, Morlet 116, *DBS* s.n. Gumbel.

Guncelinus 1148 153, 611, 612, *Guncel'* 896 bis, (filius) *Gunt'* 320, (Conannus filius) *Guncel'* 179, (Herbertus filius) *Gunt'* 454, (Herberti filii) ∼ 502, 895, (Herebertus filius) ∼ 30, (heredes) ∼ 583, 603,

(heredes Hugonis) *Guncel'* 167, (Hugonis filii) *Guntsel'* 180, (Hugonis filii) *Guncel'* 183, (Hugonis filii) *Guntscel'* 424, (Rogerus filius) *Gunt'* 415, (de Rogero filio) ∼ 29, *Guncel'* Dore 857, ∼ filius Hugonis 833.—OG *Gunzelin*; Forssner 136, Morlet 118.

(uxor Ricardi filii) **Gunfridi** 1148 285.—OG *Gundfrid*; Forssner 133.[3]

Gunnild 1148 40.—ON *Gunnhildr*, ODan *Gunhild* f.; *PNDB* 277.

Gunnora 1148 288.—ODan *Gunnur* f.; *PNDB* 278 and n. 4. For early instances in Normandy see Adigard 101ff., 306ff. Note also *Gunnora*, *Gunnor* early 12th-c. *LVH* 50, 52, (de) *Gunnora* 1210–11 *PRBW* 161 (Winchester).

Gunt', see *Guncelinus*.

Gunterus filius Berengarii 1148 837, ∼ parmentarius 250.—OG *Gunter*; Forssner 136, Morlet 117.

Gunts(c)el', see *Guncelinus*.

Gupill' 1148 740, (filia) ∼ 78.—An original nickname, OFr *golpil*, *goupil* 'fox', which survives in the ModFr surname *Goupil* (Dauzat 301).[4] See also *Ulpis*, byn.

H

(uxor) **Haccheselt** 1148 363.—A phrase-name, whose first el. is *hacche*- from OE *haccian* 'to cut, hack, chop into small pieces' and the second OE *sealt* 'salt'. Cf. Gervasius *Hakesalt* 1176, Roger *Hackesalt* 1296–7 (*MED* s.v.),[5] *Hacchemus*, below, p. 212, and the names in *Hache*-, *Hak(k)e*- listed by Reaney *Origin*, 288. On *LW cch* for OE *cc* [k] see below, p. 225.

(domus) **Hachechasse** 136.—A Norman byname, *hache cassée* 'broken battle-axe', which is recorded in the latinized form (Ricardi) *Fractae Securis* 1066–79.[6] In *LW Hache*- *ch* stands for [tʃ] as in *Pancheuot*

---

[1] Early English examples are *Goislan(us)* 1086 DB L 341, 344 *ter*, 344b, 345, *Goislin(us)* 1130 P 109, 117, 154, etc., *Goislen* 1086 DB O 155b. The variation in form of the name under notice is well illustrated in the case of Goslenus (Joslenus) of Tours, steward of Anjou, who is called *Joislenus*, *Goslenus*, *Joslenus*, *Jollanus* in French charters c. 1150–60; see *France* passim. Note also *Goillano* (abl) de Autebarg by the side of *Gollano* (abl) de Autebarge Hy II *DCh* 369, 374 (L). The double consonant in *Gollan*, *Jollan* probably represents an *l mouillé*; see Pope § 696, L. E. Menger, *The Anglo-Norman Dialect* (New York, 1904), 103f.

[2] Local instances of the name are *Godnoð*, mon. Winchester, Wm. I, *BMC* 159, 220, *Godnothus de puteo* 12th c. *LVH* 123. See below, p. 415.

[3] Well evidenced in DB 1086; Ellis *Introduction* ii. 333. Note also *Gumfridus* 1201 *Cur. Rich I–1201* 443 (Wa), (Hugonem f.) *Gunfridi* 1202 *NthAss* 96.

[4] Cf. also (de Ursello) *Gopil*, (de Anfr') *Gopil* 1195 *MRSN* 159, (de filio) *Goupil* 1198 *MRSN* 382 (Normandy), (Henricus) *Gupil* 1273 *RH* i, 313 (Li), (Petrus) *Gupil* 1278/9 *RH* ii. 543 (K), (Ricardus) *Gopil RH* ii. 578 (K).

[5] An additional example is (Henry) *Hackesalt* a 1227 *Cal Chart R 1226–57* 59 (Monm.). Note also (de Roberto) *Hacckesalt* 1285 *Survey*.

[6] In a charter concerning St. Étienne de Fontenay (Calvados), *Bull. de la Soc. des antiquaires de Normandie*, 56 (1961–2), 33.

(byn.), *Ticheborne* (pl.n.); cf. also *PNDB* § 121. The use of *ch* for initial [k] before a back vowel in *-chasse* has many parallels in *LW*; see below, p. 225 and Addenda.

Hadewis 1148 834.—OG *Hadwid*, (Rom.) *Hadewi(di)s* f.; Forssner 144.

Haliprest 229.—An original byname, OE *hālig* 'holy', *prēost* 'priest'; cf. Alfwin *Haliprest* Hy I *ELPN* 153 (London), and the nickname *Helteprest* 1066 *LW* (q.v.).

Hamo filius Erneis *c.* 1110 269, (de feudo Roberti filii) *Ham'* 96.—OG *Haimo*, OFr *Hamo(n)*; Forssner 141f., Morlet 122, *DBS* s.n. Haim.

Hangere 1148 19.—ME *hangere* 'hangman'; see *MED* s.v. *hongere*. In this sense the word has not previously been recorded until *c.* 1450.

Hardi[n]gus faber *c.* 1110 128; **1148** *Herdingus* 987, *Herdi[n]g'* brachiator 109, *Hard'* brachiator 379, (filius) *Herdi[n]g'* fabri 379.—OE *Hearding*; *PNDB* 287f.

Haroldus de Chenesham **1148** 34, idem ∼ 34.—ON *Haraldr*, ODan *Harald*; *PNDB* 284ff. For a pre-conquest Norman example see Adigard 308.

(domus) **Hauoc** 123.—OE **Hafoc*; Redin 7, Tengvik 186f., *DBS* s.n. Hawk. This is the earliest example of the name on independent record.[1]

Hedricus, see *Edricus*.

Helbingus 194.—OG *Helbing*,[2] *Helbung*; Förstemann 840f.

(uxor) **Heleboldi 1148** 966.—OG *Helbold*; Förstemann 738.

Helewisa 1148 575, 577, 1055.—OG (Rom.) *Hel(e)-widis* f., OFr *Heluïs*, *Heloïs*; Forssner 145, Jacobsson 216f., *DBS* s.n. Elwes.

Helias dapifer episcopi *c.* 1110 70.—The biblical name *Elias*. It is recorded a few times in OE sources. *Helias* is the usual form in OFr.

Henricus thesaurarius 184;[3] *c.* 1110 ∼ de Dunmera 87, ∼ de Dommere 137, *Henrico* (dat) de Domera 10, *Henricus* de Port 39, 40, 51, (Adelidis soror) *Henrici* de Port 239, *Henricus* frater Debou' 144, ∼ lardarius 18, 59; **1148** ∼ 1014, (filia) *Henrici* 150, (Aluricus gener) ∼ 201, (Mathilda filia) ∼ 815, *Henricus* de

Traci 175, 258, (de) *Henrico* fabro 901, (de) ∼ filio Herefast' 258, ipse *Henricus* 258, ∼ filius Roberti scoter' 452, (filia) *Henrici* filii Turstini 398, 414, *Henricus* Gladewin' 192, 289, ∼ mercator 581, ∼ pictor 133, (de) *Henrico* presbitero 807.—OG *Henric*; Forssner 147.

(coquus) **Herberti** *c.* 1110 107, (Goisfridus filius) *Hereberti* 27, 32, *Herbertus* camerarius 24,[4] 33, 74, 111, 116, 123, 152, *Herberti* (gen) camerarii 35, 117, 292, (Ranulfus dapifer) ∼ camerarii 55, *Herebertus* camerarius 4, 13b, 48, *Herbertus* de Sancto Quintino 150, 151, *Herberto* (dat) de Sancto Quintino 149, *Herebertus* de Sancto Quintino 50, *Herbertus* filius Edwin' 252, ∼ filius Edwini 258, ∼ Gidi 185, ∼ presbiter 119; **1148** *Herebert* 259, *Herebertus* 274, (heredes) *Hereberti* 1076, (Willelmus filius) *Herberti* 121, (Willelmus filius) *Hereberti* 618, *Herbertus* camerarius 4, 38, 841, 860, 873, eidem *Herberto* 828, *Herebertus* camerarius 828, idem ∼ 38, ipse ∼ 38, *Hereberto* (dat) camerario 542, eidem ∼ 38, de ∼ 38, *Herbertus* Campion 933, *Herebertus* Corneilla 10, ∼ de Saleb' 450, ipse ∼ 451, *Herberto* (dat) de Sar' 451, *Herebertus* (abl) filio Gaufridi 800, ipse *Herbertus* 800, eidem *Herberto* 800, *Herbertus* filius Gunt' 454, (heredes) *Herberti* filii Gunt' 502, 895, *Herebertus* filius Gunt' 30, ∼ filius Radulfi 574, 596, 829, ∼ filius Saieti 1078, ∼ filius Watscon' 436, *Herbertus* filius Westman 506, *Herebertus* filius Westman 463, *Herbertus* Westman 478, (de) *Hereberto* filio Westman 38, idem *Herebertus* 38, *Herbertus* Hosatus 955, *Herebertus* lardinarius 59, ∼ 59, ∼ palmarius 84, 720, ∼ Papanholt 772, ∼ pincerna 333, ∼ prepositus 76, 157, *Hereberto* (dat) 77, *Herbertus* presbiter 908, 912, *Herebertus* presbiter 632, (filius) *Hereberti* turtellar' 290, *Herebertus* vigil 750.—OG *Her(e)bert*; Forssner 148f.

Herdingus, see *Hardingus*.

Herebert, see *Herbert*.

Herefast 1148 230, (de Henrico filio) *Herefast'* 258.—ODan *Arnfast*. The forms under notice go back to the Norman variant *Herfast*, on which see Adigard 76, 273ff.[5] The first el. shows association with the OE and ContG names in *Here-*. Note also (terra . . . Arnoldi) *Herefast* 1189–1204 *PRBW* 160 (Winchester).

---

[1] It also enters into the OE pl.ns *Hafucestun c.* 975, Hauxton (C), and *Hafecesweorð c.* 1030, Hawksworth (YW); see *PNC* 85f., *PNYW* iv. 199f., *DEPN* s.nn. Cf. below, p. 205, n. 238.

[2] The form *Helbing* is the first el. in the pl.n. *Helbingestat* 816, Helmstadt (Unterfranken), for which see Förstemann ii. (1). 1207.

[3] He was a tenant-in-chief in 1086, DB Ha 49.

[4] Cf. DB 1086, Ha 42b, 45b, 48b.

[5] Among several Norman bearers of the name we may note Herfast, chaplain to William I and subsequently bishop of Elmham and Thetford, on whom see Stenton *ASE* 642. He occurs in DB as *Herfastus episcopus* Sf 447, *Ærefastus* Nf 197b, *Arfastus episcopus* Sf 394.

(de terris) **Herefridi** *c.* **1110** 76, *Herfridus* regis serviens 44; **1148** *Herefridus* presbiter 423.—OG *Her(e)frid*; Förstemann 769, Morlet 125.[1]

Hereman' **1148** 117.—OG *Hereman*; Forssner 149f.

(de) **Hereuico** **1148** 38, *Hereuicus* clericus 31, 220, 284, ~ 31, *Herv'* clericus 40, *Hereuicus* Freschet 282, *Heruic'* Freschet 492, (de) *Hereuic'* parmentario 190, ipse ~ 190.—OG *Herewig, Herewic*; Forssner 150f.

Herfrid, see *Herefrid*.

Herleboldus **1148** 721, (filie) *Herlebaldi* 587, 588, (uxor) *Herleboldi* 795.—OG *Erlebold, Herlebold*; Forssner 78, Morlet 81.

Herluinus *c.* **1110** 108.—OG *Erlewin, Herlewin*; Forssner 79f., Morlet 81f.

Hersie (dat) filio Warner' **1148** 77.—OE *Heresige*.[2]

Heruic, see *Hereuic*.

Hiechsi 219.—OE **Hēahsige*. This is the only known example of the name. On *ie* for OE *ēa* see below, p. 224.

Hizeman 57.—OG *Hizman*; Forssner 153.

Hoellus *c.* **1110** 106; **1148** *Hoel* 257.—OBret *Houuel, Hoel*;[3] *DBS* s.n. Howel.

(Radulfus) **Holinessone** *c.* **1110** 117.—An original byname, OE *holegn*, ME *holīn* 'holly'. See Addenda.

Hoppecole **1148** 378.—Possibly an original byname, ME **hopp(e)colle*, whose first el. could be *hoppe* 'flax pod' (*c.* 1300ff., *MED*)[4] or *hoppe* 'the hop plant, the cones of the female hop plant' (1440ff., *MED*), and the second *colle* 'barrel' (*c.* 1500; a nonce-word of uncertain etymology, *MED*).[5] A later instance is probably (de Hugone) *Hoppetolle* 1210–11 *PRBW* 331 (Ha) with *t* miswritten or misread for *c*. Cf. also (de terra) *Hopcherl* late 13th *c. St Aug* 31 (K). See Addenda.

(de) **Hoppere** **1148** 696.—ME *hoppere* 'dancer' (*MED* s.v.).[6] Cf. also Thuresson 188, *DBS* s.n. Hopper.

Hotot **1148** 936.—The Norman pl.n. *Hotot*, used elliptically for *Willelmus de Hotot*; see below, p. 194.

Hubertus filius Willelmi *c.* **1110** 73; **1148** ~ clericus 960.—OG *Hubert*; Forssner 156.

(Bernardus) **Hubold** **1148** 501.—OG *Hugebald, Hubald*, used here as a patronymic; Forssner 155f., Morlet 139f.

Huchelinus parcherius 282.—OG *Hugelin*; Forssner 156f. [k] for [g] in the *LW* form is due to AN influence; see *PNDB* § 128.

Hudo molendinarius **1148** 86.—OG *Hudo*; Förstemann 921, Morlet 142.

Hugo de Chiuilli *c.* **1110** 91, ~ de Menes 163, ~ filius Albuchon 40, (uxor) *Hugonis* filii Albuchon 40, *Hugo* lardarius 16,[7] ~ Oillardus 8,[8] ~ Oilardus 17; **1148** *Hugoni* (dat) 83, (de) *Hugone* 139, (Guncel' filius) *Hugonis* 833, (Robertus filius) ~ 851, (Stephanus filius) ~ 453, *Hugo* Bel 810, (heredes) *Hugonis* burgensis 861, *Hugo* de Aucho 850, (heredes) *Hugonis* de Auco 650, *Hugo* de Goi 920, *Hugoni* (dat) de Hahela 381, *Hugo* 381, *Hugoni* (dat) de Mortemer 421, 609, *Hugo* de Porta 314, 932,[9] *Hugoni* (dat) de Pusat 494, *Hugo* drapier 994, ~ filius Brum' 561, ~ filius Cupping' 294, 362, ~ filius Chepping' 23, ~ filius Chepp' 403, (de) *Hugone* filio Chepping' 172, *Hugo* 403, (filii) *Hugonis* filii Guntsel' 180, (filius) ~ filii Guntscel' 424, (heredes) ~ Guncel' 167, (uxor) ~ filii Guncel' 183, (heredes) ~ Friedai 590, *Hugo* Hacchemus 164, 482, 539, ~ Haccemus 18, 434, 458, ~ pistor 975, 980, ~ Pofile 400, ~ scriniarius 308, ~ tornitor 313.—OG *Hugo*; Forssner 157f.

Humfridus, see *Hunfridus*.

Hunbric 161.—OE *Hūnbeorht*.

Huneman 8.—OE *Hūnmann*.

Hunfridus **1148** 1067, (uxor) *Hunfridi* 1034, *Hunfrido* (dat) 415, (Roberto filio) *Hunfridi* 223, 870, 873, 898, 899, *Hunfridus* capellanus 782, ~ de Sutton' 705, *Humfridus* de Sutton' 668, 675, *Hunfridus* monacus 554, 562, *Humfridus* monacus 565, *Hunfridus* Palefrei 263, ~ Pancheuot 641.—OG *Hunfrid*; Forssner 158f.

Huni 264.—ON, ODan *Húni*; Fellows Jensen 145f.

[1] An early Norman example is *Herfridus* à Thumelhinvilla 1035–49 *RADN* 31. OE *Herefriδ*, which is not recorded after *c.* 867, would have given **Hereuert*.

[2] The only OE bearer of the name is *Heresige*, 946 *BCS* 874 (K), a minister of King Eadred.

[3] See K. H. Jackson, *A Historical Phonology of Breton* (Dublin, 1967), 148, 271. The name means 'good-looking'.

[4] Note also OE *gehopp* 'seed-pod', clearly a cognate, and perhaps the ancestor, of ME *hoppe* 'flax pod'; on the OE word cf. H. D. Meritt, *Fact and Lore about Old English Words* (Stanford, 1954), 88.

[5] OE *cole* 'hollow, vat' in *ōden-cole* 'hollow serving as a threshing floor' and *wīn-cole* 'wine vat' (BT, Clark Hall) is

a misprint for *colc*; see F. Holthausen, *Altenglisches etymologisches Wörterbuch* (Heidelberg, 1963), s.v. *colc*, H. D. Meritt, op. cit. in last note, p. 62.

[6] The earliest example in *MED* is Waldr' *le Hoppere* 1203.

[7] Cf. (domum) *Hugonis Larderarii* 1096 *EHR* 35 (1920), 388, *Hugo Larderarius* 1100–7 ibid. 391, Winchester.

[8] His son is *Will[elmu]s filius Hug[onis] Oillardi* 1130 *P* 50 (Sr.)

[9] His name is entered in the *LVH* together with that of his wife: *Hugo de Port', Orence coniunx eius*, 73.

I

Imma 1148 917.—A variant of OG *Emma* (q.v.).

Ingelbertus 1148 937.—OG *Ingelbert*; Forssner 71f.

Ingulfus *c.* 1110 88; **1148** ∼ 712, (uxor) *Ingulfi* 212, *Ingolfus* de Auiton' 740, *Ingulfus* besmere 61, (uxor) *Ingulf* Long' 207.—ON *Ingolfr*, ODan *Ingulf* or OG *Ingulf*; *PNDB* 298. Ten bearers of the name in Normandy are listed by Adigard, pp. 364–6.

Isabel 1148 448, 1015, ∼ de Diua 315, 318.—OFr *Isabel*, a vernacular variant of *Elisabeth*, recorded at least from the end of the eleventh century (Maine, Paris). The final syllable of the parent form was re-replaced by *-bel*, evidently through association with the adj. *bel(e)*, and initial *el-* was lost by aphaeresis. See further Jacobsson 206ff., and cf. Withycombe 156f.[1]

Issiran 273.—Possibly from an unrecorded OG **Isen(h)ram, -ran*. The el. *Isen-* occurs in OG *Isenbard, -burh, -god*, which are all recorded in OE and ME sources; see Forssner 165–7.[2]

Iua 1148 6, *Iva* 789.—OG *Iva* f.; Forssner 168. See also *Iueta*.

Iuelot 1148 206.—An OFr double diminutive of *Ivo* (q.v.).

Iueta 1148 223, 254, *Iveta* 228.—An OFr diminutive of *Iva* (q.v.); *DBS* s.n. Ivatt.

(Osbertus filius) Iuonis *c.* 1110 126; **1148** (Ricardus frater) ∼ 384, (uxor) ∼ 383, (uxori) ∼ 246.—OG *Ivo*; Forssner 168f. See also *Iuelot*.

Iwen parmentarius *c.* 1110 282; **1148** (filius) *Iwein'* 1071.—MWelsh *Ywein*; Jackson 324. An earlier example is *Iuuein* 1086 DB Wa 242b; note also *Iweinus* 1130 P 116 (Li).

J

Iohannes Bensetoure *c.* 1110 264, ∼ filius Ernuceon 37,[3] ∼ filius Fulcher' 286; **1148** ∼ 148, 1065, (de)

Iohanne 159, (filia) *Iohannis* 956, (Stephanus frater) ∼ 409, 1068, *Iohannes* aurifaber 826, 847, 852, ∼ cordwanarius 1063, ∼ de Port 2, 138, 474, *Iohannis* (gen) de Port 84, *Iohanni* (dat) de Port 439, 685, (de) *Iohanne* de Port 270, *Iohannes* faber 314, 426, ∼ filius Radulfi 140, 143, 155, ∼ frater Richer' 49, 943, ipse ∼ 49, ∼ ioculator 366, ∼ Longus 1073, ∼ nepos Petri 34, 154, 859, ∼ nepos Petri merciarii 359, ∼ presbiter 504.—The biblical name.

(Alur') Iola *c.* 1110 222.—ON *Ióli*, ODan *Iuli*; *PNDB* 300. The name is used here in a patronymic function. Final *-a* is due to anglicizing.

Iudicellus *c.* 1110 102; **1148** *Iudichel* 275, 864, (de) *Iudichell'* 1048.[4]—OBret *Iudicael*; *PNDB* 301, Jackson 311.

L

Lacchewei 1148 47, (Radulfus) ∼ 74, 420, (Radulfo) ∼ 74, *Lacchewai* 617, *Lachewei* 802.—Additional references to the same man are Rad' *Lacchewhai* 1155/6 P 54, ∼ *Lachewai* 1156/7 P 105. A byname of uncertain meaning. The second el. could be OE *weg* 'track, road, path, street', ME also 'door, gate' (*NED* s.v. way, I 1f., *c.* 1250); the first, ME [latʃ-], should perhaps be compared with OE **læcc* 'stream, bog' or **læcce* 'trap' (*EPN* ii. 10).[5] If so we might have a topographical designation, a field- or road-name, here indicating place of residence or origin, though the complete absence of the preposition *de* in all *LW* and *P* forms would be remarkable.[6] An unrecorded compound of ME *lacche, lach(e)* 'a fastening for a door or gate' (*NED*, 1331ff.) and *weg* in the sense of 'door, gate', hence 'a gate with a latch, a *latchway' would be a semantically acceptable nickname for a gate-keeper. A final and perhaps preferable alternative would be a phrase-name 'latch the door';[7] the relevant verb is not, however, recorded until 1530.

Lambert, see *Lambricht*.

DB E 84.

---

[1] Dauzat's theory (p. 337) that *Isabel* is of Spanish origin and was first borne in France by the Princess Isabelle (d. 1270), a sister of St. Louis, is clearly incorrect.

[2] The el. *Isen-* sometimes appears as *Isin-* in German and French records; see Morlet 147 s.nn. *Isanbald, Isembardus, Isamberga, Isanbraht, Isingarda, Isanger,* and *Isengaudus*. A few spellings with *-ss-* have also been noted: *Issimbardus* 942, *Issenberga* 11th c. (Morlet), (Ric' filius) *Issenborc* 1198 *MRSN* 359. Loss of *n* before *r* is well evidenced in OE; see Campbell § 474, E. Tengstrand, *A Contribution to the Study of Genitival Composition in Old English Place-Names* (Uppsala, 1940), 296, n. 1.

[3] Perhaps identical with *Johannes filius Ernucūñ* 1086

[4] *Juthekel de Wintonia* is mentioned in a Winchester charter, *temp.* Henry I: *EHR* 14 (1899), 424.

[5] Cf. *DEPN* s.n. Latchingdon, and the pl.ns *Latchmere* 1392, Latchmere (Sr), *PNSr* 57f., *Latchmore* 1282, in Bramley (Ha), *VCH Hants* iv. 433, *Lechewer* 1251, Latches Fen (C), *PNC* 266.

[6] A place called **Latchway* does not seem to exist in the parts of England so far surveyed by the Place-Name Society and others. There is none in Hampshire as Mr. J. E. B. Gover kindly informs me.

[7] Cf. *Escitteport* (byn.) < **scytte-port*, below p. 211.

(Ricardus filius) **Lambricht 1148** 555, 564, (Ricardus) *Lambert* 916.—OG *Lambert*; Forssner 172, Jacobsson 127f. The second el. has been anglicized in *Lambricht*.

Lancdelere 286.—Perhaps *Lanc* < OE *Lang*[1] or **Hlanc* < OE *hlanc* 'lean, thin', with an added by-name, *delere* < OE *dǽlere* 'distributor, agent; almsgiver'. A possible alternative would be *Lanc* (as above) *de Lere*, an abbreviation for *Le[g]recestre* > Leicester, as in *Osbertus de Lerec'* 1130 P 82.

(pro terra Petri) **Lancel' 1148** 332.—OG (Rom.) *Lancelin*; Forssner 173f., Morlet 157. The name is used here as a patronymic.

Laue 246.—OE *Lāfa*; Redin 51, 123.[2]

Laurentius 1148 26.—Lat *Laurentius*; Withycombe 182f.

Lefflet 251, *Leflet* Ecregeles docter 25.—OE *Lēofflǽd* f.

Leouingus 125, 260, *Leowingus* 203, *Leuingus* 248, *Leuingius* 20, *Luuingus* bedel 278, (domus) *Lewingi* Dol 139, *Leuingus* Drache 292, (domus) *Lewingii* Mandingessone 68, *Luuingus* scalarius 283; **1148** (de) *Luuingo* 573.—OE *Lēofing*, *Lȳfing*; Redin 167f., *PNDB* 312.

Lepstanus 218, 223, (gardini) *Lipestani* Bittecat 98.—OE *Lēofstān*. On *-ps-* for *-fs-* see below, p. 226.

Lesweda 57.—OE *Lēofswīð* f. The second el. reflects late WS *-swȳð* < *-swīð*.[3]

Letard 1148 775.—OG *Leuthard*, *Let(h)ard*; Forssner 179, Morlet 160.

Lethmerus 57.—OE *Lēodmǽr*; *PNDB* 310. On *t(h)* for *d* see *PNDB* §§ 102 (3), 96. One *Lēodmǽr* was a mon. at Winchester under Cnut; *BEH* 3773–9, *SCBI* xv, 4108–22.

(Siwardi) **Leuerunessone** 53.—OE *Lēofrūn* f.

Leueua 179.—OE *Lēofgifu* f.

Leuingus, see *Leouingus*.

Leuret 150, ~ de Essewem 4.—OE *Lēofred*.

(domus) **Leurici** 111, *Leovricus* Abeaham 186, *Lowricus* presbiter de Sapalanda monacorum 160.—OE *Lēofrīc*.

Lewinus 213, *Liuuinus* 107, *Liwinus* 107, *Luwinus* 223, *Lowinus* 236, *Lewinus* Balloe 57, (domus) *Lewini* Chane 49,[4] (domus) ~ Gulee 104, *Lowinus* presbiter 170, *Leuwinus* presbiter 190, *Lewinus* presbiter 257, ~ Scottelauessone 174, ~ sutor 6, (domus) *Lewine* Waterpotes 140, *Lewinus* Wrtwos 170; *c.* 1110 ~ 71; **1148** *Luinus* budel 648, ~ Child 716.—OE *Lēofwine*.

Lewoldus 209, (domus) *Liwoldi* 89, *Luwoldus* Gustate 168.—OE *Lēofwald*.

Licgard 1148 1056.[5]—OG *Liudgard*, (Rom.) *Li(t)-gardis*, *Lichardis* f.; Förstemann 1040f., Morlet 159, Jacobsson 222f.

Lichesuster 1148 647.—A compound of OE *līc* 'corpse' and *sweostor*, *s(w)uster* 'sister; nun',[6] perhaps used as a nickname for a woman who prepared corpses for burial.

Lipestanus, see *Lepstanus*.

Liuuinus, see *Lewinus*.

Liwoldus, see *Lewoldus*.

Lodewis 1148 909, 1007.—OG *Hludowic*, *Lodewic*; Forssner 153. The immediate source of the *LW* name, in which *d* represents [ð], is OFr *Loðewis*, a form found in *ASC* (E) 1108, 1116, etc.

Lowinus, see *Lewinus*.

Lowricus, see *Leuricus*.

Lucelina 1148 930.—A derivative of OG *Luzela* f. (Förstemann 1034) with the suffix *-īna*.[7]

Lufman Cat 127.—OE *Lēofmann*.

Luinus, see *Lewinus*.

Lupsida *c.* 1110 232.—OE *Lēofsidu* f.; *PNDB* 315. On *-ps-* for *-fs-* see below, p. 226.

Lupsone 233.—OE *Lēofsunu*.

Lursius 211.—For *Lupsius* < OE *Lēofsige*?

(domus) **Lutemanni** 116.—OE *Lȳtelmann* with loss of *l* by dissimilation, as in *Litemannus c.* 1102–11 *ELPN* 54; *DBS* s.n. Lilleyman.[8]

Luuingus, see *Leouingus*.

---

[1] See *PNDB* 308. A previously unnoticed, pre-DB instance is *Lang*, mon. Æðelred I, *Num Chron*[5] 4 (1924), 253.

[2] A ME example is *Laua* de Cadatrea 1167/8 P 138 (D).

[3] See Campbell § 318. Local examples are *Æþelswyð*, *Ealhswyð*, *Wilswyð*, *Wulfswyð*, all *c.* 1030, *LVH* 64, 57, 62, 62.

[4] He is *Leofwine kana* 11th c. *LVH* 70.

[5] One *Licgeard* was a benefactress of New Minster, Winchester, *c.* 1030, *LVH* 59.

[6] Reaney *SMS* 18 (1953), 110, regards *Liche-* as an error for *Lithe-* which he would further emend to *Litle-*, hence *Litlesuster* 'little sister', but this seems quite unecessary.

[7] *Luzela* is a hypocoristic diminutive of names in *Leut-*; cf. also *Liuzilin* m., Förstemann 1034.

[8] *Litilman* was a London moneyer under Æðelstan. There is some evidence for an OE *Ludman*, on which see R. Forsberg, *A Contribution to a Dictionary of Old English Place-Names* (Uppsala, 1950), 167, but it need hardly be considered here.

Luwen 221.—OE *Lēofwynn* f.

Luwinus, see *Lewinus*.

Luwoldus, see *Lewoldus*.

M

Macher' 1148 221, (de Rogero) ∼ 221.—Perhaps OG *Marcher*[1] with dissimilatory loss of *r*; cf. below p. 226. The name is used here in a patronymic function. A possible alternative would be OG *Magher* (Forssner 286), in which case *ch* [k] for *g* in the *LW* forms might be an AN feature (*PNDB* § 128), but note also spellings like *Macbert, Machard, Machelm* (< *Mag-*) in early French sources (Morlet 164).

Mactilda 1148 106, *Mathilda* filia Henrici 815, *Matilda* 419, *Matilde* (dat) 419, *Matildis* 801, ∼ filia Godefridi 461.—OG *Mahthild* f; Forssner 181f.

(Osbertus frater) **Maiesent** c. 1110 121, 122.—OG *Magis(w)ind* f., OFr *Maissent*; Forssner 183f. Note also *Maisenda* 12th c. *LVH* 52.

Mainard' parmentarius 1148 622.—OG *Mainard*; Forssner 181, *DBS* s.n. Maynard.

Mallardus 1148 967.—An original byname, OFr *mal(l)art, maillart* 'wild duck'.[2] Cf. also the ME examples listed by Forssner (pp. 182f.), whose suggestion that the etymon is an unrecorded OG **Magilhard* need, however, not be considered.

(Lewingii) **Mandingessone** 68.—Probably OE **Manding*, an *ing*-derivative of OE *mand* f. 'basket',[3] and hence an original nickname.

Mandode 230.—Perhaps OE *Mann* (Redin 8) and the byname *Dod(d)a*, on which see *PNDB* 224.[4] The *LW*

form may, however, stand for *Manbode* with *d* for *b* by anticipatory dittography and if so the etymon is OG *Megin-, Maim-, Menbodo*, on which see Förstemann 1073, Forssner 185, Morlet 165.[5] It occurs in DB 1086 as *Manbodo* Y 324b.[6] See also *Andrebode*.

Manig' 1148 452.—ODan *Manni*; *PNDB* 324. Also in Normandy; see Adigard 225f., 367, 456ff. Cf. also *Manne* below.

(Willelmi filii) **Manne** 1148 9.—OE *Manna* (Redin 52) or ODan *Manni*, for which see *Manig* above.

Marieta filia Alurici 1148 739.—An OFr diminutive of *Maria*.

Martinus 188; 1148 (heredes) *Martini* 17, 1058, (soror) ∼ 144, (uxor) ∼ 28, 43, 56, 139, 795, 808, 825, 854, (uxori) ∼ 565, 566, 809, *Martinus* de Bintewrda 56, ∼ de Binteword' 487.—Lat *Martinus*. For pre-conquest examples see Searle 346, 349.

Mat(h)ilda, see *Mactilda*.

Merwn 1148 914.—OE *Mǣrwynn* f.; *PNDB* 326f., Reaney, *SMS* 18 (1953), 97. Another Ha instance is *Maruuen* 12th c. *LVH* 53; also as the first el. of the local name *Merewenehaia LW* I, 66 'Mǣrwynn's fenced-in piece of ground', a property in Winchester; see below, p. 238, s.n.

Michael 1148 1011.—The biblical name.[7]

Miles clericus 1148 684.—OFr *Miles, Milon* from OG *Milo*; Forssner 191, Morlet 169, *DBS* s.n. Miles.

Morell' Paginan' 1148 194.—OFr *Morel*, an original byname from *morel* adj. 'of swarthy complexion (like a Moor)'.[8] Recorded in England from 1086 onwards; see *DBS* s.n. Note also (Will') *Morel* 1207 *FineR* 456 (Winchester).

Morgellor 1148 40.—Unexplained.

---

[1] Forssner 286–7, to whose examples we may add (Symon filius) *Markere* 1167/8 *P* 146 (So), (Willelmus filius) *Marchere* c. 1150–75, BM, Add. MS. 40,000, fo. 2ᵛ (Liber Vitæ of Thorney Abbey, C), (de) *Markero* de Torneberga 1175/6 *P* 27 (Bk).

[2] On the OFr and early ModFr variant *maillart* see *FEW* vi (1). 426, and Huguet v. 109. The modern dialect of Picardy has *maillard*. The byname is well evidenced in Normandy, examples being (Gerold) *Maillart* 1195 *MRSN* 163, (de Johanne) ∼ 1198 ibid. 326, (Willelmo) *Mallart* late 12th-c. (orig.) *Jumièges* ii. 164, (Willelmo) *Maillart* ibid. 165, (Rogeri) *Malart* c. 1200 (orig.) ibid. 218. Also in Picardy: (Balduinus) *Maillart* 1218, (Pierre) *Malart* 1380; see further Morlet *Étude*, 430. Reaney, *DBS* s.n. Maylard, would derive our name from the rare OG *Madalhard* but this is an unlikely base in view of the evidence presented here and on phonological grounds. The ModFr surname *Maillard* (and *Maillart* in a *chanson de geste*) is explained by Dauzat (p. 405) from

OFr *mail* 'mallet, club'.

[3] Cf. (de Gilibert) *Mande* 1210–11 *PRBW* 27 (Ha).

[4] *Mann minister* was a benefactor of New Minster and two of his namesakes appear as lay brothers of the foundation: *LVH* 22, 63f. The name *Dod(d)a* was borne by a priest and a lay brother, *LVH* 29, 63.

[5] One of Morlet's examples is from Normandy (Jumièges).

[6] On *-an-* for *-ain-* see Kalbow 106.

[7] *Michaeli* (dat) Napario 1130 *P* 86 (Nth) seems to be the earliest recorded instance of the name in England, unless we count the appearance of *Michael*, an Italian chaplain of the Conqueror, as a witness to a Westminster charter in 1068, *Reg* i, 22. He was appointed to the see of Avranches in the same year; see D. C. Douglas, *William the Conqueror* (London, 1964), 209.

[8] Norman instances are (Odonis) *Morel* 1030 *RADN* 192, (a) *Morello* c. 1080 *AGC* 108, *Morellus* 1079–87 *AGC* 122. For more early French materi see Drevin 43.

(uxor) **Multun** 1148 1051.—OFr *molton* 'ram'; cf. *DBS* s.n. Mutton.[1]

Muriel 1148 752, 853, 1042, 1074, 1075, 1078.—OIr *Muirgel* f.[2] Common in Normandy.[3] Early examples in England include *Moriellae* (gen), *Muriellae* (gen), sister of Eudo dapifer, *c.* 1080,[4] *Muriel c.* 1120 *LVH* 53, ~ 12th c. *LVH* 136, 140, ~ filia Rad' de Sauineio 1130 *P* 96 (Sf), *Murieli* (dat) de Belcampo 1130 *P* 89 (Lei); for later material see *DBS* s.n.

Murta 1148 60.—OE **Murta* from the Germanic stem **murt-* in ModE dial *mort* 'a young salmon', Shetl *murt* 'a small being, a child'; for details see my note on the name, *SNPh* 40 (1968), 10.

N

Nicher 1148 787.—An original nickname, OE *nicor* 'water-sprite, sea-monster'; for later examples see *DBS* s.n. Niker.

Nicholaus 1148 51, 273, 758, (uxor) *Nicholai* 103, 880, *Nicholaus* presbiter 341.—Lat *Nicolaus*; Withycombe 216f., *DBS* s.n. Nicholas.

Nigellus de Cholcham *c.* 1110 205; 1148 ~ presbiter 938.—*Nigellus*, the diminutive of *Niger*, is the latinized form of OFr *Niel, Ne(i)el,*[5] originally a nickname applied to persons of dark complexion. It was very popular in Normandy and in post-conquest England.[6] The traditional derivation from OIr *Niáll*, as stated by Withycombe (p. 217) and Reaney, *DBS* s.n. Neal,

---

[1] Cf. also (Robertus) *Multon* 1181–9 *RAH* ii. 384 (Normandy).

[2] See M. Förster, *Der Flussname Themse* (Munich, 1941), 645, n. 3.

[3] e.g. *Muriel* 1035–66 *RADN* 33 (Fécamp), *Murielis* (gen) parceariae 1083–5 *AGC* 119, (filia) *Murieldis* 1180 *MRSN* 14, (de Hais) *Muriel* 1195 *MRSN* 218.

[4] W. D. Macray (ed.), *Chronicon abbatiae Rameseiensis* (RS, 1886), 207, 232.

[5] Cf. *Nielli* (gen) vicecomitis 1013 (orig.) *RADN* 109, (signum) *Negelli* 1032–5 (orig.) *RADN* 226 (Normandy). On the OFr form *Neiel* see Vallet 83, 162. Early non-latinized examples in English sources are *Neigel*, mon. Thetford, Wm. II, *BMC* 53, (at) *Neæle* Pynceune, a Norman, *c.* 1100–30 Earle 259 (D). Note also that *Nigellus* was a common Latin cognomen; see I. Kajanto, *The Latin Cognomina* (Helsinki, 1965), 228.

[6] The DB under-tenants who bore it in 1086 take up a whole page in Ellis's index (*Introduction* ii. 357–8).

[7] Only recorded as the name of an eighth-century king of Sussex.

[8] The suffix is Germanic (< *-ina*) or Romance (< Lat. *-inus*); see A. Bach, *Deutsche Namenkunde*, i (Heidelberg, 1952), § 97: 1, Lebel 43, K. Michaëlsson in *Mélanges de linguistique offerts à Mario Roques*, iv (Paris, 1952), 184f.

---

is obviously improbable, except in those parts of the North where Irish and Hiberno-Norse influence can be assumed. See also *Niger*, byn., and the semantic opposite *Blundel*, pers.n.

(Robertus filius) **Nunne** *c.* 1110 253.—OE *Nunna*; Redin 68.[7]

O

Odgaressune, see *Edgar*.

Odiham 1148 468.—The pl.n. Odiham (Ha) used elliptically for *Alwinus de Odiam* (q.v.).

Odo 275, (domus Aldredi fratris) *Odonis* 46, *Odo* de Esp[er]chefort 143, (domus) *Odonis* de Esperchefort 77, *Odo* Ticchemannessone 133; *c.* 1110 (Willelmus filius) *Odonis* 42, (Willelmo filio) ~ 107, *Odo* monetarius 129; 1148 (Ricardus filius) *Odonis* 351, (Ricardus filius) *Odoni[s]* 380, (Willelmi filii) *Odonis* 405, *Odo* presbiter 662.—OE *Od(d)a* or, as in most if not all post-conquest instances, OG *Odo*; Forssner 198f., *PNDB* 333f.

(Hugo) **Oillardus** *c.* 1110 8, (Hugo) *Oilardus* 17.—OG *Odil(h)ard*, (Rom.) *Oilard*, used here as a patronymic; Forssner 195, Morlet 175f.

(Osbertus filius) **Oini** *c.* 1110 197; 1148 *Oinus* 91, 667, (Willelmo filio) *Oin* 555, (terris . . .) *Oini* filii Erepulfi 660, *Oinus* parmentarius 299.—OG *Audin, Odin,* OFr *Oin,* a short form in *-in*[8] of names in *Aud-, Od-;* cf. Förstemann 189, Morlet 45.[9] The loss

---

[9] Early Norman examples include *Odini* (gen), son of Rainold, 1035–40 (orig.) *RADN* 375, (Bernardus filius) *Odini* 1066 Deville *Ste Trinité*, 454, *Odinus* 1077 (orig.) *Jumièges* i. 84, (Ricardus filius) *Odini* 1108 *St. Wandrille* 110, (~) *Oini* 1111–18 ibid. 112, (Willelmo filio) *Oini* 1111–18 *France* 59, *Oino* (abl) early 12th c. (orig.) *France* 127, *Oyno* (dat) de Fiscano 1150–1 *RAH* i. 22.

In England the name turns up in DB 1086 with (Hungerus filius) *Odini* (see below) and *Odinus camerarius* W 74b, Ex 16, *Oinus camerarius* Ex 3. The fact that in one entry, Do 81b, the same man is called *Odonis* (gen) *camerarii* seems to indicate that it could be used as a diminutive of *Odo* and may sometimes even have been formed directly from the latter name. Later native instances are *Oino* (dat) servienti 1130 *P* 5 (O), (Willelmus) *Oin* 1164/5 *P* 43 (Ha), (Geroldus filius) *Oin[i]* 1198 *PRS* xxiv. 114 (E). (de Ric̃) *Odyn* 1274/5 *RH* i. 497 (Nf). Cf. also the forms cited below, p. 167 nn. 1–2.

In early 12th-c. original charters, French and English, the archaic chancery form *Audinus* is used by the side of vernacular *Oin(us)*, a case in point being the name of the contemporary bishop of Évreux, who is referred to as *Audino* (abl) 1121 *Reg* ii, cxxxii, *Audini* (gen) 1126 ibid. clxxvii–viii, 1131 ibid. ccxlviii, by the side of *Oino* (abl) 1129 ibid. ccxiii, 1137 *Reg* iii, 69. Ordericus Vitalis

of the medial dental is OFr.[1] An alternative source which may have to be considered in some cases is Anglo-Scand *Oðin* < ON *Auðunn*, ODan *Øthin*; *NPN* 100ff., *PNDB* 170.[2] See also *Audoenus*.

(fratri) **Olaf 1148** 507.—ON *Óláfr*, ODan *Olaf*; *PNDB* 335. Other local instances are *Olaf LVH* 74, *Olauus LVH* 56, both late 11th- or early 12th-century.

Oricus 1148 986.—OG *Audric*, *Odric* (Förstemann 200, Morlet 44) with OFr assimilation of *dr* (*ðr*) > *rr*, as in *Or(r)icus* by the side of *Odricus* in French 11th- and 12th-century charters; see Drevin 26, 157. In OE *Ordrīc d* remains in ME. An alternative base is OG *Odelric* (Morlet 176), which was reduced to *Olric* > *Orri(c)* in OFr; cf. Drevin 44, Jacobsson 131.

Ormerus 1148 467.—OE *Ordmǣr*.

(Robertus filius) **Osberti** de Auco *c.* **1110** 75, *Osbertus* filius Alberede 3, 4, 69, ~ filius Iuonis 126, ~ filius Oini 197, ~ filius Thiardi 101, ~ filius Tihardi 122, ipse ~ 101, ~ Tiart 30, *Osbertus* frater Maiesent 121, 122; **1148** ~ 5, 111, 147, (filius) *Osberti* 1032, (de) *Osberto* 111, *Osbertus* cerarius 828, 888, ~ 828, ~ Cod 513, *Osberto* (dat) Cod 696, *Osbertus* 696, ~ filius Stiwardi 585, ~ magister 715, 728, 941, ~ monacus 1026, ~ Waspail 475.—OG *Osbert*, on which see *PNDB* 338, or in some cases perhaps OE *Ōsbeorht*.

(uxor) **Oslac 1148** 336.—OE *Ōslāc*.

(de) **Osmod 1148** 323, 324, *Osmodus* 911.—OE *Ōsmōd*.

Osmoda 1148 80, 160, 372, 404, 433, 666, 894, 970.—

ODan *Asmoth* f.; *PNDB* 168. The first el. has been anglicized.

Osmundus 1148 794.—OE *Ōsmund*; *PNDB* 340.

P

Paganus de la medehalla 12; **1148** ~ 820, (que fuit) *Pagani* 188, (filio) ~ 188, (de) *Pagano* 30, (de) ~ filio Picard' 323, *Paganus* filius Pic' 552, ~ Pic' 21, 92, 364, 367, 370, 406, 431, ~ 323, idem ~ 365, item ~ 371, iterum ~ 377, ~ fullo 610, (filia) *Pagani* fullonis 637, *Paganus* Gallus 40, 428, ~ medicus 1023.—Lat *Paganus* from *paganus* 'villager, peasant, civilian', OFr *Paien*; Tengvik 161, 193f., 223, *DBS* s.n. Pain, Reaney *Origin*, 146.

Palefrei 1148 267, (Hunfridus) ~ 263, *Palefr'* 263.— OFr *palefrei* 'saddle-horse, palfrey'. A latinized form is (Willelmo) *Palefrido* (abl) 1128 *Reg* ii, CCXI. See also *DBS* s.n. Palfrey.

Panta 1148 45.—OG *Panto* or a ME short form of *Pantulf*, a Continental name which was not uncommon in England from 1086 onwards; cf. Forssner 203.

Patricius 1148 609 *bis*, ~ Cachastra 698.—Lat *Patricius*.[5]

Pauida 1148 427, *Pauie* 396.—Note also *Pauia* 12th c. *LVH* 136. The etymon is Lat *Papia*, the OFr vernacular form of which was *Pavie*.[6] The name was borne by William the Conqueror's paternal (step)-grandmother.[7] The *LW* spelling *Pauida* shows scribal

---

consistently uses the form *Audinus* for the bishop; see his *Historia ecclesiastica*, v (Paris, 1855), 118 *et passim*.

Oin could also be latinized *Audoenus* by association with the name of the famous seventh-century bishop and patron saint of Rouen. On this stereotyped documentary form of OG *Audwin* and its variant *Audoinus* see W. Levison, *Scriptores rerum Merovingicarum*, v (1910), 536, n. The OFr vernacular form of the name was *Ouen*; see Kalbow 96, Dauzat–Rostaing s.n. St.-Ouen. The modern French surname *Ouin* is from *Audoin*; Dauzat 458. Examples of the unetymological use of *Audoenus* for *O(d)inus* are (Hungerus filius) *Audoeni* 1086 DB Ex 17, 19b by the side of (Hungerus filius) *Odini* DB Do 85, and *Audoeno* (abl) 1127 (orig.) *Reg* ii, CCV, *Audoeni* (gen) 1136 *Reg* iii, 944 with reference to the bishop of Évreux.

Bergh (p. 21) is wrong in deriving Old Provençal *Audino* from OG *Audwini*; the supposed reduction of *-wini* > *-in(i)*, which may merely be due to a change of suffix as Bach thinks, is only recorded in Alemannic; see A. Socin, *Mittelhochdeutsches Namenbuch* (Basel, 1903), 176f., J. Schatz in *Zeitschr. für deutsches Altertum*, 72 (1935), 154f., E. Schröder, *Deutsche Namenkunde* (Göttingen, 1944), 74, A. Bach, *Deutsche Namenkunde*, i (Heidelberg, 1952), § 98.

[1] The form *Ohin* fil. Godold 1186–8 *BuryS* 45 (Sf), *Ohinus*, ibid. 47, shows loss of the intervocalic consonant and subsequent insertion of a hiatus-filling *h*.

[2] Note especially *Oinus dacus* 1066 DB E 25. *Odin(us)* 1086 DB Ch 269 is probably Scand. *Opinus* 12th c. *LVH* 65 (son of Robert and Æmma) is OG or Scand.

[3] See on him below, p. 168, n. 1.

[4] I. Kajanto, *The Latin Cognomina* (Helsinki, 1965), 311. On the meaning of *paganus* see further E. Löfstedt, *Late Latin* (Inst. for samenlignende kulturforskning, Ser. A: 25, Oslo, 1959), 75–8.

[5] Cf. *Patric* de Cadurc' 1130 *P* 80 (Gl), a Frenchman from Sourches (Maine), (Willelmus) *Patric* 1130 *P* 66, *Patricius*, a boy at Hyde Abbey, *c.* 1130–40 *LVH* 40. OFr examples are *Patricius* filius Ingelbaldi 1077 C. Métais (ed.), *Cartulaire de l'abbaye cardinale de la Trinité de Vendôme*, i (Paris, 1893), 409, ~ Fulchoii filius 1098 ibid. 407 (St. Ouen), (Willelmus) ~ 1066–83 *AGC* 95 (Caen).   [6] Jacobsson 240f.

[7] In Norman sources her name usually appears in its traditional Latin form, e.g. *Papię* (gen) comitissę 1017–25 (orig.) *RADN* 118. The vernacular variant is recorded in an original charter of 1037–48: *matris meę Paveię*, *RADN* 274.

association with Lat *pavidus* 'timorous'. For additional examples of the name see *DBS* s.n. Pavey. The etymology proposed by Reaney (ibid.) is incorrect.

Peitewinus 1148 69, *Peiteuin'* 82, (de) ∼ 82.—OFr *peitevin* 'a man from Poitou'; *DBS* s.n. Poidevin.

Peni 1148 5.—An original byname, OE *peni(n)g*; *DBS* s.n. Penney.

Petita 1148 40.—A fem. nickname from OFr *petit* 'little'; *DBS* s.n. Pettit. See also *Petit*, byname, p. 215. A Norman example is (Herveio filio) *Petite* 1180 *MRSN* 3.

Petrus 134; 1148 (Gaufridus filius) *Petri* 509, (Radulfus filius) ∼ 386, 397, (Ernaldus frater) ∼ 842, 1045, (Ernoldus frater) ∼ 135, 977, 981, 1060, (Iohannes nepos) ∼ 34, 154, 859, *Petrus Agnell'* 585, (terram) *Petri de Valuin'* 476, *Petrus* Estreis 790, *Petro* (dat) filio archidiaconi 872, (terra) *Petri* Lancel' 332, *Petrus* merciarius 35, 136, 200, 210, 238, 265, 515, 557, 863, (Ernaldus frater) *Petri* merciarii 904, (Iohannes nepos) ∼ merciarii 359, *Petrus* napier 937, ∼ sellarius 516, ∼ Tresor 151.—Lat *Petrus*.

Philippus 1148 247, 292, (de) *Philippo* 292, *Philippus* de Fuleflod' 291, 293, ∼ de Vallo 393, ∼ filius Sanson' 227.—Lat *Philippus*.

(de Pagano filio) **Picard'** 1148 323, (Paganus filius) *Pic'* 552, (Paganus) ∼ 21, 364, (Pag') ∼ 92, 367, 370, 406, 431.[1]—OFr *picart* 'a man from Picardy' rather than OFr *picart*, *pichart* 'spear' (also adj. 'pointed'), which would, however, have a semantic parallel in *Picot* (q.v.). As an alternative etymon Reaney, *DBS* s.n. Pickard, postulates an OFr pers.n. *Pic-hard*, but this is unnecessary and improbable.

Picot pincerna *c.* 1110 291; 1148 ∼ sannarius 184, (de) *Pic'* saln' 644.—An original byname, OFr *picot* 'pointed weapon'; see also *DBS* s.n. Pickett.[2]

Pieferret 1148 774.—OFr *pié ferré* 'ironshod foot', probably a nickname for one who wore or manu-

factured hobnailed boots, is well evidenced in early French sources: *Pié-Ferré*, 1292 Paris (Pachnio 30), *Pieferé* 13th c., Eu (Seine-Maritime).[3] A semantic cognate is ME *P(i)edefer c.* 1190ff., ModE *Pettifer*; *DBS* s.n.[4]

Pilluc 187.—Apparently a derivative in -*uc* of an OE *Pilla*, a hypocoristic form of names in *Pīl-*. See further my note, *SNPh* 40 (1968), 11.[5]

Piterun 1148 269.—Perhaps from an unrecorded OE *Peohtrūn*, late OE *Pihtrūn* f., a compound with the rare and archaic el. *Peoht-*; cf. Searle 387 and my comments, *NoB* 33 (1945), 86.

Pontius 1148 558.—Lat *Pontius*, OFr *Ponz*; *DBS* s.n. Points, Jacobsson 84f. Early examples are *Ponz* 1086 DB Br 61, Walterus fil. ∼ DB O 154b.

Porcell' 1148 278.—OFr *porcel* 'pig'; *DBS* s.n. Purcell.

Porcus 1148 613.—Lat. *porcus*, OFr *porc* 'hog'. Cf. the Norman byn. (Gautier) *Le Porc* 1332 *Cartulaire de l'abbaye de La Luzerne* (Saint-Lô, 1878), 181 (Manche).

Portereue 1148 804.—OE *portgerēfa* 'portreeve, mayor'. Evidently not a real (by)name but merely the title of the official in question. Cf. Tengvik 265f.

Posta 1148 1072, 1073.—A derivative of OE *post* 'post, pillar'. See also *Post*, byn.

(domus) **Poti** 137; 1148 (Willelmus filius) *Pot* 488.—An original byname, OE *pott* 'pot', and used as such in (God) *Pot c.* 1110 (q.v. below). Cf. *DBS* s.n. Pott.[6]

Pucheshele 265.—Clearly a pl.n., used here elliptically to denote a person from the locality in question; cf. below, p. 199. It has not been identified.[7]

Pupelina 1148 119.—OFr *Po(u)peline* f. Cf. OFr *popelin* 'child', ModFr (16th c.) *poupeline* 'doll'; *FEW* ix. 601ff. Norman examples of the name are

---

[1] Earlier examples are (seruitium) *Picardi* 1121 *AC* 8 (Winchester), *Picard' c.* 1123 *AC* 19, (terra) *Picardi* Archar' 1130 *P* 83 (Nth), *Picard'* de Domfront, a Norman (E or Ht), 1130 *P* 53. Our man is *Pag' filius Pichardi* 1160/1 *P* 57 (Ha). His son, *Radulfus filius Pagani Pichard*, is mentioned in *Malmesbury Reg*, 35 (late 12th c.).

[2] There are several bearers of the name and byname in DB 1086 (Ellis *Introduction* ii. 367, Tengvik 379), among them the notorious sheriff of Cambridgeshire. On *Picot de Sai* (Orne) see Loyd 96. There is no need to assume, with Reaney, the existence of an OFr pers.n. *Pic* (+suffix).

[3] See M.-T. Morlet in *Rev. internat. d'onomastique* 12 (1960), 219.

[4] A latinized variant of this byname is seen in *Herbertus pedes ferri* 12th c. *LVH* 126.

[5] Cf. also (de tenemento) Leofwini *Pilloc*, (quod fuit)

Leofwine *Pilloc*, 12th c. J. Stevenson (ed.), *Chronicon monasterii de Abingdon*, ii (RS, 1858), 330, 332, Gilbertus *Pilloc* a 1225 W. H. Hart (ed.), *Historia et cartularium monasterii S. Petri Gloucestriae*, ii (RS, 1865), 232, Henr' *Pilloc*, Henr' *Pille* 1278/9 *RH* ii. 806 (Oxford). Could we in fact be concerned here with a real nickname, *Pilla*, *Pilluc*, related to OE *pīl*?

[6] Reaney's alternative suggestion that ME *Pot(te)* is an aphetic form of *Philpot* seems unnecessary.

[7] There is no corresponding place in Ha. Puxol (Fareham parish) is *Pukesole* 1233 (ex inf. Mr. J. E. B. Gover). In the pl.n. under notice the second el. is WS -*hēale* > ME -*hēle*, dat. sg. of *healh* 'nook, corner of land, watermeadow'. The first could be an OE *pūc*, which is presupposed by ModE *pouk*, *powk* 'a small blister, pustule' (*NED*, *EDD*), perhaps used as a nickname.

(Ernaldo filio) *Popelinę* c. 1050 *RADN* 285, (mansuram) *Popeline* 1180–9 *RAH* ii. 366, (de Ansch') *Poupeline* 1198 *MRSN* 348. For later ME instances see Reaney *Origin*, 228.

R

(Robertus filius) **Radulfi** *c.* 1110 47, 54, *Radulfus* Brito 31, ∼ clericus 243, ∼ de Felgeriis 13a, ∼ de Mortuomari 141, 142, *Radulfo* (dat) de Mortuomari 148, *Radulfus* de Tuberilli 118, ∼ Escouell' 118, ∼ filius Raingard' 288, ∼ Holinessone 117, ∼ homo Herberti camerarii 292, ∼ presbiter 177, ∼ Rosell' 20, (filius) *Radulfi* Roselli 1, 5, 19, (terra) ∼ Roselli 80, (filius) ∼ Russel 199, 200, 201, 216, *Radulfus* taneator Cattessone 208; **1148** ∼ 357, (Herebertus filius) *Radulfi* 574, 596, 829, (Iohannes filius) ∼ 140, 143, 155, (Robertus filius) ∼ 892, *Radulfus* aurifaber 115, (de heredibus) *Radulfi* camerarii 72, (heredes) ∼ camerarii 806, 918, (uxor) ∼ camerarii 978, *Radulfus* capellanus 1003, ∼ caretarius 657, 822, ∼ carnifex 677, ∼ clericus 14, 654, 659, 1001, ∼ cocus 61, ∼ Cointe 890, 896, ∼ Cuinta 1021, ∼ Cuinte 974, 995, (de) *Radulfo* Cuinta 39, (de) ∼ 896, *Radulfus* 39 *bis*, ∼ de Bichint' 591, ∼ de Bosco 359, (uxori) *Radulfi* de Clera 945, *Radulfus* de Dummera 641, ∼ de Morsted' 742,[1] ∼ de Oili 122, ∼ de Ouint' 759, ∼ de Port 138, *Radulfo* (dat) de Port 473, *Radulfus* de Walteruile 879, (terris . . .) *Radulfi* de Wingeham 63, *Radulfus* Duchet 306, ∼ filius Amfridi parmentarii 636, (de) *Radulfo* filio Burewoldi 292, *Radulfus* filius Cheppi[n]g' 466, ∼ filius Petri 386, 397, ∼ filius Sewala 718, ∼ 719, ∼ filius Suarling' 124, ∼ filius Vlfi 125, ∼ Lacchewei 74, 420, ∼ 420, *Radulfo* (dat) Lacchewei 74, *Radulfus* Lupus 569, ∼ nepos Godefridi 642, ∼ presbiter 976, ∼ sacrista 300, ∼ Sciteliure 1031, ∼ Soggera 747.—OG *Radulf*; *DBS* s.n. Ralf.[2]

Raimbaldus 205; *Reimboldus* **1148** 843.—OG *Rainbald*; Forssner 209, *DBS* s.n. Rainbow.

Raimerus **1148** 923.—OG *Ragimer*, *Raimar*; Forssner 207, Morlet 183.

(Willelmus filius) **Raimundi** **1148** 800, *Reimundus* 357, ∼ parmentarius 40, *Raimundus* parmentarius 85, 734, 777.—OG *Raimund*; Forssner 207, Morlet 185, *DBS* s.n. Raymond. Note also (de domibus que

fuerunt) *Reimundi* 1174–88 *PRBW* 159, (Petro filio) ∼ ibid. (Winchester), the reference being to R. parmentarius.

(Ricardus filius) **Rainer'** 1148 376.—OG *Rainer*; Forssner 210, *DBS* s.n. Rayner.

(Radulfus filius) **Raingard'** *c.* 1110 288.—OG *Raingard* f.; Förstemann 1229, Morlet 184.[3]

Rand' Bonus Homo 1148 481, ∼ de Morsteda 630,[1] ∼ presbiter 543.—OG *Randulf*; Förstemann 1247f., Morlet 187. Reaney, *DBS* s.n. Randolph, incorrectly derives the name from a nonexistent ON *Rannulfr.[4]

Rannulfus Crispus *c.* 1110 80, *Ranulfus* dapifer Herberti camerarii 55, *Rannulfus* de Curleio 175, *Ranulfus* filius Roberti Dop 281, *Rann'* Pasturellus 82.—OG *Hrannulf*, *Rannulf*; Forssner 211f., Morlet 135.

Raulot 1148 246.—OFr *Ra(o)ul* < OG *Radulf* with the OFr diminutive suffix -*ot*.

Reginaldus de Sagio 1148 186, 226, 228, 411, 417, 440, 621, ∼ de Sag' 156, ipse ∼ 228, ∼ filius Edulfi 594, ∼ Longus 388.—OG *Re(g)inald*; Forssner 208, *DBS* s.n. Reynold.

Reimboldus, see *Raimbaldus*.

Reimundus, see *Raimundus*.

Ricardus capellanus comitis de Mellent *c.* 1110 2, ∼ de Curci 45, 53, ∼ Dublel 290, ∼ faber 127, ∼ prepositus 113, 189, 204, ∼ tailator 36; **1148** *Ricardus* 139, 501, 956, 1050, (de) *Ricardo* 139, (Walteri filii) *Ricardi* 205, 559, (Waltero filio) ∼ 562, *Ricardus* acularius 20, ∼ Baganorus 38, (filia) *Ricardi* budel 432, *Ricardus* carnifex 59, ∼ clericus 44, 48, 53, ipse ∼ 48, ∼ cocus 664, (Andreas filius) *Ricardi* cordwanarii 628, *Ricardus* coruesarius 926, 1010, ∼ coruesarius 1024, ∼ Cuillebrant 560, ∼ de Baiaco 7, 10, idem ∼ 8, ∼ de Braio 309, ∼ de Exon' 438, ∼ de Haia 1067, ∼ de Limesia 536, (de) *Ricardo* de Limesia 535, ∼ (dat) de Limesia 544, (hospicium . . .) *Ricardi* de Ricarduill' 821, (uxor) ∼ filii Gunfridi 285, *Ricardus* filius Lambricht 555, 564, ∼ Lambert 916, ∼ filius Odonis 351, ∼ filius Odoni[s] 380, ∼ filius Rainer' 376, ∼ filius Robert[i] Petit 226, ∼ filius Turoldi 25, ∼ frater Iuonis 384, ∼ fundor 182, 229, 231, 255,[5] ∼ furbar' 831, ∼ Galne 779, ∼ Grailepeis 823, ∼ Loer' 483, item ∼ 484, ∼ Longus 534, item ∼ 535, ∼ lorimer 443, 745, (de) *Ricardo*

---

[1] These entries may refer to the same person, the scribe having mixed up the names *Radulf* and *Randulf*.

[2] Note that ON *Rǫðulfr* (rare), ODan *Rathulf* is an adoption of the ContGerm name; see *Personnamn* (*Nordisk kultur*, vii (Stockholm, 1947)), 87, 132, 223.

[3] A later example is (terra que fuit) *Reingard'* a 1206 Urry *Canterbury*, 326, 359 (Canterbury).

[4] This misleading etymology is repeated in his *Origin*, 125, 328.

[5] * Riꝯ* (dat) *Fundori* 1156/7 *P* 104 (Ha).

lorimer 443, *Ricardus* le meddere 180, ∼ medicus 1044, ∼ Niger 224, 251, *Ricardo* (dat) Nigro 38, *Ricardus* pictor 382, ∼ Pinguis 110, ∼ presbiter 322, 590, (de) *Ricardo* Tistede 881.—OG *Ricard*; Forssner 213f., *DBS* s.n. Richard.

(Willelmus filius) **Richefemme 1148** 181.—An OFr nickname, *riche femme* 'rich, noble woman'; cf. the ModFr surname *Richomme*, Dauzat 520.

(pro) **Richer' 1148** 1027, (Iohannes frater) ∼ 49, 943, ∼ presbiter 989.—OG *Richer*; Forssner 214f., *DBS* s.n.

Richild 1148 835.—OG *Richild* f.; Forssner 215.

Robertus c. 1110 97, (Emma uxor) *Roberti* 94, *Roberto* (dat) de Seifrewast 107, (Ranulfus filius) *Roberti* Dop 281, *Robertus* filius Durandi 267, ∼ filius Dur' 71, ∼ filius Fulcheredi 52, (de feudo) *Roberti* filii Ham' 96, *Robertus* filius Nunne 253, ∼ filius Osberti de Auco 75, ∼ filius Radulfi 47, 54, (Emma uxor) *Roberti* filii Wasferi 99, *Robertus* filius Wimundi 7, 41, 62, 65, ∼ frater Warini 176, ∼ Fresle 181, ∼ Maleductus 45, 53, 56, (pater ipsius) *Roberti* 53, (filius) ∼ Marmion 230, *Robertus* pistor filius Willelmi 73, ∼ scaldeator 167; **1148** ∼ 5, 754, 862, ∼ Abendon' 679, ∼ Bell' 316, (de) *Roberto* Bontens 937, *Robertus* Crassus 316, ∼ de Baioc' 1001 *bis*, *Roberto* (dat) de Campesiet 704, *Robertus* de Columbiers 875, (filia) *Roberti* de Diua 34,[1] *Robertus* de Hungerford 123, *Roberto* (dat) de Hungerfort 738, ∼ de Inglesh' 417, *Robertus* de Ingl' 1, 26, 55, 66, 127, 506, 553, 579, 602, item ∼ 580, *Roberto* (dat) de Ingl' 555, (de feudo) *Roberti* de Oili 25, *Robertus* de Pont' 270, ∼ de Ponte 830, ∼ de Sancto Pancratio 31, 260, 345, 356, 670, 692, 700, ∼ 316, idem ∼ 693, *Roberto* (dat) de Sancto Pancratio 283, (de) ∼ de Sancto Pancratio 316, ∼ (dat) de Sifrewast 288, *Robertus* de Turwill' 416, ∼ elemosinarius 441, 451, 495, 726 *bis*, idem ∼ 716, (de) *Roberto* elemosinario 716, *Robertus* faber 177, ∼ 220, (de) *Roberto* fabro 220, *Robertus* filius Cupp' 395, ∼ filius Estm' 369, ∼ filius Hugonis 851, *Roberto* (dat) filio Hunfridi 223, 870, 873, 898, 899, *Robertus* filius Radulfi 892, ∼ frater Goda Hacchemus 568, (Emma uxor) *Roberti* fratris Warini 479, *Robertus* Grifin 798, *Roberto* macone 96, *Robertus* Marc' 517, ∼ Mart' 9, ∼ la Martra 67, ∼ Martre 310, ∼ Matre 443, ∼ Mieta 208, ∼ Norreis

660, 676, 678, 710, *Roberto* (dat) Norreis 73, 659, 672, 673, 674, 675, 717, ∼ 661, eidem ∼ 677, *Robertus* Oisun 40, 870, 877, 881, ∼ Oison 983, idem ∼ 882, ∼ parmentarius 373, (Ricardus filius) *Robert[i]* Petit 226, *Robertus* Pinguis 533, 559, 566, 687, 698, 996, ∼ presbiter 595, ∼ Putheld' 236, ∼ Quadde 541, ∼ Rust 178, (Henricus filius) *Roberti* scoter' 452, *Robertus* sellarius 305, ∼ sutor 1025, ∼ taleator 134, ∼ Trotardin 59, ∼ Turlux 1074, (uxor) *Roberti* unctarii 61, *Robertus* 61, ∼ Wint' 173.—OG *Robert*; Forssner 216f.

Rogerus Amberlang' *c.* 1110 249, ∼ filius Armerlanc 20, ∼ 20, ∼ episcopus Salesberie 75, ∼ filius Geroldi 34, ∼ frater abbatis 72, 73, ∼ Patinus 43, ∼ Siccus 23; **1148** ∼ 26, (de) *Rogero* 26, *Rogerus* 451 *bis*, 856, (Willelmus filius) *Rogeri* 434, 464, 508, 519, *Rogerus* Abonel 971, 973, 991, (uxor) *Rogeri* aurifabri 323, (uxor) ∼ 323, *Rogerus* Blundus 368, ∼ cocus 803, 931, (uxor) *Rogeri* coci 605, *Rogerus* de Forest 498, ∼ de Haia 38, 90, 91, 104, 903, 913, 1043, idem ∼ 38, 73 *bis*, (de) *Rogero* de Haia 73, (que fuit) *Rogeri* de Meleford' 799, *Rogero* (dat) de Port 580, 581, eidem ∼ 582, 583, *Rogerus* de Sagio 74, ∼ de Wdecota 33, ∼ dispensator 779, ∼ filius Chepping' 462, ∼ filius Chupping' 1080, ∼ filius Gunt' 415, ipse ∼ 29, (de) *Rogero* filio Gunt' 29, *Rogerus* Lippe 361, (de) *Rogero* Macher' 221, *Rogerus* Mercherel 57, ∼ molendinarius 874, ∼ palmarius 142, ∼ parmentarius 735, ∼ pictor 27, 379, ∼ pistor 342, ∼ Pofil 391, ∼ tinctor 52, 77, 663, idem ∼ 77 *bis*, ipse ∼ 78, (de) *Rogero* 78, *Rogerus* vinetarius 571, ∼ 573, (de) *Rogero* vinetario 573, *Rogerus* Witepe 480.—OG *Roger*; Forssner 217f.

Rotrogus 1148 893.—OG *Hrodroh*, *Rotroc*; Forssner 220f., Morlet 138.

Rualdus filius Faderlin *c.* 1110 29; **1148** ∼ 988.—OG *Hrod(w)ald*, (Rom.) *Roald*; Förstemann 916, Morlet 138. Cf. also *Roaldus* 1086 DB Lei 233, *Ruald* Adobed DB D 114b, *Ruthald c.* 1100 *LVH* 72, *Ruold se cniht c.* 1120 Earle 259 (D), *Ruald'* Croc 1130 *P* 17, 39 (Ha).[2]

Rucche 1148 225.—Probably an original byname, OFr *rusche* 'bee-hive; a kind of basket', Norm. dial. *ruche* 'a measure for grain, half a bushel'; *FEW* x. 581ff.

---

[1] *Rodbertus de Diue, LVH* 50.
[2] Some of the bearers may have come from Brittany where the name appears to have been popular. Of Breton origin was clearly *Rualdus filius Wigani*, an important landowner *temp.* Henry I; see *EHR* 14 (1899), 418–19, 1130 *P* 46, 99, 155; note also *Rualdus constabularius* (of

Duke Conan IV) *c.* 1170 *RAH* i. 441, *Ruaud'* Brito 1198 *MRSN* 299. The ninth- and eleventh-century forms quoted by J. Loth, *Chrestomathie bretonne* (Paris, 1890), 161, could in fact all go back to OG *Rodald*. On *Rud-* by the side of *Rod-* (< OG *Hrōd-*) in West Frankish sources see Kaufmann *Unters.* 246, *Erg.-Bd* 202.

S

(domus) **Safugel** 81.—OE *Sæfugel*; *NPN* 115.[1]

Saier, see *Seiher*.

Saiet c. 1110 256; 1148 (heredes) *Saieti* 848, (Herebertus filius) ∼ 1078.—OE *Sægeat*; *PNDB* 353. Note also *Saiet*, *Saied*, mon. Winchester, Henry I, *BMC* 298, 104, *Saiet*, do., Stephen, *BMC* 129, *Saietus* monetarius 1130 *P* 40.

Saieua c. 1110 175; 1148 ∼ 242.—OE *Sægifu* f.; *PNDB* 353.

Samuel 1148 251, *Samueli* (dat) 451, (de) *Samuele* 451 bis.—The biblical name; Withycombe 250f.

Sanson 1148 129, *Sansoni* (dat) 128, (Philippus filius) *Sanson* 227, ∼ monetarius 64, 118,[2] ∼ 65.—The biblical name; Withycombe 250, *DBS* s.n. Sampson. A pre-conquest Norman instance is *Sansonis* (gen) *de Turri* 1030 *RADN* 192.

(uxor) **Sauar'** 1148 126.—The abbreviation probably stands for *Sauarici*, the latinized genitive of OG *Savaric*, on which see Forssner 223, Morlet 195, Tavernier-Vereecken 175.[5]

Sawalo c. 1110 287, ∼ presbiter 105, *Sawale* presbiter 219, *Sawalus* presbiter 36, *Sewal* presbiter 215; 1148 (Radulfus filius) *Sewala* 718.—OG (Rom.) *Saxwalo*, *Saswalo*; Forssner 223, Morlet 193f.[3] The reduction of [ks] to [s] and the subsequent effacement of the spirant are due to OFr sound-development; see *PNDB* §§ 112, 142.[4] The el. *-wala*, *-walo*, a weak variant of OG *-walh*, occurs in some names in OFr and Flemish records; see also Mansion 42 (on *Adalwala*) and Tavernier-Vereecken 38.

Sawardus, see *Sewardus*.

Sawinus 180, 217, ∼ frater Wnstani 175; c. 1110 ∼ 115, 212; 1148 *Sewinus* 741, ∼ de Barra 744, (terra) *Sewini* de Pol 742.—OE *Sæwine*. If *Sewinus de Barra* was a Norman we have in his case OG *Sewin* or

(Rom.) *Seiuin* (< OG *Sigwin*), for which see Morlet 196, 199.

Scerpt 1148 757.—For *Scerpa*, *-e*? If so we have OE *Sce(a)rpa*, an original byname from OE *scearp* 'sharp, quick, smart', as in *healðegen Scearpa* 1026 *KCD* 742. On late WS *ea* > *e* after initial *sc* see Campbell § 312.

Scorphanus c. 1110 195, *Escorfan* 38; 1148 *Scorfan* 563.—The same man is mentioned in the 1130 Pipe Roll: *Scorfano* (dat) 4, 5, 76, 108. It is interesting to note that two fictitious characters in the OFr *chanson de geste* 'Floovent' are called *Escorfan*: a Saracen king and a Duke of Brittany. The form *Escorfant* occurs in another OFr poem and there are at least some eighteen persons in the French medieval epics called *Escorfaut*, including eight Saracens, one king of Saxony, one Persian giant, etc.[6] The name has not been explained. See Addenda.

(Lewinus) **Scottelauessone** 174.—Evidently, as Reaney suggests,[7] an OE *Scotlaf*, the first member being OE *Scott* 'Scot', which, though used by itself as a pers.n. and byname,[8] is not recorded as an el. in OE dithematic names. A close semantic parallel is provided by the numerous names in *Peoht-*; see Searle 387 and *Piterun* above.

Seburga c. 1110 234; 1148 *Seburg'* 839.—OE *Sæburh* f. The 1110 example is the earliest occurrence of the name on record. Other Ha instances are *Sæburh* 12th c. *LVH* 125, (Wluuinus &) *Sæbu[r]ch uxor eius*, *LVH* 124. Cf. *DBS* s.n. Seaber.

(Gaufridus filius) **Segar'** 1148 1046.—OE *Sægar*; *PNDB* 352f., *DBS* s.n. Sagar.

Segrim 1148 337, 725.—ON *Sægrimr*, perhaps an Anglo-Scand formation; *PNDB* 353,[9] Fellows Jensen 284, *DBS* s.n. Seagrim.

Seiher 1148 1083, (de) *Saiero* 484.—OG *Sigiheri*, (Rom.) *Saiher*, *Saier*. In OFr, *Sigi-* became *Sei-* (Pope § 228), of which *Sai-* is an AN variant (*PNDB* § 38).[10] Cf. Ekwall *Genitive*, 89, *DBS* s.n. Sayer.

---

[1] Other Ha instances are *Sæfugel* 11th-c. *LVH* 64, *Sefuel* 12th-c. *LVH* 126.

[2] A moneyer named *Sanson* worked under Stephen, but his mint is uncertain; *BMC* ii, p. 381. See further below, p. 415 and Table 43.

[3] Pre-conquest Norman examples are *Sauuali* (gen) laici 1024 *St. Wandrille* 39, (signum) *Sasuuali* 1027–35 (orig.) *RADN* 216, *Sauvalus*, *Sagualus* 1050–66 (13th c.) *RADN* 383. *Sasuualo* is well evidenced in DB 1086.

[4] The form (Willelmus filius) *Sahuala* 1086 DB Sf 412 illustrates the intermediate stage [χ] that preceded the complete effacement of pre-consonantal [z] < [s].

[5] The first el. may be a Rom. form of OG *Swāba-*; see Kaufmann *Erg.-Bd* 333.

[6] Langlois 198–9; note also Rob' *Escorfaut* 1203 *MRSN*

529 (Coutances).

[7] *SMS*, 18 (1953), 101.

[8] Recorded as a pers.n. from 1082 onwards, as a byn. from c. 1100; see *PNDB* 356, n. 5, *DBS* s.n. Scott. The only pre-conquest example of the name occurs on two purported Stamford coins, Æðelred II, *BEH* 3538–9, but these are probably not English; see G. van der Meer in R. H. M. Dolley (ed.), *Anglo-Saxon Coins* (London, 1961), 175.

[9] The Lund eleventh-century moneyer mentioned *PNDB* 353, n. 2 was an Englishman, not a Dane.

[10] A great number of forms in *Sei-* (9th–11th c.) are listed by Morlet 197ff., Drevin 47. In DB 1086 we have *Seibertus* Co 125 and *Seifridus*, *Sæifridus* C 200b, by the side of *Safridus* Nt 287b.

Selida 1148 162, 935, ~ batar' 217, *Selid'* machun 297, ~ maco 340, (de) ~ Ruffo 292.—OE *Sælida*; *PNDB* 353, *DBS* s.n. Sallitt. One *Salidus* was abbot of Hyde Abbey 1149–71, *LVH* 41.

Selieua 1148 704.—OE *Sæleofu f. This name has not been recorded before.[1] *-leofu* is an irregular form, probably due to the analogy of such fem. elements as *-gifu* and *-lufu*.[2]

Seman' 1148 116, *Semannus* bolengarius 924, *Seman* harangarius 237.—OE *Sæmann*; *DBS* s.n. Seaman. Later Winchester examples are *Seman* de Thedden' 1207 *Fine R* 457, ~ Cordub' ibid.

Semitonius 1148 1084.—From Lat *semitonium* 'half-tone'; cf. MLat *semitonus* idem (Latham).

Serlo 1148 131, 756.—OG *Serlo*; *PNDB* 357f., *DBS* s.n. Searl. One *Serlo filius Pagani* is mentioned as a former house-owner outside East Gate in Winchester, a 1210–11 *PRBW* 159.

(**Emma uxor**) **Sermonar'** 1148 312, (uxor) ~ 601.—OFr *sermoneor, sermonier* 'preacher', latinized *sermonarius*.[3] ME *sermoner* is recorded from 1325 (*NED*). See also *DBS* s.n. Sermin.

Sewal(a), see *Sawalo*.

Sewardus 264; *c.* 1110 *Sawardus* 88; 1148 *Sewardus* 906, *Seward'* serviens abbatisse 586.—OE *Sæweard*; *DBS* s.n. Seward.

Sewi 1148 69, 964, (Eva uxor) ~ 699, (Godefridus filius) ~ 532, 764, 780, *Sewico* (dat) 751.—OE *Sæwig*; *PNDB* 354. In the last form, *-wic* reflects an AN spelling-pronunciation of *-wig*, see *PNDB* § 133.

Sewinus, see *Sawinus*.

Sewlf serviens 1148 1041, (iuxta domum) *Sewlfi* servientis 1001.—OE *Sæwulf*; *DBS* s.n. Self.

Sideloc 22.—OE *Sidlocc, an original byname, 'with long curls', OE *sid* 'wide, broad, spacious; (of clothes, hair, etc.) long, hanging' (BT s.v., III), *locc* 'curl'; cf. OE *sidfeax* 'with long hair' (BT). A later example is *Sideloc*, mon. Wareham, William I, *BMC* 1038–40, 1042.

(**Alwinus**) **Sidessone** 1.—Probably OE *Scid, a nickname from *scid* 'thin slip of wood, shingle, billet' with AN *s* for initial *sc*, as in the Wt pl.n. Shide,

DB *Side, Sida*; cf. below, p. 225. OE *sid*, on which see the preceding entry, would be a formally possible alternative, but does not seem to have been used with reference to persons.

Siluester 1148 61, 62, 98, 394, 412, 531, 546, 587, 597, 598, 634, 636, 640, 764, 768, (catalla) *Siluestri* 62, (de) *Siluestro* 636.—MLat *Siluester*; *DBS* s.n. Silvester, Withycombe 257.

Simenel 1148 724.—An OFr diminutive of *Simon* (q.v.). Cf. the ModFr surname *Simenel, Simonel*; Dauzat 553.

Simon *c.* 1110 114, ~ dispensator 283; 1148 ~ 258, *Symon* 359, ~ de Hangelt' 338, *Simon* dispensator 1069.—The biblical name. See also *Simenel*.

Simphorianus 1148 311.—Lat (Greek) *Symphorianus*. The name of a saint who is supposed to have been martyred at Autun in the second or third century and whose cult spread throughout France.[4] See Addenda.

Sired parmentarius 1148 334.—OE *Sigered*; *PNDB* 360f., *DBS* s.n. Sired.

(**domus**) **Siremani** 95.—OE *scirmann* 'governor of a shire, sheriff, steward'; cf. Æþelwine *scirman* 1017–20 *ASWrits* 26 and see also Tengvik 268. An alternative source would be an OE *Scirmann, a compound of the name-themes *scir* 'bright' and *mann*.

Sitcelane 1148 108.—This might be an unidentified local name (road- or field-name) from OE *sic* 'a small stream, a piece of meadow along a stream' (*EPN* ii, 121f.) and OE *lanu* 'lane, narrow road'. If so *tc*, which stands for [ts], would be an AN substitute for OE [tʃ]. On the occasional use of pl.ns in a personal-name function see below, p. 199.

(**domus**) **Siwardi** Leuerunessone 53; *c.* 1110 *Siuardus* Mus 192; 1148 *Siwardus* de Hedeleia 620, ~ monetarius 112, 512,[5] (domum) *Siwardi* monetarii 511.—OE *Sigeweard*.

Smiewinus 198.—OE *Smeawine*; *PNDB* 366, *DBS* s.n. Smewing. On *ie* for OE *ea* see below, p. 224.

Sonricus hosarius 57.—Probably an OE *Sunnric, the first el. being OE *sunne* 'sun' as in OE *Sunngifu* f., *Sunnhild f., and *Sunnwine*.[6] There is no corresponding OG name. See also *Sunabella*.

---

[1] It may survive in the ModE surname *Sealeaf* as Reaney thinks, *DBS* s.n., but the ME forms adduced by him are all from OE *Sælufu* f., on which see *PNDB* 353.

[2] A clear case of the use of *-leofu* is *Eadleofu* f., 969 (orig.) *AS Ch* 46. The grammatically correct form occurs in *Ælfleof*, a nun at Romsey, *c.* 1030 *LVH* 62.

[3] Not recorded in classical or medieval Latin.

[4] J. Baudot and L. Chaussin, *Vie des saints*, viii (Paris,

1949), 418ff. Relics of the saint were preserved at Hyde Abbey (and at New Minster?), Winchester; see *LVH* 151.

[5] *Siward*, mon. Winchester, Stephen, *BMC* 130–1. See below, p. 416 and Table 43.

[6] *Sunngifu*, which was borrowed in ON as *Sunnifa*, is well evidenced from 1066 onwards; Forssner 226, Boehler 117, Fellows Jensen 271f. *Sunnhild is attested by the ME forms *Sunild'* 1201 *Pleas before the King or*

Spilemanus brandwirchte 294; *c.* **1110** *Spileman'* presbiter 244; **1148** ~ 240.—OE *Spilemann*,[1] from **spilemann* 'player, jester', probably a native formation from *spilian* 'to sport, play' and hence a synonym of OE *spilere*. See *ELPN* 64f., M. Förster, *Anglia*, 62 (1938), 68, *DBS* s.n. Spillman.

Spiringus **1148** 927, *Spirig'* 215.—An *ing*-derivative of OE *spīr* 'spike, blade', a later Hampshire instance being (de Willelmo) *Spiring* 1210–11 *PRBW* 114. See also *DBS* s.n.

Stanulfus, see *Steinulfus*.

Steinulfus 234, (domus) *Stanulfi* presbiteri 45.—ON *Steinolfr*; *PNDB* 373f. Not found in Denmark or Normandy. *Stanulf* may be OE **Stānwulf*.

Stephanus **1148** 643, 644, 865, 900, 939, (de) *Stephano* 900, (terra) *Stephani* archidiaconi 817, *Stephanus* de Crichelad' 316, *Stephano* (dat) de Crech' 319, ~ 316, 317, *Stephanus* filius Hugonis 453, ~ frater Iohannis 409, 1068, ~ Mucheto 89, ~ Sarazinus 951.—Lat *Stephanus*; Withycombe 260, *DBS* s.n. Stephen.

Stigandus *c.* **1110** 261, ~ clericus 242; **1148** ~ 88, ~ archidiaconus 688, 762, ~ 783, ~ 784, *Stigando* (dat) 784, ~ archidiacono 783, *Stigandus* filius Goscelini 197, ~ maco 807, *Stigando* (dat) maconi 806, (managium) *Stigandi* 806, *Stigandus* parmentarius 387.—ON *Stigandr*; *PNDB* 374f., Fellows Jensen 266. Six pre-conquest Norman bearers of the name are listed by Adigard 138f., 315ff.

Stiward, see Occupational Bynames.

Strod **1148** 796.—An original byname, OE *(ge)strod* 'confiscation, robbery, plunder, booty'.

(Radulfus filius) **Suarling'** **1148** 124.—ON **Svartlingr* or OE *swertling* 'titlark'; *PNDB* 379. One *Swartl[ing]*

was a *puer* at New Minster, Winchester, *c.* 1070, *LVH* 35.[2]

Suein' *c.* **1110** 241.—ON *Sveinn*, ODan *Swen*; *PNDB* 380f., *ELPN* 81, *DNS* s.n. Swain. For an early Norman example see Adigard 318.

Sueta *c.* **1110** 202.—OE *Swēta*; Redin 54.[3]

Suift **1148** 760.—OE *Swift*; Redin 26, *DBS* s.n. Cf. also (de duabus terris que fuerunt Willelmi) *Swift* 1210–11 *PRBW* 159 (Winchester).

Sunabella **1148** 180.—ME *Sunne* f., latinized *Sunna*,[4] a short form of names in *Sun(n)-*; see *Sonricus* above. The byname is Lat *bella*, OFr *bele* 'beautiful'.

Suot 288.—OE *Swōt*; Redin 15.[5]

Surpap **1148** 965.—A nickname from OE *sūr* 'sour' and ME *pap(p)* 'soft or semi-liquid food for infants or invalids; mash, paste, pulp' (*NED* s.v. *pap*, first recorded *c.* 1430).

T

Tailebroc **1148** 75, 470, 651, *Taillebroc* 608.—A Norman nickname, the first el. being the imperative of OFr *taillier* 'to strike, cut', as in *Taillebosc*, *Taillefer*, etc.,[6] the second probably OFr *broche*, ONFr *broc*, 'spike, prong; spit; spigot', for which see *FEW* i. 543ff., Godefroy viii. 379.[7] Note also the OFr figurative expression *taillier* (or *tranchier*) *la broche (de)* 'to cut short, interrupt' (Tobler-Lommatzsch i. 1156), early ModFr *trencher la broche (à)* 'to cut short' (Huguet ii. 2), literally 'to cut off the spigot'.

(uxor) **Talazin** **1148** 542.—OWelsh *Taliessin*, MBret *Taliesin*, *Talgesin*.[8]

---

his Justices, iii (London, 1967), 52 (Y), and *Sunnild* 1209 (Nf), on which see my note, *Early English and Norse Studies presented to Hugh Smith* (London, 1963), 57. *Sunnwine* occurs in DB *TRE* (*PNDB* s.n.), later examples being (Thome filii) *Sunwine StGreg* 32, (~) *Sunwini* 43, 45, (~) *Sunewini* 46, *Sunewino* (abl) filio Godewini ibid. 52, all *c.* 1200 (K). *Sunegod*, mon. Æðelred II (and later occurrences), and *Suneman*, 963 and later (Forssner 226) are OG. *Sonulf*, 1066 and later, is < ON *Sunnulfr* (Fellows Jensen 272).

[1] Recorded as the name of moneyers at Southampton and Winchester, Æðelred II–Edw. Conf. (sometimes misread as *Swileman*) and of an eleventh-century tenant at Worcester. The **1148** man may be identical with *Spilemannus* 1157/8 *P* 175 (Winchester). Cf. also Redin s.n. *Spila* (p. 54) with references.

[2] Perhaps the same person as the defunct priest of Hyde Abbey referred to in the entry (pro) *Suartlingo sac'*

1122–3 L. Delisle (ed.), *Rouleau mortuaire de B. Vital, abbé de Savigny* (Paris, 1909), Pl. xliii, no. 183.

[3] The *LW* form may also reflect OE *Swēte* f., which occurs *c.* 1030 *LVH* 59. *Sweta c.* 1120 *LVH* 51 could be either gender.

[4] Attested by *Sunna* uxor Rogeri fabri, daughter of Thora, 1202 (Li); Fellows Jensen 271. An early OE pers.n. **Sunna* m. has been inferred from pl.ns; see *DEPN* s.nn. Sonning, Sunbury, and Sunningdale.

[5] Perhaps identical with *Swot* 11th-c. *LVH* 71.

[6] See Tengvik 388, Dauzat 561.

[7] Found as a byname in Normandy, e.g. Goiffredus *Broc* 1025 *RADN* 135, (signum) Walteri *Broc* 1092–6 *Jumièges* i. 120, Rodulfus *Broch c.* 1080 ibid. 105. Cf. also Galt' *Tailleborc* 1198 *MRSN* 439, whose second el. is OFr *borc* 'fortified town'.

[8] See M. Förster, *Der Flussname Themse* (Munich, 1941), 851, K. H. Jackson, *A Historical Phonology of Breton* (Dublin, 1967), § 605.

(Willelmus) **Tardif** *c.* 1110 268; 1148 (uxor) ∼ 858.—OFr *tardif* 'slow, sluggish'; *DBS* s.n. Tardew.

(Alwinus filius) **Tartere** 178.—OE *Tāthere* with an inorganic *r* due to anticipatory dittography or *Torthere* with *a* for *o* by scribal error. Both names are archaic and rare.[1]

Tellebiene 1148 886.—Apparently a phrase-name, OE **telle-bēane* 'count beans', from OE *tellan* 'to count, reckon' and *bēan* f., acc. sg. and pl. *bēane* 'bean(s)'. The meaning of such a nickname is not obvious, but in ME *bēn(e)* was also used as a symbol for something of little value (*MED* s.v.); hence perhaps 'one who counts trifles, hoards worthless things, a miser'. On *LW ie* for OE *ēa* see below, p. 224.

Teodericus, see *Theodricus*.

Terri trauet' 1148 219, *Terricus* vigil 354.—OFr *T(i)erri*, latinized *Terricus* < OG *Theod(e)ric* (q.v.); Forssner 231f., Morlet 69f., *DBS* s.n. Terrey.

Theduinus 1148 1061.—OG *Theoduin*; Forssner 233. There is no native equivalent.

Theodricus 235, ∼ coquus regis 185; *c.* 1110 ∼ presbiter 188; 1148 *Teodericus* molendinarius 990.—OG *Theod(e)ric*; Forssner 231f., *PNDB* 383f. This is the traditional latinized form; for the OFr vernacular form see *Terri* above.

(Osbertus filius) **Thiardi** *c.* 1110 101, (Osbertus filius) *Tihardi* 122, (Osb') *Tiart* 30.—OFr *Thiard* < OG *Theudhard*; Forssner 233.

Thomas de Sancto Iohanne *c.* 1110 30; 1148 (filii) *Thome* clerici 32, (uxor) ∼ clerici 317.—The biblical name; Withycombe 266f.

Tiart, see *Thiardus*.

(Odo) **Ticchemannessone** 133.—OE **ticcenmann* 'man who keeps or breeds kids', the first el. being OE *ticcen* 'kid', as is plausibly suggested by Tengvik (pp. 163f.). The loss of medial *n* is due to assimilation. Cf. also ME *Goteman*, *Bucswayn*; Thuresson 69.

(de) **Tiecia** 1148 79.—OG (Rom.) *Tietsa*, *Teucia*, *Tezia*, f. a hypocoristic form of names in *Theud-*; Morlet 71.[2]

Tihardus, see *Thiardus*.

(domus) **Tochi** 108; 1148 ∼ 469, *Toche* 763.—ON, ODan *Tóki*; *PNDB* 385f., *ELPN* 82, Fellows Jensen 287f., *DBS* s.n. Tookey. Also in Normandy; Adigard 148ff., 419f.

Toli 1148 510.—ODan *Toli*; *PNDB* 386, *ELPN* 82, Fellows Jensen 289f., Adigard 150, 420f. Note also (de Rogero) *Toli* 1210–11 *PRBW* 108 (Ha).

Totelbied 247.—OE *Tottel* (Redin 140) with an added byname, probably *bierd* < OE *beard* 'beard'. The loss of *r* in *bied* would be AN (Pope § 1184). On *LW ie* < OE *ĕa* see below, p. 224. An alternative source of the pers.n. is OE **Tuttel* (q.v.) with AN *o* for *u*.

Trauetier 1148 105, (Terri) *Trauet'* 219.—An occupational byname, OFr *travetier* 'shopkeeper, building contractor' (Godefroy); cf. Anglo-Lat *travetarius* 'carrier, hawker' (Latham). See also below, p. 205.

Trentemars 1148 907, 940, (filii) *Trentem'* 486, 514, (heredes) ∼ 455.—An OFr nickname, *trente mars* (acc. plur. of *marc*) '30 marks'.[3] For semantic parallels cf. the bynames of Osbertus *oitdeniers* or *octodenarii c.* 1130–42 (London)[4] and Perrot *Trentécus* 1292 (Paris),[5] as well as the material listed by Reaney *Origin*, 250.

Trewa 1148 1052.—OE **Trēowa*, an original byname from OE *trēowe*, *trīewe* 'faithful, honest'; Redin 79, *DBS* s.n. True.

Truued 1148 303.—The OFr pt. part. *tro(u)vé* 'found', used as a name in the sense of 'foundling',[6] or OFr *truvet* 'trivet' (Flanders, Picardy, 1315–1586, *FEW* xiii, 292).[7]

Turbertus 1148 310, *Tur'btus* carnifex 669, *Turb'* cocus 235, (de) ∼ War' 292.—A hybrid compound of OScand *Þor-*, *Þur-* and OG *-bert*, formed in Normandy; *PNDB* 390f., *DBS* s.n. Turbard.

Turchetillus butar' 1148 793.[8]—ON *þorke(ti)ll*, ODan *Thorkil*; *PNDB* 394f., *ELPN* 83, *DBS* s.n. Thurkell. Common in Normandy; Adigard 322–6.

Turneteil 1148 969.—The noun *turntail* 'one who turns tail, a coward' has so far not been recorded until 1621 (*NED*). The verbal phrase 'to turn tail', origin-

---

[1] *Tāthere* occurs in an eighth-century charter, in *LVD*, and in the pl.ns Tattershall (Li), Tatterford, and Tattersett (both Nf). *Torthere* is recorded only as the name of a Hereford bishop in the eighth century.

[2] Cf. also *Theodisia* in an OFr charter *c.* 1080, Drevin 48.

[3] One Robert *Trentemars* was a burgess of Winchester in 1207, *Fine R* 453. Andreas *Trentemars* is mentioned in *The London Eyre of 1244* (London, 1970), nos. 212, 282. On Walter *Trentemars* 1260 and Edmund *Trentemars*

1281–1308, both London citizens, see Ekwall *Subs R*, 193.

[4] On him see J. H. Round, *Geoffrey de Mandeville* (London, 1892), 374–5.   [5] Pachnio 49.

[6] See Lebel (p. 95) who adduces an example from 1292. Final *d* in the *LW* form would stand for AN [θ] or [ð] < Lat *-t-*; Pope §§ 346, 356, 1176.

[7] The OFr variant *trevet* occurs as the byname of Robertus *Trevet*, late 12th-c., *Jumièges* ii. 163.

[8] The same as *Turchetillo* (dat) *buter'* 1130 *P* 16 (Do).

ally a falconry term, appears in 1575 (*NED* s.v. turn, 59).

Turoldus 1148 625, (de) *Turoldo* 317, *Turoldus* carnifex 114, (de feudo) *Turoldi* de Estuna 26, (Ricardus filius) ∼ 25, *Turoldus* presbiter 190, ∼ Scuuel' 266, ∼ Scuueil' 272.—ON *Þóraldr*, ODan *Thorald*;[1] *PNDB* 390. Adigard has found 28 pre-conquest occurrences of the name in Normandy (pp. 342–7).

Turpin 1148 885.—MLat *Turpinus*,[2] OFr *Turpin*, *To(u)rpin*; Michaëlsson i. 106–8. Derivation from ON *Þorfinnr*, as proposed by Reaney, *DBS* s.n. Turpin, is clearly impossible.

Turstinus *c.* 1110 75, ∼ clericus 180, 289; **1148** *Turstinus* 641, 707, 1035, (filia Henrici filii) *Turstini* 398, 414, (Edulfus nepos) ∼ 489, 674, idem *Turstinus* 674, ∼ acularius 24, 203, ∼ clericus 221, 385, 493, 496, 510, 572, 673, 696, 701, 749, 785, item ∼ 494, idem ∼ 511, 673 *bis*, 696 *bis*, (soror uxoris) *Turstini* 496, *Turstino* (dat) 696, *Turstinus* Danais 13, ∼ Daneis 727, ∼ Deneis 710, ∼ de Aisel' 204, *Turstino* (dat) de Aisel' 205, ∼ de Fislia 448, ∼ de Ordia 400, *Turstinus* de Wordia 401, ∼ Mansel 813, 836.—ON *Þorsteinn*, ODan *Thorsten*; *PNDB* 396, *ELPN* 83f., Fellows Jensen 313ff., *DBS* s.n. Thurstan. Adigard (pp. 326–40) lists no less than 60 early bearers of the name in Normandy.

(domus) **Tutel** 114.—OE **Tuttel*, a derivative of OE *Tutta*; Redin 111, 144. See also *Totelbied*.

U

Uctredus 211.—OE *Ūhtred*; *PNDB* 398, *ELPN* 66, *DBS* s.n. Oughtred.

Udelina 1148 600.—A Romance derivative of OG *Uda* f.[3] Later Ha instances are *Udelina c.* 1200 *LVH* 142, (Hugone filio) *Udeline* 1210–11 *PRBW* 145. The corresponding masc. name is also found in Ha: (Johannis) *Udelini PRBW* 114. Cf. *Udelot* below.

Udelot 1148 751.—An OFr diminutive of OG *Ud(d)o*.

Ulf *c.* 1110 131, *Ulfus* 229; **1148** (terra) *Ulf* 410, (terra) *Ulf'* 690, (Radulfus filius) *Ulfi* 125, *Ulf* Niwem' 588.—ON *Ulfr*, ODan *Ulf*; *PNDB* 400f., Adigard 460ff.

(domus) **Ulfchetilli** 102.—ODan *Ulfk(et)il*; *PNDB* 399f., *ELPN* 84, Fellows Jensen 325ff., *DBS* s.n. Uncle.

Ulgarus wantar' 195; **1148** *Ulgerus* 1036.—OE *Wulfgār*; *PNDB* 419, *DBS* s.n. Woolgar.

Ulmarus 278.—OE *Wulfmǣr*; *PNDB* 421f., *DBS* s.n. Woolmer.

Ulsild 1148 959.—OE *Wulfhild* f. The *LW* form has *s* for *f* by scribal error.

(domus) **Ulueue** 52, (domus) ∼ Betteslaf 158; **1148** *Wluiua* 335, *Wlueua* 746.—OE *Wulfgifu* f.; *PNDB* 420, *DBS* s.n. Wolvey.

Uluricus, see *Wluricus*.

Ulwardus, see *Wlwardus*.

Unfridus Parfait *c.* 1110 112, *Unsfr'* Parfait 120.—OG *Unfrid*; Forssner 236. The inorganic *s* in the second form is an AN feature.[4]

Urandus presbiter 193.—Probably OG *Wulfhramn*, (Rom.) *Ulfrand* (Morlet 231)[5] with loss of the medial consonant and subsequent vocalization or assimilation of *l*.[6] On *Wlfram*, *Wlfrann* in ME sources see Forssner 260, *ELPN* 106, 116.

Urluid 1148 934.—This, as Professor Kenneth Jackson kindly informs me, is an OBret **Uur-luit*, from *uur* 'man' and *loit*, *luit* 'grey'. The first el. could alternatively be the intensive prefix *uur-*, *uor-*.

(de) **Urselino** Iudeo **1148** 443.—OFr *Urselin* (Morlet 209), a diminutive of OG (Lat) *Urso*. On the latter name see Forssner 236f.

V

Victricus 263.—OE *Wihtrīc*; *PNDB* 414. The name is still found in Winchester in 1207: *Victrich'*, *Fine R* 454.

Viuianus 1148 318.—Lat *Vivianus*,[7] OFr *Vivien*. The name was borne by a fifth-century Gallo-Roman saint and is well evidenced in French records from the

---

[1] Only in the pl.n. *Thoreldorp*, Torrendrup; *DaGP* 1353, s.n. Therels.

[2] A derivative of Lat *turpis* 'ugly, unsightly; unseemly, base'.

[3] For *Uda*, *Ud(d)o* see Förstemann 1472f. On the stem *Ud-* cf. Kaufmann *Erg.-Bd* 363, *Unters.* 118f.

[4] See A. Stimming, *Der anglonormannische Boeve de Haumtone* (Halle, 1899), 227f.

[5] In OFr the Germ. el. -(*h*)*ramn*, -*rann* frequently appears as -*rand*, -*rant*; see Kalbow 91f., Drevin 170, Michaëlsson ii. 119f., and cf. *Walerand* below.

[6] Cf. *Ulricus* > OFr *Ouri*; P. Fouché, *Phonétique historique du français*, iii (Paris, 1966), 855.

[7] I. Kajanto, *The Latin Cognomina* (Helsinki, 1965), 159.

ninth century onwards.[1] Cf. also Bergh 157, O. Brattö, *Studi di antroponimia fiorentina* (Gothenburg, 1953), 202f., *DBS* s.n. Vivian.[2]

W

Walderus taneator *c.* 1110 210; 1148 *Walder'* 264, (pro terra) ~ 651.—OG *Waldheri*, later *Walter*. In French (incl. Norman) and Flemish records the name always appears as *Walter(i)us*, *Gualter(i)us*, *Gauterius*, etc., with medial *t*,[3] but in Low German (Old Saxon) sources we find *Walderus* by the side of *Walterus* and it therefore seems likely that the *LW* forms under notice are in fact of Old Saxon provenance.[4] Cf. *Walderius sacerdos* 1106–24 *LVH* 38, *Walderus presbiter* early 12th c. *ELPN* 108 (London). See also *Walterus*.

(filie) **Walerand'** 1148 389.—OG *Waleramn*, *Waleran*; Forssner 241, Morlet 215. On -*rand* for -*ran* see *Urandus* above.

Walterus Chibus *c.* 1110 64; 1148 ~ de Andeleio 947, (de feudo) *Walteri* de Grainuill' 350, *Walterus* de Ticheb' 799, 827, (de terra) *Walteri* filii Ricardi 205, (de feudo) ~ filii Ricardi 559, *Waltero* (dat) filio Ricardi 562, *Walterus* draper 945, item ~ 945, ~ Martre 202, ~ Meroie 211, ~ parmentarius 992, ~ presbiter 957.—OG *Walter*; Forssner 243f. See also *Walderus*.

Walwain 1148 576.—This is the well-known Arthurian name which appears as *Walwen* in William of Malmesbury (*c.* 1125),[5] as *Walwanus* by the side of *Gualgua(i)nus*, *Gualwanus*, etc., in Geoffrey of Monmouth (*c.* 1135)[6] and as *Walwein* in Wace's *Brut* (A.D. 1155).[7] In Continental French texts the usual form is *Gauvain*.

The etymon is generally held to be OWelsh *Gwalchmei*, the second el. of which was remodelled on the analogy of names like *Owein*, *Iwain*. See the comments in *Sir Gawain and the Green Knight* (2nd rev. edn., Oxford, 1967), 76f.; cf. *DBS* s.n. Gavin;[8] and see Addenda.

(Robertus frater) **Warini** *c.* 1110 176, *Warinus* de Hantona 248, ~ prepositus 78, 79, (per) *Warinum* prepositum 20, (requisivit) ~ prepositum 59; 1148 *Warinus* 1062, (Willelmo filio) *Warini* 66, (Emma uxor Roberti fratris) *Warini* 479, *Warinus* aurifaber 866, 878, idem ~ 878, ~ filius Blachem' 374, ~ rusmangre 194.—OG *Warin*; Forssner 246f., *DBS* s.n. Wareing.

(Hersie filio) **Warner'** 1148 77.—OG *Warinher*, *Warner*; Forssner 247f., Morlet 219.

Wasco, see *Watso*.

(Emma uxor Roberti filii) **Wasferi** *c.* 1110 99.—OBret **Uuasfer*, from *uuas* 'lad, youth, servant' and *fer* 'firm, strong, sturdy'.[9]

Watso 1148 348, *Watsco* 714, (Herebertus filius) *Watscon'* 436, *Wasco* clericus 408.—OG *Wazo*; Forssner 249. *Watscon'* is short for the latinized gen. *Watsconis*. See also *Gazo*.

Wdia 1148 353.—OE *Wudia*; *PNDB* 417. See also *Widie*.

(domus . . .) **Welestani** Opchieher 90.—OE *Wilstān*[10] with AN *e* for *i* (*PNDB* § 12) or rather *Wenestan* < OE *Wynstān*, for which see *Wnstanus* below, with *l—n* < *n—n* by dissimilation. Medial *e* is inorganic; see below, p. 225. See also *Wirstanus*.

Wenestanus, see *Wnstanus*.

(Herebertus filius) **Westman** 1148 463,[11] (de Here-

---

[1] An early example is *Vivianus* comes 844–5 F. Lot and C. Brunel (eds.), *Recueil des actes de Charles II le Chauve*, i (Paris, 1943), 183. For 11th- and 12th-c. instances see P. Boissonnade, *Du nouveau sur la Chanson de Roland* (Paris, 1923), 393. One *Vivianus* witnessed a Norman charter in 1049–58, *RADN* 318 (Lisieux). The occurrences of the name in the French epic romances are listed by Langlois, p. 672.

[2] The earliest occurrences in England seem to be *Viuienes* (gen) *c.* 1100–30 Earle 258 (Exeter), *Vivienus* *c.*1100–16 T. Stapleton (ed.), *Chronicon Petroburgense* (Camden OS, 47, 1849), 175, *Vivianus* 1125–8 ibid. 158, 167 (Nth). None of these examples is noted by Withycombe or Reaney.

[3] Morlet 213, Drevin 49, *RADN* (Index), Mansion 153, Tavernier-Vereecken 41f.

[4] W. Schlaug, *Studien zu den altsächsischen Personennamen des 11. u. 12. Jahrhunderts* (Lund, 1955), 152ff. The el. *Wald-* is common in Old Saxon names.

[5] *Gesta regum* ii. 342.

[6] A. Griscom (ed.), *The Historia regum Britanniae of Geoffrey of Monmouth* (London, 1929), Index.

[7] Ed. I. Arnold (Paris, 1938–40), Index.

[8] The numerous occurrences of the name in OFr and Flemish charters, *c.* 1110–1219, have recently been listed by P. Gallais in his paper 'Bleheri, la cour de Poitiers et la diffusion des écrits arthuriens sur le Continent', *Moyen Age et littérature comparée* (Paris, 1967), 46–79 (with map).—A later English example is *Walewein* 13th-c. *LVD* 84.

[9] *Ex inf.* Prof. Kenneth Jackson.

[10] Note specially *Wilstan* leuita, ~ sacerdos *c.* 1030 *LVH* 25, 26, 61.

[11] The same man appears as *Herbertus filius Westman* in 1166/7, *P* 193 (Winchester). A pre-conquest example of the name is *Westmanus* in the Thorney Abbey *Liber Vitae*; see D. Whitelock, *Saga-Book of the Viking Society*, 12 (1940), 145. Note also (totam terram) *Wesman*, 1068 (Falaise); C. H. Haskins, *Norman Institutions* (Cambridge, Mass., 1918), 39, n. 163.

berto filio) ~ 38, (Herbertus) ~ 478, (Herbertus filius) ~ 506.—ON *Vestmaðr*, ODan *Westman*; *NPN* 175, *DBS* s.n. Westman. Also in Normandy; see note 11, p. 176, above. See Addenda.

Wibertus Saluagius *c.* 1110 3.—OE *Wīgbeorht* or perhaps rather OG *Wigbert*; *PNDB* 413.

Wiburg' *c.* 1110 206, 211.—OE *Wīgburh* f.; Boehler 126, *DBS* s.n. Wyber. No less than five bearers of the name appear at different dates in the *LVH*.[1]

Widie 1148 429.—See also *Wdia*, who may in fact be the same person. *Widia* or *Wudia* was the name of a Winchester moneyer under Cnut–Edw. Conf.; Redin 159f. The variant forms exhibit the same interchange between *i* and *u* as in OE *widu* by the side of *wudu*, no doubt as a result of association with this word. It is possible, however, that in 1148 the two forms were felt and used as entirely separate names.

Wigot de Linc *c.* 1110 154.[2]—ODan *Wigot*; *PNDB* 404, *ELPN* 84, Fellows Jensen 335f, Adigard, 369f.

Willelmus 245; *c.* 1110 (Hubertus filius) *Willelmi* 73, (Robertus pistor filius) ~ 73, *Willelmus* Bertram 156,[3] ~ Brun 294, ~ Brunus 42, ~ de Albinneio 14, 33, ~ de Anesi 115, ~ de Hoctona 196, 245, 273, 278, ~ de Meleford' 277, ~ de Ponte Archar' 49, ~ de Ponthearcar' 173, ~ de Pontearch' 82, 143, ~ de Pont' 259, ~ de Salesberie 144, ~ filius Anschetilli 46,[4] ~ filius Ansgeri 138, 170, (de filio) *Willelmi* filii Gisleberti 49, *Willelmus* filius Odonis 42, ~ filius eius 133, *Willelmo* (dat) filio Odonis 107, *Willelmus* potarius 93, 255, ~ scrutarius 284, ~ Tardif 268; 1148 ~ 40, 1083 *bis*, (que fuit) *Willelmi* 482, (Godefridus filius) ~ 5, 36, 95, 174, 321, 327, 445, 573, *Willelmus* archidiaconus 221, 222, 262, 277, 281, 667, ~ barrar' 1062, ~ Blundus 730, ~ bruwere 188, ~ briwere 199, ~ Caddus 809, ~ clericus 286, 1084, *Willelmo* (dat) clerico 167, *Willelmus* Danzel 526, 527, 549, idem ~ 550, *Willelmo* (dat) de Bradeia 507, *Willelmus* de Cadumo 413, *Willelmo* (dat) de Chaisneto 512, ~ de Chateleia 512, *Willelmus* de Corbulio 198, (uxor) *W[illelmi]* de Glauston' 985, (terra) *Willelmi* de Hoctune 838, (filio) ~ de Hoctun' 74, *Willelmus* de Hotot 814, 816,[5] ~ Hotot 1009, *Willelmo* (dat) de Ipingis 426, *Willelmus* de Piro

55, *Willelmi* (gen) de Pont 671, (de feudo) ~ Pont' 171, *Willelmo* (dat) Pontearch' 830, *Willelmus* de Rotomag' 195, ~ de Suttun' 343, ~ de Sotton' 511, ~ 672, *Willelmo* (dat) de Sutt' 672, *Willelmus* de Templo 1064, ~ de Tocho 360,[6] ~ Durage 349, (terra) *Willelmi* elemosinarii 538,[7] *Willelmus* Exon' 1081, ~ faber 179, 769, (uxor) *Willelmi* fabri 253, *Willelmus* filius Bos 66, 99, 564, ~ filius Estmer' 230, ~ filius Girardi 944, ~ filius Herberti 121, ~ filius Hereberti 618, (de feudo) *Willelmi* filii Manne 9, (filii) ~ filii Odonis 405, *Willelmo* (dat) filio Oin 555, *Willelmus* filius Pot 488, ~ filius Raimundi 800, ~ 800, ~ filius Richefemme 181, ~ filius Rogeri 434, 464, 508, 519, item ~ 465, *Willelmo* (dat) filio Warin' 66, *Willelmus* Gall' 230, ~ lorimer 218, ~ marescallus 315, 529, 1033, ~ Martel 41, 51, 54, *Willelmo* (dat) Martel 35, *Willelmus* Mart' 490, *Willelmo* (dat) *Mart'* 467, 488, 489, 492, ~ Mar' 491, *Willelmus* medicus 1028, ~ Mordant 326, ~ Novus 584, ~ palmarius 407, ~ Peuerel 946, ~ Piec 56, ~ pinctor 120, ~ Pinguis 213, 849, *Willelmo* (dat) Ping' 422, *Willelmus* Polanus 1006, ~ portarius 695, 708, 713, 716 *bis*, ~ Post' 897, ~ presbiter 599, ~ Surlaf 819, 961, ~ tanator 1047, ~ Ulpis 665, ~ vigil 1005, ~ Waranc' 766.—OG *Willelm*; Forssner 255ff., *PNDB* 415.

Wilward' 1148 706.—For *Wulward* or *Wlward* from OE *Wulfweard*. An OE **Wilweard* with the same first el. as *Wilstān* (for which see *Welestan* above) is not on record.

(Robertus filius) **Wimundi** *c.* 1110 7, 41, 62, 65, (uxor) ~ monetarii 22,[8] *Wimundus* presbiter 146; 1148 ~ 332.—OE *Wīgmund* or Norman *Wimund*;[9] *PNDB* 413, *DBS* s.n. Wyman.

Wirstanus *c.* 1110 102.—OE *Wynstān*, *Winstān* with *r* for *n* by dissimilation or OE *Wilstān* with AN confusion of the liquids.[10] See also *Welestanus* and *Wnstanus*.

(Godwinus) **Withmundin** *c.* 1110 132.—An *ing*-derivative of OE *Wihtmund*.

(domus . . .) **Wlfori** 102.—For *Wlfheri*, a latinized gen. of *OE Wulfhere*.

[1] *Wiburh* late 11th-c., p. 71, ~ *c.* 1120, p. 50, *Wiburhc* 12th-c., p. 65, *Wiburga* 12th-c., p. 137, *Wiburc*, ME, p. 145.
[2] Wigot, sheriff of Lincolnshire; see *VCH Hants* i. 535.
[3] Willelmus Bertram was a tenant-in-chief in 1086, DB Ha 47.
[4] One *Willelmus*, son of Ansketillus and Eadgyfu, is mentioned in *LVH* (p. 125, 12th c.).
[5] The pl.n. *Hotot* occurs once elliptically for *Willelmus de Hotot;* see above, p. 162.

[6] He appears as *Willelmus de Thoca* in a Winchester charter, *temp.* Henry I; *EHR* 14 (1899), 424.
[7] *Willelmus elemosinarius* occurs in a Winchester charter *c.* 1130; *EHR* 14 (1899), 423.
[8] *Wimund* was a Winchester moneyer under William I, William II, and Henry I; *SCBI* xi. 176, 177, 259, xii. 168–70. See also below, pp. 399, 410, and Tables 38, 39, and 41.
[9] Ultimately of either ON or OG provenance; Adigard 368f.
[10] See *PNDB* § 60.

Wlueua, Wluiua, see *Ulueue*.

Wluricus 149, (domus) *Vulurici* 56, *Wluricus* presbiter 7; *c.* **1110** *Uluricus* 295; **1148** *Wluricus* caretarius 1019, ∼ de Windes' 1066, ∼ parmentarius 922.—OE *Wulfrīc*.

Wlwardus bedellus 32, *Ulwardus* Cheppe 284, *Wlwardus* harengarius 33; *c.* **1110** *Ulwardus* eius filius [i.e. of Lewing Dol] 139.—OE *Wulfweard*. See also *Wilward*.

Wlwoldus 189.—OE *Wulfwald*.

Wndai 177.—OE **Wyndæg*. If not an error for *Win-*, the spelling *Wn-* reflects the OE variant *Wun-*, on which see *PNDB* 416f. This is the earliest known

example of the name, later occurrences being (Ricardi) *Windai* 1176/7 *P* 139 (Nf or Sf), *Wyndai* de Grendona 1183 (Du),[1] and *Windeh* 12th c. *LVD* (facs.) 42.

(curtillum) **Wnprice** 118.—Unexplained.

(Burewoldus filius) **Wnstani** 181, (Sawinus frater) ∼ 175, (domus) *Wenestani* 86, (domus) ∼ Sotebord 88.—OE *Wyn-*, *Wunstān*. On *Wun-* cf. *Wndai* above. See also *Welestanus*, *Wirstanus* and *Wuinestaham*.

Wuido 9.—OG *Wido*; Forssner 254.

Wuinestaham Escitteport 16.—Probably a garbled form of *Winestan* < OE *Wynstān*; see *Wnstanus* above.

---

[1] W. Greenwell (ed.), *Boldon Buke* (Surtees Soc. 25, Durham, 1852), 41. A different name is *Winedæg*, which was borne by some Canterbury and Romney moneyers, Cnut–Henry I, and by a couple of Canterbury burgesses in the 12th c., on whom see Urry *Canterbury*, *passim*.

ii. THE NAMES ARRANGED BY DATE AND NATIONAL PROVENANCE

In the main index above, which lists all the personal names in the Winton Domesday in one alphabetical sequence regardless of date and provenance, our concern has been strictly linguistic and etymological. However, if we are to trace the evolution of the local onomastic system from the eve of the conquest until the middle of the twelfth century a more varied approach to the material is necessary, based on chronology and other criteria. In the lists given below the names are consequently arranged by survey, with a further division according to national provenance and certain formal and semantic criteria.

Names of Old English and Scandinavian origin have been entered under their standard West Saxon[1] or Old Norse forms, the actual *LW* spellings being added in brackets wherever necessary or desirable for the sake of clarity. Minor orthographic variants have been disregarded. In the case of continental Germanic names where a uniform standard cannot for obvious reasons be established, the *LW* spellings have been used as they stand. Biblical and classical names present no problems; they have been listed under their *LW* forms.[2]

In the case of doubtful etymologies the *LW* form is preceded by a question mark. Alternative derivations of major significance have been indicated by the addition of the abbreviations *OE*, *OG*, or *ON*. Names which occur only as patronymics are preceded by a (p) in brackets. Unrecorded etyma, or those not found in pre-conquest sources, are marked with an asterisk.[3]

The 1066 survey contains the following Old English names of the traditional di-thematic type:

Ælfflæd f. (Alfed),[4] *Ælfgār* (Algar), *Ælfgifu* f. (Alueua), *Ælfhēah* (Elfeg), *Ælfhere* (Alfere), *Ælfmær* (Almar, Elmar, Elmer), *Ælfnōð* (Alnod), *Ælfred* (Alured), *Ælfrīc* (Aluric, Alric), *Ælfstān* (Alestan), *Ælfwald* (Alwold), *Ælfweard* (Alward), *Ælfwīg* (Alwi), *Ælfwine* (Alwinus), *Æðelflæd* f. (Ailflet), *Æðelmōd* (Almod), *Æðelsige* (Ailsi), *Æðelstān* (Estan; or *Ēadstān*), *Æðelwald* (Adelwold), *Æðelweard* (Ailward), *Æðelwīg* (Ailwi), *Æðelwine* (Ailwinus);

Beorhtmær (Brithmar), *Beorhtrīc* (Bictric), *Beorhtstān* (? Brucstan), *Beorhtswīð* f. (Brithsuid), **Beorhtwīf* f. (Brithwif), *Beorhtwīg* (Brictwi), *Beorhtwine* (Brithwinus), *Beorhtwynn* f. (Brithwen), *Brūnmann*, *Brūnstān*, **Brūnwīf* f., *Burgwald* (Burewold);

(p) *Cynesige* (? Chasie), *Ēadgifu* f. (Edewa), *Ēadrīc* (Edric), *Ēadsige* (? Edtie), *Ēadstān* (Estan; or *Æðelstān*), *Ēadwacer* (Edwacre), *Ēadweard* (Edward), *Ēadwīg* (Edwi), *Ēadwine* (Edwinus), *Ealdgȳð* f. (Aldied), *Ealdrēd* (Ald-, Eldred);

(p) *Friðuwine* (Frefhewinus), *Godmann* (Godeman), **Godnōð* (Gonnod), *Godrīc*,

---

[1] On the use of the spelling *-red* for the OE el. *-ræd* see above, p. 145, n. 1.

[2] The Latin endings of the *LW* forms quoted have been omitted except in a few cases where the non-latinized form could not be reconstructed with reasonable certainty, mainly compounds with *-wine*, latinized *-winus*, which tend to apocopate final *-e* in late OE; cf. *PNDB* § 48, *ELPN*, pp. xviiif.

[3] Note that the *TRE* portion of DB is here regarded as a pre-conquest source.

[4] In the present lists names in *Al-* have usually been taken to represent OE parent forms in *Ælf-* although several of them may in fact go back to compounds in *Æðel-* or *Eald-*; for details see the alphabetical and etymological index.

Godrūn f. (Goderun), *Godwine*, **Hēahsige* (Hiechsi), *Hūnbeorht* (Hunbric), *Hūnmann* (Huneman);

Lēodmǣr (Lethmer), *Lēofflǣd* f. (Lefflet), *Lēofgifu* f. (Leueua), *Lēofmann* (Lufman), *Lēofred* (Leuret), *Lēofrīc* (Leuric, Leov-, Lowric), (p) *Lēofrūn* f. (Leuerunessone), *Lēofsige* (? Lursi), *Lēofstān* (Lepstan, Lipestan), *Lēofsunu* (Lupsone), *Lēofswīð* f. (Lesweda), *Lēofwald* (Lewold, Li-, Luwold), *Lēofwine* (Lewinus, Li-, Lu-, Lowinus), *Lēofwynn* f. (Luwen);

Sǣweard (Seward), *Sǣwine* (Sawinus), **Scīrmann* (Sireman), (p) **Scotlāf* (Scottelauessone), *Sigeweard* (Siward), *Smēawine* (Smiewinus), **Stānwulf* (? Stanulf; ON), **Sun(n)rīc* (Sonric), (p) *Tāthere* (? Tartere; or *Torhthere*);

Ūhtred (Uctred), *Wihtrīc* (Victric), *Wilstān* (?Welestan), *Wulfgār* (Ulgar), *Wulfgifu* f. (Ulueua), *Wulfhere* (Wlfor), *Wulfmǣr* (Ulmar), *Wulfrīc* (Wluric), *Wulfwald* (Wlwold), *Wulfweard* (Wlward, Ulward), **Wyndæg* (Wndai), *Wynstān* (Wnstan, Wuinestaham, Wenestan, ? Welestan).

Monothematic names are *Æfic* (Auic), *Babba* (Babbi, gen.), *Bolla* (Bolle), *Brūn*, *Cēoca* (Ceca), *Colling*, *Cypping* (Cheping, Chiping), **Edde* f., *God* (?), *Goda* (Gode), *Goding*, **Hlanc* (? Lanc), *Lāfa* (Laue), *Lang* (? Lanc), *Lēofing* (Leowing, Leuing, Luuing), (p) **Manding* (Mandingessone), *Mann* (? Mandode), *Od(d)a* (Odo; OG), **Pilluc*, *Swōt* (Suot), *Tottel* (Totel), **Tuttel* (Tutel).

A final group of miscellaneous formations, chiefly original bynames, includes **Āncild*, *Balloc*,[1] (p) *Brūncyng* (Brunechingessone, Brincigesone), **Bullocesēage* (Bullochesiega),[1] (p) *Cyng* (Chingessone), *Dodesmere* (pl. n.), *Fugel*, **Hafoc* (Hauoc), **Hāligprēost* (Haliprest), *Lȳtelmann* (Lutemann), **Pott* (Pot),[1] *Pucheshele* (pl.n.), *Sǣfugel* (Safugel), (p) **Scīd* (Sidessone), **Sīdlocc* (Sideloc), *Spilemann*, and (p) **Ticcenmann* (Ticchemannessone).

Names of Continental Germanic provenance in **1066** are *Adelard*, (p) *Aitard* (var. *Etard*), *Andrebode*, *Coleman*, *Emma* f., *Engelric*, *Euerwin*, *Fulcard*, *Fulger* (? Fulges), *Gaufrid*, *Gilebert*, (p) *Goce*, **Godesbrand*, *Godesman*, *Helbing*, *Henric*, *Hizeman*, *Hugelin* (Huchelin), **Isenran* (? Issiran), *Mainbodo* (? Mandode), *Odo* (OE), *Raimbald*, *Theodric*, *Wido* (Wuido), *Willelm*, *Wulfram* (? Urandus).

The Biblical, Greek, and Latin (incl. OFr) element is represented by *Adam*, *Capel* (OFr),[2] *Dalphin*, *Durand*, *Eustachius*, *Hachechasse* (OFr), *Martinus*, *Paganus*, *Petrus*, and *Vitalis* (? Ficellus).

Scandinavian in origin are *Eilaf*, *Farmann*, *Gautr* (Got), *Húni*, (p) *Ketill* (Chetel), *Kol(l)sveinn* (Golsewanus), *Steinolfr*, *Tóki* (Tochi), *Þorsteinn* (Turstin), *Ulfketill*, *Ulfr*.

Chitebaue, *Climehen*, (p) *Douet* (Douetessone), (p) *Ecregel*, and *Wnprice* have been left unexplained.

In the survey of c. 1110 the class of native dithematic names includes:

Ælfgifu f. (Alueua), (p) *Ælfmǣr* (Ælmer, Almar), *Ælfred* (? Alur'; or *Ælfrīc*), *Ælfrīc* (Aluric, ? Alur'), *Ælfsige* (Elsi), *Ælfstān* (Alestan), *Ælfwīg* (Alwi), *Ælfwine* (Alwinus), *Æscwulf* (Essulf), *Æðelweard* (Eilward);

*Bealdfrið (Baluert; OG), *Beorhtwald* (Brithwold), *Beorhtwine* (Bricthwinus), *Blæc-*

---

[1] Also used as a byname. [2] Used elliptically for *Godwinus Capel*.

mann (Blachem'), (p) *Cynewynn* f. (Chiwen), *Ēadgifu* f. (Edeua), *Ēadmund* (Edmund), *Ēadred* (Edred), *Ēadrīc* (Edric), *Ēadweard* (Edward), *Ēadwine* (Edwinus), *Ealdgȳð* f. (Aldied), *Ealdred* (Aldred);

Godwine, *Lēofsidu* f. (Lupsida), *Lēofwine* (Lewinus), *Sǣburh f. (Seburga), *Sǣgēat* (Saiet), *Sǣgifu* f. (Saieua), *Sǣweard* (Saward), *Sǣwine* (Sawinus), *Sigeweard* (Siuard), *Wīgbeorht* (Wibert; OG), *Wīgburh* f. (Wiburg), *Wīgmund* (Wimund; OG, ON), (p) *Wihtmund* (Withmundin), *Wilstān* (? Wirstan; or *Wynstān*), *Wulfrīc* (Uluric), *Wulfweard* (Ulward), *Wynstān* (? Wirstan; or *Wilstān*).

Uncompounded and other formations are ME *Bredful* (Bretfol), *Brūning*, (p) *Catt* (Cattessone), *Cypping* (Chip(p)ing, Cheping), *Dēora* (? Deria), (p) *Fæderling (Faderlin), *Foxprica, *God* (?), (p) *Grēne* (Grenessone), *Hearding* (Hardi[n]g), (p) *Holegn (Holinessone), (p) *Nunna* (Nunne), *Spilemann*, *Swēta* (Sueta).

The Continental Germanic element is represented by *Adelidis* f., *Ainolf*, (p) *Albereda* f., *Alberic*, (p) *Amberlanc*, *Ansger*, *Arnulf*, *Ascelin*, *Audoenus*, *Baldewin*, *Baldfrith* (Baluert; OE), *Baldric*, *Bernard*, (p) *Bertram*, (p) *Boselin*, (p) *Emelina* f., *Emma* f., *Erchembald*, (p) *Erneis*, (p) *Ernuceon*;

(p) *Fulcher*, (p) *Fulchered*, *Gardin*, *Gaufrid*, *Gazo*, (p) *Gerold*, (p) *Gibart*, *Gilebert*, *Girard*, *Gisla* f., *Gisold* (Gesord), *Gisulf*, *Godefrid*, *Goisbert*, *Goisfrid*, *Hamo*, *Henric*, *Her(e)bert*, *Her(e)frid*, *Herluin*, *Hubert*, *Hugo*, *Ingulf* (ON), *Iuo*, *Maiesent* f.;

Odo, (p) *Oil(l)ard*, (p) *Oinus* (ON), *Osbert*, *Radulf*, (p) *Raingard* f., *Rannulf*, *Ricard*, *Robert*, *Roger*, *Ruald*, *Sawalo*, *Theodric*, (p) *Thiard*, *Unfrid*, *Walder*, *Walter*, *Warin*, *Wibert* (OE), *Willelm*, *Wimund* (OE, ON).

The following Scandinavian names occur in the **c. 1110 survey**: *Algot*, *Ásketill* (Anschetill), *Azur* (Atser), *Ingólfr* (Ingulf; OG), (p) *Ióli*, (p) *Oðin* (Oinus; OG), *Stigandr*, *Sveinn*, *Þorsteinn* (Turstin), *Ulfr*, *Wigot*, *Wimund* (OE, OG).

Biblical names are *Helias*, *Iohannes*, *Simon*, and *Thomas*, whilst (p) *Albuchon*, *Blundel*, *Constantinus*, (p) *Durand*, *Nigellus*, and *Picot* are of Latin or OFr provenance.

The small group of Celtic names includes *Hoel*, *Iwen*, *Iudicell*, and (p) *Wasfer*. *Debou'* and *Scorphan* are obscure.

In the 1148 survey the Old English dithematic names are as follows: *Ācwulf* (? Aoulf), *Ælfgār* (Alger), *Ælfgifu* f. (Alueua), *Ælfred* (Alured), *Ælfrīc* (Aluric), *Ælfwine* (Alwinus), *Æðelmǣr* (Ailmer), *Æðelmōd* (Almod), *Æðelrīc* (Ailric), (p) *Æðelstān* (Estan; or *Ēadstān*), *Æðelwaru* f. (Ailware), *Æðelweard* (Ailward), *Æðelwine* (Ailwinus);

Beorhtwine (Brictwinus), *Beorhtwynn* f. (Bricht-, Brictwen), *Blæcmann* (Blacheman), *Blīðhild f. (Blithild; OG), *Brūnhild f., (p) *Brūnmann* (Brum'), *Burgwald* (Burewold, Burold), *Colrūn f., *Dīcwine (Dicheuin), *Ēadgār* (Edgar), *Ēadgȳð* f. (Edit), *Ēadmund* (Edmund), *Ēadred* (Edred), *Ēadrīc* (Edric), (p) *Ēadstān* (Estan; or *Æðelstān*), *Ēadweard* (Edward), *Ēadwine* (Edwinus), *Ēadwulf* (Edulf), *Ealdgȳð* f. (Aldit, Eldit), *Ealdhelm* (Aldelm), *Ealdred* (Aldred), *Ealdwine* (Aldwinus), (p) *Ēastmǣr* (Estmer);

(p) *Frīgedæg* (Fri-, Friedai),[1] (p) *Glædwine* (Gladewin'), *Godrīc*, *Godwine*, *Goldburh f. (Golburg), *Heresige* (Hersie), *Lēofwine* (Luinus), *Mǣrwynn* f. (Merwn), *Ordmǣr* (Ormer), *Ōslāc*, *Ōsmōd*, *Ōsmund*, *Peohtrūn f. (Piterun);

---

[1] Also used as a byname.

*Sǣburh f. (Seburg), (p) Sǣgār (Segar), (p) Sǣgēat (Saiet), Sǣgifu f. (Saieua), *Sǣ-lēofu f. (Selieua), Sǣlida (Selida), Sǣmann (Seman), Sǣweard (Seward), Sǣwīg (Sewi, -wic), Sǣwine (Sewinus), Sǣwulf (Sewlf), Sigered (Sired), Sigeweard (Siward);

Wīgmund (Wimund; OG, ON), Wulfgār (Ulger), Wulfgifu f. (Wluiua, Wlueua), Wulfhild f. (Ulsild), Wulfrīc (Wluric), Wulfweard (Wilward).

Old English monothematic names are Ad(d)a (Ade), *Byttuc (? Bittuc), Coppa,[1] Cūfing (Chuuing), Cypping (Chepping, Cupping), Dēora (Diera), God (?), Goda, Hearding (Herding, Hard'), Lȳfing (Luuing), (p) Manna (Manne; ODan), *Murta, *Posta, *Spīring, ME Sunne f. (Sunabella), Widia (Widie), Wudia (Wdia).

Finally, there is a group of miscellaneous native names of various types, mainly original bynames:

(a) place-names: Crichel (?), Ficheldene, Froggemore, Sitcelane (?). Baganora, Lacchewei (?), and Odiham occur both independently and as the bynames of Ricard, Radulf, and Alwinus respectively.

(b) occupational bynames: ME Briwere, ME Hangere, ME Hoppere, Portgerēfa (Portereue), Spilemann.

(c) nicknames: Crabeleg, Cristescoc, *Cwaca (Cuuache), Dora,[1] Duresumer, (p) *Fæder-ling (Federling), *Fǣttig (Fati), Forst, Fugel, *Haccesealt (Haccheselt), Hoppecole, *Līcsweostor (Lichesuster), *Nicor (Nicher), *Peni(n)g (Peni), (p) *Pott, Scearpa (? Scerpt), *Strod, *Sūrpap, (p) *Swertling (Suarling; ON), Swift, *Tellebēane (Tellebiene), *Trēowa (Trewa), Turneteil.

The extensive Continental Germanic element is represented by:

(p) Abonel, Adelard, Adeleis f. (var. Adeliz), Ainulf, (p) Alberic, Albreda f., Ansere, Ansfrid, Ansger, Ansgod (ON), Atscelina f., Baldewin, Berengar, Bernard (var. Burnard), Blithild f. (OE), (p) Bos, Drogo, Ebrard, Emma f., Engelram, Erenburg f., (p) Er(e)pulf, Ernald, Erneis;

Fulco, Gaufrid, Giboda, Gilebert, Girard, Girin, Girold, Gisulf, Godard, Godebold, Godefrid, Godehild f. (Godehald), Godelina f., (p) Goislan (var. Gollan), Goscelin, Grim-bald, (p) Gumbold, Guncelin, (p) Gunfrid, Gunter, Hadewis f., Hardrada f. (? Erdrea), Helebold, Helewisa f., Henric, Her(e)bert, Herefrid, Hereman, Hereuic, Herlebold, Hubert, (p) Hubold, Hudo, Hugo, Hunfrid, Imma f. (cf. Emma), Ingelbert, Ingulf (ON), Iua f., Iuelot, Iueta f., Iuo;

(p) Lambert, (p) Lancelin, Letard, Licgard f., Lodewis, Lucelina f., (p) Macher, Mactilda f., Mainard, (p) Marcher (? Macher), Miles, Odo, Oinus (ON), Oric, Osbert, Panta, Radulf, Raimer, Raimund, (p) Rainer, Randulf, Raulot, Reginald, Reimbold, Ricard, Richer, Richild f., Robert, Roger, Rotrog, Ruald, Sauaric, Seiher (var. Saier), Serlo, (p) Sewala, Sewinus, Teoderic (var. Terri), Theduin, Tiecia f., Udelina f., Udelot, Walder, (p) Walerand, Walter, Warin, (p) Warner, Watso (varr. Watsco, Wasco), Willelm, Wimund (OE, ON).

Greek, Latin, and Biblical (including derivatives) are Adam, Alexander, Andreas, Auitia, Bartolomeus, Basilia, Beatrix, Benedictus, Bonefacius, Clemens, Cristianus, Daniel, David, Durand, Enoc, Eva, Gervasius, Isabel, Iohannes, Laurentius, Marieta, Martinus,

---

[1] Also used as a byname.

Michael, Nicholaus, Nigellus, Paganus, Papia (Pauie, Pauida), *Patricius, Petrus, Philippus, Pontius, Samuel, Sanson, Semitonius, Siluester, Simenel, Simon, Simphorianus, Stephanus,* (p) *Thomas, Turpin, Urselinus, Vivianus.*

A special category is formed by a number of Old French original bynames: *Baf* (?), *Bargelo'* (?), *Barillus, Basset, Bonafilia* f., *Brifald* (var. *Brufald*), *Brustin, Caper*[un], *Chawete, Cornilla, Crichel* (?), *Deulecreisse, Doisel, Duchet, Dulzan, Durage* (?), *Gif(f)ard, Gupill, Mallard, Morellus, Multun, Palefrei, Peitewin, Petita* f., (p) *Picard, Picot, Pieferret, Porcellus, Porcus, Pupelina* f., (p) *Richefemme* f., *Rucche, Tail(l)ebroc, Tardif, Trentemars, Truued.*[1]

Occupational terms used as personal names are *Alebast*[er], (p) *Asinarius, Sermonarius,* and *Trauetier.*[2]

The Norman place-name *Hotot* appears once for *Willelmus* (*de*) *Hotot.*

Of Scandinavian provenance are *Agemund, Arnfast* (Herefast), *Arnþórr* (Ertur, var. Ercur; OBret), *Ása* f., *Asgautr* (Ansgod; OG), *Ásgeirr* (Anser; OG), *Ásketill* (Anschetillus), *Ásmoth* f. (Osmoda), *Azur* (Ascor, Atscor), (p) *Brandr,* (p) *Farmann, Gunnhildr* f., *Gunnur* f. (Gunnora), *Haraldr, Ingolfr* (Ingulf; OG), *Ketill* (Chetel), *Kolbrandr* (Colbrand), *Kol(l)sveinn* (Colsuein), *Manni* (Manig), *Óláfr, Oðin* (Oinus; OG), **Sægrimr* (Segrim), *Stigandr,* (p) **Svartlingr* (Suarling; OE), *Tóki* (Tochi), *Tóli, Þóraldr* (Turold), *Þorbert* (Turbert, hybr.), *Þorketill* (Turchetillus), *Þorsteinn* (Turstin), *Ulfr,* (p) *Vestmaðr* (Westman).

The Celtic, mainly Old Breton, group comprises *Alan, Arthur* (Ertur, Ercur; ON), *Briauel, Conan,* (p) *Grifin, Hoel,* (p) *Iwein, Iudichel, Muriel* f., *Talazin, Urluid,* and *Walwain.* Here may also belong the obscure *Morgellor* and *Scorfan.*

iii. SOME STATISTICS (Fig. 1 and Tables 6–8)

The preceding lists will have given a good idea of the general character and structure of medieval Winchester nomenclature at the three dates covered by the *LW* surveys, and of the relative importance of its various components. However, in order to make the picture clearer and bring out more graphically the main onomastic trends operating during the period under review, a summary statistical analysis of the material has been attempted below, with the resultant data presented in tabular form and in diagrams.

The classification used in Tables 6 and 7 is that employed in the foregoing chronological survey and should be self-explanatory. Note that the *OE and ME miscellaneous* class comprises original bynames as well as some place-names used in a personal-name function, whilst the category described as *Old French bynames* includes nicknames, some occupational terms, and one place-name[3] that occur independently in the *LW* as designations for persons. Where alternative etymologies have been suggested, only one of these has been counted. Some doubtful cases are commented upon in the footnotes to Table 6. In this table, names which occur only as patronymics, and hence belong to an earlier stratum than that represented by the relevant survey, have been counted separately and

---

[1] Of the names in this group *Cornilla, Duchet, Durage, Palefrei,* and *Tardif* were used both independently and in their original function as bynames to

designate the same persons; see the list on p. 220, below.

[2] Used elliptically for *Terri trauet*[ier].

[3] *Hotot* **1148.**

TABLE 6

The number of different personal names of various categories in Surveys I and II and in 1207 (cf. Fig. 1a)

	1066	%	c. 1110	%	1148	%	1207	%
OE dithematic	82[a]	51·3	33[g]	29·8	61[l]	19·2	15	17·6
+patr.	5[b]		3		7			
OE monothematic	19[c]	11·9	6[h]	5·4	16[m]	5·0	—	—
+patr.	1		1		1			
OE and ME miscellaneous	13	8·1	3	2·7	32[n]	10·1	—	—
+patr.	4		4		3			
Continental Germanic	23[d]	14·4	48[i]	43·2	96[o]	30·2	30	35·3
+patr.	2		16		15			
Biblical, Greek, Latin	8[e]	5·0	6	5·4	42[p]	13·2	35	41·2
+patr.	—		2		1			
Old French bynames	2[f]	1·2	2[j]	1·8	36[q]	11·3	1[t]	1·2
+patr.	—		—		3			
Scandinavian	10	6·2	8[k]	7·2	23[r]	7·3	2[u]	2·35
+patr.	1		1		3			
Celtic	—	—	3	2·7	10[s]	3·1	2[v]	2·35
+patr.	—		1		2			
Unexplained	3	1·9	2	1·8	2	0·6	—	—
+patr.	2		—		—			
Totals (excl. patronymics)	160		111		318		85	
Totals: Native names %		71·3		37·9		34·3		17·6
Foreign names %		28·7		62·1		65·7		82·4

[a] Incl. four uncertain cases: *Beorhtstān, Ēadsige, Lēofsige, Wilstān.*

[b] Incl. *Cynesige* (?), *Tāthere* (?). [c] Incl. *God, Odda,* but not *Mann.*

[d] Incl. four uncertain cases: *Fulger, *Isenran, Mainbodo, Wulfram.*

[e] *Vitalis* (? *Ficellus*) is uncertain. [f] *Capel, Hachechasse.*

[g] Incl. *Ælfred* (? *Alur'*). [h] Incl. *Dēora, God,* both uncertain.

[i] Incl. *Baldfrith, Ingulf, Wibert. Walder* and *Walter* have been counted as one name, *Wimund* (< *Wīgmund*) as OE.

[j] *Blundel, Picot.* [k] *Ingulf* counted as OG. [l] Incl. *Ācwulf* (?) and *Wīgmund.*

[m] *God* (uncertain) and ME *Sunne* have been included here. *Widia* and *Wudia* are counted as separate names.

[n] Incl. *Crichel, Scearpa,* both doubtful; also OE pl.ns used as pers.ns.

[o] Incl. *Blithild, Hardrada* (? *Erdrea*), and *Ingulf. Emma* and *Imma* have been counted as one name, like *Walder* and *Walter.*

[p] Incl. *Gervasius,* of uncertain etymology.

[q] Incl. *Baf, Bargelo', Durage,* all uncertain, but not *Crichel.*

[r] *Ansgod* and *Ingulf* have been counted as OG. [s] Incl. *Arthur* (LW *Ertur', Ercur'*).

[t] *Pipard.* [u] *Anketil, Turbert;* both Norman. [v] *Alan, Brian;* both Breton.

listed as *patr.* They are not included in the totals and percentages in Table 6 and have been left out altogether in Tables 7 and 8.

By way of supplement to the statistical data derived from the three *LW* surveys of **1066, c. 1110,** and **1148,** and set out in Tables 6–8 below, a later Winchester source, which throws much light on the onomastic situation in the city two generations after the **1148** survey, has also been utilized. This is the list of 389 citizens who served as pledges for the sheriff in 1207,[1] and of whom 383 are mentioned by name. The exact figures and

---

[1] Printed in *Fine R*, 452–7.

percentages based on this document have been added in separate columns at the end of Tables 6–8. The evidence provided by Tables 6 and 7 has also been shown diagrammatically in Figs. 1 and 2.

While the number of different names recorded in the *LW* surveys can be established with reasonable accuracy, as seen in Table 6, any estimate of their actual and relative frequency in terms of the number of occurrences at the three relevant dates will be at best very approximate and tentative, since persons appearing without distinctive surnames can only rarely be identified with certainty. Table 7 is based on a rough mechanical

TABLE 7

The estimated number of occurrences of personal names of various categories in Surveys I and II and in 1207 (cf. Fig. 1b)

	1066	%	c. 1110	%	1148	%	1207	%
OE dithematic	211	67·9	52	22·8	124	13·6	20	5·2
OE monothematic	41	13·2	13	5·7	26	2·9	—	—
OE and ME miscellaneous	13	4·2	3	1·3	32	3·5	—	—
Continental Germanic	25	8·0	134	58·8	484	53·1	231	60·0
Biblical, Greek, Latin	8	2·6	9	4·0	121	13·2	119	31·3
Old French bynames	2	0·6	2	0·9	38	4·2	1	0·3
Scandinavian	11	3·5	11	4·8	67	7·3	4	1·1
Celtic	—	—	4	1·7	20	2·2	8	2·1
Totals	311		228*		912		383	
Native names %		85·3		29·8		20·0		5·2
Foreign names %		14·7		70·2		80·0		94·8

* The striking discrepancy between the totals for the two earlier surveys is largely due to the much greater number of identifiable tenants with multiple holdings at the latter date, cases in point being *Herbertus camerarius* who held no less than ten different properties, *Willelmus de Ponte Archar'* with five and *Chepingus fil. Alueue*, *Robertus fil. Wimundi*, and *Sawalo presbiter* with four each. Note also an entry like **I, 57** which lists twelve persons holding land in a certain area in 1066, but none in *c.* 1110.

count of occurrences and though people identified by various epithets have of course only been counted once, each unidentified occurrence of a name counts as one item in the statistics.[1] If allowance is made for this obvious source of numerical error, the figures may still have some value as indicating the relative importance of the various elements in the nomenclature of early medieval Winchester. The 1207 list mentions 383 different persons; the figures and percentages given for this category are therefore exact.

The frequency of the commonest names, native and foreign, in the *LW* surveys and in the Winchester list of 1207, expressed in terms of the number of occurrences and as percentages of the totals for each source, is shown in Table 8. This table includes all names that occur ten times or more in any one of the lists. They are arranged in the order of frequency with which they appear in the **1148** survey.[2]

[1] Patronymics have not been included. The 'unexplained' category has been left out.

[2] On the statistical problem involved see the remarks relating to Table 7.

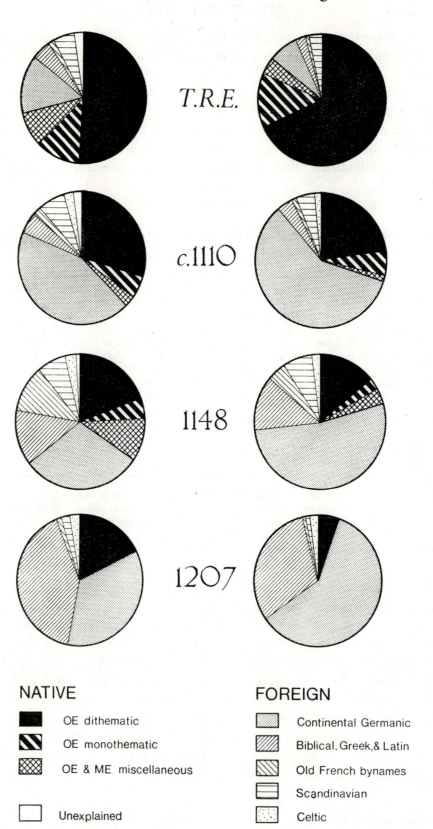

NATIVE

- ■ OE dithematic
- ◨ OE monothematic
- ▨ OE & ME miscellaneous
- ☐ Unexplained

FOREIGN

- ▨ Continental Germanic
- ▨ Biblical, Greek, & Latin
- ▨ Old French bynames
- ▤ Scandinavian
- ⸭ Celtic

FIG. 1. The categories of personal names in Surveys I and II and in 1207: (*a*), by the number of different names (cf. Table 6); (*b*), by the estimated number of occurrences (cf. Table 7).

TABLE 8

*The commonest personal names in Surveys I and II and in 1207**

	1066	%	c. 1110	%	1148	%	1207	%
Willelm	1	—	14	6·1	60	6·6	39	10·2
Robert	—	—	15	6·5	46	5·0	38	10·0
Ricard	—	—	6	2·6	38	4·1	35	9·0
Radulf	—	—	12	5·2	33	3·6	16	4·2
Roger	—	—	6	2·6	29	3·2	12	3·1
Herbert	—	—	5	2·1	20	2·2	2	0·5
Hugo	—	—	5	2·1	16	1·7	10	2·6
Johannes B	—	—	3	1·3	12	1·3	19	5·0
Anschetill ON	—	—	2	0·8	10	1·1	1	—
Drogo	—	—	—	—	10	1·1	—	—
Gaufrid	1	—	3	1·3	10	1·1	13	3·4
Henric	1	—	4	1·7	10	1·1	16	4·2
Stephan B	—	—	—	—	10	1·1	6	1·5
Turstin ON	1	—	2	0·8	10	1·1	—	—
Walter	—	—	2	0·8	10	1·1	13	3·4
Petrus B	1	—	—	—	9	1·0	15	3·9
Alwin OE	16	5·1	7	3·0	8	0·8	1	—
Godwin OE	18	5·8	5	2·1	5	—	2	0·5
Adam B	1	—	—	—	1	—	13	3·4
Leouing OE	10	3·2	—	—	1	—	—	—
Lewin OE	12	3·8	1	—	1	—	—	—

* National provenance is indicated by the abbreviations *B* = biblical, *OE* = Old English, *ON* = Old Norse after the relevant names. Names of Continental Germanic origin have been left unmarked. Note that the two Scandinavian names *Anschetill* and *Turstin* were certainly in most cases borne by Normans.

iv. THE STRUCTURE AND DEVELOPMENT OF WINCHESTER NOMENCLATURE: THE NATIVE AND FOREIGN ELEMENTS (Figs. 1 and 2; Tables 6–8)

The general trend which emerges from the statistics is the gradual shrinking of the stock of traditional OE dithematic names, the *Ælfstān* type, and its replacement by a rapidly growing number of Continental Germanic, mainly Old French, loans, as well as of biblical, Latin, and Greek names, most of them imported from across the Channel.[1] The popularity of native formations of the byname type, some of them probably of recent Middle English coinage, and the increasing use of OFr original nicknames is another significant feature of mid twelfth-century personal nomenclature. The Scandinavian element, which was reinforced by importations from Normandy, remains not inconsiderable throughout the period under review. The Celtic, mainly Old Breton, names are few in number.

The native compound names call for little comment beyond that given in the etymological section. A certain number have not been found in other sources, viz. *Beorhtwīf* f., *Brūnwīf* f., *Hēahsige*, *Scīrmann*, *Scotlāf*, *Sunnrīc* (all **1066**), *Dīcwine*, *Peohtrūn* f.

---

[1] This trend is well brought out in the interesting statistics compiled by Professor Dorothy Whitelock on the basis of the confraternity lists of Thorney Abbey, *Saga-Book of the Viking Society*, 12 (1940), 129ff. Cf. also *DBS*, pp. xixff., Reaney *Origin* 101ff.

The survival of the native personal names is dealt with at length by B. Seltén in his recent book, *The Anglo-Saxon Heritage in Middle English Personal Names; East Anglia 1100–1399* (Lund Studies in English, 43, 1972).

and *Sǣlēofu* f. (all **1148**).[1] *Brūnhild* f. (**1148**), *Godnōð* (**1066**), *Goldburh* f. (**1148**), *Sǣburh* f. (*c.* **1110**), and *Wyndæg* (**1066**) are the earliest examples of these names on record. *Colrūn* f. and *Heresige* (both **1148**) are very rare, and *Hūnbeorht* and *Tāthere* (or *Torhthere*), both **1066**, reappear after two or three centuries. A rare name is also *Wihtmund*, recorded in the patronymic *Wihtmunding* (Withmundin, *c.* **1110**), which incidentally represents a remarkable survival of an obsolescent type of word-formation.

The material is not large enough to lend itself to statistical treatment, but it may be noted that *Godwine*, *Ælfwine*, and *Ēadwine* are by far the most popular names in the native dithematic group throughout the period.[2] The occurrence of numerous compounds with the late OE element *Sǣ-* seems to reflect a prevailing fashion in early medieval name-giving.[3]

Special interest attaches to some previously unrecorded monothematic names: *Edde* f. (a hypocoristic form of *Ēadgyð* f.), *Manding*, *Pilluc*, and *Tuttel* (all *TRE*), *Byttuc* (?), *Cwaca*, *Murta*, *Posta*, and *Spīring* (all **1148**). *Cypping*, which first turns up in the *LVH c.* 1030, was evidently a popular Hampshire name; it occurs in all three surveys and was borne by a number of persons, perhaps members of the same family. *Nunna* (patr., *c.* **1110**) is an archaic name which makes a surprising reappearance.

A number of original bynames were used in a personal-name function; see the lists of miscellaneous formations, above pp. 180–2. Of these some have not been recorded before: *Āncild*, *Scīd*, *Ticcenmann* (all **1066**), *Bredful*, *Fæderling* (also **1148**), *Foxprica*, *Holegn* (*c.* **1110**), *Crabeleg*, *Duresumer* (an Anglo-Norman hybrid), *Fǣttig*, *Hoppecole*, *Līcsweostor*, *Strod*, and *Sūrpap* (**1148**).

In the case of *Brūncyng* (**1066**), *Cristescoc* (**1148**), *Hafoc* (**1066**), *Hāligprēost* (**1066**), *Nicor* (**1148**), *Peni(n)g* (**1148**), *Pott* (**1066**), and *Sīdlocc* (**1066**), the *LW* occurrences antedate those previously recorded.

Phrase-names are *Haccesealt* (also found in later sources), *Tellebēane*, and *Turneteil*, of which the last two have not been found elsewhere.

On some native occupational terms and place-names used independently as personal names see above, pp. 182–3.

As for the Continental Germanic element (see the lists, pp. 180–2, above), there can be no doubt that the majority of names in that category are West Frankish (Old French) in origin, and that they were brought to England by immigrants mainly from Normandy, Picardy, and adjacent parts of France, as is indicated by the parallel material from contemporary Norman, and occasionally Picard, sources adduced in the etymological index.[4]

---

[1] The unrecorded OE names **Bealdfrið* and **Blīðhild* f. may survive in *Baluert*, *c.* **1110**, and *Blithild*, **1148**, respectively, though OG origin seems the more probable alternative in both cases; see above s.nn.

[2] For *Ælfwine* and *Godwine* see Table 8. *Ēadwine* shows the following number of occurrences: **1066** 6, *c.* **1110** 2, **1148** 6, **1207** 0. The frequent use of *Godwine* may, as F. Barlow points out, *Edward the Confessor* (London, 1970), 127, n. 4, be due to the fact that its most famous bearer, the Earl of Wessex, was very popular in Winchester.

[3] **1066**: three different names in *Sǣ-*; *c.* **1110**: 5;

1148: 11. See also my note, *NoB* 33 (1945), 95, n. 59, and *ELPN* 58ff.

[4] With very few exceptions the names in this category are in fact recorded in the Old French sources excerpted by Morlet to whose useful repertory frequent reference is made in the etymological index. *Andrebode*, *Helbing*, and *Hizeman* (all **1066**) have so far only been found in South German documents. *Er(e)pulf* (**1148**) occurs, it is true, in two lists from St. Germain des Prés (Paris, early 9th c., probably the same person), but from *c.* 1000 onwards it is a typically Flemish name; see Mansion 43, Tavernier-Vereecken 72.

Moreover, though most names appear in the traditional Latin spellings that were the accepted standard in Continental and English chanceries and scriptoria, some forms are distinctively Old French, such as *Erneis, Girardus* (both also **1148**), *Goisbertus, Goisfridus, Maiesent, Oil(l)ardus, Thiardus* (varr. *Tihardus, Tiart*), all *c.* **1110**, *Adeleis* (var. *Adeliz*), *Girinus, Giroldus, Godehald, Goisl[anus], Hadewis, Helewisa, Lodewis, Oinus, Oricus, Seiher* (var. *Saier*), *Terri* (by the side of traditional *Theodricus*), *Tiecia*, all **1148**. *Ernuceon* (*c.* **1110**), *Abonel, Iueta, Iuelot, Raulot* and *Udelot* (all **1148**), have OFr suffixes. The occasional use of an OFr byname is of course an indication of the provenance of the personal name to which it is affixed.[1] The extensive group of original OFr bynames used independently in a personal-name function in the **1148** survey (see the list on p. 183, above) should also be noted in this connection.[2]

Many bearers of OG names were well-known Norman barons as a glance at the list of local bynames will show. Some of them may have had only slight connections with the city of Winchester and their appearance in the surveys may tend to produce some distortion of the statistics which should ideally only include genuine local residents.

Among the persons bearing OG names there were probably a fair number of Bretons and Flemings as well as some Saxons and other Germans,[3] but in the absence of specific information about their nationality this can only rarely be established on the basis of their names alone, a majority of which were current over a great part of Western Europe.[4] In addition, as has already been pointed out, the common use of stereotyped latinized spellings tends to level out any distinctive dialectal features.[5]

A decisive factor in the eventual victory of Continental names in medieval English nomenclature (Fig. 2) was of course the social prestige they enjoyed which led fathers of English or Scandinavian descent to give their children such names. In the *c.* **1110** survey we have *Herbertus filius Edwini, Radulfus Holinessone, Robertus filius Nunne* and *Rualdus filius Faderlin*. Examples abound in the **1148** list: *Hugo, Roger*, and *Radulf* were sons of *Cypping*; *Geruasius* and *Radulf* sons of *Burhwald*; *Robert* and *Willelm* sons of *Ēastmǣr*; *Reginald* son of *Ēadwulf*; *Warin* son of *Blæcmann*; *Herbert* son of *Sǣgēat*; *Godefrid* son of *Sǣwīg*; *Girard* son of *Brand* (ON); *Herbert* son of *Westman* (ON); etc. *Goda Hacchemus* had a brother named *Robert*.[6]

Of the opposite practice we have three instances *TRE: Alwinus Aitardessone* and his brother (?) *Alward filius Etardii*, and *Algar Godesbranesson*. There are no similar examples in *c.* **1110** and only one in the **1148** list: *Hersie filius Warner*.[7]

Walderus (*c.* 1110, 1148) may have been a Saxon for reasons stated s.n. *Godesbrand* and *Isenran* (both **1066**), though clearly of OG origin, have not been found in Continental records.

[1] The OFr bynames are listed below, p. 219.

[2] Some phonological criteria of OFr provenance are briefly mentioned below, p. 226.

[3] Cf. also above, p. 188, n. 4.

[4] See Mansion's useful list of 'overal voorkomende namen', pp. 63–4.

[5] A few bynames indicate nationality. *Godwinus francigena* (1066) was a Frenchman (but see Addenda to p. 211) and so were no doubt *Paganus Gallus* and *Willelmus Gallus* (1148). *Radulfus Brito* (*c.*1110) was a Breton,

Ricardus Loer' (**1148**) perhaps a Lorrainer. *Robertus Norreis* and *Turstinus Danais* (**1148**) were of Norwegian and Danish descent respectively. *Turstinus Mansel* (**1148**) was a native of Maine. *Peitewinus* and *Picard* (**1148**) probably came from Poitou and Picardy. *Deulecreisse* and *Urselinus* (**1148**) are described as Jews. If *Bargelo'* (**1148**) stands for *Bargelonensis* the man was a Spaniard. See also *Estreis*, byn.

[6] *Asmund* (< ODan Asmund), a citizen of Winchester, had two sons, *Bonifacius* and *Reimund*, mentioned *c.* 1120–30, *EHR* 14 (1899), 424.

[7] For a full discussion of the supplanting of native names by the more fashionable French ones as seen in the early London sources see *ELPN* 91ff.

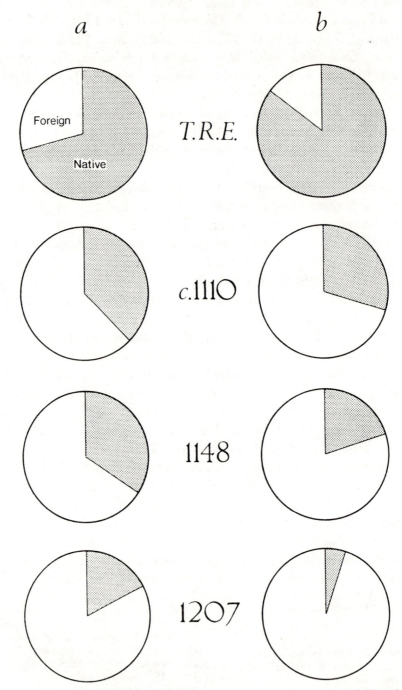

F IG. 2. Percentages of native and foreign personal names in Surveys I and II and in 1207: (*a*), by the number of different names (cf. Table 6); (*b*), by the estimated number of occurrences (cf. Table 7).

In assessing the significance of the Scandinavian element (above, pp. 180–3) it should be remembered that many of the names in this group were also used in pre- and post-conquest Normandy,[1] and that their bearers may consequently in some cases have been immigrants from that province. This is true of the majority of relevant names, exceptions being *Agemund*, *Algot*, *Arnþórr*, *Ása* f., *Asmoth* f., *Eilaf*, *Gautr*, *Gunnhildr* f., *Húni*, *Kolbrand*, *Kol(l)sveinn*, *Óláfr*, **Sægrímr*, *Steinolfr*, **Svartlingr*, and *Ulfketil*, which have not so far been found in Norman sources. Of these *Kolbrandr*, *Kol(l)sveinn*, and *Steinolfr* are West Scandinavian, *Algot*, *Asmoth*, and *Ulfketil* Old Danish, whilst the remaining ones may be either. **Sægrímr* seems to be an Anglo-Scandinavian formation.

Biblical, Greek, and Latin names form a category that grows in extent and popularity during the period under review (above, pp. 180–3 and Table 7). Some of them are occasionally found in England before the conquest, for instance *Adam*, *Daniel*, *Iohannes*, *Martin*, and *Petrus*, their bearers being priests or monks, but the great majority of those occurring in *LW* were certainly imported from the Continent. With some exceptions they owe their adoption to the fact that they were originally borne by saints. *Alexander* and *Vivianus* (both **1148**) were probably called after their namesakes in the medieval romances. *Semitonius* (**1148**), which is not recorded elsewhere, looks like a learned nick-name for an organist. *Albuchon* (patr., **c. 1110**) is an archaic Gallo-Roman name. *Marieta* and *Simenel* have OFr suffixes, and *Isabel* is an OFr variant of Elisabeth.

Of the twelve certain Celtic names[2] that occur in the *LW*, no less than six are Old Breton: *Alan*, *Conan*, *Hoel*, *Iudicel*, *Urluid*, and *Wasfer*. *Grifin* is Welsh and *Briauel* the name of a Welsh saint. *Iwen* and *Walwain* are ultimately Old Welsh, but they were also borne by two well-known characters in the medieval epic romances, and their Winchester namesakes may well have been named after these mythical heroes. This may also be true of the unexplained *Scorfan* (**c. 1110, 1148**; two persons ?), which occurs several times in the Old French *chansons de geste*. *Talazin* may similarly have been called after the legendary Welsh bard, but the name occurs also in Brittany. *Muriel* is an Old Irish feminine name which was brought to Normandy in the early eleventh century and thence to England.[3]

---

[1] And hence on the whole ultimately of Old Danish origin.

[2] *Ertur'* (var. *Ercur'*) **1148** most probably goes back to OBret *Arthur* but might alternatively represent Anglo-Scand *Ar(n)ður*.

[3] On the occurrence in Normandy of Irish personal names brought there by Hiberno-Norse vikings, see L. Musset in *Mediaeval Scandinavia*, 2 (1969), 190.

3

BYNAMES

BYNAMES or descriptive and explanatory epithets of various kinds added to Christian names were used in England since the eighth century. Their rise and development and the process by which in the course of time many of them became hereditary surnames were fully dealt with by P. H. Reaney in 1958 (*DBS*) and 1967 (*Origin*). Important observations have also been contributed by Ekwall (*ELPN*), and by Tengvik in his monograph on *Old English Bynames* (1938), where the relevant Old English and Anglo-French material up to *c.* 1100 is brought together. The Middle English occupational bynames have been collected by Fransson and Thuresson in their dissertations (1935, 1950).[1]

In the present paper only a summary treatment of the bynames in the Winton Domesday will accordingly be attempted. It may be noted that the neutral term *byname* will be used throughout in order to avoid the connotation of heredity implied in *surname* which would be anachronistic in an eleventh and early twelfth-century context. Among the Norman feudal aristocracy many bynames, notably local ones, admittedly became hereditary during the eleventh century,[2] but the *LW* surveys throw no light on this problem.

The bynames have been classified into four main groups in accordance with the system adopted by Ekwall and Reaney:

   i. local bynames
  ii. occupational bynames
 iii. bynames of relationship
 iv. other bynames, chiefly nicknames

Within each category the arrangement is alphabetical, each entry including the byname with its variant forms, if any, the personal name(s) with which it is associated,[3] and the date(s), but not a complete list of occurrences since these should be looked for under the relevant personal name in the main index.

---

[1] See also B. Seltén, 'Some notes on Middle English by-names in independent use', *English Studies*, 46 (1965), 165–81, idem, *Early East Anglian nicknames: 'Shakespeare' names* (*Scripta minora Reg. Soc. litt. hum. Lundensis*, 1968/69, 3, Lund 1969); G. Kristensson, 'Studies on Middle English local surnames containing elements of French origin', *English Studies*, 50 (1969), 465–86.

[2] Tengvik 10ff., Reaney *Origin* 300ff.

[3] The personal names are quoted in the nominative form irrespective of the case in which they occur in the surveys.

i. LOCAL BYNAMES

Abendon', *Robertus* **1148.**—Short for *Abendonensis* 'from Abingdon'.

Aisel', *Turstinus de* **1148.**—Ashley (Ha), parish and manor in King's Somborne hd.

Albinneio, *Willelmus de c.* **1110.**—Saint-Martin d'Aubigny (Manche); *VCH Hants* i. 535, Loyd 7.

Andeleio, *Walterus de* **1148.**—Les Andelys (Eure).

Anesi, *Willelmus de c.* **1110.**—Anisy (Calvados); Loyd 4f.

Auco, *Osbertus c.* 1110, *Auco, Aucho, Hugo de* **1148.**—Eu (Seine-Maritime).

Auelton', *God' presbiter de* **1148.**—Alton (Ha).

Auiton', *Ingolfus de* **1148.**—Avington (Ha).

Baganorus, *Ricardus* **1148.**—Bagnor (Brk). See also *Baganora*, pers.n.

Baiaco, *Ricardus de* 1148, *Baioc', Robertus de* **1148.** —Bayeux (Calvados).

Barra, *Sewinus de* **1148.**—La Barre-en-Ouche (Eure) or La Barre-de-Semilly (Manche). Cf. also *Ricardus de Barra* 1086 DB(So); Tengvik 70. But possibly a suburban bar, cf. **744**, n. 1.

Bichint', *Radulfus de* **1148.**—Bighton (Ha).

Bintewrda, *Binteword', Martinus de* **1148.**—Bentworth (Ha).

Bosco, *Radulfus de* **1148.**—From one of the numerous places in France called Bois or Bosc, e.g. Bosc-le-Hard (Seine-Maritime); cf. Loyd 18f.

Bradeia, *Willelmus de* **1148.**—Probably for *Bradelia*, Bradley (Ha). A pl.n. *Broadey does not exist.

Braio, *Ricardus de* **1148.**—One of several places in France called Bray (Aisne, Aube, Calvados, Oise) < Gaulish *Braium*.[1] High Bray (D), DB *Braia*, and Bray (Brk), DB *Brai*, are improbable alternatives since they would hardly be latinized as neuters.[2]

Braiosa, *Burnard de* **1148.**—Briouze (Orne); Loyd 20.

Brudefort, Adam de **1148.**—Bridford (D).

Cadumo, *Willelmus de* **1148.**—Caen (Calvados).

Cainesham, *Canesham, Aluricus de* 1066, *Chainesham, Ailwardus de* 1066, *Cainesham, Chipingus de c.* 1110, *Chenesham, Haroldus de* **1148.**—Keynsham (So).

Calp', *Drogo de* **1148.**—Possibly *Calpestret* in Winchester.[3] Cf. below, p. 233.

Campesiet, *Robertus de* **1148.**—Kempshot (Ha).

Carnot', *Ebrardus de* **1148.**—Chartres (Eure-et-Loir). The medieval Latin form is *Carnotum*.

Cederli', *Godwinus* **1066.**—Chitterley (D), DB Ex *Chederlia*; *PND* 555.

Cell', *Gaufridus de* **1148.**—Probably one of the numerous French places called (La) Celle, Celles, etc. < Lat *cella*, on which see Dauzat–Rostaing 159f., but cf. the next entry.

Cellar', *Alanus de* **1148.**—(Le) Cellier < Lat *cellarium*, the name of several places in France (Loire-Atlantique, etc.); see Dauzat–Rostaing 160. Cf. also the preceding entry.[4]

Chainesham, see *Cainesham*.

Chaisneto, *Willelmus de* **1148.**—There are several places called (Le) Quesnoy, Quesney, Quesnay in the north of France.[5] One Anglo-Norman family is known to have come from Le Quesnay in Seine-Maritime; Loyd 27f.

Chateleia, *Willelmus de* **1148.**—Perhaps Catlees, a tenement in Froyle (Ha). One Richard Catteley held a virgate there before 1415.[6]

Chenesham, see *Cainesham*.

Chinai, *Gilebertus de* **1148.**—Probably a place in France; not identified.

Chiuilli, *Hugo de c.* 1110.[7]—Quevilly (Calvados) or Le Petit-Quevilly (Seine-Maritime); J. Adigard des Gautries, *Annales de Normandie* 6 (1956), 321.

Cholcham, *Nigellus de c.* **1110.**—An unidentified English pl.n. in -*ham*(*m*). The first el. might be OE *colc* 'hollow, pool'.[8]

---

[1] Gröhler i. 155.
[2] Bray (Brk) is always *de* (*in*) *Brai* in the 1130 Pipe Roll.
[3] Now St. Thomas Street.
[4] The editor and Dr. D. J. Keene suggest that the reference may be to the *cellarium* of St. Swithun's Priory in Winchester. In the late thirteenth century one Drogo was cellarer of the foundation and is described as *Drogo de Celario Sancti Swithuni Wynton'*;

see T. F. Kirby, *Annals of Winchester College* (London and Winchester, 1892), 9, and cf. below, p. 313.
[5] From Gallo-Roman *cassanētum* 'oak-copse'.
[6] *VCH Hants* ii. 504.
[7] His widow is mentioned in the Pipe Roll of 1130: *pro . . . uxore Hugonis chiuilli* (p. 53). Note also *Nicol' de Kivel'* 1207 *Fine R* 453 (Winchester).
[8] See M. Löfvenberg's note, *PNGl* i. xii.

Chrichelada, *Alueua de* **1066,** *Crichelad', Crech', Stephanus de* **1148.**—Cricklade (W). See also *Crichel,* pers.n.

Clera, *Radulfus de* **1148.**—Clere (Ha), DB *Clere.*

Columbiers, *Robertus de* **1148.**—One of several French places called Colombiers, -ières; Gröhler ii. 202, Dauzat–Rostaing 201. Loyd (p. 30) mentions two Colombières in Calvados.

Corbulio, *Willelmus de* **1148.**—Corbeil (Marne or Seine-et-Oise).

Crech', see *Chrichelada.*

Crichelad', see *Chrichelada.*

Curci, *Ricardus de c.* **1110.**—Courcy (Calvados).

Curleio, *Rannulfus de c.* **1110.**—Corlay (Côtes-du-Nord), Corlay (Haute-Marne), or Courlay (Deux-Sèvres).[1]

Diua, *Ansgier de* **1148,** *Isabel de* **1148,** *Robertus de* **1148.**—Dives-sur-Mer (Calvados).

Dodesmere 1066.—see Personal Names.

Domera, *Dommere,* see *Dunmera.*

Dunmera, *Dommere, Domera, Henricus de c.* **1110,** *Dummera, Radulfus de* **1148.**—Dummer (Ha).

Esperchefort, *Odo de* **1066.**—Sparkford (Ha).

Essewem, *Leuret de* **1066.**—A pl.n. in *Ash-*;[2] perhaps an error for *Essewelle* > Ashwell (D, E, Hrt, etc.).[3]

Estuna, *Turoldus de* **1148.**—Easton in Fawley hd (Ha).

Exon', *Ricardus de* **1148,** *Exon', Willelmus* **1148.**—*Exonia,* the latinized form of Exeter. In the second case we have the adj. *Exoniensis.*

Felgeriis, *Radulfus de c.* **1110.**—Fougères in Ille-et-Vilaine (Brittany).

Ficheldene 1148.—see Personal Names.

Fislia, *Turstinus de* **1148.**—Fishleigh (D); PND 143.

Forda, *Brumanus de la* **1066.**—Fordingbridge (Ha), DB *Forde.*[4]

Forest, *Rogerus de* **1148.**—Probably a French place called (La) Forest, a common name in the north of France,[5] or perhaps the New Forest (Ha), *Nova Foresta* DB, *Noveforest* 1154.

Froggemore 1148.—see Personal Names.

Fuleflod', *Philippus de* **1148,** *Fuleflot, Godwinus de* **1148.**—Fulflood in Weeke parish (Ha).[6] See also *Vallo* below.

Glauston', *Willelmus de* **1148.**—Glastonbury (So). The person in question is clearly identical with Willelmus de *Glastonia* 1130 *P* 13, chamberlain of Normandy.[7] On AN *au* for *a* before *st* in the *LW* form see Pope § 1153.

Goi, *Hugo de* **1148.**—Gouy (Aisne, Pas-de-Calais, Seine-Maritime).[8]

Grainuill', *Walterus de* **1148.**—Grainville-sur-Odon (Calvados) < *Grainvilla* 1077 seems preferable in view of the early forms. The pl.n. occurs several times in various French departments.[9]

Hacche, *Hecche, Ansfridus de* **1148.**—Hatch in Cliddesden (Ha).

Hahela, *Hugo de* **1148.**—Probably an error for *La Hela*[10] and hence one of the places called Hele, DB *Hela,* in D or So.

Haia, *Ricardus de* **1148,** *Rogerus de* **1148.**—One of the French places called La Haye (Eure, Manche, Seine-Maritime, etc.). If the persons under notice belong to the family dealt with by Loyd (p. 51), we are concerned with La Haye-du-Puits (Manche).

Hangelt', *Symon de* **1148.**—Hangleton (Sx).

Hantona, *Warinus de c.* **1110.**—Southampton (Ha).

Hecche, see *Hacche.*

Hedeleia, *Siwardus de* **1148.**—Headley (Ha).

Hela, *Hugo de la* **1148.**—See *Hahela.*

---

[1] Cf. also *Thomas de Curleio* 1198 *MRSN* 346.

[2] For the spelling *Ess(e)-* for OE *Æsc-* cf. *Essulfus c.* 1110 < *Æscwulf.*

[3] No such place has so far been found in Ha. Ellisfield (Ha) is *Esewelle* in DB, but would hardly be a suitable base; see *DEPN* s.n.

[4] Dr. D. J. Keene suggests that this could refer to an area on the north side of the High Street in Winchester, which was known in the thirteenth century as *la Forde.* See also below, p. 237, s.n.

[5] Note for example Forest (Nord), Leforest (Pas-de-Calais), La Forêt-du-Parc (Eure), Forêt-la-Folie (Eure).

[6] Another early form of the pl.n. is (Siberd de) *Fulflod'* 1207 Fine R 457 (Winchester).

[7] On him see *Reg* ii, 1579.

[8] There are five places of this name in Pas-de-Calais (with various affixes); see Dauzat-Rostaing s.n. Gaugeac.

[9] See also Sanders *Baronies,* 41, n. 3.

[10] Cf. Willelmus *de Lahela* 1130 *P* 40 (Ha) and the material in R. E. Zachrisson's paper, 'The French definite article in English place-names', *Anglia,* 34 (1911), 308ff.

Hoctona, *Willelmus de c.* 1110, *Hoctune, Hoctun',* *Willelmus de* 1148.—Houghton (Ha).

Hodiam, see *Odiam.*

Hotot, *Willelmus de* 1148, *Hotot, Willelmus* 1148.—One of several places in Normandy called Hautot, Hotot, Hottot.[1] See also *Hotot,* pers.n.

Hungerford, *Hungerfort, Robertus de* 1148.—Hungerford (Brk).

Inglesh', *Ingl', Robertus de* 1148.—Inglesham (W).

Iorz, *Anschetillus de, c.* 1110, *Ansgar de c.* 1110.—Jort (Calvados); Tengvik 94.[2]

Ipingis, *Willelmus de* 1148.—Iping (Sx).

Lere, *Lanc de* 1066.—See *Lancdelere,* pers.n.

Limesia, *Ricardus de* 1148.—Limésy (Seine-Maritime).

Linc, *Wigot de c.* 1110.[3]—Lincoln (Li).

Mapeldreham, *Alueua de c.* 1110.—Mapledurham (Ha).

Masiaco, *Gaufridus de* 1148.—Perhaps Massy (Seine-Maritime). This and similar place-names, ultimately derived from Lat *Mac(c)ius, Massius,* are found in various parts of France; cf. the survey in Dauzat–Rostaing s.n. Macé.

Medehalla, *Paganus de la* 1066.—OE *meduheall* 'mead-hall'. The reference is clearly to a tavern or inn, perhaps in Winchester itself. See also below, p. 238, s.n.

Meleford', *Willelmus de c.* 1110, *Meleford, Gilebertus de* 1148, *Meleford', Rogerus de* 1148.—Milford (Ha).

Mellent, *Ricardus capellanus comitis de c.* 1110.—Meulan (Seine-et-Oise).

Menes, *Hugo de c.* 1110.—East or West Meon (Ha).

Mitlinget', *Edmundus de* 1148.—Midlington in Droxford (Ha); *VCH Hants* iii. 286.

Morsteda, *Rand' de* 1148, *Morsted', Radulfus de* 1148.—Morestead (Ha).

Mortuomari, *Radulfus de c.* 1110, *Mortemer, Hugo*

de 1148.—Mortemer-sur-Eaulne (Seine-Maritime); Loyd 70f.

Mucheto, *Stephanus* 1148.—see Other Bynames.

Odiam, *Alwinus de* 1148, *Hodiam, Alwinus de c.* 1110.—Odiham (Ha). See also *Odiham,* pers.n.

Oili, *Radulfus de* 1148, *Robertus de* 1148.—From one of several places in Calvados called Ouilly.

Ordia, *Chipingus de* 1066, *Godwinus de* 1066, *Turstinus de* 1148, *Wordia, Turstinus de* 1148.—*Chipingus* held in Headbourne Worthy (Ha) TRE.[4] In the remaining cases we have either or both of King's Worthy and Martyr Worthy (Ha).

Ouinton', *Radulfus de* 1148.—Ovington (Ha).

Papanholt, *Herebertus* 1148.—A lost place in Micheldever (Ha). It is *Papanholt* 901 *BCS* 596, *Papeholt Hereberti* 1166/7 *P* 188, and *Papenholt* in 1253; *DEPN* s.n. Papworth. It may be the present Micheldever Wood.[5]

Perci, *Emma de c.* 1110.—Percy-en-Auge (Calvados); Loyd 77.

Piro, *Willelmus de* 1148.—Either Le Poirier (Calvados, canton de Frénouville)[6] or Le Pire (Pas-de-Calais, canton de Neufchâtel).[7]

Pol, *Sewinus de* 1148.—Poole (Do) or South Pool (D).

Ponte, *Pont', Robertus de* 1148.—Possibly Pont-de-l'Arche (Eure) as in the following entry, but Pont (with various affixes) is a very common French pl.n.; see Dauzat–Rostaing 540f.

Ponte Archar', *Ponthearcar', Pontearch', Pont', Willelmus de c.* 1110, *Pontearchar', Pont', Willelmus* 1148, *Pont', Willelmus de* 1148.—Pont-de-l'Arche (Eure).

Port, *Henricus de c.* 1110, *Iohannes de* 1148, *Radulfus de* 1148, *Rogerus de* 1148, *Porta, Hugo de* 1148.—Port-en-Bessin (Calvados); Loyd 79.

Portesia, *Baldewinus de* 1148.—Portsea Island (Ha).

Pucheshele 1066.—see Personal Names.

Pusat, *Hugo de* 1148.[8]—Le Puiset (Eure-et-Loir).

---

[1] There are eight in Seine-Maritime, one in Eure, four in Calvados and three in Manche. For details see B. Holmberg, *Tomt och toft som appellativ och ortnamnselement* (Uppsala, 1946), 237ff.

[2] This is *Jort* 1049–58; see J. Adigard des Gautries, 'Les Noms de lieux du Calvados', *Annales de Normandie,* 3 (1953), 28. Note also Gaufridus de *Jort* 1154–89 *Seals* 2, Rannulfo (abl) de *Jorz c.* 1200 ibid. 260 (Lei, W).

[3] Wigot, sheriff of Lincolnshire; *VCH Hants* i. 535.

[4] DB Ha 46b.

[5] *Ex inf.* Mr J. E. B. Gover, who notes a reference to *boscus de Papenholte in hundredo de Mucheldevere* in the 1294 Assize Rolls.

[6] This is *villa quæ dicitur Pirus* 1082, (ecclesia Sancte Marie de) *Piro* 1150; C. Hippeau, *Dictionnaire topographique du Calvados* (Paris, 1883), 224.

[7] Early forms are *Pirus* 1179, *Le Pire* 1395; A. de Loisne, *Dictionnaire topographique du département du Pas-de-Calais* (Paris, 1907), 298.

[8] *Hug' de Puisato* 1153–4 *Reg* iii, 258.

Rediuers, *Baldewinus de c.* 1110.—Reviers (Calvados); Loyd 85.

Ricarduill', *Ricardus de* 1148.—Ricarville (Seine-Maritime; two places) or Richarville (Seine-et-Oise).

Rotomag', *Willelmus de* 1148.—Rouen (Seine-Maritime).

Sagio, *Reginaldus de* 1148, *Rogerus de* 1148.—Sées (Orne).

Salesberie, *Willelmus de c.* 1110, *Saleb', Herebertus de* 1148, *Sar', Herebertus de* 1148.—Salisbury (W). See also *Sar'* below.

Sancta Maria, *Anschetillus de* 1148.—A place called Sainte-Marie, of which there are several in Normandy, or possibly a reference to St. Mary's Abbey, of which Anschetil may have been a servant, see **II, 661** and cf. **731**, n. 1.

Sancto Iohanne, *Thomas de c.* 1110.—Saint-Jean-le-Thomas (Manche); *VCH Hants* i. 535.

Sancto Laudo, *Gaufridus de* 1148.—Saint-Lô (Manche).

Sancto Nicholao, *Gaufridus de* 1148.—One of the fifteen places in Normandy called Saint-Nicholas.

Sancto Pancratio, *Robertus de* 1148.—Probably Saint-Planchers (Manche) which is *parrochia S. Pancratii* in 1155.

Sancto Quintino, *Herbertus de c.* 1110.—One of several places in Normandy called Saint-Quentin.

Sancto Walarico, *Bernardus de c.* 1110.—Saint-Valéry-sur-Somme (Somme).[1]

Sapalanda *monacorum, Lowricus presbiter de* **1066.**—This is probably an unrecorded OE *scēap-land* 'sheep-land, tract of grass-land used for pasturing sheep'.[2] On AN [s] for OE [ʃ] see below, p. 225. Cf. DB *Sapeswic, Scapeuuic,* Shapwick (So, Do) < OE *scēapwīc* 'sheep farm', *DEPN* s.n. See below, p. 238, s.n.

Sar', *Godefridus c.* 1110.—Short for *Sarisberiensis* 'from Salisbury'. See also *Salesberie* above.

Seifrewast, *Robertus de c.* 1110, *Sifrewast, Robertus de* 1148.—Chiffrevast (Manche); Loyd 61, 98.

Stanam, *Edwardus de* 1148.—North or South Stoneham (Ha).

Sutton', *Humfridus de* 1148, *Suttun', Sotton', Sutt', Willelmus de* 1148.—Sutton (Ha). See Addenda.

Templo, *Willelmus de* 1148.—Several places in France were called Le Temple to indicate that they were the property of the Order of Knights Templars; Gröhler ii. 386f., Dauzat–Rostaing 672.

Ticheb', *Walterus de* 1148.—Tichborne (Ha).

Tistede, *Ricardus* 1148.—East or West Tisted (Ha).

Tocho, see *Tolcha.*

Tolcha, *Godefridus de c.* 1110, *Tocho, Willelmus de* 1148.[3]—Touques (Calvados).[4] Note also *Rog' de Tolcha* 1130 *P* 41, 163 (Ha).

Traci, *Henricus de* 1148.—One of the places in Calvados called Tracy; see Loyd 105f.

Tuberilli, *Radulfus de c.* 1110.—Possibly a corrupt form of *Tubervilla* > Thouberville (Eure).[5]

Turwill', *Robertus de* 1148.—One of several places in Normandy named Tourville; cf. also Loyd 108.

Vallo, *Philippus de* 1148.—The reference, as Dr. D. J. Keene points out, may be to a locality outside the NW. corner of Winchester which was known as *la Val* in the thirteenth century. The part of this valley that extended outside the city liberty was known as *Fulflod*; see *Fuleflod* above. The man under notice may thus have been identical with *Philippus de Fuleflod*. On the other hand, *Val* is a very common French pl.n.; see Dauzat–Rostaing 694ff. See also below, p. 237, s.n.

Valuin', *Petrus de* 1148.—Valognes (Manche).[6]

Walt', *Alexander de* 1148.—Bishop's Waltham or North Waltham (Ha).

Walteruile, *Radulfus de* 1148.—Vatierville (Seine-Maritime); Loyd III.

---

[1] See G. H. Fowler, *The Genealogist*, 30 (1914), 2f.

[2] The word *sheep-land* is not recorded until 1722 (*NED*). The medial *a* in *Sapalanda* is probably an AN inorganic vowel but could also reflect an OE gen. plur. *scēapa.*

[3] *Willelmus de Thoca, c.* 1130 *EHR* 14 (1899), 424 (Winchester).

[4] Early forms are *Toucqua* 1023, *Tolce* 1059–66, *Tocha* 1061–6; see J. Adigard des Gautries, 'Les Noms de lieux du Calvados', *Annales de Normandie, 3*

(1953), 144.

[5] *Tuberti villa c.* 1060, *Tubervilla* 1175; see Blosseville (B. E. Poret, Marquis de), *Dictionnaire topographique du département de l'Eure* (Paris, 1877), 215, J. Adigard des Gautries, 'Les Noms de lieux de l'Eure', *Annales de Normandie,* 5 (1955), 26.

[6] For early forms, e.g. *Valungia* 1055, see J. Adigard des Gautries, 'Les Noms de lieux de la Manche attestés entre 911 et 1066', *Annales de Normandie,* 2 (1951), 42.

Wdecota, *Rogerus de* **1148.**—Woodcote nr. Bramdean (Ha).

Windelesor, *Windes', Godefridus de* **1148,** *Windes', Wluricus de* **1148.**—Winsor (Ha).

Wingeham, *Radulfus de* **1148.**—Wingham (K).

Wint', *Robertus* **1148.**—For *Wintoniensis* 'from Winchester'.

Wordia, see *Ordia.*

Notes on the Local Bynames (Fig. 3)

The great majority of English place-names used as local epithets in the Winchester surveys refer, not surprisingly, to localities in **Hampshire** (fig. 3). They are as follows: Alton (*Auelton*),[1] Ashley (*Aisel'*), Avington (*Auiton'*), Bentworth (*Bintewrda*), Bighton

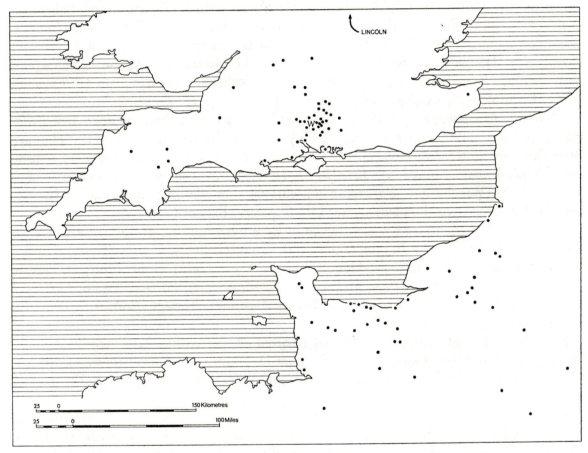

FIG. 3. Immigration and conquest: places from which the local bynames in Surveys I and II were derived (1:4 million).

Massy has not been identified. For those places where alternative identifications exist, the following have been shown: Le Poirier (Calvados), La Barre-de-Semilly (Manche), Le Petit-Quevilly and Ricardville (Seine-Maritime).

(*Bichint'*), Bradley (? *Bradeia*), Catlees (? *Chateleia*), Clere (*Clera*), Dummer (*Dunmera*; 2),[2] Easton (*Estuna*), Fordingbridge (*la Forda*), Fulflood (*Fuleflod'*; 2), Hatch (*Hacche, Hecche*), Headley (*Hedeleia*), Houghton (*Hoctona*), Kempshot (*Campesiet*), Mapledurham

---

[1] The main *LW* form is given in brackets.   [2] The figures indicate the number of persons concerned.

(*Mapeldreham*), Meon, East or West (*Menes*), Midlington (*Mitlinget'*), Milford (*Meleford*; 3), Morestead (*Morsteda*; 2), New Forest (? *Forest*; Normandy), Odiham (*Odiam, Hodiam*), Ovington (*Ouinton'*), *Papanholt* (a lost name; ? Micheldever Wood), Portsea Island (*Portesia*), Southampton (*Hantona*), Sparkford (*Esperchefort*), Stoneham, North or South (*Stanam*), Sutton, Tichborne (*Ticheb'*), Tisted (*Tistede*), Waltham, Bishop's or North (*Walt'*), Winchester (*Wint[oniensis]*), Winsor (*Windelesor, Windes'*; 2), Woodcote (*Wdecota*),Worthy (*Ordia*): Headbourne Worthy, Kings Worthy or Martyr Worthy (3).

The neighbouring counties contribute a number of local bynames. **Devon** is represented by Bridford (*Brudefort*), Chitterley (*Cederli'*), Exeter (*Exon'*; 2), Fishleigh (*Fislia*), and one of the many places called Hele (*Hahela* for *La Hela*), **Dorset** by Poole (*Pol*),[1] **Wiltshire** by Cricklade (*Chrichelada, Crech'*; 2), Inglesham (*Inglesh'*), and Salisbury (*Salesberie, Saleb', Sar'*; 3). Four Winchester citizens hailed from Keynsham (*Cainesham*, etc.) in **Somerset,** and Glastonbury (*Glauston'*) figures in the title of a Norman chamberlain. Hangleton (*Hangelt'*) and Iping (*Ipingis*) in **Sussex,** Abingdon (*Abendon[ensis]*), Bagnor (*Baganorus*), and Hungerford in **Berkshire,** and Wingham (*Wingeham*) in **Kent** complete the catalogue of places of origin.[2]

Cholcham, Essewem, and *Sapalanda*, have not been identified. *Paganus de la Medehalla* may have been a Winchester innkeeper. *Calp'* (2) may be *Calpestret*, now St. Thomas Street, in Winchester. Adjectival epithets derived from the latinized forms of place-names are *Abendon[ensis]* (Abingdon), *Exon[iensis]* (Exeter), *Sar[isberiensis]* (Salisbury) and *Wint[oniensis]* (Winchester). *Baganorus* is a curious example of a Latin ending having been added directly to the place-name, DB *Bagenore*, Bagnor (Brk).

Of identified French places which figure in local bynames (fig. 3) the majority are in **Calvados**: Anisy (*Anesi*),[3] Bayeux (*Baiaco*; 2), Caen (*Cadumo*), Courcy (*Curci*), Dives-sur-Mer (*Diua*; 3), Grainville-sur-Odon (*Grainuill'*), Jort (*Iorz*), Ouilly (*Oili*; 2), Percy-en-Auge (*Perci*), Le Poirier (*Piro*; or Le Pire, Pas-de-Calais), Port-en-Bessin (*Port*; 5), Quevilly (*Chiuilli*; or Le Petit-Quevilly, Seine-Maritime), Reviers (*Rediuers*), Touques (*Tocho, Tolcha*; 2), Tracy (*Traci*).

Manche is represented by Chiffrevast (*Seifrewast, Sifrewast*), La Barre-de-Semilly (*Barra*; or La Barre-en-Ouche, Eure), St. Jean-le-Thomas (*de Sancto Iohanne*), St. Lô (*de Sancto Laudo*), St. Martin d'Aubigny (*Albinneio*), St. Planchers (*de Sancto Pancratio*), Valognes (*Valuin*).

In **Seine-Maritime** are Bosc-le-Hard (*Bosco* ?), Eu (*Auco, Aucho*; 2), Limésy (*Limesia*), Massy (*Masiaco* ?), Mortemer-sur-Eaulne (*Mortuomari*; 2), Le Petit-Quevilly (or Quevilly, Calvados; see above), Ricarville (*Ricarduill'*; or Richarville, Seine-et-Oise), Rouen (*Rotomag'*), Vatierville (*Walteruile*).

A few places are in **Eure**: Les Andelys (*Andeleio*), La Barre-en-Ouche (or La Barre-de-Semilly, Manche; cf. above), Pont-de-l'Arche (*Ponte Archar'*; 2), Thouberville (*Tuberilli* ?). In **Eure-et-Loir** are Chartres (*Carnot'*), and Le Puiset (*Pusat*); in **Orne,** Briouze (*Braiosa*), and Sées (*Sagio*; 2); in **Seine-et-Oise,** Corbeil (*Corbulio*; or in

---

[1] Or South Pool (D).
[2] Wigot de Linc[olnia], the sheriff of Lincolnshire, is mentioned once *c.* 1110.

[3] The *LW* form is given in brackets, often in the latinized ablative. Figures refer to the number of persons involved.

Marne), Meulan (*Mellent*), and Richarville (or Ricarville, Seine-Maritime; see above). St. Valéry-sur-**Somme** (*de Sancto Walarico*) is in that department. Fougères (*Felgeriis*) is in **Ille-et-Vilaine.** (de) *Piro* may be Le Pire (**Pas-de-Calais**; or Le Poirier, **Calvados**).

A fair number of common French place-names cannot be assigned to a definite locality: Bray (*Braio*), Celle(s) (*Cell'*), Le Cellier (*Cellar'*), Colombier(e)s (*Columbiers*), Co(u)rlay (*Curleio*), La Forest (*Forest*),[1] Gouy (*Goi*), Hautot or Hot(t)ot (*Hotot*), La Haye (*Haia*; 2), Le Quesnoy, etc. (*Chaisneto*), St. Nicolas (*de Sancto Nicholao*), St. Quentin (*de Sancto Quintino*), Ste. Marie (*de Sancta Maria*), Temple (*Templo*), Tourville (*Turwill'*), Val (*Vallo*).

Chinai is probably French but has not been identified.[2]

The preposition *de* is used regularly both in English and French local bynames. It has been omitted in *Godwinus Cederli'* **1066**, *Herebertus Papanholt* **1148**, *Willelmus Hotot* **1148** (*semel*, by the side of *Willelmus de Hotot, bis*), and *Willelmus Pontearchar'*, *Willelmus Pont'* **1148** (once each, by the side of five cases with normal *de*).

Whether these cases reflect a genuine tendency to drop the preposition or whether they are merely due to scribal negligence cannot be decided on the basis of the *LW* material. There are, however, numerous parallels in DB, with both native and French place-names, and some instances of loss of the preposition have also been found in Norman eleventh-century charters.[3]

Special interest attaches to a few instances in which a place-name appears by itself in a personal-name function. These are as follows: *Baganora* **1148** (Bagnor, Brk) by the side of *Ricardus Baganorus* **1148**, *Dodesmere* **1066** (not identified), *Ficheldene* **1148** (Figheldean, W), *Froggemore* **1148** (Frogmore, Ha), *Hotot* **1148** (Hautot, etc., Normandy) by the side of *Willelmus de Hotot* (*bis*) and *Willelmus Hotot* (*semel*) **1148**, *Odiham* **1148** (Odiham, Ha) by the side of *Alwinus de Hodiam* **c. 1110**, *Alwinus de Odiam* **1148**, and *Pucheshele* **1066** (not identified). A possibly relevant example is also *Sitcelane* **1148** which may be an unidentified field-name in *lanu* 'lane, narrow road'.[4]

These cases should probably be explained as due either to a sort of deliberate scribal ellipsis or to mere accidental or negligent omission of the Christian name by the compiler or the copyist of the lists. It does not seem likely that at this early date a person should in actual, as distinct from scribal, usage have been referred to by his place of origin or residence alone.[5]

---

[1] This may be the New Forest in Ha.

[2] (Stephanus) *Mucheto* could be a French pl.n. with omission of *de*; see below, p. 214, s.n.

[3] Cf. E. Ekwall, *English Place-Names in -ing* (2nd edn., Lund, 1962), 72, n. 1. *DBS*, p. xivf. and, for the DB instances, Tengvik 30f., 125–30. Early Norman examples, all from original charters, are Osbernus *Hotot* 1069 *Jumièges* i. 81 (prob. Hautot-l'Auvray, Seine-Maritime), Wilelmus *Brietot* c. 1080 ibid. 106 (not identified), Rodbertus *Bortville* 1085 *France* 39 (not identified), Wido *Oillei* 1085 ibid. (Ouilly, Calvados), Ansfredus *Haretelville* 1086 *Jumièges* i. 113 (Heurteauville, Seine-Maritime; note that the pl.n. is in the latinized genitive; (signum) Gisleberti *Vuarenne* 1088 ibid. 118 (pl.n. in the gen). See also Ekwall *Genitive*, 76.

[4] *Crichel* **1148** belongs here if it stands for *Crichelade*, Cricklade (W).

[5] Cf. also B. Seltén, *English Studies*, 46 (1965), 171ff. The earliest example in his material of a local byname in independent use is from 1289.

ii. OCCUPATIONAL BYNAMES[1]

acularius, *Adelardus, Ricardus, Turstinus* **1148.**—MLat *acularius 'needle-maker',[2] a translation of OFr *aguillier*, which is attested as a byname in ME from 1188 onwards; see Fransson 148, *DBS* s.n. Aguilar.

adeling, see Other Bynames.

alebaster, see Personal Names.

archar', *Gilebertus* **c. 1110.**—MLat *arcarius*, OFr *archier* 'bowman, archer', also 'bow-maker'; Thuresson 161, *DBS* s.n. Archer.

archidiaconus, *Aluricus* **c. 1110,** *Stephanus, Stigandus, Willelmus* **1148.**—MLat *archidiaconus* 'archdeacon'.

asinarius, see Personal Names.

aurifaber, *Brithmarus* **1066,** *Atscor, Iohannes, Radulfus, Rogerus, Warinus* **1148.**—Lat *aurifaber* 'goldsmith', translating OE *goldsmið*, OFr *orfevre*; Tengvik 235f.

barrar', *Willelmus* **1148.**—MLat *barrarius*,[3] OFr *barrier* 'gate-keeper'; cf. the ME and ModE surname *Barrer*, ModFr *Barrier* (Dauzat s.n.). Fransson (p. 194) and Reaney, *DBS* s.n., incorrectly explain the term as denoting 'a dweller by a town gate'.

batar', *Selida* **1148.**—MLat *batarius, a latinization of the OFr noun *bateor* 'one who beats', which occurs, usually with a complement specifying the activity referred to, in various technical senses, such as 'gold-beater, silversmith, fuller, thresher' (Tobler–Lommatzsch s.v.), and was borrowed in ME as *bat(o)ur*; for examples in English sources (from 1199 onwards) see Fransson 102. In the *LW* instance the meaning may be 'coppersmith' or 'dealer in beaten copper or brassware'; see Ekwall *Subs R*, 354, *DBS* s.n. Bater[4]. The corresponding native term is ME *bēter* (< OE *bēatere*), which *MED* defines as 'one who beats cloth, a fuller; a metalworker'.

bedel, *Luuingus* **1066,** *bedellus, Aisil, Wlwardus* **1066,** *Alwinus, Bricthwinus* **c. 1110,** *bedel, Erneis* **1148,** *budel, Luinus, Ricardus* **1148.**—OE *bydel*,

MLat *bedellus*, OFr *bedel* 'beadle'; Tengvik 240, Thuresson 153f., *DBS* s.n. Beadel.

besmer', *besmera, Ailwardus* **1148,** *besmere, Ingulfus* **1148.**—ME *besmere* 'maker of besoms', a derivative of OE *besma* 'besom, broom'; Fransson 173, *DBS* s.n. Bessemer.

bolengarius, *Semannus* **1148,** *bulengarius, Edmundus* **1148.**—MLat *bolen-*, *bulengarius*, OFr *bolenger* 'baker'; Fransson 62, *DBS* s.n. Bullinger.

brachiator, *Hardingus* **1148,** *braciator, Alwinus* **1148.**—MLat *braciator*,[5] OFr *braceor* 'brewer'; Thuresson 201. Cf. *DBS* s.n. Brasseur and see *briwere* below.

brandwirchte, *Spilemanus* **1066.**[6]—OE *brandwyrhta 'sword-maker'. This is the only known example of the word; Fransson 152f., *MED* s.v. *brand*.

briwere, *bruwere, Willelmus* **1148.**—OE *brēowere, ME *brewere, briwere* 'brewer'; Fransson 77f., *DBS* s.n. Brewer. See also *Briwer'*, pers.n.

buclar', *bucl', Anschetillus* **1148.**—MLat *buclarius, a latinized form of OFr *bo(u)clier* 'buckle-maker', ME *bokeler*; Fransson 150, *DBS* s.n. Buckler. The term could probably also mean 'girdler'; see Ekwall *Subs R*, 355.

budel, see *bedel*.

bulengarius, see *bolengarius*.

burgeis, *Gaufridus* **c. 1110,** *burg[ensis], Ansfridus, Gaufridus, Hugo* **1148.**—MLat *burgensis*, OFr *burgeis* 'burgess'; *DBS* s.n. Burges.

buriman, *Edricus* **1148.**—OE *burhmann* 'citizen'. The *LW* form reflects the ME variant *buriman* (*MED* s.v. *burgh*, 5k). Cf. Sim' *Borgoman* 1207 *Fine R* 452 (Winchester).

butar', *Turchetillus* **1148.**[7]—MLat *buttarius* 'cooper',[8] a derivative of MLat *but(t)a, but(t)is* 'butt, cask, leather bottle, waterskin', OFr *bo(u)t*. Cf. the OFr and ModFr surname *Botier, Boutier* 'maker or seller of bottles.[9] The ME forms *le Buter, le Buttare, le Buttere* listed *DBS* s.n. *Butter* may belong here and need not, as Reaney thinks, be

---

[1] Including some terms denoting status: *burgeis, buriman, chenicte.*

[2] Not in Latham or Du Cange or *Mittellateinisches Wörterbuch*, i (Munich, 1967).

[3] Du Cange records one instance from Rouen 1207.

[4] Cf. also the ModFr surname *Batteur* which Dauzat, s.n., explains as 'gold-beater'.

[5] Latham s.v. *brasium.*

[6] Misdated 1103–15 by Fransson and *MED.*

[7] Perhaps the same man as *Turchetillo* (dat) *buter'* 1130 *P* 16 (Do).

[8] Latham s.v. *butta* (1136, 1230). Du Cange, i. 797, col. 3, has one Continental example which he translates 'one who loads or fills casks'.

[9] Drevin 61, G. de Beauvillé, *Rev. internat. d'onomastique*, 6 (1954), 64.

explained as 'keeper of the buttery'[1] or 'maker
or seller of butter'. The latter trade was clearly
followed by Henry *le Boterer* 1280 (*MED*) and
Will. *le Buterar'* 1327 (Fransson 68).

camerarius, *Albericus, Gaufridus, Her(e)bertus* c.
1110, *Alwinus, God', Radulfus* **1148.**—MLat
camerarius 'chamberlain'; Tengvik 240f.

campion, *Herbertus* **1148.**—ONFr *campion* 'a
combatant in the campus or arena, a champion';
DBS s.n. Champion.

cancellarius, *Edwardus* **1148.**—MLat *cancellarius*
'chancellor'; Tengvik 241.

cangeor,[2] *Andrebode* **1066.**—ONFr *cangeor,*[3] OFr
changeor 'money-changer'.

capellanus, *Hunfridus, Radulfus* **1148,** *capellanus
comitis de Mellent, Ricardus* c. **1110.**—MLat
capellanus 'chaplain'.

caretarius, *Radulfus, Wluricus* **1148.**—MLat *caret-
tarius*, ONFr *caretier*, ME *cartere* 'carter'; Thuresson 92f., *DBS* s.n. Carter.

carnifex, *Bernardus, Radulfus, Ricardus, Turbertus,
Turoldus* **1148.**—Lat *carnifex* in the MLat sense
'butcher', translating OE *flæscmangere*, ME *flesh-
mongere* or *fleshhewere*, or OFr *bo(u)chier*; Fransson
73f., *DBS* s.n. Butcher.

carpentarius, *Aoulf, Godard', Godefrid* **1148.**—
MLat *carpentarius*, ONFr *carpenter* 'carpenter';
Fransson 158f.

cerarius, *Osbertus* **1148.**—MLat *cerarius* 'maker or
seller of wax-candles'. The usual ME term is
chaundeler, candeler, on which see Fransson 72f.,
DBS s.n. Chandler.

chenicte, *Ailwardus, Godwinus* **1066.**—OE *cniht*
'servant, retainer, soldier'; Tengvik 246, *DBS* s.n.
Knight.

clericus, *Gaufridus, Turstinus* **1066,** *Alwinus, Elsi,
Gaufridus, Goisfridus, Radulfus, Stigandus, Tur-
stinus* c. **1110,** *Edwardus, Girinus, God', Here-
uicus, Hubertus, Miles, Radulfus, Ricardus, Thomas,
Turstinus, Wasco, Willelmus* **1148.**—MLat *clericus*,
OE *cleric*, OFr *clerc* 'clerk, scribe'; Tengvik 245f.,
Thuresson 221, *DBS* s.n. Clark.

cocus, see *coquus*.

coquus, *Albericus* c. **1110,** *cocus, Albericus,
Aluricus, Ernaldus, Radulfus, Ricardus, Rogerus,
Turbertus* **1148,** *coquus regis, Theodricus* **1066.**—
Lat *coquus, cocus* 'cook', OE *cōc*; *DBS* s.n. Cook.

corduanus, *Ade, Cuppingus* **1148.**—MLat *corduanus*, OFr *cordoan*, ME *cordewan* 'Cordovan
leather', used metonymically for *cordwanarius*
(q.v.).

cordwanarius, *Gilebertus, Iohannes, Ricardus* **1148.**
—MLat *cordwanarius*, OFr *cordoanier* 'cordwainer,
shoemaker'; Fransson 130f., *DBS* s.n. Cordner.
See also *corduanus* and *corueisarius*.

cornem', *Godefridus* **1148.**—Short for *corneman-
g(e)re*, OE **cornmangere* 'one who deals in corn'.
Cf. the ME examples (from 1177 onwards) collected by Fransson (p. 60).

corue(i)sarius, *Ailwardus, Ricardus* **1148.**—MLat
corve(i)sarius,[4] OFr *corveisier* 'shoemaker'; Fransson 131. See also *corduanus, cordwanarius*.

dapifer, *Edmundus* **1148,** *dapifer episcopi, Helias*
c. **1110,** *dapifer Herberti camerarii, Rannulfus* c.
1110.—MLat *dapifer* 'sewer, steward or seneschal'.

delere, *Lanc* **1066.**—See *Lancdelere*, pers.n.

diaconus, *Aluricus* **1066.**—MLat *diaconus*, OE
diacon 'deacon'; Tengvik 249f., *DBS* s.n. Deacon.

dispensator, *Simon* c. **1110,** *Rogerus, Simon* **1148.**
—MLat *dispensator*, OFr *despensier* 'steward,
bursar, butler'; Tengvik 250, *DBS* s.n. Spencer.

draper, *Walterus* **1148,** *drapier, Hugo* **1148.**—
OFr *drapier*, ME *draper* 'maker or seller of woollen
cloth'; Fransson 89, *DBS* s.n. Draper.

elemosinarius, *Robertus, Willelmus* **1148.**—MLat
elemosinarius, OFr *aumonier* 'almoner'; Thuresson
177.

episcopus *Salesberie, Rogerus* c. **1110.**—This is
Roger le Poer, who held the see of Salisbury
1102–39.

faber, *Edwinus* **1066,** *Hardingus, Ricardus* c. **1110,**
*Aelricus, Ailwinus, Bernardus, Edwinus, Henricus,
Herdingus, Iohannes, Robertus, Willelmus* **1148.**—
Lat *faber* 'smith', translating OE *smið* or OFr
fevre; Tengvik 269f.

---

[1] The keeper of a buttery, MLat *buteria, boteria*, is
called *buticularius, buticlarus*, later *butellarius, butil-
larius, botellarius*; Latham s.v. The corresponding
vernacular forms are OFr *boteiller, boutiler*, ME
boteler, etc. (*MED* s.v.).

[2] MS. *gangeor*.

[3] Norman examples are Reginaldus *le cangeor*
1137–50 *St. Wandrille* 123, Gaufr' *le Cangeor* 1203
MRSN 562. Note also Henr' *Changor* 1207 *Fine R*
452 (Winchester).

[4] Latham s.v. *cordubanum*.

feller, *Alwinus le c.* 1110.—ME *fellere* 'feller, cutter' (*MED*) with the prefixed French definite article. Cf. Osbertus *fellere c.* 1120–30, *EHR* 14 (1899), 424 (Winchester).

fenarius, *Alwinus* 1066.—MLat *fenarius* 'hay-merchant'. The corresponding native word was OE **h(ī)egmangere*, ME *heimongere*; cf. *DBS* s.n. Hayman.

fullo, *God', Paganus* 1148.—Lat *fullo* 'fuller', which translates OE *fullere* or *wealcere*, OFr *fouleor*. Fransson 100f., *DBS* s.n. Fuller.

fundor, *Ricardus* 1148.—MLat *fundor*, OFr *fondeur* 'metal-founder'; Fransson 138.

furbar', *Ricardus* 1148.—MLat *furbarius*, OFr *fo(u)rbeor* 'furbisher of armour, etc.'; Fransson 151, *DBS* s.n. Furber.

gangeor, see *cangeor*.

hangere, see Personal Names.

harengarius, *Algarus, Wlwardus* 1066, *harangarius, Seman* 1148.—MLat *harengarius*[1] 'herring-monger' from OFr *harenc* 'herring'. The corresponding native word is ME *heringmongere*; Fransson 77.

heuere, *Alwinus* 1066.—OE *hēawere* (in compounds), ME *hewere* 'a cutter of wood or stone' (*MED*); Thuresson 234, *DBS* s.n. Hewer.

hoppere, see Personal Names.

hosarius, *Sonricus* 1066.—MLat *hosarius*, ME *hosiere* 'hosier'; Fransson 115, *DBS* s.n. Hosier.

ieltfange, see Other Bynames.

ioculator, *Iohannes* 1148.—Lat *ioculator* 'jester, entertainer, jongleur', OFr *jogleor* 'minstrel, juggler'; Thuresson 189f., *DBS* s.n. Juggler.

lardarius, *Henricus, Hugo c.* 1110.[2]—MLat *lardarius* 'official who has charge of a larder'. Note however that OFr *lardier* also meant 'pork-butcher'. See also *lardinarius*.

lardinarius, *Herebertus* 1148.—MLat *lardinarius*, OFr *lardiner*, a synonym of *lardarius* above; Thuresson 121.

lignator, *Alwinus* 1148.—Lat *lignator* 'wood-cutter'. See also *feller, heuere*.

lorimer, *Anschetillus, Ricardus, Willelmus* 1148.—OFr *loremier, lorimier* 'lorimer, spurrier'; Fransson 147, *DBS* s.n. Lorimer.

machun, maco, *Anschetillus, Baldewinus, Robertus, Selid', Stigandus* 1148.—ONFr *machun*, Anglo-Lat *maco* 'mason'; Fransson 175, Latham s.v. *mazo*, *ELPN* 110, *DBS* s.n. Mason.

magister, *Osbertus* 1148.—Lat *magister*, OE *mægester*, OFr *maistre* 'teacher, schoolmaster'; Thuresson 178f., *DBS* s.n. Master.

magister monetarius, *Godwinus Socche* 1066.—See *monetarius*.

marescallus, *God', Willelmus* 1148.—MLat *marescallus*, OFr *mareschal* 'one who tends horses, a farrier'; Fransson 144, *DBS* s.n. Marshall.

meddere, *Ricardus le* 1148.—Probably ME *medere* 'maker or seller of mead'; Thuresson 202, *DBS* s.n. Meader, or possibly ME *maderere, madrer* 'one who manufactures, or dyes with, madder', an agent noun from OE *mædere, mæddre* 'madder', for which see Fransson 108, *DBS* s.n. Madder. In the latter case the *LW* form would show loss of *-er-* by haplology, *e* for *a* in the first syllable being AN or dialectal; cf. below, p. 223. Note also (de terra Osbert) *Maddere* 1174–88 *PRBW* 160 (Winchester). For the synonymous OFr term see *Waranc'* below, p. 217.

medicus, *Grimbaldus, Paganus, Ricardus, Willelmus* 1148.—Lat *medicus* 'physician'. The corresponding native term is OE *lǣce*, ME *lēche*; Fransson 187.

mercator, *Henricus* 1148.—Lat *mercator* 'merchant'. The OFr word was *marcheant*, the native term OE *cēapmann*, ME *chapman*.

merciarius, *Petrus* 1148.—MLat *merciarius, mercerius*, OFr *mercier* 'merchant', ME *mercer* 'dealer in textile fabrics, esp. silks, velvets, etc.'; Fransson 92. See also *Mercherel*, byn.

molendinarius, *Ansgod, Hudo, Rogerus, Teodericus* 1148.—MLat *molendinarius* 'miller'. On the vernacular synonyms OE *myle(n)weard, *mylnere* (ME *milner*, etc.), and OFr *molnier* (ME *mouner*), see Fransson 56ff.

monacus, *Hunfridus, Osbertus* 1148.—MLat *monachus* 'monk'.

monetarius, *Alestanus, Alwardus filius Etardii, Alwinus Aitardessone, Andrebodus* 1066, *Odo, Wimundus c.* 1100, *Sanson, Siwardus* 1148, *magister monetarius, Godwinus Socche* 1066.—Lat *monetarius* 'moneyer'. Cf. OE *mynetere*, ME *mineter*, OFr *mon(n)ier*, ME *monnyer*; Fransson 135.

---

[1] Not in Latham. Du Cange records one example from 1235 (Cluny).

[2] He is called *Hugo Larderarius* in Winchester charters *c.* 1100; see above, p. 162, n. 7.

napier, *Petrus* **1148,** *napparius, Audoenus* **c. 1110.—**
MLat *nap(p)arius,* OFr *napier* 'keeper of the
table-linen'; Thuresson 121, *DBS* s.n. Napier.

palmarius,[1] *Anschetillus* **c. 1110.** *Ailwinus, Here-*
bertus, Rogerus, Willelmus **1148.—**MLat *palmarius*
'pilgrim to the Holy Land', OFr *palmier*; Tengvik
262, *DBS* s.n. Palmer.

parcheminus, *Ainulfus* **1148.—**OFr *parchemin*
'parchment', used metonymically of a maker of
parchment. Cf. ME *parcheminer*; Fransson 128f.

parcherius, *Huchelinus* **1066.—**A latinized form of
OFr *parchier, parker* 'park-keeper'. The usual
MLat form is *parcarius.* Cf. Thuresson 105, *DBS*
s.n. Parker.

parmentarius, *Iwen* **c. 1110,** *Amfridus, Baldewinus,*
Gunter', Hereuic', Mainard', Oinus, Raimundus,
Robertus, Rogerus, Sired, Stigandus, Walterus,
Wluricus **1148.—**MLat *parmentarius,* OFr *par-*
mentier 'tailor'; Fransson 111, *DBS* s.n. Parmenter.

pasturellus, see Other Bynames.

pictor, *Henricus, Ricardus, Rogerus, Willelmus*[2]
1148.—Lat *pictor* 'painter'. The OFr term was
peintour which was borrowed as ME *peyntour,*
etc.; Fransson 177.

pincerna, *Picot* **c. 1110,** *Girinus, Herebertus* **1148.—**
MLat *pincerna* 'butler' which translates OFr
bouteiller.

pistor, *Robertus filius Willelmi* **c. 1110,** *Baldewinus,*
Hugo, Rogerus **1148.—**Lat *pistor* 'baker'. The
vernacular term was OE *bæcere,* ME *bakere.* See
also *bolengarius.*

portarius, *Willelmus* **1148.—**MLat *portarius,* OFr
portier, ME *porter* 'door-keeper'; Tengvik 265,
Thuresson 148f., *DBS* s.n. Porter.

portereue 1148.—See *Portereue,* pers.n.

potarius, *Willelmus* **c. 1110.—**MLat *pot(t)arius*
'potter', translating OE *pottere* or OFr *potier*;
Fransson 184, *DBS* s.n. Potter.

prepositus, *Ricardus* **1066,** *Gesordus, Ricardus,*
Warinus **c. 1110,** *Herebertus* **1148,** *prepositus*
Wint[oniæ], Adelwoldus **1066.—**MLat *prepositus*
'provost, reeve of a borough' translates OE
geréfa, ME *réve.*

presbiter, *Almodus, Alwinus, Burwoldus, Coleman,*
*Colswanus (Golsewanus), Godricus, Lewinus, Leuri-
cus (Lowricus), Stanulfus, Urandus, Wluricus **1066,**
Almarus, Brithwoldus, Edwardus, Elsi, Essulfus,
Herbertus, Radulfus, Sawalo, Spileman, Theodricus,
Wimundus **c. 1110,** *Baldewinus, Benedictus, Col-*
sueinus, Ernoldus, Geruasius, Gilebertus, God',
Godwinus, Henricus, Her(e)bertus, Herefridus, Io-
hannes, Nicholaus, Nigellus, Odo, Radulfus, Ran-
dulfus, Ricardus, Richer', Robertus, Turoldus,
Walterus, Willelmus **1148.—**MLat *presbyter* 'priest',
OE *préost,* OFr *prestre*; Thuresson 167f., *DBS*
s.n. Priest.

regina, *Edde, Emma* **1066.—**Lat *regina* 'queen'.

regis serviens, *Erchembaldus, Herfridus* **c. 1110.—**
The precise function of these royal officials is not
known.

rusmangre, *Warin'* **1148.—**OE **ryscmangere* 'a
seller of rushes' (used for strewing on floors);
cf. ModE *rush-dealer (NED* 1851), *rush-man* (1606),
rush-reaper (1552). See *Rus,* p. 215, and Addenda.

sacrista, *Ailwinus, Radulfus* **1148.—**MLat *sacrista*
'sacristan'.

salnarius, *sannarius, Picot* **1148.—**MLat *salinarius,*
OFr *sauneor* 'salt-boiler'; Thuresson 203.

saponarius, *Ailwinus* **1148,** *savonarius, Godricus*
1066.—MLat *saponarius, savonarius* 'soap-maker',
OFr *savonnier,* ME *sauoner*; Fransson 71f. The
native word is OE *sápere,*[3] ME *sópere.*

scalarius, *Luuingus* **1066.—**Lat *scalarius* 'ladder-
maker'.

scaldeator, *Robertus* **c. 1110.—**MLat *scaldeator,*
OFr *eschaldeor,*[4] *escaudeur* 'one who scalds pigs,
poultry, etc.' Cf. ME *scalder*; Thuresson 126.

scoter', *Robertus* **1148.—**ME *schótere* 'bowman,
archer', a derivative of OE *scéotan* 'to shoot';
Thuresson 161f., *DBS* s.n. Shooter.

scriba, *Gisulfus* **1148.—**Lat *scriba* 'scribe'.

scriniarius, *Hugo* **1148.—**MLat *scriniarius,*[5] OFr
escrinier 'cabinet-maker'.

scrutarius, *Willelmus* **c. 1110.—**Lat *scrutarius*
'dealer in second-hand clothes, ragman'.

---

[1] The word is abbreviated *palm'* in all but one case
which has *palmar'.* Hence *palmarius* has been chosen as
the standard form; cf. also Osbertus *palmari'* 1130
P 113. But *palmerius* was a common MLat variant.

[2] Willemus *pinctor* 1148 **II, 120.** In the first three
cases the MS. has *pic'.*

[3] Recorded in *Saperetun* 969 *BCS* 1239, Saberton

(Gl); *PNGl* ii. 43.

[4] Godefroy, ix. 509.

[5] Recorded once in Du Cange: *scrin[i]arius,* 1479.
In classical Latin a *scriniarius* was an official in charge
of the imperial *scrinium,* and this and cognate senses,
clearly inappropriate here, are amply attested in MLat;
see Niermeyer s.v.

scutarius, *Alanus* **1148**.—MLat *scutarius* 'shield-wright'. The OE term was *scildwyrhta*.

sellarius, *Aschetillus, Berengarius, Fulcho, Petrus, Robertus* **1148**.—MLat *sellarius* 'saddler', translating OFr *selier* or ME *sadelere*; Fransson 123f.

sermonarius, see Personal Names.

serviens, *Anschetillus, Sewlf* **1148**, *serviens abbatisse, Seward'* **1148**, *serviens episcopi, Anschetillus* **1148**. —Lat *serviens* 'servant'. See also *regis serviens*.

spileman, see Personal Names.

stiward, *Alwinus* **1148**, (*Osbertus filius*) *Stiwardi* **1148**.—OE *stigweard* 'steward'; Tengvik 272, *DBS* s.n. Steward.

sutor, *Lewinus* **1066**, *Robertus* **1148**.—Lat *sutor* 'shoemaker'. The native term is OE *sūtere*.

tailator, *Ricardus* **c. 1110**.—MLat *taillator* 'tailor', a latinization of OFr *tailleor*, on which see Fransson 110f. See also *taleator*.

taleator, *Gilebertus, Robertus* **1148**.—MLat *taleator* 'tally-cutter', or a variant of *tailator* 'tailor' (q.v.), as is suggested by Niermeyer s.v.

taneator, *Edredus, Radulfus, Walderus* **c. 1110**, *tan(n)ator, Bonefacius, Willelmus* **1148**.—MLat *tannator* 'tanner', translating OE *tannere* or OFr *taneor, tannour*, on which see Fransson 119. The variant *taneator* does not seem to have been noticed before.[1]

telarius, *Aldelmus* **1148**.—MLat. *telarius* 'weaver', OFr *telere, tel(l)ier*.

thesaurarius, *Henricus* **1066**.—Lat *thesaurarius*, OFr *tresorier* 'treasurer'. See also *Tresor*, nickname.

ticcheman, see Personal Names.

tinctor, *Ailwardus, Ailware, Drogo, Rogerus* **1148**.—MLat *tinctor* 'dyer', translating OFr *teindeor, teintur*, ME *deier* (< OE **dēagere*); Fransson 104ff.

tornator, *Elfegus* **1066**, *tornitor, Hugo* **1148**.—Lat *tornator*, OFr *tourneur* 'turner'; cf. Fransson 166. The variant *tornitor* has not been recorded before; it may, alternatively, stand for MLat *torniator* 'jouster'.

trauetier, see Personal Names.

turtellarius, *Herbertus* **1148**.—MLat **turtellarius*, from *turtella* 'cake', a latinized form of OFr *to(u)rtelier* 'confectioner'.

unctarius, *Robertus* **1148**.—MLat *unctarius*, OFr *ointier*, ME *oynter* 'seller of grease'; Thuresson 200.

vigil, *Herbertus, Terricus, Willelmus* **1148**.—Lat *vigil* 'watchman'. The OFr term is *gaite*, ONFr *waite*; Thuresson 147.

vinetarius, *Ailwardus, Edricus, Rogerus* **1148**.—MLat *vinetarius*, OFr *vinetier*, ME *vineter* 'vintner'; cf. Fransson 79.

wantar', *Ulgarus* **1066**.—MLat *wantarius* 'glover'. The vernacular terms were OE **glōfere*, ME *glover*, and OFr *gantier, wantier*.

waranc(h)ier, see Other Bynames s.v. *Waranc'*.

watmaungre, *Alwinus* **1066**.—OE **wǣtmangere* 'seller of drinks', the first el. being OE *wǣt* n. 'liquid, drink' or *wǣta* m. 'wetness, water, drink'.

Notes on the occupational bynames

The bynames listed above are nearly all latinized, the vernacular forms being retained in the following cases, (*a*) English: *besmere, brandwirchte, briwere* (var. *bruwere*), *budel, buriman, chenicte, cornem[angere], delere* (?), *feller, heuere, meddere, rusmangre, scoter, stiward*, and *watmaungre*; (*b*) Old French: *bedel, burgeis, campion, cangeor, drap(i)er, lorimer, machun*(?), *napier*, and *trauetier*. Of these *rusmangre* < OE **ryscmangere* and *watmaungre* < OE **wǣtmangere* have not been recorded before, and *brandwirchte* < OE **brandwyrhta* is a *hapax legomenon*.[2]

Of the Latin terms a few are not included in Latham's dictionary: *acularius, barrarius, batarius, buclarius, harengarius, scriniarius, turtellarius*, and *unctarius*.[3] *Taneator* and *tornitor* are previously unrecorded variants of *tannator* and *tornator*.

---

[1] But note also Mansellus *taneator* 1091 R. Charles and Menjot d'Elbenne (eds.), *Cartulaire de l'abbaye de Saint Vincent du Mans* (Le Mans, 1886, 1913), 182.

[2] *Brandwirchte* has been misdated 1103–15 by Fransson (p. 152) and *MED*.

[3] *acularius, batarius, buclarius*, and *turtellarius* are not in Du Cange or later glossaries of medieval Latin. Of *barrarius, harengarius*, and *scriniarius* Du Cange has one example each from French sources.

Occupational terms sometimes occur independently as designations for persons with omission of the Christian name. The following two examples where the reference is to the same person illustrate this phenomenon:

Alwinus *Stiward* **1148**: Osbertus *filius Stiwardi*
Terri *Trauet[ier]* **1148**: *Trauetier*

A similar instance may be *Briwer'* **1148** who is perhaps identical with Willelmus *Briwere* (var. *Bruwere*).

Other cases in point are *Alebast[er]* **1148** 'crossbowman', *Asinarius* **1148** 'donkey-driver', *Hangere* **1148** 'hangman', *Hoppere* **1148** 'dancer', *Portereue* **1148** 'port-reeve', *Sermonarius* **1148** 'preacher', (p) *Ticcheman* **1066** < OE **ticcenmann* 'keeper or breeder of kids'. The late OE pers.n. *Spileman*, **1066–1148**, was an original designation for a player or jester but had long ago lost its professional connotation; the **1066** bearer was a sword-maker and his *c.* **1110** namesake a priest.[1]

It should also be noted that some epithets classed under nicknames (below, pp. 207–17) may, by metonymy, have served to indicate the bearer's trade or occupation, examples being *Casier* 'cheese-cellar', *Cheppe* 'cap', *Cornet* 'trumpet, cornet', *Escitteport* (< *scytteport*) 'shut-gate', *Furwatel* 'cake-oven', *Patinus* 'wooden shoe', *Softebred* 'soft bread', *Waranc'* 'madder dye'.[2]

iii. BYNAMES OF RELATIONSHIP

The commonest type is the Latin patronymic formula *filius N.N.* which is abundantly attested in the three surveys and requires no further comment or exemplification here. The corresponding vernacular combination of a personal name in the genitive and *sunu* is sometimes met with in our material. In the **1066** survey we have Godwinus *Elmeressone*, Alwinus *Aitardessone*, Godeman *Brunechingessone*, Alwi *Chasiessone*, Godricus *Chingessone*, Alestanus *Douetessone*, Algar *Godesbranesson*, Siwardus *Leuerunessone*, Lewingius *Mandingessone*, Lewinus *Scottelauessone*, Alwinus *Sidessone*, and Odo *Ticchemannessone*. The *c.* **1110** list yields only four examples: God' *Ælmeressone*, Radulfus taneator *Cattessone*, Godwinus *Grenessone*, and Radulfus *Holinessone*. In **1148** we have one instance only: *Edgaresune* (*Odgaressune*), which occurs independently without a preceding pers.n. In several of the above cases the native genitive formula may owe its retention to the fact that the patronymic was unfamiliar to the scribe who was uncertain how to latinize it and hence decided to take over the form as it stood in his original.

The formula *filia N.N.* is also common, but there is only one example of the vernacular variant: *Leflet Ecregeles docter* **1066**, another difficult patronymic with which the latinizing clerk had failed to cope.

The occasional survival into the early twelfth century of the OE suffix *-ing* to express a patronymic relationship is attested by (Godwinus) *Withmundin* *c.* **1110**.

---

[1] On occupational bynames in independent use see B. Seltén, *English Studies*, 46 (1965), 176ff.
[2] See Reaney *Origin*, 245–7. The pers.n. *Hauoc*

(q.v.), an original byname, OE *hafoc* 'hawk', seems to have been borne by a hawker. Cf. also Rad' *hauoc*, a London falconer in 1130, P 148; Reaney, ibid. 245.

Other relationships are expressed by the terms *frater*, e.g. Sawinus *frater Wnstani* **1066**, Osbertus *frater Maiesent* **c. 1110**, Ernoldus *frater Petri* **1148**, etc., and *uxor* which is fairly common, often in the truncated formula *uxor Almodi*, *uxor Edrici*, etc., with omission of the Christian name. *Gener* and *pater* occur once each: Aluricus *gener Henrici* **1148**, Alwinus *pater Chepingi* **1066**, *soror* twice: Adelidis *soror Henrici de Port* **c. 1110**, *soror Martini* **1148**, and *nepos* three times: Edulfus *nepos Turstini*, Iohannes *nepos Petri mercatoris*, Radulfus *nepos Godefridi*, all **1148ff.** Two women are described as *vidua*, namely *Brithwen* **1066** and *Aldied* **c. 1110**.[1]

The compiler's need for precision sometimes led to unwieldy combinations like *Emma uxor Roberti fratris Warini* **1148**.

In some cases the patronymic function is expressed by placing the father's name in an uninflected form immediately after the name of the son. That such combinations were in fact patronymic in origin is confirmed by the following instances in which the conventional *filius* formula is employed by the side of the appositional one:

Rogerus *filius Armerlanc* **c. 1110** : Rogerus *Amberlang*
Alexander *filius Gollan'* **1148** : Alexander *Goisl'*
Hugo *filius Guntscel'* **1148** : (heredes) Hugonis *Guncel'*
Ricardus *filius Lambricht* **1148** : Ricardus *Lambert*
Paganus *filius Picard'* **1148** : Paganus *Pic'*
Osbertus *filius Thiardi* **c. 1110** : Osbertus *Tiart*
Herebertus *filius Westman* **1148** : Herebertus *Westman*

The other examples are: Willelmus *Bertram* **c. 1110**, (domus) Burewoldi *Frefhewini* **1066** (ɔ: Frethewini), Gislebertus *Gibart* **c. 1110**, Hugo *Gladewin'* **1148**, (domus) Godwini *Goce* **1066**, Astcelinus *Godeman* **c. 1110**,[2] Robertus *Grifin* **1148**, Durandus *Gumbold* **1148**, Bernardus *Hubold* **1148**, Alur' *Iola* **c. 1110**, Petrus *Lanc[elin]* **1148**, Hugo *Oil(l)ardus* **c. 1110**.[3]

It is interesting to note that, as Ekwall points out with reference to similar cases in early London sources,[4] the second element in the combination is generally not latinized and that the patronyms are mostly unusual foreign names which were no doubt liable to be mistaken for bynames. (Burewoldi) *Frefhewini* and *Oil(l)ardus* are the only latinized forms.

An unusual variant of this pattern is represented by *Rogerus Abonel* (*ter*) and *Rogerus Macher'*, both **1148**, whose patronyms occur once each independently. The scribe probably mistook them for bynames and left out the first name on the analogy of cases like those listed below, pp. 219–20.[5]

---

[1] The byname of Ulueua *Betteslaf* (**1066**) may illustrate the use of OE *lāf* 'widow'.

[2] *Godeman* may, however, be a genuine byname.

[3] Possible instances are also *Leovricus Abeaham* **1066** (for *Abraham*?) and *Rogerus Loer'* **1148** (for *Loherus*?), on which see below, pp. 207, 213.

[4] *ELPN* 128ff.

[5] The use of uninflected Christian names as bynames in medieval East Anglia is dealt with at length by Bo Seltén in his recent important book, *The Anglo-Saxon heritage in Middle English personal names*, i (Lund studies in English, 43, 1972), 54ff.

iv. OTHER BYNAMES, CHIEFLY NICKNAMES

Abeaham, *Leovricus* **1066.**—At first sight this looks like an OE pl.n. in -*ham(m)*, but an *Eahām does not exist,[1] and there are no examples in our material of the use of *ab* for normal *de* to indicate place of origin. Perhaps the pers.n. *Abraham* used here in a patronymic function (see above, p. 206, n. 3), *e* for *r* being a copyist's error. The name is not recorded before the Conquest but turns up up in DB 1086: *Abraham* presbyter Gl 162.

Abonel, *Rogerus* **1148.**—See *Abonel*, pers.n.

Adeling, *Ernoldus* **1148.**—OE *æðeling* 'man of royal blood, nobleman', ME *atheling* 'nobleman or lord, knight, warrior' (*MED*).[2]

Agnell', *Petrus* **1148.**—Lat *agnellus* 'little lamb', OFr *agnel* 'lamb'.

Amberlang, *Rogerus c.* **1110.**—See *Amberlang*, pers.n.

Bade, *Bictricus* **1066.**—Probably an OE *badda, formed from the stem in OE *bæddel* 'hermaphrodite', *bædling* 'effeminate man', ME *badde* 'bad, wicked' (1221ff.; *MED* s.v.);[3] cf. also (Robert) *Badding* 1187–1221 *ELPN* 136 (London).

Baganorus, *Ricardus* **1148.**—See Local Bynames.

Bal', *Gaufridus* **1148.**—Cf. (Ricardus) *Bal*, (Robertus) *Bal* 12th c. *LVH* 70. Probably OE *beall,[4] ME *bal* 'round body, sphere, ball' (*c.* 1200, *MED*), but we may also have OE *b(e)ald* 'bold, brave' or its OFr synonym *balt* with AN loss of the final consonant.[5]

Balloe, *Lewinus* **1066.**—For *Balloc* < OE *bealluc* 'ballock, testicle', an earlier example of the byname being (Mataðan) *Balluc*, mon. Lincoln, Cnut.[6] See also *Balloc*, pers.n. and *Taddebelloc*, byn.

Banne, *Brucstanus* **1066.**—Perhaps an OE *banna,

an agential formation from OE *bannan* 'to summon, command'. In ME *bannen* also meant 'to curse', tr. and itr., and this meaning, which is apparently due to the influence of the ON synonym *banna* (see *MED* s.v.), may well have existed in OE. The post-conquest byname (Willelmus) *Banne* 1086 DB Gl 162, He 179, (de Ricardo) *Banne* 1210–11 *PRBW* 122 (Ha), (Michael, Walkelin) *Bane* late 13th c. *StAug* 18 (K), on the other hand, is probably OFr *ban(n)e* 'hamper, pannier; tip-cart', Norm. dial. *banne* 'farm wagon',[7] as in the Picard instances (Laurentius dictus) *le Banne*, (Wiardus dictus) *li Banne*, both 1261, (Huone) *le Bane* 1260 (La Neuville-Roi, Oise),[8] and the ModFr surname *Banne* (Dauzat 24).

Bar, *Goduinus* **1148.**—OE *bār* 'boar'; *DBS* s.n. Boar.

Barbitre, *Aluinus c.* **1110.**—An OE nickname *bār-bītere 'boar-biter' is a conceivable formation though the point of it is obscure.[9] If, however, the first *r* is miswritten for *c*, we have ME *bakbitere* 'defamer, traducer' (*MED*, *c.* 1200ff.). On the syncope of medial *e* in -*bitre* see below, p. 223.

Barrat', *Girardus c.* **1110.**—OFr *barat* 'commerce; trickery, fraud', ME *barat* 'strife, trouble, combat; bargaining; deception, fraud' (*MED*); *DBS* s.n. Barrat.

Bel, *Hugo* **1148,** *Bell',* *Robertus* **1148,** *Bella, Suna* **1148.**—Lat *bellus*, OFr *bel(e)* 'beautiful, fair'; *DBS* s.n. Bell.

Bensetoure, *Iohannes c.* **1110.**—See Addenda.

Bertram, *Willelmus c.* **1110.**—See *Bertram*, pers.n.

Betteslaf, *Ulueua* **1066.**—She occurs twice in DB TRE: *Ulueua beteslau* Ha 43, *Vlueuæ* (gen)

---

[1] *DEPN*, p. xvi.

[2] On the use of the word as a title in the OE period see Tengvik 236.

[3] The ultimate etymology of these words is unknown, and even the quantity of the vowel in the two OE nouns is doubtful. BT, *NED*, and *MED* take it to be short, whereas Clark Hall, F. Holthausen, *Altenglisches etymologisches Wörterbuch* (Heidelberg, 1963), and C. T. Onions, *The Oxford Dictionary of English Etymology* (Oxford, 1966), s.v. *bad*, mark it as long. An OE verb *bædan* 'to defile' from which Holthausen would explain *bæddel*, etc., does not seem to exist; see H. D. Meritt, *Fact and Lore about Old English Words* (Stanford, 1954), 190. The OE pers.n. *Bad(d)a*, on the other hand, is a pet-form of names in *B(e)adu-*; Redin 44. Variants inferred from pl.ns are *Beadda*,

Bæddi, and *Bæddel*; see *DEPN* s.nn. Baddiley, Baddesley, and Badlesmere.

[4] Presupposed by the derivative *bealluc*.

[5] See *PNDB* § 103.

[6] *BEH* 1658, 1664.

[7] Tobler–Lommatzsch s.v. *bane*, *FEW* i. 325 f.

[8] L. Carolus-Barré (ed.), *Les plus anciennes chartes en langue française*, i (Paris, 1964), 48. The derivative *banastre* 'big basket, hamper' was also used as a nickname in OFr and ME, e.g. (Willelmo) *Banastre c.* 1200 F. Dubosc (ed.), *Cartulaire de l'abbaye de la Luzerne* (in *Archives départementales de la Manche*, St. Lô, 1878), 35 (Manche); for ME examples see *DBS* s.n. Bannister.

[9] Cf. perhaps ModE *sheep-biter* 'a dog that bites or worries sheep' (1548, *NED*).

beteslau W 74b. Round identified the byname with the Sa pl.n. Beslow, DB *Beteslawe*,[1] but the absence of *de* in all three cases and the final *f* in the *LW* spelling raise doubts about the correctness of this derivation. A satisfactory alternative is not easy to find, however. The second el. could be OE *lāf* f. 'relict, widow'[2] in which case DB *-lau* would be due to inflected *-lāfe* [lave]. The first el. might be the same as in Beslow, i.e. the gen. of OE *Betti*, pers.n., hence 'Betti's widow', but the reappearance of this archaic name in the eleventh century would be somewhat unexpected.[3] See Addenda.

Bied, *Totel* 1066.—See next entry.

Bierd, *Alwinus* 1148.—OE *beard* 'beard'; *DBS* s.n. Beard. On *ie* < *ĕa* see below p. 224. The loss of pre-consonantal *r* in *bied* is an AN feature; Pope § 1184. See also *Blachebiert, cum barba, Fulebiert* below.

Bittecat, *Lipestanus* 1066.—The second el. is OE *catt* 'cat', the first probably OE *bytt(e)* f. 'bottle, cask'; hence perhaps a sobriquet for a heavy drinker. See also *Cat* below.

Blachebiert, *Brunstanus* 1066.—OE *blæc* 'black', *beard* 'beard'; *DBS* s.n. Blackbird. See also *Bierd* above.

Blundus, *Drogo, Rogerus, Willelmus* 1148.—OFr *blund, blond* 'blond, fair'; *DBS* s.n. Blunt.

Bochenel, *Gilebertus* 1066.—Possibly a diminutive of OFr *bo(u)c* 'he-goat' with the double suffix *-in-el*.[4] Cf. early ModFr *bouquin* 'young he-goat, kid', OFr *bouquine* 'she-goat', and the French surnames *Bouquin, Bouquain, Bouquerel*; *FEW* i. 587, Dauzat 58.

Bollochessege, *Alwinus c.* 1110.—See *Bullochesiega*, pers.n.

Bontens, *Robertus* 1148.—OFr *bon tens* 'good time', a nickname for a man of a jovial disposition. *Bontens, Bontemps*[5] is a common surname in Old and Modern French; see Pachnio 19f., Dauzat 51.

Bonus homo, *Rand'* 1148.—A translation of OFr *bonhomme* 'good-natured, worthy man; commoner, peasant' or ME *godman* 'good, righteous man; male head of a household; citizen of a town; master in a craft or guild' (*MED* s.v.). See also *Godeman*, byn., and *DBS* s.n. Bonham.

Braders, *Alestanus* 1066.—OE *brād ears* 'broad arse'; cf. (Godwin) *Bredhers* 1137 *ELPN* 140 (London).

Brito, *Radulfus c.* 1110.—Lat *Brito*, OFr *Bret* 'Breton'.

Brun(us), *Willelmus c.* 1110.—OE *brūn* or OFr *brun* 'brown'; Tengvik 391, *DBS* s.n. Brown. See also *Brun*, pers.n.

Burdin, *Arnulfus c.* 1110.—MLat *burdinus* 'a small mule' was used on the Continent both as a pers.n. and as a byname.[6] Cf. also ModFr dial *bourdin* 'donkey, young ox'; *FEW* i. 633.

Buriman, *Edricus* 1148.—See Occupational Bynames.

Cachastra, *Patricius* 1148.—A Norman byname, other examples of which are (Adheliz uxor) *Cacast'* c. 1130 (Winchester),[7] (de dono Ranulfi) *Cachastre* 1172–89 *RAH* ii. 315 (Calvados), (Thom') *Cachastre* 1195 *MRSN* 272 (Normandy). The first el. should perhaps be associated with ONFr *cachier* 'to hunt, chase', ONFr *cacheor* 'hunter; race-horse', the second being the OFr suffix *-astre* which was used to form nouns and adjectives, e.g. *banastre, fillastre, folastre*, often with a pejorative connotation.[8]

---

[1] *VCH Hants* i. 429.

[2] As in *Byrhtwara Ælfrices laf* 973–87 *AS Wills* 11 (K); cf. also *Sifled relicta Lefsii c.* 975 E. O. Blake (ed.), *Liber Eliensis* (Camden 3rd ser. 92, 1962), 85.

[3] Not recorded after *c.* 840, *LVD*; Redin 126. Note, however, the occurrence in *LW* of archaic names like OE *Nunna* (*c.* 1110) and *Tāthere* or *Torhthere* (1066).

[4] On medial *e* for pretonic *i* in *Bochenel*, an OFr and AN feature, cf. PNDB § 12, Jacobsson 34. A parallel case, with *e* for *o*, is *Simenel* (< *Simon*, *-el*), on which see p. 172, above.

[5] *Bontemps* could perhaps also mean 'born at an auspicious time, on an auspicious day'; see J. K. Brechenmacher, *Etymol. Wörterbuch der deutschen Familiennamen*, i (Limburg, 1960), 183, 622 (s.n. Gutzeit). G. Serra, *La tradizione latina e greco-latina*

nell' onomastica medioevale italiana (Gothenburg, 1950), 29 and n. 1, would explain the byname as an original formula of salutation, meaning 'Good day', or the like.

[6] (signum) *Burdini* 1069–70 *Jumièges* i. 81, *Burdin* 11th-c. ibid. 133, *Burdinus clericus* 1060–1 C. Métais (ed.), *Cartulaire de l'abbaye de la Trinité de Vendôme*, i (Paris, 1893), 253, (Ugo) *Burdinus* 1062–72 C. Ragut (ed.), *Cartulaire de St. Vincent de Mâcon* (Mâcon, 1864), nos. 31, 32, (Gislebert) *Bordin* 1198 *MRSN* 485; for additional examples see Morlet 62, s.v. *Burd-*, who incorrectly takes the name to be Germanic. The antipope Gregory VIII (1118–21), a native of southern France, was nicknamed *Burdinus*.

[7] *EHR* 14 (1899), 424.

[8] See K. Nyrop, *Grammaire historique de la langue française*, iii (Copenhagen, 1936), § 186. Cf. also the byn. (Rogero) *Malfillastre c.* 1170 P. Barnes and C. F.

Caddus, *Willelmus* **1148.**—This is Willelm Cade, a money-lender of Flemish extraction, who is frequently mentioned in the 1155/8 Pipe Rolls and various other contemporary sources.[1] His byname is probably Lat *cadus* 'a large vessel for containing liquids, a jar, jug', ME *cade* 'a cask; a barrel used for herring or other fish' (*MED* 1337ff.). Cf. also *DBS* s.n. Cadd.

Campion, *Herbertus* **1148.**—See Occupational Bynames.

Capel, *Godwinus* **1066.**—See *Capel*, pers.n.

Casier, *Ascelinus* c. **1110.**—OFr *chasier*, ONFr *casier* 'a cheese-cellar, cheese-basket'.

Cat, *Lufman* **1066.**—OE *catt* 'cat'. See also *Bittecat*, byn., and *Cattessone*, pers. n.

Cecus, *Edricus* **1066.**[2]—Lat *cecus* 'blind', translating OE *blind(a)*; *DBS* s.n. Blind.

Chane, *Lewinus* **1066.**—The same man as *Leofwine kana* 11th-c. *LVH* 70. The byname may be OE *canne* f. 'can, cup', or, in view of the single *n*, possibly ON *kani* 'wooden bowl; a kind of boat', which was also used as a byname; cf. on this and on the pers.n. *Cana* DB 1066 (Sx, Sr), *PNDB* 213. Final -*a* in the *LVH* form would be due to association with Lat *canna* or to anglicizing of the alternative Scand etymon.[3]

Cheppe, *Ulwardus* **1066.**—OE *cæppe* f. 'cap'; cf. *ELPN* 144, *DBS* s.n. Capp.

Chibus, *Walterus* c. **1110.**—Other examples of the same word used as a byname are probably (Godrico) *Kebbe* 1114–30,[4] (Sæman) *Kebbe* c. 1150–75, BM, Add. MS. 40,000, fo. 2ʳ (Liber Vitae of Thorney Abbey (C)), (Willelmus) *Kibbe* 1184/5 P 122 (Wo), (Walterus) *Kebe* 1186–8 *Bury S* 44 (Sf), (Radulphus) *Kibe*, ibid. 9 (Sf), (Johannes) *Kybe*

1275 *RH* ii. 763 (O), (Durandus) *Kebe*, (Petrus) *Kebe* 1275 *RH* ii. 470 (K), (Robertus) *Kibus* 1275 *RH* ii. 482 (K). The etymon is evidently an OE **cybbe* or **cybba* (< PrG **kubbiįa-*, a *įa-* or *įan-*stem). The latinized *LW* form may alternatively go back to a variant **cybb* (< *kubįa-*); see Tengvik 302. The meaning would be something like 'a rounded object; a thick-set, clumsy person'. Native cognates are OE **cobb(e)* 'a round lump, a cob' (*EPN* i. 103, *DEPN* s.n. Cobb), ModE *cob* 'something rounded or forming a roundish lump; head or top' (*NED* s.v.). On the PrG stem **kub(b)*- and its descendants see further Pokorny i. 396.[5]

Chie, *Ailricus* **1148.**— LW *Chie* stands for [kie], perhaps OE *cēo* f. 'chough' (< PrG **kūhįōn*); Campbell § 238: 3 and, on *ie* for *ēo*, below p. 224.[6]

Child, *Luinus* **1148.**—OE *cild* 'child, young nobleman; retainer (?)', perhaps used here in some technical sense; cf. *DEPN* s.n. Chilton, *DBS* s.n. Child.[7]

Childebroder, *Alwinus* **1066.**—OE **cild-brōðor* 'brother of a *cild*'; cf. *Child* above. The precise implication of the byname is not apparent.

Chuet, *Edricus* **1066.**—No satisfactory suggestion can be offered. Hardly OE *cū* 'cow' with the OFr suffix -*et*.[8]

Cimel, *Godwinus* **1066.**—The OE form of the byname must be *čimel*, which may be a derivative with the diminutive suffix -*el* (< -*ila-*) of the West Germanic stem **kīm-*, attested by MLG *kīme* m., ModLG *kiem* (Mensing), MDu *kieme, kijme* m., ModDu *kiem*, OHG *chīmo* m., MHG *kīme, kīm*, ModG *Keim*, all meaning 'a germ, sprout, seed'.[9] The root does not seem to be recorded in English. There is also a MLG (and MDu?) *kimmel* 'a bit, gag' (Schiller–Lübben, Lasch–Borchling) of

---

Slade (eds.), *A Medieval Miscellany for D. M. Stenton* (PRS 76, London, 1960) 38 (Ch), < OFr *fillastre* 'stepson'.

[1] On Willem Cade see the articles cited by F. Barlow, above II, 809, n. 1.

[2] Identical with *Edricus cecus tegnus regis* who held *TRE* and in 1086 (DB W 74) and with the Suffolk landowner Edric of Laxfield; see D. C. Douglas, *Bury*, pp. xcff.

[3] OFr *cane* 'cane' proposed by Reaney, *DBS* s.n., is an unlikely etymon for the pre-conquest byname.

[4] W. D. Macray (ed.), *Chronicon abbatiae Rameseiensis* (RS, 1886), 256.

[5] Note also the OE pers.ns **Cybba* and **Cybbel* which have been inferred from the boundary-marks *Cybban stan* 957 *BCS* 1002 (Brk) and *Cybles weorðig*

849 *BCS* 455 (Wo), respectively; *DEPN* s.n. Cubbington. The post-conquest byname (Æluric) *Chebbel* 1087–98 *Bury* 33 (Sf) is plausibly derived by Tengvik (p. 301) and Reaney, *DBS* s.n. Keeble, from an OE **cybbel*. A recent discussion of the word-group under notice is found in A. Zettersten's *Middle English Word Studies* (Lund, 1964), 18ff.

[6] Cf. perhaps also (Alwi) *Kya* c. 1100–30 Earle 257 (D; Tengvik 363). This cannot be ON *kýr* 'cow' as is suggested by M. Förster, *Anglia*, 62 (1938), 66.

[7] For its use in OE sources as a title meaning 'young nobleman', see Tengvik 243ff.

[8] Certainly not from the pl.n. Chute Forest (W), as Tengvik thinks (p. 125).

[9] See also Pokorny i. 355. Note that OSax *kīmo* which figures in the etymological dictionaries is not on record.

unknown etymology which should perhaps be considered here.

Clawecuncte, *Godwinus* 1066.—A phrase-name, OE *clawe-* from *clawian* 'to scratch, claw', OE **cunte* 'vulva'.[1] For semantic parallels see Reaney *Origin*, 294 f. The second *c* in *-cuncte* is dittographic.

Clenehand, *God'* 1066.—OE *clǣne hand* 'clean hand'.

Cod, *Osbertus* 1148.—OE *codd*, ME *cod* 'bag, sack' and various other meanings for which see *MED* s.v.

Cole, *Gaufridus* 1148.—OFr *cole* 'cowl, hooded cloak'. Cf. (de terra Nicholai) *Cole* c. 1200 *PRBW* 159 (Winchester).

Coppa, *Eduinus* 1148.—See *Coppa*, pers.n.

Coppede, *Alestanus* 1066.—OE **coppede* 'provided with a top', here perhaps in the sense of 'tall'. The word is recorded as a pl.n. element; see *DEPN* s.v. *copp*.

Corduanus, *Ade, Cuppingus* 1148.—See Occupational Bynames.

Corneilla, *Herebertus* 1148.—See *Cornilla*, pers.n.

Cornet, *Durandus* 1148.—OFr *cornet* 'a sort of trumpet, a cornet'. Well evidenced as a byname in Normandy.[2]

Crassus, *Robertus* 1148.—Lat *crassus*, translating OFr *cras* 'fat, big'; *DBS* s.n. Crass. Note also (Johannes) *le Cras* 1285 *Survey*, and cf. *Fati*, pers.n., *Pinguis*, byn.

Crispus, *Rannulfus* c. 1110.—Lat *crispus* 'curly-headed', translating OFr *cresp(e)* or possibly OE *cyrps, crisp*; *DBS* s.n. Crisp. See also *Crul*, byn.

Crul, *Burewoldus* 1066.—ME *crul* 'curly'; *DBS* s.n. Curl. See also *Crispus*, byn.

Cuillebrant, *Ricardus* 1148.—An OFr phrase-name, the first el. being *cu(e)ille*, the imperative of OFr *cu(e)illir* 'to collect, gather up', the second OFr *brant* 'sword'.

Cuinta, *Cuinte, Cointe, Radulfus* 1148.—OFr *cointe, cuinte* 'shrewd, cunning, proud'; *DBS* s.n. Quant.

cum barba, *Gilebertus, Godricus* 1148.—The Latin phrase may stand for OE *beard* or *mid þām bearde*; cf. *ELPN* 159. See also *Bierd* above.

Cunnebried, *God'* 1066.—An OE phrase-name, **cunne-brēad*, from *cunnian* 'to test, investigate' and *brēad* 'bread'. A semantic parallel is (Walter) *le Alecunnere* 'W. the ale-inspector', 1288 (*MED*). On *ie* < *ēa* in the second el. see below, p. 224.

Danais, *Deneis, Turstinus* 1148.—OFr *daneis* 'Dane'.

Danzel, *Willelmus* 1148.—OFr *danzel* 'young man, young nobleman'. Cf. (Rodulfus cognomento) *Dancel* 1047–63 *RADN* 338 (Seine-Maritime).

Dives, *Chepingius* c. 1110.—Lat *dives* 'rich', translating OE *ēadig* or another synonym.

Dol, *Lewingus* 1066.—OE *dol* 'foolish, silly'; *DBS* s.n. Doll. Cf. also OE *Dola*, Redin 75.

Dop, *Robertus* c. 1110.—Probably, as Prof. Löfvenberg points out to me, an OE **dopp*, a strong variant of *doppa, doppe* in *dūfedoppa, fugoldoppe*. These words denote various species of waterfowl, the basic meaning being 'diver'. The same pattern of word-formation is exemplified by OE *bucc* 'male deer'[3] by the side of *bucca* 'he-goat', OE *finc* (*i*-stem) by the side of OHG *finko*.

Dore, *Guncel'* 1148.—See *Dora*, pers.n.

Drache, *Leuingus* 1066.—OE *draca* 'dragon'. ME *drake* 'the male of the duck' is not recorded until c. 1300 (*MED*); cf. *DBS* s.n. Drake.

Dublel, *Ricardus* c. 1110.—OFr *do(u)blel*, adj. 'double', sb. 'a vessel holding a double pint'; cf. ModFr dial. *doubleau* 'a jug holding two pints; (Poitou) a young man-servant, groom' (*FEW* iii, 186) and the ModFr surname *Doubleau* (Normandy; Dauzat 209).[4] For ME examples see *DBS* s.n. Dobel, and note also (Radulfus) *Dublel* c. 1127 *AC* 24 (Gl).

Duchet, *Radulfus* 1148.—See *Duchet*, pers.n.

Durage, *Willelmus* 1148.—See *Durage*, pers.n.

---

[1] The word occurs in a topographical sense in the boundary mark *to, of cuntan heale* 901 *BCS* 596, 960 *BCS* 1054, Durley parish, Ha; see H. Middendorff, *Altenglisches Flurnamenbuch* (Halle, 1902), 35, G. B. Grundy, 'The Saxon land charters of Hampshire', *Arch J* 78 (1921), 113.

[2] Andreae (gen) *Cornet*, a citizen of Bourg-l'Abbé (Calvados), 1083–5 *AGC* 119, Johannes *Cornet* 1172–8 *RAH* ii. 72 (Falaise), Lucas *Cornet* 1195

MRSN 227.

[3] *DEPN* s.v., *EPN* i. 56.

[4] OFr instances of the byname in the latinized form *Dublellus* (11th–12th c.) are listed by Drevin (p. 65); note also (Odo) *Duplellus* c. 1100 C. Métais (ed.), *Cartulaire de l'abbaye de la Trinité de Vendôme*, ii (Paris, 1894), 148, (Radulfus) *Doublel* 1198 *MRSN* 337. The sense 'twin' assumed by Drevin, Tengvik (p. 375), and Reaney, *DBS* s.n. Dobel, is not recorded.

Escitteport, *Wuinestaham* **1066.**—An OE phrase-name, **scytte-port*, from *scyttan* 'to shut, bolt' and *port* 'gate, entrance', apparently a nickname for a gate-keeper.

Escouell', see *Scuuel'*.

Estreis, Petrus **1148.**—AN *estreis*, Anglo-Lat *estresius* 'Easterling, Eastlander', i.e. 'German, esp. a native of the Baltic coast, a citizen of a Hanse town'; see *DBS* s.n. Estridge, Latham s.v. and cf. *Norreis*, byn. (q.v. below). Ekwall *Subs R*, 198, n. 51 (cf. ibid. 45–6), would explain *estreis* as an AN form of ME *ēstrish* < *ēstrichish*, a derivative of *ēstrīche* 'an eastern country' (*MED*). See also G. T. Lapsley, *EHR* 21 (1906), 511.

Etsinemeta, *Edwinus* **1148.**—This looks like a Lat phrase *et sine meta* (MLat also *mete*; Latham) 'and without limit', which gives no obvious sense, however. If the first word is OE, ME *et*, the imperative of *etan*, the phrase could mean 'eat without moderation', a possible nickname for a glutton.[1] Cf. also Edwignus *Sinemete* c. 1102–11 (London), whose byname Ekwall, *ELPN*, 167, explains as 'without food', Lat *sine* and OE *mete* 'food', or as 'one who blesses his food, says grace regularly', the first el. being a form of the ME verb *signe* 'to mark or consecrate with the sign of the cross'. The spelling *sine*, which recurs in the *LW* form, renders the latter alternative somewhat unlikely.

Flathege, *Alestanus* **1066.**—Apparently a compound of ME *flat* adj. 'level, smooth, even' and OE *hege* 'hedge, fence', the reference being to a feature of the man's place of residence. See Addenda.

Francigena, *Godwinus* **1066.**—MLat *francigena* 'Frenchman'. The corresponding OE term *frencisc*[2] occurs as the byname of *Roð' ðe Frenccisce* c. 1100–30 Earle 270 (So). See Addenda.

Freschet, *Her(e)uicus* **1148.**—OFr *freschet* 'fresh', here probably in the figurative sense 'lively, alert'.[3]

Fresle, *Robertus* c. **1110.**—OFr *frai(s)le*, *fresle* 'weak, frail'; *DBS* s.n. Frail.

Friedai, *Hugo* **1148.**—See *Fridai*, pers.n.

Fulebiert, *Aluricus* **1066.**—OE *fūl* 'foul', *beard* 'beard'. On *LW ie* for OE *ĕa*, see below, p. 224. See also *Bierd*, *Blachebiert* above.

Furwatel, *Giroldus* **1148.**—A Norman nickname, the first el. being OFr *fo(u)r* 'oven', the second ONFr *wa(s)tel*, Central Fr *gastel* 'cake'.[4] An OFr example of the same byname is (Willelmus) *Forgastel* p 1119 (Saintes).[5] 'Cake-oven' would be an apt sobriquet for a confectioner.

Gallus, *Paganus*, *Willelmus* **1148.**—Lat *Gallus* 'Frenchman' rather than *gallus* 'cock'.

Galne, *Ricardus* **1148.**—OFr *jalne*, ONFr *galne* 'yellow'; cf. the ModFr surname *Gaune*, Dauzat 283.

Gibart, *Gisl'* c. **1110.**—See *Gibart*, pers.n.

Gidi, *Herbertus* c. **1110.**—OE *gydig*, ME *gidi* 'possessed, insane; foolish, stupid'; *DBS* s.n. Giddy.

Gladewin', *Henricus* **1148.**—See *Gladewin'*, pers.n.

Goce, *Godwinus* **1066.**—See *Goce*, pers.n.

Godeman, *Astcelinus* c. **1110.**—A genuine byname, OE *gōd mann* 'bonus homo'[6] or the OE (or OG) pers.n. *Godmann* in a patronymic function; see *Godemannus*, pers.n., and *Bonus homo*, byn.

Godeswale, *Edwinus* **1066.**—For *Godesawle*, OE *gōd sāwol* 'good soul'; cf. (Godwin) *Gotsaul* early 12th c. *ELPN* 151 (London) and *DBS* s.n. Godsal.

Goisl', *Alexander* **1148.**—See *Goisl'*, pers.n.

Grailepeis, *Ricardus* **1148.**—OFr *grai(s)le* 'thin, slender', *p(e)iz* 'chest', hence 'narrow-chested'.

---

[1] For the use of Lat *sine* cf. *Bernardus sine napa* 1086 DB Ex 306b 'B. without a napkin', *Galterus sine napis* c. 1150 *Jumièges* i. 179. The preposition translates OFr *senz*, *sanz* in vernacular nicknames like *Galfridus senz Mance*, 'without sleeves', 1168/9 *P* 14 (Li), *Willelmus Sanzgunele*, 'without a tunic', 1180/81 *P* 102 (Hrt). An OE phrase *et sīn(n)ne mete* 'eat his (refl.) food' is unlikely in view of the rarity of *sīn* in OE prose and its speedy obsolescence in ME.

[2] On this see Cecily Clark, *Leeds Studies in English*, n.s. 3 (1969), 38–41.

[3] Norman examples are (Ricardi) *Freschet* 1129 *Reg* ii, p. 365, (Herberti) ~ 1137 *Reg* iii, 749, (Rob') ~ 1198 *MRSN* 399. Note also (Johannes) *Frechet* c. 1145 Drevin 66, (Aimericus) *Freschet* 1162–77 C. Urseau

(ed.), *Cartulaire noir de la cathédrale d'Angers* (Paris, 1908), 359.

[4] Cf. also (Garner) *Gastel* c. 1120 Drevin 67 (Ronceray), (Hugo) *Wastel* 1180 *MRSN* 69 (Rouen). The word was borrowed in ME as *wastel* 'bread made of the finest flour; a cake or loaf of this bread' (*NED* s.v., c. 1300); cf. also the compound *cornewastel* (1279, *MED* s.v.) and Anglo-Latin *wastellus*, *gastellus* (1190ff.; Latham).

[5] T. Grasilier (ed.), *Cartulaire de l'abbaye royale de Notre Dame de Saintes* (Niort, 1871), 171.

[6] ME *godman* also had the meanings 'male head of a household, householder (1275ff.); citizen of a town; master in a craft or guild (1389ff.)'; *MED* s.v.

Gretsud, *Godwinus* 1066.—The same man as Godwine *Great seod* 11th c. *LVH* 74; OE *grēat* 'big', *sēod* 'purse, bag'. On *LW u* for OE *ēo* in *-sud* see below, p. 224.

Grifin, *Robertus* 1148.—See *Grifin*, pers.n.

Gruti, *Ansgerus* 1148.—From an unrecorded OE adj. **grūtig*, ME **grūti*, a derivative of OE *grūt* 'groats, coarse meal'; cf. (Edwinus) *Grut* 1066 DB 67, 95 (E),[1] (Lefsi) *Grut* 1169/70 P 12 (Nf or Sf). An OE **grēotig* from *grēot* 'sand, earth' with *LW u* for *ēo*, on which see below, p. 224, is a possible alternative.[2]

Gule, *Edwinus* 1066.—Perhaps OE **gul(l)a*, the weak form of **gul(l)* 'yellow' which has been inferred from OE *gullisc* 'gilded' and is the ancestor of ME *gul(l)* 'yellow, pale'.[3] OFr *gole, gule* 'throat', though formally acceptable, would be a less likely etymon for a *TRE* byname. But cf. the next entry.

Gulee, *Lewinus* 1066.—This is probably OFr *go(u)lee* 'big mouthful; words of abuse'. See also *Gule*, byn.

Gumbold, *Durandus* 1148.—See *Gumbold*, pers.n.

Gustate, *Luwoldus* 1066.—The Lat imperative *gustate* from *gusto* 'to taste', a suitable nickname for a hospitable innkeeper.

Hacchemus (*sexiens*), **Haccemus** (*ter*), **Hachemus** (*semel*), *Goda, Hugo* 1148.[4]—The second el. is OE *mūs* 'mouse'. The first is probably *hacce-* from OE *haccian* 'to cut, hack' as in *Haccheselt* 1148, pers.n. (q.v.), a possible alternative being OE *hæcc, hæcce*, ME *hacche* 'hatch, small door, gate, wicket', perhaps in the secondary sense of 'rack or crib for hay' (*MED* s.v., 3a), which *MED* takes to be the first el. of the ME byname (Anschetil) *Hacchecoc* 1166 (loc. cit.). See Addenda.

Helteprest, *Godman* 1066, **Hieltepreost**, *Ailwinus* 1066.—OE (*se*) *healta prēost* 'the lame priest'; cf. *Haliprest*, pers.n. above, and the bynames in *-prest* listed by Reaney *Origin*, 195–6. On *LW e* and *ie* for OE (WS) *ea* see below p. 224. Note also

on *Leowerdes healta* [gewittnesse] 1050–71 Earle 253 (D).

Herra, *Alured* 1148.—OE *hearra*, ME *herre* 'master, lord'. Cf. (de Willelmo) le *Herre* 1179/80 P 56 (L). Cf. also the OE pers.n. *Hærra*, 11th c., Redin 76.[5] OE *heorra*, ME *herre* 'hinge of a door', is a possible alternative.

Hieltepreost, see *Helteprest*.

Horloc, *Borewoldus* 1066.—OE *hār locc* 'grey lock'; *DBS* s.n. Harlock. See also *Sideloc*, pers.n.

Hosatus, *Herbertus* 1148.—MLat *hosatus*, OFr *hosé* 'booted'. Cf. (Walterus) *Hosatus, Hosed* 1086 DB; Tengvik 37of., *DBS* s.n. Hussey.

Hubold, *Bernardus* 1148.—See *Hubold*, pers.n.

Hwit, *Alestanus* 1066.—OE *hwīt* 'white, fair-haired, of fair complexion'; Tengvik 319, *DBS* s.n. White.

Ieltfange, *Alwinus* 1066.—Perhaps an unrecorded OE **g(i)eld-fenga* 'tax-gatherer', from OE *g(i)eld* 'tax, tribute' and *fenga* 'one who takes something, a receiver', as in *and-fenga* 'receiver, defender, undertaker'. The second el. would have southeastern or AN *a* for *e*; see below, p. 223.

Iola, *Alur' c.* 1110.—See *Iola*, pers.n.

Iude(i)us, *Deulecreisse, Urselinus* 1148.—Lat *Iudaeus* 'Jew'.

Iunior, *Goduinus* 1148.—Lat *iunior* 'the younger', translating OE *geongra*, ME *yungre*.[6]

Lacchewei, *Radulfus* 1148.—See *Lacchewei*, pers.n.

Lamart', *Goda* 1148.—See (la) *Martra*, byn.

Lancel', *Petrus* 1148.—See *Lancel[in]*, pers.n.

Lefeller, *Alwinus c.* 1110.—See Occupational Bynames s.v. *feller*.

Lippe, *Rogerus* 1148.—OE *lippa* 'lip' or its OFr synonym *lip(p)e*; Tengvik 32of., *DBS* s.n. Lipp.

Litteprot, *Goderun* 1066.—Perhaps, as Tengvik suggests (p. 348), a hybrid compound of OE *lytel* 'little' and OFr *pro(d), pru(d)* 'advantage, profit'; see

---

[1] ModE *grouty* 'muddy, dirty' is recorded from 1744 (*NED*).

[2] ModE *gritty* 'containing grit, sandy' turns up in 1598 (*NED*).

[3] Ultimately from ON *gulr*; see R. Menner, *MLN* 59 (1944), 112. The ME word is recorded from *c.* 1350 (*MED*).

[4] Hugo *Hacchemus* is clearly the same man as Hugo *Hachemus* 1157/8 P 176 (Ha), and perhaps as *Hachemus* 1166/7 P 191 (Oakley, Ha). The name also occurs in the 1285 *Survey*: (de Galfrido) *Hachemus* (with *ch*

probably for [tʃ]). See Addenda.

[5] An Exeter moneyer under Harold I and Harthacnut. A much earlier example is *Heara* 765 *BCS* 196. This could alternatively be WS *hēar(r)a*, comp. of *hēah*, as R. E. Zachrisson thinks: *Uppsala universitets årsskrift*, 1924, *Filosofi* . . . 8, p. 125.

[6] The form (Ælfferes) *Geongran* quoted by Tengvik (p. 314) from *KCD* 1290 is not a byname. The critical text in *AS Wills* (p. 14) has *Ælfferes dohtor þa geon[g]ran* 'Ælfhere's younger daughter'.

also *DBS* s.n. Littleproud. A parallel is (Simonem) *Smalprut* 1221 *Cur* 1221–2, 56, (Ric') *Smalprout* 1278/9 *RH* ii. 703 (O). *Litte-* seems to reflect the OE variant *lўttel*, on which see Campbell § 453, Luick § 668. The second *l* is lost by dissimilation; cf. below, p. 226.

Loer', *Ricardus* 1148.—Perhaps OFr *loe(o)r* 'praiser, lauder' or 'one who rents or leases something'. Alternatively, the *LW* form may be an abbreviation of OFr *lo(h)erenc* 'Lorrainer' (Langlois 399f.) or go back to OFr *Loh(i)er* < OG *Lothar* (Michaëls-son i. 103),[1] used here in a patronymic function.

Longus, *Ailmerus, Ingulf, Iohannes, Reginaldus, Ricardus* 1148.—Lat *longus*, OE *lang* 'tall'. As a byname *(se) langa* is well evidenced in OE sources; see Tengvik 320, *DBS* s.n. Lang.

Lupus, *Radulfus* 1148.—Lat *lupus* 'wolf'. OFr *leu, lou* was a very common nickname; see Dauzat s.n. Loup, *DBS* s.nn. Lew, Low.[2]

Macher', *Rogerus* 1148.—See *Macher'*, pers.n.

Maleductus, *Robertus c.* 1110.—MLat *maleductus*, OFr *malduit* 'ill-bred, boorish'; Tengvik 350, *DBS* s.n. Mauduit. Note also Robert *Maudut c.* 1210–11 *PRBW* 160 (Winchester).

Mansel, *Turstinus* 1148.—OFr *mancel, mansel*

'inhabitant of Maine' (< MLat *[Ceno]manicellus*),[3] which is well evidenced in French and English medieval sources both as a pers.n. and a byname.[4] Drevin's suggestion (p. 69), which is also reported by Reaney, *DBS* s.n. Mansel, that the etymon is MLat *mansellus* 'a small manor', a diminutive of MLat *mansus*, supposedly used in the metonymic sense of 'tenant of a *mansellus*',[5] is clearly improbable. The MLat word survives in OFr as *masel* 'house in the country, small farm',[6] and the vernacular terms for 'tenant farmer' were *maisnier* < MLat *mansionarius* and *masuier* < MLat *mansuarius*; see *FEW* vi: 1, 253f., 256.

Mar, see *Martel*.

Marc', *Robertus* 1148.—If the form is reliable this could be OFr *marc* 'mark, a unit of weight for gold and silver'. But *c* may be a copyist's error for *t*, in which case the man under notice is most probably identical with Robertus (la) *Martra*, q.v.

Marmion, *Robertus c.* 1110.—OFr *marmion* 'a little fellow, brat, monkey' was a popular nickname in Normandy.[7]

Martel, *Edit; Martel, Mart', Mar', Willelmus* 1148.—OFr *martel* 'hammer'; Tengvik 378, *DBS* s.n. Martel.

---

[1] OFr *lo(h)erenc* occurs in England as the byname of Rogerus *Loerenc* 1166 *RBE* 320 (Bd), Johannes *Loereng* ibid. 322 (Bd). The pers.n. *Loh(i)er* is recorded in DB 1086 as *Loherus* by the side of *Loderus*, both Sf 396b.

[2] The diminutive *louet, leuet* occurs in DB 1086; Tengvik 363.

[3] Langlois 428, H. J. Wolf, *Die Bildung der franzö-sischen Ethnica* (Paris and Geneva, 1964), 15, 61. On *Cenomanicellus* see A. Dauzat, *Rev. internat. d'onomastique* 3 (1951), 7. The word survives in the ModFr surname *Manceau, Manchel*; Dauzat 411. In the *ASC* the province of Maine is *þæt land Mans* (E) 1073, (D) 1074, *þone eorldom þe Mans is gehaten* (E) 1087, *þa Manige* (E) 1091, *þa Mannie* (E) 1110–12 < *Cenomannis* (abl. plur.), *pagus Cenomannicum*; cf. A. Holder, *Altceltischer Sprachschatz* (Leipzig, 1896–1913), i. 984ff., iii. 1201f., Dauzat–Rostaing s.n. (Le) Mans.

[4] Early French instances are *Mansellus* taneator 1091, ~ vicarius 1097–1103, ~ de Recordana late 11th-c. (Les Ricordaines, Sarthe), ~ de Campanacio early 12th-c. (Champagné, Sarthe), all in R. Charles and Menjot d'Elbenne (eds.), *Cartulaire de l'abbaye de Saint Vincent du Mans* (Le Mans, 1886, 1913), 182, 176, 67, 87 (17th-c. transcript of a lost 12th-c. original). The corresponding fem. name is *Mansella* 11th-c. ibid. 136. Examples of the byname function include (Hugonis) *Manselli* 1049 (17th c.) C. Urseau (ed.),

Cartulaire noir de la cathédrale d'Angers (Paris, 1908) 98, (Goisfredo) *Mancello c.* 1063 (12th c.) *RADN* 339, (Ursel) *Mansellus* de Punctello a 1080 (copy) *France* 397 (Pointel, Orne). For ME examples see *DBS* s.n. Mansel and note also (Warinus) *Mansel* 1125–8 T. Stapleton (ed.), *Chronicon Petroburgense* (Camden OS 47, 1849), 166 (Nth), (Willelmus) ~ 1142 *Seals* 153 (Gl), *Mansel* 1185 Templars 84 (Li). Four or five English tenants surnamed *Mansel* are listed in the 1166 portion of the *RBE*. Most of the above forms as well as those adduced by Drevin occur in twelfth-century and later manuscripts and could therefore exhibit the OFr change [ts] > [s]. However, the marked pre-dominance of early spellings in *-sel* would seem to point to the existence, by the side of OFr *mancel*, of an early variant *mansel*, formed directly from the OFr pl.n. (Le) *Mans* < *Celmans* < *Cenomannis*.

[5] Also *mansellum*; see *Novum glossarium mediae Latinitatis*, Fasc. Ma (Copenhagen, 1959), col. 135.

[6] Only recorded once, in the plur. form *masiaus* (Picardy, 13th c., Tobler–Lommatzsch). Cf. also ModFr dial *masèl* (Languedoc) 'small house in the country', and *mansel* (Normandy) 'tenement, dwelling', which is a late adoption of the MLat term; see *FEW* vol. vi, pt. 1, pp. 263, 265f.

[7] (Vuillelmus) *Marmio* 1060 *RADN* 329, (Robertus) *Marmio* a 1080 *AGC* 110, (Gaufr') *Marmion* 1195 *MRSN* 227.

Martra (*la*), *Martre, Matre, Mart', Robertus;*[1] *Martre, Walterus; la Mart', Goda* 1148.—OFr *martre* 'weasel'; *DBS* s.n. Marter.[2] See also *Marc'*, byn.

Mase, *Edtie* 1066.—OE *māse* 'tit-mouse'.

Matre, see *Martra*.

Meddere, *Ricardus le* 1148.—See Occupational Bynames.

Mercherel, *Rogerus* 1148.—Probably OFr *mercier*, ONFr *merch(i)er* 'merchant' with the diminutive suffix *-el*, as in early ModFr *mercereau* 'small merchant' (1596ff.); *FEW* vi: 2, 41f.[3] On *LW ch* for [tʃ] see below, p. 225. Cf. also *mercator, merciarius*, occupational bynames.

Meroie, *Walterus* 1148.—Possibly an OFr byname, whose second el. could be OFr *o(i)e* f. 'goose' or *oie* f. '(sense of) hearing; ear', as in (Herbertus) *Maloei* 1088 *Jumièges* i. 119, (Rob') *Beloie* 1198 *MRSN* 326. The first is unexplained.

Mieta, *Robertus* 1148.—OFr *miete* f. 'crumb', as in (Ernulf') *Miete* 1161/2 *P* 67 (London), (Ern') *Miet(t)a* 1162/3 *P* 71, 1165/6 *P* 130; (Ric') *Mieta* 1180 *MRSN* 79 (Normandy).

Mordant, *Willelmus* 1148.—OFr *mordant*, adj., 'biting, sarcastic'; *DBS* s.n. Mordaunt. The corresponding noun, which meant 'metal clasp or buckle fastened to the belt', could also have been used as a byname.

Mucheto, *Stephanus* 1148.—This looks like an OFr pl.n. formed with the common Lat suffix *-ētum*, the preposition *de* having been inadvertently omitted by the copyist, but it has not been possible to identify the locality that may be referred to.[4]

Mus, *Siuuardus c.* 1110.—OE *mūs* 'mouse'; Tengvik 364, *DBS* s.n. Mowse. See also *Hacchemus* above.

Nalad, *Godwinus c.* 1110.—OE *nā lāð* 'not harmful, not unpleasant'. A later example of this byname is

(Rogerus) *Nolod* 13th c. (Nf).[5] Cf. also (Robert) *Nagod, temp.* Henry I, *ELPN* 159 (London).

Niger, *Godefridus, Ricardus* 1148.—Lat *niger* 'black, dark-complexioned', translating OE *blæc, se blaca*, or OFr (le) *neir*; Tengvik 292f., *DBS* s.n. Black. See also *Nigellus*, pers.n.

Niwem', *Ulf* 1148.—ME (*þe*) *nīwe man*, 'the new man, the newcomer'; *DBS* s.n. Newman. A later Ha example is (de Hugone) *Niweman* 1210–11 *PRBW* 17 (Crawley). See also *Novus* below.

Norreis, *Robertus* 1148.—OFr *nor(r)eis* 'man from the North, Norwegian'; *DBS* s.n. Norris.

Novus, *Willelmus* 1148.—Lat *novus* 'new, newcomer', translating ME *nīwe, newe* or OFr *nuef*, *neuf*. Cf. *Niwem[an]* above.

Oil(l)ardus, *Hugo c.* 1110.—See *Oillardus*, pers.n.

Oison, *Oisun, Robertus* 1148.—OFr *oison* 'gosling'.[6] Cf. the Modern French surname *Oison, Loison*; Dauzat 455. Note also (terra Thome) *Oisun*, (de Hugone) ~ 1210–11 *PRBW* 160, 162 (Winchester).

Opchieher, *Welestanus* 1066.—*Op-* probably stands for OE *ūp* 'up' but the second el. is obscure.

Paginan', *Morell'* 1148.—Probably OFr *paignon* 'a small loaf of bread' with *a* for *o* by scribal error. A later Norman example is (Radulfi) *Painnon* 1184.[7] Derivation from post-classical and medieval Lat *pagino* 'to compose, write, mark the pages in a manuscript',[8] in which case the *LW* form would stand for the pres. part. *paginans*, is not a satisfactory alternative. See Addenda.

Palefrei, *Hunfridus* 1148.—See *Palefrei*, pers.n.

Pancheuot, *Hunfridus* 1148.—OFr *pance*, ONFr *panche* 'paunch, belly', *volt* 'arched, vaulted'; hence 'pot-bellied'. See *DBS* s.n. Pauncefoot. A parallel is (Willelmi) *Pedivolt* 'arched foot' 1057 *RADN* 316 (Normandy), (Hugo) *Petuuolt, Pedeuolt* DB 1086 (Ca). On the last two forms see Tengvik (p. 325), who offers no explanation.

---

[1] The same man as Rotbertus *Lamartre* 1128–33 *Reg* ii, ccxi, Rob' *Lamartre* 1130 *P* 5, 30, 34. A later Winchester instance is (Martinus) *la Martre* a 1210–11 *PRBW* 160.

[2] Norman examples are (Ran') *Lamartre* 1195 *MRSN* 139, (Ran') *Le Martre* 1198 *MRSN* 422.

[3] Note also the ModFr surname *Mercereau*; Dauzat 430.

[4] There is a hamlet called Mocquet in Manche, commune of Flamanville, for which, however, no early forms are at present available. Besides, *-ētum* normally gives *-ay, -oy* in the North of France.

[5] M. Chibnall (ed.), *Select Documents of the English lands of the Abbey of Bec* (London, 1951), 107, 113.

[6] A Norman example is (Ingram) *Oison* 1131–5 *Reg* ii, 1974 (Sées), a later English one being (Martinum) *Oisun* 1198 *P* 82 (D; PRS 23). The surname of Hugo and Johannes *Osion* 1207 *Fine R* 452 (Winchester) probably stands for *Oison*.

[7] *RAH*, Introd., 343. The word is evidenced in the medieval and modern dialects of Picardy and Flanders; see *FEW* vii. 546.

[8] Souter, Du Cange, s.v.

Parcheminus, see Occupational Bynames.

Parfait, *Unfridus c. 1110.*—OFr *parfait* 'perfect'; *DBS* s.n. Parfait.

Pasturellus, *Rannulfus c. 1110.*—A latinized form of OFr *pastorel* 'young shepherd; simpleton, lout'.

Patinus, *Rogerus c. 1110.*[1]—MLat *patinus* 'wooden shoe, slipper', OFr *patin* 'patten'; *DBS* s.n. Patten. A Norman example is (Gaufr') *Patin* 1205 *MRSN* 558.

Penifeder, *Godwinus 1066.*—OE **peni(n)gfæder* 'pennyfather, miser'; *DBS* s.n. Pennyfather.

Penipurs, *Aluricus 1066.*—OE **peni(n)gpurs* 'penny purse'; Tengvik 353.

Petit, *Robertus 1148.*—OFr *petit* 'little'; *DBS* s.n. Pettit. See also *Petita*, pers.n.

Peuerel, *Willelmus 1148.*—The OFr byname *Peu(e)-rel*, a diminutive of *pevre* 'pepper'. The latinized form is *Piperellus*. See further Tengvik 326, *DBS* s.n. Peverall.

Picteurte, *Elmarus 1066.*—This is an OE phrase-name, **pice-wurte*, from OE **pic(i)an* 'to pick' and *wyrt, wurt* f. 'herb, vegetable', acc. sg. and pl. *wurte*. The first el. of the *LW* form should read *Piche-*. The loss of initial *w* before *u* in the second el. is an AN feature (*PNDB* § 55). For other bynames compounded with *Pice-*, a popular and prolific type, see Reaney *Origin*, 288, B. Seltén, *English Studies*, 46 (1965), 167f.

Piec, *Willelmus 1148.*—OE **pēac* 'knoll, hill, peak' (*EPN* ii, 60), here probably in the figurative sense of 'stout, thick-set man'. Cf. (Uluric) *Pec* 1087–98 *Bury* 39 (Sf), on which see Tengvik 325, and the ME examples discussed by Reaney s.n. Peak. The *LW* form has Ha *ie* for *ēa*; see p. 224.

Pinguis, *Ricardus, Robertus, Willelmus 1148.*—Lat *pinguis* 'fat', translating OE *fætt* or OFr *cras, gras,* or *gros*; cf. Tengvik 312. See also *Crassus*, byn.

Pofil, *Rogerus*; *Pofile, Hugo 1148.*—OFr *porfil* 'hem, braid (on a dress)' rather than *porfile* 'porphyry'. The loss of pre-consonantal *r* is AN; see Pope § 1184. Cf. (terra Radulfi) *Porfil* (?) 1285 *Survey*. See Addenda.

Polanus, *Willelmus 1148.*—MLat *polanus*, OFr *po-lain* 'colt, foal'; *DBS* s.n. Pullan. Norman examples are (Ansfredo) *Polein* 1059–66 *RADN* 414, (Adam) ∼ 1198 *MRSN* 431, 439.

Poplestan, *Alwinus 1066.*—OE *popelstān* 'pebble'.

Porriz, *Godwinus 1066.*—Possibly OE *portic* 'porch, vestibule' with *r* for *t* by scribal error and AN [-its] for OE [-itʃ]. If so a suitable nickname for a door-keeper.

Post', *Willelmus 1148.*—OE *post* 'post, pillar, door-post' or its OFr synonym *post*. See also *Posta*, pers.n.

Pot, *God' c. 1110.*—OE *pott* 'pot'. See also *Pot*, pers.n., *Waterpot*, byn.

Prichelus, *Brunild 1148.*—A phrase-name, **price-lūs*, from OE *prician* 'to prick, pierce', *lūs* 'louse'.

Prison, *Godwinus c. 1110, God' 1148.*—OFr *prison* 'prisoner'. An earlier example is (Æluuin) *Prisun* 1087–98 *Bury* 26 (Sf).

Putheld', *Robertus 1148.*—Perhaps an OE **pytt-heald*, a compound of *pytt* 'pit, excavated hole, esp. one where minerals or other materials are got' (*EPN* ii. 75) and (ge-)*heald* 'protector, guardian'; hence 'one who guards a gravel-pit', or the like.

Puttuc, *Edricus 1148.*—OE **puttoc*, ME *puttok* 'kite'; Tengvik 365, *DBS* s.n. Puttock.

Quadde, *Robertus 1148.*—A pet-form, with hypo-coristic gemination, of ME *quad, qued*, adj. 'evil, wicked, bad', sb. 'bad or wicked person' < OE *cwēad*, which is only recorded in the sense 'dung'. See *NED* s.v. *qued*.

Rosellus, *Russel, Radulfus c. 1110.*—OFr *rossel* 'red-faced, ruddy'; *DBS* s.n. Russel. Note also *Rosellus* 1086 DB E 105b (Colchester).

Ruffus, *Alwinus 1066, Ruffa, Edit*; *Ruffo* (abl), (de) *Selid' 1148.*—Lat *rufus* 'red, ruddy', trans-lating OE *rēad(a)* or OFr *ros, rossel*; Tengvik 330f. See also *Rosellus*, byn.

Rus, *Ailwardus 1148.*—OE *risc, *rysc*, ME *rusche* 'a rush'; see also *Rusmangre*, occupational byname.

Russel, see *Rosellus*.

Rust, *Robertus 1148.*—OE *rūst* 'rust', used of reddish hair or complexion; Tengvik 332, *DBS* s.n. Rust.

Saluagius, *Wibertus c. 1110.*—MLat *salvagius*, OFr *salvage* 'savage, ferocious'; *DBS* s.n. Savage.

Sar', *Godefridus c. 1110.*—See *Sar'*, local byname.

Sarazinus, *Stephanus 1148.*—OFr *Sarasin* 'Sara-cen'; *DBS* s.n. Sarson.

---

[1] In 1122 his property is referred to as *terram que fuit Rogeri Patin*; see E. J. Kealey, *Roger of Salisbury* (Berkeley, Calif., 1972), 238.

Sarz, *Godwinus* 1066.—Unexplained, but cf. *Sorz* below.[1]

Sciteliure, *Radulfus* 1148.—Perhaps a compound of OE *scitte* f. 'looseness of the bowels, diarrhoea' and *lifer* 'liver'.[2]

Scodhe, *Estanus* 1066.—This may be an OE **scōda*, a variant or derivative of **scōd* 'pod, husk', which is presupposed by ModE dial. *shood*, *shude*, *shewd* 'the husks of oats after threshing' (*NED*, *EDD*) and seems to occur as the byname of Simon *Scod* 1278/9 *RH* ii. 857 (O) and Gilbertus *Shod* 1274/5 *RH* i. 521 (Nf).[3] An alternative etymon would be an OE **scoda*, an agential noun from *scūdan* 'to run, hurry'.[4]

Scuuel', *Scuueil*, *Turoldus* 1148, *Escouell'*, *Rad'* c. 1110.—OFr *escofle*, *escufle* 'kite', or a diminutive of OFr *esco(u)ve* 'broom', attested by early ModFr *escouvelle* 'brush'.[5]

Siccus, *Rogerus* c. 1110.—Lat *siccus* 'dry', a translation of OFr *sec* 'dry, lean, emaciated'; *FEW* xi. 585.

Socche, *Godwinus* 1066.—OE **socca*, a derivative of *socc* 'light shoe, slipper', recorded as the byname of Leuuinus *Socca* 1066 DB Ex 475b (D); Tengvik 371f.

Softebred, *God'* 1066.—OE *sōfte* 'soft', *brēad* 'bread'. Evidently a nickname for a baker. Cf. Orm *Dreiebred* 1169/70 *P* 131 (St) 'dry bread'.

Soggera, *Radulfus* 1148.—OFr *soegre* (varr. *suegre*, *soigre*, *sougre*), a Norman form of standard OFr *suire* 'father-in-law'; *FEW* xii, 15. Note also that in Old Provençal the word is *sogre*. The *LW* spelling is due to the scribe's attempt at latinization.

Sorz, *Godwinus* 1066.—Possibly OFr *sort* 'deaf' with AN nom. *-s*, but the form is uncertain since

the man under notice is also called Godwinus *Sarz*. If the latter variant is the correct one, no satisfactory etymology can be suggested. See also *Surdus*, byn.

Sotebord, *Wenestanus* 1066.—OE *sōt* 'soot', *bord* 'board, table', perhaps an opprobrious nickname for a slovenly shopkeeper or landlord.

Spich, *Aldwinus* 1148.—OE *spic* 'fat bacon'.[6]

Stud', *Alnodus* 1066.—Perhaps, as Tengvik suggests (p. 367), OE *stūt* 'gnat', final *d* for *t* being an AN inverted spelling.

Surdus, *Godefridus* 1148.—Lat *surdus* 'deaf', translating OE *dēaf* or OFr *sort*. See also *Sorz*, byn.

Surlaf, *Willelmus* 1148.—OE *sūr hlāf* 'sour bread'; cf. OE *hwītelāf* 'white bread'.

Taddebelloc, *Alueredus* 1066.—OE **tād(e)-bealluc* 'toad-ballock', from OE *tāde* f. 'toad' and *bealluc* 'ballock, testicle'. See also *Balloc*, pers.n. and byn.

Tardif, *Willelmus* c. 1110.—See *Tardif*, pers.n.

Toi, *Alurici* (gen.) 1066.—Possibly a latinized genitive of OE *tōa*, the wk. masc. sg. of *tōh* 'tough, tenacious'.[7] For the use of this word as a byname see *DBS* s.n. Tough.

Tresor, *Ansgod*, Petrus 1148, *Treisor*, *Clemens* 1148.—OFr *tresor* 'treasure', also 'treasurer'; *DBS* s.n. Treasure.

Trotardin, *Robertus* 1148.—An OFr formation from the verb *troter* 'to trot' with the suffix *-ard* to which has been added the diminutive ending *-in*.[8] Cf. (Rog') *Trotard'* 1207 *Fine R* 452, (Joh') *Trottard'* ibid. 455 (both Winchester) and the OFr byname (Rogeri) *Trotin*, 1198 (Normandy).[9]

Turlux, *Robertus* 1148.—Cf. (Godefr') *Torlosc* 1195 *MRSN* 172. The second el. of this Norman byname is probably the adj. *lois*, fem. *lo(i)sche*

---

[1] Not the Norman pl.n. Sars-le-Bois (Pas-de-Calais), as Tengvik thinks (p. 129).

[2] A possible first el. is also OE *scite* 'dung, excrement'; *EPN* ii. 112.

[3] Continental cognates are MLG *schōde* (Lasch-Borchling), MHG *schōte* (Lexer) 'seed-pod, husk, shell'; see also Pokorny i. 952.

[4] Only recorded in the pres. part. *scūdende*; Sievers-Brunner § 385, Anm. 1. Formal parallels would be OE *loca* 'lock, bolt', *sprota* 'sprout', from *lūcan*, *sprūtan*.

[5] On *escufle* see *FEW* xi. 319. Note also (Willelmus) *Escofle* c. 1100, D. C. Douglas, *The Social Structure of Medieval East Anglia* (Oxford, 1927), 268 (Nf). An alternative source of *LW Scuuel* would be an OE **scufl*, a variant of *scofl* 'shovel', which is postulated by

Luick §§ 78, Anm. 2, 379. OE *scofl* cannot, as Reaney suggests, *DBS* s.n. Shovel, be the direct ancestor of the *LW* form.

[6] A later instance is (Johannes) *Spich* 1217–34 R. R. Darlington (ed.), *Cartulary of Worcester Cathedral Priory* (London, 1968), 212.

[7] Weak adjectives with or without the definite article were often used as bynames in OE; the relevant cases are listed by Tengvik, p. 282.

[8] On the suffix *-ard* see Lebel 85. A good semantic parallel to the name under notice is OFr *Amblard(us)* 'one who ambles along' (Lebel, loc. cit.).

[9] On *Trotin* see K. Michaëlsson in *Mélanges de linguistique offerts à Mario Roques*, iv (Paris, 1952), 184, with additional examples.

(< Lat *luscus*) 'squinting, short-sighted'.[1] The first might be OFr *tor* 'bull'. On *x* [ks] for *sc* in -*lux*, which is due to ME metathesis, see Campbell § 440, Jordan § 182, Anm. 1.

Ulpis, *Willelmus* **1148.**—Lat *vulpis* 'fox', a side-form of *vulpes*, as in (Fulcoius) *Vulpis* 1089 (Condé-sur-Sarthe, Orne).[2] Initial *v* was left out by the *LW* scribe on the mistaken analogy of the names in *Ul(u)-* < OE *Wulf-* which exhibit the AN change *wu-* > *u-*; for examples see above, p. 175.

Verbula, *Ailricus* **1148.**—MLat *verbula* 'little words', plur. of *verbulum*.

War', *Turbertus* **1148.**—If not an abbreviation for *waranc'*, on which see the following entry, this could be OE *wær*, wk. masc. *wara*, 'wary, astute, prudent', as in *Edsige ware*, mon. Cnut, Exeter, *BMC* 74.

Waranc', *Edwardus, Willelmus* **1148.**—Probably OFr (Northern) *waranc(h)e*, (Central) *garance*, MLat *warantia* 'madder, madder dye'[3] or short for the corresponding agent noun ONFr **waranc(h)ier* 'one who manufactures, or dyes in, madder' which is attested by Old Picard *warancheur* (with a different suffix),[4] and by the byname (Rad') *Warantier* 1207 *Fine R* 457 (Winchester).[5] The noun survives in Modern French as *garancier* (1614ff.). Note also the ModFr surname *Garancier*, (Northern) *Garancher*; Dauzat 278. ME semantic equivalents of the term are the occupational bynames *Madrer, Madster*; Fransson 108.

Waspail, *Osbertus* **1148.**—OFr *gaspail*, ONFr *waspail* 'what is thrown away in threshing and winnowing, chaff; wastefulness'. The word is well evidenced as a byname in OFr sources, probably in the sense of 'squanderer, wastrel'.[6] An early ME example is (Rogerus) *Waspail* 1130 *P* 21 (W). Note also the Ha pl.n. Hartley Westpall, *c.* 1270 *Hertlegh Waspayl*, on which see *DEPN* s.n.

Waterpotes, *Lewine* (gen) **1066.**—OE **wæterpott* 'vessel for holding water'. ME *waterpot* is not recorded until 1382 (*NED*).

Watmaungre, *Alwinus* **1066.**—See Occupational Bynames.

Witegos, *Adam* **1066.**—OE *hwītegōs* 'white goose'. Another early instance is (Edwinus filius) *Witegos* 1095–1107 Urry, *Canterbury* 386 (Canterbury).[7]

Witepe, *Rogerus* **1148.**—OE **hwīt(e)pēa* 'white peacock'; cf. *DBS* s.n. Paw, Peacock.

Withmundin, *Godwinus c.* **1110.**—See *Withmund(in)*, pers.n.

Wridel, *Edwinus* **1066.**—This is either an OE **wridel*, an -*ila*-derivative of *wrīðan* 'to turn, twist, bind, tie', perhaps the name for an implement, or an adj. **wridol* 'twisting, turning' formed from the same verb with the suffix -*ula*. Cf. also OE *wride* 'a winding, a twist' in pl. ns; *EPN* ii. 279.

Wrtwos, *Lewinus* **1066.**—OE **wyrt-*, **wurt-wōs* 'herb sap, vegetable juice'.

Notes on the nicknames

Of the native nicknames the majority are identical with recorded OE or ME words:[8] *æðeling* (Adeling, **1148**), ME *badde* (Bade, **1066**), ME *bakbitere* (? Barbitre, **1066**), ME *bal* (Bal, **1148**), *bār* (Bar, **1148**), *bealluc* (Balloe, **1066**),[9] *beard* (Bierd, Bied, **1066**, **1148**), *brūn* (Brun, *c.* **1110**; OFr), ME *cade* (Caddus, **1148**), *canne* (? Chane, **1066**; ON),

---

[1] (de Godefr') *Lusco* 1195 *MRSN* 182, (Nicolaus) *Luscus* 1210 L. V. Delisle, *Cartulaire normand de Philippe Auguste* (Caen, 1852), no. 201, (Bonhome) *Luscus* 1177/8 *P* 80 (Wa ?). On the use of the fem. form *losche* with masc. nouns see Pope § 783 (i).

[2] *Cahiers Léopold Delisle*, 12 (1963), 26. Note also (Rainaldo) *Vulpe* 1138 C. H. Haskins, *Norman Institutions* (Cambridge, Mass., 1918), 92 (Rouen). *Vulpis, Ulpis* probably translates OFr *golpil, goupil* 'fox', which occurs in *LW* as a pers.n.; see *Gupill'* 1148, above p. 160.

[3] See *FEW* xvii. 622, Latham s.v. The corresponding verb is recorded in the Northern form *waranchier* (Hainaut, Flanders; 1283ff.)

[4] Jehan le *Warancheur* 1290; Morlet *Étude*, 153, 421.

[5] The 1207 form probably owes its medial *t* to scribal association with Anglo-Lat *warantia*.

[6] (Petrus) *Gaspallus* 1092 C. Métais (ed.), *Cartulaire de l'abbaye cardinale de la Trinité de Vendôme*, ii (Paris, 1894), 70, (Henr') *Waspail* 1180 *MRSN* 78, (Radulfus) ~ 1180–2 *RAH* ii. 205 (Normandy), (Rad') ~ 1157/8 *P* 120 *et passim*, (Fulcone) ~ 1171–83 *Seals* 199 (Gl), (Osb') *Waspaille* 1207 *FineR* 454 (Winchester).

[7] The printed edition has *Pitegos* with the common scribal confusion of *P-* and insular *W-*.

[8] The *LW* form and the date of its occurrence are given in brackets. The existence of alternative derivations is indicated by the abbreviations OE, OFr, ON.

[9] Also used independently as a pers.n.

catt (Cat, **1066**), *cæppe* (Cheppe, **1066**), *cēo* (? Chie, **1148**), *cild* (Child, **1148**), *codd* (Cod, **1148**), *coppede* (Coppede, **1066**), ME *crul* (Crul, **1066**), *dol* (Dol, **1066**), *dora* (Dore, **1148**),[1] *draca* (Drache, **1066**), *Frīgedæg* (Friedai, **1148**),[2] *gōd mann* (? Godeman, **c. 1110**), ME *gul* (? Gule, **1066**), *gydig* (Gidi, **c. 1110**), *hearra* (Herra, **1148**), *hwīt* (Hwit, **1066**), *hwītegōs* (Witegos, **1066**);

lippa (Lippe, **1148**; OFr), *māse* (Mase, **1066**), *mūs* (Mus, **c. 1110**), ME *nīwe man* (Niwem', **1148**), *pēac* (Piec, **1148**), *popelstān* (Poplestan, **1066**), *portic* (? Porriz, **1066**), *post* (Post', **1148**; OFr), *pott* (Pot, **c. 1110**),[1] *puttoc* (Puttuc, **1148**), *risc*, **rysc* (Rus, **1148**), *rūst* (Rust, **1148**), *spic* (Spich, **1148**), *stūt* (Stud', **1066**), *tōh* (? Toi, gen., **1066**), *wær* (? War', **1148**), ME *waterpot* (Waterpot, **1066**).

Derivatives are *Coppa* (< copp, **1148**),[1] *Quadde* (< cwēad, **1148**), *Socche* (< socc, **1066**).

In a few cases an unrecorded OE word has been inferred from a *LW* form: *banna* (Banne, **1066**), *cæppel* (? Capel, **1066**; OFr), *cimel* (Cimel, **1066**), *cybb(e)* (Chibus, **c. 1110**), *dopp* (Dop, **c. 1110**), *grūtig* (Gruti, **1148**), *scōd(a)* (Scodhe, **1066**), *wridel, -ol* (Wridel, **1066**).

Compounds formed of known OE words, but most of them probably coined *ad hoc* and hence of an ephemeral character, include: *brādears* (Braders, **1066**), *byttecatt* (Bittecat, **1066**), *bullocesēage* (Bollochessege, **c. 1110**),[2] *cildbrōðor* (Childebroder, **1066**), *clǣnehand* (Clenehand, **1066**), *fūlbeard* (Fulebiert, **1066**), *gieldfenga* (Jeltfange, **1066**), *grēatsēod* (Gretsud, **1066**), *healt (se healta) prēost* (Helteprest, Hieltepreost, **1066**), *hwītepēa* (Witepe, **1148**), *peni(n)gpurs* (Penipurs, **1066**), *pyttheald* (? Putheld, **1148**), *scittelifer* (Sciteliure, **1148**), *sōftebrēad* (Softebred, **1066**), *sōtbord* (Sotebord, **1066**), *sūrhlāf* (Surlaf, **1148**), *tādebealluc* (Taddebelloc, **1066**), *wyrtwōs* (Wrtwos, **1066**).

Some of the above may well have existed as common nouns in OE, notably *hwītepēa* 'white peacock', *peningpurs* 'money-bag', *sūrhlāf* 'sour bread', *wyrtwōs* 'vegetable juice'.

The following compound bynames have survived as modern surnames: *blǣcbeard* (Blachebiert, **1066**), *hārlocc* (Horloc, **1066**), *gōd sāwol* (Godeswale, **1066**), *peni(n)gfæder* (Penifeder, **1066**).

Phrase-names consisting of a verbal element and an object noun are *clawe-cunte* (Clawecuncte, **1066**), *cunne-brēad* (Cunnebried, **1066**), *hacce-mūs* (Hacchemus, **1148**),[3] *pice-wurte* (Picteurte, **1066**), *price-lūs* (Prichelus, **1148**), and *scytte-port* (Escitteport, **1066**). To the same category belong the following personal names which originated as nicknames: *Haccesealt* (Hacchesclt), *Tellebēane* (Tellebiene), and *Turneteil*, all **1148**.[4]

An interesting type is represented by the formula *nā lāð* (Nalad, **c. 1110**), evidently a favourite expression of the person on whom it was conferred as a nickname; cf. also *Gustate*, **1066**.

Lȳtelprod (Litteprot, **1066**) is an Anglo-French hybrid. *Baganorus* (**1148**) is derived from the pl.n. Bagnor (Brk).

No satisfactory explanations have been found for *Bensetoure* (**c. 1110**)[5], *Chie* (**1148**),

---

[1] Also used independently as a pers.n.
[2] Also used independently in **1066**.
[3] Alternatively OE **hæcc(e)-mūs* 'hatch-mouse'.

[4] On names of this type see now B. Seltén, *Early East Anglian Nicknames: 'Shakespeare' Names* (Lund, 1969).
[5] But see now Addenda to p. 207.

Chuet (**1066**), *Opchieher* (**1066**), and *Sarz* (var. *Sorz*, **1066**); those proposed for *Abeaham* (**1066**), *Betteslaf* (**1066**), and *Lacchewei* (**1148**)[1] are conjectural.

Of Old French bynames the **1066** list has five somewhat uncertain cases: *Bochenel, Capel* (OE), *Gule* (OE), *Gulee, Sorz*, to which we may add the hybrid *Litteprot* noted above. In **c. 1110** occur *Barrat, Brun* (OE), *Burdin, Casier, Dublel, Fresle, Marmion, Parfait, Prison* (also **1148**), *Russel*, and *Tardif*.[1] The **1148** survey supplies no less than 43 (45)[2] examples: *Bel, Bontens, Cachastra, Cole, Corneilla,*[1] *Cornet, Cuillebrant, Cuinta,* (and varr.), *Danais, Danzel, Duchet,*[1] *Durage,*[1] *Estreis, Freschet, Furwatel, Galne, Grailepeis, Lippe* (OE), *Loer', Mansel, Marc', Martel, Martre* (and varr.), *Mercherel, Meroie, Mieta, Mordant, Mucheto, Norreis, Oison, Paignon* (Paginan'), *Palefrei,*[1] *Pancheuot, Petit, Peuerel, Pofil(e), Post* (OE), *Prison, Scuue(i)l, Soggera, Tresor, Trotardin, Turlux, Waranc', Waspail.*

The majority of the above forms go back to well-evidenced OFr (or later) words. *Bochenel* and *Trotardin* are normal suffixal derivatives. *Cuillebrant* is a phrase-name of a familiar type. *Pancheuot* and *Peuerel* are well-known Norman sobriquets that have survived as English surnames. *Furwatel*, though not in the dictionaries, is recorded elsewhere in a Continental French source, and *Grailepeis* and *Turlux* are clearly two more of 'those nicknames that the Normans loved to inexorably bestow on one another'.[3]

Marc' may be an incorrect spelling for *Mart[re]*. The etymologies suggested for *Cachastra* and *Durage* are conjectural, and no explanation has been found for *Meroie* and *Mucheto*.

The stock of nicknames in the *LW* also includes a number of Latin epithets, most of them appearing in the **1148** survey. They translate vernacular terms, sometimes English but in the later surveys mainly Old French, and are as follows: (*a*) **1066**: *Cecus, Francigena, Gustate, Ruf(f)us*; (*b*) **c. 1110**: *Brito, Crispus, Dives, Maleductus, Patinus, Pasturellus, Rosellus, Salvagius, Siccus*; (*c*) **1148**: *Agnellus, Bellus, Blundus, Bonus homo, Caddus, Crassus, Cum barba, Gallus, Hosatus, Iude(i)us, Iunior, Longus, Lupus, Niger, Novus, Pinguis, Polanus, Ruffus, Sarazinus, Surdus, Verbula, Vulpis* (Ulpis). *Etsinemeta* (**1148**) may be an Anglo-Latin hybrid.

In assessing the role played by formations of the nickname type in the period under review, account must also be taken of the numerous cases in which a nickname had come to be used independently in a personal-name function. This process had in fact been going on since early OE times and is a significant factor in the evolution of medieval English nomenclature. Of special interest as throwing light on the genesis of this class of names are a number of instances in which the same person is apparently referred to alternatively by personal name and nickname, or by nickname alone. The following examples of this phenomenon are found in our material:

Balloc **1066**	Lewinus *Balloe* **1066**
Bullochesiega **1066**	Alwinus *Bollochessege* **c. 1110**
(curtillum) *Capel* **1066**	(domus) Godwini *Capel* **1066**

[1] Also used independently as a pers.n.
[2] The second figure includes *Lippe* and *Post* which are probably English.

[3] J. H. Round, *Feudal England* (London, 1894), 194.

Ceca **1066**[1]	Godwine *Ceoca*, a Winchester moneyer *TRE*
(domus) *Poti* **1066**	God' *Pot* **c. 1110**
Cornilla **1148**	Herebertus *Corneilla* **1148**
Coppa **1148**	de Eduino *Coppa* **1148**
Dora **1148**	Guncel' *Dore* **1148**
Duchet **1148**	Radulfus *Duchet* **1148**
Durage **1148**	Willelmus *Durage* **1148**
(heredes) *Fridai* **1148**	Hugo *Friedai* **1148**
Lacchewei **1148**	Radulfus *Lacchewei* **1148**
Palefrei **1148**	Hunfridus *Palefrei* **1148**
(uxor) *Tardif* **1148**	Willelmus *Tardif* **c. 1110**

The native and OFr names that had clearly originated as nicknames are included in the statistics above (pp. 183–6) among 'OE and ME miscellaneous' and 'OFr bynames' and figure under the same heads in the chronological lists (pp. 180–3). OFr nicknames used as personal names are particularly numerous in the **1148** survey and represent a variety of morphological and semantic types.

Although, as is well known, the precise meaning of a nickname can hardly ever be ascertained, a classification of the material surveyed in the present chapter into a few broad semantic categories may be useful and will be attempted below. Cases of uncertain etymology have been left out,[2] but the groups include original bynames used in a personal-name function. These are marked (p). Native names are given in their reconstructed OE or ME form.

1. **Physical characteristics**: *Basset* (p), *Bealluc*, *Beard*, *Bel*, *Blæcbeard*, *Blund*, *Brādears*, *Brūn*, *Bulloceseage*, *Cecus*, *Clænehand*, *Coppede*, *Crabeleg* (p), *Crassus*, *Crispus*, *Crul*, *Cum barba*, *Cwaca* (p), *Fǣttig* (p), *Fresle*, *Fūlbeard*, *Galne*, *Gif(f)ard* (p), *Grailepeis*, *Gule*, *Hārlocc*, *Healt(a) prēost*, *Hwīt*, *Lippa*, *Longus*, *Marmion*, *Morellus* (p), *Niger*, *Pancheuot*, *Pēac*, *Petit*, *Pinguis*, *Rosellus*, *Ruffus*, *Rūst*, *Scittelifer*, *Siccus*, *Sīdlocc* (p), *Surdus*, *Tādebealluc*.

2. **Mental and moral characteristics**: *Badde*, *Barrat*, *Bona filia* (p), *Bontens*, *Bonus homo*, *Brifald* (p), *Cuinta*, *Dives*, *Dol*, *Dulzan* (p), *Freschet*, *Gōdmann*, *Gōdsāwol*, *Gydig*, *Lȳtelprod*, *Maleductus*, *Mordant*, *Parfait*, *Peni(n)gfæder*, *Salvagius*, *Tardif*, *Trēowa* (p), *Waspail*.

3. **Indications of social status, etc.**: *Æðeling*, *Ancild*, *Cild*, *Cildbrōðor*, *Danzel*, *Fæderling* (p), *Hāligprēost* (p), *Hearra*, *Iunior*, *Līcsweostor* (p), *Mercherel*, *Niweman*, *Novus*, *Pasturellus*, *Prison*, *Richefemme* (p), *Soggera*, *Truued*.

4. **Nationality**: see above, p. 189, n. 5.

5. **Animals**: *Agnellus*, *Bar*, *Bochenel*, *Burdin*, *Byttecatt*, *Catt*, *Chawete* (p), *Corneilla*, *Dop*, *Dora*, *Draca*, *Fugel* (p), *Gupill*, *Hafoc* (p), *Hwītegōs*, *Hwītepēa*, *Lupus*, *Mallard* (p), *Martre*, *Māse*, *Multun* (p), *Mūs*, *Oison*, *Palefrei*, *Polanus*, *Porcellus* (p), *Porcus* (p), *Puttoc*, *Sǣfugel* (p), *Stūt*, *Turlux*, *Ulpis*.

---

[1] His identity with the moneyer is probable but not certain.

[2] As have also a number of nicknames whose etymology is reasonably clear but whose semantic content could not be defined with sufficient accuracy for the purpose of the classification adopted here.

6. **Articles of clothing** : *Capel, Caperun* (p), *Cæppe, Cole, Hosatus, Patinus, Pieferret* (p), *Pofil.*

7. **Various objects** : *Bal, Barillus* (p), *Cade, Canne, Casier, Codd, Cornet, Doisel* (p), *Dublel, Duresumer* (p), *Furwatel, Grēatsēod, Holegn* (p), *Hoppecole* (p), *Marc, Martel, Mieta, Paginan', Parcheminus, Peni(n)g* (p), *Peni(n)gpurs, Picot* (p), *Popelstān, Post', Pott, Risc (Rysc), Rucche, Scīd* (p), *Sōftebrēad, Sōtbord, Spic, Sūrhlāf, Sūrpap* (p), *Trentemars* (p), *Tresor, Waranc', Waterpot, Wyrtwōs.*

8. **Miscellaneous** : *Frīgedæg, Gulee, Gustate, Nā lāð, Nicor* (p), *Peuerel, Verbula.*

9. **Phrase-names** : see above, p. 218.

4

NOTES ON THE PHONOLOGY OF THE NAMES

IN the following notes only some of the more important orthographic and linguistic features of the onomastic material in the *LW* will be briefly commented upon.[1]

Very little specific information about the dialect of Winchester and of Hampshire generally in the late Old English and early Middle English periods is at present available. We have as yet no survey of the place-names of mainland Hampshire although those of the Isle of Wight, where special conditions prevailed, have been dealt with at great length by Kökeritz.[2]

The ME texts assigned to the area in question[3] are too late to yield any useful data about the regional dialect at the time with which we are concerned here. To what extent a local variety of late West Saxon may have developed in the ancient capital and the surrounding district, possibly incorporating both south-eastern and south-western traits, cannot at present be determined. However, as will be seen below, a study of the names in the *LW* seems to reveal the presence of some features apparently characteristic of the local dialect, although in view of its paucity and other obvious limitations the material in question can at best only warrant very tentative conclusions. Moreover, in assessing the value of the spellings in our record as phonological evidence, allowance must always be made for the influence exercised by the scribal and linguistic habits of the Anglo-Norman clerks who were partly or wholly responsible for the compilation of the surveys. Reference to this important factor will be made frequently in the notes below.[4]

i. VOWELS AND DIPHTHONGS

OE *ā* remains unchanged: *Bar* (byn.), *Braders* (byn.), *Haliprest*, *Nalad* (byn., nā lāð), *Surlaf* (byn., -hlāf), etc. In the byname *Horloc* (hārlocc) the first *o* is probably due to anticipation of the second.[5]

In *watmaungre* (byn.) we have a very early instance of AN *au* < *a* before nasal groups; see Luick § 414, 2, Pope § 1152.

OE *æ* is mostly *a*, as in *Adeling* (byn., æðeling), *Ail-* (Æðel-), *Al(e)-* (Ælf-), *Auic* (Æfic), *Blacheman*, *Gladewin*, *Waterpot* (byn.). The traditional digraph is used in

---

[1] In quoting name forms the Latin endings have usually been left out. Dates are only given in a few cases. As far as phonology and orthography are concerned, it has not been possible to discover any significant differences between the three *LW* surveys.

[2] *The Place-Names of the Isle of Wight* (Uppsala, 1940).

[3] Jordan 5ff. MS. *e* of the *Poema Morale* (early 13th c.) may be of Ha provenance; see Hallqvist 64. The *Codex Wintoniensis* (BM, Add. MS. 15,350), a

Winchester cartulary from *c.* 1130–50, exhibits virtually no significant deviations from standard late WS orthography; for a detailed analysis of the vowel system see R. A. Williams, 'Die Vokale der Tonsilben im Codex Wintoniensis', *Anglia*, 25 (1902), 392–517.

[4] Cf. also the analysis of AN influence on DB personal names in *PNDB* 40f., 44–129.

[5] For an identical example, *Horloch*, London 1187, see *ELPN* 180.

Ælmeressone (c. 1110). In some cases we have *e*, as in *Cheppe* (byn.), *Elfeg*, *Elmar*, *Elmer*, *Elsi(e)*, *Essulf*, *Federling* (also *Faderlin*), *Penifeder* (byn.), *Hecche* (pl.n.) by the side of *Hacche*. This may be an AN spelling for *æ* or partly reflect south-eastern *e* for *æ*, which perhaps also occurred in Ha; see *PNDB* § 6 with references and, for Sx examples, Rubin 33ff.

On AN *au* for *a* before *st* in *Glauston'*, Glastonbury (OE Glæstinga-), see Pope § 1153.

The interchange of *ei* and *ai* in *Eilward*, *Ailward*, *Lacchewei*, *Lacchewai*, *Saier*, *Seiher*, may be an AN feature; see *PNDB* § 38. *Etard*, *Chenesham* (pl.n.) by the side of *Aitard*, *Chainesham* illustrate the AN change *ai* > *e*.[1]

OE *ǣ*[1] (< WG *ai*+*i*) occurs in the el. *Sǣ-*, which is often written *Sa-*, as in *Safugel* 1066, *Saiet*, *Saieua*, *Saward*, *Sawinus* c. 1110 (*Saiet*, *Saieua* also 1148), and in the by-name *Clenehand*.

ǣ[2] (< WG *ā*) is *e* in *Merwn* (Mǣrwynn). As a second el. *-mǣr* is *-mar* in *Almar*, *Elmar*, *Brithmar*, *Ulmar*, and *-mer* in *Ailmer*, *Elmer*, *Estmer*, *Lethmer*, *Ormer*. The elements *-flǣd* and *-rǣd* have always *e*. In *watmaungre* (byn., wǣt-) the vowel may have been shortened.

It seems reasonable to assume that the South-East Midland or East Saxon change of *ǣ*[1] and *ǣ*[2] > *ā* could occasionally also take place in Ha; there are traces of it in Sr, for which see Sundby 143 with references.

The result of *i*-mutation of PrOE *a* before nasals is *a* (< *æ*) in the pl.n. *Campesiet* > Kempshot and in *Ieltfange* (byn., gieldfenga). This is a well-attested feature of the dialects of K, Sx, Sr, and Ha; cf. Sundby 135. *Peni* and *Penifeder* (byn.) have normal *e*.

Unstressed medial *e* is syncopated in *Barbitre* (byn., -bītere), *rusmangre*, and *watmaungre* (bynames, -mangere), a late OE change for which cf. Luick § 345: 1, Campbell § 392. On *-re* for *-er* in *Edwacre*, *Sciteliure* (byn., -lifer) see *PNDB* § 67.

Bollochessege (byn., Bulloces-), *Borewold* (Burh-), *-sone* (-sunu), *Sonric* (Sunnric) have AN *o* for *u*.

OE *y̆* is represented by *u*, evidently an AN spelling for [y̆], in *Brudefort* (pl.n., Brȳda-), *budel* (byn., bydel), *Cupping* (Cypping), *Lutemann* (Lȳtelmann), *Luuing* (Lȳfing, or Lēofing; cf. below), *Palliesputte* I, 165 (pl.n., -pytt), *Putheld* (byn., pyttheald ?), *Rus* (byn., rysc), *rusmangre* (byn., rysc-).[2]

I-spellings include *Chip(p)ing*, *Gidi* (byn., gydig), *Litteprot* (byn., ly̆tel-), *Escitteport* (byn., scytte-),[3] and *e* for *y* occurs in *Cheping*, *Meleford* (pl.n., Mylen-), *Mensterstret* II, 789 (Mynster-), *Wenestan* (Wyn-), and in *Aldied* (-gȳð), *Lesweda* (late WS -swȳð <-swið; Campbell § 318), *Brithwen*, *Chiwen*, *Luwen* (-wynn).

The prevailing local sound was no doubt *y̆*, as in the neighbouring counties of Sussex (western part), Surrey, Wiltshire, and Dorset where the ME place-name material exhibits a marked preponderance of *u*-spellings; see Rubin 106–11, Sundby 41, 50–1, *PNW*, pp. xx–xxi. The other variants are probably to some extent due to AN sound-substitution (cf. *PNDB* §§ 19–21), but we should perhaps, as Kökeritz points out, *SNph* 10

---

[1] *Scuueil* (byn.) and *Treisor* (byn.) by the side of *Scuuel*, *Tresor* are AN inverted spellings with *ei* for *e*.
[2] In *Rus* and *rusmangre* we may of course have [u] < [y] before [ʃ]; Jordan § 43: 2.

[3] In *Edit*, *Aldit*, *Eldit* (-gȳð) the vowel of the second el. may have been unrounded in OE owing to reduction of stress; see *PNDB* § 20.

(1937/38), 91, 93, reckon with sporadic isolative unrounding of *ў* > *ĭ* in Ha, and the *e*-spellings may partly reflect the change *ў* > *ĕ* which is evidenced in various southern dialects; see Kökeritz, p. xcviii and, for *e* in Do, Sr, and Sx, Sundby 53–6, Rubin 111–12.

The WS diphthong that arose by fracture before *l*-groups is usually *a* (< *æ* < *ea*) in *LW*: *Balloc, Aldelm, Aldied, Aldred, Aldwinus*. In the four examples in *Ald-* lengthening has not taken place; cf. *ELPN* 186. The normal development before lengthening groups is seen in *Eldit, Eldred, Putheld* (byn., -heald ?), with *ę̄* < *ǣ* < *ēa*.

In *Taddebelloc* (byn., -bealluc), *Helteprest* (byn., healt-), *Haccheselt* (-sealt), *e* < WS *ea*, unless merely an AN spelling for late OE *æ*, may reflect the change *ea* > *e* in southern dialects, for which see Hallqvist 12, 27f. Note also *Hieltepreost* (byn.; healt-) with *ie* for *ea*.

OE *ēa* (< WG *au* and as the result of secondary lengthening of *ĕa*) appears as *ie* in a number of cases: *Bullochesiega* (-ēage), by the side of *Bollochessege* with normal late WS *ē* < *ēa* before *g*, *Campesiet* (Kempshot, pl.n.; -scēat), *Cunnebried* (byn., -brēad), *Hiechsi* (Hēahsige), *Piec* (byn., *pēac), *Smiewinus* (Smēawine), *Tellebiene* (Telle-bēane), and *Bierd, Bied* (byn., bĕard), *Blachebiert* (byn.), *Fulebiert* (byn.). These spellings evidently reflect the change *ēa* > *ie* which is well evidenced in various Saxon counties; see Kökeritz, pp. xciif., Löfvenberg 8, Hallqvist 20, 53ff., Sundby 152ff. (note especially the Ha material, p. 154).

The common el. *Ēad-*, on the other hand, is always *Ed-*; note also *Estmer* (Ēast-), *Gretsud* (byn., grēat-), *heuere* (byn., hēawere), *Softebred* (byn., -brēad).

OE *Hĕarding* is *Harding* or *Herding*. The byname *Braders* (-ears) may have had secondary OE *ēa*; see Luick § 268, *ELPN* 187.

The traditional spelling of the diphthong *ēo* survives in *Hieltepreost* (byn.), *Leouing*, *Leovric*. The late OE monophthong is represented by *e* in *Ceca* (Cēoca), *Leuing, Leuret, Leuric, Lewinus*, and other names in *Lēof-, Hali-, Helteprest* (byn.), *Menes* (pl.n., Mēon). Other variants are *u* in *bruwere* (byn., *brēowere), *Luuing* (partly Lȳfing), *Lufman, Lupsida, Lupsone, Luinus, Luwen, Luwold, Gretsud* (byn., -sēod),[1] *o* in *Lowric, Lowinus*, and *i* in *Briwer'* (also *briwere*, byn.), *Lipestan*, and *Liwold*.

The precise phonetic value of these spellings is somewhat uncertain. The *i*-forms seem to reflect a widespread tendency in late OE for *ēo* > *ī*, on which see *PNDB* § 34, *ELPN* 189f., whereas *u* and *o* are usually taken to stand for [ŏ̄]; cf. Sundby 81 with references, Kökeritz, p. xcv. An additional variant is *ie* in *Selieua* < Sǣlēofu and *Diera* < Dēora.

Unaccented final *-a* in weak masculine names and bynames is often retained: *Ceca, Coppa, Diera, Dora, Goda, Herra* (byn.), *Murta, Posta, Selida, Sueta, Trewa, Wdia*. Reduction to *-e* is seen in *Ade, Bade* (byn.), *Banne* (byn.), *Bolle, Cuuache, Dore* (byn.), *Drache* (byn.), *Laue, Lippe* (byn.), *Quadde* (byn.), *Socche* (byn.), *Wdie*.

Final *-u* is reduced to *-e* in *-sone, -sune* < OE *-sunu* (for examples see above, p. 205) and

---

[1] *Burnard* (with *u* for ø) by the side of *Bernard* goes back to anglicized *Beornhard*, perhaps with secondary lengthening of *eo* before *rn*, or, if *u* stands for [y], to a variant with late OE *Byrn-* < *Beorn-*; cf. PNDB §§ 29–31.

Ailware < *Æðelwaru* f.[1] In Scand weak names masc. *-i* and fem. *-a* are preserved: *Huni, Manig,*[2] *Tochi, Toli, Asa* f. *Toche* (**1148**) has *-e* < *-i* or < anglicized *-a*.

The element *-wine* is practically always latinized *-winus,* but final *-e* remains in the non-latinized forms *Alwine* Bierd **1148**, *Edwine* presbiter *c.* **1110**, (domus) *Lewine* Waterpotes **1066**. *Dicheuin* **1148** may be a genuine case of apocope, like *feller* (occup. byn., *c.* **1110**) < OE **fellere*; cf. *PNDB* § 48.

The element *-sige* is usually reduced to *-si* (see below, p. 227), but note *Elsie* clericus *c.* **1110**, *Hersie* **1148**; see also *PNDB* § 47.

The insertion of inorganic vowels in consonant groups is a common feature of *LW* phonology, examples being *Baldewin, Brunestan, Burewold, Colerun, Erepulf, Fareman, Gladewin, Huneman, chenicte* (byn.) < OE *cniht.* This is at least partly an AN phenomenon; see *PNDB* §§ 51–2, Campbell § 367.

ii. CONSONANTS

The OE voiceless stop *c* [k] is generally written *ch* before front vowels in accordance with AN orthographic practice, as in *Cheping, Chiping, Chetel, Drache* (byn.), *Nicher, Prichelus* (byn.), *Tochi,* and occasionally before back vowels and consonants (by the side of normal *c*), e.g. *Chainesham* (pl.n.), *Chateleia* (pl.n.), *Chrichelada* (pl.n.), *Chane* (byn.), *Fulcho.* The affricate [tʃ], which the Normans replaced by [ts] in most positions, is represented by *c* initially and finally: *Ceca, Porcestr'* **II, 925,** *Ciricestria* **II, 656,** and the names in *-ric.*[3] In intervocalic position it is usually written *cch,* as in *Hacche, Hecche* (Hatch, pl.n.), *Ticchemannessone,* but *ch* is also found, as in *Ticheb'* (Tichborne, pl.n.), and even occurs initially in *Child* (byn.), *Childebroder* (byn.), and finally in *Spich* (byn.). The OE geminate stop *cc* is written *cch* in *Bucchestret* **II, 264,** *Haccheselt, Socche* (byn.).

The consonant group [çt] in the elements *Beorht-* (*Briht-*) and *Wiht-* is represented by *c(h)t* or *th.* The palatal spirant [ç] is rendered by *ch* [k] in *Hiechsi,*[4] velar [χ] by *c* in *Uctred.*

For OE [ʃ] traditional *sc* is sometimes used, as in *Escitteport* (byn., scytte-), *Sciteliure* (byn., scitte-), but AN *s(s)* is more common: *Sireman* (Scīr-), *Campesiet* (Kempshot, pl.n.; -scēat), *Essulf* (Æsc-), *Fislia* (Fishley, pl.n.), *Flesmangerestret* **I, 181** (flǣsc-). Another variant is *sch* in *eschamel* **I, 23** < OE *sc(e)amol* 'bench, table', *escheopes* **I, 27** < OE *sc(e)oppa* 'booth'.

The unvoicing of final *d* in *Ailflet, Lefflet, Aldret, Leuret, Fulebiert* (byn.), *Lethmer,* etc., and in the pl.ns *Brudefort, Esperchefort,* and *Fuleflot* is mainly AN; see *PNDB* § 102. In *Stud* (byn.) *d* is apparently an inverted spelling for *t.*

For OE [ð] and [þ] in medial and final positions the Normans used the symbols *d* and, finally, also *t,* with the same phonetic value as the corresponding OE spirants, examples being *Aldied* (-gȳþ), *Alnod* (-nōþ), *Adeling* (byn., æðeling), *Childebroder* (-brōðor), *Lesweda* (-swīþ), *Aldit, Edit* (-gȳþ); cf. also the OFr forms *Lodewis, Pieferret, Truued.*

Initial [þ] is *t* as in *Turstin,* etc.

---

[1] Names in *-gifu, -lēofu, -sidu* were always latinized and hence afford no examples of this change.

[2] *-ig* is an inverted spelling reflecting the late OE change *-ig* > *-ī*; *PNDB* § 134.

[3] A possible instance of *-iz* for OE *-ic* [itʃ] is *Porriz* (byn.) if < OE *portic.*

[4] In *Hiechsi* (< OE Hēahsige) we may have OE [ks] < [χs]; Campbell §§ 416, 481 (4).

The el. *Æðel-* > *Ægel-* > *Ail-* by a native sound-change described by Ekwall, *ELPN* 197.[1]

A variety of spellings are employed to render the affricate [ts]: *Ascelin, Astcelin, Azelin, Atscelina, Atser, Ascor, Atscor, Guncelin, Guntsel', Goce.*

The OE change *fs* > *ps*, on which see *PNDB* § 90, is evidenced in the el. *Lēof-*, examples being *Lepstan, Lipestan, Lupsida, Lupsone, Lursius* (for *Lupsius* ?).[2]

Loss of consonants takes place medially in clusters, e.g. *Burewold* < Burhwald (with subsequent insertion of an inorganic vowel), *Golburg* < Goldburh, *Ormer* < Ordmǽr, *Ulgar* < Wulfgār, and before a consonant group in *Lesweda* < Lēofswīð (*PNDB* § 93). In *Lewinus* and *Lewold f* has been assimilated to a following *w*. Assimilation of *dn* > *nn* is seen in *Gonnod* < Godnōð, of *nd* > *n(n)* in *Godesbran* < -brand, of *nm* > *m(m)* in *Bruman* < Brūnmann, *Ticchemann* < Ticcenmann. The loss of *r* in *Bictric* < Brihtrīc, *Matre* (byn.) by the side of *Martre*, and of *l* in *Alfed* < Alfled, *Lutemann* < Lȳtelmann, *Litteprot* (byn.) < Lȳtelprod, is due to dissimilation. The final consonant is lost in *Hunbric* and *Godehal*, and an inorganic *h* appears initially in *Hedrici* (gen.) and *Hodiam* (pl.n., Odiham).

Finally some miscellaneous Romance features will be briefly mentioned.[3] Initial *w*- in *Watso, Willelm*, and other ContGerm names is North French (incl. AN),[4] examples of Central French *g*- being *Gazo, Giboda*. Also North French and AN are initial *c* [k] in *campion* (byn.), *cangeor* (byn.), *Caper[un], Casier* (byn.), *ch* [tʃ] in *Albuchon, Mercherel* (byn.), *Pancheuot* (byn.), *g* in *Galne* (byn.), as well as the effacement of pre-consonantal *r* in *Pofile* (byn.) and *Bied* (byn.). An OFr prosthetic *e* is added in *Escitteport* (byn., scytte-), *Escorfan* by the side of *Scorfan, Esperchefort* (pl.n., Spearcan-), *eschamel* **I, 23** (OE sceamol), and *escheopes* **I, 27** (OE sceoppa).

---

[1] This is not an AN change as has usually been assumed. For the traditional view see *PNDB* 104ff., Campbell § 484, n. 5.

[2] Note also *Ælpstan* 12th-c. *LVH* 66, *Alpstanus*

stretbidel 12th-c. *EHR* 14 (1899), 423 (Winchester).

[3] Note also the OFr forms listed above, pp. 189, 219.

[4] Also *Furwatel* (byn.) < ONFr *-wa(s)tel*, Central French *-gastel*.

5

LATINIZATION, ANGLICIZING, AND INFLEXION

MASCULINE names, both native and non-native, ending in a consonant, are very often latinized and follow the second declension: nom. -us,[1] gen. -i, etc. Names in -wine are latinized -winus, the only exceptions being those noted above, p. 225. Names in -here and -sige, on the other hand, usually remain unlatinized: Alfere, OG Ansere, Ailsi, Elsi(e), Hersie, Hiechsi. Exceptions, both somewhat uncertain, are Lursius < Lēofsige (?) and Wlfori (gen.) < Wulfhere (?).

OE and Scand weak names are not latinized.[2] On the retention or reduction of their unaccented final vowels see above, pp. 224–5. OG weak names were latinized according to the third declension: Hugo, Hugonis, etc., exceptions being Andrebodus, Sawalus (by the side of Sawalo).

Feminine names whose second el. ends in a vowel are regularly latinized according to the first declension: Alueua (gen. Alueue) and other compounds in -gifu, Lupsida (< Lēofsidu), Selieua (< Sǣlēofu). An exception is Ailware < Æðelwaru. Those ending in a consonant, i.e. compounds with the second elements -burh, -flǣd, -gȳð, -hild, -rūn, -swīð, -wīf, -wynn are not latinized, the only exceptions being Lesweda (< Lēofswīð) and Seburga (< Sǣburh). The same is true of OG names, where latinization only occurs in Helewisa, Mactilda, Mat(h)ilda and, in accordance with a different but common Continental pattern, Adelidis and Matildis. Of the three Scand names in our material Gunnora (< Gunnur) and Osmoda (< Asmoth) are latinized, Gunnild is not.

Weak fem. names of various provenance are latinized according to the first declension: Edde (gen),[3] Emma (gen. Emme), Gisla, Imma, Iua, Iueta, Pauida (by the side of non-latinized Pavie), Petita, Pupelina, Suna. In OG names -a was of course the etymological vowel.

Occasionally there may be some doubt about the true gender of a name in -a, since the ending might be that of an OE weak masc. or of a latinized fem. form, cases in point being Goda, (domus . . .) Gode (gen), Sueta.

Bynames of various types ending in a vowel were sometimes latinized as fem. weak nouns: besmera by the side of besmere < OE besmere, cuinta (varr. cuinte, cointe) < OFr cuinte, cointe, martra (var. martre) < OFr martre, soggera < OFr soegre, sougre.

Anglicizing, which usually involves the replacing of a foreign name theme by the corresponding native one, has taken place in Baluert (?, -ferð for -frid), Burnard (Beorn- for Bern-), Lambricht (-briht for -bert), Osmoda (Ōs- for Ás-). The OE ending -a replaces Scand -i in Iola, and is used in OG Giboda, Panta, Sewala.

---

[1] -ius occurs in Chepingius, Leuingius.
[2] Exceptions to this general rule are Babbi, Toi (byn.), genitives of Babba, Tōa. Chibus (byn.) probably goes back to an OE *cybbe (-iḁa-stem). Odo is mainly OG but may in some cases represent OE Od(d)a.
[3] OE *Edde, latinized *Edda, gen. Eddę.

The native gen. ending *-es* has been preserved in a number of patronymics, for which see above, p. 205. The French definite article is used in the bynames *le feller*, *la Martra*, *le meddere* and in the local names *la Forda*, *la Hela*,[1] *la Medehalla*.

---

[1] MS. *Hahela*.

6

LEXICOGRAPHICAL NOTES

Sometimes the occurrences of native words in *LW* antedate those recorded in the *MED* and *NED*. The more important cases are listed below.[1]

LW	MED *or* NED
bretfol (pers.n.) *c.* **1110**	*bredful c.* 1200, *MED*
cornemongere (byn.) **1148**	*cornmongere* 1177, *MED*
crul (byn.) **1066**	*crul* 1191, *MED*
cunte (in *Clawecuncte*, byn.) **1066**	*cunte c.* 1230, *NED supp*
feller (byn.) *c.* **1110**	*fellere* 1390, *MED*
flat (in *Flathege*, byn.) **1066**	*flat c.* 1330 (Scand. loanword), *MED*
gruti (byn.) **1148**	*grouty* 1744, *NED*
hangere (pers.n.) **1148**	*hongere c.* 1400 (in concrete senses; in sense of 'hangman' 1450), *MED*
hoppere (pers.n.) **1148**	*hoppere* 1203, *MED*
leg (in *Crabeleg*, pers.n.) **1148**[2]	*leg* 1168 (Scand. loanword), *MED*
pap (in *Surpap*, pers.n.) **1148**	*pap c.* 1430, *NED*
penipurs (byn.) **1066**	*pennypurse* 1473, *NED*
scoter' (byn.) **1148**	*shooter* 1297, *NED*
turneteil (pers.n.) **1148**	*turntail* sb. 1621, verbal phrase 1575, *NED*
waterpot (byn.) **1066**	*waterpot* 1382, *NED*

A certain number of previously unrecorded OE words, or unrecorded compounds of known words, have been derived, with varying degrees of probability, from the onomastic material in *LW*. They are as follows: *āncild* 'only child' (**1066**, p. 149), *begēate* f. 'acquisition, property' (**1066**; in *Godebiete*, p. 158), *dopp* 'diving bird' (*c.* **1110**, p. 210), *fæderling* 'relative on the father's side' (*c.* **1110**, p. 156), *gieldfenga* 'tax-gatherer' (**1066**, p. 212), *hwītepēa* 'white peacock' (**1148**, p. 217), *ryscmangere* 'rush-monger' (**1148**, p. 203), *scōd* 'pod, husk' (**1066**, p. 216), *sūrhlāf* 'sour bread' (**1148**, p. 216), *ticcenmann* 'one who tends or breeds kids' (**1066**, p. 174), *wætmangere* 'seller of drinks' (**1066**, p. 204), *wyrtwōs* 'herb sap' (**1066**, p. 217).

Reconstructed words whose semantic content can only be indicated more or less approximately are *banna* (**1066**, p. 207), *cimel* (**1066**, p. 209), *cybb(e)* (*c.* **1110**, p. 209), *wridel* (*wridol*, **1066**, p. 217).

Some contributions to Old French lexicography may be gleaned from the lists of by-names, pp. 183, 204, 219.

A few previously unrecorded Medieval Latin occupational terms are listed on p. 204.

---

[1] *LW* occurrences already noted by Reaney in *DBS* have not been included here. Cf. also the list compiled by Tengvik (pp. 23ff.).
[2] Note also (Lefwin) *Leg* 1176 *ELPN* 157.

PART III

THE EARLY PLACE-NAMES OF WINCHESTER[1]

THE importance of place-names in the study of the topography and early history of Winchester can scarcely be overstated. Of the fifty-seven names discussed in the following entries, thirty-one occur in the Winton Domesday and illuminate many varied aspects of the early medieval city and its immediate surroundings.

The street-names provide both the earliest and at the same time the largest group of such names available from any English town before the thirteenth century. Five are known from the tenth century, nine from the eleventh (if the names from Survey **I** are included as a reflection of the lost *TRE* survey), and a further five from the twelfth. To these streets, six other names may be added, known only from thirteenth-century or later sources, but of a form which suggests an early and perhaps even a pre-conquest origin. Outside the city the main roads were *stræte*, the suburban lanes *twicene*; inside the walls all the ways of which we have record were *stræte*. In four cases the first element derived from an OE genitive plural in *-ena* or *-era*; in five cases the first element was a personal name (once perhaps the name of an animal), and in fourteen names it was a descriptive noun.[2] The five street-names which derive from manufacturing activities are especially important in any discussion of the early commerce of the city.[3]

The other early place-names, of which fifteen occur in the Winton Domesday, are more varied in character but scarcely of less interest. Thirty-three are considered here in all; early names not found in the Winton Domesday and names known only from later sources but possibly of early origin being also included. Three of these place-names are known from the tenth century, seven from the eleventh, thirteen from the twelfth century, and ten from the thirteenth or fourteenth centuries. They include six guildhall-names, four mill-names, nine area-names, seven house-names, four names relating to defences—gates, bars, and ditches—and three names of water-courses.[4] The area-names,

---

[1] This part could not have been written without the characteristically generous contribution of personal- and place-name scholars. The initial lists were compiled from Mr. J. E. B. Gover's typescript *Place-Names of Hampshire*, augmented from Dr. D. J. Keene's files of Winchester topography. Professor Kenneth Cameron, Dr. Olof von Feilitzen, and Dr. K. I. Sandred commented in detail on these lists. Their remarks, especially those of Dr. von Feilitzen, have sometimes been reproduced verbatim in the entries. Professor Dorothy Whitelock, Mr. J. E. B. Gover, Professor Otto Lehmann-Brockhaus, and Mr. Alexan-

der Rumble were kind enough to comment on particular forms or to check individual occurrences. Final responsibility for the entries must however rest with the compilers.

[2] Streets qualified only by an adjective of direction such as 'north' have not been included. See, e.g., *BCS* 605 (Sawyer 1443) and cf. Ekwall *SNCL* 41.

[3] See below, pp. 427–39.

[4] As with streets, topographical features qualified only by an adjective of direction, e.g. 'North Gate', 'West Gate', have not been included.

especially *Coiteburi, Denemarche, Erdberi,* and *Wlveseia,* are of particular value for the early topography of the city, while the guildhall-names, four of which occur in the Winton Domesday, have long been famous among the earliest indications of urban institutions.[1]

In the lists which follow, headnames in bold type are from the Winton Domesday and are the forms of Survey **II** (1148) unless otherwise stated. References to specific entries in the survey(s) have only been given for place-names other than street-names, '1066', '*c.* 1110', and '1148' being used in the street-name section to indicate both the approximate date of the form and the source, Survey **I** *TRE*,[2] Survey **I** *modo*, and Survey **II**, respectively. Headnames in italic indicate early names not occurring in the Winton Domesday which are included here because they may have been in use as early as the twelfth or thirteenth centuries. Thirteenth-century and later names in *-lane* have not been included.

---

[1] See below, pp. 335–6.
[2] In this context *TRE* and '1066' must be taken to refer to the Edwardian survey perhaps to be dated *c.* 1057: see below p. 407 and cf. p. 10, above.

1

STREET-NAMES

Abonestrete [Worthy Lane]: see *Bonestrete*.

Altus vicus [High Street]: see *Magnus vicus*.

Alwarnestret [subsequently *Fleshmongerstret* 1293–4 onwards and now St. Peter Street, *Proc Hants FC* 24 (1967), 82–5]: 1148, *Alwarenestret c.* 1110, *Aylwarestrete* 1279 *Cal Chart R*, *Alwardstrete* 1268 *Cal Pat R*, *Alwarestrete c.* 1319 Stowe 846, *Alwarestret c.* 1329 ibid. The first element is no doubt OE *Æðelwaru* f. pers.n., the forms *Alwarnestret c.* 1110, *Alwarnestret* 1148 being due to the analogy of street-names like *Scowrtenestret* and *Sildwortenestret*, whose first members have the weak gen. plur. in *-ene*. Note also *Brudenestret*, *Colobrochestret*, and perhaps *Wunegrestret* below, and see Ekwall *SNCL* 18–19.

Athelyngestret [Upper High Street]: 1330 Stowe 846, *Hathelingestret* 1227 *Cal Chart R*. The first element is OE *æðeling* 'man of royal blood, nobleman' (Ekwall *SNCL* 81–2) and the meaning might be 'street of the princes or æthelings'. But Ernoldus Adeling had three properties in this area in 1148 (**II, 243, 248,** and **271**), so that the street-name should probably be interpreted in a particular rather than a general sense.

Bonestrete [Worthy Lane]: *c.* 1322 Stowe 846, *Abonestrete c.* 1391 ibid. First el. is OE *bān* n. 'bone'. The street ran across the site of a Roman cemetery containing in this area mainly inhumation burials.

(la) Broctwychene [Wales Street and/or Water Lane]: 1272–3 PRBW, *(la) Bruoctwychen'* 1286–7 ibid., *Broctwychen'* 1289–90 ibid. 'Brook lane'. The first el. is OE *brōc* m. 'brook'. For the second el. see below, *Sevetuichne*.

Brudenestret [Staple Gardens]: 1148, 1227 *Cal Chart R*, 1280 Ass, 1330 Goodman *Chartulary*, 1352 *Cal Pat R*, *Bredenestret c.* 1110, 1182 *P*, *Bredin-* 1178 *P*, *Briddenestrate* 1256 Ass, *Briden-* 1294 WCA St. John's Hospital Rental. The first el. could perhaps be OE *brȳd* f. 'bride' with an analogical weak gen.pl. in *-ena*, ME *-ene* (for regular *brȳda*), as in the London street-name *Wyvenelane* 1328ff. 'lane of the women (or wives)';

see Ekwall *SNCL* 123 and *Alwarnestret* above. The meaning of such a name is not obvious but cf. Bride Lane in Gloucester, *PNGl* ii. 127. A possible alternative would be OE *breden, briden, bryden* adj. 'made of, covered with boards or planks', the reference being to some kind of wooden pavement (?); see *EPN* s.v. and note the place-names Bridenbridge (Wo, lost; *PNWo* 359–60) and Bredenbury (He; *DEPN* s.n.) which show a similar interchange of *i*, *e*, and *u* in the first syllable. Note also the church of St. Mary Bredin, otherwise *Bredene cherche*, in Canterbury, described on two occasions as *ecclesia lignea*: Urry *Canterbury*, 213. This interpretation makes good sense archaeologically, since corduroy roads of various kinds were a feature of early medieval towns in northern Europe, although they do not seem to have been recognized so far in England, at least in the south.

Bucchestret [Busket Lane]: *c.* 1110, 1148, *Bukerestreta c.* 1130 *Reg*, *Buockestrete* (sic) 1172 Goodman *Chartulary*, *Buckestrete* 1208–9 *PRBW*, *Buxstrete* 1280 Ass, *Bulkestret* (sic) 1283 WCL Records I, no. 87, *Bukkestrete c.* 1322 Stowe 846. The interesting early spelling *Bukerestreta* might seem to indicate that the first el. is the gen.sg. or pl. of ME *būkere, bouker* 'one who cleans and bleaches cloth' (Fransson 109–10, *MED* s.v. bouker) hence 'the street of the bleacher(s)', but all the other forms point to OE *bucca* 'he-goat', or *Bucca*, pers.n. or byname.

Calpestret [St. Thomas Street]: *c.* 1110, 1148, 1203 FF, 1271, 1299 Ipm, 1279 *Cal Chart R*, etc. The meaning is obscure. *Drogo de Calp'* (**II, 525** and **838**) might be a member of a family that had given its name to the street, or perhaps vice versa. *Calp'* could possibly represent the name of a locality in France; cf. Caup (Lot-et-Garonne), *Dictionnaire des postes et des télégraphes* (Paris 1905), 341, for which no early forms are, however, available.

Ceap strǣt [High Street]: see *Magnus vicus*.

(Super) cheshulluo [Chesil Street]: 1155–82 Godstow Cart, *Cheshulle* 1259 *Selborne Charters*, 1543 FF, *Chushulle* 13th-c. St. Denis Cart, 1291 *Tax*,

1297 HMC vi, *Chishull* 1352 *Cal Pat R*, (*in vico de*) *Chesehull'* 1396–7 *PRBW*, *Cheshull* 1563 FF, *Chesehull juxta Winton* 1578 FF. 'Gravel hill'. The first element is OE **cis* m. 'gravel'; *DEPN* and *EPN* s.v. Cf. the identical place-name Chishall (E), on which see *PNEss* 520–1. The street runs along a steeply rising bank of river gravel on the east side of the Itchen river. The form *Cheesehill* 1750 Godson Map, 6″ OS, is probably a back-formation influenced by the location of the Cheese Fair on the hill above, but the possibility of a derivation from OE *cȳse, cīese* m. 'cheese' should perhaps not be ignored.

Colobrochestret [Colebrook Street]: 1148, *Colbrokenestret* after 1148 Welbeck MS, *Colbrokestret* 1210–11 *PRBW*, *Colbrokstret(e)* 1263–4 *PRBW*, *Colebroke-* 1311 Ipm, etc. The street seems to have taken its name from a backwater of the Itchen river which must have had the name 'cool brook', v. OE *cōl*, adj., *brōc* m.

Flesmangerestret [Parchment Street now represents the 13th-century and earlier Fleshmonger Street in question here, but from the later 13th century the name was applied to the street formerly called *Alwarnestret* (q.v.), now St. Peter Street]: c. 1110, 1148, 1210–11 *PRBW*, (*to*) *flæs[c]mangere stræte*, (*andlang*) *flæscmangara stræte* 996 KCD 1291, *Flesmongere-* 1191 Holtzmann, *Flesshe-mongere-* 1227 *Cal Chart R*, (*in*) *vico Carnificum* 1323 *Reg Assier*, *Fleshmongerestret* c. 1378 Stowe 846. 'The street of the butchers', v. OE *flæsc-mangere* 'butcher'; Ekwall *SNCL* 41–2; Fransson 74.

(*in vico*) **Fullonum** [unknown, possibly an alternative name for *Tannerestret* or *Bucchestret*]: 1102–5 *Reg*. 'Street of the fullers'. The only occurrence of the name. See also above, p. 9, n. 1.

Gerestret [Trafalgar Street]: c. 1110, 1148, *Garstrete* 1172, c. 1250 Goodman *Chartulary*, 1207 *Fine R*, etc. *Kerstreta* 1171 P, *Grastrete* 1208–9 *PRBW*, 1311 Ipm, *Carstrete* 1396 *Cal Pat R*. Probably 'Grass street', first el. OE *gærs, græs* n.; see *MED* s.v. *gras*, where the Winchester street-name is included.

Goldestret [Southgate Street]: c. 1110, 1148, 1258 *Cal Chart R*, etc., *Gold-* 1225–8, c. 1270 *Selborne Charters*, etc. The first el. is probably OE *gold* n. 'gold', hence perhaps 'goldsmiths' street'. OE *golde* f. 'gold-coloured plant, marigold' seems less likely, *EPN* s.v. For the presence of goldsmiths in

this and neighbouring streets, see below, p. 439 and Fig. 23a.

Hathelingestret [Upper High Street]: see *Athelynge-stret*.

Jewry Street: see *Scowrtenestret* and above, **II, 443**, n. 3. The name Jewry Street does not come into use until the 13th cent.

(In) Magno vico [High Street]: 1148, 1203 FF, 1256 Ass, (*on þa*) *ceap stræt*, (*andlanges þære*) *ceap stræte* 909 BCS 630, (*andlang*) *cypstræte* 996 KCD 1291, (*on*) *cypincge* c. 1000 Ælfric, (*in parte meridiana*) *popularis plateae* c. 1000 *Vita Dunstani* (auct. B),[1] (*iton* [sic] *þa*) *cypinge*, (*anlang*) *cypinge* 1012 KCD 720, (*in hoc*) *vico*, (*in*) *mercato* c. 1110, *civitatis . . . fori* 1141 *Gesta Stephani*, (*in*) *alto vico* 1280 Ass, (*in*) *summo vico* c. 1285 *Selborne Charters*, *Alta Strata* 1349 *Cal Pat R*, *Hei stret* 1523 *Black Book*. The earlier name is from OE *cēap* m. 'market'; Ekwall *SNCL* 41.

Mensterstret [Little Minster Street]: 1148, *Munstrestret* 1285 Appendix I, below, *Minesture-* 1299 Ipm, *Ministere-* 1318 Goodman *Chartulary*, *Ministrestrete* c. 1321 Stowe 846, etc. From OE *mynster* n. 'monastery'. This street was originally the nearest to the cathedral and led directly to the gate of the monastery. The street to the east now known as Great Minster Street only emerged in the later 14th or 15th century. In 1437 Little Minster Street was *Ministerstret* and Great Minster Street was the *vicus iuxta cimiterium Sancti Swithuni Wyntonie*, *Black Book*.

Paillardestwichene [Canon Street]: 1208–9 *PRBW*, *Pailardestvichene* 1210–11 ibid., *Paylardestwychene* 1400 *Reg Wykeham*. The second element is from OE *twicen(e)* f., here in the sense of 'a lane joining two roads', as in *Sevetuichne* (q.v.). The first element is ME *payllart, palȝard* (< OFr *paillart*) 'a professional beggar or vagabond; a low or dissolute person; a lecher' (*NED* s.v. *palliard*), perhaps used as a nickname as was frequently the case with the OFr word. But compare below (*la*) *Twychene* and *Beggars Street* [St. John's Street to the north of Bubb's Cross] 14th c., -*Lane* 18th c., both of which are also just outside the city wall.

Scowrtenestret [Jewry Street]: 1148, *Scowertenestret* c. 1110, *Schortenestreta* 1191 P, *Schortenestret(e)* 1202 P, 1297 HMC vi, c. 1325 Stowe 846, *Shortene-* 1256 Ass, 1280 *Cal Pat R*. 'Street of the shoemakers', v. OE *scōhwyrhta* m. 'shoemaker'; BT s.v.

---

[1] The *popularis platea* was probably not in High Street, but a market-place outside West Gate, at the junction of *Wodestret*, *Athelyngestret*, and the modern Sussex Street; see below, pp. 265, 285, and 330, n. 1.

Sevetuichne (-ena) [approximately St. Michael's Road–St. Michael's Passage]: 1148 **II, 1001,** *Suvetvichene* 1210–11 *PRBW, Sewinestwichene* 1217 Southwick Cart, *Sevetwychene* normal form by late 13th c. PRBW. The second element is OE *twicen(e)* f. 'a place where two roads meet'; according to M. Löfvenberg, *Studies on Middle English Local Surnames* (Lund, 1942), 216, and *SMS* 19 (1956), 126–7, *twicen(e)* could also mean 'narrow alley or lane'. The word is probably used here in the sense of 'a lane joining two roads'. The first element is OE *Sǣwine* m. pers. n. Cf. also the identical Oxford street-name *Sewenestuchene* 1270 *PNO* 43.

Sildwortenestret [Upper Brook Street]: 1148, *(to, andlang) scyldwyrhtana strǣte* 996 *KCD* 1291, *Seldwritene-* c. 1230 *Selborne Charters, Schilwrhitte-* 1241 ibid., *Suldworthene-* 1247 ibid., *Shuldwrtene-* 1258 ibid., *Shuldwryghte-* 1334 HMC vi, *Schuldwryghte-* 1337 WCA Stake Roll, *Shulworthestret* 1396 Stowe 846, the normal form in the 14th c., *Sheldwroght-* 1352 *Cal Pat R.* 'Street of the shield-makers', *v.* OE *scildwyrhta* m. 'shield-maker'; Ekwall *SNCL* 41–2.

Snidelingestret [Tower Street]: 1148, *Snithelinga stret* c. 1110, *Snithelingstret* c. 1270 WCL Records 1, no. 74, *Snythelyngestret* 1337 HMC vi, *Snythelingstret* c. 1360 Stowe 846. The first el. may be the gen. of an OE plur. **Sniðelingas* from OE **sniðel,* ME *snithel,* NE dial. *sniddle* 'coarse grass, rushes, sedge' (*NED* s.v.), hence 'people living at a place overgrown with coarse grass, etc.' Parallels would be Rising (Nf), ME *Risinges,* Saling (E), DB *Salinges,* which probably mean 'people by the brushwood' and 'dwellers at the willows'; see E. Ekwall, *English Place-Names in -ing* (Lund, 1962), 24, 60; *DEPN* s.nn. See Addenda.

(on þa) strǣt midde [a lost street, probably *not* High Street]: 909 *BCS* 630. Translated by Birch *Ancient Manuscript,* 32, as 'the mid-street', and interpreted by F. J. Baigent (ibid., appendix following p. 32) as a reference to High Street, the mid-street is perhaps to be identified with the street which formed the southern boundary of the original New and Nunnaminster precincts and is represented today by the passage leading from Water Close to Wolvesey. See below, p. 322, n. 8.

Tannerestret(e) [Lower Brook Street–Tanner Street]: c. 1110, 1148, 1210–11 *PRBW, (on) Tænnerestret* 990 *KCD* 673, *Tannarestret* 1172 Goodman *Cartulary, Tannerestret* 13th- and 14th-c. St. Denis Cart, Stowe 846, *Tanner-* 1256 Ass, 1352 *Cal Pat R.* 'Street of the tanners', OE *tannere* m.

(la) Twychene [Swan Lane]: c. 1322, c. 1336, c. 1368 Stowe 846. 'The Lane'. For OE *twicen(e),* see above *Sevetuichne. La Twychene* was known as Beggars Lane in the 16th c. (WCL), when there was a house there called *The Swan* (WCM 1321).

Wudestret [Romsey Road]: c. 1220 St. Denis Cart, *Wodestret* c. 1343 Stowe 846. The name means 'the street where wood was sold' or possibly 'the street leading to the wood' (Ekwall *SNCL* 77), either of which makes good sense in relation to this street.

Wunegrestret [Middle Brook Street]: 1148, *Wenegenestret* c. 1110, *Wenegere-, Wengarestret* 1210–11 *PRBW, Wynegere-* 1221 *Selborne Charters, Wonegere-* 1238 ibid., *Wynegare-* 1243 ibid., *Wonegar-* 1279 *Cal Chart R,* c. 1285 *Selborne Charters,* 1352 *Cal Pat R, Wonegare-* 1299 Ipm, c. 1330 Stowe 846. First el. OE *Winegār* pers.n., recorded in the boundary mark *to Winagares stapule* 1032 (12th c.) *KCD* 746 (Brk), and possibly in the DB place-name Wingerworth, *PNDb* (EPNS 28), 330. The Winchester street-name and the DB place-name might alternatively contain an OE **Wyngār* with the common and productive element *Wyn(n)-.* The vowel variation in the first syllable of the Winchester name reflects the rounding of *win- > wyn-,* ME *wun- (won-),* which is evidenced in a number of counties, including Hampshire. (On *Wun-* by the side of *Wyn-* in OE sources, see *PNDB* 416–17. Note also the forms for Wonston (Ha), Winstone (Gl), and Woolland (Do); *DEPN* s.nn.). The second *n* in *Wenegene-* may be due to scribal error (dittography) or to assimilation of *n–r > n–n.* Association with the gen.plur. forms in *-ene-,* for which see above *Alwarnestret,* should perhaps also be considered.

PLACE-NAMES OTHER THAN STREET-NAMES

(de) Balchus [on north side of High Street, near the entry to *Flesmangerestret*]: 1148 **II, 52,** *le balche(us)* c. 1110 **I, 19.** The place *ubi latrones ponebantur in prisone* (**I, 19**). The meaning is probably the 'balk- or beam-house' (i.e. one constructed of strong timber), first element OE *balc(a)* m., ME *balk(e)*; second el. *hūs* n. Cf. the synonymous Colchester name *Balkerne* 1154ff., whose second element is OE *ærn* n. 'house'; *PNEss* 370. See also *MED* s.v. 3a, where the reference is over two centuries later than the occurrence here. The meaning may be interpreted as a fenced gaol compound or prison cage, see below, pp. 305–6. A derivation from Lat. *balchio* 'house with a balcony' (Du Cange) is to be rejected.

Bardich [part or the whole of the boundary ditch of the western suburb, see below, *Grenedych*]: c. 1327 Stowe 846. The meaning is 'the ditch with a bar across' (?) or 'which bars the way' from ME *barre, bar(r)* 'a barrier, obstruction or barricade, esp. outside the gate of a walled city; also the gate itself' (*MED* s.v.). Cf *le Barrestret* 1286, 1335 (in Droitwich), *PNWo* 21, 285 n. For discussion of this boundary and the city bars, see below, p. 264.

Black Ditch [watercourse west of the Itchen river, north of the city]: 1753 WCA Abbotts Barton estate map, (*innan*) *blacan lace*, (*of*) *blaca lace* 961 *BCS* 1076. The second el. is OE *lacu* f. 'stream'.

Chenictehalla [possibly the same property as *Chepmanneshal'*, q.v., on the north side of High Street]: 1066 **I, 10.** See also the separate name, *la chenictahalla* 1066 **I, 34.** 'The hall of the *cnihtas* (knights)', OE *cniht*, gen.pl. *-a*.

Chepmanneshal' [possibly the same property as *chenictehalla* of **I, 10,** q.v. on the north side of High Street]: 1156 *P*, *Chepmannessela* 1158 *P*, *Chepmaneshela* 1160 *P*, *Chupmanneshalle* 1212 Appendix I, below. This was the place *ubi linei panni venduntur* (**II, 69**). The name means 'The hall of the merchant(s)', *v*. OE *cēapmann*. On the singular form of the first element see Ekwall *SNCL* 14–15. On the question of the identification of this property with the *Chenictehalla*, see above **I, 10, n. 1; II, 69, n. 1.**

(in porta de) Chingeta [King's Gate]: 1148 **II, 928,** *kinggeshiate* 1198 FF, (*extra Portam*) *Kingate* 1210–11 *PRBW*, *Kinghete* 1242 Close R, *Kynggate* 1266 *Black Book*. 'The king's gate'. The second element is OE *geat* n.

Coiteburi [Coitbury: an undefined area north of High Street lying between Lower Brook Street and Eastgate Street, see above **II, 687,** note 2]: 1148 **II, 687,** *Coitburiam* 1207 *Rot Chart*, *Coytebury* c. 1363 Stowe 846. This name seems to be comparable to the small group of London names in -*bury* (Aldermanbury, Bucklersbury, Lothbury), where the final element is OE *burg* f. 'fort', later 'a court, manor-house' or 'large farm'. These names 'doubtless denoted large houses or groups of houses, manors and heads of sokes, residences of wealthy people' (Ekwall *SNCL* 194 and 195–7). The first element is possibly a pers.n.

(on) costices mylne [a mill a short distance upstream from Durngate, possibly to be identified with Durngate Mill, see below, p. 283]: (*of*) *costices mylne* 961 *BCS* 1076. The first el. may be a pers.n. **Costic*, a derivative of OE **Cost*, which has been inferred from *Costesford* 675 *ASC*, probably Cosford (Sa). See *DEPN* s.n. Costessey.

Creprestr(e) [the mill of Cripstead, near St. Cross]: 1208–9 *PRBW*. The form is unchanging throughout the Middle Ages. The second el. is OE *trēow* n. 'tree', the first possibly OE *crēopere* 'cripple'. 'Cripstead' survives as a lane-name in St. Cross.

Denemarche [a low-lying meadow north of the walled city]: 1280, 1306 Ass, 1365 Hyde Cart, *DeneMarch'* 1281 Ass, *Danemarche* 1281 *Cal Pat R*. The early spellings with 'ch' show that this must be, as in March (*PNC* 253), a locative form in -*i* with palatal *c* of OE *mearc* f. 'boundary', and this is confirmed by (*andlang*) *mearce* 961 *BCS* 1076, which describes the southern boundary of Easton as it appears to run towards the Fulflood valley along the north side of the area known in the 18th century as *Danemark Mead*. The first el. seems to be OE *denu* f. 'valley', thus 'boundary in a valley'. On the forms with *a* see above, p. 223, and for the boundary, below, p. 257. For medieval and later traditions associating *Denemarch* with the site of the fabulous contest between Colbrand the Dane and Guy of Warwick, which have probably favoured the form *Dane-* in late and post-medieval spellings, see *Milner*[3], 109–12 and cf. Rudborne in *Anglia Sacra*, i. 212.

Derniata [Durn Gate]: 1165 *P*, *Dernegata* 1166 *P*, *Dernegate* 1167 *P*, *Durnegate* 1205–22 Goodman *Chartulary*, 1261 Ipm, etc. The first element is OE *dierne* adj. 'secret, hidden'; the second el. is OE *geat* n. Cf. Derngate in Northampton, *PNNp* 7.

Erdberi [a piece of ground within the western suburb. The word sometimes seems to refer to the suburban bank and ditch and is the origin of the second element in Oram's Arbour]: 1182–3 *P*, *Erdberia* 1188–9 *P*, *Urdburi* 1250–60 *Selborne Charters*, *Wrothbur'* 1280 Ass, *Urthbury* 1287 WCL Custumal, *hurb[er]y* c. 1321 Stowe 846, *herthbur'* c. 1326 ibid., *Erbery* 1417 WCA Tarrage, *The Harbor* 16th-c. WCA Tarrage. OE *eorðburg* f. 'earthwork'; *EPN* s.v., and cf. *Antiquity*, 17 (1943), 62–3 for a list of comparable examples, sometimes applied to prehistoric earthworks. This may also originally have been the case here, for the piece of ground to which the name is attached occupies the NW. corner of the Iron Age ditched and banked enclosure, the defences of which were not remodelled to form part of the boundary of the city liberty until the early twelfth century. (H)*arbour* usually derives from OE *herebeorg*, *EPN* s.v., but in this case looks like a later popular etymology. The 13th-century spelling *Urd-* is AN and is found in the south for OE *eo* in ME.

Flodstoc [the mill of Floodstock, on the city wall over the stream at College Bridge]: 1208–9 *PRBW*, *Flodstock* 1289–90 *PRBW*, *Floudstok* 1306–7 ibid. The first element is presumably OE *flōd* mn. 'flowing, stream', much less likely *flōde* f. 'water channel'. The second element is the common OE *stoc* 'secondary settlement, outlying farmstead', conceivably here with reference to extra-mural settlement subsequent to that of the walled area. The stream which worked this mill was one of the principal millstreams of the city, and was probably of pre-conquest origin (see below, p. 283).

(de la) Forda [perhaps Fordingbridge (Ha), but possibly a locality in Winchester]: 1066 **I, 3**, *la Forde* 1256, 1280 Ass. The latter form was the name of an area on the north side of High Street at the point where a number of streams ran across the road. The name also occurs in the late 9th- or early 10th-century bounds of Ealhswith's estate, (*up of þæm*) *forda* 909 BCS 630, with reference apparently to the same general area, but on the south side of High Street (cf. below, p. 322). The property (**I, 3**) occupied *TRE* by *Brumanus de la Forda* lay on the north side of High Street, probably to the west of the entry to Tanner Street (see below, p. 244) and thus close to the area of *la Forde*.

(de) Fuleflod' [*Fulflood*, a stream and area-name in the suburbs north-west of the walled city]: 1148 **II, 291**, (*to þære*) *fulan flode*, (*of þære*) *fulan flode* 961 BCS 1076, (*de*) *Fuleflot* 1148 **II, 245**, (*de*) *Fulflod'* 1207 *Fine R.* The first el. is OE *fūl* 'foul, dirty', the second OE *flōd* 'stream'. The name refers to a stream, now in an underground pipe, which drained the valley north-west of the city, and also, as an area-name, to that part of the valley which extended outside the city liberty. See above, p. 194, s.v. and cf. p. 239, s.n. *Vallo*.

(pro, de) gihalda [a guildhall on the south side of High Street, on or near the site of the royal palace (see below p. 336)]: 1148 **II, 140**, **143**, and **155**.

(terra) Godebieta [Godbegot, on the north side of High Street, between Royal Oak Passage and St. Peter Street]: 1148 **II, 42**, (*Ælfrices*) *gode begeaton* 1052–3 Sawyer 1153, (*domus*) *Godebiete* 1066, c. 1110 **I, 23**, *Godebyhute* 1294 HMC vi, *la Goudebyȝete* 1327 Obed R, *la Godbeyit* 1352 *Cal Pat R*, (*curiam in*) *Goudebegete* 1402 *Black Book*, *Goudbeyete* 1412 ibid., *Goodbegat* 1535 *VE*. This name, which is fully discussed above, pp. 158–9, probably means something like 'the good bargain'.

(le) Grenedych [part or the whole of the boundary ditch of the western suburb, see above, *Bardich*]: c. 1378 Stowe 846. 'The green ditch'.

hantachenesele [a guildhall in Colebrook Street *ubi probi homines Wint' potabant Gildam suam*]: 1148 **II, 712**. The only occurrence of this name describes a structure already out of use (*solebat ibi esse*) in 1148. The final el. appears to be OE *sele* m. 'hall'. Charles Gross (*The Gild Merchant* (Oxford, 1890), i. 196) interpreted the first el. as *hanse* and cited examples to show that *hanse* means 'payment, toll, entry-fee' and is frequently synonymous with 'guild'. In his glossary (ibid. ii. 407) he suggested further that the meaning was 'the hall of the cnihten hanse (?)', but in both places he gave the original form incorrectly as *hantachensele*. Gross's view cannot be supported. The first el. is clearly *hanta* not *hansa*, and the misreading of *s* for *t* is not a very likely scribal error.

Moreover the gen. pl. of *cniht*, normally *cnihta*, but occuring as *chenicte*, *chenicta* in Survey **I** (**I**, 10 and **34**, see above *chenictehalla*), could only reach *-chene-* by a scribal omission of several letters. Gross's view thus requires a degree of manuscript corruption beyond that normal in the other names. No satisfactory etymology can, however, be suggested, although it may be worth noting that *hantachene-* looks like a weak gen. pl. in *-ene-*, such as may be seen in some of the Winchester street-names, cf. *Alwarnestret*, above, p. 233.

(le) hauekheye [the site of the Hawk Mews, in the area of Gladstone Street, west of Sussex Street]: *c.* 1352 Stowe 846, *le haukhey c.* 1378 ibid., *Hawkehei* 1546 *Black Book*. Another form is *la haucose c.* 1342 Stowe 846. The first el. is from OE *hafoc* m. 'hawk', the second is OE *(ge)hæg* 'enclosure', thus 'hawk enclosure'. Also known as *(haias de) Parroc*, q.v.

(Domus) Hauoc [a property outside West Gate, possibly the same as *(le) hauekheye*, q.v.]: 1066 **I, 123.** For the pers.n., see above, p. 161 s.n., and for the property, see **I, 123,** n. 1. *Hafoc* was an original byname from the OE common noun *hafoc* and could have been used metonymically as a nickname for a hawker, as may be the case here. A parallel example is the Londoner named *(Rad')* *Hauoc* who owed the Exchequer 'two gerfalcons and two Norwegian hawks' and who clearly owed his nickname to his trade: Reaney *Origin*, 245, quoting *Pipe Roll 31 Henry I*, p. 148.

Hyda(m) [the site outside North Gate to which the New Minster migrated *c.* 1110]: 1114 *Reg*, *(Abbas de) Hida* 1156 P, *(Abbacia de la) Hyde* 1219 *Book of Fees*, *(Abbatia Sancti Petri de) Hyda (extra Wynton')* 1262 FF. This name is OE *hīd* 'hide, measure of land', and is the piece of land *in qua nunc sedet abbatia* (1114).

Lortebourne [the stream serving the cathedral priory, now called Lockburn]: 1337 *Obed R*, *Lorteborne* 1390 ibid., *Lourtebourne* 1398 *Reg Wykeham*. The second element is OE *burna* 'stream, brook'. The first element is OE **lort(e)* 'dirt, mud', see *EPN* s.v. ME *Lort(e)burne* was a common pl.n., which is found in different parts of England. In the present case it could refer to a watercourse utilized as a sewer. See further E. Ekwall, *English River-Names* (Oxford, 1928), 259; R. Forsberg, *A Contribution to a Dictionary of Old English Place-Names* (Uppsala, 1950), 158–61.

Lousfeyre [a fair held at the place where linen cloths were sold, i.e. at *Chepmanneshal'*, q.v.]: 1330 Good-man *Chartulary*. In the 13th century this tenement was known as *Luggesour*, *Lungesour* 1284–5, 1284–6 P, *Longover* 1326–7 *Cal Mem R*. The meaning may be 'clothes market' (?), cf. *Lousy Fair*, but the sense of the early form of the tenement name is uncertain. Cf. perhaps Forsberg *Contribution*, 182ff. See also below, p. 515, n. 2.

(de la) medehalla [a tavern, inn, or even a guild-hall, perhaps in Winchester itself]: 1066 **I, 12.** OE *meduheall* 'mead-hall'. See above p. 195, s.n.

Merewenehaia [an enclosure in the middle of High Street near the entries to Colebrook and Tanner Streets, see above, **I, 66,** n. 1]: *c.* 1110 **I, 66,** *merwenhaye c.* 1329 Stowe 846, *Merewenehay c.* 1370 ibid., *Merewynhay c.* 1370 ibid. The meaning is 'Mǣrwynn's fenced-in piece of ground', where *Mǣrwynn* is a known local name, see above p. 165, s.v. *Merwn*.

(apud) Palliesputte [a triangular piece of land with houses, at the limits of the city liberty, on the east side of the road to Basingstoke, 700 m north of North Gate]: *c.* 1110 **I, 165,** *Pollespitte* 1196 FF, *Pallesputte c.* 1327 Stowe 846. The first el. is probably ODan *Palni*, Anglo-Scand *Palli(g)*, on which see *NPN* 108, *PNDB* 343; the second OE *pytt* m. 'pit, pond', hence 'Palli's pit'.

(haias de) Parroc [the name for the King's Hawk Mews]: 1201 *Rot Litt Claus*, *(la) Parrok* 1222 ibid. The meaning is 'enclosed ground, paddock'. Also known as *(le) hauekheye*, q.v.

(de) Sapalanda [unknown, an estate of the monks of St. Swithun's(?), or perhaps more likely a locality in Winchester in or near *Brudenestret*]: 1066, *c.* 1110 **I, 153–4, 159–61.** This is probably an OE **scēap(a)-land* 'sheep-land, tract of grass-land used for pasturing sheep', for which see above, p. 196, s.v. The name may possibly refer to a once open area within the North Gate, perhaps used as a sheep market: see below, pp. 285–6.

(molendina de fonte) segrim [Wharf Mill]: 1208–9 *PRBW*, *molendina segrim* 1227 PRBW, *Segremys-myllys* 1482, WCL Registers. 'Segrim's mills'. The pers.n. occurs in Winchester in 1148 (**II, 337, 725**), see above, p. 171, s.n., but the mill was probably named from the spring called *Segrimys-well* 1482 WCL Registers.

Thomeseiete [(? St.) Thomas Gate, the principal entry to New Minster, in Market Street in the area of the junction with Market Lane]: *c.* 1110 **I, 64,** *Thomae Aete c.* 1221–3 *Malmesbury Reg*, *Thomeshet* 13th-c. St. Denis Cart, *Thomasyate*

1349 Hyde Cart, (*ad ianuas portae dicti novi Monasterii qui nunc vocatur*) *Thomasesgate* 14th-c. (prob. relying on 12th-c. source) *LVH*. The second el. is *-iete* < OE *geat* n. 'gate'.

(de) Vallo [perhaps the locality outside the north-west corner of the city known as *la Val* in the 13th century]: 1148 **II, 393.** See above p. 196, s.n. and cf. *Fulflood*, above pp. 194 and 237, s.n.

Wlveseia [Wolvesey, the bishop's palace]: 1208–9, 1210–11 *PRBW, Wolves'* 1138 (13th c.) *Worcester ann, Wlvesey* 1233 *Selborne Charters, Wulvesye c.* 1260 ibid., *Wulveseye* 1284 *Cal Chart R,* 1307 *Cal Pat R, Wolveseie c.* 1296 *Reg Pontissara, Wolveseye* 1320 *Cal Chart R.* The second el. is OE *ēg, īeg* f. 'island'. The first el. is probably *Wulf* pers.n., so the meaning would be 'Wulf's island', with reference to an area of higher or firmer ground which appears here between the streams in the valley floor and became the site of the palace.

PART IV

WINCHESTER IN THE ELEVENTH AND TWELFTH CENTURIES

1

INTRODUCTION

i. TERMS OF REFERENCE

FULL as they are, the two surveys present only a limited picture of Winchester in the eleventh and twelfth centuries. They are essentially financial and tenurial records of the city at three dates: in the time of King Edward (perhaps more precisely *c.* 1057, as we shall see), in the time of Henry I, and in 1148. Other matters are only touched on incidentally, if at all, so that even major facts of the city's topography must be obtained from different sources. The evidence available is extensive, varied, and almost entirely complementary to that of the surveys. By using these sources in combination, it is possible to reach a wider and more firmly based knowledge and understanding of the city's development in the eleventh and twelfth centuries than the surveys alone would allow.

In this part an attempt will therefore be made to examine the evidence of the surveys in the context of all that is at present known of the city in this period from other written sources, and from the evidence of archaeology, topography, and surviving buildings. Using this broad basis, the surveys will themselves be subjected to a detailed analysis designed so far as possible to disentangle the social and economic geography of this distant period, and to follow the changes that took place in Winchester in the crowded century between about 1050 and 1148. An attempt will also be made to set the city in the context of the contemporary countryside, but this should not be seen as more than a sketch of what might one day be possible, given extensive research, on the lines adopted here, into the development of each of the neighbouring settlements.

In space, therefore, our principal subject is the walled city and its ancient suburbs. The wider area cannot be seen in the same detail. Nor is it yet possible to make many useful comparisons with other towns of the same period, where detailed work needs still to be done. We are nevertheless aware that comparative studies are undoubtedly the most fruitful line of advance, and will have much to contribute to an understanding not only of Winchester in particular, but of contemporary urban development in general.

In time our detailed study extends from the reign of the Confessor to that of Henry II. We have not dealt with the tenth-century city, nor with the conditions under which Winchester returned to urban life at the end of the ninth century, except in so far as an outline of these problems is needed to explain the situation in the eleventh and twelfth centuries. The nature of the evidence is such that the later periods will more often illuminate the earlier. The materials presented in this volume should thus form the basis upon which future discussion of the tenth-century city must rest. Nor have we dealt with matters relating to the period after the later twelfth century, except where these help to explain an earlier situation, or to confirm trends already discerned.

Detailed discussion of the architectural development or archaeological investigation of individual buildings or areas of the city will not be found in this volume. Where this evidence exists, the broad outlines necessary for a description of the evolution and character of the urban scene and of its components will be given; for details, reference will be made to other volumes of Winchester Studies.

A few words of caution should perhaps be given. We have approached these surveys in a positive manner and have sought to extract from them as much as we could reliably learn, at least in so far as our own insight, such as it is, has allowed. Due weight must be placed throughout on the qualifications, 'probably', 'possibly', 'perhaps', and on the conditional mood in which much of what we have written has had to be cast. Second, there has been no space here for detailed criticism of the sources which lie behind our comments on the situation in Winchester before *c.* 1050. This criticism, particularly in relation to the Anglo-Saxon charters and other documents essential to the study of the three great minsters, will be found in due course in the relevant subsequent volumes of Winchester Studies.

ii. TOPOGRAPHICAL RECONSTRUCTION AND DISTRIBUTION MAPS

On the basis of a relatively limited number of accurately located properties, and with reasonable suppositions as to the order and method of survey, it is possible to draw up a schematic map of Survey **II** for purposes of geographical analysis (Fig. 19). Where a given number of entries fall into a known length of street, one half of the group can be assigned to one side of the street and the second half to the other. Distribution diagrams compiled in this way will approximate to reality. This method will obviously work best with the simple north–south streets within the walls, less well with the complex blocks of High Street, and only with difficulty in the suburbs, where changes from street to street, and on occasion the limits of the area surveyed, are both uncertain. The topographical basis of this reconstruction is sound enough, however, for the north–south streets within the walls and for High Street, to support comparisons of the density of occupation and of the frontage-width of properties between different parts of the city.[1] Outside the walls, by contrast, the distributions shown in the figures are very approximate.

In the figures representing the distribution of multiple rents and the great fiefs in 1148 (Figs. 18 and 19) the succession of properties in the suburbs has therefore been

[1] On this, see further below, p. 375 and Fig. 17.

reconstructed in a purely diagrammatic way, and in an only slightly more representative form for High Street, *Bucchestret*, and *Colobrochestret* within the walls.

The distribution maps illustrating separate aspects of the evidence provided by the surveys (e.g. Figs. 13, 21–3) have been based on the topographical reconstruction of Survey **II** shown in Figs. 18 and 19. An attempt has been made in these smaller maps to show the actual approximate location of entries shown only in diagrammatic bar-form in Figs. 18 and 19, and this attempt follows the interpretations suggested below in the discussion of the order of survey. Where the distribution maps show evidence derived from Survey **I**, this has been plotted using the available evidence of correspondences between the entries in Surveys **I** and **II** (Table 9), together with such indications as exist of the order in which Survey **I** was undertaken (Fig. 4).

iii. THE ORDER OF THE SURVEYS (Fig. 4 and Table 9)

The inquirers employed by Henry I *c.* 1110 and by the bishop in 1148 adopted the same general approach to their surveys of the city and suburbs of Winchester. They began within the walls on the north side of High Street. They then passed to the south side of High Street and, having finished there, surveyed the streets to the north of High Street from west to east, and the streets to the south of High Street from east to west. The suburbs were each surveyed in their appropriate place as the survey within the walls came to the gate leading into that suburb. On both occasions the treatment of High Street suggests that in all streets the normal method of inquiry was to survey the full length of one side of the street from one property to the next, and then to cross over and do the other side in the opposite direction. This method of perambulation, expressed by the word *ethergingis* in Survey **I**, and the order of progress from street to street, were closely followed by other surveyors of the city of Winchester in the later Middle Ages. Such were the assessors of tarrage in 1417 and the collectors of lay subsidies in the fourteenth and fifteenth centuries.[1] The order of survey was primarily a matter of convenience to the surveyors as they walked about the city, but it is evident that a traditional order of progress from street to street was established at least as early as the beginning of the twelfth century (Fig. 4).

These general points of resemblance between the twelfth-century surveys and those of the later Middle Ages suggest that the later surveys may illuminate the earlier in particular details. In the later surveys the entire block to north or south of High Street, between High Street and the parallel back street, was included in the survey of High Street. The length of the north–south street between High Street and the back street was known as 'the entry' to that particular street, and formed part of the same administrative area as the High Street frontage itself. In the High Street section of Surveys **I** and **II** there may well therefore be included not only properties fronting on to the High Street, but also properties fronting on to the entries to the north–south streets, and even on to the High Street side of the back street. Some of the references to the *callis regis* may thus refer to the entries themselves.[2]

[1] See *SMW*. For an account of the route followed by the assessors of tarrage, see T. Atkinson, *Eliza-* *bethan Winchester* (London, 1963), 17–29.

[2] e.g. **I**, **19**, **20**, and **23**. See also below, pp. 280–2.

In the later surveys High Street was considered to extend from West Gate as far east as the entry to Tanner Street on the north, and the western entry to Colebrook Street on the south. The south side of what is now known as Broadway was occupied by St. Mary's Abbey, and the north side, from the entry to Tanner Street eastwards to the city wall, was surveyed as part of the aldermanry of Colebrook Street. High Street may thus have been regarded as having a similar eastern limit in the twelfth century.

The physical contrast between Broadway and the rest of High Street was even more marked in the Middle Ages than it is today, for the street leading to East Gate and the city bridge was carried over low-lying marshy ground on a causeway intersected by a number of streams.[1] Early settlement in High Street, and hence the area to which that street-name was applied, may have been limited by the west end of the causeway. On the other hand Survey I begins *a porta orientali* as if the gate did mark the east end of the High Street area, and in the tenth century the street which defined the northern boundary of Nunnaminster was known as *ceap stræt*.[2] Nor is this ambiguity entirely resolved by the fact that, on the south side of High Street, Survey I stopped near the western entry to Colebrook Street, or by the possibility that some of the properties under *Bucchestret* in Survey II lay on the north side of High Street between Tanner Street and East Gate.

The strip of properties extending south from High Street between the modern Little and Great Minster Streets, which had once formed part of the royal palace site, was included in the High Street section of the 1417 survey.

So far as the north–south streets are concerned, the later surveys, as they run on from one street to the next, show that properties fronting on to those sides of the back streets furthest from High Street may be included under the heading for one or other of the north–south streets.

Of the suburbs, only the western and northern were included in the later surveys,[3] but here too the order of progress seems to have been the same as in the twelfth century. In the fourteenth and fifteenth centuries the three streets outside West Gate were surveyed in order from south-west to north-east, after which the surveyors made their way from the north end of the modern Sussex Street directly into the suburb outside North Gate.

A reconstruction of the routes taken by the surveyors, so far as this is possible, may now be given. Figure 4 shows these routes diagrammatically, with the positions of those entries which can be positively identified. Table 9 lists the correspondences which can be established between the entries in the two surveys.

The order of survey: Survey I

The surveyors began at the east end of the north side of **High Street** and passed in order the entrances or entries to *Wunegrestret* (**I, 10?**), *Flesmangerestret* (**I, 19–21**), *Alwarnestret* (**I, 23**), and property between *Snidelingestret* and *Brudenestret* (**I, 35–6**). On the south side of High Street they began next to West Gate (**I, 39–40**), continued east

[1] See below, p. 283.

[2] See above, p. 234, s.n., and below, pp. 278, and

322, n. 8.

[3] On the reason for this, see below, p. 255.

past the royal palace (**I, 57–61**) and *Thomeseiete* (**I, 64**), and ended at *Merewenehaia* (**I, 66**) by the western entry to Colebrook Street. If the order of the main survey of High Street was followed, the lands of the barons and tenants surveyed from east to west (including a property **I, 71** at the entry to *Tannerestret*) lay on the north side of High Street, while the lands of the rent-payers, surveyed from west to east, lay on the south side.

Outside West Gate the survey began on the south side of the gate (**I, 81**). No entries can, however, be safely allotted to the modern Romsey Road or Upper High Street. The entries around **I, 93** and **I, 107**, both near St. Valery's church, were perhaps in Sussex Street (medieval name not known). Most of this street was probably surveyed from south to north and all the properties as far as **I, 116** seem to have been on its west side. After **I, 116** the surveyors crossed to the east side to **I, 117** which was probably towards the north end of the street. They then perhaps dealt with the remaining properties in the street finishing with **I, 123** which may have been next to **I, 116**.

There is no evidence of the order of survey in **Snidelingestret** or **Brudenestret**.

The **lands of the barons** following the *Brudenestret* entries probably lay exclusively in *Brudenestret*, where properties under this heading can be identified in Survey **II**, the order of survey here being probably the same as in Survey **II**.[1]

The entries **outside North Gate** relate only to encroachments on to the street or the city ditch (**I, 163–5**).

The survey of **Scowrtenestret** probably deals only with the west side of the street, to which in Survey **II** the king's rents were confined. In **Alwarnestret** the order of Survey **I** cannot be established, since there is no consistent pattern in the identification of properties between the two surveys. In **Flesmangerestret** three properties towards the south end of the west side were surveyed from north to south. Two properties towards the end of the entries under **Wunegrestret** may be on the west side of the street (**I, 191** and **195**), since they were mentioned under *Sildwortenestret* in Survey **II**. In **Tannerestret** the order of survey was probably the same on both occasions.[1] In **Bucchestret** Surveys **I** and **II** followed the same order.[1]

In Survey **I**, entry **245** was on the west side of **Calpestret**. In **Goldestret** Surveys **I** and **II** followed the same order.[1] No conclusions are possible with regard to **Gerestret**.

The order of survey: Survey II

From a starting-point on the north side of **High Street** next to West Gate (**II, 3**), the surveyors worked eastwards, passing in succession properties between *Snidelingestret* and *Brudenestret* (**II, 10–24**), between *Brudenestret* and *Scowrtenestret* (**II, 32–4**), the entry to *Alwarnestret* (**II, 42–3**), the entry to *Flesmangerestret* (**II, 52–9**), and the entry to *Wunegrestret* (**II, 69**).

Property **II, 111** near *Thomeseiete* is the first in this survey which can be identified as lying on the south side of High Street, but **II, 90, 105,** and **106** may have been in the same area, and a number of the preceding properties may also have been on the south side of the street.

[1] See Fig. 4.

After *Thomeseiete* there are a number of properties in which moneyers had interests (**II, 112, 118,** and possibly **115** and **117**) and so the surveyors perhaps continued along High Street towards the church of St. Laurence, past the area in which both earlier and later the activities of the mint were situated. Properties in High Street had an average frontage width of about 25 feet in 1148[1] and this would allow about 15 tenements between the site of *Thomeseiete* and the west end of the church of St. Laurence. There were 17 tenements in this length of frontage in 1417 and in 1870. This number of entries from *Thomeseiete* would bring the survey to item **128,** and with items **127–8** there is a break in the succession of entries in the bishop's fief. The surveyors may then, like their successors in 1417, have gone to the south end of the modern Great Minster Street, and have surveyed from south to north those properties which had developed on part of the site of the royal palace. The property at the north end of this block was probably the *gihalda* (**II, 140** and **143**). These separate references to the *gihalda* suggest that the surveyors were here dealing with a complex and subdivided group of properties. **II, 138** and **139** were later described as being in High Street and so were not perhaps part of a strict south to north progression in this part of the survey. They may even have been in the block between the entries to *Mensterstret* and *Calpestret*. The group of properties thus conjectured to be on the site of the former royal palace corresponds almost exactly with the largest group of the bishop's rents *de .B.*

This reconstruction of the order of survey leaves 26 properties at ground level to occupy the remaining length of the High Street frontage up to West Gate. The seven upper rooms (**II, 152–8**) were perhaps over some of these 26 properties, but the reference to the *gihalda* among them (**II, 155**) suggests that they may have been near **II, 140–3**. There is, however, no obvious explanation as to why the entries relating to these seven rooms should have been separated from the other references to the *gihalda*.

An alternative reconstruction would identify the properties from which rents add up to nine marks (**II, 160–6, 168,** and **170**) with the later site of the mint, east of the church of St. Laurence. This would, however, leave no more than seven entries for the length of High Street between the palace site and West Gate, where Survey **I** records at least eighteen properties.

Outside West Gate (for the surveyors have now returned to the west end of High Street) a tentative reconstruction of the order of survey is possible. The entries may be divided into three groups according to the three main streets of the suburb: (*a*) **II, 177** to **220,** (*b*) **II, 221** to **262,** and (*c*) **II, 263** to **304.** Since the two properties near St. Valery's church (**II, 267** and **288**) occur in the group which would correspond to the modern Sussex Street, and two of the three properties of Ernold Atheling (**II, 243** and **248**) occur in the group which would correspond to *Athelyngestret* (now Upper High Street), the three streets of the suburb appear to have been surveyed in order from south-west to north-east, commencing with *Wodestret* (now Romsey Road). At West Gate the surveyors began with a small group of properties in the king's fief (**II, 177** to **180**) which probably corresponded to the small area on the south side of the gate with which in 1417 the collectors of tarrage (a king's rent) began their survey of the suburb.

---

[1] See below, p. 377.

The next block of property (**II, 181** to **196**) lay in the bishop's fief and probably occupied the rest of the south side of *Wodestret*, which the bishop took into his liberty of the soke in the thirteenth century. The north side of *Wodestret* remained in that part of the city held direct from the king and in the remaining entries which fall into group (*a*) there were numerous rents to the king in 1148. The north side of the street was surveyed from west to east and the last property in this group was probably opposite the starting-point (**II, 220**). *Athelyngestret* was probably surveyed from south to north on its west side and then from north to south on its east side. According to this reconstruction Richard the fusour's properties (**II, 229, 231,** and **255**) form a convenient group midway along each side of the street. In the modern Sussex Street the order of survey is not clear, except that the surveyors probably finished at the north end of the street.

The survey was thence continued into the suburb **outside North Gate.** The bishop's properties, which occupy the first part of the section, probably lay in the west and south parts of the suburb, and the abbot's properties which follow probably lay near Hyde Abbey to the north and east. In the distribution maps, this latter group of properties (**II, 321** to **357**) have been assumed to lie equally on both sides of the modern Hyde Street, beginning on the west side from south to north and then running from north to south on the east side.

As in Survey **I** there is no evidence for the order of survey in **Snidelingestret** or **Brudenestret.**

In **Scowrtenestret** the surveyors began at the north end of the street and worked down the west side. They then surveyed the east side from south to north, beginning with **II, 449.**

The survey of **Alwarnestret** ended near the north wall of the city (**II, 508**), and the simplest way of achieving this would have been to continue directly from the north end of **Scowrtenestret** (**II, 472**), southwards down the west side of *Alwarnestret*, and then back northwards up the east side of the street.

In **Flesmangerestret**, however, the surveyors started at the south end of the west side (**II, 510–15**) and seem to have worked up and down the street, finishing opposite their starting-point (**II, 539–40**). This discontinuity may represent a point at which the surveyors broke off their work, or the division between two separate circuits.

The west side of **Sildwortenestret** was surveyed first, since two properties on the east side (**II, 562** and **563**) fall into the second half of this group of entries. If the surveyors continued directly from *Flesmangerestret*, they would have begun at the south end of *Sildwortenestret*.

The surveyors continued directly into **Wunegrestret**, where they surveyed the west side from south to north (**II, 571** and **584**) and then dealt with the east side, probably from north to south (cf. **II, 599**).

In **Tannerestret** the west side of the street was surveyed first, possibly from south to north (**II, 617**). With **II, 632** the surveyors reached the north end of the east side of the street.

The order of survey in **Bucchestret** is difficult to reconstruct because at least one street, possibly the north part of *Bucchestret* itself, was incorporated into the Black

Friars' precinct in the thirteenth century.[1] The properties on the north side of the lower end of the High Street, between the entry to *Tannerestret* and East Gate, may have been included under this heading in Survey **II,** for in the later medieval surveys they are included with *Bucchestret* in the aldermanry of Colebrook Street. The water on which **II, 680** lay was one of many streams in this part of the city. Property **II, 687** was probably situated in the north part of this area, and the surveyors moved from there towards the city wall at East Gate (**II, 691–5**), possibly along an intra-mural street to which *Bucchestret* was joined at its north end. The twelve final properties under *Bucchestret* may have lain along the north frontage of what is now Broadway, between East Gate and Tanner Street.

In **Colobrochestret** the surveyors began by East Gate.

Of the two principal streets **outside East Gate,** St. John's Street and Chesil Street, the latter was surveyed in the second half of this group of entries (**II, 782**). There is no evidence that properties on the site of the fair on St. Giles's Hill were included in this survey.

The reference to a house *iuxta murum* (**II, 797**) under **Mensterstret** might mean that the strip of ground inside the city wall between South Gate and King's Gate was included under this heading, as it was in the later medieval surveys. If part of the site of the former royal palace was covered by this section of the survey, one might have expected a more distinctive block of the bishop's rents to be recorded here.[2]

Property **II, 838** can be located within fairly close limits on the west side of **Calpestret,** and **II, 850** was on the same side of the street, near the corner at the north or south end. The position of these two properties in the succession of entries suggests that the east side of *Calpestret* was surveyed first and that the west side was surveyed from south to north.

The surveyors carried directly on from *Calpestret* into **Goldestret** (**II, 851–5**), where they presumably began at the north end of the east side.

The two headings '**Outside South Gate**' probably represent a rough division of properties according to the two streets outside South Gate and King's Gate. One reconstruction of the order of survey is suggested here, but others are possible. Having finished *Goldestret* the surveyors started outside South Gate and worked along the lane outside the wall towards King's Gate (**II, 928**). They may then have returned along the other side of the lane to survey the street outside South Gate from north to south. They next crossed into the street outside King's Gate, possibly via an east–west lane to the south of the modern Romans Road.[3] In Kingsgate Street they worked from south (**II, 960**) to north as far as *Sevetuichne,* where the entries under the second heading '**Outside South Gate**' commence (**II, 1001**). The surveyors appear to have continued towards King's Gate, perhaps, since **1001** may be next to **1041,** up the east side of the street and down the west. They then probably turned east into the modern College Street (**II, 1054**).

The survey concluded with **Gerestret** within the walls.

---

[1] See below, p. 353.
[2] Cf. above, p. 246 and below, pp. 299–301.
[3] Romans Lane was known as *Mullelane* in the

fourteenth century; in the nineteenth it was replaced by Romans Road, about 20 yards to the north, Goodman *Chartulary,* no. 445.

TABLE 9

Correspondences between the entries in Survey I and Survey II

There are no ascertainable correspondences in the following areas:

Outside North Gate
Scowrtenestret
Colobrochestret
Outside East Gate
Mensterstret
Outside South Gate (i)
Outside South Gate (ii)

For the remaining areas the relevant entries in Survey II are listed in sequence in the left-hand column and the corresponding entries in Survey I in the right-hand column.

— · — · — approximate correspondence

————— direct correspondence

------- possible correspondence

TABLE 9 (*cont.*)

High Street

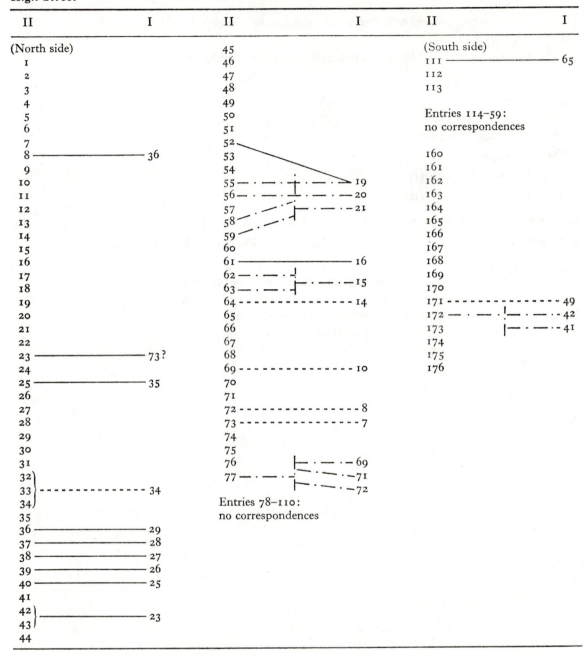

II	I	II	I	II	I
(North side)		45		(South side)	
1		46		111 ——————— 65	
2		47		112	
3		48		113	
4		49			
5		50		Entries 114–59:	
6		51		no correspondences	
7		52			
8 ——————— 36		53		160	
9		54		161	
10		55 — · — · — 19		162	
11		56 — · — · — 20		163	
12		57 — · — · — 21		164	
13		58		165	
14		59		166	
15		60		167	
16		61 ——————— 16		168	
17		62 — · — · —		169	
18		63 — · — · — 15		170	
19		64 - - - - - - - 14		171 - - - - - - - 49	
20		65		172 — · — · — 42	
21		66		173 — · — · — 41	
22		67		174	
23 ——————— 73?		68		175	
24		69 - - - - - - - 10		176	
25 ——————— 35		70			
26		71			
27		72 - - - - - - - 8			
28		73 - - - - - - - 7			
29		74			
30		75			
31		76 — · — · — 69			
32 ⎫		77 — · — · — 71			
33 ⎬ - - - - - - - 34		— · — · — 72			
34 ⎭					
35		Entries 78–110:			
36 ——————— 29		no correspondences			
37 ——————— 28					
38 ——————— 27					
39 ——————— 26					
40 ——————— 25					
41					
42 ⎫ ——————— 23					
43 ⎭					
44					

TABLE 9 (*cont.*)

Outside West Gate		*Snidelingestret*		*Brudenestret*	
II	I	II	I	II	I
Entries 177–256:		Entries 358–78:		393	
no correspondences		no correspondences		394	
		379 ——————— 128		395	
257		380 - - - - - - - - - - - - 129		396	
258		No more correspondences in		397	
259		this street, 381–92		398	
260				399	
261 ——————— 110				400	
262				401	
263				402	
264				403 - - - - - - - - - - 134	
265				404	
266				405 - - - - - - - - - - 133	
267				406 ⎞	⎧ 141
268 ⎫ ——————— 108				407 ⎟ —————	⎨ 142
269 ⎭				408 ⎟	⎩
270				409 ⎠	
271				410	
272				411	
273				412	
274				413	
275 - - - - - - - - - 102				414	
276				415	
277				416	
278				417	
279				418 ⎫ ————— 145	
280				419 ⎭	
281				420 ——————— 147	
282				421 ——————— 148	
283				422	
284				423	
285				424	
286				425	
287				426	
288 ——————— 107				427	
289					
290					
291					
292					
293					
294					
295					
296					
297					
298					
299					
300					
301					
302					
303					
304					

TABLE 9 (*cont.*)

Alwarnestret		Flesmangerestret		Sildwortenestret	
II	I	II	I	II	I
473		510 ——————— 183		Entries 541–58:	
474		511 ——————— 182		no correspondences	
475		512 ——————— 181			
476		513		559	
477		514		560	
478				561 (*Wunegrestret*)	
479		No more correspondences in		562 - - - - - - - - - - - - - 191	
480		this street, 515–40		563 - - - - - - - - - - - - - 195	
481				564	
482				565	
483				566	
484 or 501 - - - - - - - - 178				567	
485					
486 or 487 ——— 174 or 175					
487 or 486 ——— 175 or 174					
488 - - - - - - - - - - - - - 174					
489					
490					
491					
492					
493 ——————— 180					
494					
495					
496					
497					
498					
499					
500 - - - - - - - - - - - - - 177					
501 or 484 - - - - - - - - 178					
502					
503					
504					
505					
506					
507					
508					
509					

TABLE 9 (*cont.*)

Wunegrestret		Tannerestret		Bucchestret	
II	I	II	I	II	I
568		608 - - - - - - - - - - - - - 205		667	
569		609		668	
570 —————— 186		610		669	
571				670	
572 —————— 194		Entries 611–42:		671	
573		no correspondences		672	
574				673	
575		643		674	
		644 - - - - - - - - - - - - 212		675	
No more correspondences in		645		676	
this street, entries 576–607		646 —————— 213		677	
		647		678	
		648		679	
		649		680 —————— 223	
		650		681	
		651		682	
		652		683	
		653		684	
		654		685	
		655		686	
		656		687	
		657		688 - - - - - - - - - 218 or 236	
		658		689	
		659		690 —————— {228	
		660		691 {229	
		661		692	
		662		693	
		663		694	
		664		695	
		665		696	
		666		697	
				698	
				699	
				700	
				701	
				702	
				703	
				704	
				705 —————— 234	
				706	
				707	

TABLE 9 (cont.)

Calpestret		Goldestret		Gerestret	
II	**I**	**II**	**I**	**II**	**I**
822		851		1068 or 1072 - - - - - - - 285?	
823		852		1069 ——————— 283	
824		853		1070	
825		854		1071 ——————— 282	
826 ——————— 261		855		1072 or 1068 - - - - - - - 285?	
827 ——————— 262		856		1073	
828		857		1074	
829		858 ——————— 268		1075	
830 ——————— 259		859 ——————— 269		1076	
831		860 ——————— 270		1077	
832		861 ——————— 271		1078	
833		862		1079	
834		863		1080	
835		864		1081	
836		865 ——————— 272		1082	
837		866		1083	
838 ——————— 245		867		1084	
839		868		1085	
840		869		1086	
841		870			
842		871			
843		872			
844		873			
845		874			
846		875 ⎫ ——————— 278			
847		876 ⎭			
848 ——————— 256		877			
849		878			
850		879			
		880 ——————— 280			
		881			
		882			
		883			
		884			
		885			
		886			
		887			
		888			
		889			
		890			
		891			
		892			
		893			
		894			
		895			
		896			
		897			
		898			
		899			

iv. THE LIMITS OF THE URBAN AREA (Figs. 5 and 6)

There can be no doubt that the surveys of *c.* 1110 and 1148 were dealing with an urban area clearly distinguished from the surrounding countryside. This area extended well beyond the walls of the city, but the surveys themselves are uninformative as to its outer limits. Outside North Gate encroachments at Palliesputte (**I, 165**), at the limits of the later medieval suburb, were within the cognizance of Henry I's commissioners. Outside West Gate the same commissioners perhaps took as their limit the boundary ditch known from later sources. A church and houses at least five hundred yards to the south of King's Gate were included in the second survey (**II, 960**).

From the thirteenth century, evidence for the limits of the liberty of Winchester is more frequent and more precise. In that period of definition the distinction between the city and soke of Winchester became increasingly clear. The citizens of Winchester held the city at farm from the king. The soke was held by the bishop and administered by his bailiff. With the exception of the precinct of the cathedral priory and the bishop's palace of Wolvesey, the city included the area within the walls and most of the northern and western suburbs. Outside North Gate the precinct of Hyde Abbey, including the parish church of St. Bartholomew, was outside the city liberty and came to be considered as part of the abbot's hundred of Micheldever. The eastern and southern suburbs, together with the south part of the area outside West Gate, an area of at present unknown extent outside North Gate, and the site of the bishop's fair on St. Giles's Hill, made up the soke.[1]

The soke owed its origin as a liberty distinct from that of the city to the overwhelming predominance of the bishop and the cathedral as landlords outside the East and South Gates of the city. This situation is revealed most clearly in the survey of 1148. Elsewhere in Winchester the tenurial heterogeneity typical of a borough was much more marked, and the considerable estate of the bishop scattered over those parts of Winchester which were to be recognized as the city never came to be regarded as part of the jurisdiction of the soke.[2]

The first steps towards the formal definition of the soke appear to have been taken by Bishop Peter des Roches in 1231–3, immediately after his return from the Holy Land and on his attainment of supreme political influence. They were probably part of a major reorganization of the administration of the episcopal estates at that time.[3] In November 1280 a Winchester jury summarized the stages in the evolution of the soke for the justices on eyre. Up to the time of King John, they said, the city and all its surburbs were in the hands of the kings of England. Bishop Peter des Roches appropriated the

[1] The Tarrage Survey of 1417 is the best source for the extent of the city liberty in the Middle Ages. The limits of the soke can be reconstructed by comparing that survey with the liberty boundaries recorded in early Ordnance Survey maps. In the fifteenth and sixteenth centuries, part of the parish of St. Bartholomew, Hyde, and some properties on the road to Andover lay in the soke. For a fuller discussion of details and problems, see *SMW*.

[2] For a discussion of the evidence of rents and fiefs

in this matter, see below, p. 356–8.

[3] The bishop's pipe roll for 1231–2 contains evidence of an attempt to set the income from Winchester on a firmer basis. In that roll the heading *Ministerium Wintonie* was last used for the Winchester account. The heading *Soccagium* was first used in the following year. For changes on the rest of the episcopal estates see J. Z. Titow, *Winchester Yields: A Study in Medieval Agricultural Productivity* (Cambridge, 1972), 9.

suburbs outside the South and East Gates, and Bishop William Raleigh (1244–50) appropriated half the street outside West Gate and half the street outside North Gate.[1]

The boundaries of city and soke as reconstructed from later medieval and post-medieval evidence are shown in Fig. 5.[2] Together they represent approximately the extent of the urban area in the twelfth century.

Winchester was omitted from Domesday Book, but the gap in the Hampshire survey gives no indication of the outer limits of Winchester, for the manor of Chilcomb, held by the bishop for the support of the monks of St. Swithun, abutted Winchester on virtually every side. By the later tenth century the *terra suburbana* of Chilcomb, *quae undique adjacet civitati*, was supposed to have formed part of the original royal endowment of the church in the seventh century, and was already identified as the source of supplies for the monastic table.[3] In 1086 the Chilcomb estate, temporarily in the bishop's hands but clearly intended for the support of the monks, still preserved its original integrity as the sole component of the hundred of *Falemere*, apparently independent of the hundreds of *Falelie* and *Bitelsiete*, into which fell the other lands of the church of Winchester to east and west of the river Itchen respectively.[4] Later this Chilcomb estate, by then known as the manor of Barton, lay partly in the hundred of *Falle* (Fawley) and partly in the hundred of *Buttesgate* (Buddlesgate) and centred on the farmstead at Priors Barton, immediately south of the city (Fig. 5). In the early thirteenth century the manor of Barton included the tithings of Sparsholt, Weeke, Drayton, St. James, Fulflood, Bradley, Chilcomb, Hangelcomb, Winnall, Morstead, Ovington, Compton, and possibly Littleton,[5] in a ring around the city. Ovington, detached from the main block of the Barton estate, was not originally a part of it, for it was included in the Old English list of places which together with the single hide of Chilcomb made up the hundred hides of the Chilcomb or Fawley Hundred. Merdon (now Hursley parish) was subtracted from the estate during the episcopate of Henry of Blois.[6] The list of the tithings of which Barton was composed in the thirteenth century shows that the manor abutted on its inner edge on to the boundaries of the city and soke as they were in the later Middle Ages.[7]

The origin of the ancient estate of Chilcomb is unexplained. Tenth-century tradition and descriptions suggest that it was intimately associated with Winchester and the

[1] PRO, Just. 1/784, m. 33. This statement is the most comprehensive made by Winchester jurors on this subject. In 1272 they said that the aldermanries of Thomas le Marescal and Gilbert le Cordwaner, outside West Gate and North Gate respectively, had been appropriated by Peter des Roches (ibid. 780, m. 21). The matter was also raised at the inquiry into the city fee farm in 1285, see Appendix I. 2, pp. 512–13, below. Cf. *VCH Hants* v. 47.

[2] See *SMW*.

[3] The relevant charters are Sawyer 325, 376, 817, 818, and 821. See H. P. R. Finberg, *The Early Charters of Wessex* (Leicester, 1964), ch. VII, and cf. the review by Dorothy Whitelock, *EHR* 81 (1966), 103. For the boundaries of the estate west of the river Itchen see *Arch J*, 78 (1921), 162–73.

[4] *VCH Hants* i. 459–64.

[5] The 1248 roll is the earliest surviving account for the priory estates (WCL, Computus Roll A). Littleton was accounted for separately in this and in all subsequent rolls, but in the account for the Barton rents of assize in 1248 Littleton is entered with a note that nothing was received, as if in earlier years it had been accounted as part of the manor of Barton.

[6] Goodman *Chartulary*, 7.

[7] Rents from Kingsgate Street in the soke and from the parish of St. Mary de Vallibus in the city were entered in the accounts of the manor of Barton, but the jurisdiction of the manor court did not extend into these liberties. This system of accounting is analogous to that of the bishop's soke, the annual accounts for which included rents from properties situated in the city liberty.

West Saxon kings at an early date, and that it may have been comparable to the *territoria* around certain towns in Gaul in the Merovingian and Carolingian periods.[1] These *territoria* seem frequently to have been 'three miles' (Roman miles, i.e. about 4·5 kilometres) in radius and were regarded as part of the town or at least closely associated with it. Shortly after the translation of St. Swithun in 971 a blind man had his sight restored at a stone cross known as the King's Stone which stood three miles from Winchester and within sight of the city.[2] At the time of the translation itself the people of Winchester walked barefoot three miles from the city to meet the reliquary of the saint which was being brought from King Edgar's *villa* where it had been made.[3] The territory surrounding and associated with Winchester thus appears to have been clearly defined and would have approximately corresponded in extent to the Chilcomb estate. There may be a significant pointer to the origin of such a dependent territory in the statement in the *Textus Roffensis* that the peace of the king's court should extend from the gate where he resides for three miles, three furlongs, nine acres' breadth, nine feet, nine hands' breadth, and nine grains of barley,[4] for Winchester was pre-eminently a royal city. In the later Middle Ages, however, the manor of Barton, the home farm of the cathedral priory, had little more than a geographical association with the urban area.

In the tenth century the land immediately north of the walled area of the city was included within the bounds of the bishop's estate of Easton, outside the ancient Chilcomb estate, but within the new hundred centred upon it. In 961 the Easton boundary followed the river Itchen almost up to the north-east corner of the city wall. It then turned west along a boundary (*andlang mearce*), probably now represented by Swifts Lake and Hyde Abbey mill-stream, and still remembered in the name Danemark.[5] The boundary then followed the Fulflood stream west as far as the Roman road to Cirencester, along which it turned in a north-westerly direction.[6] This means that most of the street outside the North Gate lay without the urban area. The land ceded to New Minster on the occasion of its move to Hyde in 1110 was therefore taken out of the bishop's Easton estate.[7]

Topographical and archaeological evidence relating to the extent of Winchester in the twelfth century is discussed in detail below. At two points, however, this evidence suggests a different arrangement from that seen in the liberty boundaries of the thirteenth century and later. On topographical grounds, the churches of St. James and St. Faith might be taken to represent the limits of the western and southern suburbs respectively, and lines for the suburban boundaries leading up to them can be suggested (Fig. 5). Winnall church might have occupied a similar position. There is strong documentary evidence associating these three churches with the city rather than with Chilcomb for, with the church of St. Giles, they appear among the Winchester churches confirmed by Alexander III to the cathedral priory in 1172. This list included only those churches

[1] Anne Lombard-Jourdan, 'Oppidum et banlieu', *Annales: Économies, Sociétés, Civilisations*, 27 (1972), 373–95.

[2] Wulfstan, *Narratio Metrica*, bk. II, lines 706–73, esp. 714–18.   [3] Ibid., lines 22–34.

[4] F. Lieberman, *Die Gesetze der Angel-Sachsen* (Halle, 1903–16), i. 390; see also L. J. Downer (ed.),

Leges Henrici Primi (Oxford, 1972), 120–1.

[5] See above, p. 236, s.n.

[6] Sawyer 695; *Arch J* 81 (1924), 88–92.

[7] *Regesta*, ii, no. 1070. The land described as Wrdie was subsequently known as *Litelwordy* and Abbotts Barton, see below, pp. 266–7.

within and immediately without the walls; these churches were distinct from the chapels within the Chilcomb estate which were confirmed by Bishop Henry of Blois and Henry II to the priory on separate occasions.[1] In the later Middle Ages, however, and probably by the latter part of the thirteenth century, the churches of St. James, St. Faith, and Winnall lay within the manor of Barton, which had thus encroached on the urban area as the population of the city declined.

It is possible that before the growth of the suburbs the churches of St. James, St. Faith, Winnall, and St. Giles had served small rural settlements within the Chilcomb estate, close to but distinct from the city.[2] The churches of St. James and St. Anastasius, also at the suburban limits, were associated with chapels still further distant from the city walls, the White Minster and the chapel at Weeke respectively. These chapels may also denote early settlements and may even have been the parents of the churches founded closer to the city at the suburban limits. These points have important implications for study of the settlement pattern in the immediate neighbourhood of the city before the development of Winchester as a thoroughly urban centre in the tenth century.

Domesday Book records nine churches within the manor of Chilcomb and these nine were a distinctive feature of that estate early in the twelfth century.[3] Previous attempts to identify the nine churches have included those of St. James, St. Faith, and Winnall,[4] which on the evidence cited above lay within the urban area of Winchester at that time. Ten churches known to have existed in the twelfth century lay within the Chilcomb estate. They are the churches of Chilcomb, Morestead, St. Catherine on the Hill, the White Monastery, Compton, Hursley, Weeke, Littleton, Sparsholt, and Lainston. All of them, except the last two, can be identified as being in the possession of the cathedral priory in the twelfth or thirteenth century.[5] Of the ten churches only those of St. Catherine on the Hill and Lainston are not recorded in documentary evidence for the twelfth century.[6] The excavators of St. Catherine's church suggested that it was founded before 1100.[7] It therefore seems likely that the church of Lainston, a small settlement, probably subsidiary to Sparsholt, in a remote and woodland area of the Chilcomb estate, was an addition to the original nine. This identification of the nine churches implies that the strictly urban area of Winchester had already been enlarged to its maximum extent by 1086.

[1] Goodman *Chartulary*, nos. 3, 4, and 42. Innocent III's confirmation of 1204 reaffirms that of Alexander III and by also including a confirmation of the chapels of Chilcomb makes it clear that St. James, St. Faith, and Winnall were associated with Winchester rather than Chilcomb.

[2] Evidence of pagan Anglo-Saxon cemeteries has been recovered from the neighbourhood of the churches of St. James and St. Giles: Audrey Meaney, *A Gazetteer of Early Anglo-Saxon Burial Sites* (London, 1964), 101.

[3] *VCH Hants* i. 463; *Winchester ann*, s.a. 1122.

[4] e.g. *St. Catharine's Hill*, 192.

[5] Goodman *Chartulary*, nos. 3 and 451. In the fourteenth century the priory had an annual pension of 2s. from Sparsholt church: WCL, Records vol. i, fo. 38, no. 119.

[6] For Sparsholt church see *Curia Regis Rolls 1203–5*, p. 118, and for the others Goodman *Chartulary*, no. 3.

[7] *St. Catharine's Hill*, 256–7.

2

GENERAL TOPOGRAPHY

i. THE SITE (Fig. 33)

THE site of Winchester had been continuously settled for over a thousand years when Survey **I** was compiled during the reign of Henry I.[1] It was the setting successively of a major Iron Age settlement of near-urban status, of the fifth-largest town of the Roman province, and of a royal and ecclesiastical centre of non-urban and almost ceremonial character in the early kingdom of Wessex. Winchester returned to urban life in the reign of Alfred, as the largest of the fortified places designed to defend Wessex from Danish attack. It was the town of this period, with its planned system of regular streets and refurbished defences, which provided the setting for the Winchester of the surveys.

The city stands at a natural focus of communications, at a point where a prehistoric route from east to west along the downland ridges crossed a north–south route along the Itchen valley. This natural focus was emphasized by the pattern of Roman roads which approached the city from all directions, and which down to the present century have formed the basis of most long-distance routes. To these must be added the Itchen river which with improvement has at times been navigable for barges as high as Winchester since at least the end of the twelfth century, and probably from the late Saxon period.

The city is situated in the bottom and on the lower slopes of the Itchen valley, at the point where a spur of the western downland breaks forward to provide both the narrowest natural crossing of the marshy flood plain, and the easiest approach to the river. Here too the western slopes are at their gentlest and offer the largest area of raised ground for permanent settlement. East of the river the bluff of St. Giles's Hill rises abruptly from the valley floor, and settlement on this bank of the river has always been constricted to a narrow shelf below the hill.

In the eleventh century the urban area on the western bank was still principally contained within the Roman defences of the second and third century A.D., but outside each of the gates there were substantial suburbs often arranged in close relationship to the lines of the Roman roads. The eastern half of the walled area of 58·2 ha (143·8 acres) lies on the valley floor at about 36 m O.D. About 475 m to the west of East Gate the ground within the walls begins to rise in a steady slope (about 1 in 12) which brings the highest part of the walled area to about 60 m O.D.

In the valley bottom the subsoil is alluvial chalk brash, which drains easily, but the sloping western half of the city lies on a terrace of impervious, sticky, 'clay-like' river-gravel which here covers the chalk. The gravel dies away uphill, so that over the greater

[1] For the background to this section see M. Biddle *et al.*, *Pre-Roman and Roman Winchester* i, *Venta Belgarum* (Winchester Studies 3, i, forthcoming).

part of the western suburb the chalk is immediately below the surface. To some extent these factors had been masked already in the eleventh century by the accumulated deposits of a thousand years of settlement, but the contrast between the two areas of the city was still apparent. On the slopes of the western part of the walled area, surface water could neither drain into streams nor soak easily into the soil, and so flowed away down the sloping streets into a stagnant pool to the east of New Minster.[1] In the lower eastern area, the city was traversed by many streams, flowing from north to south along the streets, bridged at frequent intervals, and set with mills. The River Itchen, crossed by the city bridge immediately outside East Gate, flowed directly below the eastern walls.

Of the ecology of the landscape of which Winchester formed a part little is yet known at this period. In general the higher lands immediately to the east and west of the city seem to have been well wooded; the lower ground particularly in the upper Itchen valley and the vale of Chilcomb was more densely settled and cultivated. More detailed information of the composition of the tree-cover and the extent and character of open land must await the results of botanical enquiries now in train.[2]

ii. THE SUBURBS AND APPROACHES TO THE CITY (Figs. 6 and 33; cf. Figs. 25–7)

The evidence of the two surveys suggests that, as in the later Middle Ages, the inhabitants of the suburbs were on average poorer than those who lived within the walls, and that on the whole land was cheaper there.[3] By 1066 the built-up area of the suburbs, extending far from the city gates, appears to have reflected the prosperity of the city of which they were an integral part. There are grounds for believing that at an earlier period there may have been a ring of independent hamlets around the city, each of which impinged upon and became part of the area which was eventually incorporated into the suburbs.[4] Apart from population, two other factors affected the growth and form of the suburbs: the natural topography of the Itchen valley which encouraged linear expansion to north and south, rather than up the steep slopes to east and west; and the approach roads along which the suburban houses were usually aligned.

The approach roads in the immediate vicinity of the city followed the same lines in the Middle Ages as they do today, but the actual use of some of these twelfth-century routes from other centres to Winchester was quite different (Figs. 7 and 33). On the west side of the city the route from Salisbury followed the Roman road through Somborne until the thirteenth century.[5] Half a mile outside the suburb it was joined by the road from Romsey and the New Forest, and approached West Gate along the street known in the thirteenth century as *Wodestret* (now Romsey Road). The other main street of the western suburb, known as *Athelyngestret* in the thirteenth century (now Upper High Street), was presumably used only for journeys to and from the neighbouring woodland

---

[1] *Arch J*, 119 (1962), 157–8, 170, 179, 182.

[2] See A. C. Barefoot *et al.*, *Botanical and Environmental Studies* (Winchester Studies 10, forthcoming).

[3] See below, pp. 375–82.

[4] This hypothesis, which may concern a crucial point in the evolution of Winchester, and depends on several congruent historical, topographical, and archaeo-logical lines of argument, will be developed more fully in Winchester Studies 4. See also above, pp. 256–8.

[5] In 1200 William Briwere had a licence to fortify a castle in Hampshire at either Ashley or Stockbridge (*Rot Chart* 70). He chose Ashley, which lies nearer the line of the Roman route from Salisbury.

villages of Crawley and Sparsholt, until the main route from Salisbury via Stockbridge was established in the thirteenth century.[1] A part of this road between Crawley and Sparsholt parishes may, however, be the *herpathe* of a dubious tenth-century charter.[2]

The principal street of the suburb outside North Gate ran along a valley terrace just to the west of the line of the Roman road from Silchester and London. The Roman road was, however, itself apparently still used in the late Saxon period as far south as Martyr Worthy.[3] In the Middle Ages the road outside North Gate seems to have carried no more than local traffic from the densely populated upper Itchen valley, the villages on the north side of which were linked by an important late Saxon road (*bradan hærpath*), and possibly from Basingstoke.[4] The main road from Newbury, Oxford, and the Midlands joined the Roman road from Cirencester two miles out of Winchester, left it again just before the city, passed along the western flank of the northern suburb, and entered the city through West Gate.[5] Topographical considerations suggest that this route may antedate the growth of the northern suburb, whose form it does not appear to have influenced. Before the rebirth of urban life in Winchester, the road from the upper Itchen valley may have followed the line of Worthy Lane and joined the route from the Midlands to enter the city by West Gate, for the direct line of the Roman road to North Gate was lost in the post-Roman period. Hyde Street, which runs at its north end some three hundred feet west of the line of the Roman road, appears to branch off Worthy Lane, and may have developed as a link between Worthy Lane and North Gate in connection with the growth of the suburb of which it was to be the principal street. It was certainly functioning as an approach to the city by the early tenth century, at least for traffic bringing produce from the villages to the north, since the market-place within North Gate formed by that time an integral part of the intra-mural street grid.

The importance of the east–west axis of High Street in early Winchester is further demonstrated by the convergence on East Gate of major routes from north and south. In the Middle Ages the main route from London ran through Alton and Alresford and entered Winchester by East Gate.[6] The approach to the Itchen bridge would have been along St. John's Street, either via Easton and Winnall, or directly from Alresford over St. Giles's Down. The former would have avoided the steep slope of St. Giles's Hill and may have been the more commonly used, especially since Easton Lane has been worn more deeply into the hillside at Winnall than any other road near the city, apart from Romsey Road to the west. There is, however, no direct evidence for a road along the south side of the Itchen valley corresponding to the *bradan hærpath* north of the river, although its existence may be presumed. In the tenth century the *hærpath* coming from

[1] Stockbridge occupies a major crossing of the river Test at a point where the later medieval roads from London and Winchester to Salisbury converge. The establishment of a market and a borough there attracted traffic en route from Winchester to Salisbury. For the origin of the borough see M. W. Beresford, *New Towns of the Middle Ages* (London, 1967), 449.

[2] Sawyer 381. [3] Sawyer 273 and 309.

[4] Sawyer 273 and 309; cf. below, p. 383.

[5] Routes from Titchfield Abbey to the Midlands and the North passed through Winchester, Whitchurch, Newbury, and Oxford: Welbeck MS. 1.A.2. (BM, Loans 29/56).

[6] F. M. Stenton, 'The Road System of Medieval England', D. M. Stenton (ed.), *Preparatory to Anglo-Saxon England* (Oxford, 1970), 241. For the importance which was attached to this route see *Cal Chart R 1257–1300*, p. 122.

the direction of London passed from Bishop's Sutton along the north boundary of Tich-borne.[1] Where it crossed the boundary between Easton and Avington, a mile to the east of Magdalen Hill Down, it was known as *portstret*.[2] This is the only indication that the three miles of straight road, running due west to Winchester, into and through the site of

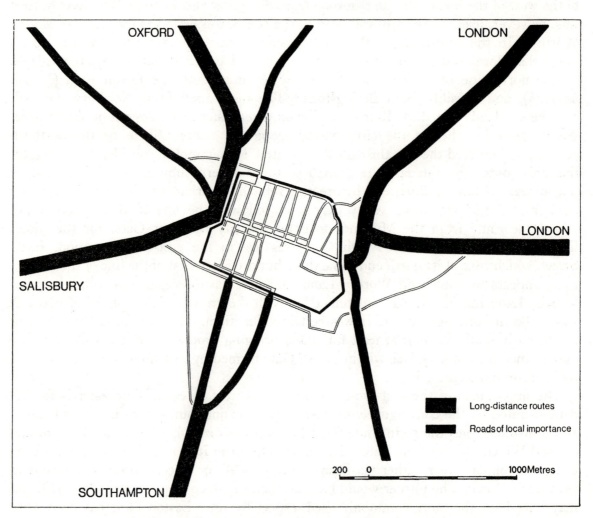

FIG. 7. The medieval approaches to Winchester (1:25,000).

St. Giles's fair, are of ancient and possibly Roman origin. It seems likely that in the late Saxon period this straight road branched off the road through Ovington parish (now the A31), while the latter continued in a south-westerly direction over Fawley Down to Twyford, a route which was commonly followed in the eighteenth century.

[1] The modern road through New Alresford dates from the establishment of the new borough in the thirteenth century.

[2] Sawyer 695 and 699. In his reconstruction of the bounds of Avington, G. B. Grundy identified the *hærpath* as the road in the valley by the river, but his later view that the identical *portstret* of the Easton bounds was the modern road from Winchester to Alresford fits much better with the succession of common points on the boundary between Easton and Avington and with the circuit of Avington as a whole: *Arch J*, 78 (1921), 94–9; ibid. 81 (1924), 88–92.

To the south of East Gate, Chesil Street, the termination of the Roman road from Portchester, carried traffic from Portsmouth, Bishop's Waltham, and the Meon valley.

In the thirteenth century traffic from Southampton approached Winchester from the south along the Roman road on the west side of the Itchen valley and entered the city through South Gate.[1] Some six miles south of the city this road was known as *stræte* in the tenth century.[2] There are some indications that, close to the city, the earliest Roman route may have followed the line of Kingsgate Street. The name King's Gate may itself denote an association between this gate and the early Anglo-Saxon royal palace,[3] and there thus remains the possibility that at the time of the surveys Kingsgate Street was the principal approach to the city from the south.

The form of the suburban boundaries and the extent of the built-up area in the thirteenth and fourteenth centuries suggest that the suburban population of Winchester was concentrated along the principal approach roads to the city. It also seems that traffic to large but distant centres was no more important and possibly less important in encouraging suburban growth than traffic to the villages in the immediate hinterland of the city (cf. Figs. 7 and 25–7).

Apart from the approach roads, the only consistent features of the suburban street pattern were the lanes or 'twichens' which ran along the outer edge of the city ditch (cf. Fig. 25). These survive in Swan Lane (*la Twychene*) outside North Gate, Sussex Street outside West Gate, and in St. James's Lane, Canon Street (*Paillardestwichene*), and College Street on the south side of the city.[4] Two such lanes were probably closed before *c.* 1110: the street along which the burgesses had taken their horses to water (**I, 163**) seems to have been an extra-mural lane on the east side of North Gate; and the street destroyed by the construction of the king's ditch (**I, 81**) may have been a lane on the south side of West Gate. Other suburban streets (such as *Sevetuichne* and perhaps other lanes outside South Gate) functioned as links between the principal suburban routes. There were other suburban streets with special functions, such as the street leading from *Wodestret* (now Romsey Road) to the great bridge over the castle ditch.[5]

The layout of the eastern suburb was constricted by the steep slope of St. Giles's Hill. The modern Water Lane seems to be the result of colonization of the bank of the river which, as the evidence for the bridge outside East Gate suggests,[6] was wider in the twelfth century than now. The *hollustreet*,[7] on the site of the modern Magdalen Hill, parallel to and uphill from St. John's Street, may represent the back road mentioned in 1148 (**II, 768–9**), but was not made into a major road until modern times.

The suburbs were bounded by ditches and earth banks which are best recorded in the western and northern suburbs. A length of the earthwork enclosing the pre-Roman

[1] South Gate was distinguished from King's Gate as *versus Suhampt'* in 1242, *Close R 1237–42*, p. 449.

[2] Sawyer 418.

[3] See above, p. 236, s.n., and below, p. 290.

[4] For the early names, see above, p. 234–5, s.nn.

[5] St. Denis Cartulary, fo. 119ᵛ. The Palm Sunday processions from the cathedral and Hyde Abbey to St. James's church were to meet *supra castellum* and *ante portam castelli*, presumably in *Wodestret*. This arrangement, made in 1114, suggests that the lane connecting the castle gate and bridge to *Wodestret* was already in existence: see below, p. 303 and n. 4. Other minor lanes in the western suburb were closed before *c.* 1110; see **I, 91** and **107**.

[6] See below, p. 271, n. 9.

[7] HRO, Magdalen Hospital Deeds. This street or lane is first recorded in 1235–6, PRBW 1235–6, Soke account.

settlement on the slope of the hill to the west of the walled area was re-dug as a bank and ditch in the twelfth century, and served as part of the boundary of the western suburb.[1] The medieval earthwork extended south and west to *Wodestret*, and north-east to join Hyde Street at *Palliesputte*, where in the fourteenth century it was known as the king's ditch or *Bardich*.[2] By the late twelfth century, land within the western suburb between *Wodestret* (now Romsey Road) and *Athelyngestret* (now Upper High Street) was known as *Erdberi*, a name which, in the forms *Urthbury* or *herthbur'*, was in the thirteenth and fourteenth centuries also applied to the earthwork which enclosed the suburb itself and land outside it.[3] The *Urthbury* ditch may have been one of the two ditches in the western suburb mentioned in Survey **I (I, 123)**.

Little is known of the physical features which formed the boundaries of the other suburbs. Before 1208–9 land outside East Gate was occupied *fossato et barris civitatis*,[4] but no surviving or recorded topographical features indicate the position of these works, other than the boundaries of the liberty of the soke. On the south side of the city two topographical features suggest the boundaries of a large suburb extending from South Gate to the church of St. Faith. Kingsgate Street itself represents this line on the east, and a cart track or drove-way leading from the church of St. Faith to the south-west corner of the city wall and thence to the church of St. James suggests the west side (Fig. 5).[5]

It seems possible that these two roads developed along, and either just inside or just outside, the line of an earthwork of the sort which marked the limit of the western suburb. The drove-way from St. Faith to St. James was clearly an important route between different parts of the manor of Barton, avoiding the city. Neither route represents the line of any known liberty or parish boundary, and by the later thirteenth century they lay within the separate jurisdictions of the soke and the manor of Barton. Any suburban limits which they represent can only be earlier than that date.[6] Significantly, the Priors Barton farmstead lay just outside these apparent limits.

On the approach roads themselves the suburban limits were represented by bars. There were bars at the north end of Hyde Street in the fourteenth century; and in the eastern suburb the area at the southern end of Chesil Street is still known as Bar End. It is not known whether these bars were substantial barriers, simple gates, or only booms.[7]

A more notable feature of the entries to the suburbs were the churches which were sited there. St. Anastasius lay just inside the bank and ditch on the road from Weeke to West Gate. St. James stood near the entry to the western suburb from Salisbury. St. Faith stood just within the possible limits of the early southern suburb discussed above, and Winnall church may once have occupied a similar position to the north-east. By the

---

[1] *VI Interim*, 254–9.

[2] e.g. Stowe 846, fo. 29; for the early names, see above, pp. 236 and 238, s.nn.

[3] See above, p. 237, s.n.; Appendix I. 1, p. 509, n. 5 and *SMW*.

[4] *PRBW 1208–9* 77.

[5] This track existed in the early sixteenth century (WCL, Register of the Common Seal, vol. ii, fo. 25ᵛ) and is clearly shown in later maps, e.g. WCA, Survey

of Manor of Thurmonds, 1639; WCL, Survey of Priors Barton, 1751; HRO, Winchester, St. Faith Tithe Award Map, 1846.

[6] This hypothesis remains no more than a possibility. Kingsgate Street is a perfectly feasible road in its own right and the cart track from St. Faith to St. James may have developed as a by-pass round the city.

[7] Cf. Urry *Canterbury*, 196–7.

mid-thirteenth century the churches of St. James, St. Faith, and Winnall stood within the manor of Barton, and their parishes extended out from, rather than into, the suburbs. These three churches may thus have originated as the nuclei of detached hamlets, but the most outstanding feature of their location in the twelfth century was their proximity to the suburbs and they were regarded then as churches of the city rather than of the surrounding countryside.[1]

St. Faith and St. James appear to have occupied salient positions at the entry to their suburbs. A triangular piece of land in a similarly salient position was a feature of the entry to the northern suburb at *Palliesputte*, although there is no evidence that there was a church there.

The suburban ditches may never have done more than mark off the urban area from the surrounding countryside; and the bars themselves seem to have had no defensive function. Nothing is known of the structure of the churches at the suburban limits. At some period they might have performed a defensive function, but the common association of churches with town gates and other places important to travellers provides a sufficient devotional and economic reason for their existence. Suburban ditches might hinder an attack, but at all periods the principal defences of the city were its walls.

The character of the suburbs, with their streets, lanes, houses, shops, gardens, and churches, was much the same as the city within the walls. A group of twelfth-century pits observed just within the ancient city liberty on the north side of *Wodestret*[2] demonstrates that the western suburb was intensively occupied at that date far out from the city gate. On the evidence of the king's properties in Survey **I** this would appear also to have been the case in the mid-eleventh century. The suburb outside West Gate appears in the surveys to have been the most prosperous. Since it was the only one of the suburbs to contain properties in the king's fief, it was probably the earliest to grow, and may even have been defined as early as the first half of the tenth century. The heterogeneity of land tenure in the western suburb in 1148 suggests that of all the suburbs this had undergone the longest period of development.[3] In some parts of this suburb there was, however, a considerable expansion of the built-up area between King Edward's reign and the early twelfth century.[4] Between 934 and *c.* 939, at the request of the citizens, the bishop dedicated a church on the south side of the market place (*popularis platea*) outside West Gate.[5] At least three other churches, St. James, St. Valery, and St. Leonard, are known to have been in existence here in the twelfth century.[6] There were, however, considerable areas of open land in the western suburb, set well back from the street frontages, and the sale of corn *de Erdberi* in the late twelfth century[7] shows that then, as in the later Middle Ages when the population had declined, agriculture was practised within the suburban boundary.

[1] See above, pp. 257–8.

[2] By M. Biddle and D. J. Keene in 1970. See Winchester Studies 5, Gazetteer.

[3] For the evidence of rents and fiefs, see below, pp. 375–82.

[4] See, for example, I, 117–22 and cf. below, p. 351 and Table 12b.

[5] W. Stubbs (ed.), *Memorials of St. Dunstan* (RS, 1874) 14, 15, 21. The church may have been that later known as St. Martin in the Ditch. For the date of the dedication, see below, p. 330, n. 1.

[6] For St. Valery see I, 107. Henry of Blois seized the chapel of St. Leonard from Hyde Abbey (*Monasticon*, ii. 437), see below, p. 320.

[7] *Pipe Roll 29 Henry II*, p. 147.

The suburb outside North Gate probably developed later than the western suburb, for in 961 nearly all of the modern Hyde Street lay outside the limits of the city.[1] The northern suburb contained a pre-conquest church, and if the houses at *Palliesputte* (**I, 165**) were part of the suburban development rather than a detached hamlet, the built-up area of the suburb was already as extensive, by the early twelfth century, as it was ever to become. There were houses worth 7s. a year near the site of Hyde Abbey at the time of its move in 1110,[2] and the establishment of the abbey no doubt increased the prosperity of the area.

The evidence for the evolution of the northern suburb is so closely associated with the acquisition of land to the north of the city by New Minster, and the minster's eventual migration there, that it is best to consider the two matters together. In 983 New Minster had acquired an extensive piece of meadow on the north side of the city, bounded by the River Itchen on the east, and later known as Hyde Moors.[3] The dimensions given in the grant suggest that the west boundary of the meadow was represented by the line of Hyde Abbey mill-stream, and that the church and principal buildings of the abbey were therefore erected on land which already belonged to the community. At the time of the move the abbey acquired from the bishop the houses worth 7s., the manor of Worthy with its church and parochial rights, and the land known as *Hida*, in which in 1114 the abbey was said to stand. King Henry I acted as intermediary in this transfer, which was recorded in a royal charter of 1114.[4]

Later sources state that the Worthy of the 1114 charter was Little Worthy, also known as Abbott's Barton.[5] The Abbott's Barton farm-lands fell within the limits of the bishop's estate of Easton as defined in 961, and could thus have been granted to Hyde Abbey by the bishop about 1110.[6]

It is not certain whether the abbey at this stage acquired the whole suburb under the title of the land called Hyde, or merely the agricultural land outside it, together with 7s. rent from suburban houses. The record of rents in 1148, when most of the northern suburb lay within the abbot's fief, shows that by that year the abbey had acquired

---

[1] See above, p. 257 and Fig. 5.

[2] See below, n. 4.

[3] *Liber de Hyda*, 228–31 (Sawyer 845). This land was the southernmost tip of an extensive estate, including Micheldever and Abbots Worthy to the north of the city, and is recorded under Abbots Worthy in Domesday Book, *VCH Hants* ii. 470. See Figs. 5 and 6.

[4] *Regesta*, ii, no. 1070, *Monasticon*, ii. 444. The clause *in qua nunc sedet abbathia*, in relation to the land known as Hyde, may mean that no distinction was made between Hyde Moors and the land newly acquired by the abbey, or that the abbey precinct already included land on the west side of the mill-stream.

[5] The contemporary index to the late fourteenth-century Hyde Abbey register, referring to the charter of 1114 now missing from the register, explains: *Wordia alias Litilwordy quae nunc dicitur berton*, BM, Harl. MS. 1761, fo. 31ᵛ. There has subsequently been

some confusion between this Worthy and Abbots Worthy. The latter belonged to New Minster before the conquest and lay within the bounds of Easton in 961: see the account of the endowments of the abbey printed in *Monasticon*, ii. 435–6 from the sixteenth-century BM, Cotton MS. Vesp. D ix, and *Regesta*, ii, no. 1070. The parish church of Worthy was almost certainly not that of St. Bartholomew in Hyde Street, but may have been the church in the Abbott's Barton water-meadows dedicated to St. Gertrude: Goodman *Chartulary*, p. 170. The site of this chapel is marked on a plan of Abbott's Barton farm surveyed in 1753 in WCA and may be observed on the ground today.

[6] J. H. Round suggested that the Worthy of the 1114 charter was identical with the Worthy which the bishop held for the monks of the Cathedral in 1086, *VCH Hants* ii. 466. But the Abbott's Barton lands were probably still associated with Easton in 1086 and there is no evidence that Easton was ever assigned for the upkeep of the monks.

extensive rights in the suburb, presumably from the bishop. Two further acts of Henry I suggest that the abbey acquired these rights within a few years of the move. In a diploma which can probably be dated to 2 February 1116 Henry I, on the recommendation of the bishop, granted the *libertatem vici extra portam borialem* to the abbey.[1] This grant, intended as compensation for the damage inflicted on the abbey by William I, presumably confirmed and consolidated the possession of the land and rights in the suburb which the abbot had acquired from the bishop. Before 1133, and probably immediately consequent upon the acts of 1114 or 1116, Henry I issued a precept to the sheriff of Hampshire and the collectors of Winchester to the effect that the abbey's land of Hyde (in view of the recipients of the writ at least a part of which must have been within the urban area) and the land of the exchange (probably Alton and Clere) were to be free of geld.[2] If New Minster had not moved to Hyde, the land of the northern suburb—like that in the suburbs to the south and east of the city—would probably in 1148 have been for the most part in the fiefs of the bishop and prior.

The abbot does not appear to have acquired the whole suburb, for in the second survey a number of properties at the beginning and end of the section outside North Gate (**II, 305–16, 320,** and **356**) were in the bishop's fief. These properties probably lay towards the city wall in the area where those parts of the bishop's soke outside North Gate which can be identified in the later Middle Ages also lay.[3] This area was south of the line of the Fulflood stream and may mean that the land of *Hida* acquired by the abbot was strictly that part of the northern suburb which had once been part of the bishop's rural estate.

At the time of Survey **I** the abbot owned the landgable of houses at *Palliesputte* (**I, 65**). It seems most likely that he acquired this landgable after the migration of the abbey and that therefore the first survey was made in or after 1110.

The abbot's liberty of Hyde Street survived into the thirteenth century, for in 1234–5 he claimed jurisdiction in matters of tenure there,[4] but by the latter part of the century this jurisdiction was limited to the precincts of the abbey, and to the abbey lands outside the suburb.[5]

Little is known of the other suburbs in the twelfth century and earlier. Two plots of ground outside the south gate of the city were the subject of an exchange in *c.* 970–5.[6] In the mid-twelfth century the built-up area of this suburb extended at least as far as the houses and church recorded five hundred yards south of King's Gate (**II, 960–3**). In the later Middle Ages Kingsgate Street, because of its proximity to the college and the cathedral, was more populous than the street outside South Gate. The greater number of parish churches outside King's Gate, compared with South Gate (Fig. 10), and the concentration of officials and craftsmen outside King's Gate in 1148 (Figs. 21 and 23),[7] suggest that this may also have been the case in the eleventh and twelfth centuries.

The evidence for the early growth of the suburbs in the tenth and eleventh centuries

---

[1] *Regesta*, ii, no. 1125.
[2] Ibid., no. 1886.
[3] See Appendix I. 2, pp. 512–13, and *SMW*.
[4] *Curia Regis Rolls 1233–7*, no. 1218. The Abbot did not cite the diploma of 1116 as the basis for his

claim but relied upon Henry II's confirmation of the charter of 1114, for which see *Monasticon*, ii. 446.
[5] *Monasticon*, ii. 447.
[6] *AS Ch*, no. XLIX (Sawyer 1449).
[7] See below, pp. 387 and 433–4.

is clear. The western suburb was probably the first to develop and may have formed part of the urban area from the beginning of the tenth century. The other suburbs expanded outwards into the rural estates of the mother church of Winchester, in the case of the northern suburb apparently after 961. As a whole, the suburbs may well have reached their maximum extent and density of population in the twelfth century, for all the later evidence points to their steady decline.

iii. SUBURBAN PROCESSIONS (Fig. 33)

The scanty evidence for liturgical processions beyond the confines of the mother church of Winchester throws some light on the topography of the city and the surrounding area, and on their unity in the early Middle Ages.[1]

The migration of New Minster to a site outside the city walls led to a dispute over the arrangements for the Palm Sunday procession to the church of St. James, in which the monks of both Old and New Minsters took part. The settlement of this matter, embodied in a royal charter of 1114, contains the only circumstantial details of a liturgical procession in early medieval Winchester.[2] Before the migration to Hyde, the monks of the two minsters apparently formed a single procession from the centre of the city. From now on the main procession of 'New Minster', accompanied by its relics and led by the prior, was to proceed independently from Hyde and join the procession from the cathedral, which included the abbot of Hyde and a few of his monks, at a place above and in front of the castle gate. This point was presumably in *Wodestret*, by the street leading to the castle gate. The united procession was then to make a station (*stationem*) at the church of St. James and to return to a place in front of West Gate near the street of St. Valery (the modern Sussex Street). At this point the procession was to divide and the abbey procession, now led by its abbot, was to return to Hyde, presumably by a route outside the city walls along the street of St. Valery.

The blessing of the palms and the procession on Palm Sunday were a well-established feature of carolingian liturgy and of the liturgies of the tenth-century reform;[3] it is not surprising to find evidence for them in tenth-century Winchester. The *Regularis Concordia*, drawn up in Winchester about 970 for the governance of monastic life there and in the other centres of reform in England, describes the order of a Palm Sunday procession to a church where the palms were blessed. The procession then returned to a place before the doors of the mother church, where the respond *Ingrediente Domino* was intoned as the doors were opened and the procession entered.[4] It seems likely that the church in Winchester at which the palms were blessed was the church of St. James. In at least one of the carolingian processions, the stational church was outside the walls of the city.[5]

[1] Processions within the precincts of the three ministers, for example that on the death of a brother of Old Minster in the eleventh century, have not been considered here; C. H. Turner, 'The churches in Winchester in the early eleventh century', *JTS* 17 (1916), 65–8; cf. below, pp. 291, 315–16.

[2] *Regesta*, ii, no. 1070; the full text is printed in *Monasticon*, ii. 444–5, and in *Reg Pontissara* 439–41.

[3] A. Baumstark, 'La Solennité des palmes dans l'ancienne et la nouvelle Rome', *Irénikon*, 13 (Amay-sur-Meuse, 1936), 3–24. K. Hallinger, *Gorze-Kluny* (Studia Anselmiana, 22–3 and 24–5, Rome, 1950–1), 919–25.

[4] Thomas Symons (ed.), *Regularis Concordia* (London, 1953), 34–5.

[5] At Metz in *c.* 750: T. Klauser, 'Eine Stationliste der Metzer Kirche aus dem 8. Jahrhundert', *Ephemerides Liturgicae*, 44 (Rome, 1930), 162–87.

The choice of a church in an elevated position outside the walls would correspond most satisfactorily with the original events which were being commemorated, and with the order of the fourth-century Palm Sunday procession in Jerusalem, from which the carolingian practices were ultimately derived.[1] There can in any case be little doubt that by the middle of the eleventh century the liturgical celebration of Easter held an important place in the life of the western suburb of Winchester.[2]

The early twelfth-century description of the Palm Sunday procession in Winchester, particularly in its emphasis on the *statio* at St. James's and the halt outside West Gate, suggests that it corresponded rather more to the procession elaborately described by Lanfranc in his Monastic Constitutions[3] than to that described in the *Regularis Concordia*. Archbishop Lanfranc appears to have been responsible for the introduction of the Blessed Sacrament into the procession, a feature which soon became characteristic of Palm Sunday processions in England and Normandy.[4] He was probably also responsible for the elaboration of the procession in other ways, such as the introduction of the four distinct halts, including that at the gate of the city (not the mother church) at which the *Ingrediente Domino* was intoned.[5] Lanfranc's innovations first took effect in England at Canterbury. Before Lanfranc's time the details of the Canterbury procession were almost identical to those outlined in the *Regularis Concordia*.[6] By 1114, Winchester, as well as Canterbury, would appear to have adopted the Lanfrancian order.[7]

The *Regularis Concordia* mentions a second procession to a church other than the mother church: at Candlemas, to the church where the candles were blessed.[8] It is not known whether in Winchester this church was in the town or within the monastic precinct. In the fourteenth century the parish church of St. Clement owed an annual payment of two pounds of wax to the cathedral, the only specific payment of this kind from a church in the city,[9] but it is not necessarily significant in this context.

---

[1] A. Baumstark, op. cit. p. 268, n. 3 above. For the topographical setting of the procession in Jerusalem described by Etheria see F. Chabrol and H. Leclercq (ed.), *Dictionnaire d'archéologie chrétienne et de liturgie* (1907–53), s.v. Palme.

[2] I, 105.

[3] David Knowles (ed.), *The Monastic Constitutions of Lanfranc* (London, 1951), 22–6.

[4] For this and its possible connection with the Eucharistic controversy see ibid. 151–2 and Edmund Bishop, 'Holy Week Rites of Sarum, Hereford, and Rouen Compared', in his *Liturgica Historica* (Oxford, 1918, repr. 1962).

[5] It is interesting to note that in the depiction of Christ's entry into Jerusalem in the Winchester Psalter (Francis Wormald, *The Winchester Psalter* (London, 1973), fig. 22) the upper storeys of the city gate are occupied by six beardless figures and a bearded man gesticulating. They may be intended to represent the choir of boys which sang the *Gloria Laus* from the top of the gate as described in several accounts of Palm Sunday processions.

[6] R. M. Wooley (ed.), *The Canterbury Benedictional* (HBS 51, London, 1917), 22–8.

[7] There is a detailed order for a Palm Sunday procession, including a station at a place outside the gates of a city, in the late twelfth- or early thirteenth-century gradual which probably belonged to the monastic cathedral of Downpatrick in Ireland: Bod., Rawlinson MS. C. 892, fos. 44–49. This gradual had some dependence on a Winchester archetype, and its version of the Palm Sunday rites could well represent the practice at Winchester. Unfortunately the order contains no precise topographical information and in any case appears to allow for adaptation to more than one locality. For the provenance of this gradual and its association with Winchester, see D. H. Turner (ed.), *The Missal of New Minster Winchester* (HBS 93, London, 1960), Appendix, p. 3, and idem, 'The Crowland Gradual: An English Benedictine Manuscript', *Ephemerides Liturgicæ*, 74 (Rome, 1960), 168–74. A short extract from the order for the procession has been printed in Karl Young, *The Drama of the Medieval Church* (Oxford, 1933), i. 92, where the attribution to Winchester is made without reservation.

[8] Thomas Symons (ed.), *Regularis Concordia* (London, 1953), 30–1.

[9] WCL, Records, vol. i, fo. 38, no. 119.

Later medieval evidence indicates something of the routes of other processions from the cathedral to churches and other places in the immediate vicinity of the city. In the fourteenth century the cathedral priory had rights of station on their feast days at the churches of St. James, St. Faith, St. Giles, and St. Catherine on the Hill.[1] There was a processional way on St. Giles's Hill in 1491, and Minster Lane, directly opposite the west door of the cathedral, was also a 'procession way' in the fifteenth century. There were free-standing crosses just outside West Gate, at the junction of the modern Andover Road and Worthy Lane, in the open space at the north end of St. John's Street, and perhaps also in Water Lane and at Bar End.[2] The Butter Cross in High Street may also have originated as a processional cross.

It is possible that in the early Middle Ages the close association of certain of the more distant outlying churches with the mother church of Winchester was emphasized by their inclusion in liturgical processions. The nine churches of the Chilcomb estate, which formed a recognized group in the late eleventh and early twelfth centuries,[3] could perhaps have been included in processions, as were churches up to five or six kilometres distant from the mother churches of Metz and St. Riquier in the eighth and ninth centuries.[4]

iv. THE RIVER ITCHEN (Figs. 32 and 33)

The River Itchen has probably been diverted and controlled in the neighbourhood of Winchester ever since a settlement was established there in the valley bottom. The erection of mills and the cutting of the leats associated with them in the late Saxon period probably modified the course of the main stream to a considerable extent.[5] There seem to have been even more extensive works on the river some miles to the south of Winchester in the tenth or eleventh centuries, for the Anglo-Saxon boundaries of land at Stoneham included both the old and new courses of the Itchen.[6] The new waterway may have been cut to improve navigation, but there is no other evidence for this use of the river before the episcopate of Godfrey de Lucy (1189–1204). King John confirmed to Bishop Godfrey the duties on certain articles of merchandise coming to or going from Winchester to the sea *per trencheam quam dictus Wintoniensis Episcopus fecit fieri*.[7] Bishop Godfrey appears to have enjoyed rights over the passage of water in the Itchen[8] similar to those of his

[1] WCL, Records, vol. i, fo. 38, no. 119.

[2] For details see *SMW*. These places would have marked stages in the processions of Rogationtide and Corpus Christi. The latter was in many respects the successor of the Palm Sunday procession and was very popular with the citizens of Winchester, cf. *Black Book*, 73–4, 131, 145, 170.

[3] See above, p. 258. The *novem ecclesiis quae de maneriis monachorum fuerant* were the subject of a dispute between the monks and the bishop in 1122. The uncanonical procession which the monks performed as a protest on this occasion was, however, probably limited to the confines of the monastery, *Winchester ann*, 46.

[4] For Metz: T. Klauser, op. cit. on p. 268, n. 5 above and T. Klauser and R. S. Bour, 'Un Document

du ixe siècle: notes sur l'ancienne liturgie de Metz et sur les églises antérieures de l'an mil', *Annuaire de la Société d'Histoire et d'Archéologie de la Lorraine*, 38 (1929), 497–643. For St. Riquier: Edmund Bishop, 'Angilbert's Ordo' in his *Liturgica Historica* (Oxford, 1918, repr. 1962), and for the identification of the places named, F. Lot, *Hariulf: Chronique de l'abbaye de Saint Riquier* (Collection de textes pour servir à l'étude et à l'enseignement de l'histoire, Paris, 1894).

[5] See below, p. 282.

[6] *Of þære ealdan Icenan on ufwyrd þonæ orcerd on þa niwan ea*, Sawyer 1012.

[7] *Reg Pontissara* 741–3. This charter is not entirely above suspicion.

[8] In 1446 Bishop Beaufort ratified a charter of de Lucy dated 1202 allowing Hugh de Chikehull, lord

successors, who in the later Middle Ages controlled the entire flow of water from Alresford pond to Itchen Ferry by Southampton.[1] Godfrey de Lucy was responsible for the foundation of New Alresford. The tradition that he had the artificial pond at Alresford constructed as a reservoir for a waterway extending to Winchester and thence to the sea may therefore be correct.[2] The Itchen canal does not seem to have continued in use, for by 1275 its course was obstructed by a number of mills belonging to the bishop,[3] and this state of affairs persisted into the seventeenth century.[4]

v. THE CITY BRIDGE (Fig. 32)

The crossing of the River Itchen immediately east of the city was a dominant factor in the growth of settlement on the site of Winchester. The present city bridge lies some 16 m north of the line of the Roman road, which had itself probably crossed the river by a timber bridge carried on stone piers.[5] This timberwork would not long have outlasted the end of regular maintenance, and the present line may have begun as a ford upstream from the turbulence caused by the ruins of the Roman structure.

The date when a bridge was first built in this upstream position is not recorded, but it must have been considerably before the second half of the eleventh century when Winchester tradition was already attributing its construction to St. Swithun (d. 862).[6] A post-conquest *Vita* of St. Swithun (traditionally ascribed to Goscelin of St. Bertin's, d. *c.* 1099)[7] describes this bridge as *pontem . . . ad orientalem portam civitatis arcubus lapideis opere non leviter ruituro*.[8] Such words written for an audience of the late eleventh or early twelfth century seem likely to be an accurate description of the bridge as it then stood.[9]

The structure may have been already old. A ten-line poem, now extant only in a copy of the first half of the twelfth century, appears to purport to be an inscription, apparently

of the manor of Wollston, free passage on the river Itchen by Southampton: WCL, Register of the Common Seal, vol. i, fo. 71.

[1] In the sixteenth century the bishops appointed an officer who had the custody of the pond and of the river down to Itchen Ferry, e.g. WCL, Register of the Common Seal, vol. ii, fo. 95[v].
[2] M. W. Beresford, *New Towns of the Middle Ages* (London, 1967), 442. For the tradition, see Milner[3] i. 173–4.
[3] *VCH Hants* v. 451 and PRO, C143/3/11.
[4] E. Course, 'The Itchen Navigation', *Proc. Hants FC* 24 (1967), 113–26.
[5] For the position of the Roman road, see Winchester Studies 3 (forthcoming). The existence and likely character of the Roman bridge can be inferred from the evidence for the country as a whole presented by D. P. Dymond in *Arch J* 118 (1961), 136–64.
[6] See the poem *Unum Beati Swithuni Miraculum*, printed by A. A. Locke, *in Praise of Winchester* (London, 1912), 124–5, from a copy added in the first quarter of the twelfth century to BM, MS. Royal 15 C. vii, fo. 125[r–v]. An earlier copy exists as an

integral part of Bodleian, MS. Auct. F. 2. 14, fo. 49[v], a manuscript dated by N. R. Ker to the second half of the eleventh century (Ker *Catalogue*, 354; *Libraries*, 179).
[7] *BHL* 7943. The attribution to Goscelin has been questioned by P. Grierson, *EHR* 55 (1940), 533 n., 540 n., but the *Vita* occurs in manuscripts of the earlier part of the twelfth century. On Goscelin's works see now F. Barlow (ed.), *The Life of King Edward the Confessor* (London, 1962), 91–111, who accepts Grierson's doubts, but points to Goscelin's apparent close connections with the Winchester monasteries (p. 99).
[8] E. P. Sauvage, *AB* 7 (1888), 378, lines 16–18; see also J. Earle, *Gloucester Fragments*, i (London, 1861), 70. William of Malmesbury's account (*Gesta Pontificum*, 161) is derived from the *Vita*.
[9] Three stone arches found below Bridge Street in 1878 show that the medieval bridge was on the line of the present bridge (erected 1813), but that it extended much further east, across ground now completely occupied by buildings to either side: Winchester City Library, drawing by T. Stopher inserted into his copy of Milner[2]. For discussion see Winchester Studies 5 (forthcoming).

on the East Gate, recording the construction of the bridge by Bishop Swithun in A.D. 859, in the seventh indiction.[1] Although the date is internally consistent and perfectly possible,[2] the language of the poem may suggest that it was probably not composed before the tenth century, when the writer could of course have drawn on earlier material. Unlike the longer poem, *Unum Beati Swithuni Miraculum*, it contains nothing of the miraculous, and does not attribute to Swithun the construction of the gate as well as the bridge. It provides a factual account and an appeal for the traveller's prayers for Swithun, *antistes quondam*.[3] The restraint of the text leaves the impression that it was composed before the growth of the saint's cult which followed the translation of 971.

Whether the poem ever appeared on the gate must be doubtful; it was perhaps more in the nature of an exercise. But it may provide evidence both of the existence of the bridge as early as the mid tenth century, and of a rather precise tradition then current of its construction during the episcopate of Swithun between 852 and 862–3.

vi. THE CITY WALL AND GATES (Figs. 25–7 and 32)

The defences of the Roman town were completed in the third century A.D. by the addition of a stone wall around the entire circuit and by the construction of at least four and possibly five stone gates. Excavation on all four sides of the city has shown that the line of the Roman wall was exactly followed by all subsequent defences.[4] The wall was strengthened in the later fourth century by the addition of an unknown number of bastions for the mounting of defensive artillery, and it was perhaps because of this modernization that the defences remained of sufficient importance in the seventh or eighth century for the systematic blocking of the south gate to have been worth undertaking, first by a ditch and subsequently by a stone wall.[5] There seems every likelihood that the entire Roman wall was not only visible, but still an effective barrier, when it was taken as the basis for the defensive circuit of the late ninth century.

In the Burghal Hidage 2,400 hides were assigned to Winchester for the maintenance (?) and defence of its wall.[6] From the statement at the end of one version of that document that every hide was represented by one man, and that every pole of wall ($16\frac{1}{2}$ feet) was manned by four men, it follows that the length of the defences then in question was $(2,400 \div 4) \times 16\frac{1}{2}$ feet, or 9,900 feet (3,017 m). The actual length of the Roman circuit, measured as far as possible around the inner face of the wall, is 9,954 feet (3,034 m), an almost exact correspondence. If this second figure is converted to hides, on the basis that $16\frac{1}{2}$ feet = 4 hides, then that actual length of the defences would be equivalent to

[1] Printed by A. A. Locke, *In Praise of Winchester* (London, 1912), 129, from the copy added to BM, MS. Royal 15 C. vii, fo. 124ᵛ, in a hand of the first half of the twelfth century. The poem begins *Hanc portam presens cernis quicumque viator* and is written in dactylic hexameters, with a heavily spondaic scansion.

[2] Swithun was bishop 852–62; *indictio septima* is correct for 24 Sept. 858 to 23 Sept. 859.

[3] On this evidence alone, the poem post-dates both the alleged date of construction of the bridge in 859 and Swithun's death in 862. It was thus in no way

intended as a building or dedication inscription, but rather as a memorial.

[4] A detailed account of the Roman defences will be found in Winchester Studies 3 (forthcoming).

[5] *X Interim*, 117–18.

[6] *AS Ch* 246–9 and 494–6; for the best text see now David Hill, 'The Burghal Hidage: the establishment of a text', *Med Arch* 13 (1969), 84–92. It was A. J. Robertson in *AS Ch* 495 who first pointed out the 'striking' correspondence between the town wall of Winchester and the Burghal Hidage figures.

2,413·1 hides. It is clear from the document as a whole that such large figures were rounded off to the nearest fifty or a hundred hides, so that in the case of Winchester the actual length of the defences on the ground agrees exactly with the quoted hidage of 2,400.[1]

These figures leave little doubt that the Roman wall formed the basis of the late Saxon defences. When the precise coincidence of the physical remains of the Roman and later medieval walls is taken into consideration, together with the fact that the late Saxon street plan fills the entire walled area of the Roman town, and that a late Saxon intra-mural street ran around the inside of the greater part of the Roman circuit,[2] the identity of the Roman and late Saxon defensive lines becomes a certainty.

In the form in which it now exists the Burghal Hidage appears to have been drawn up between 914 and 918,[3] but there are good grounds for believing that in Wessex the burghal fortresses were in being by 892.[4] The Winchester street plan can probably be dated to before c. 904.[5] This and other actions taken before the death of Alfred (899), such as the establishment of a mint and the initial moves towards the foundation of New Minster,[6] are all aspects of the deliberate creation of an urban community. Together they suggest that the arrangements for maintaining and manning the defences of the city had been undertaken before the king's death, and probably between c. 880 and 892, by which time the defences of the rest of Wessex were in order.[7]

The area of Winchester thus enclosed by the end of the ninth century was 58·2 ha (143·8 acres), the same as that of the walled Roman city of five hundred years earlier, and easily the largest in area of the thirty-three places listed in the Burghal Hidage.

Of the late Saxon wall itself very little is known. By c. 900 the defence near East Gate was the *cyninges burg hege*;[8] in 901, and on the south, it was *(binnan) wealle*;[9] by 975–9, again on the south, it was *(to ðan) ealdan portwealle*,[10] and c. 994 the eastern defences were *muri, moenia*,[11] but these references give little idea of the actual nature of the fortifications. On the five occasions on which they are mentioned in the Winton Domesday, the word used is *murus*,[12] which can probably be taken to mean an actual stone wall. There is no direct archaeological evidence that the late Saxon and Norman wall was of stone, rather than a timber replacement on the Roman line, but large areas of herring-bone flintwork in the outer face of the surviving south-eastern stretch of the wall by The Weirs suggest extensive repairs in either the Anglo-Saxon or early Norman periods.[13] The idea of a late Saxon stone wall, whether in part simply the Roman wall

---

[1] For what it is worth, the percentage 'error' between the quoted (2,400) and the 'actual' hidage (2413·1) is 0·55.

[2] See below, pp. 278–9.   [3] See Addenda.

[4] Stenton *ASE* 264–5.   [5] See below, pp. 277–8.

[6] See below, pp. 313 and 396.

[7] It may be possible to narrow the date to c. 880–6, on the grounds that by 886 Alfred had turned his attention to the restoration of London and is unlikely to have done so until the defences of Wessex were in order: see Martin Biddle, op. cit. on p. 276, n. 6, below, pp. 248–51.

[8] Sawyer 1560, *BCS* 630; Birch *Ancient Manuscript*, 32–3 and 96.

[9] Sawyer 360, *BCS* 596.

[10] Sawyer 1376, *KCD* 1347, *AS Ch*, no. LIII.

[11] Wulfstan *Narratio metrica*, bk. I, lines 497 and 580.

[12] I, 240; II, 691, 692, and 694, all referring to the east wall; and II, 797, the south wall.

[13] For the problems of dating herring-bone work, see J. Taylor and H. M. Taylor, 'Herring-bone masonry as a criterion of date', *JBAA*³, 27(1964), 4–13. The herring-bone work in question is not Roman, for the face is set well back from the Roman line. Dated buildings provide no evidence that the technique was used in this form in Winchester in or after the twelfth century.

refaced, or in part rebuilt on Roman foundations, finds support in the tenth- or eleventh-century stone walls now recognized as additions to earlier earthen defences at, among others, Cricklade, Hereford, Lydford, South Cadbury, Wareham, and Wallingford.[1]

A system of one or more external ditches completed the defences at these places, and Winchester was probably no exception. There was certainly a ditch around the Roman town, from which the material of the ramparts was taken, but it has seldom been observed, having been removed in most places by the much larger ditch of the later Middle Ages. The early medieval ditch system has suffered the same fate, but there is written evidence for its existence in Survey **I**, and archaeological and topographical considerations show something of its character. Ditches outside the west and north gates are mentioned on several occasions *c.* 1110 and in one case the wording probably implies the existence of a ditch *TRE*.[2] The Easton charter of A.D. 961 describes a boundary which ran across the north side of the city, about 150 m in advance of the wall: the intervening space was perhaps at least partly occupied by the ditch system.[3] The presence of more than one ditch is suggested by the discovery at 10 City Road in 1971 of a broad, flat-bottomed ditch which lay just north of the outer lip of the wide later medieval ditch and approximately 40 m in front of the city wall. At this distance the newly discovered ditch can scarcely have been the innermost ditch. This view is perhaps reinforced by the reference in Survey **I, 163** to a house outside North Gate which had been built since the time of King Edward on the site of a lane *per quem burgenses ducebant equos suos ad aquare.* This lane was most probably a direct continuation eastwards of Swan Lane, and part therefore of the system of lanes or *twicene* which ran round the outside of the city to north, west, and south.[4] The new house also lay on the ditch, *super fossatum*, presumably on its northern lip. If this is correct the ditch in question was about 33 m north of the city wall, and like that at 10 City Road is unlikely to have been the innermost ditch, for late Saxon town ditches seem usually to have been far too small to fill the intervening space. The ditch at 10 City Road, which was *c.* 7 m wide, was difficult to date, but the few fragments of pottery from the silting suggest that it was open in the tenth to twelfth centuries.[5]

Late Saxon Winchester was probably therefore defended by a system of multiple ditches in front of the city wall. Although most of the detailed evidence relates to the northern defences, the position of the external lanes or *twicene*, which lie at a regular distance of about 45 m from the wall, suggests the presence on the north, west, and south sides of the city of a wide strip of ground which may originally have been occupied by

[1] The evidence is summarized with further references in C. A. Ralegh Radford, 'The Later Pre-Conquest Boroughs and their Defences', *Med Arch* 14 (1970), 83–103; Hereford: *CA* 33 (July 1972), 256–8.

[2] **I**, 117, 122, 163, and **164**. For the possible existence of the ditch in 1066, see **I, 163**. The 'two ditches' of **I, 123** are probably the ditch of the city liberty and the partly-silted northern ditch of the Iron Age settlement, rather than any part of the ditch outside the city wall (see above, **I, 123**, n. 3). For the Iron Age ditch, which was still a considerable obstacle in the eleventh–twelfth centuries, see Winchester

Studies 3 (forthcoming), Iron Age Gazeteer, Site 1.5.

[3] Sawyer 695. See above, p. 236, s.v. *Denemarche*, and cf. pp. 257 and 266–7.

[4] See above, p. 263.

[5] For 10 City Road, see *X Interim*, 120–1, and Winchester Studies 5 (forthcoming). Note that **I, 117** and **122** refer to a ditch on the west side of the city, and that **I, 222**, where the house sat part on the street and part on the ditch, may show like **I, 163**, that street and ditch (? outer ditch) lay close together; but see **I, 122**, n. 3 for an alternative interpretation.

such a ditch system as that described.[1] This area may originally have been royal land in the same sense as the wall itself and the streets of the town: the northern ditch of Survey **I** was the *fossatum regis*.[2] Whether this description would originally have extended to the whole of the strip 150 m wide between the north wall and the boundary of Easton, and whether this would have included an area of cleared ground beyond the outer ditch, are problems related to the late ninth-century defences which cannot be discussed here.

By 1066 there were at least four gates in the circuit of the Winchester defences, and there may have been six. The documentary, archaeological, and topographical evidence for the existence, location, and even the character of these gates is considerably more extensive than that relating to the wall. The behaviour of the present-day roads approaching the city from the west and north suggests that the medieval and therefore presumably the Saxon gates occupied on these sides precisely the same position as their Roman forerunners, whose location is accurately indicated by the known courses of Roman roads and streets. The situation at the East Gate is rather different, for there the river crossing has shifted northwards since the Roman period and this has caused a corresponding northward displacement in the site of the gate.[3] At South Gate there have been complex changes, so that the Saxon and later gate lay immediately west of the Roman gate, which seems to have been entirely blocked in the post-Roman period.[4] The behaviour of the internal street pattern, in continuous use since the tenth century and in the case of High Street since even earlier, confirms the proposed location of the West, South, and East Gates, and even adds a little to our knowledge of the location of North Gate, within which there was originally an open area, possibly a market.[5]

The East, West, and South gates are all first mentioned about the middle of the tenth century,[6] but the North Gate does not appear before Survey **I** (*c.* 1110), where however the street outside the gate suggest the latter's existence by at least 1066.[7] All four gates occur in Survey **II,** where a further gate makes its first appearance, in the presence of two separate but identical headings for the two lists of properties *Extra portam de Sud*.[8] The first of these headings seems to refer to South Gate, while the second presumably refers to King's Gate, *Chingeta*, which is however only named in an entry in the first list.[9] The sixth gate is first mentioned in the Pipe Roll for 1165 as *Derniata*, now Durngate.[10]

Although North Gate does not appear in the available sources before *c.* 1066, there seems every reason to suppose that it was in existence as early as the West, South, or East Gates, for it would have been needed for local traffic on the route north up the Itchen valley.[11] The existence of this gate by the late ninth century may also be implied by its

---

[1] There seem never to have been ditches in the valley bottom, neither along the eastern parts of the northern and southern defences, nor in front of the east wall, where the River Itchen served the same purpose.

[2] **I,** 163 and **164.**

[3] See above, p. 271.

[4] *X Interim*, 117–18.

[5] See below, pp. 285–6.

[6] East Gate, *c.* 946–55, Sawyer 463, *BCS* 758; West Gate, *c.* 950, W. Stubbs (ed.), *Memorials of St. Dunstan* (RS, 1874), 14; South Gate, *c.* 964–75, Sawyer

1449, *BCS* 1163. East Gate is also mentioned *c.* 994 in Wulfstan (*Narratio metrica*, bk. I, lines 573–4), before *c.* 1050 in another poem (see above, p. 271 and n. 6), and a further reference in a third poem may relate to before 971 (see above, p. 272 and n. 1). The gates of Winchester are referred to in *ASC*, s.a. 1006.

[7] **I,** 163–5.

[8] Rubrics before entries **II, 900** and **1001.**

[9] **II, 928**; see also above, p. 236, s.v.

[10] See above, p. 237, s.v.

[11] See above, p. 261.

symmetrical relationship to the open area, possibly a market, formed by the internal street pattern at this point.[1]

The main approach-roads from north and south, as well as from east and west, converged on the East and West Gates and thus on the axis of High Street, a fact which suggests that the North and South Gates played a secondary role as regards long-distance traffic. Even today, there is no satisfactory north–south route through the walled city. Like South Gate, North Gate may even have been blocked during the post-Roman period. Nevertheless the existence of properly re-organized and probably refurbished defences by the end of the ninth century should imply that some at least and perhaps all four of the principal gates were in use, or had been brought back into use, by that time.

King's Gate and Durngate, both with names of OE origin as the early forms show, are probably earlier than the mid-twelfth century. Little can be said of Durngate, except that it lay on a by-pass route between a heavily occupied quarter of the city and, across the river, the suburb of Winnall and the main road to London along Easton Lane.[2] The development of this suburb, whose inhabitants used the gate frequently in the later Middle Ages, would obviously have increased the need for Durngate, as would the growth of dense urban conditions in the Tanner Street area by about the middle of the eleventh century. If, however, Durngate mill was in existence by 961, as seems likely,[3] then the gate may well be as early and have given access not only to the mill, but also to the village from which the Winnall suburb grew.

King's Gate may be of even earlier origin. The suburb outside this gate seems always to have been the more important of the two southern suburbs,[4] while the name itself probably implies some connection with the royal palace a short distance to the north. There are some grounds also for believing that a Roman gate, perhaps immediately east of King's Gate, may have been the principal south gate of the Roman town. When the blocking of the Roman gate by South Gate is taken into consideration,[5] it may well seem that King's Gate was already the principal entry into the area of the royal palace and Old Minster during the period before the rebirth of urban conditions in Winchester at the end of the ninth century. King's Gate lay on the direct route south to the port and industrial centre of Hamwih, which was at the height of its development in the eighth and ninth centuries, and provided a striking contrast and complement to the royal and ecclesiastical character of Winchester.[6]

There is some evidence for the nature of these gates in the late Saxon and Norman periods. Lodges, presumably for a porter, were present at both the West and East Gates, and at the latter there was a church above the gate.[7] Wulfstan, writing in 993–4, records that this gate was dedicated to St. Michael, so that the church was probably in existence by that time.[8]

[1] See below, pp. 281–2 and 285–6.
[2] See above, p. 261.   [3] See below, p. 283.
[4] See above, p. 267.
[5] X Interim, 117–18.
[6] P. V. Addyman and D. H. Hill, 'Saxon Southampton: a review of the evidence', Proc. Hants FC 25 (1968), 61–93, and 26 (1969), 61–96. For the comparison, see Martin Biddle, 'Winchester: the development of an early capital', in H. Jankuhn (ed.), Vor- und Frühformen der europäischen Stadt im Mittelalter (Göttingen, 1973), ii. 246–7.
[7] II, 3 and 695. The lodge at East Gate had gone out of use by 1148, as the steps up to the church may also have done. The rent of 15d. in King's Gate (II, 928) may suggest that there was also a lodge there.
[8] Wulfstan, Narratio metrica, bk. I, lines 573–4.

At least three other churches stood by or over the city gates. St. Swithun over King's Gate is first mentioned in the later thirteenth century;[1] St. Mary over North Gate appears first about 1340;[2] while St. Mary by West Gate, although only recorded about 1270,[3] was certainly in existence a century earlier, as drawings of its now destroyed chancel arch make clear.[4] Churches seem also to have stood at the limits of the suburbs.[5]

Although definite evidence of pre-conquest date is rare, the close association of gates and churches seems to be a regular feature of some late Saxon towns: St. Michael's church at Oxford and St. Martin's church at Wareham, both of Anglo-Saxon date, provide two of the better known examples. Of these Winchester churches, one at least was in existence by the late tenth century and another by the twelfth, but it is extremely unlikely that further evidence relating either to these, or to the other two churches, will ever be forthcoming.

West Gate still retains a considerable part of its twelfth-century structure showing typical Norman ashlar of small squared stones with diagonal tooling and wide joints. The north-west quoin may be even earlier, for it has been cut to take the south springing of the mid twelfth-century chancel arch of St. Mary by West Gate, while its masonry consists of large adze-dressed blocks, quite different to the Norman work elsewhere in the gate. This quoin may possibly be part of the pre-Norman gate, and if so must be of Anglo-Saxon rather than Roman date.[6]

vii. THE STREETS WITHIN THE WALLS (Figs. 25–7 and 32)

The survival of the Roman defences, the lines of some of the approach-roads, and the positions of some of the gates contrasts strongly with the disappearance of the Roman street plan within the walls. Excavations since 1961 have recovered the outline plan of the Roman streets, and already by 1963 it was clear that the streets in use today, although forming a remarkably rectilinear plan, are not of Roman origin. Subsequent research, both archaeological and documentary, has shown that the existing pattern was laid out as a planned system not later than the mid tenth century and probably before c. 904.[7] The street plans of Winchester and of the other larger burhs listed in the Burghal Hidage can best be seen as the result of a deliberate policy of urban formation in response to the military situation during the latter part of Alfred's reign (871–99). In these places rectilinear street plans seem to be a deliberate expression of the organization and apportionment of the land for permanent settlement. In this context, the Winchester street plan

[1] *Reg Pontissara* ii. 598.

[2] Reg Orleton, quoted Milner[2] ii. 304.

[3] *Reg Pontissara* ii. 598. *Orientalem* here is probably an error for *occidentalem*.

[4] *Archaeologia*, 16 (1812), 361, Pl. lxiii.

[5] See above, pp. 264–5.

[6] One chamber of what may be the early medieval south gate was found about 1925 on the west side of Southgate Street, just inside the line of the Roman town wall: *X Interim*, Fig. 6.

[7] Martin Biddle and David Hill, 'Late Saxon planned towns', *Antiq J* 51 (1971), 70–85. The detailed evidence relating to the Winchester street-plan was given in full in this article (pp. 70–8), and only an outline description need be given here, together with additional evidence, relating mainly to the intra-mural street, and to changes in the street plan in the period covered by the Winton Domesday. For a full account of the street-names, see above, pp. 233–5.

should probably be regarded as essentially contemporary with the re-organization and refurbishing of the defences between *c.* 880 and 892.[1]

High Street seems to have been the pre-existing axis around which the street pattern was laid down. Although very little is known of Winchester before 900, it seems clear that High Street was already the principal route through the town between the two gates by which long-distance traffic from all directions entered the city. In the higher western part of the walled area, High Street has worn a deep depression into the hillside, a depression that extends well behind, and may therefore antedate, the existing frontages which themselves have remained unchanged since the late Saxon period. At its eastern end High Street was already *ceap stræt* by *c.* 900, and the street as a whole was usually called by this name, or by its Latin equivalents *forum* or *mercatum*, 'market', as late as the twelfth century.[2] It seems probable that it first began to function as a street market, an *Einstrassenanlage*, serving the pre-urban community long before the laying out of the street system.

The late Saxon street pattern has four main components: High Street, the back streets, the north–south streets, and the intra-mural street that runs along the inside of the city wall (Fig. 25). The two back streets run parallel to High Street to north and south at a distance of about 31 m. The north–south streets are regularly spaced and run parallel one to another in two separate series, one to the north and the other to the south of High Street.[3] The intra-mural street survives today most clearly in North Walls and St. Swithun Street, but may originally have been continuous, even perhaps where the cathedral precinct abutted directly on to the defences in the south-eastern part of the city (Fig. 32).[4]

Excavations at Castle Yard in 1971 showed that an intra-mural street had originally followed the inside of the defences where they break west to form a large salient at the south-west corner of the walled area.[5] At this point the intra-mural street had forked west from one of the north–south streets, and had been metalled nine times before both it and the north–south street were abandoned and blocked by the construction of the

---

[1] See above, p. 273, esp. n. 7, for the possibility that the reorganization was complete or at least well under way by 886. Detailed study of the boundaries and later extensions of the three minsters in the south-eastern quarter of the city shows that the rectilinear street plan originally extended over the greater part of that area, where today it has entirely vanished. The original layout was gradually eroded: by the establishment of New Minster *c.* 901–3, by the extension of the Old, New, and Nunnaminster enclosures in the 960s, and by the expansion of the royal palace *c.* 1070. Only the later stages in this process can be described here (p. 280). The detailed evidence for the original extent of the rectilinear plan, for the elements (High Street and mid-street) that preceded it, and for the relationship between the minsters and the streets will be presented in Winchester Studies 4. But see also below, pp. 280, 293–4, 313–14, 322, 323, and n. 12.

[2] Sawyer 1560, *BCS* 630; Birch *Ancient Manuscript*, 32–3 and 96.

[3] *Bucchestret*, which was not specifically discussed in the previous article (see above, p. 277 n. 7), probably ran north in the twelfth century across the land later occupied by Blackfriars (*SMW*, s.v. Blackfriars). It was therefore the easternmost of the north–south streets on the north side of High Street.

[4] In addition to these four major components, there were probably many minor lanes within the walled area, as in the western suburb (cf. I, 91 and 107). These minor lanes probably ran north and south from High Street into the blocks between High Street and the back streets (I, 28, 45, and 53), or east and west between the north–south streets, or at least into the blocks between them (I, 135). They were apparently mentioned in the surveys only when they had been closed, and there may have been many more of them. Some lanes not mentioned still exist today (cf. Fig. 32), but could be of later medieval origin (cf. St. Pancras's Lane, *IX Interim*, 109).

[5] *X Interim*, 101–4.

Norman castle in 1067. This part of the intra-mural street presumably continued around the inside of the salient to join the westward continuation of St. Swithun Street, west of South Gate, where in the seventeenth century there was an exit to South Gate from the south-east corner of the castle, and where a lane still in use in the nineteenth century remains today as a private entry. Tower Street (*Snidelingestret*) completed the intra-mural ring on the west.

On the east of the city Colebrook Street (east) alone survives as part of the intra-mural ring. The southward continuation of this street (Mant's Lane) is modern, but the Colebrook Street property in Survey **II**, *ubi callis regis solebat esse* (**II, 716**), may have lain on the original southward continuation of this street towards the Wolvesey boundary.[1] North of High Street there was a very long narrow strip inside the city wall which was recognized as king's ground in the Middle Ages, and was probably the city's *magna placea* on the east side of the land acquired by the Black Friars in 1235.[2] From the thirteenth century the west side of this strip was defined by the wall of the Blackfriars' precinct. Since the latter was extra-parochial, the strip itself was subsequently included in the nearest accessible parish, that of St. Peter Colebrook, as the modern parish boundaries demonstrate.[3] Eastgate Street, more or less on the line of this strip of ground, was laid out about 1844 and is thus entirely modern. The strip recalls those areas of royal land behind the fortifications of other towns, such as Oxford and Canterbury, where they were apparently intended to allow access to the walls for purposes of defence.[4] This function was recalled in Winchester in 1258 when the Greyfriars were allowed to enclose the ground between their house and the city wall (i.e. the street now known as North Walls), on condition that they would allow access for repair or in time of war.[5] By the later Middle Ages, however, much of the intra-mural strip had already been colonized by houses built against the city wall: the large number of properties in *Snidelingestret* (Tower Street) in Survey **II**, and some of the properties entered under *Bucchestret* (**II, 691, 692,** and **694**), and *Mensterstret* (**II, 797**), suggest that this colonization was well under way, if not essentially complete, by the middle of the twelfth century.[6]

The existence of an intra-mural street and open space, providing direct access to the wall for the greater part of its length, emphasizes the close relationship between the street plan and the defences, and strengthens the probability that the refurbishing of the defences and the laying out of the streets took place at the same time. This combination reflects most sharply the insistent demands of the military situation in Wessex in the years following 880.

The street system was therefore old when Survey I was drawn up about 1110, and

[1] The land which later became Wolvesey may have been in lay hands until the 970s (see below p. 323), but nothing is known of the possible, and perhaps likely, continuation of the intra-mural street from the north-east corner of the Wolvesey area around to the south-west corner at the boundary of the monastic precinct of Old Minster.

[2] WCM 1144. See **II, 687**, n. 2.

[3] *SMW*, s.v. Coytebury and Blackfriars. There is no evidence to support the suggestion that this strip

may have formed part of the estate which Ealhswith seems to have given for the foundation of Nunnaminster, see below, p. 322.

[4] H. E. Salter, 'A Lecture on the Walls of Oxford', in *Records of Medieval Oxford* (Oxford Chronicle Co. Ltd., 1912), 76–84, esp. p. 78. See also Urry *Canterbury*, 45.

[5] *Cal Chart R 1257–1300*, p. 12.

[6] For *Snidelingestret*, see Table 26 on p. 377, and Fig. 19.

many changes had already taken place. Those recorded in the surveys belong mostly to the period between 1066 and *c.* 1110 with which Survey I is concerned, and give an impression of rapid change, due mainly to the immediate impact of the Norman conquest. In this discussion, it will be useful to consider both the streets within the walls and the suburban streets. Ten closures are recorded in Survey I, four in the suburbs and six within the walls. Of the internal streets, only two were major north–south streets,[1] the other four being minor lanes.[2] In the suburbs, two of the closures affected lengths of the external 'twichens',[3] the other two being minor lanes.[4] Of the seven *vici* recorded as closed in Survey I, two were destroyed by the building of the castle in 1067,[5] one for the construction of the kitchen of the extended royal palace about 1070,[6] three for private advantage in the period 1066–*c.* 1110,[7] and one seems to have been blocked before 1066.[8] Three lanes (*viculum, venella*) were also shut.[9] By contrast, Survey II records only one closure.[10] And only one other major change is known in the century before 1066, when the back street north of New Minster and the street which formerly marked its eastern boundary must have been closed in Edgar's extension of that monastery between 963 and 970.[11] Survey I may thus have caught the city in a moment of unwonted change: both before and after, the pattern seems to be one of steady but not rapid evolution.

This view is confirmed by the records of encroachments in the two surveys, for while some encroachments occur only in Survey I,[12] and another only in Survey II,[13] there seems to be at least some correspondence between the nine encroachments listed in Survey I under High Street, and the eight under the same heading in Survey II.[14] The preponderance of encroachments listed under High Street, and their continuing financial significance, even if only at a low level, contrast with the smaller number of encroachments in the suburbs, and the failure to maintain any continuing record of their financial implications. Of those encroachments listed under High Street in Survey I, part or the whole of six belong to the period 1066–*c.* 1110,[15] while two had taken place before then.[16]

---

[1] I, **40** and **60**.

[2] I, **28, 45, 53**, and **135**; for discussion, see above, p. 278, n. 4.

[3] I, **81** and **163**, see above, p. 263.

[4] I, **91** and **107**.

[5] I, **39, 40** (see below, p. 303), and **81**.

[6] I, **60** (see below, p. 293).

[7] I, **28, 53** (before *c.* 1100), and **163**.

[8] I, **135**.

[9] One went before *c.* 1100 (I, **45**), and the other two in the period between 1066 and *c.* 1110 (I, **91** and **107**).

[10] II, **716**. The contrast may be partly due to the different nature of the two surveys, for Survey I was solely concerned to record matter affecting royal rights. Nevertheless the intention of Survey II to discover *de quocunque tenet* probably ensured that closures and significant encroachments were recorded where they were known to have occurred since the time of Survey I. It is thus striking that with the possible exception of the encroachments in High Street, Survey II does not record the closures or encroachments listed in Survey I.

[11] Sawyer 807, *BCS* 1302. See below, pp. 313–14, where the streets bounding the New Minster site are further discussed. See also Fig. 9, *c.* 963–1066, which shows that the eastward continuation of the back street was probably blocked by the northward expansion of Nunnaminster, cf. below, p. 322.

[12] Outside West Gate: I, **83, 90, 101**, and **122**; outside North Gate: I, **165** (if the meaning here is 'on top of', rather than 'beside').

[13] Outside South Gate (probably in *Paillardestwichene*): II, **925**.

[14] I, **19, 20, 23, 52, 59, 64, 65, 73**, and **78**; II, **17, 43, 56, 87, 88, 98, 105**, and **106**. The approximate correspondences are I, **23** with II, **42–3**; I, **19–21** with II, **52–9**; and I, **59** and **64** on the south side of High Street in its eastern half with II, **106, 105**, and **98**, respectively, in the same area. I, **65** is identical with II, **111** (see above, I, **65**, n. 1), but there is no mention in the later entry of the encroachment recorded in Survey I.

[15] I, **19, 20, 52, 59, 73**, and **78**.

[16] I, **20** and **23**.

In Survey **II**, there is only one High Street encroachment that seems certainly unrecorded in the earlier survey and was probably therefore of more recent occurrence.[1] Like the closing of streets, the record of encroachments in the two surveys suggests a period of fairly rapid change in the decades after the conquest, preceded and followed by a slower evolution.

The two surveys show some difference in the Latin terminology for the streets. In Survey **I**, the streets closed are all *vici* or *viculum/venella*;[2] the encroachments outside West Gate are all *in (de) vico regis*;[3] but the encroachments listed under High Street are *in (de) calle regis*.[4] There are two exceptions: in one case under High Street, the result of encroachment was that *vicus regis ibi est strictior*;[5] and at *Palliesputte* houses on the road to Basingstoke were *in calle regis*.[6] In Survey **II** *vicus* occurs once only, in the heading for High Street, *In magno vico*,[7] otherwise *callis* is used exclusively.[8] Taking the two surveys together, the following pattern emerges:

	vicus	*callis*
Closures	7	1
Encroachments	5	17

from which it seems possible that *callis* is being used in the sense of 'highway', as in the modern distinction between 'closing a street [*not* a *or* the highway]' and 'obstructing the highway [*rarely* street, *more frequently* road]'. In later medieval Winchester the distinction was between *vicus* and *via*. In the surveys *via* occurs in one context only, probably with the meaning 'right of way', which is closely related to the sense of 'highway' discussed here.[9]

It is clear therefore that High Street encroachments *in (de) calle regis* need not have been in High Street itself, but could as well have lain in the entries to the north–south streets, for these entries were normally included with High Street in later Winchester surveys.[10] This seems to have been the case with the Godbegot encroachments,[11] and with those in the neighbourhood of *Thomeseiete*,[12] and may have been the case at what seems to be the entry to *Flesmangerestret*.[13]

As noted above, Survey **II** does not record the encroachments mentioned in Survey **I**, except in High Street, and then not always. Encroachments could therefore be quickly forgotten and there must have been many of which no written record now exists. Unrecorded encroachment on to the back of the defences, presumably before 1066, can be detected from the surveys and also from archaeological evidence.[14] The same fate seems to have overtaken the market place inside North Gate, whose loss can probably be placed

---

[1] **II**, **17**. **II**, **87** and **88** may also be recent encroachments.

[2] See above, p. 280, nn. 5–9. In addition, in **I**, **80/81**, *vicus* is used of High Street, and in **I**, **162** it occurs probably with reference to *Brudenestret*.

[3] See above, p. 280, n. 12.

[4] See above, p. 280, n. 14.

[5] **I**, **73**.

[6] **I**, **165**.

[7] **II**, before entry **1**.

[8] See above, p. 280, n. 14, and **II**, **716** and **925**.

[9] **II**, **766–9**.

[10] See above, p. 243.

[11] **I**, **23** and **II**, **43**.

[12] **I**, **59**, **64**, and **65**; and **II**, **98**, **105**, **106**, and **111**.

[13] **I**, **19** and **20**; **II**, **56**.

[14] See above, p. 279. At Tower Street buildings on the west side of *Snidelingestret*, encroaching on the back of the defences, can be dated to the middle of the eleventh century: Winchester Studies 5 (forthcoming).

before 1066, since there is no record in either of the surveys of its existence or of encroach-ment upon it.[1]

While it is therefore clear that there have been changes in the width of the Winchester streets due to encroachment, many of these changes seem to have concerned the entries to the north–south streets where their effect is only too obvious today. Elsewhere the street frontages seem to have remained remarkably constant, at least from the eleventh century, if not from the moment when they were first laid out.[2] Measurements of the existing widths, from frontage to frontage, suggests that the north–south streets were intended to be between 24 feet and 30 feet (7·3 and 9·1 m) in width.[3] By contrast High Street is nowhere less than 30 feet (9·1 m) wide today, and measurements suggest an original average width of at least 40 feet (12·2 m), with some areas considerably wider.[4] The back streets to north and south of High Street average in width between 10 and 15 feet (3·0 and 4·6 m), and the intra-mural streets about 20 feet (6·1 m). There was therefore something of a hierarchy of streets in medieval Winchester, and this pattern may reflect conscious decisions concerning the width of the streets and their intended function when they were first laid out before the end of the ninth century.[5]

The streets of Winchester are thus among the most important sources for the history of the city. They not only allow the original late Saxon pattern to be described, and some-thing of the factors behind it to be understood; they also show something of the complex evolution of the city in the years immediately before and after the Norman conquest, and emphasize that the medieval city was then already ancient.

viii. MILLS AND WATERCOURSES (Figs. 8, 25–7, and 32–3)[6]

Winchester was well supplied with water. Apart from the main stream of the Itchen on the east side of the city, there was a complex network of subsidiary channels and mill-leats within the city walls. Some of these streams were taken out of the Itchen as much as a mile north of Winchester and rejoined the main river up to a mile south of the city. A tributary stream rising at Headbourne Worthy was the principal water supply for Hyde Abbey, and powered the Abbey mill before flowing into this subsidiary system.

The mill on the main river outside East Gate was in existence by 940[7] and was probably in the possession of Wherwell Abbey by 1086.[8] There was a mill to the north outside

---

[1] See above, p. 261, and below, p. 285. The evidence for the former existence of this market is topographical; the pattern of the streets in this area, and their re-lationship to North Gate, suggest the former existence of a rectangular open space within, and symmetrically placed in relation to, North Gate.

[2] For detailed discussion, see the reports of excava-tions on the Assize Courts and Lower Brook Street sites in Winchester Studies 5 (forthcoming).

[3] Measurements were taken from the O.S. 1:500 plans of 1869–71.

[4] At the Pentice the width decreases to about 26 feet (7·9 m) perhaps because of an encroachment associated

with the extension of the Norman royal palace c. 1070 or its destruction in 1141.

[5] Regulations regarding street widths can be found in both English and continental laws of the twelfth century and later: e.g. L. J. Downer (ed.), Leges Henrici Primi (Oxford, 1972), 248–9, § 80. 3.

[6] For general surveys of the mills of medieval Win-chester see VCH Hants v. 48, 49; J. S. Furley, 'Some points relating to the mills of Winchester in the middle ages', Wessex, vol. ii, no. 1 (1931), pp. 60–9.

[7] Sawyer 463.

[8] See below, p. 356.

Durn Gate by 1165[1] and at Segrim's Well to the south by 1208.[2] These three mills were mainly powered by the flow of the main stream outside the east wall of the city, but the last caught some water from the system within the city. *Costices mylne*, a short distance upstream from Durn Gate, probably enjoyed the same water supply in 961.[3] Outside the city to the south, and powered by the subsidiary streams running through the city as well as by the main river, were the mills of Floodstock, Priors Barton, Cripstead, and Sparkeford, all in existence by 1208.[4] The mill at Floodstock may have been one of the sheriff's mills before Wolvesey, granted to the bishop and church of Winchester by John de Port in about 1155.[5]

The maintenance of a sufficient head of water to power the mills at Floodstock, Barton, Cripstead, and Sparkeford was only made possible by a sophisticated system of leats within the walled city. Parts of this system were already in existence by the late ninth century, for three mill-streams in the eastern part of the town are mentioned in the bounds of the land of Queen Ealhswith at this period.[6] It is reasonable to suppose that the Brooks system (the streams running down *Sildwortenestret*, *Wunegrestret*, *Tannerestret*, and *Bucchestret*), which is well documented as an integral part of the street pattern in the later Middle Ages, was laid out or formalized at the same time as the streets themselves, in other words shortly before the bounds of Ealhswith's lands were described.[7] The mill acquired by New Minster in 901, described as the southernmost mill within the city wall, would have been an integral part of this system.[8] Black Ditch, the channel which supplied most of the water for the Brooks system, certainly seems to have been in existence by 961.[9]

The causeway in the lower part of the town which formed the continuation of High Street across marshy ground to East Gate and the crossing of the main river was perhaps formalized in this period.[10] It would also have provided a seat for mills and at least two mills (**II, 697** and the mill at Newbridge) appear to have existed there in the twelfth century.

Further details of this system are preserved in the surviving records of Bishop Æthelwold's monastic planning of the 970s. King Edgar is credited with having introduced a fine stream of water into New Minster during this period.[11] New Minster had a mill which stood on ground ceded to the Old Minster. A watercourse with at least two mills on it flowed through the ground between New Minster and Nunnaminster, and one of those mills may have been on the site of that known as Postern Mill in the later Middle Ages. There was also a watercourse adjacent to the land which Æthelwold enclosed with a wall extending from the Minster to the old town wall.[12] This stream may have been the one which drove the Floodstock mill and which still flows between Wolvesey and the

---

[1] *Pipe Roll 11 Henry II*, p. 41. Durn Gate mill may be identical with *costices mylne* named in the bounds of Easton in 961, Sawyer 695, see above, p. 236, s.n.

[2] *PRBW 1208–9*, 78. [3] Sawyer 695.

[4] *PRBW 1208–9*, 78 and 79. A pair of twelfth-century stone arches carry the city wall over running water at the site of Floodstock mill, evidence that the mill existed by that period.

[5] Goodman *Chartulary*, no. 453.

[6] Birch *Ancient Manuscript*, 32, 96.

[7] See above, pp. 277–8.

[8] Sawyer 360.

[9] *Blacan lace* named in the bounds of Easton, Sawyer 695, see above, p. 236, s.n.

[10] See above, p. 244.

[11] *LVH* 8.

[12] The relevant charters are Sawyer 1376, 1449. See also *I Interim*, 175, and below, pp. 308, 317, and 323–4.

Cathedral Close. In addition, Æthelwold himself caused a stream of fresh running water to be brought through the monastery buildings for sanitary purposes.[1] The Lockburn, which ran out of *Colobrochestret*, through the reredorter of the Norman cathedral priory, and past the college to the south of the city, may be the descendant of this stream, as Winchester tradition seems long to have held.

The two twelfth-century surveys mention only the mill of St. Mary's Abbey within East Gate (**II, 697**). In the later Middle Ages the abbey mill stood in the south part of the monastic enclosure, but Speed's plan of Winchester shows an additional mill on the stream against the east wall of the precinct.[2] Other mills known to have stood within the city walls in the twelfth century were the mills at Coitbury[3] and the mill at Newbridge in High Street at the entry to Tanner Street.[4]

Four millers are identified in the 1148 survey (**II, 86, 331, 874,** and **990**). None of them had more than one property and the tenements of three of them may have been close to the mills which they worked. Ansgod, a tenant of the abbot of Hyde outside North Gate (**331**), may have worked the abbey mill. Hudo, a tenant of the bishop towards the east end of High Street (**86**), may have been in charge of the mill at Newbridge. Theoderic, a tenant of the bishop in the south part of Kingsgate Street (**990**), could have been in charge of one of the mills in that area, perhaps Sparkeford mill. In each case this would be the earliest evidence for the existence of these three mills.

Private houses in Winchester drew their water from wells or, in the low-lying parts of the town, from private channels leading out of the public watercourses.[5] Each of the great establishments had its own water supply. The castle no doubt relied on wells.[6] By the fourteenth century the cathedral priory had a separate self-contained supply of drinking water carried by stone conduit and lead pipe from the Itchen at Easton mill.[7] At the bishop's palace of Wolvesey, water was brought in through a system of lead pipes and stone chambers, still in working order, installed by Bishop Giffard (1100–29), or early in the episcopate of Henry of Blois (1129–71).[8] In the later thirteenth century the cathedral priory was responsible for the upkeep of the conduit in Wolvesey.[9] This suggests not only that the priory and bishop's palace were supplied from the same source but also, as the analogies of Gloucester and Canterbury indicate, that the piped supply to the priory was in existence by the early twelfth century. St. Mary's Abbey enjoyed piped water in the later Middle Ages, but its source and date of installation are unknown.[10]

---

[1] Wulfstan *Narratio Metrica*, epis., lines 38–40:
  dulcia piscosae flumina traxit aquae,
  secessusque laci penetrant secreta domorum,
  mundantes totum murmure coenobium.
Cf. Quirk *OM* 43–4.

[2] There is no written evidence for this mill.

[3] King John's charter to the citizens of Winchester in 1215 confirmed them in the possession of the seat of the two mills of Coitbury: *Rot Chart* 217.

[4] *Cal Chart R 1327–41*, p. 393.

[5] A series of these channels has been excavated in *Tannerestret*. See Winchester Studies 5, forthcoming, and *II–VIII Interim*.

[6] A twelfth-century well within the north keep has been excavated, *VIII Interim*, Fig. 2, VI. The tradition that the castle ditch was fed by streams of running water has little foundation, although Edward I's queen did have a garden with running water in the castle: Colvin (ed.), *Kings Works*, ii. 863.

[7] *Obedientiary Rolls*, 210; W. R. W. Stephens and F. T. Madge (ed.), *Documents relating to the history of the Cathedral Church of Winchester in the Seventeenth Century* (HRS, 1897), 92.

[8] *VII Interim*, 324–5.

[9] *Reg Pontissara* 656, 755.

[10] Evidence from excavations by Winchester City Rescue Archaeologist, Summer 1973.

The Norman royal palace and its Anglo-Saxon predecessor may have been served by a channel taken out of the stream in *Sildwortenestret*, which in the fourteenth century was distinguished from the other brooks by the name *Kingesbroke*.[1]

Figure 8 shows the watercourses of Winchester as they seem to have been in the later Middle Ages, and probably were in general much earlier. Mills which are known to have been in existence by the twelfth or early thirteenth century are shown, as are later mills on the sites of which twelfth-century or earlier mills may have stood.[2]

The extent and complexity of the system of watercourses in early medieval Winchester bear witness, as does the street grid within the walls, to the intensity of urban growth and the conscious planning of the framework of the city from the end of the ninth century onwards.

ix. MARKETS (Fig. 8)

The streets of Winchester were its market-place.[3] The commercial pre-eminence of High Street is emphasized by the name *ceapstræt*, by which it was known already at the beginning of the tenth century,[4] and the only references to markets in the surveys occur under High Street in Survey **I**. A market was established on the north side of the street near the 'three minsters' between 1066 and *c.* 1110 (**I, 35**), and on the south side of the street, in the area later occupied by part of the royal palace, the five mints closed by order of the king were *in mercato* (**I, 58**). In the thirteenth century the north–south streets or 'blind streets' (*horbes rues*) were recognized as market areas similar to but lesser than High Street.[5]

In the later Middle Ages certain market functions were distinctly localized within High Street. With regard to the sale of meat at least, this was also the case in the eleventh and twelfth centuries.[6] The market at the 'three minsters' may have specialized in other produce, possibly fish.

Urban markets were often sited near important gates. The *popularis platea* outside West Gate, where Bishop Ælfheah the Bald consecrated a church between 934 and *c.* 939,[7] may well have been a market-place at the external road junction. A cross stood there in the later Middle Ages.[8]

The symmetrical setting of *Scowrtenestret* and *Brudenestret* in relation to North Gate suggests that there was originally an open area or market-place within the gate (cf. Figs. 8 and 25). The area was subsequently colonized, except for roads leading from the two streets to the gate, and from *Scowrtenestret* direct to the city wall. The lack of any reference in the surveys to encroachment in this area probably indicates that the colonization had taken place before *c.* 1066. The eastern half of the colonized area was made up

[1] See *SMW*.

[2] See also Figs. 25–7 and 32–3. The sources for Fig. 8 were Godson's map of 1750, and two early eighteenth-century plans of the watercourses above and below Winchester. Medieval written evidence for mills and waterways, where it exists, agrees with this picture.

[3] In a thirteenth-century inquisition the gates of the city were described as *iuxta mercatum Wynton: Abbreviatio Placitorum*, 47. Evidence for the penning

of animals in *Gerestret* and in the street beneath the castle in the early tenth century has been recovered in excavation: *III Interim*, 242; *VIII Interim*, 286–7.

[4] See above, p. 278.   [5] Furley *Usages*, 35.

[6] See below, p. 431 and for the markets of the later medieval city, *SMW*.

[7] See below, p. 330, n. 1.

[8] *SMW* 711. There were animal pens there in the thirteenth century, Furley *Usages*, 35.

almost entirely of Wherwell Abbey tenements (probably **II, 428–33**), and since the abbey does not seem to have increased its estate in the city after the early eleventh century[1], the encroachment may well have taken place by then. The church of St. Saviour, unlikely to have been founded after the middle of the twelfth century, stood in the western half of the colonized area on the approximate site of the modern Theatre Royal. An area of medieval metalling discovered in 1960 due north of *Brudenestret*, and behind the probable site of the church,[2] perhaps represented the surfacing of this market-place. In the later Middle Ages neither *Snidelingestret* nor *Brudenestret* extended as far north as the city wall, and the ground within the wall, to the north of the streets, may have had a special identity in an earlier period. It is possible that it was the *Sapalanda* ('sheepland') of the first survey, perhaps a sheep-market.[3]

In suitable places, markets sometimes encroached on open ground, apparently without any formal authority. A considerable part of the site of the former royal palace, which had been granted to the bishop and cathedral, was encroached upon in this way. In the fourteenth century the cattle-market stood where The Square now is, and a reference in the Customs of Winchester to penning cattle in *Mensterstret* implies that this was also the case in the previous century.[4]

X. THE FAIR (Fig. 8)

Daily exchanges of goods manufactured in Winchester and of food and raw materials brought in from the countryside took place in the city's markets, but yearly sales and purchases were made at the fair in September.[5] In the thirteenth century, Winchester fair was one of the five or six great fairs of England and the only one of the first rank south of the Thames. Merchants from all over Britain and western Europe came to the fair, most of them from London, the Midlands, Lincoln, and York in England, and from northern France, Normandy, and Flanders on the continent. The prosperity of the fair appears to have been based on a large trade in the staple products, wool, cloth, and livestock, and perhaps also on considerable transactions in agricultural produce, to which was added an extensive turnover in manufactured items, spices, and other luxuries. By the reign of Richard I this prosperity was nearing a peak which was probably achieved before the middle of the thirteenth century.[6]

In 1096 William II granted to Bishop Walkelin and the monks of the church of Winchester a fair of three days at the church of St. Giles on the eastern hill of Winchester. During this period the bishop was to enjoy all the profits and revenues which belonged to the king in the city.[7] In 1110 Henry I extended the period to eight days in exchange

[1] See below, p. 356.

[2] *Winchester 1949–60*, ii (forthcoming).

[3] See above, p. 238, s.n.

[4] Furley *Usages*, 35. See *SMW* and discussion of the site of the palace, below, p. 301. *Mensterstret* is the present Great Minster Street, see above, p. 234, s.n.

[5] A more extensive study of the topography and trade of Winchester fair will appear in *SMW*.

[6] In 1189 the receipts of the bishopric from the fair totalled £146. 8s. 7d., *Pipe Roll 1 Richard I*, p. 5. The annual average for the two years 1238 and 1239 was £163. 17s. 10½d., and for the two years 1241 and 1242, £111. 18s. 10½d.; in 1250, £162. 1s. 7d. was received: PRO, E 372/85, rot. 3; 87, rot. 3d; and 95, rot. 6. All later receipts suggest a continuous decline. The series of receipts recorded in the Bishop of Winchester's pipe rolls does not begin until 1288.

[7] *Regesta*, i, no. 377.

for the lands taken for the site of Hyde Abbey.[1] Stephen granted six days more in 1136.[2] In March 1155 Henry II, ignoring Stephen's grant, doubled the period allowed by his grandfather.[3] In spite of the terms of the early charters the fair was regarded as the exclusive right of the bishop, although he paid the cathedral priory an annual sum of 25 marks, increased by Henry of Blois to 30 marks.[4] During the sixteen days of the fair the bishop's jurisdiction on St. Giles's Hill, in the city, and within a circuit of seven leagues, appears to have been absolute.

One of the principal reasons for the success of St. Giles's Fair was no doubt the judicial and administrative framework provided by the bishop, and the protection he was able to offer to merchants coming from a distance.[5] During the disturbances of Stephen's reign, Henry of Blois was active in the interests of merchants travelling to his fair, and in this he appears to have been following his brother and successive counts of Champagne[6] in a policy to which much of the prosperity of the great fairs of Champagne was due.[7]

In the thirteenth century, merchants descended from the hill with their goods after the sixteenth day and continued the fair in the city for the rest of September.[8] This may also have been the custom in the twelfth century and underlines the possibility that even before 1096 there may have been an annual September market or fair at Winchester, perhaps originally devoted mainly to the sale of agricultural produce.[9]

The site of St. Giles's Fair came to be regarded as part of the bishop's soke of Winchester, and may be defined by the rectangular area of the soke extending on to St. Giles's Hill, surrounded on three sides by the prior's manor of Barton (cf. Fig. 5). Within the fair there was a regular system of streets along which, by the thirteenth century, permanent shops, houses, and store houses, including some structures in stone, had been erected. The buildings were possibly less substantial in the twelfth century, for three fires are recorded as having devastated the site.[10] The fair was focused on the church of St. Giles, next to which stood the episcopal court-house known as the Pavilion. Traces of the grid of streets were preserved in field boundaries on St. Giles's Hill into

[1] *Regesta*, ii, no. 947. [2] *Regesta*, iii, no. 952.
[3] *Cal Chart R 1300–26*, pp. 355–6. The witnesses to the charter provide the date range 1154–61. All of them, with the possible exception of Hugh, archbishop of Rouen, witnessed charters at the great council held at the end of March 1155 in London at which many bishops and abbots sought renewal and confirmation of their charters. Hugh was the beneficiary of one of the charters issued on that occasion and was present at the coronation at Westminster in December 1154. See R. W. Eyton, *Court, Household and Itinerary of King Henry II* (London, 1878), 6–9, and L. Delisle and E. Berger, *Recueil des actes de Henry II, roi d'Angleterre et duc de Normandie* (Paris, 1909–27), i. 94–5.
[4] Goodman *Chartulary*, no. 6.
[5] For the organization and customs of St. Giles's Fair, the outlines of which can be traced back to the first half of the thirteenth century, see G. W. Kitchin (ed.), *A Charter of Edward the Third Confirming and Enlarging the Privileges of St. Giles Fair, Winchester*,

A.D. 1349 (Winchester Cathedral Records, 2, London and Winchester, 1886); *Reg Pontissara* 722; BM Egerton MS. 2418, fos. 59ᵛ–60ᵛ; and the summary in *VCH Hants* v. 36–41.
[6] H. W. C. Davis, 'Henry of Blois and Brian Fitz-Count', *EHR* 25 (1910), 297–303.
[7] See, for example, R. H. Bautier, 'Les Foires de Champagne. Recherches sur une évolution historique', *Recueils de la Société Jean Bodin*, 5, *La Foire* (Brussels, 1953), 97–147.
[8] *Close R 1256–9*, p. 430; *Cal Pat R 1259–60*, pp. 436–7. See also below, Appendix I. 2, p. 518.
[9] For the Anglo-Saxon evidence for annual trading, see F. Harmer, 'Chipping and Market: a Lexicographical Investigation', in Cyril Fox and Bruce Dickins (ed.), *The Early Cultures of North-West Europe* (Cambridge, 1950), 335–60; and for a valuable discussion of the origin of the north-west European fairs, R. H. Bautier, op. cit. in n. 7, above.
[10] In 1162, 1197, and 1198, *Winchester ann*, s.a.

the nineteenth century, when the fair still operated on a much reduced scale. If the prosperity of Winchester had not faded away after the thirteenth century, the *nova villa*, as at least a part of the fair was known in 1287,[1] would have survived as a substantial, regularly-planned suburb on the eastern side of the city.[2]

Although St. Giles's Fair was the principal manifestation of the commercial greatness of Winchester in the twelfth century, it is not mentioned in either of the surveys.

---

[1] WCL, Custumal, fo. 17ᵛ.

[2] The fair at Troyes was frequently devastated by fires in the twelfth century, by the end of which many stone houses were being built. The fair was held in the suburb west of the *cité* and of the palace of the counts of Champagne. This suburb shows every sign of regular rectilinear planning. See E. Chapin, *Les Villes de foires de Champagne des origines au début du XIVᵉ siècle* (Bibliothèque de l'École des Hautes Études, Paris, 1937), 108–20; and Miss Chapin's map of Troyes, also reproduced in F. L. Ganshof, *Étude sur le développement des villes entre Loire et Rhin au Moyen Âge* (Paris and Brussels, 1943), plate 35. The superficial area of the western suburb of Troyes (55·2 ha) was rather more than twice that of the site of St. Giles's Fair, Winchester (26·8 ha), thus indicating the relative scale of trade at the two fairs. The total area occupied by the city and suburbs of Troyes (99 ha) was, however, less than that of the walled area and suburbs of Winchester in the twelfth century (195·7 ha).

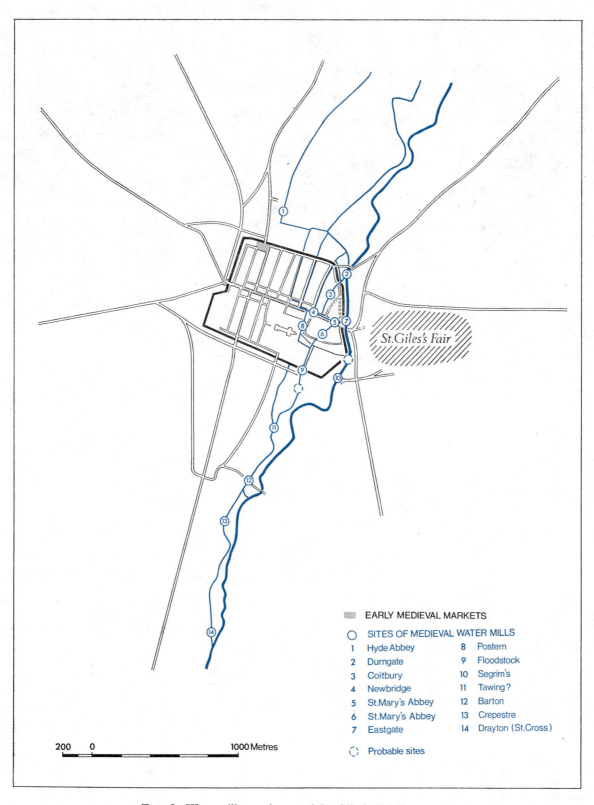

EARLY MEDIEVAL MARKETS

○ SITES OF MEDIEVAL WATER MILLS

1	Hyde Abbey	8	Postern
2	Durngate	9	Floodstock
3	Coitbury	10	Segrim's
4	Newbridge	11	Tawing?
5	St.Mary's Abbey	12	Barton
6	St.Mary's Abbey	13	Crepestre
7	Eastgate	14	Drayton (St.Cross)

◌ Probable sites

200   0   1000 Metres

St.Giles's Fair

FIG. 8. Watermills, markets, and St. Giles's Fair (1:25,000).

3

PUBLIC BUILDINGS

i. THE ROYAL PALACE (Figs. 9, 25, and 26)

The pre-conquest palace

THE arguments which suggest the existence of a royal residence in the centre of Winchester from the middle of the seventh century, if not before, need not be repeated here.[1] The palace is apparently referred to for the first time only in the later tenth century,[2] and there is little direct evidence regarding its location or use during the Anglo-Saxon period. The Winchester annals[3] say that Cnut *regni sui solium habuit in Wintonia.*[4] And at Winchester on Easter Monday 1053 Godwine was carried dying, after a seizure at the king's table, *into ðæs kinges bure, in regis cameram.*[5]

The site of the palace lay immediately west of the Old Minster, in the area east of Little Minster Street, and south of the New Minster cemetery. This much is made clear by the extension of the site northwards for the construction of William the Conqueror's hall about 1070.[6] The Anglo-Saxon palace thus lay within 40 m of the west front of the seventh-century church, and in the immediate vicinity of the west-work dedicated in

---

[1] Martin Biddle, 'Felix urbs Winthonia', in D. Parsons (ed.), *Tenth-century Studies* (London and Chichester, 1975), 123–40: idem, 'Winchester: the development of an early medieval capital', in H. Jankuhn, W. Schlesinger, and H. Steuer (ed.), *Vor- und Frühformen der europäischen Stadt im Mittelalter* (Abh. der Akademie der Wissenschaften in Göttingen, Philolog.-hist. Klasse, 3 Folge, 83), i (Göttingen, 1973), 229–61.

[2] Æthelwold (bishop 963–84) was said to be living in the royal palace (*de palatio regis, regis in obsequio*) in the 970s (i.e. after the translation of St. Swithun in 971): Lantfred, prose account of the miracles and translation of St. Swithun, written before c. 998, BM, Royal MS. 15 C. vii, fo. 26ᵛ, printed from Vatican MS. *Reginae Sueciae* 566 (formerly 769) in the excerpt from Lantfred in *Acta Sanctorum, Julii*, i (1746), 331–7, and therefore omitted by E. P. Sauvage, *AB* 4 (1885), 397, where it would have been bk. II, cap. x, according to Sauvage's division. See also Wulfstan, *Narratio metrica*, bk. I, cap. xiii, line 1393. There appear to have been royal residences at King's Worthy and at King's Somborne, north and west of the city respectively (below, p. 466), and it is sometimes clear that reference is being made to one or other of these places. There is no such indication in relation to the references now under discussion.

[3] The *Winchester annals* are a source of uneven value, in which the pre-conquest entries were probably compiled in the later twelfth century. In so far as

'Winchester and its cathedral are the centre of everything' (*Winchester ann*, p. xiii) they have some worth as a local record which preserves a good deal of purported fact for which there is no other source. They must however be treated with caution. The post-conquest entries in the printed version were compiled at different dates, those relating to the third quarter of the thirteenth century being virtually contemporary. For the post-conquest period the annals again provide what is often the only record of Winchester events.

[4] *Winchester ann*, s.a. 1017. The word *solium*, 'dwelling', has a Vulgate meaning 'throne'. It is used in both senses in Wulfstan (*Narratio metrica*, epis., line 64 and bk. I, line 805). In the annal for 1017 either meaning seems to imply residence in Winchester. The same source (s.a. 1040, 1042) refers to Queen Emma living in the city, and to the Confessor dining *in curia matris*. This may refer to Emma's own residence (possibly I, 75), rather than to the royal palace, but the queen mother could easily have resided in the latter (cf. *ASC*, s.a. 1035 (C, D), 1036 (E)). Winchester was closely associated with the later Saxon queens, for both Emma and Edith received it as a morning-gift, and remained there after the death of their husbands (E. A. Freeman, *History of the Norman Conquest* (Oxford, 1867–79), i. 306 n.; ii. 62; iii. 66, 640).

[5] *ASC*, s.a. 1053 (C, cf. D); Florence of Worcester (as p. 319, n. 5), s.a. 1053.

[6] See below, pp. 292–4.

980.[1] The name *Chingeta*, 'king's gate', applied to the eastern of the two gates in the south wall of the city, probably reflects the use of this gate as a direct approach to the palace from the south.[2]

No excavations have yet taken place on this supposed site and, in default of archaeological evidence, further information regarding the pre-conquest palace can only be derived from the presence of the king in Winchester, from meetings of the *witan*, or from the keeping of the royal treasure there. The Anglo-Saxon kings can be shown to have been present in the city on many occasions, but it will be sufficient to examine the reign of Edward the Confessor. Nevertheless the supposed consecration of Egbert in Winchester in 828, the presence of Alfred in 896 and of later kings at the dedication of New Minster in 903, and at the rededication of Old Minster in 980, and the early and frequent practice of royal burial in Winchester, suggest the existence of a royal residence within the city, or in its immediate environs, by the ninth century if not before.[3]

Edward the Confessor was possibly in Winchester on eight occasions: in 1042, for his coronation on Easter Day 1043, in November that year, in 1044(?), twice during 1045(?), again in 1046(?), and at Easter 1053.[4] On the second and last of these dates there were probably meetings of the *witan*,[5] but since unfortunately it was not the practice in this period to name the place of issue of charters, and since there is no justification for assuming that those which concern estates in one neighbourhood were necessarily brought before a witan meeting there, Oleson's suggestions are unconvincing.[6]

The Confessor's presence in the city at Easter 1043 and Easter 1053 may suggest that an Easter crown-wearing in Winchester formed a regular part of royal ceremonial by his reign, but crown-wearings as such do not seem to have been a feature of the celebration of the three great feasts in the tenth century. Nevertheless the rank and numbers of those attending, *omnes primates aegregii et duces eximii, prepotentes milites . . . populusque infinitus*, would certainly have necessitated proper accommodation on a 'palatial' scale.[7] There appears, however, to be no evidence to show where these ceremonies were then held.

This evidence alone would be sufficient to suggest the existence of a pre-conquest palace in Winchester, but it can be supplemented by indications that Winchester was already the permanent repository of the king's treasure. The reality of a centralized pre-conquest treasury is a matter on which there is a considerable divergence of opinion.[8]

[1] See below, p. 307.

[2] II, 928; see also above, p. 236, s.n.

[3] *Winchester ann*, s.a. 828; *BCS* 602, Sawyer 370; Wulfstan, *Narratio metrica*, epis., lines 63–5. Among the Anglo-Saxon kings buried in Winchester were Cynegils (d. 643, translated from Dorchester ?), Cenwalh (d. 674), Cynewulf (d. 786), Æthelwulf (d. 858, trans. from Steyning), Alfred (d. 899), Edward the Elder (d. 924), Eadred (d. 955), Eadwig (d. 959), Edmund Ironside (d. 1016, translated from Glastonbury?), Cnut (d. 1035), and Harthacnut (d. 1042).

[4] T. J. Oleson, *The Witenagemot in the reign of Edward the Confessor* (Oxford, 1955), Appendix T, and see below, p. 466, n. 7. For 1042, see *Winchester ann*, s.a.

[5] Oleson, Appendix O.

[6] Oleson, 45–7.

[7] Richardson and Sayles, 142, 405–6 n., quoting *Vita Oswaldi* (J. Raine (ed.), *Historians of the Church of York*, i (RS, 1879), 425, corrected by BM, Cotton MS. Nero E. i, fo. 9ᵛ). See also M. Biddle, 'Seasonal festivals and residence' in M. W. Barley (ed.), *The Archaeology and History of the European Town* (London, Council for British Archaeology, forthcoming).

[8] V. H. Galbraith, *Studies in the Public Records* (London, 1948), 41–6; Barlow *English Church*, 120–4, fully documents what may be called the minimal view. For the middle line, see Stenton *ASE* 643–4.

Here, however, we are concerned only with the existence of a treasury in Winchester, and what that implies for the palace there. There is definite evidence for such a treasury from the reign of Cnut, for it was on his death that all his best valuables there (*ealle þa betstan gærsuma*) fell first into the hands of Queen Emma, and were then seized by Harold.[1] Fifty-two years later William Rufus went straight from his coronation at Westminster to view the treasury and the riches (*þa madme hus 7 þa gersuman*) which the Conqueror his father had accumulated in Winchester.[2] Henry I rode to Winchester to secure the treasure within hours of Rufus's death,[3] and Stephen in his turn, and Matilda after him, did the same.[4] Although by the 1130s, and probably by 1100, the treasury had been moved from the old royal palace to the castle,[5] it was still to contemporaries both rich and ancient, *ditissimum . . . aerarium, quod tota ex antiquissimis regibus Anglia copiose referserat.*[6]

This evidence, all well known, is in fact remarkable alike for its consistency and its isolation. There is no such information for London. Although there must have been some store of treasure at Westminster in the reign of the Confessor, there is nothing to suggest that it was of more than local importance.[7] Winchester was thus not only the most ancient, but also the principal repository of the king's treasure, and Westminster (or possibly The Tower) did not supplant Winchester in this respect until the 1180s.[8]

For the existence at Winchester before the conquest of a working treasury, as distinct from the central depository of the realm, it is not necessary to argue here.[9] Nor is this the place to enter the tangled discussion concerning the origin and independence of a royal writing-office,[10] or the character and location of the *haligdom*,[11] although in purely physical terms it seems highly probable that the late Saxon palace included its own chapel,[12] distinct from the seventh-century Old Minster, now rebuilt, whose role had long before developed on quite different lines. There must, of course, have been close connections

---

[1] *ASC*, s.a. 1035 (C, D). See Addenda.

[2] Ibid., s.a. 1086 (E). William of Malmesbury (*Gesta regum*, bk. iii, cap. 283, perhaps following the Chronicle) says that Rufus *omnem illum thesaurum Wintoniae totis annis regni cumulatum ab arcanis sacrariis eruit in lucem.*

[3] Ordericus Vitalis, *Ecclesiastica Historia* (ed. A. Le Prévost, Paris, 1838–55), iv. 87.

[4] See below, p. 305.

[5] See below, pp. 304–5.

[6] *Gesta Stephani*, cap. 4; cf. *Historia Novella*, cap. 463.

[7] This is the straightforward interpretation of Ailred of Rievaulx's tale; it seems doubtful whether a popular story written down a century after the event would be given any credence except for the almost total lack of hard evidence (Barlow *English Church*, 123–4). Anglo-Saxon England was not run 'from a box under the bed', although the royal house-keeping at Westminster may have been.

[8] R. A. Brown, ' "The Treasury" of the late Twelfth Century', in J. Conway Davies (ed.), *Studies Presented to Sir Hilary Jenkinson* (Oxford, 1957), 35–47, esp. 38–44.

[9] For Henry the treasurer, and other royal officials mentioned in the surveys, see below, pp. 387–92.

[10] V. H. Galbraith, *Studies in the Public Records* (London, 1948), 36–42; Barlow *English Church*, 123–34; R. A. Brown, *The Normans and the Norman Conquest* (London, 1969), 69–74.

[11] Cyril Hart, 'The *Codex Wintoniensis* and the king's *haligdom*', *Agric HR* 18 (1970), suppl. 7–38, esp. 18–20, sees a central chancery and archives 'stored at Winchester during the whole of the three centuries following . . . 854' (p. 19). This view is in contrast to the current general position which favours, as with the treasury (see above, p. 290, n. 8), a minimal view of the chancery's development, at least until the very last years of the Anglo-Saxon kingdom, see Barlow *English Church*, 133–4, or P. Chaplais, 'The Anglo-Saxon Chancery: from the Diploma to the Writ', *Journal of the Society of Archivists*, 3 (1966), 160–76.

[12] This chapel *could* be the otherwise unrecorded church of St. George known from the route followed by funeral processions *c.* 1000 to lie in the general area of the palace: Worcester Cathedral Library, MS. F 173, fo. 21, printed and discussed by C. H. Turner in *JTS* 17 (1916), 65–8.

between the Old and New Minsters and the Winchester palace. They stood within a few paces of each other, and the *Codex Wintoniensis* may indicate the access enjoyed by Winchester clerics to royal records, perhaps in the course of providing whatever secretariat was required.[1]

It may thus be thought that the evidence for a pre-conquest palace in the heart of Winchester, although mostly circumstantial, is nevertheless compelling. We know almost nothing of the urban palaces of the Anglo-Saxon kings, although the evidence available for rural palaces,[2] and the illustrations in the Bayeux Tapestry of the Confessor's palace at Westminster,[3] may lead us to suppose a considerable complex of stone structures, probably not out of scale beside the two great churches of the Old and New Minsters. The palace of Otto the Great at Magdeburg, residence of Edith, daughter of Edward the Elder, and now shown by its recent discovery and excavation to have been one of the most remarkable creations of its age, should remind us of how much may still remain to be discovered in a period for which the English, like the German, written sources are in many respects meagre.[4]

The Norman palace

By 1086 the New Minster had acquired the manors of Alton and Clere (Kingsclere, Hants) from the Conqueror *pro excambio domus regis, . . . pro excambio terrae, in qua domus regis est in civitate*.[5] The sequence of events can be established from a series of documents copied into the *Liber Vitae* of New Minster. Here a memorandum in a fourteenth-century hand records that the domestic buildings (*officine*) of New Minster were destroyed by fire on 23 April 1065. According to this source William I obtained the site of the burnt-out buildings in exchange for the manors of Alton and Clere and in the fourth year of his reign (1069–70) built his *palacium cum aula sua* on the same site. The memorandum in question may have been in origin a twelfth-century document, but it cannot have been

---

[1] Hart, *Agric HR* 18 (1970), suppl. 18–20. There seems no real evidence for supposing that royal records were housed in the Old Minster rather than in a palace chapel, although the rebuilding of the minster in the later tenth century would have provided ample space, e.g. in the upper levels of the west work (see below, p. 307). It is perhaps relevant in this context to recall that according to the *Dialogus de Scaccario* the sacristan of Westminster Abbey by ancient privilege supplied the ink for the Exchequer. It has been conjectured, however, that the *Dialogus* originally read 'W.' at this point and not *Westmonasterii*, the reference being to the sacristan of Winchester Cathedral. This emendation was rejected by Poole, principally on the grounds that there was no connection between Winchester Cathedral and the royal palace, and in this he was reluctantly followed by Johnson. Poole's argument is, however, not only incorrect, but can be reversed on the grounds that at the time the *Dialogus* was written the connection between Winchester and both the treasury and the exchequer was older than and as close as the relation-

ship between those offices and Westminster Abbey. The sacristan at Westminster may thus have succeeded his counterpart at Winchester in a privilege which perhaps provides a small link between Winchester and the early royal administration (A. Hughes, C. G. Crump, and C. Johnson (ed.), *Dialogus de Scaccario* (Oxford, 1902), 65 (lines 26–7), 170; G. J. Turner, 'The Exchequer at Winchester', *EHR* 19 (1904), 286–7; R. L. Poole, *The Exchequer in the Twelfth Century* (Oxford, 1912), 79; C. Johnson (ed.), *Dialogus de Scaccario* (London, 1950), 12, n.).

[2] Reviewed in M. Biddle, 'Archaeology and the beginnings of English Society', in P. Clemoes and K. Hughes (eds.), *England Before the Conquest* (Cambridge, 1971), 399–402.

[3] R. A. Brown, 'The architecture', in F. M. Stenton (ed.), *The Bayeux Tapestry* (2nd edn., London, 1965), 80.

[4] See now Ernst Nickel in H. Jankuhn (ed.), op. cit. above, p. 289, n. 1.

[5] *DB*, fo. 43.

drawn up before 1143, since it includes events up to that date.[1] It is consistently incorrect in its quotation of calendar years, and two charters of William I's reign, also both recorded in the *Liber Vitae*, suggest that it may be confused, or at least incomplete, in its account of the land occupied by the new buildings of the palace. The first of these charters is a text in an eleventh-century hand which purports to be the original record of the grant of *c.* 1070 by which William gave Alton and Clere in exchange for the cemetery of the New Minster *quam ego ad aulam meam faciendam mutuo ab abbate accepi.*[2] The information that the Conqueror's hall was built on the cemetery of New Minster is confirmed by a New Minster grant of 1082–8,[3] and is implied by the terms of Henry I's confirmation of his father's grant in (?) 1116.[4]

That the situation was even more complex is shown by the entries in Survey **I**. These entries all concern an area on the south side of High Street, where twelve houses had been destroyed since the time of the Confessor *quia in eorum terris fuit facta domus regis.*[5] Some of these properties had been on the royal fief and some on the fief of the abbot of New Minster, but all had been taken into the king's house.[6] Five *monete* adjacent to these properties had also been destroyed by the king's order, probably to make way for the palace,[7] and a street had been blocked by the construction of the king's kitchen.[8]

The surviving records thus suggest that the land acquired by the Conqueror was made up of a number of different parcels, a strip of built-up land on the south side of High Street, the cemetery of New Minster, and perhaps also part of the site of the minster's domestic buildings. The exact location of these parcels can be quite closely determined using a variety of evidence, written, archaeological, and topographical, and by examining

---

[1] *LVH* 1–3. For further discussion of this memorandum and the inconsistency of the dates it gives, see below, p. 297, n. 3, and p. 300, n. 1, especially the latter for the date 1143 quoted here. The memorandum states that the *officine* of New Minster were burnt on the feast of St. George (23 Apr.), 1066, in the twenty-fourth year of Edward the Confessor, and the second year of Abbot Ælfwig. These indications are not consistent, for on any reckoning of the beginning of the year, Edward was dead by 23 Apr. 1066. His twenty-fourth year must, moreover, be calculated from his accession (? 8 June 1042), since if calculated from his coronation it would fall after his death: 24 Edward was thus June 1065 to 4/5 Jan. 1066. This would agree with what is known of Ælfwig's abbacy (D. Knowles, C. N. L. Brooke, and V. C. M. London (eds.), *The Heads of Religious Houses: England and Wales 940–1216* (Cambridge, 1972), 81), which may have begun at the end of 1063, his second year being more or less equivalent to the calendar year 1065, but Edward's twenty-fourth regnal year will still not fit a fire on 23 Apr. 1065. It is therefore necessary to suppose an error not only in '1066', but also in '24'. Edward's twenth-third year calculated from his coronation would have been 3 Apr. 1065 to 4/5 Jan. 1066; calculated from his accession it would have been June 1064– June 1065. On either basis it would agree with a fire on 23 Apr. 1065 in Ælfwig's second year. Since the facts

most likely to be correct are the day the fire occurred, the identity of the abbot (with perhaps the year of his abbacy), and the king's reign, if not his regnal year, 1064 and 1065 are the only possibilities, and the second the more likely. Errors in the other two dates given in calendar years in this memorandum suggest that these dates may all be insertions, and that no particular trust should be placed on '1066' in the present context.

[2] *LVH* 110–13; *Regesta*, i, no. 37. Although there seems no good reason for following Birch in regarding this entry in the *Liber Vitae* as the original record, personally attested by a ragged cross in the Conqueror's own hand, there seems equally little reason for the comment '? spurious' of the *Regesta*.

[3] *LVH* 163–4: *terra cimiterii aecclesiae nostrae in qua aula eius constructa est.*

[4] Ibid. 291; *Regesta*, ii, no. 1126: *terra illa in qua edificavit* [sc. *Willelmus*] *aulam suam in urbe Wintonie.* The land *ubi domus meus sedet in Wintonia* had always been free of gelds, murder-fines, pleas, and plaints (*LVH* 291), as had apparently the cemetery before it (ibid. 112), and these liberties were extended to the holding of Alton and Clere at the time of the exchange.

[5] I, 80/1.

[6] I, 57.

[7] I, 58, see below, pp. 397–9.

[8] I, 60, n. 1, cf. **59** and **61**; see also above, p. 280.

the problem both in the light of the pre-existing topography, and from a knowledge of the arrangement and tenurial situation following the destruction of the palace in 1141. The evidence is complex and can only be given here in outline.[1]

By 1066 the cemetery of New Minster seems to have extended across the whole north side of the pre-conquest palace, and was itself bounded to the north by a line of properties on the south side of High Street (Fig. 9).[2] The cemetery appears to have been separated from the monastic enclosure to the east by a street running south from High Street past the doors of the two minsters. There are good grounds for believing that the domestic buildings of New Minster lay at this time east of the street, immediately north of the church.[3] Later evidence relating to the site of the palace after its destruction suggests that the street was taken into the palace precinct at the time of its extension in *c.* 1070, but that the precinct itself did not extend east of the street.[4] If this was the case, the statement of the memorandum in the *Liber Vitae* that the Conqueror took the site of the minster's burnt-out domestic buildings for the construction of his palace and hall cannot be correct,[5] for this site will have lain outside and to the east of the greatest known extent of the palace. The memorandum appears, however, to have been confused on this point, as has already been shown. The alternative version, provided by the more nearly contemporary documents discussed above, that it was the cemetery of New Minster which was taken over for the extension of the palace, appears by contrast to be correct.[6]

The properties destroyed on the south side of High Street can also be identified with some certainty from records of later royal interest in their site, long after the destruction of the palace in 1141.[7] It is thus possible to establish that the area acquired by William I about 1070 for the construction of a new palace and hall extended from the northern boundary of the Anglo-Saxon palace north to High Street. It incorporated an already existing street to the east, and extended west as far as the limit of the New Minster cemetery, where there was perhaps already a lane running south to the north-west corner of the older palace and beyond (Fig. 9, *c.* 1110). The new site measured 110 m each way (1·2 ha), and may have more than doubled the area of the older palace. The complexities of its former tenure (one-quarter divided between the fees of the king and the abbot of New Minster, and three-quarters lying within the minster's precinct) are more than sufficient to explain the doubts expressed by the jurors of the county when they claimed in 1086 that the abbot had wrongly received Alton in exchange for the king's house, *quia domus erat regis.*[8]

In default of excavation, nothing is known of the composition or layout of the Norman palace, and there exists only Gerald the Welshman's comment: *domos regias apud*

[1] A full discussion will appear in Winchester Studies 4.

[2] See below, p. 315.

[3] See below, p. 315.

[4] This was the street blocked by the king's kitchen, see above, p. 293, n. 8.

[5] *LVH* 2.

[6] For the effect of this transaction on New Minster, see below, pp. 316–17.

[7] See below, pp. 299–301 and Appendix I. 1, p. 510, n. 1. For the interest of the castle (i.e. presumably of the constable) in the tenement at the extreme east end of this group of properties (now part of 28 High Street), see *SMW* 147–8, quoting WCA, Enrolments, m. 11, 11d. This relationship presumably reflects the constable's wider interests in the site of the former palace.

[8] *DB*, fo. 43.

Wintoniam . . . regiae Londoniensi non qualitate non quantitate secundas.[1] This statement can only be checked today by a comparison of the areas involved. The area of the Winchester palace during the Norman period, including a minimal figure for the Anglo-Saxon palace, the full extent of which southwards is unknown, was about 2 ha, compared with about 3·1 ha for the palace of Westminster at its greatest extent in the fourteenth century.[2] In this respect therefore Gerald's remarks may not be exaggerated.

There is little evidence relating to the use of the Winchester palace during the Norman period. The only document known to have been issued there is a diploma in favour of Abbot Baldwin of Bury St. Edmunds, dated 31 May 1081, *apud Wintoniam in palatio regio*.[3] Nor is the evidence about the king's treasure any more helpful. The treasure was certainly kept in the castle by 1135, and had probably been moved there before 1100,[4] but whether the move was made for security as soon as the castle had been built, or whether the treasure remained in the palace during the latter part of the eleventh century, is not recorded, although the building of a new hall *c*. 1070 implies that there was no intention initially of running down the old palace in favour of a new residence in the castle. In the years when the Conqueror's hall was new, and the Norman cathedral beginning to rise, appearances must have been quite the reverse.

These were the years when the Norman kings were frequently in Winchester. Of the twenty-one Easters of the Conqueror's reign, ten were spent in France, five in Winchester, and the remaining six in unknown places. These feasts apart, William is only known to have been in Winchester at Whitsun 1081.[5] William II's movements are more obscure, but he was certainly in Winchester after his coronation in 1087, at Easter 1095, again at Easter 1100, and perhaps immediately before his death that August. His charters suggest further visits in 1087–9 (twice?) and in 1093. He had intended to celebrate Easter at Winchester in 1097, but was delayed in France by bad weather on the crossing; his arrival in England two years later about Easter Day 1099 might again suggest the intention of celebrating the feast in Winchester, close to his likely ports of landing.[6] With Henry I the situation is much clearer: of his thirty-five Easters on the throne, seventeen were celebrated in France, six in Winchester, ten elsewhere in England (never more than once in any one place, except three times at Woodstock), and in two years there was no ceremony. Henry was also in Winchester in August 1100 on his accession, in July, August, and October 1101,

[1] Giraldus Cambrensis, *Vita S. Remigii*, cap. 27, in *Opera* (ed. J. F. Dimock, RS, 1877), vii. 46. Gerald was writing *c*. 1198, when he was about fifty years old. Although not a contemporary witness, he had been under the patronage of Henry of Blois and was thus in a reasonable position to know the facts. Gerald's reference to the London palace should certainly refer to Westminster by the date he was writing.

[2] Calculated from Colvin (ed.) *King's Works*, plan box, plan III. The boundaries of the eleventh- and twelfth-century palace are not known.

[3] *Bury*, 50–5 (n. 7), esp. p. 55, n. 3, and on the authenticity of the charter, pp. xxxii–xxxiv. This is apparently only the second occurrence of the word *palatium* in relation to the Winchester palace, the terminology of which is as follows: *c*. 1000, *de palatio regis*,

regis in obsequio (poet.); 1017, *regni solium* (fig.); *c*. 1070, 1082–8, *c*. 1116, 1212, *aula*; 1081, *in palatio regio*; 1086, *c*. 1110, *domus regis*; *c*. 1114–33, *domus mea propria*; *c*. 1143, *palacium cum aula, palacium regis cum aula, aulam . . . et palacium*; *c*. 1198, *domos regias*.

[4] See below, pp. 304–5, and cf. above, p. 291.

[5] *Regesta*, i, pp. xxi–xxii, and the charters calendared in that volume are the principal source; see also F. M. Powicke and E. B. Fryde, *Handbook of British Chronology* (London, 2nd edn., 1961), 31, for absences abroad; and D. C. Douglas, *William the Conqueror* (London, 1964), 449–53, and *passim*.

[6] Sources as for William the Conqueror, but see also E. A. Freeman, *The Reign of William Rufus* (Oxford, 1882), s.v. 'Winchester', and *ASC*, s.a. 1095, 1100.

possibly in 1106 and 1107, in 1111, in August 1114, after the middle of September 1115, in February and in April–May 1121, possibly in 1122, in January and at Whitsun 1127, in September–October, and at Christmas 1129, in the middle months of 1130, and in April–May and in June 1133.[1]

The famous annal for 1086 which describes how the Conqueror 'wore his royal crown three times a year as often as he was in England: at Easter at Winchester, at Whitsuntide at Westminster, at Christmas at Gloucester', and how 'on these occasions all the great men of England were assembled about him',[2] is fully borne out, if only as regards Winchester, by the more detailed evidence of the chronicles and charters. The custom was not perhaps introduced by the Conqueror,[3] nor did it lapse with his reign. Both William II and Henry I maintained their father's practice, at least until the earlier years of Henry's reign. On the day of his coronation Henry I issued a writ ordering certain gifts to be made to the monks and chanters of Westminster, Winchester, and Gloucester, on all those feasts on which, as his predecessors had done, he wore his crown in their churches.[4] The first four Easters of his reign (1101–4) were spent in Winchester, and the Easter of 1108, but there was then an interval of fifteen years before he next celebrated Easter in the city in 1123. It was to be fifty-three years before a king again celebrated the feast in Winchester in 1176, and during this period only eighteen other royal visits are recorded, seven by Henry I,[5] five by Stephen, and six by Henry II.[6]

It looks very much as if the close connection between Winchester and the ceremonial of the king's court lapsed during the latter part of Henry I's reign. By this time the treasury, as we shall see, may have been located in the castle, where there is archaeological evidence for extensive alterations and additions during the first part of the century. A decline in the use of the old palace may have been hastened both by the growth of more suitable accommodation in the castle, and by the king's choice of other venues for his Easter courts. If this led to the decay of the palace, perhaps from an unwillingness to maintain two royal dwellings in the same city, it will have reacted in turn on the suita-

[1] *Regesta*, ii, pp. xxix–xxxi; see also the index of the *Regesta* for charters given at Winchester on dates quoted here but not included in the itinerary.

[2] *ASC*, s.a. 1086 [1087]; trans. G. N. Garmonsway, *The Anglo-Saxon Chronicle* (London, 1953), 219–20; cf. William of Malmesbury, *Vita Wulfstani* (ed. R. R. Darlington, Camden 3rd ser. 40, 1928), 34. For a slightly variant tradition, see *Winchester ann*, s.a. 1073. Crown-wearings were suitable occasions for other ceremonies, particularly the marriage and coronation of queens (Richardson and Sayles, 409). It is not known whether such events took place in Winchester, although there were certainly councils and other meetings there on several Easters (e.g. 1072, 1103, and 1133), presumably to take advantage of the presence together at one time of a large number of important persons.

[3] Above, p. 290, esp. Biddle, op. cit. in n. 7.

[4] *Regesta*, ii, no. 490; Richardson and Sayles, 217.

[5] Symeon of Durham (*Historia regum*, cap. 214, in *Opera omnia* (ed. T. Arnold, RS 1885), ii. 283)

writes of Henry's visit to Winchester after Michaelmas 1129 in terms appropriate to the kind of gathering that attended a crown-wearing (*comitantibus archiepiscopis, episcopis, abbatibus, et pene totius Angliae primatibus*). There seems to be no other evidence for regular visits to Winchester at this season, although Professor Barlow has pointed out (*Edward the Confessor* (London, 1970), 186) that Edward the Confessor's celebration of Easter at Winchester could have been connected with treasury accounting. If this were the case a king's presence at or after Michaelmas, for the principal audit of the year, would seem likely, at least on occasion. The only recorded possibilities are, however, Oct. 1101, Sept. 1115, and Sept.–Oct. 1129.

[6] *Regesta*, iii, pp. xxxix–xliv, xlviii; L. F. Salzman, *Henry II* (London, 1917), 241–51. In the latter part of his reign Henry II was frequently in Winchester, at Easter 1176, 1179, and possibly 1188, at Christmas 1178 and 1181, and on nine other recorded occasions between 1176 and his death in 1189.

bility of Winchester for these ceremonies. When Richard I was crowned in Winchester on the Octave of Easter 1194, he moved down from the castle to spend the night before his coronation in the cathedral priory, from whence he went in procession to the church the following morning.[1] By this time the old palace had long been destroyed, but if it was already in decay, or in other ways unfitted for royal accommodation, by the middle or latter part of Henry I's reign, the ceremony of crown-wearing would have involved a long procession from the castle, rather than the very short route from the old palace to the cathedral. The arrangements for Richard I's coronation show that this was a significant consideration, although not one which would affect the king's presence in the city, and residence in the castle, on other occasions.

The evidence for the decline in royal use of the palace may help to explain some peculiarities in its later history. Among the more striking points is the lack of contemporary comment on its destruction. This is recorded only in the memorandum in the *Liber Vitae* to which reference has already been made.[2] On Saturday 2 August 1141[3] Winchester was burnt by Henry of Blois's forces, together with most of its churches, St. Mary's Abbey, *et totum palacium Regis cum aula sua*.[4] If the palace had still been a major royal residence, it is most unlikely that its burning would have passed unnoticed by all except a local record specifically concerned with parochial reorganization consequent upon the damage to the city.

It is also remarkable that there appears at first sight to be no comment upon the part played by the palace during the events in Winchester which led up to its destruction. It is possible, however, that the palace was no longer a royal house, and that its buildings, and even the land on which they stood, had passed to the bishop. This seems at least to be the implication of such evidence as survives. Most striking is the description by the author of the *Gesta Stephani* of Henry of Blois's residences in Winchester: 'castellum . . . episcopi, quod venustissimo constructum cemate in civitatis medio locarat, sed et domum illius, quam ad instar castelli fortiter et inexpugnabiliter firmarat',[5] words which imply two distinct buildings, of which one must be Wolvesey, while the other can only have been the royal palace.[6]

[1] Roger of Hoveden, *Chronica* (ed. W. Stubbs, RS, 1868–71), iii. 246.

[2] *LVH* 2–3.

[3] This date, and the date of Thursday, 31 July, given a few lines earlier for the arrival of the empress's forces in Winchester, are both correct for the year 1141, although 1140 is given in the text (*LVH* 2, line 16). The true date of these events is, of course, 1141.

[4] This statement is not entirely trustworthy. For reasons which will become apparent, it is unlikely that the palace was itself burnt by Henry of Blois's forces rather than by those of his opponents. The document omits the burning of Hyde Abbey, and probably exaggerates the extent of the destruction of the city and churches. The former can perhaps be explained by supposing that the document was solely concerned with the earlier history and proposed reorganization of land in the central area of the city. For the latter see below, p. 386, and cf. *Gesta Stephani*, cap. 65, *Historia Novella*, cap. 499; Continuator of Florence of Worcester, *Chronicon ex chronicis* (ed. B. Thorpe, London, 1848–9), ii. 133. For Hyde Abbey, see below, pp. 318–19.

[5] *Gesta Stephani*, cap. 63. R. H. C. Davis has attributed the authorship of the *Gesta* to Robert of Lewes, an associate of Henry of Blois and himself bishop of Bath from 1136 onwards (*EHR* 77 (1962), 209–32). This attribution enhances the value of the *Gesta*'s evidence regarding Henry of Blois, and the fact that the bishop of Bath held a property in Winchester (**II, 476**) might give added weight to the *Gesta*'s comments on the situation in the city.

[6] This interpretation has been put forward independently by R. H. C. Davis, *King Stephen 1135–1154* (London, 1967), 64, n. 24.

The problem is to identify which is which. The matter is discussed below in some detail in connection with the bishop's palace at Wolvesey.[1] Assuming that the author of the *Gesta* was consistent in his use of *castellum*, it appears that this building should be identified with the royal palace, and that the *domus* should therefore be equated with Wolvesey. The position of the castle *in civitatis medio* supports this view.

The account given by the *Gesta* of the course of events in Winchester in August 1141 shows that while both the *domus* and the *castellum* were besieged, it was on the *castellum* that action was concentrated.[2] It was from here that fire-brands were launched by the bishop's forces, and the identification of the *castellum* with the centrally-placed royal palace makes it easier to understand how these could have set fire to the city, for Wolvesey is sited too far away from the built-up area for this to have been probable. The *Gesta*'s reference to the use of fire is paralleled by William of Malmesbury's statement that the brands were thrown *ex turre pontificis*.[3] This evidence implies that the *turris* formed part of the castle and was thus located at the royal palace, rather than at Wolvesey, as has previously been believed. It is possible that the bishop had more than one *turris* in Winchester, but the normal meaning of the word at this date is 'keep', in the sense in which this is applied today to the principal component of a twelfth-century castle. It is perhaps unlikely that the bishop possessed two such structures in a single city. The Winchester annal describing Henry of Blois's construction of a *turris fortissima* in 1138 is likely therefore to refer to the same building as the *turris pontificis* mentioned by Malmesbury, and now apparently to be identified as forming part of the *castellum* at the royal palace.[4]

The evidence would seem to suggest, therefore, that Henry of Blois had acquired the royal palace by 1138, and that he then constructed a keep there and carried out various alterations which converted it into a building which the author of the *Gesta* could call a castle, *venustissimo constructum cemate*.[5]

[1] See below, pp. 325–7. The interpretation now offered is different from that which has been put forward (e.g. in *II–IX Interims*) with regard to Wolvesey, and differs from the generally accepted tradition that Wolvesey was the centre of the fighting. The evidence relating to the royal palace has never been discussed in detail, however, and it is now apparent that the two buildings cannot be considered in isolation one from the other. It is worth noting, with regard to the royal palace, that even if the traditional view of Wolvesey's part in the actions of 1141 were to be maintained (on the basis that the *castellum* and Wolvesey are to be equated), the *Gesta*'s description of the *domus* (which would on this view be the royal palace) still implies that Henry of Blois had carried out alterations and additions there. Either interpretation leads therefore to the conclusion that the bishop had undertaken building works at the royal palace. The matter can probably be settled by excavation of the royal palace site, and of the unexcavated south-western quarter of Wolvesey: see Addenda to p. 324, n. 3.

[2] *Gesta*, cap. 63–5; see below, p. 325, Table 10.

[3] *Historia Novella*, cap. 499: *ex turre pontificis iaculatum incendium in domos burgensium*; cf. *Gesta*,

cap. 65: *ignibus foras* [sc. *ex castello*] *emissis maiorem civitatis partem . . . in fauillas penitus redegerunt*.

[4] *Winchester ann.*, s.a. For a further discussion of this annal and its interpretation, see below, pp. 325–6.

[5] *Gesta*, cap. 63. These words do not necessarily relate only to Henry of Blois's works (as K. R. Potter's translation implies, p. 84), but more probably to the impression given by the building complex as a whole, which must by now have consisted of many periods. The clause, quoted in full on p. 297, is fraught with difficulties, and it should be noted that the same editor's translation of *locarat* is perhaps not entirely satisfactory. The primary meaning of *locāre* given by Ducange is to 'hire', 'lease', or 'rent', *conducere*; the secondary meaning is 'to occupy', or 'live in', *habitare*. The pluperfect *locarat* might thus be translated 'had leased' or 'had occupied', 'had been living in'. The former would have interesting implications for the nature of the bishop's interest in the palace, but would probably not be sufficient to explain the control he exercised over its site and buildings. The latter, following only a few words after the *Gesta*'s account of Henry's flight from the city, seems more appropriate.

If the bishop had thus acquired the royal palace, it would help to explain a passage written by Gaimar in 1139, the straight forward interpretation of which is that there was then a chained copy of the Anglo-Saxon Chronicle in the bishop's residence at Winchester, and that it was believed to have been placed there by Alfred.[1] Whether Alfred's involvement was more than a tradition is immaterial, for if the book had been chained *en l'eveskez* long before 1139, it cannot have been in either of the Norman halls at Wolvesey, both of which had been recently built.[2] The book could, however, quite properly have been kept in the royal palace, and if this were now in the bishop's hands, Gaimar's use of *eveskez* may have been quite correct and comparable to the use of the phrase *castellum episcopi* by the author of the *Gesta*.

A further piece of evidence for the use of the royal palace by the bishop concerns its final demolition (as opposed to its burning). Gerald the Welshman recounts how Henry of Blois seized the opportunity to demolish the royal buildings, because they stood inconveniently close to his cathedral, and how he carried away their materials to build his own residence in the city.[3] This was, Gerald claims, an abuse of his public authority, carried out suddenly and in haste. Whatever one makes of Gerald's comments, it remains that Henry had the power to carry out the demolition. It must have followed his acquisition of the site in the 1130s and may have taken place between the burning of the palace in August 1141[4] and the reorganization of its site in 1143.[5] This was the opportunity the bishop seized *raptim et subito . . . et in majorem publicae potestatis offensam*.

The evidence relating to the bishop's interest in the palace extends beyond its buildings to the land on which they stood (Fig. 19). An analysis of the properties in High Street in 1148 shows that the street frontage formerly occupied by the palace on the south side of the street was then apparently in the bishop's fief.[6] The strip of land forming the western margin of the palace site (subsequently the Constabulary, the area between Little and Great Minster Streets) seems also to have been in the bishop's hands by this time.[7] Since there had previously been palace buildings on the south side of High Street, and probably also along the western strip, the properties listed in the 1148

---

[1] Geffrei Gaimar, *L'Estoire des Engleis* (ed. A. Bell, Anglo-Norman Text Society, Oxford, 1960), lines 2334–40. See U. T. Holmes and M. A. Klenke, *Chrétien, Troyes and the Grail* (Chapel Hill, N.C., 1959), 14–15, and cf. Martin Biddle, 'Wolvesey: the *domus quasi palatium* of Henry de Blois in Winchester', *Château Gaillard*, 3 (ed. A. J. Taylor, London and Chichester, 1969), 32, n. 17.

[2] See below, pp. 326–7.

[3] Loc. cit. above, p. 295, n. 1:

domos regias apud Wintoniam, ecclesiae ipsius atrio nimis enormiter imminentes, . . . quoniam cathedrali ecclesiae . . . nimium vicinae fuerant et onerosae, . . . funditus in brevi, raptim et subito, nacta solum temporis opportunitate, dejecit; et in majorem publicae potestatis offensam, ex dirutis aedificiis et abstractis domos episcopales egregias sibi in eadem urbe construxit.

[4] We cannot be absolutely certain that the palace was burnt on the same day as the other parts of the city

(see above, p. 297, nn. 3 and 4). If it was the building held by the bishop's forces, from which were thrown the fire-brands which caused the other destruction in the city, it is unlikely that it was destroyed by his own forces on the same occasion. Nevertheless, the equation of the royal palace with the *castellum*, and the siege of the latter, provides an obvious explanation of how the royal palace came to be burnt at some stage in the fighting. It may be noted that Robert, earl of Gloucester, was lodged in the immediate area during the latter part of the siege (*in vicino sancti Swithuni hospitatus*: *Historia Novella*, cap. 500; and see **II, 139** for one of his own properties here).

[5] See below, p. 300; and for further comment on the date of the demolition and the use made of the materials, p. 326.

[6] **II, 112–26**; see above, p. 246, and below, pp. 353–5 and Appendix I. 1, p. 510, n. 1.

[7] **II, 129–37**; see above, p. 246, and below, p. 354 and Appendix I. 1, p. 510, n. 1.

survey can only have come into being after the burning and subsequent demolition of the palace.

It was to regularize the parochial difficulties, which had arisen from this destruction and as a result of the burning of city churches, that the bishop called a diocesan synod on 12 November, probably in 1143.[1] At this meeting it was decided that all the land which William the Conqueror had received in exchange from New Minster for the building of his hall and palace should be assigned in perpetuity to St. Laurence's church. The memorandum recording these decisions breaks off at this point, but had it continued it might have clarified some of the uncertainties which arise when the extent of St. Laurence's parish is compared with our other information relating to the land acquired by the Conqueror. When it first becomes possible to establish the limits of the parish in the eighteenth century, its extent includes a small part of the High Street frontage and the whole of the Constabulary strip discussed above, but excludes the north-western angle of the cathedral cemetery, which was extra-parochial.[2] There have certainly been many changes in the boundaries of the parish, but there is good evidence for the boundaries of the cathedral cemetery in the mid fourteenth century, which shows that there was encroachment on to the cemetery in the area of the present Square (cf. Fig. 32).[3] The early boundaries of the cemetery and the later boundaries of the parish suggest therefore that the land assigned to St. Laurence's church in 1143 can never have included *all* the land (*tota illa terra*) once occupied by the Conqueror's hall and palace, but must have excluded that part which had formerly been the New Minster cemetery, while including the greater part (or originally the whole) of the area acquired by the Conqueror along High Street.[4] There was also added to the parish, for reasons not now obvious, the western strip later known as the Constabulary.

These considerations show that the bishop was able to make fundamental rearrangements in the layout of the site of the former palace. It was divided up, by and large, into

[1] *LVH* 1–3. This memorandum, already discussed in various contexts above (p. 293, n. 1, and p. 297, n. 3), was probably in origin a record of the meeting, the date of which is given as 12 Nov. 1150, in the fourteenth year of Henry of Blois's consecration. The bishop's fourteenth year was, however, 17 Nov. 1142 to 16 Nov. 1143, so that the date cannot stand as it is given. The memorandum is in error on both previous occasions where it has used the calendar year, although in both cases the other indications of date appear correct or at least reconcilable. It seems possible therefore that the calendar years were inserted subsequent to the drawing up of the original, perhaps even in the fourteenth century when the document was finally copied in the form in which it survives. Henry of Blois's movements give little help in deciding between 1143 and 1150 (see below, p. 320, n. 2 and p. 493), but the stage of redevelopment reached in this area by the time of Survey **II** in 1148 may suggest that the earlier date is preferable. There is moreover independent evidence that a legatine council was held at Winchester in September 1143 (T. Arnold (ed.), *Symeonis monachi historia regum . . . continuata* (RS, 1882–5), ii. 315). Bishop Henry was present at a council in London on 10 Nov. 1143 (*Waverly ann*, s.a.) and at a legatine council on 30 Nov. 1143, also in London (L. Voss, *Heinrich von Blois* (Berlin, 1932), 48, n. 44). It is possible that the business of the Winchester parishes was transacted on the occasion of either the September council, or one of the earlier gatherings in Winchester that year (Voss, op. cit. 46–8), and that the Hyde author or copyist confused this meeting with a record of the earlier of the November councils in some local source, such as the Waverley annals. Chronological confusion might also arise from the fact that there was probably a considerable gathering of clergy and laity in Winchester on the occasion of Bishop Henry's translation of the relics of the kings and bishops, perhaps in 1150 (*Winchester ann*, s.a.; another cathedral priory source dates the translation to 1158: Goodman *Chartulary*, no. 4). Lena Voss (op. cit. 87) accepted 1150 without comment as the date of the meeting to reorganize the Winchester parishes, as did J. H. Round, *Geoffrey de Mandeville* (London, 1892), 127, n.

[2] William Godson, *Map . . . of Winchester* (Basing, 1750).   [3] *I Interim*, 180–1; and see also *SMW*.

[4] Above, p. 294.

the units out of which it had been formed. Those areas that had been urban property in the fiefs of the king and the abbot of New Minster were returned to urban uses, but in the bishop's fief. The New Minster cemetery reverted to ecclesiastical use, but since the rest of the minster's site had been returned to the cathedral when the minster moved to Hyde Abbey in 1110,[1] the old cemetery now became an extension of the cathedral cemetery, which thus included from this time the entire site of New Minster. The third component of the Conqueror's palace, namely the ancient palace of the Anglo-Saxon kings, disappeared without trace. The northern part of its site must have been taken into the cathedral cemetery, west and north-west of the west front of the Norman cathedral. The southern part, stretching for an unknown distance southwards towards the city wall, was taken into the cathedral precinct to form part or the whole of the great court and gardens west of the cloister.[2] The completion of these new arrangements was probably marked by the construction of the Close Wall, as it exists today along Symonds Street and St. Swithun Street, together with its former extension north from the minster gate towards St. Laurence church, along the boundary between the Constabulary and the cathedral cemetery (Fig. 9, c. 1148, cf. Fig. 32).[3]

By 1148 the properties in the bishop's fief on parts of the site of the former palace seem to have been extensively developed and were held by relatively wealthy and prominent people.[4] By the early thirteenth century, however, these properties were once more in the royal fief, and it may perhaps be assumed that Henry of Blois lost possession of them at the time of the Treaty of Winchester in November 1153, on Henry II's accession, or during his exile in France in the years before 1158.[5]

The evidence shows that Henry of Blois exercised full control over the site and buildings of the royal palace in the centre of Winchester, but does not provide any indication as to when he or William Giffard, his predecessor as bishop (1100–29), had acquired this authority. The regular sequence of Easter crown-wearings was broken after 1108, and although Henry I was frequently in Winchester after that year, he may well have resided at the castle. The move of New Minster to Hyde Abbey in 1110, and the return of its site to the cathedral, caused great changes in the area immediately east of the palace,[6] but there is no reason to suppose any connection between this event and a change in the status of the palace. At the time of Survey I, in c. 1110 or perhaps as late as 1115,[7] the properties on the king's fief held by royal officials were noticeably concentrated in High Street, to either side of and opposite the palace, or in the streets immediately to the west (Fig. 21, inset). By 1148, the more complete picture provided by Survey II shows a looser distribution which perhaps reflects the decline and destruction of the palace, but does not suggest any concentration of officials' interests around the castle (Fig. 21).[8]

[1] Below, p. 317.

[2] T. D. Atkinson, 'Winchester Cathedral Close', *Proc Hants FC* 15.1 (1941), Pl. II, opp. p. 12.

[3] Visible details of flintwork and ashlar show that the present Close Wall is in origin a twelfth-century structure. Since this was written, the position of its 'extension' northwards, called 'Constable's Wall' has been re-interpreted: see Addenda and cf. above, p. 299.

[4] II, 112–26, 129–37, and notes to the entries. For

John son of Ralph holding the guildhall on the site of the palace in 1148 (II, 140, 143, and 155), see below, pp. 336, 423.

[5] See below, pp. 353–4; and Appendix I. 1, p. 510, n. 1. For the possibility that his castle on the palace site was slighted in 1155–6, see below, pp. 326, n. 5.

[6] Below, p. 317.

[7] For this date, see below, p. 410.

[8] See also below, pp. 387–92.

The distribution of properties held by royal officials perhaps implies that the palace was still the principal royal residence as late as the middle of Henry I's reign. It was probably declining, however, during Henry's later years, being gradually replaced by the royal residence in the castle. When Stephen entered Winchester in December 1135 to secure the royal treasure, he was warmly greeted by the bishop, his brother.[1] It seems most likely that it was on this occasion, or shortly afterwards, that Henry of Blois obtained the ancient palace from the king's hands.[2]

ii. THE CASTLE (Figs. 26, 27, and 32)

The date of the original construction of Winchester castle was obscured for many years by E. A. Freeman's view that the name *Guenta* used in this context by William of Poitiers referred not to Winchester but to Norwich. This interpretation was rejected by Professor Frank Barlow in 1964, and there need now be no hesitation in accepting that Winchester castle was built, or at least commenced, between Christmas 1066 and the following February.[3] The existence of the castle by the beginning of the 1070s is further shown by a contemporary record of the Easter council held there in 1072 *in capella regia, quae sita est in castello*, to discuss the dispute that had arisen between Canterbury and York over the primacy.[4]

Although this is the sum of the reliable documentary evidence relating to the castle before the early years of the twelfth century,[5] quite detailed information regarding its arrangement and development is now available as a result of excavation.[6] South of West Gate the Roman defences swung westwards to form at the south-west corner of the town a large salient, 244 m from north to south and 61 m wide. This area was as fully occupied as any other part of Winchester during the late Saxon period, and was traversed by a north–south street, and surrounded to north, west, and south by an intra-mural street running just within the line of the Roman walls.[7] The castle was formed within this salient by the construction of a line of bank and ditch cutting off the area from the remainder of the city. The Roman town wall, still in use, became the defensive perimeter of the castle to north, west, and south; the new earthworks formed the fourth side.[8]

[1] *Gesta Stephani*, cap. 3.

[2] Sometime between 1114 and 1133 Henry issued a precept that the land of Hyde and that taken in exchange by the abbey should be as free of gelds and other charges as the original site of the abbey, and as *domus mea propria et homines qui in ea manent* (*Regesta*, ii, no. 1886; *Monasticon*, ii. 445). The *homines* may have been royal servants, thus implying royal use of the palace and some permanent staff as late as the second half of the reign. The clause may, however, suggest that there were already by this time other persons dwelling in the palace and enjoying its liberties. It is perhaps striking the single word *homines* is used, rather than *homines mei*. Such a situation could only have arisen with royal permission. See Addenda.

[3] F. Barlow, 'Guenta', *Antiq J* 44 (1964), 217–19.

[4] The phrase quoted appears in a clause at the end of the confirmation of this council issued at Windsor the following Whitsun (D. Wilkins, *Concilia*, i (1737),

325); best text in T. A. M. Bishop and P. Chaplais (eds.), *Facsimiles of English Royal Writs to A.D. 1100* (Oxford, 1957), Pl. xxix opp. Both this confirmation and the document drawn up to record the decisions taken in the chapel of Winchester castle survive in the original (Canterbury Cathedral Archives, MSS. Ch. Ant. A1) (the confirmation) and A2 (the Winchester record). The latter (not containing the clause in question) was reproduced by *The Palaeolographical Society*, vol. i, pt. 10 (London, 1880), pl. 170.

[5] The *Winchester ann* (s.a. 1072) record the captivity of Stigand *in Wintoniae oppido*, information which is repeated by later writers of equally uncertain reliability (*Anglia Sacra*, i. 250).

[6] A full account will appear in Winchester Studies 6. See also *II Interim* and *VI–X Interims*.

[7] See above, pp. 278–80.

[8] William of Poitiers was precisely correct in stating that the castle was built within the walls: *Gesta*

The area taken for the new castle and its eastern defences was about 2·3 ha (5·7 acres). The destruction was considerable, and is vividly revealed by the streets and buildings found in excavation buried beneath or within the Norman ramparts. These events are barely reflected in the written record, for the well-known reference in Survey **I** to the *vicus* destroyed *quando rex fecit facere suum fossatum*[1] falls in the section relating to the area outside West Gate, and must imply the suppression of an extra-mural street, probably a lane or 'twichen' running from north to south outside and parallel to the west side of the salient. This would imply that the ditch outside the city wall was widened in connection with the building of the castle. Only one entry seems to reflect the destruction within the walls: the street or *vicus* next to West Gate, on the south side of High Street, which by *c.* 1110 had been taken into a house belonging to Hugh son of Albuchon and Henry de Port.[2] This street is probably to be identified with the north–south street found in excavation below the castle earthworks, but there remains the question of why the survey contains no specific account of properties along it, since the excavations showed that the area had been fully developed. A simple but probably incorrect answer might be that there had been no properties in the street owing rents or services to the crown in the time of the Confessor. It is perhaps more likely that the street had been simply obliterated, and that the surveyors of *c.* 1110 saw no point in repeating information from the *TRE* survey that was of no possible relevance.[3] Even the name of the street has now been lost.

Before 1155 there is virtually no documentary evidence relating either to the topography of the castle or to the 'king's houses' within it.[4] From then onwards, with the commencement of the surviving series of Pipe Rolls, work on some part of the structure is recorded in almost every year.[5] These entries show that there was concentrated within the castle in the second half of the twelfth century 'that complex of halls, chambers and chapels which constituted a medieval palace'.[6] The problems are to decide how early this complex was formed, and the relationship which it bore to the royal palace in the centre of the city.[7]

Archaeological evidence, although as yet confined to the northern end of the castle, provides a clear picture of the development of that part of the structure during the later eleventh and twelfth centuries. Whether or not a motte at the south end of the site formed part of the original layout, the northern end of the defended area was reasonably open, and here an apsidal stone chapel was built in the years immediately after 1067.[8] There are unlikely to have been two chapels within the castle so soon after its construction.

Guillelmi, bk. ii, cap. 36 (ed. Raymonde Foreville, *Les Classiques de l'histoire de France au Moyen Âge* (1952), 238).

[1] **I, 81.** [2] **I, 40.**

[3] This was not the case in High Street, in relation to the properties removed to make way for the extension of the palace (**I, 57**), since the surveyors were there under some obligation to make their figures tally with those of the *TRE* survey (**I, 80/1**).

[4] The existence of the castle gate in approximately its later position by 1114 is shown by the agreement that

the Palm Sunday processions from Hyde Abbey and the cathedral should meet *supra castellum* and *ante portam castelli* on their way to St. James's church. Since they must have been moving west along *Wodestret*, the agreement probably also implies the existence by this date of a street leading from the gate into *Wodestret*. See above, pp. 263 and 268.

[5] Colvin (ed.) *King's Works*, ii. 854–7.

[6] Ibid. 855.

[7] See above, pp. 296–7.

[8] *VIII Interim*, 290, Fig. 2, pls. xli, xlii; *X Interim*, 104–9.

This, and the quality of the masonry, the presence of internal wall-paintings, and the use of coloured glass in the windows, combine to suggest that this building should be identified with the *capella regia* of 1072.

Within a very short time the northern apex of the castle was strengthened by the construction of an earthen platform revetted by timber to the west and south.[1] The chapel lay immediately adjacent to the timber revetment, which was curved to avoid the north-east angle of the nave. The chapel's situation was now unfavourable, and became more so when the timberwork was soon replaced by a stone retaining-wall, although this wall was again angled to avoid the nave and chancel. Finally, the earthen platform was replaced by an immense stone keep, the chapel supressed, and the area south of the original platform filled to a depth of 3 m, burying the chapel walls. The construction of the keep can probably be attributed to Henry I. It marks the completion of the first stage in the development of a strong-point at the northern end of the castle, designed to command and control the West Gate of the city.[2]

The archaeological evidence demonstrates the importance and scale of these otherwise unrecorded changes through which the castle passed in the later eleventh and twelfth centuries. It shows the development of a complex defensive system apparently based on strong-points at the north and south ends of the site. The former was certainly an addition, and there is no reason to suppose that the southern motte was necessarily part of the original plan. The evidence both written and structural also suggests that provision was made from the castle's earliest years for the accommodation of the royal household. Where there was a *capella regia*, in which both the Conqueror and his queen took part in the council of 1072, there is likely also to have been a royal hall and chambers.

The extension of the royal palace in the centre of the city by William the Conqueror shows that the relationship between the palace and the castle was not a simple one.[3] The Norman castle and its new royal buildings were not intended to replace the ancient palace, although they may have done so for a short period while the palace was being enlarged and rebuilt.

The location of the treasury between 1066 and 1141, for which there is a little evidence, clarifies, to some extent, the relative functions of these two royal houses. Before 1066 the treasure can only have been kept in the central palace, for the castle had not been built. After the destruction of this palace in 1141, and for as long as the treasury remained in Winchester, it must have been located in the castle, except perhaps from the later years of the civil war.[4] The problem is to decide where it was in the seventy-five years between 1066 and 1141. The earliest indication is provided by Ordericus Vitalis. Writing about 1130 of the events following the death of William Rufus, he describes Henry hurrying *ad arcem Guentoniae ubi regalis thesaurus continebatur*.[5] Here the meaning of *arx* is almost certainly 'castle', rather than a general reference to the walled town, and this view is perhaps supported by a plea of *c.* 1111 made before the queen *in curia domini*

---

[1] A penny of William I's third type of *c.* 1070–2 (?) was found below this earthwork, ibid. 105.

[2] *VIII Interim*, 291–2.

[3] See above, p. 295.

[4] R. A. Brown, ' "The Treasury" of the later twelfth century', in J. Conway Davies (ed.), *Studies Presented to Sir Hilary Jenkinson* (Oxford, 1957), 35–49.

[5] Ordericus Vitalis, *Ecclesiastica Historia* (ed. A. Le Prévost, Paris, 1838–55), iv. 87.

mei et mea apud Wintoniam in thesauro, said by the Abingdon Chronicle to have been held *in castello*.[1] Although the Chronicle is not an entirely reliable source, and the phrase *in castello* could be an addition, there is nevertheless some further evidence to show that the treasury was already located in the castle by the end of Henry I's reign.

In 1135 William of Pont de l'Arche, sheriff of the counties of Hampshire and Wiltshire and custodian of Winchester castle, delivered to Stephen on his accession *ditissimum regis Henrici aerarium . . . cum castello*, having previously refused Henry of Blois's request *ut castellum sibi traderet, thesauros aperiret*.[2] In 1141 Henry handed over to the empress Matilda *castello et regni corona . . . thesaurisque, quos licet perpaucos rex ibi reliquerat*.[3] The sequence of action implied by the second of these entries, the association of the castle and treasury in each of them, and the force of *ibi* in the third, all suggest that the treasury was located within the castle, and had been there since before the death of Henry I. The association of the custody of the castle and of the treasury is also of interest in view of the connection which the constable of the castle enjoyed in later times with parts of the site of the former palace.[4] Although this connection may simply reflect the assignment to the constable of rents from the site, it may imply an older arrangement in which he was responsible for the security of the treasury while it was still located within the ancient palace.

From the admittedly scanty evidence it would seem that some accommodation for the royal household was provided within the castle from the time of its original construction. But the extention and rebuilding of the central palace about 1070 must imply that the Conqueror intended to make that complex, rather than the new castle, his principal residence in the city, and may also mean that the treasury was still in its former location. By 1135, however, and perhaps as early as 1100, the treasury was in the castle, a change which may reflect the growing importance of the castle as seen in the major structural alterations and additions of Henry's reign. These developments would have resulted in a corresponding reduction in the status and use of the central palace. They may thus account for the situation in which by the early 1140s[5] the bishop seems to have obtained a substantial degree of control over its site and buildings.

iii. GAOLS (Fig. 32)

In the reign of King Edward thieves were imprisoned in the king's *balchus* on the north side of High Street, near the entry to *Flesmangerestret*. By the time of Survey **I** this structure, which seems to have stood in the open street, had been incorporated into a neighbouring property and was occupied by butchers (**I, 19**), but the site or place-name

[1] *Regesta*, ii, no. 1000; J. Stevenson (ed.), *Chronicon Monasterii de Abingdon* (RS, 1858), ii. 116.

[2] *Gesta Stephani*, cap. 4; cf. *Historia Novella*, cap. 460, 463. William of Pont de l'Arche is described in both sources as *custos* of the treasury, and by the former as *custos et resignator*. See also *Gesta*, cap. 77, where *castellum ipsius* and *castello illius* can only refer to Winchester. Recent views would see William of Pont d l'Arche not as the treasurer, but as the more

powerful of the two chamberlains: Richardson and Sayles, 200.

[3] *Gesta*, cap. 59.

[4] See below, p. 510, n. 1.

[5] See above, pp. 297 ff. For the subsequent history of the castle see Colvin (ed.) *King's Works*, ii. 855–64; and for the treasury in Winchester in the second half of the twelfth century, R. A. Brown, op. cit. above, on p. 304, n. 4.

was still a landmark in 1148 (**II, 52**). The name[1] suggests a timber structure of beams or stakes which may have formed a prison cage or cage and pillory such as were common in the later Middle Ages,[2] and such as stood in the market square in Winchester in the sixteenth century for the short-term accommodation of prisoners.[3]

The medieval county gaol stood on the west side of *Scowrtenestret* and its custody, together with the custody of the castle gate in Winchester, pertained to land at Woodcote in the parish of Bramdean. In the thirteenth century this land was said to have been held for the service of the custody of the gaol since the Norman conquest. Milo the porter held Bramdean in 1086 and had a *haga* in Winchester worth 3*s*.[4] Milo evidently had the custody of the castle gate and his *haga* may thus have represented the site of the gaol. The surveys contain no explicit reference to the county gaol, but a property in *Brudenestret* which might have backed on to the gaol was held for the service of victualling the prison, a service which appears to have been added to the other customs due since the time of King Edward (**I, 144**). If the prison in question was indeed the one in *Scowrtenestret* this would be the earliest reference to an English county gaol.[5]

There were at least three other gaols in Winchester. The castle contained a gaol, and in the thirteenth century the guildhall where the city court met was sometimes known as the gaol of the city.[6] The bishop maintained a gaol in his palace at Wolvesey.[7]

In 1417 the gallows stood just within the suburban boundary on the road to Andover. There is evidence that the gallows occupied the same position in the thirteenth century and possibly before.[8]

iv. THE OLD MINSTER AND THE NORMAN CATHEDRAL (Figs. 9, 25–7, and 32)

The church later known as the Old Minster was founded by Cenwalh of Wessex in or about A.D. 648 and dedicated to St. Peter and St. Paul.[9] A cruciform structure with north and south porticus opening off the nave, and an eastern arm, perhaps apsidal, it was built just south of the Roman forum, astride an east–west street of the Roman town, and on a site which lies today immediately north of the nave of the present cathedral.[10]

[1] See above, p. 236, s.n. We are most grateful to Prof. E. L. G. Stones and Dr. A. J. Taylor for discussing this matter, and to Mr. R. E. Latham for confirming that no examples of *balcheus, balchus* are to be found among the materials of the complete Medieval Latin Dictionary. The OE origin of the word seems inescapable. Prison cages, in the sense of fully enclosed structures, were made in the Middle Ages; see for example, Edward I's orders for the confinement of the Countess of Buchan at Berwick, discussed in D. Dalrymple, *Annals of Scotland* (3rd edn., Edinburgh, 1819), ii. 11–12.

[2] R. B. Pugh, *Imprisonment in Medieval England* (Cambridge, 1968), 102, 112–13, 347, 357.

[3] *VCH Hants* v. 6; and *SMW*.

[4] See *SMW*, s.v. 'gaol'; J. H. Round in *VCH Hants* i. 438; *Book of Fees*, i. 78; *Rot Chart* i. 126.

[5] Cf. Pugh, op. cit. above, n. 2, 57–8.

[6] See *SMW* 186; Colvin (ed.) *King's Works*, ii. 855.

[7] See Addenda.

[8] *SMW* 798. In 1272 a man being taken from the goal to be hanged escaped to the church of St. Mary outside West Gate which was on the way to where the gallows were later known to have been: PRO, Just. 1/780, m. 20d.

[9] *ASC*, s.a. 648 (F); the other versions of the Chronicle record the fact under 641, 642, or 643 in their general account of Cenwalh's reign, but there is no reason to doubt F's date, which appears to accord with his relatively late conversion. Only F records the dedication, to St. Peter, which Bede gives as St. Peter and St. Paul (*HE* iii. 7). The latter is used sufficiently often in later cathedral documents to suggest a strong tradition that it was originally the full dedication, although afterwards usually shortened to St. Peter.

[10] For a full account of the site and of the sequence of chuches revealed by excavation in 1962–9, see *Winchester Studies* 4, *The Old and New Minsters*

Wini, the first bishop of Winchester, was not consecrated until about 660, so that if the date of the original foundation of the Old Minster is correct, the church was in use for some years before becoming a bishop's see. It seems possible that its original function was to serve an adjacent royal residence, and that its elevation to the status of a cathedral was not at first envisaged.[1]

Apart from the succession of bishops, little is known of the history of the church in seventh, eighth, or ninth centuries. Later records show that it was the scene of royal ceremonial and of a long sequence of royal burials,[2] and there is evidence for the translation to Winchester of relics such as the body of Birinus from Dorchester on Thames.[3] In 860 the city was taken by a Danish army, but the attackers were soon routed and the church does not seem to have been harmed.[4]

It is not until the second half of the tenth century that we have a reasonable amount of evidence for the history of the Old Minster. The community was reformed by Æthelwold (bishop 963–84), shortly after his consecration at the end of 963: the church was probably the scene of the promulgation of *Regularis Concordia* a few years later; and on 15 July 971 the body of Swithun (bishop 852–62) was translated from its original grave outside the west door of the early church. The translation seems to have been the signal for a great rebuilding which took place in two stages.[5] Between, apparently, 971 and a dedication in 980 the church was extended westward over the site of St. Swithun's grave. Following this dedication, the Old Minster was extended eastward, and the eastern part of the original structure was entirely remodelled to form the principal crossing and high altar of the new church. The completion of these works was marked by a second dedication in 993–4, during the episcopacy of Ælfheah (984–1005).[6]

In its final form the church was 76 m in length. Its most remarkable feature was the west-work dedicated in 980. Standing on a base 25 m square, this structure was probably between 40 and 50 m high. The royal palace lay immediately opposite, and the New Minster with its new tower stood a short distance to the north (Fig. 9, c. 963–1066). Together they formed a group of buildings on a monumental scale apparently unequalled elsewhere in the country until the rise of Westminster in the middle and latter part of the eleventh century. West-works of the kind built at Winchester, which seems to have been similar to the surviving example at Corvey on the Weser, were sometimes arranged to accommodate the throne of the local ruler at first- or second-floor level, in a position from which he could observe the whole or greater part of the interior of the church.[7] This may well have been one of the functions of the Winchester west-work. It seems probable too that the juxtaposition of palace and Old Minster was a convenience on those

in Winchester, by Martin Biddle and Birthe Kjølbye-Biddle (in preparation). Preliminary accounts may be found in *II–VIII Interims*.

[1] See above, p. 289, and further references given there in n. 1.

[2] See above, p. 290, n. 3.   [3] Bede, *HE* iii. 7.

[4] The Annals of St. Bertin's show that 860 is acceptable as the date of this event rather than the looser 'in the time of' Æthelberht of *ASC*, s.a.

[5] R. N. Quirk, 'Winchester Cathedral in the tenth century', *Arch J* 114 (1957), 28–68, analysed the documentary sources for the translation and rebuilding, and reached conclusions which have been thoroughly substantiated by subsequent excavation.

[6] See above, p. 306, n. 10. A summary account of the architectural sequence as revealed by excavation will be found in *VIII Interim*, 317–21.

[7] Felix Kreusch, *Beobachtungen an der Westanlage der Klosterkirche zu Corvey* (Beihefte der Bonner Jahrbücher, 9, Cologne–Graz, 1963).

occasions such as Easter when the king wore his crown in the cathedral.[1] When the close association of the royal family with both the Old and New Minsters is recalled, it can be seen that in this sense at least the three buildings were parts of a single complex.

The monastery attached to Old Minster was rebuilt during Æthelwold's episcopate, and arrangements were made for the supply of water to the monastic buildings and for their drainage. The boundaries of the monastic precinct were also defined or redefined, a dispute with New Minster over land at the north-east corner of the cathedral property was settled by an exchange, and the three monasteries, the Old Minster, the New Minster, and the Nunnaminster, were brought into a single enclosure marked by ditches, fences, and walls. Æthelwold's intention was to provide the conditions under which monks and nuns could dwell in peace and solitude, *a civium tumultu remoti*.[2]

By the end of the tenth century the Old Minster and its monastic precinct had taken their final form (Fig. 9, *c*. 963–1066). Throughout the eleventh century, until the first consecration of the new Norman church in 1093, the Old Minster played a role of exceptional importance as the principal church of Wessex, as the scene of royal burials in the earlier part of the century, as a place of coronation and crown-wearing, and as the centre of pilgrimage to the tomb and relics of St. Swithun.[3]

The Old Minster had stood in its final form for less than a century when Walkelin, the first Norman bishop, began the construction of a new cathedral in 1079.[4] The monks entered their church on 8 April 1093, presumably on the day of its dedication, and the following July, on the feast of St. Swithun, the saint's feretory was brought from the Old Minster into the new cathedral.[5] The demolition of the Old Minster began the next day on Walkelin's instructions, and was completed the same year, apart from one porticus and the high altar,[6] under which in the following year, 1094, relics of St. Swithun and of many other saints were found.[7]

The fact that the western end of the Old Minster lies partly under the nave of the Norman cathedral[8] shows that the dedication of 1093 cannot have been a dedication of the entire Norman church, for its nave could not have been completed before the demolition of Old Minster had begun. This dedication may thus have marked the completion only of the eastern arm, crossing, and transepts of the new church, together with part of the eastern three or four bays of the nave to form an abutment for the construction of the central tower.

The work needed to finish the nave was probably put in hand almost immediately

[1] See above, pp. 295–6, cf. p. 290.

[2] The evolution of the monastic precinct and its boundaries will be discussed in detail in Winchester Studies 4. A shorter account, with references, may be found in Martin Biddle, 'Felix urbs Winthonia', in D. Parsons (ed.), *Tenth-Century Studies* (London and Chichester, 1975), 123–40.

[3] For royal ceremonial see above, pp. 290, 295–7. The cult of St. Swithun will be described by Daniel Sheerin, *Ecce patronus adest: texts and studies concerning the origin and development of the cult of St. Swithun* (in preparation).

[4] *Winchester ann*, s.a. For William II's grant of

stone from the Isle of Wight, see *Regesta*, ii, p. 405, no. 412d, and for the story of William I's gift of timber from *Hanepinges* (Hampage Wood), see *Winchester ann*, s.a. 1086.

[5] Ibid., s.a. There were two feasts of St. Swithun, 2 July, the day of his death, and 15 July, *translatio*. The latter is probably meant, being by this date the principal feast.

[6] Ibid., *sequenti vero die, iussu domini Walkelini episcopi, coeperunt homines primum vetus frangere monasterium*.

[7] Ibid., s.a.

[8] *VIII Interim*, 315–17, Fig. 10.

after the dedication of 1093. The foundations of the northern tower of the Norman west front were placed partly in the open trench from which the foundations of the Anglo-Saxon west-work had been quarried away in the course of demolition. This trench was also used for the reburial of well over a thousand bodies, presumably those disturbed in digging the foundations of the new nave across the graveyard to the south of the Old Minster.[1] The date of the completion of the nave is not recorded. It seems likely that it was during William Giffard's episcopate (1100–29), and probably before 1122–4, when the bishop and monks were in dispute over the restitution to the community of certain lands and rights of patronage which Walkelin had taken before 1086 for building the cathedral, and had promised would be restored upon its completion.[2] This event may have been marked by the dedication of an altar to St. Swithun on 27 June about the year 1121.[3] It is striking that so important an act took place only a few days before the two feasts of the saint (2 and 15 July), and two days before the feast of St. Peter and St. Paul on 29 June, which was specially observed at Winchester, perhaps because it represented the original dedication of the Old Minster.[4] If the dedication of the altar to St. Swithun did mark the final completion of the new church, it is easy to see why a demand would then arise for the return of the lands taken to finance its construction.

The site chosen for the Norman cathedral lay south and east of the Old Minster, and the orientation of the new building was considerably south of east. It seems probable that both the site and the alignment were conditioned by the pre-existing boundaries of the royal palace to the west, and the monastic precinct of New Minster to the north (Fig. 9 c. 1110). If the piece of land projecting from the southern boundary of the New Minster was to be avoided, the length of the new cathedral could only be accommodated by

[1] Ibid.

[2] Goodman *Chartulary*, no. 1. In *DB* (fo. 41) the lands of the monks held by the bishop, from which he enjoyed the revenue, totalled £332. 15s. 0d. in value and although slightly different figures might be obtained (not however varying by more than £7), this figure compares well with the 300 librates of land said in Giffard's charter of restitution (Goodman *Chartulary*, no. 1; *Gesta pontificum*, bk. ii, cap. 77) to have been taken by Walkelin for building the church. The date range of this charter is 1123–9, but it was presumably drawn up in or after 1124 when the bishop and monks were reconciled and the bishop granted them a charter (*Winchester ann.*, s.a. 1122, 1124). A second charter of Giffard, relating to the restitution of rights of patronage in certain churches may be dated 1126–9 through the mention of Prior Ingulf (Goodman *Chartulary*, no. 2).

[3] Goodman *Chartulary*, no. 32. The dedication was attended by a large congregation of ecclesiastical and lay persons who had come together for this purpose. The date is given by Goodman as '*c.* 1121', but is in fact uncertain and depends on the mention of Prior Hugh, who is apparently otherwise unrecorded but regarded by the editors of the *Monasticon* (i (1817), 201) as intervening between Eustace (d. 1120) and Geoffrey III (d. 1126). Neither Eustace nor Hugh is

mentioned by D. Knowles, C. N. L. Brooke and V. C. M. London (*The Heads of Religious Houses, England and Wales, 940–1216* (Cambridge, 1972), 80), who regard the Geoffrey III of the *Monasticon* as the same person as Geoffrey II. If Knowles and Brooke are correct, and Hugh is not a figment, then he can only have followed their Geoffrey II (d. 1126) and have preceded Prior Ingulph who became abbot of Abingdon in 1130. The date of Giffard's restitution to the monks would favour an earlier date, if indeed the dedication is to be connected with the completion of the nave, but the tone of Goodman *Chartulary*, no. 32 might perhaps suit best the period of harmony in or after 1124. There is, however, no evidence that relations were bad before the dispute of 1122–4, and it is perhaps better to regard so important a dedication as being in some way connected with the completion of the nave. Since there were apparently no grounds for a dispute between bishop and monks, at least on this matter, at an earlier date, the completion of the nave and the date of Goodman *Chartulary*, no. 32 are perhaps best placed before 1122–4.

[4] Note for example the blue capitals marking this feast in the Winchester Kalendar, BM, Arundel MS. 60, fo. 4ᵛ (F. Wormald, *English Kalendars before A.D. 1100* (HBS 72, London, 1933), 147).

turning the whole axis of the building slightly to the south. This arrangement perhaps also allowed the new nave to pass between the Old Minster and its monastic buildings. It is clear that these were south of the Anglo-Saxon church, and must have been separated from it by a space, since the ground immediately south of the church was occupied by part of the cemetery.[1] Although the east range of the Norman cloister is of very early date, it appears to be structurally subsequent to the south transept. This may suggest that the Anglo-Saxon monastic buildings were retained in use in the area which became the cloister garth of the Norman monastery, while the ranges of the new cloister were constructed around them. Some such provision would certainly have had to be made for the accommodation of the community in the period of perhaps more than twenty years during which the new cathedral and its monastery were being built. Although little is known of the structural history of the Norman monastery, its buildings were probably complete before Giffard's death in 1129, and perhaps very much earlier.[2]

It was not only in the conditions governing the choice of its site that the Norman cathedral was influenced by its predecessor. The immense size of the new church, 162 m (533 ft.) in length, was undoubtedly a response to the eminence of the city in royal and ecclesiastical affairs. No other church in England or Normandy even approached this scale until the second half of the twelfth century and then only rarely. At the time of its building Winchester cathedral was surpassed in length only by St. Hugh's construction of the third church of Cluny in 1086–1109. And both of these far exceeded the other churches of Western christendom.[3] The plan of the new cathedral may also have owed something to Old Minster, for the Norman west front was almost a western transept, and must have been intended to provide a western entrance to the cathedral even more monumental than the west-work of Old Minster. Both structures were important components of the group of buildings facing the palace. This alone may have required a certain ceremonial character in the new design, and may even have conditioned its siting, for it is noticeable that the Norman west front projected little further west than the Anglo-Saxon west-work, and despite the changed alignment of the new cathedral occupied very nearly the same position as its predecessor. It is not perhaps impossible or even unlikely that there was some spatial relationship between the palace and the cathedral, such as an axial arrangement of entrances, which was as far as possible to be preserved in the new scheme.

The Norman west front, perhaps incorporating twin towers as in the Conqueror's two great abbeys in Caen, occupies a transitional position in the development of Anglo-Norman romanesque architecture. It is more advanced than any earlier or contemporary structure in Normandy, recalling in its projection to north and south the west front of Lincoln of c. 1072–92, but it scarcely approaches the scale of the western transepts of

---

[1] This is clear from the reference to burials south of the church in Wulfstan and Lantfred: Quirk *OM* 38–9; cf. Wulfstan, *Narratio metrica*, bk. I, lines 461–4; Lantfred, bk. I, ch. ii (p. 23, lines 5–7).

[2] *Winchester ann.*, s.a. 1128 mentions the cloister, refectory, dormitory, and infirmary, and the chapter house is mentioned s.a. 1124.

[3] Cluny III was about 187·3 m long, Canterbury (including the east end of the early twelfth century) 138 m, Norwich 138 m, St. Albans 122 m, Old St. Peter's 120 m, the great churches of the route to Compostella, between 98 m and 110 m, S. Ambrogio, Milan, 102 m, Abbaye aux Hommes 90 m, Abbaye aux Dames 82 m.

Ely (planned by *c.* 1174?) or Bury St. Edmunds (*c.* 1182 onwards), in which this very English feature is seen to its fullest extent. The Winchester sequence shows the importance of pre-conquest influence in the development of this aspect of Anglo-Norman architecture,[1] but it is much less certain whether the architectural connection reflects any continuity in the liturgical function of western structures. It seems, for example, most unlikely that the Norman west end was intended to house a royal pew, for this would have been excessively far from the centre of the church. It may however have provided an external gallery, which looked out over the space between the cathedral and the palace, and which could have been used for royal appearances on the occasions of crown-wearing and other great ceremonial.[2] The length of the nave, and the unencumbered passage offered by the aisles of nave and transepts, seem however to reflect changes in liturgical practice, and perhaps suggest the greater frequency of processions to different altars or stations *within* the cathedral, rather than to a series of separate churches in the vicinity.[3] The great size of the church, providing ample accommodation for a large congregation, may also reflect a wish to combine the functions of the Old and New Minsters. The move of the latter to Hyde, and its relegation to a secondary role in the religious life of the city, followed the commencement of the cathedral nave, which may even have been far advanced at the time, if not actually complete.

   Although the scale and character of the Norman cathedral reflect the importance of the city when the church was designed and built, the uses to which it was put reflect only the waning importance of Winchester as a royal centre. Until 1108 the court normally celebrated Easter in the city, and the king wore his crown in the cathedral, but this practice was not regularly maintained after that year. In August 1100 William II was buried in the cathedral after his fatal accident in the New Forest; this was the last royal burial in Winchester. But if the royal connection was in decline, the church remained a centre of pilgrimage to the shrine of St. Swithun, and the place of burial of the earlier Wessex and English kings. Although Norman taste and liturgical practice had demanded a new cathedral, there is no suggestion that the replacement of the Anglo-Saxon church was in any way an attempt to suppress a focus of Anglo-Saxon society. The bodies of the

[1] A. W. Clapham, *English Romanesque Architecture before the Conquest* (Oxford, 1930), 38; Geoffrey Webb, *Ely* (Cathedral Books, 1950), 8.

[2] When the empress Matilda was received in Winchester by Henry of Blois in March 1141 she was saluted by the citizens as their lady and their queen *fori civitatis*, according to the author of the *Gesta Stephani* (cap. 59). This event may be the same as her reception in Winchester Cathedral on 3 Mar. 1141, *honorifica facta processione*, recorded by William of Malmesbury, *Historia Novella*, cap. 491, in which case the salutation may have taken place in the High Street (which as a market street might be described as *forum*), or perhaps in the square between the lathedral and palace, the empress accompanied by the bishop appearing to the people from a gallery as suggested. The fact that the bishop bade the people salute her suggests a formal meeting (*publica audientia*, *Gesta*,

cap. 59), rather than a continuing acclamation in the course of a moving procession. Matilda was not the only royal person acclaimed by the citizens of Winchester, for Stephen was received by them in 1135 (*Historia Novella*, cap. 461; cf. *Gesta*, cap. 3, *cum dignioribus Wintoniae civibus*). Whether Winchester claimed some traditional right to acclaim a new sovereign, as did the citizens of London (P. E. Schramm, *Geschichte des Englischen Königtums im Lichte der Krönung* (Weimar, 1937), 156–7), does not emerge, although it seems likely that it would in fact have had the older claim. The juxta-position of cathedral and palace with the square between them may suggest that there was some actual provision for just such ceremonies.

[3] As seen in the route taken by funeral processions *c.* 1000, C. H. Turner, *JTS* 17 (1916), 65–8. See also above, pp. 268–70.

kings and bishops were translated into the new cathedral where they still remain; the feretory of St. Swithun was placed with all honour in the new church;[1] outside, over the site of the demolished west-work of the Old Minster, a memorial forecourt was created in which the stone coffins of the most important of the earlier burials were preserved in position around the site of St. Swithun's original grave, itself now marked by a new monument.[2] Suppression of the past was not indeed required, for the immense new church was itself a monument to the Norman acquisition of the Old English kingdom, and even of the relics of its departed saints and kings. It seems probable that this was in part actually the intention of the new design.

The boundaries of the cathedral precinct seem to have remained unchanged from the time of Æthelwold until the early twelfth century (Fig. 9; compare *c.* 963–1066 and *c.* 1110). In 1110, when the New Minster was moved to Hyde outside the North Gate, the site previously occupied by the minster in the centre of the city, immediately adjacent to the northern boundary of the cathedral precinct, was acquired by the cathedral.[3] The greater part of this land was left outside the precinct to serve as the town cemetery, but the portion projecting southward to the east of the Norman transept was cut off from the remainder and was eventually enclosed within the cathedral precinct. Thirty years later, after the events of 1141, the cathedral also acquired the greater part of the site of the former royal palace, and here too the area concerned was almost entirely given over to use as the town cemetery.[4] The building of the Close Wall probably followed this second acquisition, and with its construction the outlines of the cathedral area reached very much the pattern they still follow today (Fig. 9, *c.* 1148). The cathedral enclosure was now complete on all sides,[5] and the entire site of New Minster, which had originally been formed at the beginning of the tenth century partly from cathedral land, had now reverted to the older foundation, and was to remain for more than seven centuries the burial ground of the city.

After the death of Walkelin in 1098, the see was held by only two bishops in the succeeding seventy years, by William Giffard from 1100 to 1129, and by Henry of Blois from 1129 to 1171. The influence of these men on the growth and completion of the cathedral and its precinct we have already seen. Giffard was also responsible for the extensive rebuilding necessitated by the fall of the central tower in 1107.[6] Henry of Blois does not seem to have contributed greatly to the fabric of the cathedral, but was active in other ways, in the translation of relics and the establishment of chantries,[7] in the enlargement of the cathedral treasury,[8] and probably in administration of the cathedral lands, some of which he appropriated for his own use, but eventually for the most part restored.[9]

[1] *Winchester ann*, s.a. 1093.
[2] *VI Interim*, 275–8, Pls. LXIII–IV.
[3] See below, p. 317.
[4] See above, p. 301.
[5] The fence along the north side of the cathedral, defining the northern limit of 'Paradise', and marking (except in its eastern third) the ancient boundary between the Old and New Minsters, was not replaced by a stone wall until the thirteenth century: *IX Interim*, 123–4.
[6] *Winchester ann*, s.a.

[7] Ibid., s.a. 1150; in the fourteenth-century cartulary of the priory this translation is said to have taken place in 1158: Goodman *Chartulary*, no. 4, which also contains the references to the chantries; cf. also ibid., no. 5.
[8] Edmund Bishop, 'Gifts of Bishop Henry of Blois . . . to Winchester Cathedral', *Liturgica Historica* (Oxford, 1918, repr. 1962), 392–401.
[9] Goodman *Chartulary*, nos. 3, 7, 14, 26, and 42. For the cathedral priory as a Winchester landowner, see below, p. 355.

Survey **II** provides what is probably the earliest record of some of the monastic officers of St. Swithun's. The sacrist appears on several occasions.[1] His holding of property in *Mensterstret*, next to the city wall, and in King's Gate, probably reflects the monastery's responsibility, known from later sources, for the upkeep of the gate and the city wall nearby. The sacrist's frequent occurrence by comparison with the other monastic officials —he is the only property-owner of any significance—may also reflect his responsibility for the day-to-day maintenance of the fabric.[2] The infirmarer,[3] the cellerarian (or a family connected with the cellar),[4] and possibly the hordarian[5] may also be mentioned.[6] The survey shows no trace of any formal assignment of property-revenue to the individual offices of St. Swithun's or any other Winchester monastery.

V. NEW MINSTER AND HYDE ABBEY (Figs. 9, 25–7, and 33)

The circumstances surrounding the foundation of New Minster are obscure.[7] The community, whatever its antecedants may have been, does not appear until 901, the year in which the building of the church may have been begun. Although Grimbald probably had a residence on the site for himself and a few companions during Alfred's reign, there is little evidence that the king intended initially that this should form the nucleus of a new monastery. The first steps may have been taken shortly after Edward the Elder's accession, but Grimbald is not among the witnesses to the grants purporting to have been made to the community in 901 and the foundation may have followed his death, on 8 July that year. The new church was dedicated in 903 to the Holy Trinity, St. Mary, and St. Peter.[8] The ceremony may have been accompanied or followed by the issue of a formal charter of foundation,[9] and by an acknowledgement of the steps taken to provide the land occupied by the new monastery in the middle of the city.[10]

The site lay on the north side of Old Minster. The precinct was defined to the west, north, east, and partly to the south by streets which were later absorbed into the precinct

---

[1] **II, 791** and n. 1, **796–8, 818,** and **928.** The mention of two sacrists in **II, 791** may imply the existence of a sub-sacrist.

[2] The relative importance of the sacrist's office may be emphasized by the possible identification in Survey II of the sacrists of all three of the Winchester monasteries; see **II, 300** and **722** and cf. below, pp. 321 and 323, where the other identifiable monastic officers of Hyde Abbey and St. Mary's are also listed.

[3] **II, 61.**

[4] **II, 1002**; cf. p. 193, s.n. Cellar'.

[5] **II, 320,** see esp. n. 2; the identification is very uncertain.

[6] No monastic almoner can be certainly identified: William (**II, 538**) was probably a royal almoner, and Robert (**II, 441,** etc.) cannot be identified.

[7] For the interpretation followed here, see Philip Grierson, 'Grimbald of St. Bertin's', *EHR* 55 (1940), 529–61. The matter is further discussed with additional topographical information in Martin Biddle, 'Felix urbs Winthonia: Winchester in the age of monastic reform', in D. Parsons (ed.), *Tenth-Century Studies* (London and Chichester, 1975), 123–40, and will be reconsidered in detail in Martin Biddle and Birthe Kjølbye-Biddle, *The Old and New Minsters in Winchester* (Winchester Studies 4, in preparation).

[8] *ASC* [F], s.a. There is some uncertainty over the dedication, which may not at first have included St. Mary (cf. *BCS* 602, Sawyer 270). The New Minster is described as the *monasterium Sancti salvatoris* in an original (?) charter of 925×933 (*BCS* 648, Sawyer 1417), and by the refoundation of the 960s (*BCS* 1190, Sawyer 745) seems to have been regarded as dedicated to St. Saviour, St. Mary, and St. Peter, although the Holy Trinity appears in later documents, both before and after the move to Hyde. See further, *LVII* viii.

[9] *BCS* 602, Sawyer 370; cf. *LVH* 214–17.

[10] *BCS* 605, Sawyer 1443; best edition by F. E. Harmer, *Select English Historical Documents of the Ninth and Tenth Centuries* (Cambridge, 1914), no. 16; cf. *BCS* 1338 for a second fragmentary version.

and do not survive today. The area enclosed was about 1·6 ha. The formation of the precinct, around a nucleus consisting of the site of Grimbald's *monasteriolum* with its church and stone dormitory, involved the acquisition of land from the bishop and community of Old Minster, as well as a considerable area purchased at a high price from those *circummanentibus iure haereditatis*.[1] For reasons which are not now fully apparent the church was itself built against the southern boundary of the site, immediately adjacent to the north side of Old Minster.

The complexity of the steps that had to be taken to provide a suitable site, its cost, and the lack of freedom evident and accepted in the location of the church, all suggest an urgent purpose behind the new foundation. This purpose has never been satisfactorily explained. The idea of an educational foundation must be discounted. No great weight can be given to the view that New Minster was *originally* intended as a royal burial-church, even if it did in the event provide the last resting place of Alfred and his children. Yet the construction of a new church alongside the existing cathedral demands explanation, and the dissimilarity in the plan and scale of the two churches may provide a clue. Old Minster was still at this date much as it had been built two hundred and fifty years before, a small church with an over-all area of 354 sq. m. It was by now probably crowded with internal fittings, altars, and tombs. New Minster was by contrast a large church, with an aisled nave alone occupying more than 790 sq. m, and with an eastern complex of unknown extent. Unlike Old Minster, it could accommodate a congregation of considerable size.

In 1110, when New Minster migrated to Hyde, the freedom which the citizens had enjoyed to choose burial at New Minster was specifically mentioned and extended to the new site.[2] This was presumably an exception to the otherwise strict control which the cathedral exercised over burial in the city, and from which in the later Middle Ages exemption had to be sought and presumably purchased.[3] This privilege was apparently well established at New Minster before the move, and there is no reason to suppose that it was then a recent introduction.

The character of the church itself and the citizen's right of burial in its cemetery may thus suggest that a close relationship existed between New Minster and the people of Winchester from a time early in the monastery's history, and possibly from the moment of its foundation. Edward's purpose (and perhaps his father's wish) in establishing a new church in the centre of the city, so close to the existing cathedral, may therefore have been to provide for the needs of the new burh and its rapidly growing population. While Old Minster remained the bishop's see, New Minster was to be the burh church.

During the first half of the tenth century New Minster was closely associated with the royal house. Alfred's body was translated to New Minster from his original grave in Old Minster, and laid to rest beside his wife Ealhswith. Edward the Elder and two of his sons were also buried there, and later Eadwig (d. 959), with whose burial the use of the church for royal interments came to an end.[4] Its principal treasure was the tomb and

[1] *LVH* 4; cf. *BCS* 602.
[2] *Reg Pontissara* 441.
[3] The rights of the prior and convent of St. Swithun over the parish churches of the city and suburbs were described in full in 1331. An original record of these rights is in WCL, Records, vol. i, fo. 38, no. 119, see also BM, Add. MS 29436, fos. 67–71.
[4] *LVH* 5–7.

shrine of St. Grimbald,[1] but from an early date the house also possessed relics of St. Josse (Judoc).[2] The history of its buildings in this period is obscure. The church may have been completed by the dedication of a tower to St. Mary in 908, but this event seems more likely to refer to Nunnaminster.[3] Edmund (939–46) may have intended to carry out further works, but was apparently prevented by his early death.[4]

The monastery of New Minster was reformed by Æthelwold in 964, and placed under Æthelgar, who was brought from Abingdon as the new abbot.[5] During the rearrangement and extension of the sites of all three minsters over the next few years, the precinct of New Minster was enlarged to the west, north, and east, increasing its area to 2·5 ha (Fig. 9, c. 963–1066), *ut omnia secundum sanctissimi patris Benedicti institutum intra monasterium haberentur*.[6] Boundary disputes with the Old Minster and Nunnaminster were settled at the same time,[7] and the conventual buildings were restored and re-planned on regular lines.[8] In 966 Edgar seems to have given some formal recognition to these events in a statement which was later drawn up as the famous 'Golden Charter', virtually an instrument of refoundation, reflecting (cap. xii) not only the efforts of Æthel-wold to secure the privacy of the monasteries, but also the reconstruction of the New Minster buildings in accordance with the newly imposed rule.[9] Most of these buildings probably lay to the north of the church, but the infirmary (*domus infirmorum*) mentioned in the 'Golden Charter' may perhaps be identified with the claustral building found east of the church in 1970 (Fig. 9, c. 963–1066).[10]

Between 979/80 and 988, perhaps towards 988, a great tower was added to New Minster at the expense of King Æthelred, probably at the west end of the church, and perhaps before the west front.[11] The tower is described in a notoriously obscure passage of the *Liber Vitae* analysed in detail by the late Roger Quirk.[12] His conclusions suggest a tower of six storeys embellished with external sculpture throughout its height, the decoration at each level apparently reflecting the dedication of the corresponding storey. The west-work of Old Minster was dedicated in 980.[13] The New Minster tower, at least 20 m in height and standing only 20 m from the west-work, can only have been constructed in a spirit of ostentatious competition with the older community.

The extended precinct now contained at least two cemeteries, one to the west of the church and claustral buildings, and a second north-east of the church. There were several chapels within the precinct by the end of the century: St. George (in the western

---

[1] Grierson, op. cit. (above, p. 313, n. 7), pp. 557–8.

[2] LVH 6; Grierson, op. cit. 556.

[3] See below, pp. 321–2.

[4] LVH 6–7.

[5] ASC, s.a. 963 [E], 964 [A].

[6] LVH 8; cf. BCS 1302, Sawyer 807, of 963 × 970.

[7] BCS 1163, Sawyer 1449; best edition AS Ch, no. XLIX, where the charter is regarded as representing a slightly later stage of events than BCS 1302.

[8] LVH 8: *redintegrando omnia monastici ordinis domicilia regulari perfectioni*.

[9] BCS 1190, Sawyer 745; cf. LVH 232–46. This document should perhaps be regarded not as a charter or a copy of one, but rather as a record of what happened in 966, drawn up later at the instance of Æthel-wold, and therefore to be dated 966 × 984: F. Wormald in *Romanesque and Gothic Art* (Acts of the Twentieth International Congress of the History of Art, Princeton, 1963), i. 24–6.

[10] IX Interim, 118–23, Fig. 8, Phase D.

[11] This position is suggested by the location of a church or chapel of St. Mary the Virgin and all Holy Virgins at about this point in the sequence of the route followed by Winchester funeral processions c. 1000, for this was the dedication of the lowest storey of the New Minster tower: C. H. Turner, JTS 17 (1916), 65–8.

[12] R. N. Quirk, 'Winchester New Minster and its tenth-century tower', JBAA³ 24 (1961), 16–54.

[13] See above, p. 307.

cemetery or possibly in the palace),[1] St. Gregory (at the west end of the church), St. Thomas (on the north side of the precinct, near *Thomeseiete*), and St. Maurice with St. Pantaleon (perhaps to be identified with the later church of St. Maurice just outside the precinct to the north, but apparently closely related to it).[2]

New Minster was now at its zenith, with the buildings and site at their fullest extent. In Cnut's reign the king himself presented the minster with a great gold cross, and after his death his widow gave the so-called 'Greek Shrine', with the head of St. Valentine and further relics.[3] In the reign of Edward the Confessor the relics of St. Grimbald were translated for a second time, from the silver shrine in which they had been placed in the time of Bishop Ælfheah I (934–51), to a yet more fitting receptacle.[4] The minster was, however, on the eve of its decline.

The domestic buildings (*officine*) of New Minster were destroyed by fire on St. George's Day 1065.[5] The fire ran across the south-west corner of the buildings and then eastwards up to the monastery gate, known in the twelfth century as *Thomeseiete*.[6] The community were faced with an immediate problem of reconstruction, but whether work actually began on the site of the burnt-out buildings is unknown. Four or five years later in 1069–70, when William I extended the royal palace northwards to High Street, he took in the cemetery which then formed the western third of the New Minster precinct (Fig. 9, cf. *c.* 963–1066 and *c.* 1110).[7] The later memorandum in the *Liber Vitae*, which provides the only continuous account of these events, claims that William acquired the site of the burnt-out buildings of the monastery for the extension of his palace, but this appears to be incorrect, the contemporary sources referring only to the loss of the cemetery land in exchange for the manors of Alton and Clere.[7] The site of the burnt-out *officine*, on the north side of the church, remained within the New Minster precinct (Fig. 9, *c.* 1110).

The reduced enclosure now contained only 1·4 ha, less than the original precinct at the time of the minster's foundation a century and a half before. In this restricted area provision had now to be made both for the conventual buildings and for a cemetery. The first problem appears to have been solved by reconstructing and greatly enlarging the existing claustral block lying to the east of the church, and perhaps originally built in the 960s as the infirmary.[8] The extension of this complex northwards—conditions eastwards were unsuitable, as we shall see—involved the suppression of an existing chapel and the use of part of a cemetery (Fig. 9, *c.* 1110).[9]

Space for burial was now restricted. Before the loss of the western area to the palace, the minster seems to have had at least two cemeteries. The larger lay apart from the church and monastery, to the west of the street giving access to the palace and the two churches. The second lay around the north side and east end of the New Minster church and extended north-eastward in the direction of St. Maurice's church (Fig. 9, *c.* 963–1066).

[1] See above, p. 291, n. 12.

[2] C. H. Turner, *JTS* 17 (1916), 65–8.

[3] *LVH* lxiii–lxv, 151–3, 161–3; *ASC* [F], s.a. 1041. For the relics in the great cross, see also below, p. 320, n. 6.

[4] Grierson, op. cit. (above, p. 313, n. 7), p. 558.

[5] *LVH* 2; for the date see above, p. 293, n. 1.

[6] See above, p. 238, s.v. *Thomeseiete*.

[7] See above, pp. 292–4.

[8] *IX Interim*, 118–23.

[9] *I Interim*, 159–72.

The former was perhaps the lay cemetery in which the citizens had right of burial. The latter was perhaps in part the monastic cemetery. It was the north-eastern part of this second cemetery which was now required for the extension of the monastery's domestic buildings. There thus remained only the area immediately adjacent to the east end of the church, and the larger space to the north of the nave which appears to have been the site of the original domestic complex burnt down in 1065.[1] The large-scale reconstruction of the domestic buildings east of the church may therefore reflect a decision to use the site of the burnt-out buildings as the principal cemetery of the reduced precinct.[2]

The New Minster now occupied a cramped site. The domestic buildings stood along the low-lying eastern margin of the precinct, beside the watercourse running between New Minster and Nunnaminster.[3] The area was dank and fetid:

aqua etiam, quae per devexos civitatis vicos a porta confluens occidentali, circa situm monasterii . . . in paludem horridam congregata, et in lutum ex flacone diutina condensata, foetorem ex se intollerabilem emittens, et sua corruptione aerem vicinum inficiens, fratribus in loco memorato Deo servientibus plurima infirmitatum gravamina frequenter inferebat.[4]

Later it was also remembered that New Minster had lain so close to the cathedral that the singing and the bells of one confounded the singers and the ringing of the other, and that a man could scarcely pass between the two buildings.[4] But it is quite clear that these latter memories refer to the Old and New Minsters (Fig. 9, c. 963–1066), and not to the New Minster and the Norman cathedral, which by 1110 had stood for some seventeen years at a reasonable distance to the south (Fig. 9, c. 1110, cf. c. 963–1066).

Because of the restricted site and unhealthy conditions, and on account of *alia multa incommoda*, the monastery was moved about 1110 to a new site at Hyde outside the north gate of the city.[5] As part of the agreement entered into shortly after the move, the site in the middle of the city formerly occupied by the minster was transferred to the bishop and cathedral.[6] The land acquired from them about 901 as part of the original foundation thus reverted now to their ownership. With the exception of the small rectangular area projecting southwards from the eastern end of the New Minster precinct, which was now incorporated into the cathedral monastery, the remainder of the site became part of the cathedral yard and was used for burial until the nineteenth century (Fig. 9, c. 1148).

[1] The discovery of a few burials immediately north of the New Minster nave in 1963 (*II Interim*, 211, Pl. LVII, lower, Trench VIII) does not invalidate the suggestion that the original domestic buildings were north of the nave. At Old Minster, for example, a cemetery along the south side of the church intervened between the church and the domestic buildings of the monastery, which were thus situated at some distance to the south. A similar situation has been observed at Glastonbury and at Abingdon, and may have been fairly common (Martin Biddle in *Med Arch* 12 (1968), 64–5). The attached cloister of the post-conquest period does not seem to have been characteristic of Anglo-Saxon monasteries.

[2] This conclusion has not been tested by excavation, and remains an hypothesis.

[3] See above, p. 315, n. 7, for earlier arrangements concerning this watercourse.

[4] BM, Cotton MS. Vespasian. D. ix, fo. 30ᵛ, printed and discussed by R. N. Quirk in *I Interim*, 179–80, 182. Cf. the shorter versions given by William of Malmesbury, *Gesta regum*, bk. ii, cap. 124, and *Gesta pontificum*, bk. ii, cap. 78.

[5] *Winchester ann*, s.a.; Hyde annals, s.a. (Hyde Cart fo. 17); *Waverley ann*, s.a. 1111. These annals represent three different verbal traditions, the third agreeing in all respects with Roger of Hoveden (*Chronica* (ed. W. Stubbs, RS, 1868–71), i. 168).

[6] *Monasticon*, ii. 444, nos. x and xii; best printed text in *Reg Pontissara* 439–41; see also *Regesta*, ii, no. 1070.

The new cathedral must have been approaching completion in 1110, and its great size, and the timing of the New Minster move, may reflect a wish to combine in the Norman church the public functions of the Old and New Minsters.[1] The layout and scale of the former must have been known from the commencement of works in 1079, but it is uncertain whether this indicates that the removal of New Minster was already envisaged. The inconvenience of New Minster's position will have been apparent since the fire of 1065 and William I's acquisition of more than a third of its site four years later. It is not perhaps impossible that these events, and the decisions to rebuild the cathedral and remove New Minster to Hyde, all formed part of a long-term design conceived in the 1070s and brought to completion nearly forty years later.

Henry I was in a real sense the founder of Hyde Abbey, for the migration of New Minster was undertaken on royal initiative and under strict royal control. About 1110 the king caused the community to move with its relics to the new site at Hyde in the north suburb.[2] Here the New Minster already owned an extensive tract of water-meadow immediately to the north of the city,[3] and it was on the western edge of this land, on a specially prepared platform of clay, that the abbey church and principal conventual buildings were erected.[4] The new site was conveniently situated towards the principal group of the minster's rural estates centring on Micheldever, six or seven miles to the north of Winchester.

By 1110, or within a few years of that date, further lands for the precinct of the new monastery were acquired from the episcopal estates surrounding the city,[5] the king acting as an intermediary. These acquisitions were formally recognized in a charter of King Henry drawn up on 13 September 1114.[6] They consisted of the land called Hyde where the abbey now stood, houses worth 7s. a year, probably in Hyde Street, the manor called Worthy (now Abbotts Barton), and the parochial rights of the church of Worthy, which may have been the church dedicated to St. Gertrude in the meadows to the north of Abbotts Barton. The Hyde Abbey estates now extended north from the city wall without a break through Abbotts Barton and Abbots Worthy to Micheldever. The newly acquired lands were free of geld, and at the request of the bishop the king granted to the abbey the liberty of the street outside the North Gate of the city. Survey **II** records the extensive territorial rights of the abbey in this northern suburb.[7]

The physical separation of the two minsters meant that new arrangements were now necessary for those occasions, such as the annual Palm Sunday procession, when the two communities acted together. These arrangements were confirmed in the charter of 1114.[8]

In 1141 Hyde Abbey was burned during the great siege, together with St. Mary's Abbey within the walls, many parish churches, and the better part of the city. The most reliable sources imply that this burning took place during the general conflagration

---

[1] See above, p. 311.

[2] *Winchester ann*, s.a.

[3] Later known as Hyde Moors, see above, p. 266.

[4] This platform was observed in 1787–8, see below, p. 321, n. 4.

[5] At the time of the move to Hyde the bishop still held the estates surrounding Winchester which nominally belonged to the cathedral priory, see above, p. 309 and n. 2.

[6] See above, p. 266, n. 4.

[7] For Hyde Abbey and the development of the northern suburb, see above, pp. 266–7.

[8] For the procession, see above, pp. 268–9.

caused by the firebrands shot from the bishop's tower in the middle of the city,[1] and later Hyde tradition blamed the bishop for the fire at the abbey.[2] If the fire started near the centre of the city, however, it would have had to progress almost half a mile, as well as crossing the city wall and ditch, in order to damage the abbey. The disposition of the opposing forces during the siege was extremely complex, and the fire at Hyde may therefore have been the result of some other skirmish rather than the bishop's projectiles. The empress occupied the royal castle and the eastern part of the city, and with the support of the citizens presumably controlled most of the area within the walls. The bishop's men held his tower or castle, probably on the site of the royal palace, and his house at Wolvesey, together with the western part of the city, by which the chronicler may have meant the western suburb overlooking the royal castle. Other forces on the side of the bishop and the royal party, including the Londoners, controlled the approach roads to east and west.[3] The monks of Hyde almost certainly supported the empress rather than the bishop, and the abbey may have been burned in a clash between the bishop's forces on the west and those of the empress on the east, or by troops supporting the bishop from outside the city.

The abbey's greatest loss in the fire was the cross donated by Cnut, which collapsed beneath the ashes. Soon after the siege the remains of its materials, including precious metals to the value of thirty marks of gold and more than five hundred marks of silver, were recovered from the ruins on the orders of the bishop, and used as payment for the knights he had hired at great expense.[4] One twelfth-century source claims that other treasures were taken from the abbey for the bishop on the same occasion,[5] and later sources developed this into an elaborate list of the ornaments he had seized.[6]

The events of 1141 were, however, simply the high point in a quarrel between the bishop and the monks of Hyde. Since the death of Osbert about 1135, the office of abbot had been vacant and Bishop Henry had probably appropriated the abbey's revenues to his own use. After the fire the bishop held the abbey for another year, and then appointed Hugh, his own candidate, to the abbacy.[7] The abbey did not prosper under

[1] *Gesta Stephani*, cap. 65 and *Historia Novella*, cap. 499.

[2] Hyde Cart, fo. 17[r-v].

[3] The occupation of the royal castle by the empress is recorded in *Winchester ann*, *Gesta Stephani*, and *Historia Novella*. The annals record that the forces of the empress occupied the eastern part of the city, from which the attack on the bishop's *castellum* and *domus*, recorded in the *Gesta*, must have been launched. St. Mary's Abbey could easily have been a base for this attack: the firing of the nunnery would then have been an attempt to relieve the pressure on Wolvesey. The occupation of the western part of Winchester by the bishop's forces is specifically recorded in the annals alone. The account in both the *Gesta* and the *Historia Novella* show that the forces of the royal party controlled the area outside the city to east and west. For the bishop's tower and its location, see above, p. 298 and below, pp. 325–6.

[4] *Historia Novella*, cap. 499, *Winchester ann*, s.a.

1141. For the hiring of the knights, *Gesta Stephani*, cap. 65.

[5] Continuator of Florence of Worcester, *Chronicon ex chronicis* (ed. B. Thorpe, London, 1848–9), ii. 133–6. This source also gives the amount of silver recovered as £500, rather than marks.

[6] The two accounts printed by the editors of the *Monasticon*, ii. 437 and 445, are in substantial agreement. The former, printed from BM, Cotton MS. Vesp. D. ix, fos. 33–4 (not identified as the source by the editors of the *Monasticon*), is a sixteenth-century copy of what appear to be fifteenth-century memoranda concerning the history of the cathedral and Hyde Abbey. The latter is an addition in a later fifteenth-century hand, made on fo. 3 of the Hyde Cart.

[7] D. Knowles, C. N. L. Brooke, and V. C. M. London (eds.), *The Heads of Religious Houses, England and Wales, 940–1216* (Cambridge, 1972), 80–2. The account of the vacancy and Abbot Hugh's succession rests only on the fifteenth-century annals of Hyde (Hyde

Hugh,[1] and it was at this time, probably in 1144–5 during the time of Pope Lucius II, that Henry of Blois first put forward his scheme for elevating the bishopric of Winchester to metropolitan rank, above the other sees of south-central England, and making the abbot of Hyde a suffragan bishop.[2]

After the accession of Pope Eugenius III the monks of Hyde were able to prosecute their case against Bishop Henry and Abbot Hugh. The matter came to a head during the visit or visits which Henry of Blois made to the papal court at Rome between the latter part of 1148 and 1150, following his condemnation at the council of Rheims during the spring of 1148. By his skilled diplomacy and the distribution of gifts Bishop Henry managed to maintain his position and receive absolution, but he failed in a further attempt to achieve metropolitan status.[3]

Henry of Blois seems never to have established with Hyde the friendly relations which he eventually achieved with the cathedral priory.[4] If the later Hyde source is to be believed the bishop seized further Hyde properties after 1161, including the churches or chapels of St. Bartholomew, St. Leonard (in the western suburb), St. Helen in or near Winchester, and the chapel of Worthy.[5]

Hyde Abbey's fortunes took a turn for the better in 1182 when miracles associated with the relics of St. Barnabas marked the beginning of a rebuilding programme,[6] and from

Cart, fo. 17), and on the fifteenth-century (?) account of Bishop Henry's devastations printed by the editors of the *Monasticon*, ii. 437, for which see above, p. 319, n. 6.

[1] No new monks entered the community under Hugh, *LVH* 41. The fifteenth-century source provides a fuller account of his mismanagement, *Monasticon*, ii. 437.

[2] The only record of the proposal to elevate the abbot of Hyde is in *Winchester ann*, s.a. 1143, in which the proposal is attributed to some time during the papacy of Innocent II, who died on 24 Sept. 1143. The annalist admitted, however, to imperfect knowledge: he provides a very uneven account of the ten years following 1141. The acquisition of the office of legate in 1139 had been Bishop Henry's first answer to the election of Theobald as archbishop of Canterbury. Soon after learning of the death of Innocent II, Henry set out for Rome in an attempt to renew his legatine authority, but had gone no further than Cluny when Pope Celestine II died, on 8 March 1144 (*Waverley ann*, 229, and T. Arnold (ed.), *Symeonis Historia Regum continuata per Johannem Hagulstadensem*, ii (RS, 1885), 315–16). Henry failed to obtain the office of legate from Celestine's successor, Lucius II (d. 15 Feb. 1145), who appears nevertheless to have sent him the *pallium* (W. Stubbs (ed.), *Radulfi de Diceto Decani Lundoniensis Opera Historica* (RS, 1876) i. 255). St. Bernard's letter to Lucius II obliquely refers to Henry of Blois's metropolitan ambitions (B. S. James (trans.), *The Letters of St. Bernard of Clairvaux* (London, 1952), no. 204). The Winchester annalist may therefore be confusing Henry's undoubted

success at establishing his authority over the English church under Innocent II, with his later attempts to raise his see to metropolitan rank.

[3] *Winchester ann*, s.a. 1149 and 1151; M. Chibnall (ed.), *The Historia Pontificalis of John of Salisbury* (London, 1956), 10, 78. For Henry's visit or visits to Rome, see Chibnall, *Historia Pontificalis*, Appendix I, 91–4, and W. J. Millor, H. E. Butler, and C. N. L. Brooke (eds.), *The Letters of John of Salisbury*, i, *The Early Letters* (London, 1955), Appendix, 253–4.

[4] See above, p. 312. Bishop Henry is usually supposed to have presented a restored version of the great cross to Hyde in 1167 (*Liber de Hyda*, p. li, and *VCH Hants* ii. 117–18), but the sole authority is the statement under that year in *Winchester ann: Magna crux consecrata est ab Henrico episcopo*. This cross, recorded in a cathedral priory source, is almost certainly the elaborate *crux nova et magna* which heads the list of ornaments given by Henry of Blois to the cathedral (Edmund Bishop, 'Gifts of Bishop Henry of Blois, . . . to Winchester Cathedral' in his *Liturgica Historica* (Oxford, 1918, repr. 1962), 392–401).

[5] *Monasticon*, ii. 437; see above, p. 319, n. 6. For the chapels of St. Leonard and St. Helen, see Goodman *Chartulary* no. 394, and *SMW*.

[6] *Winchester ann*, s.a. The community did not perhaps acquire its relics of St. Barnabas until the twelfth century, for the notice of them in the twelfth-century list of New Minster or Hyde Abbey relics is an addition, or even a secondary addition, to the original list (*LVH* 152–3; cf. BM, Stowe MS. 944, fo. 55ᵛ). The additions were made following the list of relics contained in the great cross and do not necessarily relate

then on the abbey was frequently known by its dedication to this apostle. A cross of the abbey was seized and destroyed by peasants in 1187.[1]

Little is known of the development of the abbey buildings in the twelfth century. The principal structures were probably complete before 1141 and the cloisters may have been finished in the ten years before the siege.[2] Surviving fragments of the western boundary wall and of a great hall, possibly the almoner's hall,[3] near the main entrance towards Hyde Street, include twelfth-century work. The plan of the abbey church, the west front of which was approached directly from Hyde Street, is known in block outline (Fig. 27).[4] In the forecourt stood the parish church of St. Bartholomew, which may have served the northern suburb since before the arrival of the abbey at Hyde.[5]

The surveys provide no record of any of the officials of New Minster, but in Survey **II** the sacrist of Hyde is probably to be found holding land on the abbot's fief in the western suburb,[6] while *ministri* of the abbot are in the northern suburb,[7] where a hordarian, conceivably an official of the abbey or of the cathedral priory, is also located.[8]

vi. THE NUNNAMINSTER (ST. MARY'S ABBEY) (Figs. 9, 25–7, and 32)

St. Mary's Abbey, otherwise Nunnaminster or the *monasterium sanctimonialium*, is the least known of the three Winchester monasteries. It lay to the south of High Street, east of New Minster, and seems to have been founded and dedicated to St. Mary by Ealhswith, Alfred's queen (d. 902–3 ?), and perhaps completed by her son, Edward the Elder.[9] The dedication of a tower by Plegmund *c.* 908 in honour of Mary, the mother of God, may have marked the finishing of the church.[10] In the time of St. Eadburga (d. *c.* 951–3) there was an oratory or chapel dedicated to St. Peter in or near the nunnery

---

to it. Barnabas was commemorated at New Minster in the eleventh century, but three of the saints whose relics are included in the additions to the list (Leonard, Blaise, and Frideswide) were not commemorated in any of the eleventh-century New Minster kalendars, although their names were added to one of them in the thirteenth century (Francis Wormald (ed.), *English Kalendars before A.D. 1100*, i, *Texts* (HBS 72, London, 1933)).

[1] Hyde Cart, fo. 18.

[2] A number of capitals, perhaps formerly part of the abbey cloister, survive in St. Bartholomew's church at Hyde. They are described and illustrated by C. J. P. Cave, 'Capitals from the Cloister of Hyde Abbey', *Antiq J* 25 (1945), 81, and Pls. IV–VIII. The capitals are usually dated to the 1130s because of their similarity to those from Reading Abbey, see G. Zarnecki, *English Romanesque Sculpture, 1066–1140* (London, 1951), 37, and Lawrence Stone, *Sculpture in Britain: the Middle Ages* (Harmondsworth, Middlesex, 1955), 58.

[3] This structure, which survived into the nineteenth century, has traditionally been identified as the abbot's hall, e.g. *Monasticon* ii. 43, but was probably too far away from the main church to have fulfilled this function.

[4] Henry Howard, 'Enquiries concerning the Tomb of King Alfred, at Hyde Abbey, near Winchester',

Archaeologia, 3 (1798), 309–12; see also Alfred Bowker, *The King Alfred Millenary: A Record of the Proceedings of the National Commemoration* (London, 1902), 66–8, plan facing p. 62.   [5] See below, p. 330.

[6] **II**, 300; for sacrists and other officials of the Winchester monasteries cf. above, p. 313, esp. nn. 1–6 and below, p. 323.

[7] **II**, 349.

[8] **II**, 320, see esp. n. 2 and cf. above, p. 313. For the abbey as a property-owner in Winchester, see below, pp. 355–8.

[9] The tradition that Alfred shared in the foundation appears to be based on the use made by the editors of the *Monasticon* (ii. 451, n.b) of a corrupt passage from William of Malmesbury (cf. *Gesta pontificum*, bk. ii, cap. 78). Ealhswith is regarded as the sole founder by *LVH* 5 (written *c.* 1020–30 and perhaps based on an earlier text of Æthelred's reign) and all other sources, none of them earlier than the thirteenth century in their present form, take the same view (*Monasticon*, ii. 451, n.c., 453, num. I; cf. *VCH Hants* ii. 122, and Birch *Ancient Manuscript*, 3–6). The tradition that the foundation was completed by Edward the Elder rests only on the authority of Leland, but may be acceptable if the dedication of a tower in 908 refers to this church (see next note).

[10] *The Chronicle of Æthelweard* (ed. A. Campbell, London, 1962), 52. Most writers have taken this annal

garden.[1] This chapel was probably identical with the later parish church of St. Peter in *Colo-brochestret*.[2] The first foundation, described by William of Malmesbury as a *monasteriolum*, was in some decay (*pene destructum*) at the time of the second foundation by Æthelwold *c*. 964.[3] How much Æthelwold undertook is uncertain: if William of Malmesbury is to be believed, the bishop founded and built the monastery on the site of the earlier *monasteriolum*.[4] Between 963 and 970 Nunnaminster shared with the Old and New Minsters in the general rearrangement and consolidation of their sites (Fig. 9, *c*. 963–1066). The boundaries of the nunnery were extended over adjacent land from which secular dwellings had been removed, and the Nunnaminster and the two other minsters were brought into a single enclosure defined by walls and fences.[5] At about the same time, there was a series of exchanges between the three minsters in an attempt to settle differences between them, the Nunnaminster receiving two mills in return for the loss of a watercourse.[6] By these arrangements, undertaken at the height of the reform period, Æthelwold sought to secure for the three communities the seclusion needed to follow their calling *a civium tumultu remoti*.[7]

The lands that were thus extended and enclosed during the 960s, and which were ever subsequently to form the precinct of St. Mary's Abbey until the Reformation, were apparently based on an estate which had originally belonged to Ealhswith. The bounds of this property, in a form which suggests that they date from before the queen's death in 902–3(?), are preserved by an entry in a tenth-century hand added to an eighth-century book of prayers which probably belonged to the nunnery.[8] The bounds enclose the greater part of the area later occupied by St. Mary's Abbey and suggest that Ealhswith provided the site for the foundation of the house.

For two centuries after the reforms of Æthelwold, the history of Nunnaminster is a blank, and the succession of its abbesses is virtually unknown.[9] In the late eleventh or early twelfth century its buildings were remodelled. The abbey church probably shared in the reconstruction and appears to have been rededicated in 1108.[10] In August 1141, during the fighting between Henry of Blois and the empress's forces under Robert of Gloucester, the abbey was burnt down by firebrands thrown from the bishop's keep.[11]

to refer to Nunnaminster, but P. Grierson in *EHR* 55 (1940), 557 relates it to New Minster. The lowest porticus of the New Minster tower of the 980s was dedicated to the Virgin and her Holy Virgins, and the original dedication of New Minster included both the Holy Trinity and St. Peter, in addition to St. Mary (*LVH* viii). The dedication of a tower in 908 is therefore more likely to refer to St. Mary's Abbey. See Addenda.

[1] See Addenda.   [2] See Addenda.

[3] *Gesta pontificum*, bk. ii, caps. 75 (p. 167) and 78 (p. 174). *ASC* s.a. 963 (E), a twelfth-century Peterborough addition, implies that this took place in 963–4, in the same year as the reform of the Old and New Minsters, but the basis for this statement is unknown. See also Ælfric, Life of Æthelwold, cap. 16 (M. Winterbottom (ed.), *Three Lives of English Saints* (Toronto, 1972), 24, cf. p. 47).

[4] *...fundatum et factum monasterium...; construxit in eadem urbe sanctimonialium cenobium Adelwoldus*: *Gesta pontificum*, bk. ii, caps. 75 and 78.

[5] *BCS* 1302, Sawyer 807.

[6] *BCS* 1163, Sawyer 1449, cf. *AS Ch*, no. XLIX.

[7] *BCS* 1302, Sawyer 807.

[8] BM, Harl, MS. 2965, edited by Birch *Ancient Manuscript*. The bounds are printed on p. 96, and discussed on pp. 32–3, with map and unpaged appendix by F. J. Baigent following p. 32; see also *BCS* 630, Sawyer 1560. Baigent's solution of these bounds is not satisfactory. A new solution, taking the points in a clockwise direction and not requiring an extension north of High Street, will appear in Winchester Studies 4.   [9] *VCH Hants* ii. 126.

[10] Excavations in 1973 by the Winchester City Rescue Archaeologist revealed the south-west corner of the late Saxon monastic block, to which a vaulted under-croft (perhaps for the frater) had been added in the early Norman period. See Addenda.

[11] *Historia Novella*, cap. 499; *Gesta Stephani*, cap. 65; *LVH* 2; *Winchester ann*, s.a. For the identification of the *turris pontificis*, see above, p. 298.

There is no record of the rebuilding which must have followed within a few years, but it is doubtful if the monastic life was seriously interrupted.[1] In 1148 the business affairs of the nunnery as a city landlord show no sign of the recent disturbances, even among its properties in *Colobrochestret*, where damage and disruption would have been worst if the destruction was as serious as the chroniclers imply (Fig. 9, c. 1148).[2]

A few of the abbey's officers and servants are mentioned in Survey **II**. The sacrist and steward holding property on the abbess's fief in Colebrook Street were presumably abbey officials,[3] the abbess's gardener dwelling outside South Gate may have tended the abbey's vineyard there,[4] and two other servants can probably also be identified.[5]

vii. THE BISHOP'S PALACE (WOLVESEY) (Figs. 9, 25–7, and 32; Table 10)

The first mention of the bishop's *aula* occurs c. 1000 with reference to the time of Bishop Æthelwold.[6] It is mentioned again under 1042[7] and in the reign of Stephen, Henry of Blois (bishop, 1129–71) built a new residence.[8] Excavations from 1963 to 1971 at the Norman palace of the bishops at Wolvesey,[9] in the south-eastern corner of the walled city (Fig. 9, c. 1148), showed that the twelfth-century structures were preceded by an earlier complex beginning in the later tenth century.[10] These earlier buildings, established on a site that seems previously to have been open fields, probably formed part of the late Saxon episcopal residence.[11]

Wolvesey stands in an enclosure of some 3·6 ha, defined by the walls of the city to the east and south. The remaining sides are also marked by walls, of which that to the north was built or rebuilt in 1377–8 on the line of much older boundary.[12] The western wall, which separates Wolvesey from the cathedral precinct, is not older in its present form than the eighteenth century, but the boundary may be much older. Between 975 and 979 the Old Minster acquired two acres of land and an adjacent stream 'within the space extending to the old town-wall' which Bishop Æthelwold had enclosed with a wall for the monastery.[13] This transaction seems to reflect the final stages in the creation of the Old Minster precinct, and was a consequence of the rearrangement of the lands of the three Winchester monasteries undertaken by Æthelwold between 963 and 970 to secure privacy for the reformed monastic life of the three houses.[14] The present-day boundary between the bishop's palace and the cathedral precinct probably follows the

[1] No trace of destruction was observed in the recent excavations.   [2] See below, pp. 356 and 386.

[3] **II, 722** and **723**.

[4] **II, 961** and n. 2.

[5] **II, 586** (*serviens abbatisse*); **II, 661** and **731**, n. 1 (*Anschetillus de Sancta Maria*). For officers and servants of the cathedral priory and Hyde Abbey, see above, pp. 313 and 321.

[6] See Addenda.

[7] *Winchester ann*, s.a.: *in domo episcopi*.

[8] Ibid., s.a. 1138. The difficulties surrounding the interpretation of this and other references to Henry of Blois's works are discussed below, pp. 325 ff.

[9] The name occurs first, in the form *Wlveseia*, in the early thirteenth century (see above, p. 239, s.n.). The earlier references to the bishop's house are not specifically identified, however, and thus give rise to difficulties which are discussed below, pp. 325 ff.

[10] Preliminary reports will be found in *II–X Interims*. A full account will appear in Martin Biddle *et al.*, *Winchester Castle and Wolvesey Palace* (Winchester Studies 6, in preparation).

[11] *X Interim*, 326–8.

[12] PRBW 1377–8 (HRO, MS. Eccl. 159385, m. 33). This wall apparently follows the north side of 'mid-street', forming the southern boundary of Ealhswith's land as recorded in *BCS* 630 (Sawyer 1560) of a date earlier than 902–3 (?) (see above, p. 235, *stroet midde* and p. 322, n. 8).

[13] *AS Ch*, no. LIII (Sawyer 1376).

[14] *BCS* 1302 (Sawyer 807); and *BCS* 1163, *AS Ch*, no. XLIX (Sawyer 1449).

course of Æthelwold's wall, which would also have served to demarcate, perhaps for the first time, the enclosure of the palace (Fig. 9, *c.* 963–1066).

The creation of a separate residence for the bishop would thus seem to be part and parcel of the general reform of the Winchester monasteries during Æthelwold's episcopate, and to have resulted from the need to sever the more worldly life of the bishop's house from the seclusion of the cloister.[1] Very little is known of the layout of the bishop's palace at this period. The buildings so far identified lay in the northern part of the Wolvesey enclosure, beneath the north range of the Norman palace, and extending further north into an unexcavated area where their remains must have been destroyed by the later moat. The buildings examined formed an east–west range, bounded by a ditch to west and south. The western end of the range contained a masonry chapel, originally apsidal at each end, but subsequently extended by a small rectangular eastern porticus. The line of the chapel was extended eastward by a range of timber buildings of which very little has survived. These structures may be identified as part of a pre-conquest episcopal palace, partly by their obvious ecclesiastical character,[2] partly by the subsequent continuous use of the site for the bishop's residence, and partly by datable finds of pottery, coins, and other objects demonstrating occupation in the later tenth and eleventh centuries.

Continuity in function seems also reflected in the stages by which the palace was rebuilt and extended in the post-conquest period. The site had been arable since long before the establishment of the late Saxon complex. The fields to the south continued in use, and when the first Norman hall was built, it was aligned on the field boundaries and not on the existing buildings (Fig. 9, *c.* 1110). The decision to place the new hall to the south-west of the older structures seems to imply, however, that the latter remained standing. The new hall was a large ashlar-cased building of T-shaped plan, with its principal rooms at first-floor level above a solid substructure. The style of the masonry suggests a date near the beginning of the twelfth century, and hence in the episcopate of William Giffard (1100–29).[3] Although it is normal to call such a building a hall, it seems probable that it was a complete residence on an exceptionally grand scale, incorporating the bishop's private appartments, a function it continued to perform until the seventeenth century. The present chapel, over the eastern part of the cross-block at the south end of the hall, probably occupies the site of the original chapel. It enhances the impression of a private residence rather than a public hall. A piped water-supply was also laid on at this time, terminating in a well-house near the north-east corner of the new building.[4]

There is no contemporary record of the construction or use of the first or west hall, despite its size and magnificence.[5] In the late 1130s and early 1140s, however, when both

---

[1] For the residence of Æthelwold in the royal palace in the 970s, see above, p. 289, n. 2.

[2] For an identical two-apsed building, apparently serving as a chapel in the New Minster cemetery, see Fig. 9, *c.* 963–1066, and cf. *III Interim*, 258–60.

[3] *VIII Interim*, 322–3. See Addenda.

[4] *IX Interim*, 130; *X Interim*, 330–2. In the later Middle Ages the water piped to Wolvesey may have been taken out of the cathedral's supply, see above, p. 284.

[5] It was 53 m in length, the largest known non-

monastic domestic structure of its date in England, apart from Westminster Hall. The construction of Winchester House, Southwark, the London palace of the bishops of Winchester, has also been attributed to William Giffard (S. Toy in *Surrey Archaeological Coll.* 49 (1944–5), 75–81). So has the building of the great hall at Taunton Castle, another of the bishopric houses (C. A. R. Radford and A. D. Hallam, 'The History of Taunton Castle in the Light of Recent Excavations', *Proc. Somerset Archaeological and Nat. Hist. Soc.* 98 (1953), 55–96).

the city and its bishop played a central role in events before and during the civil war, the bishop's house and castle are several times mentioned, unfortunately never by name. Two buildings were involved, as the author of the *Gesta* makes clear.[1] One of these must have been the complex later known as Wolvesey, and the other was probably the former royal palace.[2] The references may be tabulated as in Table 10.

Any interpretation depends on the assumption that the author of the *Gesta* was consistent in his usage of *castellum*, and correct in his implication of two distinct buildings (2A and B). It would then follow that it was the *castellum*, not the *domus*, which was

TABLE 10

The bishop's domus *and* castellum *in Winchester, 1138–41*

	Date	A	B	Source
1	1138	*domum quasi palatium*	*cum turri* [sic] *fortissima*	*Winchester ann*, s.a.
2	1141	*domum illius*	*castellumque episcopi*	*Gesta*, cap. 63
3			*ad obsidendum episcopi castellum*	*Gesta*, cap. 64
4			*episcopi castellum . . . obsidebant*	*Gesta*, cap. 65
5			*ad episcopi obtinendum castellum*	*Gesta*, cap. 65
6			*ignibus foras* [sc. *ex castello*] *emissis*	*Gesta*, cap. 65
7	1141		*ex turre pontificis*	*Historia Novella*, cap. 499

heavily besieged and from which fire was thrown by the defenders (2–6). This latter point leads to the equation of the *castellum* of the *Gesta* with the place described by William of Malmesbury whence firebrands were thrown *ex turre pontificis* (7).

The well-known Winchester annal for 1138 has always been taken to refer to a single structural complex, a *domus* which included a *turris fortissima*, a keep (1A and B),[3] and it has been assumed that this complex was at Wolvesey.[4] There has been some difficulty in identifying the *turris* at Wolvesey, although various solutions have been suggested.[5] The evidence of the *Gesta* may now suggest, however, that the annal is more complex than has been realized. The emphasis of the whole annal of some fourteen lines is on the places where fortifications were built or strengthened and on the persons who undertook them. Henry of Blois's works are recorded in the first sentence, with Winchester at the beginning and in most detail. The passage should perhaps be translated:

1138. This year Bishop Henry built a palatial house and a strong tower in Winchester; and castles at Merdon, Farnham, Waltham, Downton, and Taunton. Bishop Roger of Salisbury . . .

The force of *cum*, in the phrase *cum turri* [sic] *fortissima*, appears here to be 'with' or

---

[1] *Gesta Stephani*, cap. 63: *castellumque episcopi . . ., sed et domum illius.*

[2] This matter is discussed at length, from the point of view of the royal palace, on pp. 297–9, above, esp. p. 298, n. 1.

[3] *Winchester ann*, s.a.: *Hoc anno fecit Henricus episcopus aedificare domum quasi palatium cum turri* [sic] *fortissima in Wintonia.*

[4] See, for example, Martin Biddle, 'Wolvesey: the *domus quasi palatium* of Henry de Blois in Winchester', *Château Gaillard*, 3 (ed. A. J. Taylor, London and Chichester, 1969), 28–36.

[5] Ibid. 35; cf. *V Interim*, 274–5. See now *X Interim*, 329.

'together with' in the sense of 'and', rather than 'in connection' or 'in company with'. If this view is acceptable, the annal cannot be used as evidence that the *domus* and *turris* were part of the same complex. The annal and the *Gesta*, far from contradicting each other, seem thus to be in agreement.

Bishop Henry may therefore have had two separate and distinct residences in Winchester: a *castellum* and a *domus*. The *castellum* was in the middle of the city, and may perhaps be identified with the (former) royal palace, north and west of the cathedral.[1] The *domus* could in this case only be identified with Wolvesey, and the various references provide some additional information. The annal for 1138 shows that the works on which the bishop was then engaged at the *domus*, or had recently completed, were on such a scale that they appeared to represent the construction, rather than the extension or rebuilding, of the now palatial house. By 1141, when it too was besieged, the bishop had fortified this house *ad instar castelli*.[2]

The evidence of the structure shows that Henry's works at Wolvesey continued for another thirty years, until the end of his episcopate. Additional documentary evidence is lacking however, with one exception. Writing about 1198 Gerald the Welshman, who had been under Henry of Blois's patronage, recorded that the bishop had demolished the royal palace and *ex dirutis aedificiis et abstractis domos episcopales egregias sibi in eadem urbe construxit*.[3] No date is attached to these events, for which there seem now to have been two possible occasions. When the bishop built his *turris* in 1138, apparently transforming the old royal palace into what could be called a castle, there must have been considerable alterations; but the rubble from any demolitions would probably have been needed for the new *turris*. Three years later in 1141 the royal palace was destroyed by fire in the fighting of that summer, probably as a result of its use as a castle by the bishop's forces. By 1148, and probably by as early as 1143, the site had been subdivided and redeveloped, and by this time the palace buildings must have been cleared away.[4] It was probably in the years between 1141 and 1143, therefore, that Henry of Blois obtained the materials of the royal palace for use in further works at Wolvesey.[5]

The structural sequence of the buildings at Wolvesey, as now understood as a result of the excavations of 1963–71,[6] appears to conform well with the sequence of events revealed by the documentary evidence discussed above.[7] The isolated western hall or

---

[1] See above, p. 298. At Glastonbury Henry built *quoddam regale palacium quod vocabatur castellum*: Adami de Domerham, *Historia de rebus gestis Glastoniensibus* (ed. T. Hearne, Oxford, 1727), ii. 316.

[2] *Gesta Stephani*, cap. 63: *domum illius, quam ad instar castelli fortiter et inexpugnabiliter firmarat*.

[3] This passage is quoted and discussed above, p. 299.

[4] This matter is discussed in detail above, pp. 299–301.

[5] The expenditure of £6. 1s. on the demolition of the bishop's castle or castles is recorded under Hampshire in the Pipe Roll for 1155–6 (*Pipe Roll 2 Henry II*, p. 54: the abbreviation of *castellum* makes it unclear whether *castello* or *castellis* is intended, both being perhaps more likely than the genitive singular, *castelli*). This may refer to any one or to all three of his castles in Hampshire. If it includes Winchester, it follows from what has been argued here that the payment related to the castle formed out of the old royal palace and not to Wolvesey. It is not impossible that the bishop left his *turris* of 1138 standing after the demolition of the other buildings on the royal palace/bishop's castle site in 1141–3, and that this *turris* was eventually felled in 1155–6. But there is no evidence that this happened. The slighting of Henry of Blois's castles is further discussed in Martin Biddle, op. cit. above, on p. 325, n. 4.

[6] See above, p. 323, n. 10.

[7] The outline which follows supersedes the previous interpretations as given in *II–IX Interims* and in Martin Biddle, op. cit., above, on p. 325, n. 4. For the new interpretation, see *X Interim*, 328–32.

residence of the early twelfth century, attributed to William Giffard (Fig. 9, *c.* 1110), was augmented some decades later by a separate eastern hall of grand proportions.[1] The two halls, facing each other across an open courtyard, were subsequently linked together by the construction of curtain walls closing the north and south sides of the courtyard, and enclosing a new court to the south of the eastern hall (Fig. 9, *c.* 1148). This action rendered the house defensible for the first time, and may reasonably be associated with the steps taken by the bishop in or before 1141 to strengthen the house *ad instar castelli*. If this is correct, the building of the eastern hall can probably be associated with his construction of a *domus quasi palatium* in or before 1138.

The building of the curtain walls was followed by the erection of a garderobe tower at the south-east corner of the eastern hall. This tower was built of reused materials, the first part of the palace to be so. It was followed by a major phase of reconstruction which saw the building of Wymondestour around a core formed by the earlier garderobe tower, the construction of a large keep-like structure further north, and the insertion of internal ranges across the north side of the courtyard, and in the interior of the southern court, against the south end of the eastern hall. This phase also made use of older materials, including a series of plain column shafts in the walls of the 'keep'.

The construction of the eastern hall had respected the site of the southern range of the late Saxon palace, although the north end of the hall had been built across the now-silted boundary ditch running along the south margin of the earlier buildings. Nor did the subsequent construction of the curtain wall linking the northern ends of the two halls necessarily involve the demolition of the late Saxon structures. They would now have been left outside the perimeter of the Norman house, however, and would presumably have been demolished (if indeed they had survived until this moment) to clear a field of fire outside the northern curtain.

By this time, therefore, there would have been old building materials available on site, from which the garderobe tower forming the first stage of Wymondestour could have been built. It would thus be unwise to see in this early tower one of the structures erected with materials from the old royal palace. It is quite another case, however, with the major phase of reconstruction which follows. Even in the areas excavated, and with little knowledge of what may have been added above ground level, these form a series of impressive additions to the fabric. In these new buildings it seems reasonable to see the *domos episcopales egregias* erected by Henry of Blois at least partly from the materials of the old royal palace and apparently in the years following 1141.

The only other major changes to the house during Henry of Blois's lifetime were the construction of a new north range and the reconstruction of the eastern hall, which was now raised to first-floor level. These works were probably begun after the bishop's return

[1] Unlike the western hall, the east hall was at ground-floor level and contained a true hall 27 m in length, as well as a two- or three-storied chamber-block at the south end. Entrance to the building seems to have been through the formal façade at this end, and the impression is given of a public hall rather than a solely private residence. The building of a second hall of this character may perhaps be explained by Bishop Henry's many public duties in the 1130s, as bishop, papal legate, administrator of the vacant see of Canterbury, and as his brother's chief agent. The porch and stairs added to the north end of the west hall, before the linking of the two halls, belongs to this same phase of increased magnificence and improved amenity.

from exile at Cluny in 1158.[1] Thirteen years later, when Bishop Henry lay dying *in pallacio ... episcopi* in August 1171, surrounded by the brethren of his cathedral priory,[2] the house of which he was the true creator had reached its greatest extent and almost its final form. In the succeeding five centuries during which it remained the city residence of the bishops of Winchester, alterations and additions were restricted to repairs and to improvements in general amenity. The only exception was the reconstruction of the eastern hall in an aisled form in the thirteenth century.[3]

Of the retinue which filled this immense house in the twelfth century, we have only the barest outline. Survey **II** does, however, provide some information. The bishop's justiciar, probably his chancellor, and one of his servants, are specifically mentioned.[4] In addition other sources reveal something of the clerical retinue of Henry of Blois among those who held land in Winchester in 1148: Jocelin de Bohun (by then bishop of Salisbury),[5] Robert of Lewes (by then bishop of Bath),[6] Hugh du Puiset,[7] Robert of Inglesham, and Osbert, probably also of Inglesham,[8] Richard the priest,[9] and the clerks, William, Iudichel, and Jordan Fantosme.[10]

viii. HOSPITALS (Fig. 33)

By the middle of the twelfth century, two substantial hospitals stood outside the walls of Winchester. In about 1136 Bishop Henry founded the Hospital of St. Cross for the reception of the poor, on a site near the river a mile to the south of the city.[11] The Hospital of St. Mary Magdalen, for the care of lepers and other sick persons, was established before 1148 on the downs nearly one and a half miles to the east of the city in a remote situation at the junction of the three parishes of Easton, Chilcomb, and Winnall.[12] By 1148 both hospitals had acquired a number of properties in Winchester,[13] and there is some evidence of the way in which places in St. Cross were offered to the inhabitants of Winchester by that date.[14] In both cases the sites seem to have been chosen because they were well beyond the limits of the suburbs of Winchester, and so there are no references to the hospital buildings in the surveys. The surviving evidence suggests that the major periods of construction in both hospitals came after the date of Survey **II**, at St. Cross between about 1160 and the early thirteenth century,[15] and at St. Mary Magdalen in the 1170s.[16]

There was probably at least one smaller hospital in existence by 1148, and possibly as early as *c.* 1110. The establishment later known as the Sustren Spittal, situated outside King's Gate and dependent upon the cathedral priory, may be the hospital mentioned in **II, 1054**; it was possibly the same hospital which held land outside West Gate at the time of Survey **I**, but this was more likely a private foundation.[17]

[1] *III Interim*, 260; *IX Interim*, 128–9.
[2] *Reg Pontissara* 628
[3] *IX Interim*, 129.
[4] **II, 89** and **665**; **1001**; **208** and **442**.
[5] **II, 51**.   [6] **II, 476**.
[7] **II, 494**.   [8] **II, 1** and **715**.
[9] **II, 322**.
[10] **II, 167** and **864**.
[11] *VCH Hants* ii. 193–4.
[12] See **II, 276**, n. 2.

[13] For the St. Cross properties, see **II, 9**, n. 2; and for those of St. Mary Magdalen, **II, 276**, n. 2.
[14] See **II, 963**, n. 1.
[15] *VCH Hants* v. 59–69.
[16] *Vetusta Monumenta*, iii (London, 1796), 1–12 and Pls. I, II, and III: Schnebbelie's drawings from which the plates were made are in the library of the Society of Antiquaries, Hants Red Portfolio, i. 10, 11, and 12.
[17] See **II, 1054**, n. 1 and cf. **I, 117**.

In later medieval tradition St. Beornstan, bishop of Winchester in 931–4, was said to have founded a *xenodochium* before the gate of the city. This establishment came to be identified with St. John's Hospital in the High Street towards East Gate. St. John's was flourishing by 1219, but no earlier references to it have been identified.[1]

The sites of such charitable institutions would, like those of the parish churches, normally have been free of rents and services and so could escape mention in the surveys. The monk's hospital of **II, 1054** was only mentioned in 1148 because a rent due from land belonging to the hospital had lapsed.

Survey **I, 101** records the charitable erection of five cottages for the poor in the western suburb of the city in the early years of the twelfth century. Such informal establishments may have been common.

ix. LESSER CHURCHES (Figs. 5, 6, 10, 12, 25–7, 32, and 33)

By the late thirteenth century there were fifty-seven parish churches within the area covered by the surveys (Fig. 10). This total includes the outlying churches of St. James, St. Faith, Winnall, and St. Giles, and the churches over the city gates, but excludes St. Catherine's on the Hill, the church of St. Mary in the cathedral cemetery, and the chapel of St. John's Hospital.[2] There is documentary or architectural evidence that thirty-four churches of this fifty-seven were in existence in the twelfth century,[3] and on general grounds it seems likely that almost all of the fifty-seven were established by the middle of the twelfth century, by which date a formal parochial system seems already to have existed in the city. Forty churches were said to have been burned during the siege of 1141.[4] Yet only four separate churches are mentioned in Survey **I** and four more in Survey **II**.[5] In each of these cases, except for St. Peter *in macellis* and perhaps for the church over East Gate, the reference in the surveys is the earliest documentary evidence for the existence of the church. The recording of churches was incidental to the main purpose of the surveys and they were only mentioned if rents were due from them, if they held land which was subject to investigation in the survey, or if the structure of the church was a necessary landmark in the definition of a property.

No more than ten or eleven of these twelfth-century churches can be proved to have been in existence before the Norman conquest. The pre-conquest origins of St. Mary Tanner Street, St. Pancras, and St. Maurice have been demonstrated by excavation.[6] Between 934 and *c.* 939 Bishop Ælfheah I at the request of the citizens and in the

[1] See *SMW*. For a possible alternative origin of St. John's Hospital, see below, p. 336.

[2] This total also excludes the friars' churches, the hospitals of St. Cross and St. Mary Magdalen, the chapels in the royal castle and in Wolvesey palace, and any other chapels within the precincts of the cathedral or abbeys, such as the chapel on the site of the grave of St. Swithun adjacent to the cathedral. The churches of Winchester will be discussed in full in *SMW*. For a late thirteenth-century list which includes most of the parish churches, see *Reg Pontissara* 597–9. See also, Goodman *Chartulary*, lvi–lix.

[3] The number may be thirty-eight, see below, p. 330,

n. 7. For two further possibilities, see **I, 10** and **71**.

[4] Continuator of Florence of Worcester, *Chronicon ex chronicis* (ed. B. Thorpe, London, 1848–9), ii. 133.

[5] See **I, 10, 23, 71**, and **107**; and **II, 511, 632, 695**, and **960**.

[6] For St. Mary and St. Pancras, see *X Interim*, 312–13 and 318–20; for St. Maurice, *Winchester 1949–60*, iii, forthcoming. Excavations on the site of St. Maurice revealed a small pre-Norman church, and a pre-conquest inscription in Scandinavian runes was found built into the church tower in 1970: see now B. Kjølbye-Biddle and R. I. Page in *Antiq J* 55 (1975), 389–94.

company of the young Dunstan dedicated a church by West Gate, probably identical with St. Martin in the Ditch.[1] St. Peter in *Colobrochestret* was probably in existence by the middle of the tenth century.[2] St. Peter *in macellis* was founded by the reeve Æthelwine before 1012.[3] St. Michael Kingsgate Street has a pre-conquest sundial,[4] and a fragment of pre-conquest sculpture was recovered from the site of St. Ruel. There is alternate quoining and the probable remains of a late Saxon doorway in the nave of St. Bartholomew, Hyde. The existence of the church of St. James in *c.* 970 is implied by the record in the *Regularis Concordia* of a church to which the monks processed on Palm Sunday,[5] and the pre-conquest origin of the church over East Gate is suggested by the dedication of the gate to St. Michael recorded *c.* 994.[6] The existence by 1148 of several other churches can perhaps be inferred from the distribution of certain properties of priests and clerks in Survey II.[7] A number of churches which did not long survive the conquest or which cannot now be identified are recorded in late Saxon sources, but some if not all of these were within the precincts of the Old Minster, the New Minster, or the Nunnaminster.[8]

A number of the dedications recorded in the twelfth and thirteenth centuries clearly belong to the period of the Norman conquest and after. Dedications to St. Valery, St. Leonard, St. Faith, St. Margaret, St. Anastasius, St. Giles, and perhaps the three to St. Nicholas, are in this group. The dedication to St. Petroc may date from 1177, when the saint's relics were displayed in Winchester, although St. Petroc had been venerated in the city in the mid-eleventh century.[9] The churches themselves, however, were not necessarily founded in this period, for rededications were possible.[10] The other dedications could all have been made in the Wessex of the tenth and early eleventh centuries, but those to St. Boniface and St. Alphege (Ælfheah II, bishop of Winchester 984–1005) may be

[1] W. Stubbs (ed.), *Memorials of St. Dunstan* (RS, 1879), 14, 15, 261. Ælfheah became bishop in 934. The events described here took place before *c.* 939 when Dunstan was ordained priest.

[2] See above, p. 322 and nn. 1–2.

[3] See **I, 23**. Excavations revealed part of the plan of the pre-conquest church: *Winchester 1949–60*, i. 43–5.

[4] A similar sundial is built into the surviving tower of St. Maurice's church; for both, see A. R. and P. M. Green, *Saxon Architecture and Sculpture in Hampshire* (Winchester, 1951), 58–9, pl. XIX.

[5] Thomas Symons (ed.), *Regularis Concordia* (London, 1953), 34–5; *Regesta*, ii, no. 1070. See p. 268.

[6] **II, 695**; cf. Wulfstan, *Narratio metrica*, bk. I, lines 573–4. There are no later references to this church, which presumably belonged to St. Mary's Abbey. The *capella sancte Marie ultra portam Orientalem* in the thirteenth-century list (*Reg Pontissara* 598) probably represents a scribal error for the church of St. Mary at West Gate, for which see below, p. 333.

[7] See below, p. 395 and Tables 32–3. If all the possibilities suggested in the tables are accepted, a further four would be added to the list of churches known to have existed in the twelfth century, making a total of thirty-eight.

[8] C. H. Turner, 'The churches in Winchester in the early eleventh century', *JTS* 17 (1916), 65–8; see also

above, pp. 268 and 315–16. The church dedicated to St. Maurice and his companions, with St. Pantaleon and all martyrs, might have been identical with the church known later as St. Maurice's, see above, p. 329, n. 6. Another early church, which may also have stood within the precincts of the minsters, was the *monasterium* purchased by St. Oswald when he was a young priest, perhaps shortly before 950 (J. Raine (ed.), *The Historians of the church of York*, i (RS, 1879), 410–11). St. Peter in *Colobrochestret*, situated at the south-east corner of the precinct of St. Mary's abbey was probably a similar case: see above, p. 322 and nn. 1–2. A pre-conquest cross-base formerly at Priors Barton and now in the City Museum may have come from the church of St. Faith near Priors Barton, and may possibly indicate a pre-conquest origin for that church: *Proc Hants FC* x (1922), 219–20.

[9] F. Wormald, 'The English saints in the litany in Arundel MS. 60', *AB* 64 (1946), 79; P. Grosjean, 'Vies et miracles de Saint Petroc: I, Le dossier du manuscrit de Gotha', *AB* 74 (1956), 131–88.

[10] The church of St. Petroc fell into ruins in the late fourteenth century. After its restoration in the fifteenth century it was rededicated to St. Thomas the martyr. See *Reg Wykeham* ii. 166–7 and 545–7; *Reg Wolsey* 56; and *SMW*.

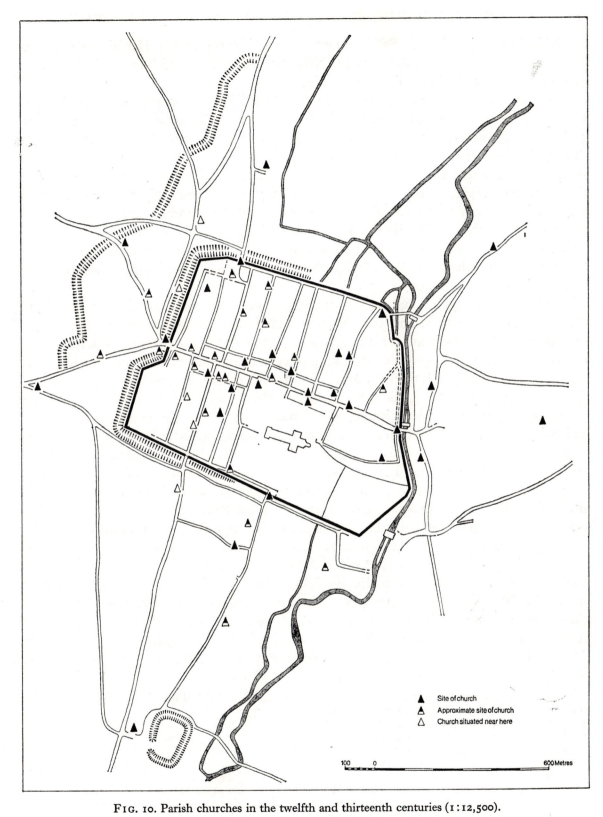

Fig. 10. Parish churches in the twelfth and thirteenth centuries (1:12,500).

The positions of two churches named in the late thirteenth-century list, St. Nicholas outside the wall and St. Helen, cannot be even approximately indicated.

particularly noted. That to St. Clement presumably represents Danish or seafaring influence. One of the dedications to St. Nicholas was in the neighbourhood of the fish-market, a connection also evident in London.

A parochial system seems to have been established before the siege of 1141. In 1143 Bishop Henry convened in the cathedral an assembly of ecclesiastics, rectors of churches, and laity, in order to reach a permanent settlement concerning the churches burned during the siege, and their parishioners.[1] It was ordained that the site of the royal palace should be assigned to the church of St. Laurence, next recorded in 1147.[2] The record of the other decisions has been lost, but the intention of the assembly to assign disputed areas within the city to individual churches for parochial purposes seems clear. So far as the mother church of Winchester was concerned, the establishment of full parochial rights was an undesirable development on the part of the city churches: even in late thirteenth-century lists, the Winchester churches, as *capelle*, are distinguished from the *ecclesie* of the rural parishes.[3]

Surviving wills suggest that burials were not commonly made in city churches until the late fifteenth century, and the excavation of St. Mary Tanner Street, where only one burial was found, supports this conclusion. On the other hand there is written evidence that in the 1360s burials were already taking place at the church of St. Pancras, a wealthier and more spacious church than St. Mary's, and some twenty graves have been excavated there.[4] An account of the rights of St. Swithun's Priory over the churches in the diocese drawn up in 1331 stated that burials could not take place in the churches of the city and suburbs without the licence of the prior or sacrist.[5] Of the Winchester churches recorded in this document only the three suburban churches of St. James, St. Anastasius, and St. Giles were said to have cemeteries. The early development of cemeteries in the suburbs[6] may reflect a distinction between the parish or lesser churches within and without the walls in this matter of burial rights, but could merely result from the less crowded condition of the suburbs. Baptismal rights may have been established earlier than burial rights, for a font was erected in the church of St. Mary Tanner Street by the early thirteenth century if not before.[7] Yet proximity to the mother church could inhibit the development of even this specially valued privilege, and in 1349 the abbess of St. Mary's Abbey objected strongly to the construction of a *baptisterium* in the parish church of St. Peter Colebrook Street.[8] At the time of Survey II the lesser churches of Winchester would thus appear to have been the focal points of a parochial system within the city in which rights of burial and baptism were as yet reserved by the mother church.[9]

[1] *LVH* 2, 3. The account of this meeting is inserted in a fourteenth-century hand into an otherwise mainly eleventh-century manuscript, but there is no evidence that it distorts the events it records in the light of later conditions. For the problems associated with this account and the date of the synod, see above, pp. 293, 297, n. 3, 300, n. 1.

[2] When the Abbey of Tiron was confirmed in its possession: J. H. Round (ed.), *Calendar of Documents preserved in France*, i. 368. The church of St. Laurence was later the possession of Hyde Abbey, perhaps on account of the original tenurial associations of its site; *VCH Hants* v. 75.

[3] *Reg Pontissara* 597–9.

[4] *VIII Interim*, 309–10.

[5] WCL, Records, vol. i, fo. 38.

[6] Excavation in 1972 showed that the cemetery of St. Anastasius (now St. Paul's Church) may have been in use as early as the beginning of the twelfth century.

[7] *VIII Interim*, 302–4.   [8] Reg Edington, fo. 21.

[9] On the sizes of twelfth-cent. parishes, see below, pp. 498–9.

As in London, Canterbury, and Lincoln,[1] many of these churches were no doubt essentially private foundations, perhaps intended as chapels for the owners of substantial town houses and their dependants (Fig. 12). In a rapidly changing urban situation the town house and its associated land could soon be split up among a number of different tenancies, while the chapel came to be used by all the surrounding householders and so emerged as a parish church. The foundation of one such church appearing in the surveys is recorded,[2] and the surveys themselves throw some light on the matter. In Survey **I**, two of the four churches mentioned are said to pertain to individual houses,[3] and a third is said to belong to a private individual.[4] In Survey **II**, two churches were situated within groups of tenements which may represent the subdivision of earlier large town houses and their associated land.[5]

Some churches may have been founded for the use of guilds: the church in Survey **I** belonging to Cheping son of Alveva was associated with a guildhall, and there is later evidence that at least two other churches were associated with guildhalls.[6] The excavation of the church of St. Mary Tanner Street and the area surrounding it has also provided a pointer to this private origin of a parish church. In the earlier periods of the church one doorway appears to have opened into a plot belonging to a substantial house 15 m to the south, while the other opened on to a lane or passage leading to the street; the latter was the only door which remained in use throughout the life of the church.[7]

In this period a church could be a source of profit, like any other piece of real estate, and this, rather than spiritual needs, was probably the reason for some foundations. Of these two motives, financial and spiritual, the former perhaps predominated in the foundation of those churches at the city gateways where travellers paused on entering or leaving the city and, like Harold at Bosham, might say a prayer for a successful journey. St. Mary Westgate, the twelfth-century arch of which survived into the nineteenth century, was adjacent to and partly built into the structure of the gate.[8] There were churches of St. Mary over North Gate, and St. Swithun over King's Gate, and a church over East Gate. The association between churches and gateways was common in medieval towns, and in Winchester this principle was extended to the entries to the suburbs, where the churches of St. Anastasius, St. James, St. Faith, and St. Martin, Winnall, were situated. Two churches had special functions in the twelfth century. St. Bartholomew in the north suburb, a pre-conquest foundation, was included in the precinct of Hyde Abbey following the move of New Minster to Hyde in 1110, and was subsequently subordinated to the abbey. St. Laurence lay within the site of the royal palace with which it may have been associated before the fire of 1141.

[1] On the question of the foundation of churches in towns, see C. N. L. Brooke, 'The Missionary at Home: the Church in the Towns, 1000–1250', in C. J. Cuming (ed.), *Studies in Church History*, 6 (Cambridge, 1970); J. W. F. Hill, *Medieval Lincoln* (Cambridge, 1965), 130–52; Urry *Canterbury*, 207–13.

[2] See **I, 23.**

[3] **I, 23** and **71.**

[4] **I, 10.**

[5] **II, 511** and **960.** The former may have originated as the chapel of the town house of the abbess of Wherwell (cf. Fig. 12).

[6] In the later thirteenth century, both St. Peter Whitbread and St. Petroc stood near former guildhalls which were by that time in private possession: see *SMW*. The fraternities associated with the churches of St. Maurice and St. Mary Kalendar were in existence before 1237: Goodman *Chartulary*, no. 470. These guilds may, of course, have grown up long after the churches were founded, but cf. below, p. 427.

[7] *IX Interim*, 107.

[8] *Archaeologia*, 16 (1812), 361, pl. lxiii: Society of Antiquaries, Hants Red Portfolio, ii. 26.

In the fourteenth century the patrons of Winchester parish churches were the bishop, the prior of the cathedral, the abbot of Hyde, the abbesses of St. Mary's, Winchester, and Wherwell, the prior of St. Denis near Southampton, and the archdeacon of Surrey.[1] Most of the advowsons were probably in ecclesiastical hands by the mid-twelfth century. A few of these churches, like the chapel of the abbess of Wherwell at her town house in *Flesmangerestret*,[2] may have been founded by ecclesiastical bodies. Lay foundations, which may have been the majority, presumably came into ecclesiastical possession by donation, and perhaps in some cases by reversion to the ecclesiastical lord of the land on which the church stood.[3] St. Peter *in macellis* came into the possession of the cathedral along with a substantial part of the property with which it was originally associated.[4] At the time of Survey **I**, at least one of the four churches mentioned was in lay possession. In 1148 Wherwell and St. Mary's Abbey apparently each possessed a church, and a third may have been in the possession of its priest. When, before 1142, St. Denis Priory acquired the churches of St. John and St. Peter outside East Gate they were both in the possession of Stigand the chaplain.[5]

The distribution of the parish churches apparently reflected that of the population (Fig. 10). Churches were more frequent within the walls than without, and there was a tendency towards concentration in High Street. A number of churches were situated towards the rear of the properties with which they were associated. Examples of this are the two St. Peters, St. George, St. Nicholas, St. Clement, St. Andrew, and possibly St. Paul in High Street, and St. Pancras in Wongar Street (*Wunegrestret*). This remote and enclosed situation might be taken to emphasize the private origin of these churches, but others of apparently similar origin, such as St. Mary Tanner Street, were situated directly on the street frontage. The position of the church may rather reflect the intensity of building on the street frontage at the time of its foundation. By the early twelfth century the churches in High Street at least were hemmed in by houses and shops (cf. Fig. 12). All the churches of which the alignments are known, with one exception,[6] were aligned according to the street grid and property boundaries, rather than on a true east–west axis.

The small size of the early churches may also suggest their private origin. The nave of St. Mary Tanner Street in the twelfth century measured 4 m by 5 m, and the early naves of St. Pancras and St. Peter *in macellis* were about the same width, the nave of St. Pancras being about 3 m longer.[7] Archaeological and architectural evidence demonstrates that Winchester parish churches, and in particular their naves, were being enlarged from at least as early as the later eleventh century. The parishes themselves, however, did not increase in area until after the depopulation occasioned by the visitations of the plague in the mid-fourteenth century. Since the population of Winchester

---

[1] *VCH Hants* v. 75–6. For the archdeacon's church, see **II**, 817, n. 1.

[2] **II**, 511.

[3] Possible examples are the churches of St. Peter and St. Paul at the west end of High Street, and the church of St. Michael in *Scowrtenestret*, both of which stood on the fief of the abbot of Hyde and are later recorded in his possession.

[4] See below, p. 340 and Fig. 12.

[5] See **II**, 688, n. 1.

[6] The church excavated in Staple Gardens, possibly identical with St. Mary in *Brudenestret*: see *Winchester 1949–60*, i. 166–76. The arguments there produced against this being the church of St. Mary have little substance; cf. *SMW*, s.v. 'parish churches'.

[7] The areas of the original naves of St. Mary and St. Pancras were thus 20 sq. m and 32 sq. m, respectively.

almost certainly fell after the twelfth century, the resources available to the individual churches in their parishes during this early period of enlargement were probably declining or at least static. The enlargement of the parish churches in the later eleventh and twelfth century might thus represent their adaptation to a parochial function, and to a congregation larger than the private group for which they were originally intended.

X. GUILDHALLS (Fig. 32)

The identities of the eleventh- and twelfth-century guildhalls in Winchester remain as obscure as the functions of the associations of *chenictes* themselves. Survey **I** mentions two halls on the north side of High Street where *chenictes* had met or drunk their guild in the time of King Edward, but this practice does not appear to have continued into the twelfth century.[1] It is possible that, as at Canterbury, there was a connection between one of these associations of *chenictes* and the merchants of the city, for there are some grounds for identifying the *chenictehalla* of **I, 10** with Chapman's Hall, which was in existence by 1130, and where linen cloths were sold in 1148.[2] In the second survey the *hantachenesele* where the *probi homines* of Winchester used to drink their guild is mentioned under *Colobrochestret*, but again there is no indication that this practice continued at the time of the survey.[3]

The drinking of ale and the foundation of a church at one of the halls on the north side of High Street suggest that for their members these early guilds were social and religious institutions which provided an important framework for daily life in the town.[4] The surviving records of other pre-conquest guilds show that one of their functions was to provide benefits for their members similar to those arising from kinship obligations, a particularly valuable social service in a rapidly expanding city where a substantial proportion of the population were recent immigrants.[5] In these circumstances the guilds themselves could have been as ephemeral or as fluid in their organization as many town fraternities of the later Middle Ages. The halls themselves need hardly have differed from substantial domestic halls, and on the dissolution or amalgamation of a guild could have easily passed into private use, as two guildhalls, one of them possibly identical with **I, 34,** are known to have done in the thirteenth century.[6] Conversely, there is no evidence to suggest that the early twelfth-century stone-vaulted structure which survives in St. Thomas Street,[7] as fine a private hall as is known from the period, was ever used by a guild.

---

[1] **I, 10** and **34**; cf. above, p. 236, s.n. *chenictehalla*. The *medehalla* of **I, 12** might indicate another hall in this area, cf. above, p. 238, s.n. For comparable guilds in London and Canterbury, see F. M. Stenton, 'Norman London', in D. M. Stenton (ed.), *Preparatory to Anglo-Saxon England* (Oxford, 1970), 32–3; and Urry *Canterbury*, 124–31. The London guild of *cnihtas* was also obsolescent in the early twelfth century. For other Winchester guilds of this period and before, see below, p. 427.

[2] See **II, 69**, and n. 1; cf. above, p. 236, s.n. *chepmanneshal'*. There is, however, no recorded connection between Chapman's Hall and the merchant guild of the city, for which see below, p. 427.

[3] **II, 712**; cf. above, p. 237, s.n.

[4] **I, 10**.

[5] For an over-all account of pre-conquest guilds, see Barlow *English Church*, 196–8, and the references there cited.

[6] The other guildhall was in *Calpestret* near the church of St. Petroc, perhaps dedicated *c.* 1177, with which it may have been associated. This guildhall had passed into private use by *c.* 1270, *Selborne Charters*, 80 and *SMW*.

[7] Now part of 24 St. Thomas Street; for plan see *VCH Hants* v. 8, 9.

In the later Middle Ages the boundary between social and religious associations and municipal authority was often ill-defined, and this may also have been the case in the eleventh and twelfth centuries, with the reservation that municipal authority itself was considerably less distinct at that time than in the later period. A possible association between one of the early halls and the merchants of Winchester has been mentioned. The two halls on the north side of High Street were held freely from King Edward and the hall in Colebrook Street was in the king's hands in 1148.[1] The king was lord of the city and these guilds may have been linked with the organization of town life. In the thirteenth century the Winchester merchant guild was made up of four 'houses' (*meisons*),[2] a division which may reflect separate earlier associations in the nature of guilds.

In the 1148 survey a *gihalda* is mentioned in three associated entries which probably all refer to the same building.[3] This *gihalda* lay on the south side of High Street and, according to the context of the survey, was probably on or near the site of the demolished royal palace, at that time in the possession of the bishop.[4] In the thirteenth century the gaol of the city of Winchester, later known also as the hall of pleas, where the court of the mayor and bailiffs met, and as *le Gildehalle*, occupied a first-floor position towards the north-west corner of the site of the royal palace, just west of the church of St. Laurence. This site, with its royal associations, might have been suitable in 1148 for a hall of the merchant guild, a body co-extensive at a later date with those citizens of Winchester who enjoyed the privilege of having their pleas heard in the city court. There is some evidence that this guildhall was under royal supervision in 1148.[5] In 1361 the town court was removed to a site at the entry to *Calpestret*, where the Old Guildhall, erected in 1711, now stands.[6]

A problem relating to the evolution of the municipal organization of Winchester on which the twelfth-century surveys throw no clear light is that of St. John's Hospital.[7] Above the twin infirmaries of the hospital there was a hall where in the fourteenth and fifteenth centuries the *burghmote*, the assembly of the commonalty or *probi homines* of Winchester, met three times a year.[8] The administration of St. John's Hospital was supervised by the municipal authorities, and the fraternity of St. John which met there included among its members the leading figures in city affairs.[9] No reference to St. John's can, however, be conclusively identified in the surveys. The area in which the hospital lay was, however, within the aldermanry of Colebrook Street in the fourteenth century, and it may therefore be possible that the *hantachenesele*, where the *probi homines* used to drink their guild, entered under *Colobrochestret* in the 1148 survey, was identical with the hall at St. John's Hospital.[10]

[1] Urry *Canterbury*, 126, cites similar cases in Canterbury and Dover.   [2] Furley *Usages*, 39.
[3] II, 140, 143, and 155.
[4] See above, p. 298.
[5] See below, p. 423.   [6] *SMW* 186.
[7] For the traditional origin of the hospital, see p. 329, above.

[8] Furley *City Government*, 65–6.
[9] For the details of the constitution of St. John's Hospital, first recorded in 1219, see *SMW* and cf. *Proc Hants FC* 19 (1955), 20–34.
[10] II, 712; but this suggestion does not fit well with the order of survey, see above, p. 248.

4

PRIVATE HOUSES

ALTHOUGH the two surveys were intended as records of rents and services rather than buildings, and consequently provide little direct information on the nature and distribution of the different types of private house, some general conclusions are possible. Many different kinds of structure were mentioned incidentally, and using the evidence of the groupings of rents it is possible to reconstruct some physical developments in the house or plot layout at an early period.

i. TERMINOLOGY (Figs. 11–13 and Table 3)

In Survey **I** the two terms generally used to describe houses are *domus* and *mansura*, and each appears almost exclusively in different parts of the survey (Table 3). *Domus* is used to describe the built-up properties in High Street, outside West Gate, and in *Brudenestret*. No one term is generally used to describe properties in the other streets, but *mansura* is used in the plural in those cases where a single rent was owed by one person from more than one house. This might have been so already in the time of King Edward (e.g., **I, 142** and **177**), but more frequently was the result of the amalgamation of houses into one ownership. Thus in a single entry under *Bucchestret*, Luwinus rendered 5*d*. and customs, and Lepstanus rendered 12*d*. and customs *TRE*, but in *c.* 1110 Gisulf owed the same from two *mansurae* (**I, 223**). This implies that in most entries in those streets where the property was not otherwise defined, and where a single person owed a single rent, the property was regarded as a *mansura*. A further or alternative implication is that the *mansura*, almost always mentioned in the plural, was a relatively small but self-contained and independent dwelling-house. This interpretation is supported by the fact that three *mansurae* were contained, along with other structures, within the *domus* known as *Godebiete* in High Street (**I, 23**).

It might be argued that the usage of *domus* and *mansura* reflects a division of the survey of the city between two panels of commissioners. There certainly are differences in the forms of the entries and in the scope of the inquiry in different parts of the survey,[1] but Table 3 shows that these differences do not correspond exactly with the changing use of *domus* and *mansura*. In the 'lands of the barons' in *Brudenestret* both words were used, and so probably do not each represent terms favoured by separate groups of surveyors.

The *domus* appears to have been a substantial house or establishment. Godbegot, measuring 132 feet (40·23 m) from east to west along High Street and 148 feet 6 inches (45·26 m) from south to north, contained a church, shambles, and subsidiary dwellings,

---

[1] See above, pp. 12–13.

and was certainly a considerable unit (Fig. 12).[1] At least one other *domus* had a church, and several *domus* were in multiple occupation, but, as will be argued below, single establishments of the size of Godbegot were probably exceptional at the date of Survey **I**. The term *domus* could also denote a single structure forming part of a larger house, as in later medieval building terminology. Thus one of the three *mansurae* in Godbegot is also described as *domus*. But in the formal sense in which *domus* appears to be used on most occasions in Survey **I**, the term seems to mean a large house as opposed to the smaller *mansurae* in the north–south streets.

In Survey **II** *domus* does not appear to have been used in the formal sense of Survey **I**, but in the ambiguous later medieval and modern sense of 'house' or 'building'. In the descriptions of brew-houses in Survey **II**, the fittings and utensils for brewing are distinguished from the *domus* or structure (**II, 62, 568, 591,** and **856**). The term *domus* also appears to be used frequently with specific reference to the house as a structural feature. A *domus* might be cited as a property boundary (**II, 511** and **1001**): there are *domus* next to the city wall or gates (**II, 691, 694, 695, 708,** and **796–9**), and encroaching on to the street (**II, 925**), but on other occasions there appears to be no special reason for the use of the term.

Mansio was the common term for a dwelling house in Survey **II**, and like *mansura* in Survey **I** was mainly used in the plural. An obscure term which relates to dwellings is *managium*. *Managia* were frequently held free of rent as part of a larger property, from the remainder of which rent was due. Thus outside West Gate, the wife of Godwin of Fulflood owed 4*s.* rent to the prior, had 34*d.* rent from the property, and held her *managium* quit (**II, 245**). The term may denote the dwelling place of the landlord, in this case the wife of Godwin of Fulflood, within the property. In such situations the landlord may have deliberately arranged for the rent due from one part of the property to be supported by that part of the tenement which he did not occupy, but from which he himself drew rent.[2] The term *hospicium*, possibly used in a specialized sense in Survey **II**, is discussed below.[3]

The word *terra* was frequently used in both surveys. In most instances it has the general meaning of 'real estate', hence on occasion *terra* appears to be synonymous with *mansura*.[4] Empty plots were described as *vasta terra* (**II, 54** and **517**), *vasta platea* (**II, 728**),[5] and *curtilla* (**I, 117–22**; **II, 193** and **685**). *Gardina* and *prata* are also mentioned (**I, 98**; **II, 357** and **674**).[6]

Apart from the general terms discussed above, a number of specific kinds of structure are mentioned in the two surveys (Figs. 11 and 13). *Bordelli* (**I, 84** and **101**; **II, 585**) were no doubt the simplest form of dwelling-house. Stalls (*estals*) encroaching on to the street in front of houses were less permanent structures than *domus*, and were particularly associated with butchers, who have traditionally displayed their goods in front of their

[1] Goodman *Goodbegot*, 2–5; cf. *KCD* 720, Sawyer 925.

[2] For an apparently unspecialized use of the term *managium*, see M. Gibbs (ed.), *Early Charters of the Cathedral Church of St. Paul, London* (Camden 3rd ser. 58, 1939), no. 121.

[3] See p. 389.

[4] Cf. **II, 656**, n. 1.

[5] For waste properties in general in the surveys, see below, p. 386.

[6] The terms *gardinum* and *pratum* both occur in both the entries in Survey **II**.

houses.[1] The shambles by the church in Godbegot were no doubt similar structures
(**I, 23**; **II, 43**). *Seldae* were more substantial. The *selda* where linen cloths were sold
(**II, 69**) was a large property, and another *selda* (**II, 148**) was worth 10*s.* a year in rent.[2]
In the thirteenth century the *seldae* in St. Giles's Fair appear to have been large structures
containing many individual booths or *fenestrae*, each let separately.[3] The twelfth-century
seldae in the city may have been similar. One group of shops (*escheopes*) is recorded in
Survey **I, 27**.

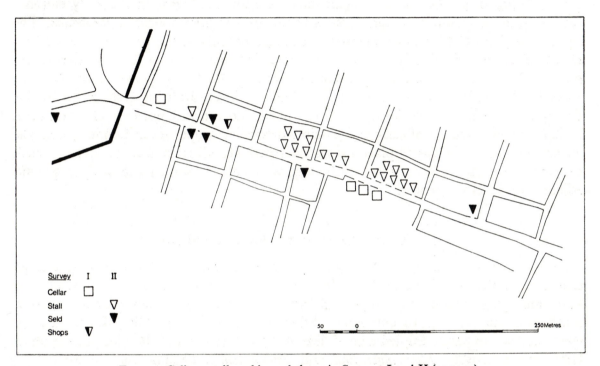

FIG. 11. Cellars, stalls, selds, and shops in Surveys I and II (1:5,000).
The number of cellars taken into the Norman extension of the royal palace on the south side of High Street is not known.
Three are shown.

Of parts of houses, there are mentions of a kitchen (**II, 403**) and of a range of upper
rooms or solars (**II, 151–8**). In Survey **I** a number of cellars (*cellarii*) are recorded
(Fig. 11), one near West Gate belonging to King Edward (**I, 38**), and others belonging to
the burgesses near the royal palace on the south side of High Street (**I, 61–3**). After the
siege of 1141 the Londoners pillaged many of the houses and cellars in Winchester.[4] These
cellars were not necessarily below ground,[5] since at least five of them were converted
into forges between the reign of Edward the Confessor and the early twelfth century.
Many of the surviving twelfth-century stone undercrofts in this country, now partly or

---

[1] The following entries refer to stalls: **I, 20** and
21; **II, 27, 43, 45, 48, 49, 54, 56**, and **58**. See also
Fig. 11 and below, pp. 431–3.

[2] For selds, see **I, 71**; **II, 33, 69, 148, 165**, and
180; and cf. Fig. 11.

[3] The *fenestrae* were possibly window-like openings

with folding shutters; cf. *VCH Hants* v. 37.

[4] *domibusque et cellariis: Gesta Stephani*, cap. 67.

[5] There was a *domus subterranea* in London *c.* 1100;
B. W. Kissan, 'An early list of London properties',
Trans. London and Middlesex Archaeological Society,
N.S. 8 (1940), 57–69.

wholly underground, were originally surface structures,[1] and it is possible that the Winchester cellars were similar, used for the safe keeping of the occupants and their goods in the way that the simple sense of the word *cellarium* suggests.

In Domesday Book the words normally used to describe urban properties were *haga*, *mansura*, and occasionally *domus*. The thirty-one *mansurae* which Wherwell Abbey owned in Winchester in 1086 appear to correspond to the abbey's properties recorded in Survey **II**, and were probably the same size as the average urban tenement of the later Middle Ages (cf. Fig. 12). These same tenements were known as *hagae* in the early eleventh century,[2] and a synonymous term also used in pre-conquest sources is *praedium*. The term *haga* (from OE *haga* m. 'enclosure, messuage') occurs in the property-name *Merewenehaia* (**I, 66**). Nothing is known of the nature of this property, but the vacant plot outside West Gate where the royal hawk-mews had stood was known as the *haias de Parroc* or *le hauekheye* in the thirteenth and fourteenth centuries, suggesting that by this date the term denoted an enclosure relatively unencumbered with houses.[3] The term *burh*, which denotes a number of early and possibly defensible properties in London, occurs as an element in two Winchester place-names, *Coiteburi* (**II, 687**) and *Erdberi*.[4] In the twelfth century each of these Winchester burhs appears to have been a piece of open ground adjacent to the city defences.

ii. EARLY TENEMENTS (Figs. 12 and 19)

At least three early tenements in High Street were several times larger than the average tenement of the later Middle Ages. In 1012 the *praedium* later known as Godbegot measured 132 feet (40·23 m) along High Street and 148 feet 6 inches (45·26 m) from south to north (**I, 23**). In 996 King Æthelred granted to the Old Minster a *haga* which appears to have occupied a good deal of the western end of the block facing on to High Street between *Flesmangerestret* and *Sildwortenestret*.[5] The seld in Survey **II** where linen cloths were sold, Chapman's Hall, as represented by the block of property acquired by St. Swithun's Priory in 1330, was of a comparable size, with a frontage on to High Street of perhaps a hundred feet (**II, 69**). In the early twelfth century two of these tenements and one other in High Street contained churches which may have originated as the private chapels of the owners of the properties (**I, 10, 23, and 71**). Furthermore, the landlords of two of these tenements exercised a private jurisdiction over their tenants (**I, 23 and II, 69**), and sake and soke is mentioned in connection with one other house in Survey **I** (**I, 279**).[6] Normally such jurisdictions disappeared as tenements were divided, family estates disintegrated, and municipal authority was consolidated, but in special circumstances a strong landlord could preserve his liberty against encroachment. Thus

[1] P. A. Faulkner, 'Medieval Undercrofts and Town Houses', *Arch J* 123 (1966), 120–35.
[2] See below, p. 356.
[3] For these names, see above, p. 238, s.nn.
[4] See above, pp. 236 and 237, s.nn.
[5] *KCD* 1291, Sawyer 889.
[6] For similar private jurisdictions in twelfth-century London, see F. M. Stenton, 'Norman London', in D. M. Stenton (ed.), *Preparatory to Anglo-Saxon England* (Oxford, 1970), 33–5. Stenton's reference to the bishop's soke in Winchester in the twelfth-century (ibid. 33, n. 4) in fact relates to the bishop's soke in the suburbs of the city in the thirteenth century, discussed above, pp. 255–6.

the prior of St. Swithun's still exercised the manorial jurisdiction of Godbegot in the sixteenth century,[1] and in 1330 the lord of the Clothselde, usually a wealthy Winchester merchant, still enjoyed a special jurisdiction over his tenants (**II, 69**).

There is some evidence for the once widespread existence of such large tenements in the city. In Survey **II** tenements from which rents were due to the king, the bishop, the prior of St. Swithun's, the abbot of Hyde, and the abbesses of St. Mary's, Wherwell, and Romsey, occur in groups throughout the city and suburbs. These rents may represent the units into which a larger tenement, or in the case of very large groups of rents, several larger tenements, had been divided. Unfortunately neither the nature of the large tenements nor the date of their origin is known. And the nature of the rents is equally uncertain. By 1148 almost all the land in the city and suburbs belonged to one of these fiefs. By 1066 the fiefs of the king and of the abbeys of Wherwell and Romsey, the only fiefs for which there is evidence at this date, appear to have already achieved the form which they took in 1148.

The ecclesiastical landlords may have acquired considerable parts of the fiefs by purchase or endowment from lay lords, just as they acquired the advowsons of parish churches in this period.

In 1148 there were still some substantial blocks of property in private possession, and the identities of others may have been lost by successive alienations and divisions. The Worthy estate in *Brudenestret*, recently in lay hands, covered four entries in Survey **II** (**II, 406–9**), as did Roger de Port's fief in *Wunegrestret* (**II, 580–3**), while William Martel's fief in *Alwarnestret* covered five entries (**II, 488–92**). Two of the groups of properties surveyed in 1148 included churches whose advowsons were later recorded as belonging to the owners of the rents. Survey **II** thus appears to preserve in its grouping of rents the outline of an earlier arrangement in which the 'urban manor', with the territorial lordship and perhaps the private church of its rural counterpart, may have been a common and easily recognizable feature (Fig. 12).

Figure 19 shows, for the streets where reconstruction is possible, the distribution of fiefs according to the entries in the second survey. The private fiefs and the smaller blocks of property belonging to the great lords are perhaps most representative of the size of early tenements as units of occupation. Even allowing for the uncertainties in this form of reconstruction, the early tenements in the side streets appear to have been comparable in size to Godbegot. Private jurisdictions were probably already disappearing in the twelfth century and by 1148 there would have been little physical evidence of the earlier layout of these tenements. The evidence of the fiefs of the king and of Wherwell and Romsey Abbeys, already quoted, indicates that the subdivision of the large tenements had taken place by 1066, for the number of Winchester properties which these fiefs contained at that date was approximately the same as the number they contained in the twelfth century. The nine *hagae* in Tanner Street which King Æthelred granted to his thegn Æthelweard in 990 might even represent the division of one of these large properties.[2] Traces of this early pattern of occupation may hardly have outlasted the twelfth century.

---

[1] Goodman *Goodbegot*, 13–17, 24–37.   [2] *KCD* 673, Sawyer 874.

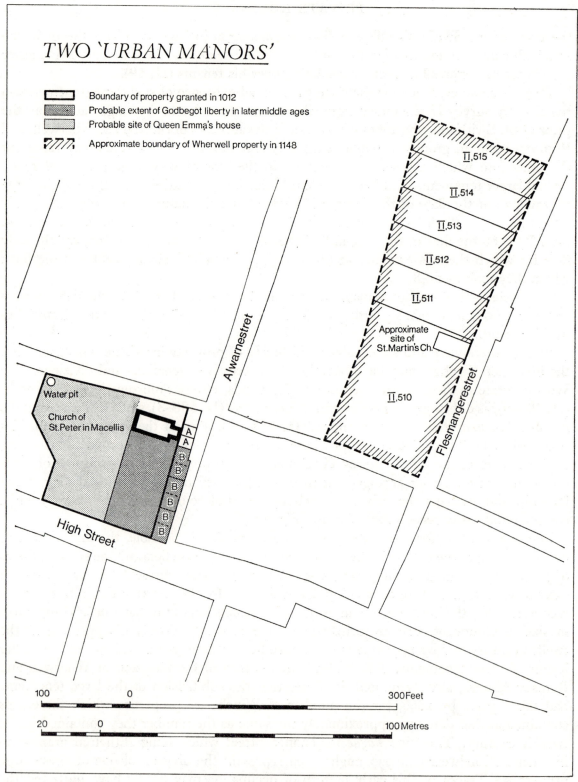

FIG. 12. Two 'urban manors': Godbegot, and the property of the abbess of Wherwell in *Flesmangerestret*
(1:1,250).

See **I, 23**, n. 1 (pp. 37–8), for discussion of the Godbegot property. (A: two shambles encroaching on the street and taken
into the church by *c.* 1110; B: three *mansurae* taken out of the street *TRE*, and perhaps represented by six stalls in 1148).
The extent of the Wherwell property is based on the average frontage represented by the entries in *Flesmangerestret* (cf.
Table 26). **II, 510** seems to have been on the south side of the church, and the other divisions are shown accordingly.

iii. THE SUBDIVISION OF TENEMENTS (Fig. 13)

This subdivision of tenements was evidently a function of the expansion of the population of Winchester in the tenth and eleventh centuries. Further subdivisions in the later eleventh and twelfth centuries are recorded in the surveys. A group of houses in the

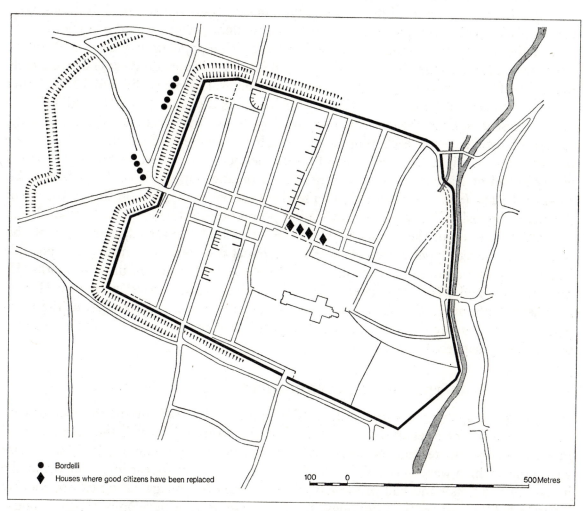

●   Bordelli

◆   Houses where good citizens have been replaced

100   0   500 Metres

FIG. 13. The subdivision of properties in the eleventh and twelfth centuries (1 : 10,000).
The Fig. shows the *bordelli* outside West Gate *c.* 1110, and the houses where good citizens were replaced by poor men between *TRE* and *c.* 1110. The blocks of Romsey Abbey and Wherwell Abbey property, shown in heavy outline as subdivided by the late eleventh century, have been reconstructed on the evidence of Survey II.

middle part of the north side of High Street went into multiple occupation between the reign of King Edward and *c.* 1110, when the surveyors noted that the household of a single good citizen had been succeeded by a number of poor men (**I, 13a, 16, 17,** and **18**). A landlord might also let out part of his property, and thus in *Brudenestret* the daughter of Henry son of Thurstin received rent from one part of her property there and kept her household in another house on the same property (**II, 414**). Similarly, Drew let out and lived in separate parts of the same tenement (**II, 401**).

Accommodation could also be let furnished: the sister of the wife of Thurstin the clerk lived in part of Thurstin's house in *Alwarnestret* and had household-goods belonging to her sister; and in *Bucchestret* a man rented a house and goods for 16*s.* (**II, 496** and **699**). The *catalla* mentioned in these entries may, however, have been specialized equipment of a semi-permanent nature, such as the brewing utensils mentioned elsewhere in Survey **II**.[1] In the later Middle Ages, dye-houses, brew-houses, and bakeries were commonly let with a comprehensive range of equipment provided by the landlord.[2]

A further way to accommodate and profit from a rising population was for landlords to erect rows of houses to let. The rows of four and five *bordelli* outside West Gate were early examples of those rows of cottages common in medieval towns (**I, 84** and **101**).[3] Other references to several houses on a single piece of ground (e.g. **I, 98, 107,** and **117–22**) may represent similar though superior developments. In Survey **II** there are some groups of regular rents, each rent large enough to represent the market-value of the property, which might represent rows of houses deliberately erected for profit. The abbot of Hyde had at least four adjacent rents of 9*s.* on the north side of High Street (**II, 11–14**; the 11*s.* (xi s.) rent from **II, 15** may be a scribal error), and on the south side of the street the bishop had a number of similar properties, in the neighbourhood of, if not occupying, the site of the former royal palace. Here he had four adjacent rents of 10*s.* (**II, 146–9**), seven upper rooms let nearby for equal fractions of as near £2 as possible (**II, 152–8**), and a group of seven or more tenements let for rent in units of marks (**II, 160–6, 168,** and **170**). Moreover, many of the individual entries in Survey **II** may represent single properties on which there were several houses or cottages, as the comparison of this survey with the suggested population of the city and with later medieval evidence may suggest.[4]

iv. THE AMALGAMATION OF TENEMENTS (Fig. 19)

Although landgable rents are not denoted by name in the 1148 survey, they can usually be identified by their relatively low value or by the position in which they are recorded in each entry. Some tenements clearly owed landgable to more than one lord,[5] and there were others which were in two fiefs.[6] Such tenements usually appear in the survey at the junction of two fiefs,[7] and had presumably been created by amalgamating two previously separate holdings or parts of holdings. In the course of such developments early house plots or property boundaries could easily be obliterated in a way which is well documented for the later medieval city. These tenements were virtually confined to the side streets within the walls. In High Street the market demand for individual properties was perhaps

---

[1] See below, p. 431.

[2] See *SMW.*

[3] For an excavated Winchester example of the thirteenth century, see *VI Interim,* 265–6; *VII Interim,* 308–9.

[4] See below, pp. 440–1.

[5] The following tenements appear to be in this category in Survey II: High Street, **81**; Outside West Gate, **180**; *Brudenestret,* **397** and **418**; *Scowrtenestret,*

442; *Alwarnestret,* **501**; *Flesmangerestret,* **512** and **520**; *Sildwortenestret,* **557**; *Wunegrestret,* **570** and **605**; *Tannerestret,* **657**; *Bucchestret,* **674**; *Gerestret,* **1082**.

[6] The following tenements are in this category in Survey II: High Street, **9** and **25**.

[7] Of the tenements listed above, n. 5, the following are at the junction of fiefs recorded in the surrounding entries: **180, 418, 442, 557, 570, 657, 1082**.

so high as to prevent amalgamation, and in the suburbs there was perhaps sufficient land available to allow a house to be enlarged without acquiring an adjacent property. This apparent fluidity in size and layout may have been an important characteristic of private houses in the side streets within the walls.

V. HOUSE TYPES: THE PHYSICAL EVIDENCE

One standing building and the results of archaeological excavation, together with fragmentary information from several other houses, provide fairly complete evidence for the plans of seven private houses in eleventh- and twelfth-century Winchester.[1]

The whole body of archaeological evidence from the city shows that throughout the Middle Ages most private houses were built of timber. The characteristic house of the eleventh and twelfth century appears to have been constructed of massive timber posts, with scantlings of up to 300 × 400 mm (approximately 12 by 16 inches), set in large foundation pits or trenches. Such structures could easily have been of two storeys. They seem usually to have been about 5 m (16½ feet) wide and their bay length, based on the spacing of the major posts, was probably about 2·5 m (8 feet).[2] In some of these houses the infilling between the major posts was probably composed of interlocking quarter-cut boards set vertically, a technique widely used at this period in northern Europe.[3] All the buildings of this type so far discovered were placed on the street frontage, some parallel to it and some at right angles. The houses parallel to the street, measuring 7·6 m (25 feet) or less in length,[4] appear to have been somewhat shorter than those set at right angles, whose length was between 10·5 and 11·5 m (35 and 37½ feet).[5] The houses lying parallel to the street were set back about 2·5 m (8 feet), and the intervening space was probably occupied by subsidiary structures, perhaps of one storey only, which in *Tannerestret* appear to have been built over channels carrying water from the stream running down the middle of the street.[6] The front ends of the houses lying at right angles to the street may sometimes have been similarly differentiated from the rest of the structure.[7]

These houses appear to have been equally well adapted to an industrial or to a purely domestic use.[8] The first construction of two of them can be dated to the late tenth or early eleventh century.[9] In one of these cases, a house parallel to the street succeeded an

---

[1] For most of the archaeological evidence see *II–IX Interims*. Archaeological evidence not published in the interim reports, or reinterpreted since publication, is frequently drawn upon in this section. The final report of the archaeological evidence from Lower Brook Street, together with a discussion of the houses of medieval Winchester, will appear as Winchester Studies 5, *The Brooks and other town sites of medieval Winchester*.

[2] *III Interim*, 248–9, Fig. 3, Pl. LXXIV; *IX Interim*, 102–3, 110–11, Fig. 2, Pls. XXXIII, XXXIV*b*, and XXXVI*a*.

[3] Boards of this type were found reused in the lining of a water-channel in *Tannerestret*.

[4] Houses VI, VII, and IV/VIII in *Tannerestret* (*III Interim*, 248–9, Fig. 3), and possibly House XII in the same street, although the full length of this structure was not excavated (*IX Interim*, 110–11, Fig. 2).

[5] Houses II and III in *Gerestret* (*III Interim*, 243, Pl. LXXXII) and Houses IX and X in *Tannerestret* (*IX Interim*, 102–3, Fig. 2).

[6] See above, p. 284, n. 5.

[7] Houses IX and X in *Tannerestret*: see above, n. 5.

[8] Houses IX, X, and XII in *Tannerestret* (*VIII Interim*, 298–302, Fig. 8; *IX Interim*, 102–3, 110–11).

[9] Palaeomagnetic dating of samples from the earliest floors of House II in *Gerestret* suggests a date of *c.* A.D. 1000, cf. *III Interim*, 243, Pl. LXXXII. Radiocarbon dating of a timber post from House XII in *Tannerestret* suggests that this structure underwent a major reconstruction shortly before the middle of the eleventh century.

earlier and much slighter post-structure set at right angles.[1] Buildings of this kind perhaps represent the first specifically urban house type in early medieval Winchester and with minor modifications they remained in use as late as the thirteenth century. Their dimensions are similar to those of many village houses of the same period,[2] but at least in the earlier Middle Ages they may be distinguished from the rural examples by their regular alignment on the street frontage, and perhaps also by their more substantial and elaborate structure.[3] During the thirteenth and early fourteenth centuries houses of post-in-trench construction were replaced by buildings with a fully framed structure incorporating a ground-sill.[4] In a further development, these framed houses were raised on a low stone ground wall.[5]

Stone houses solidly built of flint rubble with ashlar dressing represented a different social level. The complete plans of three twelfth-century houses of this kind are known from Winchester, and one of them (in St. Thomas Street) still stands two storeys high. All three were set back from the street, in contrast to the timber houses which were closely set along the frontage or a couple of metres behind it. The internal dimensions of the stone houses were similar to those of the timber houses: if the timber houses were also of two storeys, the total floor-space of these two types cannot have differed greatly. Two of the stone houses, one excavated in *Tannerestret*[6] and the other still standing in *Calpestret* (i.e. the St. Thomas Street house),[7] were set at right angles to the street immediately behind the built-up frontage, which was itself in each case probably occupied by a timber structure. The internal dimensions of the *Tannerestret* house were 4·4 by 11·5 m (14½ by 38 feet), and of the *Calpestret* house 5 by 7·9 m (16½ by 26 feet), providing an internal floor-space on each floor of 50·6 and 39·5 sq. m, respectively. The *Calpestret* house, with its ground floor vaulted in two quadripartite bays, was more elaborate than the *Tannerestret* house, which probably had a simple barrel vault. Unlike the *Calpestret* house, the *Tannerestret* house appears to have had an internal stair. In both cases the lower storey, which was at ground level, could have been used for either storage or accommodation. In the second half of the twelfth century an elaborate fireplace was inserted in the lower storey of the *Tannerestret* house, suggesting that it was then used principally for accommodation. These houses were perhaps characteristic of the dwellings of the more substantial citizens. An almost exact duplicate of the *Tannerestret* house was built in the thirteenth century, little more than 20 metres away, on the same side of the street.[8]

The third stone house stood about 25 m to the east of *Snidelingestret*, roughly parallel

[1] House XII in *Tannerestret*: *X Interim*, 314–18.

[2] Maurice Beresford and John G. Hurst (eds.), *Deserted Medieval Villages* (London, 1971), 114–15, Figs. 17–22.

[3] Ibid. 89–97, 124–7. A regularity of house layout in relation to the street pattern is, however, a distinctive feature of a number of medieval villages by the twelfth and thirteenth centuries: ibid. 124–7. The excavated area of the late Saxon town of Thetford appears to display a much less regular pattern than Winchester: B. K. Davison, *Med Arch* 11 (1967), 189–208.

[4] House XII in *Tannerestret*: *VIII Interim*, 307–8, Fig. 8.

[5] *III Interim*, 247; Keene *Brooks Area*, 119–21.

[6] *II Interim*, 197–9, Fig. 4, Pls. XLVIIb, XLVIII, and L; cf. *VII Interim*, Fig. 3.

[7] There are drawings and a plan of this structure in *VCH Hants* v. 8–9. For its relation to the local topography, see the OS 1:500 plan of Winchester, surveyed in 1869–70.

[8] House III: *III Interim*, 248, Fig. 3, Pl. LXXIV.

to it on a north–south alignment.[1] It was set well back from what Survey **II** suggests was a frontage densely built-up with poor-quality houses. To the north the house abutted on what appears to have been a small stone chapel, perhaps that of St. Mary in *Brudenestret*, and both may have served to enclose a small courtyard towards *Snidelingestret*.[2] This spacious layout was characteristic of the houses of the wealthiest citizens in the fourteenth century,[3] and this may also have been the case in the twelfth century. This stone house was one of the longer examples, measuring 5 by 10·4 m (16½ by 34½ feet) internally, and having a floor area of 52 sq. m on one floor. In this case the lower storey appears to have lain entirely underground and can only have been used for storage. It is possible, however, that this house had two storeys above ground, in addition to the cellar, and thus contained considerably more accommodation than the other two examples.[4] The close association with a chapel, which may have originated as the private chapel of the occupant, is also perhaps a pointer to the relatively high status of this property.[5]

These three stone houses occur in streets of widely differing general character and this may indicate the extent to which, in the side streets at least, houses of different types and sizes were intermingled. The stone house in *Tannerestret* was certainly a close neighbour of timber houses of varying sizes. No certain identifications may be made between the properties on which these stone houses stood and the entries in the two surveys. It may be significant, however, that the schematic reconstruction of properties in Fig. 19 suggests that the stone house in *Calpestret* may have been equivalent to **II, 848** or **849**. Between the reigns of Edward the Confessor and Stephen, the property represented by **II, 848** was probably held by a succession of moneyers, and in 1148 it was next to a property (**II, 847**) belonging to a goldsmith.[6]

The structure of the *Calpestret* house indicates that it may date from the early years of the twelfth century. Archaeological evidence suggests that the *Tannerestret* house was probably built before the middle of the twelfth century, and that the house in *Snidelingestret*

---

[1] *Winchester 1949–60*, i. 166–70, Fig. 58.

[2] The layout of the house and chapel shows that they originally faced towards *Snidelingestret*. This street was depopulated sooner than *Brudenestret*, with which the tenement appears eventually to have been associated. The only church in *Brudenestret* was apparently that of St. Mary, which was said to have been in ruins by 1452 (*Archaeologia*, i (1790), 91). Although this is the only record of the church of St. Mary in *Brudenestret* so far discovered, this identification of the chapel seems more reasonable than its equation with the church of St. Odulf (similarly recorded only once and not associated with any particular street in the city) put forward in *Winchester 1949–60*, i. 172. See also *SMW*.

[3] Keene *Brooks Area*, 105–6.

[4] In the excavation report (see above, n. 1) this structure is consistently described as an upper-halled house, with the cellar as the lower storey. It is clear from the published section, however, that the cellar was entirely below ground from the time it was

built. If the excavator's interpretation of this building as a two-storied structure is correct, there can only have been one storey available for domestic use, and that would have been at ground level. Since there was some evidence for an external staircase, there may in fact have been two storeys above ground, thus making a total of three storeys including the cellar, but this possibility is not considered in the excavation report.

[5] But see below, p. 348, n. 1.

[6] The identification of the properties on which the other two stone houses stood is even less clear. The *Tannerestret* house *may* have stood on the property represented by **II, 615** or **616**, and the *Snidelingestret* house *may* have stood on that represented by **II, 379, 380**, or **381**. The interpretation of the evidence of Survey **II** in *Winchester 1949–60*, i. 171–6 is unreliable, but the author is probably correct in stating that by the later thirteenth century the property on which the house stood had come into the possession of the archdeacon of Winchester. See *SMW* 247.

should be roughly dated to the same century.[1] Two-storied stone houses of this type, sometimes described as 'Norman town houses', are usually thought to be a twelfth-century innovation. But first-floor halls were a characteristic of Anglo-Saxon domestic architecture,[2] and the Winchester stone houses were clearly related in their size and proportions to the pre-conquest timber houses in the city. The *cellarii* in High Street in the reign of Edward the Confessor (**I, 61–3**) are most probably to be interpreted as masonry, perhaps barrel-vaulted structures, used as shops or storehouses, and with a chamber or hall above.[3] The masonry structure buried below the castle earthworks in 1067 may also have been such a domestic building.[4] Two-storied stone halls may thus have had an Anglo-Saxon origin.

Oak shingles are the earliest roofing material for which there is evidence in medieval Winchester. They have been recovered from eleventh- and twelfth-century contexts and appear to have remained in use, at least for smaller buildings, into the fourteenth century.[5] Until the end of the twelfth century some private houses may have been roofed with thatch, but by the fourteenth century the Winchester by-laws appear to have followed the London building regulations in forbidding its use.[6] Blue slates from Devon and Cornwall were used on royal buildings in Winchester during the reign of Henry II,[7] but their use on private houses seems only to have developed in the thirteenth century. Slates were the characteristic roofing material of later medieval Winchester, even on the smallest structures, and did not give way to clay tiles until the later fifteenth century, although clay ridge-tiles were in use from the early thirteenth century, perhaps in combination with slate or shingles.[8]

The types of houses discussed here, both timber and stone, probably represent the dwellings of the middle and upper ranks of Winchester society. The smallest dwellings have either not been present in the areas excavated or have left few archaeological traces. One site in *Tannerestret* has produced evidence—not yet fully interpreted—for a timber building of probable twelfth-century date, measuring about 5 m (16½ feet) square.[9] Houses of this size may well have been the usual accommodation for the poorest Winchester families in the early Middle Ages, and units of these dimensions may have been combined to form the rows of cottages recorded in Survey I.[10]

[1] The published evidence for the *Snidelingestret* house (see above, p. 347, n. 1), allowing for the revisions in the dating of Winchester medieval pottery which have taken place since publication, suggests that it was built after the eleventh century and was demolished in the fifteenth century. It is thus possible that the construction of the house and chapel was associated with the tenure of the property by the archdeacon of Winchester in the thirteenth century.

[2] R. A. Brown, 'The Architecture', in F. M. Stenton (ed.), *The Bayeux Tapestry* (2nd edn., London, 1965), 79–81. See also in general P. V. Addyman, 'The Anglo-Saxon House: a New Review', *Anglo-Saxon England*, 1 (1972), 273–307, which, however, barely touches the question of first-floor halls.

[3] Cf. above, pp. 339–40.

[4] *VIII Interim*, 268, Pls. XLIa, XLIIa.

[5] Some typical shingles are illustrated in *I Interim*, Fig. 11. For their use in later medieval Winchester, see Keene *Brooks Area*, 122–3, and *SMW*.

[6] Keene *Brooks Area*, 122.

[7] Colvin (ed.) *King's Works*, ii. 855.

[8] Keene *Brooks Area*, 123.

[9] *IX Interim*, 107–8, Fig. 2, pl. XXXIIb. This structure appears to have fulfilled from the beginning an industrial function.

[10] A row of cottages constructed in *Tannerestret* in the late thirteenth or early fourteenth century contained three individual family units, each about 5 m square (i.e. 25 sq. m): *VI Interim*, 265–6, Fig. 3, Pl. LVIII.

5

LAND OWNERSHIP

i. THE GREAT FIEFS

Introduction

MOST of the land surveyed in 1148 pertained to seven great fiefs belonging to the king, the bishop, the prior of St. Swithun's, the abbot of Hyde, and the abbesses of St. Mary's, Wherwell, and Romsey. These lords were not necessarily the only recipients of income from the properties in their fiefs, and indeed in many instances their own rents were eclipsed by the sums that their tenants received, but the distribution of their rents is important evidence for the territorial interests of these great lords in Winchester. This distribution in some cases probably represents an apportionment of the land in the city at the time of the reorganization under Alfred,[1] and may in addition lead to an understanding of some aspects of suburban development. In the case of four of these fiefs the situation in the mid twelfth century can be compared with evidence for earlier or later periods. The king's landgable rents were surveyed in 1285,[2] as well as in *TRE*, *c.* 1110, and 1148; the bishop's income from properties in Winchester was accounted for in the episcopal Pipe Rolls, the earliest of which to survive covers the year 1208–9;[3] and the Winchester properties of Wherwell and Romsey Abbeys were described in Domesday Book.

Figures 14 and 15 show the distribution of these seven great estates in Winchester in terms of their holdings and the amount of rent they received from each part of the city; Tables 11–19, 21, and 22 demonstrate their territorial distribution and relative importance; and Figs. 16 and 19 shows this same distribution in plan and diagrammatic form.

The general sense of both surveys seems to be that unless there is a positive indication to the contrary each entry describes a built-up tenement. The paragraphing of the surveys therefore probably provides the most reliable means of identifying individual tenements for the purposes of counting, and this method has normally been adopted in the following discussion. In both surveys, however, there is a significant minority of cases where it is clear that a single entry represents more than one habitation. Individual habitations may be identified where there are references to more than one *domus*, *mansura*, or *terra* in a single entry, and where a single tenement clearly contained separate parts in separate tenure. In a few cases a divided landgable rent allows one to be fairly certain that a tenement was in the hands of more than one occupant.

We may suspect that the actual number of habitations was even more in excess of the number of entries than this direct evidence suggests, but we have no precise method of

---

[1] See above, pp. 273 and 277–8.
[2] See below, Appendix II. 2, pp. 516–18.
[3] *PRBW 1208–9*, 76–9.

quantifying this impression.[1] In addition to the habitations, a number of separate parcels may also be identified, usually waste lands or empty houses. In Survey **II** the number of tenements more nearly approaches the number of parcels and habitations than in Survey **I**, perhaps because the paragraphing of the latter was sometimes conditioned by the layout of a possible Edwardian exemplar. Table 12*b* contains the numbers of tenements, parcels, and habitations on the king's fief at the three dates recorded in the surveys. This provides the only quantitative means of comparison between the royal fief *TRE* and at later dates.

The king's fief (Figs. 14–16 and 19; Tables 2, 3, 11, 12*a* and *b*, 15–19, 21, and 22)

In almost every case the compilers of Survey **I** simply enumerated the rents due to King Edward and stated that the present tenant owed the same, so that no monetary comparison between *TRE* and *c.* 1110 is possible. Landgable rents from properties in High Street and outside West Gate, rarely specified in Survey **I**, were probably included in the *consuetudines* due to the king from these properties. By 1148 the king's dues from these areas were expressed in monetary terms. Apart from these limitations, the surveys show the same pattern of distribution of the king's landgable rents in Winchester (cf. Table 2). The king had no property in the southern and eastern suburbs, and almost nothing in the northern suburb or in Colebrook Street. He received most from High Street and the western suburb, and in the twelfth century from *Calpestret, Bucchestret, Tannerestret,* and *Brudenestret,* with lesser sums from the other streets.

Between the reign of King Edward and the date of Survey **I** the king appears to have lost control of twenty-seven or more of the properties in High Street from which he had once received customs (not counting those tenements taken into the royal palace). He also lost control of six tenements outside West Gate and three 'on the lands of the barons' in *Brudenestret.*[2] A comparison of the number of tenements in which the king possessed, or had once possessed, rights or rents in *c.* 1110 with the number of tenements on his fief in 1148 shows that, in High Street at least, Henry I probably recovered most of the tenements that had once been lost (Table 2). Some allowance must probably be made, however, for the subdivision of royal tenements in High Street between *c.* 1110 and 1148, so that in the absence of a monetary comparison there is no clear indication of the extent to which the crown permanently lost its estate in High Street. Nevertheless, it seems unlikely that the royal tenements could have been subdivided to such an extent that the thirty-five remaining in royal hands in *c.* 1110 could be represented by the seventy-six tenements in royal possession in 1148, particularly since the usual landgable assessment for each tenement appears to have been 6*d.* at both dates.

There is evidence that some of the royal properties on the south side of High Street to the west of the palace site may not have been recovered by Henry I. King Edward had at least eighteen tenements there (**I, 39–56**; the location of tenements 'on the lands of the barons' is not known). Henry I had customs from no more than nine of these, and in 1148 only seven of the twenty-nine tenements in that area were in the king's fief (**II, 141–51** and **159–76**). There may, however, be an alternative explanation for the loss

---

[1] See below, pp. 440–1.   [2] See above, Table 2.

of these tenements. The bishop had rents from twenty-two of them in 1148 and may here, as elsewhere in High Street, have encroached on royal property after c. 1110.[1] The bishop probably lost these tenements after 1154, along with most of his other property in High Street, but there is no sign that the king subsequently recovered any of his rights in them.

There can be no doubt, however, of the essential territorial stability of the royal fief in the eleventh and twelfth centuries. The numbers of entries recording properties on the king's fief in the two surveys (Table 2) are very similar. In High Street and outside West Gate the number of royal tenements increased between c. 1110 and 1148, in the former case possibly, and, in the latter almost certainly, because of the subdivision of properties represented by single entries in the earlier survey. In several of the side streets within the walls there was a significant reduction in the number of royal tenements over the same period. Since there was a fall of a similar order in royal rent receipts in the same streets, it is likely that these tenements were entirely lost to the king's fief, perhaps in the absence of a strong royal authority under Stephen.

This territorial stability may be contrasted with the considerable changes in the intensity of the use or occupation of the land comprising the royal fief in the century covered by the surveys. These changes can be detected by identifying the numbers of individual parcels of property and of individual habitations on the royal fief (Table 12b). Between *TRE* and c. 1110 the numbers of parcels and habitations on the whole of the king's fief rose by about thirteen per cent. This increase was virtually confined to the suburb outside West Gate, and was accounted for mainly by the construction of houses on plots which had not previously been built-up. Between c. 1110 and 1148, however, the numbers of parcels and habitations on the king's fief declined by much the same amount as they had risen in the previous half century. This decline was most marked in *Calpestret*, *Tannerestret*, *Bucchestret*, and *Wunegrestret*, and to a lesser extent outside West Gate and in *Goldestret*. In *Wunegrestret* and *Goldestret* the fall in numbers may be accounted for by those tenements which were lost altogether from the king's fief, and for these areas it could be argued that the decline was caused simply by the transfer of property from the king's fief into other hands. But in the other areas the decline in the number of parcels and habitations was in excess of the number of tenements entirely lost. The decline in the number of habitations was particularly marked in *Tannerestret* and *Bucchestret*. Outside West Gate the decline was perhaps relatively insignificant when considered as a proportion of the total number of properties on the royal fief in that area. Within the limits of this selective and possibly unreliable evidence it appears that those areas of the city where the decline in the number of habitations was most marked between c. 1110 and 1148 were among those which had achieved their maximum development before the Norman conquest. Those of more recent growth, such as the western suburb, seem not to have suffered from this decline. This may mean that in the first half of the twelfth century there was some shift in the focus of settlement away from *Tannerestret* and *Bucchestret*, and possibly also from *Calpestret*, in favour of the western suburb. As a whole, so far as its total stock of houses and properties was concerned, the city perhaps reverted to its former condition in the reign of the Confessor.

[1] See below, p. 354.

The individual landgable payments were small and nearly all were between 4*d.* and 12*d.* Three standard units of assessment appear to have been used (Table 3). In High Street the unit was 6*d.* and outside West Gate it was 4*d.* In the side or north–south streets within the walls assessments based on units of 6*d.* and 4*d.* occur, but an assessment based on a unit of 5*d.* is most common. Between *TRE* and *c.* 1110 the landgable assessments of most of those curtilages outside West Gate where houses had been erected during the period were increased (**I, 119–21**). The curtilages had originally been assessed at 2*d.* In three out of four cases this sum was doubled, and in the fourth quadrupled. These new sums were clearly in proportion to an assessment of 4*d.* for a built-up property. This distribution is evident at all three dates covered by the surveys, and may represent the relative values of land in the three areas when the assessments were originally made.

With the exception of *Mensterstret* (now Little Minster Street) and *Bucchestret*, continuity is the most distinguishing feature of the king's landgable estate in Winchester in the twelfth and thirteenth centuries. The total landgable assessed in 1148 approximates closely to the total landgable in 1285 and to the total *terragium* which the city bailiffs collected in 1355.[1] The proportions of the whole due from the individual streets were approximately the same in *c.* 1110, 1148, and 1285 (Fig. 14*a*). There is a contrast, however, between the slight over-all decline in the totals during the short period *c.* 1110 to 1148 and the over-all stability in the period 1148 to 1285. The civil-war disturbances of 1141 no doubt had a more drastic effect on the royal revenues than the occasional losses and defaults which inevitably occurred over the longer period.

Some of the 1148 assessments of landgable evidently remained the same throughout the rest of the Middle Ages. Three tenements (**II, 571, 572,** and **604**) in *Wunegrestret*, for example, may be identified in the 1285 list of landgable rents, and two of them (**II, 571** and **604**) may be identified with tenements of the same assessment in the Tarrage Survey of 1417.

In *Mensterstret* (now Little Minster Street) the sum of 11*s.* 7*d.* assessed in 1285 was very much more than the twelfth-century total. This may have been because rents from a part of the site of the royal palace, apparently in the bishop's hands by 1148,[2] were included in the *Mensterestret* total in 1285. That part of the palace site which lay towards High Street, and was known as the Drapery, was accounted for separately from the landgable rents in 1285.[3] But rents totalling 15*s.* 6*d.* from that part of the palace site which lay next to *Mensterstret* were being received by the constable of Winchester castle in 1212,[4] and as late as 1327 were still regarded as distinct from the landgable rents and pertaining to the castle rather than to the city.[5] When rents from the constabulary were included in the general landgable or tarrage assessment of 1417, they were included under High Street rather than under Minster Street.[6] If a part of the palace site was responsible for the Minster Street increase, it was probably therefore not that from which rents to the constable of the castle were due.

---

[1] In 1355 the receipts *de terragio* totalled £7. 5*s.* 5*d.*: Furley *City Government*, 179.

[2] See above, pp. 246 and 299, and below, pp. 354–5.

[3] See Appendix I. 2, pp. 513–14.

[4] See Appendix I. 1, p. 510.

[5] PRO, C 143/193/10.

[6] See *SMW*, s.v. 'Tarrage survey'.

The reason for the drastic fall in revenue from *Bucchestret* by 1285 is more obvious. A large area near *Bucchestret*, possibly including the north part of the street itself, was taken into the precinct of the Black Friars in the thirteenth century and at least two of the tenements acquired by the friars are known to have owed rents to the king.[1]

The bishop's fief (Figs. 14–16 and 19; Tables 11, 13–19, 21, and 22)

In 1148 the largest and most valuable fief was the bishop's. The fief extended throughout almost the whole of the surveyed area and was particularly important in the suburbs. *Mensterstret*, *Calpestret*, *Goldestret*, and *Gerestret* in the south-western quarter of the walled city formed the only area where the fief was insignificant. In all, the bishop received £69. 7s. 6¾d., 2 bizants, and 2½ lbs. of pepper from 402 properties. More than half of the total came from High Street, where only just over a seventh of the bishop's properties were situated. The southern suburb containing more than a quarter of his properties produced but an eighth of his rent. Most of the rest of the bishop's revenue came from the western and eastern suburbs and from *Tannerestret*. The individual rents varied from small sums, usually between 1s. and 3s. and equivalent to the king's landgable rents, to amounts of several pounds. The higher rents were almost all from High Street.

There were few charges on these rents. In *Calpestret* the bishop paid 2s. 6d. to the prior, and in *Goldestret* 7½d. to the king.

The revenue which the bishop could expect from rents in Winchester in 1148 was nearly two and a half times the sum he could hope for—and more than three and a half times the sum he actually received—in the early thirteenth century. A street-by-street comparison of the episcopal revenues in 1148 and 1210–11 is shown in Table 13 (cf. Fig. 14a). This dramatic decline in revenue must have resulted from the loss of some considerable source or sources of income between 1148 and 1208–9.[2] Bishop Henry enjoyed an exceptional and even quasi-royal position in Winchester during the reign of Stephen, and may in consequence have enjoyed revenues from properties which were more properly the king's. The bishop may therefore have lost a considerable income from Winchester properties following the accession of Henry II in 1154.

The distinctive classes of rent due to the bishop in 1148 were those which were *de .B.* and *de terra Baronum*.[3] Table 14 and Fig. 14 show the totals of these rents street by street. Leaving aside High Street for the time being, a comparison of these figures shows that the rents *de .B.* and *de terra Baronum* largely account for the differences between the revenues of 1148 and those of 1210–11. Other changes are within the limits which could be explained by natural lapses of rents of assize, acquisition of individual properties by the bishop, and the consolidation of interests in those suburbs which were to become the bishop's soke.

In High Street between 1148 and 1208–9 the bishop lost rent worth nearly £40 a year. Little more than a third of this can be accounted for by his rents *de .B.* It is fairly clear, however, that the bishop lost a rent of 12 marks, not described as *de .B.*, from

---

[1] Ibid., s.v. 'Black Friars'.

[2] *PRBW 1208–9* simply gives the total of rents of assize due as £27. 16s. 3½d. *PRBW 1210–11* records that the same total was due, and for the first time gives

the totals due from individual streets.

[3] For the use of these terms in Survey **II**, see above, pp. 19–25.

the tenement in the king's fief later known as Chapman's Hall (**II, 69**). The later history of this property is well documented, but there is no record of the bishop's interest in it after 1148. This raises the possibility that the bishop lost all his revenues from properties in High Street which were on the king's fief. Excluding rents *de .B.* from tenements on the king's fief, these revenues totalled £14. 2s., and with the rents *de .B.* would account for nearly three-quarters of the bishop's loss in High Street. It is also possible, as suggested above, that between c. 1110 and 1148 the bishop had enlarged his fief at the king's expense on the south side of High Street between West Gate and the royal palace.[1] The bishop's rents from this area, apart from those *de .B.*, totalled £11. 6s. 8½d. If he subsequently lost these properties also, the decline in episcopal revenues from High Street by the early thirteenth century would be accounted for almost entirely.[2]

These specific suggestions in explanation of the decline of the bishop's revenue must remain hypotheses, for there is no instance in which those classes of rent enjoyed by the bishop in 1148 and discussed above can be shown to have been resumed by the king.

Nevertheless, there is sufficient evidence to suggest some connection between royal interests in Winchester and the bishop's rents *de .B.* and *de terra Baronum*. Bishop Henry apparently controlled the site of the royal palace, destroyed in 1141, and previously little-used for several years.[3] Six or seven years after the siege the site had probably been recolonized, and properties there would have been producing rent which should have been included in the 1148 survey. The largest block of properties from which rents *de .B.* were due to the bishop appears to have occupied the palace site (**II, 112–40**; cf. Fig. 19). These properties probably occupied the High Street frontage and the strip of land running south along the western margin, later known as the Constabulary. By the early thirteenth century these properties were once more in the possession of the king.[4]

In their general distribution the rents *de .B.* and *de terra Baronum*, both paid to the bishop, display a similarity to royal interests in the city, for they occur only in those areas where the royal fief also lay (Fig. 19). They are thus virtually confined to what might be termed the original royal borough, the streets within the walls and the western suburb, and are absent from the suburbs to the south and east. The single rent *de terra Baronum* from a tenement outside North Gate (**II, 356**) was apparently near the city wall and not far distant from the only tenement in the northern suburb on the royal fief in 1148 (**II, 351**). The link with the royal fief can be demonstrated even more precisely, for most of the rents *de .B.* and *de terra Baronum* came from properties which were either adjacent to tenements in the royal fief, or were included in blocks of episcopal property adjacent to the royal fief. The one significant exception to this was the group of rents *de .B.* on the west side of *Tannerestret*. The procedure by which rents from royal property may have been claimed by the bishop is not clear. There does not, for example, appear to be any link between the tenements 'on the lands of the barons' in Survey **I** and the bishop's rents *de terra Baronum* in Survey **II**. The bishop had no rents *de terra Baronum*

---

[1] See above, p. 351.

[2] The loss of £39. 19s. 8d. rent from properties in High Street would be accounted for by the following sums: £13. 11s. 3d. from rents *de .B.*, £14. 2s. from tenements on the king's fief, and £11. 6s. 8½d. from the

tenements to the west of the royal palace; a total of £38. 19s. 11½d.

[3] See above, pp. 298–301.

[4] See Appendix I. 1, p. 510 and above, p. 352.

from High Street in 1148, and in *Brudenestret* he had a rent *de terra Baronum* from only one **(II, 421)** of the eight properties which can be identified with five tenements 'on the lands of the barons' in Survey **I**. The bishop had no other rents from this group of tenements in 1148.

There is a clear distinction between the distribution of the rents *de terra Baronum* and those *de .B.* The former were confined almost exclusively to the western suburb, *Snidelingestret*, and *Brudenestret*. If the order of survey suggested above is correct, most of the rents *de terra Baronum* in the suburb were due from properties close to West Gate. Rents *de .B.* were nearly all due from High Street and from the streets within the walls to the east of *Scowrtenestret*. The contrast between these distributions argues against the forms being synonymous, but it could be merely the result of differences in scribal practice and in the method of compiling the survey.[1] There are no obvious explanations for this pattern of distribution, except possibly in the case of the apparent link between the rents *de .B.* and the site of the royal palace. *De .B.* may mean *de Baronibus*, or be an extreme abbreviation of *de terra Baronum*. The two terms may thus have the same meaning, but even if this were so the pattern of their distribution could be no more easily explained. Indeed explanations regarding the site of the former royal palace would be yet more difficult.[2]

The prior's fief (Figs. 14–16 and 19; Tables 11, 15–19, 21, and 22)

The prior's fief was about a third of the bishop's in value and comprised about half the number of properties. An income of £28. 3s. 8d. was due from 203 properties whose distribution was almost as widespread as those of the bishop. More than a third of this income was due from the eleven properties in High Street; the rest was largely due from the more densely populated streets within the walls, except *Scowrtenestret*, and from the eastern, western, and southern suburbs. The rents themselves were mainly between 1s. and 5s., although there was a significant number of 5d. rents. Rents of £1 and over were only due from High Street. The charges on these properties were small, 9s. in all, and mostly due to the bishop or the king.

There appears to be no significant difference between the distribution of the properties of the prior and the bishop in the suburbs. Such a difference might, for example, have indicated where the priory manor of Chilcomb originally came up to the city walls.

The fief of the abbot of Hyde (Figs. and Tables as before)

The abbot of Hyde drew £11. 4s. 3½d. from ninety-five properties. Nearly half of this income came from his eighteen properties in High Street. Elsewhere, his principal interests were in the northern and western suburbs and in *Scowrtenestret*. He had no rent south of High Street. The individual rents ranged mainly from 1s. to 4s., with a number still smaller. Higher rents were due only from High Street. The highest of these, a rent of 14s., was no longer received in 1148.

---

[1] See above, pp. 19–25 and cf. Tables 4 and 5.   [2] See above, pp. 24–5.

The fief of the abbess of St. Mary's (Figs. and Tables as before)

The abbess of St. Mary's received £6. 1s. 9½d. from thirty-four properties. £5. 4s. of this came from the six tenements in High Street and 11s. 8½d. from the eighteen properties in *Colobrochestret*. The abbess also had scattered properties in *Sildwortenestret* and *Bucchestret*, and a block of property with a church outside South Gate. The individual rents were rarely more than 1s. except in High Street, where most were between 2s. and 4s. and two reached £1.

The fief of the abbess of Wherwell (Figs. and Tables as before)

The estate of Wherwell Abbey was entirely within the walls and comprised twenty-one properties principally in two groups in *Scowrtenestret* and *Flesmangerestret*, but also in *Brudenestret* and *Alwarnestret*. Three of these properties each produced two rents, and two others each represented the amalgamation of two properties (**II, 419, 428, 501, 513,** and **521**). Wherwell Abbey owned twenty-nine *hagae* in Winchester in the early eleventh century.[1] By 1086 this number had increased to thirty-one *masurae*,[2] then worth 30s., but said to have been worth 50s. in 1066. There was in addition a mill worth 48s., but not mentioned in the Winchester surveys.[3] By 1148 the properties had still not recovered their pre-conquest value: a total of £2. 2s. 2d. was due from a maximum of twenty-five identifiable houses or holdings, although a total of £2. 3s. 10d. was claimed or had recently been received.

The fief of the abbess of Romsey (Figs. and Tables as before)

The Romsey Abbey estate was also entirely within the walls and comprised twelve properties, ten of them in *Calpestret* and *Goldestret*, one in *Wunegrestret*, and one, made up of three lands, in *Gerestret*. In 1086 the abbey had fourteen burgesses in Winchester, rendering a total of 25s.[4] The same number of houses or holdings can be identified in Survey **II**, but they produced no more than £1 rent, of which only 19s. 2d. was actually received.

General comment on the great fiefs

The distribution of the great fiefs reflects the distinct territorial interests of their lords. By the thirteenth century Winchester was a city of two lords, the king and the bishop, and the basis of this dual jurisdiction can be seen in their fiefs of 1148. The king's fief, confined to the prosperous and densely-populated walled area and to the western suburb, might be expected to represent the area of earliest urban development. It was precisely these areas which later formed the major part of the liberty which the citizens of Winchester held from the king. The bishop's fief was more widespread than the king's, but in the thirteenth century the bishop was to be able to consolidate his jurisdiction only over those parts of Winchester where his fief and the other fief pertaining to the mother church of Winchester, that of the prior, predominated to the exclusion of the king.

---

[1] *KCD* 707, Sawyer 904.

[2] The abbess's own house, probably situated in the area of **II, 510–11**, may have been additional to this total: *DGSEE*, 354.

[3] *VCH Hants* i. 475.

[4] Ibid. 474.

Thus outside North Gate the abbot of Hyde, a much less powerful lord, could later estab-lish his liberty over no more than the precinct of his abbey, so that most of this suburb, where the fiefs of the bishop and abbot predominated to the virtual, but not entire, exclusion of the king, came to form part of the liberty of the city rather than part of the soke of the bishop. Those parts of the northern and western suburbs which did become part of the bishop's soke no doubt contained those portions of the bishop's fief recorded there in Survey **II**.

This pattern of development emphasizes the strength of the king's authority as lord of Winchester in the twelfth and thirteenth centuries, for in 1148 the value of his estate was less than a seventh of the value of the bishop's, and in the early thirteenth century probably less than half. For a brief period Henry of Blois appears to have enjoyed a quasi-royal authority in Winchester under a weak, or at least fraternal, king. This episode may even heighten the impression of the fundamental strength of the crown given when a new king reasserted royal authority to the full in the years after 1154.

The other great fiefs were more localized. The prior had a considerable estate in the suburbs, but within the walls his properties were concentrated near the priory in *Men-sterstret*, *Calpestret*, and *Goldestret*. The abbot's lands lay near Hyde Abbey. Within the walls the abbot's properties lay principally in *Scowrtenestret* and in High Street near the entry to *Scowrtenestret*, easily accessible from the abbey via North Gate. The abbess's lands lay almost exclusively in the immediate vicinity of St. Mary's Abbey in *Colo-brochestret*. Most of the lands of the abbesses of Wherwell and Romsey were concen-trated in single streets, presumably near their town houses.

Virtually nothing is known of the date and manner in which these lands were acquired.[1] The Wherwell estate appears to have been virtually complete by the first half of the eleventh century. The king's and Romsey Abbey's estates were apparently complete by 1066. The eastern and southern suburbs probably grew up on land which in the tenth century had long belonged to the mother church of Winchester, while most of the northern suburb developed within a rural estate of the bishop.[2]

On the other hand, some of the properties recorded as part of the great fiefs in 1148 were relatively recent acquisitions. The site of Hyde Abbey outside North Gate belonged to the bishop before the New Minster moved there in 1110, and the distribution of Hyde Abbey lands within the walls in 1148 suggests that they represent endowments of the neighbouring Hyde Abbey rather than of New Minster. Indeed there are no properties in 1148 which by their situation within the city might be thought to have belonged originally to New Minster.[3] A number of properties in Survey **I** appear to have belonged to the abbot in the time of King Edward (**I, 57, 69, 71, 72,** and **147**) and at least the first of them lay near New Minster. The stages by which the abbey acquired its estate in the northern suburb are well documented.[4] St. Swithun's Priory also acquired some of

---

[1] Cf. above, p. 349, and below, pp. 453, 456–7.

[2] See above, pp. 257, and 266.

[3] It is unlikely that New Minster owned no property in Winchester apart from its site. This raises the possi-bility that there was an exchange of tenements between New Minster and Old Minster when the former moved

to Hyde. Hyde Abbey was not recorded in the surveys as a landlord in the southern suburb, where New Minster had acquired property in the 970s: see above pp. 267, n. 6 and 308, n. 2.

[4] See above, pp. 266–7.

its Winchester lands in the late eleventh and early twelfth centuries (e.g. **I, 16, 28**, and **93**).

Some parts of the great fiefs may date back to an apportionment of the land of Winchester among the great lords of the region in the reign of Alfred. Considerable changes had, however, been effected by a continuing process, of endowment and other acquisition, which was to continue throughout the Middle Ages, but which seems on the available evidence to have been already of long standing by the middle of the twelfth century.

Some limited but valuable conclusions on the economic development of Winchester in the eleventh and twelfth centuries may be drawn from the evidence of these fiefs. The incomplete evidence for the king's estate suggests that it was static during the later eleventh and early twelfth centuries, but that it underwent a distinct decline during the reign of Stephen. The Wherwell and Romsey estates appear to have reached a peak of development during the reign of Edward the Confessor, but had declined noticeably by 1148.

A comparison of the total rent which made up the great fiefs with the total rent due to other landlords, both in individual streets and in the city as a whole, shows that by the middle of the twelfth century, if not before, the seven great fiefs were overshadowed in monetary terms by the estates of private landlords.[1] The only possible exception was the bishop's fief in the southern and eastern suburbs, and perhaps for a short period in High Street. The Winchester property-market was thus overwhelmingly secular. In territorial predominance, nevertheless, the seven great fiefs were unmatched by any of the private estates.

---

[1] See Figs. 15 and 16 and Tables 21–3. These exaggerate the situation somewhat, since a proportion of the rent received by private landlords was in some cases paid to one of the lords of the seven great fiefs (see below, pp. 370–4).

TABLE 12a

The king's rents TRE, c. 1110, 1148, and 1285 (cf. Fig. 14a)

Key numbers on Fig. 14a	Streets	Rents TRE.[1] Total (s. d.)	Number	c. 1110 Total (£ s. d.)	Number	1148 Total (£ s. d.)	Number	1285 Total (£ s. d.)	Number
1	High Street	—	—	2 9[2]	6	1 11 0	61	1 19 8	56
	Outside West Gate	3 11	8	4 11[2]	9	18 2	59	19 2	42
	Outside North Gate	—	—	—	—	6	1	—	—
2	Snidelingestret	—	—	2 8	7	3 2	7	2 4	8
3	Brudenestret	—	—	13 7	10	7 3	9	9 4	10
4	Scowrtenestret	—	—	10 0	9	6 2	7	8 5	10
5	Alwarnestret	—	—	5 10	7	5 6	7	5 2	5
6	Flesmangerestret	—	—	3 7	3	1 7	2	—	—
7	Sildwortenestret	—	—	—	—	4 3	7	4 1	6
8	Wunegrestret	—	—	10 5	13	2 11	4	2 6	3
9	Tannerestret	—	—	14 3	17	10 9	4	7 6	6
10	Bucchestret	—	—	1 2 8½	33	18 1¼	24	1 4	3
11	Colobrochestret	—	—	—	—	—	—	—	—
	Outside East Gate	—	—	—	—	—	—	—	—
12	Mensterstret	—	—	—	—	6	1	11 7	13
13	Calpestret	—	—	1 8 8	27	18 1	17	12 5	14
14	Goldestret	—	—	11 6	14	5 9½	9	8 2	13
	Outside South Gate i	—	—	—	—	—	—	—	—
	Outside South Gate ii	—	—	—	—	—	—	—	—
15	Gerestret	—	—	1 0 8	14	9 8	12	9 10½	7
	Totals	—	—	£7 11 6½[3]	169	£7 3 4¾	231	£7 1 7½	196

[1] So far as can be deduced from the text, the rent totals TRE were the same as in c. 1110, except outside West Gate.

[2] Many of the landgable rents for these areas appear to have been included under the heading of customs.

[3] This total is not strictly comparable with those for 1148 and 1285: see note 2 above.

Note: The number of rents will not necessarily correspond to the number of tenements (cf. Table 2).

TABLE 12*b*

The king's tenements TRE, c. *1110, and 1148, calculated according to entries in the surveys,*
parcels, and habitations

	TRE			c. 1110			1148		
	Entries	Parcels	Habita-tions	Entries	Parcels	Habita-tions	Entries	Parcels	Habita-tions
High Street	77	72	72	62	74	72	76	78	76
Outside West Gate	40	48	42	43	77	77	58	70	70
Outside North Gate	—	—	—	—	—	—	1	1	1
Snidelingestret	7	7	7	7	7	7	7	7	7
Brudenestret	9	10	10	9	10	10	9	9	9
Scowrtenestret	8	10	10	8	11	11	7	7	7
Alwarnestret	7	8	8	7	8	8	7	7	7
Flesmangerestret	3	3	3	3	3	3	2	2	2
Sildwortenestret	—	—	—	—	—	—	7	10	10
Wunegrestret	13	15	15	13	15	15	5	6	6
Tannerestret	18	23	23	18	23	23	15	16	10
Bucchestret	25	33	33	26	35	35	24	31	27
Colobrochestret	—	—	—	—	—	—	1	1	—
Outside East Gate	—	—	—	—	—	—	—	—	—
Mensterstret	—	—	—	—	—	—	3	3	3
Calpestret	24	33	33	25	33	35	17	18	18
Goldestret	14	14	14	16	16	16	10	10	10
Outside South Gate i	—	—	—	—	—	—	—	—	—
Outside South Gate ii	—	—	—	—	—	—	—	—	—
Gerestret	13	14	14	14	15	15	13	13	12
Totals	258	290	284	251	327	325	262	289	275

TABLE 13

The bishop's rents in 1148 and 1210–11 (cf. Fig. 14a)

Key numbers on Fig. 14a	Streets	Total in 1148[1]			Total rent of assize 1210–11[2]			Total rent from tenements let at will in 1210–11[2]		
		£	s.	d.	£	s.	d.	£	s.	d.
1	High Street	40	0	6½		17	4		—	
	Outside West Gate	5	2	6		17	4		—	
	Outside North Gate	1	4	10½	1	7	11½		—	
2	*Snidelingestret*	1	15	0		—			—	
3	*Brudenestret*	1	1	4		—			—	
4	*Scowrtenestret*	1	2	0		—			—	
5	*Alwarnestret*		14	7¾		—			—	
6	*Flesmangerestret*		11	9		—		1	7	6
7	*Sildwortenestret*		6	7		—			—	
8	*Wunegestret*		13	1		12	11½		12	2
9	*Tannerestret*	2	7	5½		15	6		—	
10	*Bucchestret*		8	3		1	0		—	
11	*Colobrochestret*		1	1		5	0		—	
	Outside East Gate	2	19	6½	5	8	5½	2	5	6
12	*Mensterstret*		5	10		—			—	
13	*Calpestret*	1	0	0		—			—	
14	*Goldestret*		10	2		—			—	
	Outside South Gate i	4	9	11 ⎫	6	6	11½	1	19	6
	Outside South Gate ii	4	10	5 ⎭						
15	*Gerestret*		2	7	1	10	4		—	
	Totals	£69	7	6¾	£18	1	0[3]	£6	5	8[3]

[1] For notes on totals see Table 11.

[2] Taken from *PRBW 1210–11*.

[3] A total of £9. 2s. 8½d. of these receipts was in default.

TABLE 14

The bishop's rents de .B. *and* de terra Baronum *in 1148* (cf. Fig. 14a)

Key numbers in Fig. 14a	Streets	Rents *de .B.*		Number of rents	Rents *de terra Baronum*[1]		Number of rents	Total number of bishop's properties
		Total			Total			
		£	s.	d.		£	s.	d.			
1	High Street	13	11	3	38	—			—	71
	Outside West Gate	1	2	0	1	3	1	5	16	37
	Outside North Gate	—			—		13	4	1	14
2	*Snidelingestret*	—			—	1	7	4	20	25
3	*Brudenestret*	—			—	1	1	4	13	12
4	*Scowrtenestret*	—			—	1	2	0[2]	6	6
5	*Alwarnestret*		9	8¾	8		2	6	2	10
6	*Flesmangerestret*	—			—		1	3	1	9
7	*Sildwortenestret*			4	1	—			—	6
8	*Wunegrestret*		3	0	1	—			1[3]	15
9	*Tannerestret*		14	5	12		2	0	1	27
10	*Bucchestret*		5	11	4	—			—	9
11	*Colobrochestret*	—			—	—			—	2
	Outside East Gate	—			—	—			—	32
12	*Mensterstret*		4	6	2	—			—	4
13	*Calpestret*	1	18	0	2	—			—	2
14	*Goldestret*	—			—	—			—	2
	Outside South Gate i	—			—	—			—	62
	Outside South Gate ii	—			—	—			—	55
15	*Gerestret*			7	1		2	0	1	2
	Totals	£18	9	8¾	69	£7	13	2	62	402

[1] Including *de t .B.*   [2] Plus 1 bizant.   [3] ½ lb. of pepper.

TABLE 15

The seven great fiefs in 1148: the total number of their tenements in each street

Streets	The seven fiefs														Tenements not in the seven fiefs	Totals	
	King		Bishop		Prior		Abbot		Abbess		Wherwell		Romsey				
	A	B	A	B	A	B	A	B	A	B	A	B	A	B		A	B
High Street	76	76	71	58	13	6	18	18	6	1	—	—	—	—	9	193	168
Outside West Gate	58	58	37	26	21	21	13	12	—	—	—	—	—	—	11	140	128
Outside North Gate	1	1	14	14	—	—	29	29	—	—	—	—	—	—	9	53	53
Snidelingestret	7	7	25	24	2	2	1	1	—	—	—	—	—	—	1	36	35
Brudenestret	9	9	12	11	5	5	1	1	—	—	2	1	—	—	8	37	35
Scowrtenestret	7	7	6	4	—	—	23	23	—	—	6	6	—	—	5	47	45
Alwarnestret	7	7	10	8	4	4	2	2	1	1	1	—	—	—	15	40	37
Flesmangerestret	2	—	9	9	9	7	—	—	—	—	12	12	—	—	3	35	31
Sildwortenestret	7	7	6	5	5	5	2	2	3	1	—	—	—	—	7	30	27
Wunegrestret	5	5	15	14	14	12	—	—	—	—	—	—	1	1	8	43	40
Tannerestret	15	15	27	27	10	7	6	6	—	—	—	—	—	—	4	62	59
Bucchestret	24	24	9	6	3	2	—	—	2	1	—	—	—	—	8	46	41
Colobrochestret	1	—	2	2	—	—	—	—	18	18	—	—	—	—	4	25	24
Outside East Gate	—	—	32	32	24	22	—	—	—	—	—	—	—	—	3	59	57
Mensterstret	3	3	4	3	20	20	—	—	—	—	—	—	—	—	7	34	33
Calpestret	17	17	2	—	11	11	—	—	—	—	—	—	1	1	—	31	29
Goldestret	10	10	2	2	19	19	—	—	—	—	—	—	9	8	10	50	49
Outside South Gate i	—	—	62	62	31	31	—	—	4	4	—	—	—	—	4	101	101
Outside South Gate ii	—	—	55	55	9	9	—	—	—	—	—	—	—	—	3	67	67
Gerestret	13	13	2	2	3	2	—	—	—	—	—	—	1	1	1	20	19
Totals	262	259	402	364	203	185	95	94	34	26	21	19	12	11	120	1149	1078

Notes. The figures in column A represent the total number of holdings in a fief. Tenements which lay in two or more of the fiefs will thus be counted more than once in the totals. The figures will not necessarily agree with those in Table 11 since some tenements which were part of a fief did not provide a rent.

The figures in column B are made up only of those tenements where the lord of one of the seven fiefs appears to have received the landgable. No tenement is counted more than once. In a few cases the attribution to one lord or another is not conclusive and some tenements appear to owe landgable to more than one lord. Nevertheless the figures in this column represent the distribution of territorial lordship more accurately than those in column A.

TABLE 16

The seven great fiefs in 1148: the total number of tenements of a fief in each street as a percentage of the total number of tenements in that fief (cf. Fig. 14b)

Key numbers on Fig. 14b	Streets	Fiefs													
		King		Bishop		Prior		Abbot		Abbess		Wherwell		Romsey	
		A	B	A	B	A	B	A	B	A	B	A	B	A	B
1	High Street	29	29	18	16	6	3	19	19	18	4	—	—	—	—
	Outside West Gate	22	22	9	7	10	11	13	13	—	—	—	—	—	—
	Outside North Gate	<0.5	<0.5	3	4	—	—	30	31	—	—	—	—	—	—
2	Snidelingestret	3	3	6	7	1	1	1	1	—	—	—	—	—	—
3	Brudenestret	3	3	3	4	2	3	1	1	—	—	10	5	—	—
4	Scowrtenestret	3	3	1	1	—	—	24	24	—	—	29	32	—	—
5	Alwarnestret	3	3	2	2	2	2	2	2	3	4	5	—	—	—
6	Flesmangerestret	1	—	2	2	4	4	—	—	—	—	57	63	—	—
7	Sildwortenestret	3	3	1	2	2	3	2	2	9	4	—	—	—	—
8	Wunegrestret	2	2	4	4	7	6	—	—	—	—	—	—	8	9
9	Tannerestret	6	6	7	7	5	4	6	6	—	—	—	—	—	—
10	Bucchestret	9	9	2	2	1	1	—	—	6	4	—	—	—	—
11	Colobrochestret	<0.5	—	<0.5	1	—	—	—	—	53	69	—	—	—	—
	Outside East Gate	—	—	8	9	12	11	—	—	—	—	—	—	—	—
12	Mensterstret	1	1	1	1	10	11	—	—	—	—	—	—	—	—
13	Calpestret	7	7	<0.5	—	5	6	—	—	—	—	—	—	8	9
14	Goldestret	4	4	<0.5	1	9	10	—	—	—	—	—	—	75	73
	Outside South Gate i	—	—	15	17	15	17	—	—	12	15	—	—	—	—
	Outside South Gate ii	—	—	14	15	4	5	—	—	—	—	—	—	—	—
15	Gerestret	5	5	<0.5	1	1	1	—	—	—	—	—	—	8	9
	Totals	101	100	96	103	96	99	98	99	101	100	101	100	99	100

Note. For the difference between column A and column B see the note to Table 15. The figures in column A are adopted in Fig. 14b since they provide a better picture of the composition of the individual fiefs than those in column B.

TABLE 17

The seven great fiefs in 1148: the total rent of a fief in each street as a percentage of the total rent of that fief (cf. Fig. 14b)

Key numbers on Fig. 14b	Streets	Fiefs						
		King	Bishop	Prior	Abbot	Abbess	Wherwell	Romsey
1	High Street	22	58	43	44	86	—	—
	Outside West Gate	13	7	9	9	—	—	—
	Outside North Gate	< 0·5	2	—	22	—	—	—
2	*Snidelingestret*	2	3	1	1	—	—	—
3	*Brudenestret*	5	2	3	1	—	12	—
4	*Scowrtenestret*	4	2	—	17	—	21	—
5	*Alwarnestret*	4	1	1	1	—	10	—
6	*Flesmangerestret*	1	1	5	—	—	57	—
7	*Sildwortenestret*	3	< 0·5	1	2	3	—	—
8	*Wunegrestret*	2	1	3	—	—	—	4
9	*Tannerestret*	8	3	5	3	—	—	—
10	*Bucchestret*	13	1	< 0·5	—	1	—	—
11	*Colobrochestret*	—	< 0·5	—	—	10	—	—
	Outside East Gate	—	4	5	—	—	—	—
12	*Mensterstret*	< 0·5	< 0·5	4	—	—	—	—
13	*Calpestret*	13	1	3	—	—	—	8
14	*Goldestret*	4	1	7	—	—	—	70
	Outside South Gate i	—	6	4	—	2	—	—
	Outside South Gate ii	—	6	5	—	—	—	—
15	*Gerestret*	7	< 0·5	1	—	—	—	18
	Totals	101	99	100	100	102	100	100

TABLE 18

The seven great fiefs in 1148: the total number of tenements of a fief in each street as a percentage of the total number of tenements in that street (cf. Fig. 15)

Key numbers on Fig. 15	Streets	King		Bishop		Prior		Abbot		Abbess		Wherwell		Romsey		Tenements not in the seven fiefs		Totals %	
		A	B	A	B	A	B	A	B	A	B	A	B	A	B	A	B	A	B
1	High Street	45	45	42	35	8	4	11	11	4	1	—	—	—	—	5	5	115	101
	Outside West Gate	45	45	29	20	16	16	10	9	—	—	—	—	—	—	9	9	109	99
	Outside North Gate	2	2	26	26	—	—	54	54	—	—	—	—	—	—	17	17	99	99
2	*Snidelingestret*	20	20	71	68	6	6	3	3	—	—	—	—	—	—	3	3	103	100
3	*Brudenestret*	26	26	35	32	14	14	3	3	—	—	6	3	—	—	22	23	105	100
4	*Scowrtenestret*	16	16	13	9	—	—	51	51	—	—	13	13	—	—	11	11	104	100
5	*Alwarnestret*	19	19	27	22	11	11	5	5	3	3	3	—	—	—	43	43	111	103
6	*Flesmangerestret*	6	—	29	29	29	23	—	—	—	—	39	39	—	—	10	10	113	101
7	*Sildwortenestret*	23	26	20	19	20	19	7	7	10	4	—	—	—	—	23	26	103	101
8	*Wunegrestret*	13	13	38	35	35	30	—	—	—	—	—	—	3	3	20	20	109	101
9	*Tannerestret*	25	25	46	46	17	12	10	10	—	—	—	—	—	—	7	7	105	100
10	*Bucchestret*	59	59	22	15	6	5	—	—	4	2	—	—	—	—	20	20	111	101
11	*Colobrochestret*	4	—	8	8	—	—	—	—	75	75	—	—	—	—	17	17	104	100
	Outside East Gate	—	—	56	56	42	39	—	—	—	—	—	—	—	—	5	5	103	100
12	*Menstrestret*	9	9	12	9	61	61	—	—	—	—	—	—	—	—	21	21	103	100
13	*Calpestret*	59	59	7	—	38	38	—	—	—	—	—	—	3	3	—	—	107	100
14	*Goldestret*	20	20	4	4	39	39	—	—	—	—	—	—	18	16	20	20	101	99
	Outside South Gate i	—	—	61	61	31	31	—	—	4	4	—	—	—	—	4	4	100	100
	Outside South Gate ii	—	—	82	82	13	13	—	—	—	—	—	—	—	—	4	4	99	99
15	*Gerestret*	68	68	11	11	16	11	—	—	—	—	—	—	5	5	5	5	105	100
	Totals %	24	24	37	34	19	17	9	9	3	2	2	2	1	1	11	11	106	100

Note. The figures express percentages of the total number of tenements in the streets as defined in the notes to Table 20. For columns A and B see the note to Table 15. The figures in column B are adopted in Fig. 15 since they provide a better picture of the composition of the individual streets than those in column A.

TABLE 19

The seven great fiefs in 1148: the total rent of a fief in each street as a percentage of the total rents from that street (cf. Fig. 15)

Key numbers on Fig. 15	Streets	The seven fiefs							Other landlords	Totals %
		King	Bishop	Prior	Abbot	Abbess	Wherwell	Romsey		
1	High Street	1	21	6	3	3	—	—	66	100
	Outside West Gate	2	13	6	3	—	—	—	75	99
	Outside North Gate	1	10	—	19	—	—	—	71	101
2	Snidelingestret	2	29	7	2	—	—	—	60	100
3	Brudenestret	3	9	7	1	—	2	—	77	99
4	Scowrtenestret	2	6	—	10	—	3	—	79	100
5	Alwarnestret	2	6	2	1	—	2	—	86	99
6	Flesmangerestret	1	6	13	—	—	11	—	69	100
7	Sildwortenestret	3	5	4	3	3	—	—	82	100
8	Wunegrestret	2	10	14	—	—	—	1	74	101
9	Tannerestret	3	14	8	2	—	—	—	74	101
10	Bucchestret	8	3	1	—	2	—	—	87	101
11	Colobrochestret	—	2	—	—	25	—	—	74	101
	Outside East Gate	—	28	14	—	—	—	—	59	101
12	Mensterstret	1	5	16	—	—	—	—	79	101
13	Calpestret	7	8	6	—	—	—	1	78	100
14	Goldestret	2	3	13	—	—	—	4	78	100
	Outside South Gate i	—	28	7	—	1	—	—	64	100
	Outside South Gate ii	—	34	10	—	—	—	—	56	100
15	Gerestret	12	3	6	—	—	—	5	74	100

TABLE 20

Tenements and their rents in 1148 (cf. Fig. 17b)

Key numbers on Fig. 17b	Streets	Number of tenements[1]	Number of rents	Total rent			Average rent product per tenement (shillings)[5]	Average size of rent (shillings)[5]
				£	s.	d.		
1	High Street	168[2]	360	190	0	6½[3]	23	10·6
	Outside West Gate	128	236	39	2	9½	6	3·3
	Outside North Gate	53	86	12	13	9	5	3·0
2	*Snidelingestret*	35	56	6	1	11	3	2·2
3	*Brudenestret*	35	64	11	4	11½	7	3·5
4	*Scowrtenestret*	45	73	17	14	10[4]	8	4·9
5	*Alwarnestret*	37	66	11	5	0¾	6	3·4
6	*Flesmangerestret*	31	57	10	12	3	7	3·7
7	*Sildwortenestret*	27	50	6	14	9	5	2·7
8	*Wunegrestret*	40	64	6	14	4	3	2·1
9	*Tannerestret*	59	99	18	4	5	6	3·7
10	*Bucchestret*	41	70	11	2	11¼	5	3·2
11	*Colobrochestret*	24	35	2	7	5½	2	1·3
	Outside East Gate	57	97	10	18	4½	4	2·2
12	*Mensterstret*	33	42	6	9	9	4	3·1
13	*Calpestret*	29	54	12	14	9	9	4·7
14	*Goldestret*	49	73	16	4	5	7	4·4
	Outside South Gate i	101	151	15	16	10½[4]	3	2·1
	Outside South Gate ii	67	108	13	4	3½	4	2·4
15	*Gerestret*	19	29	3	12	2	4	2·5
	Totals	1078	1870	£423	0	8½	Median: 5	Median: 3·1

[1] With the exceptions recorded in note 2, below, each entry in the survey is taken to represent a tenement.
[2] Stalls from which weekly rents were due, the lodge at West Gate, and the *Balchus* are not included.
[3] Excludes weekly rents and tolls.   [4] Plus 1 bezant.
[5] For discussion of these figures see p. 380.

The Ownership of Property in Winchester in 1148

a. The Distribution of Tenements by Fiefs

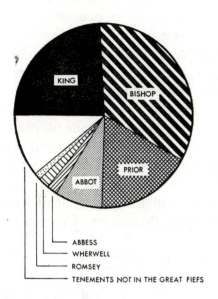

FIG 16

TABLE 21

The tenements in each fief in 1148 as a percentage of the total number of tenements in the city (cf. Fig. 16a)

Fief	Total number of tenements	Percentage of total for the city
King	259	24
Bishop	364	34
Prior	185	17
Abbot	94	9
Abbess	26	2
Wherwell	19	2
Romsey	11	1
Other landlords[1]	120	11
Totals	1078	100%

[1] Tenements not in any of the seven great fiefs.

b. Rents Received by Landlords

TABLE 22

The rent in each fief in 1148 as a percentage of the total rents in the city (cf. Fig. 16b)

Fief	Total rent			Percentage of the total rent in the city
	£	s.	d.	
King	7	3	4¾	2
Bishop	69	7	6¾	16
Prior	28	3	8	7
Abbot	11	4	3½	3
Abbess	6	1	9½	1
Wherwell	2	2	2	< 0·5
Romsey	1	0	0	< 0·5
Other landlords[1]	297	17	9	70
Totals	£423	0	7½	100%

[1] Rent not received by any of the seven great fiefs.

ii. PRIVATE LANDLORDS (Figs. 15 and 16; Tables 11, 21, and 22)

In the twelfth century the Winchester property-market appears to have operated mainly among private landlords. In every part of the city private landlords received a rent-total considerably greater than that received by all seven of the great fiefs (Figs. 15 and 16). In most areas this total was more than twice that received by the great lords, the only exceptions being High Street, where the bishop seems to have had an unusually high revenue, the southern suburbs, where he also had a high revenue, and *Snidelingestret*, again substantially in the bishop's fief (Table 11). But the individual estates of the private landlords ranked low in 1148 by comparison with the seven great fiefs, both in numbers of holdings, and in totals of rent received (Table 23): the richest of the private landlords, Robert of Inglesham, comes about halfway between the abbot of Hyde and the abbess of St. Mary's. One hundred and ninety private landlords owning more than one property are considered here. Of these, only seventy-two had rent receipts greater than those of the abbess of Romsey, who was by far the poorest of the seven great lords, a figure that is probably less than 8 per cent of the total of eight or nine hundred private individuals recorded in Survey **II**. Furthermore, the estates of nearly all the private landlords were burdened with outgoing payments to a far greater extent than those of the seven great fiefs.

There were some difficulties in the choice of the sample of 190 private landlords, principally arising from uncertainty over the identification of individuals, but the sample is probably representative of the class. The rents received and paid by each of these landlords have been tabulated, and the balance of rent remaining to them, or the deficit, has been calculated (Table 23). The sample can for the most part only be analysed from the point of view of the monetary interest, for the real value of property occupied by the landlord for his own commercial or domestic purposes cannot be estimated.

The rentrolls of a few private landlords on the king's fief in *c.* 1110 can be partially reconstructed from the evidence of Survey **I**. This survey does not, however, indicate how much these men paid from their properties to landlords other than the king. Herbert the chamberlain[1] received rent of £27. 10s. 9d. a year from ten properties. He probably paid a rent of unknown amount from one of these tenements to William d'Aubigny. The son of Ralf Rosell[2] probably received £11. 16s. rent from three tenements in High Street, but we do not know how much he received from the three tenements which he held on the king's fief elsewhere in the city. Robert Mauduit[3] received £6. 16s. from three tenements; Henry de Port[4] £5. 19s. from three tenements; Robert son of Ralf[5] £4. 14s. from two tenements; and Anschetil de Jort[6] £2. 2s. from two tenements in High Street, plus an unknown sum from two other tenements. On the whole these receipts seem higher than the receipts of private landlords in 1148 (Table 24). Herbert the chamberlain received three times more than the wealthiest private landlord of Survey **II**, Robert of Inglesham, but in 1148 Herbert's son[7] received only £4. 2s. from seven properties. This fall in income may reflect a general economic trend, perhaps associated

---

[1] I, Preface, n. 2.   [2] I, 1, n. 1.   [3] I, 45, n. 1.   [4] I, 39, n. 2.
[5] I, 47, n. 2.   [6] I, 9, n. 1.   [7] II, 4, n. 1.

with the effects on the city of the siege of 1141.[1] In Herbert's case, however, we may see in particular the results of a slackening of the link between the royal court and the city after the early years of the reign of Henry I.[2] Royal officials might still need a house in Winchester, but there was perhaps no longer the need for a substantial income from property there. This in its turn would have a deflationary effect on the price of property as a whole.

TABLE 23

The estates of private landlords holding more than one property in 1148

Their properties		Their rents	
Number of properties	Number of landlords	Balance of rent	Number of landlords
14	1	£8 1s. 0d.	1
13	2	£7 to £8	1
12	1	£6 to £7	none
11	2	£5 to £6	2
10	1	£4 to £5	1
9	2	£3 to £4	2
8	4	£2 10s. to £3	none
7	2	£2 to £2.10s.	3
6	5	£1.10s. to £2	7
5	11	£1 to £1.10s.	18
4	19	10s. to £1	30
3	35	Less than 10s.	74
2	105	Deficit {less than 10s.	43
		10s. to £1	5
		over £1	3
	190		190

The number of private individuals who appear from Survey **II** to have had any extensive interest in property is very small. The 190 with more than one property represent less than a quarter of the total number of individuals identified in the survey. They were probably a much smaller proportion of the total number of heads of households in the city.[3] More than half the 190 had no more than two properties. By contrast, the fifteen private landlords who each held between seven and fourteen properties probably formed a distinctive group. A similar picture emerges from an analysis of the balance of rent remaining to each landlord. Nearly two-thirds of the sample had a balance of less than a £1, or a deficit of less than 10s. The ten who had a balance of more than £2 may perhaps be identified as a distinctive group of the richest private landlords (Table 24). On the whole, the same individuals appear to have been both the richest landlords and to have held the largest number of properties, although there are some significant exceptions. Pain son of Picard[4] had twelve properties, but a balance of only 12s. 9d. from

[1] See below, pp. 386 and 489.
[2] See above, pp. 295–7; below, pp. 472–3, and for the reflection of this in the interests of royal officials
in the city, p. 387, and Fig. 21.
[3] Cf. below, pp. 440–1.
[4] II, 21, n. 1.

receipts of £2. 16s. 6d. Robert Norreis[1] had a balance of only 13s. from receipts of 17s. 8d. Some landlords had a large revenue from relatively few properties, although in these cases the discrepancy was not so extreme. Samson the moneyer, for example, had a balance of £3. 19s. 4d. out of receipts of £6. 7s. 4d. from a total of five properties,[2] and Robert the Weasel[3] had a balance of £2. 7s. 2d. out of receipts of £4. 12s. 8d. from five properties. Samson's properties were in a group to either side of the central area of High Street: a small portfolio of well-chosen properties could evidently provide a good annual income.

TABLE 24

The ten richest private landlords in 1148

Name	Rent received			Rent paid			Balance			Number of properties
	£	s.	d.	£	s.	d.	£	s.	d.	
Robert of Inglesham	8	18	10		17	10	8	1	0	13
William Martel	7	16	3			6	7	15	9	10
Thurstin the clerk	7	4	9	1	10	11¾	5	13	9¼	14
Godfrey son of William	5	10	4		8	8	5	1	8	9
Widow of Martin of Bentworth	5	19	2½	1	15	9	4	3	4½	11
Samson the moneyer	6	7	4	2	8	0	3	19	4	5
Herbert the chamberlain	4	2	0		8	8	3	13	4	7
Ernald brother of Peter the mercer	3	15	0	1	7	6	2	7	6	8
Robert the Weasel	4	12	8	2	5	6	2	7	2	5
Robert of St. Pancras	3	7	0	1	0	9	2	6	3	11

The interests of the ten richest landlords throw some light on the means of advancement in mid-twelfth-century Winchester (Table 24). Three of them, William Martel,[4] Thurstin the clerk,[5] and Herbert the chamberlain,[6] were royal officials. Two more, Robert the Weasel[7] and Robert of St. Pancras,[8] appear to have had connections with the court. One other, Samson,[9] was a moneyer. Ernald[10] was the brother of a wealthy Winchester merchant, who himself had nine properties with a balance of £1. 3s. 1d. rent. This group also includes the widow of a Winchester butcher.[11] Robert of Inglesham may have been the clerical retainer of Henry of Blois shortly to become archdeacon of Surrey.[12] Nothing beyond the evidence of the survey is known of Godfrey son of William.[13] This suggests that their interests may have been confined to Winchester. Local interest is indeed an important characteristic of the group as a whole. Six of the ten are not known outside Winchester, and Thurstin the clerk appears to have made his career in the county administration.

Conspicuously absent from the ranks of the richer landlords was the local baronial family of Port.[14] John de Port had a balance of 4s. 2d. out of receipts of 5s. 2d. from seven properties. Roger de Port had rents, probably landgable, worth 4s. from four properties with no outgoings. Hugh and Adelaide de Port each had two properties with balances

[1] II, 73, n. 5 (13 properties).   [2] II, 64, n. 1.   [3] II, 9, n. 1.
[4] II, 35, n. 2.   [5] II, 221, n. 1.   [6] II, 4, n. 1.   [7] II, 9, n. 1.
[8] II, 31, n. 3.   [9] II, 64, n. 1.   [10] II, 135, n. 1.   [11] See above, pp. 27–8.
[12] II, 1, n. 1.   [13] II, 5, n. 1.   [14] II, 2, n. 1, and 479, n. 2.

of 1s. 9d. and 3d., respectively. This comparatively extensive family estate, made up of fifteen properties, perhaps represented an ancient family inheritance, the owners of which no longer had much direct interest in Winchester affairs.

Several burgesses of middle rank may be identified among the private landlords. Herbert the reeve[1] had three properties, received £1. 16s. 10d. rent, and paid 11s. 8½d. Raymond the parmenter[2] had a balance of £1. 1s. 10d. out of receipts of £1. 19s. 6d. from four properties. The ancestors of some important thirteenth-century Winchester families may also be identified among the private landlords. Herbert son of Westman,[3] who was to be a moneyer of Henry II, had a balance of 7s. 1d. out of receipts of £1. 1s. from four properties. Robert Oisun[4] had six properties, but received a total of only 10s. from a single rent, while he paid out 11s. 6d.

TABLE 25

Private landlords with properties in High Street in 1148

Balance of rent	Total number of landlords	Landlords with properties in High Street	Percentage with properties in High Street
Over £2	10	9	90
£1–£2	25	14	56
10s.–£1	30	12	40
Less than 10s.	73	26	36
Deficit	52	11	22
Total	190	72	38

Fifty-one of the 190 landlords in the sample had a deficit. Forty-one of these had no more than two properties, five had three, three had four, and two had six properties. Clearly those with a deficit were usually the smaller landlords, but the example of Robert Oisun shows that those who paid out more than they received were not necessarily poor or insignificant property-owners. Siward the moneyer[5] had an over-all deficit of £1. 1s. 3d. from his three properties, and Richard of Limésy, apparently a member of a well-connected family,[6] had a deficit of 4s. 5d.

For private landlords, as well as for the lords of the seven great fiefs, property in High Street was the most desirable. As Table 25 shows, it was a characteristic of the estates of the richer landlords.

Of the ten richest, only Thurstin the clerk had no property in High Street, and the less valuable estates contained a progressively smaller proportion of High Street property. Nevertheless, more than a third of all the private landlords owning more than one property had one of them in High Street.

The estates of the more important private landlords were widespread throughout the city, while the smaller and less valuable estates were more localized. So far as the smaller

[1] II, 76, n. 1. [2] II, 40, n. 3. [3] II, 38, n. 5. [4] II, 40, n. 2.
[5] II, 112, n. 1. [6] II, 535, n. 2.

estates of two or three properties are concerned, this pattern is probably exaggerated by the difficulty of identifying individuals, but the example of the estate of Pain son of Picard, which was large and of relatively little value,[1] appears to justify this conclusion. Pain's estate was virtually confined to the north-west quarter of the city.

In the fourteenth and early fifteenth centuries the number of private landlords with estates widespread throughout the city and suburbs was very small. Such landlords were mainly interested in their properties as an investment and as a source of income.[2] In 1148 Robert of Inglesham and the nine other richest property-owners were probably good examples of this class of *rentier* landlords.

In the later Middle Ages, most Winchester private landlords owned relatively compact estates confined to one or two areas of the city or scattered up and down both sides of a single street. There seems to have been a strong link between the composition of these estates and the commercial or manufacturing interests of their owners.[3] Examples of this class in the mid-twelfth century are less easy to identify, although Herbert son of Westman and Robert Oisun may be representative. Herbert had a property in High Street near the entry to *Scowrtenestret* (**II, 38**), another in *Scowrtenestret* itself (**II, 463**), and two apparently opposite one another in *Alwarnestret* (**II, 478** and **506**). Robert Oisun had a group of four properties towards the south end and on both sides of *Goldestret* (**II, 870, 877**, and **881–2**), one in High Street almost opposite the entry to *Goldestret* (**II, 40**), and one outside South Gate (**II, 983**). In both these cases the High Street property perhaps served as a market outlet, conveniently situated for commercial interests themselves centred elsewhere.

The richer private landlords of the twelfth century were probably better off than any private landlords in later medieval Winchester, and this pin-points the early prosperity of the city. John Gabriel was one of the half-dozen wealthiest merchants in *c.* 1330, and was elected mayor in 1320, 1328, and 1334. In 1331 the annual value of his rents and tenements in the city and suburbs was £9. 6s. 8d.[4] Mark le Fayre was almost certainly the wealthiest merchant and landowner of fourteenth- and fifteenth-century Winchester. In 1417 his thirty-five tenements in the city had a nominal annual rental value of £32. 9s. 11d. Between 1426 and 1431 the average annual receipt from these properties, by then in the possession of his son-in-law, was £26, of which on average a balance of £18 remained after deductions for quit-rents and repairs.[5] The estates of Herbert the chamberlain (the elder) in Survey **I** and Robert of Inglesham in Survey **II**, even in their twelfth-century values, are directly comparable with these estates of the later Middle Ages.

[1] See above, p. 371, and n. 4.

[2] Keene *Brooks Area*, 148–62.

[3] Ibid.

[4] Keene *Brooks Area*, 132–3 and 204–5. PRO, C 143/226/17: the estimate of the value of Gabriel's estate in this *inquisitio ad quod damnum* was probably to some extent conventional, but it differs sufficiently from estimates of the estates of other Winchester landlords of the same period in other *inquisitiones* for it to approximate to the real value.

[5] The 1431 rental for these properties has been published: D. May, 'The Somer Rentals in the Winchester City Archives', *Proc Hants FC* 18 (1954), 325–31. The values for 1426–31 have been calculated from the Somer account rolls in WCA.

iii. THE INTENSITY OF DEVELOPMENT BY 1148

Introduction

The survey of 1148 conveys a strong impression of the varied nature and intensity of development among the streets and areas of the city. There are four ways of measuring these differences: by estimating the mean frontage-width of properties in individual streets (Fig. 17a): by analysing the number of rents due from individual properties (Fig. 18); by comparing the degree to which the seven great fiefs were intermingled (Fig. 19); and by assessing the average value of properties in each street (Figs. 17b and c). Of these four approaches, the first three should indicate the intensity of land use, the comparative density of settlement, and the degree to which the property-market had operated in the different parts of the city. The fourth indicates variations in property-values from street to street in 1148. A comparison of this with the other approaches may illustrate some important characteristics of the different patterns of settlement in the city.

The width of properties on the street frontage (Fig. 17a and Table 26)

Since the area covered by each street heading can be defined with some precision,[1] it is possible to work out for most of the streets within the walls the mean length of street-frontage occupied by the entries in Survey **II**. Actual tenement frontages probably differed considerably above and below the mean figure, and in the north–south streets there was probably a very considerable difference in frontage-size between the more spacious properties towards the city walls, and the more closely-packed properties towards High Street. But the length of the areas along and within which these properties lay can be quite precisely defined in terms of street-frontage, and since the archaeological evidence suggests that in 1148, as in later periods, houses were already concentrated on the street frontages,[2] the average frontage-width is a reliable index of the density of building in a given street. On the whole, only the straight length of a street-frontage is included in the frontage total. This assumes that the tenement layout was simpler than it probably was, but avoids the difficulty of allowing for corner properties. Although the back streets parallel to High Street are known to have been occupied by separate properties in the later Middle Ages, the comparison between the north–south streets will not be distorted because these were spaced at approximately equal intervals at their High Street ends. Such problems make the calculation of a figure for High Street particularly difficult, even if allowances are made for properties in the entries to the side streets. In general the later medieval pattern of occupation has been followed in reconstructing the available frontage-lengths. There has therefore been no need to allow for properties ranged along the intra-mural lanes, except possibly in the case of *Mensterstret*. The number of properties, the frontage-lengths, and the street-averages are shown in Table 26, followed by notes on the problems of individual streets.

Reliable figures for the north and south suburbs cannot be provided, since the attribution of properties to individual streets is uncertain. There is very little evidence, in particular to the south of the city, for the extent of the built-up area outside the walls.[3]

[1] See above, pp. 242–4.   [2] *IX Interim*, 98–9, 115; *X Interim*, 310–18.
[3] See above, pp. 265–7.

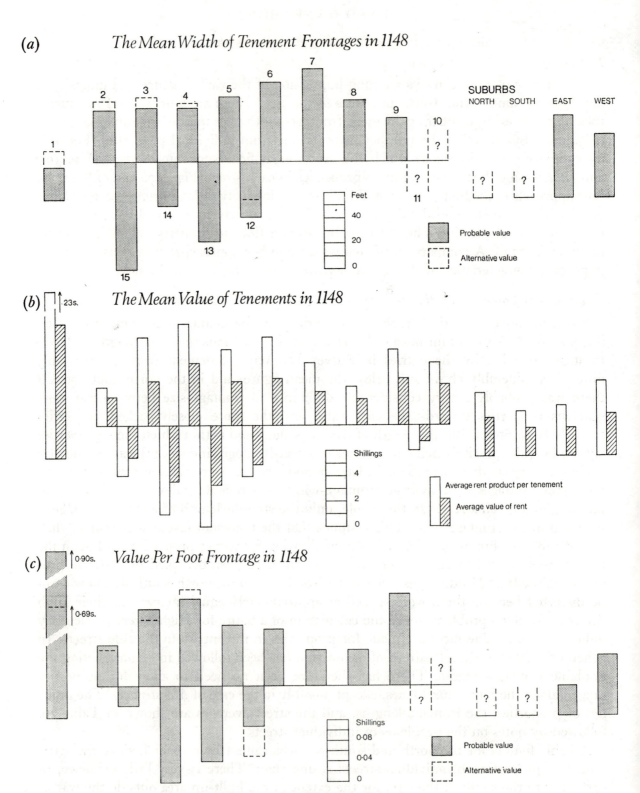

(a) *The Mean Width of Tenement Frontages in 1148*

(b) *The Mean Value of Tenements in 1148*

(c) *Value Per Foot Frontage in 1148*

FIG. 17 *a, b, c.* Tenements in 1148.

The representation of the south suburb is based on the combination of the figures given under the two headings 'outside South Gate' in Tables 20 and 26. To identify the streets on this Figure see the key numbers also given on those tables.

TABLE 26 (cf. Fig. 17 *a* and *c*)

Tenement frontages and their value in 1148

Key numbers on Fig. 17*a*	Street	Frontage in feet	Number of properties	Average frontage in feet[1]	Value of property per foot frontage (shillings)[1]
1	High Street *a*	4020	161	25	0·90
	b	6000	161	38	0·69
	Outside West Gate	6400	128	50	0·12
	Outside North Gate	?	53	?	?
2	*Snidelingestret a*	1440	35	41	0·08
	b	1680	35	48	0·07
3	*Brudenestret a*	1480	35	42	0·15
	b	1780	35	51	0·13
4	*Scowrtenestret a*	2050	45	46	0·17
	b	1840	45	42	0·19
5	*Alwarnestret*	1840	37	51	0·12
6	*Flesmangerestret*	1880	31	62	0·11
7	*Sildwortenestret*	1900	27	73	0·07
8	*Wunegrestret*	1940	40	48	0·07
9	*Tannerestret*	2050	59	34	0·18
10	*Bucchestret*	?	41	?	?
11	*Colobrochestret*	?	24	?	?
	Outside East Gate	3740	57	65	0·06
12	*Mensterstret a*	1450	33	44	0·08
	b	900	33	30	0·14
13	*Calpestret*	1660	28	63	0·15
14	*Goldestret*	1700	48	35	0·19
	Outside South Gate i	?	101	?	?
	Outside South Gate ii	?	67	?	?
15	*Gerestret*	1640	19	86	0·04

[1] For the calculation of these values, see below, p. 380.

Where there are alternative lengths, the first is the more likely and has been adopted in the reconstruction diagrams.

High Street. Stalls, encroachments, and the seven upper rooms have been excluded from the total number of properties. The frontage length under *a* represents the High Street frontage between West Gate and the entry to Tanner Street only, and includes a single measurement from High Street south to the corner of the Close wall at Minster gate to allow for that part of the royal palace which was built upon by the thirteenth century. In order to arrive at the total under *b* an allowance for the entries to the side streets has been added to the first total.

Outside West Gate. The frontages of both sides of the three streets in the western suburb are included in the total. The length of the street which runs parallel to the city wall is measured from West Gate to its junction with the street leading from North Gate.

Snidelingestret and Brudenestret. By the later Middle Ages both these streets stopped short of the north wall of the city and were connected with North Gate by lanes running into *Scowrtenestret* (Jewry Street). Excavation in 1960 revealed a medieval metalled surface in line with and to the north of the present end of *Brudenestret* (Staple Gardens), and it is possible that the original *Snidelingestret* and *Brudenestret* extended as far as the city wall. The alternative frontage lengths are for the short later-medieval streets and the possibly longer early-medieval streets, respectively.

Scowrtenestret. The shorter frontage is based on a simple measurement of the north–south length of the street as far as the city wall. The longer frontage includes allowances for the way from North Gate into *Scowrtenestret*, and for the south and west sides of the island of property within North Gate.

Tannerestret. The east side of the entry from High Street to *Tannerestret*, which lay in Tanner Street aldermanry in the later Middle Ages, is included in the frontage length.

Mensterstret. The east side of the street was occupied by the royal palace and St. Swithun's Priory, and so is not included in the frontage measurements. The shorter length consists of the west side of the street only. The longer length includes an allowance for the properties against the city wall between *Mensterstret* and King's Gate (cf. **II**, 797).

Outside East Gate. The frontage lengths here are uncertain. The figure given allows for St. John's Street as far north as the sharp turn uphill to the east, and for Chesil Street as far south as Bar End. In the later Middle Ages the built-up area extended considerably further north.

Even taking possible variants into account, Table 26 shows that the most densely-occupied streets within the city were those which led to the city gates, a fact which emphasizes the importance of incoming traffic for Winchester's prosperity. High Street was probably the most densely occupied of all; *Goldestret*, *Tannerestret*, and *Scowrtenestret* were next; *Snidelingestret* and *Brudenestret*, relatively densely populated, were fairly easily accessible from both West Gate and North Gate, and included many of the 'lands of the barons'. *Mensterstret* was near the royal palace and cathedral, and was relatively accessible. The western suburb, where the numbers of houses were increasing in the late eleventh century, was comparatively more densely occupied than at a later date. If the properties under the second heading 'outside South Gate' lay to the north of *Sevetuichne*, the area outside King's Gate must have been one of the more densely occupied parts of the city, as the concentration of craftsmen there also suggests.[1]

This pattern can be compared with that of the late thirteenth and early fourteenth centuries. *Snidelingestret*, *Brudenestret*, and the western suburb had declined drastically by then. *Scowrtenestret* and *Alwarnestret*, relatively densely occupied in 1148, contained the homes of Jews and wealthy merchants. *Tannerestret* was still densely occupied, but *Goldestret* had lost its earlier concentration of population.[2]

Some comparisons in the size of tenements are possible between Winchester and other towns in the twelfth century. Table 26 shows that in the more densely built-up areas an average-sized tenement probably had a frontage of between 30 and 40 feet (9 and 12 m). In the north–south streets the depth of these properties was probably between 100 and 150 feet (30 and 46 m), although some may have extended from one street to the next.[3] These dimensions correspond approximately to those of the tenements, as opposed to the smaller cottages, in the more densely built-up part of the city in the fourteenth century.[4] In twelfth-century London and within the walls of Canterbury about 1200, frontages seem also to have been about this size.[5] In Lincoln between 1066 and 1086, 166 messuages occupying an area of about 14 acres (5·6 ha) were destroyed.[6] Each messuage will therefore have covered on average about 400 square yards (330 sq. m.), and could have measured 36 by 100 feet (11 by 30 m). The average size of tenements and the density of housing in the central areas of at least four English cities in the twelfth century were thus evidently similar.

Multiple rents due from tenements (Fig. 18 and Table 27)

Table 27 shows the proportion of entries in each street in Survey **II** from which more than one rent, or more than two rents, were due. A multiplicity of rents due from a single property does not necessarily mean that the property was in multiple occupation, except where the separate rents were due to one landlord. The number of rents due from a single property thus represents the value of the property as a source of income to a number of

---

[1] See below, p. 439.

[2] See *SMW*.

[3] It is possible that the confusion which arose over **II, 563** (cf. **I, 195**) was because the property extended from *Sildwortenestret* to *Wunegrestret*.

[4] See *SMW*, and below, p. 381, n. 2.

[5] Urry *Canterbury*, 249–88 (Rental D); F. M. Stenton, 'Norman London', in D. M. Stenton (ed.), *Preparatory to Anglo-Saxon England* (Oxford, 1970), 47.

[6] Francis Hill, *Medieval Lincoln* (Cambridge, 1965), 55.

individuals, and the intensity with which the property-market had operated in that area, rather than the number of persons actually inhabiting the property. If the conditions of the late thirteenth and early fourteenth centuries are applicable to twelfth-century Winchester, reserved rents were due in greater numbers from substantial houses than from small properties. But on the whole, since there are so many variables, this indicator of

TABLE 27

Multiple rents in 1148 (cf. Fig. 18)

Street	More than one rent		More than two rents	
	No.	%	No.	%
High Street	107	61	41[2]	23[2]
Outside West Gate	83	70	16	12
Outside North Gate	30	57	5	9
Snidelingestret	17	48	2	5
Brudenestret	20	57	6	17
Scowrtenestret	21	48	5	11
Alwarnestret	23	62	8	22
Flesmangerestret	18	58	4	13
Sildwortenestret	17	63	6	22
Wunegrestret	20	50	6	15
Tannerestret	28	47	9	15
Brudenestret	20	49	10	24
Colobrochestret	13	54	1	4
Outside East Gate	27	47	4	7
Mensterstret	15	45	—	—
Calpestret	21	75	3	11
Goldestret	25	52	2	4
Outside South Gate i	49	49[1]	5	5[1]
Outside South Gate ii	32	48[1]	7	10[1]
Gerestret	10	45	1	5

[1] The percentages for the south suburb as a whole are 49% with more than one rent and 7% with more than two rents.

[2] Might be more representative for the north side of High Street only. This figure is probably distorted by large numbers of the bishop's rents.

the relative prosperity of different parts of the city is the least reliable. In the analysis of the proportion of properties from which more than two rents were due, High Street stands high, together with *Alwarnestret* and *Sildwortenestret*, which later, on the basis of their frontage-widths, appear to have been among the less densely-occupied streets. *Bucchestret* appears somewhat more developed in this respect than High Street. In the analysis of the proportion of properties from which more than one rent was due, *Calpestret* and the suburb outside West Gate stand higher than High Street, *Alwarnestret*, or *Sildwortenestret*. The general pattern, it is clear, was for about half or more of all the houses in Winchester to be held by some form of subtenancy.

The intermingling of fiefs (Figs. 15, 18 and 19; Tables 18 and 19)

The degree to which the seven great fiefs intermingled is shown in Fig. 15 and Tables 18 and 19. Figure 19 shows the details of this intermingling house by house for the walled area and suburbs, while Fig. 18 shows properties from which one rent, or more than one rent, was due. The areas where in 1148 tenure was most heterogeneous, and where multiple rents were due from single tenements, were presumably those where property had been most in demand. On these grounds High Street and the suburb outside West Gate appear to have been the most intensively developed. The complexity of rents and tenures on the north side of High Street indicates that that side of the street was probably the most developed area of the whole city. The south side of High Street appears by contrast to have been relatively undeveloped, although this appearance may in part have been created by colonization of the site of the royal palace in the six or seven years before Survey **II** was made.

The value of property in 1148 (Figs. 17b and c; Tables 20 and 26)

An assessment of variations in property-values in 1148 may be based on the mean rent-product of the individual tenement, or on the mean value of the individual rents from street to street. These values are given in Table 20 and are represented diagrammatically in Fig. 17. The results obtained by the two methods are virtually identical.

The mean rent-product of tenements has been calculated by dividing the total rent recorded for each street in Survey **II** by the number of tenements in the street. In arriving at the total rent for each street no account has been taken of the fact that in some tenements landlords paid rents as well as receiving them: to assess the true rent-product of these tenements it would be necessary to subtract the rent paid by these landlords from that which they received. In many cases, however, this calculation would result in a negative rent (e.g. **II, 167–70**), and the obvious value of the tenement to the landlord himself could not be estimated. The straightforward sum-total of all the rents recorded for each tenement is therefore the best method of arriving at an approximate indication of the total rent-product of a property. This method will exaggerate the value of those tenements, mainly in High Street, from which many rents were due. Nevertheless, the fact that many rents were due from a single tenement is an important indication of its value.

Apart from High Street the mean rent-value of tenements varied from 2s. in *Colobrochestret* to 8s. in *Scowrtenestret* and 9s. in *Calpestret*. Other areas with high values were *Brudenestret*, *Flesmangerestret*, *Goldestret*, outside West Gate, *Alwarnestret*, and *Tannerestret*. Areas with low values, in addition to *Colobrochestret*, were *Snidelingestret*, *Wunegrestret*, the east and south suburbs, *Mensterstret*, and *Gerestret*.

The mean value of tenements in High Street was 23s., and the range in value of individual tenements was much greater there than elsewhere, extending from 6d. to £8. 9s. Thirty-three per cent of the tenements in High Street each produced more than 20s. rent; these were responsible for 81 per cent of the total rent-product of the street. The mean value of the remaining tenements was 7s. so that even those of low value in High Street stood relatively high by comparison with the rest of the city.

The mean value of the individual rent in each street has been calculated by dividing the total rent-product of each street by the total number of rents recorded there. This produces almost exactly the same topographical distribution of property-values as the first method, although the variation from street to street is usually less marked. A difference which may be noted between the results of the two methods is that by the second method *Brudenestret* and the eastern suburb both appear to be slightly less prominent as areas of high and low property-values respectively.

Conclusion

The first three analyses alone show that High Street was among the most densely-occupied and economically desirable areas of the city. The suburb outside West Gate was the most developed of the suburbs in the twelfth century, and the high degree to which fiefs were intermingled there suggests that this development had been in progress for a long time. The analyses produce contrasting rankings for the north–south streets within the walls. *Alwarnestret* and *Flesmangerestret*, for example, appeared to have been less built-up than other streets (Fig. 17*a*; Table 26), but exhibited to a considerable degree the intermingling of fiefs (Fig. 19; Tables 18 and 19), and contained a relatively high proportion of properties from which more than two rents were due (Fig. 18; Table 27). This contrast may result in part from the fact that both streets were equidistant from the centres of the great fiefs represented there;[1] it may also mean that the properties there were relatively large, and yet were, or had been, much in demand and could produce a good income.

These conclusions are supported by the analysis of property-values. The correlation between a high density of occupation, indicated by the mean frontage-width of tenements, and a high property-value is obvious for High Street. It is also clear for *Tannerestret*, *Scowrtenestret*, and *Goldestret*, and perhaps also for the western suburb and *Brudenestret*. Conversely, there are areas where a low density of occupation corresponds with a low property-value. *Gerestret*, *Mensterstret*, *Wunegrestret*, the eastern suburb, and perhaps also *Colobrochestret* and much of the southern suburb, are good examples of this, although in the last two cases density of occupation cannot easily be estimated. The opposite principle, however, applies in other areas. In *Calpestret* and *Flesmangerestret*, and to a lesser extent in *Alwarnestret* and *Sildwortenestret*, properties appear to have been relatively large and of high value. In *Snidelingestret* they were probably relatively small and of low value.

This apparent paradox may reveal some of the fundamental characteristics of settlement in the different parts of the city. In later medieval Winchester, certain streets were characterized by a preponderance of large houses and others by a preponderance of cottages, while in a third group of streets, consisting of the prosperous commercial and industrial areas, large houses and cottages were more or less equally intermixed. This ranking of areas corresponded to the social and economic status of their inhabitants.[2] The twelfth-century evidence for density of occupation and the value of individual tenements may represent a similar situation. If this is correct, High Street and *Tannerestret*, for example, would contain a mixture of large and small houses, the value of the smaller houses in High Street being forced up by the market-demand for property

---

[1] See above, pp. 356–8.
[2] See *SMW*. The distribution of the larger houses

(described in the sources as tenements) and cottages can be determined from the tarrage survey of 1417.

there. Prosperous tradesmen were perhaps the characteristic inhabitants of these areas.[1] *Snidelingestret* and possibly also the group of properties under the second heading 'outside South Gate' may have been inhabited by relatively poor families living closely together. In the case of the group 'outside South Gate' this appears to be corroborated by the occupations of the inhabitants, several of whom were among the lower ranks of the leather and victualling trades.[2]

The houses in those areas grouped above with *Gerestret* were perhaps relatively small, widely spaced, and not much in demand. By contrast, *Calpestret*, *Flesmangerestret*, and *Alwarnestret* probably contained the most spacious private houses in the city, the homes of the leading inhabitants. In these areas were also concentrated the properties of the barons, magnates, royal officials, and goldsmiths in 1148, and those of the moneyers in the early twelfth century.[3]

Finally, we may compare property-values per foot-frontage from street to street (Fig. 17c; Table 26). These figures have been obtained by dividing the total rent-product of a street (Table 20) by its frontage length in feet (Table 26), a process similar to the basis of modern rating-valuation. The value for each street will reflect the market-value of property, rather than the size or desirability of houses. Thus property was valued higher in *Goldestret* than in *Calpestret*, although in the latter the individual tenement brought in on average more rent. The values of property per foot-frontage in the individual streets show quite clearly that commerce and ease of access dictated the market-value of property in mid twelfth-century Winchester. Investment in property brought the greatest return in High Street. The next most valuable areas were the streets leading from High Street to the city gates: *Goldestret*, *Tannerestret*, and *Scowrtenestret*. Values tailed off in the areas to either side of these streets. Property in *Goldestret*, which continued the main road leading from Southampton, was the most valuable after that in High Street. With the exception of *Tannerestret*, the more valuable of the side-streets were near the north–south axis formed by *Goldestret* and *Scowrtenestret*. *Tannerestret*, with its industrial character, differed from the other more prosperous streets within the walls, and the value of its property stood in sharp contrast to adjacent streets, at least those to the west. *Snidelingestret* and *Wunegrestret* contained relatively small properties of low value. Of all the streets which can be valued in this way, *Gerestret* contained property of the least value. This street was also one of the first in which the decay of properties may be traced in the thirteenth century.

iv. TENEMENTS ATTACHED TO RURAL ESTATES (Fig. 20 and Table 28)

Twenty-five rural estates can be identified in Hampshire to which tenements in Winchester were attached in the period before 1148. Dependent tenements were one of the ways in which rural estates could participate in the privileges of a borough. They could provide the lord of the estate with access for his produce to the largest market in the region, together with the town house that was necessary for the maintenance of his social

---

[1] See below, p. 439, and Fig. 23.
[2] See below, p. 433, and Fig. 23.
[3] See below, pp. 387, 410, and 439, and Figs. 21–3.

great fiefs in 1148 (1:5,000)

dths of the properties, Table 26. Outside North Gate and South Gate (i and
identify the streets on this Figure, cf. *either* Fig. 32 *or* the entry numbers
urvey II on p. 69, above.

position; or they could ensure a regular source of income from houses and other properties in the town. These properties were administered as part of the rural manor, even where the landlord owned a considerable number of other tenements in the city. The rents from the tenements dependent on Headbourne Worthy and Alresford were due, for example, to the reeves of those manors and not directly to the cathedral priory or the bishop. The jurisdiction of the manor may also have extended over its urban appendages.

The groups of tenements dependent on individual rural estates varied from single houses to eight or nine *hagae*. Most of them were recorded in Domesday Book, but the dependent tenements of the estates in Tisted, Kilmeston, and Hurstbourne, recorded in pre-conquest sources, were not mentioned in 1086; nor were tenements of Overton, Polhampton, Lasham, Odiham, Wolverton, and Alresford recorded in Surveys I and II. Domesday Book may thus not have been a complete record of this, as of other matters, but it is also likely that some of the early connections between the city and country estates may have lapsed by the late eleventh century, for only a few of the dependent tenements recorded in 1086 can be identified in 1148. By the date of the Domesday survey it would appear that the dependent tenements were as subject to the forces of the urban land-market as other tenements in Winchester. The evidence for the dependent tenements is summarized in Table 28.

Manors with appendages in Winchester were scattered throughout Hampshire as far as the county boundaries. They lay mostly in the northern part of the county, although there were groups on the river Test, and in the area of the upper Itchen and Meon valleys to the east and west of the city. A single manor lay at the edge of the New Forest. This distribution marks out that central and northern part of the county which lay particularly within the scope of Winchester's influence. But the relatively even spread, and the lack of any concentration in the immediate area of the city, or on the lines of main routes to the city, indicate a relationship that was probably based on more than simple economic or commercial factors. Perhaps the link between some of these manors and their urban tenements may initially have been the means by which the inhabitants of the county were guaranteed accommodation within the defences of Winchester in times of trouble.

Within the city there was a marked concentration of dependent tenements in the north-west quarter of the walled area, to the west of *Scowrtenestret*. The other tenements were situated in *Alwarnestret*, *Tannerestret*, *Calpestret*, and outside East Gate. Basingstoke had four properties somewhere in the suburbs. Three reasons for this pattern may be suggested. It could simply reflect the deficiencies of the record; or it may mean that for some reason the connection between the manor and its urban appendage survived longer in the north-western part of the city than elsewhere; or, since the majority of manors with urban tenements lay to the north of the city, the tenements themselves may have been situated near the northern entrance to the city. The location of the Alresford property in the eastern suburb appears to support the third of these suggestions, but the location of the Eversley tenement in *Calpestret* does not.

TABLE 28

Tenements in Winchester attached to rural estates in Hampshire (cf. Fig. 20)

Place	Property in Winchester[1]	Value	Lord	Source[2]	Notes
Wallop (Over Wallop)	2 *hagae*	65*d*.	King	*VCH* i. 453a	
Clatford	7 *hagae*	10*s*.	King	*VCH* i. 453b	
Basingstoke	4 *suburbani*	Used to pay 12*s*. 11*d*.	King	*VCH* i. 456a	Cf. II, 434
Faccombe (by Netherton)	6 *domus*	Not given	King	*VCH* i. 456b	
West Meon	8 *hagae*	6*s*.	Bishop of Winchester	*VCH* i. 461b	
Houghton	3 *burgenses*	30*d*.	Bishop of Winchester	*VCH* i. 462b	The burgesses are not said to be in Winchester
Mottisfont	1 *haga*	30*d*.	Archbishop Thomas of York	*VCH* i. 468b	
Eversley	1 *haga*	7*d*.	Westminster Abbey	*VCH* i. 472b	See **I, 262**
Preston Candover	1 *haga*	17*d*.	Earl Roger of Shrewsbury	*VCH* i. 477b	
Bramley	3 *burgenses*	22*d*.	Hugh de Port	*VCH* i. 479b	Winchester is not mentioned, but a space is left for the insertion of the name of the borough
Corhampton	1 *domus*	5*s*.	Hugh de Port	*VCH* i. 481a	
Headbourne Worthy	8 *hagae*	65*s*. 4*d*.	Ralf de Mortimer (from Old Minster)	*VCH* i. 489b	See **I, 141–2** and **II, 406–9, 502,** and **608**
King's Somborne	9 *mansiones burgensium*	12*s*. 2*d*.	William de Ow	*VCH* i. 491b	The houses are not said to be in Winchester
Worthy	1 *masura*	Pays nothing	Bernard Pancevolt	*VCH* i. 494b	
Stratfield Saye	1 *haga*	Not given	Hugh son of Baldri	*VCH* i. 496a	
Bramdean	1 *haga*	3*s*.	Milo the porter	*VCH* i. 503b	See above, p. 306
Norton (in Wonston)	5 *hagae*	10*s*.	Ode of Winchester	*VCH* i. 504a	
Dummer	3 *hagae*	2*s*.	Ode of Winchester	*VCH* i. 505a	
Minstead	1 *haga*	12*d*.	Sons of Godfric Malf	*VCH* i. 515b	
West Tisted	1 *haga* in W. pertaining to the 7 hides at Tisted	—	King Eadred granted to Æthelgeard	Sawyer 488 (946 × 55 for this postscript)	
Kilmeston	1 *haga* in the town within the south wall	—	King Edgar, to Æthelwulf for 3 lives with reversion to Old Minster	Sawyer 693 (961)	Winchester is not named
Hurstbourne	13 *predia*	—	King Edgar, to monks of Abingdon	Sawyer 689 (961)	
Overton	1 *terra*	—	King	**I, 152**	
Polhampton	1 *domus*	—	King	**I, 156**	
Lasham	2 *mansurae*	30*d*.	King	**I, 157**	
Odiham	—	—	King	**II, 387, 392,** and ? **830**	
Wolverton	1 *terra*	Waste		**II, 435**	
Alresford	*terra*	5*s*.	Bishop of Winchester	**II, 742**	

[1] The Winchester properties of Romsey and Wherwell Abbeys, enumerated in Domesday Book, are not included in this table, for by virtue of their size they seem to represent urban estates of an altogether different character. They are discussed on pp. 356–8, above. The identification of place-names is based on that in *VCH Hants* from which the list in *DGSEE*, 354 occasionally differs for no good reason. The three *mansurae* entered under Awbridge and Houghton in *DB*, and identified as Winchester tenements in *DGSEE*, were probably not urban dwellings.

[2] References to Domesday Book are given to the translation in *VCH Hants* i. 449–526. References to Anglo-Saxon charters are given to Sawyer, with the purported date of the charter in brackets. References to the Winton Domesday are given in the usual form.

FIG. 20. Manors with urban property in early medieval Hampshire (1:500,000; cf. Table 28).

The inset shows the location in Winchester of those properties which can be identified, and indicates the direction of the manors to which they were attached. The Winchester evidence is given in Table 28, and the tenements in Twynham and Southampton are recorded in the Domesday Book.

Labels on map:

Polhampton
Wolverton
Eversley
Overton
Basingstoke
Worthy
Odiham
Lasham
Alresford

Basingstoke
Neatham
WINCHESTER
Southampton
Titchfield
Twynham

Legend:
■ Boroughs in Domesday Book
▲ Markets in Domesday Book
● Manors with urban property

5   0   20 Kilometres
5   0   15 Miles

V. WASTE LANDS

In 1148 thirty-four properties were recorded as either wholly or in part waste.[1] Almost all of them lay within the walls and the majority of them lay in the side streets north of High Street. High Street contained only one waste property, and the two in the suburbs lay on the south side of the city. On the whole the waste properties appear to have been situated in the less densely-occupied areas within the walls. If extensive areas of the city had been laid waste during the siege of 1141, they had been largely rebuilt by 1148, for the survey records no concentration of waste properties near the two castles or the royal palace, where the fighting was presumably thickest. Hyde Abbey was burnt during the sieges, but there were no waste properties outside North Gate in 1148.

Survey I records only three waste properties, all outside West Gate.[2] Only one of these was waste in the early twelfth century, for the other two were built on after the time of King Edward. The contrast with the relatively large number of waste tenements in 1148[3] suggests that the siege of 1141 may have been a factor in creating the waste properties recorded in Survey II. This does not, however, alter the fundamental fact that by 1148 there was little evidence of any devastation which may have been caused by the seige.

[1] The waste properties in Survey II were: in High Street, **91**; in *Scowrtenestret*, **434–6**, **468**, and **472**; in *Alwarnestret*, **474**, **475**, and **509**; in *Flesmangerestret*, **513**, **517**, **518**, **521**, **533**, and **538**; in *Sildwortenestret*, **552**; in *Wunegrestret*, **603**; in *Tannerestret*, **645–9**; in *Bucchestret*, **671**, **676**, **678**, **680**, **682**, and **704**; in *Colobrochestret*, **728**; in *Calpestret*, **830**; in *Goldestret*, **867**; outside South Gate, **1030** and **1054**; and in *Gerestret*, **1069** and **1082**.

[2] I, **82**, **117**, and **122**.

[3] In Survey I, properties waste in the early twelfth century accounted for 0·3 per cent of the total properties recorded; in 1148 waste properties formed 3 per cent of the total.

6

ORGANIZATION AND SOCIETY

i. OFFICIALS, BARONS, AND MAGNATES (Fig. 21; Tables 29 and 30)

THREE distinct groups of landlords in Winchester reflect the character of the city as a royal capital. Officials of the royal household and administration, barons, and magnates, defined here as bishops, abbots, and earls,[1] were each involved in the life of the city in different ways, which are reflected in the surveys by the holding of property.[2]

The royal officials formed the largest group and as individuals held the most properties. The holders of the largest estates, such as Herbert the chamberlain and Thurstin the clerk, were local men who owned land in Hampshire and adjoining counties. Some royal officials perhaps resided in the city for much of their time, others such as Thomas of St. John or Wigod of Lincoln, who each had a single property, probably visited it only on business. The properties of the officials lay in all but two of the streets within the walls, and in the suburbs outside West Gate and King's Gate. This widespread distribution reflects the local interests of the larger property-owners among them. Only one property, that of the chancellor, lying outside King's Gate and not far from the royal palace, appears to have been in any way an official residence.

The barons were the second largest of the three groups. As individuals, most of them held no more than one or two properties, although local landlords such as the de Ports had quite extensive estates in the city. In 1148 their properties lay principally in the western suburb and in the streets to the north of High Street.

None of the magnates held more than three properties, for their interests were solely those of occasional visitors to the capital and to the king's court. The distribution of their properties in 1148 is similar to that of the barons, and taken together the two groups seem to have favoured the streets near the site of the royal palace to the south of High Street, and *Flesmangerestret* and *Alwarnestret* to the north. The evidence of the first survey suggests that *Brudenestret* should be included with these streets, and that *Calpestret* and *Goldestret* were even more favoured at the time when the palace was still the focus of royal interest in the city. In 1148 magnates, barons, and even officials had their properties on the whole in the quiet, relatively unpopulated streets away from the commercial bustle of High Street, and apart from the concentrations of craftsmen. They had few properties, for example, in *Tannerestret*, although *Bucchestret* seems to have been an exception.[3] Those areas favoured by the barons and magnates in the twelfth century were precisely those where the Jews and the wealthiest merchants of the city lived in the thirteenth and early fourteenth centuries.[4]

---

[1] The somewhat artificial distinction between 'barons' and 'magnates' is introduced in an attempt to differentiate between those important men whose interest in Winchester had a national basis and those whose interests may have been more local.

[2] See Tables 29–30.

[3] For the distribution of craftsmen, see Fig. 23 and pp. 427–39.

[4] See *SMW*.

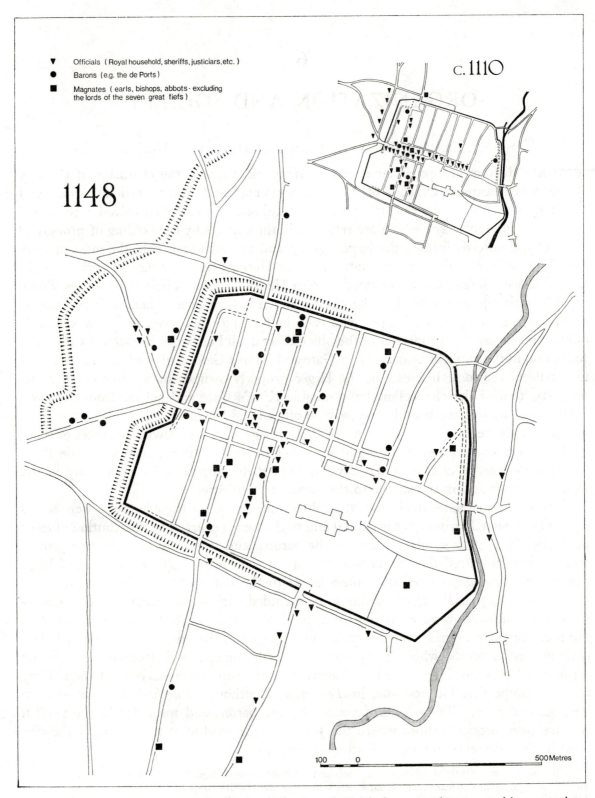

FIG. 21. Winchester as a royal capital—the properties of royal officials, barons, and magnates: (*a*), *c.* 1110, inset (1:25,000; cf. Table 29); (*b*), 1148 (1:10,000; cf. Table 30).

Something can be said of the actual residences or hospices of visiting magnates or barons. The bishops of Durham and Worcester had their houses in the northern suburb near North Gate.[1] In 1114–15 Abbot Faricius of Abingdon acquired a *hospitium* there which stood on land for which he owed the bishop of Winchester 12*d*. rent.[2] Between Hyde Abbey and the city wall, the earl of Gloucester had a house which he granted to Keynsham Abbey between 1166/7 and 1183, on condition that the canons of Keynsham provided him with lodgings when he came to Winchester.[3] About 1137 the monks of Glastonbury were provided with a hospice in the southern suburb by their abbot, Henry of Blois,[4] and the bishop of Exeter had a property not far away.[5] Anselm lodged in a house somewhere in the suburbs of Winchester in 1093.[6] Between 1143 and 1166 the bishop was concerned with the hospice of the monks of Eynsham in *Alwarnestret*.[7] When the knights of the Temple came to Winchester they lodged in a house in *Calpestret* which their servants or tenants kept ready for them.[8] The bishop of Bath appears to have had a similar arrangement at a house in *Alwarnestret*, where his *hospes* owed him rent of half a mark.[9]

Lesser men also had *hospitia*. Robert, son of William of Pont de l'Arche, held a *hospicium* of John de Port outside West Gate in 1148, and in the same year Richard of Ricardville had lately owned a *hospicium* in *Mensterstret*.[10] Other properties belonging to magnates, simply recorded as lands or rents in the surveys, may have been let on conditions which allowed their owners to lodge there when visiting the city: properties of the count of Meulan, of the earls of Leicester, Warwick, and Clare, of William Peverel, of bishops and abbots, and even of the men of Caen, may have fallen into this category.[11] But a number of these were undoubtedly no more than sources of income, and some hospices may have been omitted from the surveys because they were free of all services. The Winchester houses of both the abbess of Wherwell and the abbot of Abingdon were free of all customs and gelds.[12]

The number of hospices in the city may have been increasing in the first half of the twelfth century, and the location of many of them in the suburbs suggests that it was only there that, by that date, there was space for substantial residences. In the latter part of the twelfth century, Winchester declined as a royal centre and distant magnates appear no longer to have maintained houses there. A distant landlord could even have difficulty in collecting his rents, for when the abbot of Malmesbury granted his Winchester properties to Hugh Camberlane in the late twelfth century, he insisted that Hugh should send the annual rent of the property to Malmesbury at his own expense.[13] In the thirteenth century the earls of Chester had an inn in *Shortestrete* (Jewry Street), but by

[1] **I, 163.**

[2] J. Stevenson (ed.), *Chronicon Monasterii de Abingdon* (RS, 1858), ii. 111–12.

[3] Robert B. Patterson (ed.), *Earldom of Gloucester Charters: the Charters and Scribes of the Earls and Countesses of Gloucester to A.D. 1217* (Oxford, 1973), no. 102. See also **II, 139** and **475.**

[4] **II, 963.**

[5] **II, 952.**

[6] R. W. Southern (ed.), *The Life of St. Anselm*

Archbishop of Canterbury by Eadmer (London, 1962), 65–6.

[7] **II, 477**

[8] **II, 838.**

[9] **II, 476.**

[10] **II, 270** and **821.**

[11] **I, 2** and **279**; **II, 51, 229, 451, 585, 946,** and **1073.**

[12] *VCH Hants* v. 475; *Regesta*, ii, no. 1110.

[13] J. S. Brewer and C. T. Martin (eds.), *The Register of Malmesbury Abbey* (RS, 1879–80), ii. 35. See **II, 21.**

TABLE 29

The properties of royal officials, barons, and magnates in Survey I (cf. Fig. 21a)

Name	Office	Date of holding property and/or of death	Properties
Royal officials[1]			
Alberic the chamberlain	Queen's chamberlain	1086 and *c.* 1110	102
Bernard the queen's chancellor	Chancellor of Queen Matilda	d. 1148	83
Erchembald the king's sergeant	A royal sergeant	before *c.* 1110	107
Geoffrey the chamberlain	A royal chamberlain	temp. William II and *c.* 1110	246, 270, 272
Gisulf	The king's scribe	*c.* 1110	223; cf. II, 680
Henry de Port	Sheriff of Hants, 1101–6?	*c.* 1110	39–40, 51
Henry the larderer	A royal larderer, son of Hugh	*c.* 1110	18, 59
Henry the treasurer[2]	A royal treasurer	*TRE*, 1086, d. before *c.* 1110	184
Herbert the chamberlain	Chamberlain of the royal treasury under William II, and royal treasurer under Henry I	d. before 1130	4, 13b, 24, 33, 35, 48, 74, 111, 116–17, 123, 152, 292
Herfrid the king's sergeant	A royal sergeant	*c.* 1110	44
Hugh the larderer	A royal larderer, father of Henry	After *TRE*, before *c.* 1110	16
Hugh Oillard	Probably a royal constable	*c.* 1110, d. before 1130	8, 17
Oin the napier	Probably a royal napier	*c.* 1110, probably d. before 1130	6
Robert Mauduit	A royal chamberlain	*c.* 1110, d. *c.* 1129	45, 53, 56
Simon the dispenser	A royal dispenser	*c.* 1110	283; cf. II, 1069
Theodoric the king's cook[2]	A royal cook	*TRE*	185
Thomas of St. John	Sheriff of Oxon., *c.* 1110–17	*c.* 1110	30
Wigod of Lincoln	Sheriff of Lincs., 1115–21	*c.* 1110	154
William d'Aubigny	The royal master butler	*c.* 1110, d. 1139	14, 33
William of Houghton	A royal chamberlain	*c.* 1110 and 1135, d. before 1148	196, 245, 273, 278; cf. II, 74 for his son
William of Pont de l'Arche	Sheriff of Hants and Berks., and a royal chamberlain	*c.* 1110, d. before 1148	259
William son of Ansger	Possibly a justiciar in Essex	*c.* 1110, d. *c.* 1122	79, 138, 170
For the Bishop of Salisbury, chancellor and chief justiciar, see below.			
Barons			
Baldwin of Reviers		*c.* 1110	260
Herbert of St. Quentin		*c.* 1110 and 1121?	50, 149–51
Ralph of Mortemer		*c.* 1110	141–2, 148
Robert Marmion		*c.* 1110	230
Roger son of Gerold		*c.* 1110	34
Magnates			
Bishop of Durham		before *c.* 1110	163
Bishop of Salisbury	(Also chancellor and chief justiciar)	*c.* 1110	75, 108 (cf. II, 268–9)
Bishop of Worcester		*c.* 1110	163
Abbot of St. Edmunds		*TRE*, *c.* 1110 and 1148	280; cf. II, 880
Abbot of Westminster		Possibly *TRE*, *c.* 1110 and 1148	262; cf. II, 827
Count of Meulan		*c.* 1110	158
Earl of Warwick		*c.* 1110, d. 1119	279

[1] The royal officials include household officers, but exclude the reeves and other local officers of the city.
[2] A royal official *TRE*.

TABLE 30

The properties of royal officials, barons, and magnates in Survey II (cf. Fig. 21b)

Name	Office	Date of holding property and/or of death	Properties
Royal officials[1]			
Alwin the chamberlain	Chamberlain of Queen Matilda	before 1148	**128**
The chancellor	Presumably the royal chancellor	1148	**1018**
Gisulf the scribe	A royal scribe	before 1148	**680**; cf. I, 223
Grimbald the physician	Henry I's doctor	d. 1137/8	**827**
Herbert the chamberlain	A royal chamberlain?	1148	**4, 38, 542, 828, 841, 860, 873**
John son of Ralph	Sheriff of London in 1158	1148	**140, 143, 155, ?159**
Richard the fusour	Fusour of the Exchequer	1148	**182, 229, 231, 255**
Richard of La Haye	Steward to Duke Henry	1148	**1067**
Robert d'Oilli	A royal constable	d. 1142	**25**
Simon the dispenser	A royal dispenser	before 1148	**1069**; cf. I, 283
Thurstin the clerk	Clerk of William of Pont de l'Arche; sheriff of Hants, 1155–9	1148, d. by 1160	**221, 385, 493–4, 496, 510–11, 572, 673, 696, 701, ?707, 749, 785**
William the almoner	A royal almoner?	1148	**538**
William of Glastonbury	Chamberlain of Normandy	? before 1148	**985**
William the Marshal	A royal marshal?	1148	**315, 529, 1033**
William Martel	A royal steward and sheriff of Surrey	1148	**35, 41, 51, 54, 467, 488–92**
William of Pont de l'Arche	Sheriff of Hants and Berks., and a royal chamberlain	d. before 1148	**171, 671, 830**
Barons			
Bernard of Briouze		1148	**817, 872**
Henry de Tracy		1148, d. by 1165	**175, 258**
Hugh of Mortemer		1148	**421, 609**
John de Port		1148, d. 1167	**2, 84, 138, 270, 439, 474, 685**
Peter of Valognes		1148, d. 1158	**476**
Ralph de Port		1148	**473**
Richard of Limésy		1148	**535–6, 544**
Roger de Port		1148	**580–3**
Walter of Grainville		?1148	**350**
Walter son of Richard		d. 1138	**205, 559, 562**
William Brewer		1148	**188, 199**
William of Chesney		1148	**512**
William Peverel		1148	**946**
Magnates			
Bishop of Bath		1148	**476**
Bishop of Exeter		1148	**952**
Bishop of Salisbury		1148	**51, 268–9** (cf. I, 108), **691**
Abbot of St. Edmunds		1148	**880**; cf. I, 280
Abbot of Glastonbury		1148, acquired c. 1137	**963**
Abbot of Westminster		1148	**827**; cf. I, 262
Earl of Gloucester		1147	**139, 475**
Earl of Hertford		1148	**585**
Earl of Leicester		1148	**717, 857, 892**
Hugh of Le Puiset	Bishop of Durham, 1153–95	1148, d. 1195	**494**

[1] The royal officials include household officers, but exclude the reeves and other local officers of the city. For an additional possibility, cf. **II, 631**, n. 1.

the fourteenth century the city of Winchester lacked large houses for accommodation of distinguished visitors, and in 1327 the citizens petitioned the king that his ministers should not live outside the liberty when he came to stay in the city.[1] We have come a long way from the situation in the mid ninth century, when the bishop held land in Berkshire partly in return for entertaining the king's visitors to Winchester.[2]

ii. THE CLERGY (Tables 31–3)

Even with the bishops and other ecclesiastical magnates excluded, the clergy form the largest single identified occupational group recorded in the surveys. The number of clergy shown in Table 31 suggests the ecclesiastical, political, and administrative importance of Winchester, as well as the number of its parish churches, and so reflects the size and prosperity of the city as a whole.

Apart from the ecclesiastical magnates, four classes of secular clergy are identified in the surveys: archdeacons, priests, clerks, and chaplains. A single archdeacon, Aluric, with a property in *Alwarnestret*, is recorded in Survey I in the reign of King Edward.[3] By the time of the 1148 survey the division of the diocese into two archdeaconries, Winchester and Surrey, was probably well established, and in part accounts for the number of archdeacons recorded. Of the three archdeacons identified in this survey, William[4] and Stigand[5] were alive in 1148, while Stephen had probably died some years previously.[6] Hugh of Le Puiset, who had a property in *Alwarnestret* may, however, have been archdeacon of Winchester in 1148.[7] William could have been the archdeacon of London, in which case Stigand may be identified as archdeacon of Surrey, but these identifications are by no means certain.[8] Both William and Stigand held relatively large estates, mostly in the suburbs. Robert of Inglesham, who may have been identical with a later archdeacon of Surrey, was the wealthiest private landlord in 1148.[9]

The priests and clerks recorded in the surveys appear to have differed by more than clerical rank. In 1148 the clerks were on average markedly more wealthy than the priests, even if we exclude Thurstin the clerk, whose estate in the city was exceptionally large.[10] Thurstin was a royal official in minor orders. Herbert, the royal chamberlain, one of the largest Winchester property owners *c.* 1110, was likewise of clerical status, although this

[1] *Cal Pat R 1272–81*, p. 360; PRO, C 143/193/10.
[2] *BCS* 474, Sawyer 307, discussed in H. P. R. Finberg, *The Early Charters of Wessex* (Leicester, 1964), 203; cf. C. Hart, *Agric. HR* 18 (1970), Suppl. 13.
[3] I, 176.   [4] II, 222.   [5] II, 688.
[6] II, 817. Stephen's first and last occurrences as archdeacon were in 1107, or earlier, and in *c.* 1128, respectively.
[7] II, 494. Hugh was probably made archdeacon of Winchester in or after 1142 when Jocelyn, a predecessor in the office, became bishop of Salisbury. Hugh was active on the bishop of Winchester's behalf in southern England in the latter part of 1148 and in 1149, while the bishop was paying a visit to Rome, and so could well have held the office of archdeacon at the time of the survey (*Gesta Stephani*, cap. 113; T. Arnold (ed.), *Symeonis Historia Regum Continuata per*

Johannem Hagulstadensem, ii (RS, 1885), 322, and cf. above, p. 320). Hugh was described as archdeacon of Winchester on his election to Durham in 1153 (W. Stubbs (ed), *Gervasii Cantuariensi Opera Historica*, ii (RS, 1879), 157). There is no evidence that he was archdeacon as early as 1139, as was suggested by Goodman *Chartulary*, p. 4; cf. G. V. Scammell, *Hugh du Puiset, bishop of Durham* (Cambridge, 1956), 7.
[8] If Hugh did not hold the office of archdeacon at the date of the survey, William and Stigand would probably have been the two archdeacons of the diocese and one of them would soon have been succeeded by Hugh. In either case this necessitates some revision of the list published in Le Neve *Monastic Cathedrals 1066–1300*, 92.
[9] II, 1, n. 1, and Table 24.
[10] II, 221.

TABLE 31

The clergy in Surveys I and II

| | Survey I — TRE | | | | | | | | | | Survey I — modo, c. 1110 | | | | | | | | | | Survey II, 1148 | | | | | | | | | |
| | Arch-deacons | | Priests | | Clerks | | Chaplains | | Total clergy | | Arch-deacons | | Priests | | Clerks | | Chaplains | | Total clergy | | Arch-deacons | | Priests | | Clerks | | Chaplains | | Total clergy | |
	A[1]	B[1]	A	B	A	B	A	B	A	B	A	B	A	B	A	B	A	B	A	B	A	B	A	B	A	B	A	B	A	B
High Street, north	—	—	3	3	—	—	—	—	3	3	—	—	2	2	—	—	1	1	3	3	—	—	1	1	4	7	—	—	5	8
High Street, south	—	—	2	2	—	—	—	—	2	2	—	—	1	2	—	—	—	—	1	2	—	—	—	—	1	1	—	—	1	1
Outside West Gate	—	—	—	—	—	—	—	—	—	—	—	—	2	2	—	—	—	—	2	2	1	4	3	3	3	4	—	—	7	11
Outside North Gate	—	—	—	—	—	—	—	—	—	—	—	—	—	—	—	—	—	—	—	—	—	—	3	3	1	1	—	—	4	4
Snidelingestret	—	—	1	1	1	1	—	—	2	2	—	—	1	1	—	—	—	—	1	1	—	—	1	1	1	3	—	—	2	4
Brudenestret	—	—	1	1	1	1	—	—	2	2	—	—	2	3	1[2]	2[2]	—	—	3	5	—	—	1	1	1	1	—	—	2	2
Scowrtenestret	—	—	2	2	—	1	—	—	2	3	—	—	1	1	—	—	—	—	1	1	—	—	—	—	—	—	—	—	—	—
Alwarnestret	1	1	—	—	—	—	—	—	1	1	—	—	1	1	1	1	—	—	2	2	—	—	3	3	2	5	—	—	5	8
Flesmangerestret	—	—	—	—	—	—	—	—	—	—	—	—	—	—	—	—	—	—	—	—	—	—	1	1	3	5	—	—	4	6
Sildwortenestret	—	—	—	—	—	—	—	—	—	—	—	—	—	1	—	—	—	—	—	1	—	—	1	1	—	—	—	—	1	1
Wunegrestret	—	—	2	2	—	—	—	—	2	2	—	—	1	1	—	—	—	—	1	1	—	—	3	3	1	1	—	—	4	4
Tannerestret	—	—	—	—	—	—	—	—	—	—	—	—	—	—	—	—	—	—	—	—	—	—	2	2	2	3	—	—	4	5
Bucchestret	—	—	2	2	—	—	—	—	2	2	—	—	2	3	—	—	—	—	2	3	2	2	—	—	2	4	—	—	4	6
Outside East Gate	—	—	—	—	—	—	—	—	—	—	—	—	—	—	—	—	—	—	—	—	1	3	2	2	1	2	1	1	5	8
Mensterstret	—	—	—	—	—	—	—	—	—	—	—	—	—	—	—	—	—	—	—	—	1	1	1	1	—	—	—	—	2	2
Calpestret	—	—	2	2	—	—	—	—	2	2	—	—	2	2	—	—	—	—	2	2	—	—	—	—	—	—	—	—	—	—
Goldestret	—	—	1	1	—	—	—	—	1	1	—	—	—	—	—	—	—	—	—	—	—	—	5	6	1	1	—	—	6	7
Outside Southgate i	—	—	—	—	—	—	—	—	—	—	—	—	—	—	—	—	—	—	—	—	—	—	1	1	1	1	—	—	2	2
Outside Southgate ii	—	—	—	—	—	—	—	—	—	—	—	—	—	—	—	—	—	—	—	—	—	—	—	—	1	1	1	1	2	2
Gerestret	—	—	3	3	—	—	—	—	3	3	—	—	1	1	1	1	—	—	2	2	—	—	—	—	1	1	—	—	1	1
Totals[3]	1	1	13	19	1	1	1	1	15	21	—	—	12	17	3	6	1	1	16	24	3	10	24	28	13	38	2	2	42	78

[1] A = number of individuals, B = number of occurrences.   [2] Elsi (I, 148–9) is counted here as a priest (cf. I, 71, n. 4).

[3] Totals under A represent the number of individuals. They will not necessarily equal the sum of the figures in the column above, since an individual may occur under more than one street.

is not explicitly stated in the survey.[1] Several of the other clerks may have been involved at a lower level in royal, ecclesiastical, or household administration. William, for example, may have been associated with the bishop's household.[2] A bureaucratic career clearly offered more chances for material advancement than the pastoral ministry. Some clerks, however, like the majority of priests, held no more than one property and may have been involved in parochial work. Of the three priests who held more than one property in 1148, Herbert,[3] who held three, appears to have been a parish priest, but Richard,[4] who held two properties, may have been a member of the bishop's household.

Between c. 1110 and 1148 there was a significant increase in the number of clerks relative to the number of priests. There is even some slight sign of an increase between the reigns of King Edward and of Henry I. These increases perhaps represented an enlargement of the bureaucratic element in the population of Winchester between the reign of the Confessor and the middle of the twelfth century, although the number of parish clergy in minor orders may also have risen.

Three chaplains each occur once in the surveys. Richard served the count of Meulan,[5] and Humphrey was probably the chaplain of the abbess of St. Mary's.[6] Nothing is known of Ralph,[7] unless the apparent proximity of his property to the church of St. Michael outside King's Gate suggests that he was associated with that parish.

The surveys contain some evidence for the families of the clergy. Between the time of King Edward and c. 1110 the son of a priest succeeded his father in a tenement,[8] and in c. 1110 another son of a priest was a property-owner.[9] No children of priests were recorded in 1148, although Peter the son of the archdeacon held a tenement.[10] Several clerks were married. We hear of the wife and sons of Thomas the clerk,[11] and Herbert the chamberlain and Thurstin were both succeeded in their offices by their sons.

The distribution of the properties of the clergy reflects, on the whole, their wealth as represented by the number of properties which they held. In Survey I the properties of the clergy were distributed fairly evenly over the city. Of the priests in c. 1110, only those two who had more than one tenement held property in High Street.[12] The absence of priests as property-holders in High Street was even more marked in 1148, but the wealthier clerks were better represented there, for five of the eight who had more than one property had a holding in High Street.[13] There is at this date a sharp contrast with Survey I in the absence of priests and clerks from the streets to the south of High Street, in the south-west quarter of the city. This was an area characterized by the houses of magnates and wealthy citizens,[14] but this character had not changed significantly between the dates of the surveys, and had even become a little less marked, so that it cannot provide an explanation for the apparent migration of clergy from the area. Elsewhere within the walls, and in all the suburbs, the properties of priests and clerks were evenly distributed.

This generally even distribution of the holdings of the priests, and the fact that most of them are recorded no more than once, are significant pointers to their parochial

---

[1] I, Preface. [2] II, 167. [3] II, 632, 908, and 912. [4] II, 322 and 590.
[5] I, 2. [6] II, 782. [7] II, 1003. [8] I, 190.
[9] I, 169. [10] II, 872. [11] II, 32. [12] I, 36 and 71.
[13] II, 14, 31, 32, 40, and 44. [14] See above, pp. 373 and 387.

associations. Several priests can be associated with specific churches. In *c.* 1110 Elsi had rent from a church, probably St. George's, and the property to which it belonged in High Street.[1] In 1148 Herbert held a land which belonged to the church of St. John in *Tannerestret,*[2] and a priest and a clerk each held property near the church of All Saints in Kingsgate Street.[3] In the latter case the priest paid a rent of 3*d.* to the owner of the church, perhaps for his dwelling.

TABLE 32

The clergy in 1148: possible associations between priests and parish churches

Survey II	Street	Name of priest	Church
190	Outside West Gate	Turold	Opposite St. Martin
241	Outside West Gate	Godwin	Opposite St. Anastasius or St. Leonard
473	*Alwarnestret*	Ernold	Near St. Michael
504	*Alwarnestret*	John	Opposite St. Michael
543	*Sildwortenestret*	Randulf	Near St. Ruel
599	*Wunegrestret*	William	Near St. Pancras
632	*Tannerestret*	Herbert	Near St. John
662	*Tannerestret*	Odo	Opposite St. George
807	*Mensterstret*	Henry	Near St. Martin
957	Outside South Gate i	Walter	Near All Saints

TABLE 33

The clergy in 1148: possible associations between clerks and parish churches

Survey II	Street	Name of clerk	Church
408	*Brudenestret*	Wazo	Near St. Mary
497 **503**	*Alwarnestret*	Girin	Near St. Martin Opposite St. Michael
540	*Flesmangerestret*	Edward	Opposite St. Martin
646	*Tannerestret*	God'	Opposite St. Mary
960	Outside South Gate i	Hubert	All Saints

Many of the priests's houses, standing on land pertaining to their churches and free of rent, were probably omitted from the surveys, along with the majority of the parish churches themselves. Yet in Survey **II** a number of priests and clerks appear in entries representing properties which seem to have been close to parish churches. These parish priests would thus perhaps have lived in houses where there was no tenurial link with the church, or where such a link had been broken. This was a not uncommon situation in later medieval Winchester and presumably reflected the pressures of the property-market in a densely built-up city.[4] Table 32 shows the churches with which some of the priests may have been associated, and Table 33 shows the churches with which some of the clerks may have been associated.

[1] I, 71.   [2] II, 632.   [3] II, 957 and 960.   [4] See *SMW*, s.v. 'parish churches'.

Only in the case of All Saints is there any clear suggestion that the church was served by a clerk as well as a priest, and so it is possible that some parish churches were staffed by no more than a clerk in minor orders.

No real estimate is possible of that proportion of the total population of the city which was made up of parish clergy and clerks, since a considerable number cannot have been recorded in the surveys. In 1148 the archdeacons, priests, clerks, and chaplains represented 4 per cent of the named individuals, and less than 0·5 per cent of the estimated total of the population.[1] In about 1400 the equivalent body of clergy perhaps represented about 1 per cent of the estimated total population of the city.[2] The figure would perhaps have been a little higher in the twelfth century.[3]

iii. THE MINT (Fig. 22 and Tables 34–45)[4]

Introduction

The first coins to carry the mint-signature of Winchester were issued at the very end of Alfred's reign, probably after c. 895.[5] Issues of Beorhtric, Egbert, and Æthelwulf have been attributed to Winchester, but it is possible that the refoundation of the city in the 880s and 890s may provide the most likely moment for the establishment of the mint.[6] No coins bearing the name of Winchester are known from the reigns of Edward the Elder, Edmund, or Eadred, but coining is unlikely to have been interrupted at this period, and in the intervening reign of Æthelstan eight different moneyers (but probably not more than six in any one issue) produced at least two types carrying the city's signature.[7] From Eadwig to Harold II every Anglo-Saxon king except Edmund Ironside minted coins in Winchester, and this practice continued after the conquest until the end of John's re-coinage (c. 1207), following which, with the exception of a miniscule issue in the winter of 1217, there was an interval of forty years before the final period of activity in 1248–50.[8]

From the time of Æthelstan's Grateley decree in c. 925–35 there were to be six money-ers working in Winchester,[9] a number which rose to as many as fourteen (not necessarily all active at the same moment) in the *expanding cross* issue of 1050–3 (?).[10] Of the sur-viving coins from the period between 975 and 1066, about 7 per cent came from the

---

[1] See below, pp. 440–1.

[2] Based on the 1379 clerical poll tax roll in WCL, and on the estimated total population of Winchester in c. 1400. See below, p. 440, and, for further details, *SMW*.

[3] J. C. Russell estimated that in 1377 the clergy represented about 1·5 per cent of the total population of England. The figures which he suggested for 1086 would give a percentage of 0·4: *British and Medieval Population* (Albuquerque, 1948), 42–5, 54, 145; see also idem, 'The Clerical Population of Medieval England', *Traditio*, 2 (1944), 177–212.

[4] This section has benefited immensely from the kind and detailed criticism of numismatists: we would thank especially the late Mr. Derek Allen, Mr. Christopher Blunt, Mr. Michael Dolley, Mr. F. Elmore Jones, the late Commander R. P. Mack, and Mr. Ian Stewart. Miss M. M. Archibald and Mr. Elmore Jones generously provided information from their (unpublished) work on the new Lincoln and Prestwich hoards. Dr. Olof von

Feilitzen's comments on the personal names have been of the utmost value.

[5] R. H. M. Dolley and C. E. Blunt, 'The Chrono-logy of the coins of Ælfred the Great 871–99', in R. H. M. Dolley (ed.), *Anglo-Saxon Coins* (London, 1961), 87.

[6] Michael Dolley, 'The location of the pre-Ælfredian mint(s) of Wessex', *Proc Hants FC* 27 (1970), 57–61.

[7] *English Hammered Coinage*, i. 93–4. See now C. E. Blunt, 'The Coinage of Athelstan', *BNJ* 42 (1973), 35–160.

[8] Mrs. Yvonne Harvey's detailed study of the entire surviving product of the Winchester mint will appear as Winchester Studies 8.

[9] ii Athelstan 14. § 2: F. L. Attenborough (ed.), *The Laws of the Earliest English Kings* (Cambridge, 1922), 134–5.

[10] See Table 37, and cf. Michael Dolley, *The Nor-man Conquest and the English Coinage* (London, 1966), 13, for the later issues.

Winchester mint, which thus ranked fourth in the country, after London (24 per cent), York (10 per cent), and Lincoln (9 per cent).[1] After *c.* 1075, with the reduction of moneyers at the northern mints of York, Lincoln, and Chester, Winchester with a complement of six moneyers[2] seems on this basis to have ranked third after London and Canterbury.[3]

Knowledge of Henry I's coinage is incomplete, but Winchester still had more named moneyers during the reign (16) than any other mint except London (37). Yet it seems clear that its position may have been declining in relation to the coinage as a whole, due to the increasing importance of mints such as Lincoln, Norwich, and Thetford, the last of which seems also to have had sixteen moneyers operative at one time or another during this reign. Nevertheless, Henry I's possibly short-lived last type was struck by seven Winchester moneyers,[4] and Stephen's first issue by as many.[5] Winchester now ranked about fourth among English mints, equal with Canterbury and York, but clearly subordinate in this reign to Lincoln and Norwich with twelve and eighteen known moneyers respectively, and London with twenty-three.[6]

There is unfortunately insufficient evidence for the 1140s and 1150s when Winchester's position was probably still further eroded by the sack of the city in 1141. Its reduced position is confirmed in Henry II's reign, for although there is some evidence that Winchester had a theoretical complement of eight royal moneyers as late as 1180–1, only four are known for the *cross-and-crosslets* ('Tealby') coinage of 1158–80, and these four operated simultaneously only in Class A of *c.* 1158–61.[7] The number of known moneyers again rose as high as seven for limited periods of the *short-cross* coinage, although four or even less was the usual maximum.[8] Comparison between mints on the basis of the numbers of moneyers named suggests that Winchester had sunk to sixth or seventh place during the Tealby coinage,[9] but recovered to play an important role after the recoinage of 1180, exceeding that of York and Lincoln, perhaps because the bulk of the royal treasure was still kept in the city.[10] Four moneyers took part in the final coinage of 1248–50, as was also the case at the fifteen other provincial mints.[11]

The workshops of the mint, TRE and c. 1110

Before the rebuilding of the mint associated with the short-cross coinage, the moneyers appear to have worked individually in separate workshops[12] which they held on their own account. These workshops were nevertheless situated fairly close together in the same part of High Street. Sometime before the compilation of Survey I, and perhaps as

[1] H. Bertil A. Petersson, *Anglo-Saxon Currency* (Lund, 1969), 140–1, Tables 42 and 43.

[2] Dolley, *The Norman Conquest*, 13, but see *BMC Norman kings* clxxxvi, clxxxviii, ccxlviii, and cf. Michael Dolley in *Seaby's Coin and Medal Bulletin*, 605 (Jan. 1969), 11–15.

[3] *BMC Norman kings* clxxxviii.

[4] Ibid. ccxlix, Type XV, of 1134/5 (?), cf. Dolley, *The Norman Conquest*, 27–8, and below, Table 41.

[5] *BMC Norman kings* ccxlix, Type I, of *c.* 1135–41 (?), to which Stiefne must be added: see R. P. Mack in *BNJ* 35 (1966), 45.

[6] The figures are taken from *English Hammered Coinage*, i. 151–2; but see also H. R. Mossop, *The*

Lincoln Mint *c.* 890–1279 (Newcastle, 1970), Pls. LXXXVI–VII.

[7] *BMC Henry II* clxvi–clxviii; see also ibid. lxxvii–lxxxi for the farm paid by Winchester and other cities for the right to have moneyers to a given number.

[8] *English Hammered Coinage*, i. 168–70.

[9] *BMC Henry II* clxxxii–iii.

[10] *English Hammered Coinage*, i. 169–70. For the treasure, see above, p. 291.

[11] Charles Johnson (ed.), *The De Moneta of Nicholas Oresme* (London, 1956), App. II, p. 100, cf. pp. 53–5; *English Hammered Coinage*, i. 171.

[12] See below, p. 422, esp. n. 6.

early as 1066, five moneyers' workshops (*monete*) in High Street were destroyed by the king's order.[1] This entry follows immediately upon the list of properties removed to make way for the extension of the royal palace, and precedes entries referring to the king's kitchen,[2] from which it is clear that the workshops lay on the south side of High Street, in the block to the east of St. Laurence's church (Fig. 9, *c.* 963–1066).

The five *monete* might perhaps be equated with the workshops which had become redundant in Winchester during the latter part of Edward the Confessor's reign, when the city shared in the general process of restricting the privilege of coining to a fixed number of individuals.[3] The reduction from ten known moneyers in 1053–6(?)[4] to six in 1070–2(?) might even seem almost to account for the five *monete*, but it is doubtful if this is the correct explanation. As will be seen, the forges which seem to represent the mint in *c.* 1110 were then recent developments, as if the process of minting had been moved from elsewhere in the period since 1066. In addition, it seems possible to identify at least two and possibly four of the five moneyers whose *monete* were destroyed by the king's order, and one of these, Godnoth, was minting as late as the beginning of William I's third issue in *c.* 1070.[5] The five *monete* seem likely therefore to have been active, or recently active, in the early years of the Conqueror's reign, and thus to represent the moneyers surviving after the Confessor's reduction rather than those who had then been closed.

The surviving coins do not on the other hand indicate any decrease in the activity of the Winchester mint early in the Conqueror's reign,[6] and if the five *monete* represented the entire establishment, it must have been replaced without delay on another site. There is however no suggestion that the five *monete* were the only moneyers' workshops in the city, and the surveys of *c.* 1110 and 1148 give no hint that the mint at these dates was represented by a single structure or closely knit group of buildings. The evidence points rather to the reverse, to a number of individual units, physically and tenurially distinct, even if lying fairly close together in the same part of High Street.

Although the first survey does not specifically say so, there seems in fact little doubt that the five workshops were destroyed to make way for the extension of the royal palace

---

[1] *Et in mercato fuerunt v monete que sunt diffacte precepto regis* (**I, 58**). The phrase *in mercato* seems here to mean 'in the High Street', cf. *ceap straet*, see above, p. 233, s.n.   [2] **I, 57**, and **59–61**.

[3] Michael Dolley, *The Norman Conquest and the English Coinage* (London, 1966), 12–13; cf. idem, *Yorkshire Philosophical Society, Annual Report 1971* (1972), 98–100, for the York evidence for reduction.

[4] See Table 37. It will be noticed that eleven moneyers are also known for the *small flan/short cross* issue of 1048–50 (?). The fourteen moneyers known for the intervening *expanding cross* issue must surely include changes from one moneyer to another during the life of the issue.

[5] The entry in Survey **I** referring to the destruction of the mints (**I, 58**) is preceded by an entry (**I, 57**) listing the twelve *burgenses* whose houses were encroached upon, and presumably destroyed, for the extension of the *domus regis*. These twelve names include Lethmerus and Gonnod who may be identified with the Ladmær and Godnoth who minted for Edward the Confessor and William I (Types II and III), respectively. The name Lethmerus occurs once only in the two surveys, while Gonnod (who appears also in **I, 182** as a *TRE* tenant) is the earliest recorded occurrence of this name. Lewinus Balloe and Alestanus Hwit could be the Leofwine and Ælfstan or Æthelstan who both struck coins for Edward the Confessor, although there are several persons with these personal names in the surveys, and it is only the fact of their occurrence here that raises the possibility of this identification. The cases of Gonnod and Lethmerus suggest, however, that the five destroyed mints were located in, or attached to, houses held by the twelve burgesses, or were rented from them.

[6] William I's third issue, the *canopy* type of 1070–2 (?), is the first of his issues for which six moneyers are known, the first and second issues being known from four and five moneyers respectively: *BMC Norman kings* ccxlviii.

in *c.* 1070, and that the *preceptum regis* refers to this event rather than to a deliberate reduction in the number of moneyers in the latter half of the Confessor's reign. This view is supported by the position of the entry referring to the *monete*, and by the identification of moneyers in the preceding list of burgesses whose houses had been removed to make way for the enlarged palace.

The most obvious points about the location of the moneyers' workshops, or at least some of them, in the period down to 1070 are that they lay in the busiest street of the city, and were outside and not within the precincts of the royal palace. While there is no evidence to show where the workshops had been at any earlier date, the subsequent history of the mint shows a clear preference for this area, for in 1179–80, if not by 1148, the mint returned to the site occupied by the five workshops before their destruction more than a century before.

At the north-east corner of the extended precinct of the palace, and in the immediate area of *Thomeseiete*, there were in *c.* 1110 a series of at least eighteen forges (*forgiae*) whose entries in the first survey follow immediately upon the record of the destroyed mints.[1] All the forges seem to be recent developments, twelve of them encroaching on the highway,[2] and six occupying sites which in 1066 had been merchant houses or warehouses (*cellarii*).

Their annual values range between 3*s.* and 8*s.*, confirming the impression given by the encroachments that the forges were relatively small properties, workshops rather than substantial tenements. Seven of the forges were held *c.* 1110 by Robert son of Wimund.[3] The identity of this Wimund is scarcely in doubt; apart from a Wimund *presbiter* holding land in the north-west part of the city in *c.* 1110,[4] the only other occurrence of the name in Survey **I**, with the exception of Robert's father, was the Wimund *monetarius* whose wife held an unoccupied property on the north side of High Street.[5] Wimund was a Winchester moneyer under William I, William II, and Henry I, his latest known coins being of Henry I Type VIII of 1116–19 (?).[6] The references to *Robertus filius Wimundi* and to *uxor Wimundi*, without any references to Wimund himself, suggest that he was dead by the time of the first survey.

The remaining eleven forges were held by or from persons with no discoverable connection with the coinage: Walter Chibus held four from Boselin's son; another four were held by Gilbert Gibart; two by Henry the larderer; and one by the monks of the cathedral priory.[7] This does not necessarily mean that the forges were unconnected with the mint, for each of these holders, including also Robert son of Wimund, received rents from their forges, which may therefore have actually been occupied by moneyers

---

[1] **I, 59**, and **61–5**.

[2] For a discussion of encroachment see above, pp. 280–1. It seems probable that these encroachments were comparatively recent at the time of the survey, and one had been licensed by Warin, a reeve of Henry I's time, see above **I, 20**, n. 4. One of the forges in **I, 59** is not specifically recorded as an encroachment, but being immediately adjacent to the royal kitchen is not likely to be older than the extension of the palace area in *c.* 1070.

[3] **I, 62** and **65**; cf. **I, 7** and **41**.

[4] **I, 146**.

[5] **I, 22**.

[6] *BMC Norman kings* ccxlviii; Michael Dolley, *The Norman Conquest and the English Coinage* (London, 1966), 24.

[7] Unless the monks were holding the forge in which the one moneyer perhaps coining for the bishop of Winchester was at work (cf. *BMC Henry II* xcviii–ci, clxvii).

of whose tenancy no other record exists. That moneyers did on occasion have to rent their workshops, can be seen from other evidence,[1] and Survey **I** may perhaps suggest that it was the normal practice in Winchester at this time.

The forges of *c.* 1110 were recent developments of a workshop character; they lay near to the old site of at least a part of the mint; and seven of them were held by a man likely to have been the son of a moneyer recently dead. It is hard to avoid the conclusion that the forges were in fact the moneyers' workshops. If this is correct, it is noteworthy that even after the expansion of the palace, the mint remained outside its precinct, and occupied an area in the busiest street of the city. There is still a clear impression that at this date the mint consisted of quite separate structures and properties, lying more or less together in the same area; there is no sign of a special building to house the mint as a whole.

Moneyers and their properties TRE

There can be no certainty that all the individual *monete* forming the Winchester mint were to be found in this area, for the houses of those moneyers specifically named in

TABLE 34

The mint: moneyers of Edward the Confessor named in Survey I, TRE

Survey I forms	Coin forms	Street	Entry	Text
Alestanus	Ælfstan Æthelstan Æstan	*Brudenestret* ('lands of the barons')	**I, 154**	A. fuit *monet'* TRE . . .
Alwardus filius Etardii	Ælfweard	Outside West Gate	**I, 107**	Terra A.f.E. reddebat omnes consuetudines *TRE*, et fuit *monet'* regis E
Alwinus Aitardessone	Ælfwine	High St. (N)	**I, 11**	A. A. fuit quidam *monetarius TRE* . . .
Andrebodus Andrebode	Anderboda	High St. (N) *Tannerestret*	**I, 29** **I, 212**	A. fuit *monetarius TRE* . . . A. *cangeor* . . .
Godwinus Socche	Godwine	High St. (N)	**I, 15**	G. S. fuit *TRE magister monetarius,* . . .

Survey **I** lay in several parts of the city, both in the time of Edward the Confessor and *c.* 1110. Five moneyers are named *TRE* (Table 34).

This list raises a number of difficult problems. There seems to be no period during Edward's reign when five moneyers with these names were ever active together; at the one moment when four of them were minting simultaneously, there were five or six other active moneyers who are not specifically named in Survey **I**. In fact only two of Edward's issues were struck by as few as five moneyers, and in these cases only two of those mentioned in Survey **I** or their namesakes were concerned. If the five named moneyers of Survey **I** cannot therefore represent the full complement of moneyers for any one issue,

---

[1] *Pipe Roll 26 Henry II*, p. 82 (Northampton). A moneyer's workshop, apart from the furnace, was a simple, easily mobile affair. Any metal-working furnace would probably suffice. See W. C. Wells, *Notes on Mediaeval Moneyers* (repr. from *Spink's Numismatic Circular*, London, 1939), 8–16.

there may be other moneyers to be identified *TRE* among persons of the same name in the survey. On general grounds alone, it would seem likely that this should be so, for the moneyers must have been a relatively wealthy group in the population, and ought to be well represented in the relatively large number of properties enumerated in Survey **I**. Moneyers did not, however, hold property solely from the king: Godwinus Socche's land in High Street was on the bishop's fief.[1] At least eight other moneyers of Edward's reign cannot be concealed in Survey **I** for their names do not occur.[2] While some of these may have been dead before the moment crystallized as *TRE*—on which the evidence of the moneyers will be seen to have some bearing—their periods of activity show that this cannot be the sole explanation. Some moneyers, it might seem, held no royal land, and do not therefore appear in Survey **I**. The survey may however include moneyers who struck in several or even many issues, as well as those who had ceased minting before the time represented by the *TRE* portion of the survey. Ælfweard is a case in point: he is described in the survey as a moneyer of King Edward, but the latest known coins bearing his signature are of Harold I's *jewel-cross* issue of *c.* 1036–7.[3] If he was indeed a Winchester moneyer of Edward the Confessor, there must be coins with his signature awaiting discovery. These are in any case likely to come from the earlier issues of the reign, whereas the *TRE* survey seems on balance, as will appear, to reflect the composition of the mint just after the middle of the reign, when Ælfweard was almost certainly not active.[4]

This raises the general question of why five moneyers should be specifically identified in the survey, if one of them was not active at the same time as the others, and if, as seems possible, there were other moneyers who were included in the survey, but not differentiated. The form of the entries relating to the five named moneyers may be significant: *monetarius* is not used here as a byname, but always in the form *N. . . . fuit monetarius T.R.E.* or *N. . . . fuit monetarius regis Edwardi*, in contrast to all other personal descriptions in the surveys, where the epithet is used as a byname without the verb.[5]

---

[1] **I, 15.** See below, p. 402, n. 4, and pp. 403, 422.

[2] Ægelwine, Brand, Brihtwold, Frithemund, Loc (for Æthelstan or Æstan Loc), Spræclinc, Spileman (*not* Swileman, see Table 37, n. 1), and Widia (for Godwine Widia). Spileman does occur once *TRE* (~ *brand-wirchte*, **I, 294**), but there is nothing to associate him with moneying, and the *presbiter* of the same name *c.* 1110 (**I, 244**) is out of question.

[3] **I, 107.** Peter Seaby, 'The Sequence of Anglo-Saxon Coin Types, 1030–50', *BNJ* 28 (1955–7), 145.

[4] Not only was Ælfweard not working in Winchester during this reign, but as will be seen below (pp. 402 and 407) the entry mentioning him (**I, 107**) is different in form from those relating to the other named moneyers, among whom Ælfweard was furthermore the only one to render royal customs. While these discrepancies may reflect his position as a retired moneyer, it is not clear why in this case he should be specifically mentioned. Two alternative explanations may be possible. Like Odo *monetarius* in *c.* 1110 (see below, p. 409 and Table 38) he may have had some connection with the Winchester mint other than that of actual coining, possibly in the provision of dies (see below, p. 409, n. 10). A second possibility is that he was an active moneyer of another mint, like Sanson in 1148 (see below, p. 415 and Table 43). Moneyers named Ælfweard struck for the Confessor at Bristol, Canterbury, London, and Shaftesbury. Only the London Ælfweard was at all prolific, and he struck in the *sovereign/eagles* type of 1056–9 (?), as well as in the two preceding and three following issues. It is possibly significant in relation to these suggestions that Ælfweard was succeeded in his property (**I, 107**) by William son of Odo (see **I, 42**, n. 1), perhaps a member of the family of goldsmiths who also provided the dies for the coinage, and had interests in London and elsewhere (cf. below, p. 409, n. 1).

[5] The only other cases where the verb is used with a noun to qualify a person or persons are **I, 53** and **57**, both referring to matters subsequent to the *TRE* survey. In contrast to the usage of this survey, *monetarius* occurs only as a byname in *c.* 1110 and 1148 (**I, 22** and **129**; **II, 64, 112, 118, 511**, and **512**).

It has been suggested elsewhere that the *TRE* portion of Survey **I** is based on a written survey of the Confessor's reign.[1] If this view is correct, *TRE* implies not a generalized memory of the earlier situation, but a precise occasion, even if the date in years was omitted from the record of the *TRE* inquiry, as it was from that of *c.* 1110. If such an earlier inquiry was concerned, as it must have been, with the king's interests in the city and its inhabitants, the recording of moneyers, from whom a variety of payments was due,[2] may have been one of its features. It is possible therefore that the entries regarding moneyers were originally in the present tense, *N . . . est monetarius* (supposing the earlier survey to have been in Latin), and that this was changed to the past tense, along with the verbs *tenere*, *habere*, etc. when the earlier text was used *c.* 1110 as the basis for the *TRE* entries. In this context it is possibly significant that the entry relating to Ælfweard is in a different form. This may only reflect the distinction between entries beginning *Domus . . .* and those commencing with the name of the holder,[3] but it is not impossible that for some reason now unknown the verb in the *TRE* text was in this case already in the past tense, and reflected the fact that Ælfweard was no longer an active moneyer at the time.

If it is true that the text of the *TRE* survey listed moneyers for specific financial reasons, it becomes even more necessary to account for the failure of that text to identify the other moneyers active at the time it was drawn up. Here there can only be speculation: the *c.* 1110 text may omit items of information of this kind because they were of little or no recognizable financial importance by the reign of Henry I; or the *TRE* text may never have included the names of other moneyers, perhaps because they held their principal tenement on another fief.[4] In this case the *TRE* text might have listed these moneyers elsewhere, but if it did so, the information was not relevant *c.* 1110, and was not recorded. Even in its surviving form however the *TRE* survey shows a special interest in moneyers, more of whom are specifically named than the practitioners of any other trade or occupation, apart from the thirteen priests. This situation is not maintained *c.* 1110, when the two moneyers are well down the list, nor in 1148, when the moneyers are numerically insignificant compared with the totals recorded for other trades and occupations.[5] The surveyors' interest in moneyers may seem to have declined since the conquest, but it does not necessarily follow that the importance of moneyers as a source of royal revenue had fallen. In 1148 the moneyers seem to have formed one of the highest-ranking groups in the social and economic hierarchy of the city.[6]

There may be an alternative reason why five moneyers, and only five, were specifically named *TRE*. The problem is particularly acute because, as will be seen, it seems possible that the survey includes other moneyers of the period whom it does not specifically identify. Of the five moneyers listed in Table 34, only Alwardus (or rather, his land) is said to have rendered customs *TRE*; Alwinus held a house belonging to the royal manor

[1] See above, pp. 9–10.
[2] See D. F. Allen's remarks in *BMC Henry II* lxxvii–lxxxviii, which, although mainly concerned with the *cross-and-crosslets* coinage, are relevant to earlier periods.
[3] See above, pp. 12–13, cf. pp. 337–8.

[4] Cf. Godwinus Socche, **I, 15.** In 1148 Sanson *monetarius* held land on the bishop's fief (**II, 118** and possibly **129**) as well as on the king's (**II, 64** and **65**).
[5] See below, Table 47, *c.* 1110, Table 48, and cf. Table 50.
[6] See below, pp. 443–4, Table 52.

of Basingstoke; Godwinus held a house on the bishop's fief; and Andrebodus[1] and Alestanus held property, but the payment of customs is not mentioned. Alwardus (Ælfweard), the one member of this group who did render custom, is an exception on other
grounds, as we have already seen.[2] The simplest explanation of this pattern may be that
moneyers as a class were regarded as the king's men. If they held royal land and rendered
custom, they were royal burgesses and there was no further need to identify them as
moneyers. If, however, they held land not on the royal fief (either exclusively or, as in
the case of Andrebode, as well as royal land), then they had to be listed and identified.
Such an interpretation would imply that all the moneyers active at the period of a survey
(whether *TRE*, *c.* 1110, or 1148) are included, whether silently or specifically, in the
survey in question. It would thus help to explain why such a high proportion of moneyers
do seem to be identifiable as the following pages will show.

It is noteworthy in this context that Andrebodus, who is described as a moneyer in the
usual way in **I, 29,** was only identified with the byname *cangeor* in **I, 212.** A moneyer
could therefore be identified on one occasion only, and that in connection with his
principal residence; when his name occurred elsewhere in the survey, whether in the *TRE*
text, or in the compilation of *c.* 1110, it might not be specifically distinguished as that of
a moneyer, and might even carry a byname or nickname not given in the entry referring
to his activity as a moneyer.

It follows from these arguments that the *TRE* text of Survey **I** may well include
further references to the five named moneyers; and also that other moneyers not specifically described may in fact occur in the survey as holders of land or tenants or recipients
of rent. It is clear that this may apply equally well to the survey of *c.* 1110, but there we
shall find a different use of the word *monetarius*, as well as other changes.

It may therefore be worthwhile to try to identify, among the many persons named in the
TRE portion of Survey **I,** those who were perhaps identical with Winchester moneyers
of the same name in the reign of Edward the Confessor. There are many difficulties,
and the attempt could not have been made without Dr. Olof von Feilitzen's study of the
personal names in Part II, for the OE names used by Edward's moneyers are rendered
by the survey into very varying Latin forms. The basis of the suggested identifications
are first, identity of name; second, occupation of a property held in *c.* 1110 or even 1148
by a known moneyer or person likely to have been connected with the coinage; third,
family relationship to other persons bearing the names of known moneyers; fourth,
occupation of a property next to, or in the immediate vicinity of, properties occupied
by known moneyers, or less certainly, by other persons possibly identifiable as moneyers.[3]

On this basis there seem to be in the *TRE* portion of Survey **I,** in addition to the five
named moneyers, another nine persons who can with some confidence be identified

---

[1] *Andrebode cangeor* rendered customs on **I, 212,**
but *cangeor* is a vernacular byname and may not have
the force of an official title, as *monetarius* may perhaps
have had. The argument being developed here suggests that it was precisely because this property was
on the royal fief that Andrebode was not on this
occasion described as a *monetarius*.

[2] See above, p. 402, and below, p. 407.

[3] The attempt to identify moneyers has revealed a
wide range of possible family and tenurial relationships.
These cannot be discussed in detail in this volume,
but will be given in full by the present writers in Mrs.
Yvonne Harvey's forthcoming study of the Winchester
mint (Winchester Studies 8).

TABLE 35

The mint: moneyers of Edward the Confessor probably identifiable in Survey I, TRE[1]

Survey I forms	Coin forms	Entry	Street	Notes
Brithmarus	Beorhtmær (Brihtmær)	**I, 166**	*Scowrtenestret*	*aurifaber*; next to an Alwinus
		I, 217	*Bucchestret*	A Sawinus held part of this property *TRE* (see below). A Lepstanus held the next property *TRE* (Table 36)
Brunstanus				
Blachebiert	Brun[stan?]	**I, 256**	*Calpestret*	Saiet, probably Henry I's moneyer, held this property *c.* 1110 (Table 39). See also below, Lewinus
Brunestanus		**I, 17**	High St. (N)	An Alestanus held a house on this property *TRE*
Edwinus	Eadwine	**I, 66**	High St. (S)	Close to the forges of *c.* 1110 (**I, 59, 61–5**)
Godemannus	Godmann	**I, 107**	Outside West Gate	A tenant of the property held by Alwardus (Ælfweard) the moneyer, *TRE* (Table 34). See also below, Lewinus
Lethmerus	Ladmær (?)	**I, 57**	High St. (S)	A burgess who held a property removed to make way for the extension of the royal palace *c.* 1070, in the area of the five *monete* destroyed at that time. The only occurrence of this name in the survey. See above, p. 398
Lewinus (etc.)	Leofwine	**I, 107**	Outside West Gate	A tenant of the property held by Alwardus (Ælfweard) the moneyer *TRE* (Table 34). See also above, Godemannus
Luwinus		**I, 223**	*Bucchestret*	A Lepstanus held part of this property *TRE* (Table 36); next to an Alwinus *TRE* in a property held by an Alur' Iola (?Aluricus) *c.* 1110
Lewinus presbiter		**I, 257**	*Calpestret*	Although described as *presbiter*, it is noteworthy that this Lewinus held a property next to a Brunstanus *TRE* (see above), and that this latter property was held *c.* 1110 by Saiet, probably Henry I's moneyer of that name (Table 39)
Sawinus	Sæwine	**I, 217**	*Bucchestret*	A Brithmarus held part of this property *TRE* (see above); next to the property held by a Lepstanus *TRE* (Table 36)
Sawinus frater Wnstani		**I, 175**	*Alwarnestret*	Wynstan was a *TRE* moneyer, see below

[1] Where two entries are given under any one name, it should not necessarily be concluded that the individuals concerned are identical, but simply that two possibilities exist, one or both of which may be correct. If both possibilities seem strong, this may be some evidence for the identity of the two persons, but there is, unless stated, no other ground for this supposition. It must be noted that any of these persons may have held other properties in the city, but that no attempt has been made to include in the list properties other than those for which there seems some evidence to suppose a moneying connection.

Survey I forms	Coin forms	Entry	Street	Notes
Sewardus	Sæweard	**I, 264**	*Calpestret*	This is the only occurrence of this name in Survey **I** *TRE*. A God' (?Godric, Godwine) also held part of this property *TRE*, which is close to the properties **I, 256–7**, where there may be moneying connections *TRE* (see above, Brunstanus and Lewinus)
Wuinestaham				
Escitteport	Wynstan	**I, 16**	High St. (N)	Between the properties held *TRE* by Godwinus, *magister monetarius*, and Brunestanus (see above)
(Sawinus frater) Wnstani		**I, 175**	*Alwarnestret*	Sawinus was a *TRE* moneyer, see above

with moneyers of the same name striking for Edward the Confessor, and a further six individuals who might possibly also have been moneyers (Tables 35 and 36).

The distribution of the properties listed in Tables 34–6 shows a tendency for the holdings of the moneyers or presumed moneyers to lie together in a few clearly-defined areas of the city (Fig. 22a). A group of properties on the north side of High Street opposite the site of the five *monete* of **I, 58,** and close to the forges of *c.* 1110, is particularly clear; other groups seem to occur in *Tannerestret* and *Bucchestret*, also in an area close to the workshops of the mint; with a further group in *Calpestret*, an important property outside West Gate, and a few scattered tenements. The distribution can only give an outline of the situation, for some properties held by moneyers must be unidentified, and some properties will have been incorrectly assumed to have moneying connections.[1] There is the additional problem that some of these properties can only represent land held by moneyers in a purely private capacity as a source of income, and will have no other relevance to the mint. With these limitations, however, the distribution gives some indication of the areas in which Edward the Confessor's moneyers lived and worked in Winchester.

The absolute separation of these two activities is by no means certain. By *c.* 1110 the eighteen forges, if correctly identified as mint workshops, would seem to have provided ample accommodation for the presumed complement of six moneyers. If we were also to assume that the five *monete* destroyed *c.* 1070 represented all, or the greater part, of the workshop plant of the mint at that time, then it would seem clear that moneyers did not strike in or at their own homes. It is possible, however, that the forges of *c.* 1110 and the *monete* of an earlier period represent only the more industrial side of the process, and that other aspects of the work went on in the moneyer's house in the normal medieval manner. At this period the moneyers were also exchangers, Andrebodus the moneyer was also *Andrebode cangeor*.[2] The process of exchanging, whereby in return for his new coin the moneyer obtained old silver for reminting, involved the storage of large quantities

[1] An illustration of the difficulties is given by **I, 86–91** outside West Gate, a group of properties where the names not only hint at moneying connections, emphasized by their occurrence as a group, but also compare closely with **I, 14–17** on the north side of High Street, where the connection with moneying is not in doubt.

[2] **I, 212.** The MS. reads *gangeor*. See also above, p. 201, s.v. *cangeor*.

TABLE 36

The mint: moneyers of Edward the Confessor possibly identifiable in Survey I, TRE

Survey I forms	Coin forms	Entry	Street	Notes
Ceca	Godwine Ceoca (?)	**I, 171**	*Scowrtenestret*	The only occurrence of this name in the surveys. Close to Brithmarus (Table 35) and Luwoldus, see below
Colling'	Coll(?) only	**I, 206**	*Tannerestret*	The only possible name in the surveys which might produce the shortened version *Coll* of the coins. It occurs once only
Godricus Chingessone	Godric	**I, 128**	*Snidelingestret*	Next to Odo *monetarius c.* 1110 (Table 38)
Lepstanus	Leofstan	**I, 218**	*Bucchestret*	Next to the property held *TRE* by a Brithmarus and a Sawinus (Table 35)
		I, 223	*Bucchestret*	A Luwinus held part of this property *TRE* (Table 35); next to an Alwinus *TRE* in a property held by an Alur' Iola (?Aluricus) *c.* 1110. The only other occurrence of Lepstanus in Survey **I** is outside West Gate (**I, 98**)
Luwoldus Gustate	Leofwold	**I, 168**	*Scowrtenestret*	Next to an Alwinus and next but one to Brithmarus *aurifaber* (Table 35)
		I, 209	*Tannerestret*	Close to Andrebode *cangeor* (Table 34), and Colling', see above
				The only other occurrence of this name in the surveys is **I, 89** (*TRE*), outside West Gate
Leouingus	Lyfing Leofing Lifinc	**I, 125**	*Snidelingestret*	Close to Godricus (see above) and to a property (**I, 129**) held by Odo *monetarius c.* 1110 (Table 38)
Leuingus		**I, 248**	*Calpestret*	In a street with moneying connections. **I, 256–7, 264** (cf. Table 35)
(domus) Lewingii Mandingessone		**I, 68**	High St. (N)	This property, on the 'lands of the barons' in High St. is near the east end of the street on the north side, and must be close to or in among the group of properties with moneying connections, **I, 11, 15, 16** (?), **17** (?)

of old and new bullion, and there can be little doubt that this was safer in the moneyer's house than in a workshop. The *monete* and the forges were, however, separate from the moneyers' houses, and it may be necessary to account for their existence by supposing that after exchange at the moneyer's house, the old silver was moved as required to the workshop for melting down, assaying, and recoining, before being returned to the house for safe keeping. That moneyers' other properties should be situated close to those which they rented or owned as workshops, as Fig. 22 suggests, thus seems reasonable enough, although there is not the slightest indication that their own houses had anything to do with the actual process of coining.

Tables 34–6 suggest that it may be possible to identify as many as twenty of the twenty-eight moneyers who struck for Edward the Confessor in Winchester. Their known periods of activity may in turn indicate the actual date at which the *TRE* survey was undertaken. Table 37 shows the moneyers named, or probably or possibly identifiable, against the types they struck, and lists as well the moneyers who do not appear in the survey.

The table suggests that nine of the ten moneyers of the *trefoil-quadrilateral* types of 1046–8 may have been identified, and that the *TRE* survey should be dated to those years. On the other hand these nine include only two of the five named moneyers of Table 34, and even if coins of Æthelstan of this type should be found, the absence of Anderboda seems difficult to explain. It may be better to look for a period of perhaps several issues over which the majority if not all of the moneyers striking have been potentially identified in the survey, and in which most of the five named moneyers are known to have been active. Four of these five moneyers struck coins of the *pointed helmet* and *sovereign/eagles* types of 1053–6 (?) and 1056–9 (?). Ælfweard did not, but as discussed above there are some grounds for supposing that he was not active at the time of the survey. These types were also struck by Brihtmær and Leofwold, the former identified with reasonable certainty in the survey and the latter less securely. The second type was also struck by Spræclinc, this being the first in which he is known to have been active. Spræclinc cannot be identified in the survey, and his distinctive name cannot be hidden under a variant form. With the exception of this moneyer, those known to have struck the *hammer-cross* and subsequent issues of the Confessor can also be identified in the survey, but the correspondence between these moneyers and the four named moneyers of Table 34 who were active in the *sovereign/eagles* type diminishes progressively. It seems hard to avoid the conclusion that the *sovereign/eagles* type of *c.* 1056–9 offers the best correspondence with the moneyers named or identifiable in the survey, and that the date of the survey should be placed shortly after 1056.[1] If, as seems to be the case, Spræclinc's career as a moneyer was just beginning at this time, his omission from the survey is understandable. His activity may have begun during the issue of this type, but subsequent to the survey, and if he held his property on a non-royal fief, he would not therefore be mentioned. Certainly he cannot yet have acquired wide interests in the city or he would surely have held some royal land, and this he did not. His career continued until at least William II Type II of 1089–92 (?), a period of some thirty years.

Moneyers and their properties c. *1110*

Only two moneyers were specifically identified by the inquiry of c. 1110, and one of them may have been already dead at the time of the survey.

[1] **I, 75**, the *domus Emme regine*, may have retained this name after Queen Emma's death in 1052; the entry is of no help in assessing the date of the *TRE* survey.

TABLE 37

The mint: the types struck by Edward the Confessor's and Harold II's Winchester moneyers in relation to the identification of moneyers in Survey I, TRE (cf. Fig. 22a)

Moneyers	1042-4 (?) Pax	1044-6 (?) Radiate/Small Cross	1046-8 (?) Trefoil-Quadrilateral	1048-50 (?) Small Flan/Short Cross	1050-3 (?) Expanding Cross	1053-6 (?) Pointed Helmet	1056-9 (?) Sovereign/Eagles	1059-62 (?) Hammer Cross	1062-5 (?) Bust Facing/Small Cross	1065-6 (?) Pyramids	1066 Pax
Certainly identified											
Ælfweard	—	—	—	—	—	—	—	—	—	—	—
Ælfwine	—	—	x	—	x	x	x	x	x	x	x
Anderboda	—	—	—	—	—	x	x	x	x	x	x
Godwine	x	—	x	x	x	x	x	x	—	—	—
Æthelstan (Ælfstan, Æstan)	x	—	—	x	x	x	x	—	—	—	—
Probably identified											
Brihtmær	—	—	—	—	—	x	x	x	—	—	—
Brun	—	—	—	x	—	—	—	—	—	—	—
Eadwine	x	—	x	x	x	—	—	—	—	—	—
Godmann	x	—	—	—	—	x	—	—	—	—	—
Ladmær	x	x	x	x	x	x	—	—	—	—	—
Leofwine	—	x	x	x	x	—	—	—	—	—	—
Sæwine	x	—	x	—	—	—	—	—	—	—	—
Sæweard	x	—	—	—	—	—	—	—	—	—	—
Wynstan	—	—	—	—	—	x	—	—	—	—	—
Possibly identified											
Ceoca (Godwine Ceoca?)	x	—	x	—	—	—	—	—	—	—	—
Coll (Colling?)	—	—	—	x	—	—	—	—	—	—	—
Godric	—	x	x	x	x	—	x	—	—	—	x
Leofstan	x	x	—	—	—	—	—	—	—	—	—
Leofwold	—	—	—	—	—	m²	x	x	x	x	x
Lyfing	x	x	x	x	x	x	x	x	x	x	x
Not in Survey I											
Ægelwine	x	x	—	x	x	x	—	—	—	—	—
Spileman[1]	x	—	—	—	—	—	—	—	—	—	—
Widia (and Godwine Widia)	—	x	—	—	x	x	—	—	—	—	—
Loc (and Æthelstan/Æstan Loc)	—	—	x	x	x	—	—	—	—	—	—
Frithemund	—	—	—	—	—	—	—	—	—	—	—
Brand	—	—	—	—	x	—	—	—	—	—	—
Brihtwold	—	—	—	—	x	—	—	—	—	—	—
Spræclinc	—	—	—	—	—	—	x	x	x	x	x

[1] This is undoubtedly the correct reading of the name often quoted as Swileman, as Dr. Olof von Feilitzen points out.

[2] A *Pointed Helmet–Sovereign Eagles* mule of Leofwold occurred in the Walbrook hoard (*Inventory*, no. 255).

Odo is unknown as a Winchester moneyer of Henry I, no coins with his signature being on record, but it seems probable that he is to be identified with Odo, or Otto, son of the goldsmith of the same name in whose family the office of die-cutter was in all probability already an hereditary sergeanty.[1] At the time of the *TRE* survey several of the properties near **I, 129** appear to have had some connection with moneyers,[2] but there is no sign that this was still the case *c.* 1110, and by 1148 Odo's property had passed to his son Richard.[3]

Odo son of Odo was succeeded in his *ministerium cuneorum*[4] by his son William at some date between 1116 and 1127. A William son of Odo appears in *c.* 1110 holding part of **I, 107**, a property that had formerly been held by Ælfweard the moneyer.[5] The same

TABLE 38

The mint: moneyers of Henry I named in Survey I, modo

Name	Entry	Street	Text
Odo	**I, 129**	*Snidelingestret*	Modo Odo *monetarius* . . .
Wimundus	**I, 22**	High St. (N)	Modo habet uxor Wimundi *monetarii* . . .

William may also be the holder of a half share in **I, 42** on the south side of High Street, between West Gate and the palace.[6] This property was next to a tenement held by Robert son of Wimund, probably the moneyer of the same name,[7] and in 1148 both properties were apparently held by Hugh son of Chepping, whom there is some reason to identify with Stephen's moneyer of the same name.[8]

If, as seems likely, Odo *monetarius* is to be identified with Odo the die-cutter, then the family had interests in Winchester over at least two generations. William son of Odo the die-cutter had probably been succeeded by his own son William before 1148, a situation that may be reflected in Survey **II** where the properties, which may be identified as those formerly held by William son of Odo *monetarius*, were no longer held by the family.[9] Whether the family's interest in Winchester implies that there was an official connection between the office of the die-cutter and the Winchester mint, or whether the interest was purely private, cannot now be established, although the usual view would be that the engraving of the dies was at this period confined to London.[10]

[1] See above, **I, 42**, n. 1; cf. D. F. Allen in *BMC Henry II* cxii–cxiii. The possible connection adduced in **I, 42**, n. 1 between Odo *monetarius* of Winchester and the Odo who was a Bury St. Edmunds moneyer in Henry I Type XIV of 1131–4 (?) may find some support in the numismatic evidence. Mr. F. Elmore Jones points out that of the three known coins of this mint and moneyer, one (coll. F. Elmore Jones, ex. P. W. Carlyon-Britton, cf. *Num Chron* 4th ser. 1 (1901), 392) is of an unusual style which is found at other mints, and notably at Winchester. The coin may have come from the Canterbury hoard of 1901 (*Inventory*, no. 71), as did the second of the three known coins of this mint and moneyer (also coll. F. Elmore Jones); *BMC*

Norman kings, no. 113, may perhaps be identified as the third example, but this is far from certain. See also Addenda.

[2] **I, 125** and **128**; cf. Table 36.

[3] **II, 380**.

[4] *Rymer's Foedera*, i (1869), 9; cf. *Regesta*, ii, no. 543.

[5] See Table 34.

[6] This William is apparently distinct from William son of Odo son of Ticcheman, see above **I, 42**, n. 1.

[7] See Table 39.

[8] **II, 172**. See Table 44.   [9] **II, 172** and **288**.

[10] The latest evidence for die-cutting in Winchester is the lead trial-piece of the moneyer Æstan for Edward

The second of the two persons named as a *monetarius c.* 1110 is of almost equal interest, in this case as an indication of the actual date at which this inquiry was undertaken. The form of entry **I, 22** suggests that Wimund was already dead at the time of the survey, and the references to Robert son of Wimund in connection with forges, discussed above, supports this view. Wimund's latest known coins belong to Henry I Type VIII of 1116–19 (?), his career (supposing only one moneyer of his name to be involved) having begun thirty years before during the striking of William I Type VIII in 1083–6 (?).[1] The latest possible date for Survey **I** is apparently given by the reference to Bernard as *cancellarius regine* in **I, 83**, for he was consecrated bishop of St. David's in September 1115.[2] The difficulty may however be minimal, for the exact chronology of Henry I's coinage is somewhat uncertain. If Wimund died early in the issue, when the bulk of the coins would be struck, and if the issue began as little as a year earlier than supposed, a satisfactory correspondence would emerge, and the inquiry of '*c.* 1110' would then seem to have been undertaken in 1115.

If we now attempt to identify Henry I's other moneyers in Survey **I** *modo*, on the lines followed for Edward the Confessor's reign in Tables 34–7 above, it should be possible to examine the distribution of their interests in the city, and may be possible to adduce further evidence regarding the date of the survey.

Sixteen moneyers may have struck coins for Henry I in Winchester.[3] Of these, four do not appear in Survey **I**,[4] but one is certainly identified and six may be identified with some probability (Table 39), and a further five with less certainty (Table 40). The distribution of their properties follows the pattern established for Edward the Confessor: a group on the north side of High Street, with other groups in *Bucchestret* and *Calpestret*, and with scattered interests elsewhere, especially now in *Brudenestret* and *Scowrtenestret* (Fig. 22*b*). This correspondence, sometimes extending to individual properties, suggests a high degree of continuity and coherence among the families and business interests of Winchester moneyers over a period of about sixty years.

In Table 41, which shows the types struck by each of Henry I's Winchester moneyers, the moneyers have been arranged according to whether they are certainly, probably, or possibly identifiable in Survey **I**, or were altogether omitted.

Knowledge of Henry I's coinage is still incomplete, but the table shows that the survey omits four of the twelve moneyers known in Henry I's last five types, while

---

the Confessor's *pointed helmet* type of *c.* 1053–6, R. H. M. Dolley, 'A piedfort lead trial-piece of Edward the Confessor', *BNJ* 27 (1952–4), 175–8. Æstan might be identifiable under the name Alestanus in Survey **I** *TRE* (see Table 34), but no properties held by an Alestanus were in *Wunegrestret* (Middle Brook Street), where this trial-piece was found, and the only Estanus held land in *Gerestret* (**I, 285**).

[1] Michael Dolley, 'More thoughts on the Winchester mint under William II', *Seaby's Coin and Medal Bulletin*, 605 (Jan. 1969), 11–15.

[2] See above **I, 83**, n. 1.

[3] To the list of seventeen given in *English Ham-*

mered Coinage, i. 148, Ainulf should be added, and Snirwood and Wulwine (see next n.) deleted. The status of Æstan and Edwine is uncertain (see p. 415, n. 4).

[4] Alwold, Engelram, Sawulf, and Tovi. A 'Snirwood' and a Wulwine are also quoted by North in *English Hammered Coinage*, i. 148, but no further authority can be found for Wulwine, who like 'Snirwood' appears to rest on an apparently unique coin of Type I (Drabble sale, lot 637) reading +SHIRPOD—NC, which could equally well be of Lincoln (H. R. Mossop, *The Lincoln Mint c. 890–1279* (Newcastle, 1970), Pl. LXXXV, 10, with a footnote to the effect that the attribution is doubtful).

TABLE 39

The mint: moneyers of Henry I probably identifiable in Survey I, modo

Survey I forms	Coin forms	Entry	Street	Notes
Chepingus filius Alueue	Kippig	**I, 134**	*Brudenestret*	**I, 134** was held in 1148 by Hugh son of Cheppingus (**II, 403**). Note also Chepingus' interest in **I, 10** (see below, Godwinus) and in **I, 71** and **73**, also on the north side of High St., the latter held in 1148 by Hugh son of Cheppingus (**II, 23**)
Chepingius dives		**I, 87**	Outside West Gate	This property lay in a group with possible but undefinable moneying connections *TRE* (see above, p. 405, n. 1). Perhaps the same as **II, 294**, held by Hugh son of Cheppingus in 1148, although that property was not on the king's fief. Chepingius the rich may be identifiable with Chepingus son of Alveva, see **I, 10**, n. 6
Edwinus (Herebertus filius) Edwini	Edwine[1]	**I, 252** **I, 258**	*Calpestret*⎫ *Calpestret*⎭	These properties lie to either side of **I, 256** and **257** with probable moneying connections both *TRE* and *modo* (see below, Saiet; Table 35; and Table 40, Alwinus)
Godwinus	Godwine	**I, 172**	*Scowrtenestret*	Next to Ceca (Ceoca) *TRE* (Table 36), but there is nothing else to identify this particular Godwinus with the moneyer of the same name
Godwinus Prison		**I, 10**	High St. (N)	Next to Alwinus *monetarius TRE* (Table 34), and note the interest of Chepingus son of Alveva in this property
		I, 228 **I, 238**	*Bucchestret*⎫ *Bucchestret*⎭	These properties lie in a street with probable moneying connections both *TRE* and *modo* (Tables 35–6 and 40)
Lewinus	Lefwine	**I, 71**	High St. (N.)	The only occurrence of this name *c.* 1110. Note the interest of Chepingus son of Alveva in this property
Saiet		**I, 256**	*Calpestret*	The only occurrence of this name in Survey I. A property held by Brunstanus *TRE* (Table 35) and by Saiet's heirs in 1148 (**II, 848**), in a street with other probable or possible moneying connections both *TRE* and *modo* (see this Table and Tables 35–6)
Stigandus	Stigant	**I, 261**	*Calpestret*	This is the only occurrence of this name in Survey I, apart from the clerk, perhaps the later archdeacon, of **242**. The property lies among several others with apparent moneying connections both *TRE* and *modo* (see this table and Tables 35–6). It may perhaps be identified with **II, 826** which was held in 1148 by Johannes *aurifaber* (**II, 826**, n. 1). For Stigand, see **II, 88**, n. 1

[1] For Edwine as a moneyer, see below, p. 415, n. 4.

TABLE 39 (*cont.*)

Survey I forms	Coin forms	Entry	Street	Notes
Wimundus	Wimund	**I, 22**	High St. (N.)	For this tenement, the property of the *uxor Wimundi monetarii*, see Table 38
(Robertus filius) Wimundi		**I, 7**	High St. (N.)	Probably the site of forges in 1148 (**II, 73**)
		I, 41	High St. (S.)	Held by Hugh son of Cheppingus in 1148 (**II, 172**)
		I, 62 **I, 65**	High St. (S.) ⎫ High St. (S.) ⎭	Forges, see above, p. 399. **I, 65** was the site of a *fabrica* or *forgia* in c. 1110 × 1148 and was held in the latter year by Osbertus, probably Henry II's moneyer of the same name (**II, 111**, n. 2, and also Table 45).

TABLE 40

The mint: moneyers of Henry I possibly identifiable in Survey I, modo

Survey I forms	Coin forms	Entry	Street	Notes
Ainolfus	Ainulf	**I, 23**	High St. (N.)	The only occurrence of this name in Survey I. The property is Godbegot, and the next tenement was that of the *uxor Wimundi monetarii* (Tables 38–9)
Alestanus (Son of Leuret)	Æstan[1]	**I, 150**	*Brudenestret*	It is possible that this moneyer may be identifiable under the Latin form Alestanus, of which this is the only occurrence in c. 1110. Two persons named Chip(p)ingus had an interest in this property in c. 1110, but neither of them may be certainly identified as the moneyer Kippig, who was probably Cheping son of Alveva (see Table 39 and **I, 10**, n. 6)
Aluricus	Alric	**I, 263**	*Calpestret*	The only occurrence of this name in c. 1110. The next property was held in part by Sewardus *TRE* (Table 35). For the possible moneying connections of properties in this street, see this table and Tables 35–6 and 39.
Alwinus bedellus	Ailwine, Alwine, Ælfwine	**I, 168**	*Scowrtenestret*	Held by Luwoldus *TRE* (Table 36) in a street with apparent moneying connections both then and *modo* (Table 39)
		I, 221	*Bucchestret*	Among properties with apparent moneying connections both *TRE* and *modo* (Tables 35–6 and 39)
clericus		**I, 257**	*Calpestret*	For the possible moneying interest of this property, see Table 35, Lewinus
Eilwardus filius Chiwen	Ailward	**I, 254**	*Calpestret*	The only occurrence of this name c. 1110. This property lies in a group with apparent moneying interests both at this date and *TRE* (this table and Tables 35–6 and 39)

[1] For Æstan as a moneyer, see below p. 415, n. 4.

apparently including all those known from the earlier part of the reign. In the present state of research it is not possible to use the table to control the date of 1115 for the *modo* portion of Survey **I** suggested above on the basis of Wimund's activity as a moneyer.[1]

Before concluding this account of the moneyers perhaps to be identified in Survey **I**, it may be useful to consider briefly whether any of the moneyers of Harold II, William I,

TABLE 41

The mint: the types struck by Henry I's Winchester moneyers in relation to the identification of moneyers in Survey I, modo (cf. Fig. 22b)

Moneyers	1100/1 (?)	1101-4 (?)	1104-7 (?)	1107/8 (?)	1108-10 (?)	1110-13 (?)	1113-16 (?)	1116-19 (?)	1119-22 (?)	1122-4 (?)	1124/5 (?)	1125-8 (?)	1128-31 (?)	1131-4 (?)	1134-5 (?)
	I	II	III	IV	V	VI	VII	VIII	IX	XI	X	XII	XIII	XIV	XV
Certainly identified															
Wimund	x	—	—	—	x	—	—	x	—	—	—	—	—	—	—
Probably identified															
Edwine[1]	—	—	—	—	—	—	—	—	—	—	—	—	—	x(?)	—
Godwine	x	x	—	x	x	x	—	—	—	—	x	—	—	x	x
Kippig	—	—	—	—	—	—	—	—	—	—	—	—	—	—	x
Lefwine	x	—	—	—	—	—	—	—	—	—	x	—	x	x	—
Saiet	—	—	—	—	—	—	x	—	x	—	x	—	x	x	x
Stigant	—	—	—	—	—	—	—	—	—	—	x	—	x	x	—
Possibly identified															
Æstan[1]	—	—	—	—	—	—	—	—	—	—	—	—	—	—	—
Ailward	—	—	—	—	—	—	—	—	—	—	—	—	—	—	x
Ailwine	—	—	—	—	—	—	—	—	x	x	—	—	—	—	—
Ainulf	—	—	—	—	—	—	x	—	—	—	—	—	—	—	—
Alric	—	—	—	—	—	—	—	—	—	—	—	—	—	x	x
Not in Survey I															
Alwold	—	—	—	—	—	—	—	—	—	—	—	—	—	—	x
Engelram	—	—	—	—	—	—	—	—	—	x	x	x	x	x	—
Sawulf	—	—	—	—	—	—	—	—	—	—	—	x	x	x(?)	—
Tovi	—	—	—	—	—	—	—	—	—	—	—	—	—	—	x

[1] For Edwine and Æstan, see p. 415, n. 4. Their status as moneyers of Henry I at Winchester is uncertain.

or William II may be included, apart from those who survived to strike in Henry I's reign, or had already begun coining for Edward the Confessor.

The six Winchester moneyers known for Harold II had all previously struck for the Confessor. Two of these are named in the *TRE* survey, three are possibly identifiable, and one does not occur.[2] Of the twelve moneyers who are known to have struck for William the Conqueror in Winchester, seven of the same name had previously struck for the Confessor, and five of these also for Harold II. Of these seven, all except one are perhaps to be identified in the *TRE* entries.[3] Only two of the five new moneyers

[1] See Addenda.

[2] Ælfwine and Anderboda; Godric, Leofwold, and Lyfing; Spræclinc is omitted.

[3] Ælfwine, Æstan, Anderboda, Godwine, Leofwold, and Lyfing; Spræclinc is omitted.

TABLE 42

The mint: moneyers of Henry I probably or possibly identifiable in Survey II, 1148 (excluding Kippig and Saiet who also struck for Stephen, and for whom see Table 44) (cf. Fig. 22c)

('Possible' identifications are preceded by a '?')

Survey II forms	Coin forms	Entry	Street	Notes
Ailwardus	Ailward	**II, 36**	High St. (N.)	The property held *TRE* by Andrebodus *monetarius* (**I, 29**)
Alwinus				
Alwine Bierd	Ailwine, Alwine, Ælfwine	**II, 69**	High St. (N.)	Chapman's Hall, probably to be equated with **I, 10**, where both Chepingus son of Alveva and Godwinus Prison had an interest *c.* 1110
?Alwinus camerarius		**II, 128**	High St. (S.)	In 1148 this property, formerly held by Alwinus *camerarius*, was held quit by Gaufridus *burgensis*, who paid a substantial rent to Sanson, probably the same person as Sanson *monetarius* (Table 43), presumably for another part of what had become one property
?Engelramus	Engelram	**II, 589**	*Wunegrestret*	The only occurrence of this name in the surveys
?Estan'	Æstan	**II, 375**	*Snidelingestret*	Alueua *filia Estan'* held this property in 1148. This is the only occurrence of the name Estan' in Survey II
Godwinus				
?Goduinus Bar	Godwine	**II, 825**	*Calpestret*	Next to Iohannes *aurifaber* in **II, 826**, a property which seems to have been held *c.* 1110 (**I, 261**) by a Stigandus (Table 39)
Godwinus Prison		**II, 690**	*Bucchestret*	In 1148 the Abbess of St. Mary's paid the king 10*d. pro terra God' Prison* which may be identified with **I, 238**. Godwinus Prison is probably to be identified with the Henry I moneyer Godwine (Table 39)
?Stigandus	Stigant	**II, 88**	High St. (S.)	Close to forges in **II, 90** and in an area of the city clearly associated with moneying. No other Stigandus in Survey II seems a likely candidate, but it should be noted that in Survey **I** Stigandus, if correctly identified, held property in *Calpestret* (Table 39). See **II, 88**, n. 1

appearing in the Conqueror's reign may be identifiable, Wimund who struck also for William II and Henry I,[1] and Godnoth whose property on the south side of High Street lay in the area of the five *monete*, and whose house was removed *c*. 1070 to make way for the extension of the palace.[2]

Eight Winchester moneyers are known to have struck coins for William II. Although six of them had the same names as William the Conqueror's moneyers, they may not in each case be the same person.[3] Two new moneyers appear in this reign, Aldwine who cannot be identified in Survey I at either date, and Edwine, who with three other moneyers of William II continued to strike in Henry I's reign.[4]

Moneyers and their properties in 1148

Two moneyers were specifically named by the inquiry of 1148 (Table 43).

Sanson is not known as a Winchester moneyer, but a moneyer with this name struck irregular coins of Stephen's first issue with the mint signature ANTOI, ANT, or AN, as well

TABLE 43

The mint: moneyers of Stephen named in Survey II, 1148 (cf. Fig. 22c)

Name	Entry	Street	Text
Sanson	II, 64	High St. (N.)	Sanson *monet'* . . .
	II, 65	High St. (N.)	Item Sanson . . .
	II, 118	High St. (S.)	Sanson *monet'* . . .
Siwardus	II, 112	High St. (S.)	Siwardus *monet'* . . .
	II, 512	*Flesmangerestret*	Siwardus *monet'* . . .
			cf. **II, 511**, usque ad domum Siwardi *monet'* . . .

as further coins of Henry II's *cross-and-crosslets* type.[5] Considerable doubt has been expressed over the attribution of these coins to Southampton, and Canterbury has been suggested as an alternative.[6] The presence of Sanson in Winchester, with three properties in precisely the area favoured by moneying interests for at least a century, must raise again not only the question of the Canterbury attribution, but also the nature of the connections between the Winchester mint and Southampton during this period.[7]

[1] See Tables 38–9. The three new moneyers of William I not apparently identifiable in Survey I are Brunic, Goldinc, and Siward.

[2] I, 57; see above, pp. 397–8. A Gonnodus, possibly the same man, also held *TRE* a property in *Flesmangerestret* (I, 182), which in 1148 (II, 511) was next to the house of Siward *monetarius*.

[3] Æstan, Godwine, Leofwold, Lyfing, Spræclinc, and Wimund. Lyfing, for example, seems either to have had an interrupted career or to represent two successive moneyers of the same name, Michael Dolley, *Seaby's Coin and Medal Bulletin*, 605 (Jan. 1969), 11–15.

[4] Æstan, Godwine, and Wimund. See Tables 38–40. Edwine's status as a moneyer of Henry I rests on Brooke in *English Coins*, 90, and on a record of a possible coin of this moneyer of Type XIV in the Watford hoard (*Inventory*, no. 372). It may be relevant

that Table 39 suggests that a property which might have been Edwine's was held *c*. 1110 (? 1115) by his son, and that Edwine was therefore perhaps dead by this date. An earlier and a later moneyer of this name might be involved. Æstan's status in Henry I's reign is even more uncertain, and rests solely on *English Coins*, 90. Table 40 shows that his identification in Survey I *modo* is problematical.

[5] *BMC Norman kings* xci–xciv, 381–2; *BMC Henry II* clxiv, 146, no. 749.

[6] *BNJ* 28 (1955–7), 541; ibid. 35 (1966), 75–7. See also *BMC Norman kings* xcii–xciii.

[7] Mr. F. Elmore Jones points out that the numismatic evidence still favours the Canterbury attribution, and that as the Southampton mint seems to have closed finally in Cnut's reign (*BNJ* 39 (1970), 10–11), it is unlikely to have been reopened in 1141 to strike

Siward, the other moneyer named in Survey **II**, had his house in *Flesmangerestret*,[1] and a second interest on the south side of High Street in the area of the forges recorded *c.* 1110 and subsequently.[2] Seven other Winchester moneyers are known to have struck coins for Stephen, and six of these can perhaps be identified in Survey **II** (Table 44). The seventh, Alwold, does not appear in the survey. Of these eight moneyers, seven were active in Type I (*c.* 1135–41),[3] and another in Type VII (*c.* 1153–8).[4] Tables 39 and 44 suggest that Kippig, a moneyer of Henry I and of Stephen's Type I, is to be identified with Chepingus *filius Alueue*, and that his son Hugh was Stephen's Type VII moneyer of the same name. Chepingus was apparently dead by 1148 and the suggested identifications would allow his office to have been taken over by his son Hugh before the issue of Type VII about 1153, for which Hugh is at present the only known Winchester moneyer.

By the reign of Stephen the concentration of moneyer's interests upon the central area of High Street was even more strongly marked than in earlier periods (Tables 43–4, cf. Fig. 22c). Although some moneyers still held properties in the side streets, the former importance in this respect of *Calpestret* and the *Bucchestret* area had declined. The tendency for moneyers to have an interest in the workshop area on the south side of High Street, in addition to an important holding on the north side of the street, or in one of the side streets, is confirmed, and appears to reflect the separation between the industrial aspects of coining and the residences of the moneyers which has already appeared in the earlier surveys.[5]

Moneyers who were active in the middle or later part of Henry I's reign, who did not continue to strike for Stephen, may also be identifiable in Survey **II** (Table 42, cf. Table 41). These indications are naturally less clear than those relating to Stephen's moneyers who were active close to the time of Survey **II**. It is nevertheless noticeable that in most cases these properties continued to have some moneying connection in 1148, or can be equated with moneying interests at the time of Survey **I** *modo*, in the first half of Henry's reign, and even earlier.[6]

The continuity in moneyers' interests noted between *TRE* and *c.* 1110 can thus also be seen between the latter date and 1148, and extends even to the properties then held by men who were subsequently to strike for Henry II (Table 45). In two cases, the properties of Anderbodus *TRE*, the continuity of moneying interests can probably be established for the best part of a century (Table 42, **II, 36,** and Table 44, **II, 643–4**). There are some indications that this situation arose from sons succeeding their fathers as moneyers, or

---

an irregular issue by one or at the most two moneyers (see below, p. 419, n. 8). The evidence for a *Sanson monetarius* in Winchester cannot be dismissed, however, and as Mr. Elmore Jones himself has shown an emergency mint of short duration was opened (in Wilton) after a much more limited disaster in Winchester in 1180 (see also below, p. 419, n. 8). While it is clear that coining facilities were then still probably available in Wilton (which had been striking earlier in Henry II's reign), the physical plant was not so elaborate that it could not have been constructed at short notice in Southampton, when conditions in Winchester were very insecure in 1141. See Addenda.

[1] See Addenda.
[2] See **I,** 65, n. 1, and **II,** 111, n. 2.
[3] Alwold, Geffrei, Kippig, Rogier, Saiet, Siward, and Stiefne.
[4] Hugh.
[5] See above, pp. 405–7.
[6] In Table 42 there are two entries under Godwinus. Godwinus Prison, who appears also in Table 39, may be the moneyer active in the earlier part of Henry I's reign (Table 41). It seems unlikely that the moneyer of the same name who struck in Types XIV and XV was the same person; Goduinus Bar is a possible identification for this later moneyer.

TABLE 44

The mint: moneyers of Stephen probably identifiable in Survey II, 1148 (cf. Fig. 22c)

Survey II forms	Coin forms	Entry	Street	Notes
Cheppingus	Kippig	—	—	Cheppingus was apparently dead by 1148. For his son's properties see below, Hugo filius Cheppingi, and for his own properties in *c.* 1110, see Table 39
Gaufridus	Geffrei	**II, 101**	High St. (S.)	Among properties with probable moneying connections (**II, 90, 91, 95, 96, 104, 111,** and **112**)
Hugo filius Cheppingi	Hueo	**II, 23**	High St. (N.)	An important interest in this property was held in *c.* 1110 by Chepingus son of Alveva (Table 39, cf. **I, 134**)
		II, 172	High St. (S.)	This property was held in *c.* 1110 by Robert son of Wimund and William son of Odo (**I, 41** and **42**: see Table 39; **I, 42**, n. 1; and p. 409, above)
		II, 403	*Brudenestret*	A property held *c.* 1110 by Chepingus son of Alveva (**I, 134**), who also held **I, 73**, for which see **II, 23** (above and Table 39). Hugh apparently lived at **II, 403** where he had his *coquina* and his *managium*
Rogerus de Haia	Rogier Rogirus	**II, 38**	High St. (N.)	Herbert son of Westman, Henry II's moneyer, was an undertenant in this property in 1148 (Table 45 and **II, 38**, n. 5). It is equivalent to **I, 27** and close to **II, 36** which is to be identified with **I, 29**, the property of Andrebodus *monetarius TRE*
		II, 73	High St. (N.)	Forges in this property were held by Roger de Haia in 1148. It is the same as **I, 7**, held by Robert son of Wimund in *c.* 1110 (Table 39)
		II, 90	High St. (S.)	Roger de Haia held forges in this property in 1148
		II, 91	High St. (S.)	Note Roger de Haia's interest in these properties
		II, 104	High St. (S.)	adjacent to, and in an area of, moneying connections
Saietus	Saiet	**II, 848**	*Calpestret*	This property can be equated with **I, 256** (Table 39). By 1148 it was held by Saiet's heirs. This is the only occurrence of the name in Survey **II**, apart from a Herebertus *filius Saieti* in **II, 1078**. The moneying connections of *Calpestret*, *TRE* and *modo*, make the equation with Saiet the moneyer highly probable
Stephanus	Stiefne	**II, 643** **II, 644**	*Tannerestret*	These properties may be equated with **I, 212** held by Andrebode *cangeor*, the moneyer, for whom see Table 34 and above, pp. 403 and 405.
		II, 865	*Goldestret*	Next to Warinus *aurifaber* (**II, 866**)
Stephanus Mucheto		**II, 89**	High St. (S)	Between Stigandus (**II, 88**, see Table 42) and Roger de Haia's forges (**II, 90**, see above and below, p. 419)

TABLE 45

The mint: future moneyers of Henry II's cross-and-crosslets ('Tealby') coinage probably identifiable in Survey II, 1148 (cf. Fig. 22c)[1]

Survey II forms	Coin forms	Entry	Street	Notes
Herebertus filius Westman	Herbert	**II, 38**	High St. (N.)	For Herbert son of Westman as a moneyer, see above **II, 38**, n. 5. For Roger de Haia's (perhaps Stephen's moneyer, Rogier) substantial interest in this property and the long-established moneying connections of this area see Table 44, and Table 42, 'Ailwardus'
Osbertus	Hosbert (Osebern[2])	**II, 111**	High St. (S.)	Equivalent to **I, 65** where in *c.* 1110 and subsequently there were forges or a *fabrica* (**I, 65**, n. 1)
Osbertus cerarius		**II, 828** **II, 888**	*Calpestret* *Goldestret*	This man appears to be identical with the Osbert of **II, 111**; see n. 2 to that entry; and for the possible moneying connections of this area, cf. **II, 826** and **I, 261** (Table 39)
Ricardus filius Odonis	Ricard	**II, 380**	*Snidelingestret*	Equivalent to **I, 129** held *c.* 1110 by Odo *monetarius*, presumably Richard's father. See above **I, 42**, n. 1 Note also the interest of Ricardus Niger and Ricardus Baganorus in **II, 38**. There is no other reason for supposing that either of these Richards had anything to do with moneying
Willelmus filius Bos	Willem	**II, 66**	High St. (N.)	Next to Sanson *monetarius* in **II, 64–5** (Table 43)
		II, 99	High St. (S.)	Among properties with probable moneying connections in 1148: **II, 94** and **104**, Roger de Haia, and **II, 101**, Gaufridus (Table 44). It may be worth noting that there were forges in **I, 64** held from *filio Boselini c.* 1110, although if **II, 111** equals **I, 65**, it is not clear that **II, 99** can be equated with **I, 64**. Note also Willelmus's interest in **II, 564** in *Sildwortenestret*, where there appear to be no other moneying interests

[1] In this table the identification of Herebertus as Henry II's moneyer seems certain, the identification of Osbertus highly probable. Ricardus and Willelmus were obviously more difficult to identify, but a thorough check of all the persons with these names in Survey II revealed only five possibilities in each case, and further consideration suggested only Richard son of Odo, and William son of Bos as likely identifications.

[2] Mr. Elmore Jones informs us that a die duplicate of *BMC Henry II* no. 771* has recently come to light in a private collection. It shows clearly that the name of the moneyer is Osebern and not Osebert as read from 771*. In the light of this correction, Dr. von Feilitzen prefers to regard Hosbert and Osebern as two different moneyers. The moneyer Osbern of the succeeding *short-cross* coinage seems thus to have begun striking in the previous type.

at least from the retention of moneying within a single family. The most obvious cases are the families of Chepingus,[1] Odo,[2] and perhaps Saiet,[3] but there are probably others where the relationships can no longer be established, and are reflected only in the descent of properties. Continuity of *use* between *c.* 1110, 1148, and even later can perhaps be demonstrated in the case of **II, 111**, a property where there were forges held by Robert son of Wimund in *c.* 1110 (**I, 65**).[4] There was subsequently a *fabrica* on this site, which was later described as a *forgia* when the property was granted to the Priory of St. Denis. The Osbertus who held this property in 1148 may in turn be identifiable with Henry II's moneyer Hosbert (Table 45).

Forges occur only twice in Survey **II**, and in both cases they were held by Roger de Haia from Girinus *pincerna* (Table 44). Those in **II, 73** on the north side of High Street appear to have been held *c.* 1110 by Robert son of Wimund (**I, 7**), and thus demonstrate the same kind of continuity already seen in **II, 111**. There seems little doubt that the workshops of the mint in 1148 were still in the area to which they had moved before *c.* 1110, probably after the extension of the royal palace over their original site *c.* 1070.[5] The palace had however been destroyed in 1141 during the rout of Winchester, and by 1148 its site was being redeveloped.[6] Moneyers were by now moving back into this area on the south side of High Street (**II, 112** and **118**, cf. Table 43 and Fig. 22*c*), and re-occupying the site that had been occupied eighty years before by moneyer's houses and the five *monete*.[7] This tendency was brought to a logical conclusion in 1179–80 when the *monetaria* or mint for the new *short-cross* coinage was set up here in exactly the area taken into the royal palace a hundred and ten years before.[8]

During the time of Henry II's *cross-and-crosslets* coinage, however, the pattern of the earlier twelfth century still prevailed (Table 45). Moneyers of this coinage appear to have held properties on the north side of High Street, in some of the side streets, and in that

---

[1] Chepingus *filius Alueue* (Table 39)—Hugh son of Chepping (Table 44).   [2] Above, **I, 42**, n. 1.
[3] Above **I, 256**, n. 2, where Aluric the goldsmith *might* be identifiable with the Aluricus of **I, 263** (Table 40).
[4] Above, **I, 65**, n. 1.   [5] See above, pp. 399–400.
[6] See above, pp. 299–301.
[7] The area formerly occupied by the northern extension of the royal palace appears to be represented in Survey **II** by **II, 112–29**. In these eighteen properties in 1148 there were two named moneyers (one with two properties), one moneyer probably identified (**II, 128**), and one goldsmith (**II, 115**). There was also a Hereman (**II, 117**), who should perhaps be noted as the only person of this name in the surveys, in view of the possibility that a moneyer Hereman may have been recorded for Henry II's *short-cross* coinage at Winchester (*BMC Henry II* clxvii); the name is, however, most probably a misreading of Herebert.
[8] See below, Appendix I. 2, p. 514, n. 1. £12. 16*s.* 2*d.* was spent in 1179–80 on the construction of the *cambium regis* in Winchester, and the daily salaries of the *cambitores* were paid from 27 December 1179 (*Pipe Roll 26 Henry II*, p. 131). Since the fire which destroyed

the *monetaria* in 1180 did not take place until the 1/2 or 14/15 July (*Winchester ann*, s.a.), it seems probable that the reconstruction of the mint, and particularly the erection of a centralized building, took place before, and not as a consequence of, the fire. In any case there was time for Winchester moneyers to issue *short-cross* coins of Type I*a* before the fire (J. D. Brand and F. Elmore Jones, 'The Emergency Mint of Wilton in 1180', *BNJ* 35 (1966), 116–19). There were serious fires in Winchester or at St. Giles's Fair in 1102, 1162, 1180, 1197, and 1198 (*Winchester ann*, s.a.), and considerable destruction resulting from the rout of Winchester in 1141 (see above, pp. 297, 318–19, 323, 489 and n. 8). The destruction of the mint is only recorded on the one occasion in 1180. There is no evidence to support the traditional view that the mint was also burnt in 1102 (Milner³ i. 152), but it seems possible that the destruction of the palace in 1141 may have damaged the moneyers' workshops immediately to the east. This is at least the argument behind the suggestion that the mint was then transferred for a short period to Southampton, where coins with the mint-signature ANTOI, ANT, or AN were issued by Sanson and perhaps Willem (see above, p. 415, and n. 7; cf. *English Coins*, 92, 99).

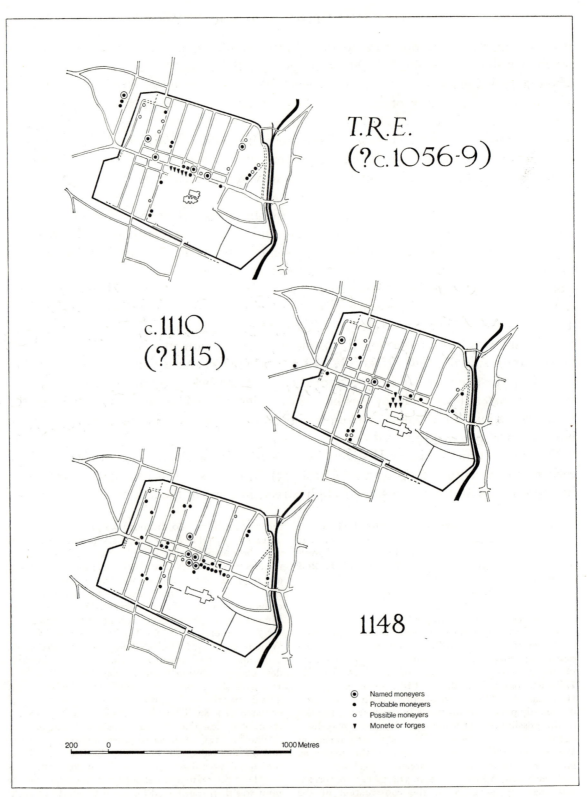

	Named moneyers
	Probable moneyers
	Possible moneyers
	Monete or forges

FIG. 22. Mints and moneyers' interests in Winchester (1:20,000): (*a*), *TRE, ?c.* 1056–9 (cf. Tables 34–7); (*b*), *c.* 1110, ?1115 (cf. Tables 38–41); (*c*), 1148 (cf. Tables 42–5).

Figure 22*a* includes the five *monete* on the south side of High Street destroyed *c.* 1070 (?) for the Norman extension of the royal palace. Figure 22*c* includes moneyers of Henry I who seem still to have had interests in Winchester as late as 1148 (Table 42), as well as future moneyers of Henry II who appear already to have had interests in the city by that date (Table 45).

part of the south side of High Street, east of the former site of the palace (**II, 99** and **111**), where the workshops of the moneyers seem to have lain since the latter part of the eleventh century.[1]

The status and offices of moneyers

The two surveys make it quite clear that the Winchester moneyers were of burgess rank. This is apparent not only from their extensive interest in urban properties, but also in Survey **I** from the explicit description of the holders of land in High Street as *burgenses*.[2] This must apply to at least three of the moneyers in Table 34, to Wimund in Table 38, and to all those moneyers in Tables 35, 36, 39, and 40 whose properties were in High Street and whose identification can be accepted. In addition the description of the former holders of land on the site of the extended royal palace as *burgenses* (**I, 57**) would appear to emphasize this statement with regard to Lethmerus (Table 35) and Gonnod.[3] It is also clear from **I, 162** that Alestanus in Table 34, Chepingus in Table 39, and a second Alestanus (perhaps to be identified with Æstan) in Table 40 should probably be regarded as *burgenses*. It thus seems likely that all or most Winchester moneyers were of burgess rank both *TRE* and *c.* 1110. They were, moreover, in economic (as perhaps in social) terms the most prominent of the various occupational groups in the city in 1148, and of closely comparable economic status with the royal officials. Unlike the latter, however, the moneyers' interests did not extend to the surrounding countryside, but were entirely confined to the city itself.[4]

The moneyers of Winchester were in some way related to the goldsmiths. Both had considerable property in *Calpestret*, although by 1148 moneying interests were declining there, while there was still a clear concentration of goldsmiths in that street and in *Goldestret* (Fig. 22c, cf. Fig. 23a). Brithmarus *aurifaber* of **I, 166** may have been Edward the Confessor's moneyer (Table 35); Saiet's nephew Aluric the goldsmith may himself have been a moneyer, as his uncle certainly was.[5]

The connection was probably a reflection of the arrangements for exchanging old silver for recoinage. Since at this date the exchequer was not involved in providing the moneyer with a working capital of royal bullion, and since the function of exchanging was the moneyer's prerogative,[6] he was inevitably involved in many of the same technical activities as a goldsmith,[7] and it should occasion no surprise if they were sometimes one and the same individual, or had close family or business contacts one with another. The case of Andrebodus, *monetarius* and *cangeor* in the time of King Edward, illustrates one aspect of this situation with particular clarity (Table 34), while the family of Odo *monetarius*, if correctly identified, shows the interrelations of goldsmith, die-cutter, and moneyer within a single family over several generations.[8]

There is finally the question of Godwinus Socche *magister monetarius*.[9] It seems certain

---

[1] For the Winchester mint under Henry II, see *BMC Henry II* clxvi–clxviii, and *passim*. The later history and production of the Winchester mint from 1180–*c.* 1207 and in 1217–18 and 1248–50 will be considered in detail in Winchester Studies 8, see above, p. 396, n. 8.
[2] **I, 80/81.**
[3] Above, p. 398, n. 5.

[4] On this see further below, pp. 444, 447, Fig. 24 and Tables 50–2.
[5] Above, **I, 256**, n. 1; see also above, p. 419, n. 3.
[6] See the very clear discussion of this problem by D. F. Allen in *BMC Henry II* lxxxviii–xciv, esp. p. xciii.
[7] For goldsmiths, see below, p. 439.
[8] See above, **I, 42**, n. 1.
[9] **I, 15.**

from the abbreviated form of *monetarius*, that this, rather than *monetariorum*, is the correct extension. At the time of Survey **I** *TRE* he seems to have been active as long as, if not longer than, any of Edward the Confessor's moneyers then striking (Table 37). That this made him the senior moneyer seems likely; that it gave him any authority over the others, as the extension *magister monetariorum* might imply, finds no other support in the survey.

The terms used for the mint and moneyers' workshops

In the *TRE* portion of Survey **I** the only word used to denote a mint or moneyer's workshop is *moneta*, given in the plural *monete*.[1] The term *forgia*, *forgie* occurs only in the *modo* entries of Survey **I**, and on two occasions in Survey **II**.[2] It seems likely that the absence of the word *forgia* in the *TRE* entries reflects the usage of the original text lying behind these entries in Survey **I**, and that *monete* was the Latin equivalent of OE *mynet-smiþþe* f. 'mint' from *mynetian*, 'to coin' or 'mint'.

It has been argued above that the *forgie* in Surveys **I** and **II** were moneyers' workshops.[3] In one case it is clear from the descent of the property that the terms *forgie* (in the plural), *fabrica*, and *forgia* (in the singular) could all be used to describe the same entity.[4] In Survey **I** the eighteen forges are grouped into six entries. It seems probable that each entry represents a single workshop, within which there could be a varying number of forges, from one to six as the case might be.

The earliest recorded term used in Winchester for the mint as a whole appears to be *monetaria*.[5] It is possibly no coincidence that this term first appears in 1180 immediately after the reorganization of the mint which seems to have put an end to the scattered workshops of individual moneyers, and to have brought the whole operation for the first time into a single building.[6]

iv. THE ADMINISTRATION OF THE CITY (Table 46)

The two surveys and a few other contemporary documents provide some evidence for the government and local administration of the city in the eleventh and twelfth centuries.

The daily lives of the citizens were regulated in the early twelfth century, and no doubt before the conquest, by a recognized body of custom of which very little is known in detail from this period.[7] Later similarities between the customs of London and Winchester and their bracketing together in early grants of privileges to other towns[8] suggest that even in the tenth century the customs of the royal city had been as well defined as those which the burgesses of London declared for their city, and which were included

---

[1] **I, 58.**   [2] **I, 59** and **61–5**; **II, 73** and **90.**
[3] See above, pp. 399–400.   [4] **I, 65**, n. 1.
[5] *Winchester ann*, s.a. 1180.
[6] In the years before 1180, the Winchester moneyers were expressly forbidden to work together in a single building: see **II, 38**, n. 5, and *BMC Henry II* ciii, cvi. There appears to be no evidence that they were kept separate in any other city. As the late Mr. Derek Allen pointed out to us, this may underline the local peculiarities characteristic of the production of medieval

money in England, at least in the earlier part of the period. The relatively full documentation available for the Winchester mint should not lead us to suppose that Winchester practice was necessarily general practice.

[7] Henry II's charter of 1155–8 confirmed the citizens in all the customs and liberties which they had enjoyed in the reign of Henry I.

[8] e.g. to Wilton in 1129–35, Taunton in 1135–9, and Gloucester in 1155; A. Ballard, *British Borough Charters, 1042–1216* (Cambridge, 1913), 12.

in the laws of Æthelred II.[1] The customs were no doubt vouchsafed by the body of citizens which met three times a year in the *burghmote*, an extensive group which, however, probably did not include all the male householders in the city.[2] One of the first occasions on which we meet members of this group is when we read of the eighty-six of the 'better burgesses' on whose sworn testimony Survey **I** was based. Two precepts of Henry I addressed to the sheriff of Hampshire, the reeve of Winchester, and the burgesses of the city, confirming Hugh the larderer's grants of property there to the cathedral priory, illustrate a further aspect of the responsibility of this body of citizens.[3] Hugh's gifts had taken place in the presence of the *probi homines* of the city who were to give judgement if any dispute arose. The responsibility for bearing witness enjoined on the inhabitants of boroughs in the Anglo-Saxon laws was developing into the right of adjudicating in matters of tenure.

In a less formal setting the *probi homines* no doubt acted for the city as a whole, as when Bishop Henry *cum dignioribus Wintoniae civibus* met King Stephen after his coronation.[4] They were a cohesive social group as the existence of a guildhall where they used to drink together indicates (**II, 712**).[5]

It seems likely that by the twelfth century a smaller body than the *burghmote* met more frequently for the transaction of business on the same lines as the London court of husting,[6] but such a meeting cannot be identified in Winchester before the early thirteenth century.[7] Later in the thirteenth century the court of the mayor and bailiffs, also known as the king's court of the city of Winchester, met regularly in the guildhall or hall of pleas in High Street. In this connection it may be significant that in 1148 a guildhall which was probably identical with this one was held by John son of Ralf, a royal official and perhaps a reeve of the city (**II, 140**).

The king's reeve (*prepositus*) was the principal officer involved in the government of the city. Table 46 shows the known reeves of Winchester during the eleventh and twelfth centuries. The *Portereue* of **II, 804** was perhaps already a personal name, for it is the only occurrence of the vernacular title in the surveys, and this form occurs as the byname of several persons who were neither reeves nor bailiffs during the thirteenth and fourteenth centuries. By the latter part of the reign of Henry I, if not by the date of Survey **I**, there were at least two royal reeves in Winchester, although they seem frequently to have acted and to have been addressed independently. In Survey **I** we have Warin, Gesord, and Richard, *prepositi*, all property-owners, although only the first is recorded in the survey as having acted in an official capacity. There were always two reeves in

---

[1] A. J. Robertson, *The Laws of the Kings of England from Edmund to Henry I* (Cambridge, 1925), 71–9. Tait *Medieval Borough*, 124.

[2] This was the practice in the thirteenth and fourteenth centuries: Furley *City Government*, 65. This court or assembly is first specifically referred to as *burgemoto Wintonie* in 1212, *Curia Regis Rolls 1210–12*, p. 291.

[3] *Regesta*, ii, nos. 803–4.

[4] *Gesta Stephani*, cap. 3. A similar group, the *primates urbis*, were addressed by Duke William in 1066 and after consulting with Queen Edith, in whose

dower Winchester lay, they submitted to the Conqueror: Catherine Morton and Hope Muntz (eds.), *The Carmen de Hastingæ Proelio of Guy Bishop of Amiens* (Oxford, 1972), 40–1.

[5] For a possible association between this and other guildhalls, see above, p. 336.

[6] Tait *Medieval Borough*, 40–1.

[7] In *c.* 1212 a case was heard *in halimoto Wintonie*, *Curia Regis R 1210–12*, p.290. That this hall-moot was a more restricted session than the *burghmote* is suggested by the parallel relationship of the London folk-moot to the husting.

those witness-lists of twelfth-century conveyances in Winchester in which reeves appear, the earliest of which can probably be dated to *c.* 1130. In the thirteenth century the city normally had two reeves, or bailiffs (*ballivi*) as they came increasingly to be called, although there seems sometimes to have been a larger number.

As in Canterbury[1] and in thirteenth-century Winchester, so in early medieval Winchester the reeves were local men, or at least local property-owners. Æthelwine, *praefectus* of the city, built the church of St. Peter in a property in High Street before 1012 (**I, 23**).

TABLE 46

The reeves of Winchester in the eleventh and twelfth centuries: a chronological list in their probable order of succession

Date	Name	Source
Before 1012	Æthelwine praefectus	Sawyer 925; see **I, 23**, n. 5
TRE	Adelwoldus (holding property)	**I, 23**, and **38**
1105	Geraldus	*Regesta*, ii, no. 687
1107–22	Geraldus	Ibid., no. 1380
1103–6	Gaufridus	Ibid., no. 803
1100–6	Ricardus	Ibid., no. 804
c. 1110	Ricardus (holding property)	**I, 113, 189**, and **204**
c. 1110	Gesordus (holding property)	**I, 20**
c. 1110	Warinus (encroachments and holding property)	**I, 20, 59, 78**, and **79**
c. 1130	Godwinus and Godefridus (witnesses)	*EHR* 14 (1899), 423
1148	Herebertus (holding property)	**II, 76**
1156–7	Stigand (rendering farm; he appears to be dead by 1159)	**II, 88**, n. 1
Before 1180–1	Stephanus filius Pagani *and* Willelmus filius Baldewini (witnesses)	BM, Egerton MS. 3031, fo. 36ᵛ
After 1168	Johannes filius Radulfi *and* Nicholaus vinetarius (witnesses)	**II, 140**, n. 1

Adelwoldus, reeve under Edward the Confessor, gave to his parents the three houses in High Street in which they lived (**I, 23**). Warin, Gesord, and Richard were property-owners in *c.* 1110, as was Herbert in 1148.

The reeves probably supervised the assembly of *probi homines*, and it was no doubt in exercising one aspect of this office that they headed the witness lists of conveyances. Stigand the reeve issued a document acknowledging that a conveyance had taken place in his presence.[2] Above all, however, the reeve was the king's representative in the city. He was responsible for the collection of landgable and other customs (**I, 27, 29, 32**, and **44**), and for the toll of a penny a week from each butcher's stall (**I, 19**). Appendix I. 2 shows the sources of income which the reeve's successors, the bailiffs, collected for the king in the thirteenth century. The reeves perhaps looked after certain other properties of the crown (**I, 38**). Another of their important functions was the regulation and collection of rents from encroachments on to the king's highway (**I, 20** and **59; II, 56**).

Normally the reeve rendered an account for this money to the sheriff of Hampshire, who accounted for the farm of the city at the exchequer. In 1156 and 1157 Stigand the reeve[2] himself accounted for the farm: this situation, exceptional in the context of the

[1] Urry *Canterbury*, 82–7.　　[2] See **II, 88**, n. 1.

rest of Henry II's reign, may represent the survival of irregular practices from the reign of Stephen. The charge of Winchester would have been one of the sheriff's most important duties, and this explains why Hugh de Port, the sheriff, was described in 1096 as *vicarius* of Winchester.[1] Conversely the office of reeve was of some importance in the county, and its holder was sometimes used by the king in judicial matters outside the city.[2] Beornulf, the earliest known reeve (*wīcgerēfa*) of Winchester, who died *c.* 896, was lamented as one of King Alfred's best thegns,[3] as befitted the custodian of the focal point in the defence of Wessex.

The reeves maintained a small staff, for in *c.* 1130 we hear of their clerk, William son of Osbert.[4] The collectors of geld, scots, and aids were perhaps subordinate to the reeve, after whom they were addressed in royal precepts,[5] although they probably accounted directly to the sheriff. In *c.* 1130 Nigel the collector occupied a lowly position in a list of witnesses.[6]

Three entries in Survey **I** show that the king's justiciar sometimes acted in cases which might normally concern the reeve. Each of these entries (**I, 43, 53,** and **135**) concerns an encroachment which resulted in the complete closure of a street, and it was probably the scale of these alterations to the street pattern which brought the case before the justiciar. The terminology of the entries suggests that proceedings before the justiciar were more formal than those before the reeve. Local justiciars were introduced and widely used by the Norman kings.[7] Richard de Courcy, who acted as justiciar in Winchester before *c.* 1100, seems to have had no other local interests and was mainly involved in the administration of Normandy.[8] Herbert the chamberlain, who although he was not described as justiciar may have acted as such on occasions,[9] did, however, have strong local interests. The day-to-day administration of the king's interest in the city was in the hands of the reeves under the supervision of the sheriff. Exceptional matters were dealt with by a local justiciar.

During the reign of Stephen the office of local justiciar in other cities and counties was a valuable prize for barons and bishops alike.[10] The exceptional position of Bishop Henry with regard to Winchester is underlined by the fact that in 1148 he had his own justiciar to administer his interests there and that in one instance his justiciar appears to have been responsible for a royal property (**II, 89** and **665**).[11]

At neighbourhood level the unit of administration in thirteenth-century Winchester was the aldermanry (*aldermanria*), often described in the assize rolls as the ward (*warda*). From the thirteenth-century evidence it appears that each street, at least within the walls, constituted an aldermanry, and that as the population of the city declined adjacent streets were amalgamated to form more extensive aldermanries. In 1340 there were eight aldermanries within the walls, and the western and northern suburbs formed a ninth. By

---

[1] *Regesta*, i, no. 379.
[2] *Regesta*, ii, no. 687.
[3] *ASC*, s.a. 897 (A).
[4] *EHR* 14 (1899), 423.
[5] *Regesta*, ii, no. 1110.
[6] *EHR* 14 (1899), 423.
[7] H. A. Cronne, 'The office of local justiciar in England under the Norman Kings', *Univ. of Birmingham Historical Journal*, 6 (1958), 18–38.
[8] See **I, 45**, n. 4, and *Regesta*, i, *passim*.
[9] e.g. *Regesta*, ii, no. 1380, in which he takes precedence over the sheriff and the reeve of Winchester.
[10] Cronne, op. cit. above, n. 7; Richardson and Sayles, 174.
[11] See below, p. 490.

1417 the number of aldermanries in the city had fallen to six, and to five by 1524.[1] It is possible that the *custodia episcopi Salesberie* obscurely mentioned in the first survey (**I, 108**) is an early reference to a ward outside West Gate, but it seems unlikely that the head of the royal administration should have been directly responsible for so small a unit as a single ward, even in a capital city.

There is no evidence that the aldermanry or ward court was ever as important in Winchester as it was in Canterbury or London.[2] In the reign of Henry I, Godwin an alderman headed the list of witnesses to a sale of land in *Bucchestret*,[3] as if the witnesses for such transactions were originally provided on an aldermanry basis, or were attending an assembly of the aldermanry. This is, however, the only known transaction in which a Winchester alderman occupies such an important position among the witnesses.[4] In the thirteenth century the role of the Winchester aldermen in the publication of conveyances was a minor one.[5]

In the later Middle Ages the beadles were officers subordinate to the aldermen, with local police responsibilities.[6] The beadles recorded in the two surveys were for the most part very localized property-holders, and the occurrence of *Alpstanus stretbidel* among the witnesses of *c.* 1130[7] suggests that in the twelfth century too they operated within the aldermanry or street. The 'king's beadles' appear to have been responsible for the property known as the *Balchus* in 1148 (**II, 52**), where there may perhaps have been some connection between the former use of this prison and their police authority.

There is some evidence for other minor responsibilities. Each of the city gates presumably had its porter. The porter's lodge at West Gate, mentioned in 1148, still survives today (**II, 3**). William the porter held a number of properties near the East Gate, of which he had charge (**II, 695**). A William the gatekeeper (*barrar'*) held property (**II, 1062**) near King's Gate or the gate of Wolvesey Palace. The responsibility of keeping watch for breaches of the peace appears to have been that of individual householders under the supervision of the aldermen, as in the later Middle Ages,[8] for a number of property-holders were specifically not exempted from this responsibility.[9] There are in addition three occurrences of the byname 'watchman' (*vigil'*) in 1148 (**II, 354, 750,** and **1005**), each of them outside a separate gate of the city. The duties of these watchmen were probably distinct from those of the householders' watch, and may have arisen in response to the disturbances of Stephen's reign.

The authority of the royal administration was overriding in Winchester but there were also other jurisdictions within the urban area. That of the bishop was the next most important, and its development in the thirteenth century led to the administrative fission of the city and the soke.[10] The abbot of Hyde exercised a similar authority in the northern suburb in the twelfth century.[11] Other lords probably had less well-defined rights over their own fiefs and even over individual houses.[12]

[1] For the evolution of the Winchester aldermanries, see *SMW*.   [2] Urry *Canterbury*, 92–104.
[3] *EHR* 14 (1899), 424.
[4] For references, see Table 46.
[5] Furley *Usages*, 43. For the evolution of public conveyancing practice in Winchester, see *SMW*.
[6] Furley *City Government*, 145.
[7] *EHR* 14 (1899), 423.
[8] Furley *City Government*, 146.
[9] See above, p. 15, and **I, 33–4, 45–6, 69, 71, 76–9, 133, 154, 158.**   [10] See above, p. 255.
[11] See above, pp. 266–7.   [12] See above, pp. 340–1.

v. GUILDS

There were several guilds in twelfth-century Winchester apart from those whose guildhalls have been discussed above.[1] In the time of King Edward the Confessor there was a guild of the men living in the western suburb, known apparently as the Easter guild, which owned property there (**I, 105**).[2] There may have been some connection between this guild and the city merchant guild which later owned property in the same area.

The *gilda mercatorum* itself is first mentioned in the charter of Henry II granting freedom from toll to its members in 1155–8,[3] but there is no evidence that will allow the guild merchant to be identified with any of the guilds mentioned in Surveys **I** and **II**. The charter was addressed to the citizens of the guild of merchants alone. In a separate charter of about the same date Henry II confirmed the citizens of Winchester as a whole in the enjoyment of the liberties which they had had in the time of King Henry I.[4] This may mean that the charter to the citizens of the guild of merchants was the first recognition of the existence of that guild and that the guild itself had come into being since the reign of Henry I. The guildhall of the merchant guild may be mentioned in Survey **II**.[5]

This does not mean, however, that at an earlier date Winchester traders did not form associations in order to protect their own interests. A possible connection between Chapman's Hall and a guild of *cnihtas* has been suggested above;[6] and by 1130 the weavers and fullers of Winchester each had their own guilds.[7]

The religious connotations of several of the early guilds have been mentioned above.[8] In this connection it is worth noting that there was a guild of priests (*mæssepreosta gylde*) and a guild of deacons (*diacona gylde*) in Winchester in the later tenth century.[9] But we have no means of knowing how long these bodies survived, or whether they were connected in any way with the religious fraternities in the city during the thirteenth century.[10]

vi. TRADES (Fig. 23; Tables 47–9)

By the late tenth century Winchester had so developed as a centre of manufacture and consumption that at least three of the streets within its walls were distinguished by their concentrations of specialist tradesmen. The street of the tanners (*Tænnerestret*) is recorded in 990, and the streets of the shield-makers (*Scyldwyrhtana stræt*) and of the butchers (*Flæscmangere stræt*) in 996.[11] The other street-names recorded in Survey **I** date back no doubt to the same period. Of these only *Scowrtenestret*, the street of the

---

[1] See pp. 335–6.

[2] There may be a parallel to this association in the London guild of English *cnihtas*, responsible for the suburban area of Portsoken, and tracing its origins back to the reign of King Edgar. For a discussion of the evidence relating to this guild, see *AS Writs* 231–5.

[3] *Archaeologia*, 49 (1885), 214. Furley *City Government*, 178.

[4] Ibid.

[5] See above, p. 336.

[4] See p. 335.

[7] See below, p. 438.

[8] See above, p. 435.

[9] *AS Wills* 24–7, 126–7.

[10] For the fraternities at the churches of St. Mary Kalender and St. Maurice, each presided over by a prior and including a number of priests, see Goodman *Chartulary*, no. 470, and *Cal Pat R 1350–4*, pp. 368–73.

[11] See above, pp. 234–5.

shoe-makers, clearly suggests the occupation of its early inhabitants. *Goldestret* may mean the street of the goldsmiths,[1] and it is possible that *Gerestret* was so named from a hay-market held there, although the name may have derived from the grassy nature of the locality.[2] Corroborative evidence that these trades were carried on in or near their respective streets exists only for the tanners, the butchers, and the goldsmiths.[3] It may be significant that four out of the probable total of five trades which gave their names to streets, tanning, shield-making, shoe-making, and butchery, used noisome animal products as raw materials.

The two twelfth-century surveys provide the only comprehensive evidence for the trades of early medieval Winchester, and can be supplemented by no more than a few records of individuals and a list of witnesses from the area of *Bucchestret* in *c.* 1130.[4] Comparable information of a less complete nature is available from the public records and from local conveyances for the thirteenth century, but a comprehensive picture of the trades of medieval Winchester can only otherwise be obtained from the city records of the fourteenth century. Even so, the twelfth-century surveys have serious limitations as evidence for trades and craftsmen. The survey of *c.* 1110 dealt only with the king's properties and is not very informative for areas of the city outside High Street and the western suburb. The second survey is apparently complete in its coverage of properties, but since it often fails to name and may frequently even fail to indicate the existence of tenants on the lowest rung of the tenurial ladder, it is of restricted value as a record of the artisan population, many of whom must have been tenants-at-will or for terms of years. This limitation presumably also applies to the earlier survey. Only the wealthier craftsmen will therefore be recorded in the surveys and this seems to be clearly demonstrated, as will be shown, in the cases of the leather and clothing trades in 1148.

Tables 47–9, and Figs. 23*a* and 23*b* show the occurrences and distribution of the trades in Winchester. Officers of the royal administration and household, and officers of other households, whose interests reflect Winchester's position as a capital city, are not included,[5] nor are the priests and clerks who form numerically the largest single professional group identified in the surveys.[6] The moneyers also form a special group and are dealt with elsewhere.[7]

Fifteen different occupational bynames are recorded for *TRE*, thirteen for *c.* 1110, and forty-eight in 1148, thus further indicating the fuller coverage of Survey **II**. The surveys mention sixty-two different occupational bynames, but their uneven coverage is demonstrated by the fact that eight occupational bynames are recorded solely for *TRE*, seven solely for *c.* 1110, and thirty-six solely in 1148. Apart from the trades of smith (*faber*) and baker (*softebred*, *pistor*), which are recorded for all three dates, the two groups of trades recorded for *TRE* and for *c.* 1110 are entirely different.

---

[1] Or perhaps 'marigold street', but cf. above, p. 234, s.n.

[2] See above, p. 234; and cf. E. Ekwall, *Street Names of the City of London* (Oxford, 1965), 96–7, s.n. Gracechurch Street.

[3] See below, pp. 431, 434, and 439. For the doubtful possibility that the name *Bucchestret* might have to do with the cleaning and bleaching of cloth, see above, p. 233, s.n.

[4] *EHR* 14 (1899), 424. The witness's trades were: *fellere*, *tinctor*, *faber*, *taleator*, and *tannator*. A *faber* occurs in another Winchester witness list of the same period, ibid. 423.

[5] See above, pp. 387–92.

[6] See above, pp. 392–6.

[7] See above, pp. 396–422.

TABLE 47

The trades in Survey I: individuals identified by occupational bynames or names denoting commercial activities, and their distribution by streets

	Total number of individuals in each trade	Occupational bynames or names denoting commercial activities	High Street (N.)	High Street (S.)	Outside West Gate	Smidelingestret	Terra baronum (Brudenestret)	Scowrtenestret	Wunegrestret	Tannerestret	Bucchestret	Calpestret	Goldestret	Gerestret	Total number of occurrences
TRE	2	Harengarius	2	—	—	—	—	—	—	—	—	—	—	—	2
	1	Aurifaber	—	—	—	—	—	1	—	—	—	—	—	—	1
		Brandwirchte	—	—	—	—	—	—	—	—	—	—	—	1	1
		Faber	—	—	1	—	—	—	—	—	—	—	—	—	1
		Fenarius	—	—	1	—	—	—	—	—	—	—	—	—	1
		Gustate (innkeeper?)	—	—	—	—	—	1	—	—	—	—	—	—	1
		Heuere	—	—	1	—	—	—	—	—	—	—	—	—	1
		Hosarius	—	1	—	—	—	—	—	—	—	—	—	—	1
		Savonarius	1	—	—	—	—	—	—	—	—	—	—	—	1
		Scalarius	—	—	—	—	—	—	—	—	—	—	—	1	1
		Softebred (baker ?)	—	—	—	—	—	—	—	—	—	—	1	—	1
		Sutor	1	—	—	—	—	—	—	—	—	—	—	—	1
		Tornator	—	—	1	—	—	—	—	—	—	—	—	—	1
		Wantar'	—	—	—	—	—	—	1	—	—	—	—	—	1
		Watmaungre (water-seller?)	—	—	—	—	1	—	—	—	—	—	—	—	1
		Number of separate trades in each street	3	1	4	—	1	2	1	—	—	—	1	2	16

A total of 15 trades, distributed between 16 individuals

	Total number of individuals in each trade	Occupational bynames or names denoting commercial activities	High Street (N.)	High Street (S.)	Outside West Gate	Smidelingestret	Terra baronum (Brudenestret)	Scowrtenestret	Wunegrestret	Tannerestret	Bucchestret	Calpestret	Goldestret	Gerestret	Total number of occurrences
c. 1110	8	Carnifex	8	—	—	—	—	—	—	—	—	—	—	—	8
	3	Taneator	—	—	—	—	—	—	—	2	1	—	—	—	3
	2	Coquus	—	—	2	—	—	—	1	—	—	—	—	—	3
		Faber	—	—	—	2	—	—	—	—	—	—	—	—	2
	1	Archarius	—	—	1	—	—	—	—	—	—	—	—	—	1
		Feller	—	—	1	—	—	—	—	—	—	—	—	—	1
		Lauandaria	—	—	1	—	—	—	—	—	—	—	—	—	1
		Parmentarius	—	—	—	—	—	—	—	—	—	—	—	1	1
		Pistor	1	—	—	—	—	—	—	—	—	—	—	—	1
		Potarius	—	—	1	—	—	—	—	—	—	1	—	—	2
		Scaldeator	—	—	—	—	—	1	—	—	—	—	—	—	1
		Scrutarius	—	—	—	—	—	—	—	—	—	—	—	1	1
		Tailator	1	—	—	—	—	—	—	—	—	—	—	—	1
		Number of separate trades in each street	3	—	5	1	—	1	1	1	1	1	—	2	26

A total of 13 trades, distributed between 24 individuals

A stricter comparison of the trades at the three dates represented by the surveys may be obtained by considering from Survey **II** only those occupational bynames which occur on the king's fief. There were twenty-three separate trades on the king's fief in that survey, compared with thirteen in *c.* 1110 and fifteen *TRE*. But eight of the trades recorded for *c.* 1110 did not occur on the king's fief in 1148, and nineteen of the twenty-six

TABLE 48

The trades in Survey II: individuals identified by occupational bynames or names denoting commercial activities, and their distribution by streets

Total number of individuals in each trade	Occupational bynames or names denoting commercial activities	High Street (N.)	High Street (S.)	[Great Minster Street]	Outside West Gate	Outside North Gate	Snidelingestret	Brudenestret	Scowrtenestret	Alwarnestret	Flesmangerestret	Sildwortenestret	Wunegrestret	Tannerestret	Buchestret	Colobrochestret	Outside East Gate	Mensterstret	Calpestret	Goldestret	Outside South Gate i	Outside South Gate ii	Gerestret	Total number of occurrences
13	Parmentarius	2	—	—	3	1	3	—	—	—	—	—	—	2	—	—	3	—	—	—	2	—	—	16
9	Faber	1	1	—	5	1	1	1	—	—	—	—	—	—	—	—	2	1	—	—	1	—	—	13
7	Cocus	1	1	—	1	—	—	—	—	—	—	1	1	2	—	—	—	1	—	—	2	—	—	9
5	Aurifaber	1	1	—	—	1	—	—	—	—	—	—	—	—	2	—	—	1	—	3	—	—	—	8
	Carnifex[1]	2	1	—	—	—	—	—	—	—	1	—	—	—	—	—	—	—	1	—	—	—	1	5
	Sellarius	—	—	—	1	3	—	—	—	—	—	—	—	—	—	—	—	2	—	—	—	1	—	5
	Maco	—	1	—	1	3	—	—	—	—	—	—	—	—	—	—	1	—	—	—	—	2	—	8
4	Cordwanarius	2	—	—	2	—	—	—	—	—	—	—	—	1	—	—	—	—	—	—	—	1	—	6
	Molendinarius	1	—	—	—	1	—	—	—	—	—	—	—	—	—	—	—	—	1	—	1	—	—	4
	Pictor	1	1	1	—	—	2	—	—	—	—	—	—	—	1	—	—	—	—	—	—	—	—	5
	Tinctor	4	—	—	—	—	—	—	—	—	—	1	—	4	—	—	—	—	—	—	—	—	—	9
3	Acularius	4	1	—	1	—	1	—	—	—	—	—	—	—	—	—	—	—	—	—	—	—	—	5
	Brachiator/Bruwere[2]	—	—	—	2	—	1	—	—	—	1	—	1	—	—	—	1	—	—	—	—	—	—	6
	Carpentarius	—	—	—	2	2	—	—	—	—	—	—	—	—	—	—	—	1	—	—	—	—	—	3
	Lorimer	—	—	—	2	1	1	—	1	—	1	—	—	—	—	—	—	—	—	—	—	—	—	5
	Mercator/Merciarius/Mercherel[2]	2	—	1	4	1	1	—	1	—	1	—	—	—	—	—	1	—	—	1	4	2	—	13
	Pistor	1	1	—	—	—	—	—	—	—	—	—	2	—	—	—	—	—	—	—	4[*]	1	—	8
	Vinetarius	—	1	—	—	—	—	—	—	—	—	—	2	—	1	—	—	—	—	—	—	—	—	4
	Waranchier	—	—	—	1	1	—	—	—	—	—	—	—	1	—	—	2	—	—	—	—	—	—	3
2	Besmere	1	—	—	—	—	—	—	—	—	—	—	—	—	—	1	1	—	—	—	1	—	—	3
	Bulengarius	—	—	—	—	—	—	—	—	—	—	1	—	—	—	—	1	—	—	—	—	—	—	2
	Caretarius	—	—	—	—	—	—	—	—	—	—	—	—	1	—	1	—	—	1	—	—	2	—	3
	Coruesarius	—	—	—	—	—	—	—	—	—	—	—	—	—	—	—	—	—	—	—	2	2	—	4
	Drapier	—	—	—	—	—	—	—	—	—	—	—	—	2	—	—	—	—	—	—	2	—	—	2
	Fullo	—	—	—	—	—	—	—	—	—	1	—	—	—	1	—	—	1	—	—	—	1	—	3
	Tannator	—	—	—	—	—	—	—	—	—	—	—	—	—	1	—	—	—	—	—	—	1	—	2
	Turtellarius/Furwatel	—	—	—	1	—	—	—	—	—	—	—	—	—	—	—	—	—	—	—	1	—	—	2
1	Trades in which only one individual was concerned[3]	T	—	—	B F H I J L M P	O S	—	—	—	—	—	C C	—	M	K	—	—	D	E G	E E	N	R Q	A	23
	Number of separate trades in each street	13	7	2	19	11	5	1	1	1	3	4	4	7	4	1	6	5	5	4	11	10	2	179

{ High Street (S.) 7 + [Great Minster Street] 2 } 17

A total of 47 trades, distributed between 125 individuals

[1] Not including shambles, stalls, etc.
[2] Not including references to breweries, chattels, etc.
[3] Identified by letters as follows: A asinarius, B batar', C buclar', D butar', E cerarius, E cerarius, F cornemangere, G furbar', H harangarius, I lignator, J meddere, K parcheminus, L rusmangre, M sannarius, N sparonus, O scrionarius, P sourarius, Q sutor, R telarius, S tornitor, T unctarius

trades recorded in Survey **I** for *TRE* and *c.* 1110 together did not occur on the king's fief in 1148. The significance of these figures may be that the variety of trades practised on the king's fief by the early twelfth century was similar to that of the mid-twelfth century, rather than that there had been a considerable expansion in the range of commerce and manufacture between the two periods. A demonstration of the defects of a simple comparison of the two surveys is that fullers, who were relatively numerous in Survey **II**, do not appear in Survey **I**, although we have a reference to a street of fullers in the city at about the same date as Survey **I** was compiled.[1]

The sample of trades in Survey **I** is too small to show any meaningful distribution within the city, but may be usefully compared with the later evidence. Since the residences of individuals can rarely be identified, the distribution of trades in 1148 represents the total number of properties held by individuals with occupational bynames. In later medieval Winchester, except in the cases of a few very wealthy merchants, there was a close correlation between an individual's commercial interests and the distribution of his properties; this was presumably also the case in the twelfth century.

The surveys contain evidence of a more precise nature for brewing and butchery. Ten entries under High Street in 1148 refer to stalls or shambles. The four from which no rent was received during Lent were evidently butchers' stalls. From one of these four stalls and from one of the other six, toll was due. It thus seems likely that all the stalls, shambles, and other properties from which toll was due represented butchers' establishments.

The hire of brew-houses and their utensils is mentioned in two entries, and in another the tenure of chattels is associated with brewing. It is possible that all the references to the tenure of chattels indicate that ale was brewed on the premises, although in some cases similar equipment for other processes such as dyeing[2] may have been on hire, or the chattels may even have been domestic furnishings.[3] The surveyors may have recorded this information with a view to making assessments for brewgable, which is otherwise hardly mentioned in the surveys.

Most of the trades recorded in 1148 fall easily into the small number of well-defined groups identified in Table 49 (cf. Fig. 23).

The trades providing food, drink, and such other household requirements as grease, salt, candles, and soap are the most various group. Of the victualling trades the butchers were the most localized, for their stalls are only recorded on the north side of High Street, principally in the neighbourhood of the entries to *Alwarnestret* and *Flesmangerestret*. The church in the entry to the former street was later known as St. Peter *in macellis*, and before *c.* 1110 two shambles were demolished here in order to extend the chancel of the church.[4] The butchers had perhaps originally congregated near the entry to *Flesmangerestret*, but by the beginning of the twelfth century had already set up their stalls further to the west in High Street, a movement which eventually became a migration and at the end of the thirteenth century resulted in the change of the name *Alwarnestret* to

---

[1] See above, p. 234, s.n. (*in vico*) *Fullonum*.

[2] The word *utensilia* can also denote looms, but brewing equipment seems more likely in this context. In later medieval Winchester dye-houses were fre-

quently sold or let with all their utensils, principally vats and tubs: see *SMW*, s.v. 'dyeing'.

[3] Cf. above, p. 344. **II, 496** might be such a case.

[4] See above, **I, 23**, n. 5, and Fig. 12.

Flesmangerestret.[1] The five named butchers held few properties in 1148. Nevertheless the supply of meat to the royal household, for example, could be a lucrative source of trade and perhaps Martin of Bentworth, not named as a butcher, but with interests in butchers' stalls as well as in many other properties, was involved in such an enterprise.[2]

TABLE 49

The trades in Survey II, 1148, grouped as shown in Figs. 23a and 23b

Fig. 23a	CLOTH WORKERS	Fig. 23b	BUTCHERY AND BREWING
	Drapier		Brachiator
	Fullo		Briwere
	Parmentarius		Carnifex
	Telarius		
	Tinctor		OTHER VICTUALLING TRADES
	Waranchier		Bulengarius
			Cerarius
	LEATHER WORKERS		Cocus
	Cordwanarius		Cornemangere
	Coruesarius		Furwatel
	Lorimer		Harangarius
	Parcheminus		Meddere
	Sellarius		Molendinarius
	Sutor		Pistor
	Tannator		Sannarius
			Saponarius
	GOLDSMITHS		Turtellarius
	Aurifaber		Unctarius
			Vinetarius
	METAL WORKERS		
	Batar'		SERVICE TRADES
	Buclar'		Acularius
	Faber		Asinarius
	Furbar'		Besmere
			Butar'
	BUILDING WORKERS		Caretarius
	Carpentarius		Rusmangre
	Lignator		Scriniarius
	Maco		Scutarius
	Pictor		Tornitor
	MERCHANTS		
	Mercator		
	Mercherel		
	Merciarius		

Ale was probably brewed for sale in many of the larger houses, as in the later Middle Ages. The references to brew-houses or brewing in 1148 all appear to be cases of sub-letting. There seems to be no particular pattern in the distribution of the known brew-houses, except that many of them were near High Street.

Fish must have been an important part of the diet, yet apart from two dealers in herrings in the time of King Edward, and another in 1148, there is no record in the surveys of the

---

[1] See above, pp. 233–4.   [2] See above, pp. 27–8.

trade in fish. In the thirteenth and fourteenth centuries the fishmongers had their stalls west of the butchers in High Street,[1] and it is possible that some of the stalls mentioned in 1148 belonged to fishmongers rather than butchers.

Taken altogether the victualling trades were concentrated in High Street and the western suburb, to some extent in the north-east quarter of the walled area, and, if the reconstruction of the order of survey is correct, in the suburb outside King's Gate. The cooks and bakers are the most numerous of the named trades and apart from those who might have worked in large households, their trade was probably with the poorer artisan section of the community who did not have elaborate kitchens. There is some correlation, particularly outside King's Gate, between the distribution of the properties of victuallers, especially cooks and bakers, and those belonging to workers in the clothing and leather trades. The vintners probably enjoyed the highest status of all the victuallers, and one of them was a reeve of Winchester in the twelfth century.[2]

The group classified as service trades were not very numerous and provided for miscellaneous household wants such as floor-covering, brooms, tubs, furniture, needles, and transport. Their properties were principally in High Street and the western suburb. The shield-maker could perhaps have been classified as a leather worker. The needle-makers probably worked in bone rather than metal. The turners, of whom one is recorded *TRE* and another in 1148, probably made the wooden bowls which the evidence of archaeological deposits with preserved organic materials suggest were widely used. They must also have made the elaborate turned rails characteristic of romanesque furniture, and also evidenced in the archaeological record.

No potters were recorded in 1148. William the potter who held property in the west suburb in *c.* 1110 was a royal servant and a benefactor of St. Swithun's Priory, and so cannot be classed as a tradesman.[3] The nearest deposits of potting clay known to have been worked during the Middle Ages are three miles south of the city, and the nearest kiln so far discovered and known to have been in operation at the time of the surveys was at Michelmersh, six miles to the west. There was probably, however, a considerable pottery industry somewhere in the neighbourhood, for the distribution of the eleventh-century fabric known as 'Winchester Ware' is virtually confined to the city. The less sophisticated fabrics seem also to be of restricted distribution, so that the evidence may suggest that potters are one of the trades actually present but omitted by the surveys, perhaps because of their lowly social status.

Building workers were comparatively numerous. Most private houses were probably constructed of wood rather than stone, but the predominance of masons over carpenters perhaps reflects not only their more elevated status but also the great activity in public building in Winchester in the late eleventh and twelfth centuries. The relatively large number of individual painters recorded is worth notice, but it is not clear what sort of painting they practised. The properties of building craftsmen were widely scattered in 1148, but some of them appear to have been grouped in the neighbourhood of the cathedral or near Hyde Abbey. The presence of a *heuere* in the western suburb *TRE*, a *feller* in *c.* 1110, and a *lignator* in 1148, underlines its proximity to the woodland on the

---

[1] See *SMW*, s.v. 'fishmongers'.   [2] See above, p. 424, and cf. Table 46.   [3] **I**, 93, n. 1.

west side of the city, and the possibility that there was a wood-market or at least a concentration of woodworkers there, as the later medieval name *Wodestret* suggests.

Goldsmiths apart, metal working in the second survey is almost entirely represented by the nine blacksmiths. The three trades of bucklemaker, furbisher, and beater are represented only in four properties. The blacksmith to whom St. Swithun appeared in a vision in *c.* 968 is the earliest known Winchester craftsman.[1] The quantity of iron available and the quality of the smiths' work in later tenth-century Winchester is indeed well attested by the elaborate coffin-fittings excavated from graves in the Old and New Minster cemeteries. In the twelfth century the blacksmiths' main source of trade was apparently shoeing horses, for most of their properties were in the suburbs and were often close to the city gates, where horses could be shod at the beginning or end of a journey. Their properties within the walls were also near the gates, as well as in High Street. The number of their properties in the western suburb emphasizes the importance of the western approach to Winchester. Robert the smith had two properties on either side of the street immediately outside West Gate in 1148, and there was a smith outside West Gate *TRE*, and another in *Snidelingestret* in *c.* 1110.

A wide range of trades connected with the manufacture of leather and leather objects is recorded in the surveys. Leather-making is a smelly process which requires a large supply of water, and the tanners and the parchment-maker in the surveys occupied principally the two best-watered streets in the city, *Tannerestret* and *Bucchestret*, which lay to the leeward of the main inhabited area. The tanner outside King's Gate could also have had easy access to running water. The tanners were not significant property-owners, but by the middle of the twelfth century they already appear to have been moving out of *Tannerestret* into the area of *Bucchestret* to the east, where they mostly lived in the later Middle Ages.[2] Two of the properties excavated in *Tannerestret* (Lower Brook Street) contained substantial timber-lined pits of eleventh-century date which would have been suitable for such leather-making processes as bating or tanning, and at the same date both properties included wide timber-lined water-channels where skins could have been washed. By the end of the thirteenth century both these properties were occupied by cloth workers. In *c.* 1110 two tanners held properties in *Tannerestret* and one in *Bucchestret*. In 1148 there was one tanner and a parchment-maker in *Bucchestret*, but none in *Tannerestret*. This migration was perhaps caused by an increase of population within the walled area, and by the superior claims of cloth workers to the clean water supply in *Tannerestret*.

Other leather workers were not tied to the water supply to the same extent. Three types of shoe-maker were recorded in 1148, cordwainers, corvesers, and a cobbler (*sutor*), and they appear to have ranked in that order of prosperity. Their properties were principally in High Street and the western and southern suburbs. The cordwainers, whose work was presumably the most elaborate, had most of their properties in High Street and outside West Gate. The corvesers and the cobbler were outside South Gate and King's Gate. No shoemakers were recorded in *Scowrtenestret* in the surveys, although

---

[1] Wulfstan *Narratio Metrica*, bk. I, lines 1–198, which implies, but does not state, that the smith was a Winchester man.   [2] See *SMW*, s.v. 'leather-workers'.

a lorimer held property there in 1148. This suggests that we have here a third instance of occupational migration within the city since the tenth century. The other properties of lorimers and that of the saddler were outside the walls. Cordwainers evidently enjoyed a special status among the Winchester leather workers, and may have controlled the trade in finished products.

In the provision of raw materials and the organization of production the cloth trade was probably one of the most complex in the city. Most of the necessary entrepreneurial activity was presumably undertaken by the greater merchants of Winchester, those *prudeshommes* who, at least by the early thirteenth century, were members of the merchant guild and enjoyed the freedom to buy and sell in the city and elsewhere.[1] Unfortunately men of this standing can rarely be identified in the surveys, although Chapman's Hall, with its market for linen cloths and its church on the north side of High Street, probably served some of them as both a commercial and a social centre in the twelfth century (**II, 69**).[2] Osbert the linen draper was responsible for this property in 1157–8, and in the thirteenth century the church was known as St. Mary of the linen cloth.[3] In that century the principal market for wool was on the south side of High Street, at the eastern end of the site of the royal palace. The Drapery, occupying the structure of the old mint, adjoined it on the west,[4] but there is no sign in 1148 of any development in the wool or woollen-cloth market which foreshadowed these arrangements. Two drapers had properties outside South Gate in 1148 but neither held more than one property.

The individual craftsmen who are recorded seem to occur numerically in inverse ratio to their economic and social status in the city. Thus in Survey **II** one weaver, two fullers, two dealers or dyers in madder, four dyers and thirteen parmenters can be identified. The parmenters, whose properties were widespread, probably carried on a substantial trade in clothing for which there would have been ample opportunity among the many large households of the city. The *Tannerestret* properties of Mainard and Ralf son of Ansfrid (**II, 622** and **636**) perhaps indicate an entrepreneurial interest in cloth production. Raymond the parmenter appears to have been a considerable property-owner.[5] The parmenters may in fact have been responsible for most aspects of the tailoring trade, for the *tailator* of *c.* 1110 and the *taleator* of *c.* 1130 were perhaps concerned rather with the cutting of tallies than of cloth. In many thirteenth-century towns the dyers alone among the cloth-manufacturing trades achieved economic and social prominence, presumably by virtue of their special skills in preparing dyes, and as a result of the commercial contacts necessary for the acquisition of their raw materials.[6] This was probably also the case in twelfth-century Winchester, for they are recorded relatively frequently as property-owners and one of them, Roger, held five properties.[7] In the early thirteenth century, dyers were not subject to those commercial and social restrictions which excluded practising fullers and weavers from the franchise.[8]

By the later thirteenth century, there appear to have been a number of weavers in the

[1] A. F. Leach (ed.), 'The Laws of the Weavers and Fullers of Winchester', in *Beverley Town Documents* (Selden Society, 14, 1900), 134.

[2] See above, p. 335.

[3] *Pipe Roll 4 Henry II*, p. 176; *Reg Pontissara* 599.

[4] See Appendix I. 2, pp. 513–14.

[5] **II, 40**, n. 3.

[6] E. M. Carus-Wilson, *Medieval Merchant Venturers* (London, 1954), 222–6.

[7] **II, 52**, n. 1.

[8] See above, n. 1.

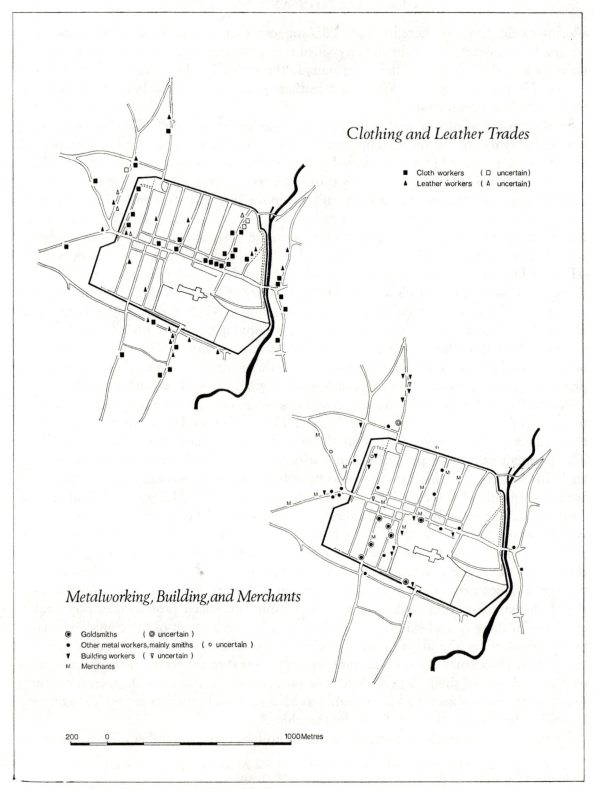

Clothing and Leather Trades

■ Cloth workers (□ uncertain)
▲ Leather workers (△ uncertain)

Metalworking, Building, and Merchants

◉ Goldsmiths (◎ uncertain)
● Other metal workers, mainly smiths (○ uncertain)
▼ Building workers (▽ uncertain)
M Merchants

200   0   1000 Metres

Fig. 23 (a)

Fig. 23. Trades and their distribution in 1148 (1:20,000; for the groupings, cf. Table 49).

Butchery and Brewing

ᵇ   Butchers

▪   Butchers' shambles and stalls
    (▫ uncertain)

ᴮ   Brewers

●   Brewhouses (○ uncertain)

Victualling and Services

▪   Victualling trades (▫ uncertain)
    [including Brewers & Butchers but not brewhouses]

◆   Service trades and miscellaneous (◇ uncertain)

200   0   1000 Metres

Fɪɢ. 23 (*b*)

suburbs of the city, for the creation of the bishop's soke, a suburban jurisdiction, deprived the city authorities of dues collected from looms.[1] A century earlier, weavers may have been taking advantage of cheaper housing and of the possibilities of additional employment in agriculture in the suburbs, for the single weaver identified in 1148 had a holding in the southern suburb, probably outside King's Gate.

The properties of the dyers and fullers were located near the well-regulated streams of the north-east quarter of the walled area, where there was also open meadow ground (**II, 674**) on which tenters could be erected for drying and stretching cloth. By 1148 *Tannerestret* had clearly become an area producing cloth rather than leather. Dyers also held properties in High Street, but these were principally at the east end of the street near the entry to *Tannerestret*. There is a single early twelfth-century reference to a Fullers' Street in Winchester.[2] It probably lay in the north-east quarter of the city, and may have been a temporary alternative name for *Tannerestret* or *Bucchestret*.[3]

Although the weavers' and fullers' crafts were of relatively low status, they were each prosperous enough to render a yearly payment of one mark of gold or £6 in silver to the royal exchequer for their guilds. This payment, first recorded in 1130 and regularly made throughout the reign of Henry II,[4] no doubt guaranteed such rights as these craftsmen enjoyed against the encroachments of wealthier and more privileged citizens. The weavers' payment was doubled in 1165–6.[5] This is important testimony of their prosperity in the twelfth century, for they now paid the same as the London weavers, and no other urban cloth workers' guild increased its payments to the crown in this period. Significantly, there is no record of a Winchester guild of dyers at this time.

As already noted there is little evidence in the surveys of greater commerce. Peter the mercer was a considerable property-holder, principally in the western suburb and in High Street.[6] Henry the merchant, and Roger Mercherel, if he was a merchant, each had but a single holding.[7] The great merchants of the city cannot have been distinguished by occupational bynames. Something of the interests of smaller men can be determined from the distribution of their properties.[8]

The presence of the court and royal administration, as well as the commerce and manufactures of the city, made Winchester an important centre for the money market. The special need for cash by both sides during the reign of Stephen may have helped to line the pockets of a number of Winchester citizens as they did those of Gervase of Cornhill in London.[9] By 1148 at least two Jews had established themselves in *Scowrtenestret*[10] (later to be known as Jewry Street), and by the end of the century the Jewish community in Winchester was one of the wealthiest in England.[11] William Cade, the great

---

[1] See Appendix I. 2, pp. 512–13.

[2] *Regesta*, ii, no. 729 and p. 311, no. xxviii. See also above, p. 234.

[3] A comparable case concerns *Wunegrestret* in the fourteenth century, which was known to one out-of-town property owner as *Dierstret*, the single known occurrence of this name: *SMW* 379.

[4] *Pipe Roll 31 Henry I*, p. 37 and *Henry II, passim*. For the weavers' guilds of this period at London, Lincoln, Oxford, Huntingdon, Nottingham, York, and

Gloucester, see Carus-Wilson, *Merchant Venturers*, 225–6.

[5] *Pipe Roll 12 Henry II*, p. 105.

[6] **II, 35**, n. 1.   [7] **II, 581** and **57**, respectively.

[8] See above, p. 374.   [9] *Regesta*, iii, no. 243.

[10] **II, 443** and **444**.

[11] H. M. Chew, 'A Jewish Aid to Marry, 1221', *Transactions of the Jewish Historical Society of England*, 11 (1924–7), 99–111; *Miscellanies of the Jewish Historical Society of England*, 1 (1925), lix.

financier whose main interests were in Kent, had a house in Winchester in 1148.[1] Walter Chibus, who held moneyers' forges near *Thomeseiete* in c. 1110 was said to have been a usurer,[2] and Conan, a property owner in the southern suburb and the first known inmate of St. Cross Hospital, was a money-lender (*fenerator*).[3]

Goldsmiths were a surprisingly numerous group, and in 1148 had most of their properties in *Goldestret*, *Calpestret*, and *Mensterstret*, towards the former site of the royal palace and the cathedral, and among the houses of royal officials, barons, and magnates. Most of their trade was probably in the manufacture and sale of jewellery, and perhaps also in the cutting of seal dies and other fine metal work,[4] for both of which they were ideally situated. They may also have been involved in money-lending or pawn-broking. The one goldsmith recorded on the first survey in the reign of King Edward held property in *Scowrtenestret*, later favoured by the Jews.

As a whole the distribution of named trades in Winchester in 1148 points to the well-defined character of certain areas of the city. At all three dates represented by the surveys High Street and the western suburb contained the widest range of occupations. Within High Street itself there were several marked areas of specialization. There were concentrations of craftsmen, particularly in the clothing and leather trades, in *Tannerestret*, *Bucchestret*, and in the suburb outside King's Gate. There was, however, no necessary correlation between the concentrations of craftsmen and the density of population in individual streets. The average frontage widths of properties in *Tannerestret*, and perhaps outside King's Gate as far south as *Sevetuichne*, were relatively small, but so also were the frontages in *Goldestret* and *Scowrtenestret*, where there were no concentrations of craftsmen. Clearly our knowledge of the occupational structure of the twelfth-century city will always be imperfect. The vitality and variety of the trades in early medieval Winchester cannot, however, be denied and their dynamism is well demonstrated by the three cases of significant occupational migration which had taken place by the middle of the twelfth century. This was probably characteristic of a period of expansion and prosperity, and the apparent migration of shoemakers may have been connected with suburban growth. In Winchester this organic process continued, with regard to some trades at least, into the fourteenth century.[5] With the exception of the high number of goldsmiths, the trades of twelfth-century Winchester display no characteristic which may be attributed to the royal connections of the city. Royal requirements may have been important in stimulating manufactures and commerce in the tenth century, but by the time of the surveys Winchester, with its substantial population, had generated its own economic momentum.

[1] Hilary Jenkinson, 'William Cade, a financier of the twelfth century', *EHR* 28 (1913), 209–27. After his death Cade was remembered for the capital which he had supplied for trade and commerce, rather than for his financial arrangements with the crown, and this may suggest the principal interest of the Winchester money-lenders: C. H. Haskins, 'William Cade', ibid. 730–1.

[2] I, 64, n. 4.

[3] See II, 963, n. 1.

[4] For the cutting of seal-dies by goldsmiths, see H. S. Kingsford, 'Some English Medieval Seal Engravers', *Arch J* 97 (1940), 155–79.

[5] See *SMW*; the most significant changes in occupational location in the later Middle Ages concern the cloth-finishing industry, which underwent considerable expansion.

vii. THE POPULATION OF WINCHESTER IN THE TWELFTH CENTURY

It is possible to make some estimate of the population of the city on the basis of the 1148 survey. That survey is a record of rents rather than of households, but it is reasonable to assume that each individual entry represented a built-up tenement which in turn represented at least one house or household. The occasional references to waste land, curtilages, and meadow imply that the entries in the survey normally relate to built-up properties. In a few cases it is clear that the entries represent more than one house, and it is possible that this was quite common in the more densely built-up areas. The simplest assumption, however, is that each entry represented one house. On this basis there were about 1,100 houses in Winchester in 1148.

In a well-developed town it seems likely that the number of families was 9–10 per cent in excess of the number of houses.[1] Each family contained perhaps on average 4·5 persons.[2] This produces a total for mid-twelfth-century Winchester of about 5,500 persons. This total may usefully be compared with a more securely-founded calculation for Winchester in the early fifteenth century, using the same multipliers. According to the Tarrage Survey there were about 800 houses in the city in 1417. The population of the city alone was thus about 4,000. Fourteenth- and sixteenth-century subsidy lists show that the soke contained at that time at least a third of the total urban population. In the early fifteenth century Winchester thus contained about 6,000 persons, excluding clerics and the garrison of the royal castle.[3]

Yet at this date Winchester had been subject to a more or less continuous economic decline since 1148 and had suffered severely in the plagues of the fourteenth century. By 1417 the built-up area was considerably less extensive than it had been in 1300.[4] It could be argued that over-all demographic growth in the second half of the twelfth and in the thirteenth century resulted in an absolute increase in the population of Winchester, in spite of its decline relative to other English cities, to such an extent that even after the plagues the population was about equal to its level in 1148. On the other hand the 1148 survey and such other twelfth-century documentary and archaeological evidence as we have suggests that in the mid twelfth century the built-up area was as extensive as in 1300, if not even larger. This is evident both in the extent of the built-up area in the suburbs and in the intensity of occupation of individual streets within the walls. If we therefore assume for Winchester a pre-plague population of 8,000, it seems likely that in the mid twelfth century the true figure would have been in excess of this.

Assuming that the later medieval evidence for family size and the ratio between houses and households is applicable to the twelfth century, the simplest explanation of the apparent contradiction between this total and that calculated on the basis of the 1148 survey, is that the number of houses was considerably in excess of the number of entries in the survey, perhaps by as much as forty to fifty per cent.[5] This may not be an impossible figure, for the fifty-seven separate entries for the relatively densely-built-up

[1] Roger Mols, *Introduction à la démographie historique des villes d'Europe du XIVe au XVIIIe siècle,* ii (Louvain, 1955), 131–40.

[2] Ibid. 100–30.

[3] This will be more fully argued in *SMW.*

[4] Based on the reconstruction of the later medieval tenement pattern in *SMW.*

[5] A population of 8,000 would occupy 1,600 houses, according to the multipliers adopted here.

Tanner Street in the Tarrage Survey of 1417 accounted for seventy-nine houses.[1] Three of the entries in the survey were gardens, and so the number of houses was 46 per cent in excess of the number of built-up properties. This excess is largely to be accounted for by the numbers of cottages in rows on single properties. That may also have been the case in the twelfth century. Unfortunately there is no means of calculating the ratio between the number of houses and the number of entries in the 1148 survey.

viii. SOCIAL STRUCTURE IN 1148 (Fig. 24; Tables 50–2)

Inadequate though it may be for the purpose, the survey of 1148 provides the earliest comprehensive evidence for the social structure of medieval Winchester. The eight hundred or nine hundred persons named in the survey probably represent less than half the total number of the heads of households in the city in the mid twelfth century.[2] Of this eight or nine hundred only about a quarter can be identified as members of a particular occupational group. The sample on which any conclusions are to be based is therefore small. It represents principally the wealthier citizens, and the available information means that there is little more than property-holding from which to deduce the social and economic hierarchy of the city—and less than a quarter of the individuals in the survey held more than one property.

The lords of the seven great fiefs will not be considered in this discussion, for they stood above and apart from the social life of the citizen community. We should not forget, however, that Winchester was the centre of the extensive estates of the bishopric and the cathedral, and of the lesser estates of Hyde Abbey and St. Mary's, and that expenditure in the city markets by these institutions and by the royal household must have been an important factor in the formation and increase of the wealth of the citizens. We shall see that the royal officials with their strong local interests occupied what was probably a significant social position among the community. The service of the bishop, the prior, the abbot, or the abbess may equally have been a means of advancement for Winchester laymen.

The individual occupational and social groups identifiable in Survey **II** have been discussed in the preceding sections.[3] Their relative wealth and importance may be assessed according to the number of individuals forming each group, and the frequency of their occurrences (Table 50), and according to the total rent which each received and the total balance or deficit remaining to them after the subtraction of their rent payments (Table 51). The characteristics of each group may be demonstrated by expressing their rent receipts and balances as an arithmetic mean (Table 52); and this information can also be presented in a distribution diagram (Fig. 24).

[1] See *SMW*. The number of entries in the Tarrage Survey as a whole (809) is almost exactly the same as the total number of houses it records (806), since many of the entries record gardens alone.

[2] See above, pp. 440–1.

[3] See above, pp. 387–439. The groups are identified and classified in the following tables: magnates, barons, and royal officials, Table 30; clergy, Table 31; trades-men and merchants, Tables 48 and 49. The seven moneyers considered here are made up of those named in Survey **II** (Table 43), and those who minted at any time during Stephen's reign and are probably identifiable in Survey **II** (Table 44). Chepping, who by 1148 had been succeeded in his properties by his son Hugh, also a moneyer of Stephen, has not been counted in the group of moneyers.

TABLE 50

Occupational groups: numbers of constituent individuals and their occurrences

Occupational group	Number of individuals	Number of occurrences	Mean number of occurrences
Magnates	10	16	1·6
Barons	13	29	2·2
Royal officials	16	53	3·3
Clergy	41[1]	65	1·6
Moneyers	7[2]	19	2·7
Merchants	3	13	4·3
Cloth workers	25	34	1·4
Leather workers	18	24	1·3
Goldsmiths	5	8	1·6
Metal workers	12	16	1·3
Building workers	13	17	1·3
Butchers and brewers	8	11	1·4
Other victuallers	28	36	1·3
Service trades	13	17	1·3
Sub-total for tradesmen	122	163	1·4
Total	212	358	1·7

(Tradesmen bracket: Cloth workers through Service trades)

[1] Not including Thurstin the clerk, here counted as a royal official.   [2] See p. 441, n. 3.

TABLE 51

Occupational groups: rent-receipts, payments, and balances

Occupational group	Receipts £	s.	d.	Payments £	s.	d.	Balance Credit £	s.	d.	Deficit £	s.	d.
Magnates		19	10		8	8		11	2	—		
Barons	2	6	1		8	9	1	17	4	—		
Royal officials	24	11	0	4	6	5¾	20	4	6¼	—		
Clergy	11	14	0	4	17	9	6	16	3	—		
Moneyers	13	10	0½	7	8	3	6	1	9½	—		
Merchants	3	19	0	2	17	5	1	1	7	—		
Cloth workers	5	8	11	3	13	9¼	1	15	1¾	—		
Leather workers		15	6	4	3	7½				3	8	1½
Goldsmiths	1	15	8	1	8	3½		7	4½	—		
Metal workers		13	5	1	19	5				1	6	0
Building workers	1	10	7		18	0		12	7	—		
Butchers and brewers		19	4		17	2		2	2	—		
Other victuallers	6	4	2	4	9	3	1	14	11	—		
Service Trades	2	14	8	1	12	10½	1	1	9½	—		
Sub-total for tradesmen	20	2	3	19	2	4¾		19	10¼	—		
Total	£77	2	2½	£39	9	8½	£37	12	6	—		

(Tradesmen bracket: Cloth workers through Service Trades)

As one might expect, the social groups of lower status were larger than those above them. Magnates and barons were followed in a descending social scale by royal officials, clergy, and tradesmen, in groups of increasing size. The moneyers, a group considered separately here because of their special interest, and the merchants, for whom there are unusual difficulties of identification, probably stood at the head of the main body of tradesmen.

Most of the occupational groups recorded in Survey **II** were considerably larger than those recorded in Survey **I**, the result of the greater coverage of the later survey. The

TABLE 52

The ranking of the occupational groups

A. By mean rent receipts	£	s.	d.	B. By mean rent balances	£	s.	d.	
Moneyers	1	18	7¼	Royal officials	1	5	3½	Credit
Royal officials	1	10	8¼	Moneyers		17	4¾	Credit
Merchants	1	6	4	Merchants		7	2	Credit
Mean for all groups		7	3¼	*Mean for all groups*		3	6	Credit
Goldsmiths		7	1½	Clergy		3	4	Credit
Clergy		5	8½	Barons		2	10½	Credit
Other victuallers		4	5	Service trades		1	8	Credit
Cloth workers		4	4¼	Goldsmiths		1	5¼	Credit
Service trades		4	2½	Cloth workers		1	5	Credit
Barons		3	6½	Other victuallers		1	3	Credit
Mean for all tradesmen		3	3½	Magnates		1	1½	Credit
Butchers and brewers		2	5	Building workers			11½	Credit
Building workers		2	4¼	Butchers and brewers			3¼	Credit
Magnates		1	11¾	*Mean for all tradesmen*			1¾	Credit
Metal workers		1	1½					
Leather workers			10	Metal workers		2	2	Deficit
				Leather workers		3	9	Deficit

number of royal officials in Survey **II** was, however, considerably smaller than in Survey **I**, especially when we remember that five of the sixteen mentioned in Survey **II** were in fact dead by 1148. This fall in number should reflect the decline of Winchester as a royal capital and is presumably evidence also of a changing society in the city. Nevertheless, on the evidence of Survey **II**, the royal officials were still among the most important members of the community in 1148.

One source of difficulty with these analyses arises from the varying degree of completeness with which we have been able to identify the occupational groups among the individuals recorded in the survey. The groups of high social status, magnates, barons, and royal officials, have perhaps been fully identified by the use of other documentary sources. The evidence of the coinage has aided the identification of virtually all the moneyers. For the other groups we rely, however, on the bynames given in the text of the survey, which denote the occupation of the individual in no more than a minority of cases. For these groups, principally tradesmen, our totals of individuals are therefore underestimates of the actual figures. The proportion of society made up by its lower ranks must therefore have been much larger than our figures indicate, and the moneyers must have formed a very small group indeed. Of all the lower-ranking groups identified here, the clergy probably approach nearest to completeness.

We may now turn to the structure of Winchester society as revealed by the holdings and rents of the different groups. The different analyses produce very similar results. In 1148 magnates and barons were not significant members of city society, whatever power they may otherwise have wielded nationally and in the countryside around. Their properties were simply places to stay when they visited Winchester, neither sources of income nor investments in the economic life of the city. They represented a political rather than a social interest in urban affairs. The remoteness of the two leading lay magnates, the earls of Gloucester and Leicester, from Winchester life in 1148 may perhaps be demonstrated by the fact that the rents from their fiefs in the city were not specified in Survey **II**. We may form some idea from other sources of the money rents which the two earls received from these properties in the mid twelfth century,[1] and it is clear that they cannot be regarded as important landlords in the city. In the reign of Henry I the situation may have been different. In 1130 a number of magnates were pardoned relatively large sums of the city's aid.[2] This suggests that at that date magnates, even excluding the bishop of Winchester, owned a good deal of the wealth of the city. The apparent withdrawal of this wealth was perhaps associated with the slackening of the bond between Winchester and the monarchy, and with the dislocation caused by the siege of 1141.

The royal officials and moneyers were by far the most obviously wealthy of the private property-owners in Winchester.[3] Of the two groups the royal officials were probably the richer and in addition to their strongly marked interest in the city, several of them were also landowners elsewhere in Hampshire and in other counties. The moneyers' interests, along with those of virtually every other group of private landlords in the survey, except for the magnates and barons, appear by contrast to have been confined to Winchester alone. It is not really possible to say whether the merchants also belonged to this élite group, since very few individual merchants can be identified in the survey. The high position occupied by the merchant group in these tables is due solely to the wealth of Peter the mercer.[4] Peter's brother, Ernald,[5] was, however, one of the wealthiest of the private landlords in 1148, and it is probable that he, along with some of the other wealthy private landlords whose interests or occupations are not recorded, belonged to the

---

[1] See **II**, 139, n. 2, and **717**, n. 2.

[2] *Pipe Roll 31 Henry I*, p. 41. The 33 pardons allowed accounted for £57. 15s. out of a total aid of £80. The bishop of Salisbury, the earls of Gloucester, Leicester, and Warenne, and the count of Meulan were pardoned a total of £16. 8s. 4d. The bishop of Winchester was pardoned £12 and the abbess of St. Mary's £1.

[3] A special difficulty of identification concerns the royal officials and moneyers. Here, particularly in the case of the moneyers, we may have included individuals who did not in fact belong to the group. In theory this could affect the estimation of the status of the group on the basis of its rent-receipts and balances. In practice there is little significant difference. If we exclude Herbert the chamberlain, William the al-

moner, and William the marshal from the royal officials, the average rent-receipt and rent-balance for that group would be £1. 10s. 1d. and £1. 4s. 6d. credit, respectively, and its position in the hierarchy in Table 52 would not be affected. The exclusion of moneyers not certainly identified would elevate that group to an undisputed top position in Table 52. The average rent-receipt and rent-balance of the only two moneyers named in Survey **II** would be £3. 8s. 8d. and £1. 9s. 0½d., respectively. If we exclude the three more doubtful identifications (Gaufridus, Saiet, and Stiefne), the average rent receipt and balance of the moneyers would be £3. 6s. 3d. and £1. 10s. 4½d., respectively.

[4] See above, p. 372.   [5] See above, Table 24.

merchant body of the city. Within at the most a decade of the survey this group, which probably included the moneyers and some of the wealthier tradesmen, was sufficiently distinctive and sufficiently numerous to be granted formal recognition by the crown.[1]

The remaining occupational groups, the clergy and the tradesmen, stood at a distinctly lower level than the royal officials and the moneyers.[2] Their mean rent-receipts and credit balances were much lower;[3] the range in value of their receipts and balances was much smaller; and a far greater proportion of both groups had a *small* total receipt, credit, or deficit, than the royal officials and moneyers.[4] The interest of most of the members of these groups in their properties was not that of a *rentier* landlord. Of the tradesmen, the goldsmiths, the cloth workers, the victuallers, and the practitioners of the service trades were clearly the wealthier groups; the building workers, metal workers, and leather workers were the poorer. Leather workers were indeed perhaps the lowest ranking of all the groups identified here.

Some of the individual trades appear to have ranked higher than the groups of trades of which they formed a part. The size of the sample, and the nature of the arithmetic mean, require that such conclusions should be treated with extreme caution, but it may be significant that the mean receipts of the fullers and dyers, 9s. and 7s. 10d. respectively, were higher than those of any other group of tradesmen, including the goldsmiths. The cooks, with a mean receipt of 5s. 10d., also ranked high. The mean balance of rent received by the cooks, 5s. 4d., puts them above the clergy and all other tradesmen, including the fullers and dyers, who had balances of 3s. 6d. and 2s. 7d. respectively.

The hierarchy that we have just described is defined solely by property-holdings and rents and may not therefore represent the true relative wealth of individuals. Real estate may have represented a higher proportion of the total wealth of certain groups than of others. Clothiers, for example, with their workshops, dye-houses, and tenter grounds, may have had to invest more in real property than the goldsmiths whose wealth may have consisted largely of movables. Apart from these two examples it is difficult to say where such allowances might be made: probably, however, as in these cases, the order of the hierarchy would not be affected.

The surveys throw a little light on family successions and the interlocking interests out of which the social hierarchy evolved. The moneyers provide the best examples, partly because we are better informed about them than any other contemporary group of Winchester citizens. The families of Odo and Cheping included moneyers in at least two generations.[5] In numerous properties, links with moneyers seem to recur at different dates, implying sales, transactions, alliances, and other arrangements between individuals and families, by which one moneyer might take over the business as well as the property of another. This pattern may also have been typical of other occupations. In the guilds of eleventh- and twelfth-century Winchester we have further important evidence for communities of interest extending beyond the family and involving social as well as commercial matters.[6]

---

[1] See above, p. 427.
[2] Among the clergy we may have an outstanding exception in Robert of Inglesham: see above, p. 372 and Table 24.
[3] Table 52.
[4] Fig. 24.
[5] See above, pp. 409, 416.
[6] See above, pp. 335–6 and 427.

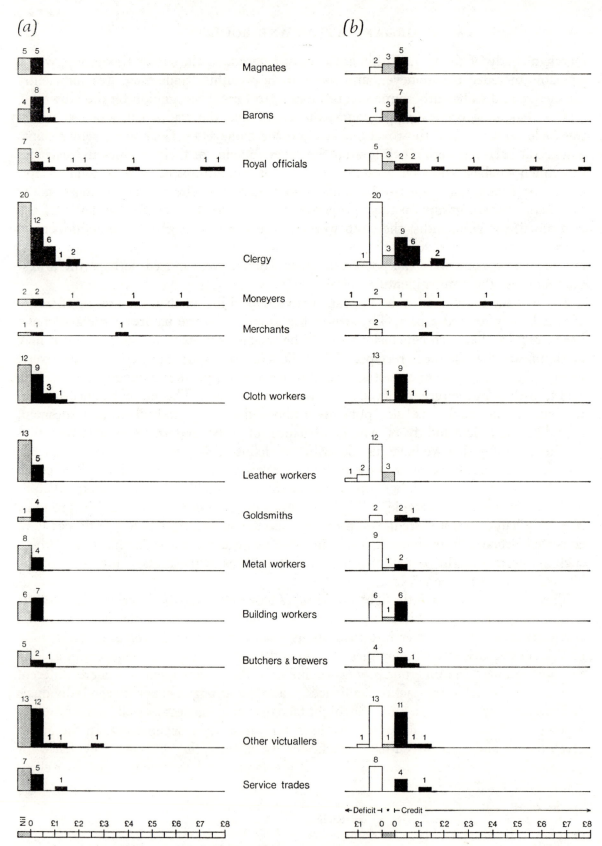

FIG. 24. Occupational groups and their rents in 1148: (*a*) the distribution of total rent receipts; (*b*) the distribution of rent balances.

The figures above the columns denote the number of individuals in each class. In (*b*) the stippled columns (marked by the asterisk on the scale) include those individuals whose receipts and payments balanced exactly, and those for whom neither receipts nor payments in money were recorded.

Several key families in the later hierarchy of the city appear in the surveys. The two moneying families already mentioned may have been particularly important in the first half of the twelfth century, and the ancestors of three of the leading dynasties of early thirteenth-century Winchester may be identified in Survey **II**. The descendants of Hugh son of Chepping, moneyer of Stephen, probably included the wealthy John Kipping[1] who was a reeve of the city in the early thirteenth century, his contemporary, Nicholas Cupping,[2] and the Nicholas Cupping[3] who was mayor in 1243 and a moneyer in the re-coinage of 1248. Herbert son of Westman, probably a moneyer of Henry II, was perhaps the father of Elias Westman, the earliest named mayor of Winchester.[4] Robert Oisun[5] may have been the father of Thomas Oisun,[6] an early mayor of the city, and the grand-father of Hugh Oysun,[7] mayor before 1228.

In 1148 the moneyers were probably typical of the upper ranks of the social and economic hierarchy of the citizens. The tenure of their office was probably a mark of their wealth rather than the original means of its acquisition. Their commercial interests probably extended far beyond the coinage, and we have one example of a chandler who probably later became a moneyer,[8] but the moneyers and other citizens of comparable wealth perhaps represented the highest rank of those whose interests were confined to the city and its commercial activity. Above them were the royal officials who moved also in the migratory and more elevated world of the royal court, and some of whom were important landlords outside the city. Tenure of royal office had probably always been a mark of high status among Winchester citizens, although in 1148 this situation was changing. The men of commerce had probably also enjoyed their relatively high rank for a considerable period, as the evidence of Survey **I** suggests, particularly in the variety of trades and in the importance of the moneyers of the Confessor's reign.[9]

There are, however, traces of an earlier situation in which Hampshire landowners may have played a relatively larger and more prominent part in the affairs of the city than they did in 1148. These signs include the contrast between the size and the value of some of the city estates in 1148, particularly those of the baronial family of Port,[10] and of the abbesses of Wherwell and Romsey,[11] and the numerous links between rural estates and urban tenements.[12] The changing status of the reeves of Winchester may provide a concrete illustration of this development.

In the reign of Alfred, the reeve of Winchester was one of the king's principal thegns. A century later one of the reeves owned a very large and valuable property in High Street. The Winchester reeves of the early twelfth century may have retained something of this

---

[1] *Fine R* 452; alias John son of Kipping, see the Queen's College, Oxford, MS. 1017.

[2] *Fine R* 452.

[3] WCM 1149; Charles Johnson (ed.), *The De Moneta of Nicholas of Oresme and English Mint Documents* (London, 1956), 100.

[4] See **II, 38**, n. 5. He may have been preceded in the office by Thomas Oysun see below, n. 6.

[5] **II, 40**.

[6] See **II, 40**, n. 2, and **139**, n. 2. He witnessed a document as mayor in the late twelfth or early thirteenth century, possibly even before 1207 when Elyas

Westman is first known to have held the office: WCM 12108; see also *Proc Hants FC* 20 (1956), 51, n. 22.

[7] He occurs as Hugh Osion in 1207, *Fine R* 457. John Osion occurs on the same page of the same list. For Hugh's mayoralty see *Selborne Charters*, ii. 75.

[8] See **II, 111**, n. 2.

[9] See above, pp. 400–7 and 428–31.

[10] See above, pp. 372–3. John de Port was disposing of property in the southern suburb within a few years of 1148: Goodman *Chartulary*, no. 453.

[11] See above, p. 356.

[12] See above, pp. 382–4, Table 28, and Fig. 20.

status, but later in the century, as in the thirteenth, they appear to have been drawn from the ranks of the commercial citizens.[1] Tradesmen also aspired to be county landowners, perhaps for commercial as well as social reasons. At the end of the twelfth century, Pentecost, a leading citizen who owned many rents and houses in the city and at St. Giles's Fair, is recorded as holding land at Morestead from the cathedral priory.[2] Substantial holdings of agricultural land were characteristic of the leading citizens of the thirteenth century, including the members of the Oysun family, and there were some cases where successful merchants evolved into country gentry.[3] Although there is no evidence for this trend before the late twelfth century, it is possible that the chief merchants of Winchester were already acquiring country properties in 1148.

[1] See above, p. 424.

[2] For Morestead, see J. T. Appleby (ed.), *The Chronicle of Richard of Devizes* (London, 1963), 58–9. For his properties in Winchester, see St. Denis Cart, fo. 117, and *Cal Chart R 1226–57*, p. 40.

[3] See *SMW*, and for later thirteenth- and early-fourteenth-century examples, Keene *Brooks Area*, 155.

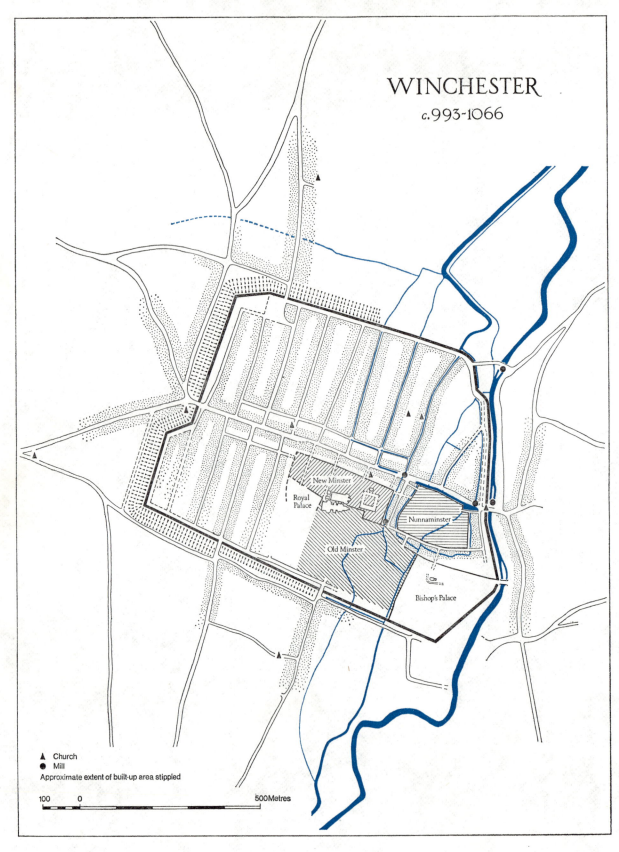

WINCHESTER
*c.*993-1066

▲ Church
● Mill
Approximate extent of built-up area stippled

100   0   500 Metres

New Minster

Royal
Palace

Nunnaminster

Old Minster

Bishop's Palace

FIG. 25. (1:10,000).
Only parish churches known to be of pre-conquest origin are shown.

PART V
GENERAL SURVEY AND CONCLUSIONS

1

THE LATE SAXON 'BURH'

(Fig. 25)

LATE Saxon Winchester was a centre of outstanding and perhaps unique importance in the fabric of the kingdom, a centre which is exceptionally well documented for its period, both in written records and in the available results of archaeological inquiry.

The single most important source for the study of the late Saxon city is the survey of royal rents and services taken in the time of King Edward the Confessor and now surviving only in the use made of it by the compilers of Survey I in *c.* 1110.[1] The existence of a written Edwardian survey finds confirmation not only in the completeness and accuracy with which names of half a century earlier could be recalled and recorded *c.* 1110, but also in the form of the latter record in which the 'twelfth-century details appear both second and secondary'.[2] Moreover, it can be dated. The moneyers named in the *TRE* entries, and those who may probably or possibly be identified as moneyers (as well as consideration of known moneyers who do not appear), suggest that the survey was compiled either in 1046–8, or more probably in 1056–9, perhaps *c.* 1057.[3] The *TRE* details of other towns recorded in Domesday Book show that the Edwardian survey of Winchester is unlikely to have been unique. It is remarkable in being the sole survivor, and as such the earliest lengthy account of any English or north European town.

As it now survives the *TRE* survey is limited to royal interests. Whether it originally listed the holdings of other lords is unknowable, and perhaps unlikely. But it is fairly certain that it was once a more extensive description of royal holdings: there must have been details of the landgable-payers who were later listed as displaced by the king's house,[4] there may have been entries for the streets destroyed by the castle,[5] and there are hints that the listing of moneyers was fuller and more formal in the earlier record, and perhaps related to the king's interest in the coinage as a source of revenue.[6] The *TRE* survey shows, for all its limitations, that Winchester in the reign of the Confessor was a large and complex city by the standards of its time. It is clear too that the size and complexity were the product of a long evolution.

[1] See above, pp. 9–10.
[2] Sally Harvey, *EHR* 86 (1971), 770.
[3] See above, p. 407.

[4] I, 57, 61, and 80/1.
[5] See above, p. 303.
[6] See above, pp. 401–3.

The defences of Roman *Venta* survived to form the frame for early medieval Winchester. The Roman approach roads and gates or sites of gates continued to direct entry into the walled area.[1] Outside the eastern gate the River Itchen, something of a hindrance on the important east–west route through the walled city, was bridged in stone at an early date, possibly in the third quarter of the ninth century.[2] Within the walls in the seventh to ninth centuries there seem to have been large open spaces, at least partly under cultivation, and three—perhaps four—components of settlement: a royal dwelling, the episcopal community, a limited number of enclosed private dwellings, and perhaps some service population along the eastern part of the axial route which later became *ceap stræt* and is now High Street.[3]

This was a royal and ecclesiastical community, but there is nothing to show that it was a town. Comparison with *Hamwih* (Anglo-Saxon Southampton), which was apparently urban by this date, emphasizes the non-urban character of contemporary Winchester.[4]

Nevertheless it was within this framework that a new town was founded in the late ninth century. Around the pre-existing axis of High Street a new street grid was laid out, linked to the defences by an intra-mural street running within the walls around most, and perhaps all of their circuit.[5] A complex series of water-courses, closely related to the new layout of the streets, and designed to provide both a supply of water and motive power for the city's several mills, may have been constructed about the same time, and was certainly in existence by the late ninth century.[6] The initial purpose behind the new foundation was military effectiveness.[7] The new *burh* was one of Alfred's fortresses for the defence of Wessex against Danish attack: refurbishing of the Roman walls must have been one of the first tasks. No trace of this work has yet been found. The recutting of the city ditch, the digging of an outer ditch, and the reconstruction in stone of the city gates were all undertaken during the late Saxon period, but how early is unknown.[8]

It is certain that Alfred had founded several of the Wessex *burhs* before 892, and likely that the refoundation of Winchester, with the refurbishing of its defences and the laying out of its streets, was carried out between *c.* 880 and 886.[9] The physical task involved in laying out the streets was alone considerable: some 8·63 km (5·4 miles) of surfacing had to be laid, involving the use of 8,000 tonne (7,870 tons) of flint cobbles.[10] These figures make no allowances for the external streets, which are likely to be the work of later decades.

---

[1] See above, pp. 260–3, 276.   [2] See above, p. 272.

[3] For a general survey of Winchester in the post-Roman period, see Martin Biddle, 'Winchester: the development of an early capital', in H. Jankuhn, W. Schlesinger, and H. Steuer (eds.), *Vor- und Frühformen der europäischen Stadt im Mittelalter* (Abh. der Akademie der Wissenschaften in Göttingen, Philolog.-hist. Klasse, 3 Folge, 83), i (Göttingen, 1973), 229–61, esp. 237–47. For the palace and cathedral, cf. also above, pp. 289, 306–7.

[4] Biddle, op. cit. in last note, 247, and cf. P. V. Addyman, 'Saxon Southampton: a town and international port of the 8th to 10th century', ibid. 218–28.

[5] See above, pp. 277–9.

[6] See above, pp. 282–5.

[7] Martin Biddle and David Hill, 'Late Saxon planned towns', *Antiq J* 51 (1971), 70–85, esp. 82–5.

[8] See above, pp. 273–4, 277.

[9] See above, p. 273 and n. 7.

[10] High Street, as the pre-existing axis, is omitted from these figures, even if (as seems likely) it was also relaid at the same time. On the other hand, the streets that originally continued the grid over the south-east quarter of the city, and were later lost by the foundation and expansion of the minsters, are included. For the possible widths of streets, see above, p. 282.

The extent of the new town was dictated by the existing Roman defences, but the fact that the new street-plan filled the entire walled area, and was intimately linked to the defences by the intra-mural street, shows that the intention was eventually to use the whole of the available space. As growth in the next century showed, this was a reasonable decision. With an enclosed area of 58·2 ha (143·8 acres), Winchester was easily the largest of the Alfredian *burhs* of Wessex.[1] Lack of knowledge of the defended area of contemporary urban places outside Wessex, and difficulties in defining the area at all if defences were not present (for example, at Ipswich), make further comparison problematical. York in the late ninth century may have covered an area of 35 ha (87 acres), and London was perhaps twice that size.[2] Winchester was thus one of the largest, possibly the largest, urban centre in England at this date.

With the exception of Southampton, the nearest places of any size were Chichester, Wallingford, and Wareham at a distance of between 40 and 60 km (25 and 40 miles).[3] In the immediate area of the walled city there were a number of villages and lesser settlements forming a ring around the town. Some of the nearer of these places may later have been absorbed by the expansion of the suburbs, but their origins go back perhaps to the pagan Saxon period, when Winchester seems to have provided a focus for the settlement of the region.[4] Both these inner places and the more distant villages of the surrounding valley and downland were linked to Winchester by roads that preserved the main routes of the Roman system while extending it with new lines that reflect the increasingly dense settlement of the area in the post-Roman centuries.[5] Some three miles or so from the city the traveller to Winchester passed a marker—a cross known as the King's Stone is on record at one point—an indication perhaps that he was entering the territory dependent on the city.[6] The origin of this ancient division is unknown, but the area involved seems to have corresponded approximately with the ancient estate of Chilcomb, traditionally granted to Old Minster by the West Saxon King Cenwalh at the time of the minster's foundation in the mid seventh century. At an earlier date the estate was presumably a possession of the West Saxon kings and may have represented the Roman or sub-Roman *territorium* of *Venta*. That it was still of some importance in terms of land-ownership and administration in the tenth and eleventh centuries is made clear by its assignment to Old Minster for the maintenance of the monastic table, and by its subsequent treatment in Domesday Book.

[1] The following are the approximate figures for the areas of the larger *burhs* listed in the Burghal Hidage:

Burh	Assessment (Hides)	Area	
		Hectares	Acres
Winchester	2400	58·2	143·8
Wallingford	2400	41·0	101·4
Southwark	1800	30 (?)	75 (?)
Buckingham	1600	?	?
Wareham	1600	37·2	91·8
Chichester	1500	40·5	100
Cricklade	1500	29·2	72·2

The course of the burghal defences at Buckingham is unknown. The Southwark area, which seems too low for the assessment, is based on the hypothetical outline in Martin Biddle and Daphne Hudson, *The Future of London's Past* (Worcester, 1973), Fig. 9. 4.

[2] For York, see *City of York*, ii, *The Defences* (RCHM, 1972), 7–8, 58 (Fig.); and for London, Biddle and Hudson, op. cit. in last note, paras. 4. 35 and 44, and cf. Fig. 9. 4.

[3] For the situation in the twelfth century, cf. below, p. 502.

[4] Biddle, op. cit. (above, p. 450, n. 3) pp. 237–41.

[5] See above, pp. 260–3.

[6] See above, pp. 256–7.

The refoundation of the city in the 880s was followed by a corresponding development in its ecclesiastical affairs. For two and a half centuries Old Minster had been the only religious community—perhaps the only church—in Winchester. But, shortly after 900, two other minsters were established, New Minster in 901–3 and Nunnaminster about the same time, both in the south-eastern quarter of the city.[1] While both monasteries reflect and emphasize the increasing importance of the city as an urban centre, New Minster may have been the direct result of the refoundation of the city, and may perhaps have been intended from the start to provide for the needs of the growing population. No other explanation seems adequately to explain the construction of a great new church, of a size suitable for a considerable congregation, in immediate and awkward proximity to the ancient cathedral.

While nothing is yet known of the foundation of lesser churches at this early date—the earliest we have on record was founded between 934 and c. 939[2]—the apportionment of land within the walls of the city and the development of properties had proceeded at such a pace that complex arrangements had to be made c. 901 to provide land for the site of New Minster, much of the area being already developed, presumably in the previous twenty years.[3] The land of the new borough had perhaps initially been parcelled out in large grants to individual lay and ecclesiastical lords. That this was the case is perhaps suggested by the distribution of the territorial interests of the great lords in 1148, and especially by the way in which their fiefs were intermingled throughout the city. The subdivision of these early parcels seems clearly reflected in Survey II. Originally they may have represented large tenements which were in some ways comparable to a rural manor, being associated both with a territorial jurisdiction and sometimes with a private church, whose advowson may later be found belonging to the owner of the rents. The evidence is obviously patchy and incomplete, but if it does provide an explanation for the blocks of adjacent properties in single lordship revealed by Survey II, then it is clear that large tenements were once widespread throughout the walled city, and were probably a feature of the western suburb. It is more economical to suppose that they preserve the outlines of an earlier pattern of land-holding, perhaps that of the newly founded borough of the 880s, than to imagine that such agglomerations could have been formed by c. 1000 through the operation of an active urban land-market working on an earlier and much more subdivided pattern.[4]

Without extensive excavation designed to reveal the framework of land apportionment in the earliest stages of the Alfredian *burh*, it is impossible to be sure what arrangements may have been made to parcel out the land along the new streets. The imposition of a regular and rectilinear street layout itself suggests that division of the walled area and the apportionment of land was a controlling factor in the planning of the new foundation, and the evidence of the large tenements may hint at the way in which the detailed allocation was carried out.

The encouragement of settlement in the new *burh* would have been a major problem,

[1] See above, pp. 313–15, 321–2.
[2] See above, pp. 329–30.
[3] See above, p. 314. Some of this area may, however, have long been occupied by properties or parts of properties associated with the postulated early use of High Street as a through route and market street, before the new developments of the late ninth century.
[4] Fig. 19; cf. above, pp. 340–1.

comparable in its difficulties, as it may have been comparable in its solution, to the problems facing Edward I in the creation of the Welsh new towns, four centuries later.[1] The Winchester evidence as we now have it may allow a possible reconstruction. When the refoundation of the city was contemplated *c.* 880, the greater part of the walled area was unencumbered by buildings, a deduction which can be made from the fact that it was then feasible to lay out a new street-pattern, an undertaking that would have been virtually impossible if the ground was already covered by buildings. The negative evidence of archaeology supports the view that there were large open areas in the ninth century and earlier. Moreover, the existing royal, ecclesiastical, and private enclosures were small enough to be incorporated within the new pattern.[2] It seems probable also that the greater part of the walled area and of the later western suburb was royal land, and had been so since the establishment of the Wessex monarchy some four centuries earlier.[3] The land outside the walls to the south and east belonged to the cathedral church and had probably formed part of its original endowment in the seventh century. To the north the Crown seems to have retained possession of the land running up to the limits of the city until well into the tenth century, possibly because of its proximity to a royal residence at Kings Worthy.[4]

The way was thus open for laying out a new pattern within the walls. It looks as if, once the streets had been marked out, and perhaps laid, the frontages and the land behind them were parcelled out in large blocks. The parcels probably varied in size— one in High Street for which there is good later evidence was 0·2 ha (0·49 acres or 2,400 square yards); another in *Flesmangerestret* may have been as large as 0·43 ha (1·06 acres or 5,200 square yards)[5]—but were apparently large enough to permit subsequent subdivision as a series of adjacent tenements.[6] This latter evolution was perhaps encouraged by landlords hoping for future profit who could offer generous terms to prospective builders and occupants, or could themselves build for rent or as a speculative investment. Landlords could in turn have been encouraged to undertake their initial expenditure by the terms of the original grants. The complexities of tenure and the associated financial transactions revealed by the *TRE* survey as existing *c.* 1057 (?) show that the operations of the Winchester land-market were then already of long standing and considerable intricacy. The good evidence available for this later period is consistent with an original situation on the lines of that reconstructed here.

If this was the course adopted to ensure a viable community for the new borough, we still have little means of knowing how rapidly its development proceeded. Initially,

[1] Maurice Beresford, *New Towns of the Middle Ages* (London, 1967), 55–225, *passim*.

[2] This statement will be argued in detail in discussion of the evolution of the palace and minster sites in Winchester Studies 4.

[3] The eastern and southern suburbs were probably church land from a very early date, as is strongly suggested by the total absence of royal holdings there *TRE, c.* 1110, or in 1148: see above, pp. 265–8 and cf. Fig. 19. Within the walls, the precinct of Old Minster was presumably alienated by the crown at the foundation of the church in the mid-seventh century,

and may have been further increased, at the expense of royal land, at the time of the establishment of the bishopric *c.* 660. Private estates within the walls must represent further alienations, for longer or shorter periods, and may have been resumed, or exchanged for holdings along the new streets.

[4] Cf. below, pp. 465–6.

[5] Cf. Fig. 12.

[6] An average Winchester tenement in the more densely occupied areas of the city later occupied between 400 and 500 square yards (330 and 420 sq. m.): see above, p. 378.

perhaps, the large tenements were provided by their owners with a principal dwelling and a private church. There would then be ample room for the temporary accommodation of people and livestock from the neighbouring estates of the lord in times of trouble. Defence was after all the initial impulse in the establishment of the *burhs*, and the protection of the countryside for some twenty miles around their primary duty.[1] Temporary refuge would have had to be organized on some workable system of which the large tenements may be in part a reflection. Certainly, the properties in Winchester dependent on rural manors may originally have functioned in this way, and it is interesting to note that they are to be found well away from the central area of the city. They thus suggest that early development was widespread within the walls.[2] The later importance of High Street and the streets leading to the city gates, and the density of their development, suggest that these were perhaps the areas of earliest development.[3] If some such mechanism as that outlined here did lie behind the recreation of a populous centre in the late ninth century, the process would not have occurred overnight. The evidence for the tenth century suggests that the development of the new borough continued for many decades.

The reform of the Winchester monasteries in 964 was followed during the next few years by the adjustment and enlargement of their boundaries and by their enclosure within a single precinct.[4] The ground immediately adjacent to the monasteries was cleared of houses, and the whole area walled or fenced to provide privacy and peace from the rush of the city (*a civium tumultu*).[5] The buildings of all three minsters were reconstructed and enlarged during the latter part of the century and, perhaps as a result of the reform of Old Minster, a separate residence was provided for the bishop in the southeastern corner of the city.[6] Nothing is known of the royal palace at this period apart from the fact of its existence.

It seems clear from this evidence that conditions along High Street, adjacent to New Minster and Nunnaminster, were crowded in the 960s, although perhaps no more so than they were *c.* 901 when New Minster was founded.[7] The reform of the monasteries made it essential to erect a barrier between them and the bustle of the city, and this was achieved, but probably only at the expense of worse crowding in the city centre. The whole of the back street south of High Street, from the later Little Minster Street eastwards, was lost in the process, together with parts of various north–south streets, a total minimum length of 600 m (2,000 feet).

The intensification of religious life in the three minsters would have made a considerable impact on the economy of the secular community. Major building works were under way for thirty years from the 960s, and during Æthelwold's episcopate (d. 984) were probably in progress at all three minsters simultaneously. The artistic output of the Winchester *scriptoria* and other *ateliers* was now at its height.[8] Their productions reflect

[1] Stenton *ASE*, p. 264.
[2] See above, pp. 382–5 and cf. Fig. 20.
[3] See above, p. 378, 381.
[4] See above, pp. 308, 315, 322. For a more detailed study, see Martin Biddle, '*Felix urbs Winthonia*: Winchester in the age of monastic reform', in D. Parsons (ed.), *Tenth-century Studies* (London and Chichester, 1975), 123–40.

[5] *BCS* 1302, Sawyer 807.
[6] See above, p. 324.
[7] See above, p. 314.
[8] T. D. Kendrick, *Late Saxon and Viking Art* (London, 1949), 1–54; Margaret Rickert, *Painting in Britain: the middle ages* (London, 1954), 42–52; and cf. Francis Wormald, 'The "Winchester School" before St. Æthelwold', in Peter Clemoes and Kathleen

THE LATE SAXON 'BURH'

a conspicuous consumption of precious materials by the monastic community that clearly extended far beyond the range of stuffs indicated by the few surviving fragments. These works suggest, as little else can today, the scale of services involved in the support of the artists and craftsmen, and indeed of the whole economically non-productive monastic community of which such specialists, whether or not themselves in orders, formed an integral part.

The emergence by the end of the tenth century of street-names—which in some cases indicate the trades carried on along the various streets—must show, on any estimate of the chronology of name-formation, that the localization of trades was already far advanced in late tenth-century Winchester.[1] Archaeological evidence for this process is still limited, since it can come only from large-scale area excavations in the ordinary parts of the late Saxon city, away from the south-east quarter, and only one such excavation of sufficient scale has yet been carried out, in *Tannerestret* (Lower Brook Street) in 1965–71. Here the results showed that the building up of the street frontage had begun in the tenth century and had been completed by the mid eleventh, but did not reveal definable evidence of industrial activity, for example of tanning, before the eleventh century. All the evidence we have, whether from archaeology, or from Surveys I and II and other sources, suggests a steady and continuous intensification of the built-up area within the walls during the tenth century, beginning with High Street and the other streets leading to the gates and continuing with the remaining streets to north and south.

The origin of the suburbs during this period is itself a reasonable indication that space was becoming scarce to find within the walls.[2] While there may have been other advantages to be gained from living outside the gates, the initial impulse seems likely to have been the ready availability of land. Direct documentary evidence for the emergence of the suburbs is slight, and there has so far been too little excavation in these areas to be of much assistance. Nevertheless, a pattern is clear. The western suburb was apparently the first to develop, perhaps as early as the beginning of the tenth century. It was followed, perhaps in the second half of the century, by the other suburbs. Their maximum extent was probably reached in the twelfth century. The early date of the western suburb is suggested by its tenurial complexity,[3] by the extent of royal holdings (absent from the southern and eastern suburbs, and represented in the north suburb in 1148 by only a single property), by the dedication of a church there in 934–c. 939, and perhaps by its role in the Palm Sunday procession.[4] It seems natural too that the first suburb should develop around the approaches to the city of the most important long-distance routes.[5] Although there is little direct evidence for the evolution of the other suburbs, it must seem probable that they emerged during the long peace of the tenth century, rather than in the years of renewed Danish attack that saw the arrival of the millennium. Winchester men must then have been glad enough, as in 1006, to stay within their gates.[6]

The Winton Domesday provides direct evidence for the condition of the city only at the end of the Anglo-Saxon period and then only for those properties on the king's fief.

Hughes (eds.), *England before the Conquest* (Cambridge, 1971), 305–13.

[1] See above, pp. 233–5, 427–8.

[2] See above, pp. 263–8.
[3] Cf. Fig. 19.
[4] See above, pp. 268–9.
[5] See above, pp. 260–1.
[6] *ASC*, s.a. 1006 (C, D, E, F).

Nevertheless by a close comparison of Survey **I** with Survey **II** we may deduce that in the latter part of King Edward's reign the pattern of land-holding within the city walls, and the general state of development reflected in that pattern, was similar in its essential outlines to the situation more completely recorded in 1148. This conclusion is obviously of great importance in understanding the growth of Winchester in the first half of the eleventh century, although there is hardly any evidence on which we may base the chronology of that growth before *c.* 1057, when King Edward's presumed survey was probably drawn up.

The seven great fiefs, within which virtually all land in the city lay in 1148,[1] had probably come into being by *c.* 1057. The king's fief within the walls contained almost exactly the same number of properties *TRE* as in *c.* 1110 and slightly more than in 1148.[2] The distribution of these properties from street to street was also very much the same at the three dates represented by the surveys. This implies not only that the king's fief was territorially static, but that outside its boundaries and partly demarcated by them there were in the late Saxon period other fiefs which were equally well defined as to their physical extent. These conditions probably also obtained in the western suburb for, although the king's properties there increased in number between the dates of Survey **I** and Survey **II**, it seems likely that their territorial limits *TRE* and in 1148 were similar. The evidence for the other fiefs is less direct. The city estates of the abbeys of Wherwell and Romsey were very much the same size *TRE*, in 1086, and in 1148,[3] and it is a reasonable deduction that their distribution was probably also the same at all three dates. We are less well informed as to the fiefs of the bishop and the abbot of New Minster, although their existence *TRE* is clearly recorded in Survey **I**.[4] It may be a fair assumption however that the distribution of these two fiefs, both within the walls and outside West Gate, was the same *TRE* as in 1148, except for the site of the conqueror's palace, the bishop's lands *de .B.* and *de terra baronum*, and perhaps also the abbot's land in *Scowrtenestret*.[5] The same is probably true of the fiefs belonging to the monks of the cathedral and the abbess of Nunnaminster.

Figure 19, compiled solely on the evidence of Survey **II**, may therefore be taken in general as a diagrammatic representation of the distribution of the major fiefs within the walls and outside West Gate in the reign of Edward the Confessor, as well as in the middle of the twelfth century.

In considering the origin of this distribution we have trodden even further along the path of speculation. There are a number of tenth- and early eleventh-century charters which record, on their face value at any rate, the alienation of royal properties in Winchester. It is therefore at least possible that the six great fiefs (other than the king's) were created over a long period as a result of royal grants. Romsey Abbey, for example, may have acquired its Winchester property from the king soon after its foundation in the early tenth century, or on its reform in *c.* 967. Wherwell abbey may have acquired its tenements from King Æthelred, or perhaps from his mother, soon after its foundation

---

[1] See above, pp. 349–58.
[2] See above, p. 351, Tables 2 and 12*b*.
[3] See above, pp. 356–8.

[4] See, for example, **I, 15, 35, 57,** and **69–72.**
[5] See above, pp. 292–4, 353–5, 357.

c. 980 (?). The thirteen *prædia* in Winchester pertaining to Hurstbourne Tarrant, and granted to Abingdon Abbey in 961, probably represent a donation of a similar nature, which was however resumed after the death of King Edgar.[1]

The fiefs of the Winchester monasteries were considerably larger and may have been created piecemeal. New Minster cannot have acquired its properties before its foundation at the beginning of the tenth century, but the major part of the Winchester properties of the bishop and of Old Minster may have been acquired as part of a royal apportionment of the lands of the borough among the great lords of the region at the time of Alfred's refoundation of Winchester in the 880s. On the other hand, Old Minster and New Minster both appear to have benefited from royal and private grants of land in Hampshire as a whole throughout the tenth century, and could equally well have acquired property in Winchester in the same manner. Some of these Winchester tenements may have been acquired from the king along with the rural estates of which they formed part, in the manner of the Abingdon grant. The king may even have exercised some discrimination in the alienation of his property, for it is clear from the surveys that in the eleventh and early twelfth centuries his fief predominated in High Street, the most valuable area of the city.[2]

Nearly all the recorded alienations of royal property in Winchester, and certainly all the extensive ones, seem to have taken place in the tenth century and were probably characteristic of a relatively early stage in the city's development.[3] The succession of alienations, if such it was, had clearly come to an end by *c.* 1057, for the king's fief was static from that date onwards;[4] alienation may have ceased by the early eleventh century.

We have so far discussed the fiefs simply as whole estates. In charting the growth of Winchester, it is important to establish by what date the fiefs had themselves been subdivided to the extent recorded in the 1148 survey.[5] The evidence of the royal fief, scattered throughout the walled area, together with that of the Romsey and Wherwell fiefs, shows that this stage of development had almost certainly been achieved throughout the walled area by the end of Edward the Confessor's reign, if not, as the evidence for the Wherwell fief may suggest,[6] considerably earlier in the century. The Godbegot tenement in High Street provides a concrete instance of this process of subdivision. Here a large property appears to have been divided into two tenements between 1012 and 1052. The encroachments at Godbegot provide further evidence of the pressure on space in High Street in the reign of King Edward. The colonization by Wherwell properties of the postulated early market inside North Gate is an additional and perhaps very early example of this pressure.[7]

---

[1] *BCS* 1080 (cf. 1144), Sawyer 689, and *KCD* 1312, Sawyer 937; see also Table 28.

[2] See above, pp. 350–3 and Fig. 15.

[3] The royal grant of Eversley to the abbot of Westminster in 1053 × 66 (probably 1053 × *c.* 1057 in view of the evidence of Survey I) included only one tenement in Winchester; see I, 262, n. 1.

[4] See above, pp. 350–3. The losses from the king's fief which were incurred between *c.* 1057 and *c.* 1110, and which were subsequently recovered, may be classified as encroachments rather than alienations.

[5] For which, see above, pp. 340–4 and Fig. 13.

[6] If we accept at face-value the statement dated 1008, recording the nunnery's possession of twenty-nine messuages in Winchester, in the postscript to the admittedly dubious confirmatory charter of King Æthelred to Wherwell: (*KCD* 707, Sawyer 904).

[7] See above, pp. 281–2, 285–6, and cf. I, 23, n. 1, and Fig. 12.

The monetary revenues which these great lords received from their Winchester lands in the Confessor's reign were probably much of the same order if not actually higher than the sums recorded in 1148.[1] Their rent receipts from Winchester properties were considerably higher in proportion to the size of their estates than the nominal sums the king received. There is no pre-conquest evidence for the rent receipts of the landlords lower down the tenurial scale, but we may suspect that many of them enjoyed rent-rolls comparable to those recorded in *c.* 1110 and 1148.

Outside the walls the built-up area of the suburbs was still expanding on the eve of the conquest, but was probably nearing its maximum extent. Outside West Gate there were still tenements and curtilages in that undivided state which had probably long ceased to be typical of the walled area, although a number of tenements appear to have been in multiple occupation and were soon to be divided, and the curtilages were soon to be built up.[2] The suburbs, in particular the western suburb, appear to have had vigorous lives of their own. The existence of the Easter Guild of the men outside West Gate shows that their inhabitants may have led an existence which was in many respects consciously independent of the city within the walls.[3] The western suburb, the only suburb which contained properties in the king's fief, was probably the first to grow and the first to be considered as part of the urban area. The other suburbs probably grew by encroachment upon the ancient estate of the church outside the walls. We know that most of the area later covered by the northern suburb lay outside the limits of the city in the 960s. But this is the only evidence for the extent of the suburbs on the north, east, and south of Winchester before the twelfth century,[4] although it is likely that they were already flourishing by the date of the Norman Conquest.

On the eve of the conquest the city within the walls, with the exception of its public buildings, must have presented much the appearance it was to retain for the greater part of the Middle Ages. Street frontages were continuously built-up; much, perhaps most, of the encroachment that could reasonably be allowed on streets and open spaces had already taken place, and at least one of the types of private house which was to be most characteristic of the city in later years had already evolved.[5] Further development and evolution were to take place at the private level within a structural framework which was already well established by 1066.

The parish churches serving this community reflected its vitality and its growth.[6] Ten or perhaps eleven are known to have been founded before the Norman Conquest. Since six may be identified as tenth- or early eleventh-century foundations, it is probably reasonable to see the establishment of these churches as characteristic of the early phases of the city's growth. Four of the pre-conquest foundations including two of the tenth century or earlier were situated in the suburbs, so that it might seem that the suburbs did not lag far behind the walled area in their development. In six out of the possible eleven cases the evidence for suggesting a pre-conquest foundation is architectural or archaeological alone. If more church fabrics survived above ground, or more were excavated,

---

[1] See above, pp. 356, 358.
[2] See above, pp. 265, 344, and Table 12*b*.
[3] See above, pp. 427, and **I, 105,** n. 1.
[4] See above, pp. 266–8.

[5] See above, pp. 345–8.
[6] For the parish churches in general, see above, pp. 329–35.

it seems likely that we would be able to add considerably to the stock of pre-conquest foundations, and to suggest that a substantial proportion, if not the majority, of the fifty-seven parish churches which existed in the city by the late thirteenth century, were founded before the Norman Conquest. The foundation of these churches may have been undertaken for a variety of motives, but few can be proved. On the Winchester evidence we may suggest that the prevailing purpose was the fulfilment of a community need, whether that community was a family, a neighbourhood, or a guild association. The enlargement of the original fabric of these churches, a process which continued even when the population and wealth of the city had ceased to grow, may reflect their adaptation to a wider parochial function. This was presumably a gradual process, but if the suggestion that New Minster was originally established as a great church to serve the borough has any value,[1] the reform of New Minster in the 960s and its enclosure within a monastic precinct may have served as a stimulus to the parochial evolution of the lesser churches within the city.

The variety of crafts and trades practised in Winchester on the eve of the Norman Conquest must have been one of the most strikingly urban features of the community.[2] The basic trades of the city's economy were probably those concerned with providing food and with the manufacture and working of leather, wood, and iron. Survey I may present a biased picture, but it is possible that the Winchester clothing industry had not yet achieved in King Edward's reign the significance which it enjoyed in the twelfth century.[3] The evidence of street-names suggests that butchery, tanning, and shield-making were each established in their own well-defined areas of the city by the late tenth century. This may also have been the case with goldsmithing and shoe-making. Archaeological evidence confirms the location of tanning in *Tannerestret* in the eleventh century. Other localizations, such as the fishmongers on the north side of High Street towards West Gate, and the woodworkers in the western suburb, perhaps in the street later known as *Wodestret*, may also have been established before the conquest.[4] Certainly, the moneyers were already located in the central part of High Street which they favoured throughout the two following centuries. This latter group figures prominently in Survey I, and we may probably identify in it the commercial élite of the city, with interests extending far beyond the simple production of coin.[5]

The physical fabric of the city implies the existence of a number of trades not specifically recorded in the *TRE* survey. Masons, carpenters, plasterers, and other specialists, as well as labourers, must have been required in considerable numbers during the building programmes of the latter part of the tenth century, as they would have been in the building works of a century later.[6] Most of the private houses in the city were built of wood, but the parish churches and probably a significant number of private buildings were constructed of stone.[7] There would have been a steady demand for masons as well as carpenters.

As a royal and ecclesiastical centre Winchester would have fostered a considerable

[1] See above, pp. 313-15.
[2] For trades in general, see above, pp. 427-41, and Tables 47-9.
[3] No clothing workers were recorded *TRE*.

[4] See Table 47 and I, 30, 33, 91, and 105.
[5] See above, pp. 444-7.
[6] See above, pp. 307, 315, and cf. below, p. 471.
[7] See above, pp. 345-8.

demand for high-quality products. In the tenth century some of the craftsmen who catered for these requirements, such as the goldsmiths, were probably associated with or even members of the ecclesiastical communities or the royal household,[1] but by the reign of the Confessor it seems likely that even goldsmiths worked in a relatively free and open market in the city.[2] We are best informed as to the elaborately wrought and richly decorated reliquaries and crosses made for the Old and New Minsters,[3] but the archaeological evidence shows that jewellery and other personal ornaments were produced in precious metals for the wealthier members of Winchester society.[4] Bronze-working, too, reached a high standard. Three late Saxon bronze strap-ends discovered in different parts of the city show that this type of object was produced in some numbers, apparently for a secular market, in a well-defined style clearly related to that of the Winchester manuscript decorations of the same period.[5] The strap-ends were produced according to different grades of elaboration and expense. The same varied demand is also evident at this period in the range of decorated iron coffin-fittings made for burials in the great minsters.[6] Fine pottery was also produced for this specialized Winchester market which dealt in objects beyond those needed simply for everyday use.[7]

The localization of trades implies also a localization of marketing within the streets which functioned as a whole as the market-place of the city. High Street (*ceap stræt*) was the principal market from an early date. By the late Saxon period there were specialized areas within High Street for the sale of meat and possibly fish, and for the minting and perhaps the exchange of coin.[8] The provisioning of the city and the distribution of its products implied a good deal of traffic with the surrounding countryside,[9] and it is in this trade that markets outside West Gate and inside North Gate may have been especially important from an early date. The North Gate market, which was perhaps particularly associated with the sale of sheep, had probably to a great extent disappeared beneath encroachments by 1066.[10] Bynames indicating places of origin may illustrate something of the close relationship between Winchester and the immediately surrounding countryside. Two of the seven English places occurring in local bynames *TRE* were within a mile of the city.[11]

The *TRE* bynames of origin show something also of the wider contacts of the city with the rest of Wessex. They provide no evidence for the strong link with the northern and eastern parts of Hampshire which they demonstrate in the twelfth century, but since

---

[1] Dunstan and Æthelwold were remembered as workers in precious metals (W. Stubbs (ed.), *Memorials of Saint Dunstan Archbishop of Canterbury* (RS, 1874), 21, 79, 169–70; J. Stevenson (ed.), *Chronicon Monasterii de Abingdon* (RS, 1858), i. 344, and ii. 278) and there were three *aurifices* among the brothers of Old Minster in the late tenth century (*LVH* 25). King Edgar's reliquary for St. Swithun appears to have been fabricated in the royal household (Wulfstan *Narratio Metrica*, p. 141).

[2] There are no *aurifices* in the later part of the list of the brothers of Old Minister in *LVH* 24–30.

[3] See above, pp. 257, 316.

[3] These include gold braids, a silver-gilt strap-end, silver and bronze garter-hooks, silver rings, and a silver brooch; see *III Interim*, 262–4 and Winchester Studies 7.

[5] For the largest and most elaborate of these bronze strap-ends, see *VII Interim*, 326–8, Pl. LXVII, and for the whole group, Winchester Studies 7.

[6] Winchester Studies 4.

[7] See above, p. 433.

[8] See above, pp. 397–407, 431–3.

[9] See above, pp. 260–3.

[10] See above, pp. 285–6.

[11] Worthy and Sparkeford. The other five places were Ashwell, Chitterly, Cricklade, Fordingbridge, and Keynsham. See also above, pp. 193–7.

the evidence of the city tenements attached to rural estates shows that the link was in existence before the conquest, we may attribute the absence of byname evidence to the deficiencies of the record.[1] What little we know about the movements of the late Saxon kings suggests that journeys in a north-westerly direction from Winchester to Chippenham, Calne, Bath, and Gloucester must have been common. The occurrence of Keynsham and Cricklade among Winchester bynames *TRE*,[2] and the widespread use of Bath stone for building in southern England during the pre-conquest period,[3] show that these journeys probably followed well-established routes of migration and commerce. The occurrence of at least one Devon name[4] among the local bynames *TRE* suggests that sea-borne traffic with Exeter and its hinterland was already a feature of Winchester's inter-regional commerce.

The miracles associated with the relics of St. Swithun and their translation attracted many pilgrims to the city from *c.* 970 onwards. The places of origin of many of these pilgrims are recorded, and throw some light on Winchester's sphere of influence. Wulfstan's poem on the miracles, written in 993–4, mentions pilgrims from London, Kent, East Anglia, the Midlands, the North, and the West Country, as well as from abroad. Eighteen of the thirty-seven pilgrims whose places or areas of origin are recorded by Wulfstan came from London, impressive testimony both of the size of that city and of its special relationship with Winchester, a relationship which is more easily defined at a later period.[5]

To whatever extent it was already overshadowed by London, Winchester was clearly a major regional centre in the pre-conquest period. Again this is a situation which is more easily defined at a later period, but we may cite the evidence of the surviving coins from the period between 975 and 1066,[6] and of the number of moneyers at work in the city during this period,[7] to establish the degree of Winchester's regional pre-eminence as a commercial centre. An annual fair was probably already being held at Winchester by this time.[8]

Southampton was Winchester's principal link with sea-going trade. The Solent had long been one of the main areas of embarkation for the Continent,[9] and Southampton had been a populous trading and industrial centre for more than two centuries before Winchester began to develop an urban character in the late ninth century.[10] The contrast between the two settlements in this early period is strikingly demonstrated by coin finds. The continuous series of Anglo-Saxon coins found in Winchester does not begin until the second half of the ninth century. This was the very period at which the long series of coins found in the neighbourhood of St. Mary's Church, Southampton (the site of

---

[1] See below, pp. 382–5, 497, Table 28, and Fig. 20.
[2] See above, p. 460, n. 11.
[3] E. M. Jope, 'The Saxon Building-Stone Industry in Southern and Midland England', *Med Arch* 8 (1964), 91–118.
[4] Chitterly, see above, p. 460, n. 11.
[5] Wulfstan *Narratio Metrica*, *passim*; and see below, pp. 502–3. See Addenda.
[6] See below, pp. 468–9.
[7] See above, pp. 396–7.
[8] See above, p. 287.

[9] Philip Grierson, 'The Relations between England and Flanders before the Norman Conquest', *Trans. Royal Hist. Soc.*[4] 23 (1941), 71–112, reprinted with additions in R. W. Southern (ed.), *Essays in Medieval History* (London, 1968), 61–92.
[10] P. V. Addyman and D. H. Hill, 'Saxon Southampton: A Review of the Evidence. Part I: History, Location, Date and Character of the Town', *Proc Hants FC* 25 (1968), 61–93; *idem*, 'Part II: Industry, Trade and Everyday Life', ibid. 26 (1969), 61–96.

the early settlement), was coming to an end.[1] In the tenth century the settlement at Southampton migrated to the western water-front, where the later medieval town was situated,[2] but its function as a port presumably continued to flourish and serviced the increasing trade generated by Winchester.[3] The Southampton traffic was probably of some significance in encouraging the growth of the south suburb of Winchester.

The best-recorded overseas contacts of Winchester in the tenth and eleventh centuries were those at an ecclesiastical level with the county of Flanders.[4] Winchester is also involved by implication in the political ties between Flanders and England at the same period.[5] That these contacts may have been paralleled in commerce is suggested by the discovery in Winchester of small quantities of pottery of this period from Flanders, Lotharingia, and Saxony.[6] The trade with Flanders was presumably carried on along a route connecting the English south-coast ports with the crossing of the Channel to Wissant or Bruges.[7] Trade with Normandy via the Seine had perhaps already developed by the eleventh century when there is evidence for this commerce from Southampton.[8] It has recently been suggested that much of the great wealth of England in the first half of the eleventh century may have been derived from the export of wool, silver from the Harz mountains being one of the principal imports in return.[9] Flanders would probably have been the main area of exchange in this commerce. As one of the principal royal administrative and moneying centres, and the heart of what was probably an important wool-producing area, Winchester's own trade with Flanders and north-west Germany may well have included this traffic in wool and precious metal. There is hardly any evidence for trade between Winchester and Scandinavia in this period, in spite of the political contacts which existed.[10] Some traffic with Burgundy, the Mediterranean, and Rome may be assumed, but it was probably slight. The discovery in the city of two eleventh-century Byzantine lead seals and two Byzantine copper coins suggest that there were definite links between Winchester and the Levant in the late Saxon and early Norman periods, even if these links were only represented by official visits and pilgrimages.[11]

Before the Norman Conquest, this complex and diverse community had clearly evolved its own hierarchy and social forms. It enjoyed its own distinctive customs as a borough

---

[1] Addyman and Hill, op. cit. above, p. 461, n. 10.

[2] P. V. Addyman, op. cit. above, p. 450, n. 4.

[3] There is a good evidence for its flourishing state in the first half of the eleventh century: Colin Platt, *Medieval Southampton: a port and trading community, A.D. 1000–1600* (London, 1973), 6–11.

[4] Philip Grierson, op. cit. above, p. 461, n. 9.

[5] Ibid.　　　　　　[6] Cf. below, pp. 478–9.

[7] The account of Earl Godwin's expedition from Bruges to England in *ASC* s.a. 1052 [C, D; cf. E] provides a vivid picture of the sea-route along the south coast between Portland and Sandwich.

[8] Platt, op. cit., p. 6. Rouen merchants were trading in London by *c.* 1000 (A. J. Robertson (ed.), *The Laws of the Kings of England from Edmund to Henry I* (Cambridge, 1925), 73. See also Addenda.

[9] P. H. Sawyer, 'The Wealth of England in the eleventh century', *Trans. Royal Hist. Soc.*[5] 15 (1965), 145–64.

[10] For a tenth-century strap-end decorated in the Jellinge style found in Winchester, see *III Interim*, 262. Contact at a relatively high social level in the first half of the eleventh century and even the actual presence of Scandinavians are evidenced by a few artefacts in metal and bone found in the city and by a hogback tombstone and a carved stone frieze from Old Minster (T. D. Kendrick, *Late Saxon and Viking Art* (London, 1949), 100; *IV Interim*, 325, 329–32). For a runestone, see above, p. 329, n. 6. For personal-name fashions, see below, p. 463.

[11] For the seals and coins, see below, p. 478 and notes. *ASC* records two visits to Jerusalem in the period to which the seals belong: that of Earl Swein who set out from Bruges and died in Constantinople in 1052 (s.a. [C]), and that of Bishop Aldred of Worcester in 1058 (s.a. [D]). Note also Ulf and Madselin, friends of Aldred, who set out for Jerusalem just after the conquest: *AS Wills*, no. xxxix.

and was probably administered by a well-defined body of officers. The borough was the king's and its chief officer was his reeve, or reeves, who collected his rents and some other revenues, regulated encroachments, and supervised the borough courts. The wards under their aldermen (who perhaps exercised some form of judicial authority) were probably also in existence, along with a number of lesser officers first recorded in the twelfth century.[1] Among the citizens themselves there were at least four associations or guilds, organized perhaps on a neighbourhood or social basis, and owning halls where convivial meetings were held. Such associations were probably typical of an urban community, and in Winchester there were guilds of priests and deacons as well as lay-men.[2] In no case can a connection be proved between one of these guilds and a commercial or manufacturing interest, nor is it necessary to postulate such a link to explain their existence. But the possibility that one of the guildhalls on the north side of High Street *TRE* was identical with the structure later known as Chapman's Hall, where linen cloth was sold, may throw some light on the possible origin or evolution of one of these associations.[3]

With at least one group of burgesses, the moneyers, we may be reasonably certain that there was already established before the conquest that nexus of family relationships, property holding, obligation, and interest in economic affairs which characterized the higher ranks of urban society in the Middle Ages. No direct successions can be established of moneying or other leading families from the reign of King Edward into the twelfth century, but since several of Edward's Winchester moneyers continued to mint after the conquest,[4] and several properties remained in the possession of a single family over the same period,[5] we may conclude that there was an element of continuity in the social hierarchy of the city in the second half of the eleventh century. The fortunes of some of the leading families which can be identified at a later date were thus probably being laid before the conquest.[6]

The population of Winchester in the middle of the eleventh century was perhaps almost entirely composed of Englishmen, many of whom may have been relatively recent immigrants from the villages of Hampshire and the rest of Wessex. The pattern of immigration suggested by the bynames of origin and the manors to which tenements in the city were attached probably reflects the structure of the trading and marketing complex centred on Winchester, but the relatively widespread distribution of places of origin in Wessex indicates that the city's position as the royal capital of that ancient kingdom was an important factor conditioning immigration, if only at a relatively high social level. In the personal names of the citizens, however, there is evidence for two alien influences, which in a minority of cases may indicate the actual presence of a foreign element. The overwhelming majority of personal names, 85 per cent of the individuals recorded as property-holders *TRE*, were of Old English origin.[7] A small group, 4 per cent of the *TRE* property-holders, were named after the Scandinavian fashion which could easily have been adopted by English members of Winchester society (although in no case can this be

---

[1] See above, pp. 422–6.
[2] See above, p. 427.
[3] See above, p. 335 and **I, 10**.
[4] See above, pp. 413–15.

[5] See below, pp. 410, 416–19.
[6] Cf. below, pp. 475–6.
[7] These percentages are based on those in Table 7, to the nearest whole number.

demonstrated or disproved). A larger group, 8 per cent of the *TRE* property-holders, bore names of Continental Germanic origin, which may have reflected an essentially Norman, Flemish, or perhaps Lotharingian tradition. Many of this group may have been Englishmen by birth,[1] but one had a French byname and may thus be identified as a foreigner.[2] The fact that the two royal servants named in the *TRE* survey bore Germanic names[3] may mean that they belonged to a foreign element associated with King Edward's household. A royal or possibly a trading connection may explain the French birth of one of the Englishmen.[4]

One of the most important aspects of late Saxon Winchester was its character as an ecclesiastical centre. Its three great minsters towered over the rest of the city, and their precincts together with that of the bishop's residence occupied more than a quarter of the walled area.[5] The traveller passing beyond the limits of the city immediately entered the extensive estates of the mother church of Winchester, or those of New Minster.[6] Since the 960s the precincts of the three minsters had been walled off from the rest of the city and the members of their communities, who were probably drawn from higher ranks of society than all but the most influential of the Winchester burgesses, led enclosed and regulated lives. These communities may have been largely self-supporting so far as their everyday needs were concerned, although the concentration of their revenues in the city, their luxury requirements, and their need for servants, probably did much to stimulate trade and employment. There were other ways too in which the three minsters came into direct contact with the citizens of Winchester. The great churches of the Old and New Minsters, and possibly also that of Nunnaminster, were directly accessible from the rest of the city. Before the reform New Minster may have served the urban community as a whole,[7] and the canons of both Old and New Minsters may have served the growing number of lesser churches in the city.[8] The relics of St. Judoc in New Minster and subsequently of St. Swithun in Old Minster attracted citizens and pilgrims and their money. From the period of reform onwards, the direct impact of the great minsters on the everyday lives of the citizens was largely restricted to the principal festivals of the year. The drama, the liturgy, and the processions extended the awareness of the citizens beyond the restricted limits of their daily lives, and were important factors in confirming the identity of the city and its unity with the surrounding countryside.[9] These were benefits which the parish churches, even if they were sometimes served from the minsters, and even if their priests and clerks formed united bodies in the city,[10] could not provide.

The less obvious activities of the minsters—the music, writing, painting, and manuscript production which in Winchester characterize the later tenth and early eleventh

[1] One was probably the son of an Englishman: see I, 133, and cf. p. 174, s.n. *Ticchemannessone*.

[2] Gilbert Bochenel: **I, 40.**

[3] Henry the treasurer and Theoderic the king's cook: **I, 184–5.**

[4] Godwin the Frenchman: **I, 55** and **57**; but see p. 189, n. 5, and Addenda to p. 211, *Francigena*.

[5] See Fig. 9, *c.* 963–1066 and cf. Fig. 25.

[6] Except for a narrow wedge of royal land north of the city, see below, pp. 465–6.

[7] See above, p. 314.

[8] This can be no more than supposition. The church which the young Oswald purchased in Winchester is perhaps more likely to have been one of the lesser churches within the precincts of Old or New Minster, than one of the developing parish churches of the city: see above, pp. 329–35.

[9] See above, pp. 268–70.

[10] See above, p. 427.

century rather than the reign of King Edward[1]—probably contributed also to the character and distinction of the city as a whole. Some works, such as King Edgar's shrine for the relics of St. Swithun, or the cross which Cnut gave to New Minster,[2] were probably commissioned from the craftsmen of the city. It was perhaps as a result of such commissions that the sophisticated style of the monastic workshops came to be reflected in items produced for a larger market.[3] At the aristocratic level of society, where most of the members of the communities probably moved, there was a considerable exchange of ideas between clergy and laity. Ælfric's sermons, perhaps compiled while a monk at Winchester, were one of the means by which such ideas may have percolated down to the burgess community.[4]

The bishop, the prior of Old Minster, the abbot of New Minster, and the abbesses of Nunnaminster, Romsey, and Wherwell[5] also exercised as landlords and residents a direct influence on the lives of the citizens. At the end of King Edward's reign other ecclesiastical lords, including the archbishop of York and the abbots of Westminster and St. Edmunds, had properties in Winchester[6] which were no doubt intended to provide residences for the occasions when church or secular councils met in the city. On these occasions the clerics must have been one of the most conspicuous elements in the population.

In these terms the royal presence in the city was probably not so significant as the ecclesiastical. Indeed a number of essentially royal responsibilities in the capital of the kings of Wessex were deputed to the more institutionalized and less peripatetic ecclesiastical authority. These included the reception of important visitors from abroad,[7] local defence, relief from the ravages of attack,[8] and perhaps the maintenance of the royal residence in the absence of the king.[9] The extensive royal endowments of Old Minster immediately outside the city may in part have been intended to enable the bishop and the church to fulfil this role. There was in addition a close physical association between the royal residence in the city and the cathedral church of Old Minster. In the later tenth century the west end of the minster, directly opposite the palace, seems to have been specially designed to accommodate the monarch on ceremonial occasions. Old Minster and New Minster, with their tombs of kings and relics of the saints, enshrined the heart of the Old English kingdom.[10]

The palace in the centre of the city was not the only royal residence in the Winchester region. To the north of the city there was a narrow wedge of royal territory which did not come into the possession of the church in the Anglo-Saxon period.[11] This included Kings Worthy, two miles from Winchester, where there was probably a royal residence: King Æthelstan held a meeting of his *witan* at Worthy.[12] Still further north, on the route

[1] For the apparent lack of distinction of Winchester in this period, see Barlow *English Church*, 225.

[2] See above, pp. 257, 316–19.

[3] See above, p. 460.

[4] For a useful summary of the evidence on this topic, see Ælfric, 11–21.

[5] See above, pp. 353–8.

[6] Tables 28–9.

[7] See above, p. 392.

[8] King Eadred left £200 to the bishop of Winchester to purchase for the people of Hampshire relief from want and the ravages of the heathen army, with another £200 to be kept at Winchester for whichever shire might need it (*BCS* 912–14, Sawyer 1515).

[9] See above, p. 289, n. 2, for Bishop Æthelwold's occupation of the royal palace.

[10] See above, pp. 307–8, 314–15.

[11] Represented by the manor of *Bertune* (Barton Stacey) in *DB: VCH Hants* i. 452.

[12] *in villa omnibus notissima que Porcig Þorðig nuncupatur* (*BCS* 675, Sawyer 413).

to Bath and Gloucester, there was an important royal residence at Andover, twelve or thirteen miles from Winchester.[1] King Edgar held a meeting of the *witan* there[2] and Andover was the scene of another meeting of the *witan* on the eve of the dedication of Old Minster in 980.[3] The location of these meetings suggests that a royal residence near the city was sometimes preferred to the palace within, and that the palace itself may only have been used on formal or ceremonial occasions. This preference appears also to have been exercised in or soon after 971, when King Edgar gathered into his presence at the *villam . . . quam magnam vocitare solent*, the smiths who were to make the reliquary of St. Swithun.[4] This royal establishment appears to have been situated somewhat more than three miles to the west of the city and may possibly be identified with King's Somborne. In the ninth and early tenth centuries there were other royal residences in Hampshire, at Micheldever and Southampton.[5] Over the period between the beginning of Egbert's and the end of Æthelstan's reign royal charters would appear to have been dated from Southampton almost as frequently as from Winchester.[6] It is important to remember, however, that these impressions are based on a very small and possibly unrepresentative sample. Comparable information is almost entirely lacking for the later Saxon kings, so that even if one may suspect that the king was in the Winchester area, his actual place of residence cannot be determined.[7]

   Kings Worthy (as part of Barton Stacey), Andover, and King's Somborne may be identified from Domesday Book as members of that group of royal manors in Hampshire which contributed to the maintenance of King Edward and his household either in kind or according to a standard money render.[8] Some of the other manors in this group, and others alienated before King Edward's reign, may also at one time have included royal residences,[9] but they need have done no more than provide money and supplies for the king when he was in the Winchester area.

[1] The royal manors of Barton Stacey and Wherwell (the nunnery was not founded there until *c.* 980(?)) formed a continuous tract of royal territory along the Roman road between Winchester and Andover. Easton, which included the land along the first mile of this road out of Winchester, appears to have remained in royal hands until 961: see above, p. 257, Figs. 5 and 6.

[2] A. J. Robertson (ed.), *The Laws of the Kings of England from Edmund to Henry I* (Cambridge, 1925), 31.

[3] Wulfstan *Narratio Metrica*, p. 67, epis. 75–84. Andover was also the scene of the meeting in 994 between King Æthelred and Olaf Tryggvason (*ASC*, s.a.).

[4] Wulfstan *Narratio Metrica*, pp. 141–2, and see above, p. 257.

[5] A charter of King Æthelred was dated 862 *in villa regali que appellatur Mycendefr* (*BCS* 504–5, Sawyer 335). For charters, including forgeries, dated at Southampton (*Omtun, in villa regali quae appellatur Hamptone, in pago/loco qui dicitur Hamtun*), see *BCS* 389, 390, 391, 393, 431, 596, 598, 601, and 602, Sawyer 272–3, 275–6, 288, 360, 366, 369, and 370.

[6] Making some allowance for forgeries, there may survive from this period three or four royal charters dated at Winchester and three, providing good evidence

for three separate meetings, dated at Southampton. For the Winchester charters see *BCS* 447, 594, 622, and 702, Sawyer, 322, 359, 385, and 425.

[7] After the reign of Æthelstan, the place of making the grant is rarely named in the dating clauses of Anglo-Saxon charters. The identification of the occasions on which Edward the Confessor was present at Winchester in T. J. Oleson, *The Witenagemot in the reign of Edward the Confessor* (Oxford, 1955), 45–7 and Appendix T, must be treated with extreme caution, for the dating clauses of none of the charters cited include the place at which the donation was made (see also above, p. 290).

[8] For the identification of this group and the *firma unius noctis* in Hampshire, see *VCH Hants* ii. 401–3, and cf. in general, J. H. Round, *Feudal England: Historical Studies on the XIth and XIIth centuries* (London, 1895), 109–15.

[9] Among King Edward's manors the more likely sites are Basingstoke, the centre of a group of six hundreds, and perhaps Eling, from which Henry I set sail in 1129–30 (*Pipe Roll 31 Henry I*, p. 39). Kingsclere, associated with Basingstoke and Hurstbourne Tarrant in the render of the farm of one night to King Edward, was described as *regia . . . villa* in

The nature of King Edward's establishment in Winchester is difficult to determine. After the Norman Conquest and the enlargement of the royal palace, the royal administration, including the treasury, was a significant and permanent presence in the city, and the royal officials were among the wealthiest private landlords.[1] King Edward probably maintained a treasury in Winchester,[2] although no more than two royal officials, Henry the treasurer and Theoderic the king's cook, can be identified in the *TRE* survey.[3] It is possible that a permanent, and specifically royal, administrative establishment was developing in the city in Edward's reign. If so, this was a development which continued even more rapidly following the conquest.

To describe in outline the topography, economy, and society of late Saxon Winchester is one thing; to compare the city with the other towns of contemporary England on any sort of quantitative basis is a task of a quite different order. And yet to reach an understanding of the urban component in a culture, or of the true nature and function of an individual town, comparison is essential. Description is only the groundwork of such an inquiry. Period by period in this concluding section we shall make a first attempt to see Winchester within the total context of contemporary English urban society. It will be a difficult and premature task, for the materials—on urban size or on mint-output, for example—are not yet all available, or available in a suitable form. This attempt will have served a purpose if it allows others to avoid the pitfalls into which we have inevitably fallen.[4]

A brief comparison has already been made between the enclosed areas and the assessments of the larger *burhs* of Alfredian origin.[5] The growth of suburbs during the tenth and eleventh centuries makes it difficult to establish the exact area of a town during this subsequent period. The extent of suburban occupation is rarely if ever accurately definable in the present state of knowledge, except for the later Middle Ages, and then only seldom.[6] A comparison between late Saxon towns on the basis of occupied area is not therefore practicable. Nor can the number of lesser or parish churches be used as an index of the size and wealth of the population at this early period,[7] for the dates of their foundation are usually unknown. In both these matters archaeological evidence is of increasing importance, but is not yet available in sufficient quantity.[8]

Two lines of inquiry may offer more hope of success: the number of tenements in the city, and the output of its moneyers.

Domesday Book provides evidence of varying difficulty for the number of houses in English towns *TRE* and *TRW*.[9] Neither London nor Winchester are described and the evidence is therefore useless for present purposes unless some figure can be found for the

c. 994 (Wulfstan *Narratio Metrica*, p. 157). Both Kingsclere and Hurstbourne included royal residences in the reign of Henry II (Colvin (ed.) *King's Works*, 940–1, 963, 1005). Of the alienated manors, the most likely sites may be Wherwell (see above, p. 466, n. 1) and Odiham. The latter belonged to Earl Harold *TRE* and was the site of a royal residence in the early twelfth century (Colvin (ed.) *King's Works*, 766).

[1] See below, p. 444.
[2] See above, p. 291.

[3] Table 29.
[4] This discussion of the ranking of the late Saxon town is followed by similar discussions for *c.* 1110 and *c.* 1148, below, pp. 483–8 and 499–505.
[5] See above, p. 451.
[6] See below, pp. 483–5.
[7] But for the situation *c.* 1110, cf. below, p. 486.
[8] Cf. the remarks in Martin Biddle and Daphne Hudson, *The Future of London's Past* (Worcester, 1973), paras. 4. 44–5, and 6. 3.
[9] Stephenson *BT*, Appendix III.

number of tenements in Winchester *TRE*. This may be possible. The figures set out in Table 12*b* show that the number of properties on the king's fief was similar *TRE* and in 1148. This holds true whether the count is based on survey entries, parcels, or habitations.[1] The ratio of the king's holdings to the rest of the city can be derived directly from Survey **II**: any attempt to establish the size of the city *TRE* can only be based on the assumption that this ratio was approximately the same at the two dates in question. It is difficult to know whether this assumption can be justified. But we have argued that the constancy of the pattern formed by the king's holdings is in itself an indication that the city had reached *TRE* much the same stage of over-all development as is shown by Survey **II** in 1148.[2] If this is correct, the ratio in 1148 may be used to estimate the size of the city *TRE* and *c*. 1110, from the size of the king's holdings at those dates, but the results must not be treated as more than a broad indication of the real situation.

On this basis Winchester appears to have had about 1,130 tenements *TRE*[3] and would thus rank fourth, after London (first, presumptively), York (second, with 1,890 tenements), and Norwich (third, with 1,320 tenements), but about equal with Lincoln (1,150 tenements), and considerably above Oxford (990) and Thetford (943).[4] This is a ranking which appears to conform well to the independent evidence of the coinage. In terms of the number of moneyers striking in the *sovereign/eagles* type of 1056–9 (?), and in the succeeding *hammer-cross* type of 1059–62 (?), Winchester and Lincoln seem to have ranked third, about equal (nine moneyers each in the former type, seven and twelve respectively in the latter), with London in first place (seventeen and thirteen moneyers respectively) and York second (eleven moneyers in each type).[5] The relative output of their moneyers as reflected in the surviving coins of the period 973–1066 may be a rather better guide to the ranking of these cities: by this test, Winchester ranks fourth with 7 per cent, following London (24 per cent), York (10 per cent), and Lincoln (9 per cent).[6] When this latter evidence is presented on a graph, type by type, York and Lincoln can be seen to follow each other quite closely throughout the period, with London well above, except in the years 973–82 and 1053–66, and Winchester usually in fourth place.

---

[1] For discussion, see above, pp. 349–51.

[2] See above, p. 351.

[3] The figures for the composition of the king's fief in 1148 are given in Table 12*b*. Similar figures for the remainder of the city can be derived from the same survey. They produce the following ratios for the relationship of the king's fief to the remainder of the city in 1148:

entries	262:816 (1:3·13)	total 1078
parcels	289:872 (1:3·02)	total 1161
habitations	275:825 (1:3·00)	total 1100

Similar figures for the composition of the king's fief *TRE* are also given in Table 12*b*. Using the ratios established for 1148, the following figures emerge for the relationship of the king's fief to the remainder of the city *TRE*:

entries	258:808	total 1066
parcels	290:876	total 1166
habitations	284:852	total 1136

For the situation in *c*. 1110, see below, p. 481, n. 6.

[4] For the figures used here, see Stephenson *BT*, Appendix III, and note that they include persons (e.g. *homines*, *burgenses*) as representing *mansiones*.

[5] For London, see Michael Dolley, *The Norman Conquest and the English Coinage* (London, 1966), 13; York, *idem*, 'The mythical Norman element in the 1882 Bishophill (York) find of Anglo-Saxon coins', *Yorkshire Philosophical Society Annual Report* (1971), 88–101, esp. 99; Lincoln, H. R. Mossop *et al.*, *The Lincoln Mint c. 890–1279* (Newcastle upon Tyne, 1970), 13–15, Table 1; Winchester, above, p. 407, Table 37.

[6] H. Bertil A. Petersson, *Anglo-Saxon Currency* (Lund, 1969), 140–1, Tables 42 and 43. Petersson's figure for Winchester includes Southampton (ibid. 90), for which a separate figure is not quoted.

Separate figures are not available for Norwich,[1] but its mint seems to have been of lesser importance throughout this period and not to have reflected fully the economic status of a city whose importance is clear on other grounds.

The congruent evidence presented here suggests that Winchester occupied about fourth position among English towns towards the end of the Anglo-Saxon period. It was clearly subordinate in these terms to London, York, and probably Norwich, but was roughly comparable to Lincoln. These five cities seem by contrast to have been of considerably greater size and wealth than their nearest rivals. Changes took place within this group after the conquest, and by the middle of the twelfth century its supremacy was being challenged by the rising power of other centres.

[1] Petersson includes Norwich in his East Anglian district, with seven other mints including Thetford (ibid.). There seem to have been five moneyers active in Norwich in the latter part of Edward the Confessor's reign and under Harold II.

2

THE ANGLO-NORMAN CITY

(Fig. 26)

WHATEVER the destruction caused in Hampshire and neighbouring counties by the march of William's forces,[1] Winchester itself surrendered without a contest in November 1066. The leading citizens (*primates urbis*) consulted with Queen Edith, in whose dower the city lay and who was apparently in residence, and having reached their decision, went out with gifts to meet their conquerors.[2] By his annexation of the heart of the Old English kingdom, William opened the way for a flank march around London and his coronation in Westminster Abbey on Christmas Day 1066.

The absence from Domesday Book of any detailed account of Winchester makes it difficult to assess the immediate effects of the conquest in its economic and social impact on the city.[3] By the date of Survey **I,** nearly fifty years after Hastings,[4] some of the results are clear enough, but the immediate impact must be traced today in the changes wrought on the physical fabric of the city.

Within some two months of the surrender the south-western corner of the walled city was embanked to form the site of the new castle, a street outside the walls, a street and a lane within the walls, and the houses along them (including a masonry building), being swept away in the process.[5] By 1072 the castle contained at least one stone structure, a richly appointed chapel, which was a sufficient setting for the important Easter council in that year.[6]

The enlargement of the Anglo-Saxon royal palace in the centre of the city, to something like double its former size, took place about 1070.[7] This too involved the blocking of streets and the destruction of existing property, including twelve burgess houses on the south side of High Street and five *monete*,[8] as well as the secularization of the greater part of the New Minster cemetery.[9] The resulting dislocation affected an even greater area: eastwards along High Street houses or warehouses (*cellarii*) belonging to the burgesses of King Edward's time were occupied *c.* 1110 by forges which seem to have been the displaced workshops of the Winchester moneyers.[10] And the restriction of its precinct set

[1] F. H. Baring, 'The Conqueror's footprints in Domesday', *EHR* 13 (1898), 17–25; reprinted with additions and alterations in his *Domesday Tables* (London, 1909), 207–16; idem, 'William the Conqueror's March through Hampshire in 1066', *Proc Hants FC* 7, ii (1915), 33–9; see now, Finn *Norman Conquest*, 19–23, 64–71.

[2] Catherine Morton and Hope Muntz (eds.), *The Carmen de Hastingae Prælio of Guy Bishop of Amiens* (Oxford, 1972), 40–1. See also above, p. 423 and n. 4.

[3] But see above, p. 356, for the effect on Wherwell Abbey property in the city, and cf. below, p. 481.

[4] For the date of Survey **I** *modo*, see above, pp. 9 and 410.

[5] See above, p. 302.

[6] Ibid., and n. 4.

[7] See above, pp. 292–4.

[8] See above, pp. 397–8.

[9] See above, pp. 293–4.

[10] See above, p. 399.

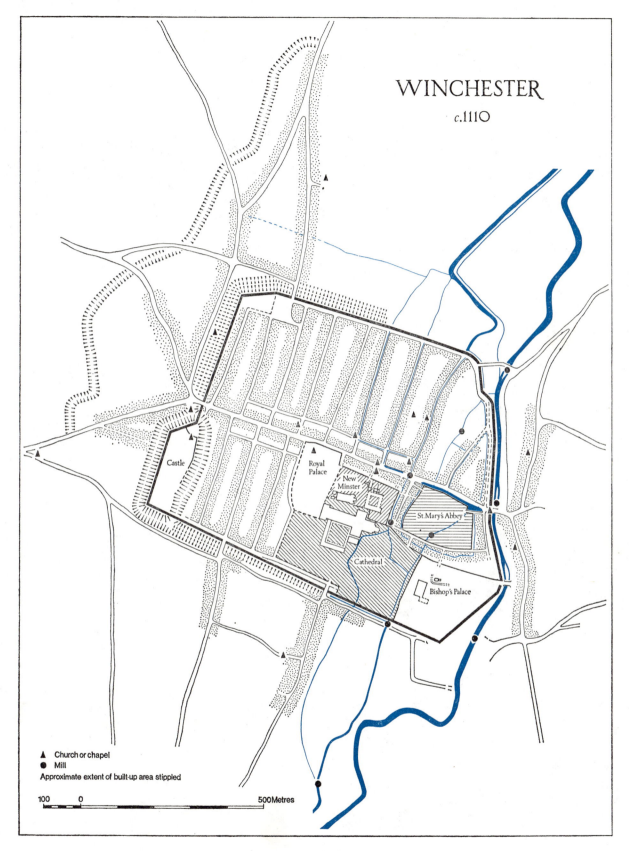

WINCHESTER
*c.*1110

Castle

Royal
Palace

New
Minster

St. Mary's Abbey

Cathedral

Bishop's Palace

▲ Church or chapel
● Mill
Approximate extent of built-up area stippled

100   0   500 Metres

FIG. 26. (1:10,000).

Parish churches known to have been in existence by *c.* 1110 are shown. The castle chapel and the church of St. Laurence,
which may have originated as the chapel of the extended Norman royal palace, are also shown.

New Minster on a course that was to lead within forty years to the migration to Hyde.[1] The loss of the minster's cemetery and its desecration by the extension of the royal palace can scarcely have been welcomed. The citizens had long enjoyed the right freely to choose burial in the New Minster cemetery, a relationship which may reflect the original purpose of the minster's foundation as the *burh* church. When finally the move to Hyde took place, this right was expressly preserved in relation to the new site.[2]

Amid the striking impression made by the reconstruction and expansion of the royal buildings, the disruption caused by their construction must not be entirely forgotten. It is nevertheless hard to evaluate. William acquired the New Minster land by exchange, whether compulsory or not. But we know nothing of how lesser property-owners and tenants were treated. By 1070 there may have been time and reason to reach agreements: this can scarcely have been the case in 1067 when buildings in the south-western corner of the city were cleared to make way for the castle. In these actions we can see some urban reflection of the damage caused by the conquest in the surrounding countryside.[3]

Unlike the rural areas, the city must have benefited almost immediately from the massive investment in public works which was to continue unabated for the next fifty or sixty years. The enlargement of the royal palace, and the construction of a new hall and accompanying buildings,[4] later described (although not by an eye-witness) as second neither in design nor size to those at London,[5] was rapidly followed by the rebuilding of the cathedral.[6] By the second decade of the twelfth century, when this immense church was approaching completion,[7] further works were already in progress, the building of Hyde Abbey, the reconstruction of Nunnaminster, and the rebuilding of the bishop's palace at Wolvesey.[8] It is hard to avoid the impression that the royal works at castle and palace in the 1060s and 1070s, the forty-year campaign at the cathedral, and the subsequent activity at Hyde, Nunnaminster, and Wolvesey, had each in their turn represented the maximum building effort practicable at any one time. Whether or not the sequence in which the extension of the palace preceded the rebuilding of the cathedral, which was itself followed by the move of New Minster to Hyde, formed part of a long-term design carried out over forty years—and thus must remain uncertain[9]—the availability of finance, men, and materials will have imposed their own limitations, especially on the rate of progress.

Whatever the doubts regarding any over-all concept in planning or architectural terms, there can be no doubt that the reconstruction of palace and cathedral demonstrated, and were intended to demonstrate, the success and finality of the Norman acquisition of the Old English state, and in particular the annexation of its royal capital. Although nothing is yet known of William's palace hall, it is probably no coincidence that it was at Winchester rather than London that he chose to have it built.[10] The existence of a relatively

[1] See above, pp. 317–18.   [2] See above, p. 314.

[3] See above, p. 470, n. 1.

[4] The kitchen is specifically mentioned, and the various words used to describe the palace (see above, p. 295, n. 3) suggest the whole complex of buildings which went to make up an early royal residence.

[5] i.e. Westminster. See above, p. 295 and n. 1.

[6] See above, pp. 308–12.

[7] See above, p. 309.

[8] See above, pp. 318, 322, 324.

[9] See above, p. 311.

[10] William I acquired stone from Caen for works at Westminster, but their nature is unknown: Colvin (ed.) *King's Works*, i. 491.

new hall at Westminster may have had little to do with this decision, and did not deter William Rufus from its rebuilding thirty years later. It is, however, the reconstruction of the cathedral which provides the clearest indication of its builders' purpose. By 1079 Old Minster was barely a century old in its final form, a church of considerable size and of monumental aspect. That it was nevertheless old-fashioned both in liturgical terms and in architecture cannot be doubted. It was replaced by a new cathedral of quite exceptional proportions, equalled in its time only by Cluny III, and over half as large again as the Confessor's new church at Westminster.[1] If the architectural style and liturgical planning of the new church reflect the tastes of its Norman builders, its grand scale suggests the special place of the city in the kingdom, and its siting emphasizes the ceremonial relationship between the cathedral and the palace.[2]

As the eleventh century came to an end, and the cathedral neared completion, the monumental architecture of the new royal and ecclesiastical buildings in the centre of the city bore witness on a scale nowhere else attempted to the measure of the Norman domination. Here, as probably in the later years of Anglo-Saxon rule, the Norman kings wore their crown at Easter, on the most important feast of the Christian year.[3] Here too was the principal repository of the king's treasure, now evolving into a working department, and here (or perhaps in the castle) sessions of the Exchequer were being held soon after the beginning of the twelfth century.[4]

It is important that some characterization of this moment should have been attempted, for it was almost at once to pass. The last royal burial to take place in Winchester was that of William Rufus in August 1100,[5] and although the cathedral would in future be the occasional setting of royal ceremonial, this would reveal the inconveniences arising from the abandonment of the old royal palace, as at the coronation of Richard I in 1194,[6] or would arise from reasons of dynastic expediency or public security, as with the baptism of Prince Arthur in 1486, or the marriage of Queen Mary to Philip of Spain in 1554. During the first decade of the twelfth century the custom of the royal court in celebrating Easter at Winchester (when the king was in England) was also broken,[7] and by the end of Henry I's reign the castle seems to have replaced the royal palace, not only as the repository of the treasure, but also as the king's residence in the city.[8] The severing of the close tie between residence and cathedral is probably as sharp an indication as any that the nature of the relationship between Winchester and the crown had undergone an

---

[1] Cf. the remarks by A. W. Clapham in *Archaeologia*, 83 (1933), 236.

[2] See above, p. 311.

[3] See above, p. 296.

[4] See above, p. 291 and the references cited in nn. 1–8, and cf. p. 292, n. 1. For the latest survey of this question, see E. J. Kealey, *Roger of Salisbury* (Berkeley and Los Angeles, Calif., 1972), 42–62, esp. the Abingdon and Plympton cases discussed on pp. 46 and 61–2, and the charter printed on p. 245, with its notes.

[5] The Norman kings were usually buried in abbeys of their own foundation, even if, as in the case of William I and Henry I, this involved delays and the transportation of the body over long distances. William I was buried in the Abbaye aux Hommes,

the monastery of St. Stephen at Caen; Henry I at Reading; Stephen at Faversham. William II is the only exception. Whether his burial at Winchester should be seen as the last in an earlier tradition, or simply as a convenience, following his death in the New Forest, is uncertain. It may be that Winchester Cathedral, the first part of which was dedicated in his reign, and for which he had given stone (see above, p. 308), and may have made other grants (see below, p. 478), was felt to be particularly appropriate for his burial. The circumstances and the ceremony were, however, equally inauspicious; *Gesta Regum*, cap. 333 (p. 379).

[6] See above, p. 297.

[7] See above, p. 296.

[8] See above, pp. 296–7, 303–5.

essential change. Henceforth the castle, strengthened and remodelled on frequent occasions from at least as early as the beginning of the twelfth century, was to be the sole royal house in Winchester. By the second half of the century there is ample evidence for the existence within its walls of that whole 'complex of halls, chambers, and chapels which constituted a medieval palace'.[1]

At the same time as Winchester was declining to the status of an important but no longer exceptional residence, the position of the bishop and his cathedral church seems to have been on the increase, and perhaps not only in architectural and topographical terms. The results of this shift in emphasis would be seen most clearly in the part played by Henry of Blois in the city's affairs in 1141, and in his ordering of the 1148 survey, but the change was already apparent in the episcopate of his predecessor, William Giffard (1100–29). The completion of the Norman cathedral and its monastic buildings, probably before the end of Giffard's reign, was accompanied by the acquisition of an extensive area to the north of the church, following the move of New Minster to Hyde in 1110.[2] This process was completed after the destruction of the royal palace in the 1140s. Simultaneously, the physical development of the bishop's palace at Wolvesey was taking place.[3] A stone hall of very considerable size was added to the pre-existing late-Saxon complex by Bishop Giffard, probably not much later than *c.* 1110. Apparently intended as a residential block, and incorporating a new chapel, this hall was itself a palace by the contemporary standards of the continent.

Within eighty years of the conquest the greater public buildings of Winchester had been entirely rebuilt. The royal palace had passed through the period of its greatest development, and had vanished entirely. Such fundamental changes do not seem to have affected the general fabric of the city, where by contrast the dominant theme is one of continuity. This may in part reflect the inadequacy of the record: were we able to follow the structural history of many separate houses, and to treat the result numerically, a different picture might emerge. But there is no archaeological evidence of any major change in house type or building technique at the time of the conquest, or until the technical innovations of two or more centuries later. Although the houses of the greater officials, barons, and magnates may have been built or rebuilt to suit Norman taste, there is no reason to suppose this would necessarily have had any rapid influence on the general stock of domestic housing.[4]

Survey **I** does seem, however, to reflect a phase of fairly rapid change in the streets of the city between 1066 and *c.* 1110, a change more rapid than that of the succeeding half-century.[5] While many of these changes, whether the blocking of streets and lanes or encroachments upon them, were expressly or probably the result of the construction or extension of the greater public buildings, others resulted from the extension of private houses, and perhaps from pressure on space in the commercial areas in and immediately adjacent to High Street. These pressures were already apparent before the conquest, as may be seen in the encroachments at Godbegot, or in the colonization by Wherwell properties of the postulated early market inside North Gate.[6] Earlier still, the reorganization

---

[1] See above, p. 303. [2] See above, p. 317. [3] See above, p. 324.
[4] See above, p. 345–8. [5] See above, p. 281. [6] See above, **I**, 23, n. 1, and pp. 281–2, 285–6.

of the monastic precincts during the 960s and 970s had greatly altered the streets in the south-eastern quarter of the city.[1] In all other essentials, however, the street plan remained, and has remained, as it was first laid down towards the end of the ninth century. Only on the site of the former royal palace were there any further changes of importance during the twelfth century, when the area was recolonized after the events of 1141, but apparently before the survey of 1148.[2]

The defensive circuit remained unaltered but was strengthened in the area of the castle, probably in 1067, by the digging of a new and presumably enlarged ditch.[3] Evidence for work elsewhere on the defences in the Norman period is entirely structural, but sufficient has been noted—at West Gate, at the site of Floodstock mill, and near the south-east corner of the city wall[4]—to show that the walls and gates were not neglected. If the evidence of reconstruction at West Gate is of general relevance, the defences may even have been considerably remodelled during this period.

By contrast with the greater buildings of church and state, the remainder of the city, in its defences and in its streets, presents a picture of continuous evolution from the pre-conquest period, with renewal and the intensification of commercial pressures as the main agents of change and growth.

An outstanding feature of the Hampshire Domesday is the fall in value of many estates between 1066 and the time when their subsequent owners received them, followed by their ensuing recovery before 1086.[5] The comparative figures for Winchester do not exist, but the sequence of sequestration and rebuilding that we have seen, together with the effect of massive capital investment in new works, suggests that the fortunes of the city may have mirrored those of the county, and may possibly have recovered even more quickly. No monetary comparison is feasible between the rents due to King Edward and those owed to King Henry I in Winchester.[6] Only in relation to the Wherwell estate can we make a direct comparison between *TRE* and 1086. Here the value had decreased from 50s. to 30s., and had still not recovered its *TRE* value by 1148, while the comparable estate of Romsey Abbey declined in value after 1086.[7] The sample is, however, far too small to provide any over-all picture. As far as the evidence goes, it suggests that these three fiefs were complete by the middle of the eleventh century, that the Wherwell and Romsey estates were then at the peak of their development, and that the king's fief remained static until it underwent a distinct decline in Stephen's reign. In so far as this evidence can be applied to Winchester as a whole, it reinforces the impression obtained from several different sources that the city was highly developed both in its economy and in the intensity of its settlement before the conquest, and that its subsequent history, at least from the early twelfth century, was a gradual decline.

The clearest indication of the social impact of the conquest is provided by the changes in the giving of personal names.[8] In the time of King Edward over 70 per cent of the

---

[1] See above, p. 278, n. 1.
[2] See above, pp. 299–301.
[3] See above, p. 303.
[4] See above, pp. 273, 277, 283.
[5] R. Welldon Finn in *DGSEE* 315–18; cf. Finn *Norman Conquest*, 64–71.

[6] There had been some development on the royal fief by *c.* 1110, notably outside West Gate, but the crown also lost control of some properties, not all of which were subsequently recovered; see above, pp. 350–1.
[7] See above, p. 356.
[8] See above, pp. 183–91 and cf. Figs. 1 and 2.

Winchester citizens recorded in Survey **I** bore native names; by *c*. 1110 this figure had been halved.[1] The corresponding increase in foreign names was almost entirely accounted for by names of Continental Germanic origin, names, that is, of essentially Norman fashion. To what extent this does indeed reflect changing fashion, rather than an actual change in the composition of the population, it is hard if not impossible to define. In Winchester especially, in what was in many ways the leading city of the kingdom, social pressures would have worked with particular speed to encourage the adoption of new modes. Royal officials were the foremost men in city society, and the principal merchants would have come into close and frequent contact with the royal household.

By contrast with these changes in nomenclature, there is in Survey **I** a good deal of evidence for continuity of tenure within a single family,[2] and the cases where a Norman lord held property in *c*. 1110 do not necessarily imply changes in occupancy. Nevertheless, taking only those persons identifiable as of Norman family, and omitting all those bearing Norman names but not otherwise identified (and hence conceivably of English origin), it is possible to see that by *c*. 1110 Normans had replaced Anglo-Saxons as payers of landgable in 19 per cent or 57 out of the 296 separately enumerated properties. It is of course impossible to decide whether this scale of replacement on the king's fief was representative of the situation in the city as a whole, or whether it had been influenced by royal initiative. It is moreover a minimum picture, for some (but how many is uncertain) of the further 42 per cent or 125 landgable-payers with Norman names, would have been of Norman stock.[3] The actual level of replacement of English by Norman tenants must lie somewhere between the 19 per cent quoted above and the total of 61 per cent of Winchester citizens who in *c*. 1110 bore Norman names and were the principal tenants of land on the royal fief.

The evidence for continuity of English tenure between *TRE* and *c*. 1110 is somewhat easier to handle, for few if any Norman tenants would have born English names. The figure will again be a minimum, because it is uncertain how many Englishmen are concealed within the 42 per cent of otherwise unidentified landgable-payers with Norman names. Just over 27 per cent of those paying landgable on royal land in Winchester in *c*. 1110 had Old English names, some 80 cases out of the 296 entries in the survey. These include at least eight instances of sons succeeding their fathers,[4] and two where an Englishman had been succeeded by his wife.[5]

The distribution of these English tenants on the royal fief is very uneven: there were very few in High Street and *Goldestret* (absolutely, and as a percentage both of the entries in the street, and of the total of English names), whereas outside West Gate, perhaps in

---

[1] Table 6. The proportions are even more striking if calculated on the basis of the estimated number of occurrences: 85 per cent *TRE* compared to 30 per cent *c*. 1110 (Table 7).

[2] e.g. **I**, **85**, n. 1, but the best evidence is provided by the moneyers, whose continuity of interest in specific properties and areas of the city can be demonstrated; see above, pp. 410, 416–19, 421 and Tables 34–6 and 38–40. The moneyers may, however, be a special case, an instance of continuity in administrative practice,

rather than representative of any general continuity in tenure.

[3] For some examples of Englishmen with Norman names, cf. **I**, **133, 208, 252** (and **258**), and **253**.

[4] **I, 85, 133, 135, 139, 150, 155, 190,** and **203**.

[5] **I, 160** and **184**. In the latter case, it must remain uncertain whether Henry the treasurer was an Englishman or a Norman follower of the Confessor: continuity between *TRE* and *c*. 1110 is unaffected.

Brudenestret (if the 'lands of the barons' are included), in *Tannerestret*, and above all in *Bucchestret*, there were concentrations of Englishmen amounting in the last case to at least 61 per cent of the entries for the street, and as many as 20 per cent of the English landgable-payers recorded in Survey **I**. The conclusions seem evident: there was a considerable degree of continuity in Winchester society between *TRE* and *c.* 1110, but by the latter date English occupancy of the greater streets—High Street and the north–south axis of *Scowrtenestret* and *Goldestret*—was limited. This is not to say that English tenants were now necessarily of lower status than before, or were especially associated with industrial activities, as their presence in *Tannerestret* or *Bucchestret* might seem at first sight to suggest. Their importance in *Brudenestret* and on the 'lands of the barons' there indicates that their status may not have declined, an impression which is strengthened by the standing of individual Englishmen,[1] and by the connection between English tenants and the coinage.[2] Of the sixteen moneyers who struck coins for Henry I in Winchester, eleven bore OE names, a further three may have been English, and only two, neither of whom is known to have struck coins before *c.* 1113, had OG names.[3] The moneyers were obviously a special case, but in Winchester they would have helped to maintain the position of the English community.

The strength of English continuity at a relatively high level of urban society may suggest that the changes seen in the guilds of the city about the time of the conquest were due more to the unstable nature of these associations, than to any real breakdown in the forms of Anglo-Saxon community life.[4] The evidence for a general continuity must not conceal, however, the very real and sudden changes that had taken place. The principal streets of the city were no longer the residence of the leading men of the English community.

Whatever the short-term effects of the conquest on the commercial and social life of the city, an over-all impression of economic prosperity is provided by the survey of *c.* 1110. It is a prosperity, moreover, which seems to derive directly from an economic basis already long established before the date of the survey.

The pressure for space apparent in the commercial areas of the city before the conquest has already been mentioned. The subdivision of tenements in High Street between *TRE* and *c.* 1110 may be a further example of this same pressure,[5] and, as with the changes to the streets, so too this subdivision seems to perpetuate trends which were already established in pre-conquest times.[6] The importance of the suburbs was increasing in *c.* 1110. The northern suburb may have extended by this date as far north as *Palliesputte* (**I**, 165). And in the western suburb there is clearer evidence not only for an increased intensity of development in the period up to *c.*1110, but also for the appearance of rows of houses or cottages to let.[7] This latter situation may be a new factor,

---

[1] Cf. **I**, **10**, **71**, **73**, and **134**, for example, for Cheping son of Alveva.

[2] See above, pp. 407–15.

[3] See Table 41. Stigant, Tovi, and Wimund may have been English; Ainulf and Engelram are OG names. Cf. above, pp. 147 f., s.nn.

[4] See above, pp. 335–6 and 427.

[5] See above, p. 343.

[6] See above, pp. 340–1, 457.

[7] See above, p. 344. The importance of the western suburb is seen also in the number of its churches: it contained at least seven, compared with two in the northern suburb, two (four, if Winnall and St. Giles are included) in the eastern suburb, and six (three of which were outside King's Gate) in the two southern suburbs together.

but one that seems to have been confirmed by the time of Survey **II**. It was to become a characteristic feature of the medieval town.

The variety of trades recorded in the survey of *c.* 1110 strengthens the impression of a varied and extensive commercial life, but the evidence is such that it is not possible to make any real comparison with *TRE* or 1148.[1] The list of thirteen trades revealed by the occupational bynames is incomplete, but can be extended both by reference to trades known to have been established in the city already before the conquest, and by consideration of the archaeological evidence. The investment in major building that was so marked a feature of Winchester in the half century following the conquest finds, for example, little reflection in the *c.* 1110 survey, although it must be remembered that this survey deals only with the king's fief. The many trades that would have been involved in the supply and implementation of so large a programme would have included masons, glaziers, sawyers, carpenters, joiners, plasterers, smiths, plumbers,[2] coopers, carriers, painters, lime burners, and other specialists, as well as labourers. The archaeological evidence shows the presence also of iron and bronze working (including the more specialized work of bell-founding which was perhaps undertaken by out-of-town craftsmen), and to this the coinage adds the assaying of silver and probably implies the working of gold, in view of the business connections of the moneyers. Weavers, dyers, fullers, and millers (or at least mills) are known from other evidence, but have left little trace at this date in the archaeological record. Bone-working, including comb-making, is also apparent in the archaeological evidence, although on no large scale. There is evidence for extensive pottery making. From all these sources some forty trades can be accounted for without adding minor specializations, a total nearly as large as that recorded in 1148.[3] It seems certain that this figure for *c.* 1110 is an underestimate; a more accurate picture may prove feasible when the archaeological evidence has been further studied. The differences in the trades recorded on the king's fief *TRE, c.* 1110, and in 1148 suggest only that as great a variety of trades was practised there *TRE* or *c.* 1110, as in 1148, when twenty-three separate trades were recorded.[4] Little can be said of the distribution of trades in the early twelfth century, but what information there is confirms the pattern already observable before the conquest: tanners held property in *Tannerestret* and *Bucchestret*, and the butchers had their stalls in High Street, and had already begun their slow migration westwards.[5] Millers, by contrast, had to remain close to their source of energy; we hear little of them in early twelfth-century Winchester, but earlier evidence suggests that there were at least seven mills within or immediately adjacent to the walled area.[6]

The commercial activity of the city would have been most obvious in its markets, which in the Norman period were the same as before the conquest, principally in High Street, but also perhaps outside West Gate and inside North Gate.[7] There had been

---

[1] See above, pp. 428–31 and Table 47.

[2] Their importance in the roofing of the new buildings scarcely needs stressing. The provision of piped water to the bishop's palace and perhaps to the cathedral priory in the earlier part of the twelfth century demonstrates the scale and sophistication of their work in both design and execution. The Wolvesey supply is still operative today. See above, p. 284.

[3] See above, pp. 428–31 and Table 48.

[4] See above, p. 431.   [5] See above, pp. 429, 431.

[6] See above, pp. 282–4.

[7] See above, pp. 285–6.

encroachment on to the North Gate area *TRE*, but the continuing use of the name *Sapalanda* 'sheep-land' (?) may imply that some market function still persisted as late as *c.*1110.[1] In High Street the destruction of burgess houses, by implication *in mercato*, to make way for the extension of the palace *c.* 1070 may have restricted market activities in that part of the street, and may perhaps be reflected not only in the westward migration of the butchers' stalls, but also in the emergence since the time of King Edward of a new market further west up High Street 'at the three minsters'.[2]

By the beginning of the twelfth century the annual fair in September may already have been the most striking demonstration of the city's commercial life. Held on the eastern hill the fair probably had by this time a long history as a regional marketing centre and its European connections, not specifically recorded before the early thirteenth century, were perhaps already developing much earlier. William II's grant to the bishop and monks of the cathedral in 1096 of a three-day fair at the church of St. Giles probably represents therefore not the beginning of the fair, but rather an assignment of revenue from an existing source, made over to the cathedral at a critical stage in its reconstruction. In 1110 this grant was extended to eight days in compensation for land taken for the site of Hyde Abbey, and further extended to fourteen days in 1136.[3] These cumulative grants to the bishop—of rights in the fair and further rights over the city during the same period—are possibly significant of the changing balance of authority in the city. There were specific reasons why the bishop should have been granted extra revenue in 1096 and 1110, but the fraternal grant in 1136 may have opened the way for Henry of Blois's exceptional position reflected in the 1148 survey.

The goods which reached Winchester from the Continent as a result of overseas trade were not those which can be expected to have left much trace in the archaeological record, nor have excavations yet been undertaken on the site of the fair itself.[4] The city's more distant contacts in this period and even before the conquest are nevertheless reflected in a remarkable way by the two Byzantine lead seals found under controlled archaeological conditions in widely separated parts of the city, and dating to *c.* 1059–64 and *c.* 1060–80, and by the discovery of two eleventh-century Byzantine coins.[5] Other eleventh- and twelfth-century coins also reached the city from the Continent,[6] as did small quantities of imported pottery.[7] The latter includes red-painted pottery of French origin, and glazed ware of Andenne type, probably from the area forming present-day Belgium. The imported pottery need not represent a shift in the centre of trading

---

[1] See above, p. 238, s.n.

[2] **I, 35.**

[3] See above, pp. 286–7, 308–9.

[4] Two thirteenth-century Irish pennies have been found on the site of the fair: *The Hampshire Observer*, 7 June 1930.

[5] For the two seals and their archaeological contexts on sites in *Gerestret* and *Tannerestret*, see *II Interim*, 195–7, and *The Numismatic Circular*, 71 (1963), 93–6, and 72 (1964), 49–50. Two Byzantine copper coins, both probably of the eleventh century, have been found in Winchester. One of them came from a stratified context, probably of the twelfth century, in

Tannerestret, on a property adjacent to and perhaps even associated with the property where one of the Byzantine lead seals was found.

[6] For full details, see Winchester Studies 8, in preparation. The coins include an eleventh-century denier of Le Mans and a Norman denier of the same period.

[7] Reliable statements regarding the changing pattern of medieval pottery imports can be derived only from a full statistical analysis of the material found in recent excavations. This is in progress and will appear in due course in Winchester Studies 7.

contacts compared with the pre-conquest period, when pottery imports of Rhineland origin were also present, for the development of early medieval pottery in northern and north-western France is still highly obscure and many of the unidentified fabrics found in Winchester in pre-conquest contexts may be of French origin. Nevertheless, Rhineland contacts were declining or had even ceased so far as Winchester was concerned by soon after the conquest, perhaps as a result of the capture of this trade by London. Contacts with Normandy and northern France may, by contrast, and through geographical proximity, have been continuous.

Limited as it is to the king's fief, Survey **I** may give a one-sided picture of the social structure of Winchester in *c.* 1110. Distributions such as that of royal officials, barons, and magnates (Fig. 21) show at this date only their distribution on the royal fief, and as such indicate the extent and location of that estate rather than a true distribution of the persons concerned. With this limitation clearly in mind, we may still see that *c.* 1110 the uppermost level of the social hierarchy was strongly influenced by the two centres of royal activity, the palace and the castle. There is a notable concentration of royal officials in the streets between these places, in the High Street, and in the western suburb on the main road to the North. To what extent this distribution had been affected by the con-struction of the castle, and thus represented a change from the pre-conquest situation, we cannot tell. But it is worth remarking that twenty-one royal officials are listed *c.* 1110, and only two *TRE*.[1] Does this indicate a new and perhaps more permanent concentration of royal officials and hence of royal administration in the city since the conquest—a circumstance parallel to the great development of the royal buildings—or does it simply reflect the failure of the *TRE* survey, or the references to it in the *c.* 1110 survey, to record titles of office, and our relative inability to identify pre-conquest individuals? It is difficult to be sure, but the possibility of a considerable post-conquest development in the permanent functioning of royal administration in the city does seem clear.

If this is so, there had clearly been some change of character, and not only of nationality, in the composition of the uppermost levels of Winchester society since the conquest. If we look at the clergy, by contrast, the evidence of Survey **I** suggests a rather stable situation between *TRE* and *c.* 1110, with very little variation in the numbers represented on the royal estate.[2] This, of course, provides only an indication of the clergy in the open community, and as such may support in a general way the view that the greater number of Winchester's lesser churches were of pre-conquest origin. The evidence tells nothing of developments that may have been taking place in the monastic communities, and in the clerical staff of the royal and episcopal households. The importance of Winchester as a centre for church councils in the 1070s,[3] the regular Easter crown-wearings, and the immense building programme at the cathedral and later at Hyde, St. Mary's, and Wolvesey all argue for the significance and perhaps increasing importance of Winchester as an ecclesiastical centre, and thus for the role of the clergy in city society. It is probably a further indication of Winchester's role in ecclesiastical affairs that church magnates—

[1] See above, Table 29, and cf. pp. 387–92.
[2] See above, Table 31 and cf. p. 394.
[3] Councils in 1070, 1072, and 1076: F. M. Powicke and E. B. Fryde, *Handbook of British Chronology* (2nd edn., London, 1961), 549.

bishops and abbots—acquired residences in the city and suburbs in the late eleventh and twelfth centuries.[1] These trends seem broadly to reflect the conditions arising from the Norman policy of transferring diocesan centres—and thus ecclesiastical administration—to important towns, a development seen most clearly in Lincoln, Norwich, and Old Sarum.

The leading men of the community were already a recognized body by the time of the conquest, the *primates urbis* who surrendered the city in 1066, or the *probi homines* or *digniores cives* of the following century.[2] From this group the reeves were presumably drawn, and also the aldermen, and all the greater property-owners would supposedly have taken part in its deliberations. These were perhaps also the *meliores burgenses* from whom the jurors for Survey **I** were chosen. This term may imply that there were burgesses who were not within the citizen body that met three times a year in the *burghmote*.

Unfortunately the evidence of Survey **I** is not sufficient to permit the identification of occupational groups and their ranking, as can be done with Survey **II,** but a few family relationships can be established, especially among the moneyers.[3] That the latter were of burgess rank is clear, but whether they enjoyed *c.* 1110 the dominant position among the locally-based occupational groups that they occupied in 1148 cannot be shown, although the distribution of their properties in the principal streets of the city may suggest that they did.[4]

Complex ties united the citizens, beyond those of economic status and a shared interest in a stable and well-ordered community. The patterns of kinship which were one of the most important threads in the social fabric in the later history of the city are only faintly discernible in the evidence we possess for the early twelfth century, but were certainly no less important. The origins of families that were prominent in the thirteenth century can be seen not only in 1148, but occasionally as early as the beginning of the century. Such was the Cheping family.[5] Other kin-groups which may not have survived into later periods can with some probability be seen in existence in the eleventh and twelfth centuries, as moneying interests passed from generation to generation, not always in the direct line.[6]

There was also the social life of the guilds, well developed before the conquest, but little documented, and possibly of changing pattern, as associations dissolved and reformed.[7] By the early twelfth century there may already have been links between one or more of these associations and the emergent governing body of the city.[8]

The hints that we possess do not suggest that the society of Winchester in the early twelfth century was markedly different from that in 1148, although it should probably be assumed that the royal connection was more intimate at the earlier date and may have been to some extent residual by the later. But it must be remembered that the information for a quantitative comparison between *c.* 1110 and 1148 does not exist and that impressions are an imprecise guide. What we can never clearly know is the character of the mass of the inhabitants who went unrecorded. We may realize from the numerical difference

[1] See above, p. 389.
[2] See above, pp. 422–3.
[3] See above, pp. 409–15, 421–2, 475.
[4] See above, Fig. 22 and Tables 38–41.

[5] I, 10, n. 6; cf. II, 23, n. 1; and see above, pp. 445–7.
[6] See above, pp. 419–22.
[7] See above, pp. 335–6.
[8] See above, p. 427.

between recorded individuals and the likely total population in 1148 not only the in-completeness of Survey **II**, but also how much less adequate is the survey of *c.* 1110, which deals only with the royal fief, perhaps one quarter of the city as described in the later survey.

We have little sure information about the farm of Winchester in the later eleventh and early twelfth centuries.[1] The failure of Domesday Book to provide any continuous account of the city means that there is no immediately obvious, direct basis for making a comparison, however uncertain, between Winchester and the other cities of the king-dom.[2] Yet, as we have already stressed, the comparative study of these towns and their regions is essential if we are to approach any real understanding of the nature and extent of the urban component in early medieval society, and of the changing status of individual towns.

We may begin with the evidence of recorded Domesday population in the country as a whole around 1086.[3] This shows that Hampshire, Surrey, and Sussex had a density of 5–7 recorded adults per square mile. These counties were relatively less populated than the area of the Thames estuary or the shires spread out from Lincolnshire to Somerset along the Jurassic ridge; and markedly less populated than Norfolk or Suffolk with a density of 12 or more recorded adults per square mile. If this pattern is examined in detail for the south-eastern counties alone, it still holds broadly true;[4] but Hampshire, unlike Surrey and Sussex, is not distinguished by a single area of population above a density of 5–10 recorded adults per square mile, at least according to the method of distribution adopted by *The Domesday Geography of South-East England*.[5]

The urban element has been disregarded in these figures taken from *The Domesday Geography*. It may therefore be interesting to attempt a comparison between the urban and rural populations. If, for example, the holdings on the king's fief in Winchester *c.* 1110 bore the same proportion to the rest of the city then as they did in 1148, one would expect a total of about 1,300 habitations at the earlier date.[6] This is a high figure, an increase of some 15 per cent over the situation *TRE*, and it only holds good if the ratio

---

[1] But see below, pp. 500, 506, and Table 53.

[2] There is of course a good deal of scattered infor-mation about Winchester in Domesday Book; see above, pp. 292 and 382–3, and cf. Table 28.

[3] H. C. Darby (ed.), *An Historical Geography of England before A.D. 1800* (Cambridge, corrected reprint, 1969), 208–13, esp. the caveats on p. 210, and Fig. 25.

[4] *DGSEE* 585–90, Figs. 168–9.

[5] Using the figures 'adjusted for serfs', ibid., fig. 169. The unadjusted figures show a population density of 12 per square mile in the Whitchurch–Litchfield area some ten miles north of Winchester: ibid. 312, Fig. 94.

[6] For the basis of this calculation, see above, p. 468 and n. 3, where the figures for 1148 are quoted and the possible position *TRE* is derived from them. Using the ratios established for 1148, the following figures emerge for the relationship of the king's fief to the remainder of the city *c.* 1110:

entries	251:786	total 1037
parcels	327:988	total 1315
habitations	325:975	total 1300

The discrepancy between the total for parcels or habitations and that for entries is so marked as to suggest that the paragraphing of the putative Edwardian exemplar may have imposed a straight-jacket on the form of the *c.* 1110 survey, with the result that the entries of the latter conceal a much larger actual number of property units. The situation is also evident, although not so marked, in the *TRE* figures (above, p. 468, n. 3), and presumably indicates that develop-ment had even then taken place within a more tradi-tional framework represented by the paragraphing of the survey as we have it. For the problems caused by the scribe's attempt to indicate the original (?) para-graphs of the *TRE* survey in writing the *c.* 1110 text, see below, Appendix II. 2, pp. 524–6.

between the king's fief and the remainder of the city was constant at the three dates. If the increase in properties—parcels or habitations—detectable on the king's fief c. 1110 was confined to that fief, or even exceeded the increase elsewhere in the city, the total will have been falsely enlarged. If the figure of 1,300 habitations is accepted, it would mean that Winchester accounted for about an eighth of the total rural and urban population of the mainland county at the turn of the eleventh and twelfth centuries.[1] This figure far exceeds the proportion of urban to rural population recorded for any other town in the south-eastern counties in 1086: only Wallingford with about a thirteenth and Oxford with about a sixteenth of their county populations begin to approach it.[2] Such a figure is of course affected by the density of rural population, and it has already been pointed out that Winchester did not lie in the most densely populated area of the country. The point is more clearly demonstrated by Chester, where the recorded population for the county as a whole is very low. This results in a percentage of urban to rural population of 15·3 per cent, the only figure to exceed that of Winchester. More instructive is the contrast between Norwich/Norfolk at 4·7 per cent in an area with a population density of more than 12 persons per square mile, and Winchester/Hampshire at 12·4 per cent, in an area with a density of between 5 and 7 persons per square mile. It is clear from this example that urban population is not simply proportional to total population at this period, whatever may be the long-term trend. The figures emphasize the extra attraction that Winchester must have exercised up to this time, in order to have become so marked a concentration of population. And the force of this argument in a local context is in no way diminished by the tendency of the relatively low total population of the county to enhance the position of Winchester by comparison with urban communities in areas of the country with a denser recorded population.

In the countryside around the city, Domesday Book recorded the densest and most

---

[1] The total recorded population may be found for this purpose by using the figures in *DGSEE* 314 and 351–2, together with the c. 1110 figure for Winchester habitations given above, p. 481, n. 6:

(i) As quoted in DB		(ii) Adjusted for servi; Southampton minimum
Rural	8835	7684
Southampton	230	182
Twynham	99	99
Winchester c. 1110	1300	1300
	10,464	9265

The Winchester figure is 12·4 per cent of (i) and 14·0 per cent of (ii).

[2] The figure can be simply calculated from the tables, etc. in *DGSEE*, omitting the rural element from the borough totals when calculating the percentages. The recorded urban populations of the larger urban places as a percentage of the total rural and urban recorded population of their counties are as follows (figures have *not* been 'adjusted for servi'):

	%		%
Winchester	12·4	Southampton	2·2
Wallingford	7·5	Guildford	2·0
Oxford	6·0	Southwark	1·2
Lewes	4·1	Hertford	1·1
Canterbury	3·8	Berkhampstead	1·1
Sandwich	3·1	Buckingham	1·0
Chichester	2·9		

It must be remembered that these figures share all the uncertainties of Domesday statistics, and especially of its urban information, and that no figure is possible for London. These percentages may be of some value if they are used solely as a guide to the broad pattern of differing relationship between town and country, but they cannot, without some elaborate weighting that would exceed the reliability of the evidence, be used to rank the towns in any exact order. Even if the Winchester percentage were reduced by using the c. 1110 figure for entries (1,037), rather than that for habitations (1,300), the resulting figure of 10·2 per cent would still place the city at the top of the list, with about a tenth of the total recorded urban and rural population of the mainland county.

extensive distribution of *servi* in the south-eastern counties.[1] No other city of major importance was similarly situated: London, Oxford, and Canterbury were in areas of low or negligible densities of servile population. The significance of this fact for Winchester is hard to assess. We may be seeing a reflection of a pre-conquest situation, but this may have been enhanced by the dislocation caused by the conquest in the relatively huge concentration of population which the city then represented. Displacements in the upper levels of urban society may have caused widening disruption as their effects passed down the social ladder towards those least able to cushion the shock of rapid change.

The evidence for population densities and the distribution of *servi* obviously touches upon the question of the relative wealth of the English counties in 1086. This is an area where Domesday studies have made little advance, principally because of the intractable nature of Domesday values.[2] All that can usefully be said here is this: the varying density of plough-teams supports the evidence of population density in suggesting that Hampshire was not one of the wealthiest counties in late eleventh-century England, at least in the south-east.[3] Its plough-teams, like its population, were concentrated in the middle and upper reaches of the rich river-valleys of the Test, the Itchen, the Meon, and to a lesser extent the Avon.[4] Elsewhere there were vast open spaces. It was probably this concentration of activity in the valleys, and comparative under-use of the higher chalk downland and Tertiary sands and gravels to the south and extreme north-east, which accounted for what may be the comparative lack of wealth in the county, as it surely accounted for the relatively low density of population.

Population figures as insecurely based as the estimate given above of the number of habitations in early twelfth-century Winchester may of course be an especially uncertain guide to the relative status of a city in which the economic importance of the court and its permanent officials must be given full weight. Some indication of their exceptional significance in Winchester's economy is provided by an examination of the pardons to the aid of 1130.[5] The royal officials and magnates were certainly no less prominent in the city c. 1110,[6] and may have been of even greater importance then and earlier, if the evidence for the slackening of the bond between court and city in the early twelfth century is recalled.[7] The basic economy, aspects of which may be expressed by the size of the occupied area, the number of inhabitants, the number of churches, and such indicators of commercial activity as might be quantifiable, for example the production of coinage, was undoubtedly strengthened by the presence of the royal court and the royal officials, and by the importance of Winchester as an ecclesiastical centre. These factors, and the activity they attracted in commerce and public works, seem to have boosted the life of the city, so that it came to occupy a higher rank in the hierarchy of English towns than it would have done had it served solely as the principal marketing and commercial centre for Hampshire and its region.

As soon as any attempt is made to compare the towns and cities of Norman England one with another, the inquiry comes up against the lack of precisely quantifiable evidence,

[1] *DGSEE* 589–95, esp. Figs. 171 and 172.
[2] Finn *Norman Conquest*, xi, 6–18.
[3] *DGSEE*, Fig. 170.
[4] Ibid., Figs. 92–5, cf. Fig. 98.
[5] See below, p. 504.
[6] See above, pp. 387–92 and Table 29.
[7] See above, pp. 295–6, 301–2.

whether in relation to Winchester, or to the other cities of the realm. By the later twelfth century the urban area of Winchester may be set out as follows:[1]

	hectares	acres
The walled city	58·2	143·8
The suburbs		
North	19·6	48·4
South	49·2	121·6
East	21·1	52·1
West	20·7	51·1
City and suburbs	168·8	417·0
The fair	26·8	66·2
Total area	195·6	483·2

It will be argued below that there is no evidence to suggest that the city expanded during the later twelfth century.[2] The figures given here may therefore reasonably be applied to Winchester at the beginning of the century. The size of the *walled* city is clearly no guide for this period, whether or not it may be a useful indicator at an earlier date. For the most striking fact about these areas is that the suburbs appear to cover nearly three times the area of the walled city; even if the great size of the southern suburb is discounted, the early twelfth-century suburbs were still probably twice as large as the walled area.

Some English cities of Roman origin were contained within the circuit of their ancient walls throughout the Middle Ages. Others, such as York, Lincoln, or Chester expanded beyond their Roman defences, and were eventually provided at least in part with new walls enclosing a greater area. Such expansion and refortification is more marked a feature of Continental urban evolution, and has left its mark in the successive lines of concentric defences to be seen, for example, in towns of Roman origin such as Cologne or Paris, or in medieval towns like Bruges and Ghent. Such an outer circuit may have been emerging piecemeal in Winchester by the early twelfth century, and have left its traces in the bank and ditch of the western suburb, cast up about this time, and in the other hints that survive of suburban bars and boundaries.[3] Such an evolution did actually take place in some English towns, as at Northampton in the same period as the tentative moves at Winchester, or at Bristol in the next century.

In Winchester we can see a situation in which expansion and the internal development of the suburbs had reached a point by the early twelfth century where suburban defences were becoming necessary. Before these defences had evolved into a continuous circuit, however, the period of expansion had come to an end, and had even been reversed. In this, as in so many other points, there seems to be a reasonably clear indication of the city's growth and increasing prosperity up to the early twelfth century, followed by a slow but steady decline.

---

[1] For discussion of the walled area and suburban limits, see above, pp. 263-8, 273; for the fair, see p. 288, n. 2.

[2] See below, p. 494.
[3] See above, pp. 263-4.

The extent and importance of the suburbs means that it is at present virtually impossible to make any safe comparison between Winchester and other towns in the early twelfth century on the basis of urban area alone. The detailed evidence for suburban areas has not yet been brought together in such a way, and with sufficient chronological precision, to make a comparison of this kind reliable.

A comparison based on the number of houses may be slightly more practicable. If the figure of 1,300 tenements *c.* 1110 is acceptable as a basis for comparison with the Domesday figures for borough houses, Winchester would rank second after London (first, presumptively), about equal with Norwich (1,270), but before York (1,181), and Lincoln (fifth, 910), and far above Thetford (sixth, 720) or Gloucester (seventh, 508).[1]

This is a ranking entirely consistent with the evidence of the coinage as it is at present understood.[2] The basic statistical appraisal now available for the surviving coins of the period 975–1066 does not unfortunately yet extend into the post-conquest period.[3] It seems certain that this approach to the ranking of early medieval towns will be of increasing value as it takes in a greater period, particularly now that the intimate association between moneyers and the commercial life of their city has been demonstrated from the Winchester evidence.[4] In the period between *c.* 1075 and the end of Henry I's reign Winchester seems to have occupied in the coinage a position second only to London. In the latter half of this period its position was certainly being eroded by the increase in other centres, but no firm figures are available to permit a more exact judgement based either on the size of moneyers' 'colleges' or on surviving production. Furthermore, Winchester's exceptional position in the earlier part of this period is due as much to the reduction in moneyers at York and Lincoln as to any clearly marked increase (so far as is yet known) in its own coinage. If there was such an increase, it may have been at least partly attributable to the local need for coin to service the capital investment by the early Norman kings in the West Saxon capital, and to pay the large wage and supply bills resulting from the works programme. Such a need could have been met by an increase in exchange arising from the presence in the city of the newly rich Anglo-Norman aristocracy.

A more accurate knowledge of the date of foundation of lesser churches in Winchester and elsewhere might also contribute to an understanding of the ranking of towns at this period. A close relationship seems to exist in some of the pre-conquest towns of eastern

---

[1] Stephenson *BT*, Appendix III, p. 221, cf. pp. 152–4. Like all Domesday statistics, those given by Stephenson do not exactly agree with those compiled by other workers, for example in the *Domesday Geographies*. The figure for York is the only serious problem that may affect the ranking used here. If the 400 *mansiones non hospitatae quae reddunt meliores .i. denarium et aliae minus* are omitted, York is reduced to 781 houses (*recte* 778½, see H. C. Darby and I. S. Maxwell (eds.), *Domesday Geography of Northern England* (Cambridge, 1962), 154–6), with the result that it falls to fifth place, Winchester second, about equal with Norwich, and Lincoln fourth. The only factor which encourages much reliance on these figures is the comparative isolation of the leading towns as a group distinct from towns of the rank of Gloucester and below; cf. Stephenson's remarks *BT* 152, esp. n. 2. The inadequacy of the Domesday record of towns is only too clearly seen in the case of the Hampshire boroughs of Southampton and Twynham, but other descriptions are even more inadequate, e.g. Rochester, or totally lacking. However, the figures provide only one contributory thread in the discussion here, and they are consistent with the general pattern.

[2] See above, pp. 396–7.

[3] See above, p. 468, n. 6, and pp. 468–9.

[4] See above, pp. 421–2, 447.

England between the number of parish churches, the average size of parishes, and the average number of households they contain.[1] A closer dating of church origins can come only from excavation. It has been amply demonstrated in Winchester by the adjacent churches of St. Mary in Tanner Street and St. Pancras, both of which, although first recorded in the later twelfth century, have proved to be of pre-conquest date.[2] Some ten or eleven of Winchester's lesser churches are now known to have been in existence before 1066, and almost all of the final total of fifty-seven parish churches may have been constructed before the middle of the twelfth century, by which time a parochial system seems already to have been established.[3] If, furthermore, the six churches so far excavated provide any basis for judgement, many of the fifty-seven could turn out to be of Anglo-Saxon origin.[4] No figure for the turn of the eleventh and twelfth centuries is yet possible, but it is clear that Winchester was comparable in the number of its lesser churches to the other leading centres of this period, to Norwich with forty-six churches in 1086, Lincoln with not fewer than thirty-five by about 1100, or York with perhaps as many.[5] As on every other available basis of comparison, London stands on its own. There were at least a hundred churches within its walls in the late twelfth century. Since, however, the parochial development of the City was probably different from that of other towns only in scale and not in character, London may also have been pre-eminent in the number of its churches in the early twelfth century, and perhaps even earlier.[6]

No exact ranking is of course possible. These figures are broad approximations, and show only that by this test as well Winchester was among the three or four leading cities in the land. No more accurate picture emerges from a study of the size of urban castles,[7] or of the destruction caused by their construction—only a general confirmation that Winchester was burdened with one of the larger castles, and disrupted more than most, but less than Lincoln or Norwich, by its construction. Some 880 m (2,900 feet) of Winchester streets were obliterated by the building of the castle, about 530 m within the walled area, and the remainder without.[8] Allowing for development on one side only of the intra-mural street, and of the street (*twicene*) which probably ran along the outer lip of the late Saxon city ditch(es),[9] these streets provided about 780 m of street frontage inside the walls, and 350 m outside, figures which suggest that some sixty houses may

---

[1] See below, pp. 498–9.

[2] *IX Interim*, 104–7, 111–15; *X Interim*, 312, 318–20.

[3] See above, pp. 329–35, and 395–6.

[4] St. Mary in Tanner Street, St. Maurice, St. Pancras, St. Peter *in macellis*, St. Rumbold, and a church possibly to be identified with St. Mary in *Brudenestret* (see above, p. 347) have been excavated. The first four have all been shown to be pre-conquest; the fifth is uncertain; the sixth is not earlier than the late eleventh century.

[5] Norwich: *ex inf*. Mr. Alan Carter, Norwich Survey; Lincoln: Francis Hill, *Medieval Lincoln* (Cambridge, 1965), 147. York presents a problem: there were at least 14 churches by 1100, but this seems likely to be a serious underestimate, due to the lack of church excavations in the city until recently. Some thirty-seven churches were apparently in being by

1200, and one suspects this larger total may reflect an increase in the survival of records, rather than necessarily in the founding of churches; cf. *VCH York* 365–404, esp. 365.

[6] Brooke *Missionary*, 66–8.

[7] The list of castle areas in E. S. Armitage, *The Early Norman Castles of the British Isles* (London, 1912), 396–7 needs revision in the light of increased knowledge of the topographical development of the individual castles. In any case, local features greatly influenced the size of castles: at Winchester, for example, the Roman town wall provided a ready-made boundary on three sides, and was presumably a considerable factor in deciding the original size and layout of the fortification.

[8] See above, pp. 278–9 and 302–3.

[9] See above, pp. 274–5.

have been involved, fifty or so within the walls and perhaps fifteen on the extra-mural street.[1] This estimate should be compared with the 166 houses destroyed at Lincoln and the 113 destroyed at Norwich, recorded in Domesday Book. The next highest known figure is the 51 houses destroyed in making Shrewsbury castle.

None of these tests is conclusive, and most are highly questionable, but all suggest that in this limited period Winchester seems to have vied with Norwich for second place to London. Only in the complement of its moneyers was Norwich clearly the lesser place. This last factor may emphasize the probability that Winchester was now enjoying its exceptional position by virtue of its status as a political and administrative centre.

A precise comparison in monetary terms is difficult, for Winchester is the only major town whose borough farm in 1086 is not recorded or readily deducible.[2] Nearly fifty years later the city's contribution to the aid of 1130 was 120 marks, second only to that of London at 180, well above that of Lincoln, double the contribution of York and approaching three times that of Norwich.[3] But Winchester's position in the assessments of 1130 was exceptionally high for any second city of the kingdom at this period, and we may suspect that it was due especially to the presence in the city of royal officials, barons, and other magnates.[4] A ranking on the basis of borough farms, which would perhaps reflect more directly the trade and commerce of the city,[5] might produce a slightly different picture. Yet it is difficult to believe that Winchester's position in relation to other towns was superior in 1130 to that in 1086. At the earlier date the royal connection with the city was at its height, while York was devastated; by the later date the royal connection was in decline, while York had had half a century to recover. The other arguments brought forward here regarding the rank of Winchester in the late eleventh and early twelfth centuries may thus support the suggestion that the Winchester farm in 1086 was considerably in excess of the apparent value of the £80 blanch allowed for the city against the county farm in the reign of Henry II. Converted to tale according to the principles apparently in use at the time of the Domesday survey, this figure would represent a farm of £100, thus ranking Winchester third equal to Lincoln, a little below York, and very slightly above Norwich.[6] There may even be something in the suggestion that the full value of the Winchester farm before the reign of Henry II was as high as £120 blanch (£126 or £150 by tale), which would rank the city second only to London.[7] But whatever scale of conversion is used, Winchester would not have ranked so prominently in 1086 according to the alternative values for its farm postulated here, as it did in the aid of 1130. As we have seen, there are grounds for believing that this early aid reflects the city's exceptional role as a royal centre.

[1] For an estimate that a property in the more densely built-up areas occupied between 30 and 40 feet of frontage, see above, p. 378. The average figure for the whole city, derived from Table 26, is, however, 49 feet, and so 50 has been used in estimating the possible number of intra-mural houses destroyed by the castle. The archaeological evidence has shown that the northern end of the north–south street buried by the castle was densely built-up, but whether these conditions prevailed further south is unknown. It has been assumed that outside the walls properties may have averaged twice the average intra-mural frontage.

[2] See above, p. 5 and n. 2. See also below, Table 53.

[3] See below, Table 54 and n. 3.

[4] See below, p. 504.

[5] For the relative values of the revenues contributing to the Winchester farm in the late thirteenth century, see below, Appendix I. 2. For the components of the Canterbury farm in the thirteenth century, see Urry *Canterbury* 43–4.

[6] See below, Table 53 and n. 5.

[7] See above, p. 5 and n. 2.

Winchester's position in *c.* 1110 was enhanced by comparison with the period before the conquest. In terms of relative status the city seems to have gained by the devastation of the North and the consequent reduction in rank of York and perhaps Lincoln; by contrast Norwich was now coming to the fore. It looks as if Winchester had generally improved its position through the conquest and by the Norman investment in the city as a capital centre. This enhancement, as we shall see, did not long endure.

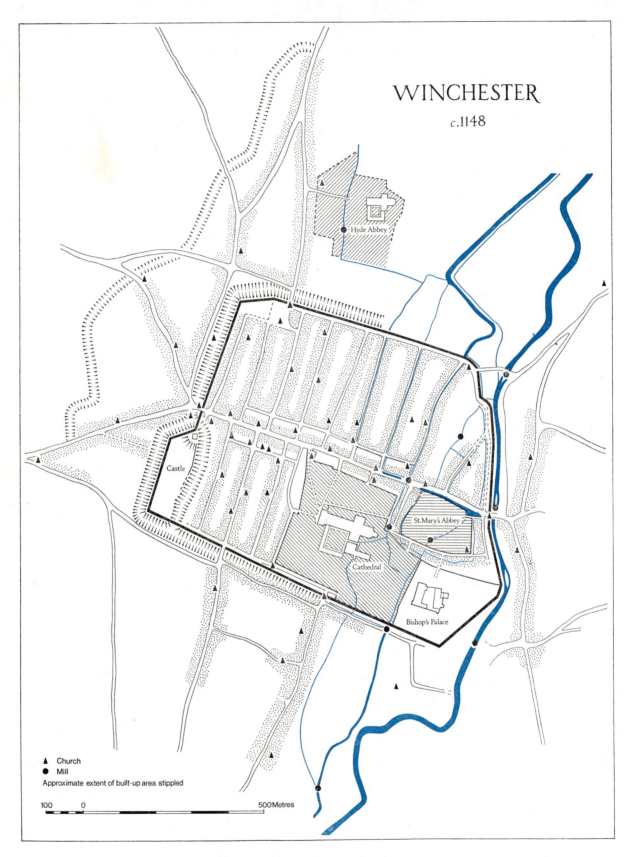

WINCHESTER

*c.*1148

Hyde Abbey

Castle

St.Mary's Abbey

Cathedral

Bishop's Palace

▲ Church
● Mill
Approximate extent of built-up area stippled

100   0   500 Metres

FIG. 27. (1:10,000).

Parish churches are shown as in Figure 10.

3

WINCHESTER IN THE REIGN OF STEPHEN

IF at any one period it became clear that Winchester was no longer a royal capital it was during the reign of Stephen. Already under Henry I there had begun that slackening of the association between Winchester and the monarchy which was to mark the start of the decline of the medieval city. By the second decade of the twelfth century the Easter crown-wearing at the ancient capital had ceased to be a regular feature of royal ceremonial, and as his reign progressed Henry's visits at other times of the year became less frequent. On these latter occasions he probably stayed in the castle, for by the end of his reign the Winchester palace had apparently ceased to be used as a royal residence.[1] The castle was compact, readily defensible, with easy access to hunting country, but it can at first have had little provision for ceremonial. It was an ideal strong point and administrative centre, protecting the king's interests in a city he rarely visited. Yet even towards the end of Henry's reign, Winchester was still a meeting place for the principal men of the kingdom, and they contributed substantially to the wealth of the city. The disturbances of Stephen's reign, in particular the burning of the royal palace in 1141 and its subsequent demolition, were perhaps the decisive factors which finally destroyed any prospect of the monarchy returning to Winchester on its old basis.[2]

In this special sense the siege of 1141 was clearly a significant incident in the decline of Winchester. Within seven years of the siege, however, the record of waste properties seems hardly to reflect the scale of the devastation that is said to have taken place.[3] The city may have been rapidly rebuilt, or the conflagrations may have been more confined to the immediate neighbourhood of the two monasteries said to have been burned, and perhaps also the royal palace, than the chroniclers' accounts suggest.[4] But even in *Colobrochestret*, next to St. Mary's Abbey, there is little evidence of devastation in the 1148 survey, and none of the archaeological excavations in the city has produced evidence of a general burning in the twelfth century. That more than forty churches were damaged in the siege is not impossible,[5] but the city's principal losses may well have resulted from looting by the victors rather than from the widespread destruction of buildings.[6] The disturbances may also have accelerated certain social changes in the city.[7] Large-scale fires were not uncommon in Winchester and other cities in the twelfth century:[8] the physical effects of the 1141 siege were perhaps no more than a magnified version of a

[1] See above, pp. 295–7.
[2] For the wealth of the magnates in the city in 1129–30, and the effect of these changes on the status and fortunes of Winchester, see below, pp. 504–5.
[3] See above, p. 386.
[4] See above, pp. 297–9, 318–19, 322–3.
[5] See above, p. 329.
[6] See above, p. 339, and cf. p. 319.
[7] See below, p. 504–6.

[8] Six major fires are recorded at Winchester and St. Giles's Fair during the twelfth century, in addition to that of 1141: *Winchester ann*, s.a. 1102, 1161, 1162, 1180, 1197, and 1198. See also above, p. 419, n. 8. The Winchester annals also record eleven fires at London, three at Canterbury, and two each at Lincoln, Gloucester, and Exeter in the same period. See also, J. H. Harvey, 'The Fire of York in 1137', *The Yorkshire Archaeological Journal*, 41 (1963–6), 364–7.

relatively frequent occurrence from which, in terms of short-term material prosperity at least, the city quickly recovered.

At the beginning of Stephen's reign Winchester was still the seat of the financial administration of the kingdom, and was to remain so for nearly another fifty years. In 1148 the royal officials formed one of the wealthiest and most distinctive groups of property-owners in the city, but they were clearly a less numerous body than in c. 1110. Their reduction in numbers was no doubt a symptom of the disruption of administrative procedures in Stephen's time, but probably also reflected the loosening of ties between the royal household and the city begun in the previous reign.[1]

During the episcopate of Henry of Blois the departure of the king from Winchester was to some extent balanced by the authority, wealth, and patronage of the bishop. In addition to the power which he wielded by virtue of his ecclesiastical offices and personal wealth, Bishop Henry exercised during his brother's reign a major political and administrative authority over the counties within his diocese, and in Winchester occupied an almost regal position. Within a few years of Stephen's accession Henry of Blois was in control of the royal castle, the royal treasure, and perhaps also the royal palace. For a few years until the siege of 1141 the bishop seems to have controlled two residences in central Winchester, where his influence had now entirely supplanted that of the king. In March 1141 he surrendered the castle and the king's treasure to the Empress Matilda, but probably recovered possession later in the same year after her defeat. The bishop did not surrender to her the royal palace, over which he exercised a special control, and so for a short time a tactical polarization actually emerged between the bishop's focus of power, in the centre and south-eastern part of the city, and the royal castle to the west. It may have been at the palace in 1138 that he built the strong keep which was to be one of the strongholds for his forces in the city during the siege of 1141. Furthermore he was said to have been responsible for the sudden and hurried demolition of the palace buildings.[2] In 1148 the bishop still controlled the site of the palace and was landlord of the numerous tenements which seem to have been established along its northern and western margins, in those very parts of the site which by the early thirteenth century were once more in the possession of the crown.[3] The remainder of the site was taken into the cathedral precinct which then attained much the extent it has maintained to the present day. By these actions Bishop Henry was perhaps fulfilling with characteristic thoroughness a role which his predecessors, certainly before the conquest,[4] would have played in the life of the city.

By 1148 Henry of Blois also received substantial revenue from properties in Winchester which do not seem rightly to have belonged to the bishopric, and may have been held by a delegation of royal authority or even actually belonged to the king.[5] In one instance the bishop's justiciar appears to have been responsible for a property in the king's fief.[6] By contrast, the king's ancient revenue from property in the city, principally in the form of landgable rents, was well defined in the 1148 survey and the bishop was probably a careful custodian of these royal interests. The crown, whoever held it, was the undisputed

---

[1] See above, pp. 433, 472–3.   [2] See above, pp. 297–301, 324–6.   [3] See above, pp. 301, 352–4.
[4] See above, p. 465   [5] See above, pp. 353–5.   [6] II, 89.

lord of the city, although the effective presence of the bishop and his officers probably meant much more to the citizens from day to day in terms of practical lordship. But this was a situation which would not outlast the accession of the Angevin dynasty.

The bishop's direct and even controlling interest in city property extended beyond the estates of the bishopric and the crown to the lands of Hyde Abbey and the cathedral priory. He appropriated the abbey estates for six years from 1135 and apparently used the income mainly for his own advantage.[1] We are perhaps more accurately, if a little less directly, informed of his actions concerning the cathedral estates. He took the priory estates into his own hands and probably at the same time ordered the compilation of the great Winchester cartulary, now known as the *Codex Wintoniensis*. This work set the title to the lands of both bishopric and priory on a new footing. He also drew up a scheme for the management of the priory lands and the assignment of their revenues, and in the reign of Henry II he formally returned these lands to the priory.[2]

The palace of Wolvesey in the south-east corner of the city provided the formal setting for the bishop's public duties. Here Henry of Blois matched Bishop Giffard's buildings with a magnificent hall which seems to have been intended for public functions, and by stages elaborated a series of separate structures into a compact and defensible palace of courtyard plan.[3] By 1148, when the bishop's survey of Winchester was undertaken, the work at Wolvesey must have been the major building project in the city.

Other public building works in Winchester in Stephen's reign were almost certainly minor in comparison to the work at Wolvesey. There is no substantial work of this period in the cathedral. Damages sustained at Hyde Abbey and St. Mary's Abbey in 1141 were probably repaired and there may well have been regular work at the royal castle, for the pipe rolls show that the pattern of substantial annual expenditure there was already established in the first year of Henry II's reign.[4]

The bishop's patronage left its mark on Winchester in other ways. He founded St. Cross Hospital for the relief of the poor (although its thirteen residents do not seem necessarily to have been poor men), and probably founded St. Mary Magdalen Hospital for lepers.[5] Henry of Blois was well known for his connoisseurship: it seems likely that he was the principal patron behind the great burst of artistic activity associated with Winchester in the middle and the second half of the twelfth century.[6] His gifts to the cathedral included fine metalwork, enamels, hangings, vestments, and books.[7] He almost certainly commissioned at Winchester the elaborately tooled bindings for two or possibly three books.[8] He probably also commissioned the illuminated Winchester Psalter for his personal use.[9] The major part of the great Winchester Bible was probably completed at Winchester during his episcopate,[10] and there are other fine manuscripts which may be

[1] See above, pp. 319–20.
[2] Goodman *Chartulary*, nos. 3, 4, and 7, and for a later reference to Henry of Blois's constitutions for the priory, ibid., no. 176. [3] See above, pp. 326–8.
[4] See above, p. 303, and Colvin (ed.) *King's Works*, ii. 855–64. [5] See above, pp. 328–9.
[6] For a summary of the evidence, see T. S. R. Boase, *English Art 1100–1216* (Oxford, 1953), 169–80.
[7] Edmund Bishop, *Liturgica Historica* (Oxford, 1918,

reprinted 1962), 392–401. [8] See below, pp. 534–40.
[9] Francis Wormald, *The Winchester Psalter* (London, 1973), 125.
[10] One of the two volumes into which the work was originally divided appears to have been complete by 1180 × 86. Much of the work in this volume and the second volume probably belongs to the period 1140–60. See Walter Oakeshott, *The Artists of the Winchester Bible* (London, 1945), 1–22, and idem, *Sigena:*

closely associated with this group.[1] It is possible that the four painters recorded in the 1148 survey were associated with work of this nature in decorating either manuscripts or buildings.[2] The bishop also perhaps encouraged in the city a wider range of intellectual activity. One of his clerks, Jordan Fantosme, author of the French metrical account of the Anglo-Scottish war of 1173–4, was a pupil of Gilbert of la Porée and ran the school of Winchester at a house facing the cathedral.[3] Two more distinguished chroniclers were closely associated with Winchester in the twelfth century. Robert of Lewes, a protégé of Henry of Blois and probably author of the *Gesta Stephani*, had property in *Alwarnestret* in 1148[4] and Richard of Devizes was at work in the cathedral priory at the end of the century.[5] There are also grounds for associating Henry of Blois with the patronage of Chrétien of Troyes, who was certainly at one time attached to the court of the bishop's nephew Henry the Liberal, count of Champagne, and some of whose works seem to display a knowledge of the Winchester region.[6] John *ioculator* (**II, 366**) was perhaps a lesser minstrel with a more direct interest in Winchester.

The compilation of the Winton Domesday fits well into the context of what we know of Henry of Blois and his position in Winchester in 1148. His survey of the city is just one of four great written surveys of real property which he is known to have had made. As abbot of Glastonbury he arranged for the compilation of a book of the abbey lands which had been alienated and subsequently recovered;[7] the *Codex Wintoniensis*, recording the cathedral estates, has already been mentioned; and Henry also had drawn up a survey of the rents of the abbey of Cluny.[8] Of these records, only the Winchester survey of 1148 included any mention of properties in which Henry of Blois himself had no direct interest. Some reasons why this survey should have included every property in the city may be suggested. In the first place the bishop was by far the largest landlord and appears in 1148 to have held a number of properties which did not strictly belong to the bishopric.[9] The most practical method of identifying the tenements he did hold may have been to survey the entire city. But Henry also had a strong interest in the estates of the cathedral priory and Hyde Abbey, and was perhaps in addition responsible for the royal properties in the city. Together with the properties which he held as bishop, these three estates accounted for 28 per cent of the total rent receipts, and 84 per cent of the tenements recorded in the survey[10], thus reinforcing the motive for undertaking a survey of the whole city.

The ordering of the 1148 survey may equally well have been motived by Bishop Henry's

---

Romanesque Paintings in Spain and the Winchester Bible Artists (London, 1972), especially p. 142.

[1] Boase, op. cit. above, p. 491, n. 6.

[2] See above, p. 433.

[3] See **II, 864**, n. 1; *VCH Hants* ii. 253–7; and R. Howlett (ed.), *Chronicles of the Reigns of Stephen, Henry II and Richard I*, iii (RS, 1886), lxi–lxii.

[4] See **II, 476**, n. 1. The year of the survey was probably that in which the first part of the *Gesta* was written: R. H. C. Davis, *EHR* 77 (1962), 209–32.

[5] J. T. Appleby (ed.), *The Chronicle of Richard of Devizes of the time of King Richard the First* (London, 1963), xi–xviii and xxiv–xxvi; and idem, 'Richard

of Devizes and the Annals of Winchester', *Bulletin of the Institute of Historical Research* 36 (1963), 70–7.

[6] Urban T. Holmes and M. Amelia Klenke, *Chrétien, Troyes, and the Grail* (Chapel Hill, N.C., 1959), chapters 1 and 2 and especially pp. 23–4 citing *Cligés* for Chrétien's knowledge of the Winchester region.

[7] T. Hearne (ed.), *Adami de Domerham Historia de rebus gestis Glastoniensibus* (Oxford, 1727), ii. 304.

[8] A. Bernard and A. Bruel (eds.), *Recueil des Chartes de l'Abbaye de Cluny*, v (Paris, 1894), 490–505.

[9] See above, pp. 353–5, 490–1.

[10] See above, Tables 21 and 22.

attitude of practical philanthropy towards his city, torn in relatively recent years by internal dissension and civil war. His view is on record that Domesday Book had been undertaken in order that everyone should be content with his own rights,[1] and the same reasoning may well have lain behind this survey of his own cathedral city.

The bishop's over-all interest in the properties in the city is implied in another source, the record of the great synod which he held in Winchester within a few years of the siege of 1141.[2] The purpose of this synod appears to have been to define the parochial areas of those churches which had been burned during the siege so that there should be no dispute between the rectors and their parishioners. One of the most important matters over which dispute could have arisen was the collection of tithes. In later medieval Winchester tithes from built-up tenements and from non-agricultural land appear to have been assessed on the basis of the rent-value of the property.[3] If this was also the case in the twelfth century, the 1148 survey would have provided just the evidence which was required for the assessments of tithes. The survey does not, however, seem to have been arranged with this in view, and the references to churches are few in number; nor is there any sign in the surviving text that it was used for this purpose. We should perhaps conclude that there were a number of motives behind the ordering of the survey, each of which had its own special validity to the bishop. In the event, the surviving text seems to have been used by no one other than the monks of the cathedral priory.[4]

There were particular reasons why Henry of Blois should look to his own revenues in 1148 and these may have affected his decision to have the survey compiled. The year given in the initial rubric of Survey II was probably considered to have lasted from 25 March 1148 to 24 March 1149, according to the modern calendar. The survey was thus most likely carried out after Bishop Henry had received news of his suspension from episcopal office and of the papal summons to Rome issued at the council of Rheims in March 1148.[5] He faced the double expense of a long journey and difficult negotiations at the papal court. Furthermore, the situation at home was unsettled in the latter part of 1148, and required considerable military expenditure on the bishop's behalf.[6]

Whatever the precise motivation behind the 1148 survey, the mere fact that it was carried out and was incorporated in a handsome volume, together with a copy of the text of an earlier survey of the king's properties, is an important indication of the special significance of the relationship between Bishop Henry of Blois and the royal city of Winchester in the middle of the twelfth century. It was a time when the bishop still seems to have hoped for the elevation of his see to metropolitan status.[7]

The city portrayed in 1148 had continued to thrive since the early years of the century. The size of its population, probably more than 8,000 persons,[8] its physical extent, and the

---

[1] *Dialogus de Scaccario*, 63.

[2] For the date and record of this synod, see above, p. 300 and n. 1.

[3] Even for the later Middle Ages the evidence for the basis of the assessment of tithes in Winchester is rare and difficult to interpret. Tithes were assessed on the basis of the rent-value of property in eighteenth-century Winchester. The case will be argued in *SMW*. In London some tithes at least were being assessed on

this basis by the thirteenth century: A. G. Little, 'Personal Tithes', *EHR* 60 (1945), 67–88 and J. A. F. Thomson, 'Tithe Disputes in later Medieval London', *EHR* 78 (1963), 1–17.   [4] See above, p. 1.

[5] M. Chibnall (ed.), *The Historia Pontificalis of John of Salisbury* (London, 1956), 10. See also above, pp. 18, 320.   [6] *Gesta Stephani*, 141–2.

[7] See above, p. 320.

[8] See above, p. 440.

variety and intensity of its settlement were characteristic even in modern terms of an urban centre, and in the twelfth century must have denoted a town of major importance.[1]

Evidence for the size of the built-up area in the mid twelfth century is limited, but sufficient to show that with the possible exception of the eastern suburb and the site of St. Giles's Fair,[2] the inhabited area of the city was by now at its maximum extent. Houses had been built at the limits of the western and northern suburbs by the early twelfth century.[3] To the south there were houses by the church of All Saints in 1148, an area apparently occupied by open gardens in 1287.[4] It was probably in the first half of the twelfth century that the bank and ditch enclosing the western suburb were constructed.[5] By this date the total area covered by the walled city and suburbs, excluding the site of St. Giles's Fair, was probably 168·8 hectares (417·0 acres).[6]

The built-up area within the walls seems also to have achieved its maximum extent and density by the middle of the twelfth century. There are two concrete instances of the pressure on building space in the city centre at this time. By 1148 the former High Street frontage of the royal palace, probably then occupied by fifteen tenements, was as intensively built-up as at any time in the city's history.[7] These tenements had presumably been constructed within the previous six or seven years since the destruction of the palace. In *Tannerestret* we may compare the situation recorded in 1148 with the evidence for the physical development of eight or nine properties, occupying a total frontage of some 95 m (315 feet) on the west side of the street, which has been recovered by archaeological excavation.[8] From the date of the first alignment of structures on to the street frontage, probably early in the tenth century, the area covered by buildings on these excavated tenements steadily increased. By the late eleventh or early twelfth century the frontage of this part of the street was continuously built up, and by the early thirteenth century if not before the built-up area was at its maximum extent. After the frontages had been fully occupied, further expansion was accommodated by building back from the street, at the rear of the tenement plots, and lanes were created to provide access to these areas from the street. Excavation has also shown that St. Pancras Lane in *Tannerestret*, which originally provided access to the rear of a tenement and was subsequently developed as a way through to the parish church of St. Pancras, had probably come into existence by the end of the eleventh century.

The two surveys provide what may be more general evidence of the pressure on building space in their records of encroachments on to streets. Even if we discount the encroachments associated with the construction of the royal castle and the enlargement of the palace, this expression of development in the fabric of the city suggests a greater activity in the period up to *c.* 1110 than in the period before 1148.[9]

---

[1] For the status of Winchester in relation to other English towns, and its long-term development in the twelfth century, see below, pp. 499–506.

[2] See below, p. 497.

[3] See above, pp. 265–6.

[4] **II, 962**, n. 2, and WCL, Custumal, fo. 31.

[5] See above, p. 264.

[6] See above, p. 484, and for the limits of the suburbs in the twelfth century, see also above, pp. 263–6.

Much of this area, even within the walls, was not built over. If we attempt to allow for this by excluding half the area of the southern suburb, which was probably the least built-up of all the suburbs, the figure is 144·2 hectares (356·2 acres).

[7] See above, p. 246.

[8] See *II–X Interims*.

[9] See above, pp. 280–1.

The evidence of Survey **II** for the average frontage-width of tenements and for the subdivision of large early properties[1] shows that by 1148 the intensity of settlement witnessed by the development of the palace site and the excavated houses in *Tannerestret* was widespread throughout the city and certain areas of the suburbs. In *Tannerestret* the average frontage-width of the eight or nine excavated properties was similar to, if not actually larger than, the average for the whole street calculated from the evidence of the 1148 survey.[2]

For *Tannerestret* and *Wunegrestret* we may compare the density of settlement in the street as a whole in 1148 with that about 1300, for we are well informed as to the density and extent of habitation in these two streets at the beginning of the fourteenth century.[3] By that date the precinct of the Grey Friars occupied 100 m (328 feet) and 128·75 m (423 feet) respectively on the two street frontages. Elsewhere the frontages were continuously built up with private houses, and several tenements included structures at the rear of their plots. The average frontage-width of the tenements was 11 m (36 feet) in *Tannerestret* and 12·3 m (40 feet) in *Wunegrestret*. These figures are almost exactly the same as those for 1148 based on a total frontage-length which includes the land later occupied by the friars.[4] In these two streets the inhabited area appears to have been at least as intensively settled in 1148 as in *c.* 1300, and was considerably more extensive.

The choice of this site near the city wall for the Grey Friars' precinct suggests that by the middle of the thirteenth century it was relatively unencumbered by dwellings, and had perhaps even lost population over the previous century. This was also the case with *Snidelingestret*, which was densely populated in 1148,[5] but contained empty plots of land *c.* 1270, and seems to have been largely uninhabited by the early fourteenth century.[6] *Gerestret* underwent a similar change.[7] *Colobrochestret* may have been an exception to the general rule within the walls, for more properties were recorded there in 1417 than in 1148.[8]

Each of the streets in mid-twelfth-century Winchester had its own well-defined character.[9] High Street was without doubt the heart of the community. Here, in the principal market-place of the city, settlement was more intense and property-values higher than

---

[1] See above, pp. 340–4, 375–8.

[2] There is some difficulty in estimating the number of tenements excavated. The earliest precise documentary evidence suggests that in *c.* 1300 the excavated area included eight tenements (Keene *Brooks Area*, Fig. 36). Archaeological evidence suggests that one of these may have represented the amalgamation of two earlier tenements. Eight properties would have an average frontage of 13 m (42 feet), nine properties an average frontage of 11·5 m (38 feet). In 1148 the average frontage for the whole of *Tannerestret* was 10·4 m (34 feet): see above, Table 26. This implies that a significant number of properties in *Tannerestret* had frontages narrower than those in the excavated area, as may well have been the case. The 1148 figures, however, take no account of properties which may have fronted solely on to side lanes. If there was a significant number of such tenements the average frontage calculated from

the record evidence would be an underestimate.

[3] Keene, *Brooks Area*, Fig. 36.

[4] See Table 26.

[5] See above, pp. 378–82, and Table 26.

[6] See *SMW*, and for some particular references: WCL, Records 1, fo. 23, and Stowe 846, fo. 17.

[7] See below, p. 506, n. 7.

[8] The Tarrage Survey of 1417 records 76 properties in *Colobrochestret* against 24 in 1148, an increase of 217 per cent. In most streets fewer properties were recorded in 1417 than in 1148, or the numbers were about the same. None of the increases was of the same order as that for *Colobrochestret*. The total number of properties recorded in the two surveys (excluding the south and east suburbs which were not included in the Tarrage Survey), was slightly higher in 1148 than in 1417. This topic will be pursued in *SMW*.

[9] See above, pp. 381–2, 439.

anywhere else. The next most densely populated streets were those leading from High Street to the gates of the city: within the walls, as well as in the suburbs, population was concentrated along the radii of communication, even when, as in the case of *Tannerestret*, the passage through the city wall was little more than a postern. Property-values in these streets were high. By contrast property-values in some of the less densely inhabited streets were also high, perhaps because they contained some of the most imposing and desirable residences in the city. *Calpestret* is the most striking example of this group of streets, and still contains a fine example of a two-storied hall, constructed in, or more probably well before, the middle of the twelfth century.[1] In a third group of streets, of which *Snidelingestret* and possibly the street outside King's Gate as far south as *Sevetuichne* are the best examples, houses were small, poor, and closely packed. There was thus a considerable variety in the density of population within the walls, and the example of the street outside King's Gate shows that parts of the suburbs were more densly populated than some of the streets within the walls. The streets outside West Gate formed the most prosperous of all the suburbs.

The 1148 survey records a wide variety of trades and manufactures.[2] The total number of trades represented is greater than in the earlier survey, but it is by no means certain that the range of trades had expanded since the eleventh century. The most numerous bodies of tradesmen were clearly those concerned with the provision of food and drink and the manufacture of cloth and leather. Butchers, some other victuallers, and some of the clothing and leather trades were clearly associated with particular areas of the city, although there is evidence that the expansion of the city and changing local conditions had resulted in the migration of three of the trades in this group in the period before 1148. Butchers had begun to move westwards from what appears to have been their original position to a less congested part of High Street; shoemakers had dispersed themselves from *Scowrtenestret*, perhaps into the suburbs, and tanners had begun to move from *Tannerestret* into a less populous area to the east. The tenacity with which certain occupations remained in one place is best illustrated by the moneyers whose principal association was with the central part of High Street at all three periods covered by the surveys.[3] For certain groups of trades, principally those associated with the manufacture of cloth and leather, it is possible to discern an economic and presumably social hierarchy reflected in the pattern of property holding. The distribution of these properties may also help to distinguish the more entrepreneurial and retail branches of certain trades from those more solely concerned with manufacture. This point is best illustrated within the leather trade by the example of the cordwainers, corvesers, and the cobblers. In the case of a few of the wealthier inhabitants, tentatively identified as merchants, but not so named in the survey, it may be possible to distinguish their commercial from their domestic establishment, as seems to be also the case with the moneyers.[4]

Apart from the existence of the moneyers, the goldsmiths, the three Christian moneylenders, and the Jews, there is little direct evidence for the higher commerce of twelfth-

[1] For a plan of this hall, see *VCH Hants* v. 9; see also above, p. 346.
[2] See above, pp. 427–39.
[3] See above, p. 419.
[4] See above, pp. 374, 405–7.

century Winchester.[1] Men who might have traded in livestock, wool, and agricultural produce between Winchester and its surrounding countryside, and in these and other articles wider afield, are not easily identified in the survey. The interests of some of the wealthier private landlords may have lain in this direction, but only in the case of Martin of Bentworth, who owned stalls and whose wealth was in striking contrast to that of the butchers named in the survey, do we have even indirect evidence of their commercial activity.

The close relationship between Winchester and the surrounding countryside, in which marketing must have played a major part, is clearly demonstrated in the links between a substantial number of properties in the city and the rural manors to which they were attached.[2] The distribution of these manors suggests that the relationship between Winchester and the northern and eastern parts of the county was particularly strong, a feature which is also evident in the distribution of places from which bynames recorded in the two surveys were derived.[3] These bynames also indicate close contacts with the rest of Wessex, and with Exeter and its hinterland. The link with Exeter was presumably based on the coastal trade which is well documented later in the twelfth century.[4]

Winchester's long-distance trade, both inland and overseas, probably expanded throughout the twelfth century, for the bishop's receipts from the annual fair of St. Giles appear to have reached a peak in the first half of the thirteenth century.[5] The continued expansion of the eastern suburb in that century, and the establishment of permanent structures on the site of the fair itself, both developments which appear to have been contrary to the general trend in the city at this period,[6] also testify to the growth of the trade of the fair long after 1148.

Archaeological evidence for the foreign trade of Winchester in the middle and later twelfth century is notably rarer than for the immediately preceeding period.[7] Some pilgrimage traffic to the Holy Land originated in, or passed through the city. Henry of Blois entrusted his newly found hospital of St. Cross to the Knights Hospitallers in 1136. Situated just outside Winchester, on the main road to Southampton, the hospital could in some way have been associated with the passage of pilgrims.[8]

By 1148 the essential outlines of the social system which characterized the later medieval city seem already to have emerged. The principal feature of this system was inequality in the distribution of wealth among the citizens, and this inequality may be represented in their property holdings as recorded in Survey **II**.[9] By the middle of the twelfth century, magnates and barons may be classed as occasional visitors rather than as members of city society. Royal officials on the other hand were clearly one of its wealthiest and most prominent groups and the same may have been true of certain members of the bishop's

[1] See above, pp. 438–9.
[2] See above, pp. 382–5.
[3] See above, pp. 197–9 and Fig. 3.
[4] E. M. Jope and G. C. Dunning, 'The use of blue slate for roofing in medieval England', *Antiq J* 34 (1954), 209–17.
[5] See above, pp. 286–8.

[6] See above, pp. 255, 287–8. By the late thirteenth century there appears to have been a substantially larger number of tenements in the eastern suburb below St. Giles's Hill than there was in 1148. See *SMW*.
[7] See above, pp. 478–9.
[8] See above, p. 328.
[9] See above, pp. 441–8.

retine. At a more strictly local level the moneyers seem to have held a similarly prominent position, but their prominence may be partly due to the fact that they are the one readily identifiable section of the citizen body. With its involvement in commerce and finance this body may already have dominated the day-to-day economic and social life of the city. Several families belonging to this oligarchical group may be identified in the surveys, together with the ancestors of some other important families of the later twelfth and thirteenth centuries.[1] Below this level the records of property holding show something of the hierarchy of trades, in which the cloth-workers probably occupied a notable position. Our knowledge of the guilds of the fullers and weavers in the twelfth century confirms both their prosperity and their subordinate position. At the lowest level of all was the largest body of the population, those individuals at the bottom of the tenurial ladder who were not named in the surveys.

The twelfth-century guilds provide important evidence for the cohesion of the upper ranks of this society.[2] The mid-twelfth century, like the period covered by Survey **I**, appears to have been a time of change in this respect. By 1148 the *probi homines* of Winchester had ceased to drink their guild at the *hantachenesele* in the area of *Colobrochestret*, and a guildhall, probably that where the city court later met, had been established at the north-west corner of the site of the former royal palace. This latter guildhall was probably the hall of the guild of merchants, a body which could well have come into existence by this date. It is just possible that the *hantachenesele* was identical with the later hall of St. John's Hospital where the *burghmote* met, so that in 1148 there may already have been established that duality of associations and meeting-places which characterized the civic life of Winchester in the later Middle Ages. At least it is virtually certain that the germs of the later municipal organization were already present. It is tempting to associate these developments with the social and economic stresses which may have arisen from the rapidly changing status of the city in the mid-twelfth century, and with the opportunities presented by the local disturbances and general insecurity of Stephen's reign.

At a local level the parish churches were probably the most important centres of social life. The full complement of 57 parish churches which may be identified in Winchester in the later Middle Ages had probably been achieved by the middle of the twelfth century, when the population of the city may have already reached its peak, and when a parochial system was already in being.[3] Most of these churches were perhaps essentially private foundations which gradually evolved a parochial function but remained strictly subordinate to the mother church of Winchester.[4] The large number of churches clearly reflected the size and wealth of the city and may have been a characteristic of some early medieval urban communities. If the twelfth-century population of Winchester was about 8,000 persons,[5] each parish would have contained about 140 individuals or 30 families. Further, each parish within the walls would have covered on average an area of about 1·6 ha (4 acres), or 1·1 ha (2·8 acres) if the extra-parochial areas of the monastic precincts, the cathedral cemetery, the bishop's palace, and the royal castle are excluded. The

---

[1] See above, p. 447.
[2] See above, pp. 335–6, 427, 480.
[3] See above, pp. 329–30, 440–1.

[4] See above, pp. 332–3.
[5] See above, pp. 440–1.

comparable figures for London, which in the twelfth century had about 100 parish churches within its walls,[1] were 1·3 ha (3·3 acres)[2] or 1·2 ha (3 acres).[3] At Lincoln each of the 15 parishes within the walled area outside the Bail[4] covered an average of 1·62 ha (4 acres) or 1·57 ha (3·9 acres).[5]

Comparison of the number of tenements recorded in the 1148 survey with the number of parish churches may throw some light on the conditions which led to their establishment, and on their relationship to the community. For each of the 57 parish churches there were 19 tenements in the 1148 survey. The same ratio applies when calculated separately for the suburbs as a whole, or for the walled area alone.[6] The ratios for individual streets show, however, considerable variation around this mean.[7] In High Street—the wealthiest and most densely-populated of the streets—there were about eleven recorded tenements to each parish church. In *Tannerestret* and *Snidelingestret*, both relatively densely-populated and neither conspicuously wealthy, the ratios were 29·5 to one and 35 to one, respectively. In *Calpestret*, a wealthy but not densely populated area, the ratio (14·5 : 1) was significantly below the mean. In the neighbouring street of *Goldestret*, where there were many more tenements, each smaller and less valuable than its counterpart in *Calpestret*, the ratio of tenements to churches (24·5 : 1) was significantly higher than the mean. These figures must be used with extreme caution. In some streets the pattern cannot be accurately determined, or does not appear to conform with that outlined here, and the nature and density of settlement in certain areas of the city may well have altered significantly between the period in which the parish churches were established and the date of the survey. Nevertheless, parish churches appear to have been more numerous in the wealthier rather than in the simply more populous areas of the city. This situation probably reflects the significance of private patronage in the establishment of churches, and may indicate one aspect of the problems of spiritual care in towns, problems which the friars did much to remedy in the thirteenth century.

Such a large number of parish churches clearly required a substantial body of clergy to serve them: the clergy formed the largest single occupational group identified in the surveys. The parish priests and clerks who seem to have formed the majority of this group were of relatively humble status, in striking contrast to some of the clerks who followed a bureaucratic career and were among the wealthier inhabitants of the city.[8]

By the middle of the twelfth century, Winchester had enjoyed a long history as a distinctively urban centre, but its status as a city, particularly in relation to other English towns, was undergoing a critical change. In attempting to define the status of the city in the twelfth century we rely principally on the evidence of the borough farms

---

[1] Brooke *Missionary*, 66–8.

[2] Based on the entire area within the walls: 133·5 ha (330 acres).

[3] Based on the area within the walls, less the extra-parochial areas of the precincts of St. Paul's, St. Martin le Grand, the priory of Holy Trinity, Aldgate, and the Tower.

[4] Sir Francis Hill, *Medieval Lincoln* (Cambridge, 1965), 147.

[5] In calculating the smaller figure the area of the

bishop's palace has been excluded.

[6] The two unlocated churches, St. Helen and St. Nicholas outside the wall, are both assumed to have been suburban, cf. Fig. 10. Churches over the gates of the city are counted as intra-mural since they were entered from inside the walls.

[7] For the number of tenements in individual streets, see Table 20, and for the number of churches, Fig. 10.

[8] See above, pp. 392–6.

and aids. This evidence is unsatisfactory in many respects, for some boroughs often paid a substantial lump sum in return for what appears to have been the continuance of an artificially low farm, and we know little of the principles which lay behind the assessments of aid, and the variations in their application between one town and another. In Tables 53 and 54 the farms and aids of the principal towns are presented as a percentage of those of

TABLE 53

The farms of the larger English towns in the eleventh and twelfth centuries

(expressed as a percentage of the farm of London, together with their rank order)[1]

1066[2]		1086			Henry II[6]			Richard I		
Rank	Town[3]	Rank	Town[4]	Percent-age	Rank	Town[7]	Percent-age	Rank	Town[8]	Percent-age
1	London	1	London	100	1	London	100	1	London	100
2	Droitwich	2	York	36	2	Southampton	58	2	Lincoln	57
3	York	3 (3 =)	Lincoln	33	3	Lincoln	33	3	Winchester	48
4	Canterbury	(3 =	Winchester[5]	33)	4	Winchester	27	4	Dunwich	38+
5	Chester	4 (5)	Norwich	33	5	Dunwich	22+	5	Northampton	38
6	Leicester	5 (6)	Thetford	28	6	Grimsby	20	6	Norwich	36
7	Gloucester	(6	Winchester[5]	28)	7	Norwich	20	7	Grimsby	35
8 =	Lincoln	7 =	Wallingford	27	8	Northampton	18	8	Southampton	34
8 =	Norwich	7 =	Colchester	27	9	Wallingford	16	9	York	33
8 =	Oxford	9	Chester	25	10	Leicester	14	10	Wallingford	27
8 =	Shrewsbury	10 =	Oxford	25	11	Cambridge	12	11	Cambridge	20
8 =	Thetford	10 =	Gloucester	25	12	Dover	10	12	Derby	19
8 =	Wallingford	12	Droitwich	23	13	Gloucester	10	13	Gloucester	18
		13	Canterbury	21	14	Canterbury	9			

[1] The percentages are derived from the sums given in the table of borough farms in Tait *Medieval Borough*, 184. Each of the sums in Tait's table has been converted to its equivalent by tale according to the principles enumerated in S. Harvey, 'Royal Revenue and Domesday Terminology', *Econ H R*, 2nd ser. 20 (1967), 221–8. Towns are ranked according to the amounts of their farms and percentages are given to the nearest whole number. Some towns whose percentages are equal may therefore have differing rank positions in the table. All the towns appearing in Table 54 are also recorded in this table or in its notes.

[2] Percentages cannot be calculated for 1066 since the farm of London is not known.

[3] Dunwich ranked thirtieth with Buckingham. The farms of Exeter, Northampton, and Winchester are not known.

[4] Dunwich (17+%) ranked sixteenth, Northampton (10%) twenty-ninth, and Exeter (6·5%) thirty-fifth.

[5] Based on the allowance of £80 blanch for the farm of the city against the Hampshire account in the pipe rolls of Henry II: see above, p. 487. This sum may not in fact represent the value of the Winchester farm before the latter part of the reign of Henry I. The higher percentage in this column is based on the rate for conversion of blanch to tale apparently used in 1086: see Harvey, op. cit. in n. 1. The lower percentage is based on the rate of 1s. in the pound common in the twelfth century.

[6] The farms of Gloucester and Northampton were raised during the reign, and those of Southampton and Wallingford fell. The earlier values used in this table are first recorded for each of these four towns in the pipe rolls of 11, 4, 2, and 6 Henry II respectively.

[7] The farms of Exeter, Oxford, and York are not known.

[8] Exeter (4%) ranked twenty-sixth. The farms of Canterbury and Oxford are not known.

London. This method assists in identifying the hierarchy of English towns, and avoids some of the difficulties of a simple ranking. The general agreement between the two tables and between the different aids in Table 54 indicates that the farms and aids provide a substantially reliable picture.

There are at present no other bases of general comparison for English towns in the twelfth century. Changes in the topographical extent of settlement are important in understanding the development of Winchester itself, and provide dramatic evidence of the expansion of such other towns as Bristol and Northampton in the twelfth century.[1] Sufficient evidence has not been collected, even for the over-all areas of individual urban

[1] See the comparative sketch plans in Martin Biddle and Daphne Hudson, *The Future of London's Past* (Worcester, 1973), Fig. 2.

TABLE 54

The aids and tallages of the larger English towns in the twelfth and early thirteenth centuries
(expressed as a percentage of the aid of London, together with their rank order)

	Towns[1]	Henry I and Henry II[2]							Richard I and John	
		1129–30[3]	1158–9[4]	1160–1[5]	1164–5	1167–9[6]	1172–3[7]	1176–7[8]	1194–1206 mean[9]	1213–14[10]
Percentages	York	33	19	20	60	54	—	20	22	25
	Norwich	25	60	30	30	32	20	10	13	—
	Lincoln	50[11]	19+	30	40	38	40	15	21	37·5
	Northampton	8	19	16	20	22	30	30	11	20
	Dunwich	—	—	—	—	22	—	15	—	—
	Exeter	17	38	12	—	22	6	10	—	15
	Winchester	67	16	18	12	18	8	15	26	10 (?)[12]
	Gloucester	12·5	10	10	12	12	11	10	9	—
	Oxford	17	11	8	10	8	6	10	6	15
	Canterbury	17	4	4	8	12	7	10	—	15
	Bristol	—	—	—	—	—	—	—	22	37·5
Rank	London	1	1	1	1	1	1	1	1	1
	York	4	5=	4	2	2	—	3	3	4
	Norwich	5	2	2=	4	4	4	7=	6	—
	Lincoln	3	4	2=	3	3	2	4=	5	2=
	Northampton	14	5=	6	5	5=	3	2	7	5
	Dunwich	—	—	—	—	5=	—	4=	—	—
	Exeter	6=	3	7	—	5=	10=	7=	—	6=
	Winchester	2	7	5	6=	8	6	4=	2	9= (?)[12]
	Gloucester	10	9	8	6=	10	5	7=	8	—
	Oxford	6=	8	9	8	13	10=	7=	10	6=
	Canterbury	6=	14	11=	9=	9	7=	7=	—	6=
	Bristol	—	—	—	—	—	—	—	4	2=

[1] With the exception of Bristol, the towns are listed in their rank order after London, based on the mean of their aids for the reign of Henry II given in Stephenson *BT*, Appendix VI, p. 225. Chester, for which of course there are no comparable figures available, would almost certainly have ranked in this group of towns: cf. Table 53.

[2] Calculated from the figures in Stephenson *BT*, Appendix IV, pp. 222–3. Only those aids for which there are figures for both London and Winchester are included here.

[3] The twelve towns ranking after London in the reign of Henry I included Colchester (17%, sixth equal), Worcester (12·5%, tenth equal), Wallingford (12·5%, tenth equal), and Cambridge (10%, thirteenth). See Stephenson *BT*, Appendix V, p. 225.

[4] The towns ranking after London and above Canterbury included Newcastle upon Tyne (6%, tenth equal), Worcester (6%, tenth equal), Hereford (5%, twelfth equal), and Shrewsbury (5%, twelfth equal).

[5] Worcester (5%, tenth) ranked between Oxford and Canterbury.

[6] Ipswich (9%, eleventh) and Berkhamstead (8+%, twelfth) ranked between Gloucester and Oxford.

[7] Ipswich (7%, seventh equal) and Corbridge (7%, seventh equal) ranked with Canterbury; and Cambridge (6%, tenth equal) ranked with Exeter and Oxford. The lack of information for York in this year means that the true rank of each town was probably one position lower than the figures in this column indicate.

[8] Bedford (10%, seventh equal) ranked with Norwich, Exeter, Gloucester, Oxford, and Canterbury.

[9] Based on the totals given in S. K. Mitchell, *Taxation in Medieval England* (ed. Sidney Painter, New Haven, Conn., 1951), 313. The records of the contributions of London during this period are irregular, but there are reasonable grounds for assuming that the capital would usually have provided £1,000: ibid. 294; *Pipe Roll 6 John*, p. 98; and cf. S. K. Mitchell, *Studies in Taxation under John and Henry III* (New Haven, Conn., 1914), 68, n. 278.

[10] *Pipe Roll 16 John*, passim. See also Mitchell *Studies in Taxation*, 116–18. The tallage for this year has been chosen for analysis because its records are the most complete and perhaps the most representative for the latter part of John's reign.

[11] Based on the total of £60 (90 marks) in *Pipe Roll 31 Henry I*, p. 121. Stephenson *BT*, Appendix V, gives 80 marks.

[12] Based on the attribution to the citizens of Winchester of 200 marks *de ultimo taillagio dominicorum R.*: *Pipe Roll 16 John*, p. 128. The same entry, *de ultimo taillagio dominicorum R.J.*, appears in the first roll of Henry III's reign: *Pipe Roll 2 Henry III*, p. 12. The reference cannot be to the Winchester tallage in 12 John, and no Winchester tallage appears on the pipe rolls for 13 or 14 John. The entry may refer to a tallage assessment on the missing pipe roll for 15 John. The position of Winchester in the tallage of 1213–14 (16 John) may not, therefore, be correctly represented by the figures in this table. In the tallage for the expedition to Ireland in 1210, Winchester ranked with Exeter, above Northampton, Gloucester, Oxford, and Lincoln. The figures for Bristol, however, show that towns with Irish connections bore particularly heavy charges in this tallage. Winchester may have ranked relatively high in the list of assessments for this reason. See *Pipe Roll 12 John*, passim.

settlements, for reliable comparisons to be made with other towns. Numismatic evidence, which is now beginning to be used on a fully quantitative basis for the pre-conquest period, can so far provide no more than the simplest of comparisons for the twelfth century.[1]

It is quite clear that in the long term Winchester lost its relatively high position among English towns between the twelfth century and the first half of the fourteenth century. In the reign of Henry II the borough aids show that Winchester ranked at least among the first eight, and probably among the first six.[2] The borough farms suggest a higher rank, but Winchester appears to have occupied sixth or seventh place among the towns with mints.[3] In 1334 Winchester ranked about fourteenth. By that date the city had been overtaken by its immediate rival, New Salisbury, by towns of the east coast and East Anglia, Newcastle, Yarmouth, Boston, Lynn, and Ipswich, and by Shrewsbury.[4] In the context of the expanding economy and population of England in the twelfth and thirteenth centuries this fall in rank need not necessarily have been accompanied by a decline in the absolute size of the city, but the contraction of the built-up area over the same period suggests that with Winchester this was in fact the case.

In the twelfth century Winchester occupied the position of regional capital for central southern England. With the possible exception of Southampton, to be discussed below, the nearest centres of comparable size and wealth, London, Bristol, and Oxford, were between 80 and 110 km (50 and 70 miles) distant. Winchester thus served a region of some 50 km (30 miles) radius. The other towns and cities listed in Tables 53 and 54, from Exeter in the south-west to York, Norwich, and Canterbury in the north and east, appear to have served regions of similar size.

Southampton was an important urban centre, closely linked with Winchester and probably heavily dependent upon it.[5] In the twelfth century a large proportion of its overseas trade must have been generated by Winchester, or at least channelled through the regional capital. In the reign of Henry II the borough farm of Southampton was second only to that of London, but the difficulties experienced in collecting the full amount,[6] the limited topographical extent of the town, in comparison to Winchester,[7] and its relatively small contribution to the borough aids, all indicate that Southampton actually ranked some way below Winchester.

To the north-east, London exercised an exceptionally powerful influence. This is clearly demonstrated by the bynames which illustrate the migration of population to

---

[1] See above, pp. 396-7, 468-9.

[2] The twelve largest towns in late twelfth-century England were probably London, York, Bristol, Lincoln, Norwich, Northampton, Winchester, Chester, Oxford, Gloucester, Canterbury, and Exeter. After London the order is uncertain, but York and Bristol should probably be set above Lincoln, Norwich, Northampton, Winchester, and possibly Chester, which should in turn probably be set above Oxford, Gloucester, Canterbury, and Exeter. See Table 54 and notes thereto. Newcastle probably also occupied a high position.

[3] See Table 53, and above, p. 397.

[4] W. G. Hoskins, *Local History in England* (London,

1959), appendix, p. 176. To Hoskins's figure of 1,030s. for the tax quota of the city of Winchester should be added 220s. for the soke of Winchester, likewise assessed at a tenth and comprising the south and east suburbs of the city. The assessments for both the city and the soke are to be found in PRO, E 179/173/20.

[5] See now, Colin Platt, *Medieval Southampton the port and trading community*, A.D. 1000-1600 (London, 1973), especially pp. 6-11.

[6] Tait *Medieval Borough*, 170.

[7] The walled area of Southampton covered 19·8 ha (48·9 acres) as opposed to Winchester's 58·2 ha (143·8 acres).

Winchester. North-eastern Hampshire was an important source, but migration from villages any nearer to London must have been rare, in striking contrast with those areas to the north, west, and south-east of Winchester which were not directly affected by the attraction of London.[1] The greater city may even have drawn some of its population from Winchester and its immediate neighbourhood.[2] The two cities had many commercial links,[3] and the rapid growth of London was a real threat to Winchester's prosperity, not only because it attracted the royal court and eventually the royal administration away from the ancient capital, but also because it was an exceptionally powerful commercial magnet. It is just possible that the archaeological evidence for the overseas trade of Winchester reflects this situation. Winchester's diminishing contacts with Flanders and north-west Europe in the twelfth century may have been caused by the more exclusive attraction of this trade to London. In the thirteenth century, when pottery suggesting overseas trade is once more found in Winchester, it is clearly derived from trade with the wine-producing areas of south-west France in which London was not such a direct competitor.[4] The rivalry of the two cities found expression in their conflicting claims to precedence at coronations,[5] and in the twelfth century came to a head at the siege of 1141 when the victorious Londoners looted the houses of the Winchester citizens.[6]

The degree of London's predominance is clearly shown in Tables 53 and 54. Not even the wealthiest provincial centre was ever valued at more than two thirds the assessment of London for both aids and farms, and a valuation of between a third and a half was probably more characteristic. The remainder of this group of provincial centres was composed of those towns whose assessments for aid was between 10 and 25 per cent that of London. On the basis of borough farms they were slightly larger in relation to London. Below this level were some fifteen towns which might be defined as regional centres of lesser significance.[7] In the borough aids of Henry II's reign Winchester's assessment was between 15 and 20 per cent that of London. By 1334 this figure had fallen to about 6 per cent,[8] but this must to some extent be offset by the widening difference in wealth between London and the provincial towns in general, which appears to have come about by the fourteenth century. We may be able to detect, in the percentages shown in Table 54, that the gap between London and the provincial towns was already widening during the twelfth century. In the reigns of Richard I and John the wealthier towns represent a smaller proportion of the assessment of London than they did in the period up to 1167–9. The percentages in Table 53 do not display the same development, for the London farm was substantially reduced under Richard I, but they do indicate

[1] See above, p. 497 and Fig. 3. This effect may however be intensified by the relative sparseness of settlement in the south-west part of Surrey: cf. *DGSEE*, Figs. 110 and 168.

[2] *De Winton'* was a common surname in London from the late twelfth century onwards: *ELPN* 121. For migration from Hampshire to London at the end of the thirteenth century, see Ekwall *Subs R* 49–71.

[3] Most strikingly evidenced by the adjournment of the London court of Husting during St. Giles's Fair: *VCH Hants* v. 36.

[4] *Winchester Studies* 7.

[5] First recorded at the second coronation of Richard I in Winchester in 1194: W. Stubbs (ed.), *Chronica Magistri Rogeri de Houedene*, iii (RS, 1870), 248; see also, *VCH Hants* v. 36.

[6] See above, p. 339.

[7] Stephenson *BT*, Appendix VI, p. 225.

[8] Based on London's quota of 1,100 marks at a fifteenth, converted to the rate of a tenth at which other towns were assessed: J. F. Willard, 'The taxes upon movables of the reign of Edward III', *EHR* 30 (1915), 69–74.

that the farms of the provincial towns as a whole covered a significantly wider range of values at the end of the twelfth century than in 1086. We may tentatively conclude that the hierarchy of English towns became more distinctive in the course of the twelfth century, and that as their populations increased by geometric progression, so the differences between the larger and the smaller towns became more obvious.

On the evidence of the borough aids Winchester declined from second to sixth or lower rank among English towns between 1130 and the reign of Henry II. This decline is all the more remarkable, for Winchester's contribution to the aid of 1129–30, at 67 per cent that of London, represented a higher proportion of London's assessment than that of any other town during the twelfth century. Winchester's high rank at the end of Henry I's reign, perhaps still fourth as it had been before the conquest, is confirmed by the numismatic evidence.[1] But even by 1135 Winchester had been overtaken as a minting centre by Norwich and recently equalled by Thetford, and it is important to remember that York and to a lesser extent Lincoln were still recovering from the devastations of the 1070s. There are, however, grounds for believing that this fall in rank according to the assessments for aid between 1130 and the reign of Henry II bore a simple relationship neither to Winchester's position as a market-centre nor to a decline in the size and wealth of its burgess population. The fall in rank may have been related rather to the nature of the assessment for aid itself, and to the change in the status of Winchester as a royal centre during the reign of Stephen. A large proportion of Winchester's assessment for aid in 1129–30 was contributed by individuals whose principal association with the city was in connection with its character as a royal capital. The pardons of contributions to the aid recorded on the pipe roll show that at least 37 per cent of the assessment was due from a group of seven magnates, and at least 24 per cent from eight royal officials.[2] If we exclude the 16 per cent of the total assessment contributed by the bishop and abbess of Winchester, we are left with a minimum of 45 per cent of the aid contributed by a group of people whose principal estates and local interests were in many cases centred far from Winchester. A comparison of Winchester with other towns on the basis of the aid of 1129–30 thus provides an exaggerated picture of the wealth of its burgesses and its economic status. The pardons show that as a result of the uncertainties of Stephen's reign a high proportion of the wealth formerly resident in the city was likely to have been withdrawn and never to have returned.

These pardons are the only evidence we have for the distribution of individual payments among the populations of the towns which were assessed for aid in 1129–30.[3] If we assume that to some extent at least they represent the actual distribution of payments, a useful comparison between Winchester and some other important towns may be made. Even if we exclude the bishop of Winchester and the abbess of St. Mary's,

---

[1] See above, pp. 396–7.

[2] For the total amount pardoned and the sums pardoned to the magnates, see above, p. 444 and n. 2. The royal officials were pardoned a total of £19. 10s. 4d., *Pipe Roll 31 Henry I*, p. 41.

[3] The largest proportion of any aid in this year was pardoned to Winchester. Oxford was pardoned 69 per cent, Canterbury 61 per cent, and London 28 per cent.

Most of the other provincial centres were pardoned between 10 and 20 per cent of their aids. At York nothing was pardoned. It seems likely that the persons who were pardoned did not altogether escape payment, but were simply excused accounting to the sheriff. The burgesses of Wallingford, however, appear to have entirely escaped payment of their aid of £15 on account of their poverty; see *Pipe Roll 31 Henry I, passim*.

the magnates as a group appear to have made a far larger contribution to the aid of Winchester than to that of any other town for which there is evidence, a striking contrast to the position of the magnates as landlords in Winchester in 1148.[1] At Canterbury the 60 per cent of the city's aid pardoned to magnates was composed of 58 per cent pardoned to the archbishop, and 2 per cent to the earl of Gloucester.[2] At Oxford a single magnate, the bishop of Salisbury, was pardoned 12 per cent of the aid.[3] Similarly at Lincoln the bishop was pardoned 17 per cent of the aid,[4] and at Gloucester the earl was pardoned 11 per cent out of the total of 12 per cent pardoned to the magnates.[5] Only at London did the number of magnates equal that at Winchester: eight magnates were pardoned a total of 13 per cent of the city's aid.[6] All the magnates pardoned at London were 'out-of-town' lords. If we take the directly comparable group in Winchester, by omitting the bishop and the abbess, the proportion of the city's aid pardoned to magnates, 21 per cent, still considerably exceeded the figure for London. Given their limitations, these figures indicate that late in the reign of Henry I Winchester was still as important a meeting place for the leading men of the kingdom as London. There was an important contrast between the two cities, however, for it would appear that the magnates contributed more to the total assessment of Winchester's aid than they did to that of London, and this may reflect differences in the relative distribution of wealth between the two cities. Under Henry II pardons of contributions to borough aids were not issued on such a large scale, but it may be representative of the reduced state of Winchester that in 1160–1, the only aid of the reign for which a significant number of Winchester pardons were issued, no magnates or royal officials were pardoned the city's aid, while members of these groups were still being pardoned contributions to the aid of London.[7]

The departure of the court and the royal administration, an extended process of disengagement which was only really complete by the early years of the fourteenth century, was an important factor in the long-term decline of the city, for it was presumably accompanied by a reduction both in the amount of money spent in the city's markets and in the demand for housing and other accommodation. These effects, probably accentuated by the seige of 1141, are first to be seen in the 1148 survey. The king's revenue from property, in the side streets at least, fell significantly between c. 1110 and 1148, and it seems likely that the decline in the number of habitations on the royal fief over the same period was representative of the city as a whole;[8] the Romsey Abbey estate in the city was worth less in 1148 than in 1086;[9] and, although the Wherwell Abbey houses were worth more in 1148 than in 1086, they had not recovered their 1066 value.[10] Of the private estates, the properties of Herbert son of Herbert the chamberlain were fewer in number in 1148 and less valuable than his father's in c. 1110.[11] More reliable is the evidence of the seven rents or totals of rent from properties in High Street which may be identified in

---

[1] There is no direct evidence as to the basis of the assessment of individual contributions to the borough aids in the reigns of Henry I and Henry II, but this contrast suggests that the value of a person's movable goods was more significant for his assessment than the value of his real property.

[2] *Pipe Roll 31 Henry I*, p. 68.

[3] Ibid., p. 6.

[4] Ibid., p. 121.

[5] Ibid., p. 80.

[6] Ibid., pp. 149–50.

[7] *Pipe Roll 7 Henry II*, pp. 18, 57.

[8] See above, pp. 350–1.

[9] See above, p. 356.

[10] See above, p. 356.

[11] See above, pp. 370–1.

both surveys. In *c.* 1110 St. Mary's Abbey received rents of 8*s.*, £4, and £1 from three tenements (**I, 8, 25,** and **36**). From the corresponding tenements in 1148 (**II, 72, 40,** and **8**) it received 6*s.*, £3. 1*s.*, and 13*s.* 6*d.* respectively, representing a fall in value of between a third and a quarter. In *c.* 1110 the cathedral priory received rents of £1. 3*s.*, £1. 17*s.*, £4, and £5. 12*s.* from four tenements (**I, 14, 15, 26,** and **28**). From the corresponding tenements in 1148 (**II, 64, 62, 39,** and **37**) it received £1, £1. 12*s.* 6*d.*, £1. 4*s.*, and £3. 18*s.* respectively. In each of these seven cases there was a fall in the value of the rent, although not always of the same order of magnitude.

By the early years of Henry II, Winchester's economy had no doubt recovered from the worst effects of the siege of 1141. The increasing prosperity of the Winchester clothing industry,[1] the borough farms, and the tallages of 1194–1206,[2] suggest that the fortunes of the city may even have improved in relation to those of several other English towns in the second half of the twelfth century. It is tempting to associate this apparent development, particularly with regard to the city's ranking on the basis of its farm, with the growth of the annual fair at Winchester. But the tallages of Richard I and John were much more varied and irregular in their assessments than the aids of Henry II and so are probably a less reliable index of the relative prosperity of towns. Winchester's assessment in the tallage of 1213–14 may be much more representative of its true relative position and this indicates some decline in the city's fortunes since the reign of Henry II. Furthermore, the account for the city farm, still nominally £142 blanch as in Henry II's time, was frequently in arrears during the reign of John.[3] The city's difficulties with the farm were so acute that in 1205 the sums which the fullers and weavers had paid for their guilds, together with four marks a year which the citizens owed to the king for a house in the city, were amalgamated with the farm, subsidizing it to the extent of £20. 13*s.* 4*d.* a year.[4] Such evidence as there is for property-values also suggests a decline in the prosperity of the city during the second half of the twelfth century. The rent receipts of the Templars from their properties in the city fell between 1148 and 1185,[5] and the properties of Thomas Brown, which came into royal possession in 1180, were valueless by 1197.[6]

The city continued to fare badly in the thirteenth century. The sieges of 1216 and 1217 caused considerable destruction in the suburbs and some permanent depopulation in the streets near the royal castle.[7] This devastation was no doubt the immediate cause of the *paupertas et destructio* which were cited in 1228 as one of the reasons for the reduction of the farm to £80 a year.[8] This was the very period at which the trade of St. Giles's Fair was reaching its maximum. In the twelfth century the expansion of the annual fair may not even have fully counterbalanced the slow decline in the permanent population and wealth of Winchester.

---

[1] See above, p. 438.
[2] See Tables 53–4.
[3] *Pipe Roll 6 John*, pp. 131–2.
[4] *Pipe Roll 7 John*, p. 128.
[5] See **II, 25,** n. 1.
[6] See below, Appendix I. 1, p. 510, n. 3.
[7] The results of this devastation may be seen in the numerous waste properties, apparently concentrated where the fighting was thickest, recorded in the Winchester accounts in PRBW for 1215–16 and 1218–19.

[8] *Close R 1227–31*, pp. 57–8, 129. The Memoranda Roll for this year includes some account of the arrears of the farm since the reign of John: PRO, E 159/9, m. 2d.

We may perhaps best draw together the main threads of the arguments developed in this concluding part by constructing a possible model for the development of Winchester in the tenth, eleventh, and twelfth centuries.

Between the end of the Roman period and the late ninth century, the city of Winchester was not an urban settlement in the modern sense of the term, but rather a royal and ceremonial centre in the midst of what appears to have been a countryside of relatively dense settlement. The port of Southampton contained the only major concentration of population, manufactures, and commerce in the region.

The disturbed conditions of the second half of the ninth century, together with Alfred's establishment of a system of defence based on fortified places, the greatest of which was Winchester, provided the first impetus towards the re-emergence of recognizably urban conditions in the city. It was apparently at this date that Winchester was provided with the grid of streets within its walls which was to continue to serve the city without major alteration into modern times. In these early years, crisis and royal policy may have encouraged the inhabitants of the surrounding villages not only to seek temporary refuge in the city, but also to take up permanent residence, and this may in turn have resulted in a relatively rapid change in the distribution and balance of population within the region. The subsequent growth of the city appears to have been continuous throughout the late Saxon period, and should probably be seen within the context of the contemporary expansion of population and economic life in the country at large. As the countryside grew more prosperous, so marketing and migration to the city increased. There may have been a spurt of growth associated with King Edgar's monastic and monetary reforms, but otherwise Winchester seems to have experienced a more or less steady development. The chronological distribution of coins found in the city suggests that this was the case, and may indicate that expansion was particularly rapid from the latter part of Cnut's reign.[1]

Over this period Winchester evolved from being solely capital of Wessex to the position of a great provincial town in a more or less united kingdom of England. The city retained nevertheless its character as a major royal centre, and eventually emerged as the administrative capital of the kingdom. It is the city at this stage in its development which is represented by the *TRE* portion of Survey **I**.

But even in the tenth century, London and York exceeded Winchester, and Lincoln was probably equal to it in size while, in the reign of King Edward, Norwich was emerging as a rival. The growth of Winchester failed to match its political importance, both because of its geographical position, and because of the relatively limited capacity of its hinterland to sustain expansion.

The city's political importance attracted a new injection of wealth and investment in the years following the Norman Conquest, and the relative stability of southern as opposed to northern England meant that for a limited period it rose to second rank among English towns. The increasing activity of the royal and perhaps also of the ecclesiastical administration brought wealth to Winchester. Survey **I** *modo* depicts the city towards the end of this phase, and contains clear evidence of expansion since the reign of Edward the Confessor.

[1] For the evidence and further discussion, see Winchester Studies 8, in preparation.

From about the date of Survey **I** in *c.* 1110 the close link between Winchester, the monarchy, and the royal administration began to slacken. This process marked the first stage in the slow decline of the city throughout the remainder of the Middle Ages. In Survey **II,** compiled in 1148, there is some evidence that this decline was already under way. We must take into account the probability that Winchester was in a depressed state in 1148 as a result of the effects of the anarchy, and in particular of the siege of 1141. Nevertheless, the city does seem to have declined over the twelfth century as a whole, so that if there was any improvement after the reign of Stephen, it probably amounted to little more than a slower rate of decline.

A direct result of the confusion of Stephen's reign is probably to be seen in the removal from Winchester of a good deal of official and aristocratic wealth. This may have caused a relatively rapid structural change in the city's economy and national position, but probably had only longer-term effects on the permanent population. Winchester was thus in decline during a period when the population and economy of the country as a whole was expanding rapidly. Trade at the city's annual fair of St. Giles, which was itself a reflection of that national economy, appears to have been expanding at the same time as the city itself was in decline. This paradox goes far towards illuminating the special character of Winchester as a royal city in the early Middle Ages.

APPENDIX I

THIRTEENTH-CENTURY SURVEYS OF WINCHESTER

Edited and translated by D. J. KEENE

---

1. THE SURVEY OF 1212

INTRODUCTION

THIS inquiry into the alienated properties of the crown in Winchester was undertaken as part of a general survey of knight's fees and sergeanties carried out by the sheriffs of each county in the summer of 1212. Properties which were still held in the king's demesne, such as the mint or the landgable rents, were not included. None of the rents mentioned here ever came to be regarded as part of the city fee farm and the crown appears to have lost control over six of the nine holdings within a few years. This survey is the only surviving list of royal holdings in Winchester made between the survey of 1148 and that of 1285.

The text of this Winchester extract follows that of the whole survey of 1212 printed from the original returns by the Deputy Keeper of the Records,[1] and has been checked against the original manuscript[2] and a thirteenth-century copy.[3] The nature and purpose of the 1212 survey has been fully discussed in the introduction to the complete edition.[4]

TEXT	TRANSLATION
Civitas Wintonie	The City of Winchester

In civitate Wintonie est quedam terra quam Rex Henricus, pater domini regis, dedit Wassall' cantatori et heredibus suis, reddendo annuatim ad scaccarium dimidiam libram scimini.[5]

In the city of Winchester there is a piece of land which King Henry, father of the present king, gave to Vassal the chanter and his heirs, rendering half a pound of cummin annually at the exchequer.[5]

[1] H. C. Maxwell Lyte (ed.), *Liber Feodorum. The Book of Fees commonly called the Testa de Nevill, reformed from the earliest MSS.*, pt. i, *1198–1242* (London, 1920), 77.

[2] PRO, E198/2/4.   [3] PRO, E198/2/5.

[4] *Liber Feodorum*, 52–64.

[5] This land lay in the western suburb in *Erdberi* (see above, p. 237, s.n.). From 1183 to 1189 the sheriff of Hampshire collected 5s. a year from the sale of corn

de Erdberia (*Pipe Roll 29 Henry II*, p. 147; *Pipe Roll 1 Richard I*, p. 5). By Michaelmas 1190 the king had granted this income to *Vassallo cantori* by charter (*Pipe Roll 2 Richard I*, p. 138). The ½ lb of cummin was still being rendered to the king in 1248–51 when Emma, daughter of William Vassal, sold the property to John son of Gregory the baker (*Selborne Charters*, ii. 80). For the later history of the property see *SMW* 698.

Dominus rex habet quoddam tenementum in civitate Wintonie ubi aula sua fuit antiquitus et valet per annum xv s. et vi d., quos constabularius Wintonie rescipit, set nescimus per cuius liberacionem.[1]

Dominus Rex Johannes dedit Willelmo tailatori suo quandam domum in Wintonia que fuit de dominio suo, que vocatur Chupmanneshalle.[2]

Dominus Rex Henricus, pater domini regis, dedit G. filio Petri quandam domum in civitate Wintonie que fuit Thome le Brun', quam dominus rex habuit de excaeta cum aliis terris suis in Wintonia.[3]

Heredes Arturi de parrok tenent quandam terram vacuam de eodem tenemento per liberacionem Willelmi Eliensis episcopi qui fuit cancellarius Regis Ricardi, set non scimus per quod servicium.[4]

Thomas Silvestr' tenet quandam terram de eodem tenemento per liberacionem eiusdem episcopi, set nescimus per quod servicium.[5]

Idem Thomas tenet quandam terram de eodem tenemento quam Nicholaus de Limeseye tenuit per liberacionem eiusdem episcopi.[5]

Petrus Piscator tenet quandam terram de eodem tenemento per liberacionem baronum de scaccario et reddit ad scaccarium annuatim iiii s.[6]

Dominus rex habuit de escaeta quandam terram vacuam in vico Judeorum quam dedit Alano Sparue, servienti G. filii Petri.

The king has a tenement in the city of Winchester where his hall stood a long time ago. It is worth 15s. 6d. a year and this sum is received by the constable of Winchester, but we do not know who authorised this.[1]

King John gave to William, his tailor, a house from his demesne in Winchester called Chapman's Hall.[2]

King Henry, father of the present king, gave to G[eoffrey] fitzPeter a house in the city of Winchester which had belonged to Thomas Brown and which the king had as escheat with his other lands in Winchester.[3]

The heirs of Arthur of Parrok hold a vacant piece of land belonging to the same tenement by the authority of William, bishop of Ely and chancellor of King Richard I, but we do not know for what service.[4]

Thomas Silvester holds a piece of land belonging to the same tenement by the authority of the same bishop, but we do not know for what service.[5]

The same Thomas holds a piece of land of the same tenement, which Nicholas of Limésy held by the authority of the same bishop.[5]

Peter the fisher holds a piece of land belonging to the same tenement by the authority of the barons of the exchequer, and renders 4s. a year at the exchequer.[6]

The king had by escheat a vacant piece of land in Jewry Street which he gave to Alan Sparrow, servant of G[eoffrey] fitzPeter.

---

[1] The site of the Norman royal palace appears to have been in the possession of the bishop of Winchester in 1148 and the greater part of the area was included in the cathedral cemetery (see above, p. 301). Certainly by the thirteenth century, and probably early in the reign of Henry II, the crown had recovered possession of the properties which had developed on the northern part of the palace site in High Street and on its western margin. The major part of the land subsequently assigned to the constable of Winchester castle lay on the west side, between the modern Little Minster Street to the west, the cemetery to the east, and the city hall of pleas (cf. II, 140) to the north. This was the area where, in the thirteenth and fourteenth centuries, tenements said to be in the Constabulary or owing rents to the castle were situated (see *SMW* and, for specific references, Stowe 846, fos. 5ᵛ, 10ᵛ, 23ᵛ, 24, 20, 31ᵛ, 37, 91). Before 1398 a small property on the High Street frontage at the extreme east end of the palace site was said to belong to the castle of Winchester (*SMW* 147–8; WCA Enrolments, m. 11, 11d), but this may simply be a reference to the Woolseld, which was associated with the castle for a short period in the middle of the fourteenth century, when the materials from its demolition were taken there (PRO, E101/561/39). In 1148 the bishop's rents from the properties which were probably equivalent to the Constabulary (II, 129–43) totalled 87s. In 1327 the rents from the Constabulary were valued at 109s. 2d. (PRO, C143/193/10). The constable may have succeeded to the rents which the bishop received in this area. The tenement worth 15s. 6d. in 1212 may have been only one of the group of properties which later became known as the Constabulary.

[2] See below, p. 515 and n. 2.

[3] The land of Master Thomas Brown, the famous exchequer official, came into the king's possession on his death in 1180. Annual sums varying from 4s. to 12s. were collected from Brown's property in Winchester between 1180 and 1195. Brown's houses were repaired in 1191–2 but by 1197 no rent could be collected because the buildings had fallen down (*Pipe Rolls, 26 Henry II–9 Richard I, passim.*)

[4] In 1190–1 Arthur of Winchester agreed to pay 13s. 4d. to have part of Brown's land in the city (*Pipe Roll 3 Richard I*, p. 91).

[5] In 1190–1 Thomas son of Silvester agreed to pay 60s. to have part of Brown's land in Winchester (*Pipe Roll 3 Richard I*, p. 91).

[6] *Petrus Pisco* paid this rent in 1209 and 1210 (*Pipe Roll 11 John*, p. 167; *Pipe Roll 12 John*, p. 185).

2. THE SURVEY OF 1285

INTRODUCTION

i. *The text*

This verdict of twelve jurors of Winchester of the time of Edward I is now among the Ministers' and Receivers' Accounts in the Public Record Office,[1] and was found in the middle of the last century among the Miscellaneous Exchequer Records of the Queen's Remembrancer's Office. Joseph Hunter brought the document to the notice of Edward Smirke who printed a considerable portion of it with some commentary in the *Archaeological Journal*.[2]

The text is written on one side of a substantial skin measuring 330 mm in width by 502 mm in length. The first eight paragraphs are written across the full width of the skin while the rest of the text is written in five adjacent columns which occupy the lower half of the skin. There is evidence at the bottom for eight tags from which the seals of the jurors were suspended. Six tags survive; fragments of seals adhere to three of them, and one tag to which no seal fragments now adhere probably once carried two seals. There are slits for a tag which has been lost and there was space for a further tag towards the bottom right-hand corner of the skin which has been torn away. The manuscript is written in a hand of the later thirteenth century. There is every sign that this document is the sworn return to an inquiry issuing from the Exchequer.

ii. *The date and purpose of the manuscript*

Smirke tentatively associated this return with the judicial inquiries made at Winchester in 1280, when indeed the episcopal appropriation of the suburb, the question of the abbot of Hyde's liberty, and Reginald son of Peter's tenure of *le muwes* were among the business dealt with.[3] The exchequer background of the document, however, and the complete contrast of its content and format with those of eyre *veredicta*, mean that Smirke's conclusion must be rejected.[4]

The greater part of the document consists of a detailed specification of the sources of income which made up the fee farm of the city and the other revenues which the king enjoyed there. Even the paragraphs dealing with encroachments on the city liberty are primarily concerned with their financial implications. In December 1264 Henry III granted the city of Winchester to its citizens, at a reduced farm of 100 marks a year, for a term of twenty-one years, to run from the previous Michaelmas.[5] As this term drew to its close the new king, always jealous of encroachments on his rights, took up the matter of the Winchester farm, especially since it might be argued that his father's reduction, granted between the battles of Lewes and Evesham, had been made under duress. In October 1284 Edward granted the custody of the city to four citizens at the old farm of £80 a year.[6] A year later he agreed that the citizens of Winchester were to be quit of the twenty marks a year which they might be considered to owe for the term of King Henry's charter. At the same time the mayor and citizens asked that the city should be restored to them at the £80 farm. Because of the pressure of other business, possibly his intended visit to Gascony, Edward ordered the barons of the exchequer to commit the city to the citizens for that farm or another *ad regis et dicte civitatis utilitatem*, or to assign the city to a warden. The barons were to make a written report to the king.[7] The present document was probably

[1] PRO, SC6/1283/9, pt. 2, no. 206.

[2] *Arch J* 7 (1850), 374–83.

[3] W. Illingworth (ed.), *Placita de Quo Warranto* (Rec Comm, 1818), 766; PRO, Just 1/784, m. 33.

[4] I am grateful to Mr. C. A. F. Meekings for discussing this point.

[5] *Cal Pat R 1258–66*, p. 391.

[6] PRO, E159/58, m.2d.

[7] PRO, E159/59, m.16, 16d. H. Rothwell (ed.), *The Chronicle of Walter of Guisborough* (Camden 3rd ser. 89, 1957), 223.

the return made on this occasion to the exchequer inquiry and the sum-total it gives, £78. 4s. 8d., was no doubt the reason why the farm continued at £80 a year.

The years 1284–5 were a period of extensive exchequer inquiries initiated under the so-called 'Statute of Rhuddlan' and generally known as Kirkby's Quest. Borough farms could fall within the cognizance of this inquest and, in the summer of 1285 the treasurer, John de Kirkby, presided at an inquiry in London which apparently concerned the farm of that city. A more precise connection between the Winchester document and the wider exchequer inquiry lies in the matter of the tallies produced against various sheriffs of Hampshire, for the articles of Kirkby's Quest specified that tallies concerning debts owed to the king and paid to sheriffs were to be produced before the inquiry.[1]

Two subsequent events support the suggestion that this Winchester verdict was given in Michaelmas term 1285. In February 1286 King Edward granted the Drapery, recovered by the judgement of the King's Court against Richard de Wherwell and others, to Richard de Merewell in return for an annual payment of £10 in addition to the £9 which had been paid before.[2] This grant evidently took place after the verdict of the Winchester jurors. Similarly the verdict probably dates from before the occasion when the pilch of grey fur due from the Linenseld was redefined as one of seven tiers (*fessis*), at some time during Michaelmas term 1285.[3]

The inquiry did not cause any large-scale survey to be undertaken in Winchester. An examplar for the paragraph on Bishop Raleigh's appropriation of the suburb probably existed in the city archives.[4] The list of persons who owed landgable rents is unlikely to have been made in 1285 since two of them, Peter Saer and Richard de Froxfel, died before November 1279.[5] This part of the verdict was no doubt copied from the most recent of the rolls of *terage* which the bailiffs of the city were supposed to keep at this time.[6] Other details of the farm could have been discovered from the bailiffs' annual account rolls.

The details of this document will be discussed in a wider context in *The Survey of Medieval Winchester* (Winchester Studies 2, forthcoming). The text is printed here principally because of the list of landgable payments, omitted by Smirke, which forms the only detailed later record comparable to the enumeration of the king's rents in the two twelfth-century surveys. Two of the properties described (the Old Mint or Drapery, and the great house of Roger Dalerun) formed part of the site of the Norman royal palace. The house where the linen cloths were sold was identical with the Chapman's Hall recorded in Survey **II**.

TEXT

Veredictum xii juratorum Winton'

[1] Dicunt quod tempore Henrici patris domini Regis Edwardi qui nunc est Willemus de Ralige tunc Winton' episcopus[7] appropriavit[8] sibi medietatem vici extra portam borialem Winton' et medietatem

TRANSLATION

Verdict of the twelve jurors of Winchester

[1] They say that in the reign of Henry [III], father of the present King Edward, William Raleigh, then bishop of Winchester,[7] appropriated[8] for himself half of the street outside the North Gate of Winchester

---

[1] H. C. Maxwell Lyte (ed.), *Inquisitions and Assessments relating to Feudal Aids*, i (London, 1899), viii–xvii.

[2] *Cal Pat R 1281–92*, p. 224.

[3] PRO, E159/59, m. 17d. Nine years' arrears of this rent are recorded for the first time in the Pipe Roll for 1285–6.

[4] See below, n. 8.

[5] PRO, Just 1/784, m. 33.

[6] Furley *Usages*, 28–9.

[7] He possessed the temporalities of the see 1244–50.

[8] Between *appropriavit* and *manent* the statement is almost word-for-word the same as that made before the itinerant justices in November 1280 (PRO, Just 1/784, m. 33). The rents for looms also appear in the Winchester Usages which were probably drawn up in the 1270s (Furley *Usages*, 28–9). For the appropriations of the suburb and the evolution of the bishop's soke see above, pp. 255–6, and *SMW*.

vici extra portam occidentalem Winton', que solebant esse in manibus eiusdem Henrici regis et pre-
decessorum suorum et pertinentes civitati sue
predicte; et per quod^a tenentes medietatem dictorum
vicorum a tempore illo subtraxerunt et se separa-
runt ab omnibus honeribus dictum regem et
civitatem predictam contingentibus. Unde per illam
appropriationem magna utensilia in quibus operantur
burelli et chalones in magna parte in illam libertatem
sic appropriatam se subtrahunt. Et quod quodlibet
tale utensile debet domino regi quinque solidos per
annum in illa libertate et infra^b quinque leucas circa
Winton'. Et similiter quodlibet utensile in quibus
operantur duplici chalones xii d. Et in quibus operantur singuli chalones vi d. per annum. Et quia in illa
libertate sic appropriata nichil solvunt eo quod ballivi
Winton' non habent ingressum in illam libertatem ad
districtiones faciendas sicut prius facere consue-
verunt fere omnes operarii burellorum et chalonum
a civitate se subtraherunt et ibi manent;^{1} et omnes
alii tenentes domini episcopi adeo liberi sunt sicut alii
de Gilda Mercatoria ad emendum et vendendum
omnimodo mercandisas ad magnum dampnum civitatis
predicte.

[2] **Item,** abbas de Hyda appropriavit sibi totam
abbatiam et curiam suam que pertinens est
civitati in precinctu libertatis eiusdem ad appro-
priand*um* hundred*o* suo de Mucheldevere, ita
quod coronatores necnon^c ballivi civitatis predicte
possunt facere suum officium de felonibus et male-
factoribus sicut solent et debent, et quam plures
tenentes domini regis sectam domino Regi debentes
et alia honera et servitia facientes.^{2} Dictus^d abbas
loca et tenementa illa sibi appropriavit et predicta
penes se inclusit per murum ad dampnum et detre-
mentum [*sic*] etcetera.^{e}

[3] **Item,** cum coronatores civitatis Winton' venirent
ad abbatiam de Hyda et vellent videre quendam
mortuum, scilicet bernarium domini regis, et suum
facere officium, predictus abbas et sui non permi-
serunt sed dominum W. de Suttone coronatorem
totius comitatus fecerunt venire per quandam poster-
nam que se ducit ad Bertonam, que est in hundredum
de Mucheldever, ad predictum officium faciendum in
preiudicium libertatis predicte.

[4] **Item,** dicunt quod quedam magna domus in
Winton' que vocatur vetus monetrium, ubi nunc

and half of the street outside the West Gate.
These areas used to be in the hands of King Henry
and his predecessors and pertained to his city. As a
result of this appropriation the tenants of those parts
of the streets removed and separated themselves
from the jurisdiction of the king and the city, and
the great looms on which burels and chalons are
made are for the most part being removed into the
appropriated liberty. The king is owed five shillings a
year for each of those looms in that liberty and within
five leagues around Winchester. Similarly for each of
the looms on which double chalons are made 12*d*. is
owed. For each of the looms on which single chalons are
made 6*d*. a year is owed. Because they pay nothing in
the appropriated liberty, and because the bailiffs of
Winchester do not have entry there to make distraints
as they used to do, nearly all the makers of burels
and chalons have removed themselves from the city
and dwell in the liberty.^{1} All the other tenants of the
bishop are as free as the men of the guild merchant
to buy and sell all manner of merchandise, causing
great loss to the city.

[2] **Item,** the abbot of Hyde took into his hundred of
Micheldever the whole of the abbey and his enclosure,
which pertains to the city and is within the precinct
of its liberty. As a result neither the coroners nor the
bailiffs of the city can carry out their duties concerning felons and wrongdoers as they are accustomed and
ought to do, and many of the king's tenants who owe
suit to him and perform other honours and services
[have been removed from the liberty of the city].^{2}
The said abbot appropriated those places and
tenements and enclosed them within his control by
a wall to the loss and detriment, etc.

[3] **Item,** when the coroners of the city of Winchester
came to Hyde Abbey and wished to view a dead man,
the king's dog-keeper, and to carry out their office,
the abbot and his men would not allow them but
caused Sir W. de Sutton, coroner of the whole
county, to come by a postern which leads to Barton
in the hundred of Micheldever to perform the said
office, to the prejudice of the liberty of the city.

[4] **Item,** they say that a certain great house in
Winchester called the Old Mint, where the Drapery

---

^{a} quos *MS.* ^{b} circa *has been struck through* ^{c} et *struck through* ^{d} *The initial letter
is very uncertainly formed* ^{e} *This and the next paragraph appear in the reverse order in the manuscript but
are marked* a *and* b *respectively in the margin.*

^{1} See p. 512 n. 8.
^{2} The copyist of the Latin text has presumably left out a phrase here.

stat draperia civitatis eiusdem, fuit aliquando in manibus antecessorum domini regis. Et cum Normannia defforceretur domino regi Johanni, quidam Walterus de Pavely, tunc maior civitatis Rotomagensis fideliter adherens predicto domino regi ut ligio domino suo, fuit totaliter destructus et a rengno regis Francie exulatus; per quod predictus dominus rex Johannes contulit eandem domum predicto Waltero pro dampnis et jacturis quas pro ipso sustinuit.[1] Idem vero Walterus obiit absque herede de corpore suo, per quod dicta domus per mortem eiusdem Walteri fuit escaeta iterum domini regis et sic stetit per multum temporis vacua et fere ruinosa usque ad mortem domini regis predicti. Unde dominus Henricus rex fecit eam extendere ad certum valorem per sacramentum legalium virorum, et fuit extensa ad sex libras et tradita civibus Winton' pro predicto redditu. Postea cum firma civitatis deteriaretur per appropriationem predicti suburbii, per quod cives eiusdem civitatis noluerunt nec potuerunt eandem firmam tenere, idem dominus Henricus rex assignavit predictas sex libras eidem firme una cum aliis redditibus, terragiis, et aliis rebus quas habuit in manu sua in civitate eadem. Processu vero temporis quidam Nicholaus Kopping' tunc maior Winton' nitebatur expellere tenentes dicte domus et removere draperiam in alium locum. Promisit domino regi lx s. per annum ultra predictas sex libras. Et cum dominus rex videret quod non posset tenentes expellere absque iniuria eisdem facienda,[a] non concessit predicto Nicholao quod postulavit. Tamen predicti sexaginta solidi per eundem Nicholaum sic promissi solvuntur ad scaccariam domini regis quolibet anno per manus ballivorum Winton'.[2] Unde dicta domus reddit per annum ix li., scilicet vi li. firme civitatis et lx s. ad scaccariam predictam.

[5] **Item,** dicunt quod magna domus quam Rogerus Dalerun modo tenet solebat esse in manibus ante-

of the city now stands, was at one time in the hands of the king's ancestors. When Normandy was seized from King John a certain Walter de Pavely, at that time mayor of the city of Rouen and a faithful adherent to the king as his liege lord, was entirely ruined and exiled from the kingdom of the king of France. King John conferred this house on Walter in recompense for the losses and trials which he had suffered on his behalf.[1] This Walter died without any heirs and so the house was once more the king's escheat and stood for a long time empty and almost in ruins until the death of the king. King Henry [III] had the value of the house assessed by the oath of law-worthy men. It was valued at six pounds and let to the citizens of Winchester for that rent. Afterwards, when the farm of the city was reduced by the appropriation of the suburb, and the citizens were neither willing nor able to continue the farm, King Henry assigned the six pounds to the farm together with other rents, terrages, and other possessions of his in the city. After a while a certain Nicholas Kopping', then mayor of Winchester, tried to expel the tenants of the house and remove the Drapery into another place, and he promised the king 60s. a year on top of the six pounds. When the king saw that he could not expel the tenants without causing them injury, he did not grant Nicholas what he asked. However, the 60s. promised by Nicholas is being paid at the royal exchequer annually by the bailiffs of Winchester.[2] And so this house renders £9 a year: £6 to the farm of the city and 60s. to the exchequer.

[5] **Item,** they say that the great house which Roger Dalerun now holds used to be in the hands of the

---

[a] iniuriam . . . faciendam *MS.*

[1] The Mint had probably once been a part of the Norman royal palace and was worth 9 marks a year in 1215 when King John granted it to William (not Walter) de Pavilly (*Rot Litt Claus* i. 214, 219, 225). Pavilly was an important baronial family in the district of Rouen but no member of it is otherwise known to have held the office of mayor of Rouen (cf. the list of mayors in A. Chéruel, *Histoire de Rouen pendant l'époque communale, 1150–1382,* i (Rouen, 1843), app. iii). The Drapery was moved into the Mint after c. 1207 when coins ceased to be struck in Winchester, but the building may have been restored to its original function for a short period in 1248–50, when the mint was temporarily re-established during

the production of the long-cross coinage (H. Ellis (ed.), *Chronica Johannis de Oxenedes* (RS, 1859), 291). In later documents, as in this one, the Old Mint and the Drapery are considered to be identical.

[2] In July 1242 the king ordered the Drapery to be moved back into High Street where it had been in the reign of John (*Close R 1237–42,* p. 449). An annual payment of 60s., from the citizens of Winchester, 'in order that the Drapery in the Mint be removed to High Street', was due at the exchequer from the year 1242–3 (PRO, E372/88, m. 24). Nicholas Kopping', who appears to have been the initiator of this move, was mayor for the year 1242–3 and possibly also for the year before (WCM 1149).

cessorum domini regis et tradita fuit eodem tempore cuidam Ricardo Brian pro l solidis quos vicecomes Suthanton' qui pro tempore fuerit modo recipiet. Set nesciunt si habeat war' etcetera.[1]

[6] **Item,** dicunt quod quedam magna domus cum pertinentiis in qua venduntur panni linei in Winton' solebat esse in manibus antecessorum domini regis donec dominus rex Johannes eandem domum cum libertatibus, consuetudinibus, et aliis pertinentiis suis dedit Willelmo cissori suo pro servitio suo, reddendo inde domino regi et heredibus suis unum peliceum de griso per annum. Postea vero Willelmus filius dicti Willelmi feofavit de dicta domo Hugonem de Stoke. Et heredes Hugonis de Stoke feofaverunt Willelmum de Dunstaple qui nunc tenet.[2]

[7] **Item,** dicunt quod quedam terra extra portam occidentalem Winton' que vocatur le muwes, in qua sita est quedam domus et quoddam columbare, que[a] solebat esse in manibus antecessorum domini regis. Et quod dominus rex Johannes, qui frequenter et multum morabatur in castro Winton', eandem terram sibi comparavit et domum ibidem construxit ad mutandum aucipites suos et eam tenuit et inde seysitus obiit. Et dominus Henricus rex fuit etiam seysitus, quousque eandem terram tradidit cum pertinentiis suis de sua mera voluntate Reginaldo filio Petri qui eam nunc tenet. Set utrum inde habeat warentum vel non ignorant.[3]

[8] **Item,** de talliis contra diversos vicecomites: unam proponunt contra Philipum de Hoivile[b][4] continentem

king's ancestors and was let at the same time to a certain Richard Brian for 50s., which the sheriff of Hampshire for the time being now receives. But they do not know whether he has any warrant etc.[1]

[6] **Item,** they say that a certain great house with appurtenances in which linen cloths are sold in Winchester used to be in the hands of the king's ancestors until King John granted it with its liberties, customs, and other appurtenances to William, his tailor, in return for the service of rendering to the king and his heirs one pilch of grey fur a year. William, son of the said William, afterwards enfeoffed Hugh de Stoke of the house. The heirs of Hugh de Stoke enfeoffed William de Dunstaple, who now holds.[2]

[7] **Item,** they say that a piece of land outside the West Gate of Winchester, called *le muwes*, on which a house and dovecot were situated, used to be in the hands of the king's ancestors. King John, who used frequently to stay a long time in Winchester castle, acquired the land and built a house there for the mewing of his falcons. He held it and died seized of it. King Henry was also seized of it and so far as the land was concerned leased it of his own free will to Reginald son of Peter, who now holds it. They do not know, however, whether he has any warrant or not.[3]

[8] **Item,** concerning tallies against divers sheriffs, they show one against Philip de Hoivile[4] for 40s.;

---

[a] *This word appears to be otiose*   [b] Houule *MS. His name frequently appears as* Hoyvile

---

[1] This was Roger Dalerun's house at the east end of the Drapery. It was later known as *la Wolselde* for which a rent of 50s. was owed to the crown. The site had once been part of the royal palace; by 1235–6 the great house there with land to east and west had been granted to Richard Brian for a rent of 50s. by the mayor and citizens (PRO, Just 1/775, m. 11d.). See *SMW* 149.

[2] This property was identical with the seld where linen cloths were sold of Survey II (69), otherwise known as Chapman's Hall. King John granted the 20 marks rent which he had from the house to Henry Burchard in 1204–5 (*Pipe Roll 7 John*, p. 128) and in 1207 ordered the seisin of the house which had belonged to Burchard to be delivered to his sergeant, Ralph the parmenter (*Rot Litt Claus* i. 82). William, the king's tailor, possessed the house by 1212 (see above, p. 510) and in the royal charter of 1215 recording the grant to him the rent of a pilch of grey fur was specified (*Rot Chart* 213). In 1276 Edward I assigned the rent, which had lately been in arrears, to his clerk, Adam de

Wintonia (*Cal Pat R 1272–81*, pp. 61 and 133; *Cal Close R 1272–9*, p. 313). By 1283 it had been discovered that William de Dunstaple owed the rent (*Cal Close R 1279–88*, p. 220). At this time the property was generally known to the Exchequer as *Luggesour, Lungesour,* or *Longover* (e.g. PRO, E372/130 m. 24, E372/131, m. 8, and *Cal Mem R 1326–7*, p. 155), a name probably connected with the *Lousfeyre* (clothes market ?) recorded as being held there in 1330 (Goodman *Chartulary*, 73, no. 149). See also p. 512, and n. 3

[3] The royal hawk mews outside West Gate were in fact constructed for Henry II (Colvin (ed.) *King's Works*, ii. 1006). The site of the mews was granted to Reginald son of Peter, lately sheriff of Hampshire, in 1263 (*Cal Pat R 1258–61*, p. 305 and W. Illingworth (ed.), *Placita de Quo Warranto* (Rec Comm, 1818), 766), but his family was already connected with the property, for in 1248 Herbert son of Peter had bequeathed it to Reading Abbey (BM, Harl. MS. 1708, fo. 114[v]). See *SMW* 716.

[4] Sheriff 1280–2 and 1305–6.

xl s. Item, aliam contra Willelmum de Wintreshulle[1] continentem c s. Item, tertiam contra Jacobum le Savage[2] continentem c s. Item, quartam contra eundem continentem xxx s. Item, quintam contra H. de Farly[3] continentem xxv s. vi d. Item, sextam contra Her*ewardum* de Mareys[4] continentem xiii li. vi s. viii d. Item, septimam contra Radulfum de Midlincton continentem xl s. Item, tres tallias de auro reginae[5] continentes xi li. xiii s. Item.

another against William de Wintreshulle[1] for 100s.; a third against James le Savage[2] for 100s.; a fourth against the same for 30s.; a fifth against Henry de Farly[3] for 25s. 6d.; a sixth against Hereward de Mareys[4] for £13. 6s. 8d.; a seventh against Ralph of Midlincton for 40s.; and three tallies for the queen's gold[5] containing £11. 13s. Item.

[9] **Item,** de redditibus pertinentibus ad firmam Winton'

    [i] Dicunt de Draperia per annum vi li.
    [ii] De redditibus fullonum x li.[6]
    [iii] De redditu assiso de langabulo:

[9] **Item,** concerning the rents pertaining to the farm of Winchester

    [i] They say from the Drapery, £6 annually
    [ii] From the rents of the fullers, £10[6]
    [iii] From the rent of assize of landgable:

Extra portam occidentalem

Terra Gilberti le Sclatiere iuxta portam occidentalem	iiiid.
Terra Thome le Marechal iuxta eandem terram	iid.
Terra eiusdem Thome iuxta eandem terram	iiiid.
Terra Roberti Vigerus que fuit Laurentii de Anne	iid.
Terra Willelmi le Bathiere	iiiid.
Terra Hugonis le Gozmongere	iiiid.
Terra Walteri de Vallo	iid.
Terra Willelmi Dunstaple	iid.
Terra Nicholai de Berton	iiiid.
Terra Ricardi le Waite	viiid.
Terra Johannis de Ichene	iid.
Terra Paulini Clerici	iiiid.
Terra Cecilie Prince	iiiid.
Terra Ismane Artur	vid.
Terra Roberti de Halle	xvid.
Terra Amicie de Anne	iiiid.
Terra Ricardi le Worckman	iiiid.
Tres terre Thome de Chulewarton'	xvid.
Terra Cecilie Squir	iid.
Terra Ivonis Coleman	iiiid.
Terra Willelmi le Arblaster	iiiid.
Terra Matille Pikard	viiid.
Terra Willelmi le ffustir	vd.

Terra dicti Willelmi	iiiid.
Terra Rogeri Capellani	iiiid.
Terra Petri Saer	iiiid.
Terra Roberti Servientis	viiid.
Terra dicti Roberti	iiiid.
Terra Clemencie Servientis	iid.
Terra Albr*ede* de Sar'	iid.
Terra Roberti Servientis	vid.
Terra Willelme Champeneys	iid.
Terra Petri Saer	iid.
Terra eiusdem Petri	xxxiid.
Terra Rogeri Davy	xviiid.
Terra dicti Rogeri	vid.
Terra dicti Rogeri	iiiid.
Terra Ricardi le Bathiere	iiiid.
Alia terra dicti Ricardi	iid.
Terra Willelmi Tinctoris	iiiid.
Terra Walkelini Sutoris	iid.
Terra Walteri le ffeure	vid.
Summa xix s. iii d.	

Calpestret

De Edelina de Cruce	xd.
De Roberto Hacckesalt	xiid.
De Andrea Beaubelet	xxvd.
De Ricardo de Werewelle	iis.
De eodem apud Gyaldam[7]	viiid.
De Andrea Silviestre	vid.
De Thoma Champeneys	iiiid.
De Ricardo Russel	iid.

De Waltero Puke	xiid.
De Nicholao le Rus	iiiid.
De Matilla Pikard	vid.
De Roberto Hacckesalt	iiiid.
De Johanne le Clopt	vid.
De Ricardo Fige	xxviid.
Summa xii s. v d.	

Snythelingestret

Terra Johannis Botman	viiid.
Terra Petri Sair	iiiid.
Terra Willelmi de Kaneford	iid.
Terra Samueli le Cutelir	iid.
Terra Willelmi Swen[a]	vid.
Terra Walteri de la Tur	iid.
Terra eiusdem	iid.
Terra Walteri de Val	iid.
Summa ii s. iiii d.	

Brudenestret

Terra Ang*ne*te la Peynturesse	iiiid.
Terra Walteri de la Tur	xiid.
Terra Johannis de Niubur'	id.
Terra Ade de Norhamton	id.
Terra Magistri Valentini	xiiiid.
Terra Abbatis[b] de Nately	iiis.
Terra Ricardi de ffroxfel pro venella	vid.

---

a An interlinear vac' *appears to denote this entry.*

b Abb'i *or* Alb'i *MS.*

[1] Sheriff 1259–61 and 1270–2.
[2] Sheriff 1256–8.
[3] Sheriff 1249–56.
[4] Sheriff 1262–4.
[5] The payment made to the queen regnant on the issue of royal charters. The exchequer had been responsible for its collection since 1207.

[6] In the twelfth century the Pipe Rolls record the fullers as paying £6 for their guild. In 1327 the fullers' rent was also assessed at £10 (PRO, C143/193/10).
[7] The guild had its hall on the west side of *Calpestret*. See *SMW* 620–1.

Terra Ricardi de Herbeldon'	xvd.
Terra Ade Sweng'	xvd.
Terra Radulfi Poxfil[a]	viiid.
Summa ix s. iiii d.	

Shortenestret

De Johanne de Burne	id.
De Willelmo[b] de Buckingeham	xd.
De Is' de Niubur'	xviiid.
De Thoma le Charpenter	xxvd.
De abbatissa sancte Marie	vd.
De Galfrido Aurifabro	viid.
De Galfrido Hachemus	vd.
De Hachechu' filio Doulegard	xxid.
De Swetemanno pro ii terris	iiiid.
De Petro Carpentario pro terra Jospini filii Glorie	iiiid.
Summa viii s. v d.	

Alwarestret

De Nicholao de Lymesy	xvd.
De Petro Westman	xiid.
De Henrico de Durnegate	xxvd.
De Henrico le Macecrer	viiid.
De Nicholao Lanario	iid.
Summa v s. ii d.	

Munstrestret

De Johanne Cobbe que fuit Roberti Carp'	vid.
De Petro Clerico	xiid.
De Henrico le Macecrer	xiid.
De Willelmo Page	xiid.
De Ricardo Cobbe	vid.
De Philipo Coco	xxid.
De Stephano Dees[c]	iiiid.
De Willelmo Bringe	vid.
De Waltero de Pones	xiid.
De Ada de Norhamton	xviiid.
De Johanne Dun	xiid.
De Johanne Vesin	xiid.
De Laurentio de Anne	vid.
Summa xi s. iii d.[1]	

Shuldwortestret

De Henrico Clerico	vid.
De Gilberto Bonseriaunt	iiiid.
De Reginaldo Cobbe	xiiiid.
De Henrico Kawet	xd.
De Martino Dore	viiid.
De Nicholao le Rus	viiid.
Summa iiii s. i d.	

Wonegerestret

De Rogero le Lung'	viiid.[2]
De Amicia filia Warrini	xiiiid.[3]
De Willelmo le Rus	viiid.[4]
Summa ii s. vi d.	

Tannerestret

De Galfrido Gostardard	xxiid.
De Ada le Muner	vid.
De Thoma le Paumer	xd.
De Galfrido le Tainturor	xxd.
De Ricardo Kachelove	xxd.
De Ricardo Russel	xiid.
Summa vii s. vi d.	

Buckestret

De Anketillo Husario	vid.
De Henrico Cobbe	iiiid.
De Henrico Prior	vid.
Summa xvi d.	

Gar'stret

De Stephano ffromund	vs. vd.
De Henrico Brian	vid.
Terra eiusdem cuiusdam venelle	xiid.
Terra Ingeleyse	viid. obolum
De Edmundo Picard	xiid.
De Matilla Picard	vid.
De Henrico Strut	xd.
Summa ix s. x d. obolum.	

Goldstret

De Willelmo filio Willelmi	viiid.
De Johanne le Bathiere	xiid.
De Ivone Coleman	vd.
De Galfrido Pistore	viiid.
De Thoma Champeneys	viiid.
De Willelmo Martin	viiid.

De Ricardo de Werewelle	xviiid.
De Willelmo Dureward	xd.
De Johanne Fromund	xd.
De Willelmo Muntagu	iiiid.
De Johanne Edgar	iiiid.
De terra Milonis de Chartres	id.obolum
De terra Johannis Anfrey	id. obolum
Summa viii s. ii d.	

Memorandum quod domus ubi Cokerellus judeus mansit debet de langabulo per annum ii s., qui per multum temporis per ballivos Winton' non fuerant levati

Memorandum: that the house where Cokerel the Jew dwelt owes 2s. a year landgable which has not been collected by the bailiffs of Winchester for a long time.

In Mangno Vico

De Johanne Vincent	vid.
De Simone de Winton'	vid.
De Willelmo de Dunstaple	vid.
De Johanne Botman	vs.
De Aluredo Pictore	vid.
De Waltero de Hou	vid.
De Johanne Botman	vid.
De Margeria ffromund	xviiid.
De Thoma le Paumer	vid.
De eodem Thoma	iiiid.
De Edmundo de Grunstede	iiiid.
De Waltero de Val	vid.
De Thoma Palmigero	iiiid.
De monachis sancti Barnabe[5]	xviiid.
De terra monachorum sancti Swithuni	iis.
De Roberto Wolward	iid.
De Henrico Strut	iid.
De Michele Parmentario	iiiid.
De Petro Westman	iid.
De monachis de Quarer'	vid.
De Thoma Ville	vid.
De Rogero Dalerun	vid.

---

[a] *Possibly a scribal error for* Porfil: *see above, p. 215, s.n.* Pofil   [b] Johanne *struck through*   [c] *The initial* D *is uncertainly formed*

[1] The correct total is 11s. 7d.
[2] See **II, 571.**
[3] See **II, 572.**
[4] See **II, 604.**
[5] The monks of Hyde Abbey.

De Ada Povere	vid.	De Willelmo de Lauinton	vid.	De Willelmo de Templo et	
De Johanne Cobbe	vid.	De abbatissa sancte Marie	xd.	W. Cutelir	ixd.
De Mabilla vidua	vid.	De Ricardo de Stogbrige	xiid.	De novem terris vacuis	
De Willelmo Prior	vid.	De Johanne le Lung	vid.	retro Draperiam	iiii s. vid.
De heredibus Galfridi Barn'	vid.	De Roberto de ffarham	vid.	De Rogero Dalerun ad	
De Emma de Chireton'	vid.	De Willelmo de Templo	ixd.	shoppam	vid.
De Gerewas' Capellano	vid.	De Stephano de Exton	ixd.	De Willelmo Kuarcoto	vid.
De Willelmo le Rus	vid.	De Willelmo le ffeure	vid.	De Petro Buffo	vid.
De Johanne Longo	vid.	Johannes Smay	vid.	De H. de Durnegate	vid.
De Philipo de Candevere	vd.	De Laurentio de Anne	xiid.	De W. Speciario	vid.
De Alexandro de Merewelle	vid.	De Willelmo de Dunstaple	iiiid.	De eodem pro terra	
De Petro Curtario	vid.	De Henrico Clerico	vid.	Henrici Molend'	vid.
De Hugone Kawet	vid.	De Samuelo le Cutelir	iiid.	Summa xxxix s. ii d.[a]1	

[iv] Item, de consuetudinibus ville predicte:[2]

de consuetudine burellorum et chalonum per annum lx s.

de consuetudine portarum a festo sancti Michelis usque festum sancti Egidii cum fferiis sancti Barnabe et sancti Swithuni[3] iiii li.

de consuetudine pesagii per idem tempus xl s.

de consuetudine piscium per idem tempus iiii li.

de consuetudinariis[4] et minutis consuetudinibus per idem tempus lx s.

de placitis et perquisitis per idem tempus c s.

Summa xxi li.

[v] Item, ab incrastino exaltationis sancte Crucis usque festum sancti Michelis, ut in pesagio lane, et consuetudine intrantium et exeuntium, et placitis et perquisitis, et de consuetudinibus portarum et aliis promissionibus mercatorum et escaetis, l marcas[5]

Summa l marcas.

Summa summarum lxxviii li. iiii s. x d.[6]

[iv] Item, from the customs of the town:[2]

from the custom of burels and chalons annually 60s.

from the custom of the gates between Michaelmas [29 September] and the feast of St. Giles [1 September], with the fairs of St. Barnabas and St. Swithun[3] £4

from the custom of pesage for the same period 40s.

from the custom of fish for the same period £4

from collectors of customs[4] and from petty customs for the same period 60s.

from pleas and perquisites for the same period 100s.

Total £21

[v] Item, between the day after Holy Cross day [i.e. 15 September] and Michaelmas [29 September], from the pesage of wool, custom paid by persons entering and leaving the city, pleas and perquisites, the customs at the gates and other promises of merchants and of escheats, 50 marks[5]

Total 50 marks

Sum Total £78. 4s. 10d.[6]

[a] *The total is written over an erasure*

1 The correct total is £1. 19s. 8d.
2 For these payments see Furley *City Government*, 97–8 and the bailiffs' account of 1354–5, ibid. 179–80.
3 The bishop's fair at St. Giles's church on the hill to the east of Winchester began on the vigil of the feast of St. Giles (31 August) and in the thirteenth century lasted for sixteen days, during which the bishop received all the revenues of the city. Thus the king did not receive the revenues from the customs enumerated here between 31 August and 15 September. After the sixteen days of the bishop's fair the merchants were supposed to descend with their goods into the city and carry on trading there (*Close R 1256–9*, p. 430). The king's receipts during this latter part of the fair, between 15 September and 29 September, are recorded in [9] [v]. See also below, n. 5.
4 *Consuetudinarius* usually means 'customary tenant', but this meaning seems unlikely in the context.
5 See above, n. 3. The exceptionally high receipts due to the king recorded in this paragraph make it clear that Winchester fair was not limited to the period during which the bishop enjoyed its revenues, but lasted throughout the month of September.
6 The correct total is £77. 8s. 3½d.

[10] Et sciendum est quod antequam P. de Rupibus episcopus Wint'[1] appropriavit sibi suburbium Winton' omnes et singuli suburbani[a] qui operabantur burellos solebant reddere pro utensile suo v s. per annum. Et quilibet operator chalonum in quo operabantur magni chalones xii d., et quilibet operantes parvos chalones vi d.

[10] And be it known that before Peter des Roches, bishop of Winchester,[1] appropriated the suburb of Winchester every one of the inhabitants of the suburb who made burels used to pay 5s. a year for his loom. Each maker of chalons paid 12d. a year [for the loom] on which great chalons were made, and each maker of small chalons [paid] 6d.

Nomina xii juratorum

Willelmus le Specir
Adam Povere
Ricardus de Stogbrig'
Johannes Russel
Johannes Moraunt
Johannes le Cras
Hugo de ffulfloud
Andreas Beaublet
Willelmus Scrut[b]
Willelmus de Occly
Walterus de Kaperigge
Thomas le Paumer.

[a] suburbany MS.   [b] MS. may read Strut.

[1] He possessed the temporalities of the see 1206–38. He appropriated the suburb in 1232–3, and the citizens of Winchester were already complaining of their loss of revenue in 1234. See above, pp. 255–6, and *Curia Regis R 1233–7*, p. 227.

APPENDIX II

THE MANUSCRIPT OF THE WINTON DOMESDAY

1. The manuscript and the handwriting *by* T. J. BROWN
2. The corrections *by* MARTIN BIDDLE
3. The binding *by* H. M. NIXON
4. Fragments of a tenth-century sacramentary from the binding *by* the late FRANCIS WORMALD

---

1. THE MANUSCRIPT AND THE HANDWRITING

by T. J. BROWN

(*Frontispiece*, Plates I–III)

THE MANUSCRIPT[1]

THE manuscript is written on thirty-three leaves of vellum, measuring 251 × 174 mm. The written area occupies 185 × 125 mm. There are twenty-nine lines to the page in double column.

Material

The membrane is of medium quality and thickness. There are original holes in the fore-edges of fos. 2 and 10. Small holes occur as follows: two in the text on fo. 5; one in the upper margins of fos. 6 and 11, and in the outer margin of fo. 14; two in the text of fo. 24; one in the text of fo. 27; and two in the outer margin of fo. 30. There is a small cut in the lower margin of fo. 8.

Quiring

There are four quires, each of four folded sheets (fos. 1–8, 9–16, 17–24, and 25–32). The last leaf (fo. 33) is a singleton. The pages in the first half of each quire are lettered *a–f*, starting on the first verso and finishing on the fourth recto. These 'signatures' face one another and are written in ink in quires I–III, in plummet, and considerably larger, in quire IV. The letters are placed at the foot of the manuscript, in the gutter, except on fos. 17ᵛ and 18ʳ, where they are near the fore-edge. There are no quire-numbers, but catchwords occur at the ends of quires II, III, and IV (fos. 16ᵛ, 24ᵛ, and 32ᵛ).

Arrangement

The first sheet in each gathering is arranged with the hair-side outwards, and hair always faces hair and flesh faces flesh within the gathering, except in quire II where the second and third sheets both have their flesh-sides facing outwards.[2]

---

[1] For pedigree of the manuscript and other details, see above, pp. 1–3.

[2] On the reason for this, see below, p. 521, n. 2, and further, pp. 523–4.

Pricking and ruling

The gatherings were pricked after folding and the pattern of holes is the same throughout, with no pricking in the inner margin. The leaves were ruled on both sides in plummet, with vertical lines for the columns, those on the extreme left and right being double. The first quire was pricked for an extra vertical line between the columns, but this has been ruled only on fos. 1ʳ–4ᵛ and 8ᵛ.

HANDWRITING

All the writing of both surveys—text, guide-letters for initials, directions for rubrics, and rubrics—was apparently done by the same scribe; but the authorship of the initials is uncertain. There is a marked contrast between the careful, more or less pure book-hand of the first page of Survey I (fo. 1ʳ) and the less careful, more mixed script of the end of Survey II (fos. 32ʳ–33ʳ); but the end of Survey I (fos. 11ᵛ–12ᵛ) scarcely differs from the beginning of Survey II (fos. 13ʳ–14ʳ), and even the opening pages of the two surveys (fos. 1ʳ and 13ᵛ) are extremely close.[1] The main transition from a slower, solider hand to a lighter, hastier one is carried out gradually over three successive openings at the beginning of Survey II (fos. 13ᵛ–14ʳ, 14ᵛ–15ʳ, 15ᵛ–16ʳ). That the whole manuscript was written at the same time follows, in any case, from its structure: Surveys I and II share the second of four more or less identical quires (see above).[2] Notably similar throughout the volume are the two sorts of abbreviation stroke, the Tironian sign for *et*, and the sign for final *-us*; the hyphens; the appearance of round *d*, of suprascript *a* (fos. 1ʳb27 and 19ʳa3), and of suprascript *i* (fos. 8ᵛb7, 11ʳa1 and 29, 13ᵛa18 and 27, and 14ʳb29). In both surveys the guide-letters for initials, placed at the outermost edges of the pages, and the directions for the rubrics are usually in the same colour of ink as the corresponding parts of the main text. They often use the simple form of *a* which occurs as a suprascript letter in the main text (fos. 3ʳb, 3ᵛa, and 32ʳ); and the current, lattice-like form of *w* commonly used in the directions in Survey II (fos. 24ᵛb, 28ʳa, and 31ᵛb) also occurs once as a guide-letter in Survey I (fo. 10ʳa). In Survey I the directions are written along the outer edges, excepting one along the bottom edge of fo. 11ᵛ; in Survey II they are written along the top or bottom edges, excepting two along the outer edges of fos. 23ᵛ and 27ʳ. Most of these directions have, as intended, been more or less completely trimmed away by the binder.[3]

The rubrics—all in red excepting two shorter ones on fos. 5ᵛ and 13ᵛ, which are in alternate black and red letters—are mostly in a capital script more or less approximating to rustic capitals (twenty-eight examples at fos. 3ᵛ, 8ʳ–13ᵛ *passim*, and 17ʳ–32ᵛ *passim*); but five are in minuscule (fos. 1ʳ, 5ʳ, 5ᵛ, 7ᵛ, and 13ᵛ). Notably similar throughout the capital rubrics are the letters *E*, *N*, *R*, and *T*, three of which occur in the same form throughout Survey I, in the formula *TRE*. Each of the two long rubrics in minuscules (fos. 1ʳ and 13ᵛ) is perfectly comparable with the main text of the page on which it occurs. The initials—red in Survey I, alternately red and blue in Survey II, and none of them flourished—are apparently by the same hand throughout the manuscript, to judge in particular by the variant forms of *A* and the form of *W*. There seems to be no means of establishing whether or not the initials were painted by the scribe who wrote the main text, the guide-letters, the directions for rubrics, and the rubrics themselves.

[1] *The New Palaeographical Society*, 1st ser. ii, pt. 1 (London, 1903–12), pl. 212, the editors of which concluded that 'the same hands appear in both Surveys, though the writing is rather more regular in the early part of the volume'.

[2] And a lengthy section of Survey II (**II, 806–89**) is written over an erased portion of Survey I, the vellum having been re-used in quire IV, instead of in what seems to have been its original position at the beginning of quire II; see below, pp. 523–4.

[3] Directions or remains of them survive at fos. 3ᵛ, 8ʳ, 9ʳ, 9ᵛ, 10ʳ, 10ᵛ, 11ᵛ, 19ᵛ, 22ᵛ, 23ᵛ, 24ʳ, 24ᵛ, 25ʳ, 27ʳ, 27ᵛ, 29ᵛ, 30ᵛ, 31ᵛ, 32ᵛ.

Nothing in the palaeography of the manuscript contradicts the conclusion that it was written as soon as Survey **II** had been completed, in 1148; and it looks as if the scribe belonged to the group—whoever they were—who normally wrote charters for Henry of Blois during the latter part of his long reign at Winchester. The script of our manuscript is neither the grandiose, papalizing script of the confirmation issued by Bishop Henry to Oseney Priory in 1143, in his capacity as legate,[1] nor the rapid documentary script of his notification of a confirmation to Sherborne Abbey in [1154–71].[2] The latter has much in common with the informal, very practical script, with its 'advanced cursive forms' due to 'common pressure of official business', that was written by some of Mr. T. A. M. Bishop's *scriptores regis*—scribes who worked for Henry I, especially towards the end of his reign, and for Stephen.[3] This script apparently originated in Henry I's chancery, and Mr. Bishop has noted that 'some of the fluency and informality of some Chancery writing can be seen, before the middle of the twelfth century, in the original charters of certain great personages.'[4] The handwriting of our scribe is of a kind commonly found, as Dr. N. R. Ker has said, in documents and cartularies written in the period between 1125 and 1160: 'the script is fundamentally book-hand, with certain current modifications which would not be found normally in a literary manuscript, chiefly the rounded instead of the upright *d*, the nota 7 instead of the ampersand, long tailed forms of *f*, *r*, and *s*, and unusually long ascenders.'[5] In both surveys, round *d* is freely used as an alternative to straight *d*, and the Tironian sign for *et* is normal; long forms of *f*, *r*, and *s*, and a comparable, pointed form of *p* occur in both, but more often in Survey **II**; but long ascenders are not found, except in the first lines of the rubrics at fos. 1ʳ and 13ᵛ. A confirmation by Bishop Henry to the church of Sherborne in [*c*. 1150–70], in practically pure book-hand, except for long *r*, resembles the most formal part of Survey **I** (fos. 1ʳ–2ᵛ).[6] More similar to the handwriting of Survey **II** is a grant by Baldwin of Portsey to Sherborne Abbey in [*c*. 1154–70], with long *f*, *r*, and *s*, and pointed *p*.[7] A much more striking example of the same contrast may be seen in two confirmations by King Stephen, one to Sawtry Abbey in [1146–54], in a somewhat literary hand, the other to Buildwas Abbey in 1139, in an advanced documentary hand.[8] The variation in formality between the beginning and the end of our manuscript is less than, or at most equal to, the variation—between one document and another—to be found in the work of contemporary scribes working for the royal chancery.[9]

2. THE CORRECTIONS IN THE WINTON DOMESDAY

by MARTIN BIDDLE

(*Frontispiece*, Plates I–III)

THERE are rather more than 240 corrections of various kinds scattered throughout the thirty-three folios of the manuscript, which shows evidence of the whole sequence of writing and correction usual in the production of literary manuscripts. It is clear that great care has been taken to produce an exact copy of the examplar of Survey **I** and of whatever preliminary recension lies behind Survey **II**.

[1] H. E. Salter, *Facsimiles of early charters in Oxford muniment rooms* (Oxford, 1929), no. 69.

[2] Ibid., no. 17.

[3] T. A. M. Bishop, *Scriptores regis* (Oxford, 1961), 12–14, and e.g. Pls. VIII and XV (Scribe xi).

[4] Ibid. 13.

[5] N. R. Ker, *English manuscripts in the century after the Norman Conquest* (Oxford, 1960), 18–19.

[6] Salter, *Oxford charters*, no. 18.

[7] Ibid., no. 20.

[8] *Palaeographical Society*, 2nd ser., Pl. 21; Bishop, *Scriptores*, nos. 381 and 362.

[9] Bishop *Scriptores*, Pls. II and XXXI (a), III and XXXIV (a), IV and XVI.

The corrections appear to be of little help in elucidating the text. Except where they relate to personal names or sums of money, they have not normally been mentioned in the footnotes if extending only to one or two letters. But they do provide information about the way in which the manuscript was produced and something about the nature of the materials that lie behind the present version.

The corrections take the form of erasures (about 187), insertions and other additions (about 45), and expungings (12). There are twenty-one short gaps in the MS. and these are confined entirely to Survey **II**. Nothing need be said about the erasures or insertions themselves, but the expungings show some variation: in three cases individual letters were expunged by a dot below them (e.g. *anteq*, **I, 53**), in two cases a pair of words were deleted by underlining (e.g. *et nullam*, **I, 8**), and on seven occasions letters or words were crossed through, five times by the rubricator (probably the scribe of the text himself) correcting the main body of the text (e.g., ~~T.R.E. Modo cam tenet~~ **I, 68**).

Most of the corrections in Survey **II** are short: of the 142 erasures, eighty-two concern single letters only, forty-seven deal with part of a word, a word, or a pair of words, eight involve the erasure of either one or two lines, and only five involve whole entries (**II, 238** and **788**) or groups of entries (**II, 203–5, 243–5**, and **806–89**). The situation in Survey **I** is rather different, even when allowance is made for the fact that it is only three-fifths the length of Survey **II** (1,392 column-lines, compared with 2,320 in Survey **II**). Of the forty-six erasures in Survey **I**, twenty-six deal with single letters, ten with individual words or a pair of words, two involve the erasure of one or two lines, and a further two require the rewriting of whole entries, while as many as six erasures concern groups of from two to seven entries (**I, 30–1, 75–6, 80–3, 142–3, 148–54**, and **204–5**). Survey **I** required fewer minor corrections than Survey **II**, but it contained as first written a number of major errors that involved substantial erasure and rewriting. Survey **II** was by comparison free of major error, but needed extensive minor emendment.

Survey **II** contains, however, one very extensive erasure: both columns on both sides of fo. 29 have been entirely erased and rewritten, and this erasure continues on to fo. 30^r, to include the whole of the left-hand and two-thirds of the right-hand column. The entire text of **II, 806–89** is thus written over some previous matter. Although this earlier material cannot now be made out, even with the help of an ultraviolet lamp, it is possible to see that each entry was distinguished by a paragraph sign (e.g. fo. 29^r a1), a feature which otherwise occurs only against the first 206 entries of Survey **I**. In that survey the longest erasure involves the whole of the right-hand column of fo. 8^v, now occupied by the seven entries **I, 148–54**. This is the last folio of the first quire of four bifolia (fos. 1^r–8^v), and the erased column is hence the last column of text in this quire.

If we return to the erased portion of Survey **II**, it will be found to involve the right-hand leaves of the two inner bifolia of the quire IV. Should this quire be detached, opened out and folded back on itself, the erased folios would become the left-hand leaves of the two *outer* bifolia, and fos. 29^r–30^r would become the first three pages of the quire. Furthermore, this refolding would not disturb the correct sequence of the hair and flesh sides of the bifolia.

It may therefore be suggested that fos. 29^r–30^r originally carried the text of that part of Survey **I** which followed upon the erased last column of the first quire (fo. 8^v, right-hand col.), and occupied the first five-and-two-thirds columns of the second quire. The erased portion on fos. 29^r–30^r would thus roughly correspond to **I, 155–203** on fos. 9^r–10^r of the present text. The whole erasure from the top of the right-hand column of fo. 8^v to two-thirds down the right-hand column of f. 30^r (**II, 889** is the last written over an erasure), would have involved six and two-thirds columns, with about fifty-six entries. This erasure of the material on the first leaves of the original second quire, and the re-use of the vellum in quire IV, may account for the dislocation in the sequence of hair and flesh faces noted in quire II, resulting from the introduction of two new bifolia. The interest of this erasure is not only that it demonstrates the value of vellum and the care taken to re-use it wherever possible, but also reveals, as unfinished or altered products so often do, the methods used and the sequence followed in the preparation of the manuscript.

The writing of the text of Survey **I** appears to have begun with the insertion of paragraph signs in the left-hand margin of each column as it was reached. That this could be done in advance of the writing of each entry suggests that the text of Survey **I** being copied was laid out in much the same form as the present version. The practice was, however, a constant source of error: against **I, 136–9**, for example, the original paragraph signs had to be erased and replaced (due to an error in **I, 135**) when the entries themselves came to be written. Eventually, after the rewriting following upon the great erasure discussed above, paragraph signs were abandoned. They end with **I, 206** at the foot of fo. 10ʳ. Their curious history may perhaps suggest that they were not present in the exemplar being copied, but were an attempt at clarification added when the writing of the present MS. was begun.

Some corrections were made by the scribe of the main text as he went along. One such is the erasure underlying the rubric *A porta Occidentis usque ad portam Orientis* on fo. 3ᵛ. In this case ultra violet light shows *domu'* after *Orientis*, so that the scribe seems to have forgotten the rubric and written the first two lines of **I, 39**, realized his mistake, and immediately erased them to leave a gap for the rubricator. That he did this immediately is shown by the fact that the following entry (**I, 39**) has not been altered. Other cases of immediate correction occur in **I, 184** and **II, 238**, while the great erasure of fos. 8ᵛ and 29ʳ–30ʳ must also belong in this category, the scribe realizing that he had made some major error only when he reached most of the way down the second column of fo. 30ʳ. It follows from this that none of these corrections would be in the hand of a corrector, even if there was a distinct person, but all in the hand of the main scribe.

When the main text was complete, or possibly quire by quire, it was read through and marked for correction. The marks showing that a correction was needed were made in the margins and not usually in the text itself. Many of them may have been cut off in trimming the pages, and of those that are detectable most have been erased, so there are few to see today (**I, 162**; **II, 245, 316**, and **387**, all erased; **I, 23, 43, 64, 75**?, and **573**, unerased). It does not seem to have been usual in this MS. to write the correct text in the margin for the corrector to follow, as was often the case with literary manuscripts, although this was done occasionally (**II, 397?, 622, 734?**, and **749?**). The corrector was presumably intended to go back to the original. And the evidence of the handwriting suggests that the corrector was in fact the scribe of the main text himself.[1]

When the corrections were made, the marginal indications to the rubricator were not always changed in conformity with the new arrangement of the lines. It is interesting to note that this was done for **I, 39** and for the whole of the rewriting of the great erasure, while it was not done for **II, 203–4** and **243–5**. The erasure of the marginal indications to corrections marked the completion of this stage of the manuscript.

The individual bifolia were presumably folded to produce quires of eight folios before writing began. There is certainly evidence that the quires had been folded before rubrication, for fo. 31ᵛ shows the erasure of the red marks which were the result of turning the page when the ink of the red initials of both columns of fo. 32ʳ was still wet.[2] It is even possible that the quires had been sewn by this stage,

---

[1] I am grateful to Professor Julian Brown for specific comment on this point. Such differences as there are between the handwriting of the main text and the corrections are probably due to the cramping and extra abbreviation required to make room for the insertion of a missing passage, and to the fact that there are internal changes in the handwriting of the text scribe, over the course of the manuscript. See above, pp. 521–2.

[2] These marks do not seem to be the result of offsetting, and the evidence of erasure (which is unlikely to have been done later) is quite clear.

but the manuscript had certainly not been bound, for that would have involved the trimming away of many of the indications for the rubricator.

The rubrications were written in gaps left in text, usually in accordance with indications written in the margins, but in the case of the three longest texts the rubricator probably worked from the originals themselves. On several occasions, especially in Survey **I**, the rubrications had to be written over erasures caused by a failure to leave the necessary blank space. In seven places the rubricator made corrections in red to the main body of the text, mostly very minor, and involving five expungings and two minute improvements to an individual letter and a mark of abbreviation respectively (**I, 108; II, 310**). The rubricator (probably the text scribe himself) must have read the entire text with care as he went along, but there is no indication in his corrections that he was working back to the originals on which the present text was based.

After the completion of the rubrication, this was itself checked and corrected. It is not possible to be sure whether the corrections were made as the work proceeded or subsequently, but where initials have been erased and rewritten, the final result seems to be the work of the rubricator of the initials himself.[1] In two cases (**II, 726 and 990**), where *ob'* (for *obolum*) at the beginning of a line has been mistaken for (*R*)*obt'* (for *Robertus*) waiting to be rubricated, a blue initial has been erased, causing a break in the proper sequence of red and blue. Here the error was only detected after the rubricator had finished his work. Sometimes it was simply a matter of changing the wrong initial in the right colour (**II, 733**, *B* to *G*), and once the wrong initial was erased, and the correct initial written in the margin to replace the wrong marginal indication that had been followed, but the rubricator never replaced the erased initial (**II, 902**). In this last example there might be perhaps some slight indication that the rubricator's work was checked by another person, for the rubricator's subsequent completion.

The corrections made to the main text by the rubricator, and those made to the rubrications, do not necessarily mark the completion of the checking and correction. Throughout the manuscript, hyphens are found written with a very thin pen at the end of lines terminating in a broken word. Since these hyphens also occur in the rewritten passages (e.g. **I, 81–3**), at least some of them came late in the sequence of checking and correction.

Finally the quires were sewn and trimmed, and in the process, and perhaps deliberately, many of the correction marks and indications for the rubricator were wholly or partly removed. The volume was then provided with the richly decorated blind-stamped binding which it still retains.

It will appear from what has been said that the manuscript of the Winton Domesday is the product of a highly organized scriptorium. The manuscript presents a consistent whole. There were, however, many mistakes in the copying and despite all the care taken in production, a good many errors still remain, particularly in spelling, grammar, and more understandably in the personal names, as the footnotes to the text make clear. But the trouble taken to produce an accurate and legible text is manifest, and in this as in the magnificent binding with which the text was provided, we can see something of the importance which contemporaries attached to these surveys of their city.

Study of the corrections may also provide some information about the nature of the materials that lie behind the present manuscript of the two surveys. Since the manuscript is a unity, it follows that the first survey must be a copy written in or after 1148 of an earlier document prepared presumably at the time of the first survey *c.* 1110. From what has been said above, it would seem that the exemplar of Survey **I** was complete and reasonably legible, for the present text of this survey contains no gaps and required fewer minor corrections than Survey **II**. There is also some indication in the attempt to write the paragraph signs in advance of the main text that the entries in the examplar were laid out in much the same

---

[1] It should be noted that it is impossible to be sure of the authorship of the rubricated initials, although they themselves all seem to be by the same hand: see above, p. 521.

way as in the present manuscript. The differences in rubrication between the two surveys may also suggest that the earlier version of Survey **I** was quite closely followed.

There must on the other hand be some reason for the number of occasions on which the scribe omitted to leave blanks for the rubricated headings in Survey **I**. There is already some suggestion in the hesitant use of paragraph signs that the original text was being in some way rearranged or at least clarified at the time of copying. It may perhaps be that the lesser headings now rubricated—principally the street-headings—were originally written to the left of the main text, and so easily missed by a scribe working down the columns. Their insertion into the main text could give rise to much confusion. If these headings were originally written in black, whether in the main text or to one side, the change to red, perhaps for clarification, would be a further source of error.

When the original of Survey **I** was copied about 1148 the arrangement of its headings may thus have been changed; it may follow that the headings are not quite so reliable as the rest of the text as evidence for what was actually contained in the original version. The headings are however very simple, so that it is only in their spelling and in their precise position in relation to the immediately adjacent entries that any uncertainties should arise. That these headings are not entirely additions of *c.* 1148, but were part of the original version, seems otherwise probable, however, since without some indication in the text the changes from street to street would not have been recoverable from the succession of entries.

The version behind the present text of Survey **II** seems to have been rather different. The presence of twenty-one short gaps shows that the examplar was not complete in every detail, or, but less likely, that it was in places illegible. That it was not as legible as the original version of Survey **I** might be suggested by the greater number of small errors throughout the text.[1]

The layout of this survey is not so complex as that of Survey **I** and the scribe had few difficulties in following his original. In only three cases were the rubricated headings written over erasures (**II, 304/5, 788/9,** and **1000/1001**), and on the first and third of these occasions the error was discovered immediately. The materials given to the scribe for copying were perhaps in the form of fairly roughly written, but clearly arranged, lists giving the results of the inquiry street by street.

3. THE BINDING OF THE WINTON DOMESDAY

by H. M. NIXON

(Plates IV–X)

THE manuscript was re-bound in the middle of the nineteenth century,[2] but the original blind-tooled leather covers have been preserved. They are now onlaid to the covers of a binding of brown calf, which measures 253 × 182 × 12 mm. The disposition of the larger rosette (Pl. X, tool 5) on the first cover suggests that the covers are in their original positions (Pls. IV and V).

Preserved separately are twenty-six vellum leaves from a tenth-century sacramentary, which formed the original 'boards' of the binding, together with a blank vellum leaf which was one of the original paste-downs. These were removed from the covers of the original binding between 1773 and 1790.

---

[1] These might just be due to the carelessness of the scribe, but in that case he had grown more careless as the manuscript progressed.

[2] Possibly in or soon after 1851. The minutes of the Council of the Society of Antiquaries record a decision on 6 May 1851 to spend £60 on binding manuscripts. The leather and lettering of the new binding resembles that of other manuscripts known to have been bound at this period.

They have been inlaid and bound up as Society of Antiquaries MS. 154*. Their text is discussed in the next Appendix.

The use of vellum leaves from a tenth-century sacramentary as the stiffening material of the covers is the most remarkable feature of the binding. It has been treated as axiomatic that, 'until about 1500, almost the sole material for the boards of English books was wood, leather being a rare exception'.[1] 'Pasteboards', Mr. Bernard Middleton goes on to say, 'did not come into use in England before the first quarter of the sixteenth century, though they were used in the East centuries earlier', and this has long been the accepted view.[2] Yet the note by Gustavus Brander and the lacing-holes in the leaves where the two main bands, the headband, and the tailband were attached, as discussed below, make it quite clear that three hundred and fifty years earlier, a Winchester binder made up the 'boards' of this unusually slim volume by pasting together vellum leaves from an undistinguished-looking out-of-date service book.

The survival of these leaves, despite the fact that Brander removed them from the original covers and the book was again rebound, probably c. 1851, enables us to reconstruct the structure of the original binding with reasonable certainty. When in doubt I have made use of the *Hegesippus* at Winchester Cathedral, probably bound at Winchester c. 1150, and of Mr. Graham Pollard's admirable paper on the construction of English twelfth-century bindings.[3] He was dealing there mainly with the undecorated leather bindings of the period, but he pointed out that the three surviving English blind-tooled romanesque bindings (Hobson XVII, XXII, and C; see Table 56), which have not undergone restoration, exhibit the same sewing and forwarding techniques as the undecorated bindings.[4]

DESCRIPTION

Sewing (Fig. 28)

The four gatherings, each of eight leaves, would have been sewn on two whittawed leather thongs, probably using a sewing frame. The single leaf at the end may originally have had a conjugate blank leaf, in which case this pair would have been sewn as a fifth gathering.

It is not now possible to see the original sewing-holes in the folds of the gatherings, but the lacing-marks of the board-leaves discussed below show that there were only two bands. It is likely that the thongs on which the book was sewn were not double, but single with a horizontal split, to permit figure-of-eight sewing in the middle of the thong where it crossed the backs of the quires. The projecting ends of the thongs, or 'slips', were also evidently divided into two and laced into the 'boards'.

When the sewing was completed the quires would have been joined about 15–20 mm from the head and the tail by kettle-stitches. Starting from the position of one of these in the first or last quire, the thread would pass from outside into the centre of the quire, and would run along the fold until the

[1] B. C. Middleton, *A History of English Craft Bookbinding Technique* (London, 1963), 62; cf. Graham Pollard, 'The construction of English twelfth-century bindings', in *Library*, 5th ser. 17 (1962), 8, 13. Mr. Pollard describes the boards of the thirteenth-century English blind-tooled binding at St. John's College, Cambridge (Hobson C: for reference, see below, p. 536 n. 2) as being made 'from a bit of a second-hand tanned-leather saddle'. BM, Egerton MS. 2900 (Hobson XIX), which is probably French, has similar 'boards' of hide.

[2] Strickland Gibson in 'The Localization of books by their bindings' (*Transactions of the Bibliographical Society*, 8 (1907), 29) suggests they were first used in Europe on Italian books of the second half of the

fifteenth century. But Sir Henry Thomas in his *Early Spanish Bookbindings* (London, 1939) cites two Spanish examples which he attributes to the second half of the fourteenth century (Pls. LXXX and LXXXI). These two books and the mid-fifteenth-century binding over pasteboards illustrated on his Pl. XCIV are all probably blank books acquired ready bound, rather than texts sent for binding after they were written. Of the one hundred bindings he illustrates (nearly all before 1500), one is in limp vellum, three have pasteboards, and the other ninety-six have wooden boards.

[3] See above, n. 1.

[4] XVII and XXII have the typical wooden boards of the period; C has leather 'boards'.

first thong was reached. It would then pass to the outside of the quire, go through the split in the thong, be looped right round the whole thickness of the thong, and return through the split to the centre of the quire, completing the figure of eight. The thread would then run along the inside of the fold to the second thong, repeat the figure-of-eight stitch, and finally emerge from the inside of the fold at the position of the other kettle-stitch (Fig. 28).

It would then pass into the next quire, which would be sewn in the same manner in the opposite direction. When the thread emerged next to the point where it started in the first quire, it would be knotted to its original end, thus forming the first kettle-stitch, and would then pass into the third

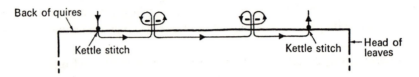

FIG. 28. The stitching of the quires of the Winton Domesday.

quire. Subsequently each quire would be joined to the preceding one at the kettle-stitches, at both head and tail, by linking the thread through the sewing of the preceding section before passing it into the next one. On its final emergence it would be knotted at the kettle-stitch.

The 'boards' (Fig. 29 and Table 55)

With the twenty-seven leaves now inlaid and bound up separately as MS. 154* is a note signed by Gustavus Brander, who purchased the Winton Domesday in 1773. Part of this reads:

> On opening the Covers of the Winchester Doomsdey I found that each Cover was Stiffen'd with 13 pieces of Parchment/in the whole 26 leaves/pasted together; wch. on Separating proved to be part of an Antient Missal in the Saxon Character & as legible as when first wrote.[1]

The text of the twenty-six leaves is discussed in the next Appendix. Here we are concerned with their use as the stiffening material of the covers. The twenty-seventh leaf, which Brander preserved, but does not mention, was one of the original paste-downs of the volume. According to a note in MS. 154*, the leaves were bound in their present form in 1919, and they are now arranged in the order in which they stood in the sacramentary (fos. 1–26), with the end-leaf as fo. 27.

The presence of four groups of lacing-holes on one or other of the long edges of all of the sacramentary leaves confirms the general truth of Brander's statement, while proving that it is not quite accurate. Each group has four holes and these holes take one or other of two easily distinguishable patterns, shown as *A* or *B* (Fig. 29).

They clearly indicate where these board-leaves were attached to the two main bands, to the head-band, and to the tailband. The two patterns can be easily distinguished by the fact that in *A* all four groups of holes form parallelograms of comparatively eccentric shape, while in *B* one of the centre groups (marking the position of one of the two main bands) forms a rectangle. All leaves that were in one board will therefore show pattern *A*: those that were in the other, pattern *B*.[2] This shows that Brander may well have written his note some little time after the leaves were removed from the binding, for the pattern of holes makes it clear that the surviving twenty-six leaves were not equally divided,

---

[1] For the full text of Brander's note, see below, p. 541; and for the circumstances of his acquisition of the MS., see above, p. 3.

[2] There has naturally been some distortion of the vellum leaves in separating and mounting them and some variation is observable in the distance between the four groups of holes. But the groups themselves retain their individuality.

with thirteen in each board, as Brander said. Pattern *A* occurs on fourteen leaves; pattern *B* is found on only twelve.

The holes approximately alternate in being on the fore-edge and in the fold of the leaves, as they are now (and were originally) bound up. The patterns also show that the leaves were sometimes reversed, sometimes turned upside-down, and sometimes both reversed and turned upside-down, when they were used in the covers. The leaves for each board were clearly all pierced at the same time with a bodkin to make these holes, and Mr. Roger Powell, who is widely experienced in repairing old vellum manuscripts, was able to show me from which side each leaf had been pierced, with certainty for twenty-one out of the twenty-six leaves.

Table 55 shows the information for each of the board-leaves as now separated and bound up in the order they originally occupied in the sacramentary. The dotted lines indicate one or more missing leaves, as shown by breaks in the text.

The alternation of fold and fore-edge in fos. 1–7 (all pattern *A*) and fos. 21–6 (all pattern *B*) originally suggested that these leaves at least were in their original order when the binder was making up his boards, and that he first made them up into pairs. If he took the top leaf off the pile and pasted it, then pasted the next leaf and turned it over so that the two pasted sides adhered to one another, and then made more pairs in this way, this alternation would be produced. The pairs could then be pasted together in the same way to build up the boards. But if he proceeded in this methodical way, each of the pairs would also have a recto facing a verso and would be the same way up as well as showing the same pattern of lacing-holes. Table 55 shows that the only consecutive pairs of leaves which conform to this are fos. 1 & 2, 3 & 4, 12 & 13, 25 & 26. This is not adequate proof of any fixed procedure, and the mixture of patterns *A* and *B* in fos. 8–20 is in itself evidence that the leaves of the sacramentary had not been gathered in their correct order after the bifolia had been cut into single leaves.

The position of a number of the leaves in the boards can, however, be ascertained from other evidence. As already noted the fourteen leaves with lacing-hole pattern *A* (fos. 1–7, 9, 12, 13, 16–18, 20) must have been in one board and the twelve with

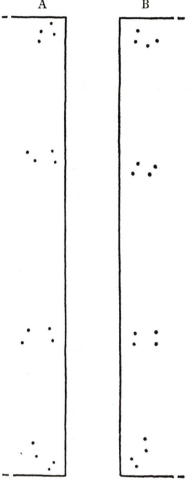

A   B

FIG. 29. The lacing-holes in the board-leaves of the Winton Domesday (cf. Table 55).

pattern *B* (8, 10, 11, 14, 15, 19, 21–6) in the other. I first thought that leaves with pattern *A* were in the first cover. In fos. 9, 12, and 13 is a circular hole about 2 mm in diameter, probably made by the larva of a furniture beetle. If these leaves were arranged in the first board (two pierced by the bodkin from the recto, one from the verso and all three upside down) this wormhole would have been about 10 mm from the head and 50 mm from the fore-edge of the board. In exactly the same position in the first leather cover (Pl. IV) can be seen the hole made by a bookworm piercing the shoulder of the dragon in a circle (tool 1). Unfortunately, no amount of experimenting with dummy leaves marked with lacing-holes and knife-slashes would produce these wormholes at the head of the first 'board'. If the pattern A leaves were in the upper cover, these wormholes were at the foot.

We can, however, tell which were the innermost surviving leaves in the covers. As described below (p. 532), fos. 17 & 20 (pattern *A*) and 19 & 21 (pattern *B*) have diagonal knife-slashes made when the corners of the turn-ins were mitred. The depth of the knife cuts in the corners of the leaves shows that fo. 20 was next to the paste-down of one cover, with fo. 17 beneath it, while on the other cover fo. 19 was the nearest of the surviving leaves to the paste-down with fo. 21 below it.

TABLE 55

The lacing-holes in the board-leaves of the Winton Domesday (cf. Fig. 29)

Folio	Hole pattern	Present position of holes	Pierced from	Way up (If *A* in upper board)
1	A	Fore-edge	Recto	Correct
2	A	Fold	Verso	Correct
3	A	Fore-edge	Verso	Upside-down
4	A	Fold	Recto	Upside-down
5	A	Fore-edge	Verso	Upside-down
6	A	Fold	Verso	Correct
7	A	Fore-edge	Verso	Upside-down
8	B	Fold	Verso	Correct
9	A	Fore-edge	Recto	Correct
10	B	Fore-edge	Verso	Upside-down
11	B	Fold	Verso	Correct
12	A	Fore-edge	? Recto	Correct
13	A	Fold	Verso	Correct
14	B	Fold	Verso	Correct
15	B	Fore-edge	Verso	Upside-down
16	A	Fore-edge	? Recto	Correct
17	A	Fore-edge	Verso	Upside-down
18	A	Fold	Verso	Correct
19	B	Fore-edge	? Verso	Correct
20	A	Fold	? Verso	Correct
21	B	Fold	? Verso	Correct
22	B	Fore-edge	Verso	Upside-down
23	B	Fold	Verso	Correct
24	B	Fore-edge	? Recto	Upside-down
25	B	Fold	Recto	Upside-down
26	B	Fore-edge	Verso	Upside-down

Note. In the column showing the side of the leaf from which it was pierced by the bodkin, a '?' denotes that this could not be established with certainty by inspection of the holes themselves, but is established by the pattern of the holes. The broken lines indicate one or more missing leaves.

The surviving blank leaf

The twenty-seventh leaf bound up with the twenty-six from the sacramentary is of markedly thinner vellum and has not been written on. It was evidently used as a paste-down of the original binding of the *Domesday*. It still has some leather adhering to its present recto close to the original fore-edge, and the stain from this turn-in is visible at head and tail, as well as on the fore-edge. The present verso has apparently been scraped at some time. The leaf is transparent and it has set-off from the rubrics of at least two leaves of the sacramentary—and the set-offs have originally been on different sides of the leaf. The scraping of the present verso partly hides this, but when the leaf is held up to the light they read from opposite sides. The present verso was evidently originally in contact with the verso of leaf 20 (the innermost of the pattern *A* leaves) and rubrics in lines 5, 6, and 14 from that page are clearly readable from the present recto. But the rubric *seq:*

ēi euān, which can be read from the present verso, does not occur on the surviving leaves. I suggest that it occurred on a thirteenth leaf, which has not survived, but was the innermost leaf of the board with pattern *B* leaves. Leaf 27 was therefore first used as a paste-down at one end of the book, with its present verso in contact with the verso of leaf 20. It then came loose, and was re-used at the other end of the book with its recto pasted on to the 'board' and over the leather turn-in. This leather probably adhering to the verso from its previous use was then scraped off.

Lacing-in

At first sight the holes in the board-leaves look too small to have had leather thongs laced through them, but Mr. Powell assures me that a split leather thong will go through a surprisingly small hole and that when the leaves were removed from the boards, separated and flattened, he would expect them to revert to a size little larger than was originally made by the bodkin. Most of them are also slightly elongated in a direction compatible with their having had a thong passed through them.

The technique used at this period on bindings with wooden boards involved making tunnels in the edge of the board next to the spine through which the thongs passed. The thong then surfaced in a groove on the inside or outside of the board,[1] before being secured by a peg driven through the thickness of the board. This method could not be used on pasteboard. With boards of hide (e.g. Hobson XIX; BM, Egerton MS. 2900) the individual thong starts on the outside, passes through a slit to the inside, and then passes to the outside of the board again, very much in the modern manner of attaching paste-boards. This was evidently the technique used on the Domesday, except that the thong was divided into two, and each of these two 'slips' passed through separate holes.

Cutting of the edges

The leaves would then have been trimmed flush with the edges of the 'boards' at head, tail, and on the fore-edge. This absence of 'squares' is a characteristic feature of twelfth-century bindings.

Headband, tailband, and tabs (fig. 30)

The main difference in the original appearance of the binding and that which it now presents would be the presence of the typical twelfth-century 'tabs' projecting from the spine at the head and tail. Mr. Pollard suggests that these tabs, which could be either square or half-moon shaped, may have been used to pull out individual volumes packed fore-edge downwards in a chest. He discusses them under the term 'secondary sewing', which would consist of the attachment of the headband, the tailband, and the tabs at head and tail.[2] If the tabs were similar to those of the *Hegesippus* (a slightly taller and considerably thicker book) they would have been of fairly thick soft whittawed leather, the width of the spine, and about 60 mm long. Of this length about 40 mm would lie along the spine from near or a little beyond the kettle-stitch to the head or the tail; the 20 mm projection at each end would be cut into roughly semicircular shape and possibly that at the head would be pierced to take a marker.[3]

---

[1] Mr. Pollard describes this groove as being normally on the inside of the board, but notes that occasionally it is found on the outside. Both the surviving English blind-tooled twelfth-century bindings with wooden boards which are unrestored have these grooves on the outside. They are clearly visible on the London binding of the *Inquisitio* of the Knights Templar (*English Binding*, Pl. 6) and can also be seen on the Winchester *Hegesippus*.

[2] Mr. Pollard talks of 'lining pieces', which form the basis of the tabs. This term, however, suggests a piece of leather which runs the full length of the spine

between the backs of the sections and the outer leather covering of the book, projecting at head and tail to form the tabs. Mr. Pollard admits (*Library*, 5th ser. 17 (1962), 12) that such an arrangement is unusual, and that the normal arrangement is that found on the Winchester *Hegesippus* and the London *Inquisitio*, which both have a separate tab at each end, running under the outer leather covering only as far as, or a little beyond, the kettle-stitch. I have therefore talked of tabs, rather than lining pieces.

[3] Cf. Pollard, *Library*, 5th ser. 17 (1962), 16. There is such a hole on the tab at the head of the *Hegesippus*.

The head- and tailbands would have been of split whittawed leather of about the same thickness as the main bands. After sewing, the projecting split thongs would have been laced diagonally into the inner angles of the board-leaves in the same manner as the slips of the main bands. A small equilateral triangle, with sides of approximately 6 mm, was cut off the inner corners of the board-leaves at head and tail to facilitate the attachment of the head- and tailbands.

The sewing of the head- and tailbands would also serve to attach the tabs to the book, but probably not in exactly the way described by Mr. Pollard.[1] In the *Hegesippus* we do not find the thread from the headbands running along inside the centre of each gathering as far as the kettle-stitch. Instead we only find about 15 mm of thread inside each section beginning about 3–5 mm from head or tail. The sewing is of green, pinkish-red, and white thread, surviving now along part of the headband as one turn of green, one red, five greens, two reds, four whites, three reds, three whites, two reds,

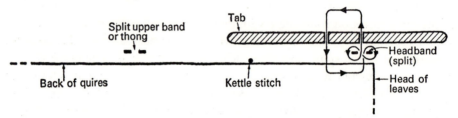

FIG. 30. The sewing of the head- and tailbands and the tabs of the Winton Domesday,
as suggested by the evidence of the *Hegesippus*.

four greens, one red, and three greens. The sewing is functional and not merely decorative, and approximately every other thread goes into the centre of the section. Basically the thread is sewn figure-of-eight-wise round the split band and when it is opposite the centre of the section it passes up through the tab, along the outside of the tab for about 15 mm, down through the tab behind the headband into the centre of the section, along inside the section for 15 mm, and up through the centre of the split band (Fig. 30). A figure-of-eight turn is then taken round its headband and its process continues. The end of the tab nearest to the kettle-stitch would be left free, but once the book was covered it would be held in position by the covering leather.

Covering

The next stage would consist of covering the book with the chocolate-brown tanned leather (probably calf) of which the sides are still preserved in the present nineteenth-century binding. The leather (as can be seen from the set-off on the surviving paste-down) was cut to allow for fairly wide turn-ins (40–50 mm) at the head, tail, and fore-edge of the boards. Where the leather, turned in at the head and tail, met that on the fore-edge, the overlap was cut away diagonally with a sharp knife. This technique (mitring the corners) is confirmed by two diagonal knife-cuts visible at the angles away from the lacing-holes on fos. 17 & 20 (pattern *A*) and 19 & 21 (pattern *B*). These leaves are evidently the survivors of the innermost board-leaves from each end although, as noted above, one or two leaves are missing from the end from which the pattern *B* leaves come.

Next to the hinge the leather from the turn-ins at head and tail was cut away somewhat carelessly. The paste-down shows that at one end of the board the leather runs nearly parallel to the hinge and finishes about 10 mm from it, while at the other it diverges at quite a marked angle, finishing about

---

[1] In the method which he describes (*Library*, 5th ser. 17 (1962), 12), the sewing thread passes up through the tab above the headband, runs along the outside of the tab to a point near the kettle-stitch, passes through the tab and is linked round the kettle-stitch, and then returns inside the section to the headband.

25 mm from the hinge. The turn-ins were presumably pasted to the board-leaves and the one surviving paste-down was certainly pasted over the turn-ins.

Decoration

The decoration of the covers was then carried out with metal tools of the type still used by bookbinders. Two such tools, engraved respectively with David harping and a griffin, are preserved in the Department of Medieval and Later Antiquities at the British Museum and are believed to date from the twelfth or early thirteenth century.[1] They are engraved metal dies, respectively 4 mm and 10 mm thick, with the designs in intaglio, and have a tapered tang attached to their upper surface to fit into a wooden handle. They would probably have been warmed before being impressed on the leather, and the leather would probably have been damped to retain the impression.

Some care has been taken in setting out the design on the first cover of the Winton Domesday, although the upper of the two circles is too far over to the right and in the lower circle the round dragon tool (**1**) is off-centre and two of the lobe-shaped dragons (**2**) overlap. Less care has been taken with the simpler rectangular design on the second cover, especially with the inner frame of the bird and curve tool (**8**).

Ten tools have been used on the two covers (see Pl. x):

1. Circular dragon (diameter 25 mm)
2. Lobe-shaped dragon (length 27 mm)
3. Concentric circles (diameter 5 mm)
4. Segment of circle with acanthus scroll (9 × 36 mm)
5. Circular eight-petalled rosette (10 mm)
6. Rectangular, two birds with human heads back to back (18 × 23 mm)
7. Square, deer running to left, with horseshoe marking on shoulder (18 × 18 mm)
8. Rectangular, feeding bird leaning over a semicircle (16 × 23 mm)
9. Rectangular, goat running to left with foliage (18 × 21 mm)
10. Arched, feeding ram (17 × 20 mm)

Of these ten tools, three appear to be peculiar to the Winchester group of bindings. These are **1**, the circular dragon; **4**, the segment of a circle with an acanthus scroll; and **9**, the goat with foliage. The other seven are all similar to tools found on the Paris bindings for Prince Henry, discussed below, which I consider to be earlier than the Winchester group. Tool **4**, the segment of a circle, makes the Winchester covers which incorporate circles more effective than the similar designs of other Romanesque binders. Hobson suggested[2] that the goat (**9**) might be Capricornus, the sign of the Zodiac. Tool **10**, the feeding ram, could equally well represent Aries. Its horns are unmistakable. The animal in the similar arched tool used by Prince Henry's first binder (and which seems also to appear on the bindings of Hobson's rowel spur group)[3] has been variously interpreted as a bear and a tiger, but certainly does not have horns.

On the first cover (Pl. iv) tools **1–6** were used as follows: two circles, one above the other, each composed of nine contiguous impressions of **4**; within each circle, **1** in the centre and eleven impressions of **2** placed radially. On either side eight spaced impressions of **6**, tooled with the heads towards the spine and the fore-edge respectively. At the head two impressions of **2**, within two of **1**, beneath each of which is **5**. At the foot is the same pattern in reverse, except that the circular dragons on **1** are the same way up as at the head. Part of the right-hand impression of **1** at the foot has been

---

[1] They are illustrated as nos. 1 and 2 on Pl. VII of G. D. Hobson, 'Some early bindings and binders' tools', in *Library*, N.S. 19 (1938), 202–49.

[2] *English Binding*, 4.

[3] *Jahrbuch der Einbandkunst*, Jahrg. 3 & 4 (1929–30), Taf. 13, A42 = C14.

replaced upside down when the book was rebound. In the centre, between the circles, two impressions of **3**, with on either side three of **2** and one of **5**.

There may have been a border of small circular tools all round the cover. Portions of nine impressions of **5** are visible down the fore-edge and eight (out of eleven?) of **3** remain along the spine, with one more above and below the row of **6** next to the spine.

On the second cover tools **3, 7–10** were used in a rectangular design (Pl. v); where arranged in horizontal bands, they are the correct way up; when they are arranged on their sides in vertical columns, the top of the tool is towards the nearest edge, as on the first cover.

In the centre are five spaced pairs of impressions of **7** forming two vertical columns; outside this is a frame of contiguous impressions of **8**, with three impressions above and below, seven (on their sides) to the right, and seven-and-a-half similarly on the left, so that the rectangle they form is somewhat distorted; an outer frame is formed by eleven contiguous sideways impressions of **9** to either side and five spaced impressions of **10** at head and tail. The bands of leather left plain between and outside the rows of tool impressions have been tooled with **3**. There are eighteen of these evenly spaced in the centre panel, arranged to form six horizontal rows of three, or three vertical rows of six; there are twenty-two between the inner and outer frame, with six evenly spaced at the top and bottom, while the vertical arrangement on each side was two/three/two; in the outer border there were probably originally eight evenly spaced impressions of the tool at head and tail, and the same two/three/two arrangement next to the fore-edge and spine, but owing to the loss of some of the leather from the edges of the cover some of these are now missing.

Clasps

There is no sign that the book had any clasps. The *Hegesippus* has the remains of two clasps hinged on the upper cover and fastening to pins on the lower, but they may be later additions.

PLACE OF ORIGIN OF THE BINDING

Two other twelfth-century bindings have survived on which some of the same tools have been used.

One of these is a twelfth-century Hegesippus, *De excidio Judeorum*, from the Phillipps, William Morris, Yates Thompson, and Dyson-Perrins collections, which is now in the Library of Winchester Cathedral, MS. XVII (Pls. VI and VII). Its early provenance is not known,[1] but it is bound in the same tanned leather as the Domesday, is tooled with seven of the same tools, and has such similar designs on both covers that they must both have been bound by the same binder at very much the same date. It is decorated with tools **1, 2, 3, 4, 6, 7, 8, 11, 12,** and **13** shown on Pl. x.

The other is a considerably larger book (Pls. VIII and IX), bound not in brown tanned leather with a smooth surface, but in tanned leather stained pink with a rough surface, and with very worn impressions of the tools (Fig. 31). It is not possible to be quite definite in the identification of the tools used, owing to the state of the leather, but the covers seem to show tools **1, 2, 4,** and **6**, all used on both the Domesday and the *Hegesippus*, and **11**, which is found only on the *Hegesippus*. Tool **2**, the lobe-shaped dragon, is of a very common twelfth-century type and versions of **6**, the man-headed

---

[1] A detailed comparison of the annotations in the *Hegesippus* with those in other Winchester manuscripts provides no indication that the *Hegesippus* was ever in the library of the cathedral priory, Hyde Abbey, or St. Mary's during the Middle Ages. The comparison was made with those manuscripts still in the cathedral library, with those that have migrated to the library of Winchester College, and with those cathedral, Hyde Abbey, and St. Mary's books listed in Ker *Libraries* and now in the British Museum. The kind assistance of Mr. J. M. G. Blakiston, formerly Fellows' Librarian, Winchester College, in making these comparisons is greatly appreciated.

birds, are found elsewhere. But **1**, the circular dragon, and **11**, the cock, do not occur outside this group, nor does **4**, the segment of a circle with an acanthus scroll, which is comparatively well preserved and shows no discernible differences. The other tools used on these large covers are shown as nos. **14–19** on Pl. x; none is found on any other known binding. As it has not been possible to take rubbings, they have been reproduced from drawings.[1]

(a)   (b)

FIG. 31. The binding of the *Codex Wintoniensis* (BM, Add. MS. 15350): the layout and elements of the tooled decoration (1/4).

(a) Original second cover (cf. Pl. IX).   (b) Original first cover (cf. Pl. VIII).

The importance of this last binding is that it covered until recently an undoubted Winchester book, the Cartulary of St. Swithun's, or *Codex Wintoniensis* (BM, Add. MS. 15350), which probably dates from about 1150. If then, as I think we may, we follow Weale and Hobson in believing that the cartulary's binding was decorated with some of the same tools as the other two books, we have a group of three bindings which all show the same basic designs—circles on the first cover and a rectangular arrangement on the second cover—and two of which cover manuscripts produced in Winchester

---

[1] With the binding is preserved a note by Mr. Graham Pollard in which he convincingly demonstrates that the book was rebound in the fourteenth century— it now has raised bands. It is almost certain, in my opinion, that the covers were then reversed, and that the cover with the three circles (Pl. VIII) was originally the first cover, although before the recent removal it was the second. The cover with the rectangular design shows some tools upside down whichever way you look at it (Pl. IX). Most twelfth-century tooled bindings normally have the tools the correct way up or on their sides. I have not noticed any, however, with those in the vertical columns upside down.

around the year 1150. The most obvious place for these three books to have been bound, as Weale suggested,[1] was Winchester and he was strongly supported in this view by G. D. Hobson, the foremost authority on these early blind-tooled bindings, which he termed Romanesque.[2] Hobson devoted Appendix F of *English Binding before 1500* to a discussion of English culture in the twelfth century, and concluded that in the second half of the century England was a home of art and letters, no less likely to lead the continent of Europe than to follow it; he expressed a firm conviction that the Winchester bindings were the earliest of all the Romanesque group. In his later work he produced evidence, discussed below, which seems to make it almost certain that Paris had the priority, and it will be as well now to consider this 'probably Winchester' group of bindings in their European setting.

French Romanesque bindings

Nearly all the Romanesque bindings described by Weale were in British libraries, and so it was assumed at first that the majority of them had been bound in this country. In 1929, when Hobson listed forty-seven examples, he suggested that twenty-six of these might be English. But by 1934, when his list had extended to ninety, he confessed that his earlier views 'like Miss Elizabeth Bennet's original opinion of Mr. Fitzwilliam Darcy ... were ill-founded and formed upon mistaken premises', and that the greater part of these bindings were produced in Paris for those attending its schools, and were not, as had been previously thought, monastic.

Some of these Paris bindings may be as early as 1137, for there is a series of glossed books of the Bible at Montpellier and Troyes (all from Clairvaux) which were made for Henry, son of Louis VI and brother of Louis VII of France, three of them containing the inscription *Henricus regis filius*. In 1137, on Louis VII's accession, Prince Henry became *regis frater*, but he may of course have continued to use the earlier style. Relying on Dr. Glunz, Hobson maintained that the state of this gloss was consistent with two of the Prince's books having been bound in 1137, but I understand from Dr. R. W. Hunt that this argument is no longer considered tenable. The bindings, however, are certainly not likely to be later than 1145, when Prince Henry entered the monastery of Clairvaux.

If, therefore, the Winchester group date from around 1150–as I believe[3]—the Paris bindings from the shop which worked for Prince Henry are earlier. Further support for this precedence was given by Dr. Rosy Schilling when she suggested that three bindings in the monastic library at Engelberg by the same Paris binders may well have been there since 1143.[4]

[1] W. H. J. Weale, *Bookbindings and rubbings of bindings in the National Art Library, South Kensington*, ii, *Catalogue* (London, 1894), Rubbings 10, 11; i, *Introduction* (London, 1898), xxiii. W. H. J. Weale and L. Taylor, *Early stamped bindings in the British Museum* (London, 1922), no. 3. The *Hegesippus* is referred to in a footnote. Its binding was first illustrated in *Illustrations from one hundred manuscripts in the library of H. Y. Thompson* iv (London, 1914), 19, Pls. I and II.

[2] Hobson first discussed Romanesque bindings in his Sandars Lectures for 1927, which were published as *English Binding before 1500* (Cambridge, 1929). He modified his views somewhat in 'Further notes on Romanesque bindings', *Library*, N.S. 15 (1934), 161–211, which lists ninety bindings of this type, and in 'Some early bindings and binders' tools', ibid., N.S. 19 (1938), 202–49, he extended the list to 106. Two more have since been published: an early

thirteenth-century *Processionale* in the Hofer collection at Harvard, which was no. 108 in Dorothy Miner's Baltimore binding exhibition catalogue of 1957 (pl. XXVI); and the glossed *Gospels of St. Matthew and St. Mark*, also early thirteenth century, which was sold at Sotheby's as Lot 1, 31 May 1960 (illustrated in the catalogue). The latter binding was discussed by A. R. A. Hobson in *The Burlington Magazine*, 102 (1960), 263–4. It is now part of the Henry Davis Gift to the British Museum.

[3] Hobson never quite admitted French priority, but had to fall back on an unsolved hypothesis of Jewish craftsmen (which is briefly discussed below) and the suggestion that the three surviving bindings of the Winchester group were not necessarily the first to be made there (Hobson, 'Further Notes', 177).

[4] *Jahrbuch der Einbandkunst*, Jahrg. 3 & 4 (1929–30), 22.

Prince Henry's binders

The manuscripts that belonged to Prince Henry are the work of at least three scribes and it is clear that two, or possibly three, binders were at work. The bindings are very close in style, but two different sets of similar engraved tools were in use. No bookbinder will willingly equip himself with two sets of tools of the same design in the same size, and since the two sets do not intermingle we may reasonably assume two binders. In his final classification of the Romanesque bindings in 1938 Hobson made an unquestionably valid distinction between Prince Henry's first and second binders—he records six bindings from the first and eight from the second—but his next group, the architectural bindery with the 'rowel spur', seems, as Dr. Schilling pointed out,[1] to have used a number of tools identical with those of the Prince's first binder. The tools used in these three—or two—binderies may have been the main source of the designs for the Winchester group, although both may derive from a common archetype.

English Romanesque bindings

In Hobson's final revised classification of 1938, the number of bindings he was prepared to attribute to England was reduced to those shown in Table 56—the Roman figures refer to the list which he began in 1929 in *English Binding before 1500*, reprinted nearly double the size in the *Library* in 1934, and to which he made fifteen additions in 1938.

TABLE 56

English Romanesque bindings: Hobson's classification

	WINCHESTER	
V	Winton Domesday. *c.* 1150	Society of Antiquaries, MS. 154
XXI	Cartulary of St. Swithun's, Winchester. *c.* 1150	British Museum, Add. MS. 15350
XXII	Hegesippus. *c.* 1150	Winchester Cathedral Library, MS. XVII
	LONDON	
XVII	Knights Templar *Inquisitio.* 1185	Public Record Office, E 164/16
XVIII	Petrus Comestor. Late 12th cent.	British Museum, Egerton MS. 272
XXIV	Petrus Lombardus. Late 12th cent.	Bodleian, MS. Rawl. C. 163
	DURHAM	
VI–IX	Puiset Bible, 4 vols. Late 12th cent.	Durham Cathedral Library, A.II.1
	OXFORD	
XVI	*Summa super Gratiani decretum.* Early 13th cent.	British Museum, Add. MS. 24659
	LATER MISCELLANEOUS	
C	*Miscellanea medica.* 13th cent.	St. John's, Cambridge, MS. 132
CVI	*Sermones Odonis Abbatis, c.* 1300	Durham University Library, V.II.8

Oxford bindings

This makes a not very grand total of thirteen bindings, but even this may err on the side of national optimism. No. XVI[2] is probably English, but Hobson's only reason for attributing it to Oxford was

---

[1] Op. cit. 19. Her plates illustrate the majority of the tools used in these binderies, but there are rather more reproductions on Pls. XXVI and XXVII of Aleksander Birkenmajer, *Oprawa rękopisa 2470 Bibljoteki Jagiellónskiej* (Krakow, 1925). They are not allotted to their respective owners on the plates. The first binder owned nos. 1, 2, 3, 4, 5, 16, 17, 21, 22, 23, 24, 26, 27, 29, 31, 33, 35, 37, 42, 43, 44, 45, 46–49, 54, 55, 57. The remainder are the second binder's. The bindings illustrated by Birkenmajer on Pls. XVIII–XXV are all by Prince Henry's first binder, except for Montpellier MS. 231 (Pls. XX and XXI) which is the work of the second binder.

[2] Misprinted 'XIV' in the 1938 classification.

the belief that a well-engraved tool of a swan found on the binding was used again on some Oxford bindings of the fifteenth century. Examination of impressions of the two tools side by side, using BM, Egerton MS. 2892 for the fifteenth-century example, confirms that the identical tool seems to have been used.[1] But as Hobson said in 1929[2] 'the evidence in favour of . . . Oxford is, I regret to say, particularly weak', for if a tool survives for two or three hundred years it may well have been in several places during this time. And Mr. Graham Pollard's very thorough investigations into early Oxford bindings have produced no sign of any decorated bindings before the middle of the fifteenth century.

Durham bindings

Nor is the evidence for Durham as a producer of blind-tooled Romanesque bindings as strong as was thought, for Hobson's VI–IX are the four great volumes of the bible of Bishop Hugh of Le Puiset, nephew of Henry of Blois. And it no longer seems to be quite so certain that this bible was written at Durham. There are three other twelfth-century blind-tooled Romanesque bindings there in the cathedral library, and they all seem to be Parisian (Hobson XII, XIII, and XIV). Should the Puiset bible prove to have been written in France, it was probably bound there.

In 'Some Early Bindings and Binders' Tools', Hobson mentioned two later English Romanesque decorated bindings. One of these (C) is a thirteenth-century manuscript at St. John's College, Cambridge. It shares with the binding (XVI) which Hobson attributed to Oxford the peculiarity of having 'boards' of cowhide instead of wood, but the decorated outer covering is of vellum. Dr. Neil Ker interprets the inscription *Iste liber pertinet domui de Mersay* as indicating that it came from Mersea Priory, Essex. The other (CVI) is now at Durham in the university library, but there is no evidence that it was bound there. Its earliest known owner was George Davenport, librarian to John Cosin, bishop of Durham, in the seventeenth century, but there is nothing to connect it with Durham at an earlier period. The manuscript it covers does, however, appear to be English *c.* 1300. Durham Cathedral Library also owns what could be the only fourteenth-century blind-tooled English binding, on a thirteenth-century Stephen Langton, *Super Ecclesiasticum.*[3] Both the place of origin and the date of this binding appear to be speculative, but it draws attention to an otherwise total absence of any English blind-tooled leather bindings in the fourteenth century. In both France and Germany bindings of this type, with rather dull vertical rows of not very interesting tool-impressions, bridge the gap between the Romanesque tooled work of the twelfth and thirteenth centuries and the new efflorescence of this technique about 1450.

Winchester and London bindings

The total absence in England of any fourteenth-century blind-tooled bindings (with this one possible exception) made me wonder at one time whether there had been any earlier English examples at all. But with this sceptical approach, I still remain convinced that Hobson was correct in identifying two twelfth-century groups, each of three books, as English: the earliest, which we may now date *c.* 1150, from Winchester; and a second group, bound in London, *c.* 1185. The majority of the tools used in both groups are clearly based on French models, but the London bindings have several tools which

---

[1] Mr. Pollard in 'The names of some English fifteenth-century binders' (*Library*, 5th ser. 25 (1970), 201–2) decided that this tool was not the original, but a very close copy. He suggested that the fifteenth-century Oxford binder who used it was Thomas Hokyns. But binders' tools have a very long life, if not constantly in use. The bindery at Windsor Castle has many of the tools from King George III's private bindery at Buckingham House (now Palace). Some of these,

known from the toolcutter's address which was stamped on them to have been engraved before 1800, were used over one hundred and fifty years later to repair bindings from the King's Library at the British Museum which had originally been tooled with them at Buckingham House.

[2] *English Binding*, 5.

[3] Ibid., Appendix C, 34–5, Pl. 31.

are unique, including two triangular ones—a crane with lowered head and a heron killing a fish—and a fine lobe-shaped example with two monsters on either side of a tree, on which stands a bird with raised wings. Both the London and Winchester groups also include quite different types of manuscript from the standard glossed Biblical texts found in the Paris bindings. There are three registers of property—the *Inquisitio Terrarum* of the Knights Templar in London (Hobson XVII), the Winton Domesday (V), and the cartulary of St. Swithun's, Winchester (XXI).

London bindings

On the three bindings of the London group thirty-six tools were used, thirty-one of them on a twelfth-century manuscript of the *Sententiae* of Peter the Lombard in the Bodleian Library (MS. Rawl. C. 163; Hobson XXIV),[1] which Miss de la Mare tells me appears to be English and could be as early as 1185. This binding, like the three in the Winchester group, has a circular design on one cover and a rectangular disposition of the tools on the other, but here the circle is found on the second cover, the opposite of the Winchester practice. The other two London bindings are on smaller books and are very similar to one another in design; both covers of both books have a rectangular lay-out similar to the upper cover of the Bodleian book. On both of them eleven tools were used which are found on the Bodleian binding. The *Inquisitio Terrarum* of the Knights Templar, which is in the Public Record Office,[2] and must date from 1185, or very shortly after, has five tools not found on the Bodleian binding. Three of these were used on the third London binding which covers a *Petrus Comestor* from the library of the Augustinian priory of St. Mary Overy in the British Museum.[3] The late Professor Francis Wormald told me that this manuscript could also just be as early as 1185, so we may take this as the approximate date of this London group. This means that there may be a gap of thirty-five years between the Winchester and the London bindings. Such a gap may, perhaps, account for the differences between the two sets of tools. Only the commonest of the Romanesque tool-types occur in both groups: Winchester tools (Pl. x) **2**, the lobe-shaped dragon; **3**, the small concentric circles; **5**, the small circular rosette; and **17**, the small lion passant found only on the St. Swithun's cartulary, although here the resemblance in the tools—particularly in the treatment of the tails—is close. We may be dealing with the few survivors of relatively prolific shops with considerably larger stocks of tools, some of which were of the same type. Nineteen tools were used on the three Winchester books and thirty-six on the London ones, but the four volumes of the Puiset Bible at Durham show impressions of nearly fifty. On the other hand it is quite possible that the binder of the London group had never seen any of the Winchester bindings and that the designs for his tools (and possibly the tools themselves) came independently from France.

A Jewish craftsman at Winchester?

On p. 174 of his 'Further Notes on Romanesque Bindings', G. D. Hobson suggested that the Winchester binder may have been a Jew, since his fount of tools showed a total lack of Christian subjects. 'None of the three books in Winchester bindings' he wrote 'is religious in character, and one of them (XXII), the Latin adaptation of Josephus's *De Bello Judaico* which was attributed to Hegesippus, may well have found a home in a Jewish library. Winchester was known as the English Jerusalem and the Jewish community there was the wealthiest and most important in the country.'

---

[1] Pls. 1 and 2 in Strickland Gibson's *Some Notable Bodleian Bindings* (Oxford, 1901–4). The lower cover is reproduced in *English Binding*, Pl. 8.

[2] E 164/16. *English Binding*, Pls. 6 and 7. Hobson XVII. For the date of the inquisition see *Templars*, xxi–xxii.

[3] Egerton MS. 272. W. Y. Fletcher, *English bookbindings in the British Museum* (London, 1895), Pl. II. Hobson XVIII.

By the early thirteenth century the Jewish community in Winchester was indeed large and wealthy. The Jews were already established in the city, if only in a small way, by 1148, but the epithet 'the English Jerusalem' is an expression of the chronicler's irony rather than a precise characterization of Winchester in the late twelfth century.

None of the Winchester books is specifically Christian, for the St. Swithun's cartulary is essentially a secular document, even if it was produced for a monastery. The Prince Henry binders in Paris, some of whose tools I have suggested the Winchester binder copied, took the trouble, quite often, but by no means always, to give prominence to certain of their religious tools on suitable books. On the glossed St. Matthew at Montpellier (Hobson IV) Prince Henry's first binder placed his tool of St. Matthew's symbol of the angel or winged man in the centre of the first cover. His binding on the glossed St. Mark at Troyes (Hobson XLII) has all four of the evangelists' symbols prominently displayed in the centre of the first cover, with St. Mark's winged lion at the top. The British Museum's St. Luke (Hobson XX), from the same shop, has the evangelist's winged ox in the centre of the front cover; in the same position is the figure of St. Paul on the glossed Epistles at Engelberg (Hobson LI) by the same binder; and a second copy of the Epistles at Engelberg (Hobson LIV), from the 'rowel spur' shop, probably identical with Prince Henry's first bindery, has a different St. Paul tool in the same position.

On three examples by Prince Henry's second binder which give similar prominence to a single tool, it is always in the centre of the second cover: St. Luke and St. John on the Gospels at Troyes (Hobson LXXX and XL) and David on the glossed Psalter at Montpellier (Hobson III).

This shows that Prince Henry's binders sometimes at least gave thought to the tools they were using, so that the Winchester binder was just as probably a Christian who did not feel that any of the three surviving bindings from his shop called for a specifically Christian tool. It does not seem particularly likely (though it is not impossible) that a Jewish craftsman would use leaves from an out-of-date Christian service book for the boards of a binding. Hobson's suggestion, based almost entirely on negative evidence, must remain no more than a possibility.

Conclusions

There seems no reason to doubt that the Winton Domesday was bound in Winchester and that it was bound very soon after it was written. Two of the three books on which the same group of binders' tools were used have a Winchester provenance, although it must be realized that the *Hegesippus* has nothing but its binding to connect it with the city.[1] Winchester, *c.* 1150, was exactly the place where work of this class was likely to be done, and there is no evidence that any tooled leather bindings were produced elsewhere in England before the London group of *c.* 1185. Winchester had the very strong Norman connections which would make natural the adoption of a comparatively modern technique developed in France, and Henry of Blois is exactly the type of person to have attracted a craftsman capable of doing this kind of work into his service. We are hardly likely to discover whether the binder was a Frenchman or an Englishman, but it seems rather more probable that he came to Winchester from France bringing with him tools and a technique which he had acquired in Paris.

The close similarity of the tools to those of Prince Henry's binders confirms the dating and, if the Winton Domesday was prepared for the use of Henry of Blois and was not subsequently used by anyone else, there would be no likelihood of its receiving an elaborate binding after his departure in exile to France in 1155.

[1] It was only given to the Cathedral Library in 1947; see above, p. 534, n. 1.

4. FRAGMENTS OF A TENTH-CENTURY SACRAMENTARY FROM THE BINDING OF THE WINTON DOMESDAY

by the late FRANCIS WORMALD[1]

(Plate XI)

THE twenty-six leaves of a sacramentary which were pasted together to form the 'boards' of the twelfth-century leather binding of the Winton Domesday have been carefully described by Dr. Neil Ker in his catalogue of *Medieval Manuscripts in British Libraries*.[2] All were mounted, and inset in paper, in their present form in 1919. The written space of each page measures 250 × 150 mm and there are twenty-seven lines to a page on fos. 1–19, and twenty-six on fos. 20–6. The writing is in black with rubrics in red, which has faded. The circumstances in which the leaves were first identified are recorded as follows in a note at the beginning of the volume (fo. iii[r]) signed by Gustavus Brander (1720–87), a former owner:

On opening the Covers of the Winchester Doomsdey I found that each Cover was Stiffen'd with 13 pieces of Parchment/in the whole 26 leaves/pasted together; wch. on Separating proved to be part of an Antient Missal in the Saxon Character & as legible as when first wrote.

The Ingenious Mr. West author of the Antiquities of Furness Abby having seen them, says they are part of an Antient Sacramentary as is Evident from the Stile & Arrangemt. of the Prayers, Collects, Preface & Lessons, the Saints Served are only those who are found in the first Calendar of the Church.

The Saxons paid no honors to British Saints & the use of these Offices was Prior to the time of the Saxon Saints being admitted into the Roman Calendar, wch. Mr. West esteems as a Negative proof of the leaves being a high Antiquity—The leather or outside Cover is very Curiously Stamped all over with a variety of Beasts & Birds in the Grotesque the Manuscript purchas'd of the Collection of James West Esq: President of the Roy[l]. Society after his Decease.[3]

From this it is clear that when found the fragments were made up of thirteen bifolia. Unfortunately there is no record of their actual arrangement, nor is it known how many bifolia made up a gathering. As has been seen the identification of the text as a sacramentary was due to the Revd. Thomas West, S.J. (1720–79), who was consulted by Gustavus Brander.

The text is written throughout in a large caroline minuscule by a single scribe. Occasionally the letter-forms have an insular look. This is particularly noticeable in the rubric at the beginning of the *Liber Comitis* on fo. 24[v] (Pl. XI) with its ascenders with wedge-shaped serifs and rather high *e*. There is also a tendency to use a majuscule *R* at the end of words, and less frequently in the middle of words.[4] The *g* is occasionally very insular. In fact, the whole of the script has rather a tentative look

[1] The text of this note was prepared shortly before Professor Wormald's death, and was not revised by him. Nothing has been added to it, but references and titles in the detailed description of the contents have been checked by B. C. Barker-Benfield. In the titles, square brackets [ ] indicate letters which are now cut away or illegible; pointed brackets ⟨ ⟩ indicate words which have been supplied but are omitted in the manuscript; round brackets ( ) are used for the expansion of abbreviations which are uncertain (otherwise, they are silently expanded). *Ad com.* or *ad compl.* have been expanded as *ad complendum* (see *Greg* p. xxv), although *ad completum* appears on fos. 6[v] 6 and 10[v] 14, *ad commun.* at 12[v] 21, and *ad complendum* is never written out in full. In general, the MS reading

is given, e.g. *post Theophania, die dominico*, without editorial comment or emendation. The usage of the MS. is followed in extensions.

[2] N. R. Ker, *Medieval Manuscripts in British Libraries*, i, *London* (Oxford, 1969), 307–8. Now bound separately as Society of Antiquaries of London, MS. 154*. On the use made of these leaves in the binding of the Winton Domesday, see above, pp. 526–31.

[3] On Gustavus Brander and his acquisition of the MS. at the sale of James West's Museum of Curiosities, see above, p. 3. A copy of the catalogue carries the handwritten note '24 Saxon Deeds were pasted on the Cover', apparently the earliest reference to these fragments (see above, p. 3, n. 5).

[4] See particularly fos. 18[r], 18[v], 20[v].

as if the scribe were feeling his way in a new type of handwriting. The spelling is marked by the habit of duplicating certain consonants, such as *circumcissionis* for *circumcisionis*, *summamus* for *sumamus*, *immitemur* for *imitemur*, *quadragessimales* for *quadragesimales*.[1] It will be recalled that such duplications are a feature of earlier insular manuscripts.[2] Another feature is that certain sounds have been spelt with an æ dipthong giving such oddities of spelling as *proueniræ* for *prouenire* (fo. 5^r 18) and *perueniræ* for *peruenire* (fo. 12^v 23). It is used throughout the manuscript for such words as *præces*, *terrænis* and *præcæpit*.

All the prayers and lections have been provided with initial letters, usually occupying the height of two or three lines. They are drawn in ink in an extremely undistinguished style which makes it difficult either to place or to date them within any recognizable art-historical category. Their main element of decoration is a form of the long-and-short leaf as is found in many tenth-century English manuscripts. There is only one initial which has any kind of animal ornament (fo. 7^v). This is a *D* at the beginning of the line, which has a rudimentary dog's head as a terminal. There are two larger initials on fo. 18^v for the *Exultet*, but their ornament is not revealing and consists of rather rudimentary interlace.

A number of additions have been made to the original text. The most extensive is a mass for the feast of St. Scholastica in the lower margins of fos. 6^v and 7^r. It is of the eleventh century. A secret for Thursday in the fourth week of Lent omitted by the original scribe has been added in the margin of fo. 12^r in an eleventh-century hand which looks a little earlier than the Scholastica addition. Three other additions should be noted: on fo. 5^r the word *effectum* has been added in an insular minuscule; the *Exultet* (fos. 18^v–19^v) has been provided with neumes; and on fo. 2^v 11 and 12 stress accents have been added.

A very small part of the whole remains. The contents divide into three main groups:

1. fos. 1^r–19^v, containing with some gaps the masses from Holy Innocents day (27 December) to Easter Saturday, ending with the *Exultet*;
2. fos. 20^r–24^r, lections for the Common of Saints, followed by a group of special masses for the dead;
3. fos. 24^v–26^v, lections for the masses of Christmas and the feast of the Holy Innocents.

In general both the text of the masses and their rubrics follow the Gregorian Sacramentary and, as far as can be ascertained, approximate to Gamber's H type.[3] It cannot have been a pure Hadrianum because the group of special masses and the prefaces have been incorporated, and this suggests a developed text. Much more unusual is the introduction into a sacramentary of the lections. This suggests that we see here a tendency towards the making of a full missal. The musical portions of the mass are not included, but we have the combination of sacramentary and lectionary.

There are two questions which must be asked. The first is the date of the manuscript, and the second is its country of origin. Dr. Ker in his description has dated it to the end of the tenth century. This is certainly a possible date, but the rather tentative aspect of the script suggests that it may be as early as the third quarter of the century. On the other hand it is most unlikely to be much earlier, because the caroline minuscule did not reach England until this time. As we have seen, there are certain features which suggest an English origin. If this can be accepted, the fragments would represent an early example of the kind of sacramentary in use in Winchester at the period of the Æthelwold reform.

---

[1] See fos. 1^r 26, 1^v 20, 4^v 11, 10^v 6.

[2] E. A. Lowe, *Codices Latini Antiquiores*, ii, *Great Britain and Ireland* (Oxford, 1935), viii.

[3] See K. Gamber, *Sakramentartypen* (Texte und Arbeiten herausgegeben durch die Erzabtei Beuron I, Heft 49/50, Beuron, 1958), 159–65.

A rather more detailed description of the contents of these fragments is appended here. References are made to the following works in abbreviated form:

Frere   W. H. Frere, *Studies in Early Roman Liturgy*, iii, *The Roman Epistle-Lectionary* (Alcuin Club Collections 32, Oxford, 1935). The numbers given here refer to Frere's list on pp. 1–24.

Gel. Fr.   K. Mohlberg, *Das fränkische Sacramentarium Gelasianum in alamannischer Überlieferung* (*Codex Sangall. No. 348*). *St. Galler Sakramentar–Forschungen I*, 2nd edn. (Liturgiegeschichtliche Quellen, Heft 1/2, Münster in Westfalen, 1939). The numbers given here refer to sections, not pages.

Greg   H. A. Wilson (ed.), *The Gregorian Sacramentary under Charles the Great* (HBS 49, London, 1915). The numbers given here refer to pages.

Klauser   Th. Klauser (ed.), *Das Römische Capitulare Evangeliorum*, i, *Typen* (Liturgiegeschichtliche Quellen und Forschungen, Heft 28, Münster in Westfalen, 1935).

L   H. Lietzmann (ed.), *Das Sacramentarium Gregorianum nach dem Aachener Urexemplar* (Liturgiegeschichtliche Quellen, Heft 3, Münster in Westfalen, 1921). The numbers given here refer to sections.

R de J   H. A. Wilson (ed.), *The Missal of Robert of Jumièges* (HBS 11, London, 1896). The numbers given here refer to pages.

[Holy Innocents. *Ad complendum*]
fo. 1ʳ 1–3. *R de J* 149; *Greg* 15 (L 12.3)
Alia
fo. 1ʳ 4–8. *R de J* 149; *Greg* 15 (L 12.4)

Pridie kalendas ianuarias id est xxx⟨i⟩ die mensis [*decembris natale*] *Sancti Silues*[*tri*]
fo. 1ʳ 9–11. *R de J* 149; *Greg* 15 (L. 13.1)
Super oblata
fo. 1ʳ 12–14. *R de J* 149; *Greg* 16 (L 13.2)
A[*d*] *compl*(*endum*)
fo. 1ʳ 15–16. *R de J* 149; *Greg* 16 (L 13.3)

Kalendas ianuarias oct[*auas*] *Domini* [*ad*] *Sanctam Mariam ad* [*Martyres*]
fo. 1ʳ 17–22. *R de J* 52, *Dominica I. post Natale Domini*; *Greg* 16 (L 14. 1)
[*S*]*uper* [*oblata*]
fo. 1ʳ 23–5. *R de J* 53, *Dominica I. post Natale Domini*; *Greg* 16 (L 14.2)
Praefatio
fo. 1ʳ 26–1ᵛ 6. *R de J* 52, *Octauas Domini*; *Greg* 256, *In Octauas Domini*
Ad com[*plendum*]
fo. 1ᵛ 7, 8. *Greg* 16 (L 14.3)
[*Alia*]
fo. 1ᵛ 9–11. *Greg* 16, *Oratio in alia Dominica* (L 15.1)
Item alia
fo. 1ᵛ 12–15. *Greg* 16, *Item in alia Dominica* (L 16.1)

In uigilia Theophania D[*omini*]
fo. 1ᵛ 16–19. *R de J* 54; *Gel. Fr.* 91

Super oblata
fo. 1ᵛ 20–22. *R de J* 54; *Gel. Fr.* 92. MS. has *summamus* for *sumamus*
Praefatio
fo. 1ᵛ 23–7, ends incompletely. *R de J* 54; *Gel. Fr.* 93

[*Epiphania Domini*]. The text begins imperfectly
fo. 2ʳ 1–3. *Greg* 18 (L 18.6), *Alia* ⟨*oratio*⟩
Ali[*a*]
fo. 2ʳ 4–7. *R de J* 55, *Super populum*; *Greg* 18 (L 18.7)

In octabas Theophania
fo. 2ʳ 8–11. *R de J* 55; *Gel. Fr.* 112
Super oblata
fo. 2ʳ 12–15. *R de J* 55; *Gel. Fr.* 113
Ad [*complendum*]
fo. 2ʳ 16–19. *R de J* 55; *Gel. Fr.* 114
Super popul[*um*]
fo. 2ʳ 20–21. *R de J* 55, under *Epiphania Domini*; *Gel. Fr.* 115

Dominica .i. post natale Domini
fo. 2ʳ 23–7. *R de J* 52; *Greg* 16 (L 14.1)
Super [*oblata*]
fo. 2ᵛ 1–3. *R de J* 53; *Greg* 16 (L 14.2)
Praefatio
fo. 2ᵛ 4–9. *R de J* 53; *Greg* 256. Ms. reads *aecclessiae* for *ecclesiae*
Ad compl(*endum*)
fo. 2ᵛ 10–13. *R de J* 53; *Greg* 163; *Gel. Fr.* 71

Dominica .ii. post natale Domini
fo. 2ᵛ 14–16. *R de J* 53, *Dom. I. post Octabas Domini;*
    Greg 164; *Gel. Fr.* 85
Super ob[lata]
fo. 2ᵛ 17–20. *R de J* 53, *Dom. I. post Octabas Domini;*
    Greg 164; *Gel. Fr.* 87
Praefatio
fo. 2ᵛ 21–5. *R de J* 53, *Dom. I. post Octabas Domini;*
    Greg 257, *Dom. II. post Natale Domini; Gel. Fr.*
    88 *Ad compl(endum)*
fo. 2ᵛ 26–7. *R de J* 53, *Dom. I. post Octabas Domini;*
    Greg 164, *Dom. II. post Natale Domini; Gel. Fr.* 89

[Dominica .i. post] Theop[hania]
fo. 3ʳ 1–4. *R de J* 56; *Greg* 164
    Super oblata
fo. 3ʳ 5–6. *R de J* 56; *Greg* 164
    Praefatio
fo. 3ʳ 7–17. *R de J* 57–8 (Preface for *Dom. IV. post*
    Theoph.); *Greg* 259 (Preface for *Dom. III.*
    post Theoph.). MS. reads *summus* for *sumus* in
    line 9
    Ad compl(endum)
fo. 3ʳ 18–20. *R de J* 56; *Greg* 164

Dominica .ii. post Theoph[ania]
fo. 3ʳ 21–4. *R de J* 56; *Greg* 164
    Super oblata
fo. 3ʳ 25–6. *R de J* 56; *Greg* 164
    Praefatio
fo. 3ʳ 27–3ᵛ 7. *R de J* 57, *Dom. III. post Theoph.;*
    Greg 259, *Dom. IV. post Theoph.*
    Ad com(plendum)
fo. 3ᵛ 8–10. *R de J* 56; *Greg* 164

Dominica .iii. post Theophania
fo. 3ᵛ 11–14. *R de J* 57; *Greg* 165
    Super oblata
fo. 3ᵛ 15–17. *R de J* 57; *Greg* 165
    Praefatio
fo. 3ᵛ 18–4ʳ 2. *R de J* 58, *Dom. V. post Theoph.* MS.
    has *i[u]efabile* for *ineffabile* in lines 19–20, *con-*
    fussione for *infusione* in line 22, and *summimus* for
    sumimus in line 24
    Ad com(plendum)
fo. 4ʳ 3–4. *R de J* 57; *Greg* 165

Feria .iiii. post Theophania (for *Feria* read *Dominica*)
fo. 4ʳ 5–9. *R de J* 57; *Greg* 165
    Super oblata
fo. 4ʳ 10–12. *R de J* 57; *Greg* 165
    Praefatio
fo. 4ʳ 13–17. *R de J* 59, *Dom. VI. post Theoph.;*
    Greg 260, *Dom. VI*

Ad c[omplendum]
fo. 4ʳ 18–20. *R de J* 58; *Greg* 165

Dominica [.v. post Th]eophania
fo. 4ʳ 21–3. *R de J* 58; *Greg* 165
[Su]per o[blata]
fo. 4ʳ 24–6. *R de J* 58; *Greg* 165
    Ad compl(endum)
fo. 4ʳ 27–4ᵛ 1, *R de J* 58; *Greg* 165

Dominica .vi. post Theoph[ania]
fo. 4ᵛ 2–5. *R de J* 59; *Greg* 166
Super oblata
fo. 4ᵛ 6–7. *R de J* 59; *Greg* 166. MS. has *emundet*
    for *mundet*

xviiii. kalendas februarias id est xiiii. die mensis
    ianuarii natale Sancti Felicis
fo. 4ᵛ 8–11. *R de J* 151; *Greg* 18–19 (L 19.1). MS.
    has *immittemur* for *imitemur*
Super oblata
fo. 4ᵛ 12–14. *R de J* 151; *Greg* 19 (L 19.2). MS. has
    adsumme for *assume* or *adsume*
    Ad comp[lendum]
fo. 4ᵛ 15–16. *R de J* 151; *Greg* 19 (L 19.3)

xvii. kalendas februarias id est xvi. die mensis
    ianuarii natale Ma[rcel]lini [pape]
fo. 4ᵛ 17–20. *R de J* 152; *Greg* 19 (L 20.1)
    Super o[blata]
fo. 4ᵛ 21–3. *R de J* 152; *Greg* 19 (L 20.2). MS. has
    subfragantibus for *suffragantibus*
    Ad com[plendum]
fo. 4ᵛ 24–6. *R de J* 152; *Greg* 19 (L 20.3)

xv. kalendas februarias id est xviii. die mensis
    ianuarii natale Sancte Prisce
fo. 5ʳ 1–4. *R de J* 153; *Greg* 19 (L 21.1)
    Super oblata
fo. 5ʳ 5–8. *R de J* 153; *Greg* 19 (L 21.2)
    Ad compl(endum)
fo. 5ʳ 9–11. *R de J* 153; *Greg* 20 (L 21.3)

xiii. kalendas februarias id est xx. die mensis
    ianuarii natale Sancti Fabiani
fo. 5ʳ 12–15. *R de J* 153; *Greg* 20 (L 22.1)
    Super oblata
fo. 5ʳ 16–18. *R de J* 154; *Greg* 20 (L 22.2). MS. has
    adsumme for *adsume*; *prouenirae* for *prouenire*
    Ad com[plendum]
fo. 5ʳ 19–21. *R de J* 154; *Greg* 20 (L 22.3). MS.
    originally omitted *effectum*, added later in an
    insular minuscule

In eodem die natale Sancti S[ebas]tiani
fo. 5ʳ 22–6. *R de J* 154; *Greg* 20 (L 23.1). MS. has
　immitatione for *imitatione*; *tribuae* for *tribue*
Super oblata
fo. 5ʳ 27–5ᵛ 2. *R de J* 154; *Greg* 20 (L 23.2)
Praefat[io]
fo. 5ᵛ 3–8. *R de J* 154; *Greg* 258
Ad compl(endum)
fo. 5ᵛ 9–12. *R de J* 154; *Greg* 20 (L 23.3)

⟨*xii.*⟩ *kalendas februarias xxi. die ianuarii natale*
　Sanctae Ag[netis] martyr[is]
fo. 5ᵛ 13–17. *R de J* 154; *Greg* 21 (L 24.1)
　Super [oblata]
fo. 5ᵛ 18–20. *R de J* 154; *Greg* 21 (L 24. 2)
Pr[aefatio]
fo. 5ᵛ 21–6ʳ 2. *R de J* 154–5; *Greg* 258.
A⟨d⟩ comp[lendum]
fo. 6ʳ 3–6. *R de J* 155; *Greg* 21 (L 24.3)

xi. kalendas februarias id est xxii. die mensis ianuarii
　natale Sancti Vincenti⟨i⟩ mart[yris]
fo. 6ʳ 7–10. *R de J* 155; *Greg* 21 (L 25.1)
Super ob[lata]
fo. 6ʳ 11–13. *R de J* 155; *Greg* 21 (L 25.2)
Praefatio
fo. 6ʳ 14–21. *R de J* 155; *Greg* 258. MS. and *R de J*
　have *rapidi* for *rabidi* and *interitus* for *interritus*
Ad com[plendum]
fo. 6ʳ 22–5. *R de J* 155; *Greg* 21 (L 25.3)

v. kalendas februarias id ⟨est⟩ xxxviii (sic, for *xxviii*)
　mensis [ianuarii] natale Sancte Agn[etis]
fo. 6ʳ 26–6ᵛ 2. *R de J* 157; *Greg* 21 (L 26.1)
[Super oblata]
fo. 6ᵛ 3–6. *R de J* 157; *Greg* 22 (L 26.2)
Ad completum (sic)
fo. 6ᵛ 7–9. *R de J* 157; *Greg* 22 (L 26.3). There are
　some differences owing to scribal ignorance
　(*caelebrantes* for *celebritatis*)

M(en)s(is) fe(b)r(uarii) .iiii. non[as] yppapanti ad
　Sanctam Mariam. oratio ad co[llectam]
fo. 6ᵛ 11–13. *Greg* 22 (L 27.1). Not found in *R de J*
Missa ad Sanctam Ma[ri]am
fo. 6ᵛ 14–19. *R de J* 159; *Greg* 22 (L 27.2)
Super oblata
fo. 6ᵛ 20–22. *R de J* 159; *Greg* 22 (L 27.3)
Praef[atio]
fo. 6ᵛ 23–4. *Greg* 259
Ad com(plendum)
fo. 6ᵛ 25–7ʳ 1. *R de J* 160; *Greg* 22 (L 27.4)
Super populum
fo. 7ʳ 2–7. *R de J* 160, n. 2; *Greg* 23 (L 27.5)

In the lower margins of fos. 6ᵛ and 7ʳ a mass of
St. Scholastica has been added in an eleventh-
century caroline minuscule: Collect, *R de J* 161;
Secret, *R de J* 162; Post-communion, *R de J*
162

Nonis februariis id est .v. die mensis februarii natale
　Sancte Agathe
fo. 7ʳ 8–12. *R de J* 160; *Greg* 23 (L 28.1)
Super oblata
fo. 7ʳ 13–16. *R de J* 160; *Greg* 23 (L 28.2). MS. has
　defferimus for *deferimus*, and *patracinio* for
　patrocinio
Praefatio
fo. 7ʳ 17–26. *R de J* 160; *Greg* 260.
Ad compl(endum)
fo. 7ʳ 27–7ᵛ 2. *R de J* 161; *Greg* 23 (L 28.3)
Alia
fo. 7ᵛ 3–5. *R de J* 161; *Greg* 23 (L 28.4)
Al[ia]
fo. 7ᵛ 6–9. *Greg* 23 (L 28.5)
Alia
fo. 7ᵛ 10–12. *Greg* 23 (L 28. 6)

xvi. kalendas martias i[d est .xiiii.] die mensis
　februarii natale Sancti V[alentini]
fo. 7ᵛ 13–16. *R de J* 163; *Greg* 24 (L 29.1)
Super oblata
fo. 7ᵛ 17–19. *R de J* 163; *Greg* 24 (L 29.2)
Ad com(plendum)
fo. 7ᵛ 20–22. *R de J* 164; *Greg* 24 (L 29.3)

.iiii. idus martias natale Sancti Grego[rii] papae
fo. 7ᵛ 23–6. *R de J* 166; *Greg* 24 (L 30.1). MS. has
　aput for *apud*
[Super oblata]
fo. 7ʳ 27. *R de J* 166; *Greg* 24 (L 30.2)

Here is a gap of some leaves

[Hebdomada .ii. in Quadragesima. Sabbato]
[Praefatio]
fo. 8ʳ 1–6. *R de J* 71; *Greg* 235. MS. has *terraenis*
　for *terrenis*, and agrees with *Greg* in having
　rubor for *robur*
Ad compl(endum)
fo. 8ʳ 7–9. *R de J* 71; *Greg* 35 (L 51.3)
Super populum
fo. 8ʳ 10–12. *R de J* 71; *Greg* 35 (L 51.4)

Die dominica ad Sanctum Laurentium foris murum
fo. 8ʳ 13–15. *R de J* 71; *Greg* 35 (L 52.1)
Secreta
fo. 8ʳ 16–18. *R de J* 71; *Greg* 35 (L 52.2)

[Praefatio]
fo. 8ʳ 19–8ᵛ 2. *R de J* 72; *Greg* 264. MS. has *propentius*
    for *propensius*
Ad compl(endum)
fo. 8ᵛ 3–5. *R de J* 72; *Greg* 36 (L 52.3)

Feria .ii. ad Sanctam Mariam
fo. 8ᵛ 6–8. *R de J* 72; *Greg* 36 (L 53.1)
Super oblata
fo. 8ᵛ 9–10. *R de J* 72; *Greg* 36 (L 53.2)
Praefatio
fo. 8ᵛ 11–18. *R de J* 72; *Greg* 265
Ad compl(endum)
fo. 8ᵛ 19–20. *R de J* 72; *Greg* 36 (L 53.3)
Super populum
fo. 8ᵛ 21–3. *R de J* 72; *Greg* 36 (L 53.4)

Feria .iii.
fo. 8ᵛ 24–6. *R de J* 73; *Greg* 36 (L 54.1)
Super oblata
fo. 8ᵛ 27–9ʳ 3. *R de J* 73; *Greg* 36 (L 54.2). MS. has
    ab salutaria for *ad salutaria*
Praefatio
fo. 9ʳ 4–11. *R de J* 73; *Greg* 265
Ad compl(endum)
fo. 9ʳ 12–13. *R de J* 73; *Greg* 36 (L 54.3)
Super populum
fo. 9ʳ 14–15. *R de J* 73; *Greg* 36 (L 54.4)

Feria .iiii. ad Sanctum Sixtum
MS. omits the Collect
[Super oblata]
fo. 9ʳ 16–18. *R de J* 73; *Greg* 37 (L 55.2)
Praefatio
fo. 9ʳ 19–25. *R de J* 73; *Greg* 265
Ad com(plendum)
fo. 9ʳ 26–9ᵛ 1. *R de J* 73; *Greg* 37 (L 55.3)
[Super populum]
fo. 9ᵛ 2–4. *R de J* 74; *Greg* 37 (L 55.4)

Feria .v. ad S[anctos] Cosmam et Damianum
fo. 9ᵛ 5–9. *R de J* 74; *Greg* 37 (L 56.1)
Super oblata
fo. 9ᵛ 10–12. *R de J* 74; *Greg* 37 (L 56.2)
Praefatio
fo. 9ᵛ 13–21. *R de J* 74; *Greg* 265
Ad com[plendum]
fo. 9ᵛ 22–4. *R de J* 74; *Greg* 37 (L 56.3)
Super populum
fo. 9ᵛ 25–7. *R de J* 74; *Greg* 37 (L 56.4)

Feria .vi. ad Sanctum Laurentium
fo. 10ʳ 1–3. *R de J* 74; *Greg* 38 (L 57.1)
Super oblata
fo. 10ʳ 4–6. *R de J* 74; *Greg* 38 (L 57.2)

Praefatio
fo. 10ʳ 7–20. *R de J* 74–5; *Greg* 265–6
Ad com(plendum)
fo. 10ʳ 21–2. *R de J* 75; *Greg* 38 (L 57.3)
Super populum
fo. 10ʳ 23–5. *R de J* 75; *Greg* 38 (L 57.4)

Sabb(atum) ad Sanctam Susannam
fo. 10ʳ 26–10ᵛ 1. *R de J* 75; *Greg* 38 (L 58.1)
Super [oblata]
fo. 10ᵛ 2–4. *R de J* 75; *Greg* 38 (L 58.2)
Praefa[tio]
fo. 10ᵛ 5–14. *R de J* 75; *Greg* 266
Ad completu[m] (sic)
fo. 10ᵛ 15–16. *R de J* 75; *Greg* 38 (L 58.3)
Super p[opulum]
fo. 10ᵛ 17–19. *R de J* 75; *Greg* 38 (L 58.4)

Die dominico ad Hie[rusalem]
fo. 10ᵛ 20–22. *R de J* 76, *Dominica IIII. in Quadra-*
    gesima; *Greg* 39 (L 59.1)
[Super oblata]
fo. 10ᵛ 23–4. *R de J* 76; *Greg* 39 (L 59.2)
Prae[fatio]
fo. 10ᵛ 25–11ʳ 5. *R de J* 76; *Greg* 266
Ad com(plendum)
fo. 11ʳ 6–8. *R de J* 76; *Greg* 39 (L 59.3). MS. reads
    semper fideli mente
Super populum
fo. 11ʳ 9–13. *R de J* 76; *Greg* 39 (L 59.4)

Feria .ii. ad sanctos .iiii. coronatos
fo. 11ʳ 14–16. *R de J* 76; *Greg* 39 (L 60.1)
Super oblata
fo. 11ʳ 17–18. *R de J* 76; *Greg* 39 (L 60.2)
Praefatio
fo. 11ʳ 19–26. *R de J* 76; *Greg* 266.
Ad com(plendum)
fo. 11ʳ 27–11ᵛ 1. *R de J* 76; *Greg* 39 (L 60.3)
Ad com[plendum], sic, for *super populum*
fo. 11ᵛ 2–4. *R de J* 77; *Greg* 39 (L 60.4)

Feria .iii. ad Sanctum Laurentium in Damascum.
fo. 11ᵛ 5–8. *R de J* 77; *Greg* 40 (L 61.1)
Super oblata
fo. 11ᵛ 9–11. *R de J* 77; *Greg* 40 (L 61.2)
Praefatio
fo. 11ᵛ 12–22. *R de J* 77; *Greg* 266, 267
Ad compl(endum), sic MS.
fo. 11ᵛ 23–5. *R de J* 77, *Super populum*; *Greg* 40
    (L 61.4) *Super populum*
Super populum, sic MS.
fo. 11ᵛ 26–7. *R de J* 77, *Ad complendum*; *Greg* 40
    (L 61.3), *Ad complendum*

Feria .iiii. ad Sanctum Paulum
fo. 12ʳ 1–5. *R de J* 77; *Greg* 40 (L 62.1)
[*Alia*]
fo. 12ʳ 6–9. *R de J* 77; *Greg* 40 (L 62.2). MS. has
terraenis for *terrenis*. In the margin is added in an
eleventh-century English hand the secret: *R de J*
78; *Greg* 40 (L 62.3)
Praefatio
fo. 12ʳ 10–24. *R de J* 78; *Greg* 267. MS. has *expullit*
for *expulit*
Ad compl(endum)
fo. 12ʳ 25–7. *R de J* 78; *Greg* 40 (L 62.4). MS. has
tuaeantur for *tueantur*
Ad com[plendum], sic, for *super populum*
fo. 12ᵛ 1–3. *R de J* 78; *Greg* 41 (L 62.5)

Feria .v. ad Sanctum Silues[trum]
fo. 12ᵛ 4–7. *Greg* 40 (L 63.1). *R de J* 78 has a different
collect agreeing with *Gel. Fr.* 412
Super [oblata]
fo. 12ᵛ 8–10. *R de J* 78; *Greg* 41 (L 63.2)
Praefati[o]
fo. 12ᵛ 11–21. *R de J* 78; *Greg* 267
Ad commun[ionem], sic MS.
fo. 12ᵛ 22–4. *R de J* 79; *Greg* 41 (L 63.3). MS. has
peruenirae for *peruenire*
Su[per] populum
fo. 12ᵛ 25–13ʳ 1. *R de J* 79; *Greg* 41 (L 63.4)

Feria .vi. ad Sanctum Eusebium
fo. 13ʳ 2–4. *R de J* 79; *Greg* 41 (L 64.1)
Su[per oblata], possibly *Sec[reta]*
fo. 13ʳ 5–6. *R de J* 79; *Greg* 41 (L 64.2)
Praefatio
fo. 13ʳ 7–20. *R de J* 79; *Greg* 267. MS. and *R de J*
have *adsumpte* for *assumpte*
Ad compl(endum)
fo. 13ʳ 21–3. *R de J* 79; *Greg* 41 (L 64.3)
Super oblata, sic, for *super populum*
fo. 13ʳ 24–6. *R de J* 79; *Greg* 42 (L 64.4)

Sabb(atum) ad Sanctum Laurentium foris murum
fo. 13ᵛ 1–4. *R de J* 79; *Greg* 42 (L 65.1)
Sec[reta]
fo. 13ᵛ 5–7. *R de J* 80; *Greg* 42 (L 65.2)
Praefatio
fo. 13ᵛ 8–17. *R de J* 80; *Greg* 267–8. MS. has *ut
quid ad haec* for *ut qui ad haec*, and *eficatiam* for
efficaciam
Ad compl(endum)
fo. 13ᵛ 18–19. *R de J* 80; *Greg* 42 (L 65.3). MS. has
operationis tuae for *operationis suae*
Super populum
fo. 13ᵛ 20–24. *R de J* 80; *Greg* 42 (L 65.4). MS. has
ualeamus as O against *mereamur* as *R de J* and C

Dominica de passione sancta ad Sanctum Petr[um]
fo. 13ᵛ 25–8. *R de J* 80; *Greg* 42 (L 66.1). MS. and
O have *largiente*
Super oblata
fo. 14ʳ 1–3. *R de J* 80; *Greg* 42 (L 66.2)

Praefatio
fo. 14ʳ 4–9. *R de J* 80; *Greg* 268
Ad compl(endum)
fo. 14ʳ 10–12. *R de J* 80; *Greg* 42 (L 66.3)

Feria .ii. ad Sanctum Chrisogono, sic MS.
fo. 14ʳ 13–15. *R de J* 81; *Greg* 43 (L 67.1)
Super oblata
fo. 14ʳ 16–18. *R de J* 81; *Greg* 43 (L 67.2)

Praefatio
fo. 14ʳ 19–25. *R de J* 81; *Greg* 268
Ad compl(endum)
fo. 14ʳ 26–7. *R de J* 81; *Greg* 43 (L 67.3). MS. has
ad medelam for *et medelam*
Super populum
fo. 14ᵛ 1–4. *R de J* 81; *Greg* 43 (L 67.4). MS. has
inerendo for *inherendo*

Feria .iii. ad Sanctum Ciriacum
fo. 14ᵛ 5–7. *R de J* 81; *Greg* 43 (L 68.1)
Super oblata
fo. 14ᵛ 8–11. *R de J* 81; *Greg* 43 (L 68.2)
Praefatio
fo. 14ᵛ 12–19. *R de J* 81; *Greg* 268. MS. has *inpediri*
for *impediri*
Ad compl(endum)
fo. 14ᵛ 20–22. *R de J* 82; *Greg* 43 (L 68.3)
Super populum
fo. 14ᵛ 23–6. *R de J* 82; *Greg* 43 (L 68.4)

Feria .iiii. ad Sanctum Marcellum
fo. 14ᵛ 27–15ʳ 3. *R de J* 82; *Greg* 44 (L 69.1). MS. agrees
more closely with *Greg* and L against *R de J*
Super oblata
fo. 15ʳ 4–5. *R de J* 82; *Greg* 44 (L 69.2)
Praefatio
fo. 15ʳ 6–11. *R de J* 82; *Greg* 268. MS. omits the
opening phrase
Ad compl(endum)
fo. 15ʳ 12–15. *R de J* 82; *Greg* 44 (L 69.3)
Super populum
fo. 15ʳ 16–19. *R de J* 82; *Greg* 44 (L 69.4). MS. has
sperante for *sperandae* and *aeffectum* for *affectum*
(*R de J*) or *effectum* (*Greg* and L)

Feria .v. ad Sanctum Appollonarem
fo. 15ʳ 20–23. *R de J* 82; *Greg* 44 (L 70.1)
Super oblata
fo. 15ʳ 24–15ᵛ 2. *R de J* 82; *Greg* 44 (L 70.2). MS. has
tribuae for *tribue*

Prefatio

fo. 15ᵛ 3–8. *R de J* 83; *Greg* 268. MS. has *defferre* for *deferre*

Ad compl(endum)

fo. 15ᵛ 9–11. *R de J* 83; *Greg* 44 (L 70.3)

Super populum

fo. 15ᵛ 12–15. *R de J* 83; *Greg* 45 (L 70.4)

Feria .vi. ad Sanctum Stephan[um]

fo. 15ᵛ 16–20. *R de J* 83; *Greg* 45 (L 71.1). MS. has *gratiam tuam* as in *R de J*, added in the margin by an eleventh-century hand

Super oblata

fo. 15ᵛ 21–4. *R de J* 83; *Greg* 45 (L 71.2). MS. has *salutari* for *saluari*

Prefatio

fo. 15ᵛ 25–16ʳ 8. *R de J* 83; *Greg* 269

Ad compl(endum)

fo. 16ʳ 9–11. *R de J* 83; *Greg* 45 (L 71.3)

Super populum

fo. 16ʳ 12–14. *R de J* 83; *Greg* 45 (L 71.4). In the MS., *de* of *concede* has been added in an English hand of the tenth century

Sabb(atum) ad Sanctum Petrum quando elim(osina) datur

fo. 16ʳ 15–19. *R de J* 83; *Greg* 45 (L 72.1)

Super oblata

fo. 16ʳ 20–22. *R de J* 84; *Greg* 45 (L 72.2). MS. has *tanti mysterii* with L's *r* and *p*

Praefatio

fo. 16ʳ 23–16ᵛ 3. *R de J* 84; *Greg* 269. MS. has *accussat* for *accusat*

Ad compl(endum)

fo. 16ᵛ 4–6. *R de J* 84; *Greg* 45 (L 72.3)

Super populum

fo. 16ᵛ 7–10. *R de J* 84; *Greg* 46 (L 72.4). MS. has *perducat* for *proficiat*

Die dominico in palmis ad Sanc[tum] Iohannem in laterani[s]

fo. 16ᵛ 11–17. *R de J* 84; *Greg* 46 (L 73.1). MS. has *summere* for *sumere* and *subirae* for *subire*

Super ob[lata]

fo. 16ᵛ 18–21. *R de J* 85; *Greg* 46 (L 73.2)

Praef[atio]

fo. 16ᵛ 22–7. *R de J* 85; *Greg* 269

Ad com(plendum)

fo. 17ʳ 1–3. *R de J* 85; *Greg* 46 (L 73.3)

Feria .ii. ad Sanctam Praxidis, sic MS.

fo. 17ʳ 4–6. *R de J* 85; *Greg* 46 (L 74.1)

Super oblata

fo. 17ʳ 7–9. *R de J* 85; *Greg* 47 (L. 74.2)

Praefatio

fo. 17ʳ 10–17. *R de J* 85; *Greg* 269

Ad compl(endum)

fo. 17ʳ 18–20. *R de J* 85; *Greg* 47 (L 74.3)

Super populum

fo. 17ʳ 21–3. *R de J* 85; *Greg* 47 (L 74.4)

Feria .iii. ad Sanctam Priscam

fo. 17ʳ 24–7. *R de J* 85; *Greg* 47 (L 75.1)

Super oblata

fo. 17ᵛ 1–2. *R de J* 86; *Greg* 47 (L 75.2). MS. has *propitius* for *propensius*

[Praefatio]

fo. 17ᵛ 3–12. *R de J* 86; *Greg* 269

Ad compl(endum)

fo. 17ᵛ 13–15. *R de J* 86; *Greg* 47 (L 75.3)

Super populum

fo. 17ᵛ 16–18. *R de J* 86; *Greg* 47 (L 75.4)

Feria .iiii. ad [Sanctam] Mariam maior[em]

fo. 17ᵛ 19–21. *R de J* 86; *Greg* 47 (L 76.1)

Super [   ], cut away in MS.

fo. 17ᵛ 22–6. *R de J* 86, *Secreta*; *Greg* 47 (L 76.2), *Alia*

Super oblata

fo. 17ᵛ 27. *R de J* 86; *Greg* 48 (L 76.3). Ending lost

There is a gap of some leaves here

[Feria .vi. in Parasceue]

fo. 18ʳ 1–5. *R de J* 90; *Greg* 53 (L 79. 18). This is the last prayer of the *orationes solempnes* on Good Friday

Ordo

fo. 18ʳ 6–26. A long rubric, see M. Andrieu, *Les Ordines Romani du haut moyen-âge* iii (*Spicilegium Sacrum Lovaniense. Études et documents*, fasc. 24), (Louvain 1951), p. 519 (ordo xxxii. 9–14, 16–18). The script is in capitals with the cues to the texts in minuscule

Benedictio ce[r]ei

fo. 18ᵛ 1–19ᵛ 27. *Exultet iam angelica turba*, as found in *Greg* 151–3, but replacing the passage *Apis ceteris que subiecta sunt homini . . . aliae collectis e foliis nectar includunt* (152. 29–153. 5) with *Apis corporis minima quant[i]tate, ingenio mirabilis naturali* (fo. 19ᵛ 21–2). Ends imperfectly at *uirgo permansit* (153.8)

fo. 20ʳ 1–12. Lection, Sapientia iii. 3–8, beginning imperfectly; probably for *in natali plurimorum martyrum*. Frere, cliii (*a*)

Sequentia Sancti euangelii secundum Matheum

fo. 20ʳ 13–20ᵛ 5. Matthew x. 16–22. In the Gospel lists this lection is used for martyrs (see Klauser, p. 186)

Lectio epistole beati Pauli apostoli ad Efessios ad apostolos, sic MS.
fo. 20ᵛ 6–13. Ephesians ii. 19–22. Frere cxlviii (*a*), *in natali Apostolorum*

Sequentia sancti euangelii secundum Lucam
fo. 20ᵛ 14–21ʳ 7. Luke xxii. 24–30. Klauser, p. 191. Lection used *in natali pape*

In natali uirginum. lectio libri sapientie, sic MS.
fo. 21ʳ 8–21ᵛ 7. Ecclesiasticus li. 1–12. Frere, cliv(*a*)

Sequentia sancti euangelii secundum Matheum
fo. 21ᵛ 8–22ʳ 5. Matthew xiii. 44–52. Klauser 187.

Special Masses

Missa pro defuncto baptizato
fo. 22ʳ 6–12. *Greg* 213 (CIIII)
Super oblata
fo. 22ʳ 13–16. *Greg* 214 (CIIII)
Infra actionem
fo. 22ʳ 17–22. *Greg* 214 (CIIII)
Missa in anniuersarium [unius?] defuncti, sic, for *ad complendum*
fo. 22ʳ 23–6. *Greg* 214 (CIIII). The incorrect rubric relates to the following mass, where it is repeated

Missa in anniuersarium unius defuncti
fo. 22ᵛ 2–5. *Greg* 215 (CVI)
Super oblata
fo. 22ᵛ 6–10. *Greg* 215 (CVI)
Infra [actionem]
fo. 22ᵛ 11–16. *Greg* 215 (CVI)
Ad comp[lendum]
fo. 22ᵛ 17–20. *Greg* 215 (CVI)

Missa pl[urimorum] defu[nctorum]
fo. 22ᵛ 21–4. *Greg* 215 (CVII)
Super oblata
fo. 22ᵛ 25–23ʳ 2. *Greg* 216 (CVII)
Infra actionem
fo. 23ʳ 3–8. *Greg* 216 (CVII)
Ad compl(endum)
fo. 23ʳ 9–13. *Greg* 216 (CVII)

Item alia missa
fo. 23ʳ 14–19. *Greg* 216 (CVIII)
Super oblata
fo. 23ʳ 20–23. *Greg* 216 (CVIII)
Infra actionem
fo. 23ʳ 24–23ᵛ 5. *Greg* 216 (CVIII). MS. has *imploramus* for *immolamus*

Ad compl(endum)
fo. 23ᵛ 6–9. *Greg* 216 (CVIII)

Item alia missa
fo. 23ᵛ 10–13. *Greg* 217 (CVIIII)
Secr(eta)
fo. 23ᵛ 14–17. *Greg* 217 (CVIIII)
Ad com(plendum)
fo. 23ᵛ 18–23. *Greg* 217 (CVIIII)

Missa in cimiteriis
fo. 23ᵛ 24–24ʳ 4. *Greg* 217 (CX)
Super oblata
fo. 24ʳ 5–10. *Greg* 217 (CX)
Infra actionem
fo. 24ʳ 11–19. *Greg* 217 (CX)
Ad compl(endum)
fo. 24ʳ 20–25. *Greg* 218 (CX)

Lections
(for fo. 24ᵛ, see Plate XI)

fo. 24ᵛ 1–3. *In Christi nomine. Incipiunt lectiones anni cyrculi lib[er] comitis. In uigilia natalis Domini ad Sanctam Mariam ad [ ] lectio epistole beati Pauli apostoli ad Romano[s]*
fo. 24ᵛ 4–14. Romans i. 1–6. Frere i

Sequentia sancti euangelii sec[undum] Mat[heum]
fo. 24ᵛ 15–26. Matthew i. 18–21. Klauser, p. 186, *in uigilia natalis Domini*

Lectio epistole beati Pauli apostoli ad Titum
fo. 25ʳ 2–12. Titus ii. 11–15. Frere ii, *ad sanctam Mariam de nocte*

Sequentia sancti euangelii secundum Iohannem, sic MS.
fo. 25ʳ 13–25ᵛ 18. Luke ii. 1–14. Klauser, p. 189, *in natale Domini ad Sanctam Mariam maiorem*

Lectio epistole beati Pauli apostoli ad Titum
fo. 25ᵛ 19–26ʳ 2. Titus iii. 4–7. Frere iii, *ad Sanctam Anastasiam*

Sequentia sancti euangelii secundum Lucam
fo. 26ʳ 3–18. Luke ii. 15–20. Klauser, p. 189, *in natale Domini ad Sanctam Anastasiam*

Initium sancti euangelii secundum Iohannem
fo. 26ʳ 19–26ᵛ 18. John i. 1–14. Klauser, p. 191, *in natale Domini ad Sanctum Petrum*

Sequentia sancti euangelii secundum Matheum
fo. 26ᵛ 19–26. Matthew ii. 13–15. Ends incompletely. Klauser, p. 186, *in natale Innocentum*

ADDENDA

p. xxii: *Bury*.—In Part II above names cited from the 'Feudal Book of Abbot Baldwin' (*Bury*, 1–44) are dated 1087–98. Note, however, that Professor V. H. Galbraith, *Domesday Book* (Oxford, 1974), 77–8, would assign this record to the early years of Henry I.

p. 41: **42**, n. 1.—Dr. Judith Green has pointed out to us that there is no clear proof that William son of Odo, the member of the family of die-cutters who held land in London, Middlesex, Essex, and Suffolk, William son of Odo, the royal constable, and William son of Odo recorded in Survey I (who was presumably identical with the William son of Odo pardoned his contribution to the Winchester aid), are the same person. She has also drawn our attention to the William son of Odo whose name is entered on the 1130 pipe roll under Devon, where he was evidently a considerable landowner (*Pipe Roll 31 Henry I*, pp. 156 and (?) 157).

Of the numerous references to William son of Odo during the reigns of Henry I and Stephen, those concerning the Devon landlord are dealt with most easily. Round (J. H. Round, *Feudal England* (London, 1895), 487) suggested that he was the son of Odo son of Gamelin, the ancestor of the lords of the barony of Great Torrington. With hindsight we can see that the royal charter of 1123 (*Regesta*, ii, no. 1391), on which Round based his case, is by no means incontrovertible as evidence for this view. Yet before 1155–6 (see below; on internal evidence alone the date is 1155–8) William son of Odo granted land at Willand (Devon) and the church there to Taunton Priory (*Cal Chart R 1327–41*, pp. 312–13), while in 1086 Odo son of Gamelin had held Willand (*VCH Devon* i (1906), 494). The Devon family is therefore not the same as the family of die-cutters. The grant to Taunton Priory was made with the assent of William's nephew and heir William, who may have been identical with the William son of Robert son of Roger who by 1156 had acquired the Torrington estates (Sanders *Baronies*, 48, where the relationship between William son of Odo and William son of Robert is said not to be known).

But to which of these two families did the royal constable and the Winchester William son of Odo belong, or was there a third, or even a fourth family? In the 1130 pipe roll, under London, Middlesex, and Essex, the name is consistently spelt *filius Othonis*, while under Hampshire and Devon it is spelt *filius Odonis* (*Pipe Roll 31 Henry I*, pp. 41, 56, 60, 145, 151, 152, 156). Following Round in an attempt to distinguish between individuals, historians have sometimes maintained this apparent distinction in modern orthography, often with confusing results (e.g. *Regesta*, ii, nos. 1269, 1295, and index). It is interesting that the spelling *filius Othonis* occurs most frequently in connection with the family of die-cutters (e.g. *Regesta*, ii, no. 1524; ibid. iii, no. 316), but it also occurs in instances which cannot be proved to be associated with that family (*Regesta*, ii, nos. 1295, 1552), and conversely Odo the die-cutter is frequently spelt *Odo* (*Bury*, 105, 109, 127, 155). Little reliance can be placed upon variant spellings of the same name, and in this case the variation may be connected with the context in which the documents were written rather than with the identity of the individual concerned.

Nor are the topographical associations of the Williams son of Odo who witnessed royal charters much help. William son of Odo only witnessed as constable in Normandy in 1131 (*Regesta*, ii, nos. 1693, 1698), but this is no reason to believe that he was not a member of the royal household in England and that he could not be identical with the William who had property in Winchester (cf. *Dialogus de Scaccario*, p. lii, and C. H. Haskins, 'The Administration of Normandy under Henry I', *EHR* 24

(1909), 209–31). A William son of Odo witnessed several documents concerning Exeter, but of these one was issued at Winchester, one at Woodstock, and one at Taunton (*Regesta*, ii, nos. 1269, 1391, 1523; ibid., iii, no. 284). A William son of Odo had interests in Shropshire: in 1121 at Bridgnorth he witnessed a royal document concerning land there (*Regesta*, ii, no. 1295), and after 1135 he witnessed a private grant of land at Ruton to Buildwas Abbey (*Cal Chart R 1257–1300*, pp. 419–20). In general, the occurrence of William son of Odo in witness lists shows no more than that in the 1120s and 1130s a person (or persons) of that name was frequently in the presence of the king.

The evidence of the Winchester survey does, however, suggest a connection between the Winchester William son of Odo and the production of coin, and so the supposition that he and Odo *monetarius* were members of the die-cutting family has some value. There are good reasons why that family should have had interests in Winchester. Charles Johnson thought that the member of the royal household was more likely to have belonged to the Devon family than to that of the die-cutters (*Dialogus de Scaccario*, 133, n. 11), but it is not impossible that, after inheriting the *ministerium cuneorum* from his father in 1116–27 (*Regesta*, ii, no. 1524), William son of Odo should have obtained a position in the royal household.

p. 74: **38**, n. 5.—Herbert witnessed conveyances of property in High Street (cf. **43**) and *Alwarnestret* (cf. **487**) *c.* 1155–60, and of a mill at East Gate *c.* 1180: Southwick Cart iii, fos. 123^v, 136^v; BM, Egerton MS. 2104, fo. 179^{r-v}.

p. 74: **40**, n. 3.—He witnessed a conveyance of property in *Alwarnestret* and *Flesmangerestret* (see **510**, n. 1) before 1155: Southwick Cart iii, fos. 133, 141^v.

p. 74: **43**, n. 4.—Probably the *stalum quod est ante gabulum monasterii sancti petri* (i.e. the church of St. Peter *in macellis*) which Thurstin the clerk (see **221**, n. 1) purchased from Martin of Bentworth and *c.* 1155–60 granted to Blithild (see **649**): Southwick Cart iii, fos. 123^v, 136.

p. 83: **156**, n. 1.—He, or his son (?) of the same name, witnessed a Winchester conveyance after 1168, and supervised the carriage of cloth from Winchester to Ireland in 1172: J. G. Jenkins (ed.), *The Cartulary of Missenden Abbey*, iii (HMC, JP1, 1962), no. 703; *Pipe Roll 18 Henry II*, p. 84.

p. 87: **221**, n. 1.—For properties which he appears to have acquired after 1148 and then granted to *Blithilde pro seruicio suo*, see **43**, **487**, and **649**, n. 1.

p. 89: **245**, n. 1.—The Fulflood was an intermittent stream which ran from the valley on the NW. side of the W. suburb into the meadows on the N. side of the city. The name was also applied to a small hamlet outside the suburb to the NW. Godwin's property was not far from this locality. Cf. **291–3** and above, p. 237, s.n.

p. 100: **434**, n. 1.—His other sons were Roger, Geoffrey, and Reginald; with Henry they witnessed their father's conveyance of **508** before *c.* 1162–3: Southwick Cart iii, fo. 134. William witnessed a charter of Henry of Blois concerning land at Farnham, Surrey, where he appears to have had interests: HMC, *Fourth Report* (London, 1874), Appendix, p. 451.

p. 101: **441**, n. 1.—He witnessed two charters of Bishop Henry, 1143–54 and 1144–71: Lena Voss, *Heinrich von Blois* (Berlin, 1932), 159, 166. In *c.* 1154–60 *Hadewis soror elemosinarii* witnessed a conveyance of a house in *Alwarnestret* (cf. **487**), where Robert had property in 1148: Southwick Cart iii, fos. 123^v, 136^v.

p. 104: **486**, n. 1.—*Galfridus Trentemars* witnessed a conveyance of property in this street and *Flesmangerestret* (see **510**, n. 1) before 1155: Southwick Cart iii, fos. 133, 141^v.

p. 104: **487**, n. 2.—This may be the house which Thurstin the clerk (see **221**, n. 1) purchased from Martin of Bentworth, and *c.* 1155–60 granted to Blithild (see **649**): Southwick Cart iii, fos. 123ᵛ, 136. But cf. **493–4** and **496**.

p. 105: **501**, n. 1.—His wife Cristina witnessed a conveyance of property in High Street (cf. **43**) and *Alwarnestret* (cf. **487**) *c.* 1155–60: Southwick Cart iii, fos. 123ᵛ, 136ᵛ.

p. 106: **510**, n. 1.—See **221**. Cf. **511**. These properties were probably represented by the land and houses in *Flesmongurstret* which *Fulcherus monetarius* had held, and the other houses *usque ad diuisas de Flesmongerestret et de Alwerestret*, all of which Thurstin granted to Southwick Priory before 1155. In the early thirteenth century the priory had 2s. rent from the property: Southwick Cart i, fo. 38, and iii, fos. 133, 141ᵛ. *Fulcherus* was not a Winchester moneyer. A *Falche* was a moneyer of Stephen's Type I at Wilton, and a *Fulcke* was a moneyer of Type A of the 'cross and crosslets' coinage of Henry II at Wallingford: R. P. Mack, 'Stephen and the Anarchy 1135–54', *BNJ*, 35 (1966), 109; *BMC Henry II*, clxxxii. Dr. von Feilitzen suggests that *Fulcherus* was possibly identical with the Wallingford moneyer.

d. 115: **649**, n. 1.—In *c.* 1155–60 Thurstin the clerk (see **221**, n. 1) granted property in High Street (cf. **43**) and *Alwarnestret* (cf. **487**) to *Blithilde pro seruicio suo*: Southwick Cart iii, fos. 123ᵛ, 136ᵛ.

p. 118: **685**, n. 1.—Through his daughter Clemencia this property passed to the Husey family. In the thirteenth century it was probably incorporated into the Black Friars' precinct and lay close to the city wall: WCM 1141 and SMW, s.v. 'Black Friars'.

p. 125: **800**, n.1.—He granted property near here to Southwick Priory. In *c.* 1160–70 the priory granted land in *Munsterstret* which *Matilda filia Remundi* (cf. **801**) had held, together with the house which *Radulphus Hlachewei* (cf. **802**) held, to Master Hugh *de Cardonuilla* for 4s. 10d. annual rent, an increase of 8d. over the previous rent: Southwick Cart i, fo. 38 and iii, fos. 128, 136.

p. 132: **914**, n. 1.—A woman of this name witnessed a conveyance of property in High Street (cf. **43**) and *Alwarnestret* (cf. **487**) *c.* 1155–60: Southwick Cart iii, fos. 123ᵛ, 136ᵛ.

p. 134: **952**, n. 1.—Robert I (1138–55): D. W. Blake, 'The Church of Exeter in the Norman period' (unpublished, Exeter University M.A. thesis, 1970), 125 ff. In the fifteenth century the bishop of Exeter had a meadow and rent on the east side of Kingsgate Street, a little to the north of the site of the church of All Saints (see **960**, n. 1): WCM 1079–1087 and *SMW*.

p. 136: **992**, n. 1.—He witnessed a conveyance of property in *Alwarnestret* and *Flesmangerestret* (see **510**, n. 1) before 1155: Southwick Cart iii, fos. 133, 141ᵛ.

p. 156: *Ernuceon.*—Cf. *Ernuceus* 1055–1108, Sées (Orne), J. Adigard des Gautries, 'Les noms de personnes attestés à Sées de 1055 environ à 1108', *Bull. de la Soc. hist. et archéol. de l'Orne* 82 (1964), 25.

pp. 158–9: *Godebiete.*—The gender and vowel quantity of OE *begeat* 'acquisition, property', on which the authorities differ, has been inferred from the form *begeto* (with late WS *e* < *ea* after palatal *g* and -*o* for -*u*) in D. Whitelock *et al.* (ed.), *The Will of Æthelgifu* (Oxford, 1968), *c.* 990 (orig.), Hrt. The relevant line 59 runs as follows: *Eall se freot 7 eall seo ælmesse þe her gecweden is hyo wile þ hit beo heore ælmessa for þon hit wæron hire hlafordes begeto*, '. . . because they were her lord's acquisitions'. This is clearly the nom. plur. of a short-stem neuter noun *begeat*. I wish to thank Prof. Whitelock for having kindly drawn my attention to this crucial form.

pp. 160–1: *Hachechasse.*—Cf. also the byname (Guillelmus) *Hachedor* 'golden axe', 1247 (Orne), H. de Charencey (ed.), *Cartulaire de l'abbaye de Notre-Dame de la Trappe* (Alençon, 1889), 135.

p. 162: *Holinessone.*—Note also (Johannes) *Holyn* 1428 (Wo), *MED* s.v. *holin.*

p. 162: *Hoppecole.*—The ME word *hoppe* 'the hop-plant' is not recorded until the 15th c. and is usually held to be a loan from MDu, but a corresponding OE word seems in fact to be attested by the derivative *hopping* 967 (14th) *BCS* 1196, which is taken to mean 'place where the (wild?) hop-plant grows' or 'hop-garden'; see *PNSr* 62, *EPN* s.v., M. Löfvenberg, *English Studies*, 43 (1962), 41.

p. 171: *Scorphanus.*—Note also (Guibertus) *Escorfanz* 1199 (Eure-et-Loir), A. de Belfort (ed.), *Archives de la Maison-Dieu de Châteaudun* (Paris, 1881), 33.

p. 172: *Simphorianus.*—On the spread of the cult of this saint, see G. Souillet, 'Saint-Symphorien dans la toponymie', *Annales de Bretagne* 66 (1959), 463–73.

p. 176: *Walwain.*—See also M. Delbouille, 'Des origines du personnage et du nom de Gauvain', *Mélanges de linguistique française . . . offerts à M. Paul Imbs* (Strasbourg, 1973), 549–59.

pp. 176–7: *Westman.*—Other Norman examples are (de) *Wesman* Gislorde 1195 *MRSN* 187, (de) ∼ de Fierevilla 1198 *MRSN* 349.

p. 196: *Sutton.*—There are three Suttons in Ha: Bishop's Sutton (DB *Sudtone*), Long Sutton, and Sutton Scotney (both *Sudtune*, DB).

p. 203: *rusmangre.*—Another ME example is (de Alano) *Le Rusmangor c.* 1210, H. E. Salter (ed.), *Cartulary of Oseney Abbey*, ii (Oxford, 1929), 341.

p. 207: *Bensetoure.*—Possibly a field-name, a compound of OE *bēan-set* 'bean-plot' (Clark Hall) and OE *ōfer* 'river-bank' or *ŏfer* 'slope, hill' (*EPN* ii, 53 f.). For the omission of *de*, see above, p. 199.

pp. 207–8: *Betteslaf.*—Cf. (terra quam dedit) *Brungares laue c.* 1100 (12th), London, *Trans. London and Middlesex Arch. Soc.*, n.s. 8 (1940), 58.

p. 211: *Flathege.*—Cf. *Smechegge* (for *Smethegge?*) 1221–34, a field-name in Shellingford (Brk), from OE *smēðe* 'smooth', *hecg(e)* 'hedge', *PNBrk* 398.

p. 211: *Francigena.*—This term, which occurs frequently in DB, could perhaps also mean 'a free (-born) man'; see R. Welldon Finn, *An Introduction to Domesday Book* (London, 1963), 148; idem, *Domesday Book* (London, 1973), 44.

p. 212: *Hacchemus.*—Later Winchester examples, in addition to those cited, are (Geoffrey) *Hachemuz c.* 1200, (Walter) *Hakemus c.* 1249; see **II, 18**, n., **II, 434**, n. 3.

p. 214: *Paginan'.*—Another Norman instance is (Guillelmus) *Paignon*, armiger, 1417, A. L. Léchaudé d'Anisy (ed.), *Grands rôles des échiquiers de Normandie*, i (Paris, 1845), 230.

p. 215: *Pofil.*—Note also (magistro Roberto) *Porfil* 1175, W. D. Macray (ed.), *Charters and Documents Illustrating the History of the Cathedral of Salisbury* (RS, London, 1891), 39.

p. 235: *Snidelingestret.*—Note also the surname (de Thoma) *Snythelyng'*, (de Johanne) *Snethelyng'* 1332, A. D. Mills (ed.), *The Dorset Lay Subsidy Roll of 1332* (Dorset Record Soc. 4, Dorchester, 1971), 3, 5.

p. 273: n. 3.—Miss Robertson in *AS Ch.* 494 put forward 911×919, but the inclusion of the burhs at Buckingham built in 914 (*ASC* s.a. 915 (D)), and the date of 918 now accepted for the death of Æthelflæd, suggests 914×918.

p. 291: n. 1.—Edward seized Emma's treasure (*eallon þan gærsaman þe heo ahte*) in November 1043: *ASC*, s.a. 1043 (D).

p. 301: n. 3.—At the time of writing it seemed most likely that the 'Constable's Wall' mentioned in the account of the fourteenth-century dispute over the former site of New Minster and the royal palace had divided the cathedral cemetery on the east from that part of the palace site which had been assigned to the constable of Winchester castle on the west. The wall was assumed to have run along the present western boundary of the cemetery where there is a line of houses known as Constable's Row. This is the interpretation shown in Figs. 9 (*c.* 1148) and 32 and was the one suggested in *I Interim*, 180–1.

A further consideration of the statements made in the fourteenth century and of the detailed topography of the area in the later middle ages now favours a different interpretation. According to this view 'Constable's Wall' defined the western boundary of the palace site. The wall no longer survives, but it ran along the east side of the modern Little Minster Street (see *SMW*, s.v. 'Constabulary'). This wall represented the 'extension' of the Close Wall north from the minster gate mentioned on p. 301, above. It was not, however, a new construction of the mid-twelfth century, but had presumably first been built in the late eleventh century to enclose the western side of the extended precinct of the Norman palace. After the destruction of the palace in 1141, numerous private houses were constructed against the eastern side of this wall facing the cathedral cemetery. The evidence of Survey **II** indicates that this process had already begun by 1148 (see above, p. 246). In the later Middle Ages these houses were said to stand on the fief of the constable of the castle (see *SMW*).

To understand the topography of the area depicted on Fig. 9 in *c.* 1148, the wall there shown marking the east side of the Constabulary should be omitted.

p. 302: n. 2.—When New Minster moved to Hyde *c.* 1110, the abbot surrendered the *terram inter Civitatem in qua prius fuit Abbathia* to the king *ad opus . . . episcopi W. et ecclesie . . . ubi sedes est episcopalis* (*Reg Pontissara* 440, cf. above, p. 317 and n. 7). It seems possible, as Professor R. H. C. Davis points out to us, that this might have given the bishop the basis for a claim to the site of the king's palace, or at least to that part of it which the Conqueror had taken in from the New Minster cemetery *c.* 1070 (see above, pp. 293–4). Bishop Henry was energetic in reclaiming lands seized from the church by William I (e.g. *Regesta*, iii, nos. 944–9) and may well have used this pretext in securing the site of the royal palace from the king, although it should not be forgotten that New Minster had been compensated for the loss of its cemetery by William's grant of Alton and Clere (see above, p. 292). For the final division of the extended area of the palace into its original components, see above, p. 300.

p. 306: n. 7.—Regularly recorded from the late thirteenth century onwards: e.g. PRBW 1287–8, m. 32d. Bishop Ælfheah II is said to have imprisoned a thief *in neruum, in cippum, in trunco*, probably in Winchester (but not necessarily at Wolvesey): M. Winterbottom (ed.), *Three Lives of English Saints* (Toronto, 1972), 29 (Ælfric's Life of St. Æthelwold, cap. 28), 63 (Wulfstan's Life of St. Æthelwold, cap. 46). For the meaning of *in cippum, in trunco*, cf. perhaps *balchus*, above, p. 236, s.v.

p. 321: n. 10. (on p. 322).—Archbishop Plegmund attested a charter at Winchester *c.* 909 (*BCS* 622, Sawyer 385, cf. *AS Ch*, no. XX), conceivably on this occasion.

p. 322: n. 1.—Recorded in the life of Saint Eadburga by Osbert of Clare (*c.* 1140): Bodleian Library, MS. Laud Misc. 114, fos. 85–120. This source is summarized, and later lives of the saint are printed, in Laurel Braswell, 'Saint Edburga of Winchester: a study of her cult, a.d. 950–1500, with an edition of the fourteenth-century Middle English and Latin Lives', *Medieval Studies* 33 (Toronto, 1971), 292–333. Braswell gives the date of Eadburga's death as 960. This cannot be correct, for Eadburga was at least three years old in 924 when her father King Edward the Elder died, and she herself is said to have died at the age of thirty. This would put her death no later than *c.* 951. Under the year

953 the Worcester annals include a prayer addressed to Eadburga, indicating that by the fourteenth century this was believed to have been the year of her death: *Worcester ann*, s.a.

p. 322: n. 2.—The identification with a 'chapel of St. Peter's monastery near by' in Braswell, op. cit. in previous Addendum, p. 302, seems less likely. MS. Laud Misc. 114, fo. 94 reads: *ad vicinum beatri* (sic) *petri apostolorum principis monasterium*. The word *monasterium* frequently denoted a small church or chapel in early medieval Winchester, cf. above, **II, 43,** n. 2.

p. 322: n. 10.—The Worcester annals follow the later thirteenth-century Winchester annals in BM, MS. Cotton Vesp. E. iv, fos. 153–201, in the entry under the year 1108: *ecclesia Sanctae Edburgae Wintoniae dedicata est*. The reference is clearly to St. Mary's Abbey for the same annals, also following the Winchester source, refer in the same terms to the burning of the nunnery in August 1141 in a summary account of the siege of that year erroneously entered under the year 1140: *civitas Wintoniae comburitur cum ecclesia de Hida et ecclesia sanctae Edburgae* (*Worcester ann*, s.a.).

p. 323: n. 6.—M. Winterbottom (ed.), *Three Lives of English Saints*, 23–4 (Ælfric's Life of St. Æthelwold, cap. 15), 45 (Wulfstan's Life of St. Æthelwold, cap. 19): *in aula sua, in qua cum hospitibus prandebat . . . a mensa exiens ad lectulum . . . abiens ad aulam* (Ælfric, cap. 15). The context suggests that the *aula* was in Winchester and the sequence implies a sleeping-chamber distinct from and additional to the hall.

p. 324: n. 3.—For the plan of the west hall, completed by excavation in 1974, see *X Interim*, fig. 20. The T-shaped plan recalls the eleventh-century(?) *palatium Tau* of the archiepiscopal palace at Reims, so named because of its over-all shape, and the similar structure erected for the bishops of Angers in the 1130s (C. Brühl, *Palatium und Civitas*, i (Cologne, 1975), 65, 159).

p. 409: n. 1.—A fourth example has come to light in the recently-discovered Lincoln hoard and is now in the BM. It is a die-duplicate of Mr. Elmore Jones's coin (ex Carlyon-Britton) and reads (without the usual punctuation) ODDO DE SANC ED MVN. It should also be noted that an Odo (Odde) was a moneyer at Thetford in Henry I Type XV and Stephen Type I.

p. 413: n. 1.—For example, Miss Marion Archibald has recently suggested that 'Type IX is stylistically out of place between Types VIII and XI and is more suitably placed after Types V and VI': J. Casey and R. Reece (eds.), *Coins and the Archaeologist* (British Archaeological Reports 4, Oxford, 1974), 269, n. 53.

p. 415: n. 7 (on p. 416).—Mr. Ian Stewart suggests that the presence of three ANT coins in the Awbridge, nr. Romsey (Hants), hoard, otherwise containing coins of Stephen Type VII and Henry II, is a strong point in favour of Southampton, since such survivals are only likely in the immediate vicinity of the original place of issue. For *Fulcherus*, another out-of-town moneyer resident in Winchester, see **II, 510,** n. 1 (Addendum to p. 106). Other possibilities are Ælfweard and Odo, for whom see above, pp. 401, n. 1, and 409, n. 1, respectively.

p. 416: n. 1.—The three properties, **II, 510–12,** all had moneying connections: see **II, 510,** n. 1 (Addendum to p. 106); **I, 182,** n. 1 (cf. p. 415, n. 2); and **II, 512** (cf. Table 43 and p. 416).

p. 461: n. 5.—Miss Whitelock points out to us that the only Old English version of the law-code known as III Edgar not to have been influenced by Archbishop Wulfstan (BM, MS. Nero A. i, in the complete version of III Edgar) refers at c. 8.1 to 'the system of measurement as is observed in Winchester'. This text is supported by the Latin of *Quadripartitus* and both agree against the Wulfstan MSS (BM,

MS. Harley 55; BM, MS. Nero A. i, in the incomplete version of III Edgar; and Corpus Christi College, Cambridge, MS. 201) which have 'as is observed *in London and* in Winchester'. The addition suggests that the special status of Winchester was being eroded in the later tenth century by the mercantile growth of London.

p. 462: n. 8.—Flodoaldus, *qui gnarus in urbe Vuentana mercator erat* (Wulfstan *Narratio metrica*, bk. II, lines 299 ff.), was most probably, as Dr. von Feilitzen informs us, a Frenchman (Norman, Picard, etc.), for his name is the Old French form of OG *Hlōdwald*. He must have been in Winchester, if the story has any basis of truth, between 971 and 993–4.

INDEX

THE references are to pages throughout. Occurrences on a single page are listed once only.

The texts of Surveys I and II on pp. 33–141 have been indexed from the English version, with the result that names and specific terms appear here in translation. Cross-references are provided as necessary.

The personal names and bynames in the two surveys have been fully listed under their text forms on pp. 147–217, on the system described on pp. 144–6 and 192. **Bold** entries in the index indicate the head-forms under which direct reference may be made to these names on pp. 147–217. References to specific pages within this section are, however, also given in the index entries. Place-names, dealt with on pp. 233–9, are treated similarly.

It should be noted that the information available about persons mentioned in Surveys I and II will normally be found in a note to their first occurrence in the texts of the Surveys. This note will refer to all other occurrences of the same person identified in the texts, but not to mentions of this person in the rest of the book. *All* pages on which a person occurs are listed in this index.

Names in *italic* are untranslated forms, usually from quotations. Note that words in cross-references (i.e. following *see* or *see also*) have for simplicity been printed in ordinary type without regard to the head-form to which they refer.

The index assumes that where cross-references are absent epithets will always be looked up by the user:

e.g. 'Philip of Fulflood' implies '*see also* Fulflood'.

In cases of doubt the cross-reference is always given.

In explicit cross-references, the index assumes that the names given will be looked for under the appropriate variations of the head-form:

e.g. (*le*) *Bathiere*, *see* John
    Froxfield, Hants, *see* Richard
    carter, *see* Ralph

refer to John *le Bathiere*, Richard of Froxfield *or* Richard Froxfield, Ralph the carter or Ralph Carter.

Robert (**Robertus**) (*cont.*):
son of Nunna, 64
son of Osbert of Eu, 46
son of Ralf, 12, 42–3, 131, 370
fitzSiward, 48
son of William of Pont de l'Arche, 33, 65, 398
son of William de Thoca, 95
son of Wimund the moneyer, 12, 34, 41, 44, 399, 409–10, 412, 417, 419
of Abingdon, 117
of Bayeux, 70, 137
de Beaumont, *see* Robert, earl of Leicester
de Chesney, *see* Robert, bishop of Lincoln
of Chiffrevast, 50, 91
of Columbiers, 130
of Dives's daughter, 73
of Fareham, 518
de Grainville, son of Gerold de Roumare, 39
de Halle, 516
of La Haye, 74, 140
de la Huche, 106
of Hungerford, 81, 122
of Inglesham, 70, 72, 75, 77, 81, 99, 105, 109, 111–12, 120, 328, 370, 372, 374, 392, 445
of Kempshot, 119
of Lewes, *see* Robert, bishop of Bath
of Limésy, 108, 135
d'Oilli I, 72
d'Oilli II, 72, 391
de Ponte (Pont de l'Arche), 65, 90, 127
of St. Pancras, 73, 89, 91, 93–5, 117–19, 372
of Tourville, 99
de Venuiz, 33
of Winchester, 84
Archer, 102
Bontemps, 133
Dispensator, 63
Dop, 67
Fresle, 59
Grifin, 125
Hacckesalt, 516
  see also Hack-salt
Hack-mouse, 71, 110
Losinga, abbot of New Minster (1090/1–1098), 57
Marmion I, 63, 390
Marmion II, 63
Mauduit I (d. *c.* 1129), 9, 17, 41–3, 370, 390
  his daughter, 33, 41
Mauduit II (son of Robert Mauduit I, drowned in the White Ship, 1120), 41–2
Miete, 86
Norreis, 77, 116–17, 120, 372
Oison, 74, 130–1, 136, 373–4, 447
Petit, 88
Porfil, 554
  see also Pofil
Putheld, 88
Quadde, 108
Rust, 84
Trentemars, 174

Trotardin, 76
Turlux, 141
Unnellus, 80
Vigerus, 516
Wolward, 517
Rochester, Kent, 485
Rogationtide, *see* festivals
Roger (**Rogerus**), 72, 77, 102, 129, 170, 187
bishop of Salisbury (1102–39), 9, 46, 325
earl of Salisbury, 384
the baker, 94
the chaplain, 516
the cook, 112, 125, 133
  his wife, 112
the dispenser, 124
the dyer, 75, 78, 115–16, 435
  his daughter, 78
the goldsmith, his wife, 93
the lean, 38
le Lung', 517
the miller, 130
the painter, 72, 97
the palmer, 82
the tailor, 121
the vintner, 110
brother of Geoffrey, abbot of New Minster, 16, 45
son of Amerland, 37, 64
  see also Amberlang, Roger Amerland
son of Chepping, 72, 102, 141
son of Gerold de Roumare, 39, 390
son of Guncelin, 72, 99
son of Walter of Tichborne, 125
son of William, 552
  see also William son of Roger
of Forest, 105
of La Haye, the moneyer of Stephen (?), 26, 74, 77, 79, 132, 139, 372, 416–19
of Hoveden, 297, 317
of Milford, 125
of Montgomery, 102
de Port, 70, 111, 341, 372, 391
of Sées, 77–8
of Touques, 196
of Valognes, 103
of Woodcote, 73, 170, 197
Abonel, 135, 136
Amerland, 64
  see also Amberlang, Roger son of Amerland
Blond, 96
Dalerun, 512, 514–15, 517–18
Davy, 516
Lip, 95
Macher, 87
Marmion, 63
Mercherel, 76, 438
Patten, 41
Pofil, 97
White-peacock, 104
Rogier, the moneyer of Stephen, *see* Roger of La Haye
Rogirus, the moneyer of Stephen, *see* Roger of La Haye

de consuet̄ ⁊ reddd̄ · xx · sol · ⁊
aliam partem tenet · Ric̄ tai
lator · ⁊ Sauualus p̄sbr̄ · ⁊ nul
lam consuet̄ faciunt · ⁊ reddit
xv · sol ·

¶ Golseuanus p̄sbr̄ tenuit
· j · domū · T · R · E · reddentem
omnē consuet̄ · q̄ tenet Joh̄
fili ᵗnuceon · ⁊ nullā con
suet̄ redd · ⁊ reddit · xx · iij · sol ·
⁊ iiij · d ·

¶ Adeluuold p̄posit̄ Wint̄
habuit · T · R · E · unū cella
riū reḡ Eduuard · q̄ hōc escā
tan · ⁊ nullā consuet̄ inde
reddit · ⁊ reddit · xv · sol ·

A PORTA OCCIDENTIS VSQ: AD
PORTAM ORIENTIS ·

¶ Aleftanus douereffone
tenuit · T · R · E · unam domū
reddentē consuet̄ q̄ tenet
henr̄ de port · ⁊ nullā consu
et̄ fac̄ inde · ⁊ in domo illa p̄
occupauit de tra regis · q̄ erat
iuxta portā · vi · solidat · ⁊ red
dit · xxxix · sol ·

¶ Gilleb̄ bochenel · t̄n T · R · E ·
· j · domū · reddentē consuet̄ q̄
eam tenet ꝯor huḡ fili al

buchon · ⁊ n̄ redd̄ consuet̄ · ⁊
erat ibi uicus · quē hugo fili al
buchon · ⁊ henr̄ de port p̄ occu
pauerunt in domo sua ·

¶ A lxviij p̄sbr̄ tenet · j · do
mū · T · R · E · ⁊ faciebat consuet̄
n̄ tenet Rob̄ fili Wimundi ·
⁊ simil̄r redd̄ consuet̄ ⁊ reddit
· xx · sol ·

¶ Terra monial̄ reddebat · T ·
R · E · consuet̄ ⁊ de ea tenet
Witt̄s fili odonis dim̄ partē ⁊
Witt̄s Brun̄ dim̄ partē · un̄ uen
tam · Rex retinuit ⁊ nullā cō
suet̄ inde faciunt · ⁊ domū red
dit · lxviij · sol ·

¶ Dom̄ Aluric̄ de cameshā
T · R · E · reddebat consuet̄ · q̄
tenet Roḡ partū · ⁊ n̄ fac̄ cō
suet̄ · ⁊ reddit · xxviij · sol · p̄
estagium suum ·

¶ Dom̄ cuidam uidue red
debat · T · R · E · consuet̄ q̄ te
net herfrid̄ regis seruiens
⁊ fac̄ consuet̄ p̄ deprecatio
nē prepositor̄ ·

¶ Domus ftanulti p̄sbr̄ erat
quieta · T · R · E · p̄ wata ⁊ Gel
dit q̄ tenet Rob̄ cyaleduct̄

Winton Domesday, fo. 3ᵛ: Survey I, 36 (part)–45 (251 × 174 mm)

Hec est Inqsitio de t̄r̄. winton̄. quis q̄s̄ tent̄. ⁊ q̄n̄ tū ten̄. ⁊ de quociuq̄. ten̄. q̄n̄tū quisq̄. inde ʦap. pꝯ pro s̄p̄i. henr̄. Anno ab incarnat̄. d̄n̄i. m̄. c̄. xl. viii.

In magno vico.

Rob̄t de mgt̄. r. vi. d. et god̄ p̄sb̄r ten̄. de eo. ⁊ ht̄ inde xviii. s̄.

Iob̄ de port debet redde. r. vi. d.

Et ū̄r̄ porta de west est quedā logia.

Herb̄t cam. r. vi. d. ⁊ ht̄ vii. s̄ Godefr̄ fil̄ witti. ten̄. iii. t̄ras. ⁊ dicit ē̄. hetas. ⁊ ht̄ in̄. xxxix. s̄.

Tpeni ht̄ in̄. iiii. s̄. ⁊ Rob̄ ii. s̄. ⁊ Osb̄ xii. d.

Iua. r. vi. d. ⁊ ht̄ xviii. s̄.

Ric̄ de baiaco. r. vi. d.

Abbissa wint̄. r. vi. d. ⁊ ht̄. xiii. s̄. ⁊ vi. d. ⁊ id̄ Ric̄ ht̄ vii. s̄.

Iob. mart̄ ten̄. i. mans̄. de feudo witti fil̄ manne. q̄te. ⁊ i. alia de feudo r. que debet redde. r. vi. d. ⁊ de hoc deb

reddē tpo. vii. s̄. ⁊ ad hospital xx. s̄. ⁊ ht̄. xxv. s̄.

Herebt corneilla Abbi de hida. vii. s̄. ⁊ Ric̄ de baiaco eid̄. abbi. xe. s̄. ⁊ ht̄. vi. s̄.

Gilebtus cū barba eid̄ abbi. xe. s̄

Andreas eid̄ abbi. xe. s̄. ⁊ ht̄ xii. s̄.

Turstin̄ danart̄. eid̄ abbi. xe. s̄.

Rad̄ cler̄ eid̄ abbi. xe. s̄.

Ric̄ de corduan̄. eid̄ abbi. xi. s̄.

Cupping cord̄ solebat redde eid̄. abbi. xiiii. s̄ sed vast̄.

heredes mart̄n̄. ht̄ ii. s̄. de i. estal. q̄d est incalle. r.

hugo haccem̄. eid̄ abbi. iiii. d. ⁊ ht̄ iiii. s̄.

Adelard̄ acul̄ eid̄ abbi. iiii. s̄. ⁊ i hangere. eid̄ abbi. iiii. s̄

Ric̄. acular̄ eid̄ abbi. iiii. s̄.

Agar̄n̄ pic̄. eid̄ abbi. xii. d. ⁊ tpo. iiii. s̄. de. r. ⁊ ht̄ xvii. s̄.

Tc Adelard̄ acul̄ eid̄ abbi. xxx. d. ⁊ ht̄ vii. s̄.

huḡ fil̄ cheppinḡ. eid̄ abbi. iiii. s̄. ⁊ ht̄. i. m̄. de corulla. ⁊ corulla ht̄ in̄. xl. d.

Turstin̄ acular̄. eid̄ abbi. vii. s̄.

Ric̄ fil̄ turold̄. templo. ii. s̄. ⁊ ē̄. de feudo Rob̄ de oili. ⁊ r.

rog̃ recep̃ iñ · v · ſ·

Henric fil' Rob scorcer abbi
xiiij · ð · ⁊ ht̄ · vij · ſ · ⁊ manig̃
ht̄ iñ · ij · ſ·

Steph fil' hug abbi xliiij ·
ð · ⁊ ht̄ · x vj · ſ·

Herbt fil' Gunt abbi · ij · ſ·

Heredes trentem abbi · ij · ſ

Anstr de heeche abbi · xv · ð

Goda hacchem abbi · xv · ð

Hugo haccem abbi · ij · ſ·

Uxor buroldi abbi · iij · ſ·

Edit martel eid abbi xviij · ð

Matildis fil' Godefr abbi
xviij · ð · ⁊ ht̄ · iij · ſ·

Rog̃ fil' chepping abbi de
hida · ij · ſ·

Herebt fil' westma eid abbi
xxxj · ð · ⁊ ht̄ · vij · ſ · ⁊ vj · ð

Fitt fil' Rog eid abbi · iiij · ſ·
⁊ ht̄ · vij · ſ·

Et ite witt ten q̃ndã trã
ubi managiũ ſuũ eſt ſ nil
iñ ſcimuſ.

Rad fil' Cheppig eid abbi
x · ð·

Ormet eid abbi x · ð · ⁊
witto mart iij · ſ·

Odilñ eid abbi xij · ð · ⁊ ẽ
vaſta.

Tochi eid abbi · v · ð·

Tailebroc abbi · ij · ð·

Ailric chie ⁊ Burewold
abbi · viij · ð·

Bruſtin abbi · xij · ð · ⁊ ẽ vaſta·

ALWARNESTRET.

Ernold p̃sbr Rad de port
vi · ð · ⁊ id filio federling̃ · vi · ð·

Ioh̃s de port ht̄ · ij · trãs vaſtas·

Et Oſbt w aſpail ht̄ ibidẽ
· j · aliã trã de feudo com
Gloec · ⁊ ẽ vaſta·

Epc bachon ht̄ trã pet de
val tuñ ⁊ redð xron dmſt
burg xij · ð · ⁊ ipſe epc ht̄ p̃a
ibi de ſuo feudo · j · aliã ⁊
ht̄ de ſuo hoſprte dũ iñ
monachi de egglesã tenẽ
q̃ndã trã vac̃.

Herbt weſtman pon xx · ð·
⁊ epo ſar · ij · ſ · ⁊ ht̄ ibi · xviij · ð·

Emma vxor Robti tẽ wa
riñ pon xij · ð · ⁊ ht̄ · iij · ſ·
⁊ Adeleis ht̄ de ead trã xviij · ð·

Rog̃ wttepe pon xvi · ð · ⁊
epo · ij · ſ · de ẽ · B · ⁊ ht̄ · xviij · ð·

Rand bon hõ pon xv · ð · ⁊
ht̄ · iij · ſ·

Hug hacchem ht̄ trã que

Winton Domesday, fo. 22ᵛ: Survey II, 451 (end)–482 (251 × 174 mm)

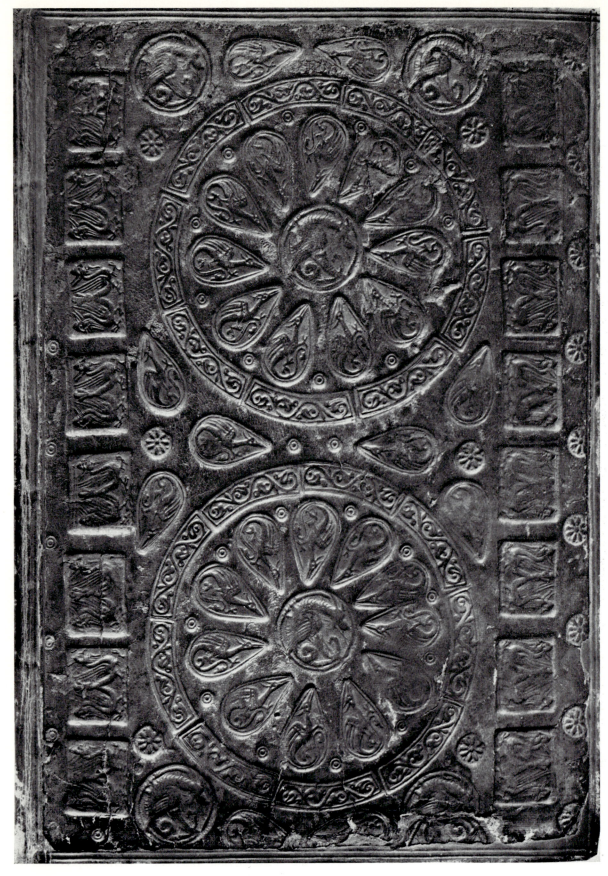

Winton Domesday, first cover (253×182 mm). *See pages* 526–40

Winton Domesday, second cover (253 × 182 mm). *See pages* 526-40

Hegesippus, first cover (288 × 207 mm). *See page* 534

Hegesippus, second cover (288 × 207 mm). *See page* 534

Codex Wintoniensis, original first cover (400×277 mm). Half-size; cf. Fig. 31*b*. *See page* 534

Codex Wintoniensis, original second cover (400 × 277 mm). Half-size; cf. Fig. 31*a*. *See page 534*

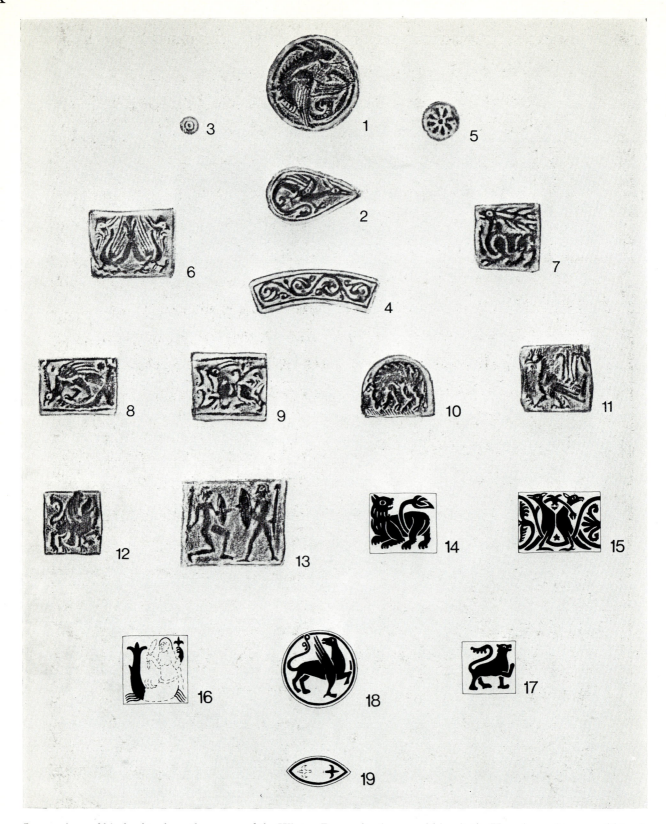

Impressions of binders' tools on the covers of the Winton Domesday (1–10, rubbings), the Hegesippus (11–13, rubbings), and the *Codex Wintoniensis* (14–19, drawings). Natural size. *See pages* 533–40

incip̄ nomine · Incipiunt lectio· anni circul̄...
comnis · in uigilia natalis d̄n̄ī ad s̄c̄tam maria ad...
lec epi t̄ȳ p āū · apl̄i · A... manū

F̄R̄S: paulus seruus · xp̄i ih̄ū
uocatus apl̄s segregatus in euangelium d...
q̄ ante p̄misēr̄at p̄phetas suos inscrip...
turis sc̄is de filio suo qui factus· e̅· ei ex...
ne dauid secundum carnem :; Qui pred̄st...
natus· e̅· filius d̄ī in uirtute secundum sp̄m
sc̄ificationis :· exsurrectionis mortuorum ih̄...
xp̄i d̄n̄i n̄r̄i :· p̄ quem accepimus gratiam
& apostolatum ad oboediendum fidei in omnib;
gentibus p̄ nomine eius :; In quibus estis & u...
uocati :· ih̄u xp̄i d̄n̄i n̄r̄i :· seq̄ sci... ...
In illo tempore · Cum ēē · desp̄on · t̄ā m...
mater ih̄u maria ioseph · antequam con...
uenirent inuenta· ē· in utero habens desp̄...
s̄c̄o· Ioseph autem uir eius cum ēē · iustus
cum nollet eam traducere & uoluit occulte
dimittere eam · Hec autem eo cogitan...
ecce angelus d̄n̄i insomnis aparuit ei dic...
Ioseph fili dauid · noli timere accipere...
mariam coniugem tuam :; Q̄d enim in...
natum· ē· despu̅ s̄c̄o· ē· :; Pariet autem fil...
& uocabis nomen eius ih̄m :· Ipse enim fa...
cium faciet populum suum a pecatis eor...

The sacramentary from the binding of the Winton Domesday, fo. 24ᵛ (written space: 250 × 150 mm).
See pages 541, 549